Labour Law
Text and Materials

Labour Law
Text and Materials

HUGH COLLINS
London School of Economics

K D EWING
King's College, London

and

AILEEN McCOLGAN
King's College, London

·H A R T·
PUBLISHING

OXFORD AND PORTLAND, OREGON
2005

Published in North America (US and Canada) by

Hart Publishing

c/o International Specialized Book Services
920 NE 58th Avenue, Suite 300
Portland, OR 97213-3786
USA
Tel: +1 503 287 3093 or toll-free: (1) 800 944 6190
Fax: +1 503 280 8832
Email: orders@isbs.com
Website: www.isbs.com

Hart Publishing, Salter's Boatyard, Folly Bridge, Abingdon Rd, Oxford, OX1 4LB
Telephone: +44 (0)1865 245533   Fax: +44 (0) 1865 794882
Email: mail@hartpub.co.uk
Website: http//:www.hartpub.co.uk

British Library Cataloguing in Publication Data

Data Available

ISBN-13: 978-1-84113-362-1
ISBN-10: 1-84113-362-0

Typeset by Forewords, Oxford, in Times 10/12 pt

Printed and bound in Great Britain by
Page Bros Ltd, Norfolk

Preface

This volume attempts to provide a comprehensive resource for students studying labour law or employment law courses. It is aimed primarily at law undergraduate studies, but we hope that it will be suitable for any students who want to learn about labour law. The volume tries to be comprehensive in the sense that it offers substantial discussion and analysis of the legal materials, together with accounts of the more important cases and legislation, and it adds criticism and perspectives drawn from a variety of disciplines. Of course, the book cannot be comprehensive in the sense of providing a highly detailed account of every aspect of the laws that might be regarded as pertinent to employment and industrial relations. We have chosen rather to focus on what seem to be to us the core issues for labour law at the beginning of the twenty-first century, whilst endeavouring to signal the presence of other aspects of the relevant law. Nor can a book of this size discuss all the relevant material in relation to the core issues, so we have added at the end of each chapter suggested additional reading, which was excluded from substantial discussion only in the interests of keeping the book within manageable proportions. Even so, we anticipate that many teachers will only tackle some of the topics, so we have endeavoured as far as possible to make each chapter self-contained.

We have endeavoured to state the law up to 1 April 2005.

Hugh Collins
Keith Ewing
Aileen McColgan

London,
September 2005.

Acknowledgements

The author and publisher gratefully acknowledge the authors and publishers of extracted material which appears in this book, and in particular the following for permission to reprint from the sources indicated.

Blackwell Publishers for permission to reprint the following: from the *Modern Law Review*: McEvoy, K., and White C. Security Vetting in Northern Ireland, (1998) 61 *Modern Law Review* 341; Wynn, M. Pregnancy Discrimination etc (1999) 62 *Modern Law Review* 435, p 442, 444; Mair, J. Maternity Leave etc , (2000) 63 *Modern Law Review* 877, 880–1.

Cavendish Publishing for extracts from: A Morris and O'Donnell (eds) *Feminist Perspective on Employment Law.*

Butterworth Heinemann for permission to reprint the following: Crouch, C. Class Conflict and the Industrial Relations Crisis etc 1977.

The Commission for Racial Equality for permission to reprint the following: Reform of the Race Relations Act 1976 1998 www.cre.org.uk; Factsheet 'Employment and Unemployment' www.cre.org.uk.

Demos for extracts from: H Wilkinson and I Briscoe *Parental Leave: The Price of Family Values.*

The Equal Opportunities Review for permission to reprint the following: Equality for Lesbians and Gay men in the Workplace (1997) 74 *Equal Opportunities Review*, p 20; Work and Sexual Orientation (1997) 74 *Equal Opportunities Review*, p 22.

The Faculty of Laws, UCL for permission to reprint the following: Arthurs, H. Understanding Labour Law etc (1985) Current Legal Problems 83.

Kluwer Law International for extracts from: "Union Exclusivity Agreements: A Comparative Overview" by K Miller *International Journal of Labour Law and Industrial Relations* vol 16 issue 4. (www.kluwerlaw.com).

Lawrence and Wishart for extracts from KD Ewing *Working Life: A New Perspective on Labour Law* (1996).

Oxford University Press Journals: A McColgan, 'Family Friendly Frolics: The Maternity and Parental Leave, etc. Regulations 1999', *Industrial Law Journal* (2000); B Hepple, 'New Approaches to International Regulation', *Industrial Law Journal* 26 (1997); B Simpson, 'A Milestone in the Legal Regulation of Pay: The National Minimum Wage Act 1998', *Industrial Law Journal* 28 (1999); B Simpson, 'Trade Union Recognition and the Law, A New Approach—Parts I and II of Schedule A1 to the Trade Union and Labour Relations (Consolidation) Act 1992', *Industrial Law Journal* 29 (2000); G Morris, 'Employment in Public Services: The Case for Special Treatment', *Oxford Journal of Legal Studies* 20 (2000); G Morris, 'The Human Rights Act and the Public/ Private Divide in Employment Law', *Industrial Law Journal* 27 (1998); H Gospel and G Lockwood, 'Disclosure of Information for Collective Bargaining: The CAC Approach Revisited', *Industrial Law Journal* 28 (1999); J Davies, 'A Cuckoo In The Nest? A "Range Of Reasonable Responses"', *Industrial Law Journal* 164 (2003); KD Ewing, 'Job Security and the Contract of Employment', *Industrial Law Journal* 18 (1989); KD Ewing, 'The Human Rights Act and Labour Law', *Industrial Law Journal* 27 (1998); KD Ewing, 'The Function of Trade Unions', *Industrial Law Journal* 34 (2005); M Connolly, 'Discrimination Law: Justification, Alternative Measures and Defences Based on Sex', *Industrial Law Journal* 30 (2001); M Freedland, 'Status and Contract in the Law of Public Employment', *Industrial Law Journal* 20 (1991); M Hall & P Edwards, 'Reforming the Redundancy Consultation Procedure', *Industrial Law Journal* 28 (1999); M Jeffrey, 'Not Really Going to Work? Of the Directive on Part-Time Work, 'Atypical Work' and Attempts to Regulate it', *Industrial Law Journal* 27

viii ACKNOWLEDGEMENTS

(1998); P Davies & C Kilpatrick, 'UK Worker Representation after Single Channel', *Industrial Law Journal* 33 (2004); P Skidmore, 'Sex, Gender and Comparators in Employment Discrimination Law', *Industrial Law Journal* 26 (1997); P Wallington, 'Policing the Miners' Strike', *Industrial Law Journal* 14 (1985); R Munday, 'Tribunal Lore: Legalism and the Industrial Tribunals', *Industrial Law Journal* 10 (1981); S Deakin & F Wilkinson, 'Rights vs Ef?ciency? The Economic Case for Transnational Labour', *Industrial Law Journal* 23 (1994).

Oxford University Press for extracts from: D Pannick *Sex Discrimination Law* (1985); H Collins *Justice in Dismissal* (1992); "Freedom of Association" by KD Ewing, in G Chambers and C McCrudden (eds) *Individual Rights and the Law in Britain* (1994); "Law, Public Services an Citizenship – New Domains, New Regimes" by M Freedland in Freedland and Sciarra (eds) *Public Services and Citizenship in European Law*.

Palgrave Macmillan for extracts from: C G Hanson, *Taming Trade Unions* (1991).

The Stationery Office for permission to reprint extracts from the following: Hobbs, S. and McKechnie, J. Child Employment in Britain etc (1997).Memorandum from the EOC to the House of Commons Select Committee on Education and Employment: Part-Time Working, vol 11. Second Report 1998–99 www.parliament.the-stationery-office.co.uk/pa/cm/cmeduemp.htm; House of Commons Select Committee on Education and Employment: Part-Time Working vol 1; 2nd report 1998–99, www.parliament.the-stationery-office.co.uk. Memorandum from Colette Fagan to the House of Commons Select Committee on Education and Employment: Part-Time Working (vol 11). Fox, A. Industrial Sociology and Industrial Relations Research Paper 3, Royal Commission on Trade Unions and Employers; Weller, P., Feldman, A., and Purdam, K. Religious Discrimination in England and Wales (2001) Home Office Research Study 220.

Taylor and Francis for extracts from: N Millward, A Bryson and J Forth *All Change at Work*; H Gospel and S Wood (eds) *Representing Workers: Trade Union Recognition*.

Sweet and Maxwell Ltd for permission to reprint the following: Pannick, D. (1983): Homosexuals, Transsexuals and the Law, Public Law 279, 281; Ellis, E. (1994): The Definition of Discrimination in European Sex Equality Law 19 European Law Review, p 573; Bowers, J. and Lewis, J. Whistleblowing (1996): Freedom of Expression etc 1 EHRLR 637; Morris, G. (1999): The European Convention on Human Rights and Employment etc 4 EHRLR, 496; Davies and Freedland Kahn-Freund's Labour and the Law 3rd edn 1983, p 18.

The Guardian for permission to reprint extracts from the following issues: 22nd July 2000; 25th November 2000; 28th September 1999; 2nd November 2000; Pannick, D. 4th October 1985; 9th September, 2000.

Trades Union Congress for permission to reprint the following: An introduction to the working families tax credit 1998, www.tuc.org.uk; A Guide to the Working Time Directive 1998, www.tuc.org.uk; Six days a Week: A guide to the Working time Regulations etc, 2000, www.tuc.org.uk; Tax credits: Briefing for MPs 2001 www.tuc.org.uk; Press Release: TUC Says 170,000 are Still Earning Less than the Minimum Wage 26 January 2001 www.tuc.org.uk; Code of Practice on Disciplinary and Grievance Procedures ACAS (2000); Briefing on the Govt.'s Proposed Amendments to the Working Time Regs 1998 www.tuc.org.uk; Press Release: 25 Jan 2000 Working Time: Govt Advice is Legally Wrong www.tuc.org.uk.

Contents

Table of cases   xvii
Table of legislation   xxxv

1   INTRODUCTION TO LABOUR LAW   1

1.1   What is labour law?   1
1.2   Methods of regulation   10
    1.2.1   Regulatory standards with criminal sanctions   10
    1.2.2   Individual civil law rights   12
    1.2.3   Collective bargaining   13
    1.2.4   Effectiveness of labour law   15
    1.2.5   The role of the State   17
1.3   Labour courts and dispute settlement   19
    1.3.1   Sources of conflict   19
    1.3.2   Alternative dispute resolution   23
    1.3.3   Other forms of alternative dispute resolution   29
    1.3.4   The ordinary courts   30
1.4   Transnational regulation   32
    1.4.1   International protection of human rights   34
    1.4.2   International protection of social and economic rights   35
    1.4.3   Transnational labour market regulation   42
1.5   Prospects for labour law   52
    1.5.1   Flexible forms of work   52
    1.5.2   Economic objectives of legal regulation   54
    1.5.3   Social exclusion   58
    1.5.4   Worker participation   61
    1.5.5   Citizenship   63
1.6   Conclusion   65

2   THE EMPLOYMENT RELATION   69

2.1   The contract of employment   69
    2.1.1   Freedom of contract   69
    2.1.2   The standard model of employment   70
    2.1.3   The legal institution of the contract of employment   73
2.2   The wage–work bargain   75
    2.2.1   Deductions for incomplete and unsatisfactory work   77
    2.2.2   Unavailability of work   87

2.2.3	Enforced idleness	90
2.2.4	The principle of mutuality or reciprocity	95
2.3	The organisational framework	95
2.4	Collective agreements	102
2.4.1	Legal enforceability	102
2.4.2	Incorporation	103
2.4.3	Enforcement by employees	104
2.4.4	Enforcement by employers	109
2.4.5	Conclusion	111
2.5	Authority and co-operation	111
2.5.1	The legal construction of hierarchy	111
2.5.2	Mutual trust and confidence or good faith in performance	113
2.5.3	Employee's duty of loyalty	126
2.5.4	Conclusion	128
2.6	Information	129
2.6.1	Dissemination of false or misleading information	130
2.6.2	Disclosure of terms of employment	135
2.6.3	Risk assessment	148
2.6.4	Disclosure of business plans to representatives of the workforce	150
2.6.5	Confidential information	150
2.6.6	Conclusion	155
2.7	The scope of employment regulation	155
2.7.1	Classification of contractual relations	157
2.7.2	Flexibility and atypical workers	166
2.7.3	Proper scope of regulation	171
2.7.4	Limits to flexibility	194
2.8	Public sector workers and public law	197
2.8.1	The approximation of public and private sectors	199
2.8.2	The retreat of public law	200
2.8.3	Government by contract	208
2.9	The adequacy of the contractual framework for employment	211

3 EQUALITY 217

3.1	Introduction	217
3.2	Prohibited grounds of discrimination	220
3.2.1	'Sex'	220
3.2.2	'Sexual orientation'	222
3.2.3	'Race'	224
3.2.4	'Religion and Belief'	227
3.2.5	'Disability'	230
3.3	Direct discrimination	235
3.3.1	Direct discrimination	235
3.4	Victimisation	256
3.5	Indirect discrimination	263
3.5.1	'Provision, criterion or practice'	266

3.5.2 The collective disadvantage test 266
3.5.3 The individual disadvantage test 271
3.5.4 Justification 273
3.6 The DDA 285
3.6.1 Justification under the DDA 285
3.6.2 Duties of reasonable accommodation 290
3.7 Exceptions 292
3.8 'Positive' discrimination 307
3.9 Prohibited discrimination 310
3.10 Sex discrimination in pay and contractual terms—the EqPA 317
3.10.1 Selecting a comparator 318
3.10.2 Sex discrimination in pay: the EqPA and the genuine material factor defence 323
3.11 Procedural and related issues 332
3.11.1 Proving discrimination 332
3.11.2 Time limits 335
3.11.3 Remedies 336
3.12 Conclusion 339

4 PROTECTING THE WORK/LIFE BALANCE? 341

4.1 Introduction 341
4.2 Part-time workers 343
4.2.1 The Part-Time Workers Directive 348
4.2.2 The Part-time Workers Regulations 2000 350
4.2.3 Impact of the Regulations 354
4.3 Time-off rights 356
4.3.1 Maternity rights 356
4.3.2 Adoptive leave 366
4.3.3 Paternity leave 367
4.3.4 Parental leave 368
4.3.5 Emergency leave 377
4.3.6 The right to request 'flexible working' 382
4.4 Minimum wage regulation 387
4.4.1 Introduction of the national minimum wage 389
4.4.2 The National Minimum Wage 392
4.4.3 Enforcement of the National Minimum Wage 397
4.4.4 Impact of the National Minimum Wage 398
4.5 The regulation of working time 401
4.5.1 The Working Time Regulations 1998 (SI 1998 No 1833) – an introduction 402
4.5.2 Annual leave 405
4.5.3 The operation of the Regulations 408
4.5.4 Working time 410
4.5.5 Exceptions to the 48 hour week 413
4.5.6 Excluded workers and working time 418

	4.5.7	Enforcement of the Working Time Regulations	422
	4.5.8	Impact of the Working Time Regulations	424
4.6	Conclusion		427

5 DISMISSAL 433

5.1	The common law of wrongful dismissal		436
	5.1.1	Compensation for wrongful dismissal	437
	5.1.2	Injunctions and declarations	463
	5.1.3	The revival of the common law	475
5.2	Statutory concept of dismissal		477
	5.2.1	Dismissal or resignation?	479
	5.2.2	Constructive dismissal	482
	5.2.3	Frustration	488
5.3	Contracting out of statutory rights		492
	5.3.1	Agreed termination and compromise agreements	494
	5.3.2	Employment	498
	5.3.3	Temporary and probationary employees	501
	5.3.4	Retirement	507
	5.3.5	The arbitration alternative	508
	5.3.6	Conclusion	509
5.4	Fairness of dismissal		511
	5.4.1	The structure of the fairness enquiry	512
	5.4.2	The range or band of reasonable responses test	515
	5.4.3	Procedural fairness	526
	5.4.4	Substantive fairness	534
5.5	Remedies for unfair dismissal		537
	5.5.1	Compliance and corrective justice	537
	5.5.2	Reinstatement	538
	5.5.3	Compensation	543
	5.5.4	Conciliation and settlements	555
5.6	Rights and reasonableness		557

6 HUMAN RIGHTS AND LABOUR LAW 561

6.1	The European Convention on Human Rights		562
	-----	-----	-----
6.2	Introduction to the Human Rights Act 1998		565
	6.2.1	The Human Rights Act and employment—the public/private divide	568
	6.2.2	The Human Rights Act and procedural fairness	573
6.3	The application of the Convention rights to employment		575
6.4	Political activities and the Human Rights Act		588
	6.4.2	Statutory restrictions on public sector workers	591
	6.4.3	Other forms of 'political' discrimination/ restrictions	595
	6.4.4	Political restrictions/discrimination and the Convention/HRA 1998	598
6.5	Workplace surveillance		601

6.5.1	The Regulation of Investigatory Powers Act 2000	608
6.5.2	The Data Protection Act 1998	610
6.5.3	The data protection principles	616
6.5.4	Enforcement of the Data Protection Principles	619
6.5.5	The DPA 1998 and protection against workplace surveillance	621
6.5.6	Workplace surveillance and the European Convention	628
6.5.7	Workplace surveillance and the Human Rights Act	633

6.6	Whistleblowing: freedom of expression in the workplace?	635
6.6.1	The Public Interest Disclosure Act	636
6.6.2	Whistleblowing and the European Convention	644

6.7	Conclusion	645

7 TRADE UNIONS AND THEIR MEMBERS 647

7.1	Trade unions and citizenship	647

7.2	What are trade unions?	649
7.2.1	Trade union objects: a source of restraint	651
7.2.2	Trade union political objects: statutory restraints	655

7.3	Trade union structure and government	659
7.3.1	Constitutional constraints	660
7.3.2	Constitutional conflicts	663

7.4	The election of trade union officers	666
7.4.1	The statutory procedures	666
7.4.2	The continuing role of the common law	672

7.5	Trade union members' rights	680
7.5.1	The right to information	681
7.5.2	The right not to strike	682
7.5.3	The right not to be excluded from membership	687

7.6	Disciplinary and expulsion procedures	693
7.6.1	Disciplinary powers	693
7.6.2	Disciplinary procedures	694
7.6.3	Disciplinary decisions	700

7.7	The adjudication of disputes	706
7.7.1	The role of external review	706
7.7.2	The role of the Certification Officer	707
7.7.3	The role of the courts	710

7.8	Conclusion	717
7.8.1	The changing direction of public policy	718
7.8.2	The changing nature of trade unionism	**719**

8 WORKER REPRESENTATION AND TRADE UNION RECOGNITION 723

8.1	Trade unions and collective bargaining	723
8.1.1	Changing public policy responses	723

| | 8.1.2 | Changing patterns of workplace representation | 726 |

8.2	Trade union membership and activities		729
	8.2.1	Access to employment	730
	8.2.2	Trade union membership, activities and services	734

8.3	Trade union representation and the right to be accompanied		752
	8.3.1	The right to be accompanied	753
	8.3.2	Scope and application	754
	8.3.3	An important qualification	755
	8.3.4	The rights and responsibilities of trade unions	757

8.4	Trade union recognition and collective bargaining		757
	8.4.1	Trade union recognition: voluntary agreements	758
	8.4.2	Trade union recognition: the statutory procedure	765

8.5	Rights of recognised trade unions		795
	8.5.1	The meaning of recognition	797
	8.5.2	Time off for trade union duties and activities	800
	8.5.3	Disclosure of information	812
	8.5.4	Trade union consultation rights	821

8.6	Other forms of workplace representation		833
	8.6.1	Staff associations: a rival to trade unionism	834
	8.6.2	Consulting employee representatives	839
	8.6.3	Information and Consultation Procedures	844

9 INDUSTRIAL CONFLICT AND THE RIGHT TO STRIKE 863

9.1	A fundamental right		863
	9.1.1	The function of industrial action	863
	9.1.2	Legal perceptions and legal challenges	867
	9.1.3	The declining prevalence of strikes and industrial action	868

9.2	The basis of legal liability		869
	9.2.1	The boundaries of liability	869
	9.2.2	Extending the boundaries of liability	872
	9.2.3	The expanded basis of liability	875
	9.2.4	Statutory immunity: where are we now?	879

9.3	Trade dispute: defining the legitimate boundaries of trade union action		880
	9.3.1	Social and political questions	881
	9.3.2	The right to strike and the changing public sector	884
	9.3.3	The Right to Strike and the House of Lords	888

9.4	Restricting the boundaries of industrial action: secondary action and other restraints		892
	9.4.1	Liability and immunity	893
	9.4.2	Withdrawal of immunity	896
	9.4.3	International solidarity action	899

9.5	Procedural restraints: ballots and notices		902
	9.5.1	The statutory duty	904
	9.5.2	Notice to the employer	904

9.5.3	Separate workplace ballots	905
9.5.4	Entitlement to vote, the voting paper and the conduct of the ballot	907
9.5.5	After the ballot: calling the industrial action	909
9.5.6	Notice of industrial action	910
9.5.7	A case for further reform?	914
9.6	**Picketing and demonstrations: reconciling conflicting freedoms**	**915**
9.6.1	Statutory protection	916
9.6.2	The Code of Practice	917
9.6.3	The scope of statutory protection: location and purpose	919
9.6.4	Liability for picketing outside the scope of statutory protection	921
9.6.5	Consumer picketing	926
9.7	**Remedies and liability: injunctions, contempt and damages**	**928**
9.7.1	Injunctions	928
9.7.2	Contempt of court	935
9.7.3	Damages	938
9.8	**Sanctions against strikers: protected and unprotected action**	**944**
9.8.1	Unfair dismissal: before the Employment Relations Act 1999	945
9.8.2	Employment Relations Act 1999: protected industrial action	947
9.8.3	Unprotected industrial action	953
9.9	**Industrial disputes and the role of the state**	**958**
9.9.1	Strategies of dispute resolution	960
9.9.2	Strategies of coercion	963
9.10	**Conclusion**	**970**

10 RESTRUCTURING THE BUSINESS 979

10.1	**Variation of jobs**	**982**
10.1.1	Flexibility under the contract of employment	983
10.1.2	Variation by collective agreement	995
10.1.3	Short-time working and employment subsidies	998
10.2	**Workforce reductions**	**1000**
10.2.1	The concept of redundancy	1003
10.2.2	Some other substantial reason	1015
10.2.3	Fairness of selection for redundancy	1019
10.3	**Redeployment**	**1024**
10.3.1	Offer of alternative employment	1024
10.3.2	Failure to consider redeployment	1027
10.3.3	A positive duty?	1028
10.4	**Insolvency**	**1028**
10.4.1	Protection of wages	1029
10.4.2	Corporate rescue	1033
10.5	**Sales of the business**	**1035**
10.5.1	Dismissals before the sale	1036
10.5.2	Dismissals after the sale	1044
10.5.3	Variation of terms by transferee	1045
10.5.4	Outsourcing	1051
10.6	**Worker participation**	**1059**

10.6.1	Individual consultation	1062
10.6.2	Mass dismissals	1063
10.6.3	Sales of the business	1065
10.6.4	Conformity to collective agreements	1067
10.6.5	Conclusion	1069
10.7	Controlling capital	1069
Index		1075

Table of Cases

Cases in bold type are extracted at the page or pages listed in bold

AB v CD [2001] IRLR 808. 649
Abadeh v BT plc [2001] ICR 156 231
Abbot v Sullivan [1952] 1 KB 189 705
***Abdulaziz, Cabales and Balkandali v UK* (1985) 7 EHRR 471** 577, **585–86**, 587
Abernethy v Mott, Hay and Anderson [1974] ICR 323 513
Abood v District Board of Education 431 US 209 (1977) 749
Abrahams v Performing Rights Society [1995] IRLR 486. 441
Abrahamsson & Anderson v Fogelqvist (Case C–407/98) [2000] ECR I–5539. . . . . 308, 309
Addis v Gramophone Co Ltd [1909] AC 488. . . . . 92, 447
Addison t/a Brayton News v Ashby [2003] ICR 667 407
ADI (UK) Ltd v Willer [2001] IRLR 542 1056
Adin v Seco Forex International Resources Ltd [1997] IRLR 280 455
AEEU and GE Caledonian (Tur1/120/2001) 838
Ahmad v The Inner London Education Authority [1977] ICR 490 882
Ahmad v UK (1982) 4 EHRR 126 . . . . 228, 563, 575, 583
***Ahmed v UK* (1998) 29 EHRR 29** 579, 594, **600**
Alamo Group (Europe) Ltd v Tucker [2003] IRLR 266 1067
Alboni v Ind Coope Retail Ltd [1998] IRLR 131 512
Alexander v Standard Telephones & Cables Ltd [1990] IRLR 55 105
***Alexander v Standard Telephones & Cables Ltd (No. 2)* [1991] IRLR 287** **105–8**, 1067
***Allonby v Accrington and Rossendale College* [2001] ICR 1189** 267, **280–82**, 283, 284, 319
***Allonby v Accrington and Rossendale College* (Case C–256/01) [2004] ECR I– ;**
    [2004] ICR 1328; [2004] IRLR 224 . . . . **176**, 193, 271, **319–20**
Amalgamated Society of Railway Servants v Osborne [1910] AC 87 655
American Cyanamid Co v Ethicon Ltd [1975] AC 396 . . . . 926, 929, 930, 931, 932, 933
***Amicus v Secretary of State for Trade & Industry* [2004] EWHC 860; [2004] IRLR 430** **305–6**
Anderson v Pringle of Scotland Ltd [1998] IRLR 64 . . . . 108, 475, 1068
Annamunthodo v Oilfield Workers' Trade Union [1961] AC 945 698
Application No 11142/84, 3 December 1986 578
Archibald v Fife Council (Scotland) [2004] ICR 954 290
Associated British Ports v Palmer [1994] ICR 97 . . . . 731, 732
Associated British Ports v TGWU [1989] ICR 557. . . . . 878, 910
Associated Newspapers Ltd v Wilson [1995] 2 AC 454. . . . . 732, 737
Associated Provincial Picture Houses Ltd v Wednesbury Corporation [1948] 1 KB 223 . . 123, 202, 712
Aston Cantlow PCC v Wallbank [2004] 1 AC 546. 568
***Attorney General v Blake* [2001] 1 AC 268** **153–54**
Attorney General v Merthyr Tydfil Union [1900] 1 Ch 516 969
Attorney General for Australia v The Queen (the Boilermakers' case) [1957] AC 288 707
Austin Rover v AUEW (TASS) [1985] IRLR 162 . . . . 935, 936
Australian Workers' Union v Bowen (No 2) (1948) 77 CLR 601 699
Aziz v Trinity Street Taxis Ltd [1989] 1 QB 463 . . . . 257, 260

Babcock FATA Ltd v Addison [1987] ICR 805 550
Badeck v Hessen (Case C–158/97) [2000] ECR I–1875. . . . . 307, 308, 309
Baldwin v British Coal Corporation [1995] IRLR 139 439
Bank of Credit and Commerce International SA v Ali [1999] IRLR 508 460
***Barber v RJB Mining (UK) Ltd* [1999] ICR 679** 73, **423–24**

Barber v Somerset County Council **[2004] UKHL 13; [2004] ICR 457** **462**
Barclay v City of Glasgow District Council [1983] IRLR 313 481
***Barretts & Baird (Wholesale) Ltd v IPCS* [1987] IRLR 3** **877–78**
Barry v Midland Bank plc [1999] ICR 859 . . . . 281, 282, 284
Barthold v Germany (1986) 13 EHRR 431 644
Barton v Investec Henderson Crosthwaite Securities Ltd [2003] ICR 1205 334
Bass Leisure Ltd v Thomas [1994] IRLR 104 1014
***Bass Taverns Ltd v Burgess* [1995] IRLR 596** **742–43**
BBC v Hearn **[1977] 1 WLR 1004; [1977] ICR 686** **883–84**, 888, 890, 891, 892, 901
BBC Scotland v Souster [2001] IRLR 150 225
Beaverbrook Newspapers Ltd v Keys [1978] ICR 582 895
***Belgian Linguistics* (1968) 1 EHRR 252** 577, **584**, 587
Bell v Lever Bros Ltd [1932] AC 161 . . . . 126, 127
Bell-Booth Group Ltd v A-G [1989] 3 NZLR 148 133
Berriman v Delabole Slate Ltd. See *Delabole Slate Ltd v Berriman*
Bessenden Properties Ltd v Corness Note (1974) [1977] ICR 821 1019
Beveridge v KLM UK Ltd [2000] IRLR 765 90
***Bilka-Kaufhaus GmbH v Weber von Hartz* (Case 170/84) [1986]**
   ECR 1607 . . . . 274, **277**, 278, 280, 281, 282, 283, 284, 325, 327, 329, 330
***Birch v University of Liverpool* [1985] ICR 470** **494**, 1002, 1023
BL Cars Ltd, MG Abingdon Plant and GMWU, AUEW, TGWU (Award No 80/65) 820
Blackpool and The Fylde College v NATHFE [1994] ICR 648 904
Board of Regents of the University of Wisconsin v Southworth, Supreme Court,
   22 March 2000 749-50
Bork (P) International A/S v Foreningen af Arbejdsledere I Danmark (Case 101/87) [1989] IRLR 41
   . . . . 1040, 1041
Bossa v Nordstress [1998] IRLR 284 219
Bottrill v Secretary of State for Trade and Industry [1999] IRLR 326 186
Bowden v Tuffnells Parcels Express (Case C–133/01) [2001] ECR I–7031 403
Boxfoldia Ltd v NGA (1982) [1988] IRLR 383 943
***Boychuck v Symons Holdings Ltd* [1977] IRLR 395** **535**, 536
***Boyle v EOC* (Case C–411/96) [1998] ECR I–6401** **362–63**, 364
***Boyo v London Borough of Lambeth* [1994] ICR 727; [1995] IRLR 50** 451-52, **465–67**, 468
Bradley v NALGO [1991] ICR 359 685
***Brassington v Cauldon Wholesale Ltd* [1978] ICR 405** **783**
***Breen v AEU* [1971] 2 QB 175** **672–76**, 677
Bristow v City Petroleum Ltd [1988] ICR 165 84
British Actors' Equity Association v Goring [1978] ICR 791 665
***British Aerospace plc v Green & Others* [1995] ICR 1006** **1021–23**, 1024
British Aircraft Corporation Ltd v Austin [1978] IRLR 332 116
British Airports Authority v Ashton [1983] IRLR 287 917
***British Airways Engine Overhaul Ltd v Francis* [1981] ICR 278** **741**
***British Coal Corp v Smith* [1994] ICR 810; [1996] ICR 515** **322**
British Fuels Ltd v Baxendale [1998] ICR 1141; [1999] 2 AC 52 . . . . 1040–42, 1046–47
British Home Stores Ltd v Burchell [1978] IRLR 379 . . . . 525, 529
***British Leyland UK Ltd v Swift* [1981] IRLR 91** **521**
British Nursing Association v Inland Revenue (National Minimum Wage Compliance Team)
   [2002] IRLR 480 . . . . **395**, 396
British Railways Board v Jackson [1994] IRLR 235 522
British Transport Commission v Gourley [1956] AC 185 440
British United Shoe Machinery Co Ltd v Clarke [1978] ICR 70 546–47
Brompton v AOC International Ltd [1997] IRLR 639 . . . . 455, 469
Brooks v BT plc [1991] IRLR 4 507
Brooks v USDAW (Decision D/31-34/03) 709
Broome v Cassell & Co [1972] AC 1130 . . . . 942, 943
***Broome v DPP* [1974] AC 587** **922–23**

Brown v AUEW **[1976] ICR 147** **677–80**
Brown v Chief Adjudication Officer [1997] ICR 266 439
Brown v Rentokil Ltd (Case C–394/96) [1998] ECR I–4185 242
Brown v TNT Worldwide (UK) Ltd [2001] ICR 182 260
Bruce v Wiggins Teape (Stationery) Ltd [1994] IRLR 536. 984
Brumfitt v Ministry of Defence [2005] IRLR 4 . . . . 250, 251
Brunnhofer v Bank der Österreichischen Postsparkasse AG (Case C–381/99) [2001] ECR I–4961. . . 331
BT plc v CWU **[2004] IRLR 58**. **905, 933–35**
BT plc v Ticehurst **[1992] ICR 383** **80-83**, 86, 97, 122
BT plc v Williams [1997] IRLR 668. . . . . 248, 249, 250
Bullivant (Roger) Ltd v Ellis **[1987] ICR 464** **151**
Burdett Coutts v Hertfordshire County Council [1984] IRLR 92 983
Burrett v West Birmingham Health Authority [1994] IRLR 7; unreported, 3 March 1994. . 253, 254
Burton and Rhule v De Vere Hotels [1997] ICR 1. . . . . 315, 316, 317
Busch v Klinikum Neustadt (Case C–109/00) [2003] ECR I–20341. 241
Byrne Bros (Formwork) Ltd v Baird [2002] ICR 667 162

Callaghan v Glasgow CC [2001] IRLR 724 291
Camden Exhibition & Display Ltd v Lynott **[1966] 1 QB 555** **109–10**
Campbell v Frisbee [2002] EWCA Civ 1374; [2003] ICR 141 . . . . 91, 153
Campion v Hamworthy Engineering Ltd [1987] ICR 966 523
Canniffe v East Riding of Yorkshire Council [2000] IRLR 555 314
Carmichael v National Power plc [1999] ICR 1226 . . . . 140, 165
Carrigan v ASLEF (EAT/564/01/RN); (Decision D/21-35/01) 709, 710
Carrington v Therm-a-Stor Ltd [1983] ICR 208 781
Carry All Motors Ltd v Pennington [1980] IRLR 455 . . . . 1007, 1008, 1009
Cases Relating to Certain Aspects of the Laws on the Use of Language in Education in Belgium.
    See *Belgian Linguistics*
Cassell v Broome. See *Broome v Cassell & Co*
Catamaran Cruisers Ltd v Williams **[1994] IRLR 384** **186, 1017–18**
Caulfield v Marshalls Clay Products [2004] ICR 1502 408
Cerberus Software Ltd v Rowley [2001] IRLR 160. 441
Champion v Chief Constable of Gwent **[1990] 1 WLR 1**. **594-95**
Chant v Acquaboats Ltd [1978] ICR 643 741
Chapman v Goonvean and Rostowrack China Clay Co Ltd [1973] ICR 310 . . . . 1008, 1009
Chappell v Times Newspapers Ltd [1975] ICR 145 473
Cheall v APEX **[1982] ICR 231; [1983] 2 AC 180** **688–89**
Cheall v UK (1986) 8 EHRR 44. 689
Chicago Teachers Union v Hudson 475 US 292 (1986) 750
Chief Constable of North Wales Police v Evans [1982] 1 WLR 1155. 207
Chief Constable of West Yorkshire Police v Khan **[2001] ICR 1065** 239, 257, **258–60**
Chubb Fire Security Ltd v Harper [1983] IRLR 311. 1018
City of Birmingham District Council v Beyer [1977] IRLR 211 733
Civil Service Union v CAC **(Award No 80/73); [1980] IRLR 274** **816–18**, 819, 820
Clark v TDG Ltd (tla Novacold) **[1999] ICR 951** **245**, 246, 290
Clark's of Hove v Bakers' Union **[1978] ICR 1076**. **830–31**
Clarke v Ely (IMI) Kynoch Ltd [1983] ICR 165 . . . . 22, 266
Clarke v Staddon (Frank) Ltd [2004] ICR 1502 408
Clarkson International Tools Ltd v Short [1973] ICR 191 546
Clay Cross (Quarry Services) Ltd v Fletcher **[1979] ICR 47** 323, **324**
Cleaning Co Ltd v Heads [1995] IRLR 4 313
Clemens v Peter Richards Ltd [1977] IRLR 332. 999
Clifton Middle School (Governing Body) v Askew **[2000] ICR 286**. **173–74**
Clouston & Co Ltd v Corry [1906] AC 122 486
Clymo v Wandsworth London Borough Council **[1989] ICR 250**. 272, **311**
Collier v Sunday Referee Publishing Co Ltd [1940] 2 KB 647 92

Collins v Royal National Theatre Board Ltd [2004] IRLR 395 289
Collins v Secretary of State for Work and Pensions (Case C–138/02) [2005] ICR 37 46
Commissioners of Inland Revenue v Post Office Ltd [2003] IRLR 199 175
Connex South Eastern Ltd v RMT [1999] IRLR 249 908
Conway v Wade [1909] AC 506 894
Cook (James W) & Co (Wivenhoe) Ltd v Tipper [1990] IRLR 386 547
Coote v Granada Hospitality Ltd (Case C–185/97) [1998] ECR I–5199 310
Copsey v WBB Devon Clays Ltd, 13 February 2004 575
Cosgrove v Caesar & Howie [2001] IRLR 653 291
Costello-Roberts v UK (1993) 19 EHRR 116 570
Cotter v NUS [1929] 2 Ch 58 . . . . 662, 663
Council of Civil Service Unions v Minister for the Civil Service (GCHQ Case) [1985] AC 374 . . **740**
Courtaulds Northern Textiles Ltd v Andrew [1979] IRLR 84 . . . . 114, 115, 486
Cowen v Haden Ltd [1983] ICR 1 1009
CRE v Dutton [1989] QB 783 227
Crédit Suisse Asset Management Ltd v Armstrong [1996] ICR 450 94
Crédit Suisse Ltd v Lister [1999] ICR 794 . . . . **1046**, 1049
Cresswell v Board of Inland Revenue [1984] ICR 508 . . . . **985–86**, 987
Crofter Hand Woven Harris Tweed v Veitch [1942] AC 435 . . . . 864, 871, 874, 893
Crossley v Faithful & Gould Holdings Ltd [2004] EWCA Civ 293; [2004] ICR 1615 . . . . **148**
Crossville Wales Ltd v Tracey (No 2) [1997] IRLR 691 551

Dacas v Brook Street Bureau (UK) Ltd [2004] ECWA Civ 217; [2004] ICR 1437 . . . . . . **191–93**
Daily Telegraph and Institute of Journalists (Award No 78/353) 820, 821
Dalgleish v Lothian and Borders Police Board [1991] IRLR 422 . . . . 154, 608
Danfoss. See Handels- og Kontorfunktionaerernes Forbund I Danmark v Dansk
    Arbejdsgiverforening (acting for Danfoss) (Case 109/88)
Darnton v University of Surrey 641
Davis v Friction Dynamics (2001) 952
Davis Contractors Ltd v Fareham Urban District Council [1956] AC 696 491
Dawkins v Antrobus (1881) 17 ChD 615 . . . . 712, 713
Dawkins v Department of the Environment [1993] ICR 517 227
De Souza v The Automobile Association [1986] ICR 514 . . . . **312**, 314
Decision D/18/03 672
Decision D/19/03 672
Decro-Wall International SA v Practitioners in Marketing Ltd [1971] 1 WLR 361 471
Defrenne v Sabena (No 2) (Case 43/75) [1976] ECR 455 . . . . 46, 50, 318, 319
Dekker v Stichting Vormingscentrum voor Jonge Volwassen (VJV-Centrum) (Case 177/88)
    [1990] ECR I–3941 241
Delabole Slate Ltd v Berriman [1985] ICR 546; [1985] IRLR 305 . . . . 513, 1048
Delaney v Staples [1992] ICR 483 . . . . 86, 441
Denco Ltd v Joinson [1991] IRLR 63 443
Dennison v UNISON (Decision D/12/03) 709
Denny, Mott & Dickson Ltd v James B Fraser & Co Ltd [1944] AC 265 491
Department of Transport v Gallacher [1994] ICR 967 812
Department for Work and Pensions v Thompson [2004] IRLR 248 . . . . **255–56**
DeSantis v Pacific Telephone and Telegraph Co Inc 608 F2d 327 (1979) 222
Devis (W) & Sons Ltd v Atkins [1977] ICR 662 . . . . 512, 547, 548, 549, 552
Devonald v Rosser Sons [1906] 2 KB 728 . . . . 71, **88–89**, 92
Dimbleby & Sons Ltd v NUJ [1984] ICR 386 . . . . 884, 897, 932
Discount Tobacco & Confectionery Ltd v Armitage (Note) [1995] ICR 431 . . . . 732, 737
Dixon v BBC [1979] ICR 281 495
Dixon v West Ella Developments Ltd [1978] ICR 856 740
Dodd v Amalgamated Marine Workers' Union [1924] 1 Ch 116 681
Doolan and others v UK [2002] IRLR 128 . . . . 34, 35
Douglas v GPMU [1995] IRLR 426 . . . . 672, 680

Douglas & Zeta-Jones v Hello Ltd [2001] QB 967 . . . . 568, 567
DPP v Jones [1999] 2 All ER 257 . . . . 922, 923
Drage v Governors of Greenford High School [2000] IRLR 314 507
Drane v Evangelou [1978] 2 All ER 437 943
Driscoll v Australian RMSN Co [1859] 1 F & F 458 92
Driskel v Peninsula Business Services Ltd [2000] IRLR 151 . . . . **250**, 252, **312–13**
Dryden v Greater Glasgow Health Board [1992] IRLR 469 . . . . **99–100**
Dudgeon v UK (1982) 4 EHRR 149 633
Duncan v Jones [1936] 1 KB 218 . . . . 923, 925
Dunnachie v Kingston-upon-Hull City Council [2004] UKHL 36; [2004] ICR 1052 . . . . **547–49**
Duport Steels Ltd v Sirs [1980] ICR 161 . . . . 876, 896
Durant v Financial Services Authority [2003] EWCA Civ 1746 . . . . 612, **613**, **613–14**, 615, 616, 622, 634

Eagland v BT plc [1992] IRLR 323 [1992] IRLR 323 141
Earl v Slater and Wheeler (Airlyne) Ltd [1972] ICR 508; [1973] 1 WLR 51 . . . . 528, 546
Eastwood v Magnox Electric plc [2004] UKHL 35; [2004] IRLR 732; [2004] ICR 1064 . 121, **457–59**,
    477, 549
EC Commission v UK (Case 165/82) [1984] ECR 3431 297
EC Commission v UK (Cases C–382/92 and C–383/92) [1994] ICR 664 839
Ecclestone v NUJ [1999] IRLR 166 . . . . **668–71**, 672
ECM (Vehicle Delivery Service) Ltd v Cox [1999] ICR 1162 1056
Edmonds v Lawson QC [2000] ICR 567; [2000] IRLR 391 . . . . **177**, 392
Edwards v Halliwell [1950] 2 All ER 1064 . . . . **661–63**
Edwards v Levy (1860) 2 F & F 94 443
Edwards v Mid Suffolk District Council [2001] ICR 616 245
Edwards v SOGAT [1971] Ch 354 . . . . 688, 704
Elliott Turbomachinery v Bates [1981] ICR 218 1009–10
Ellis v Brighton Co-operative Society Ltd [1976] IRLR 419 1016
Ellis v Brotherhood of Railway, Airline and Steamship Clerks 466 US 429 (1984) 749
Enderby v Frenchay Health Authority [1991] ICR 382 326
Enderby v Frenchay Health Authority (Case C–127/92) [1993]
    ECR I–5535 . . . . 271, 281, 283, 284, **326–27**
EOC v Birmingham. See *R v Birmingham City Council, ex parte EOC*
EOC v Director of Education [2001] 2 HKLRD 690 (HC Hong Kong) 239–40
Esterman v NALGO [1974] ICR 625 . . . . 683, **700–3**, 716, 717
Etam plc v Rowan [1989] IRLR 150 . . . . **294–95**
Euro Brokers Ltd v Rabey [1995] IRLR 206 90
European Roma Rights Centre v Immigration Officer at Prague Airport [2004] QB 811;
    [2005] 2 WLR 1 . . . . **239–40**
Evans v Elementa Holdings Ltd [1982] IRLR 43 1018
Evening Standard Co Ltd v Henderson [1987] ICR 588 90
Everson and Barrass v Secretary of State for Trade and Industry and Bell Lines Ltd (in
    liquidation) [2000] IRLR 202 1032
Express & Echo Publications Ltd v Tanton [1999] ICR 693 162
Express Newspapers Ltd v Keys [1980] IRLR 247 . . . . **881–82**
Express Newspapers Ltd v MacShane [1979] ICR 210; [1980] ICR 42 . . . . 895, 896, 971
Express & Star Ltd v NGA [1986] IRLR 222 935

Faccenda Chicken Ltd v Fowler [1986] ICR 297 . . . . **151–53**
Falconer v NUR [1986] IRLR 331 878
Farley v Skinner [2001] UKHL 49; [2002] 2 AC 732 460
Farnsworth Ltd v McCoid [1999] ICR 1047 . . . . **745–46**
Fechter v Montgomery [1863] 33 Beav. 22 92
Fender v Mildmay [1938] AC 1 993
Ferguson v Dawson & Partners (Contractors) Ltd [1976] IRLR 346 . . . . 158, 159, 160
Financial Techniques Ltd v Hughes [1981] IRLR 32 98

Fisher v York Trailer Co Ltd [1979] IRLR 385 957
Fitzgerald v Hall Russell & Co Ltd [1970] AC 984 . . . . 504, 505
Fitzgerald v University of Kent at Canterbury [2004] EWCA Civ 143; [2004] IRLR 300 506
Fitzpatrick v British Railways Board [1992] ICR 221 . . . . 130, 597, **733–34**
Fitzpatrick v Sterling Housing Association [2001] 1 AC 27 565
Ford v Warwickshire County Council [1983] ICR 273 . . . . **504–5**
Ford Motor Co Ltd v AUEFW [1969] 2 QB 302 . . . . **762**
Foreningen af Arbejdsledere I Danmark v Daddy's Dance Hall A/S (Case 324/86) [1988]
   ECR 739 . . . . 1042, 1047
Fortune v National Cash Register Co 373 Mass 96, 364 NE 2d 1251 (1977) 89
Foss v Harbottle (1843) 2 Hare 461 . . . . 661, 662, 663–64, 665
Foster v British Gas plc (Case C–188/89) [1990] IRLR 353 . . **45**
Foster v Musicians Union (Decision D/13-17/03) 709
Fradley v The Transport Salaried Staffs' Association (Decision D-28/30/03) 709
Francis v Kuala Lumpur Councillors [1962] 1 WLR 1411 471
Francovich and Bonifaci v Italy (Cases C–6/90 and C–9/90) [1992] IRLR 161 45
French v Barclays Bank Plc [1998] IRLR 646 . . . . **100–1**, 102, 460
Fullarton Petitioner [2001] IRLR 527 . . . . 773, **774**, 793

Gallacher v Post Office [1970] 3 All ER 712 . . . . **763**
Gardner (FC) Ltd v Beresford [1978] IRLR 63 . . . . 115, 756
Garland v British Rail (Case 12/81) [1982] ECR 359 280
Gascol Conversions Ltd v Mercer [1974] ICR 420 . . . . 139, 140
Gay Law Student Association v Pacific Telephone and Telegraph Co 19 FEP Cases 1419 (1979) . . 222
GCHQ Case. See Council of Civil Service Unions v Minister for the Civil Service
Geduldig v Aiello 417 US 484 (1974) **240**
General Billposting Ltd v Atkinson [1909] AC 118 91
General Cleaning Contractors Ltd v Christmas [1953] AC 180 148
GFI Group Inc v Eaglestone [1994] IRLR 119 90
Ghaidan v Godin-Mendoza [2004] 2 AC 557 . . . . 224, **565–66**, 570, 646
Gibbons v South West Water Services Ltd [1993] 2 WLR 507 338
Gilham v Kent County Council (No 2) [1985] ICR 233 523
Gill v Northern Ireland Council for Ethnic Minorities [2002] IRLR 74 597
Gill & Coote v El Vino Ltd [1983] 1 All ER 398 311
Gillespie v Northern Health and Social Services Boards (Case C–342/93)
   [1996] ECR I–47 . . . . 362, 363, 364
Gimbert (W) & Sons Ltd v Spurett [1967] 2 ITR 308 1009
Glasenapp v Germany (1987) 9 EHRR 25 . . . . 576, 598, 599, 600
Glasgow City Council v Marshall [2000] ICR 196 . . . . 326, **330–31**
Glasgow City Council v Zafar 332, 333, 334
GMB v Beloit Walmsley Ltd [2004] IRLR 18 831
GMB v Man Truck & Bus UK Ltd [2000] IRLR 636 1004
Gogay v Hertfordshire County Council [2000] IRLR 703 . . . . 90, 458, 461
Goodwin v Patent Office [1999] ICR 302 . . . . **232–33**
Goold (WA) (Pearmak) Ltd v McConnell [1995] IRLR 516 . . . . **143–44**, 446, 755
Goring v British Actors Equity Association [1987] IRLR 122 . . . . 648, 649, **652–55**
Gothard v Mirror Group Newspapers Ltd [1988] ICR 729 442
Government Communications Staff Federation v Certification Officer [1993] ICR 163 768
Grant v South-West Trains (Case C–249/96) [1998] ECR I–0621 224
Green (E) & Son (Castings) Ltd v ASTMS [1984] ICR 352 . . . . **825–26**, 827
Gregory v Philip Morris Ltd (1988) 80 ALR 455 453
Grieg v Community Industry [1974] ILR 256 223
Griffin v South West Water Services Ltd [1995] IRLR 15 . . . . 45, 1069
Griggs v Duke Power Co 401 US 424 (1971) **265**, 266
Grigoriades v Greece (1999) 27 EHRR 464 645
Groves v Lord Wimborne [1898] 2 QB 402 74

Grunwick Processing Laboratories Ltd v ACAS [1978] ICR 231 725
Gunton v Richmond-upon-Thames London Borough Council [1980]
    ICR 755 . . . . **450–51**, 464, 465, 466, 467

H K (An Infant), In re [1967] 2 QB 617. 673
Haddon v Van Den Bergh Foods Ltd [1999] ICR 1150. . . . . 522, 523
Hadjioannou v Coral Casinos Ltd [1981] IRLR 352. . . . . **519–20**
Hadmor Productions Ltd v Hamilton [1983] 1 AC 191 . . . . 890, 891
Halford v UK (1997) 24 EHRR 523 . . . . 562, 579, 609, **629–30**, 631, 632, 633
Halfpenny v IGE Medical Systems Ltd [1997] ICR 1007 358
Hall v Woolston Hall Leisure Ltd [2001] ICR 99. 76
Hallam Trustees (Diocese of) v Connaughton [1996] ICR 860 318
Hamlet v GMBATU [1987] ICR 150 . . . . **711–15**
Hampson v Department of Education and Science [1989]
    ICR 179 . . . . **273–74**, 275, 277, 280, 281, 282, 283, 284
*Handels- og Kontorfunktionaerernes Forbund I Danmark v Dansk Arbejdsgiverforening
    (acting for Danfoss) (Case 109/88)* [1989] ECR 3199. . . . . 278, 280, 325, 326, 327, 329
Hanley v Pease & Partners Ltd [1915] 1 KB 698 90
Hannam v Bradford Corporation [1970] 1 WLR 937. . . . . 699, 700
Hardy v Polk (Leeds) Ltd [2004] IRLR 420 550
Hare v Murphy Brothers Ltd [1974] ICR 603. 491
Harman v Flexible Lamps Ltd [1980] IRLR 418. . . . . **489**, 490
Harper v Virgin Net Ltd [2004] EWCA Civ 271; [2004] IRLR 390. 507
Harrison v Kent County Council [1995] ICR 434 . . . . **731–32**
Hatton v Sutherland [2002] EWCA Civ 76; [2002] ICR 613 . . . . **461–62**
Health & Safety Executive v Cadman [2004] ICR 378; [2004] IRLR 971 278
Heathmill Multimedia ASP Ltd v Jones [2003] IRLR 856 755
Hedley Byrne & Co Ltd v Heller & Partners Ltd [1964] AC 465. . . . . 132, 134
Henke v Gemeinde Schierke [1996] IRLR 701 1060
Henry v London General Transport Services Ltd [2002] EWCA Civ 488; [2002] ICR 910   104, **996–97**
Herbert Clayton and Jack Waller Ltd v Oliver [1930] AC 209 92
Hewcastle Catering Ltd v Ahmed [1992] ICR 626 76
Hicking v Basford Group Ltd (No 2) [2000] ICR 58 338
High Table Ltd v Horst [1998] ICR 409 . . . . **1014**
Hill v BFAWU (Decision D/31/02) 672
Hill v Chapell [2003] IRLR 19. 407
Hill v Parsons & Co Ltd [1972] Ch 305 . . . . 464, 469, **470–72**, 473, 474
Hivac Ltd v Park Royal Scientific Instruments Ltd [1946] Ch 169 126
Hodgson v NALGO [1972] 1 WLR 130 . . . . **664–65**
Hollister v NFU [1979] ICR 542 . . . . 998, **1015–16**
Holokrome (Award No 79/451) 821
Horkulak v Cantor Fitzgerald International [2004] EQCA Civ 1287; [2005] ICR 402 . . . 122, **455**
Horton v McMurtry (1860) 5 H & N 667 486
Howitt Transport Ltd v TGWU [1973] IRLR 25 937
HSBC v Madden [2000] ICR 1283 522
Hubbard v Pitt [1976] 1 QB 142 . . . . **926**
Hudson v GMB [1990] IRLR 67. 659
Hussman Manufacturing Ltd v Weir [1998] IRLR 288 . . . . **985**
Huvig v France (1990) 12 EHRR 528 . . . . 579, 633

Iceland Frozen Foods Ltd v Jones [1983] ICR 17 . . . . 517, 522, 523, 525, 526
Igbo v Johnson, Matthey Chemicals Ltd [1986] ICR 505 . . . . **496–97**, 498
ILO Freedom of Association Committee (Case No 1852) 309th Report of the Freedom of
    Association Committee, Vol LXXXI, 1998, Series B, no 1 738
Imperial Group Pension Trust Ltd v Imperial Tobacco Ltd [1991] 1 WLR 589; [1991] ICR 524 . 118, 122
Inco Europe Ltd v First Choice Distribution [2000] 1 WLR 586 523

Inter-City West Coast Ltd v RMT [1996] IRLR 583 907
Irani v Southampton and South West Hampshire Health Authority [1985] ICR 590 . . . **473–75**, 607
Irving v The Post Office [1987] IRLR 289 315
Isle of Wight Tourist Board v Coombes [1976] IRLR 413 114
Item Software (UK) Ltd v Fassihi [2004] EWCA Civ 1244; [2004] ICR 450 127

Jaeger 412
James v Eastleigh Borough Council [1990] 2 AC 751 . . . . **237–39**, 243, 244, 255
JämO [2000] IRLR 421 271
Janciuk v Winerite Ltd [1998] IRLR 63 450
Jaques v AUEW [1987] 1 All ER 621 711
Jiménez Melgar v Ayuntamiento de Los Barrios (Case C–438/99) [2001] ECR I–6915 241
John Brown Engineering Ltd v Brown [1997] IRLR 90 1024
Johnson v Unisys Ltd [2001] UKHL 13;
    [2001] ICR 480 . . . . **144–45**, **445–49**, 456, 457, 458, 459, 462, 477, 547, 549
Johnson v Nottinghamshire Combined Police Authority [1974] ICR 170 . . . . 1008, 1009
Johnston v Chief Constable of the Royal Ulster Constabulary (Case 222/84) [1986]
    ECR 1651 . . . . 297, **298**, 299
Johnstone v Bloomsbury Health Authority [1929] QB 333 . . . . 212, **991–94**
Jones v Associated Tunnelling Co Ltd [1981] IRLR 477 . . . . 145, **987–89**
Jones v Gwent County Council [1992] IRLR 521 . . . . **463**, 475
Jones v Post Office. See Post Office v Jones
Jones v Tower Boot Co Ltd [1997] ICR 254 . . . . **315**
Jones v University of Manchester [1993] ICR 474 . . . . 264, 266, 267, 269, **275–76**
Jørgensen v Foreningen af Speciallæger, Sygesikringens Forhandlingsudvalg (Case C–226/98)
    [2000] ECR I–2447; [2000] IRLR 726 . . . . 271, 279

Kalanke v Freie Hansestadt Bremen (Case C–450/93) [1996] ECR I–3051 . . . . 307, 309
Kampelmann v Landschaftsverband Westfalen-Lippe (Cases C–253/96 to C–258/96)
    [1998] IRLR 333 140
Kara v UK (Appl No 36528/97), 22 October 1998 . . . . 579, **582–83**, 633
Katsikas v Konstantinidis (Cases C–132, C–138, C–139/91) [1993] ECR I–6577; [1993] IRLR 179
    . . . . 1042, 1049
Kaur v MG Rover Group Ltd [2004] EWCA Civ 1507; [2005] IRLR 40 . . . . **108–9**
Kelly v National Society of Operative Printers (1915) 31 TLR 632 694
Kelly v Northern Ireland Housing Executive [1998] ICR 828 . . . . 179, 187
Kenny v Hampshire Constabulary [1999] ICR 27 290
Kent Free Press v NGA [1987] IRLR 267 935
Kerr v The Sweater Shop (Scotland) Ltd [1996] IRLR 424 85
Kerry Foods Ltd v Creber [2000] IRLR 10 1051
Khan v NIC Hygiene, Times online, 15 January 2005 337
Kidd v DRG [1985] ICR 405 . . . . 265, 267, 275
King v The Great Britain-China Centre [1992] ICR 516 . . . . **332–33**, 334
Kirby v Manpower Services Commission [1995] ICR 48 257
Kirshammer-Hack v Sidal (Case C–189/91) [1994] IRLR 185 51
Knowles v Fire Brigades Union [1997] ICR 595 . . . . **685–87**
Knox v Gye (1872) LR 5 HL 656 714
Kodeeswaran v The Attorney-General of Ceylon [1970] AC 1111 201
Kosiek v Germany (1987) 9 EHRR 328 . . . . **576**, 598, 599, 600
Kraus v Penna plc **638**
Kreil v Germany (Case C–285/98) [2000] ECR I–69 299
Krüger [1999] IRLR 808 271
Kuddus v Chief Constable of Leicester Constabulary [2002] 2 AC 122 338
Kutz-Bauer v Freie und Hansestadt Hamburg (Case C–187/00) [2003] ECR I–2741 . . . . . **279–80**
Kwik-Fit (GB) Ltd v Lineham [1992] ICR 183 . . . . **480–82**

Ladbroke Racing Ltd v Arnott [1983] IRLR 154 520
Ladup Ltd v Barnes [1982] ICR 107. 552
Lambeth London Borough Council v CRE [1989] ICR 641; [1990] ICR 768 . . . . **300–1**, 303
Landeshauptstadt Kiel v Jaeger (Case C–151/02) [2003] ECR I–8389 411
Landsorganisationen I Danmark v Ny Molle Kro (Case 287/86) [1989] IRLR 37. 1041
Lane v Shire Roofing Company (Oxford) Ltd [1995] IRLR 493 . . . . . . **158–60**, 166, 173, 179
Lange v Georg Schunemann GmbH [2001] IRLR 244. 137
Langston v AUEW [1974] ICR 180 92
Langston v AUEW (No 2) [1974] IRLR 182. 94
Langston v Cranfield University [1998] IRLR 172. 1027
Law v National Greyhound Racing Club Ltd [1983] 1 WLR 1302 202
Lawal v Northern Spirit Ltd 574
Lawlor v Union of Post Office Workers [1965] Ch 712 716
Lawrence v Regent Office Care Ltd (Case C–320/00) [2002] ECR I–7325; [2000] IRLR 608 . . 318, 319
Laws v London Chronicle (Indicator Newspapers) Ltd [1959] 1 WLR 698. . . . . . **442–43**
Lawson v Serco Ltd [2004] EWCA Civ 12; [2004] ICR 204 47
Leander v Sweden (1987) 9 EHRR 433 633
Lee v ASLEF (EAT/0625/03/RN) 691, 720
Lee v GEC Plessey Telecommunications Ltd [1993] IRLR 383 . . . . **996**
Lee v Showmen's Guild of Great Britain [1952] 2 QB 329 . . . . 700, 703
Lee Ting Sang v Chung Chi-Keung [1990] ICR 409. 190
Leech v Deputy Governor of Parkhurst Prison [1988] AC 533 202
Lees v Arthur Greaves (Lees) Ltd [1974] ICR 501 . . . . **494**
Lehnert v Ferris Faculty Association 500 US 507 (1991) 749
Leigh v NUR [1970] Ch 326 . . . . 659, 716
Lennon v Commissioner of Police of the Metropolis [2004] EWCA Civ 130; [2004] IRLR 385 . . 147–48
Leonard v Southern Derbyshire Chamber of Commerce [2001] IRLR 19. 234
Leonard v Strathclyde Buses Ltd [1998] IRLR 693 . . . . 550, 552
Lesney Products & Co Ltd v Nolan [1977] ICR 235 . . . . . . **1005–6**, 1008, 1009, 1010
Levez v Jennings (Harlow Pools) Ltd (Case C–326/96) [1998] ECR I–7835 338
Lewin [2000] IRLR 67. 270
Lewis v Motorworld Garages Ltd [1986] ICR 157 . . . . 118, **485**
Lightways (Contractors) Ltd v Associated Holdings Ltd [2000] IRLR 247 1058
Lister v Hesley Hall Ltd [2002] 1 AC 215 158
Lister v Romford Ice and Cold Storage Co Ltd [1957] AC 555 . . . . **80**, 147
Litster v Forth Dry Dock & Engineering Co Ltd [1989] ICR 341 . . . . **1039–40**
Liverpool City Council v Irwin [1977] AC 239. 147
Logan Salton v Durham County Council [1989] IRLR 99 . . . . **497-98**
London Ambulance Service v Charlton [1992] ICR 773. . . . . **803**
London Borough of Hammersmith & Fulham v Farnsworth [2000] IRLR 691 . . . . . **246**
London Borough of Harrow v Knight 644
London Borough of Newham v NALGO [1993] IRLR 83. 908
London Borough of Southwark v Afolabi [2003] ICR 800. 336
London Transport Executive v Clarke [1981] ICR 355; [1981] IRLR 166. . . . . . 469, 481
London Underground Ltd v Edwards (No 2) [1997] IRLR 157; [1999] ICR 494 . . . . 269, **275**
London Underground Ltd v Ferenc-Batchelor [2003] IRLR 252 755
London Underground Ltd v NUR [1966] ICR 170. . . . . 867, 907, 915, 976
London Underground Ltd v RMT [1996] ICR 170 867
Longley v NUJ [1987] IRLR 109 . . . . **716–17**
Lonrho Ltd v Shell Petroleum (No 2) [1982] AC 173 877
Lord Chancellor v Coker [2002] ICR 321 313
Luce v Bexley London Borough Council [1990] ICR 591 . . . . **808–9**
Lumley v Gye (1853) 2 E & B 216 . . . . **869**, 873, 874, 928
Lustig-Prean & Beckett v UK (1999) 29 EHRR 548 . . . . . . 224, 577, 579, 581, 631, 633
Lyon v St James' Press Ltd [1976] ICR 513 741–42
Lyons (J) & Sons v Wilkins [1899] 1 Ch 255 925

Macarthys Ltd v Smith (No 2) [1981] QB 180 318
McCabe v Cornwall County Council [2004] UKHL 35; [2004] ICR 1064 457–59
McClaren v The Home Office [1990] IRLR 338 . . . . **201-3**
McClelland v Northern Ireland General Health Services [1957] 1 WLR 594 . . . . . . **452**
MacDonald v Ministry of Defence [2002] ICR 174; [2003] ICR 937 . . . . 224, 601
McFeely v UK (1981) 3 EHRR 161 228
Mcgrath v de Soissons (1962) 112 LJ 60. 455
Machinists v Street 367 US 740 (1961) 749
McKay v Northern Ireland Public Service Alliance [1994] NI 103 597
McMaster v Manchester Airport plc [1998] IRLR 112 506
McMeechan v Secretary of State for Employment [1997] ICR 549 . . . . 165, **188-91**, 193, 196, 1031
McNamee v Cooper, The Times, 7 September 1966 . . . . 663, 664, 665
McVitae v UNISON [1996] IRLR 33 . . . . **694**, 695
Mahlburg v Land Mecklenburg-Vorpommern (Case C–207/98) [2000] ECR I–549 . . . . . . 361, 362
Mahmoud v Bank of Credit and Commerce International SA [1996] ICR 406;
  [1997] ICR 606; [1998] AC 20 . . . . 71, 92, 117, **118-21**, 122, 447, 459, 550
Mailway (Southern) Ltd v Willsher [1978] ICR 511 999
Malik. See *Mahmoud v Bank of Credit and Commercial International SA*
Malloch v Aberdeen Corporation [1971] WLR 1578. . . . . 205, 207, **445**, 448
Mallone v BPB Industries plc [2002] EWCA Civ 126; [2002] IRLR 452 . . . . **122–23**
Mandla v Dowell Lee [1983] QB 1; [1983] 2 AC 548 . . . . **225–27**, 272
Mann v Secretary of State for Employment [1999] IRLR 566. 1032
Marbe v George Edwardes (Daly's Theatre) Ltd [1928] 1 KB 269. 92
Market Investigations Ltd v Minister of Social Security [1969] 2 QB 173 . . . . . . 158, 159, **161**
Marley Tile Co Ltd v Shaw [1978] IRLR 238; [1980] ICR 72 744
Marschall v Land Nordrhein-Westfalen (Case C–409/95) [1997] ECR I–6363 . . . . . . 307, 309
Martin v MBS Fastenings (Glynwed) Distribution Ltd [1983] IRLR 198. . . . . 479, 481
Martin v South Bank University (Case C–4/01) [2004] IRLR 74 1052
Martins v Marks & Spencer plc [1998] ICR 1005 314
Massey v Crown Life Insurance Co [1978] ICR 590. 499
Matthews v Kent & Medway Towns Fire Authority [2005] ICR 84 . . . . **352**, 355
Meade v Haringey London Borough Council [1979] 1 WLR 637 877
Medhurst v NALGO [1990] ICR 687 685
Meer v Tower Hamlets [1988] IRLR 399 266
Merci convenzionale porto Genova SpA v Siderurgica Gabriella SpA (Case C–179/90) [1991] ECR
  I–5889 51
Merckx v Ford Motors Co (Belgium) (Case C–171/94) [1996] IRLR 467 . . . . 1049, 1050
Mercury Communications Ltd v Scott-Garner [1984] Ch 37; [1984] ICR 74 . . . . . . **885–86**, 892
Merkur Island Shipping Corporation v Laughton [1983] 2 AC 570. . . . 873, 876, 877, 893, 896, 901
Mersey Dock & Harbour Company v Verrinder [1982] IRLR 152 . . . . **920–21**
Messenger Newspapers Group Ltd v NGA (1982) [1984] IRLR 397 . . . . 935, **942–43**
Mid Staffordshire General Hospital NHS Trust v Cambridge [2003] IRLR 566 291
Middlebrook Mushrooms Ltd v TGWU [1993] ICR 612 . . . . **927–28**
Middlesbrough Borough Council v TGWU [2002] IRLR 333 827
Midland Plastic v Till [1983] ICR 118. 687
Miles v Wakefield Borough Council [1987] AC 539 . . . . 78, 79, 86, 944
Mingeley v Pennock and Ivory (tla Amber Cars) [2004] EWCA Civ 328; [2004] ICR 727 . . 165, **176–7**
Ministry of Defence v Armstrong [2004] IRLR 672. 331
Ministry of Defence v Jeremiah [1980] QB 87 311
Mirror Group Newspapers Ltd v Gunning [1986] ICR 145 . . . . **177–79**, 311
Monterosso Shipping Co Ltd v ITF [1982] ICR 675 762
Moonsar v Fiveways Express Transport Ltd [2005] IRLR 9 . . . . 251, 632
Moorcock, The (1889) 14 PD 64. . . . . 88, 991
Morgan v Electrolux [1991] ICR 369 523
Morissens v Belgium (1988) 56 DR 127 . . . . 644, 645
Morley v Heritage Plc [1993] IRLR 400 144

Morse v Future Reality Ltd (ET Case No 54571/95) 632
Moss v McLachlan [1985] IRLR 76 . . . . 924, 925, 964, 965
Mouta v Portugal (2001) 31 EHRR 47 586
MPB Structures Ltd v Munro [2004] ICR 430 408
MSF v GEC Ferranti (Defence Systems) Ltd (No 2) [1994] IRLR 113 . . . . **827–28**
MSF v Refuge Assurance plc [2002] IRLR 324 . . . . 825, 827
Murphy v Epsom College [1984] IRLR 271; [1985] ICR 80 1010
Murray v Foyle Meats Ltd [1999] ICR 827 . . . . 1006, **1011–13**

Nagarajan v London Regional Transport [1998] IRLR 73; [1999] ICR 877;
   [2000] AC 501 . . . . 237, 239, **257–58**, 259, 260
NALGO v National Travel (Midlands) Ltd [1978] ICR 598 826
National Sailors' and Firemen's Union v Reed [1926] Ch 536 894
National Union of Tailors and Garment Workers v Charles Ingram & Co Ltd [1977] ICR 530 . . 799
National Union of Teachers v Governing Body of St Mary's Church of England (Aided) Junior
   School [1997] ICR 334 45
Neale v Hereford & Worcester County Council [1986] ICR 471 523
Nelson v BBC [1977] ICR 649 . . . . 1012, 1013
Nelson v BBC (No 2) [1980] ICR 110 . . . . **551–52**, 1009, 1012
Nethermere (St Neots) Ltd v Gardiner [1984] ICR 612 . . . . **165**, 166, 168, 170, 187, 190
New Century Cleaning Co Ltd v Church [2000] IRLR 27 . . . . **169**
News Group Newspapers Ltd v SOGAT '82 [1986] IRLR 227 938
News Group Newspapers Ltd v SOGAT '82 (No 2) [1987] ICR 181 920
Niemietz v Germany (1992) 16 EHRR 7 . . . . **630**, 631, 632
Nimz v Freie und Hansestadt Hamburg (Case C–184/89) [1991] ECR I–297 . 278, 280, 326, 327, 329
NLRB v MacKay Radio and Telegraph Company 304 US 333 (1937) 954
Nokes v Doncaster Collieries Ltd [1940] AC 1014 438
North Riding Garages Ltd v Butterwick [1967] 2 QB 56 . . . . 985, **1006**, 1010
North West Thames Regional Health Authority v Noone [1988] ICR 813 333
North Yorkshire County Council v Fay [1985] IRLR 247 514
Northern Joint Police Board v Power [1997] IRLR 610 225
Norton Tool Co Ltd v Tewson [1972] ICR 501; [1973] ICR 45 . . . . 448, 543, **544–46**, 548, 549, 550
Notcutt v Universal Equipment Co (London) Ltd [1986] ICR 414 . . . . . . 440, **490–92**
Nottingham University v Fishel [2000] IRLR 471 . . . . **127–28**
NUGSAT v Albury Brothers Ltd [1978] ICR 62; [1979] ICR 84 . . . . **798–800**
NUM v Gormley, The Times, 21 October 1977 665
NUM v National Coal Board [1986] ICR 736 764
NWL Ltd v Woods [1979] ICR 867 . . . . 886, 926, **931–32**, 933

O'Brien v Associated Fire Alarms (1969) 1 AER 93 987
O'Kelly v Trusthouse Forte [1984] QB 90 . . . . **162–64**, 165, 166, 168, 175, 179, 190, 196
O'Laire v Jackal International Ltd [1990] IRLR 70 542
Ojutiku v Manpower Services Commission [1982] ICR 661 . . . . 273, 274, 283, 284
Owen v Professional Golf Association (2000) 255
Oy Lükenne AB v Liskojarvie and Juntunen (Case C–172/99) [2001] IRLR 171 . . . . . . **1056**

P, Re [2003] 2 AC 663 888
P v NAS/UWT [2003] ICR 386 . . . . **889–92**, 966
P v S & Cornwall County Council (Case C–13/94) [1996] ECR I–2143 . . . . 218, **220–21**
P & O European Ferries (Dover) Ltd v Byrne [1989] ICR 779; [1989] IRLR 254 . . . 946, **957–58**
Padfield v Minister of Agriculture, Fisheries and Food [1968] AC 997 . . . . 673, 674
Palmanor Ltd v Cedron [1978] IRLR 303 116
Palmer, Wyeth and the National Union of Rail, Maritime and Transport Workers v UK
   (2002) 35 EHRR 20; [2002] IRLR 128 . . . . 34, 35, 563, 732, 737, 738, 750, 752, 976
Parkes Classic Confectionery Ltd v Ashcroft (1973) 8 ITR 43 139
Parkins v Sodexho Ltd 638, 639

Parliamentary Commissioner for Administration v Fernandez [2004] ICR 123 331
Parry v National Westminster Bank plc [2004] EWCA Civ 1563; [2005] ICR 396 553
Paul v NALGO [1987] IRLR 413 . . . . **658**
Paul v National Probation Service [2004] IRLR 190 289
Pay v Lancashire Probation Service [2004] ICR 187 . . . . 536, **570–71**
Payne v Electrical Trades' Union, The Times, 14 April 1960 698
Peake v Automotive Products Ltd [1978] QB 233 311
Pearce v Governing Body of Mayfield Secondary School [2003]
    ICR 937 . . . . 224, **248–50**, 252, 315, **316**, 317, 571
Pedersen v Camden London Borough Council (Note) [1981] ICR 674; [1981] ICR 666 485
Pedersen (Hoj) (Case C–66/96) [1998] ECR I–7327 364
Pename Ltd v Paterson [1989] IRLR 19 84-85
Peninsula Business Services Ltd v Sweeney [2004] IRLR 49 140
Percival-Price v Department of Economic Development [2000] IRLR 380 173
Perera v The Civil Service Commission [1983] ICR 428 . . . . 264, 266
Peters v Netherlands (1994) 77A DR 75. 631
Peters (Michael) Ltd v Farnfield and Michael Peters Group Plc [1995] IRLR 190 142
Pfeiffer v Deutsches Kreuz, Kreisverband Waldshut eV (Cases C–397/01 to C–403/01)
    [2004] ECR I– ; [2005] IRLR 137 . . . . **44, 405, 414**
Piddington v Bates [1961] 1 WLR 162 . . . . **923–24**
Pink v White and White & Co (Earls Barton) Ltd [1985] IRLR 489 . . . . 1010, 1013
Polkey v AE Dayton Services Ltd [1988] ICR 142 . . . 207, **527–28**, 532, 1027, **1062–63**, 1069, 1071
Poparm Ltd v Weekes [1984] IRLR 388. 142
Port of London Authority v Payne [1994] IRLR 9 . . . . **540–41**, 542
Post Office v Fennell [1981] IRLR 221 . . . . **520**
Post Office v Foley [2000] IRLR 827; [2000] ICR 1283 . . . . 287, **522–25**, 529
Post Office v Jones [2001] ICR 805 . . . . **285–88**, 289
Post Office v Mughal [1977] ICR 763 502
Post Office v Roberts [1980] IRLR 347 . . . . **114–17**, 122, 214, 485
Post Office v Union of Post Office Workers [1974] ICR 378 743–44
Potter v Hunt Contracts Ltd [1992] IRLR 108 85
Powell v Brent London Borough Council [1988] ICR 176 475
Power Packing Casemakers Ltd v Faust [1983] ICR 292 . . . . 950, **956**
Preiss v General Dental Council 575
Presho v Department of Health and Social Security [1985] AC 310 . . . . **968–69**
Price v Civil Service Commission [1978] ICR 27 . . . . 218, 272
Priestley v Fowler (1837) 3 M & W 1 72
POA and Securicor Custodial Services Ltd (CAC Case No TUR 1/5/00) **836**, 837
Provident Financial Group Plc v Hayward [1989] ICR 160. 90

Qua v John Ford Morrison Solicitors [2003] ICR 482 . . . . **379**, 380
Quinn v Leathem [1901] AC 495 . . . . **870**, 872, 874, 893

R v A (No 2) [2002] 1 AC 45 565
R v Associated Octel Ltd [1996] 1 WLR 1543. 180
R v BBC, ex parte Lavelle [1982] IRLR 404; [1983] ICR 99 . . . . 202, 213, 445
R v Birmingham City Council, ex parte EOC [1989] AC 1155 . . . . 236–37, 239, 246, 252, 281
R v British Coal Corporation, ex parte Vardy [1993] ICR 720. . . . . 826, 829
R v CAC [2003] EWHC 1375 Admin; [2003] IRLR 460 175
R v CAC, ex parte BP Chemicals Ltd (Case Co/421/86) (Award No 86/1) (unreported) 820
R v CAC, ex parte BTP Tioxide Ltd (Award No 80/107); [1981] ICR 843 . . . . . **813**, 819, 820
R v Certification Officer, ex parte Electrical Power Engineers' Association [1990] ICR 682 666
R v Chief Constable of Thames Valley Police, ex parte Cotton [1990] IRLR 344 207
R v Civil Service Appeal Board, ex parte Attard. 202
R v Civil Service Appeal Board, ex parte Bruce [1988] AER 686 . . . . 202, 203
R v East Berkshire Area Health Authority, ex parte Noble [1990] IRLR 332 201

R v East Berkshire Area Health Authority, ex parte Walsh **[1984] IRLR 278;**
  [1984] ICR 743 . . . . 98, 201, **204–6**
R v Gaming Board for Great Britain, ex parte Benaim and Khaida [1970] 2 QB 417 673
R v Hertfordshire County Council, ex parte NUPE [1985] IRLR 258 203
R v Liverpool City Council, ex parte Ferguson, The Times, 20 November 1985 203
R v Lord Chancellor's Department, ex parte Nangle [1991] ICR 743 199
R v Lovegrove [1951] 1 All ER 804 714
R v Minister of Defence, ex parte Smith [1996] QB 517 . . . . 223, 286
R v Secretary of State for Employment, ex parte EOC [1994] IRLR 176 203
R v Secretary of State for Employment, ex parte Seymour-Smith and Perez [2000]
  ICR 244 . . . . 268, 269, 270, 279, 281
*R v Secretary of State for Foreign and Commonwealth Affairs, ex parte The Council of Civil Service
  Union* [1985] IRLR 28 202
R v Secretary of State for Trade and Industry, ex parte BECTU **(Case C–173/99) [2001]**
  ECR I–4881 . . . . **406–7**
R (BBC) v CAC **[2003] ICR 1542** **767**, 793
R (Gatwick Express) v CAC **[2003] EWHC 2035** **774–75**, 793
R (Kwik-Fit) v CAC [2002] ICR 1212 . . . . 772, 793, 794
R (Laporte) v Gloucestershire Constabulary [2004] EWCA Civ 1639 925
R (NUJ) v CAC [2005] IRLR 28 770
R (Wilkinson) v Inland Revenue Commissioners [2003] 1 WLR 2683 567
Racing Post. 769
***Radford v NATSOPA* [1972] ICR 484** 698, **704–5**, 715
***Radin (Susie) Ltd v GMB* [2004] ICR 893** **829**, 856
Railway Employees' Dept v Hanson 351 US 225 (1956) 749
***Rainey v Greater Glasgow Health Board* [1987] 1 AC 224** . . 274, 277, 280, 281, 323, **324–25**, 326, 330
Rao v Civil Aviation Authority [1992] IRLR 203 540
***Ratcliffe v North Yorkshire County Council* [1994] ICT 810; [1995] ICR 833** 318, 326, **327–29**
***Rayware Ltd v TGWU* [1989] ICR 457** **920**
***RCO Support Services Ltd v UNISON* [2002] EWCA Civ 464; [2002] ICR 751** **1057–58**
***Read (Richard) (Transport) Ltd v NUM (South Wales Area)* [1985] IRLR 67** **936–37**, 938
Readymix Concrete (South East) Ltd v Minister of Pensions and National Insurance [1968]
  2 QB 497 . . . . 158, 162, 178
Reda v Flag Ltd [2002] IRLR 747 456
Redmond-Bate v DPP, The Times, 28 July 1999 924
Redrow Homes (Yorkshire) Ltd v Wright [2004] EWCA Civ 469; [2004] IRLR 720 . . . . . 175, 179
Reed and Bull Information Systems Ltd v Stedman [1999] IRLR 299 312
Reeves v TGWU [1980] ICR 728 659
Regeling v Bestuur van de Bedrijfsvereniging voor de Metaalnijverheid **(Case C–125/97)**
  [1999] IRLR 379 . . . . **1031–32**
Rekvényi v Hungary (1999) 30 EHRR 519 599
Relaxion Group v Rhys-Harper [2003] ICR 867 310
Rewcastle v Safeway 22482/89 (IT) 254
***Richmond Precision Engineering Ltd v Pearce* [1985] IRLR 179** **1017**, 1018
Ridge v Baldwin [1964] AC 40 . . . . 200, 202, 204, 205
***Rigby v Ferodo Ltd* [1988] ICR 29** 467, **984**
Rinner-Kühn v FWW Spezial-Gebaudereinigung GmbH (Case 171/88)
  [1989] ECR 2743
  . . . . 278, 279, 280, 320, 325, 329
***RJB Mining (UK) Ltd v NUM* [1995] IRLR 556** **910**
RMT v London Underground Ltd [2001] IRLR 228 . . . . 904, 905, 976
***RMT v Midland Mainline Ltd* [2001] IRLR 813** **907–8**, 915
Robb v London Borough of Hammersmith and Fulham [1991] IRLR 72 475
***Robertson v British Gas Corp* [1983] ICR 351** 140, **997**
Robinson v British Island Airways Ltd [1977] IRLR 477 . . . . 1008, 1009
Robinson v Crompton Parkinson Ltd [1978] IRLR 61 115

Rockfon A/S v Specialarbejderforbundet I Danmark [1996] IRLR 168. 825
Roebuck v National Union of Mineworkeers (Yorkshire Area) (No 2) [1978] ICR 676 . . . **698–700**
Rommelfanger v Federal Republic of Germany (1989) DR 151 . . . . **577–79**
Rookes v Barnard [1964] AC 1129 . . . . 338, **872**, 873, 874, 942, 943
RS Components Ltd v Irwin [1973] ICR 535 513
RSPCA v Attorney General [2002] 1 WLR 448 692
Rutherford v Towncircle Ltd [2002] ICR 123 . . . . 268, 270
Rutherford v Towncircle Ltd (No 2) [2003] IRLR 858; [2005] ICR 119 . . . . . . **268–69, 270–71**

Safeway Stores plc v Burrell [1997] ICR 523 . . . . **1007-10**, 1012, 1018
Safouane & Bouterfas (1996) 227
Sagar v Ridehalgh & Sons Ltd [1931] 1 Ch 310 . . . . 71, **80**, 86
Sainsbury (J) Ltd v Savage [1980] IRLR 109 507
Sainsbury plc v Hitt [2002] EWCA Civ 1588; [2003] ICR 111 529
St John of God (Care Services) Ltd v Brooks [1992] ICR 715 1017
Salvensen v Simons [1994] ICR 409 76
Saunders v Earnest Neale Ltd [1974] ICR 565 . . . . **468**
Saunders v Scottish National Camps Association Ltd [1980] IRLR 174; [1981]
   IRLR 277 . . . . **534**, 535, 646
Scally v Southern Health and Social Services Board **[1992] 1 AC 294** . . . 118, 133, 144, **146–47**, 148
Scanfuture UK Ltd v Secretary of State for Trade and Industry 574
Scanlon v Carron (No 2), The Times, 24 July 1963 678
Schmidt v Austicks Bookshops [1978] ICR 85 . . . . 252, **253**, 254, 255
Schmidt v Secretary of State for Home Affairs [1969] 2 Ch 149 674
Schmidt and Dahlström v Sweden (1975) 1 EHRR 632 976
Schönheit v Stadt Frankfurt am Main (Cases C–4/02 and C–5/02) [2004] ECR I– 280
Scott v Aveling Barford Ltd [1978] ICR 214 116
Scott v Avery 716
Scott v Commissioners of Inland Revenue [2004] ICR 1410 338
Scott v Smith (unreported) 678
Scottbridge Construction Ltd v Wright [2003] IRLR 21 . . . . **395–96**
Scullard v Knowles & Southern Regional Council for Education & Training [1996] ICR 399 . . . 318
Secretary of State for Employment v ASLEF (No 2) [1972] ICR 19 . . . . 81, **97**, 956
Securicor Omega Express Ltd v GMB [2004] IRLR 9 . . . . 826, 829, 854
Seide v Gillette [1980] IRLR 427 227
Shamoon v Chief Constable of the Royal Ulster Constabulary (Northern Ireland) [2001]
   ICR 337; [2003] ICR 337 . . . . 239, **242–43**, 244, 313
Shirlaw v Southern Foundries (1926) Ltd [1939] 2 KB 206 694
Shotton v Hammond (1976) 120 Sol Jo 780 677
Shove v Downs Surgical plc [1984] ICR 532 454
Sidabras and D iautas v Lithuania(55480/00), 27 July 2004 . . . . 64, 577, 600
Sigurjonsson v Iceland (1993) 16 EHRR 462 747
Sillars v AEU, The Times, 21 March 1951 . . . . 678, 679
Sillars v AEU (No 2) (unreported) 678
Sinclair Roche & Temperley v Heard [2004] IRLR 763 335
Sindicato de Médicos de Asistencia Pública (SIMAP) v Conselleria de Sanidad y Consumo de la
   Generalidad Valenciana (Case C–308/98) [2000] ECR I–7963 . . . . . **404-5, 411**, 412
Sirdar v The Army Board & Secretary of State for Defence (Case C–273/97) [1999] ECR I–7403 . . 299
Smith v Gardner Merchant Ltd [1999] ICR 134 . . . . 224, 248, 249
Smith v Glasgow City District Council [1987] ICR 796 . . . . **513**
Smith v Safeway plc [1995] IRLR 472; [1995] ICR 868 . . . . 254, 255, 256
Smith & Grady v UK (1999) 29 EHRR 493 . . . . 224, 577, 631, 633
Sothern v Franks Charlesly & Co [1981] IRLR 278 479
South Ayrshire Council v Morton [2002] ICR 956 318
South Wales Miners' Federation v Glamorgan Coal Co [1905] AC 239 . . . . 870, 939
South West Launderettes Ltd v Laidler [1986] ICR 455 142

Speciality Care plc v Pachela [1996] ICR 633 752
***Spijkers v Gebroeders Benedik Abattoir CV* (Case 24/85) [1986]**
    ECR 1119 . . . . **1052–53**, 1055, 1056, 1057, 1058
Spillers-French (Holdings) Ltd v USDAW [1979] IRLR 339 828
***Spring v Guardian Assurance plc* [1995] 2 AC 296; [1994] ICR 596** 118, **130–34**, 135, 459
Spring v National Amalgamated Stevedores' and Dockers' Society [1956] 1 WLR 585 694
Squibb UK Staff Association v Certification Officer [1979] 2 All ER 452 768
Staffordshire County Council v Black [1995] IRLR 234 311
Standard Telephone and Cables Ltd and Association of Scientific, Technical and Managerial
    Staffs (Award No 79/484) 820, 821
Stansbury v Datapulse plc [2004] ICR 523 574
Stapp v Shaftesbury Society [1982] IRLR 326 506
Stedman v UK (1997) 23 EHRR CD 228, 562, 563, 575, 577, 583
Steel v UK (1998) 28 EHRR 603 927
Steel v Union of Post Office Workers [1978] ICR 181 . . . . 274, 283
Steinicke v Bundesanstalt für Arbeit (Case C–77/02) [2003] ECR I–9027 . . . . 271, 279
Stern (J & J) v Simpson [1983] IRLR 52 . . . . 479, 480
Stevenson v Teesside Bridge and Engineering Ltd (1971) 1 AER 296 987
***Stevenson v United Road Transport Union* [1977] ICR 893** **214**, 445, 698
Stewart v Cleveland Guest (Engineering) Ltd [1996] ICR 535 248
Stewart v Wadman Carpenter 314
Stokes v GMB (Decision D/24-27/03) 672, 709
***Stratford (J & T) & Son v Lindley* [1965] AC 269** **873**, 874, 875, 894, 895
***Strathclyde Regional Council v Porcelli* [1986] ICR 564** 246, **247**, 248, 249, 250, 312
***Strathclyde Regional Council v Wallace* [1998] ICR 205** 326, **329–30**
***Street v Derbyshire Unemployed Workers' Centre* [2004] ICR 213** **640–43**
Sunday Times v UK (1979) 2 EHRR 245 579
Sunley Turriff Holdings Ltd v Thompson [1996] IRLR 184 142
Sußman v Germany (1997) 25 EHRR 64 562
Sutherland v Hatton. See *Hatton v Sutherland*
Sutton v Revlon Overseas Corporation [1973] IRLR 173 1008
***Süzen v Zehnacker Gebäudereinigung GmbH Krankenhausservice* (Case C–13/95)**
    [1997] ICR 662 . . . . **1053–55**, 1056, 1057, 1058
***Swain v Denso Marston Ltd* [2000] ICR 1079** **149–50**
Sybron Corp v Rochem Ltd [1983] ICR 801 127
***System Floors (UK) Ltd v Daniel* [1982] ICR 54** **139–40**

Taff Vale Railway Co Ltd v ASRS [1901] AC 426 . . . . 867, 870, 871, 938
Taylor v Kent County Council [1969] 2 QB 560 1025
Taylor v NUM (Derbyshire Area) (No 2) [1985] IRLR 65 681
***Taylor v NUM (Derbyshire Area) (No 3)* [1985] IRLR 99** **661**, 663
***Taylor v Secretary of State for Scotland* [2000] ICR 595** **453**
TBA Industrial Products v Morland [1982] IRLR 331 506
Tehrani v UK Central Council for Nursing, Midwifery and Health Visiting 574
Tele Danmark (Case C–109/00) [2001] ECR I–6693 241
Tesco Stores Ltd v Pook [2003] EWHC 823; [2004] IRLR 618 127
TGWU v Dyer [1977] IRLR 93 799
Thibault (Case C–136/95) [1998] ECR I–2011 364
***Thlimmenos v Greece* (2001) 31 EHRR 14** 576, 586, **587–88**, 598, 599
***Thomas v NUM (South Wales Area)* [1985] ICR 886** **660**, 663
Thomas v Robinson [2003] IRLR 7 313
***Thomas & Betts Manufacturing Ltd v Harding* [1980] IRLR 255** **1027**
Thompson v Eatons Ltd [1976] ICR 336 956
Thomson (DC) & Co Ltd v Deakin [1952] Ch 646 . . . . 873, 876, 893, 894
Time Plan Education Group Ltd v NUT [1997] IRLR 457 871
Times Newspapers v Bartlett (1976) 11 ITR 106 987

Torquay Hotel Co Ltd v Cousins **[1969] 2 Ch 106** **874**, 875, 876, 877, 894, 895
Tottenham Green Under Fives' Centre v Marshall (No 2) **]1991] ICR 320** 300, **301**
Transco plc v O'Brien **[2002] EWCA Civ 379; [2002] ICR 721** **117**, 122
TSB Bank plc v Harris **[2000] IRLR 157** **134**
Tucht v Federal Republic of Germany (Appl No 9336/81) (1982). 645
Turner v London Transport Executive [1977] ICR 952 483
Turner v Sawdon & Co [1901] 2 KB 653 92
Turriff Construction Ltd v Bryant (1967) ITR 292 139
Turvey v CW Cheney & Son Ltd [1979] ICR 341 1027
Tynan v Balmer [1967] 1 QB 91 921

UK v Council (Case C–84/94) [1996] ECR I–5755 401
UKAPE v ACAS [1979] ICR 303 882
UKAPE v ACAS [1980] ICR 201 725
UNISON v UK [2002] IRLR 497 . . . . 888, 976
United Bank Ltd v Akhtar **[1989] IRLR 507** 100, **991**
United States of America v Silk 331 US 704 (1946) 159
Universe Tankships Inc of Monrovia v ITWF [1983] 1 AC 366 . . . . 892, 901
University College London Hospitals NHS Trust v UNISON **[1999] ICR 204** **887–88**
University of Manchester v Jones. See *Jones v University of Manchester*
University of Nottingham v Eyett [1999] ICR 721 148
University of Oxford v (1) Humphreys and (2) Associated Examining Board **[2000] IRLR 183** . . **1050**

Vakante v Governing Body of Addey and Standhope School (No 2) [2004] EWCA Civ 1065;
    [2005] ICR 231. 76
Venables v News Group Newspapers Ltd [2001] 2 WLR 1038. 568
Vento v Chief Constable of West Yorkshire Police (No 2) **[2003] ICR 318** **337–38**, 637
Vicary v BT plc **[1999] IRLR 680** **233–34**
Vine v National Dock Labour Board [1956] AC 488; [1956] QB 658 . . . . 453, 472
Virgo Fidelis Senior School v Boyle **[2004] ICR 1210** **338**, 637
Vogt v Germany **(1996) 21 EHRR 205** 563, **576**, 577, **579–81**, 598, 599, 600, 644
Von Colson and Kamann (Case C–14/83) [1984] ECR 1891 44

Wainwright v Home Office [2004] 2 AC 406 568
Waite v GCHW [1984] ICR 653 507
Walker v Amalgamated Union of Engineering and Foundry Workers 1969 SLT 150 698
Walker v Northumberland County Council [1995] IRLR 35 74
Wall v Standard Telephones & Cables Ltd [1990] IRLR 55 105
Wall v Standard Telephones & Cables Ltd (No 2) **[1991] IRLR 287** **105–8**, 1067
Wallace v United Grain Growers Ltd (1997) 152 DLR (4th) 1 446
Walton v Independent Living Organisation Ltd [2003] ICR 688 396
Wandsworth London Borough Council v D'Silva **[1998] IRLR 193** 98, **990**
Ward, Lock & Co v OPAS (1906) 22 TLR 327 925
Waters v Commissioner of Police of the Metropolis **[1997] ICR 1073; [2000] IRLR 720;**
    [2000] ICR 1064 . . . . 74, **261, 262, 460–61**
Weathersfield Ltd (tla Van & Truck Rentals) v Sargent **[1999] ICR 425** **225**, 236
Webb v EMO Air Cargo (UK) Ltd [1993] ICR 175. . . . . 241, 274, 281, 284
Webb v EMO Air Cargo (UK) Ltd (Case C–32/93) [1994] ECR I–3567 . . . . 241, 361, 362
Webb v EMO (No 2) [1995] ICR 1021 . . . . 219, 241, 244, 274
Weber v Universal Ogden Services Ltd (Case C–37/00) [2002] ICR 979 47
Wellman Alloys Ltd v Russell [1973] ICR 616. 448
Wendelboe v LJ Music ApS (Case 19/83) [1985] ECR 457 1041
West Midlands Co-operative Society Ltd v Tipton [1986] ICR 192 . . . . 512, 530
Western Excavating (ECC) Ltd v Sharp **[1978] IRLR 27; [1978] ICR 221** . . 116, 481, **482–84**, 486, 487
Wetherall (Bond St W1) Ltd v Lynn [1978] ICR 205. 484
Wheeler v Philip Morris Ltd (1989) 97 ALR 282 453

Whelan and t/a Cheers Off Licence v Richardson [1998] IRLR 114 550
Whent v T Cartlidge Ltd [1997] IRLR 153 . . . . **765**
White v Chief Constable of South Yorkshire Police [1999] IRLR 110 74
White v Kuzych [1951] AC 598 715
Whitehouse v Charles A Blatchford & Sons Ltd [2000] ICR 542 1037
Whitfield v Cleanaway 337
Whittall v Kirby [1947] KB 194 830
Wilkins v Cantrell and Cochrane (GB) Ltd [1978] IRLR 483 956
Willerby Holiday Homes Ltd v UCATT [2003] EWHC 2608 . . . . 943, 976
William Hill Organisation Ltd v Tucker [1999] ICR 291 . . . . **91–94**
Williams v Compair Maxam Ltd [1982] ICR 156 . . . . 28, 518, **1019–21**, 1027, **1062**, 1070
Wilson v Racher [1974] ICR 428 . . . . **443–45**
Wilson v St Helens Borough Council [1998] ICR 1141; [1999] 2 AC 52 . . 1040–42, 1046–47, 1048, 1049
Wilson (Joshua) & Bros Ltd v USDAW [1978] ICR 614 799
Wilson and the NUJ v UK (2002) 35 EHRR 20; [2002] IRLR 128 . . 34, 35, 563, 732, 737, 738, 750,
    752, 976
Wilsons & Clyde Coal Ltd v English [1938] AC 57 . . . . 72, 992
Wiltshire County Council v NATFHE [1980] ICR 455 495
Wiluszynski v London Borough of Tower Hamlets [1989] ICR 493 . . . . **78–79**, 86
Wise v USDAW [1996] ICR 691 . . . . 663, 664, 672
Woods v WM Car Services (Peterborough) Ltd [1981] ICR 666; [1982] ICR 692 . . 100, 118, **485–87**
Wragg (Thomas) & Sons Ltd v Wood [1976] ICR 313 . . . . **1025–26**

X v Austria (1979) 18 DR 75 631
X v Commission of the European Communities [1994] ECR I–4737 607
X v UK (1979) 16 DR 101 . . . . **581–82**, 583
X v Y [2004] EWCA Civ 662; [2004] ICR 1634 . . . . 535, 536, 570, **571–73**, 601, 631, 646
X and Y v Netherlands (1985) 8 EHRR 235. 577
XXX v YYY [2004] IRLR 137. 574

York Trailer Ltd v Sparkes [1973] ICR 518 543
Young, James and Webster v UK (Appl no 7601/76) (1977) XX YB 520; [1981] IRLR 408;
    (1982) 4 EHRR 38 . . . . 34, 577, 747
Young & Woods Ltd v West [1980] IRLR 201 . . . . 186, **499–500**

Zucker v Astrid Jewels Ltd [1978] ICR 1088 . . . . **743–44**

Table of Legislation

GERMANY

Basic Law 1949 580
Works Constitution Act
   art 77(3) 834

UNITED KINGDOM

Anti-Social Behaviour Act 2003
   s 57 919
Arbitration Act 1996 508
   Pt I 962
Asylum and Immigration Act 1986 76
British Telecommunications Act 1981 . . . 885
Children and Young Persons Act 1933 . 39, 407
   s 18 . . . . **39**
   s 18(1) **39**
   s 18(1)(a) **39**
   s 18(1)(aa) **39**
   s 18(1)(b) **39**
   s 18(1)(c) **39**
   s 18(1)(d) **39**
   s 18(1)(da) **39**
   s 18(1)(g) **39**
   s 18(1)(g)(i) **39**
   s 18(1)(g)(ii) **39**
   s 18(2) **39**
   s 18(2)(a) **39**
   s 18(2)(a)(i) **39**
   s 18(2)(a)(ia) **39**
Civil Contingencies Act 2004 965
   s 23(3)(b) 960, 965
Civil Jurisdiction and Judgments Act 1982 . 47
Companies Act 1986 . . . . 651, 662, 818
Conciliation Act 1896 960
Conspiracy and Protection of Property
   Act 1875 . . . . 869, 894, 960
   s 7 . . . . 921, 925
Consumer Protection Act 1987
   Pt 1 941
Contracts (Applicable Law) Act 1990 47
Contracts of Employment Act 1963 . . 136, 438
   s 4 139
Counter-Inflation Act 1973 703
Criminal Appeal Act 1907 714-15
Data Protection Act 1984 596
Data Protection Act 1998 (DPA) . . . 154, 597,
   601, 609, 611, 612, 613, 614, 615, 616, 619,
     620, 621, 623, 624, 628, 631, 633, 634, 734

   s 1 . . . . **612**
   s 1(1) 611, **612**, 621
   s 2 . . . . **612**
   s 6 628
   s 7 . . . . 616, 619, 620
   s 7(5) 620
   s 7(6) 620
   s 7(8) 614
   s 7(10) 614
   s 10 . . . . 619, 620, 621
   s 10(1) 620
   s 10(4) 621
   s 11 619
   s 12 619
   s 12A 619
   s 13 . . . . 616, 621
   s 13(1) 621
   s 13(2) 621
   s 13(3) 621
   s 14 621
   s 14(3) 621
   s 14(4) 621
   s 14(5) 621
   s 28 . . . . 612, 620, 623, 624
   s 29 . . . . 620, 624, 626
   s 29(1) 618, 619
   s 29(1)(a) 619
   s 35 619
   s 40 620
   s 42 620
   Sched 1, Pt I **616-17**
   Sched 1, Pt I, para 1 . . . . **616**
   Sched 1, Pt I, para 1(a) **616**
   Sched 1, Pt I, para 1(b) **616**
   Sched 1, Pt I, para 2 . . . . **617**
   Sched 1, Pt I, para 3 . . . . **617**
   Sched 1, Pt I, para 4 . . . . **617**
   Sched 1, Pt I, para 5 . . . . **617**
   Sched 1, Pt I, para 6 . . . . **617**
   Sched 1, Pt I, para 7 . . . . **617**
   Sched 1, Pt I, para 8 . . . . **617**
   Sched 1, Pt II 617
   Sched 1, Pt II, para 1(2) 618
   Sched 1, Pt II, para 2 . . . . . . 618, 622
   Sched 1, Pt II, para 3 618
   Sched 1, Pt II, para 3(d) 618
   Sched 1, Pt II, para 5 618
   Sched 1, Pt II, para 6 . . . . . . 619, 634
   Sched 1, Pt II, para 7 . . . . **619**

Sched 1, Pt II, para 7(a) **619**
Sched 1, Pt II, para 7(b) **619**
Sched 1, Pt II, para 8 619
Sched 1, Pt II, para 11 620
Sched 1, Pt II, para 11(2) 620
Sched 2 . . . . . . 616, 617, 618, 622, 623
Sched 3 . . . . 616, 617, 618, 622, 623, 624
Sched 7 154
Sched 7, para 2 618
Sched 12 . . . . **612**
Disability Discrimination Act 1995 (DDA) . 60,
    217, 218, 229, 231, 232, 235, 236, 245, 246,
    252, 257, 263, 285, 286, 288, 289, 290, 291,
    292, 303, 306, 310, 311, 312, 317, 331,
                                332, 607, 756
s 1 . . . . 230, 231, 232, 286
s 1(1) 230, 233
s 1(2) 230
s 2 246
s 2(1) **230**
s 3(5) **236**
s 3A(1) 245
s 3A(1)(b) 245
s 3A(2) 290
s 3A(3) 285, 286
s 3A(4) 285
s 3A(5) 236, 241, 285
s 3A(6) 288, 289
s 3B 252
s 4 . . . . 310, 311
s 4(2)(d) 311
s 4A **290**
s 4A(1) **290**, 291
s 4A(1)(a) **290**
s 4A(1)(b) **290**
s 4A(3) **290**
s 4A(3)(a) **290**
s 4A(3)(b) **290**
s 5(1)(a) 246
s 5(3) 286, 287, 288
s 6 290
s 6(1) 232, 290
s 8 336
s 16A 310
s 17A 334
s 18B 290
s 18B(2) 290
s 58 314
s 58(5) 314
s 59 292
s 64(7) 292
Sched 1 . . . . **230**
Sched 1, para 1(1) **230**
Sched 1, para 2(1) **230**
Sched 1, para 2(1)(a) **230**
Sched 1, para 2(1)(b) **230**

Sched 1, para 2(1)(c) **230**
Sched 1, para 2(2) **230**
Sched 1, para 3(1) **230**
Sched 1, para 4 232
Sched 1, para 4(1) **230**, 233
Sched 1, para 4(1)(a) **230**
Sched 1, para 4(1)(b) **230**
Sched 1, para 4(1)(c) **230**
Sched 1, para 4(1)(d) **230**
Sched 1, para 4(1)(e) **230**
Sched 1, para 4(1)(f) **230**
Sched 1, para 4(1)(g) **230**
Sched 1, para 4(1)(h) **230**
Sched 1, para 6 231
Sched 1, para 6(1) **230**
Sched 1, para 6(3) **230**
Sched 1, para 6(3)(a) **230**
Sched 1, para 8(1) **230–31**
Sched 1, para 8(1)(a) **230**
Sched 1, para 8(1)(b) **230**
Sched 1, para 8(1)(c) **230**
Sched 3, para 3 335
Education Act 1944
    s 25 582
    s 26 582
Emergency Powers Act 1920 965
Emergency Powers Act 1964 965
Employers' Liability (Compulsory Insurance)
    Act 1969 . . . . 74, 162, 158
Employment Act 1980 . . . . 666, 748, 896, 897,
                                        898, 916
    s 17 . . . . 896, 901, 932
Employment Act 1982 . 736, 748, 884, 932, 939
    s 9 945
Employment Act 1988 . . . . 666, 681, 748, 903
    s 3 683
Employment Act 1989 801
Employment Act 1990 . 683, 730, 748, 897, 898,
    945
    s 1 683
Employment Act 2002 . 366, 367, 382, 383, 530,
    755
    s 29 755
    s 31 25
    s 31(3) 533, 555
    s 32 24
    s 35 141
    s 38 141
    Sched 2, para 14 755
    Sched 2, Pt 1 530
    Sched 4 24
Employment Agencies Act 1973 193
    s 5(1)(eb) 193
Employment Protection Act 1975 . . . 724, 730,
        765, 768, 794, 801, 827, 830, 930, 967
    s 16 785

ss 17-21 812
s 53 . . . . 741, 783
s 99 . . . . 800, 821, 828, 830, 831
s 99(5) 827, 828
s 99(5)(b) 828
s 99(8) 830
Employment Protection (Consolidation) Act
    1978 (EPCA) 523, 803, 1042
s 27 803
s 55 204
s 57(1) 522
s 57(2) 522
s 57(3) 522
s 58 733
s 58(1)(b) 733, 734
s 122 188
Employment Relations Act 1975 793
Employment Relations Act 1999 . . 18, 62, 196,
    358, 380, 553, 597, 637, 707, 720, 725, 727,
    728, 734, 736, 737, 748, 753, 755, 757, 765,
    767, 768, 790, 794, 822, 833, 837, 844, 864,
             904, 908, 945, 947, 954, 966, 976
s 3 . . . . 597, 734
s 5 . . . . 822, 951
s 6 782
s 10 . . . . **753-54**, 755
s 10(1) **753**
s 10(1)(a) **753**, 755
s 10(1)(b) **753**, 754
s 10(2A) **753**
s 10(2A)(a) **753**
s 10(2A)(b) **753**
s 10(2B) **753**
s 10(2B)(a) **753**
s 10(2B)(a)(i) **753**
s 10(2B)(a)(ii) **753**
s 10(2B)(a)(iii) **753**
s 10(2B)(b) **753**
s 10(2C) **753**
s 10(2C)(a) **753**
s 10(2C)(b) **753**
s 10(2C)(c) **754**
s 10(3) 753, **754**
s 10(3)(a) **754**
s 10(3)(b) **754**, 757
s 10(3)(c) **754**
s 10(4) **754**
s 10(4)(a) **754**
s 10(4)(b) **754**
s 10(4)(c) **754**
s 10(5) **754**
s 10(5)(a) **754**
s 10(5)(b) **754**
s 10(6) **754**
s 10(7) **754**
s 11 . . . . 754, 755

s 12 . . . . 754, 755
s 13 . . . . **754**
s 13(4) 755
s 13(5) 755, 756
s 15 755
s 21 . . . . **194**, 195
s 21(1) **194**
s 21(1)(a) **194**
s 21(1)(b) **194**
s 21(1)(c) **194**
s 21(1)(d) **194**
s 21(2) **194**
s 31 193
s 71 365
Employment Relations Act 2004 . . . 691, 734,
    737, 739, 750, 751, 765, 773, 776, 778, 788,
        793, 864, 905, 908, 913, 933, 947, 951
Employment Rights Act (1996) (ERA) . . . 47,
    85, 180, 194, 218, 227, 241, 311, 334, 338,
    355, 356, 378, 397, 398, 424, 449, 477, 489,
    491, 496, 499, 523, 570, 571, 572, 573, 598,
             601, 607, 637, 782, 811
Pt X . . . 145, 375, 572, 782, 948, 1037, 1038
Pt XI 546
Pt XI, Ch VI 1043
Pt XII 1043
Pt XIV 503
s 1 . . . 107, 135, **136–37**, 139, 141, 142, 143,
                      144, 145, 987
s 1(1) **136**
s 1(2) **136**
s 1(3) **136**, 144
s 1(3)(a) **136**
s 1(3)(b) **136**
s 1(3)(c) **136**
s 1(4) **136**, 144
s 1(4)(a) **136**
s 1(4)(b) **136**
s 1(4)(c) **136**
s 1(4)(d) **136**
s 1(4)(d)(i) **136**
s 1(4)(d)(ii) **136**
s 1(4)(d)(iii) **136**, 137
s 1(4)(e) **137**
s 1(4)(f) **137**
s 1(4)(g) **137**
s 1(4)(h) **137**
s 1(4)(j) **137**
s 1(4)(k) **137**
s 1(4)(k)(i) **137**
s 1(4)(k)(ii) **137**
s 1(4)(k)(iii) **137**
s 1(4)(k)(iv) **137**
s 1(5) **137**
s 1(5)(a) **137**
s 1(5)(b) **137**

s 2. 145
s 2(1) 144
s 2(2) 138
s 2(4). 136, 138
s 3 . . . . 141, **143**, 144, 145
s 3(1) 138, **143**, 145
s 3(1)(a). **143**
s 3(1)(aa) **143**
s 3(1)(b). **143**
s 3(1)(b)(i) **143**
s 3(1)(b)(ii) **143**
s 4. 141
s 4(1) **145**
s 6. 138
s 7B 140
s 8. 135
s 11 141
s 12 141
s 13 . . . **84**, 87, 90, 135, 140, 397, 439, 441,
984, 985, 996
s 13(1) **84**
s 13(1)(a). **84**, 85
s 13(1)(b). **84**
s 13(2) **84**, 85
s 13(2)(a). **84**
s 13(2)(b). **84**, 85
s 14. . . . . **87**
s 14(4) 811
s 14(5). **87**, 959
ss 17-20 84
s 21 . . . . 84, 195
s 22. 84
s 24. 85
s 25(3) 86
s 27. . . . . **85–86**
s 27(1) **85**
s 27(1)(a). **85**
s 27(1)(b). **85**
s 27(1)(c). **85**
s 27(1)(ca) **85**
s 27(1)(cb) **85**
s 27(1)(d) **86**
s 27(1)(e). **86**
s 27(1)(f) **86**
s 27(1)(g). **86**
s 27(1)(h). **86**
s 27(1)(i) **86**
s 28 . . . . **999**
s 28(1) **999**
s 28(1)(a) **999**
s 28(1)(b) **999**
s 29(3) 959
s 31(2)(3) 999
s 43A 638
s 43B 637, 638, 643
s 43B(1)(a) 637

s 43B(1)(b) **637**, 638
s 43B(1)(c) **637**
s 43B(1)(d) **637**
s 43B(1)(e) **637**
s 43B(1)(f) **637**
s 43B(3). **637**
s 43B(4). **637**
s 43C 639, 640
s 43C(1)(b) 639
s 43D 639, 640
s 43E. 639, 640
s 43F. 639, 640
s 43G. 639, 640, 643
s 43G(1) 641
s 43G(1)(a). 640, 642, 643
s 43G(1)(a)(i). 641
s 43G(1)(a)(ii) 641
s 43G(1)(a)(iii) 641
s 43G(1)(a)(iv) 641
s 43G(1)(b). 641, 642, 643
s 43G(1)(c). 641, 643
s 43G(1)(d). 641, 642, 643
s 43G(1)(e). 641, 642, 643
s 43G(2) 640, 641, 642
s 43G(2)(a). 640
s 43G(2)(b). 640
s 43G(2)(c). 640
s 43G(2)(d). 640
s 43G(2)(e). 640
s 43G(2)(f) 640
s 43G(3) 641, 642
s 43H 639, 640
s 43H(2) 639
s 43J 637
s 44 844
s 45A. 398, 409, 423, 424, 844
s 45A(1). **409**
s 45A(1)(c). **409**
s 45A(1)(d) **409**
s 45A(1)(d)(i). **409**
s 45A(1)(d)(ii) **409**
s 47 844
s 47B 644
s 47B(1). 644
s 47C 374
s 50 597
s 55 . . . . 358, 497
s 56 358
s 57A **378**, 379, 380
s 57A(1). **378**, 379
s 57A(1)(a). **378**, 379, 380
s 57A(1)(b). **378**, 379, 380
s 57A(1)(c). **378**, 379
s 57A(1)(d) **378**, 379
s 57A(1)(e). **378**, 379
s 57A(2) 378, 379, 380

s 61 . . . . 843, 857
s 66(2) 356
s 63A. 58
s 71 . . . . 358, 359, 360, 365
s 71(1) 360
s 71(4) **360**
s 71(4)(a) **360**
s 71(4)(b) **360**
s 71(4)(c) **360**
s 71(7) 365
s 72 . . . . 358, 359
s 73 . . . . 358, 359, 365
s 73(1) 361
s 73(4) **360**
s 73(4)(a) **360**
s 73(4)(b) **361**
s 73(7) 365
s 74 . . . . 358, 360
s 75 358
s 75A 366
s 75B 366
s 76 358
s 77 358
s 78 358
s 79 358
s 80 358
s 80A 367
s 80B 367
s 80F 382
s 86 . . . . **438**, 506, 545
s 86(1) **438**
s 86(1)(a) **438**
s 86(1)(b) **438**
s 86(1)(c) **438**
s 86(2) **438**
s 86(3) **438**, 439, 442
s 86(4) **438**, 439
s 87(4) 440, 490
s 88 440
s 88(1)(b) 490
s 89 440
s 89(3) 490
s 92 . . . . 135, 479
s 93 479
s 94 . . . . 155, **493**, 496, 497, 498, 501, 572
s 94(1) **493**, 496
s 95. . . . . **478**, 495, 496, 497, 498
s 95(1) **478**, 483
s 95(1)(a) **478**, 483, 496, 497
s 95(1)(b) **478**, 496
s 95(1)(c) **478**, 482, 483
s 95(2) 478, 496
s 96 478
s 97 . . . . 441, **506**
s 97(1) **506**
s 97(1)(a) **506**

s 97(1)(b) **506**
s 97(1)(c) **506**
s 97(2) **506**
s 97(2)(a) **506**
s 97(2)(b) **506**
s 98 . . . . **511–12**, 572, 573
s 98(1) . . . **511**, 512, 522, 1015, 1037, 1038
s 98(1)(a) **511**
s 98(1)(b) **511**, 1045
s 98(2) **511**, 522
s 98(2)(a) **511**, 527
s 98(2)(b) **511**, 524, 527
s 98(2)(c) **511**, 527, 1038
s 98(2)(d) **511**
s 98(3) **511**
s 98(3)(a) **511**
s 98(3)(b) **512**
s 98(4) . . . 483, **512**, 514, 517, 520, 522, 526,
527, 528, 529, 530, 532, 533, 535, 546,
1015, 1017, 1018, 1020, 1037, 1038, 1045
s 98(4)(a) **512**, 529
s 98(4)(b) **512**
s 98A **529, 530**
s 98A(2) **529**, 530, 533
s 99 . . . . . . 356, 357, 365, 375, 516, 536
s 100 . . . . 515, 536, 844
s 100(1)(d)(e) 516
s 101 516
s 101A 398, **409**, 424, 516, 536, 844
s 101A(c) **409**
s 101A(d) **409**, 516
s 101A(d)(i) **409**
s 101A(d)(ii) **409**
s 102 516
s 103 . . . . 516, 844
s 103A 516, 642, 643
s 104 516
s 104A 398, 516
s 104B 516
s 104C 516
s 105 516
s 105(4) 424
s 105(4A) 409
s 108 . . . . **501**
s 108(1) **501**, 506
s 108(3) 501
s 109 . . . . 268, 507
s 109(2) 515
s 110 509
s 111(2) 335
s 112 . . . . **538**
s 112(2) **538**
s 112(2)(a) **538**
s 112(2)(b) **538**
s 112(3) **538**
s 112(4) **538**

s 113 . . . . 528, **538**, 540
s 113(a) **538**
s 113(b) **538**
s 114 1042
s 115 539
s 116 . . . . **538**, 540
s 116(1) **538**, 540
s 116(1)(a) **538**
s 116(1)(b) **538**
s 116(1)(c) **538**
s 116(3) 539, 540
s 117 540
s 117(3) 539
s 117(4)(a) 539
s 117(7) 540
s 119 543
s 119(1) 506
s 119(3) 552
s 120(1A) 555
s 120(1B) 555
s 122(2) 552
s 123 . . . . **543–44, 551**
s 123(1) **543–44**, 547
s 123(2) 548
s 123(3) 544
s 123(6) **551**
s 124 543
s 124(1) 552
s 124A 555
s 126 543
s 127 543
s 127A(1) 543
s 127A(3) 543
s 127A(4) 543
s 128 . . . . 162, 542
s 128(6) 142
s 129 542
s 129(9) 542
s 130 549
s 136 959
s 136(2) 959
s 138 1027
s 139 . . . . **1003–4**, 1008, 1014
s 139(1) 967, **1003**
s 139(1)(a) **1003**
s 139(1)(a)(i) **1003**
s 139(1)(a)(ii) **1004**
s 139(1)(b) **1004**, 1007, 1012
s 139(1)(b)(i) **1004**
s 139(1)(b)(ii) **1004**
s 140 959
s 140(2) 1002
s 141 . . . . **1025**
s 141(1) **1025**
s 141(1)(a) **1025**
s 141(1)(b) **1025**

s 141(2) **1025**
s 141(3) **1025**
s 141(3)(a) **1025**
s 141(3)(a)(i) **1025**
s 141(3)(a)(ii) **1025**
s 141(3)(b) **1025**
s 141(4) **1025**, 1027
s 141(4)(a) **1025**
s 141(4)(b) **1025**
s 141(4)(c) **1025**
s 141(4)(d) **1025**
s 142 1002
s 143 959
s 146 1025
ss 147-154 1003
s 155 1001
s 156 . . . . 268, 1001
s 156(1) 507
s 158 1023
s 162 1002
s 166 . . . . 1030, 1031, 1043
s 167 . . . . 1030, 1043
s 168 . . . . 1030, 1043
s 169 . . . . 1030, 1043
s 170 . . . . 1030, 1043
s 171 1001
s 182 . . . . 188, 1030, 1043
s 183 . . . . 1030, 1031, 1043
s 184 . . . . 1030, 1043
s 185 . . . . 1030, 1043
s 186 . . . . 1030, 1043
s 187 . . . . 1030, 1043
s 188 . . . . 1030, 1043
s 189 . . . . 1030, 1043
s 190 . . . . 1030, 1043
s 191 . . . . 199, 204, 754
s 192 . . . . 199, 204
s 193 199
s 194 204
s 194(6) 754
s 195 204
s 195(5) 754
s 198 140
s 199(1) 778
s 200 199
s 203 . . . . 196, **493, 495–96**, 497
s 203(1) **493**, 495, 498
s 203(1)(a) **493**, 778
s 203(1)(b) **493**
s 203(2)(e) 495
s 203(3) **495**, 498
s 203(3)(a) **495**
s 203(3)(b) **495**
s 203(3)(c) **495**
s 203(3)(d) **495**
s 203(3)(e) **495**

s 203(3)(f). 495
s 203(3A) 495
s 203(3A)(a) 495
s 203(3A)(b) 495
s 203(3A)(c) 495
s 203(3A)(d) 496
s 203(5) 508
ss 210–211 503
s 212 503
s 212(1) 503, 504
s 212(3) 503
s 212(3)(a) 503
s 212(3)(b) 503, 504, 505
s 212(3)(c) 503
s 212(4) 503
ss 213–15 503
s 216 . . . . 503, 959
s 217–19 503
ss 221–24 440
s 226 440
s 227 543
s 227(3) 506
s 230 . . . . 172, 175, 498
s 230(1) 172
s 230(2) 172
s 230(3) 175, 754
s 230(3)(a) 175
s 230(3)(b) 175
s 231 142
s 234 440
s 235 959
s 235(2A) 478
s 235(2B) 478
Employment Rights (Dispute Resolution)
    Act 1998 508
    s 12 510
Employment Subsidies Act 1978. 1000
Employment Tribunals Act 1996 476
    s 4 28
    s 18. 26
    s 18(2). 26, 555
    s 18(2)(a). 26
    s 18(2)(b). 26
Enterprise Act 2002 953, 1029, 1030, 1033, 1034
    Sched 16, para 3 1034
Equal Pay Act 1970 (EqPA) . . . 217, 218, 219,
    221, 235, 236, 261, 274, 277, 280, 310,
    317, 321, 322, 323, 324, 325, 327, 328, 329,
            330, 331, 334, 336, 352, 354, 356
    s 1(2)(a). 323
    s 1(2)(b). 323
    s 1(2)(c) 323, 330
    s 1(3) . . . 317, 322, 323, 324, 325, 326, 328,
                        329, 330, 331
    s 1(3)(a). 323
    s 1(3)(b). 323

s 1(4) 322
s 1(5). 322, 323
s 1(6) 318, 321, 322, 323
s 1(6)(c) 317
s 2(4) 336
s 2(5) 338
s 2ZA 336
s 2ZB 338
s 2ZC 338
Equal Pay (Northern Ireland) Act 1970 . 218–19
European Communities Act 1972. . . . 43, 293
    s 29(2) 194
European Parliamentary Elections Act 1978 592
Fair Employment (Northern Ireland) Act 1976
    179
Finance Act 1922 74
Finance Act 2000
    s 60 186
    Sched 8. 17
    Finance (No 2) Act 1975. 189
    Finance (No 2) Act 1987. 101
    Fire and Rescue Services Act 2004 . . . 879
    Freedom of Information Act 2000 . . . 616
    Friendly Societies Act 1974 651
    Gender Recognition Act 2004 218, 295, 296
    Health and Safety at Work etc Act 1974. 10,
        11, 12, 74, 179, 822
    s 2 . . . . 11, 16, 148
    s 2(1) 11
    s 2(2) 11, 148
    s 2(2)(a) 11
    s 2(2)(b) 11
    s 2(2)(c) 148
    s 2(4). 16
    s 2(6) 16
    s 2(7) 16
    s 3 11
    s 3(1) 179
    s 4. . . . . 11, 180
    s 5 11
    s 6 11
    s 7 11
    s 15. 11
    s 15(1) 11
    s 19. 11
    s 19(1) 11
    s 21. 11
    s 21(a) 11
    s 21(b) 11
    s 22. 11
    s 22(1) 11
    s 22(2) 11
    s 33. 11
    s 33(1) 11
    s 33(1)(a). 11
    s 33(1)(c). 11

s 33(1)(g). **11**, 12
s 33(1A) **11**
s 33(1A)(a) **12**
s 33(1A)(b) **12**
s 33(2A) **12**
s 33(2A)(a) **12**
s 33(2A)(b) **12**
Highways Act 1980
s 137. . . . . 917, **922**
House of Commons Disqualification Act
1975. 592
Human Rights Act 1998 (HRA) . . 35, 64, 128,
154, 211, 218, 220, 221, 222, 224, 256, 509,
515, 535, 536, 561, 562, 564, 565, 567,
568–69, 570, 572, 573, 574, 575, 587,
591, 598, 601, 616, 628, 631, 633, 634, 636,
646, 720, 730,732, 750, 770, 793, 916,
923, 927, 976
s 2. 571
s 2(1) **564**
s 2(1)(a). **564**
s 2(1)(b). **564**
s 2(1)(c). **564**
s 2(1)(d). **564**
s 3 . . 565, 566, 568, 570, 572, 573, 616, 628,
631, 633, 634
s 3(2)(b). 566
s 3(2)(c) 566, 568, 634
s 4(2) 567
s 4(3) 567
s 6 . . . . 568, 572, 573, 631, 633
s 6(1). 567, 572
s 6(2). **567**, 568, 570, 572, 634
s 6(2)(a). **567**
s 6(2)(b). **567**, 568
s 6(3)(a). 567
s 6(3)(b). 568
s 6(5) 568
s 7 . . . . 211, 568, 631
s 10 567
s 55 635
s 55(2)(b) 635
Sched 2 . . . . 567, 635
Immigration Act 1971 76
Income and Corporation Tax Act 1988
s 134 194
Income and Corporation Taxes Act 1970. . 986
Income Tax (Employments) Act 1943 74
Industrial Courts Act 1919 960
Industrial and Provident Societies Act 1965 651
Industrial Relations Act 1971 . . . . . . 81, 97,
178, 470, 472, 474, 483, 544, 729, 748, 765,
812, 875, 935, 939, 960
s 116. . . . . 548, 549
s 116(1) 547, 548
s 116(2). 548

s 123 548
s 123(1) 548, 549
s 134 922
s 167(1) 178
Industrial Tribunals Act 1996
s 21 485
Insolvency Act 1986
Pt 1 1031
s 8(3) 1034
s 19 1034
Sched 6 1030
Interception of Communications Act
1985. . . . . 609, 630
Jobseekers Act 1995. 60
s 14 . . . . **966–67**
s 14(1) **966**, 967
s 14(1)(a) **966**
s 14(1)(b) **966**
s 14(2). **966–67**
s 14(3) **967**
s 14(3)(a) **967**
s 14(3)(b) **967**
s 14(3)(c) **967**
s 14(4) **967**
s 14(5) **967**
s 19 . . . . **554**
s 19(1) **554**
s 19(3) **554**
s 19(4) **554**
s 19(4)(a) **554**
s 19(4)(b) **554**
s 19(5) 554
s 19(6) 554
s 35 967
Law Reform (Personal Injuries) Act 1948 . . 72
Learning and Skills Act 2000. 58
Local Government Act 1972
s 270 657
Local Government Act 1988 101
Local Government Act 2003
s 101. 1060
s 102. 1060
Local Government and Housing Act 1989
(LGHA 1989) 593
s 2. 593
s 2(2) 594
s 2(3)(a). 593
s 2(3)(b). 593
s 3. 594
Local Government (Scotland) Act 1973
s 235 657
Municipal Corporations Act 1882 205
National Insurance Act 1911 . . . . . . 74, 967
National Insurance (Industrial Injuries)
Act 1946 74

National Minimum Wage Act 1998 . . . 12, 60,
170, 174, 177, 387, 388, 647
s 1(2) 392
s 10 397
s 10(6) 397
s 11 397
s 14 398
s 17 . . . . **12–13**, 73, 397
s 17(1) **12**
s 17(2) **12**
s 17(2)(a) **13**
s 17(2)(b) **13**
s 18 397
s 19 398
s 20 398
s 21 398
s 23 398
s 25 398
s 28 397
s 34 . . . . 194, 392
s 35 . . . . 170, 392
s 37 392
s 41 . . . . 194, 392
s 43 392
s 44 . . . . 174, 392
s 45 392
s 54(3)(b) 392
Northern Ireland Act 1998 591
s 75 591
s 76 591
Official Secrets Act 1989 636
Pension Schemes Act 1993 . . . . . . 29, 1052
Pensions Act 2004 . . . . 1030, 1052
Police Act 1996
s 64 594
s 89 . . . . **923**
s 89(2) **923**
s 91 . . . . 200, 960
Police and Criminal Evidence Act 1984
s 4 965
s 24 923
Postal Services Act 2000
ss 83-84 960
Prevention of Crimes Act 1885
s 2 924
Public Interest Disclosure Act 1998
(PIDA 1998) . . 636, 637, 638, 639, 640, 641,
642, 643, 644, 645
Public Order Act 1986 922
s 14 918
Public Schools (Scotland) Teachers
Act 1882 205
Race Relations Act 1976 (RRA) . . . 217, 218,
220, 225, 226, 227, 235, 236, 239, 245, 251,
252, 256, 257, 263, 264, 265, 266, 267, 271,
274, 277, 280, 283, 284, 288, 292, 296, 299,
300, 301, 302, 306, 307, 310, 311, 312, 314,
315, 317, 332, 334, 337, 680, 757
s 1 . . . . 224, **235**, 259, 260
s 1(1) **264**
s 1(1)(a) 258, 259
s 1(1)(b) **264**
s 1(1)(b)(i) **264**
s 1(1)(b)(ii) **264**, 273, 277
s 1(1)(b)(iii) **264**
s 1(1A) **263**, 264
s 1(1A)(a) **263**
s 1(1A)(b) **263**
s 1(1A)(c) **263**, 265
s 2 . . . . **257**, 259, 260
s 2(1) 258
s 3 . . . . **224–25**
s 3(1) **224**, 225, 226, **257**
s 3(1)(a) **257**
s 3(1)(b) **257**
s 3(1)(c) **257**
s 3(1)(d) **257**
s 3(2) **225**, **257**
s 3(4) 236, 241, 267
s 3A **251**
s 3A(1) **251**, 252
s 3A(1)(a) **251**
s 3A(1)(b) **251**
s 3A(2) **251**, 252
s 4 . . . . 292, **310**, 311
s 4(1) **310**
s 4(1)(a) 302, **310**
s 4(1)(b) **310**
s 4(1)(c) 302, **310**
s 4(2) **310**
s 4(2)(a) **310**
s 4(2)(b) 302, **310**
s 4(2)(c) 302, **310**, 311, 316
s 4(2)(d) **310**
s 4A 301, **302**
s 4A(1) **302**
s 4A(1)(a) **302**
s 4A(1)(b) **302**
s 4A(1)(c) **302**
s 4A(2) **302**
s 4A(2)(a) **302**
s 4A(2)(b) **302**
s 4A(2)(c) **302**
s 4A(2)(c)(i) **302**
s 4A(2)(c)(ii) **302**
s 5 . . . . 293, 296, 301, 302
s 5(1) 293
s 5(2) **296**
s 5(2)(a) **296**
s 5(2)(b) **296**
s 5(2)(c) **296**
s 5(2)(d) 296, 300, 301

s 5(3) 296
s 5(4) 296
s 8(1) 47
s 10 292
s 11 680
s 27A 310
s 32 . . . . 314, 315
s 32(3) 314, 315
s 35 307
s 37 307
s 38 307
s 41 . . . . 273, 292
s 42 292
s 54A **334**
s 54A(2) **334**
s 54A(2)(a) **334**
s 56 336
s 56(a) 336
s 56(b) 336
s 56(c) 336
s 57ZA **334**
s 57ZA(2) **334**
s 57ZA(2)(a) **334**
s 65(2)(b) 333
s 68 335
s 74 292
s 76(6) 335
s 78 177
Redundancy Payments Act 1965. 483, 546, 1001
Regulation of Investigatory Powers Act 2000
    (RIPA) 609, 610, 611, 616, 628, 630,
                                          631, 633
s 1(3) **609**, 634
s 1(3)(a) **609**
s 1(3)(b) **609**
s 1(5) 610
s 1(6) 609
s 2(7) 609
s 2(8) 609
s 3 610
s 4 610
s 4(2) 634
s 5 610
s 78(5) 634
s 81 609
Rent Act 1977 565
Sched 1, para 2 566
Representation of the People Act 1949 . . . 680
Road Traffic Act 1972 965
Road Traffic Acts 830
Security Service Act 1989 590
Sex Discrimination Act 1975 (SDA) (amended
    1999 and 2001) . . . 178, 217, 218, 219, 220,
    221, 222, 224, 225, 235, 236, 238, 240, 241,
    242, 244, 245, 247, 248, 250, 253, 255, 257,
    261, 262, 263, 264, 265, 266, 267, 269, 270,
    271, 272, 274, 277, 280, 283, 284, 288, 292,
    296, 297, 299, 300, 306, 307, 310, 311, 312,
    313, 315, 317, 327, 329, 331, 332, 333, 334,
                    337, 355, 356, 365, 680, 741, 757
Pt 2 334
s 1 . . . . **235–36**, 259
s 1(1) 241
s 1(1)(a) 237, 238, 247, 248, 249
s 1(1)(b) 239, 325
s 1(1)(b)(ii) 325
s 1(2) **263**
s 1(2)(b) **263**
s 1(2)(b)(i) **263**
s 1(2)(b)(ii) **263**, 277
s 1(2)(b)(iii) **263**
s 2(3) 221
s 2A **221**
s 2A(1) **221**
s 2A(3) **221**
s 2A(3)(a) **221**
s 2A(3)(b) **221**
s 3 1019
s 4 . . . . 257, 259, 261
s 4(1) 261
s 4(1)(d) 261
s 4A(1) 252
s 4A(1)(a) 252
s 4A(1)(b) 252
s 4A(1)(c) 252
s 4A(3) 252
s 5(3) 222, 223, 236,
            241, 243, 244, 245, 253, 267
s 6 . . . . 310, 311, 313
s 6(2) 253
s 6(2)(b) 261, 311
s 6(2)(c) 311
s 7 . . . . **293–94**
s 7(1) 293
s 7(2) **293**, 294
s 7(2)(a) **293**, 294, 296
s 7(2)(b) **293**, 294, 297
s 7(2)(b)(i) **293**
s 7(2)(b)(ii) **293**
s 7(2)(ba) **294**
s 7(2)(ba)(i) **294**
s 7(2)(ba)(ii) **294**
s 7(2)(c) **294**, 297
s 7(2)(c)(i) **294**
s 7(2)(c)(ii) **294**, 296, 297
s 7(2)(d) **294**, 296, 297
s 7(2)(d)(i) **294**
s 7(2)(d)(ii) **294**
s 7(2)(d)(iii) **294**
s 7(2)(e) **294**, 296, 297, 300
s 7(2)(g) **294**, 297
s 7(2)(h) **294**, 297

s 7(3). **294**, 296
s 7(4). **294**, 296
s 7(4)(a) **294**
s 7(4)(b) **294**
s 7(4)(c) **294**
s 7A 295
s 7A(b) 295
s 7B **295**
s 7B(2) 295
s 7B(2)(a) **295**, 299
s 7B(2)(b) **295**
s 7B(2)(b)(i) **295**
s 7B(2)(b)(ii) **295**
s 7B(2)(c) **295**
s 7B(2)(c)(i) **295**
s 7B(2)(c)(ii) **295**
s 7B(2)(d) **295**
s 7B(3) **295**
s 10(1) 47
s 12 680
s 17 292
s 18 292
s 19 292
s 20A 310
s 41 . . . . 314, 315
s 41(3) 314
s 47 307
s 47(3) 307
s 48 307
s 49 307
s 51 292
s 51A 292
s 55 257
s 63A(2) **334**
s 63A(2)(a) **334**
s 65 336
s 65(a) 336
s 65(b) 336
s 65(c) 336
s 66 335
s 66A 334
s 76 . . . . **335**
s 76(1) **335**
s 76(5) **335**
s 82(1) **176**, 178
Social Security Act 1975
  s 19 968
  s 19(1) 968
Social Security Contributions and Benefits Act
  1992 . . . . 367, 969
  s 126 969
  s 164(4) 364
Social Security (No 2) Act 1980 969
Tax Credits Act 2002 60
Trade Boards Act 1909 388
Trade Boards Act 1918 . . . . 14, 724

Trade Disputes Act 1906 . . . . . 867, 870, 871,
  872, 875, 889, 894, 916, 920, 938, 967, 971
  s 1 . . . . 870, 871, 872
  s 2 916
  s 3 871
  s 3(2) 879
  s 4 . . . . 871, 938
Trade Disputes Act 1965 874
Trade Disputes and Trade Unions
  Act 1927 . . . . 656, 894
Trade Union Act 1871 . . . . 681, 717, 938, 939
  s 4 717
Trade Union Act 1913 . . . . 655, 656, 658, 680
Trade Union Act 1984 . . . . 656, 666, 902, 975
Trade Union and Labour Relations Act 1974
  (TULRA) 681, 729–30, 748, 879, 884,
                939, 971, 973, 974
  s 13 . . . . **875**, 879, 881, 882
  s 13(1) **875**, 877
  s 13(1)(a) **875**
  s 13(1)(b) **875**
  s 13(2) **875**, 877, 879
  s 13(3) **875**, 877, 879
  s 13(3)(a) **875**
  s 13(3)(b) **875**
  s 13(4) **875**
  s 15 916
  s 16 878
  s 17 930
  s 29(1) 886
Trade Union and Labour Relations (Consolidation) Act (TULRCA) 1992 . . . **26**, 29, 194,
  601, 659, 681, 691, 707, 719, 745, 748,
  804, 811, 819, 822, 826, 829, 879, 899, 903,
          947, 959, 962, 967, 972, 973, 974, 976
  Pt I, Ch V 686
  Pt V 686, 880, 900
  s 1 . . . . 649, **651**, 754, 839
  s 1(a) **651**
  s 1(b) **651**
  s 1(b)(i) **651**
  s 1(b)(ii) **651**
  s 2 . . . . 30, 768
  s 3 768
  s 4 768
  s 5 . . . . 30, 767, 768, 848
  s 5(a) 767
  s 5(b) 767, 768
  s 6 . . . . 30, 767, 768, 835
  s 7 768
  s 8 768
  s 9 768
  s 10 . . . . **651**
  s 10(1) **651**
  s 10(1)(a) **651**
  s 10(1)(b) **651**

s 10(1)(c) 651
s 10(2) 651
s 10(3) 651
s 10(3)(a) 651
s 10(3)(b) 651
s 15 652
s 20 . . . . 940–41, 954
s 20(1) 940
s 20(1)(a) 940
s 20(1)(a)(i) 940
s 20(1)(a)(ii) 940
s 20(1)(b) 940
s 20(2) 940
s 20(2)(a) 940
s 20(2)(b) 940
s 20(2)(c) 940, 941
s 20(3) 940
s 20(3)(a) 940
s 20(3)(b) 940
s 20(4) 940
s 20(5) 940
s 20(6) 940
s 20(6)(a) 940
s 20(6)(b) 940
s 20(7) 941
s 21 . . . . 941, 949, 954
s 21(1) 941
s 21(2) 941
s 21(2)(a) 941
s 21(2)(b) 941
s 21(2)(b)(i) 941
s 21(2)(b)(ii) 941
s 21(3) 941
s 21(4) 941
s 21(5) 941
s 21(6) 941
s 21(6)(a) 941
s 21(6)(b) 941
s 21(7) 941
s 21(7)(a) 941
s 21(7)(b) 941
s 22 . . . . 941, 954
s 22(1) 941
s 22(1)(a) 941
s 22(1)(b) 941
s 22(1)(c) 941
s 22(2) 942
s 25 . . . . 30, 707
s 28 681-82
s 28(1) 681
s 28(1)(a) 681, 682
s 28(1)(b) 682
s 28(2) 682
s 29 681
s 29(1) 682
s 29(2) 682

s 29(2)(a) 682
s 29(2)(b) 682
s 29(3) 682
s 30 . . . . 681, 682
s 30(1) 682
s 31 . . . . 30, 682
s 32 707
s 32A 682
s 37A 707
s 37B 30, 707
ss 37C–37E 707
s 46 666–67
s 46(1) 666, 667
s 46(1)(a) 666
s 46(1)(b) 666
s 46(2) 666
s 46(2)(a) 666
s 46(2)(b) 666
s 46(2)(c) 666
s 46(2)(d) 666
s 46(3) 667
s 46(4) 667
s 46(4)(a) 667
s 46(4)(b) 667
s 46(4)(c) 667
s 46(4A) 667
s 46(4A)(a) 667
s 46(4A)(b) 667
s 46(4A)(c) 667
s 46(4A)(c)(i) 667
s 46(4A)(c)(ii) 667
s 46(4A)(d) 667
s 46(5) 667
s 46(5A) 667
s 46(5B) 667
s 46(6) 667
s 47 . . . . . . 659, 666, 667, 668, 670, 672
s 47(1) 667
s 47(2) 667
s 47(3) 668, 671
s 48 . . . . 666, 667, 668
s 49 . . . . 666, 667, 668
s 50 . . . . 666, 667, 668
s 51 . . . . 666, 667, 668
s 51A 668
s 52 . . . . 666, 667
s 55 . . . . 30, 668
s 56 . . . . 668, 671
s 62 . . . . 683, 686
s 63 716
s 64 . . . . 683, 684, 685, 719, 720
s 64(1) 684
s 64(2) 684
s 64(2)(a) 684
s 64(2)(b) 684
s 64(2)(c) 684

s 64(2)(d) 684
s 64(2)(e) 684
s 64(2)(f) 684
s 64(3) 684
s 64(4) 684
s 64(5) 684
s 65 . . . . 683, 684, 685, 686, 690, 719, 720
s 65(1) 684
s 65(1)(a) 684
s 65(1)(b) 684
s 65(2) 684
s 65(2)(a) 684, 686
s 65(2)(b) 684
s 65(2)(c) 684-85
s 65(2)(d) 685
s 65(2)(d)(i) 685
s 65(2)(d)(ii) 685
s 65(2)(e) 685
s 65(2)(f) 685
s 65(2)(g) 685
s 65(2)(h) 685
s 65(2)(i) 685
s 65(2)(j) 685
s 65(6) 684
s 66 . . . . 684, 685, 719
s 66(4) 684
s 67 . . . . 684, 685, 719
s 68 811
s 72 . . . . 649, 657
s 72(1) 657
s 72(1)(a) 657
s 72(1)(b) 657
s 72(1)(c) 657
s 72(1)(d) 657
s 72(1)(e) 657
s 72(1)(f) 657, 658
s 72(2) 657
s 72(3) 657
s 72(4) 657
s 73 656
s 82 659
s 86(1) 811
s 108A 30
s 108A(2) 708
s 108A(2)(b) 709
s 108A(2)(d) 709
s 119 754
s 137 . . . . 597, 655, 730, 731, 732, 746, 748
s 137(1) 730, 731
s 137(1)(a) 730, 731, 732
s 137(1)(b) 730
s 137(1)(b)(i) 730
s 137(1)(b)(ii) 730
s 137(2) 730
s 138 . . . . 730, 731
s 139 730

s 140 . . . . 730, 731
s 141 730
s 142 . . . . 730, 731
s 143 730
s 144 . . . . 730, 796
s 145 . . . . 730, 796
s 145A 735, 739, 750-51
s 145A(1) 750, 751
s 145A(1)(a) 750
s 145A(1)(b) 750
s 145A(1)(c) 750
s 145A(1)(d) 750
s 145A(2) 750, 751
s 145A(2)(a) 750
s 145A(2)(b) 750
s 145A(3) 750
s 145A(4) 751
s 145A(4)(a) 751
s 145A(4)(b) 751
s 145A(5) 751
s 145B 739, 750-51, 783
s 145B(1) 751
s 145B(1)(a) 751
s 145B(1)(b) 751
s 145B(2) 751
s 145B(3) 751
s 145B(4) 751
s 145B(5) 751
s 145D(4) 751
s 145D(4)(a) 751
s 145D(4)(b) 751
s 145D(4)(c) 751
s 146 . . . . 730, 731, 732, 734, 735-36, 737,
739, 741, 745, 746, 751, 752, 754, 755,
781, 783, 812
s 146(1) 731, 735, 745
s 146(1)(a) 735
s 146(1)(b) 735, 745, 746
s 146(1)(ba) 735
s 146(1)(c) 735
s 146(2) 735, 743
s 146(2)(a) 735
s 146(2)(b) 735, 743, 744
s 146(2A) 735
s 146(2A)(a) 735
s 146(2A)(b) 735
s 146(2B) 735
s 146(2C) 735
s 146(2D) 735
s 146(3) 735, 749
s 146(4) 735-36
s 146(5) 736
s 146(5A) 736
s 146(5A)(a) 736
s 146(5A)(b) 736
ss 147-51 730

s 152 . . . 516, 730, 731, 732, 733, 736, 737, 746, 751, 752, 781, 812
s 152(1)(a) 732
s 152(1)(b) 732
s 152(2) 731
s 152(3) 749
s 153 . . . . 516, 730, 736
s 154 730
s 155 . . . . 551, 730
ss 156-60 730
ss 161-67 . . . . 730, 736
s 168 . 597, 744, 786, **801**, 803, 808, 810, 858
s 168(1) 754, **801**
s 168(1)(a) **801**, 808
s 168(1)(b) **801**
s 168(1)(c) **801**
s 168(2) **801**
s 168(2)(a) **801**
s 168(2)(b) **801**
s 168(3) 754, **801**
s 168(4) 754, **801**
s 168A **804–5**, 810
s 168A(1) **804**, 805, 807
s 168A(1)(a) **804**
s 168A(1)(b) **804**
s 168A(2) **804**, 805, 807
s 168A(2)(a) **804**
s 168A(2)(a)(i) **804**
s 168A(2)(a)(ii) **804**
s 168A(2)(a)(iii) **804**
s 168A(2)(a)(iv) **804**
s 168A(2)(b) **804**
s 168A(2)(c) **804**
s 168A(3) **804**
s 168A(3)(a) **804**
s 168A(3)(b) **804**
s 168A(4) **805**
s 168A(4)(a) **805**
s 168A(4)(b) **805**
s 168A(4)(c) **805**
s 168A(8) **805**
s 169 . . . . 597, 754, 786, 810
s 170 . . . . 597, 786, **807**, 808
s 170(1) **807**, 808
s 170(1)(a) 807
s 170(1)(b) 807
s 170(2) 807, 808
s 170(2A) 807
s 170(2B) 807
s 170(2C) 807
s 170(3) 807
s 170(4) 807
s 170(5) 807
s 170(5)(a) 807
s 170(5)(b) **807**
s 171 . . . . 597, 754, 786

s 172 . . . . 597, 754, 786
s 173 . . . . 597, 754, 786
s 173(1) 809
s 174 . . . . 689, **690**, 691, 692, 720
s 174(1) **690**
s 174(2) **690**
s 174(2)(a) **690**
s 174(2)(b) **690**
s 174(2)(c) **690**
s 174(2)(d) **690**, 691
s 174(3) **690**
s 174(3)(a) **690**
s 174(3)(b) **690**
s 174(3)(c) **690**
s 174(4) **690**
s 174(4)(a) **690**
s 174(4)(a)(iii) 691, 692
s 174(4)(b) **690**
s 174(4)(c) **690**
s 174(4A) **690**, 691
s 174(4B) **690**
s 174(5) 690
s 175 690
s 176 691
s 178 . . . . **798**
s 178(1) **798**
s 178(2) **798**, 801
s 178(2)(a) **798**
s 178(2)(b) **798**
s 178(2)(c) **798**
s 178(2)(d) **798**
s 178(2)(e) **798**
s 178(2)(f) **798**
s 178(2)(g) **798**
s 178(3) **798**
s 179 . . . . **102**, 110, 762, 1067
s 179(1) **102**
s 179(1)(a) **102**
s 179(1)(b) **102**
s 180 . . . . **110**, 763
s 180(1) **110**
s 180(2) **110**
s 180(2)(a) **110**
s 180(2)(b) **110**
s 180(2)(c) **110**
s 180(2)(d) **110**
s 180(3) **110**
s 181 . . . . 786, **812–13**, 815, 816
s 181(1) **812–13**, 819
s 181(2) 150, **813**, 820
s 181(2)(a) **813**
s 181(2)(b) **813**
s 181(3) **813**
s 181(4) **813**
s 181(5) **813**
s 182 . . . . 786, 813, **815**, 816, 818

s 182(1) 815
s 182(1)(a) 815
s 182(1)(b) 815
s 182(1)(c) 815, 816, 817
s 182(1)(d) 815
s 182(1)(e) 815, 816, 818
s 182(1)(f) 815
s 182(2) 815
s 182(2)(a) 815
s 182(2)(b) 815
s 183 . . . . 786, 813, 819
s 184 . . . . 786, 813
s 185 . . . . 150, 786, 813, 819, 821
s 186 796
s 187 796
s 188 . . . . 801, 823–24, 825, 826, 827, 829,
                              842, 853, 1063
s 188(1) 823
s 188(1A) 823, 830
s 188(1A)(a) 823, 824
s 188(1A)(b) 823, 824
s 188(1B) 823
s 188(1B)(a) 823
s 188(1B)(b) 823
s 188(1B)(b)(i) 823
s 188(1B)(b)(ii) 823, 842
s 188(2) 823, 827, 830, 1028
s 188(2)(a) 823
s 188(2)(b) 823
s 188(2)(c) 823
s 188(3) 823
s 188(4) 823, 827, 829, 830
s 188(4)(a) 823
s 188(4)(b) 823
s 188(4)(c) 823, 829
s 188(4)(d) 823
s 188(4)(e) 824
s 188(4)(f) 824, 829
s 188(5) 824, 827, 829
s 188(5A) 824, 844, 858
s 188(6) 824
s 188(7) 824, 830, 831
s 188(7A) 824
s 188(7A)(a) 824
s 188(7A)(b) 824
s 188(7B) 824
s 188(8) 824
s 188A 842–43
s 188A(1) 823, 842
s 188A(1)(a) 842
s 188A(1)(b) 842
s 188A(1)(c) 842
s 188A(1)(d) 842
s 188A(1)(e) 842
s 188A(1)(f) 842
s 188A(1)(g) 842

s 188A(1)(h) 842–43
s 188A(1)(i) 843
s 188A(1)(i)(i) 843
s 188A(1)(i)(ii) 843
s 189 . . . . 150, 824, 829, 853, 1063
ss 190–192 . . . . 824, 853, 1063
ss 193–194 . . . . 1063, 1064
s 195 . . . . 824, 1004, 1063
s 195(1) 1004
ss 196–198 1063
s 199 908
s 209 26
s 210 961
s 210(1) 26, 961
s 210(2) 961
s 210(3) 961
s 212 . . . . 27, 962
s 212(1) 962
s 212(1)(a) 962
s 212(1)(b) 962
s 212(2) 962
s 212(3) 962
s 212(3)(a) 962
s 212(3)(b) 962
s 212(4) 962
s 212(4)(a) 962
s 212(4)(b) 962
s 212(5) 962
s 213 962
s 214 962
s 215 963
s 218 . . . . 961, 962
s 219 . . . 879, 880, 889, 917, 930, 932, 948,
                                   950, 952
s 219(1) 879
s 219(1)(a) 879
s 219(1)(b) 879
s 219(2) 879
s 219(3) 917
s 220 . . . . 899, 916–17, 920, 921, 922, 923,
                                   924, 930
s 220(1) 916, 917
s 220(1)(a) 916
s 220(1)(b) 899, 916
s 220(2) 917
s 220(2)(a) 917
s 220(2)(b) 917
s 220(3) 917
s 220(3)(a) 917
s 220(3)(b) 917
s 220(4) 917
s 221 . . . . . 917, 925, 930, 931, 932, 933
s 221(1) 930
s 221(1)(a) 930
s 221(1)(b) 930
s 221(2) 930, 932

s 221(2)(a)	**930**
s 221(2)(b)	**930**
s 222	902
s 223	902
s 224	898, **899**, 902, 921
s 224(1)	**899**
s 224(2)	**899**
s 224(2)(a)	**899**
s 224(2)(b)	**899**
s 224(3)	**899**
s 224(3)(a)	**899**
s 224(3)(b)	**899**
s 224(4)	**899**
s 224(5)	**899**
s 224(6)	**899**
s 226	889, **904**
s 226(1)	**904**
s 226(1)(a)	**904**
s 226(1)(b)	**904**
s 226(2)(a)	934
s 226(3A)(a)	934
s 226A	904, 907, 933, 934
s 226B	904, 909
s 226C	904, 909
s 227	889, 904, 906
s 227(1)	907, 908
s 228	889, 904, **906**
s 228(1)	**906**
s 228(2)	**906**
s 228(3)	**906**
s 228(3)(a)	**906**
s 228(3)(b)	**906**
s 228(4)	**906**, 907
s 228(4)(a)	**906**
s 228(4)(b)	**906**
s 228A	**906–7**
s 228A(1)	**906**
s 228A(2)	**906**
s 228A(3)	**906**
s 228A(3)(a)	**906**
s 228A(3)(b)	**906**
s 228A(4)	**906**
s 228A(5)	**906**
s 228A(5)(a)	**906–7**
s 228A(5)(b)	**907**
s 228A(5)(c)	**907**
s 228A(5)(d)	**907**
s 229	889, 904, 908
s 230	889, 904, 908
s 231	889, 904, 909
s 231A	909, 910, 912
s 231B	909
s 232	889, 904
s 232A	907
s 232B	907, 908
s 233	889, 904, 909

s 233(3)(b)	909, 910
s 234	889, **909–10**
s 234(1)	**909**, 910
s 234(1)(a)	**909**
s 234(1)(b)	**909**, 910
s 234(2)	**909**, 910
s 234(2)(a)	**909**
s 234(2)(b)	**909**
s 234(3)	**909**, 910
s 234(3)(a)	**909**
s 234(3)(b)	**909**
s 234(4)	**909**, 910
s 234(4)(a)	**909**
s 234(4)(b)	**909**
s 234(5)	**910**
s 234(6)	**910**
s 234A	908, **911–13**, 933
s 234A(1)	**911**, 912
s 234A(2)	**911**
s 234A(3)	**911**
s 234A(3)(a)	**911**
s 234A(3)(a)(i)	**911**
s 234A(3)(a)(ii)	**911**, 912
s 234A(3)(b)	**911**
s 234A(3)(b)(i)	**911**, 913
s 234A(3)(b)(ii)	**911**
s 234A(3A)	**911**
s 234A(3A)(a)	**911**
s 234A(3A)(b)	**911**, 912
s 234A(3B)	**911**
s 234A(3B)(a)	**911**
s 234A(3B)(b)	**911**
s 234A(3B)(c)	912
s 234A(3C)	911, 912
s 234A(3C)(a)	912
s 234A(3C)(b)	912
s 234A(3C)(c)	912
s 234A(3D)	912
s 234A(3E)	912
s 234A(3E)(a)	912
s 234A(3E)(b)	912
s 234A(3F)	912
s 234A(4)	912
s 234A(4)(a)	912
s 234A(4)(b)	912
s 234A(5)	912
s 234A(5)(a)	912
s 234A(5)(a)(i)	912
s 234A(5)(a)(ii)	912
s 234A(5)(b)	912
s 234A(5B)	912
s 234A(5B)(a)	912
s 234A(5B)(a)(i)	912
s 234A(5B)(a)(ii)	912
s 234A(5B)(b)	912
s 234A(5B)(b)(i)	912

s 234A(5B)(b)(ii) 912–13
s 234A(5C) 913
s 234A(5D) 913
s 234A(5D)(a) 913
s 234A(5D)(b) 913
s 234A(6) 913
s 234A(6)(a) 913
s 234A(6)(b) 913
s 234A(7) 913
s 234A(7)(a) 913
s 234A(7)(b) 913
s 234A(7A) 913
s 234A(7B) 913
s 234A(7B)(a). 913
s 234A(7B)(b). 913
s 234A(7B)(c). 913
s 235A 889, 966
s 236 . . . . 110, 878, 902
s 236(a) 110
s 236(b) 110
s 237 . . . . 949, 954, 955
s 238 . . . . 952, 954, 955
s 238(1) 955
s 238(1)(a) 955
s 238(1)(b) 955
s 238(2). 955, 957, 958
s 238(2)(a) 955, 958
s 238(2)(b) 955
s 238(3) 955, 957
s 238(3)(a) 955
s 238(3)(b) 955
s 238(4) 955
s 238(5) 955
s 238(5)(a) 955
s 238(5)(b) 955
s 238A . 516, 948–49, 950, 952, 953, 954, 955
s 238A(1) 948
s 238A(2) 948
s 238A(2)(a) 948
s 238A(2)(b) 948
s 238A(3) 948
s 238A(4) 948
s 238A(4)(a) 948
s 238A(4)(b) 948
s 238A(5) 948, 949
s 238A(5)(a) 948
s 238A(5)(b) 948
s 238A(5)(c) 948
s 238A(6) 948
s 238A(6)(a) 948
s 238A(6)(b) 948
s 238A(6)(c) 948, 949
s 238A(6)(d) 948, 949
s 238A(6)(e) 948, 949
s 238A(7) 948
s 238A(7A) 948

s 238A(7B) 949
s 238A(7C) 949
s 238A(7D) 949
s 238A(8) 949
s 238A(9) 949
s 238B 948, 949–50
s 238B(1) 949
s 238B(2) 949
s 238B(3) 949
s 238B(4) 949
s 238B(5) 949, 950
s 238B(6) 949
s 238B(6)(a) 949
s 238B(6)(a)(i) 949
s 238B(6)(a)(ii) 949
s 238B(6)(b) 949
s 238B(7) 949
s 238B(8) 949
s 238B(8)(a) 949
s 238B(8)(b). 949–50
s 238B(8)(c). 950
s 238B(9) 950
s 238B(9)(a) 950
s 238B(9)(b) 950
s 240 960
s 241 925
s 241(1) 925
s 241(1)(a) 925
s 241(1)(b) 925
s 241(1)(c) 925
s 241(1)(d) 925
s 241(1)(e) 925
s 241(2) 925
s 241(3) 925
s 244 . . . . 880, 887, 899, 900, 901
s 244(1) . . 880, 881, 886, 889, 900, 901, 902
s 244(1)(a) 880, 887, 888, 889, 907
s 244(1)(b) 880, 888, 907
s 244(1)(c) 880, 888, 907
s 244(1)(d) 880, 888, 907
s 244(1)(e) 880, 888, 907
s 244(1)(f) 880, 888, 907
s 244(1)(g) 880, 888
s 244(3) 900, 901
s 244(5) 887, 888
s 246 . . . . 959, 972
s 254 707
ss 272-274 . . . . 199, 196
s 275 . . . . 199, 196, 740
s 276 . . . . 199, 196
s 296 736
s 296(1) 175
s 297 142
Sched A1 . . . . . 27, 765, 770, 771, 776–78
                  778–79, 781–82, 787, 794
Sched A1, para 4 788

Sched A1, para 6 . . . . 767, 835
Sched A1, para 7 767
Sched A1, para 10 788
Sched A1, para 11 788
Sched A1, para 11(2)(a) 772
Sched A1, para 12 788
Sched A1, para 14 . . . . 770, 788
Sched A1, para 15 788
Sched A1, para 15(6)(a) 794
Sched A1, para 18 . . . . 788, 794
Sched A1, para 18(3) 788
Sched A1, para 18A 788
Sched A1, para 19 . . . . 788, 794
Sched A1, para 19(2) 772
Sched A1, para 19(3) 772
Sched A1, para 19(4) 772
Sched A1, para 19B(2) **771**
Sched A1, para 19B(2)(a) **771**
Sched A1, para 19B(2)(b) **771**
Sched A1, para 19B(3) **772**
Sched A1, para 19B(3)(a) **772**
Sched A1, para 19B(3)(b) **772**
Sched A1, para 19B(3)(c) **772**
Sched A1, para 19B(3)(d) **772**
Sched A1, para 19B(3)(e) **772**
Sched A1, para 19B(4) 773
Sched A1, para 19B(5) **772**
Sched A1, para 19B(6) **772**
Sched A1, para 19B(7) **772–73**
Sched A1, para 19C 776
Sched A1, para 22 . . . . . . 773, 775, 788
Sched A1, para 22(4) 773, 775
Sched A1, para 22(4)(a) 773
Sched A1, para 22(4)(b) 773, 774, 775
Sched A1, para 22(4)(c) 773
Sched A1, para 23 775
Sched A1, para 24 789
Sched A1, para 24(4)(a) 774
Sched A1, para 25 . . . . 775, 789
Sched A1, para 25(4) 775
Sched A1, para 25(6)(a) 776
Sched A1, para 25(9) . . . 775, 776, 777, 784
Sched A1, para 26 776
Sched A1, para 26(1) **776**
Sched A1, para 26(2) **776**
Sched A1, para 26(3) **777**, 778
Sched A1, para 26(4) **777**, 778
Sched A1, para 26(4)(a) **777**
Sched A1, para 26(4)(b) **777**
Sched A1, para 26(4)(c) **777**
Sched A1, para 26(4A) **777**
Sched A1, para 26(4A)(a) **777**
Sched A1, para 26(4A)(b) **777**
Sched A1, para 26(4B) **777**
Sched A1, para 26(4B)(a) **777**
Sched A1, para 26(4B)(b) **777**

Sched A1, para 26(4C) **777**
Sched A1, para 26(4C)(a) **777**
Sched A1, para 26(4C)(b) **777**
Sched A1, para 26(4D) **777**
Sched A1, para 26(4D)(a) **777**
Sched A1, para 26(4D)(b) **777**
Sched A1, para 26(4D)(c) **777**
Sched A1, para 26(4D)(d) **777**
Sched A1, para 26(4E) **777**
Sched A1, para 26(5) **778**
Sched A1, para 26(6) **778**
Sched A1, para 26(6)(a) **778**
Sched A1, para 26(6)(b) **778**
Sched A1, para 26(7) **778**
Sched A1, para 26(8) **778**
Sched A1, para 26(8)(a) **778**
Sched A1, para 26(8)(b) **778**
Sched A1, para 26(9) **778**
Sched A1, para 26(9)(a) **778**
Sched A1, para 26(9)(b) **778**
Sched A1, para 27 . . . . 777, 778
Sched A1, para 27(1) **778**
Sched A1, para 27(1)(a) **778**
Sched A1, para 27(1)(b) **778**
Sched A1, para 27(2) **778**, 779
Sched A1, para 27(3) **779**
Sched A1, para 27A **783–84**
Sched A1, para 27A(1) **784**
Sched A1, para 27A(2) **784**
Sched A1, para 27A(2)(a) **784**
Sched A1, para 27A(2)(b) **784**
Sched A1, para 27A(2)(c) **784**
Sched A1, para 27A(2)(c)(i) **784**
Sched A1, para 27A(2)(c)(ii) **784**
Sched A1, para 27A(2)(d) **784**
Sched A1, para 27A(2)(e) **784**
Sched A1, para 27A(2)(f) **784**
Sched A1, para 27A(2)(g) **784**
Sched A1, para 27A(3) **784**
Sched A1, para 27A(3)(a) **784**
Sched A1, para 27A(3)(a)(i) **784**
Sched A1, para 27A(3)(a)(ii) **784**
Sched A1, para 27A(3)(b) **784**
Sched A1, para 27A(4) **784**
Sched A1, para 28 775
Sched A1, para 29 . . . . 775, 789
Sched A1, para 30 789
Sched A1, para 30(1) 786
Sched A1, para 31 789
Sched A1, para 31(2) 786
Sched A1, para 31(3) 786, 787
Sched A1, para 31(4) 786, 787
Sched A1, para 32 787
Sched A1, para 34 837
Sched A1, para 35(1) 769, 835
Sched A1, para 35(4) 835

Sched A1, para 35(4)(a) 835
Sched A1, para 35(4)(b) 835
Sched A1, para 35(4)(c) 835
Sched A1, para 36 769
Sched A1, para 37 769
Sched A1, paras 39-41 769
Sched A1, para 66 789
Sched A1, para 67 789
Sched A1, para 85 789
Sched A1, paras 99-103 790
Sched A1, para 104 790
Sched A1, para 107 790
Sched A1, para 110 790
Sched A1, paras 112-114 790
Sched A1, para 121 790
Sched A1, para 156 784
Sched A1, para 156(1) **781**
Sched A1, para 156(2) **781**
Sched A1, para 156(2)(a) **781**
Sched A1, para 156(2)(b) **781**
Sched A1, para 156(2)(c) **781**
Sched A1, para 156(2)(d) **781**
Sched A1, para 156(2)(e) **781**
Sched A1, para 156(2)(f) **781**
Sched A1, para 156(2)(g) **781**
Sched A1, para 156(2)(h) **781**
Sched A1, para 156(3) **781**
Sched A1, para 156(4) **782**
Sched A1, para 156(5) **782**
Sched A1, para 156(6) **782**
Sched A1, para 161 . . . . . . 516, 782, 784
Sched A1, para 161(1) **782**
Sched A1, para 161(1)(a) **782**
Sched A1, para 161(1)(b) **782**
Sched A1, para 161(2) **782**
Sched A1, para 161(2)(a) **782**
Sched A1, para 161(2)(b) **782**
Sched A1, para 161(2)(c) **782**
Sched A1, para 161(2)(d) **782**
Sched A1, para 161(2)(e) **782**
Sched A1, para 161(2)(f) **782**
Sched A1, para 161(2)(g) **782**
Sched A1, para 161(2)(h) **782**
Sched A1, para 161(3) **782**
Sched A1, para 162 . . . . 516, **782**
Sched A1, para 162(a) **782**
Sched A1, para 162(b) **782**
Sched A1, para 166B 783
Sched A1, Pt IV 790
Sched A1, Pt V 790
Sched A1, Pt VI 790, 836
Trade Union Reform and Employment Rights
Act 1993 . . . . 666, 811, 903, 966
s 14 689
Trades Disputes Act 1927 865
Truck Act 1896 . . . . 83, 84, 85

Unfair Contract Terms Act 1977 . . . 991, 994
s 1(1) 992, 993
s 1(3) 992
s 2(1) 992, 993
s 2(2) 993
s 3 98
Sched 1, para 4 993
Wages Act 1986 . . . . 54, 84
Wages Councils Act 1945 14
Welfare Reform and Pensions Act 1999 . 60, 348
Workmen's Compensation Act 1897 . . . 73, 74
Workmen's Compensation Act 1906 73

Statutory Instruments

ACAS Arbitration Scheme (Great Britain)
  Order 2004, SI 2004/753
  Sched, para 12 509
Burden of Proof Regulations 333
Child (Protection at Work) Regulations 1998, SI
  1998/276 39
Civil Procedure Rules 1998 (CPR) . . . **929**, 938
  Pt 54 (ex Order 53) 199, 204
  r 25.3(1) **929**
  r 25.3(2) **929**
  r 25.3(3) **929**
Conduct of Employment Agencies and
  Employment Businesses Regulations 2003,
  SI 2003/3319 193
County Court Rules
  O 14, r 8(1) 1023
Data Protection (Conditions under Paragraph 3
  of Part II of Schedule 1) Order 2000, SI
  2000/185 618
Disability Discrimination (Meaning of Disability) Regulations 1996, SI 1996/1455 . . . 231
  reg 3 231
  reg 4 231
  reg 5 231
Dock Workers (Regulation of Employment)
  Order 1947 878
Draft Transfer of Undertakings (Protection of
  Employment) Regulations 2005. 1036, 1042,
  1043, 1044, 1048, 1050, 1058, 1067
  reg 3 . . . . **1058–59**
  reg 3(1) **1058**
  reg 3(1)(a) **1058**
  reg 3(1)(b) **1058–59**
  reg 3(1)(b)(i) **1058**
  reg 3(1)(b)(ii) **1058**
  reg 3(1)(b)(iii) **1058**
  reg 3(2) **1059**
  reg 3(3) **1059**
  reg 3(3)(a) **1059**
  reg 3(3)(a)(i) **1059**
  reg 3(3)(a)(ii) **1059**

reg 3(3)(b) **1059**
reg 3(3)(b)(i) **1059**
reg 3(5) 1060
reg 4 . . . . 1042, 1043, **1048**
reg 4(1) 1048
reg 4(4) **1048**
reg 4(4)(a) **1048**
reg 4(4)(b) **1048**
reg 4(5) **1048**
reg 4(5)(a) **1048**
reg 4(5)(b) **1048**
reg 7 . . . . **1038**
reg 7(1) 1038, 1043
reg 7(1)(a) **1038**
reg 7(1)(b) **1038**
reg 7(2) **1038**
reg 7(3) **1038**, 1045
reg 7(3)(a) **1038**
reg 7(3)(b) **1038**
reg 8 . . . . **1043-44**, 1045
reg 8(1) **1043**
reg 8(2) **1043**, 1045
reg 8(2)(a) **1043**
reg 8(2)(b) **1043**
reg 8(3) **1043**, 1045
reg 8(4) **1043**
reg 8(4)(a) **1043**
reg 8(4)(b) **1043**
reg 8(5) **1043**
reg 8(6) **1044**
reg 9 . . . . **1050-51**
reg 9(1) **1050-51**
reg 9(2) **1051**
reg 9(2)(a) **1051**
reg 9(2)(b) **1051**
reg 9(2)(b)(i) **1051**
reg 9(2)(b)(ii) **1051**
reg 9(6) **1051**
reg 9(6)(a) **1051**
reg 9(6)(b) **1051**
reg 9(7) **1051**
reg 9(8) **1051**
reg 9(8)(a) **1051**
reg 9(8)(b) **1051**
reg 11 1044
reg 12 1044
reg 14 1051
reg 14(1)(d) 1051
Education (Modification of Enactments
  Relating to Employment) Order 1989, SI
  1989/901
    art 3 174
    art 4 174
Employers' Liability (Compulsory Insurance)
  Regulations 1998, SI 1998/2573 74

Employment Act 2002 (Dispute Resolution)
  Regulations 2004, SI 2004/752 25
    reg 3 . . . . **532**
    reg 3(2) **532**
    reg 3(2)(a) **532**
    reg 3(2)(b) **532**
    reg 3(2)(c) **532**
    reg 3(2)(d) **532**
    reg 4 532
    reg 6(4) 25
    reg 6(5) 25
    reg 6(6) 25
    reg 8 25
    reg 10 25
    reg 11(3) **533**
Employment Equality (Religion or Belief) Regulations 2003 (RBRs) . . 217, 218, 227, 228,
    229, 235, 236, 251, 257, 264, 266, 267, 271,
    284, 303, 305, 306, 307, 311, 314, 334, 337,
                                   598, 601
    reg 2(1) 228
    reg 3(1)(b) 263
    reg 3(2) 241
    reg 4 257
    reg 5 251
    reg 6 . . . . 310, 311
    reg 7 . . . . **304**
    reg 7(1) 303
    reg 7(2) 304, 305
    reg 7(2)(a) 304
    reg 7(2)(b) 304
    reg 7(2)(c) 304
    reg 7(2)(c)(i) 304
    reg 7(2)(c)(ii) 304
    reg 7(3) **304**, 305, 306
    reg 7(3)(a) **304**
    reg 7(3)(b) **304**
    reg 7(3)(c) **304**
    reg 7(3)(c)(i) **304**
    reg 7(3)(c)(ii) **304**
    reg 21 310
    reg 22 314
    reg 22(3) 314
    reg 26(1) 307
    reg 26(2) 307
    reg 26(3) 307
    reg 29 334
    reg 34 335
Employment Equality (Sex Discrimination)
  Regulations 2005 (draft) 299, 321
Employment Equality (Sexual Orientation)
  (Northern Ireland) Regulations 219
Employment Equality (Sexual Orientation)
  Regulations 2003 (SORs) . . . 217, 218, 222,
    224, 235, 236, 251, 257, 264, 266, 267, 271,
    284, 303, 305, 306, 307, 311, 314, 334, 337

reg 2(1) 222
reg 2(1)(a) 222
reg 2(1)(b) 222
reg 2(1)(c) 222
reg 3 235
reg 3(1)(b) 263
reg 3(2) 241
reg 5 251
reg 6 . . . . 310, 311
reg 7 . . . . **304**
reg 7(1) 303
reg 7(2) **304**, 305
reg 7(2)(a) **304**
reg 7(2)(b) **304**
reg 7(2)(c) **304**
reg 7(2)(c)(i) **304**
reg 7(2)(c)(ii) **304**
reg 7(3) **304**, 305, 306
reg 7(3)(a) **304**
reg 7(3)(b) **304**
reg 7(3)(b)(i) **304**
reg 7(3)(b)(ii) **304**, 306
reg 7(3)(c) **304**
reg 7(3)(c)(i) **304**
reg 7(3)(c)(ii) **304**
reg 21 310
reg 22 314
reg 22(3) 314
reg 25 293
reg 26(1) 307
reg 26(2) 307
reg 26(3) 307
reg 29 334
reg 34 335
Employment Protection (Recoupment of
    Jobseeker's Allowance and Income Support)
    Regulations 1996, SI 1996/2349 554
Employment Tribunals (Constitution and Rules
    of Procedure) (Amendment) Regulations
    2004 323
Employment Tribunals Extension of Jurisdic-
    tion Order (England and Wales) 1994, SI
    1994/1623 . . . . 86, 476
Fair Employment and Treatment Order 1998
    (FETO) 334, 336, 597, 598
Fixed-Term Employees (Prevention of Less
    Favourable Treatment) Regulations 2002, SI
    2002/2034 505
reg 3(2) 1028
reg 3(6) 1028
reg 6 516
reg 8 505
reg 8(5) 511
Health and Safety (Consultation with
    Employees) Regulations 1996, SI 1996/1513
    . . . . 16, 62, 840, 843, 844

Health and Safety (Display Screen Equipment)
    Regulations 1992, SI 1992/2792 . . 149, 607
reg 4 608
Information and Consultation of Employees
    Regulations 2004, SI 2004/3426 . . . 27, 63,
                150, 845, 847, 848, 856, 1068
Pts I–VI 856
Preamble, Recital 15 849
Preamble, Recital 18 850
reg 2 . . . . 849, 852
reg 3 849
reg 4 . . . . 849, 858
reg 4(2)(b) 849
reg 5 858
reg 7 . . . . 849, 850
reg 7(3) 849
reg 8 850
reg 8(6) 850
reg 9 859
reg 10 850
reg 11 859
reg 12 859
reg 13 859
reg 14 850
reg 14(2) 850
reg 15 . . . . 852, 859
reg 16 . . . . **851–52**, 859
reg 16(1) **851**
reg 16(1)(a) **851**
reg 16(1)(b) **851**
reg 16(1)(c) **851**
reg 16(1)(d) **851**
reg 16(1)(e) **851**
reg 16(1)(f) **851**
reg 16(1)(f)(i) **851**
reg 16(1)(f)(ii) **851**
reg 16(2) **851**
reg 16(3) **851**
reg 16(3)(a) **851**
reg 16(3)(b) **851**
reg 16(3)(b)(i) **851**
reg 16(3)(b)(ii) **851**
reg 16(4) **851**
reg 16(4)(a) **851**
reg 16(4)(b) **851**
reg 16(4)(b)(i) **851**
reg 16(4)(b)(ii) **851**
reg 16(5) **851**
reg 16(5)(a) **851**
reg 16(5)(b) **852**
reg 16(5)(c) **852**
reg 16(5)(c)(i) **852**
reg 16(5)(c)(ii) **852**
reg 17 . . . . 852, 859
reg 18 859
reg 19 852

reg 20 . . . . **852–53**, 854, 859
reg 20(1) **853**
reg 20(1)(a) **853**
reg 20(1)(b) **853**
reg 20(1)(c) **853**
reg 20(1)(c)(i) **853**
reg 20(1)(c)(ii) **853**
reg 20(2) **853**
reg 20(3) **853**
reg 20(4) **853**
reg 20(4)(a) **853**
reg 20(4)(b) **853**
reg 20(4)(c) **853**
reg 20(4)(d) **853**
reg 20(5) **853**, 854
reg 20(5)(a) **853**
reg 20(5)(b) **853**
reg 20(6) **853–54**
reg 21 859
reg 22 . . . . **854–55**, 856
reg 22(1) **854**
reg 22(1)(a) **854–55**
reg 22(1)(b) **854**
reg 22(2) **855**
reg 22(3) **855**
reg 22(3)(a) **855**
reg 22(3)(b) **855**
reg 22(4) **855**
reg 22(5) **855**
reg 22(5)(a) **855**
reg 22(5)(b) **855**
reg 22(6) **855**
reg 22(7) **855**
reg 22(8) **855**
reg 22(9) **855**
reg 23 . . . . 854, **855–56**, 859
reg 23(1) **855**
reg 23(1)(a) **855**
reg 23(1)(b) **855**, 856
reg 23(1)(c) **855**
reg 23(2) **855**
reg 23(3) **855**, 856
reg 23(3)(a) **855**
reg 23(3)(b) **855**
reg 23(3)(c) **855**
reg 23(3)(d) **855**
reg 23(3)(e) **855**
reg 23(4) **856**
reg 23(5) **856**
reg 23(5)(a) **856**
reg 23(5)(b) **856**
reg 23(6) **856**
reg 23(7) **856**
reg 24 . . . . 854, **856**, 859
reg 25 859
reg 27 857

reg 28 . . . . 857, 859
reg 29 . . . . 857, 859
reg 30 . . . . 857, 859
reg 31 . . . . 857, 859
reg 32 . . . . 857, 859
reg 33 857
reg 34 857
Sched 1 849
Sched 2 852
Local Government Officers (Political
  Restrictions) Regulations 1990,
  SI 1990/851 . . . . 593, 599
reg 3 593
Sched 594
Sched, Pt I 594
Sched, Pt II 594
Sched, Pt II, para 1 594
Sched, Pt II, para 3 594
Sched, Pt II, para 4(a) 594
Sched, Pt II, para 4(b) 594
Sched, Pt II, para 5 594
Sched, Pt II, para 6 594
Sched, Pt II, para 7 594
Sched, Pt II, para 8 594
Management of Health and Safety Regulations
  1992, SI 1992/2051 . . . . **149**
reg 3(1) **149**
reg 3(1)(a) **149**
reg 8(1) **149**
reg 8(1)(a) **149**
reg 8(1)(b) **149**
Manual Handling Operations Regulations
  1992 149
reg 4(1)(b) 149
Sched 1 150
Maternity Allowance and Statutory Maternity
  Pay Regulations 1994, SI 1994/1230 . . . 364
Maternity and Parental Leave (Amendment)
  Regulations 2002, SI 2002/2789 358
Maternity and Parental Leave, etc. Regulations
  1999 (MPLRs), SI 1999/3312 . . . 343, 356,
    358, 372, 375, 376, 377, 387, 842, 843, 844
reg 4 359
reg 5 359
reg 6 358
reg 7 358
reg 7(6) 357, 365
reg 7(7) 357, 365
reg 8 . . . . 358, 359
reg 9 360
reg 10 357
reg 13 . . . . **373**
reg 13(1) **373**
reg 13(1)(a) **373**
reg 13(1)(b) **373**
reg 14 . . . . **373**

reg 14(1) 373
reg 15 373
reg 15(a) 373
reg 15(b) 373
reg 15(c) 373
reg 15(c)(i) 373
reg 15(c)(ii) 373
reg 16 374
reg 16(a) 374
reg 16(b) 374
reg 17 . . . . 361, 374
reg 17(a) 361
reg 17(a)(i) 361
reg 17(a)(ii) 361
reg 17(a)(iii) 361
reg 17(b) 361
reg 17(b)(i) 361
reg 17(b)(ii) 361
reg 17(b)(iii) 361
reg 17(b)(iv) 361
reg 18 365
reg 18(1) 374
reg 18(2) 374
reg 18A 366
reg 18A(1) 374
reg 18A(1)(a)(ii) 366
reg 18A(1)(b) 366
reg 18A(3) 366
reg 18A(3)(a) 366
reg 18A(3)(b) 366
reg 18A(5) 366
reg 18A(5)(a) 366
reg 18A(5)(a)(i) 366
reg 18A(5)(a)(ii) 366
reg 18A(5)(b) 366
reg 19 . . . . 374, 844
reg 19(1) 374, 375
reg 19(2) 374, 375
reg 19(2)(e) 374
reg 19(2)(e)(ii) 374
reg 19(2)(f) 374
reg 19(2)(g) 375
reg 19(2)(g)(i) 375
reg 19(2)(g)(ii) 375
reg 19(4) 375
reg 19(6) 375
reg 19(7) 375
reg 19(7)(a) 375
reg 19(7)(b) 375
reg 20 . . . . 357, 844
reg 20(1) 375
reg 20(1)(a) 375
reg 20(2) 375
reg 20(2)(a) 375
reg 20(2)(b) 375
reg 20(2)(c) 375

reg 20(3) 356, 375
reg 20(3)(a) 356
reg 20(3)(b) 356
reg 20(3)(c) 356
reg 20(3)(d) 356
reg 20(3)(e) 356
reg 20(3)(e)(i) 357
reg 20(3)(ee) 357
reg 20(3)(ee)(ii) 357
reg 20(3)(ee)(iii) 357
reg 20(6) 357, 365
reg 20(6)(a) 357
reg 20(6)(b) 357
reg 20(7) 357, 365, 374, 375
reg 20(7)(a) 357
reg 20(7)(b) 357
reg 20(7)(c) 357
reg 21 358
Sched 1 375
Sched 2 . . . . 373, 374, 842
Sched 2, para 1 374
Sched 2, para 2 374
Sched 2, para 3 374
Sched 2, para 4 374
Sched 2, para 5 374
Sched 2, para 6 374
Sched 2, para 7 374
Sched 2, para 8 374
National Health Service (Remuneration and
  Conditions of Service) Regulations 1974,
  SI 1974/296 205
  reg 3(2) 205
National Minimum Wage Regulations 1999
  (NMWRs), SI 1999/584 392
  reg 2(1) 394
  reg 2(2) 397
  reg 3 394
  reg 3(3) 396
  reg 3(4) 397
  reg 4 394
  reg 6 394
  reg 6(1) 393
  reg 7 395
  reg 8 392
  reg 9 392
  reg 10 393
  reg 12 392
  reg 13 392
  reg 13(1) 396
  reg 15 . . . . 395, 396
  reg 15(1) 395, 396
  reg 15(1)(a) 396
  reg 15(1)(b) 396
  reg 15(1A) 396
  reg 16 . . . . 395, 396
  reg 17 395

reg 18 395
reg 19 395
reg 20 . . . . 393, 394
reg 20(1)(b) 393
reg 20(1)(c) 393
reg 20(1)(d) 393
reg 20(1)(e) 393
reg 21 393
reg 22 393
reg 23 393
reg 24 . . . . 393, 394
reg 25 . . . . 393, 394
reg 26A 394
reg 27 394
reg 28 . . . . 394, 396
reg 29 394
reg 38 397
1976 Order 1042
Occupational Pension Schemes (Preservation
of Benefits) Regulations 1991,
SI 1991/167 1052
Part-time Workers (Prevention of Less Favourable Treatment) Regulations 2000 (PtWRs),
SI 2000/1551 . . 73, 317, 319, 343, 350, 351,
352, 353, 354, 355
reg 2 . . . . **351, 352**
reg 2(1) 352, 353
reg 2(2) 352
reg 2(3) **352**
reg 2(3)(a) **352**
reg 2(3)(b) **352**
reg 2(3)(c) **352**
reg 2(3)(d) **352**
reg 2(4) **351**, 352, 353
reg 2(4)(a) **351**
reg 2(4)(a)(i) **351**
reg 2(4)(a)(ii) **351**, 352
reg 2(4)(b) **351**
reg 3 . . . . 352, **353**
reg 3(1) **353**
reg 3(1)(a) **353**
reg 3(1)(b) **353**
reg 3(2) **353**
reg 3(3) **353**
reg 4 . . . . 352, **353**
reg 4(1) **353**
reg 4(1)(a) **353**
reg 4(1)(b) **353**
reg 4(1)(c) **353**
reg 4(2) **353**
reg 4(2)(a) **353**
reg 4(2)(b) **353**
reg 4(3) **353**
reg 5 . . . . **350**, 353
reg 5(1) **350**
reg 5(1)(a) **350**

reg 5(1)(b) **350**, 355
reg 5(2) **350–51**
reg 5(2)(a) **351**
reg 5(2)(b) **351**
reg 5(3) **351**
reg 5(4) **351**
reg 7 516
reg 8(6) 354
Paternity and Adoption Leave (Amendment)
Regulations 2004, SI 2004/923 366
Paternity and Adoption Leave Regulations
2002 (PALRs), SI 2002/2788 (as amended
by PALRs 2004) 366, 367
reg 4 367
reg 5 367
reg 6 367
reg 8 367
reg 10 367
reg 12 367
reg 13 367
reg 14 367
reg 15 366
reg 17 366
reg 20 366
reg 22 367
reg 28 367
reg 29 367
reg 30 . . . . 366, 367
Police Regulations 2003, SI 2003/527 594
Sched 1 594
Redundancy Payments (Pensions) Regulations
1965, SI 1965/1932 1023
Safety Representatives and Safety Committee
Regulations 1977, SI 1977/500 840
reg 3 840
Servants of the Crown (Parliamentary, Euro-
pean Parliamentary and Northern Ireland
Assembly Candidature) Order 1987 . 592–93
Sex Discrimination (Northern Ireland) Order
1976 242
Social Security (Categorisation of Earners)
Regulations 1978, SI 1978/1689 194
Social Security Contributions (Intermediaries)
Regulations 2000, SI 2000/727 186
Social Security (Industrial Injuries) (Prescribed
Diseases) Regulations 1985, SI 1985/967 . 74
Social Security (Welfare to Work) Regulations
1998, SI 1998/2231 60
Statutory Paternity Pay and Statutory
Adoption Pay (General) Regulations
2002, SI 2002/2822 367
Telecommunications (Lawful Business Practice)
(Interception of Communications) Regula-
tions (LBP Regulations),
SI 2000/2699 . . . . 609, 610, 624, 628, 630,
633, 634, 635

reg 3 610
reg 3(1) 610
reg 3(1)(a) 610
reg 3(1)(b) 610
reg 3(2)(a) 610
reg 3(2)(c). 610
Trade Union Recognition (Method of
Collective Bargaining) Order 2000,
SI 2000/1300 786
Sched 786
Transfer of Undertakings (Protection of
Employment) Regulations 1981 (TUPE), SI
1981/1794 . . . 430, 764, 765, 796, 801, 822,
824, 843, 844, 1036, 1037, 1042, 1045, 1046,
1048, 1049, 1051, 1052, 1057, 1058, 1060,
1065, 1066, 1071
reg 5 . . **1038** 1039, 1040, 1042, 1045, 1046,
1049, 1052, 1065, 1067
reg 5(1) **1038**, 1039
reg 5(2) **1038**
reg 5(2)(a) **1038**
reg 5(2)(b) **1038**
reg 5(3) 1038, 1039, 1040
reg 5(4A) 1038, **1049**, 1050
reg 5(4B) **1049**, 1050
reg 5(5) **1049**, 1050
reg 6 1047
reg 7 1039
reg 8 . . . . **1037**
reg 8(1) 516, **1037**, 1039, 1048, 1050
reg 8(2) **1037**, 1040, 1048
reg 8(2)(a) **1037**
reg 8(2)(b) **1037**
reg 9 . . . . **764**
reg 9(1) **764**
reg 9(2) **764**
reg 9(2)(a) **764**
reg 9(2)(b) **764**
reg 10. . . . . 853, **1065–66**
reg 10(1). **1065**
reg 10(2) **1065**, 1066
reg 10(2)(a) **1065**
reg 10(2)(b) **1065**
reg 10(2)(c) **1065**
reg 10(2)(d) **1065**, 1066
reg 10(2A) **1066**
reg 10(2A)(a) **1066**
reg 10(2A)(b) **1066**
reg 10(2A)(b)(i) **1066**
reg 10(2A)(b)(ii) **1066**
reg 10(3). **1066**
reg 10(5). **1066**
reg 10(6). **1066**
reg 10(6)(a) **1066**
reg 10(6)(b) **1066**
reg 10(8A). **1066**

reg 10A(1). 1066
reg 11 853
reg 11(11) 1065
reg 12. . . . . 853, 1046
Transnational Information and Consultation of
Employees Regulations 1999 (TICER),
SI 1999/3323 . . . . . . 27, 62, 516, 845, 858
Sched 858
para 9(6) 858
Principle 2. . . . . **687**, 770
Principle 3. . . . . **770-71**
Working Time Regulations 1998 (WTRs) (as
amended by Working Time Regulations
1999), SI 1998/1833 . . 12, 73, 174, 343, 356,
377, 387, 397, 401, 402, 403, 404, 407, 408,
410, 413, 415, 416, 417, 418, 419, 420, 422,
423, 424, 425, 516, 536, 624, 840, 842, 843–44
reg 2 . . . . **403**
reg 2(1) **410**
reg 2(1)(a) **410**
reg 2(1)(b) **410**
reg 2(1)(c) **410**
reg 4. . . . . **402**, 413, 415, 423
reg 4(1) **402**, 413, 418, 423
reg 4(2) **402**, 418, 423
reg 4(3) 840
reg 4(4) 840
reg 5 . . . . **413**, 415
reg 5(1) 413
reg 5(2) **413**
reg 5(2)(a) **413**
reg 5(2)(b) **413**
reg 5(3) **413**
reg 6 403
reg 6(1) 418, 840
reg 6(2) 418, 840
reg 6(3) 840
reg 6(7) 418
reg 7 403
reg 8 403
reg 10 403
reg 10(1) 418, 840
reg 11 403
reg 11(1) 418, 840
reg 11(2) 418, 840
reg 12. . . . . 397, 403, 840
reg 12(1) 418, 840
reg 13. . . . . 393, 403, 405
reg 13(7) 406
reg 14 407
reg 14(4) 407
reg 15A 407
reg 16 . . . . 403, 405
reg 18 403
reg 18(2) 404
reg 18(2)(b) 404

reg 19 404
reg 20 . . . . **418**, 419, 421
reg 20(1) **418**
reg 20(1)(a) **418**
reg 20(1)(b) **418**
reg 20(1)(c) **418**
reg 20(2) **418**, 419, 421, 422
reg 21 404
reg 22 404
reg 23 840
reg 24A 404
reg 36 403
reg 38(2)(b) 423
Sched 1 . . . . 373, **408**, 516, 841
Sched 1, para 1 . . . . **408**, 841
Sched 1, para 1(a) **408**, 841
Sched 1, para 1(b) **408**, 841
Sched 1, para 1(c) **408**, 841
Sched 1, para 1(c)(i) **408**, 841
Sched 1, para 1(c)(ii) **408**, 841
Sched 1, para 1(d) **408**, 841
Sched 1, para 1(d)(i) **408**, 841
Sched 1, para 1(d)(ii) **408**, 841
Sched 1, para 1(e) **409**, 841
Sched 1, para 2 . . . . **409**, 841
Sched 1, para 3 . . . . **409**, 841
Sched 1, para 3(a) **409**, 841
Sched 1, para 3(b) **409**, 841
Sched 1, para 3(c) **409**, 841
Sched 1, para 3(d) **409**, 841
Sched 1, para 3(e) **409**, 841
Sched 1, para 3(f) **409**, 841
Sched 1, para 3(f)(i) **409**, 841
Sched 1, para 3(f)(ii) **409**, 841
Working Time Regulations 1999 . . . . 415, 422
  1974 Regulations 146
Codes of Practice
ACAS Code of Practice on Disciplinary and
  Grievance Procedures 2004 . . 755, **756**, 785
  para 100 . . . . **756**
  para 101 . . . . **756**
  para 102 . . . . **756**
ACAS Code of Practice on Disciplinary
  Practice and Procedures in Employment
  1977 . . . . 527, 753, 755 , 821
  para 10 753
ACAS Code of Practice on the Disclosure of
  Information to Trade Unions for Collective
  Bargaining Purposes 1997 . . . **814–15**, 818
  para 9 . . . . **814**
  para 10 . . . . **814**
  para 11 . . . . **814**
  para 11(i) **814**
  para 11(ii) **814**
  para 11(iii) **814**
  para 11(iv) **814**

para 11(v) **814**
para 12 . . . . **815**
para 14 . . . . **818**
para 15 . . . . **818**
ACAS Code of Practice on Time Off for
  Trade Union Duties and Activities
  2003. 797, **801–3**, **805–6**, **807–8**, **809–10**, 858
  para 11 . . . . **801**
  para 11(a) **802**
  para 11(b) **802**
  para 11(c) **802**
  para 11(d) **802**
  para 11(e) **802**
  para 11(f) **802**
  para 11(g) **802**
  para 12 . . . . **802–3**
  para 13 805
  para 15 810
  para 19 803
  para 20 803
  para 21 803–4
  para 22 805
  para 23 805
  para 24 805–6
  para 25 806
  para 26 806
  para 27 806
  para 28 810
  para 29 807
  para 30 808
  para 31 808
  para 32 808
  para 35 809
  para 36 809
  para 37 809
  para 38 809–10
  para 39 810
  para 40 810
  para 41 810
  para 42 810
  para 43 810
Code of Practice on Industrial Action Ballots
  and Notice to Employers 2000 904
Code of Practice governing staff transfers in the
  public sector 2000 1060
Code of Practice on Workforce Matters in
  Local Authority Service Contracts 797, 1060
DTI Code of Practice 2000 780
DTI Code of Practice on Picketing 1980 . . 917
DTI Code of Practice on Picketing
  1992 . . . . **918–19**, 922, 924, 927
  para 48 . . . . **918**
  para 49 . . . . **918**
  para 50 . . . . **918**, 919
  para 51 . . . . **918**
  para 62 . . . . **918**, 919

para 63 . . . . **919**
para 64 . . . . **919**
DTI Draft Code of Practice: Access to Workers
During Recognition and Derecognition
Ballots 2005 . . . . . 779, 781, 784, 785, 790
para 27 779
para 28 779
para 29 779
para 30 780
para 31 780
para 32 780
para 33 780
para 53 785
para 54 785
para 55 785
section F 785
Information Commissioner's Employment
Practices Data Protection Code . . 624, 625
Pt 3 . . . . 623, **625–26, 626–27**
para 3.2.1 . . . . **625**
para 3.2.2 . . . . **625**
para 3.2.3 . . . . **625**
para 3.2.4 . . . . **625**
para 3.2.5 . . . . **626**
para 3.2.6 . . . . **626**
para 3.2.7 . . . . **626**
para 3.2.7(a) **626**
para 3.2.7(b) **626**
para 3.2.8 . . . . **626**
para 3.2.9 . . . . **626**
para 3.5.1 . . . . **626**
para 3.5.2 . . . . **626**
para 3.5.3 . . . . **627**
para 3.5.4 . . . . **627**
para 3.5.5 . . . . **627**
Pt 4 . . . . **627–28**
para 3.4.3 . . . . **627**
para 3.4.4 . . . . **628**
para 3.4.5 . . . . **628**
para 3.5.1 . . . . **628**
para 3.5.2 . . . . **628**
para 3.5.3 . . . . **628**
para 3.5.4 . . . . **628**
para 3.5.5 . . . . **628**
para 3.5.6 . . . . **628**
para 3.5.7 . . . . **628**
para 3.6.1 . . . . **628**
para 3.6.2 . . . . **628**
para 3.6.3 . . . . **628**
para 3.6.4 . . . . **628**

UNITED STATES

Civil Rights Act 1964
Title VII 265

Constitution
First Amendment 749
Fourth Amendment 631
Fair Employment Practices Act 222
Title VII 223
National Labor Relations Act (NLRA) . . 749
s 14(b) 749
Railway Labor Act 749
Uniform Commercial Code 456

EUROPEAN UNION

Brussels Convention 1968 47
Charter of Fundamental Rights of the European Union 2000 . **6–8**, 9, 33, 35, 36, 48, 49,
64, 515, 536, 973, 1069
Ch I **6**
Ch II **6-7**
Ch III **7**
Ch IV **7–8**
art 5 6
art 5(1) 6
art 5(2) 6
art 5(3) 6
art 7 6
art 8 6
art 8(1) 6
art 8(2) 6
art 10 6
art 10(1) 6
art 11 6
art 11(1) 6
art 12 6
art 12(1) 6
art 14(1) 6
art 15 6
art 15(1) 7
art 15(2) 7
art 15(3) 7
art 21 7
art 21(1) 7
art 23 7
art 23(1) 7
art 23(2) 7
art 25 7
art 26 7
art 27 . . . . 7, 63, 1069
art 28 . . . . 7, 63
art 29 7
art 30 . . . . 7, 434–35, 503
art 31 . . . . 7, 74
art 31(1) 7
art 31(2) 8
art 32 8
art 32(1) 8
art 32(2) 8

art 33 8
art 33(1) 8
art 33(2) 8
art 34 8
art 34(1) 8
art 51 8
art 51(1) 8
art 51(2) 8
art 52 . . . . 8, 9
art 52(1) 8
art 52(2) 8
Community Charter of the Fundamental Social
  Rights of Workers 1989 . . . . . 35, 48, 406
Proposed Treaty Establishing a Constitution for
  Europe 2004 . . . . 6, 35
art II-112 9
art II-112(3) 9
art II-112(4) 9
art II-112(5) 9
Rome Convention 1980 47
  art 6 47
Single Act 1986 50
Treaty Establishing the European Community
  (EC Treaty/TEC) . . . . 42, 45, 48, 50 , 208
Preamble 50
art 2 319
art 8 46
art 10 44
art 13 . . . . 43, 49, 217
art 39 . . . . 46, 219
art 39(1) 46
art 39(2) 46
art 137 (ex art 118) . . 42–43, 48, 51, 348–9
art 137(1) 42
art 137(2) 42
art 137(3) 42, 43
art 137(4) 42, 43
art 137(5) 43
art 137(6) 42, 43
art 138 (ex art 118a) 406
art 139 48
art 141 (ex art 119) . . . 46, 50, 59, 176, 219,
  268, 270, 277, 278, 280, 308, 318, 319, 320,
    321, 322, 325, 326, 327, 329, 362, 364
art 141(1) 46, 319, 320
art 141(4) 59, 308, 309
art 251 . . . . 42, 43

Directives

Directive 75/117/EEC Equal Pay
  Directive 46, 219, 321, 364
1975 Directive 832
Directive 76/207/EEC Equal Treatment Directive (as amended by Directive 2000/78/EC)

. . 203, 219, 220, 223-24, 241, 242, 261, 279,
  299, 300, 307, 309, 314, 317, 321, 357, 361
Preamble 220
art 2(1) 220, 308, 321
art 2(2) 297, 298, 299, 321
art 2(3) 297, 299
art 2(4) 307, 308
art 3(1) 220, 321
art 3(1)(c) 321
art 4(1) 306
art 4(2) 306
art 9(2) 297, 298, 299
Directive 77/187/EEC Acquired Rights Directive 172, 173, 1035, 1039, 1040, 1047,
    1049, 1051, 1053, 1057, 1059, 1060, 1071
art 1(1) 1055
art 2(2) 173
art 3(1) 1040
art 3(3) 1047
art 4(1) 1039, 1040, 1041
art 4(2) 1048
art 5(2)(b) 1047
Directive 80/987/EEC on insolvency (as
  amended by Directive 2002/74) . . 48, 1031,
  1033, 1043
art 3 1031
art 3(1) 1031, 1032
art 3(2) 1031
art 4 1031
art 4(1) 1032
art 4(2) 1032
art 4(3) 1033
art 8a 1032
art 8b 1032
Directive 86/653/EEC on self-employed commercial agents 187
Directive 89/391/EEC on measures to encourage improvements in the safety and health
  of workers 149
art 2 406
art 2(2) 404
art 10(1) 149
art 10(1)(a) 149
Directive 91/533/EEC on an employer's obligation to inform employees of the conditions
  applicable to the contract of employment
  relationship 136, 137, 141
art 1 173
art 1(1) 140
art 1(2) 141
art 1(2)(a) 141
art 1(2)(b) 141
art 2(1) 137
Directive 92/85/EEC Pregnant Workers'
  Directive 358, 362, 363
art 2 . . . . 362, 363

art 8. 363
art 11 . . . . **362**
art 11(2) **362**
art 11(2)(b) **362**, 363
art 11(3) **362**, 363
art 11(4) **362**
Directive 93/104/EC Working Time Directive
(now, in its amended form, Directive
2003/88/EC). . . 44, 343, 401, 403, 404, 406,
407, 411, 412, 414, 417, 420, 425, 426–27
Preamble, Recital 1. 406
Preamble, Recital 4. 406
Preamble, Recital 7. 406
Preamble, Recital 8. 406
art 1(1) 406
art 1(3) 404, 405, 406
art 2. 412
art 2(1) 405
art 3. 415
art 4. 415
art 5. 415
art 6 44
art 6(2). 44
art 7 . . . . 406, 426
art 7(1) 407
art 7(2) 406
art 15 406
art 17 . . . . 406, 407, 418, 419
art 18 412
art 18(1)(b) 413
art 18(1)(b)(ii) 407
art 22(1)(d) 415
art 22(1)(e) 415
Section II 407
Directive 94/33/EC on the protection of young
people at work. **38**
art 1(1) **38**
art 1(2) **38**
art 1(3) **38**
Directive 94/45/EC European Works Council
Directive 46-48, 62, 845
Directive 95/46/EC Data Protection
Directive 154, 611, 635
Directive 96/34/EC Parental Leave Directive
(see also UNICE, CEEP and ETUC
Framework Agreement on Parental
Leave) 48, 343, 349, 372, 373, 377
Preamble 372
Directive 96/71/EC on posted workers 47
Directive 97/74/EC on European Works Coun-
cils Directive 62, 858
Directive 97/81/EC Part-time Workers
Directive 48, 343, 348, 350, 354, 849
art 5(2) 355

Directive 98/59/EC on the approximation of the
laws of the Member States relating to Collective Redundancies . . 46, **822**, 1028, 1063
art 1(1)(a). 825
art 2 . . . . **822**, 1028
art 2(1) **822**
art 2(2) **822**
art 2(3) **822**
art 2(3)(a). **822**
art 2(3)(b). **822**
art 2(3)(b)(i) **822**
art 2(3)(b)(ii) **822**
art 2(3)(b)(iii). **822**
art 2(2)(b)(iv) **822**
art 2(2)(b)(v) **822**
art 2(2)(b)(vi) **822**
art 4(1) 1064
Directive 99/70/EC on fixed-term work. 48, 495
Annex, Clause 3 495
Directive 2000/34/EC Race Equality
Directive 217, 225, 251, 272, 301, 310
Directive 2000/43/EC Racial Equality Directive
. . . . . . 49, 219, 251, 299, 302, 308, 334
art 6(2) 302, 303
Directive 2000/78/EC Employment Equality
Directive. . . 46, 49, 217, 218, 219, 228, 251,
272, 291, 293, 299, 303, 308, 310, 334, 508
Preamble, Recital 22 293
art 1. 303
art 2(b) **291**
art 2(b)(i) **291**
art 2(b)(ii) **291**
art 4. . . . . **303**
art 4(1) **303**
art 4(2) **303**
art 5 . . . . **291**, **292**
Directive 2001/23/EC Acquired Rights
Directive 1035, 1065
art 1 . . . . **1055**
art 1(1)(a) **1055**
art 1(1)(b) **1055**
art 1(1)(c) **1055**
art 3 . . . . **1036**
art 3(1) 1043, 1067
art 3(4) 1052
art 4 . . . . **1036**
art 4(1) **1036**
art 4(2) **1036**
art 5 . . . . **1043**
art 5(2) **1043**
art 5(2)(a) **1043**
art 5(2)(b) **1043**
Directive 2002/14/EC European Information
and Consultation Directive 46-48, 63,
150, 845, 846, 1064, 1068
Preamble **845–46**

Preamble, Recital 6 845
Preamble, Recital 7 845
Preamble, Recital 8 845
Preamble, Recital 9 845
Preamble, Recital 13 846
Preamble, Recital 15 846
Preamble, Recital 16 846
Preamble, Recital 19 846
Preamble, Recital 21 846
Preamble, Recital 22 846
Preamble, Recital 23 846
art 1(3) 856
art 7 857
art 8 854
art 8(1) 854
art 8(2) 854
Directive 2002/73/EC modernising the Equal
   Treatment Directive 219, 357
Directive 2002/74/EC on insolvency . . 48, 172
Directive 2002/78/EC Equal Treatment Amendment Directive . 242, 251, 252, 264, 269, 299
Directive 2003/88/EC Working Time
   Directive 404
   art 6 413
   art 7 405
   art 7(1) **405**
   art 18(1)(b)(i) **414**, 415
   art 22 . . . . **413**
   art 22(1) **413**
   art 22(1)(a) **413**
   art 22(1)(b) **413**
   art 22(1)(c) **413**
   art 22(1)(d) **413**
   art 22(1)(e) **413**
Burden of Proof Directive . . 263, 271, 333, 334
   art 4(1) 333
Proposed EC Directive on Information and
   Consultation 832

Regulations

Council Regulation 44/2001 on jurisdiction and
   the recognition and enforcement of judgments in civil and commercial matters . . 47
Council of Europe
Convention for the Protection of Human Rights
   and Fundamental Freedoms 1950 (ECHR)
   . . 4, 32, 34, 35, 220, 224, 561, 562, **563–64**,
   587, 689, 720, 730, 738, 740, 750, 924, 925,
                                          927, 975
   art 1 . . . . 569, 577, 578
   art 3 . . . . 570, 719, 973, 974, 975
   art 6 . . . . . . 562, 563, 573, 574, 575, 709
   art 6(1) **563**, 575
   art 6(2) 738

art 8 . . . . **224**, 256, 293, 561, 562, 563, 565,
   570, 571, 572, 573, 574, 575, 577, 582, 584,
   585, 586, 607, 609, 616, 628, 629, 630, 631,
               632, 633, 634, 635, 973, 974, 975
art 8(1) **224**, **563**, 571, 582, 629
art 8(2) . . **224**, **563**, 571, 579, 582, 583, 586,
                                    629, 630, 633
art 9 . 228, 229, 256, 561, 562, 575, 576, 588
art 9(1) **563**
art 9(2) **563-64**, 579
art 10 . . . . . 256, 561, 563, 570, 575, 576,
   577, 578, 579, 580, 581, 582, 586, 587,
   595, 598, 599, 600, 629, 632, 644, 645,
               916, 927, 928, 973, 974, 975
art 10(1) **564**, 578, 579
art 10(2) . . **564**, 571, 579, 582, 586, 636, 927
art 11 . . 34, 35, 561, 562, 563, 575, 576, 577,
   586, 587, 595, 598, 599, 600, 632, 692,
   720, 730, 732, 738, 739, 740, 746, 747,
           749, 752, 882, 888, 916, 927, 976
art 11(1) **564**, 976
art 11(2) **564**, 579, 586, 740, 749, 888,
                                         927, 976
art 13 629
art 14 . . . 220, 256, 293, 561, 563, 565, 571,
   572, 573, 576, 577, 582, 583, 584, 585,
               586, 587, 588, 600, 629
art 14(1) **564**
art 27(2) 579
Protocol 1, art 1 614
Protocol 1, art 2 . . . . 570, 584
Protocol 12 220
European Social Charter 1961 (revised 1996)
   35, 36, 387, 562, 719, 738, **864**, 945, 964, 973,
                                          975, 976
   art 4 . . . . 387, 440
   art 5 . . . . 730, 746
   art 6 . . . . **864**, 947
   art 6(1) **864**
   art 6(2) **864**
   art 6(3) **864**
   art 6(4) **864**, 976

INTERNATIONAL CONVENTIONS

ILO Convention No 1 (1919) on the Hours of
   Work (Industry) 36
ILO Convention No 52 (1936) on Holidays with
   Pay 36
ILO Convention No 87 (1948) on the Freedom
   of Association and Protection of Right to
   Organise . . 37, 648, 649, 719, 740, 945, 947,
               958, 964, 973, 975, 976
   art 2 740
   art 3 . . . . **648**, 945
   art 3(1) **648**

art 3(2) **648**
ILO Convention No 98 (1949) The Right to
Organise and Collective Bargaining Convention 37, 727, 738, 743, 746
art 1 . . . . **729**
art 1(1) **729**
art 1(2) **729**
art 1(2)(a) **729**
art 1(2)(b) **729**
art 2 . . . . 768, **835**
art 2(1) **835**
art 2(2) **835**
art 4 727
ILO Convention No 99 on minimum wage regulation in the agricultural sphere 388
ILO Convention No 135 (1971) The Workers'
Representatives Convention 37, 795
ILO Convention No 138 (1973) 37
ILO Convention No 155 (1981) on Occupational Safety and Health 36

ILO Convention No 156 (1981) on Workers
with Family Responsibilities 36
ILO Convention No 158 (1985) concerning Termination of Employment at the Initiative of
the Employer **435**
art 4 . . . . **435**
art 7 . . . . **435**
art 8 . . . . **435**
art 8(1) **435**
ILO Convention No 173 (1992) on Protection of Workers' Claims (Employers'
Insolvency) 1029
ILO Convention No 175 (1994) on establishing
minimum standards in part-time work . 350
ILO Convention No 182 38
ILO Declaration of Fundamental
Rights 1998 . . . . **36–7**

Introduction to Labour Law

1.1 What is labour law?

At its heart, labour law examines legal regulation of employment relations. The case for a special examination of contracts for the performance of work rests on their economic, social and political significance. For most people, employment provides the principal source of income and wealth. The legal institutions that constitute and govern the relations of production between workers and their employers provide one of the cornerstones of modern economies. From a social perspective, work not only occupies a large proportion of most people's days, but also provides one of the principal sites where we can construct social relationships and seek meaning for our lives. The consequence of unemployment is often described as 'social exclusion', which means both that the ensuing poverty prevents individuals from enjoying the benefits of society and that the unemployed are likely to experience less productive and meaningful lives. From a political perspective the employment relation lies at the centre of a fundamental conflict of interest that is intrinsic to capitalist societies. The conflict lies between the owners of capital, who invest in productive activities, and the workers, who supply the necessary labour. Employers seek to maximise the return on their investments, whereas the workers seek the highest price available for their labour, which digs into the employer's profits. As in other contractual relations, however, the parties ultimately share a common interest in the successful achievement of production and profits through the combination of capital and labour. The balance of strength between the competing interests of capital and labour always constitutes a key issue in the politics, because it contributes a vital element in the patterns of the distribution of wealth and power to which a society aspires. The law plays a pivotal role in both constituting and restricting the power of both capital and labour. Labour law is thus never far from the centre of political debate and controversy.

To examine labour law thoroughly, therefore, it is important to study the legal rules in their economic, social and political context. The details of the legal rules have a profound influence on the efficiency of the economic system, the life-chances of individuals, and the type of social justice achieved in society. For example, the rules that prohibit discrimination in access to employment on grounds such as sex, race and disability are intended to ensure that all people can contribute to the generation of wealth, promote the possibility of equality of opportunity for all citizens, and help to combat patterns of persistent social disadvantage for particular groups. Similarly, the legal rules that permit workers to take collective industrial action in order to support their claims for increases in pay and improvements in other terms and conditions have a significant influence on the distribution of wealth and power both within the firm and in society more broadly. The importance of legal rules should not be unduly exaggerated, for broader economic, social and political forces will ultimately shape a society and the experience of its citizens. For example, levels of unemployment, which depend heavily these days on global economic trends and monetary policies, have a profound influence on levels of wages, the bargaining power of workers, and, more diffusely, perceptions of social justice. Nevertheless, the rules of labour law shape how these global economic and social forces become translated into the experiences of individuals.

The appreciation of labour law as a fundamental constitutive element in modern societies implies the need to study a vast range of legal rules and institutions. We might study the rules governing access to labour markets, the regulation of any type of transaction involving work, the rules governing organisations of capital and labour, social welfare systems for handling unemployment, the supply of training and education to workers, and the links between workplace relations and broader political institutions. This large terrain trespasses over many fields that have traditionally been studied independently, such as immigration law, social security law, company law and constitutional law. At the same time, labour law requires consideration of a wide range of conceptually distinct categories of law, such as contract, tort, public law, social security law and company law. The challenge we face in this book is to provide a selective study of the key legal rules and institutions at the heart of the discipline, which forms a coherent whole, and which is also of a manageable size. When making this selection we need to strike a balance also between, on the one hand, a consideration of those legal rules which have a profound influence in shaping the economic and social system and, on the other hand, an examination of laws which have greater daily significance for lawyers. For example, the rules governing trade union organisation and industrial action structure the bargaining power of many workers in the labour market, but in practice a lawyer is far more likely to encounter the rules relating to claims for wages, unfair dismissal, and discrimination brought by individual workers. Our approach to the scope of labour law is guided by the goal of examining every aspect of the legal regulation of the employment relation, without paying heed to limits set by legal classifications and concepts. Our emphasis upon particular topics, however, depends upon a pragmatic compromise between the need to analyse the fundamental structures supported by the law whilst providing a full explanation of the rules governing common problems and disputes between employers and workers.

At the core of the subject, however, we must consider the principal legal relation through which work is performed: the contract of employment. This contract resembles other contractual relations in many respects. It contains an agreement between two parties, the employer and the employee, that involves an exchange, the employee offering to perform work in return for pay and other types of remuneration. Like other contracts, it is legally enforceable in the courts and the parties can claim compensation for breach of its terms. Yet the contract of employment is also distinctive in many respects. It is typically a long-term contract that persists over an indefinite period of time, which will be subject to modifications such as alterations in working methods and increases in pay. The contract of employment is also likely to be less specific than other types of contracts about the details of the performance required from the worker. The contract is likely to avoid precise specification of the work to be performed, but instead to grant to the employer the right to fix the details of the required performance through subsequent instructions. As a consequence, the contract of employment creates a relation of power in which the employer has the discretion, within limits, to direct labour, and the employee has the duty to obey lawful instructions. These distinctive features of the contract of employment—its indeterminate duration, its variability, its incompleteness and its construction of a relation of subordination—create the need for special regulation beyond the ordinary rules of the law of contract.

These features of the fundamental legal institution through which work is performed also help to explain the complexity of the rules to be discovered in the workplace. The contract sets a framework for the relation of production between employer and employee, but most of the details have to be constructed through further managerial directions, customs, agreements and procedures. Most employers supplement the contract with further written directions known as works rules or staff handbooks, which contain descriptions of standing instructions, procedures, facilities, opportunities and employee's rights. Where the workforce has organised a collective bargaining relationship through a trade union, a collective agreement is likely to fix pay and other benefits, to specify further rules and rights of the workers, and to establish procedures for determining further rules. As well as these written rules and agreements, settled practices are likely to develop in the performance of work, and these practices may be regarded as customary rules that the parties should observe. Whether or not all these rules are legally binding is a difficult question that will be considered in detail subsequently. The important point to be noticed here is that each workplace has a complex system of internal governance, in which the legal distinction between legally enforceable rules and mere social rules is unlikely to be significant in the daily conduct of relations of production. In other words, the 'law of the workplace' is not confined to general rules of law and special labour laws, but must also be discovered in the detailed rules and conventions of each workplace.

**[1.1] H. Arthurs, 'Understanding Labour Law: The Debate over "Industrial Pluralism"'
(1985) *Current Legal Problems* 83 (footnotes omitted)**

Put briefly, the argument is that each workplace is its own legal system, different from any other, and different as well from the legal system of the state. Whether we look at the content of the rules governing workplace behaviour, the source of those rules, the processes by which they are generated, enforced or modified—even the value system or ideology in which they are embedded—the predominant impression is the same: deed determines word, context dominates text, specific trumps general, and 'law'—as we lawyers know it—is seen, if at all, 'through a glass, darkly.' A worker arrives for work at a stipulated hour, enters the premises by a designated door, records his arrival in the prescribed manner, dons work clothes, takes tools in his hand, goes to an assigned work station, and in accordance with minutely-detailed procedures, addresses a narrow range of tasks. Virtually his every move is bounded by rules. So too his relations with fellow workers, management representatives and third persons, such as customers, which are neither wholly spontaneous nor random: they are rule bound. His remuneration and his exposure to discipline and redundancy, his enjoyment of amenities and his exposure to hardship at work, are all carefully defined by rules.

There is no point in dismissive rhetoric whose general purport is that such trivial rules do not rise to the dignity of 'law.' It matters profoundly to the worker (and his employer) whether his tea break is ten minutes or only five; whether his production quota is 110 per cent. or only 90 per cent. of what he feels capable of; whether he must silently bear his foreman's abuse or can give as good as he gets without fear of being sacked. These are 'legal' questions with an immediacy that, for the worker, far that exceeds that of the law of assault or the European Convention on Human Rights. And they are often 'legal' questions of considerable complexity: whether or to what extent plant practise tolerates blunt speech demands no less careful a balancing of interests than the limits of fair comment in the law of defamation; the complex reciprocal claims of worker and employer for pay and performance are sometimes more exquisitely arcane than feudal tenures.

If I have persuaded you that a special regime of law indeed prevails in each workplace, I must next try to show that these regimes-and others-taken collectively lend a pluralistic character to law in all industrial societies. Let me begin by more carefully identifying several of the legal regimes which emerge from, or seek to impinge upon, life at work.

First, there is the indigenous law of the workplace itself. Norms or rules are generated internally: contracts, collective agreements, arbitral awards, codes of conduct, informal understandings and, above all, customary patterns of behaviour which, though always changing, at any given moment plausibly capture what is understood to be 'the law.'

Secondly, there is what we usually refer to as 'labour law,' special rules of external, formal or state law: legislation and common law doctrine specifically intended to govern individual or collective employment relations; tort doctrine—say, 'conspiracy' or 'intimidation'—ostensibly of general application, but in practise confined to, or applied in special ways in, industrial disputes; exculpatory legislation suspending or modifying general laws as they apply in labour matters; social legislation in which entitlement is defined in relation to employment . . .

I have so far identified as important normative regimes the indigenous law of the workplace and external, but specialised, labour law. I have purposely left the least to the last: the general body of state law: the constitution, canons of contractual and statutory construction, doctrines such as *ultra vires* or natural justice, the parole evidence rule, fundamental breach or trespass *ab initio*.

The general body of state law is not, I suggest, any less political than the special rules of labour law. But its political content is generally immanent rather than overt, and becomes manifest only when the law is applied in particular circumstances. The law of assault, for example, has one significance in the context of domestic violence, a second when applied to brutal attacks upon members of racial minorities or elderly shopkeepers, and a third when invoked to regulate picketing. The law of contract which 'neutrally' defines relations between two large corporations may require special shades of meaning when used to regulate their relations with employees . . .

Each place of work, each relationship of employment, each unionised shop or factory, operates in practise within a framework of law which is in some way unique, precisely because of the indeterminate, diverse and dynamic effects of the interaction of these three regimes.

An important challenge for labour lawyers is therefore to understand how these different sources of rules interact. The legal system has to adjudicate on the interaction of the rules emanating from the contract of employment, managerial directions, the conventions of the workplace, collective agreements, special statutory regulation of employment and the general principles of public and private law. These complexities are generated in large part by the distinctive attributes of the contract of employment, but we should not forget that the social and political significance of work gives rise to demands that employment relations should not be regarded in the same light as other economic transactions.

Because work is central to people's lives, both in terms of its provision of material well-being and as a source of meaning and social integration, the idea that employment relations should be regarded merely as an economic transaction has always been contested. The economist's analysis of labour as a 'factor of production' is challenged by a rival perception that insists that the position of the worker raises profound issues concerning respect for the dignity of mankind. Under the aegis of the United Nations, the International Labour Organisation (ILO) promulgates universal standards designed to promote this humanitarian or social perspective. Its fundamental principle is: 'Labour is not a Commodity' (see P. O'Higgins, ' "Labour is not a Commodity"—an Irish Contribution to International Labour Law' (1997) 26 *Industrial Law Journal* 225). What does this slogan mean? It suggests that although the market economy drives employers to purchase labour like any other commodity used in production, the human beings who provide labour should not be treated as commodities to be bought and sold by the employer at the most favourable price. Workers should be able to choose for whom they work, and the labour market should be controlled to ensure that it produces a reasonable standard of living for a worker and dependants. More fundamentally, employers should treat workers with dignity and respect.

As well as an economic relation, therefore, labour law is centrally concerned with issues of human rights. These rights are often described as 'social rights' in order to distinguish them from the traditional civil liberties and political rights that citizens require against the abuse of state power. But the source of these social rights depends upon a similar articulation of a humanitarian concern for the dignity and autonomy of individuals. Labour law represents the field where this political tradition of respect for the individual clashes most directly with the operation of markets. Its study reveals the tensions between the two foundations of modern Western societies: the market as the powerhouse for economic growth and material well-being, and the liberal state as the protector of the rights of individuals. For example, the need for efficient use of labour in order to achieve competitive and profitable production points towards a requirement for employers to be able to hire and fire workers at will; but respect for the dignity of workers suggests that their interests in job security and being treated fairly require that constraints should be placed upon the employer's power to dismiss workers arbitrarily. Much of labour law can be analysed as the political compromises that have been struck between the need for efficient markets and the need to respect the social rights of individuals (see A.C.L. Davies, *Perspectives on Labour Law* (Cambridge, Cambridge University Press, 2004).

The importance of the political comprises that labour law represents is well illustrated by the extensive references to rights that affect the workplace contained in the

European Union's Charter of Fundamental Rights, signed at Nice in 2000. Although not legally binding on Member States, this statement of rights both describes a set of aspirations and also provides a description of fundamental principles that may be used to interpret more detailed regulation. The Charter is included as Title II in the heart of the Treaty Establishing a Constitution for Europe (CIG 87/2/04 Rev 2, Brussels, 29 October 2004), which is yet to be ratified by the Member States. Not all of the articles cited below have an obvious and immediate application to employment relations, but in fact all these concerns may arise and will be considered in this book.

[1.2] Charter of Fundamental Rights of the European Union (2000/C 364/01)

Chapter I DIGNITY

Article 5 Prohibition of slavery and forced labour
1. No one shall be held in slavery or servitude.
2. No one shall be required to perform forced or compulsory labour.
3. Trafficking in human beings is prohibited.

Chapter II FREEDOMS

Article 7 Respect for private and family life
Everyone has the right to respect for his or her private and family life, home and communications.

Article 8 Protection of personal data
1. Everyone has the right to the protection of personal data concerning him or her.
2. Such data must be processed fairly for specified purposes and on the basis of the consent of the person concerned or some other legitimate basis laid down by law. Everyone has the right of access to data which has been collected concerning him or her, and the right to have it rectified . . .

Article 10 Freedom of thought, conscience and religion
1. Everyone has the right to freedom of thought, conscience and religion. This right includes freedom to change religion or belief and freedom, either alone or in community with others and in public or private, to manifest religion or belief, in worship, teaching, practice and observance . . .

Article 11 Freedom of expression and information
1. Everyone has the right to freedom of expression. This right shall include freedom to hold opinions and to receive and impart information and ideas without interference by public authority and regardless of frontiers . . .

Article 12 Freedom of assembly and of association
1. Everyone has the right to freedom of peaceful assembly and to freedom of association at all levels, in particular in political, trade union and civic matters, which implies the right of everyone to form and to join trade unions for the protection of his or her interests . . .

Article 14
1. Everyone has the right to education and to have access to vocational and continuing training . . . .

Article 15 Freedom to chose and occupation and right to engage in work

1. Everyone has the right to engage in work and to pursue a freely chosen or accepted occupation.
2. Every citizen of the Union has the freedom to seek employment, to work, to exercise the right of establishment and to provide services in any Member State.
3. Nationals of third countries who are authorised to work in the territories of the Member States are entitled to working conditions equivalent to those of citizens of the Union.

Chapter III EQUALITY

Article 21 Non-discrimination
1. Any discrimination based on any ground such as sex, race, colour, ethnic or social origin, genetic features, language, religion or belief, political or any other opinion, membership of a national minority, property, birth, disability, age or sexual orientation shall be prohibited . . .

Article 23 Equality between men and women
1. Equality between men and women must be ensured in all areas, including employment, work and pay.
2. The principle of equality shall not prevent the maintenance or adoption of measures providing for specific advantages in favour of the under-represented sex . . .

Article 25 The rights of the elderly
The Union recognises and respects the rights of the elderly to lead a life of dignity and independence and to participate in social and cultural life.

Article 26 Integration of persons with disabilities
The Union recognises and respects the rights of persons with disabilities to benefit from measures designed to ensure their independence, social and occupational integration and participation in the life of the community.

Chapter IV SOLIDARITY

Article 27 Workers' right to information and consultation within the undertaking
Workers or their representatives must, at the appropriate levels, be guaranteed information and consultation in good time in the cases and under the conditions provided for by Community law and national laws and practices.

Article 28 Right of collective bargaining and action
Workers and employers, or their respective organisations, have, in accordance with Community law and national laws and practices, the right to negotiate and conclude collective agreements at the appropriate levels and, in cases of conflicts of interest, to take collective action to defend their interests, including strike action.

Article 29 Right of access to placement services
Everyone has the right of access to a free placement service.

Article 30 Protection in the event of unjustified dismissal
Every worker has the right to protection against unjustified dismissal, in accordance with Community law and national laws and practices.

Article 31 Fair and just working conditions
1. Every worker has the right to working conditions which respect his or her health, safety and dignity.

2. Every worker has the right to limitation of maximum working hours, to daily and weekly rest periods and to an annual period of paid leave.

Article 32 Prohibition of child labour and protection of young people at work
1. The employment of children is prohibited. The minimum age of admission to employment may not be lower than the minimum school-leaving age, without prejudice to such rules as may be more favourable to young people and except for limited derogations.
2. Young people admitted to work must have working conditions appropriate to their age and be protected against economic exploitation and any work likely to harm their safety, health or physical, mental, moral or social development or to interfere with their education.

Article 33 Family and professional life
1. The family shall enjoy legal, economic and social protection.
2. To reconcile family and professional life, everyone shall have the right to protection from dismissal for a reason connected with maternity and the right to paid maternity leave and to parental leave following the birth or adoption of a child.

Article 34 Social security and social assistance
1. The Union recognises and respect the entitlement to social security benefits and social services providing protection in cases such as maternity, illness, industrial accidents, dependency or old age, and in the case of loss of employment, in accordance with the procedures laid down by Community law and national laws and practices . . . .

Article 51 Scope
1. The provisions of this Charter are addressed to the institutions and bodies of the Union with due regard for the principle of subsidiarity and to the Member States only when they are implementing Union law. They shall therefore respect the rights, observe the principles and promote the application thereof in accordance with their respective powers.
2. This Charter does not establish any new power or task for the Community or the Union, or modify powers and tasks defined by the Treaties.

Article 52 Scope of guaranteed rights
1. Any limitation on the exercise of the rights and freedoms recognised by this Charter must be provided for by law and respect the essence of those rights and freedoms. Subject to the principle of proportionality, limitations may only be made if they are necessary and genuinely meet objectives of general interest recognized by the Union or the need to protect the rights and freedoms of others.
2. Rights recognised by this Charter which are based on the Community Treaties or the Treaty on European Union shall be exercised under the conditions and within the limits defined by those Treaties.

By virtue of Articles 51 and 52, this Charter does not create new directly enforceable legal rights, or extend the scope of European Community law, though judges and other officials might use the rights and principles it declares in the interpretation of European law. The Charter's significance lies rather in its statement of common values and principles that are shared throughout the European Union, even though many of these topics such as social security law and the law of dismissal have so far been largely reserved to regulation by Member States. The Charter also displays some of the special concerns of the European Community, such as the creation of a single market without barriers, including the free movement of workers. What should be noted especially, however, is the way in which rights of workers, such as equality of opportunity, fair treatment, collective organisation and action, and safety are regarded as part of a scheme of fundamental rights of European citizens, that is an essential part of the constitutional and social order, which will be embedded in any future Constitution for Europe. Assuming that the Constitution is ratified by Member States, the legal implications of the Charter will be further specified by an extension to Article 52 (renumbered as II-112). These provisions draw a distinction between 'rights' and 'principles' contained in the Charter, with the implication that 'rights' should always be taken into account when interpreting European Union law, whereas principles should only be an aid to interpretation for legislation intended to implement those principles. The puzzle about this distinction is that the Charter does not appear to draw a sharp distinction in its language between rights and principles.

[1.3] Proposed Treaty Establishing a Constitution for Europe (2004) Article II-112

3. Insofar as this Charter contains rights which correspond to rights guaranteed by the Convention for the Protection of Human Rights and Fundamental Freedoms, the meaning and scope of those rights shall be the same as those laid down by the said Convention. This provision shall not prevent Union law providing more extensive protection.
4. Insofar as this Charter recognises fundamental rights as they result from the constitutional traditions common to the Member States, those rights shall be interpreted in harmony with those traditions.
5. The provisions of this Charter which contain principles may be implemented by legislative and executive actions taken by institutions, bodies, offices and agencies of the Union, and by acts of Member States when they are implementing Union law, in the exercise of their respective powers. They shall be judicially cognisable only in the interpretation of such acts and in the ruling on their legality . . .

Labour law thus consists of many strands of enquiry. At its core lies the contractual relation of employment, with the relevant legal rules governing access, performance and termination. But this contractual relation can be understood adequately only in context of the other rules of the workplace, both those set by managerial direction and those established through collective agreements and conventions. These governance structures extend to the methods by which workers seek to use collective strength through trade unions in order to improve the terms and conditions of employment and to control how power is exercised in the workplace. The legal system, using primarily the instrument of legislation, seeks to channel these market relations in ways that serve broader political goals such as social justice, equality and the rights of individuals. In the final analysis, therefore, labour law concerns not merely the study of a particular kind of contractual relationship, but rather how the law seeks to control and steer relations of production for the purposes of promoting wealth, securing social justice, and guaranteeing the social rights of citizens.

1.2 Methods of regulation

Labour law uses a wide range of techniques for tackling its objectives. Indeed, one of the distinctive characteristics of this regulation has been the subtlety and variety of its methods for channelling labour markets in ways that are consistent with social and political aims. The most innovative method of regulation has been the use of collective bargaining as a source of rules to govern employment relationship. But labour law also uses private law techniques, mandatory standards backed up by criminal penalties, and occasionally public law ideas to achieve its ends. The variety of techniques is partly explained by the complexity of the subject matter: not only are there many different kinds of jobs, but also employment relations take many different forms, from the casual hourly-paid manual worker to the permanently employed, salaried and bonus-rich managing director of a large multinational enterprise. The variety of legal techniques is, however, more directly driven by considerations of effectiveness and efficiency.

Effectiveness of regulation requires employers and workers to conform to the relevant standards. But effectiveness is constantly undermined by economic incentives for evasion and avoidance. Regulation may impose additional costs upon employers, such as the cost of paying a minimum wage or adopting safety measures, so employers, ever with an eye to profitability, may be reluctant to comply with the law or least seek to minimise their costs in so doing. At the same time, employees may be reluctant to insist upon any legal rights they may be given for fear of losing their jobs to others who may be prepared to work for wages below the minimum or in unsafe conditions. The perennial difficulty that confronts labour law is to render its standards effective.

The efficiency of regulation raises a further set of problems. A government must weigh the costs of regulation against its prospective benefits. Those costs comprise not only the expense to government of administering the system, such as the costs of courts and inspectors, but also the costs imposed upon businesses, which, if significant, may reduce their competitiveness. The problem for labour law is to find techniques of regulation that minimise those costs whilst at the same time achieving as much of the intended benefits of the regulation as possible.

With these perennial problems of effectiveness and efficiency in mind, we can consider the principal regulatory techniques used by labour law.

1.2.1 Regulatory standards with criminal sanctions

Early labour legislation in the nineteenth century typically set standards which were enforceable in the magistrates' courts by criminal penalties. The tasks of monitoring and enforcement of the standards were often given to factory inspectors, who could prosecute an employer for breach of the statutory rules. This criminal law technique of regulation survives to this day primarily in relation to Health and Safety Inspectors. Although we shall not examine the important Health and Safety at Work Act 1974 in great detail, it is useful to illustrate this regulatory technique through a few extracts. The statute sets the standard of safety for the employer (section 2) (often supplemented by detailed statutory instruments (section 15)); compliance is monitored by inspectors (section 19), who may enforce the standards, usually after a warning (section 21) or an order to stop a particular activity (section 22), by bringing a prosecution. Conviction of one of the offences will lead to the imposition on the employer of a fine or imprisonment (section 33).

[1.4] Health and Safety at Work Act 1974

s.2—(1) It shall be the duty of every employer to ensure, so far as is reasonably practicable, the health safety and welfare at work of all his employees.

(2) Without prejudice to the generality of an employer's duty under the preceding subsection, the matters to which that duty extends include in particular—

(a) the provision and maintenance of plant and systems of work that are, so far as is reasonably practicable, safe and without risks to health;

(b) arrangements for ensuring, so far as is reasonably practicable, safety and absence of risks to health in connection with the use, handling, storage and transport of articles and substances . . .

s. 15—(1) . . . the Secretary of State . . . shall have power to make regulations under this section for any of the general purposes of this Part . . . [i.e. s.2 and other sections] . . . and regulations so made are . . . referred to as 'health and safety regulations' . . .

s. 19—(1) Every enforcing authority may appoint as inspectors . . . such persons having suitable qualifications as it thinks necessary for carrying into effect the relevant statutory provisions within its field of responsibility . . .

s. 21 If an inspector is of the opinion that a person—

(a) is contravening one or more of the relevant statutory provisions; or

(b) has contravened one or more of those provisions in circumstances that make it likely that the contravention will continue or be repeated,

he may serve on him a notice (in this Part referred to an 'an improvement notice') stating that he is of that opinion, specifying the provision or provisions as to which he is of that opinion, giving particulars of the reasons why he is of that opinion, and requiring that person to remedy the contravention . . .

s. 22—(1) This section applies to any activities which are being or are likely to be carried on by or under the control of any person, being activities to or in relation to which any of the relevant statutory provision apply or will, if the activities are so carried on, apply.

(2) If as regards any activities to which this section applies an inspector is of the opinion that, as carried on or likely to be carried on by or under the control of the person in question, the activities involve or, as the case may be, will involve a risk of serious personal injury, the inspector may serve on that person a notice (in this Part referred to as 'a prohibition notice') . . .

s. 33—(1) It is an offence for a person—

(a) to fail to discharge a duty to which he is subject by virtue of sections 2 to 7; . . .

(c) to contravene any health and safety regulations . . .

(g) to contravene any requirement or prohibition imposed by an improvement notice or a prohibition notice . . .

(1A) . . . a person guilty of an offence under subsection (1)(a) above . . . shall be liable—

(a) on summary conviction to a fine not exceeding £20,000;

(b) on conviction on indictment, to a fine . . .

(2A) A person guilty of an offence under subsection 1(g) . . . shall be liable—

(a) on summary conviction, to imprisonment for a term not exceeding six months, or a fine not exceeding £20,000, or both;

(b) on conviction on indictment, to imprisonment for a term not exceeding two years, or a fine, or both.

The strength of this system of regulation is that it sets general standards supplemented by detailed regulations on particular topics backed up by the threat of punitive sanctions against employers who ignore safety standards. But a weakness of this type of regulation is that it is expensive to administer, since it requires an army of inspectors to visit every workplace at frequent intervals. In practice, the small number of inspectors and the infrequency of their inspections substantially diminish the risk of prosecution. Many employers appear to make the calculation that the costs of extra safety precautions far exceed the risk of incurring the costs of a fine. To some extent this calculation can be affected by raising the level of fines, but the underlying problem of detection of breaches of the regulations cannot be solved without greatly increasing the costs of inspection. Criminal offences are also provided as a sanction under other important labour laws, such as the National Minimum Wage Act 1998 and the Working Time Regulations 1998. But in general the predominant regulatory technique has switched from criminal law to civil law.

1.2.2 Individual civil law rights

In the late twentieth century in the United Kingdom, the normal regulatory technique was to grant individual workers legal rights to seek compensation from the employer for breach of statutory standards. Some of the most important legislation that broadly follows this pattern is the law relating to unfair dismissal and redundancy, discrimination and equal pay. This technique was also developed by the courts much earlier in relation to safety legislation, where the Factory Acts, precursors to the Health and Safety at Work Act 1974, were interpreted to grant an individual employee who was injured as a result of breach of the regulations the right to claim compensation in tort. The same technique of granting individuals rights to claim compensation also comprises part of the enforcement mechanism for the National Minimum Wage Act 1998 and the Working Time Regulations 1998.

[1.5] National Minimum Wage Act 1998 section 17

(1) If a worker who qualifies for the national minimum wage is remunerated for any pay reference period by his employer at a rate which is less than the national minimum wage, the worker shall be taken to be entitled under his contract to be paid, as additional remuneration in respect of that period, the amount described in subsection (2) below.

(2) That amount is the difference between—

(a) the relevant remuneration received by the worker for the pay reference period; and
(b) the relevant remuneration which the worker would have received for that period had he been remunerated by the employer at a rate equal to the national minimum wage.

The effect of this legislation is to grant the individual employee something equivalent to a contractual right to the minimum wage, which may be enforced through the courts.

The strength of this legislation is that it grants clear legally enforceable rights to workers, and gives them the incentive to enforce those rights by bringing claims for compensation. But the effectiveness of the regulation depends crucially on the willingness of individuals to enforce their rights, and most employees will be reluctant to do so, at least until the termination of the employment relation. The daunting and expensive task for employees of going to court to enforce claims for compensation will also detract from the effectiveness of the regulation, though this problem can be reduced, as we shall see below, by the creation of inexpensive and informal specialist tribunals. A further weakness of this regulatory technique is that it is designed not to prevent breaches of standards, but rather to compensate for losses incurred by workers as a result of those breaches. The potential cost of compensation to employers no doubt encourages their compliance with the standard, but often employers may make the assessment that it is cheaper to risk the uncertain costs of potential claims than to incur the clear and immediate expense of compliance. The attraction to governments of this technique of regulation is that it avoids the cost of expensive administrative machinery such as inspectors, which perhaps explains its prevalence.

The effectiveness of individual civil law rights can be strengthened, however, by techniques of collective representation. Trade unions offer assistance to their members in pursuing their statutory rights, and may sometimes use litigation of a test case brought by an individual member to challenge a management decision. In some instances legislation has established statutory bodies that may assist individual litigants in pursuing their statutory claims. Of course, the effectiveness of these statutory bodies in supporting individual claims is severely restricted by the limited funds available.

1.2.3 Collective bargaining

For most of the twentieth century, however, the principal regulatory technique for employment was the facilitation of collective bargaining between employers and trade unions. Collective self-regulation could be achieved through collective agreements, which would set standards and fix the terms and conditions for individual contracts of employment. Collective bargaining could also establish mechanisms involving the trade union for monitoring compliance with those standards, procedures for varying the standards, and methods for resolving disputes. A collective agreement might be made either at the level of an industrial sector, thus applying to all employers in that sector to a minimum level of terms and conditions, or more commonly from the 1960s onwards, at the level of a single employer or workplace.

One significant effect of the dominance of this regulatory strategy of promoting collective bargaining or self-regulation was the relative absence of mandatory standards governing employment, either in the form of rules backed by criminal sanctions or in the form of individual rights to compensation. While most other industrialised countries introduced mandatory legislation on such matters as maximum hours or minimum wages, the United Kingdom followed a distinctive pattern of minimal direct statutory regulation of contracts of employment. For example, unlike other industrialised countries, until 1998 there was no regulation of maximum hours of work or minimum wages that applied to all workers, though particular industrial sectors such as mines were closely regulated. This pattern, sometimes dubbed 'legal abstentionism', has now, as we shall see, been reversed.

But the strategy of supporting instead the method of collective bargaining to set standards required considerable intervention by the State. The first step was to remove the legal obstacles to the establishment of collective bargaining relationships. The law needed to protect the workers' right to join a trade union, which could engage in collective bargaining on their behalf. The law also needed to protect the right of workers to take industrial action in order to back up their demands for satisfactory terms and conditions of employment, for otherwise the employer would be inclined to ignore them. The essential elements of this system of collective self-regulation in the United Kingdom were established by 1906, but only after protracted political and social struggles. The common law created by the judges in the nineteenth century, often supplemented by legislation, regarded trade unions as criminal and civil conspiracies, so legislation was required to grant immunity to trade unions in order to permit their lawful existence. Similarly, the law regarded industrial action as both a criminal and a civil wrong. For example, it was a crime under the Master and Servant Acts for a servant to leave employment without permission, and in the middle of the nineteenth century there were thousands of prosecutions a year before the magistrates. Again Parliament needed to abolish these offences (largely achieved by 1875) and to grant immunities to trade unions against civil actions (in 1906). This legislation was not without its loopholes, which were exploited from time to time by employers to fight trade unions and strikes, but for much of the twentieth century the legal system achieved the goal of permitting the development of collective bargaining for the purpose of setting terms and conditions of employment.

But the State also took a second step, which was not merely to permit collective bargaining to take place, but to promote it. After the 1914–18 war, the new Ministry of Labour encouraged industrial sectors to create Joint Industrial Councils, following the recommendation of a sub-committee of the Committee of Reconstruction chaired by J.H. Whitley. If employers failed to establish a Joint Industrial Council, the government took powers under the Trade Boards Act 1918 to impose a form of collective bargaining with the addition of independent members where no voluntary collective bargaining arrangements were in place. Although the pressure from the Ministry of Labour to establish industrial sector bargaining was not always sustained, at its peak this strategy achieved coverage through collective agreements or decisions of Trade Boards (or Wages Councils as they were called later in the comprehensive Wages Councils Act 1945) of about 85 per cent of the British workforce. These industrial sector agreements set wages and hours not only for employers in the relevant association and members of the relevant union, but also for any employers in the industrial sector or trade and any workers employed by them.

The methods by which the State promoted the development of collective bargaining or self-regulation shifted decisively after the *Report of the Royal Commission on Trade Unions and Employers' Associations* (1968, Cmnd 3623) (the Donovan Commission), when it became public policy to promote enterprise- (single-employer) or plant-level bargaining. To promote this form of collective bargaining, legislation created procedures by which trade unions might compel an employer to recognise the union and to bargain with it over terms and conditions of employment. Subsequently, the legal mechanisms for promoting industrial sector bargaining (Wages Councils) and for extending the effects of sector level agreements to all workers have been gradually dismantled. Governments have not continuously pursued a policy of promoting collective bargaining, but when they have, this support has often seemed crucial to its success in achieving coverage of the workforce and in setting high standards. Certainly the State has never been neutral about the development of collective bargaining: either promoting and channelling it, or, in some periods, seeking to confine it.

Of course, the effectiveness of collective bargaining, particularly when conducted at the enterprise level, also depends crucially on high levels of union membership among the workforce together with effective organisation and representation by officials of the union. When these conditions are satisfied, collective bargaining, viewed as a system of regulation of the employment relation, proves an effective and efficient system of regulation of the employment relation. Collective bargaining is likely to be effective where a strong union can both demand good terms and conditions and then monitor and enforce those terms subsequently. It is also efficient in the sense that the costs to the State are minimal, and the employer is permitted to use its bargaining power to insist upon terms under which the business can remain competitive. Enterprise level bargaining also has the potential advantage that the terms and conditions can be tailored more precisely than general legislative standards to the particular conditions of the business. Unlike other countries, collective agreements either at the level of industrial sector or enterprise were not legally enforceable in themselves in the United Kingdom, but they did set legally enforceable standards indirectly by often fixing the binding terms of individual contracts of employment. This enforcement mechanism provided little security against the revocation of collective agreements by employers, but in practice the standards were normally observed because they were supported by the effective social sanction of the threat of industrial action. In this way, with the support and encouragement of the State, employers and trade unions can operate their own procedures for the regulation of terms and conditions of employment.

1.2.4 Effectiveness of labour law

We have distinguished between three paradigms of regulation in labour law: mandatory standards backed by a criminal process, civil law rights supported by individual claims for compensation, and collective self-regulation. These techniques represent the major types of labour law, but other techniques are possible and may be used more frequently in the future (see Box below). In practice, with respect to any particular issue, the legal system often adopts a combination of methods. For example, in relation to health and safety issues, all three types of regulation are employed with a view to maximising the efficacy of the regulation. As well as the system of criminal penalties enforced by inspectors, the individual employee has various civil claims, including the claim for compensation for injuries. In addition, the legislation requires employers to establish Health and Safety representatives, who may ask for the formation of a committee in order to formulate and monitor health and safety policies within the workplace. Although these committees do not bargain about terms and conditions of employment, they share the feature with collective agreements that they create a collective mechanism for self-regulation and monitoring, in the hope of achieving higher levels of compliance with health and safety standards.

[1.6] Health and Safety at Work Act 1974 section 2

> **(4)** Regulations made by the Secretary of State may provide for the appointment in prescribed cases by recognised trade unions . . . of safety representatives from amongst the employees . . .
>
> **(6)** It shall be the duty of the every employer to consult any such representatives with a view to the making and maintenance of arrangements which will enable him and his employees to co-operate effectively in promoting and developing measures to ensure the health and safety at work of the employees, and in checking the effectiveness of such measures.
>
> **(7)** In such cases as may be prescribed it shall be the duty of every employer, if requested to do so by the safety representatives mention in subsection (4) above, to establish, in accordance with regulations made by the Secretary of State, a safety committee having the function of keeping under review the measures taken to ensure the health and safety at work of his employees and such other functions as may be prescribed.

The statute implies that the consultation system will be restricted to representatives drawn from a recognised trade union, but, in the absence of a recognised trade union, the duty to consult has been extended, in order to comply with European law, to either employees directly or their elected representatives: Health and Safety (Consultation with Employees) Regulations 1996, below 8.6. The system of regulation in health and safety, combining as it does all three types of regulation, is the most sophisticated used in labour law. In response to the serious problem of injuries at work, the legislation uses all the available techniques to attempt to overcome the problem of efficacy.

Yet the law of health and safety at work teaches us a solemn lesson. Despite the use of the most sophisticated and expensive regulatory techniques in labour law, it fails to meet the aspirations of the regulators. As well as the persistent problem of injuries and deaths in industry and construction work, it is estimated that about a third of workers in the EU work in discomfort stemming from noise, air pollution, extreme temperatures and faulty ergonomical design of workstations (European Foundation for the Improvement of Living and Working Conditions, *Second European Survey on Working Conditions* (Dublin, 1996)).

The important point to bear in mind always in the study of labour law is that legal regulation has to overcome substantial obstacles to achieve its goals and that rarely will legal regulation prove completely efficacious. Employers may resist or try to avoid regulation of every kind because it is perceived to impose extra costs on the business. Workers may be reluctant to seek to enforce standards owing to the fear of victimisation. Given the number and variety of workplaces, the State does not have the capacity to monitor and enforce all the standards that it seeks to promote. What we need to consider always in connection with labour law is whether changes in the design and techniques of legal regulation might serve its objectives better.

Incentives as a Regulatory Technique

As well as imposing sanctions as a deterrent to breach of regulatory standards, a government may create incentives for compliance. These incentives can take many forms. The tax system can be manipulated in order to encourage certain types of conduct. For example, workers can be offered reductions in income tax and capital gains tax if they take part of their remuneration in the form of shares in their employer's company (e.g. Finance Act 2000, Schedule 8). The object of this regulation is to encourage long-term commitment from workers to their employer by linking their economic interests to those of the owners of capital. Similarly the government can offer direct subsidies to employers to promote training, to keep workers in employment during temporary down-turns in the business, or to encourage corporate rescues of failing businesses (see Chapter 10). Another, more indirect, method of providing incentives is to permit employers to avoid state regulation and inspection provided that they adopt particular management processes. An example might be the use of a sophisticated health and safety system, which is audited and certified by independent third parties (see: N. Gunningham and R. Johnstone, *Regulating Workplace Safety: System and Sanctions* (Oxford, Oxford University Press, 1999). On the variety of modern techniques: A. Ogus, 'New Techniques for Social Regulation: Decentralisation and Diversity' in H. Collins, P. Davies, R. Rideout (eds), *Legal Regulation of the Employment Relation* (London, Kluwer, 2000) 83.

1.2.5 The role of the State

The State has always been intimately involved in the construction and steering of work relations. The private law of property, tort and contract provides support for the construction of market exchanges in the form of the wage/work bargain. The State has also always steered this market either through the imposition of mandatory standards on the parties to the exchange or through the facilitation and promotion of forms of collective self-regulation of the terms of employment. The issues of depth and form of regulatory intervention have, however, always provided a central controversy about labour law.

The fundamental question is the extent to which the State should channel and steer work relations beyond providing the rules of private law. Many employers may regard the private law rules alone as the optimal level of state support, leaving them to achieve efficient production through management of their businesses without controls and through free negotiation of the terms of employment of the workforce. This desire for autonomy, though often receiving a warm reception from governments, cannot be accepted without endangering other important goals of social justice that deeply concern the workforce, such as fair treatment, economic security, and their health and safety. Regulatory intervention is necessary to achieve such goals, but the question is what form should regulation take.

We have highlighted two central strategies, each with its strengths and weaknesses: the imposition of mandatory standards, backed by either criminal or civil sanctions, and the promotion of collective self-regulation. These strategies are not mutually exclusive. With the benefit of hindsight, however, we can see that the decline in industrial sector or trade bargaining has had the irreversible consequence that mandatory standards applicable to all, or nearly all, workers must be provided for those workers not included within effective enterprise level collective bargaining. In the last 40 years we have witnessed the emergence of an elaborate set of rights granted to individual workers, such as laws against discrimination, laws providing for compensation for unfair dismissal and redundancy, controls over working hours, and the National Minimum Wage. Although the extent and details of these rights will remain controversial since they impinge on the autonomy of businesses and in some instances impose significant costs, it seems inconceivable that this extensive regulatory scheme will be reduced. Instead, it is much more likely, especially in view of the British membership of the European Union, that mandatory regulation will be extended and strengthened.

What remains less clear is the extent to which collective self-regulation will continue to supplement and qualify the use of direct regulation of terms of employment by the State. At present, collective bargaining as a method of regulation operates only in a minority of enterprises, though it persists in the overwhelming majority of large enterprises. Stronger support for the promotion of collective bargaining by the State, as for example in the new recognition procedures of the Employment Relations Act 1999, may reverse this decline. The State may also give its support increasingly to other forms of collective self-regulation, as in the example above of health and safety committees. Whatever the form of collective self-regulation, the question arises how it should interact with the extensive system of mandatory rights of workers. Should collective self-regulation be permitted only to improve on those mandatory rights, or should it be permitted to derogate from those rights? The arguments in favour of the latter are that collective self-regulation can adjust the general principles contained in legislation in ways that are suited to the operational needs of a particular business, and that members of the workforce can trade their entitlements off against each other according to their preferences. More generally, the possibility of derogation or alienation of rights enhances the autonomy of businesses and their workforces, creating the possibility of greater efficiency and competitiveness, and reduces the paternalist role of the State. Of course, the clear danger of the possibility of derogation is that employers will use their bargaining power to force through agreements that merely remove mandatory rights. Regulatory strategy in the future thus needs to weigh the risks of derogation by collective self-regulation against the potential advantages of more responsive regulation.

1.3 Labour courts and dispute settlement

Disputes between employers and workers often prove intractable. The most obvious symptom of the problem is the employees' recourse to industrial action, either in support of a claim or as a defence against a decision made by management. Less visible, though far more numerous, are the cases where the employer disciplines or dismisses a worker, or the worker decides to quit the job, because of some disagreement. In some instances, the employer's grievance procedure or disciplinary procedure may sort out the problem. Alternatively, where the employer has recognised a trade union, they may have created a procedure for resolving disputes through negotiation or private arbitration. Yet many disputes end up either in open industrial conflict or in acerbic litigation before the courts. The special difficulty presented to the legal system by labour disputes will be examined before we consider how the legal system can develop adequate and effective institutions for dispute settlement in this context.

1.3.1 Sources of conflict

A major part of the explanation of the difficulty of labour disputes relies upon an exploration of the structural features of employment relations that create special tensions. Beyond this source of disputes, it is important to recognise two broader sources of conflict in the workplace. One concerns a contest about the link between ownership of the enterprise and the exclusive right to control its activities. The other concerns conflicts of interest within the workforce itself.

1.3.1.1 Structure of the employment relation

We have already noted some of the distinctive features of the contract of employment—its indeterminate duration, its variability, its incompleteness and its construction of a relation of subordination. These features provide an explanation of why conflicts arise and why they may prove hard to resolve. The need for modifications during the lifetime of the agreement creates the problem of 'hold-up'. Although both parties probably want the contract to persist, because the employer needs the skilled and experienced workforce as much as the employees need their jobs, they can withhold consent to changes in the terms of the contract if the modified terms are not perceived to accrue to their advantage. The parties often have competing short-term interests: the employer wants more productive work, and the employee wants better remuneration or more favourable working conditions. There is a conflict of interest, but, unlike in many other contractual relationships, the option of walking away from the proposed transaction is usually not practicable or advisable. Instead the problem has to be resolved either through negotiation or some other dispute resolution mechanism.

The contract of employment is likely to fix the principal terms such as wages, hours and the job description. But the detail of the work required, how it is to be performed and co-ordinated with other workers, how the employee will be treated at work, and how unusual contingencies such as sickness will be handled, will all often be left vague or not mentioned at all. The gaps will be filled by a mixture of directions from management and of custom and practice in the workplace. This relative degree of indeterminacy in the contract of employment creates the possibility of frequent disputes about the details of working conditions and provides no clear criteria by which such disputes may be resolved by agreement.

Added to the above difficulties, we can observe that employees may resent aspects of the relation of subordination, and in particular may resist the exercise of managerial power when its exercise is perceived to be unfair, opportunist or harsh. More fundamentally, employees may challenge the existence or scope of management's discretion over some particular matter, and again the contractual relation often provides no criteria for resolving such disputes.

Collective bargaining functions in this context both to strengthen the bargaining power of the workforce and also to provide a peaceful mechanism for the resolution of conflicts. A periodic collective agreement can settle agreed modifications of the wage/work bargain. The bargaining may resolve points of uncertainty in the terms of employment and the details of the working conditions. The collective agreement can also help to establish procedures such as grievance procedures and disciplinary procedures, which provide peaceful mechanisms for challenging the exercise of managerial discretion. At the same time, however, the collective organisation also contests at a deeper level the model of employment as merely a contractual agreement.

1.3.1.2 Ownership and control

Collective bargaining can move beyond a mechanism for setting the market price of labour to amount to an assertion that the workforce should be entitled to participate in the management of the enterprise. The collective agreement can be presented as a technique for joint self-regulation between management, as representative of the employer, and the union, as representative of the workforce. This idea of participation in management, which is sometimes described as industrial pluralism or even industrial democracy, contests what is implicit in the attitudes of many private sector employers, that is the belief that ownership of capital brings with it the right to manage the workplace unilaterally. When unions are strong, owing to high levels of membership and good organisation, they can contest this basic assumption and assert the right to participate in all aspects of running the organisation. For this purpose they require substantial information from the employer and institutional arrangements that permit union representatives to participate in making decisions. Employers are more often than not reluctant to make such concessions. The resulting conflict goes to the roots of the organisational framework. The inevitability and, more importantly, the legitimacy of conflict is sometimes explained through a contrast between a 'unitary' and a 'pluralistic' perspective or 'frame of reference'.

[1.7] A. Fox, 'Industrial Sociology and Industrial Relations', Research Paper 3, Royal Commission on Trade Unions and Employers' Associations (London, HMSO, 1966) paragraphs 7–13

In relation to industry, a crucial issue in relation to the frame of reference emerges as soon as we ask the question: 'What sort of organisation is the industrial enterprise?' A central theme of the arguments to be presented here is that much depends on whether we view it as a *unitary* or as a *pluralistic* structure.

An alternative way of presenting this distinction would be to ask: 'What is the closest analogy to the enterprise—is it, or ought it to be, analogous to a team, unified by a common purpose, or is it more plausibly viewed as a coalition of interests, a miniature democratic state composed of sectional groups with divergent interests over which the government tries to maintain some kind of dynamic equilibrium?' The answer is important, for three reasons. It determines how we expect people to behave and how we think they ought to behave. It therefore determines our reactions to people's actual behaviour. And finally, it shapes the methods we choose when we want to change their behaviour . . .

A unitary system has one source of authority and one focus of loyalty, which is why it suggests the team analogy. What pattern of behaviour do we expect from the members of a successful and healthily-functioning team? We expect them to strive jointly towards a common objective, each pulling his weight to the best of his ability. Each accepts his place and his function gladly, following the leadership of the one so appointed. There are no opposition groups or factions, and therefore no rival leaders within the team. Nor are there any outside it; the team stands alone, its members owing allegiance to their leaders but to no others . . .

Most students of industrial relations would agree that this represents a vision of what industry ought to be like which is widespread among employers, top managers and substantial sections of outside public opinion . . . Team spirit and undivided management authority co-exist to the benefit of all . . .

The whole view of industrial organisation embodied in this unitary emphasis has long since been abandoned by most social scientists as incongruent with reality and useless for the purposes of analysis . . . . We have to see the organisation as a 'plural society, containing many related but separate interests and objectives which must be maintained in some kind of equilibrium' [N.S. Ross, in E.M. Hugh-Jones (ed.), *Human Relations and Modern Management* (1958) at 121]. In place of a corporate unity reflected in a single focus of authority and loyalty, we have to accept the existence of rival sources of leadership and attachment. They need to be accepted, above all, by whoever is ruling the plural society in question . . .

The full acceptance of the notion that an industrial organization is made up of sectional groups with divergent interests involves also a full acceptance of the fact that the degree of common purpose which can exist in industry is only of a very limited nature. In the sense that the groups are mutually dependent they may be said to have a common interest in the survival of the whole of which they are the parts. But this is essentially a remote long-term consideration which enters little into the day-to-day conduct of the organisation and cannot provide that harmony of operational objectives for which managers naturally yearn.

At bottom, the conflict between the unitary and pluralist perspectives concerns the legitimacy of the distribution of power in a capitalist society. This aspect of the conflict in the workplace is often linked to theories of a broader class conflict that are thought to lie at the root of broader political struggles.

[1.8] C. Crouch, *Class Conflict and the Industrial Relations Crisis. Compromise and Corporatism in the Politics of the British State* **(London, Heinemann, 1977) 7**

> The exchange relationship around employment provides the basis for the fundamental dichotomous class model, with the class which buys labour and then deploys it being the dominant class in the unequal exchange, and that which offers labour and subjects itself to control constituting the subordinate class. The inequality of exchange implies at one and the same time an inequality of economic reward and an authority relationship; and it is in the capacity of these dimensions to have major consequences for the lives of actual persons that the tendency for class relations to assume an empirical form consists. However, this empirical form is far more complex than the simple model implies. This complexity involves consideration of two separate dimensions: the scope for a variety of concrete positions around the underlying dichotomy (the concern of stratification studies); and variation in the factors which ensure that the relationship is an unequal one (our present concern). Some of the potential sources of variation have already been mentioned. For example, as noted above, the inequality of the employment relationship may be maintained because a high rate of unemployment dramatically reduces the power of labour, or it may be that the sheer size of material resources available to capital enables it to pay large sums to secure control over labour even without high unemployment.

It is therefore a mistake to analyse the sources of labour disputes merely in terms of the effects of structural features of the contract of employment. In addition, industrial conflict often signifies a more fundamental dispute about the basic institutional arrangements for securing production in modern societies. From a pluralistic perspective, such conflict is regarded as not only endemic within business organisations, but also as the expression of legitimate interests by different groups in society. The problem confronted by labour law and the study of industrial relations is not to find a way to eliminate conflict, but rather to develop techniques such as collective bargaining and grievance procedures for providing peaceful and efficient means for the resolution of conflicts in the workplace.

1.3.1.3 Conflicts within the workforce

The above explanation of the sources of conflict in the workplace leaves out one dimension that can prove especially intractable: conflicts of interest between different groups within the workforce. The conflict may arise, for instance, over differentials in pay, the arrangement of hierarchies or selection for redundancy. The rival groups may comprise workers differentiated by skills, or members of rival unions, or men and women. An employer is likely to side with one group, so the conflict takes on the appearance of a dispute between employer and worker or employer and union, but at root it concerns a clash of interest between categories of workers or their representative unions. For example, an employer may agree with a union to select for redundancy part-time workers rather than full-time workers, as in *Clarke v Ely (IMI) Kynoch* [1983] ICR 165 (EAT). Or the employer may strike a wage bargain with the union that improves the terms and conditions of the majority of workers, but involves a disadvantage to a few. How should such conflicts be resolved? Should the law uphold the collective interest or subvert that interest by protecting the rights or expectations of the minority? We shall see that the law, in pursuing the general course of protecting the rights of individuals at the expense of collective interests, does not always appreciate the damage it may cause to the fragile solutions agreed through collective bargaining to the first and second sources of conflict described above (see: S. Leader, 'Review of *Labour Law and Freedom* by Lord Wedderburn' (1996) 25 *Industrial Law Journal* 83). But on the other hand the law's support for collective self-regulation rather than the protection of individual rights can be criticised on the ground that it thereby ignores the interests of minorities or disadvantaged groups. The following extract castigates on these grounds the policy of supporting collective bargaining rather than mandatory legal standards. This policy is dubbed 'collective *laissez-faire*', following a phrase used by Otto Kahn-Freund ('Labour Law' in O. Kahn-Freund, *Selected Writings* (London, Stevens, 1978) 1, 8).

[1.9] J. Conaghan, 'Feminism and Labour Law: Contesting the Terrain' in A. Morris and T. O'Donnell, *Feminist Perspectives on Employment Law* (London, Cavendish, 1999) 13, 23–25 (footnotes omitted)

> Many of the fundamental features of collective laissez-faire ideology express a largely hidden gendered content. The dominant assumption, for example, that voluntary collective bargaining is the most effective means of safeguarding workers' interests problematically presupposes that all workers are, or can be, effectively represented by collective bargaining and that workers' interests largely coincide. Yet the history of the trade union movement graphically reveals their persistent failure to embrace certain categories of workers (largely populated by women) or advance their interests. The pluralist reliance upon a bifurcated model of class conflict, with its implicit conception of homogeneous labour, has obscured both the complexity of conflicting interests characterising workplace relations and the hierarchical context within which such conflicts of interests are routinely played out.
>
> Equally problematic is the pluralist view of law as a largely inappropriate mechanism for the regulation of industrial relations. 'Legal abstentionism' not only fundamentally misconceived the role of the State, it also operated to distort and diminish the significance of legal regulation in the workplace with, *inter alia*, gender implications. Protective legislation, for example, governing the hours of women's work in factories, was traditionally designated as external to the system of collective bargaining and, consequently, never accorded the same legitimacy by pluralist ideology. Yet for women workers, it was clearly of considerable practical and economic significance . . .
>
> A final flaw in collective laissez faire ideology lies in its representation of the workplace as a largely autonomous, self-governing entity with relatively fixed and uncontested boundaries. In so doing, it presupposes a conceptual and practical separation of the realms of work and family life which is both artificial and misleading. In fact the spheres of production and reproduction are neither fixed nor separate but constantly changing and interacting . . . .

1.3.2 Alternative dispute resolution

The above discussion explains why labour disputes present complex and sensitive problems. If the issue comes before a court for a legal determination of the rights and obligations of the parties, the court is likely to become involved in complex issues of fairness and the breakdown of informal understandings in working relations. Its intervention in the dispute can easily become portrayed as a political issue, where the court has the unappealing role of siding with either 'the bosses' or 'the workers'. To be sure some disputes can be resolved according to the more traditional role of courts, such as the interpretation of a written contract of employment, the award of compensation for personal injury, or the interpretation of a regulatory statute. But many disputes pose far more multifaceted and controversial issues. Did the employer act fairly in dismissing the worker? Is the union's claim for increased wages justifiable? Do the workers have reasonable cause to go on strike? Is the payment system used by the employer justifiable, even though one of its effects is that female employees receive on average lower wages because of the types of jobs they perform?

Most legal systems take steps to avoid giving such questions to the ordinary courts. Legislation either creates special labour courts, such as the employment tribunals in the United Kingdom, or attempts to divert these issues into systems of alternative dispute resolution such as arbitration. This strategy is justified in part as providing a forum for dispute resolution where the adjudicator or mediator has the necessary expertise in industrial relations and employment issues to provide a constructive and acceptable solution to the parties. The strategy is also influenced by the view that the legitimacy and authority of ordinary courts might be undermined if they were given the task of adjudicating such contentious issues that often include political undercurrents. There may also be the hope that the use of alternative dispute resolution may prevent any escalation of the dispute by avoiding the zero-sum game for high stakes that typifies the litigation process before ordinary courts. Alternative dispute resolution employs many techniques including conciliation, arbitration, and informal tribunals that provide a context-sensitive method of adjudication.

1.3.2.1 Minimum statutory grievance procedures

The first and most important step in resolving any dispute arising in the workplace between an employer and an employee should be, however, the employer's own internal grievance procedure. Under such a procedure, the employee should be able to give voice to a particular complaint, and the employer should have the opportunity to resolve the matter with the minimum of expense and discord. Although most large employers operate a grievance procedure of this kind, in order to induce all employers to follow this pattern of resolving disputes internally, the Employment Act 2002 s. 32 introduced a minimum statutory grievance procedure.

The procedure requires the employee to set out the grievance in writing, and then for the employer to invite the employee to a meeting within a reasonable time after the employer has had a reasonable opportunity to consider his response. After the meeting, the employer must inform the employee of his decision and of the right to appeal. If the employee is still dissatisfied, the employee should exercise the right to appeal to a second meeting. Section 32 of the 2002 Act provides that an employee shall not present a complaint to an employment tribunal with respect to the vast majority of individual employment law rights (listed in Schedule 4 of the Act), without the employee having sent the employer a written statement of the grievance and then having waited 28 days for the employer to respond. Through administrative procedures employment tribunals simply refuse to register claims unless the employee can affirm that those conditions have been satisfied.

The purpose of this legislation is to force employees to use the internal grievance procedure of the employer's organisation prior to commencing a legal claim before a tribunal with a view both to promoting settlement of disputes before they escalate into legal proceedings and to reducing the number of claims before tribunals. The Employment Act Dispute Resolution Regulations 2004 SI 2004/752 provide exceptions to this requirement. If the employer has a collectively agreed grievance procedure, and that procedure is followed by the employee, there is no need for the employee to try to follow the statutory procedure (Regulation 10). If the employee has already been dismissed or the employment relation has otherwise terminated, the parties may dispense with the grievance procedure if it has ceased to be reasonably practicable for the employee, or his employer, to comply (Regulations 6(4)(5) and 8). Nor does the employee need to use the grievance procedure if the employer is proposing to take disciplinary action or dismissal (Regulation 6(5)(6)), because then the statutory minimum disciplinary procedure will apply (see 5.4.3. below).

The practical impact of this new statutory grievance procedure is that in general an employee needs to present an employer with a written grievance prior to commencing any legal claim in pursuit of an individual employment law right, for otherwise the employment tribunal will deny it has jurisdiction. If the employer then fails to process the grievance by holding a meeting at a reasonable time and place and reaching a decision, the employee may proceed with the claim after 28 days, and the tribunal is instructed to increase any award it makes to the employee by 10% and it may, if it considers it just and equitable in all the circumstances to do so, increase it by a further amount up to an uplift of 50%. If the tribunal considers, however, that the failure to complete the statutory grievance procedure was wholly or mainly attributable to the employee, as for example where the employee declines unreasonably to attend a meeting or even to ask for an appeal against the original decision of the employer, the tribunal has parallel powers to reduce the compensation (Employment Act 2002, s 31).

This statutory grievance procedure came into effect in October 2004. It is too soon to know whether it will have the intended effect of greatly reducing the number of claims before employment tribunals, because the dispute will be settled informally through the grievance procedure. This intended outcome will only occur if employers decide to use grievance procedures as a method for constructive resolution of disputes and for improving and explaining managerial decisions, rather than merely engaging in a formal process of backing all previous managerial decisions. But it does seem likely that the obstacle placed in the way of registering claims, which is that employees need to be able to attest that they have given the employer a written notification of the grievance and have waited 28 days, will substantially reduce the actual number of claims that enter the tribunal system.

1.3.2.2 Conciliation

The conciliation of disputes in the workplace requires an independent third person to explore the possibility of finding a consensual resolution of the conflict. In the UK, the government supplies such an independent conciliator, the Advisory, Conciliation and Arbitration Service, known as ACAS. It provides an optional conciliation service that is available to the parties to a collective industrial dispute. ACAS provided its concilation service for about 1300 industrial disputes in 2003/2004, nearly all of which were eventually settled (ACAS, *Annual Report*, 2003/4). During this concilia- tion, ACAS can provide expert advice on improvements in industrial relations, such as proposals with respect to how organisational change might be handled and how communication and consultation may be improved (see below, 9.9.1.1).

[1.10] Trade Union and Labour Relations (Consolidation) Act 1992

s. 209—It is the duty of ACAS to promote the improvement of industrial relations.

s. 210—(1) Where a trade dispute exists or is apprehended ACAS may, at the request of one or more parties to the dispute or otherwise, offer the parties to the dispute its assistance with a view to bringing about a settlement . . .

ACAS has a compulsory conciliation role, however, in connection with most individ- ual disputes, such as unfair dismissal, discrimination, equal pay, protection of wages, breach of contract, minimum wage and working time. Once a claim has been filed, it is the task of ACAS conciliation officers to attempt to persuade the parties to reach a settlement.

[1.11] Employment Tribunals Act 1996 section 18

(2) Where an application has been presented to an employment tribunal, and a copy of it has been sent to a conciliation officer, it is the duty of the conciliation officer—
  (a) if he is requested to do so by the person by whom and the person against whom the proceedings are brought, or
  (b) if, in the absence of any such request, the conciliation officer considers that he could act under this subsection with a reasonable prospect of success,
to endeavour to promote a settlement of the proceedings without their being determined by an employment tribunal.

In practice, ACAS conciliation officers become involved in nearly every individual dispute that seems likely to go to a tribunal. Out of the roughly 100,000 applications for claims brought by employees to employment tribunals in the year 2003-2004, about 42% were settled with the assistance of ACAS, with 34% of claims withdrawn or abandoned, leaving only 24% to proceed to a tribunal hearing (ACAS, *Annual Report* (London, 2004).

1.3.2.3 Arbitration

Private arbitration provides an independent person, selected by the parties, to adjudi- cate on the merits of a dispute, though without the formality and delay of ordinary courts. It may be hoped that an arbitrator will understand better the industrial rela- tions issues and the 'law of the workplace', in order to find a solution acceptable to both parties. Although many countries use arbitration as the dominant method for resolving collective industrial disputes, and some make it compulsory, in the UK this method is less common. ACAS is charged by the Trade Union and Labour Relations (Consolidation) Act (TULRCA) 1992 section 212 ([9.53] below) with the obligation to make a public arbitration service available to the parties, but there is no compulsion for them to use it. In the year 2003/2004, ACAS dealt with only 68 cases through forms of arbitration, with the bulk of these disputes concerning pay and conditions of employment (ACAS, *Annual Report* (2004) 52; [9.52] below).

In so far as UK legislation imposes compulsory arbitration on the parties to a collective dispute, this task is given to another statutory body, called since 1975 the Central Arbitration Committee (CAC). The CAC tends, however, to try to induce a negotiated settlement between the parties rather than to impose a judgment on the merits. The CAC plays a pivotal role in resolving disputes in connection with the statutory recognition procedure for trade unions who are seeking to be recognised by an employer for the purposes of collective bargaining (TULRCA 1992 Schedule A1). In addition, the CAC arbitrates disputes concerning the requirement for the employer to disclose information for the purposes of collective bargaining and in connection with complaints that the employer is not complying with a legal duty to inform and consult representatives of the workforce about the probable developments of the business and employment prospects in it (Transnational Information and Consultation of Employees Regulations 1999 SI 1999/3323; Information and Consultation of Employees Regulations 2004 SI 2004/3426).

In relation to individual disputes, again there is no tradition of using arbitrators. Employers may agree to the use of arbitration as part of a grievance procedure or a disciplinary procedure, but an employee cannot in general agree to forfeit a right to make a claim for statutory rights, even if the arbitration result is unfavourable. A recent exception is the possibility for the parties to a claim for unfair dismissal to agree in writing that their claim shall be resolved in a legally binding manner by an arbitrator appointed by ACAS (5.3.5 below). That jurisdiction has also been extended to a parent's right to ask for flexible working hours (4.3 below).

1.3.2.4 Employment tribunals

The bulk of employment disputes that enter the legal process must be brought before an employment tribunal, formerly known as an industrial tribunal. Most claims brought by individuals against their employers for breach of statutory rights and standards fall within the jurisdiction of employment tribunals. Since their creation in 1964, the jurisdiction of employment tribunals has been gradually expanded, so that now they can hear in addition to claims for numerous statutory rights some common law contract claims, such as claims for wages in debt. The principal exclusions from their jurisdiction are claims for compensation for personal injuries, claims for injunctions against collective industrial action, and any legal process contemplating the application of a criminal penalty.

In general an employment tribunal should consist of three adjudicators: a chairman, who is a qualified barrister or solicitor, and two other members, one appointed from each of two panels proposed by employers' organisations and organisations representative of employees. In order to expedite proceedings and to facilitate the determination of complex points of law, however, there are many instances when the chairman may sit alone, though the chairman has the discretion to restore the tripartite membership where he regards this as desirable (Employment Tribunals Act 1996, section 4). Employment tribunals are expected, like other tribunals, to act informally, without the requirement for legal representation, with a view to settling the dispute expeditiously. Final decisions of the tribunal may be enforced in the ordinary way as a judgment of a court through the county court system.

An employment tribunal thus represents a type of hybrid system of dispute resolution. It is partly a court, since it provides adjudication in a public forum and uses legal standards, but also partly deliberately not a court, with its majority of lay members who bring to it knowledge of the practices and standards of industrial relations, and with its informal rules of evidence and procedures. The presence of lay members in the majority of most tribunal hearings has prompted the drawing of an analogy with juries.

[1.12] *Williams v Compair Maxam Ltd* **[1982] ICR 156 (EAT)** *per* **Browne-Wilkinson J**

> The Industrial Tribunal is an industrial jury which brings to its task a knowledge of industrial relations both from the view point of the employer and the employee. Matters of good industrial relations practice are not proved before an Industrial Tribunal as they would be proved before an ordinary court; the lay members are taken to know them. The lay members of the Industrial Tribunal bring to their task their expertise in a field where conventions and practices are of the greatest importance.

Like that of a court, the procedure of an employment tribunal is adversarial, but the members of the tribunal are required to avoid formality, to ask questions of witnesses in order to clarify issues, and to avoid strict adherence to the legal rules of evidence. Tribunals have been accused of 'legalism', that is in their approach to claims they tend to analyse the issues exclusively within a legal framework and by reference to legal criteria, rather than to appreciate and give weight to the industrial relations context of the dispute. Yet, it is hard to see how employment tribunals can operate in any other way, for they are required to reach decisions in accordance with legal standards, which, as we will see, are often complex and technical.

[1.13] R. Munday, 'Tribunal Lore: Legalism and the Industrial Tribunals' (1981) 10 *Industrial Law Journal* **146, 158–9**

> The fact is that labour law possesses all the major attributes of other subjects, possibly in a more dynamic form. It has an accessible hierarchy of jurisdictions, a growing legal personnel, flourishing series of reports and a fertile fund of highly complex legislative material. Naturally, tribunals will continue to dispense with the flummery and much of the procedural and evidential paraphernalia of the law courts—in this sense, they are informal and comparatively free. But in most important respects, tribunals do closely resemble courts. Thus, if charges of legalism mean that they interpret law in legal fashion, one would expect to find these charges fully proven, for it is quite impossible to see how else tribunals could be expected to behave.

Furthermore, legalism has the virtue that it pays strict attention to the rights of individuals, not permitting them to be sacrificed for collective benefits, such as efficient production or harmonious industrial relations. The legalism of tribunals indirectly compels employers and representatives of the workforce to pay close attention to the rights and interests of individual workers, which promotes one dimension of fairness in the workplace.

Behind the criticism of legalism in tribunals, however, there lurks a more serious concern about access to justice. One potential advantage of tribunals over ordinary courts is that individual employees may be able to bring their claims without the need for incurring the expense of lawyers. Although it is permissible for an individual to present a claim without legal representation, this approach is probably not advisable. The legal issues are often sufficiently complex that legal advice, from either a lawyer or an experienced trade union representative, will become essential, but there is no legal aid for claims before tribunals (except now in Scotland). The preparation of the case in order to be able to establish the facts and to present its strengths also benefits significantly from legal advice. In addition, the employer is likely to be represented either by a lawyer or by an experienced personnel manager, which will give the employer a comparative advantage against an unrepresented claimant. For example, in a sample of cases before tribunals, unrepresented claimants against employers with legal representation won in only 10 per cent of cases, but when the positions were reversed, the claimants with legal representation won in 48 per cent of cases (H. Genn and Y. Genn, *The Effectiveness of of Representation at Tribunals* (London, Faculty of Law, QMW, 1989) 99). Although many factors may explain such outcomes, it is likely that the complexity of the legal issues addressed by employment tribunals renders it impossible for the tribunal to discuss the claim in simple, lay terms, which leads inexorably to the relative advantage of those parties who benefit from legal advice and representation.

1.3.2 Other forms of alternative dispute resolution

Labour law is replete with other forms of dispute resolution that avoid the ordinary courts. We introduce here three other permanent institutional arrangements: the Pensions Ombudsman, the Certification Officer, and the TUC Disputes Committee.

The device of creating an ombudsman for alternative dispute resolution is used in one context in relation to employment. Under the Pension Schemes Act 1993, employees who believe that they have been treated unfairly under their employer's occupational pension scheme can complain to the Pension Ombudsman. This route for alternative dispute settlement was preferred to employment tribunals because these schemes are often extremely complex and complaints may raise issues of maladministration rather than breach of legal rights. Employers may appeal against adverse determinations by the Ombudsman to the ordinary courts (see R. Nobles, 'Enforcing Employees' Pension Rights—The Courts' Hostility to the Pensions Ombudsman' (2000) 29 *Industrial Law Journal* 243).

The Certification Officer is appointed by the Secretary of State to perform numerous tasks with respect to the regulation of trade unions. Under TULRCA 1992 the

Certification Officer keeps a list of trade unions (section 2), awards certifications that a trade union is 'independent', that is not liable to interference by an employer (sections 5–6), hears complaints by individual union members about the administration of the trade union (sections 25, 31), has the power to investigate the financial affairs of trade unions (section 37B), hears complaints about breaches of the requirements for election of officials (section 55), and more generally has the jurisdiction to adjudicate on many potential disputes between a union and its members (section 108A). The Certification Officer also has less extensive powers with respect to employers' associations.

The TUC Disputes Committee is a self-regulatory mechanism adopted by trade unions that are members of the TUC, a body to which nearly all major unions are affiliated, for the purpose of resolving disputes between unions. One key issue handled by the committee concerns the problems that arise when rival unions are both seeking to recruit members in a particular enterprise for the purpose of establishing collective bargaining. A recognised union may also refer a case to the Disputes Committee when it believes that another trade union is trying to poach its members. The Committee tries to conciliate between unions before reaching a determination under rules known as the TUC Disputes Principles and Procedures. The power of the Committee depends ultimately on persuasion, because the principles are expressly stated not to be legally binding, and the Committee is unlikely to use its potential sanction of excluding a union from membership of the TUC.

1.3.3 The ordinary courts

Why are ordinary courts so often regarded as unsuitable for handling labour disputes? The historical source of the problem for ordinary courts perhaps lies in their key jurisdiction in labour disputes of being empowered to issue 'labour injunctions'. These interlocutory injunctions consist of orders to trade union officials to withdraw calls for industrial action, backed up with the potential sanctions of fines, the sequestration of the assets of the union, and possibly imprisonment of those officials for contempt of court. To the extent that courts issue such injunctions, they can be presented as intervening on the side of the employers in order to break strikes and damage the interests of workers. Far from appearing as impartial arbiters of legal rights, the courts may issue injunctions on a highly discretionary basis, with destructive effects on the union's ability to mobilise a workforce, and with consequent damage to the courts' reputation for neutrality. It is also suggested that judges like this role, being by their training and culture naturally disposed towards the protection of the interests of the owners of property and the powerful. Whatever the truth of such allegations, it is undoubtedly the case that the common law, as developed by the judges, gave them the power to stop most industrial action in its tracks by means of a labour injunction. It might be argued that the common law rules that emphasised the importance of individual freedom of contract, the freedom of markets, and the protection of individual property rights could not comprehend the possibility that collective action that interfered with these freedoms and individual rights might ever be legitimate.

[1.14] Paul Davies and Mark Freedland (eds.), *Kahn-Freund's Labour and the Law* (3rd edn., London, Stevens, 1983) 12–13

> The evolution of an orderly and (compared with many other countries) even today reasonably well-functioning system of labour relations was one of the great achievements of British civilisation. This system of collective bargaining rests on a balance of collective forces of management and organised labour. To maintain it has on the whole been the policy of the legislature during the last hundred years or so . . . However, the common law knows nothing of a balance of collective forces. It is (and this is its strength and its weakness) inspired by the belief in the equality (real or fictitious) of individuals; it operates between individuals and not otherwise. Perhaps one of the most important characteristics of civil litigation is that the public interest is not represented in the civil courts. It is this, and not only the personal background of the judiciary, which explains the inescapable fact that the contribution which the courts have made to the orderly development of collective labour relations has been slight indeed. More than that, on a number of vitally important occasions Parliament has had to intervene to redress the balance which had been upset by court decisions capable of exercising the most injurious influence on the relations between capital and labour.

Despite these reservations about the capacity of the courts for understanding the issues posed by labour disputes in ways that coincide with general perceptions of the public interest, the ordinary courts continue to occupy a commanding role in labour law. As well as their continuing jurisdiction to issue labour injunctions in collective industrial disputes, the ordinary courts provide the ultimate appeal courts in decisions taken by employment tribunals. Parties to proceedings in employment tribunals can appeal their decisions on the ground that the tribunal committed an 'error of law'. The appeal goes first to the Employment Appeal Tribunal, but then to the Court of Appeal and finally to the House of Lords. At all stages of these proceedings, references can also be made to the European Court of Justice for determinations of the meaning of European Community law. This possibility of appeal to the ordinary appeal courts gives them the power to provide authoritative interpretations of the various statutes that grant employees rights against their employers. For example, the meaning of the provisions regarding sex discrimination and unfair dismissal have been largely settled by the higher appeal courts.

To insulate, but not to ensure, the autonomy of jurisdiction over labour disputes, the Employment Appeal Tribunal (EAT), which replaced the National Industrial Relations Court in 1975, has the exclusive jurisdiction to hear appeals from employment tribunals on points of law. Like the employment tribunals, it is a tripartite body, with lay members selected from panels drawn up by employers and organisations of employees, in addition to a judge of the High Court. There is an attempt here, therefore, to create a court that is more sensitive to the industrial relations context of disputes, and thus a form of alternative dispute resolution. But the limitation of the EAT to consider only points of law and not to review the case in its entirety prevents it from departing far in its approach to adjudication from that of an ordinary court. Of course, there is some flexibility in the determination of whether an issue of law has been raised. The normal way in which a decision of an employment tribunal can be challenged is to assert that the tribunal asked itself the wrong legal question, which depends upon an interpretation of the relevant statute and the precedents set by the courts. In addition, it can be asserted that no reasonable tribunal could have reached the decision that it did by applying the correct legal test to the facts of the case, that is a claim of irrationality or perversity, which is also an error of law. These grounds for review permit the EAT to intervene quite broadly, should it so wish, but it can also prevent a flood of appeals by a restrictive definition of points of law. When an appeal is successful, the EAT will normally remit the case to an employment tribunal, sometimes with a different membership, to reconsider the facts in the light of the correct legal test.

The EAT itself is subject to appeals on points of law to the Court of Appeal and then the House of Lords. These higher courts can thus control the extent to which the EAT can expand its jurisdiction by discovering points of law. The higher courts also police the interpretations placed upon the legislation by the EAT, and can substitute their own interpretations of the legislation, without the benefit of advice from lay members on the industrial relations context. In practice, therefore, the oversight of the ordinary courts denies to the EAT the autonomy to set authoritative interpretations of labour law and to establish legal principles of good industrial relations practice.

1.4 Transnational regulation

Labour law systems in different countries diverge considerably. The sources of these differences are discoverable in such causes as different paths and stages of economic development, divergent political histories, the strength of the State, and the relative power of employers' and workers' associations. We can observe a broad spectrum of labour law systems ranging from countries which provide little more than freedom of contract between employer and employee to those that impose detailed legal regulation of every aspect of the employment relation. These national labour law systems have developed autonomously according to the political and economic histories of each country, though particular labour laws have frequently been copied from one country to another. This autonomy of national labour law systems has become increasingly subject to constraints and external pressures.

The first constraint derives from the political movement that insists that all nation States should observe certain fundamental human rights. The protection of the dignity, safety and autonomy of individuals is presented as an international legal obligation imposed upon States. Within Europe a statement of those rights was agreed in the Convention for the Protection of Human Rights and Fundamental Freedoms by the Council of Europe at Rome in 1950. These legally enforceable rights, though primarily directed at the protection of the individual citizen against the misuse of power by officials of the State, have the potential to apply to many aspects of employment relations.

A second external pressure on national autonomy in labour law systems derives from an extension of the idea of fundamental human rights to the protection of social or economic rights. These standards are most comprehensively stated in the conventions promulgated by the relevant arm of the United Nations: the International Labour Organisation (ILO). We have noted also that the Charter of Fundamental Rights of the European Union 2000 blends human rights with social and economic rights. We shall see that the possibility of legal enforcement is more precarious for social rights than the protection accorded to fundamental human rights.

Perhaps the most powerful force that challenges the autonomy of labour systems is the intensification of economic links between countries known as 'globalisation'. The economies of countries become ever more closely inter-linked as a result of improved communications and the growth of international trade. In particular, capital investors can take a global view of where best to place their investments, taking into account such factors as resources, communications, political stability, effective commercial law and labour costs. Moreover, multinational enterprises provide the organisational mechanism for taking advantage of these market freedoms and communication systems. The forces of globalisation not only undermine the autonomy of national labour law systems, but also pose a challenge to any kind of national labour standards.

[1.15] C. Crouch, 'The Globalized Economy: An End to the Age of Industrial Citizenship?' in T. Wilthagen (ed.), *Advancing Theory in Labour Law and Industrial Relations in a Global Context* (Amsterdam, North Holland, 1998) 151, 151–2

I must begin with a definition of terms. I understand *globalization* to refer to the extension of a single interlinked set of markets and organizations for the production and delivery of goods, services, finance and to some extent labour across the entire inhabited world . . . .

I use the term '*industrial citizenship*' to refer to the acquisition by employees of rights within the employment relationship, rights which go beyond, and are secured by forces external to, the position which employees are able to win purely through labour market forces. Perhaps in a post-industrial world one ought to say 'occupational citizenship' . . . .

The grounds for hypothesizing that globalization will threaten industrial citizenship are as follows. The central actors in globalization are large corporations. These have demonstrated their capacity, using both organizational and market resources, to extend their activities across the world with speed and flexibility, developing both their own internal forms of regulation and regulations taking the form of private treaties between firms. By comparison, modes of regulation achieved by political authorities or organizations engaged in collective regulation of the labour market—the two predominant sources of occupational citizenship rights—are far slower and harder to establish. It is therefore very difficult for these other actors to extend their scope over the activities of the global firms. Put another way, through the medium of its organizations, capital is able to be a strategic actor at a global level in a way that organizations that are potential guarantors of citizenship rights find it difficult to achieve.

In so far as labour laws contribute to the labour costs of employers, national legal systems come under pressure to reduce employers' costs in order to compete for capital investment. This economic pressure is described as 'regulatory competition'. The danger of regulatory competition is that it provokes a 'race to the bottom', that is a reduction of labour standards in order to attract capital investment, or, perhaps more crucially, in order to prevent capital flight to countries where labour costs are lower.

One way to avoid this race to the bottom is for countries to adopt transnational laws. If countries adopt common labour standards that impose similar costs upon employers in all or many countries, these measures remove the incentive of cheaper compliance costs to move capital away from those countries with high labour standards. Globalisation thus puts pressure on national labour law systems either to deregulate the labour market or to join with other countries in the adoption of transnational labour standards. For the United Kingdom, the major source of such transnational standards lies in the European Community.

We explain here in outline the legal significance of the three principal sources of transnational labour law: the international protection of human rights, the international protection of labour standards and social rights, and the regulation of labour markets by the European Community. The details of these international labour laws will be considered in subsequent chapters.

1.4.1 International protection of human rights

Although many Conventions and Declarations on Human Rights might be considered in this context, the European Convention on Human Rights has had the most significant impact upon labour law in the UK. As a result of protocols added to the 1950 Rome Convention, citizens of the UK gained the right to challenge national law on the ground of its inconsistency with rights protected by the Convention. In effect, the citizen could sue his or her government for failure to comply with the Convention and, if successful, would receive compensation. A losing government usually amends the relevant law, in compliance with its obligations under the international treaty, though there is no legal mechanism to force it to do so. Prior to its abolition in November 1998, the European Commission of Human Rights acted as a filter mechanism by deciding whether applications were admissible and should proceed to a full court hearing. The decisions of the Commission provide a persuasive guide to the interpretation of the Convention, but the definitive interpretation of the Convention resides in judgments of the European Court of Human Rights (ECtHR).

The most significant decisions of the ECtHR for UK labour law have been directed towards the right to belong and not to belong to a trade union through interpretations of the right to freedom of association under Article 11 of the Convention. In *Young, James and Webster v United Kingdom* [1981] IRLR 408, the Court upheld a claim of existing railway workers that their right had been violated by their dismissal for refusing to join a union pursuant to a new closed shop agreement (M. Forde, 'The "Closed Shop" Case' (1982) 11 *Industrial Law Journal* 1). In *Wilson and the National Union of Journalists; Palmer, Wyeth and the National Union of Rail, Maritime and Transport Workers; Doolan and others v United Kingdom* [2002] IRLR 128, decided 2 July 2002 (ECtHR) [8.2.1. below] the Court upheld a claim under Article 11 by an employee who refused to agree to a new contract with a wage increase on condition that he no longer would use his trade union to bargain collectively over wages on his behalf (K.D. Ewing, 'The Implications of *Wilson and Palmer*' (2003) 32 *Industrial Law Journal* 1). Few of the rights declared in the Convention are stated without qualifications, so that the crucial legal question is often directed towards the extent of permitted restrictions.

The role of the European Convention is likely to become more pervasive in its effects upon UK labour law as a result of its incorporation into national law by the Human Rights Act 1998. Claimants before any court or tribunal in the UK can rely upon the Convention rights either as a tool for the interpretation of national legislation or as the basis for a claim against a public authority that it has acted, or proposes to act, in a way which is incompatible with a Convention right. We explore the potential ramifications of the Human Rights Act for labour law throughout this work, but there is detailed discussion of its provisions in chapter 6.

1.4.2 International protection of social and economic rights

There are also many international conventions and declarations on social and economic rights. The United Nations International Covenant on Economic, Social and Cultural Rights (1966) is an international treaty which creates an obligation on signatory states progressively to realise the rights it describes, including equality between men and women, the right to work, the right to fair conditions of employment, the right to form and join trade unions, and the right to social security. Perhaps the most influential in both initially describing the scope of such rights and guiding developments in the United Kingdom has been the European Social Charter adopted by the Council of Europe in 1961 and revised in 1996. The UK has accepted 60 of the 72 rights in the 1961 Charter, but has not ratified the additional rights in the revised Charter of 1996. The European Union has also adopted statements of social and economic rights, most notably the Community Charter of the Fundamental Social Rights of Workers 1989. The Charter of Fundamental Rights of the European Union 2000 (**[1.2]** above), which is due to be integrated into the proposed European Constitution, blends both human rights and social and economic rights. These European charters emphasise such matters as safe and just working conditions, the right to bargain collectively and to take industrial action, protection against unjust discipline, and the need for government to ensure economic security through social security and welfare systems.

None of these charters, however, provides individuals with directly enforceable legal rights against either the government or an employer. Instead their principal influence depends upon political pressure and the possibility that the standards will be used as a guide to interpretation of domestic laws. Both the United Nations Covenant and the European Social Charter use a method of an expert committee reviewing national reports on compliance with social and economic rights, which then produces critical observations of the failure of the country to comply with the standards, as interpreted by the expert committee. In some legal cases, however, an acknowledged social right may influence the interpretation of a legally enforceable right. In *Wilson and the National Union of Journalists; Palmer, Wyeth and the National Union of Rail, Maritime and Transport Workers; Doolan and others v United Kingdom* [2002] IRLR 128, decided 2 July 2002 (ECtHR) (**[8.2.1]** below), the European Court of Human Rights interpreted the right to freedom of association in Article 11 of the European Convention on Human Rights in a way that acknowledged the relevance of the social right for trade unions to make representations to an employer on behalf of workers and to take industrial action in support of those claims. This approach to the interpretation of legal rights implicitly acknowledges the indivisibility and integrated character of the various instruments that proclaim the fundamental importance of protecting human rights. In the course of the book we consider the influence and implications of the European Social Charter and the Charter of the Fundamental Rights of the European Union. We concentrate our attention here, however, on the conventions of the International Labour Organisation (ILO), which provide in many areas the most detailed and comprehensive analysis of social and economic rights.

Nearly all States that are members of the United Nations are also members of the ILO. The instruments agreed by the ILO in the form of conventions can be accepted or rejected by States. As a consequence there are very few States that have ratified all the conventions. The United Kingdom has ratified about 80 conventions, that is less than one half. It has not ratified some important conventions such as the Hours of Work (Industry) Convention, No. 1 (1919), Holidays with Pay Convention, No. 52 (1936), the Occupational Safety and Health Convention, No. 155 (1981) and the Workers with Family Responsibilities Convention, No. 156 (1981). Of course, British law tracks closely the content of these conventions in most respects. But membership of the ILO does not require conformity to all its conventions.

These conventions of the ILO do not become law in the United Kingdom without legislation designed to implement them. Nor can an individual assert these rights in court, except perhaps as an aid to interpretation of domestic law, though the judges pay scant attention to the conventions when they are cited in argument. The main sanction against breach of these international standards, following an examination by a Committee of Experts, is an adverse report from an independent committee on the application of conventions and recommendations. Such a report may cause a diplomatic embarrassment, and possibly some criticism in domestic politics, but a national government may either ride out the pressure or withdraw from (or 'denounce') the convention. In the past, the reluctance of UK governments to implement conventions was justified mostly by the preference of governments to promote collective self-regulation through collective bargaining rather than the imposition of mandatory legal rules. Since 1979, however, British governments have not always accepted the content of some ILO conventions even in principle, including those that have been ratified, most notably those concerned with freedom of association for trade unions, the promotion of collective bargaining, and the protection of workers dismissed when taking industrial action. There has been a difference in philosophy, with British governments being willing to impose more restrictive conditions on trade unions than those described by ILO conventions.

In an attempt to reassert its influence in world affairs, the ILO passed a Declaration at its conference in 1998 that reaffirms its mission:

[1.16] ILO Declaration of Fundamental Rights (1998)

The International Labour Conference . . . [d]eclares that all Members, even if they have not ratified the Conventions in question, have an obligation arising from the very fact of membership in the Organization, to respect, to promote and to realize, in good faith and in accordance with the Constitution, the principles concerning the fundamental rights which are the subject of those Conventions, namely:

(a) freedom of association and the effective recognition of the right to collective bargaining;
(b) the elimination of all forms of forced or compulsory labour;
(c) the effective abolition of child labour; and
(d) the elimination of discrimination in respect of employment and occupation.

These four items represent the key labour standards from the perspective of the ILO. The Declaration is binding on all members. It is supported by a follow-up procedure to monitor compliance and to identify areas of difficulty. These core standards are based upon existing ILO conventions.

The object of the right to freedom of association is to permit workers in every country to organise trade unions for the purpose of collective bargaining. Under Convention No. 87 (1948), workers should not be subjected to any penalty by the State for joining a trade union, and trade unions should generally be free to administer their own affairs without State interference. Under Convention No. 98 (1949), workers should not be discriminated against or dismissed by their employer because of their trade union membership, or for taking part in the activities of independent trade unions. Workers' organisations should not be subject to interference (financial or otherwise) by employers (Convention No. 135 (1971)), and national governments are under a duty to take steps to promote the development of voluntary collective bargaining between trade unions and employers. These are obligations with which successive British governments have found difficulty in complying. As we shall see in chapters 7 and 8, UK law continues to be in breach of ILO standards on freedom of association in a number of respects.

The abolition of forced or compulsory labour is directed at one of the worst abuses of state power during the twentieth century: the widespread use of forced labour camps. Notorious examples include the concentration camps of Nazi Germany and the Gulag Archipelago of Stalinist Russia. In these examples, the State rounded up millions of people on the slightest pretext and forced them to work in atrocious conditions. What the Stalinists discovered, however, is that despite the usefulness of forced labour camps for the imposition of terror on the population, from an economic perspective the labour camps were highly inefficient, because the high death rates and the lack of co-operation from the workforce, combined with the huge administrative cost of running the system, made the work produced more expensive than in free labour systems. Despite the well-publicised horrors of these systems and their inefficiency, there are still countries in the world such as China which use forced labour.

Child labour is still widespread throughout the world. The ILO has tried to assert a general standard of excluding children from work until schooling has been completed at age 15 or 14 (Convention No. 138 (1973)). In many developing countries, however, children provide an essential part of the labour force, especially in agriculture. From the perspective of these developing countries, it is far from clear that the pattern of families working together in the fields to maintain their subsistence is undesirable, even though this practice obviously restricts educational opportunities. In Western industrialised countries, however, we pride ourselves on the progress we have made since Victorian times when children worked long hours in dangerous conditions in factories, mines, and sweatshops. In Europe the general standard is now set by EC law.

[1.17] Directive 94/33 on the protection of young people at work [1994] OJ L216/12

> Article 1
> 1. Member States shall take the necessary measures to prohibit work by children. They shall ensure, under conditions laid down by this Directive, that the minimum working or employment age is not lower than the minimum age at which compulsory full-time schooling as imposed by national law ends or 15 years in any event.
> 2. Member States shall ensure that work by adolescents [i.e. those between 15 and 18] is strictly regulated and protected under the conditions laid down in this Directive.
> 3. Member States shall ensure in general that employers guarantee that young people [i.e. under 18] have working conditions which suit their age. They shall ensure that young people are protected against economic exploitation and against any work likely to harm their safety, health or physical, mental, moral or social development or to jeopardise their education.

The law in the UK implements this standard through detailed legislation, which both sets general rules, and also creates many exceptions, such as juvenile actors. Although the abuses of child labour in Britain have certainly diminished since Victorian times, the problem still persists (see Box below). The ILO itself has refocused its standards with respect to child labour in ways that are compatible with the economic interests of developing countries to concentrate on the campaign to eliminate forced labour, including conscription for military service, child prostitution and pornography, drug trafficking, and work likely to harm the health, safety, and morals of children (Convention No. 182).

The final key right of the ILO is the right not to be discriminated against, or the right to equality of opportunity.. In compliance with European Community laws, legislation in the UK prohibits discrimination on many grounds including sex, marital status, race, ethnic origin, nationality, sexual orientation, disability, religion or belief, and, in 2006, on grounds of age.

The prospects for effective international labour standards or social rights look bleak, even though the forces of globalisation make the need for them all the more urgent. Multinational enterprises play a substantial role in directing capital investment throughout the world, and their power is such that many nation States are reluctant to enforce even their own domestic standards against them. Furthermore, developing countries are suspicious of international labour standards, for they may also serve the purpose of protecting the labour markets of wealthy countries from foreign competition. For this reason, efforts to incorporate international labour standards and social rights as part of the general rules governing world trade seem unlikely to be successful. Indirect forms of self-regulation may have a greater impact in practice.

Large multinational enterprises are concerned about their reputation among consumers, fearing boycotts of their products if they are demonstrated to be produced under conditions that violate basic standards, such as use of child labour or forced

Child Labour in Britain

The regulation of work performed by children is a complicated body of legislation. For most types of jobs, the Children and Young Persons Act 1933, as amended principally by the Children (Protection at Work) Regulations 1998, SI 1998/276, establishes criminal offences for breach of the rules restricting employment of children. But there are many exceptions to this regime, including licenses for children to work as actors, models and the like, and the possibility for local authorities to make exceptions through bye-laws and issuing permits. Here are some of the main rules.

Children and Young Persons Act 1933 s 18

(1) Subject to the provisions of this section and of any byelaws made thereunder no child shall be employed—

(a)   so long as he is under the age of fourteen years;

(aa)   to do any work other than light work; or

(b)   before the close of school hours on any day on which he is required to attend school; or

(c)   before seven o'clock in the morning or after seven o'clock in the evening on any day; or

(d)   for more than two hours on any day on which he is required to attend school . . . ; or

(da)   for more than twelve hours in any week in which he is required to attend school; or . . .

(g)   for more than eight hours or, if he is under the age of fifteen years, for more than five hours in any day—

    (i)   on which he is not required to attend school, and

    (ii) which is not a Sunday; . . .

(2) A local authority may make bylaws with respect to the employment of children.. and may contain provisions—

(a)   authorising—

    (i)   the employment on an occasional basis of children under the age of fourteen years . . . by their parents . . . in light agricultural or horticultural work;

    (ia) the employment of children aged thirteen years in categories of light work . . .

This legislation, together with the local authority byelaws, is extremely complicated. The body of rules represents perhaps a classic example of regulation that is so intricate and inaccessible that it is unlikely to achieve compliance. There are certainly many worrying reports of children working at night in factories, a practice unlikely to be detected by the local authority officers who are supposed to enforce the rules. On the other hand, it is important to remember that some types of casual work for limited hours may be useful for children of school age, giving them work experience and some pocket money. The following extract gives some typical individual work histories of children at school in the north of England in the period 1992-94 (before some changes in the current law), though perhaps most children in the survey had not had jobs at all except for babysitting for neighbours.

S. Hobbs and J. McKechnie, *Child Employment in Britain: A Social and Psychological Analysis* (London, The Stationary Office, 1997) Chapter 4

Jason . . . He never had a work permit. Jason started work at the age of 12 on a paper round earning £9 per week. He subsequently had another paper round at £14.00 per week and a labouring job, in which he worked three hours for £5.00. His current job in Year 10 was another paper round (six days a week for £8.00) and he kept that job over the subsequent summer. He then moved to a Sunday paper round, in which he worked only four hours and earned £18.00. He then tried working in supermarkets. In one case he earned £35.00 per week for eight and a half hours' work as a produce assistant. He was made redundant. In the other, he stacked shelves for 17 hours per week for £45 . . .

Jennifer . . . She has worked steadily since the age of 13, but continuously in the same job. Jennifer went into a local bookshop and asked if there were any vacancies. She was interviewed and taken on to work around seven or eight hours on a Saturday. The pay is £10.00 and appears to have remained unchanged throughout the whole time she has had the job. Jennifer has not had a work permit . . . She feels that having had this work is beneficial to her job prospects when she leaves school, since it shows she is responsible, willing and hardworking . . .

William. William's first job was on a milk delivery round. He earned £20.00 per week working a total of 21 hours. This job was illegal in three ways. He did not have a work permit; he was only 12 years old when he started; and he began work at 5.00 a.m . . .

P. Mizen, A. Bolton and C. Pole, 'School Age Workers: The Paid Employment of Children in Britain' (1999) 13 *Work, Employment & Society* 423, 424-5, 428
[S]urvey research has consistently revealed that between one third and one half of school age children are in paid employment at one time; and that before they leave school between two thirds and three quarters of children will have held down a paid job. Translated into 'hard' numbers, between 1.1 and 1.7 million school age children are estimated to be currently working . . .

What is also difficult to dispute is the fact that much of this involves work more usually associated with adult employment. Although newspaper delivery, the traditional preserve of working children, remains the single biggest source of employment, children below the minimum school leaving age are frequently engaged in a range of jobs stretching from washing up, serving in shops and waiting tables, through to door to door selling, working as carers, cleaners and in offices and, less frequently, on building sites and in factories. Most of these children are employed illegally, either transgressing the limitations on hours or occupying prohibited jobs, and the vast majority of child workers remain unregistered . . . [T]hese jobs are dominated by unskilled, manual work, often involving 'non-standard' employment relationships, and . . . children represent a particularly low paid and vulnerable section of the workforce . . .

[G]iven that children work in the same sectors as young workers, the hotel and catering, wholesale and retail sectors . . . , there is strong justification for believing that school age children have been caught up in employers' greater use of part-time youth and student labour more generally..

This is because children represent a useful source of additional flexible labour, particularly in those undercapitalised and intensely competitive areas of the service sector where they tend to work . . . [C]hildren are a flexible and relatively quiescent group of workers, willing to work irregular hours at short notice, and unlikely to anticipate high wages. What is more, given the constraints of schooling and the absence of direct pressures to maintain a regular wage, working children are also uninterested in full-time work or in acquiring long-term or secure employment.

labour. Some companies seek to label their products as having been produced in compliance with fair labour standards, but for this technique to be convincing it will require some mechanism of independent assessment of working conditions.

[1.18] B. Hepple, 'New Approaches to International Regulation' (1997) 26 *Industrial Law Journal* 353, 364–5

The most important current initiatives affect the exploitation of child labour. A recent ILO study [J. Hilowitz, *Labelling Child Labour Products: A Preliminary Study* (Geneva. ILO, 1997)] of six such initiatives (including 'Rugmark') shows that they share a number of features: (1) they aim to communicate to consumers the importance and social implications of purchasing the labelled products; (2) they require some form of monitoring to ensure that the desired social standards have been realised or maintained; and (3) the labelling initiative collects a levy from the retailer or importers of the products in order to improve specific conditions in the country of origin (or in the case of one Brazilian initiative expects the companies themselves to fund improvements). The levies may increase the actual unit price of the product by up to 2%. The possibility that successful boycotts might actually worsen the economic conditions of children and their families, has led some labelling initiatives to limit their goals to the improvement of working conditions rather than the total elimination of child labour, and to concentrate on positive projects to improve the health and education of children. The effectiveness of such initiatives depends on many factors such as whether there is a visible concentration of child labourers in an export industry; whether the product is desired by consumers; the degree of resistance by producers who employ children; the co-operation of exporters and importers and retail traders; and the existence of campaigning organisations within the importing country. The social labelling initiatives have met with scepticism from the European Commission which has decided not to finance or directly support them. However, they offer an opportunity for social mobilisation of consumers, workers and activists across national frontiers, provided that they are taken in conjunction with trade unions and political organisations within the affected country. This, as the sustained boycotts of South African products during the apartheid era shows, can have a mushroom effect giving moral support to the struggles of exploited workers while at the same time diminishing social and political insularity.

Another method of self-regulation is for multinational enterprises to promote a code of conduct which requires all its businesses throughout the world, together in some instances with its suppliers, to conform to some basic labour standards. But these codes are unlikely to have a major impact because the enterprise itself determines the standards and there is no mechanism of enforcement other than self-enforcement. In some cases, however, these codes have been developed in co-operation with international trade unions. If this form of self-regulation is to be effective, it seems important that these trade union organisations should be involved in determining their content and in monitoring compliance. There is a case for saying that international labour standards should support the right of international trade union organisations to be consulted by multinational enterprises about transnational employment issues, and to require these companies to negotiate about the steps required to ensure compliance with international labour standards throughout the supply chain.

1.4.3 Transnational labour market regulation

Within economic blocs, such as the North American Free Trade Agreement (NAFTA) and the European Community (EC), it is possible for the member States to develop legally binding rules to govern trade and the operation of markets, including labour markets. This regulation has a significant impact on domestic labour law systems. As a member of the EC by virtue of the Treaty of the European Community, the UK accepts the power of the institutions of the Community both to legislate and to adjudicate on Community law. The powers of the Community to legislate are, however, limited in respect of labour law matters. Nevertheless the EC exerts a growing influence on many aspects of labour law. Here we will explain the powers of EC institutions, assess the trajectory of EC labour law, and consider in particular its importance as a source of transnational labour regulation.

1.4.3.1 The competence of the EC

The limitations on the institutions of the EC to legislate and set legal standards in the field of labour law are both substantive and procedural.

[1.19] Treaty Establishing the European Community, Article 137 (formerly 118)

1. . . . [T]he Community shall support and complement the activities of the Member States in the following fields:
   —improvement in particular of the working environment to protect workers' health and safety;
   —working conditions;
   —the information and consultation of workers;
   —the integration of persons excluded from the labour market..
   —equality between men and women with regard to labour market opportunities and treatment at work.
2. To this end, the Council may adopt, by means of directives, minimum requirements for gradual implementation, having regard to the conditions and technical rules obtaining in each of the Member States . . .
   The Council shall act in accordance with the procedure referred to in article 251 after consulting the Economic and Social Committee and the Committee of the Regions.
3. However, the Council shall act unanimously on a proposal from the Commission, after consulting the European Parliament, the Economic and Social Committee and the Committee of the Regions in the following areas:
   —social security and social protection of workers;
   —protection of workers where their employment contract is terminated;
   —representation and collective defence of the interests of workers and employers. Including co-determination, subject to paragraph 6;
   —conditions of employment for third-country nationals legally residing in Community territory;
   —financial contributions for promotion of employment and job-creation, without prejudice to the provision relating to the Social Fund.
4. -A Member State may entrust management and labour, at their joint request, with the implementation of directives adopted pursuant to paragraphs 2 and 3 . . . .

5. The provisions adopted pursuant to this Article shall not prevent any Member State from maintaining or introducing more stringent protective measures compatible with this Treaty.

6. The provisions of this Article shall not apply to pay, the right of association, the right to strike or the right to impose lock-outs.

This Article of the EC Treaty divides possible areas of legislation by the European Council of Ministers into three parts or competences:

(1) Those fields that are outside the competence of the EC: pay (except discrimination in pay), the right of association, the right to strike or the right to impose lock-outs—Article 137(6).

(2) Those fields that are within the competence of the European Community, but where legislation is only permitted after a unanimous vote of Member States: for example, social security law, dismissal, collective representation—Article 137(3). To this list is added discrimination law under Article 13.

(3) Those fields which are within the competence of the European Community, where legislation can be approved by a majority vote of Member States (under the weighted voting system of Article 251): for example, health and safety, working conditions, information and consultation of workers, equal opportunity of men and women.

A further complexity of European law consists of the lack of direct effect of most legislation. EC labour law usually takes the form of a directive agreed by the Council of Ministers, which is an instruction to Member States to enact legislation (or legally binding collective agreements under Article 137(4)) in conformity with the principles laid down in the directive. In the United Kingdom, the European Communities Act 1972 permits Parliament to implement directives by means of Statutory Instruments. Unless the directive has been so implemented, however, it does not usually afford individuals legal rights. It is said that directives do not have 'direct horizontal effect'. A directive that has not been implemented, or not properly implemented, does, however, have two significant legal effects:

(1) *Interpretation or indirect effect*: the courts are under a legal obligation to interpret national law in a manner that brings its meaning into conformity with European law. Notice that this obligation applies to all UK law, including legislation that preceded EC law.

(2) *Vertical direct effect*: although directives do not have direct horizontal effect, the rights contained in directives may be claimed against the Member State, an 'organ of the State', or an 'emanation of the State' (see Box below). Thus an employee or a trade union in the public sector may be able to assert rights contained in a directive against an employer, even though the directive has not been implemented by national legislation.

[1.20] Cases C–397/01 to C–403/01 *Pfeiffer* v *Duetsches Rotes Kreuz, Kreisverband Waldshut e V* **[2005] IRLR 137 (ECJ).**

Seven rescue workers employed by the German Red Cross, a private sector body, claimed that time when they were required to be available at their place of work in case an emergency arose should be regarded as 'working time' for the purpose of the Directive on working time, 93/104, and that the terms of their employment, though apparently permitted under German law, infringed the right under Article 6(2) of the Directive to a maximum working week of 48 hours. The German labour court referred a number of issues of interpretation to the ECJ, including the questions of the direct and indirect effect of Art 6. On these issues, having concluded that German law as interpreted by the labour court was not in conformity with Art 6, the ECJ laid down the following principles of interpretation.

Judgment
It is clear from the settled case-law of the Court that, whenever the provisions of a directive appear, so far as their subject-matter is concerned, to be unconditional and sufficiently precise, they may be relied upon before the national courts by individuals against the State where the latter has failed to implement the directive in domestic law by the end of the period prescribed or where it has failed to implement the directive correctly . . .

Article 6(2) of Directive 93/104 satisfies those criteria, since it imposes on Member States in unequivocal terms a precise obligation as to the result to be achieved, which is not coupled with any condition regarding application of the rule laid down by it, which provides for a 48-hour maximum, including overtime, as regards average weekly working time . . .

It still remains to determine the legal consequences which a national court must derive from that interpretation in circumstances such as those in the main proceedings, which involve individuals.

In that regard, the court has consistently held that a directive cannot of itself impose obligations on an individual and cannot therefore be relied upon as such against an individual . . .

It follows that even a clear, precise and unconditional provision of a directive seeking to confer rights or impose obligations on individuals cannot of itslef apply in proceedings exclusively between private parties [as in this case].

However, it is apparent from case-law which has also been settled since the judgment of 10 April 1984 in Case C–14/83 *Von Colson and Kamann* [1984] ECR 1891, paragraph 26, that the Member States' obligation arising from a directive to achieve the result envisaged by the directive and their duty under Article 10 EC to take all appropriate measures, whether general or particular, to ensure the fulfilment of that obligation is binding on all the authorities of Member States including, for matters with their jurisdiction, the courts . . .

Accordingly, it must be concluded that, when hearing a case between individuals, a national court is required, when applying the provisions of domestic law adopted for the purpose of transposing obligations laid down by a directive, to consider the whole body of rules of national law and to interpret them, so far as possible, in the light of the wording and purpose of the directive in order to achieve an outcome consistent with the objective pursued by the directive. In the main proceedings, the national court must thus do whatever lies within its jurisdiction to ensure that the maximum period of weekly working time, which is set at 48 hours by Article 6(2) of Directive 93/104, is not exceeded.

A directive that has not been properly implemented by a Member State may generate two further legal consequences. The European Commission may commence proceedings against a Member State before the European Court of Justice (ECJ) for failure to implement a directive in breach of its treaty obligations. The invocation of this procedure has compelled the UK to alter national legislation on several occasions. Furthermore, an employee who lacks rights conferred by a directive owing to the failure of his Member State to implement it has in principle the right to claim compensation for any consequential losses against his government. The possibility of such claim was created by the ECJ in Cases C–6/90 and C–9/90 *Francovitch and Bonifaci v Italy*, [1992] IRLR 161 ECJ, where workers were held to be entitled to sue their government for failing to implement a directive that would have given them certain rights to guarantees of wages in the event of their employer's insolvency.

Emanations of the State

Emanations of the state include central and local government, publicly owned industries, the national health service, publicly funded schools, and regulated industries which provide public services and enjoy special powers compared to most private individuals and organisations. The test for regulated industries was proposed in the next case, which led to the inclusion of British Gas plc as an emanation of the state.

Foster v British Gas plc, C–188/89, [1990] IRLR 353 ECJ

'[A] body, whatever its legal form, which has been made responsible, pursuant to a measure adopted by the state, for providing a public service under the control of the state and has for that purpose special powers beyond those which result from the normal rules applicable in relation to individuals is included in any event among the bodies against which the provisions of a directive capable of having direct effect may be relied upon.'

The test of 'control of the state' does not require ownership, but is fulfilled by the exercise of power to regulate the business or the industrial sector. The courts adopt a purposive approach to the concept of emanation of the state, seeking to prevent governments from relying upon their own failure to implement European directives either in primary legislation or secondary regulation. Examples of emanations of the state may be found in *Griffin* v *South West Water Services Ltd* [1995] IRLR 15 ChD, and *National Union of Teachers v Governing Body of St Mary's Church of England (Aided) Junior School* [1997] ICR 334 CA, noted by J. Eady, (1997) 26 *Industrial Law Journal* 248.

Although directives are the main legislative instruments of the EC in labour law, two other sources of EC law should be mentioned. First, the Council of Ministers has the power to make regulations, which have direct horizontal effect. Regulations have been made in limited fields relevant to labour law concerned with the free movement of workers throughout the EC. Secondly, the Treaty of the European Community can itself be the source of legal rights. In particular, the ECJ has determined that Treaty provisions that are clear and can be interpreted to confer rights on individuals will be given direct effect. The most important example of such a Treaty provision in labour law is the principle of equal pay.

[1.21] Treaty of European Community, Article 141 (formerly 119)

> 141. 1.   Each Member State shall ensure that the principle of equal pay for male and female workers for equal work or work of equal value is applied.

Since this provision has direct horizontal effect (Case 43/75, *Defrenne* v. *Sabena* [1976] ECR 455 (ECJ)), it is open to applicants for claims for equal pay to rely upon it directly in employment tribunals, and for the interpretation of the principle of equal pay contained in the Treaty, tribunals can rely upon the relevant directive on equal pay (Directive 75/117).

1.4.3.2   The growing influence of EC law

The first significant effect for labour law of membership of the EC was the acceptance of the principle of free movement of workers throughout the economic area.

[1.22] Treaty of the European Community, Article 39

> 39. 1. Freedom of movement for workers shall be secured within the Community.
>
> 2. Such freedom of movement shall entail the abolition of any discrimination based on nationality between workers of the Member States as regards employment, remuneration and other conditions of work and employment . . .

The effect of Article 39, combined with detailed regulations, and read in the light of the establishment of citizenship of the European Union by Article 8 of the EC Treaty, is that it is possible for workers with EC nationalities to take up jobs, reside with their families, and take advantage of the local social security system in any Member State. In particular, EC nationals seeking work in another Member State cannot be denied jobseeker's allowance or its equivalent simply on the ground that they have not been habitually resident in the country in which the social security claim is made; rather, such benefits have to be granted to any EC national who has been genuinely seeking employment for a reasonable period in that state: Case C–0138/02 *Collins v Secretary of State for Work and Pensions* [2005] ICR 37 (ECJ). The law therefore expands the potential size of the labour market enormously.

It was correctly predicted that the equivalent provisions for free movement of capital together with free trade without tariffs within the EC would tend to intensify competition. The effect would be that Member States would be unable to protect domestic industries from foreign competition, which for inefficient industries would compel major reorganisations, mergers or closure. The foreseeable adverse effect on employment security was not, however, regarded as something that the EC should address through legislation, because in the long run the benefits of a more competitive market would improve the wealth of all the citizens of the EC. Instead, the EC Social Fund was created to grant regeneration aid to areas affected by high levels of unemployment. Nevertheless, some EC directives have introduced common standards for business reorganisations, in particular those concerned with sales of businesses (Directive 2000/78,) mass redundancies (Directive 98/59), consultation

Working Abroad

With the advent of the European Single Market and the right of free movement of workers within the EU, it seems likely that many employees domiciled or ordinarily resident in the UK will experience some period of work in another European country. The questions arise of what legal system applies to employment abroad, and in what court jurisdiction may an employee assert any claims? Answers to the latter question are relatively straightforward. Under the Brussels Convention 1968, given force in the UK by the Civil Jurisdiction and Judgments Act 1982, and now consolidated in EC Council Regulation 44/2001 of 22 December 2000 on jurisdiction and the recognition and enforcement of judgments in civil and commercial matters, an employee may make the claim in the jurisdiction either where the employee habitually carries out his work, or, if it is not possible to identify a habitual place of work, where the employer is domiciled or situated (Case C–37/00 *Weber v Universal Ogden Services Ltd* [2002] ICR 979 (ECJ)). A short-term or temporary posting abroad will not therefore prevent an employee ordinarily resident in the UK from making claims in the UK courts and tribunals. The question of the applicable law proves far more troublesome. If the employee works for a foreign company abroad, the contract of employment will almost certainly be governed by the foreign law. If the employee works in another EU country for a British company, however, the applicable law is determined by the Rome Convention 1980, given effect by the Contracts (Applicable Law) Act 1990. Article 6 of the Convention tries to reconcile the principle of permitting parties to a contract to choose the applicable law with the principle of ensuring that employees should not be disadvantaged by the employer's choice of law. The effect of Article 6 is that an employee can rely upon either the law explicitly chosen by the contract, or the law of the country in which the employee habitually carries out his work, unless it appears from the circumstances as a whole that the contract is more closely connected with another country. For example, an English employee working in France for an English company under contract of employment expressly governed by English law may be able rely upon either French law for contractual and mandatory statutory rights as the habitual place of work, or UK labour law on the basis of the express choice of law in the contract. However, in this particular example a court might conclude that in the circumstances the contract is so closely connected with UK law that only UK law should apply. Even if UK law applies, however, it may still be determined that a particular statutory right is confined to those actually working in the UK. In particular, discrimination legislation provides that it applies unless the employee does his or her work wholly outside Great Britain (Race Relations Act 1976 s.8(1); Sex Discrimination Act 1975 s.10(1)). The principal source of employment rights in the UK, the Employment Rights Act 1996, has been interpreted as a general rule only to confer rights upon employees who are actually working in Great Britain: *Lawson v Serco Ltd* [2004] EWCA Civ 12, [2004] ICR 204 (CA). But a single, short absence from Great Britain for a temporary posting abroad would not deprive the employee of protection under the 1996 Act. Special rules apply to 'posted workers', that is workers who are sent abroad by their employer under a contract with a business in another country to supply labour, or through administrative arrangements within a multinational group of companies. The state where the workers have been sent must ensure under the posted workers Directive 96/71 that these foreign workers are covered by the host state's labour standards regarding working conditions, pay, safety, discrimination. The purpose of the Directive is to prevent foreign workers from undercutting the basic labour standards enjoyed by national workers, but it also helps the posted workers themselves by permitting them to claim any superior rights such as a mandatory minimum wage notwithstanding any contrary contractual arrangement: see P. Davies, 'Posted Workers: Single Market or Protection of National Labour Law Systems?' (1997) 34 *Common Market Law Review* 571. The complexity of the above provisions perhaps represents the most forceful case for promoting further harmonisation in labour law in the EU.

and information rights of employees (Directives 2002/14, 94/45), and insolvency (Directives 80/987, 2002/74). These Directives provide workers with some substantive rights, but their principal objective is to harmonise the required procedures for these types of business reorganisations throughout EC.

As the market of the EC has become more integrated, there have been increasing calls for the introduction of a 'social dimension' to EC law. The call is in effect for the adoption of transnational labour standards, which would extend a minimum set of social and economic rights across all Member States. This movement reached its formal expression in the Community Charter of the Fundamental Social Rights of Workers (10 December 1989), a document that is not legally binding, but which may influence the interpretation of Community law. These social and economic rights have been reasserted in the Charter of Fundamental Rights of the European Union 2000 ([1.2] above).

Governments of some Member States, not least the UK, are reluctant, however, to accept an expansion of the role of EC labour law. They reject transnational regulation because in part they perceive their national regulation to represent a potential competitive advantage by imposing lower costs on employers, and in part they may be unwilling to reopen what may have been politically divisive national issues. In order to avoid some of this resistance to the social policy of the EC, a new legislative procedure, known as the Social Dialogue, has been developed under Article 139. Under this procedure, representatives of employers' associations and trade union organisations at a European level may negotiate collective agreements that fix minimum standards in the areas of Community competence delimited by Article 137. If the 'social partners' agree upon a standard, they may then ask the Council of Ministers to enact it as a directive. The Council of Ministers still has the power to reject the proposed directive, but so far it has been unwilling to do so, given that in effect the employers' associations are asking for the legislation. Although this procedure may only rarely produce agreements, it has resulted in the Directives on parental leave (96/34, 97/75), part-time work (97/81), and fixed-term work (99/70).

EC legislation has progressed rather gradually in fits and starts. The full influence of EC law upon UK labour law can only be appreciated, however, by considering as well the impact of decisions of the European Court of Justice (ECJ). We described above how the ECJ has developed the effectiveness of EC law by inventing such ideas as the indirect effect of EC law through interpretation, the direct effect of some Treaty provisions, and the vertical direct effect on 'emanations of the State'. The most remarkable impact of these constitutional doctrines in labour law has been their effect on the law of equal pay and sex discrimination. Having decided that the equal pay principle in the Treaty of the European Community could have direct horizontal effect between an employer and employee, the ECJ interpreted this principle in ways that expanded its scope considerably. The court gave the term 'pay' a broad meaning to include any benefits that might be received by the employee both during and after the termination of employment. The court also expanded the possible range of comparisons that a woman might make in order to demonstrate that she was being paid less than a man. At the same time, the court developed doctrines that served to strengthen the effect of all directives, such as the principle that Member States should provide effective remedies for claimants of rights conferred by EU law.

It seems likely that EC law will continue to grow in influence. As the market becomes more integrated owing to developments such as a single currency, the idea that each Member State should continue to retain sovereignty over the rules governing labour markets will probably appear less practicable. In order to discourage the 'race to the bottom' in regulatory standards, which is also sometimes described as 'social dumping', the economically powerful Member States will continue to press at least for the enactment of minimum standards, if not the complete harmonisation of laws. More immediately, as part of the strategy of establishing a notion of European citizenship that finds its concrete expression in the Charter of Fundamental Rights of the European Union 2000 ([1.2] above), European law is likely to affect labour law in two crucial areas: the law of discrimination and models of worker participation. The most dramatic recent development has been the use of the new Treaty power to regulate equality of opportunity beyond sex discrimination.

[1.23] Treaty of the European Community, Article 13

> 13. Without prejudice to the other provisions of this Treaty and within the limits of the power conferred by it upon the Community, the Council, acting unanimously on a proposal from the Commission and after consulting the European Parliament, may take appropriate action to combat discrimination based on sex, racial or ethnic origin, religion or belief, disability, age or sexual orientation.

Under this new Article, the Council has already agreed two directives, one implementing the principle of equal treatment of persons irrespective of racial or ethnic origin (Directive 2000/43), and the other encompassing discrimination on grounds of religion, belief, age, disability, and sexual orientation (Directive 2000/78).

1.4.3.3 The purpose of EC regulation

Given that the Member States of the EU already have extensive labour laws, what is the role for EU regulation? Should the EU seek to establish a uniform labour code for the Single Market, which would eliminate regulatory competition? Or should the EU tolerate disparities in laws subject to the establishment of a comprehensive set of minimum standards in order to prevent excessive 'social dumping'? Or should the EU confine its intervention to issues involving cross-border trade, such as the details regarding free movement of workers? Or is there a case for high labour standards across the EU in order to stimulate economic growth?

[1.24] S. Deakin and F. Wilkinson, 'Rights vs Efficiency? The Economic Case for Transnational Labour Standards' (1994) 23 *Industrial Law Journal* 289

> We now turn to a consideration of potential economic arguments in favour of transnational standards. These include the idea that harmonization is needed to establish a *level playing field* between member states by establishing *parity of costs* imposed by legislation on employers. Alternatively, harmonisation is seen as providing a *minimal floor of rights* to prevent destructive competition . . . We also consider a third possibility, namely that standards operate as *guarantors of economic participation and development* . . .

A level playing field? At first sight, this view has a certain plausibility: following the establishment of the single market in goods and services, differences in the cost structure of member states brought about by variations in relative burdens of taxation and regulation will produce 'distortions of competition'. Companies in low-cost countries will be placed at an 'artificial' competitive advantage compared to those located elsewhere in the single market. However, the view that differences in social protection are a matter for competitive forces rather than harmonization goes all the way back to the Spaak Report [Comité Intergouvernemental Créé par la Conférence de Messine, Rapport des Chefs de Délégation aux Ministres des Affaires Etrangères (Brussels, 1956)] and the report of the ILO's Committee of Experts [International Labour Office, 'Social Aspects of European Economic Co-operation' (1956) 74 *International Labour Review* 99) which preceded the signing of the Treaty of Rome in 1957. In its Explanatory Memorandum of 1990 concerning the proposals for directives on part-time and fixed term employment ('certain employment relationships'), the Commission took a similar approach in relation to differentials in wage costs:

> Wage levels, non-wage labour costs and rules on working conditions vary considerably between Member States. Broadly speaking, however, these differences do not hamper the operation of healthy competition in the Community. The differences in productivity levels attenuate these differences in unit labour costs to a considerable degree. Moreover, other production cost components tend to be higher in the less developed Member States where nominal labour costs are lowest [CVOM (90) 228—SYN 280–SYN 281, 1990, paragraph 22] . . . .

Standards as a floor of rights. In contrast to the notion of a parity of costs brought about by a level playing field, transnational standards can be seen more fruitfully as setting minimum floor below which state regulation may not fall, thereby seeking to prevent destructive competition between states. This floor of rights character of Community law is stressed in directives adopted both before and after the Single Act of 1986. The employment protection directives of the late-1970s specified that they 'shall not affect the right of Member States to apply or to introduce laws, regulation and administrative provisions which are more favourable to employees' . . . .

To some extent, the notion of standards as a floor of rights rests on an attempted reconciliation of economic and social goals of the kind expressed by the [ECJ] in its judgment in *Defrenne* v. *Sabena (No 2)* [Case 43/75 [1976] ECR 455], in which it stated that 'the aim of Article [141 on equal pay] is to avoid a situation in which undertakings established in Member States which have actually implemented the principle of equal pay suffer a competitive disadvantage in intra-Community competition as compared with undertakings established in states which have not yet eliminated discrimination as regards pay.' At the same time the Court clearly regarded social policy as not completely subsumed into an economic integrationist rationale: the Community is 'not merely an economic union, but is at the same time intended, by common action, to ensure social progress and seek the constant improvement of the living and working conditions of their peoples, as emphasized by the Preamble to the Treaty' . . .

Standards as guarantors of economic development and participation. The emphasis on standards as a floor of rights, while welcome from the point of view of clarity in social policy, is in itself a somewhat defensive response to the process of economic integration. Rather than viewing harmonisation in terms of a static end-point in which member states provide parallel forms and levels of protection, we suggest that it is potentially much more useful to see it as a dynamic process in which transnational labour standards interact with economic integration to produce a continuous upwards movement in social and economic outcomes. This involves seeing standards not as the result or output of economic growth, but . . . as an *input* into economic development of the kind needed to ensure that strategic factors do not lead either corporations or states to adopt a low wage route to competitive survival.

No doubt all of these economic arguments, together with other political consider-ations, play a role in the decisions of Member States to accede or reject proposals for directives that affect employment relations. What is common to these arguments is that they may support regulation for purposes that go beyond the facilitation of cross-border trade. But at the heart of European social policy there remains a funda-mental disagreement. Although all States share the common goal of promoting improvements in the living standards and working conditions of their citizens, the controversial question is whether this goal is best achieved either through permitting regulatory competition (as well as market competition) or through the enactment of transnational labour standards, which at least achieve some of the shared aspiration. The outcome of this disagreement is the precarious and opaque compromise repre-sented by Article 137, which in effect permits regulatory competition to operate in many aspects of the employment relation, such as pay, industrial action, collective organisation and representation, and dismissal, but simultaneously permits the impo-sition of minimum standards by a majority vote in respect of other aspects of the employment relation such as health and safety, information and consultation of workers, equality of treatment between men and women, and the hitherto unexplored category of 'working conditions'.

In concluding this assessment of the possible trajectory of EC labour law, we should note that any developments in this field need to be reconciled with the other objectives of the EC. In particular, there is potential tension between, on the one hand, labour standards and, on the other, EC rules designed to promote competitive markets and to prevent impediments to cross-border trade and movements of capital. For example, a dock work scheme in the port of Genoa, which granted a monopoly for unloading ships to the port authority and to authorised companies of dock work-ers, was held to be contrary to the competition rules of the Treaty (Case 179/90 *Merci convenzione porto Genova SpA* v. *Siderurgica Gabriella SpA* [1991] ECR I–5889 (ECJ)). But the ECJ has demonstrated a reluctance to permit competition rules to interfere with national labour laws. For example, when it was objected that the German law of unfair dismissal, by exempting small employers, was in effect giving a subsidy to employers in the form of reduced labour costs, the ECJ firmly rejected the proposition that the law amounted to a prohibited state aid to national businesses (Case 189/91 *Kirshammer-Hack* v. *Sidal* [1994] IRLR 185 (ECJ)). Even so, the poten-tial tension between national labour law standards and principles of the EC internal market may yet become a crucial battleground.

1.5 Prospects for labour law

To conclude this introduction to the subject of labour law, we introduce some of the principal themes that inform contemporary debates and that infuse each of the subsequent chapters.

1.5.1 Flexible forms of work

Whatever legal regulation of the employment relation is proposed, it will have to cope almost certainly with rapid changes in the type of work performed and the terms on which it is undertaken. In the twentieth century, business organisation tended towards large, vertically integrated systems of production, that produced goods and services for mass markets. In these large firms such as car manufacturers and banks, the business operated through a bureaucratic organisation. This organisation linked together and co-ordinated numerous jobs by means of managerial hierarchies. Employees typically joined these companies in entry positions, received training in the necessary skills for their jobs, and then, subject to good performance, remained in those jobs or received promotion and training to other jobs for much of their working careers. The jobs were typically full-time, of indefinite duration, and were expected to last until retirement, at which point most employees of these large organisations would benefit from the employer's occupational pension scheme.

Although this kind of job has certainly not disappeared, there are many signs of significant changes occurring in working relations which signal the decline of this typical pattern. People move jobs more frequently, often taking fixed-term appointments. Many more people have become self-employed in the sense that they sell their services as if they represented a separate business. Training is more often provided outside the workplace through educational institutions. Workers also have to undergo more frequent training, since they need to keep pace with changes in technology, and sometimes their jobs disappear altogether as a result of technological innovation. Hours of work have become subject to greater variability. The type of work to be performed has often become diversified, so that workers are expected to perform a wider range of tasks. With this expectation also comes more responsibility and discretion, so that the worker has to direct himself towards the most efficient use of his time.

Behind these changes in the form of work, which are sometimes described as 'flexibilisation', are some powerful economic forces that give reason to think that the changes are both permanent and evolving. Intensification of competition as a result of globalisation of capital and product markets forces employers to experiment with systems of ever more efficient use of labour. These systems often require all kinds of flexibility from employees, including variations in hours of work and job tasks. One of the principal sources of competitive advantage for businesses stems from technological innovations, which depend upon research and rapid adaptations to new types of production systems. In this 'knowledge-based' economy, employers need to reorganise their businesses in order to tap into the knowledge and innovative capacity of their employees, so that the old bureaucratic top-down command systems are no longer always the most efficient. It is also suggested that consumers now expect products that meet more precisely their desires, having ceased to be content with mass production goods of moderate quality. In order to meet this demand, employers have to be able to respond rapidly to changes in taste, to be able to customise their products, and to create production systems that achieve constant improvements in design and quality. There is little room in such production systems for the permanent job with unchanging content and moderate skills requirements.

These changes in the form of work relationships present legal regulation with difficult problems to overcome. One issue is the proper scope of legal regulation. Work may be performed through an enormous variety of contractual relations, ranging from the traditional permanent full-time job, through part-time and short-term work, to self-employment in the forms of consultancy, franchises and freelance work. The question is the extent to which legislated standards should apply to all these different kinds of working relations. For example, to what extent should protection against unfair dismissal be applied to all these different kinds of workers? Another issue is how can labour standards be defined so that they apply appropriately across all these different types of working relations. For example, the idea that there should be a maximum number of hours in a working week in order to protect the health of workers can be applied fairly simply to the traditional form of full-time employment, but how should it apply, if at all, to workers hired for a particular task, or to consultants, or to franchisees? Similarly, it may be asked how a minimum wage per hour might be applied to workers who are paid exclusively by commissions on sales or by a fixed fee for a particular piece of work.

Changes in the form of working relations present a deeper challenge to traditions of legal regulation of the workplace. Under the pattern of a job for life or for a long-term indefinite duration, many legal rights were designed to protect expectations of job security, such as the statutory rights to claim unfair dismissal and redundancy payments, and the common law protected many express contractual undertakings of job continuity. Under modern patterns of job insecurity, as exemplified by fixed-term contracts and consultancies, and rapid variations in job content in order to adapt to changing production requirements, neither party to the employment relation has the same expectations of job security and constant employment on the same job. The question arises whether the law should continue its policy of protecting job security, or whether this policy will come to be perceived as inappropriate. In addition, it can be asked whether the law should place constraints on the kinds of job packages offered by employers in order to prevent the unjustified use of insecure and casual work.

At the same time as old issues may not seem so important or need to be redefined, new issues arise from changes in working arrangements. The granting of greater autonomy to workers, that is the vesting of greater discretion and responsibility further down the organisation, creates the potential for greater stress to be experienced by workers. Work is not so easily separated from the rest of social life, because the responsibilities will be carried home. Indeed, working from home for part of the time has become more common owing to the ease of communications. Working time also becomes a less distinct sphere of social life, so that many people work longer, though flexible, hours. These types of jobs also require greater consultation between members of the workforce, both with managers and co-workers, in order to achieve efficient co-ordination of production. This consultation involves sharing information about production plans, discussing innovations and agreeing effective adaptations. Formerly these matters were within the exclusive competence of management, a privilege which was generally closely guarded. But changes in job design and working patterns involved in flexibilisation create expectations of greater participation in decision-making than formerly. How might the law respond to these new kinds of challenges? How might effective regulation prevent stress-related work, especially when work is performed unsupervised outside the workplace? How can the law ensure an appropriate scope of consultation within the workplace? These kinds of questions pose new problems for legal regulation.

1.5.2 Economic objectives of legal regulation

As well as these changes in the forms of employment relations, we should also notice an important reorientation in the perspective of governments towards legal regulation. The traditional justification for mandatory labour standards or collective bargaining was to improve terms and conditions of employment, which, as a result of the inequality of bargaining power of individual employees against their employers, tended towards poor wages, few protections against the misuse of managerial discretion, and unsafe working practices. Although this objective of improvements in terms and conditions of employment remains, it is significantly qualified by concerns about economic efficiency and the competitiveness of business.

For firms to survive and prosper in modern global markets, it is argued, what it needed is not mandatory labour standards, but rather deregulation of labour markets, thus permitting employers to discover the most productive use of labour power. This view implies a return to legal regulation through ordinary private law, that is the enforcement of the contract of employment as agreed by employer and employee. For example, it is argued that minimum wage legislation, by artificially increasing labour costs, will cause employers to reduce the number of employees or even go out of business altogether, with the undesirable effect of increasing levels of unemployment. Similarly, it is suggested that compulsory laws against unfair dismissal impose costs upon employers, which lead employers either to reduce the number of employees (an unemployment effect) or to retain unproductive workers (a productive inefficiency effect) or to lower wages in order to keep labour costs constant (an inefficient transaction, if most workers would prefer higher wages to protection of job security). On this view, therefore, mandatory labour standards both tend to backfire on the workers they are designed to help, and create inefficiencies in production. These economic arguments for deregulation of the labour market and contracts of employment became extremely influential in the 1980s. As a result some steps were taken towards deregulation such as the Wages Act 1986, and as a consequence we must pay close attention to the legal effects of individual contracts of employment.

Nevertheless, it is wrong to think that the policy of enhancing economic efficiency necessarily leads to deregulation. On the contrary, the promotion of efficiency and competitiveness in business can justify many types of legal regulation. The significance of arguments based upon economic efficiency is rather that they tend to point legal regulation in particular directions, because they often regard arguments based upon broader notions of equity and fairness as inadequate in themselves. There is no doubt that these economic considerations have a profound bearing on government policy. For example, a government is unlikely to promote regulation unless it passes an efficiency test in a 'Regulatory Impact Statement', which is an official estimate of the potential costs and benefits from a particular regulatory proposal. We can point to the kinds of legal regulation that may be supported by arguments of efficiency and competitiveness.

1.5.2.1 Labour market failure

The labour market, perhaps more than other markets, is unlikely to achieve efficient outcomes without regulatory guidance and assistance. Economists describe these imperfections in markets that prevent the most efficient results as 'market failures'. An example in the context of the labour market is labour mobility. The problem frequently occurs that workers are unable to move to the place where suitable jobs are available, perhaps because of the costs of moving home or family ties. The result is an unnecessary or inefficient level of unemployment. Regulation might reduce this market failure by notifying workers of the availability of jobs in distant locations and by providing financial assistance towards changing accommodation. The problem of labour mobility is a simple illustration of market failure. A more complex problem consists in matching skills to jobs. It is vital to ensure that workers receive the training that is appropriate for the jobs that will become available. Given that employers may not foresee the type of skill shortage and in any case will be reluctant to pay for the training of the workforce, the economic system can lose its competitiveness by failing to supply sufficient numbers of workers with the required skills. Again regulation can assist this problem both through enhancing the supply of appropriately skilled workers and by giving employers incentives to provide the necessary training.

1.5.2.2 Externalities and social costs

Another justification for the regulation of business is that certain types of costs generated by the business may not be paid for by that business but rather imposed on others or society as a whole. A business decision may therefore be efficient from the perspective of the business itself, but when the broader costs are taken into account, the decision may appear inefficient. For example, a firm may decide that it can improve its profitability by reducing the size of its workforce. These redundancies may be an efficient outcome for the firm, but when we take into account the costs of supporting unemployed workers and their dependants, we may discover that these 'social costs' far exceed the benefits to the business. Legal regulation can force employers to include some of these social costs in their calculations of efficient decisions, that is to internalise the costs of externalities. For example, the law might require employers to pay for the financial support of redundant workers through redundancy payments, severance benefits, or contributions to the social security system. The intended effect of such regulation would be to restrict workforce reductions to those cases where the benefits in terms of increased profits for the company exceed the costs of providing financial support for the unemployed workers. The objective of this regulation can be described as that of minimising social costs.

1.5.2.3 Competitiveness: capital investment

The productive efficiency of a business, that is the cost of each unit produced, depends crucially on the amount of capital investment as well as labour costs. In the familiar example of producing cars, in order to produce cars at the lowest cost, the firm has to find the optimal balance between investment in machinery and hiring labour. If labour costs are low, the incentive to invest in machinery and robots is also low. But if labour costs are high, in order to minimise unit costs, the employer may find a strong incentive to increase levels of capital investment. Using this insight, it can be suggested that in the long run there is a competitive advantage to be obtained for firms by intensive capital investment. In order to induce this beneficial long-term investment, legal regulation that increases labour costs may be desirable.

[1.25] S. Deakin and F. Wilkinson, 'Labour Law and Economic Theory: A Reappraisal' in H. Collins, P. Davies, and R. Rideout (eds.), *Legal Regulation of the Employment Relation* (London, Kluwer, 2000), 29, 60–1

> In a market environment in which competition is based upon process and product development, a low pay strategy designed to retain the profitability of increasingly obsolete equipment and product lines can bring only temporary respite. There is a limit to how far wages can be reduced in even the most segmented market, but no such limit to cost reductions from technical improvements. Similarly, at some point a product becomes so obsolete that it cannot be sold at any price. For firms and economies trapped in this downward spiral, expectations become increasingly short term and survival more and more dependent on cost cutting.
>
> Labour standards are important, then, because the ability of any one firm to adopt a high-productivity route to competitive success is limited if its rivals are able to compensate on the basis of low pay and poor working conditions. Basic levels of protection in such areas as wages, working time and conditions of employment aim to forestall destructive competition by setting a floor below which terms and conditions may not fall. Effective labour standards constitute a form of discipline for firms, requiring them to engage in continuous improvements to products and techniques in order to stay competitive. By contrast, the existence of a pool of undervalued labour offers a means by which firms can compensate for organisational and other managerial inadequacies.
>
> Labour standards do not simply permit but also effectively require firms to adopt strategies based upon enhancing the quality of labour inputs through improvements to health and safety protection, training and skills development. Low pay and poor working conditions and the absence of job security also have a negative impact on incentives for training. One orthodox explanation for low pay is that it is the result of a lack of training and skill, and that an increase in pay will further discourage employers from providing training. But a closer examination reveals again a quite different direction of causation. Firstly, low paying employers are the least likely to train. Inefficient low payers require undervalued labour to subsidise poor management or keep obsolete equipment in production and cannot afford to train except in the narrowest sense. Secondly, skill is to

an important degree a social category and jobs with poor terms and conditions of employment are unlikely to be afforded high status whatever their skill level. Employment status as well as the content of jobs determines the willingness of individuals to acquire the necessary entry qualifications by undertaking education and training.

The theory of labour law and the labour market which we have offered here, then, turns orthodoxy on its head by suggesting that in a 'free' labour market, wages are unable to perform the allocative and incentive functions which are traditionally ascribed to them, and that labour market regulation is necessary in order to restore both equity and efficiency. Our understanding of 'efficiency' refers not just to allocative efficiency in the static sense, but rather to efficiency in the sense of a dynamic process of economic growth, carried on under conditions conducive to innovation and economic sustainability.

The important thesis of the above essay is that in the long run labour standards can contribute to competitiveness better than deregulation, because they compel employers to invest in technology and product innovation in order to remain competitive. Although employers may survive in the short-term by paying low wages and meeting low labour standards, this strategy for regulation will not preserve businesses and jobs in the long run in many sectors, because employers in other countries will be able to undercut continuously those labour costs. What is needed in the long term is rather the achievement of competitiveness through superior products at low unit costs, which requires capital investment and continuous improvement in the skills of the workforce. The authors' argument is that legal regulation can rule out the low-wage, low-skill trajectory for most businesses by the imposition of mandatory labour standards.

1.5.2.4 Competitiveness: human resources management

The productive efficiency or competitiveness of a business also depends crucially on how well managers achieve the productive co-operation of the workforce. In order to produce high quality products at the least cost, managers need to achieve a kind of co-operation from employees that goes beyond obedience to orders. One need is to tap into the knowledge and skills of the workforce itself, in order to discover possible improvements in the efficiency of production and the quality of the product. Another need is for the workforce to accept flexibility, particularly functional flexibility, that is a willingness to perform a wide range of tasks according to the immediate requirements of the employer. But there are significant obstacles in the way of achieving this level of co-operation from the workforce. Workers may be unwilling to suggest improvements for fear that the employer might be able to dispense with their services or require them to accept greater responsibility or to reduce wages. Similarly, employees may fear the potential increased demands of functional flexibility and be unwilling to acquire the wide range of skills that are necessary. The question arises whether legal regulation of the employment relation might assist employers to establish relations of production which achieve the level of co-operation that is efficient, whilst at the same time providing adequate assurances and safeguards for the workforce that they will be treated fairly.

Legal rules might help to create stable institutional arrangements that might create a basis for trust and co-operation. Compulsory terms inserted into contracts might require both employer and employee to disclose certain kinds of information and to perform obligations in good faith. The law could supply models for consultation mechanisms that would meet the typical objections to such arrangements that they are easily diverted into either confrontational collective bargaining or a pointless talking shop. Legal regulation might further protect workers against an employer's opportunism by granting various types of rights, which could reinforce any contractual commitments offered by the employer. For example, if the employer offers training opportunities, the employee could have a legal right to time off to receive training in addition to a legal mechanism for enforcing the employer's promise. The general point here is that in order to ensure the stability of flexible employment relations, both employer and employee may need new kinds of safeguards for their interests, and the law may have an important role here in creating a workable institutional framework.

From an economic perspective, therefore, the prospects for labour law informed by policies of improving efficiency and competitiveness might involve extensive regulation of many aspects of the employment relation and the labour market. Such policy considerations seem likely to comprise an increasingly important element in any government's programme, though on their own they are certainly incomplete. Governments must also be concerned about 'social cohesion', that is methods for binding society together by means of shared principles and institutional frameworks that secure social justice.

1.5.3 Social exclusion

Social exclusion refers to the predicament of many groups in society, who are unable to participate in its benefits and material wealth. An inability to obtain a job is one of the prime sources of social exclusion. This inability may stem from many causes including inadequate education and training, membership of a group against which there is discrimination, and incompatible family responsibilities. Tackling social exclusion requires governments to support many social programmes, not least education and training. These programmes can intersect with regulation of the labour market, as for example where the government subsidises the wages of young workers in their first job in order to assist them in obtaining some training and work experience by exercising a right to take time off work (Employment Rights Act 1996, section 63A), or where the government supports employers' schemes for encouraging young workers to continue their education and training part-time after the school leaving age (Learning and Skills Act 2000). The most important role of government in addressing social exclusion is to raise levels of employment through its macro-economic policies.

1.5.3.1 Equality of opportunity

In relation to combating social exclusion caused by the operation of the labour market, a key principle is the idea of equality of opportunity, which states a principle of social justice that insists that jobs should be allocated on the basis of merit in the sense of ability to perform the job. The challenge for legal regulation is both to remove obstacles to equal opportunity and to assist people to take up opportunities by, for example, helping with education and training. To achieve effective equality of opportunity is, however, a complex and multi-faceted task.

To achieve effective equality of opportunity for women in the labour market, for instance, it is not sufficient merely to declare deliberate discrimination against women to be unlawful. The law needs to tackle also 'institutional discrimination', that is rules of organisations, which, though neutral on their face, have the effect of deterring or discouraging women from taking up jobs with that organisation. Such a rule might be one that requires employees to be willing to accept work in the evenings, a rule that many women may be reluctant to accept if they have other compelling family respon-sibilities. Beyond institutional discrimination, the government has to address the difficult problems of providing affordable childcare for families, in order to enable women to take up paid employment and to be better off as a result.

The range of problems that must be tackled by the law in the pursuit of effective equality of opportunity is extended, of course, by the large number of groups who may feel that they are being denied fair opportunities in the labour market. As well as women and ethnic minorities, these groups include the elderly, the young, minority religious groups, the disabled and gay men, lesbians, and bisexuals. For each group, effective equality of opportunity may require more than the prohibition of direct dis-crimination: the problems of institutional discrimination and other obstacles to labour market participation need to be overcome.

Perhaps the most controversial question in this area of equality of opportunity is the extent to which the law should permit or require employers to engage in positive discrimination in favour of a group that has historically been disadvantaged. A formal conception of equality requires the same treatment for different groups of workers, but a policy of equality of opportunity directed at combating social exclu-sion seems to support measures of positive discrimination in order realise that objective. Although UK law has not endorsed the possibility of positive discrimina-tion, it is accepted as a permitted practice under limited conditions in European law.

[1.26] Treaty Establishing the European Community, Article 141

> 141. 4. With a view to ensuring full equality in practice between men and women in working life, the principle of equal treatment shall not prevent any Member State from maintaining or adopting measures providing for specific advantages in order to make it easier for the under-represented sex to pursue a vocational activity or to prevent or compensate for disadvantages in professional careers.

1.5.3.2 Welfare to work

To address problems of long-term unemployment, the major source of social exclu-sion, the ambition of governments is to assist workers to regain employment. As well as the traditional stick of denying welfare benefits to those who are not seriously looking for a job, modern administration of the welfare system emphasises attempts to improve the prospects of the worker to obtain employment. Welfare claimants have to pass through a 'single work-focused gateway', which makes receipt of benefits conditional on attendance at a meeting with a personal advisor, who will assess the steps needed for the claimant to obtain employment. In particular, welfare benefits under the Jobseekers Act 1995 may be tied to agreement to pursue retraining or some other programme that may enable them to obtain jobs. Employers also receive various inducements to hire from the pool of long-term unemployed or young workers by receiving abatements in the employer's contributions to the social security system.

Many of the long-term unemployed are disabled, often from work-related injuries. The approach in these cases is to make receipt of welfare payments (incapacity benefit) contingent on a personal interview designed to explore what kinds of work the disabled person might be able to perform (Welfare Reform and Pensions Act 1999). In addition, a disabled person may undertake trial periods of work, and voluntary and therapeutic work, without losing the entitlement to benefit, in the hope that these experiences will facilitate a return to permanent employment (Social Security (Welfare to Work) Regulations 1998, SI 1998 No 2231). The Disability Discrimination Act 1995 should also assist these workers to obtain jobs, particularly as a result of section 6, which imposes upon employers a duty to take reasonable steps to avoid working conditions and physical arrangements which put disabled persons at a substantial disadvantage in comparison with persons who are not disabled.

Behind these welfare to work plans lies a philosophy of 'work for those who can; security for those who cannot' (Department of Social Security, *New Ambitions for Our Country: A New Contract for Welfare*, Cm 3805 (1998)), but with the important proviso that nearly everyone can work, assuming that they receive the appropriate training and guidance. To implement this policy, governments will need to intervene increasingly on the supply side of the labour market, that is to take measures designed to assist people to obtain jobs by providing training, and to regulate how work is organised in order to make it accessible and compatible with other demands on people's time. Another strand in the welfare to work philosophy is to ensure that work provides an adequate income. The National Minimum Wage Act 1998 contributes to that policy, but probably more important will be adjustments to the tax system, both to reduce taxation on low incomes and to permit 'negative income tax' under the Tax Credits Act 2002, which provides welfare benefits through the pay packet. This diversion of welfare into the wage packet helps to ensure that a low paid worker is better off in work, and increases income through more work, rather than remaining entirely or partially supported by direct welfare payments by the State. But the new approach to 'poverty traps' cannot avoid them entirely, for the element of 'means testing' required to control the cost will always drive the welfare system to withdraw benefits as wages increase.

The significance of these welfare reforms for labour law seems to be that, by ending the possibility of 'welfare dependency', access to some form of paid employment as a means of support becomes even more crucial for everyone. This pressure draws our attention even more closely to problems of equality of opportunity in obtaining work and the need to help those groups which experience discrimination or social exclusion. Another implication of these welfare reforms is that individuals will increasingly be expected to make private provision against the vicissitudes of the availability of work, inability to work through illness, or for retirement. These private arrangements may be linked to employers' schemes for fringe benefits, as in the case of occupational pension schemes. We can therefore anticipate that terms of employment that provide such benefits will become an increasingly significant dimension of working conditions as welfare provision becomes 'privatised'. Furthermore, legal regulation of such private schemes will need to ensure that they are constructed fairly, managed honestly, and provide reliable protection to the workers. Finally, it is worth noting that 'voluntary work', that is unpaid work that is undertaken as part of a welfare to work scheme, is likely to become a more substantial category of workers. Hitherto it has fallen outside the scope of labour law in the absence of a contract or recognised legal status, but such workers may reasonably expect fair treatment and deserve protection against violations of equality of opportunity principles and unfair termination of the arrangement.

1.5.3.3 The work/life balance

A recent strand in these policies designed to combat social exclusion and to achieve more effective equality of opportunity is described as 'family friendly policies'. The ambition of this policy is to make it easier for people to manage the competing demands of work and their family and civic responsibilities. Changing patterns of work may have made these competing demands even more difficult for both men and women, but the major source of concern remains the entry of women into the labour market, because they now represent about half the nation's paid workforce.

Legal regulation designed to help people achieve a practical balance between work and their other responsibilities, as well as the need for leisure time, initiates a broad agenda. It implies that jobs must pay sufficiently well to achieve a decent standard of living without requiring excessive hours of work. To achieve this goal, the regulation needs to address both minimum wages and maximum working hours. Furthermore, a practical balance between work and other responsibilities requires a rejection of an employer's unfettered right to insist upon strict performance of the terms of the contract of employment where those other responsibilities represent a compelling need for a worker to take time off. Employers have to adjust their demands to the needs of workers, rather than the other way round. Examples of such regulation include parental leave and the right to take time off work to deal with family emergencies.

1.5.4 Worker participation

We have observed that collective bargaining can play an important role in setting workplace rules, and that collective self-regulation has an equivalent, and sometimes superior, effect compared to standards established by law. Collective bargaining and other forms of worker representation can also be presented as a form of 'voice' at work, and of 'industrial democracy'. What mechanisms will provide workers with 'voice' at work? Should the law encourage forms of collective representation and, if so, what forms will be appropriate to changing work practices?

Answers to these questions must depend in large part on whether trade unions and collective bargaining will continue to occupy an important place in British industrial relations. The brute facts of union membership present a poor prognosis for collective bargaining as a comprehensive source of self-regulation and a powerful voice at work. Union membership peaked in 1979 above 13 million, but by 1997 was down to eight million and falling. By 1998 only about half of workplaces had any union members. In the other half, where a union presence might be found, there is considerable evidence that in many workplaces the union is largely inactive, and in the remainder, where unions conduct negotiations, these negotiations often deal only with a narrow range of issues, and do not necessarily include even pay. If public sector workers are taken out of these statistics on union membership and collective bargaining, because in the public sector union membership has remained high, the decline is even more dramatic; and this decline is even further accentuated if one eliminates those industries such as electricity, gas, water and transport that were formerly nationalised. The Workplace Employee Relations Survey in 1998 calculated that no collective bargaining was taking place in 80 per cent of private sector workplaces with 25 or more employees (M. Cully et al., *Britain at Work* (London, Routledge, 1999) 109).

Given this background, it seems unlikely in the foreseeable future that collective bargaining will have a significant role for most workers in setting their working conditions. It may be possible, however, for unions to reverse these trends, to arrest the decline in membership, in particular by recruiting younger workers, and to press for recognition for the purpose of collective bargaining. The law can help this process by protecting workers against anti-union discrimination and by legal imposition of compulsory recognition upon employers where the union has achieved substantial membership. The Employment Relations Act 1999 provides such a statutory recognition procedure, but does not compel employers to reach collective agreements with a recognised union. The law on its own, however, is unlikely to make any significant change in the extent and effectiveness of collective bargaining across the mass of workplaces. Any major change in the impact of collective bargaining will have to come from a reversal of social attitudes to unions, such that workers once again perceive advantages to be gained in joining unions. Recent survey evidence reveals that membership of trade unions has bottomed out at about 30% of the working population, but there is no sign of a significant reversal of the trend of decline in the influence of trade unions in the workplace (H. Kaur, *Employment Attitudes: Main findings from the British Social Attitudes Survey 2003*, DTI Employment Relations Research Series No 36 (December, 2004).

Union representation is not the only possible form of worker participation in the workplace. Many employers discourage unions but offer other types of participation, such as consultative committees. These committees are unlikely to discuss pay, but they may discuss most other aspects of working conditions, such as health and safety, product quality, training, recruitment and staffing issues, and equal opportunities policies. The membership of the committees may be determined by management or by workplace elections. It seems likely that these consultative committees will become increasingly common as managements find them a useful mechanism for sharing information, motivating the workforce and dealing with problems. The law can promote worker participation in this form by requiring employers to establish consultative committees, as in the case of European Works Councils for transnational companies (EC Directives 94/45 and 97/74, The Transnational Information and Consultation of Employees Regulations 1999, 1999 SI 3323), health and safety committees (Health and Safety (Consultation with Employees) Regulations 1996, 1996 SI 1513), and a general requirement for information and consultation with representatives of the workforce in larger undertakings (EC Directive 2002/14, The Information and Consultation of Employees Regulations 2004 SI 2004/3426) . British trade unions have in the past been suspicious of such consultative committees, because they regarded them as an ineffective substitute for collective bargaining. But consultative committees do offer the opportunity for workers to acquire information and express opinions in the workplace, which is a form of empowerment. Union members and elected representatives can often take the lead in these discussions, which can make these committees more effective in expressing the interests and concerns of the workforce. Indeed, union officials may provide indispensable experience and advice on how best to use these alternative systems of representation. Unions have also realised that these institutions for worker representation can be used to establish a presence in the workplace, with the hope that this will lead to recognition for the purpose of collective bargaining. Unions have thus become more willing to participate in consultative committees under the slogan of 'partnership'.

The idea of partnership implies an expansion of the field of worker representation beyond pay bargaining to consider the organisation of work and how best to achieve the goals of the business. Partnership also assumes a common interest between employers and workers in respect of treating workers fairly, improving their employability, and improving the profitability of the business. The slogan of partnership is not necessarily linked to union representation, as opposed to some other mechanism for selecting representatives from the workforce, though it is hard to foresee how stable and effective representative structures can be developed without the advice and experience of unions.

Pressure from the law to move in this direction emanates from the European Community, because in many Member States it has been long accepted that there may be dual channels of representation for workers, both collective bargaining about the wage/work bargain and workplace councils for consultation about broader issues such as long-term business plans. This dual approach is reflected in Articles 27 and 28 of the Charter of Fundamental Rights of the European Union 2000 ([1.2] above). In the policy statements of the European Community there is a constant repetition of a pluralist vision that promotes the right of workers to be informed and consulted about the management of the business. In its most dramatic form, this pluralist framework is expressed by the technique of the enactment of Directives by Council on the recommendation and agreement of the representatives of employers and labour through the European Social Dialogue (above *1.4.3.2*). .

1.5.5 Citizenship

Perhaps the most fundamental change that will affect labour law in the coming years is a revision of the traditional distinction between the public and private spheres. Although Western liberal States have long maintained the importance of protecting the fundamental rights of citizens in their relations with the State, a similar attention to rights has not applied in the sphere of market relations, in particular those in the form of contracts for the supply of labour. The starting-point of legal regulation of employment relations has always been rather that these are market relations, where the only relevant right is the equal right to enter freely into contracts of one's choice. On this traditional view, the powers and entitlements of employers and employees in the workplace should be established and regulated principally by agreement through a market transaction. Yet this sharp separation of a public sphere of rights from a private sphere of contractual arrangements seems now to be fundamentally challenged.

The extensive set of labour standards, framed in the form of rights of individual workers, combined with the increasing influence of transnational standards relating to civil rights and social rights, suggests a different perspective on the workplace. In this new perspective, the worker is also a citizen whilst at work. The worker is entitled to demand respect for his or her fundamental rights from the employer or any other powerful body in the workplace. These rights of citizenship are not simply the traditional values attached to liberty, privacy, and equality, but encompass social and economic rights, which enable the worker/citizen to participate fully in the advantages of a society. This expanded notion of citizenship means that civil and political rights on the one hand and social and economic rights on the other are mutually dependent and indivisible. On this reasoning, social inclusion and economic security are a precondition of effective participation in a democratic community of political equals. This indivisibility of rights explains the holistic approach adopted by the EU in the Charter of Fundamental Rights of the European Union 2000 ([1.2] above), which includes economic and social rights, and gives them equal status with civil and political rights.

On its face, the Human Rights Act 1998 appears to uphold a traditional view of rights as civil and political rights against the State. Direct claims for rights such as the right to privacy, freedom of conscience and religion, and freedom of expression are confined to proceedings against public authorities. Yet the Act is likely to create expectations on the part of all workers, whether in the public or private sector, which will be difficult to resist. The citizen as worker will demand respect for rights of citizenship not only from the State but also from employers and other bearers of private power. Furthermore, an integrated view of civil and social rights encourages courts to interpret legislation and directly enforceable legal rights in ways which fulfill the aspirations expressed in the Charters of social and economic rights. For example, the right to privacy, originally envisaged as a right against excessive intrusion by the state, can be interpreted in the light of the social right to work as providing protection against discriminatory or disproportionate barriers to gaining employment, because those barriers which create serious difficulties for a person to earn a living have adverse repercussions for individuals in the enjoyment of their private lives (see *Sidabras and Dziautas v Lithuania* (55480/00)(27/7/2004) (ECtHR)). In the legal reasoning of courts concerned with the protection of human rights, we can detect a growing disposition to interpret the broad statements of human rights in ways that will promote or protect social and economic rights, thereby revealing a greater appreciation that modern notions of citizenship embrace the idea that the well-being of individuals should be regarded as a matter of entitlement and public responsibility, not merely a matter to be left to the invisible hand of the market.

This expanded notion of citizenship applicable to economic relations in society also compels a broader perspective on the regulation of work. It requires an integration of the problems of social exclusion, equality of opportunity, and the work/life balance within discussions of labour law, because the regulation of employment relations is perceived as one strand in the endeavour to secure a richer notion of citizenship. As governments often remind us, however, citizenship also implies responsibilities as well as rights. These duties go beyond the payment of taxes and social security contributions; they require reasonable efforts (and perhaps more: N. Wikely, 'The Jobseekers Act 1995: What the Unemployed Need is a Good Haircut' (1996) 25 *Industrial Law Journal* 71) to equip oneself with the skills and knowledge required to obtain a job, and then to seek gainful employment, and in so doing to make adequate personal provision for economic security through savings and a pension.

For labour law, this expanded conception of citizenship implies three significant developments. First, it provides a justification for regulation of the employment relation to cover a wider range of issues: initiatives to promote greater and better consultation or workers or their representatives by the employer; procedures for dealing with unfair treatment of workers—not only in cases of dismissal; and the protection of workers' privacy in the face of growing surveillance practices by employers. Secondly, the exercise of managerial discretion with respect to the conduct of the business will be subject to ever closer scrutiny. It will be argued that each decision requires rational and transparent justification if it appears to have an adverse impact on the rights of individuals or groups. For example, the introduction of protection against age discrimination in 2006 will challenge a whole range of standard management practices such as hiring younger workers and imposing compulsory retirement, which will have to be justified on the ground that they are necessary for the efficient management of the enterprise. Finally, legal analysis of labour law issues is likely to become increasingly focussed on the ambit of the legal protection of individual rights. This movement is likely to be strengthened if proposals to create a new and potentially influential Commission for Equality and Human Rights come to fruition (White Paper, *Fairness for All: A New Commission for Equality and Human Rights* Cm 6185 (2004)). There is a danger that this emphasis on individual rights will obscure the importance of collective solidarity among workers in securing effective protection of labour standards. Nevertheless, the legal protection of a broader range of social and economic rights, either directly or through interpretive techniques, will compel governments to take the legitimate claims of workers much more seriously.

1.6 Conclusion

We commenced this chapter by asking 'what is labour law', but this survey of the prospects for labour law demonstrates that we must examine a rapidly shifting field. Although the politically controversial nature of labour law precludes any safe forecasts of even the near future, what seems clear is that the state will play an ever increasing role in regulating labour markets and employment relations. In determining the content of this regulation, economic considerations are likely to predominate, but there will be a countervailing force, not perhaps emanating from organisations of workers, but rather from the desire to achieve citizenship and prevent social exclusion. Yet the form of work relations seems likely to undergo constant and rapid change, so that legal regulation will need to adapt frequently to shifts in the organisation of productive activities. The same global competitive forces that compel flexibility in work relations also create the need for employers to obtain higher levels of co-operation from the workforce, which may create new opportunities for workers, perhaps assisted by the law, to have a voice in decisions that affect their working lives. To achieve all these goals efficiently and effectively, labour law will need to experiment with a wide variety of regulatory techniques and adopt both national and transnational methods. We hope that the reader will share our interest, even excitement, at the prospect of exploring these fundamental contemporary problems, and will appreciate the subtlety and complexity of the issues that must be addressed by labour law.

FURTHER READING

P. Alston, ' "Core Labour Standards" and the Transformation of the International Labour Rights Regime' (2004) 15 *European Journal of International Law* 457.

B. Bercusson, 'Democratic Legitimacy and European Labour Law' (1999) 28 *Industrial Law Journal* 153.

—— S. Deakin, P. Koistinen, Y. Kravaritou, U. Muckenberger, A. Supoit and B. Veneziani, 'A Manifesto for Social Europe' (1997) 3 *European Law Journal* 189.

D. Brodie, *A History of British Labour Law 1867-1945* (Oxford, Hart Publishing, 2003).

H. Collins, 'The Productive Disintegration of Labour Law' (1997) 26 *Industrial Law Journal* 295.

—— 'Justifications and Techniques of Legal Regulation of the Employment Relation' in H. Collins, P. Davies and R. Rideout (eds.), *Legal Regulation of the Employment Relation* (London, Kluwer, 2000) 3.

—— 'Regulating the Employment Relation for Competitiveness' (2001) 30 *Industrial Law Journal* 1.

A.C.L. Davies, *Perspectives on Labour Law* (Cambridge, Cambridge University Press, 2004).

P. Davies, 'The Emergence of European Labour Law' in W.E.J. McCarthy (ed.), *Legal Intervention in Industrial Relations: Gains and Losses* (Oxford, Blackwell, 1992).

—— 'Market Integration and Social Policy in the Court of Justice' (1995) 24 *Industrial Law Journal* 49.

—— A. Lyon-Caen, S. Sciarra and S. Simitis, *European Community Labour Law: Principles and Perspectives* (Oxford, Clarendon Press, 1996).

—— and M. Freedland, *Kahn-Freund's Labour and the Law* (London: Stevens, 3rd edn 1983) chapter 1.

—— and M. Freedland, *Labour Legislation and Public Policy* (Oxford, Clarendon Press, 1993).

S. Deakin and H. Reed, 'River Crossing or Cold Bath? Deregulation and Employment in Britain in he 1980s and 1990s' in G. Esping-Andersen and M. Regini (eds.), *Why Deregulate Labour Markets?* (Oxford, Oxford University Press, 2000).

—— and F. Wilkinson, 'Labour Law and Economic Theory: A Reappraisal' in H. Collins, P. Davies and R. Rideout (eds.), *Legal Regulation of the Employment Relation* (London, Kluwer, 2000) 29.

K.D. Ewing, *Britain and the ILO*, 2nd edn. (London, Institute of Employment Rights, 1994).

—— 'The State and Industrial Relations: "Collective Laissez-Faire" Revisited' (1998) 5 *Historical Studies in Industrial Relations* 1.

N. Gunningham and R. Johnstone, *Regulating Workplace Safety* (Oxford, Oxford University Press, 1999).

B. Hepple, ' "A Race to the Top"? International Investment Guidlelines and Corporate Codes of Conduct' (2000) 20 *Comparative Labor Law and Policy Journal* 347.

—— 'The Future of Labour Law' (1995) 24 *Industrial Law Journal* 303.

—— 'New Approaches to International Labour Regulation' (1997) 26 *Industrial Law Journal* 353.

House of Lords, House of Commons, Joint Committee on Human Rights, *The International Covenant on Economic, Social and Cultural Rights*, 21st Report of Session 2003-04, HL Paper 183, HC 1188.

K. Klare, 'Workplace Democracy & Market Reconstruction: An Agenda for Legal Reform' (1988) 38 *Catholic University Law Review* 1.

—— 'Countervailing Workers' Power as a Regulatory Strategy' in H. Collins, P. Davies and R. Rideout (eds.), *Legal Regulation of the Employment Relation* (London, Kluwer, 2000) 63.

J.K. MacMillan, 'Employment Tribunals: Philosophies and Practicalities' (1999) 28 *Industrial Law Journal* 33.

C. McCrudden, 'Human Rights Codes for Transnational Corporations: What Can the Sullivan and MacBride Principles Tell Us?' (1999) 19 *Oxford Journal of Legal Studies* 167.

S. Sciarra (ed.) *Labour Law in the Courts: National Judges and the European Court of Justice* (Oxford, Hart, 2001).

K. Stone, 'Labor and the Global Economy: Four Approaches to Transnational Labor Regulation' (1995) 16 *Michigan Journal of International Law* 987.

A. Supiot, 'The Transformation of Work and the Future of Labour Law in Europe: A Multidisciplinary Perspective' (1999) 138 *International Labour Review* 31.

G. Van Bueren, 'Including the Excluded: the case for an Economic, Social and Cultural Human Rights Act' [2002] *Public Law* 456.

Lord Wedderburn, *Labour Law and Freedom* (London, Lawrence and Wishart, 1995).

S. Wood, 'From Voluntarism to Partnership: A Third Way Overview of the Public Policy Debate in British Industrial Relations' in H. Collins, P. Davies and R. Rideout (eds.), *Legal Regulation of the Employment Relation* (London, Kluwer, 2000) 111.

The Employment Relation

2.1 The contract of employment

People work under many arrangements. Slavery, forced labour of prisoners, house-work within the family, and feudal serfdom are all institutional arrangements for work with distinctive legal frameworks. By the nineteenth century in Europe, how-ever, the preferred legal institutional arrangement for paid work was found in the law of contract. The relation between employer and labourer was analysed by lawyers as analogous to the contract for the hire of a thing. The relation was a contract for the hire of services.

2.1.1 Freedom of contract

The main significance of the contractual analysis was that it invoked the central prin-ciples of contract law: respect for the freedom to enter contracts and the freedom to choose the precise terms that form the legally enforceable obligation. Older legal reg-ulations that compelled labourers to stay in their communities, that imposed compulsory status obligations towards their superiors in a social hierarchy, and that prevented free movement of labour and freedom to contract gradually crumbled away as the nineteenth century progressed. The vestiges of restrictions on freedom to contract in Britain, that is the penal sanctions under the master and servant laws against workmen for leaving their jobs without permission, were largely abolished in 1875. Similarly, it became established in the nineteenth century that the parties to a contract for the hire of services could agree almost without legal restriction on the whole design of the economic relation: the type of work, the conditions under which work had to be performed, the duration of the relation, the allocation of risks, and the remuneration to be paid. Compared to other European countries, the common law of contract developed by the judges accorded almost complete flexibility, subject only to the restraint of trade doctrine (see box p. 91) and general rules against enforcement of illegal contracts (see box p. 76).

The legal freedom of the parties to determine the terms of their economic relation remains the fundamental principle of the law of contract governing working relations to this day. Respect for freedom of contract has three significant effects upon the shape of labour law.

First, there is great diversity in the types of contractual relations through which work is performed. For example, three secretarial and administrative assistants working for the same business may have very different contractual arrangements, even though they perform almost identical jobs. One may work under a contract of employment of indefinite duration, paid by month for a fixed number of hours. Another may be hired by the hour, according to the need of the employer, and when the assistant is willing and able to work. A third may be a self-employed temporary worker provided through an employment agency. The rates of pay are likely to differ: the second, the casual worker, will be paid least in view of the absence of any perceived commitment to work, and the third, the temporary worker, will be paid the most in cash in order to compensate for the risk of the absence of work and job insecurity, though without any of the fringe benefits earned by the first, the permanent employee, in the form of an occupational pension scheme and paid holidays. The law does not generally seek to control the choice of the parties between all these different kinds of contractual arrangements.

The second effect of the common law's respect for freedom of contract is that nearly all compulsory restrictions upon types of working relations arise from legislation rather than the common law. Legislation sometimes prohibits certain types of working relations, such as the employment of child labour, or certain terms in contracts. More commonly, legislation places additional obligations or confers additional rights on the parties to contracts for the supply of services. As a result, the bulk of specialised labour law is discovered in legislation.

Nevertheless, the third significant effect of the importance attached to freedom of contract is that the starting-point for the analysis of legal obligations arising in the context of working relations must always be the terms of any contractual arrangement. The contract of employment provides the scaffolding for the construction of the legal relation for the performance of work. The express and implied terms of the contract are legally enforceable obligations, which establish the basic structure of the rights and obligations of the employer and the worker or supplier of services. Statutory regulation often supplements, qualifies and occasionally replaces those rights and obligations, but it depends for its application on the existence of the contractual relation. Other legal obligations such as those arising in tort are also often triggered by the presence of the contractual relation. It is therefore always necessary to commence the legal analysis of work relations by ascertaining the existence and content of the contractual framework.

2.1.2 The standard model of employment

Although the common law respects freedom of contract and the consequent variety of contractual forms through which work can be performed, the courts needed to develop a standard model of rules to govern working relations, because most contractual arrangements remained until recently informal and insufficiently detailed to resolve many of the disputes that arose between the parties. Working arrangements were usually formed by oral contracts until the middle of the twentieth century, so that only some key issues such as wages and hours were expressly agreed, leaving many crucial details unresolved. The courts developed a set of default rules applicable to most working relations. This standard model of rules was described as the contract of employment. The model supplied rules to resolve disputes that arose between parties to contracts for hire of labour.

The courts' model of the contract of employment viewed the central obligations of the parties as the exchange of work for wages. Yet most contracts of employment were incomplete in the specification of the work to be provided under the contract. The job on offer might be one of 'labourer', 'mechanic', 'machine operator' or 'clerk', which merely described in general terms the type of work expected. This uncertainty was resolved by creating a standard default rule that the employer had the power to direct labour and the employee was under a correlative obligation to comply with all lawful instructions of the employer. Employers exercise this managerial power to direct labour sometimes through express instructions, but also through standard instructions in 'works rules' or 'staff handbooks' that provide an organisational framework to govern the performance of work. This legal solution to the problem of incompleteness in contracts of employment thus created—or rather consolidated—a power relation, by conferring the right to manage labour upon the employer, and by imposing a heavy duty of compliance upon the worker. This power relation was confirmed by the development of further obligations designed to resolve problems of incompleteness that placed upon the employee duties of loyalty and co-operation.

In legal terminology, this model of the employment relation was articulated as a set of implied terms. These terms were presumed to form part of every contract of employment, unless there was an express contrary agreement between the parties. Some of these terms might perhaps be justified as resting on the actual, though unexpressed, intentions of the parties. Their insertion might therefore be warranted on the traditional legal test that they were necessary to give 'business efficacy' to the contract; for an example see *Devonald v Rosser Sons* [1906] 2 KB 728 (CA), **[2.9]** below. Terms can also be implied into the contract of employment by virtue of custom in the trade or workplace; for an example see *Sagar v Ridehalgh & Sons Ltd* [1931] 1 Ch. 310 (CA), **[2.3]** below. But these days it is accepted by the courts that in fact they use a standard model of the employment relation which imposes many obligations on the parties without detailed examination of the possible intentions of the parties. These terms are sometimes described as terms 'implied by law', which captures the point that they supply the standard legal incidents of employment relations; for an example see the 'implied term of mutual trust and confidence' in *Mahmoud v Bank of Credit and Commerce International SA* [1998] AC 20 (HL), **[2.25]** below. As general implied terms or default rules, these terms implied by law express judicial preconceptions about the essential obligations arising in the context of work relations. These preconceptions both steer the interpretation of the express terms of the contract and supplement and qualify those terms.

These implied terms or default rules governing contracts of employment are constantly evolving and being refined by the courts. It is therefore difficult at any one time to give a precise and uncontentious account of their content. Nevertheless, it is helpful to provide as an introduction a rough and no doubt incomplete summary of terms implied by law, divided according to the obligations of the employer and the employee.

An employer's implied obligations include:
• To take reasonable care of the health and safety of employees;
• Not to act in a manner likely to destroy mutual trust and confidence;
• The duty to give reasonable notice of termination of the contract.

An employee's implied obligations include:
• To obey lawful orders of the employer;
• To take reasonable care in the performance of the contract;
• To act loyally towards the interests of the employer;
• To serve the employer faithfully within the requirements of the contract;
• To give reasonable notice of termination of the contract.

Each of these implied terms may be formulated by different judges in slightly varying terminology. For example, the implied term that the employer should not act in a manner likely to destroy mutual trust and confidence has sometimes been described as a duty to act in good faith or as a duty to act fairly. Since these implied terms describe what was called above judicial preconceptions about the structure and content of the contract employment, the nuances of various formulations may prove significant in the construction of a particular contract. Professor Mark Freedland has further suggested that underlying these general principles governing the construction of contracts of employment, it is useful to identify 'an overarching principle of fair management and performance' (*The Personal Employment Contract* (Oxford, Oxford University Press, 2003) pp 186–95). This overarching principle, he argues, both links together the strands in the judicial preconceptions about the content of the employment relation and serves to provide a bridge to principles underlying legislative interventions that replace or qualify the contractual framework for employment.

Although these general principles have usually been described in the common law as implied terms of the contract of employment, the standards adopted may have been determined by other branches of the law. In particular, the duties of the employer with respect to the health and safety of employees were developed through the law of negligence in tort. In the nineteenth century, the courts concluded that in principle the employer should be liable for workers' injuries incurred in the course of employment in factories and mines. But the courts introduced a notorious qualification to that principle: the employer would not be liable if the injury was actually caused by another employee (the common employment rule in *Priestly v Fowler* (1837) 3 M & W 1), which, of course, was usually the case. This qualification was removed by legislation (the Law Reform (Personal Injuries) Act 1948), though in practice the courts had by then found ways around the qualification by insisting that employers owed certain general management duties to create a safe place of work (*Wilsons and Clyde Coal Ltd v English* [1938] AC 57 (HL)). This general duty comprises diverse elements including the obligation to take reasonable care to appoint competent staff, to provide adequate tools and materials, and to create reasonably safe systems of work, including effective supervision. Whether the obligation to provide a safe place of work is based conceptually on the tort of negligence or an implied term of the contract, the content of the standards imposed by the courts on employers remains the same, because the courts use the general principles of tort law to construct the content of the implied term.

In addition to the express and implied terms of the contract, statutory employment rights have sometimes been enacted in the form that they impose a compulsory term in contracts. Such a compulsory term will override any contrary express or implied terms. For example, minimum wage legislation uses as one of its enforcement mechanisms the possibility that a worker can enforce the entitlement to a minimum wage, notwithstanding a contrary contractual agreement for a lower wage (National Minimum Wage Act 1998 section 17). A similar interpretation of the effect of maximum weekly hours regulation was accepted in *Barber v RJB Mining (UK) Ltd* [1999] ICR 679 (HC) (**[4.77]** below), where miners obtained a declaration that they were not obliged under their contracts to work the hours fixed by their contract, but could insist upon the statutory maximum fixed by the Working Time Regulations 1998. Although the use of compulsory terms as a method for the enactment of statutory employment rights provides this additional means for workers to enforce their rights in ordinary contractual disputes, for the most part statutory employment rights have been enacted as free-standing claims, which may, however, following the completion of the legal process, lead to a remedial declaration of the amendment of the express terms of the contract. For example, following a successful claim under the Part-time Workers (Prevention of Less Favourable Treatment) Regulations 2000, a tribunal may make a declaration that the terms of the part-time worker's contract should be altered to prevent unjustified less favourable terms than those enjoyed by full-time workers.

The contract of employment, as defined loosely by these ingredients of the wage/work bargain, and as supplemented by a variety of implicit obligations that resolved issues of incompleteness in the contractual arrangements, became the standard legal model under which working arrangements were conducted. The parties were generally free to reach an alternative arrangement, but the model became the presumptive legal institution that governed any economic arrangement through which an individual supplied his personal services to perform work for another.

2.1.3 The legal institution of the contract of employment

The standard model of the contract of employment became a foundational legal institution during the twentieth century. It was called initially the *contract of service* as opposed to the *contract for services*. The legal concept of the contract of employment played a central role in the development not only of labour law, but also tort law, tax law and social security law. In the law of tort, the contract of employment was used to fix the scope of the vicarious liability of employers for the negligence of agents who had caused loss to third parties. The Workmen's Compensation Acts 1897 and 1906 used the contract of service to set the outer boundaries of the compensation scheme. In taxation of personal income, the contract of employment was used to draw the line between wage earners, for whom tax should be deducted by the employer, and the self-employed who would be responsible for their own tax obligations and who could take advantage of a broader range of deductions to reduce their tax liability (Finance Act 1922 and Income Tax (Employments) Act 1943). In the social security system, the contract of employment or contract of service was used in the National Insurance Act 1911 to establish the boundaries of the new provisions regarding pensions and compulsory health insurance. The use of the contract of employment as the legal institution that determined a wide range of private and public rights and obligations was subject initially to many qualifications and exceptions in the legislation, but its role as the general determinant of the legal incidents of

---

Compensation for Workplace Injuries

Building on the Workmen's Compensation Act 1897, as part of the system known as the Welfare State, the National Insurance (Industrial Injuries) Act 1946 provides a system for compensation for injuries in the workplace, without the need to prove fault, and funded by contributions to the social security system. The Act covers injuries resulting from accidents and a list of occupational diseases (Social Security (Industrial Injuries) (Prescribed Diseases) Regulations 1985 No. 967 (as amended). Although these provisions still exist, their spirit as a collective insurance system has been changed, because the Secretary of State may recoup much of the cost of benefits paid to those injured at work from the employer (or the employer's insurer). Furthermore, owing to the somewhat narrow scope and limited amounts of compensation available under the social security system, increasingly injured workers bring tort claims for compensation. An employer is required to take out liability insurance (Employers' Liability (Compulsory Insurance) Act 1969, amended by Employers' Liability (Compulsory Insurance) Regulations 1998 SI 2573). Hence, most of the costs of compensation for workplace injuries are now shared by employers through the private insurance system. An employee's tort claim for compensation may be framed either in negligence or following *Groves v Lord Wimborne* [1898] 2 QB 402 as a breach of a statutory duty, such as those duties provided by the Health and Safety at Work Act 1974 and its accompanying specific regulations on necessary safety measures. As the modern law of negligence has expanded to include compensation not only for physical injuries but also for diseases triggered by working conditions and psychiatric illness (e.g. *White v Chief Constable of South Yorkshire Police* [1999] IRLR 110, HL), so in effect the employer's duty of care with respect to the safety of employees has expanded. It may be argued that the duty extends beyond safety to that of taking reasonable care to provide a civilised place of work that respects the dignity of individuals, as envisaged in Article 31 Charter of the Fundamental Rights of the European Union 2000 (above [1.2]). In *Walker v Northumberland County Council* [1995] IRLR 35, an employee successfully claimed damages for mental breakdown resulting from stress at work caused by the employer's breach of duty of care (see B. Barrett, 'Work-induced Stress' (1995) 24 *Industrial Law Journal* 343). The employer will also breach this duty of care if the employer knows or ought reasonably to have known that other employees may be creating the risk of physical or mental harm (*Waters v Commissioner of Police of the Metropolis* [2000] IRLR 720 (HL)). Although the general principles governing claims in tort for personal injuries are outside the scope of this work, the particular application of these principles to bullying, stress, and psychiatric harm are considered in detail below (5.1.1.5), because they provoke a complex relation between tort, contract, and statutory principles.

work and the scope of the social security system was confirmed by the Beveridge Report (*Social Insurance and Allied Services*, Cmd. 6405 (1942)) that established the general principles of what became known as the Welfare State (see S. Deakin, 'The Evolution of the Contract of Employment, 1900–1950: The Influence of the Welfare State' in N. Whiteside and R. Salais (eds.), *Governance, Industry and Labour Markets in Britain and France* (London, Routledge, 1998) 212).

This chapter examines the central aspects of this legal institution of the contract of employment. We will investigate the core economic exchange, which is the wage/work bargain, the legal aspects of the organisational framework in workplaces, the role of collective agreements between employers and trade unions in determining the content of the contract of employment, and the legal construction of the relations of authority and co-operation in the workplace, including obligations to disclose information and to respect confidences. Yet a central theme of this chapter must be an exploration of the constant tension that exists between, on the one hand, the uniform legal institution of the contract of employment with all its legal incidents and, on the other hand, the persistence of the principle of freedom of contract that permits employers to enter contracts for the supply of labour power in almost any form that they may select. This flexibility in the forms of contractual relations constantly undermines the attempt to provide a consistent and coherent regulatory scheme to govern relations at work and the social rights and obligations that arise from them. As an aspect of the diversity of employment relations, we consider whether or not public sector workers require special rules to govern their relations with the State as their employer.

2.2 The wage–work bargain

The legal construction of the core bargain of the contract of employment is the express promise to perform work in return for a promise to pay wages. The terms of this agreement that fix the nature of the work to be performed and the rate of pay become the legally enforceable obligations. In the absence of such express mutual undertakings, there may be no contract at all for want of consideration. It is therefore sometimes said that the mutuality of obligation, namely the promise to perform work in return for a promise to pay wages, is an essential element of the contract of employment.

Under the general principles of the law of contract, , if the employee performs the assigned work, but the employer fails to pay the agreed wages, the employee can in principle bring a claim for the missing wages, subject, of course, to any general defences against claims for breach of contract, such as the invalidity of the contract for fraud or its illegality (see box p. 76). Equally, if the employee fails to perform the specified work, the employer does not have to pay the wages. This general principle of 'no work, no pay' encounters many complexities, however, when applied to particular disputes arising from the course of employment. Questions include what payment

Illegality in Contracts of Employment

Under the general principles of the law of contract, a contract of employment is unenforceable if it is entered into for an illegal purpose, if it is directly prohibited by statute, or if the party seeking to enforce the contract participated knowingly in illegality during performance of the contract. The source of the illegality may be found in legislation or general principles of public policy. One common example of illegal and therefore unenforceable contracts may be those entered into in contravention of the Immigration Act 1971 and the Asylum and Immigration Act 1986. A frequent problem that arises in the context of contracts of employment is the use of schemes for tax evasion, such as the payment of workers in cash, without any formal records or tax being deducted. If an employee knows of the scheme and participates in it, the contract of employment is likely to be unenforceable on the ground of illegality, with the effect that the employee cannot claim arrears of wages. What counts as participation by an employee in a scheme to evade taxes? The test is whether the employee has actively participated in the illegality, rather than merely acquiescing to the employer's unlawful conduct: *Hall v Woolston Hall Leisure Ltd* [2001] ICR 99 CA. The mere knowledge that an employer is not paying the tax due is not sufficient to render the contract unenforceable by the employee. A more complex issue is whether an employee loses all statutory employment rights, such as claims for unfair dismissal and discrimination, if the contract is unenforceable owing to illegality. It is argued, on the one hand, that if the contract of employment is unenforceable, the statutory rights which presuppose the existence of a contractual relation should also be unenforceable; but, on the other hand, it can be asserted that statutory rights do not depend upon the enforceability of common law claims under the contract of employment and should be enforced subject to any exclusions within the statutory scheme. In connection with claims for unfair dismissal, many employees have had their claims excluded owing to their participation in tax evasion (e.g. *Salvensen v Simons* [1994] ICR 409 EAT). But the exclusion is not automatic. A statutory claim for unfair dismissal may be permitted where the legal responsibility to give correct tax returns is primarily imposed on the employer (e.g. VAT), where the employee's participation in the fraudulent scheme was not essential or significant, and where the denial of a claim for compensation for unfair dismissal could well discourage the disclosure of the fraud: *Hewcastle Catering Ltd v Ahmed* [1992] ICR 626 CA. Other statutory rights, such as rights against discrimination in the workplace, may be regarded as subsisting independently of an enforceable contract of employment. In such cases, the tribunal should only exclude the claim if it 'arises out of or is so clearly connected or inextricably bound up or linked with the illegal conduct of the applicant that the court could not permit the applicant to recover compensation without appearing to condone that conduct.' Peter Gibson LJ, *Hall v Woolston Hall Leisure Ltd* [2001] ICR 99 CA, 111. In that case the employee's awareness of the employer's breach of income tax laws did not exclude her claim for sex discrimination, whereas in *Vakante v Governing Body of Addey and Standhope School (No 2)* [2004] EWCA Civ 1065 [2005] ICR 231, a worker who deliberately concealed the fact that he did not have permission to work in the United Kingdom, in order to obtain a job, was prevented from claiming race discrimination against the employer in relation to conduct during the course of the employment.

falls due if the work is not completed, or if the work is defective, or if there is no work to be done, or if the employer forbids the employee to perform any more work.

One broad distinction between forms of employment relation provides a starting-point for answers to those questions. We can distinguish loosely between 'time-service' contracts and systems of 'performance-related pay'. The former contracts offer remuneration on condition that the employee is available to perform the allotted work at the time prescribed by the employer, and payment is calculated by reference to the amount of time that labour power is made available. Performance-related payment systems, such as piece-work, commissions and bonuses, are expressed to be contingent upon satisfactory completion of particular tasks or the achievement of particular goals. This broad distinction provides a rough answer to many questions about the allocation of risk. Under a time-service contract, the employer normally bears the risk that the work is not completed, that the work is defective, or that there is no work to be done, but is entitled to insist that the employee should remain available for work. These allocations of risks are typically reversed in contracts based upon performance-related payment systems. But these presumptions are no more than starting points for the legal analysis, which becomes more refined by an examination of the express and implied terms of the contract. In this section, we consider how the courts have construed contractual arrangements in order to allocate some of these standard risks associated with the wage–work bargain. We also examine the extent to which legislation overrides the contractual allocation of risks and in some instances the basic terms of the wage–work bargain.

2.2.1 Deductions for incomplete and unsatisfactory work

An employer's power to withhold wages is a powerful self-help remedy in response to perceived failures by the employee to perform the contractual undertaking to work. By reducing or eliminating payment, the employer forces the worker to commence a legal claim for the missing wages, an action which the employee will be reluctant to take against his current employer. The employer's entitlement to withhold wages depends upon the terms of the contract and their implications, as determined by the common law of contract. Statute provides workers with a simplified mechanism for recovering unlawful 'deductions' from pay, but provides only a marginal deterrent against misuse of the power to withhold wages. We will consider first the extent to which the common law buttresses the employer's power to use the reduction of wages in order to discipline the workforce, and then examine the extent of the statutory protection for workers against unlawful deductions.

2.2.1.1 Withholding pay at common law

The express and implied terms of the contract determine the employer's power at common law to reduce wages. Under a performance-related payment system in the contract, such as piece-work, the employer is only obliged to pay wages when the task has been completed satisfactorily. The sanction for failure to work hard is simply the refusal to pay wages on the ground that the condition for payment has not been satisfied. Under time-service contracts, however, the position is more complex, for the core of the wage–work bargain is that the employee promises to be available and willing to work according to the employer's instructions for the hours prescribed in the contract. Nevertheless, if the employer can point to a failure to work the agreed hours or to perform the agreed tasks, the employer may also withhold payment of wages. In addition, in any case of breach of contract by the employee, the employer might also seek to claim compensatory damages for losses resulting from the breach. This claim for damages might be set off against wages owed, again resulting in a reduction in payment.

Under a time-service contract, if the employee attends work, but not for all the hours prescribed in the contract, the employer has an option: either to refuse any of the work offered and thereby avoid any payment, or to accept the work offered and reduce pay on a *pro rata* basis.

[2.1] *Miles v Wakefield Borough Council* [1987] AC 539 (HL)

A local government registrar of births, deaths and marriages refused to work normally on Saturday mornings, which amounted to three hours of his normal working week of 37 hours. The House of Lords held that the employer was entitled to deduct 3/37ths of his salary. But the House of Lords also pointed out that an employer might have an option to refuse to pay any wages at all.

Lord Bridge of Harwich:
If an employee refused to perform the full duties which can be required of him under this contract of service the employer is entitled to refuse to accept any partial performance. The position then resulting, during any relevant period while these conditions obtain, is exactly as if the employee were refusing to work at all.

Lord Brightman:
If an employee offers partial performance, as he does in some types of industrial conflict falling short of a strike, the employer has a choice. He may decline to accept the partial performance that is offered, in which case the employee is entitled to no remuneration for his unwanted services, even if they are performed.

If the employee is available for work during the prescribed hours, but is unwilling to perform some aspect of the job as directed by management, the employer has the same option. Wages do not fall due unless the employee is 'ready and willing' to perform work as directed; mere attendance at the prescribed time is insufficient. The employer may refuse all performance and avoid any payment, or accept partial performance and pay for it on a *pro rata* basis. This power to withhold all payment of wages for partial defective performance is especially significant in cases of minor industrial action falling short of a strike.

[2.2] *Wiluszynski v London Borough of Tower Hamlets* [1989] ICR 493 (CA)

A local government officer participated in industrial action organised by his union which involved a refusal to answer enquiries from councillors. This refusal was a breach of contract, though it amounted only to a very small proportion of his duties. The three hours of work missed was made up after the five weeks of industrial action. The employer had warned its employees that unless they fulfilled their full range of contractual duties, they would not be paid at all for any work performed. The plaintiff worked normally during the industrial action apart from the refusal to answer enquiries from councillors, but received no pay for that period. At first instance, the plaintiff's claim for the full salary succeeded on the ground that there had been substantial performance of the job and management had acquiesced in the variation by permitting the employee to attend work. The Court of Appeal allowed the employer's appeal and held that no payment was due.

Nicholls LJ:
In my view the defendant was entitled to adopt the stance that, so long as the plaintiff continued to refuse to carry out part of his contractual duties, the defendant would not accept his services and the plaintiff would not be paid. Replying to enquiries from councillors was a material part of the duties of estate officers such as the plaintiff. The plaintiff's considered statement that he would not discharge this part of his duties was, in law, a repudiatory breach of his contract. Subject to any provision to the contrary in his contract of employment, such conduct entitled the defendant to treat the contract as terminated and to dismiss the plaintiff. The contrary conclusion would mean that the defendant would be obliged to continue to employ and pay the plaintiff even though part of the work required of him and others in his position would not be done. That cannot be right.

In my view, however, termination of the contract is not the only remedy available to an employer in such circumstances. A buyer of goods is entitled to decline to accept goods tendered to him which do not conform to a condition in the contract, without necessarily terminating the contract altogether. So with services. If an employee states that for the indefinite future he will not be performing a material part of his contractual services, the employer is entitled in response, and in advance of the services being undertaken, to decline to accept the proffered partial performance. He can hold himself out as continuing to be ready and willing to carry out the contract of employment, and to accept from the employee work as agreed and to pay him for that work as agreed, while declining to accept or pay for part only of the agreed work. I am fortified in this conclusion by observations in *Miles v Wakefield Metropolitan District Council* [above **2.2**].

In the present case the letter of 14 August can have left the plaintiff in no doubt on what was the defendant's attitude: do not come to work until you are prepared to work normally; if you do come, and you do undertake work, you will not be paid. There may be room for argument concerning the distinction between this and being suspended from duty, which the defendant explicitly stated was not the course being followed. But I do not think that this detracts from the clarity of the simple message being conveyed to the plaintiff . . .

The effect of this decision is to permit employers to withhold all payment under the contract even if the employee is working almost normally, provided that the employer makes it clear to the employee that the refusal to perform some aspect of the job as directed is regarded by the employer as a fundamental breach of contract.

A similar power to withhold wages applies to an employee's breach of an implied term regarding the quality of performance of the contract. The relevant implied term may be based upon the custom of the trade, provided that the custom is 'notorious, certain, and reasonable', or one of the general implied terms that courts insert into contracts of employment, such as the duty to perform work with reasonable care. By virtue of these implied terms an employer may be able to insist upon a reasonable quality of work, and failure to conform to this standard can be regarded as a breach of contract justifying the withholding of wages.

[2.3] *Sagar v. Ridehalgh & Son Ltd* **[1931] 1 Ch. 310 (CA)**

> A weaver claimed pay that had been deducted from wages on the ground of poor workmanship. The contract of employment was an oral agreement, but the rates of pay were fixed by collective agreement. Most mills in the locality had the custom of making deductions for work that had been performed in the view of management without reasonable care and skill, and the custom had prevailed at the defendant employer's mill for more than thirty years. There was no reference to the practice in either the oral agreement or the collective agreement. It was held, amongst other points, that the evidence established an implied term, based upon custom, that the employer could make reasonable deductions for bad work.

That decision involved an interpretation of a typical contract in the manufacturing sector that used a performance-related payment mechanism. The employer could point to defects in the pieces produced in order to justify the deductions from pay. In the case of a time-service contract, the terms of the contract may not specify in any detail the expectation of quality in performance, but the employer can rely upon the general implied terms of the obligation to take reasonable care in the performance of work and the duty to perform in good faith.

[2.4] *Lister v Romford Ice and Cold Storage Co Ltd* **[1956] AC 583 (HL)**

> The employee, a lorry driver, injured another employee when backing the lorry whilst performing his job. The injured employee successfully claimed damages against his employer. The employer (or rather its insurance company) then claimed damages against the negligent driver on the ground of breach of an implied term in the contract of employment. The House of Lords held that contracts of employment contain an implied term that an employee owes a duty to take reasonable care of his employer's property entrusted to him and generally in the performance of his duties. There was no implied term, however, that the employee was entitled to be indemnified by his employer from the employer's insurance.

Such a claim for damages against an employee is rare, because in practice the case will usually be a dispute between insurance companies about who should bear the loss, and insurance companies have agreed not to pursue such actions against employees. Nevertheless, the decision does give employers a powerful right against employees, which may affect the level of compensation in cases of dismissal for negligent damage to the employer's property or form the basis of a set-off against wages. The next case reveals how employers can withhold pay for unsatisfactory work in a time service contract on the basis of an emerging implied obligation to perform the contract faithfully.

[2.5] *British Telecommunications Plc v Ticehurst* **[1992] ICR 383 (CA)**

> Mrs Ticehurst was a manager in charge of 40 staff. Her union, the Society of Telecommunications Executives (STE), were conducting a campaign of industrial action in support of a pay claim. The union instructed its 30,000 members to take action falling

short of a strike, including the general withdrawal of goodwill, working strictly according to contractual hours, and generally not to take on tasks outside their normal duties without written instructions. The industrial action escalated into a series of one day strikes. The employers then sent a letter to all employees declaring that those employees who were not prepared to honour fully the terms of their contract and to perform all the requirements of their jobs would be sent home without pay until they were prepared to work normally. Mrs Ticehurst refused to sign an undertaking to work ' normally in accordance with the terms of my contract . . . and to take no further industrial action,' though she did state in writing that she was prepared to work normally in accordance with the contract. She was sent home without pay until the trade dispute was settled about two weeks later. The legal action was for the pay withheld. The claim was rejected by the Court of Appeal on the ground that Mrs Ticehurst had been in breach of contract by withdrawing goodwill, and that the employers were entitled to refuse to accept part performance of the contract.

Ralph Gibson LJ (giving the judgment of the court):
For my part, I would allow this appeal and, for the reasons which follow, set aside the judgment in favour of Mrs Ticehurst on the ground that not only did she not prove that she was ready and willing to work in accordance with the contract of her employment but that she was plainly evincing the intention, on her return to work, to continue in the industrial action of withdrawal of goodwill, which course of conduct amounted to a breach of the implied terms of her contract. BT were, accordingly, without bringing the contract of employment to an end, entitled to refuse to accept part-performance only by her of her contract of employment.

I have referred to the intention to continue in the action of withdrawal of goodwill, if it existed, as an intention to break the terms of her contract. It is common ground that, before 12 April, Mrs Ticehurst had been taking part in that industrial action. The advice and instructions of STE, of which the nature has been described in the account of the facts given above, called upon Mrs Ticehurst, with the intention of making BT's business unmanageable, to do many things such as (i) to require clear written instructions from her line manager in any case requiring action not covered by standing instructions; (ii) if confronted with anything which might come within the scope of the 'withdrawal of goodwill' action, to consider how much choice she had in how to do it and (by implication) to choose that option which caused the most inconvenience . . . ; (iii) with reference to many different aspects of work, not to take any course of action 'unless agreed by STE' . . .

The implied term upon which BT relies was described in [*Secretary of State for Employment v ASLEF (No 2.)* [1972] ICR 19 (CA) (**[2.11]** below)]. Although that case arose under the provisions of the Industrial Relations Act 1971, an essential issue was whether the conduct in question constituted a breach of contract according to ordinary common law principles. In April 1972 instructions to union members to work 'strictly to rule' had caused much dislocation of rail services. After resumption of normal working the unions, on the failure of further negotiations, instructed their members to resume 'work to rule'. This Court, dismissing an appeal from the NIRC, held that obedience to instructions to 'work to rule' constituted breach of contract. As to the reasons for that holding, Lord Denning MR . . . said:

'Now I quite agree that a man is not bound positively to do more for his employer than his contract requires. He can withdraw his goodwill if he pleases. But what he must not do is wilfully to obstruct the employer as he goes about his business. That is plainly the case where a man is employed singly by a single employer . . . It is equally the case when he is employed, as one of many, to work in an undertaking which needs the service of all. If he, with the others, takes steps wilfully to disrupt the undertaking, to produce chaos so that it will not run as it should, then each one who is a party to those steps is guilty of a breach of his contract. It is no answer for any one of them to say "I am only obeying the rule book", or "I am not bound to do more than a 40-hour week". That would be all very well if done in good faith without any wilful disruption of services; but what makes it wrong is the object with which it is done. There are many branches of our law when an act which would otherwise be lawful is rendered unlawful by the motive or object with which it is done. So here it is the wilful disruption which is the breach.'

Next, Buckley LJ . . . said:

Assuming . . . that the direction to work to rule avoided any specific direction to commit a breach of any express term of the contract, the instruction was nevertheless directed, and is acknowledged to have been directed, to rendering it impossible, or contributing to the impossibility, to carry on the Board's commercial activity upon a sound commercial basis, if at all. The object of the instruction was to frustrate the very commercial object for which the contracts of employment were made. It struck at the foundation of the consensual intentions of the parties of these contracts, and amounted, in my judgment, to an instruction to commit what were clearly breaches or abrogation of those contracts. These are or would be, in my judgment, breaches of an implied term to serve the employer faithfully within the requirements of the contract. It does not mean that the employer could require a man to do anything which lay outside his obligations under the contract, such as to work excess hours of work or to work an unsafe system of work or anything of that kind, but does mean that within the terms of the contract the employee must serve the employer faithfully with a view to promoting those commercial interests for which he is employed. The contrary view is, in my opinion, one which proceeds on much too narrow and formalistic an approach to the legal relations of employer and employee and is an approach which, I may perhaps add, seems to me to be unlikely to promote goodwill or confidence between the parties.

The analysis which I respectfully find most apt to define the relevant duties of Mrs Ticehurst under her contract of employment as a manager employed by BT, is that stated by Buckley LJ, namely 'an implied term to serve the employer faithfully within the requirements of the contract'. It is, I think, consistent with the judgments of Lord Denning and Roskill LJ. It was not suggested that there is any express term in the contract of employment of Mrs Ticehurst, or anything else in the general circumstances of this case, which would make it wrong to imply such a term into her contract. It is, in my judgment, necessary to imply such a term in the case of a manager who is given charge of the work of other employees and who therefore must necessarily be trusted to exercise her judgment and discretion in giving instructions to others and in supervising their work. Such a discretion, if the contract is to work properly, must be exercised faithfully in the interests of the employers.

Next, it seems to me clear that participation by Mrs Ticehurst in the concerted action of withdrawal of goodwill, as it was devised and carried out by STE and the members, would constitute a breach of that term if Mrs Ticehurst was intending to continue to participate in it. . . .

I do not accept the submission of Mr Elias [counsel for Mrs Ticehurst] that there can be no breach of the implied term for faithful service unless the intended disruption of BT's undertaking was achieved by the action taken, whether to the extent of rendering the business unmanageable or to some other level of disruption. The term is breached, in my judgment, when the employee does an act, or omits to do an act, which it would be within her contract and the discretion allowed to her not to do, or to do, as the case may be, and the employee so acts or omits to do the act, not in honest exercise of choice or discretion for the faithful performance of her work but in order to disrupt the employer's business or to cause the most inconvenience that can be caused. . . .

If on her return to work Mrs Ticehurst was evincing an intention to continue to participate in the action of withdrawal of goodwill, BT was in my judgment entitled on that ground, and without terminating the contract of employment, to refuse to let her remain at work.

Such decisions indicate that employers will often be in a strong position to insist that the employee has broken the wage–work bargain when unsatisfactory performance is offered under a time-service contract. The implied obligation appears to amount to a duty placed on the employee to perform the contract in good faith or a duty to co-operate in the performance of work in order to further the employer's business objective. The principle of 'no work, no pay' becomes 'work that does not further the employer's business objective in good faith, no pay'. These interpretations of the express and implied terms of the contract of employment plainly reinforce the managerial power to direct labour and to require co-operation from the workforce by giving management the powerful self-help sanction of the lawful refusal to pay wages. It seems possible that the duty may be more onerous for managerial employees, though this outcome may simply result from the fact that senior employees are likely to enjoy greater discretion in the determination of the tasks to be performed under their contract. This power to refuse to pay full wages in response to the implied term to perform the contract in good faith will, however, usually be subject to statutory controls over unlawful deductions.

2.2.1.2 Statutory protection against deductions

Regulation might endeavour to control the common law power of the employer to withhold wages for a number of purposes:

(a) *Transparency*: clear information to workers in advance about when wages might be reduced and by how much;
(b) *Deterrence against misuse of the power*: a deterrent sanction against the employer for abuse of the power, that is making deductions from pay when not permitted to do so under the contract;
(c) *Fairness of the power*: control over the terms of the contract to prevent the contract conferring the power to make either disproportionate deductions or deductions for trivial breaches of the employee's performance obligations.

In support of any of the above purposes, legal regulation might also create a simple, inexpensive mechanism through which an employee can challenge an unlawful deduction and recover any money due.

For nearly a century the Truck Act 1896 achieved all three of the above purposes for workmen (not white collar workers) and shop assistants. The enforcement mechanism was a prosecution brought by inspectors before a magistrates court, together with the possibility for the workman to recover any excess deduction. Though not without defects, the Truck Act 1896 provided comprehensive regulatory protection for many workers against abuse of the employer's power to enforce discipline by withholding wages until its abolition and replacement by the Wages Act 1986. With one exception, the revised law confines its regulation to the first purpose of transparency, and even that objective is qualified.

[2.6] Employment Rights Act 1996, section 13

(1) An employer shall not make a deduction from wages of a worker employed by him unless—
   (a) the deduction is required or authorised to be made by virtue of a statutory provision or a relevant provision of the worker's contract, or
   (b) the worker has previously signified in writing his agreement or consent to the making of the deduction.

(2) In this section 'relevant provision', in relation to a worker's contract, means a provision of the contract comprised—

   (a) in one or more written terms of the contract of which the employer has given the worker a copy on an occasion prior to the employer making the deduction in question, or
   (b) in one or more terms of the contract (whether express or implied and, if express, whether oral or in writing) the existence and effect, or combined effect, of which in relation to the worker the employer has notified to the worker in writing on such an occasion.

The exception to this limited control for the purpose of transparency concerns deductions made for stock shortages in the retail trade. At the time of the passage of the legislation, studies (*e.g.* T. Goriely, 'Arbitrary Deductions from Pay and the Proposed Repeal of the Truck Acts' (1983) 12 *Industrial Law Journal* 236) and cases such as *Bristow* v. *City Petroleum Ltd* [1988] ICR 165 (HL) revealed how some retail workers such as attendants at self-service petrol stations worked under contracts of employment that permitted the employer to deduct the value of stock that went missing during the worker's shift, even without the attendant's fault, as in the case of a motorist driving away without paying for petrol. As a limited exception to the general scheme of permitting freedom of contract with respect to deductions, sections 17–22 Employment Rights Act (ERA) 1996 in effect restrict deductions for cash shortages and stock deficiencies to 10 per cent of wages on any pay day, except for the final payment of wages when the employer can demand full reimbursement.

   The requirement of transparency in all other cases imposes upon employers who wish to exercise their common law disciplinary power to make deductions from pay the need to comply with the statutory requirements. The EAT has required strict conformity to section 13, which in effect demands both that the deductions rule should be a provision of the worker's contract and that the worker should have been adequately notified of its content. Tribunals can prevent deduction rules from being inserted into contracts without the express consent of the worker. For example, in

Pename Ltd v Paterson [1989] IRLR 19 (EAT), it was held that an employer had not been entitled, on the strength of a statement made in the letter confirming the applicant's employment, to deduct a week's wages from his final salary when he failed to give notice of his leaving. The employee had not put his name to the employer's declaration, and the rule could not be regarded as a contractual term so as to satisfy section 13(1)(a). Even if the rule has become a term of the contract, it may still not justify the deduction if the notification requirement in section 13(2) has not been satisfied. In *Kerr v The Sweater Shop (Scotland) Ltd* [1996] IRLR 425 (EAT), a general display within the workplace of a term, incorporated into the workers' contract, which purported to authorise the disputed deduction, was not sufficient notification. According to the EAT, section 13(2)(b) required personal, rather than general, notification of the employees affected. The requirement of transparency is also supported by strict construction of deduction rules in the contract, so that permission must be granted expressly and clearly. For example, it was held in *Potter v Hunt Contracts Ltd* [1992] IRLR 108 (EAT), that an agreement made by an employee to repay the costs of training if his employment was terminated prior to a particular date did not amount to an agreement on his part that the sums could be deducted from his wages in that event. Despite these robust interpretations of the transparency requirement, it should be observed that employers can operate a sweeping policy of making deductions provided they ensure that express rules are contained in a written contract of employment that the worker is required to sign.

An important subsidiary question is whether the ERA 1996 provisions provide an effective means of enforcement. Unlike under the former Truck Acts, there is no system of inspectors to uphold the legislation. Instead, as under the common law, workers must bring a claim in person to recover pay that has been withheld. The provisions assist enforcement by permitting claims for deductions to be brought before an employment tribunal rather than an ordinary court. The remedy awarded by a tribunal under ERA 1996 section 24, if it finds an unlawful deduction to have been made, is a declaration to that effect and an order to pay the worker the amount of any unlawful deduction.

This statutory remedy of compensation for deductions from pay has increasingly become the standard method by which employees claim any money owing from the employer, thereby avoiding claims in the ordinary courts for breach of contract. This result has been achieved by a combination of the broad definition of wages contained in the statute and the wide definition given to the concept of a 'deduction' from wages by the courts.

[2.7] Employment Rights Act 1996, section 27

(1) In this Part 'wages', in relation to a worker, means any sums payable to the worker in connection with his employment, including—
  (a) any fee, bonus, commission, holiday pay or other emolument referable to his employment, whether payable under his contract or otherwise,
  (b) statutory sick pay . . .
  (c) statutory maternity pay . . .
  (ca) statutory paternity pay . . .
  (cb) statutory adoption pay . . .

(d)   a guarantee payment . . .

(e)   any payment for time off . . . for carrying out trade union duties . . .

(f)   remuneration on suspension on medical grounds . . . and on suspension on maternity grounds . .

(g)   any sum payable in pursuance of an order for reinstatement or re-engagement . .

(h)   any sum payable in pursuance of an order for the continuation of a contract of employment . .

(i)   remuneration under a protective award . .

Any failure to pay all or part of these sums regarded as wages could be regarded as a 'deduction', even if the employer had not intended to impose a disciplinary sanction. Once the supervision of unfairness was removed as a purpose of the legislation, the narrow conception of the word 'deduction' as a disciplinary penalty became inappropriate, so that the courts were prepared to enforce the limited transparency requirement with respect to any disputes over wages. Thus, as a practical matter, most workers are likely to use this jurisdiction in any dispute with an employer over wages and other sums due, whether it be related to unauthorised disciplinary penalties, failure to pay a sum owed, or a deliberate unilateral reduction of pay by the employer. There is also a tactical advantage to workers in using this jurisdiction, which is that if an employer has a counterclaim against the worker, such as a claim for compensation for damage to property, this counterclaim has to be brought in a separate claim in the county court and cannot simply be set off against the unauthorised deduction. The employer is, however, permitted the defence that the sum deducted has already been paid or repaid (ERA 1996 section 25(3)).

The principal exception to the coverage of claims for money under this jurisdiction for deductions concerns claims on termination of employment for payments in lieu of notice. Some of these promised payments were characterised in *Delaney v Staples* [1992] ICR 483 (HL) as claims for damages for breach of contract rather than wages (see box p. 441). Claims for damages for wrongful dismissal can, however, also be brought before employment tribunals as a result of the Employment Tribunals Extension of Jurisdiction Order 1994, 1994 SI 1623. The tribunals' jurisdiction applies to claims brought by employees (as opposed to workers) for sums of less than £25,000. This jurisdiction for claims for wrongful dismissal does, however, permit the simultaneous consideration of counterclaims brought by employers.

As a consequence of these interpretations of the legislation, disputes about wages owed will normally now be handled by employment tribunals within the framework of supervision of deductions from pay. These cases represent about a fifth of the business of employment tribunals. The principal difference from the common law jurisdiction for breach of contract is the insertion of the transparency requirement, so that employers will have difficulty in relying upon obscure or implied terms (as in *Sagar v Ridehalgh* [2.3] above), or express terms that have not been expressly agreed in writing and adequately notified, in order to justify the withholding of pay. The common law cases considered above (e.g. *Ticehurst and Thompson v British Telecommunications plc, Miles v Wakefield Metropolitan District Council, Wiluszynski v London Borough of Tower Hamlets*) with respect to a refusal to pay wages in response to industrial action, however, are excluded from the tribunals' jurisdiction.

[2.8] Employment Rights Act 1996, section 14

> (5) Section 13 does not apply to a deduction from a worker's wages made by his employer where the worker has taken part in a strike or other industrial action and the deduction is made by the employer on account of the worker's having taken part in that strike or other action.

Thus the common law's support for the employer's power to withhold wages either in whole or in part in response to industrial action remains untouched by the jurisdiction over deductions.

2.2.2 Unavailability of work

Does an employee have the right to be paid even though the employer has no work to be done? In general, subject to the express terms of the contract, the employee is entitled to wages provided the employee is ready and willing to work, even if the employer does not direct the employee to perform any work. Thus the law contains a presumption in favour of the allocation of the risk of the unavailability of work to be performed onto the employer. This presumption may be adjusted, however, by variations effected by the express terms of the contract.

In time-service contracts, the employer may shift the risk back onto the employee by inserting a condition that the employee will be paid only when required, not for a regular number of hours. Such contracts can take the form of 'zero hours' contracts, or casual work. Under the express terms of such contracts, the employee is paid only for those hours that are worked, and the employer determines unilaterally when work is required. Under a zero hours contract, the employee promises to be ready and available for work, but the employer merely promises to pay for work actually performed when the employee is required. These contracts may lead to the abuse that workers can be kept hanging around at their place of work waiting for work, but not actually working, and therefore earning no money. Under arrangements for casual work, again the employer does not promise to offer any work, but equally in this case the employee does not promise to be available when required. Such arrangements probably do not amount to binding contracts at all; rather they comprise agreements about the terms of employment when and if the employee is called upon and agrees to perform work. These forms of employment secure to the employer the advantage of allocating the risk of the lack of work to be performed onto the employee, thereby permitting the employer to adjust labour costs precisely to its needs at any particular time. But this efficiency is obtained at considerable disadvantage to employees. In reality this job may provide such workers with their only source of income and they may work substantial hours for long periods of time, even though formally the job remains precarious. And in practice casual workers may feel it necessary always to comply with the employer's request to perform work for fear of losing their place in the pool of workers to whom work is offered. As well as bearing the risk of sudden diminution in income, these workers may also fail to qualify for many statutory employment rights because they lack the necessary continuous period of employment, and they are also likely to be excluded from the fringe benefits enjoyed by permanent employees.

In contracts of employment under which payment is contingent upon the completion of a task, as in the case of piece-work and commissions on sales, at first sight this arrangment permits the employer to decline to pay any wages when no work is available. But the following case illustrates the reluctance of courts to interpret contracts of employment in a way that imposes all risks of the absence of work onto the employee. The court distinguishes between the continuing existence of the contract, which is determined by the operation of its notice provision, and its mechanism for determining the amount of pay due. As long as the contract persists and the employee is able and willing to work, the employer must either provide a reasonable amount of work to be performed, so that the employee may complete the required pieces, or pay compensation instead.

[2.9] *Devonald v Rosser Sons* [1906] 2 KB 728 (CA)

The plaintiff worked as a rollerman in the defendant's tinplate factory. Under the express terms of his contract the employee was required to perform those tasks directed by the employer and he was entitled to 28 days notice of termination of employment. The employer used a piece-rate payment system for each completed box of 112 tin plates, but this payment mechanism was not specified in the written contract of employment. Following a decline in demand for its product, the employer closed the plant and two weeks later gave the employee notice of dismissal. The question before the court was what payment, if any, fell due during the six week period between the plant closure and the expiration of the notice period when the employer had not provided the employee with any work to perform. The Court of Appeal awarded the employee a sum equivalent to his average earnings prior to the plant closure for a period of six weeks. This result was achieved in part by regarding the contract of employment as a time-service contract despite the payment mechanism. Another line of argument was that although the employee bore the risk of lack of work due to some contingencies, an employee did not bear the risk of absence of work due to plant closure.

Lord Alverston CJ:
I entirely agree . . . that the implication which is to be drawn from this contract is one which, to use the language of Bowen L.J. in *The Moorcock* [14 PD 64, 68], is raised 'from the presumed intention of the parties with the object of giving to the transaction such efficacy as both parties must have intended that at all events it should have,' that 'what the law desires to effect by the implication is to give such business efficacy to the transaction as must have been intended at all events by both parties who are business men.' I am content to accept that test in deciding whether or not this contract involves the implication which is necessary to enable the plaintiff to recover. Now, in order to determine that question, the only facts that are material to be considered are that the plaintiff was in the defendants' regular employment, that he was paid by piece work, and that he was employed upon the terms of a rule which provides that 'No person regularly employed shall quit or be discharged from these works without giving or receiving twenty-eight days' notice in writing, such notice to be given on the first Monday of any calendar month.' . . . No distinction in principle can be drawn between wages by time and wages by piece. Piece work is only a method of ascertaining the amount of the wages which is to be paid to the workman. What, then, is the obligation of the employers under such a contract as the present? On the one hand we must consider the matter from the

point of view of the employers who I agree will under ordinary circumstances desire to carry on their works at a profit, though not necessarily at a profit in every week, for it is matter of common knowledge that masters have frequently to run their mills for weeks and months together at a loss in order to keep their business together and in hopes of better times. On the other hand, we have to consider the position of the workman. The workman has to live; and the effect of the defendants' contention is that if the master at any time found that his works were being carried on at a loss, he might at once close down his works and cease to employ his men, who, even if they gave notice to quit the employment, would be bound to the master for a period of at least twenty-eight days during which time they would be unable to earn any wages at all. I agree with Jelf J. that that is an unreasonable contention from the workman's point of view. In my opinion the necessary implication to be drawn from this contract is at least that the master will find a reasonable amount of work up to the expiration of a notice given in accordance with the contract. I am not prepared to say that that obligation is an absolute one to find work at all events, for the evidence shewed that it was subject to certain contingencies, such as breakdown of machinery and want of water and materials. But I am clearly of opinion that it would be no excuse to the master, for non-performance of his implied obligation to provide the workman with work, that he could no longer make his plates at a profit either for orders or for stock. It is to be observed that the question how the works are to be carried on, whether they are going to work short or full time, or whether for stock or current orders, is a matter which rests entirely in the hands of the master. The men have absolutely nothing to say to it. And it seems to me that there is nothing unreasonable in the implication that the master shall look at least twenty-eight days ahead, or, to take the extreme case, as the notice has to be given on the first Monday in the month, fifty-seven days ahead, so as to place himself in a position to provide the workman with work during the period covered by the notice.

The decision in *Devonald v Rosser Sons* therefore provides support for the idea that there may be a duty to pay wages when the payment mechanism adopted is based upon performance and there is no work to be done, provided that the employee is also under an obligation to be ready and willing to work and a duty to give notice of unavailability. Nevertheless, express terms of the contract may negative any such implication. In performance-related payment systems, the employee is also vulnerable to sharp practice by the employer in the form of termination of the employment shortly before performance entitling payment has been completed. In the United States, such sharp practice has been held to be a breach of an implied term of performance in good faith. For example, termination of employment shortly before a large commission on sales falls due may constitute a breach of an obligation to perform in good faith giving rise to liability to pay the commission (*Fortune v National Cash Register Co.*, 373 Mass. 96, 364 NE 2d 1251 (1977)). Perhaps a similar result might be achieved in the UK on the ground of a breach of the employer's implied duty not to act in a way calculated to destroy mutual trust and confidence.

These contractual allocations of the risk of the unavailability of work have been affected by legislation. In particular, in the absence of work to be performed, the employee may under certain conditions terminate the employment and claim a statutory redundancy payment. Another statutory right, known as guarantee payments, also provides a weak protection of earnings during temporary periods of under-employment or 'workless days'. These provisions are considered in Chapter 10.

2.2.3 Enforced idleness

If the employer has work to be done, does the employee have a right to insist upon being able to work rather than be idle? Is there, in short, a 'right to work'? In general, there is no obligation on the employer to direct an employee to perform work. Three exceptions qualify this general presumption.

2.2.3.1 Suspension

If the employer suspends the employee as a disciplinary measure, that is the employer requires the employee not to attend the workplace pending the outcome of disciplinary proceedings, this refusal to give the employee work may be regarded as a breach of contract unless the employer has the power to take this disciplinary measure under the terms of the contract: *Hanley v Pease & Partners Ltd* [1915] 1 KB 698. Similarly, without an express power in the contract to suspend an employee from work on medical grounds, an employee who is ready and able to work, perhaps having recovered from an illness, should be entitled to wages: *Beveridge v KLM UK Ltd* [2000] IRLR 765 (EAT). Any wages that have been withheld during suspension without express contractual provision will normally be recovered as 'deductions' from wages under ERA 1996 section 13. The exercise of an express disciplinary power to suspend the employee has to be exercised in good faith and on reasonable grounds, for otherwise the employer may be found liable for breach of the implied duty not to act in a way calculated to destroy mutual trust and confidence: *Gogay v Hertfordshire County Council* [2000] IRLR 703 (CA).

2.2.3.2 Garden Leave

The employer's refusal to provide work may be part of a 'garden leave' provision under the express terms of the contract. Under such a provision, the employer inserts a term in the contract stating that following notice of termination of the contract, the employee will not be permitted to work for another employer until the expiration of the notice period. The objective of such a clause is to prevent an employee from working for a competitor. If the employer permits the employee to work out his notice, a court will issue an injunction to prevent the employee from leaving earlier to work for a competitor: *Evening Standard Co Ltd v Henderson* [1987] ICR 588 (CA). If the employer refuses to permit the employee to work and insists that the employee should stay at home, some courts have issued injunctions to prevent the employee from working for a competitor during a notice period: *Euro Brokers Ltd v Rabey* [1995] IRLR 206; *GFI Group Inc v Eaglestone* [1994] IRLR 119. But the term of the contract providing for a long period of 'garden leave' can be challenged as a violation of the restraint of trade doctrine [see box p. 91], if the period of idleness is regarded by the court as unreasonable in length or unnecessary to protect the employer from unfair competition. Alternatively, the court may uphold the validity of the garden leave clause, but decline to enforce it by way of an injunction, if the court in exercising its discretion believes that the employer does not need such protection from competition: *Provident Financial Group Plc v Hayward* [1989] ICR 160 (CA).

Restraint of Trade Clauses

Under the restraint of trade doctrine of the common law, terms of contracts which unreasonably and contrary to the public interest prevent a worker from seeking employment or pursuing his or her calling after termination of the work relation are void and unenforceable. For example, a non-compete term in a contract which prevents a worker from setting up a rival business to his or her former employer would be unenforceable unless it was 'reasonable'. Such a restriction might be held to be reasonable if it only limited the exclusion to a particular locality for a limited period of time. The difficult question for the court is whether the term strikes a fair balance between the interests of a worker in earning a living by using his skills and knowledge against any legitimate interest of the employer to protect its intangible assets such as 'know-how' about the business and 'good-will' with customers from being used by a competitor. In *General Billposting Ltd v Atkinson* [1909] AC 118 (HL) it was apparently established that an employer cannot rely upon an otherwise reasonable and valid non-compete clause if the employer has repudiated the contract by wrongful dismissal. It is unclear, however, whether a suitably worded term protecting a legitimate interest of the employer after the termination of the employment would necessarily become ineffective in every case. In a comparable situation concerning the enforcement of a confidentiality clause after an alleged repudiation by the employer, the Court of Appeal hinted strongly that the term would remain enforceable (*Campbell v Frisbee* [2002] EWCA Civ 1374 [2003] ICR 141.) The doctrine of restraint of trade therefore aims to protect freedom to enter contracts from oppressive interference by the terms of other contracts; it does not so much restrict flexibility as enhance it by helping to preserve competition in the labour market.

2.2.3.3 *Reputation and employability*

The third exception is where the employee claims that the refusal to supply work causes the loss of an opportunity to enhance his reputation or employability. If a court finds that in the particular circumstances of the case the employee suffers such losses, the employer's refusal to supply work will be regarded as a breach of contract. The extent of these last two exceptions to the general rule that an employer is not required to provide work is explored in the following case.

[2.10] *William Hill Organisation Ltd v Tucker* **[1999] ICR 291 (CA)**

A senior dealer in a betting business resigned in order to take a job with a competitor. His work involved the complex calculation of the determination of betting odds in a new market known as 'spread betting'. Under the terms of his contract, he was required to give six months' notice of termination. Although the contract did not contain a 'garden leave' clause, the employer insisted that the employee should not work for a competitor during that period, but instead remain at home and continue to receive his wages. The employer sought an injunction to restrain the employee from working for a competitor, but the injunction was refused.

Morritt LJ (giving the judgment of the court):
When an employee has given notice to determine his contract of employment, may his employer, whilst continuing to pay his remuneration, insist that he stays away from work for the duration of the notice period, colloquially known as sending him on garden leave?

It is not disputed that he may do so if there is an express contractual term to that effect. The issue on this appeal is whether, in the absence of such a term, William Hill Organisation Ltd ('the employer'), was entitled to do so in the circumstances of this case. Mr James Goudie QC, sitting as a deputy judge of the Queen's Bench Division, considered that it was not and refused to grant an injunction to restrain its employee, the defendant, Mr Tucker, from working for a competitor during the notice period. Thus there are two points. The first is the so-called 'right-to-work' point. This obviously has ramifications far beyond this case. The second is the exercise of the judge's discretion, which is of great importance to the parties but not to anyone else. I will deal with the alleged 'right to work' first.

For the employer, it was submitted that there was no general right to work whether or not the employee was skilled. It was accepted that such a right may be implied in cases where the provision of work furthers the career of the employee or enables him to earn remuneration. It was also accepted that an employer might not capriciously deny to an employee work which was reasonably available. It was suggested that the decided cases might now be rationalised by reference to the implied obligation on both parties to a contract of employment to refrain from conduct likely to damage or destroy the mutual trust and confidence each is entitled to have in the other: *Mahmoud v Bank of Credit and Commerce International SA* [1997] ICR 606 **[[2.25]** below]. . . .

One proposition which is clearly demonstrated by all the cases to which we were referred is that the question whether there is a 'right to work' is one of construction of the particular contract in the light of its surrounding circumstances. . . .

Given that the question must be resolved by construing the particular contract of employment in the light of its surrounding circumstances, previous cases decided on their own wording and circumstances are of limited value. But in this field the cases do illustrate certain categories and trends which are of assistance. Thus, in the case of theatrical engagements, the courts have been ready to find an obligation on the part of the employer to afford the opportunity to the employee to perform the part for which he was engaged, cf *Fechter v Montgomery* [1863] 33 Beav. 22; *Marbe v George Edwardes (Daly's Theatre) Ltd* [1928] 1 KB 269 and *Herbert Clayton and Jack Waller Ltd v Oliver* [1930] AC 209. Similarly, engagement for a specific project such as employment on a specific voyage (*Driscoll v Australian RMSN Co* [1859] 1 F & F 458) or in a specific and unique post such as the chief sub-editor of a newspaper (*Collier v Sunday Referee Publishing Co Ltd* [1940] 2 KB 647) or as the manager of an overseas business (*Addis v Gramophone Co Ltd* [1909] AC 488) have been treated by the courts as giving rise to an obligation on the part of the employer not to do anything which puts the promised employment out of his power. And where the promised remuneration depends on the employer providing the opportunity to earn it, then an obligation to afford the employee an opportunity so to do is readily implied, cf *Devonald v Rosser* [1906] 2 KB 728 **[[2.9]** above] and *Addis v Gramophone Co Ltd* [1909] AC 488.

In the case of employees engaged for an indefinite term and at a fixed wage or salary, the courts have been much more reluctant so to construe the contract as to cast on the employer an obligation over and above the payment of the promised remuneration. Thus the claim for such an obligation was rejected in the cases of a representative salesman (*Turner v Sawdon & Co* [1901] 2 KB 653) and, by implication, of domestic servants (*Collier v Sunday Referee Publishing Co Ltd* [1940] 2 KB 647).

But as social conditions have changed, the courts have increasingly recognised the importance to the employee of the work, not just the pay. Thus in *Langston v Amalgamated Union of Engineering Workers* [1974] ICR 180 Lord Denning MR considered that it was open to a welder to argue that:

'. . . a man has by reason of an implication in the contract a right to work. That is he has a right to have the opportunity of doing his work when it is there to be done.'

Cairns LJ thought it arguable that the contract of employment gave the employee 'a right to attend normally at his place of work'. Stephenson LJ likewise recognised that the employee might be able to show that:

'he has a right to work out any notice which he may be given, that it is his employer's duty to allow him to exercise that right by providing him with the work, and that by continuing to suspend him on full pay, as they are doing, they are in breach of their contract of employment with him.'. . . .

It is important to appreciate the limits to the obligation for which Mr Tucker contends. It is not suggested that there is an obligation to find work if there is none to be done or none which can be done with profit to the employer. Nor does he contend that the employer is bound to allocate work to him in preference to another employee if there is not enough for both of them. He submits that if the job is there to be done and the employee was appointed to do it and is ready and willing to do so, then the employer must permit him to do so. . . .

For my part, I accept that the contract of employment in this case can and should be construed as giving rise to such an obligation on the part of the employer. First, the post of senior dealer was a specific and unique post. It is not in dispute that Mr Tucker was asked by the employer in August 1994 to investigate what was involved in setting up a spread betting business. After considering the product of his researches, the employer decided to extend its operations into that field. Mr Tucker was the only senior dealer. There were juniors below him and a manager above him but he was the person appointed to conduct this new and specialised business. No doubt every employment nowadays has a title and job description which make it sound specific and unique but I have no doubt that the post to which Mr Tucker was appointed merited that description both in substance as well as form. Secondly, the skills necessary to the proper discharge of such duties did require their frequent exercise. Though it is not a case comparable to a skilled musician who requires regular practice to stay at concert pitch, I have little doubt that frequent and continuing experience of the spread betting market, what it will bear and the subtle changes it goes through, is necessary to the enhancement and preservation of the skills of those who work in it.

Both those considerations arise from the surrounding circumstances in which the contract falls to be construed. But, thirdly, when one turns to the terms of the contract, there are further considerations pointing to the same conclusion. Not only does the contract provide for the hours and days of work so as to fill the normal working week, it specifically imposes on the employee the obligation to work those hours necessary to carry out his duties in a full and professional manner. If the work is available, it is inconsistent with that provision if the employee is entitled or bound to draw the remuneration without doing the work. To my mind, that consideration is unaffected by the provision that the duties of members of staff are as assigned by the employer or by individual managers. Not only is it followed immediately by a further stipulation requiring all staff to work such hours as are necessary for the proper performance of their duties but, in this case, the post of senior dealer in the spread betting business itself involved a broad assignment of duties. But the absence of an obligation on the employer, as contended for by Mr Tucker, would be contrary to two express terms. The first is that appearing under the heading 'Training and development'. In that part of the staff handbook, the employer declares that:

'The most important asset in any business is its employees and the [employer] is prepared to invest in its staff to ensure that they have every opportunity to develop their skills'.

The second is the express power of suspension, . . . which is limited to cases where more time is required to investigate serious allegations of breach of discipline or security. If the employer were to be entitled to keep its employee in idleness, the investment in its staff might be as illusory as the limited power of suspension would be unnecessary.

For these reasons I conclude that, on the proper construction of this contract of employment, the employer was under an obligation to permit Mr Tucker to perform the duties of the post to which it had appointed him in accordance with his contract as well during the period of his notice as before it was given. In reaching this conclusion, it is not necessary to accept or reject the propositions advanced on either side; a consideration of each plays its part in the construction of the contract but cannot be conclusive. I agree with the judge's conclusion and refusal to grant the injunction sought. In those circumstances, it is unnecessary to consider the basis on which, if he had one, he exercised his discretion.

Before parting with this case, I would add two observations. First, much of the argument was directed to the question of which party had to demonstrate a term in his favour. Did the employer have to demonstrate an express or implied term entitling him to send his employee home, albeit on full pay, for the period of his notice, colloquially known as garden leave? Or did Mr Tucker have to demonstrate an obligation on the employer to permit him to do the work? In my view, in all cases involving garden leave the first question must be that posed by Sir John Donaldson in *Langston v AUEW (No 2)* [1974] IRLR 182. Does the consideration moving from this employer extend to an obligation to permit the employee to do the work or is it confined to payment of the remuneration agreed? If the answer is in the sense of the latter alternative, then the employer is entitled to send his employee home on garden leave notwithstanding the absence of an express or implied power to do so because there is no contractual obligation to prevent him. If the answer is in the sense of the former alternative, then the employer needs a provision entitling him to send his employee on garden leave so as to absolve him from what would otherwise be a breach of contract. It is unlikely, given the hypothesis on which the point arises, that there could be an implied power for that purpose. Thus, in practice, an employer will need to stipulate for an express power to send his employee on garden leave in all cases in which the contract imposes on him an obligation to permit the employee to do the work.

Second, there appears to be a trend towards increasing reliance on garden leave provisions in preference to conventional restrictive covenants, no doubt because hitherto the courts have treated the former with greater flexibility than the latter, as explained by Neill LJ in *Crédit Suisse Asset Management Ltd v Armstrong* [1996] ICR 450. But the reported cases dealing with the court's approach to the grant of injunctions in this field show that if injunctive relief is sought, then it has to be justified on similar grounds to those necessary to the validity of an employee's covenant in restraint of trade. It seems to me that the court should be careful not to grant interlocutory relief to enforce a garden leave clause to any greater extent than would be covered by a justifiable covenant in restraint of trade previously entered into by an employee.

I would dismiss this appeal.

2.2.4 The principle of mutuality or reciprocity

The cases in this and the previous section illustrate how the risks of the wage–work bargain can be allocated according to methods of interpretation of the express terms of the contract and the insertion of terms that purport to represent the implicit intentions of the parties. The construction placed by a court on the terms of the contract determines the allocation of such risks as the unavailability of work, the need to exercise skills, and the failure to perform work tasks as directed. The respect afforded to freedom of contract both leads to the conclusion that the express contractual agreement should govern the wage–work bargain, and also requires that, as a matter of legal technique, disputes about the content of the wage–work bargain should be resolved exclusively by reference to the apparent or presumed intentions of the parties, as evidenced by the terms of the contract. The statutory protection against deductions from pay reinforces this contractual analysis by insisting, with few exceptions, that the express terms should also govern the employer's use of the power to withhold wages.

Underlying the judicial construction of the wage–work bargain, it can be suggested that the courts strive to protect what they regard as the reasonable expectations of the parties in order to give the contract business efficacy. If the employee reasonably expects the contract to provide a regular source of income, a term may be implied to pay remuneration even in the absence of work to be performed. If the employee reasonably expects to be able to perform work in order to gain experience or to enhance employability, the employer will not be permitted to force the employee into paid leave without an express term to that effect. Equally, the courts normally regard the employer's expectation that work will be performed carefully and in good faith as reasonable, so that the employer can refuse to pay for incomplete and unsatisfactory work altogether. The scope of these reasonable expectations depends in part upon the express terms of the contract, but undoubtedly the courts are willing to secure through interpretation and implied terms what they regard as a fair balance of reciprocal obligations. Professor Mark Freedland has suggested that this approach can be described by using a principle of mutuality or reciprocity (*The Personal Employment Contract* (Oxford, Oxford University Press, 2003) p129).

2.3 The organisational framework

We have already noted that contracts of employment typically provide vague or incomplete descriptions of the work to be performed by the employee. Being unsure in advance exactly what work needs to be done, the employer bargains for the right to direct labour and to monitor performance. In a small workshop, the employer can issue oral instructions and supervise performance in person. Once the business becomes larger, however, with many employees and with the employment of managers or supervisors to give instructions and to monitor the performance of work, the employment relation become embedded in an organisational framework. The organisational framework establishes hierarchies between employees, allocates responsibility and authority, and creates a set of standing orders for the direction and monitoring of work.

A work organisation may be understood as a construction made of rules. In a large organisation these rules may cover a wide range of matters including:

- Facilitation of production: rules which specify procedures to be followed, forms to be used, feed-back mechanisms, and so forth.
- Co-ordination: a framework for interaction and co-ordination between employees within the workplace. In large undertakings the purpose of these rules is to permit senior management to direct and shape the organisation. They comprise a set of standing orders to middle management and employees about how the business should be operated.
- Disciplinary codes: describing unwanted behaviour, specifying disciplinary procedures, grievance procedures and possible sanctions.
- Payment system: rules governing grading of jobs, rates of pay for jobs, methods for calculating pay, and the availability and entitlements to fringe benefits, such as sick pay, occupational pensions and sports facilities.

The most visible aspect of this construction of rules is known as the 'works rules' or 'staff hand-book'. These are booklets issued to workers, or which may be accessible to all employees through the firm's computer network. These documents contain a mixture of statements about the employer's policies, the employer's expectations from employees, explanations of procedures and the authority structure of the firm, and may describe further obligations and entitlements of employees. The form of the rule-book is not usually a written contract, but rather a document containing instructions and information.

What is the legal status of the rule-book? Is the rule-book part of the express terms of the contract of employment? Or is the rule-book merely a formal expression of the power of management to issue directions to the workforce? We need to distinguish between two possible legal effects of the rule-book. First, some or all of the rules may be incorporated as express terms of the contract of employment. Secondly, the rules, though not amounting to contractual terms, may be indirectly binding to some extent upon the parties by virtue of implied terms in the contract of employment.

In principle, if the express terms of the contract of employment purport to incorporate the rule-book as part of its terms, this express incorporation should turn the rules into statements of contractual terms. In the absence of express incorporation, however, the rule-book may still determine contractual entitlements. One possibility is that the rule-book will be regarded as a collateral contract, so that in return for the employee performing work under the contract of employment the employer agrees to be bound by the staff handbook. Another possibility is that the rule-book may become incorporated into the contract of employment as an implied term by custom and practice in the workplace over a long period of time. Alternatively, the rule-book may provide an aid to the construction of the express terms of the contract of employment. For example, the contract may appoint an employee to a position of 'administrator grade 3'; the rule-book can be used to explain the meaning of that technical terminology.

Although it is certainly possible for the rule-book to create or influence the construction of the terms of the contract of employment, it must be observed that employers generally argue that the rules of the organisation merely comprise a set of standing orders issued by management. The implied term that requires employees to conform to the instructions of management has the effect that, even if the rule-book is not expressly incorporated into the contract, an employee may be in breach of the implied duty of obedience for failing to comply with the rules. The employer can thus rely upon the rules as legal obligations even if they do not comprise terms of the contract of employment. The implied duty of obedience extends beyond a requirement of strict conformity to the rules, because the duty includes a requirement for the employee to co-operate in good faith.

[2.11] *Secretary of State for Employment v ASLEF (No.2)* **[1972] ICR 19 (CA)**

> The union instructed its members, who were railway workers, to work to rule, that is to comply strictly with the rule-book of the employers, the British Railways Board (BRB), with the objective of disrupting the railways. Under statutory powers contained at that time in the Industrial Relations Act 1971, the Secretary of State intervened to ask the court to order a ballot of the workforce. The union contended that the necessary statutory condition for the court to order a ballot, namely 'irregular industrial action short of a strike', was not satisfied, because the workers were not in breach of their contracts of employment. The Court of Appeal held that the 'work to rule' constituted breaches of contracts of employment. Although the rule-book was not itself a contractual document, the employees were in breach of an implied term of the contract. Lord Denning MR held that it was an implied term of the contract of employment that an employee must not wilfully obstruct his employer's business. Buckley LJ said that it was an implied term of the contract to serve the employer faithfully within the requirements of the contract. Roskill LJ described the implied term as a duty not to seek to obey lawful instructions so wholly unreasonably as to disrupt the efficient running of the system in which they were employed. The Court ordered that the ballot of the railway workers should be taken.

This decision reveals how the implied duty of co-operation or performance in good faith requires the employee not merely to comply with the rule-book, but in addition to interpret and apply the rules in ways which promote the objectives of the employer's business. The formulation of the implied term suggested by Buckley LJ has since been followed by the courts in the development of the implied duty of co-operation, as for example in *British Telecommunications Plc v Ticehurst* [1992] ICR 383 (CA) (**[2.5]** above).

There is a further reason why employers prefer the view that the rule-book comprises an exercise of managerial discretion. This interpretation of the legal status of the company handbook entitles the employer to vary the rules at will without the need for the consent of the employee. If the rules comprised terms of the contract, the employee would have to give consent to any variation. In general, therefore, it is no advantage to employers to have the rule-book incorporated as an express term of the contract of employment.

In contrast, for employees there may be several advantages in being able to rely upon the rule-book as an express term of the contract. One advantage is that if an employer fails to confer a benefit described in the rule-book, that failure would amount to a breach of contract. For example, if the employer omits a procedure specified in the rule-book such as a grievance procedure or a disciplinary procedure, that breach of procedure itself will amount to a breach of contract. Another advantage to employees is that, as an express term of the contract, the rule-book can be varied only by agreement between the parties. In order to avoid these possible implications of regarding the rule-book as part of the terms of the contract of employment, it is not unusual to discover statements issued by employers as part of the contract of employment that the works rules and staff handbooks are not contractual terms but merely informative documents. Such an exclusion clause should be effective, provided that the employer takes reasonable steps to draw the disclaimer to the attention of the employee, and provided that the exclusion clause passes the test of being 'fair and reasonable' in the Unfair Contract Terms Act 1977, section 3.

The courts have been asked to consider the legal status of rule-books on many occasions. It is hard to discern a consistent approach. One pattern in the legal reasoning is that the courts have distinguished between core rules and mere policy statements. Provisions in the rule-book that determine core obligations and entitlements in the wage–work bargain, such as the method for calculating wages and other benefits, hours of work, the place of work, the tasks to be performed, and disciplinary rules and procedures, will usually be regarded by a court as comprising additional express terms of the contract of employment, provided that this inference is not countered by express agreement. For example, the rules governing the disciplinary procedure were regarded as contractual terms in *R v East Berkshire Area Health Authority, ex parte Walsh* [1984] IRLR 278 (CA) (**[2.69]** below). Similarly, rules governing a profit-sharing scheme were treated as terms of the contract of employment in *Financial Techniques Ltd v Hughes* [1981] IRLR 32 (CA). But the courts frequently regard other provisions in the rule-book as policy statements or internal organisational matters that do not give employees contractual entitlements. For example, in *Secretary of State for Employment v ASLEF (No.2)* [1972] ICR 19 (CA) (**[2.11]** above), Lord Denning MR viewed the rules governing train drivers' working methods, duties and rotas as a set of instructions issued under the general prerogative of management. Similarly, the procedures by which an employer determined what action should be taken (including dismissal) with respect to long-term sick leave were regarded as falling within the employer's discretion in *Wandsworth London Borough Council v D'Silva* [1998] IRLR 193 (CA) (**[10.6]** below). If it is possible to discover a pattern in these decisions, it is perhaps that rules which provide greater specificity to express terms of the contract, such as those concerning wages and hours, are likely to be regarded as having contractual force; otherwise the rule-book is regarded by the courts as an exercise of the implied power to manage and issue instructions, so that the rules do not confer legal entitlements on employees. But this pattern should not be relied upon, because in each case the court construes the express terms of the contract to discover whether or not the particular rules in the staff handbook have been incorporated as express terms.

Employees should therefore not place much reliance upon rule-books as granting them enforceable entitlements. Nevertheless, there may sometimes be an indirect route to protect the expectations of employees generated by employers' statements of policy in the rules. If the employer exercises its discretion to change the rules during the performance of the contract of employment, an employee may assert that such a unilateral variation, though not a breach of the express terms of the contract of employment, does amount to breach of an implied term. We conclude this section by considering two cases where this indirect method of protecting the expectations of employees was attempted. The implied terms used for this purpose are standard incidents implied by law: an implied obligation not to frustrate the other party's attempts to perform the contract, and the implied term of mutual trust and confidence (2.5.2 below). The first case also illustrates how the courts usually regard rules in staff handbooks as an exercise of managerial discretion.

[2.12] *Dryden v Greater Glasgow Health Board* [1992] IRLR 469 (EAT)

The employee resigned her job as a nursing auxiliary after her employer, having consulted widely with the trade unions and staff committees, introduced a no-smoking policy in the hospital where she worked. In order to establish a claim for unfair dismissal, she had to prove that she had been 'constructively dismissed' by the employer having broken a fundamental term of the contract. The claim failed because the employee could not establish that this unilateral variation of the rules on smoking amounted to a breach of any term of the contract.

Lord Coulsfield:
The appellant's contract of employment is a standard form document, which does not contain any express clause relevant to the present issue . . .

The question whether an employer is entitled to prohibit or restrict smoking in the workplace is one which is likely to arise in a number of different contexts, and it is tempting to try to arrive at some general answer to the question whether there may be an implied contractual term which confers a 'right to smoke' on the employee. We think, however, that that temptation should be resisted. The question whether a term should be implied in a particular contract is one dependent on the particular facts and circumstances, and, while we think that there is much force in the reasoning of the Industrial Tribunal, it seems to us that they went further than is necessary for the decision of this case. It is sufficient, in our opinion, to say that the findings of fact and submissions before us form an entirely inadequate basis for holding that there was any implied contract term to the effect that smoking would, to some extent or in some way, continue to be permitted, either generally or in the particular case of the appellant. . . .

The ground of appeal set out in the appellant's notice of appeal is as follows:

'There is an implied obligation on an employer not to frustrate his employee's attempt at performing the contract. In deciding whether or not this implied obligation had been breached, the circumstances of an individual employee must be studied. The Industrial Tribunal erred in approaching this question from the point of view of the generality of the respondents' employees rather than the applicant's specific circumstances.'. . .

We are not aware of any case concerned with the present situation, in which what is sought is to treat a change in the rules governing behaviour in the place of work which affects all employees as a repudiatory breach of an implied term in relation to one employee. There can, in our view, be no doubt that an employer is entitled to make rules for the conduct of employees in their place of work, as he is entitled to give lawful orders, within the scope of the contract; nor can there be any doubt, in our view, that once it has been held that there is no implied term in the contract which entitled the employee to facilities for smoking, a rule against smoking is, in itself, a lawful rule. The appellant's argument in the present case can only succeed if it is shown that the Industrial Tribunal erred in law. The suggested error is that the Industrial Tribunal failed to approach the question from the point of view of the specific circumstances of the appellant. The Industrial Tribunal did, however, have regard to the circumstances of the appellant, along with all the other circumstances of the case. What the appellant's argument really involves, therefore, is the submission that if an employer introduces a rule which applies to all employees generally, but one with which one employee is unable to comply, the employer must be held to repudiate the contract in relation to that employee. We do not think that any of the terms implied in *United Bank Ltd v Akhtar* [1989] IRLR 507 EAT **[[10.7]** below] or *Woods v WM Car Services (Peterborough) Ltd* [1982] ICR 692 CA **[[5.26]** below], or the principles underlying them, go so far as to justify restricting the employer's ability to make and alter working rules to that extent. It may not be difficult to envisage an implied term to the effect that the employer will not change the rules of the workplace in a way which adversely affects an employee or group of employees without reasonable notice or without consultation or, perhaps, without some substantial reason. It is very much more difficult to envisage that, in the absence of a relevant particular term in the contract, it might be held that there was an implied term restricting the employer's right to change the working rules by reference to the views, or even the requirements, of each particular employee . . .

Where a rule is introduced for a legitimate purpose, the fact that it bears hardly on a particular employee does not, in our view, in itself justify an inference that the employer has acted in such a way as to repudiate the contract with that employee. There may well be rules which are unwelcome to some employees but welcome to others, and a rule banning smoking might be an example of the kind. That being so, we cannot see that there is any justification for the appellant's argument that where the employer introduces a rule which is to apply generally but with which a particular employee cannot comply, it follows that there is repudiatory conduct on the part of the employer.

Notice that the approach in the above case does not ask whether the new rule was a necessary and proportionate response to the problem of establishing a smoke-free environment in the workplace. Once the employer has established a legitimate purpose for the rule, the courts appear reluctant to tie the hands of employers in the management of the business. Nevertheless, the courts are prepared to use implied terms to impose some constraints on the discretion to change the rules.

[2.13] *French v Barclays Bank Plc* [1998] IRLR 646 (CA)

A manager was required under the terms of his contract to relocate from Oxfordshire to Essex, for which purpose he needed to sell his family home and purchase another. Under the rules of the bank in the staff manual, Mr French was offered a discretionary interest-free bridging loan to enable him to complete the purchase of a new house before selling the old one. Following a collapse in the housing market, which made it difficult for Mr French to sell his former home, the bank changed the policy stated in the staff manual, withdrew the loan, and required him to enter into a new scheme that left him worse off. One question on appeal was whether the bank was in breach of contract. Although the loan scheme was regarded as a non-contractual discretionary scheme, the bank was held liable in damages for breach of the implied term to refrain from conduct which would be likely to destroy trust and confidence.

Waller LJ:

To seek to invoke a change of policy or a change in the terms on which loans were made to employees requested to relocate which (a) has been applied to other employees over many years and (b) appeared in terms in the manual at the time when the loan was made, is conduct which would be likely to destroy the confidence and trust between the bank and its employees.

In summary, rule-books and company handbooks may sometimes confer contractual rights upon employees through a process of express incorporation or implied incorporation by custom, especially if the rules provide greater specificity to some of the core elements of the wage–work bargain. But it is more usual for courts to classify rule-books as an exercise of managerial discretion that does not confer any contractual rights. The latter interpretation permits employers to vary the rules unilaterally, without the consent of the employee. Nevertheless the rules may have significant

---

Internal Labour Markets

Economists describe the elaborate structure of payment systems in large organisations as internal labour markets. They distinguish between the external labour market, where forces of supply and demand determine wage rates, and the internal labour market, which is partly insulated from those forces. Wages are fixed within an internal labour market by a grading system, which determines wages by reference to relative wage rates for each grade, often using the technique of job evaluation. Incentives for employees to acquire skills, to work hard, and to stay with a firm derive from the possibility of promotion to higher grades (see: P. B. Doeringer and M. J. Piore, *Internal Labour Markets and Manpower Analysis* (Lexington, Mass, Lexington Books, D C Heath, 1971); O.E. Williamson, M.L. Wachter, and J. E. Harris, 'Understanding the employment relation: the analysis of idiosyncratic exchange' (1975) 6 *Bell Journal of Economics and Management Science* 250). The widespread use by employers of internal labour markets was criticised in the 1980s because these structures prevented employers from adjusting wages quickly to changing external labour market conditions, and because they obstructed individualised performance-related payment systems from being used by employers to acquire higher levels of co-operation from the workforce. In the public sector the government substantially dismantled internal labour markets by contracting out work to private companies that typically paid the lower external market rates (e.g. Local Government Act 1988). The government also encouraged the 'derigidification' of the labour market in the private sector by such measures as providing tax incentives for performance-related pay (e.g. Finance (No.2) Act 1987). (For a comprehensive discussion of government measures designed to 'derigidify' the labour market, see P. Davies and M. Freedland, *Labour Legislation and Public Policy* (Oxford, Oxford University Press, 1993) Chapter 10.) Although the use of internal labour markets may be declining, at least in their most rigid form, their existence and operation is often of the utmost practical significance to the workforce. The organisational framework creates an expectation that in return for hard work an employee can expect to reap the rewards of promotion to grades commanding higher wages and a high degree of employment security. Yet these expectations, which the employer certainly encourages, may not be protected by equivalent legal obligations.

indirect effects through the implied terms of the contract. An employee must conform to the rules in good faith in order to avoid being in breach of the implied terms of the contract of employment. Furthermore, in the striking development in the *French* case, the employer who varies the rule-book hastily without consultation, unnecessarily, for an illegitimate purpose, or in a way that imposes harsh consequences on the employee, may be found to have broken an implied obligation not to vary the rules in a way which destroys mutual trust and confidence.

2.4 Collective agreements

A collective agreement is a bargain reached between a trade union and an employer (or sometimes a group of employers). The content of a collective agreement is likely to comprise three elements. First, it usually determines for the group of employees covered by the agreement (the bargaining unit) the core aspects of their wage–work bargain, such as wage rates and normal hours of work. Secondly, the collective agreement may determine aspects of the rule-book, thus fixing how the employer should regulate the business within the scope of management's discretion. Thirdly, it is likely to contain rules about how future collective labour relations should be conducted, such as how and when bargaining should occur between the union and the employer. These three elements may be described briefly as fixing the market price of labour, joint regulation of the workplace, and procedural self-regulation of collective relations in the workplace.

2.4.1 Legal enforceability

A collective agreement is unlikely to be a legally enforceable contract itself. This absence of legal sanctions for collective agreements is due in part to statute.

[2.14] Trade Union and Labour Relations (Consolidation) Act 1992, section 179

> **(1)** A collective agreement shall be conclusively presumed not to have been intended by the parties to be a legally enforceable contract unless the agreement—
> (a) is in writing, and
> (b) contains a provision which (however expressed) states that the parties intend that the agreement shall be a legally enforceable contract.

This provision leaves open the possibility that a legally enforceable agreement might be reached, but in practice the parties to a collective agreement are unlikely to wish to use legal remedies in order to enforce the agreement. The trade union and the employer have powerful non-legal sanctions to support compliance with the terms of a collective agreement: the union can threaten industrial action, and the employer can exclude the employees from the workplace (a lock-out) or threaten deductions from pay for any refusal to work in accordance with the agreement. In addition, the use of legal sanctions such as an injunction against breach of the agreement is as likely to exacerbate and prolong conflict as to help the parties to resolve their differences with the minimum disruption to production and income. For these reasons, neither party to a collective agreement is likely to want the option of legal enforceability, so the statutory presumption merely emphasises what is likely to be the case in fact.

2.4.2 Incorporation

The absence of legal enforceability of collective agreements does not prevent them from having legal effects. A collective agreement typically creates a written document setting out the terms of the agreement. This document, like any other document, can be incorporated into a legally enforceable contract of employment by agreement between the employer and the employee. In workplaces where collective agreements have been reached, the contract of employment often incorporates the relevant collective agreement into its terms by stating expressly that the wages, hours and other conditions of employment will be set by a particular collective agreement and subsequent revisions of it. The effect of this express incorporation is that aspects of legally unenforceable collective agreements become part of the legally enforceable express terms of the individual contract of employment.

In the absence of such a term of express incorporation of a relevant collective agreement, however, the precise legal effects become harder to determine and to explain. A court may decide that a collective agreement has been incorporated into a contract of employment by implication. The legal basis for this implied incorporation presents some conceptual difficulties. An implied incorporation of the collective agreement into the contract of employment can be explained as either a 'custom of the trade' or the product of a 'course of dealing' between the parties. Writing at a time when it was much less common for the terms of individual contracts of employment to be written down, Kahn-Freund suggested a customary basis for incorporation.

[2.15] O. Kahn-Freund, 'Legal Framework' in A. Flanders and H. Clegg, *System of Industrial Relations in Great Britain* (Oxford, Blackwell, 1954) 58

> In the majority of cases . . . the parties to the contract of employment do not expressly lay down its terms, and the gap is filled by 'custom'. Here we can see the legal significance of the collective agreement. We can normally assume that its terms are the 'customary' terms and that employers and employees within its scope contract on this basis. It does not, in the writer's opinion, matter whether the worker is a member of a union party to the agreement or whether the employer is or has at any time been a member of a 'contracting' association. What does matter is whether the terms of the agreement are in fact applied in the industry and district. The wages scales and other 'codes' it contains can easily become 'crystallized custom'.

On the alternative 'course of dealing' explanation of incorporation, if it can be demonstrated that a particular contract of employment has in the past been determined in its details by a relevant collective agreement, a presumption arises that the parties to the contract of employment intended to continue that method for supplementing the content of their agreement. Both of these analyses rely heavily on past practice in order to incorporate a collective agreement into a contract of employment, and so these explanations run into difficulty when past practice is ambiguous or uncertain. In other words, these analyses attempt to incorporate collective agreements as terms implied in fact, a process that is always vulnerable to contrary evidence with respect to the intentions of the parties. English law has never taken the step of insisting that the implied incorporation of relevant collective agreements should be done as a matter of law, as one of the standard incidents of all contracts of employment.

Despite these conceptual problems, the courts usually accept without argument these days that a relevant collective agreement has been incorporated into a contract of employment, provided that there has been some reference to it in either the contract of employment or any documents issued by the employer to the employee such as a rule-book or statement about the principal terms of employment. Alternatively, if in consequence of a new collective agreement an employer introduces new terms and conditions, the employees will be regarded as having consented to the change by continuing to work normally (*Henry v London General Transport Services Ltd* [2002] EWCA Civ 488, [2002] ICR 910,CA).

A more vexing question for the court is to determine which provisions within the collective agreement have become incorporated into contracts of employment. It is usually accepted that terms of the collective agreement that set the core obligations of the wage–work bargain have been incorporated into the contract of employment. With respect to collective agreements that seek to fix aspects of the rule-book, it is routinely accepted that disciplinary procedures and individual grievance procedures become incorporated into the contract of employment. In contrast, terms in the collective agreement that are designed to regulate the collective bargaining relationship itself, which are often called the procedural aspects of the agreement, are not usually incorporated into individual contracts of employment. Outside these fairly settled areas, however, there are many instances of contested provisions of collective agreements that may or may not have been incorporated into individual contracts of employment.

2.4.3 Enforcement by employees

Just as the courts are unwilling to accept that policy statements and procedures contained in the employer's rule-book are terms of the contract of employment that confer enforceable legal rights, so too provisions in the collective agreement that seek to regulate jointly similar matters may be regarded by a court as 'inappropriate' or 'inapt' for incorporation. This judgment that some provisions of collective agreements are unsuitable for incorporation into contracts of employment in the absence of express, detailed incorporation depends in part on the language used in the collective agreement and in part on the context of the whole document.

Most of the litigation about the appropriateness of the incorporation of terms in collective agreements has concerned redundancy procedures. These collective agreements try to determine in advance how the employer should handle the need to dismiss workers for economic reasons. The agreement may establish procedures for negotiation and consultation with the union, and determine the criteria for selection for compulsory redundancy. Often the unions bargain for a seniority principle known as LIFO (last in, first out) to regulate selection for compulsory redundancy. The legal issue that arises is whether an employee can compel the employer to comply with the collective agreement by enforcing its provisions through the contract of employment. Employees with considerable seniority will be particularly concerned that the employer should comply with the LIFO principle. In the following case, the judge scrutinises a typical collective agreement governing redundancy selection with a view to reaching a determination of whether or not it confers legal rights that have been incorporated into the contract of employment.

[2.16] *Alexander v Standard Telephones & Cables Ltd (No.2)*; *Wall v Standard Telephones & Cables Ltd (No. 2)* **[1991] IRLR 287 (HC)**

> The plaintiffs in these actions had been made compulsorily redundant. They claimed that they had been selected for redundancy in breach of their contracts of employment, which incorporated a collective agreement that required selection on the basis of seniority. The employers had departed from the seniority criterion in order to retain those workers whose skills were most needed. In an earlier action ([1990] IRLR 55), the employees had failed to obtain an injunction against dismissal. This action was for damages for breach of contract. The following extracts concentrate on the *Wall* claim, but the same principles and outcome applied to the *Alexander* claim. The court had to address both the question whether the relevant collective agreement had been incorporated into the contract of employment and the question whether the particular term requiring selection by reference to seniority was appropriate for incorporation. The relevant contracts of employment had been created informally and as a result there was no evidence of a written contract that expressly incorporated any collective agreement into the contract of employment. The court therefore addressed the question whether the collective agreement regarding redundancy selection had been incorporated by implication.

> *Hobhouse J:*
> For the *Wall* action the relevant agreement is headed 'Redundancy procedure agreement between Standard Telephones and Cables plc and maintenance (AUEW, EETPU, TGWU and GMWU)'. It was signed by representatives of the company and the unions. The relevant agreement was dated 7 January 1983 and was the subject of later amendments and additions. It contains 10 numbered clauses. Having defined its application to the hourly-paid employees represented by the unions in the maintenance department, it sets out a statement of policy which recognises the need to plan employment requirements in the interests of the security of all the company's employees. It recognises that redundancy may on occasion be unavoidable and states: 'This agreement is intended firstly to provide a procedure for dealing with situations which might lead to redundancy so as to maintain security of employment as far as possible, and secondly to provide assistance should redundancy become inevitable'.

> The agreement then sets out a procedure for 'Joint consultation' which includes making provision for the three-stage procedure which will be used. This includes stage two, under which employees are to be warned that their employment will be terminated; this states

that 'the basis of selection of individuals will be that fully stated in paragraph 6 below and the warning shall be in accordance with paragraph 5 below.' It also provides that retraining and redeployment shall be discussed with those persons. The third stage involves the giving of notice in accordance with their terms of employment to the relevant individuals if, by the end of warning period, redundancy is found to be unavoidable. The agreement sets out various steps which may be taken in consultation with the shop stewards to avoid or minimise the need for redundancy. Clause 5 deals with the question of warning of redundancy.

Clause 6 is headed 'Basis of selection for redundancy'. It reads:

'When all has been done to avoid redundancy, but it is evident that some employees have to be made redundant, volunteers will be sought in the first instance and prime consideration will be given to early retirements and employees affected by ill-health.

6.1 In the event of compulsory redundancy, selection within each skill group will be made on the basis of service within the group covered by the term agreement. Skills groups are as follows:

Precision fitters.
Fitters.
Electricians.
Plumbers.
Riggers (full-time).
Boilermen/mates.

For this purpose service for ex-STC apprentices will count from completion of apprenticeship.

6.2 The mutual objective will be to ensure that a balance of skills within the department is preserved and that there is no adverse effect on the on-going business'.

(By later agreements the skill categories were redefined and it was also expressly agreed that 'basis of service' meant that employees with shorter service in any skill group would be the first to be affected by compulsory redundancy.) The remaining clauses of the collective agreement dealt with employees leaving early, temporary workers, re-employment following redundancy and transfer allowances. . . .

The principles to be applied can therefore be summarised. The relevant contract is that between the individual employee and his employer; it is the contractual intention of those two parties which must be ascertained. In so far as that intention is to be found in a written document, that document must be construed on ordinary contractual principles. In so far as there is no such document or that document is not complete or conclusive, their contractual intention has to be ascertained by inference from the other available material including collective agreements. The fact that another document is not itself contractual does not prevent it from being incorporated into the contract if that intention is shown as between the employer and the individual employee. Where a document is expressly incorporated by general words it is still necessary to consider, in conjunction with the words of incorporation, whether any particular part of that document is apt to be a term of the contract; if it is inapt, the correct construction of the contract may be that it is not a term of the contract. Where it is not a case of express incorporation, but a matter of inferring the contractual intent, the character of the document and the relevant part of it and whether it is apt to form part of the individual contract is central to the decision whether or not the inference should be drawn.

In the present cases I have concluded that the wording of the only document directly applicable to the individual plaintiffs, the statutory statements, is not sufficient to effect an express incorporation of the provisions relating to redundancy in the collective agreements: accordingly it is a matter of considering whether or not to infer that the selection procedures and the principle of seniority have been incorporated into the individual contracts of employment and this has to be decided having regard to the evidence given and an evaluation of the character of the relevant provisions in the collective agreements . . .

Turning to the collective agreements themselves it is convenient to take the *Wall* agreement first. It expressly states that it is a 'procedure' agreement. Thus, on a simplistic application of the language . . . one would conclude that it was not apt to be incorporated. However, it is of course necessary to examine the character of the agreement and its relevant parts more closely before reaching a conclusion. It is undoubtedly primarily a policy document applicable to the relationship between the unions and the company. It also is specifically concerned with procedure. Thus the third clause under the heading 'Joint consultation' lays down a procedure and it is within that scheme that individuals are to be selected for compulsory redundancy. Indeed, all the first five clauses of the agreement are clearly inappropriate for application to or incorporation in individual contracts of employment.

Clauses 7 to 10 are also inapt for such incorporation. The reference to temporary workers is merely to exclude them from the scope of the agreement. The re-employment clause merely says that the company will give consideration to re-employment, at a later date, of employees made compulsorily redundant; this is neither expressed as a contractual obligation nor could it form part of a present contract of employment. As regards transfer allowances the clause contemplates that the company may make offers of employment in another division of the company to some individuals as an alternative to redundancy and states that if such an offer should be made it will include assistance in making the transfer. This again is not apt to be a term of an existing contract of employment as it involves the choice of the company to make an offer and it is only from the making of that offer and its acceptance that any individual right can subsequently arise. As regards the provision relating to employees who leave early, it merely provides that employees will normally be required to observe their contractual obligations under their contracts of employment; therefore again it is not apt for incorporation.

In this context, where none of the other clauses of the collective agreement are apt to be incorporated into the individual contract of employment, it would require some cogent indication in clause 6 that it was to have a different character and to be incorporated into the individual contracts of employment. The plaintiffs' submissions gain nothing from the context within which clause 6 is to be found; indeed the context strongly detracts from their case. The first part of clause 6 is a statement of policy—looking for volunteers, giving priority to employees taking early retirement or affected by ill-health. Likewise paragraph 6.2 is again expressed in policy terms having regard to inter-union relationships and to the requirements of the company's on-going business; it is stated to be 'the mutual objective'. Whilst this again is not inconsistent with giving paragraph 6.1 contractual effect, it does detract from that implication. Paragraph 6.1, the critical paragraph, is expressed in terms which are capable of giving rise to individual rights. It says that selection for compulsory redundancy 'will be made on the basis of service' within the relevant group. Therefore the plaintiffs can reasonably argue that as individuals they are entitled, on account of their seniority, not to be selected. However, I consider that the wording of paragraph 6.1 is too weak, when considered in the context in which it occurs in clause 6 itself and within the context and consultation scheme of the procedure agreement as a whole, to support the inference of incorporation. Clear and specific express words of incorporation contained in a primary contractual document could displace this conclusion, but on any view the wording of the statutory statements [that is statements of the terms of contracts of employment in accordance with Employment Rights Act 1996 s.1; see below 2.31] in the present case do not suffice.

It follows that the Wall plaintiffs' case of breach of contract must fail. They cannot establish the contractual right under their individual contracts of employment which they need in order to succeed in their action for damages for breach of contract against the defendants . . .

The argument of the employees was weakened in the *Alexander* and *Wall* cases owing to the absence of any clear express incorporation of the redundancy procedure into the contracts of employment. The issue of implied incorporation became entangled with the question whether the terms of the agreement were suitable for incorporation. In other cases, however, the problem of incorporation is settled by express incorporation in the contract of employment, which seems to assist the employees in their claims to be able to rely upon provisions of the collective agreement as terms of their contracts of employment *e.g. Anderson v Pringle of Scotland Ltd* [1998] IRLR 64 (Ct Sess Outer House). Even if employees establish that the collective agreement has been expressly incorporated into the contract of employment, many provisions that it contains will still be regarded as inappropriate for transfer to the individual contract as legal entitlements. What is the basis for this judgment about whether a provision is apt for incorporation? Does the judgment turn on whether or not the provision concerns the core elements of the wage–work bargain? Or does the decision turn on whether the provision of the collective agreement is expressed in a particular way, that is with precision and in a form that describes individual entitlements? Or perhaps these determinations rest ultimately on judicial perceptions of the extent to which employers are likely to give up unilateral powers to manage the business by conferring contractual rights?

[2.17] *Kaur v MG Rover Group Ltd* [2004] EWCA Civ 1507, [2005] IRLR 40 (CA)

To ensure the company's survival, the employer entered into a succession of collective agreements, beginning with "Rover Tomorrow—The New Deal", each described as partnership agreements, in which in return from promises by the union to secure greater flexibility and cooperation on the part of the workforce, the employer agreed to protect their job security. The conditions of Mrs Kaur's employment included the term: 'Employment with the company is in accordance with and, where appropriate, subject to . . . collective agreements made from time to time with the recognised trade unions representing employees within the company.' She claimed a declaration that her terms of employment precluded compulsory redundancy dismissal in accordance with a collective agreement made at her plant in Longbridge called 'The Way Ahead Partnership Agreement', which included the provision: 'Job Security 2.1. It will be our objective to ensure that the application of the "Partnership Principles" will enable employees who want to work for Rover to stay with Rover. As with the successful introduction of "Rover Tomorrow—The New Deal", **THERE WILL BE NO COMPULSORY REDUNDANCY**. 2.2. The company recognises that its employees are the company's most valuable asset. 2.3. Any necessary reductions in manpower will be achieved in future, with the cooperation of all employees, through natural wastage, voluntary severance and early retirement, after consultation with trade unions.' The court refused to grant the declaration that the applicant had a contractual right not to be made compulsorily redundant. The Court of Appeal approved the approach of Hobhouse J in *Alexander v Standard Telephones and Cables Ltd* [2.16] above. Even in cases where there was express incorporation of the collective agreement into the individual contract of employment, the question was whether the content and the character of the relevant parts of the collective agreement were such as to make them apt to be a term of the individual contract of employment. In this case, the Court of Appeal regarded paragraph 2, viewed as a whole, as aspirational rather than a binding promise. The court emphasised that in paragraph 2.1 job security was described as an 'objective' rather than a binding commitment. In paragraph 2.3, the need for cooperation of the workforce as a whole revealed that job security was regarding as a collective matter, and so was unsuitable as a basis for individual contractual rights. The Court concluded that Paragraph 2.1 was not intended to be incorporated into the contracts of employment of individual employees and was not apt for such incorporation. In so far as it formed part of a bargain with the unions, the commitment was solely on a collective basis.

2.4.4 Enforcement by employers

The same issue of whether or not provisions in a collective agreement are appropriate for incorporation into a contract of employment can also apply to terms that impose obligations or restrictions on employees. For the most part collective agreements confer benefits on employees, so the employer has little reason to seek enforcement of its terms. Yet it is certainly possible, using suitable language that is precise and can be translated simply into individual obligations, for a collective agreement to place significant obligations upon employees via the individual contract of employment, such as express requirements to work at different tasks flexibly and to accept variable hours of work.

Collective agreements often contain a 'peace obligation', that is an agreement not to take any form of industrial action for the period of the agreement. This agreement is usually supplemented by a procedural agreement for the resolution of disputes through further negotiations or in some instances arbitration. The question arises whether the peace obligation or the procedural agreement may be legally enforceable against individual employees.

It is arguable that a peace obligation is directed solely to the collective relationship and represents a procedural undertaking at a collective level that is not suitable for incorporation into the individual contract of employment. This view has not always been accepted by the courts.

[2.18] *Camden Exhibition & Display Ltd v Lynott* [1966] 1 QB 555 (CA)

The relevant question in this case was whether the defendant employee was entitled to refuse to perform overtime work. Unless a contract of employment expressly provides for the employee to work for longer than the regular hours of employment at the request of the employer, the employee is legally entitled to refuse the extra work. But if the contract contains a term which entitles the employer to require employees to perform overtime work, then a refusal to do so may amount to a breach of the contract. In this case, the relevant collective agreement stated: 'Overtime required to ensure the due and proper performance of contracts shall not be subject to restriction, but may be worked by mutual agreement and direct arrangement between the employer and the operatives concerned'. The majority of the Court of Appeal interpreted this clause to mean that that there was a term in the contract of employment that the employees would not collectively impose a ban on overtime work, though any particular duties had to be arranged by mutual agreement. Russell LJ, dissenting, argued persuasively, however, that the collective agreement had merely refrained from setting a ceiling or restriction on overtime, leaving the matter to individual negotiation, so that even if a group of employees refused to work overtime, this action would not amount to a breach of contract.

In 1974 legislation introduced a procedural obstacle to the enforcement of peace obligations and collective dispute procedures via the individual contract of employment.

[2.19] Trade Union and Labour Relations (Consolidation) Act 1992, section 180

(1) Any terms of a collective agreement which prohibit or restrict the right of workers to engage in a strike or other industrial action, or have the effect of prohibiting or restricting that right, shall not form part of any contract between a worker and the person for whom he works unless the following conditions are met.

(2) The conditions are that the collective agreement—
(a)   is in writing,
(b)   contains a provision expressly stating that those terms shall or may be incorporated in such a contract,
(c)   is reasonably accessible at his place of work to the worker to whom it applies and is available for him to consult during working hours, and
(d)   is one where each trade union which is a party to the agreement is an independent trade union;
and that the contract with the worker expressly or impliedly incorporates those terms in the contract.

(3) The above provisions have effect notwithstanding anything in section 179 [[2.14] above] and notwithstanding any provision to the contrary in any agreement (including a collective agreement or a contract with any worker).

This section appears to block an employer's attempt to enforce a peace obligation or a dispute resolution procedure through the individual contract of employment without an express written agreement with the union to that effect. Even if such an agreement were concluded, it is unclear what benefit might accrue to an employer. A court would certainly not grant an injunction against an individual employee for refusing to work, if that would amount to an order to force the employee to resume work. Such an order would be tantamount to an order for specific performance of a contract of employment, which is both contrary to the equitable principles governing such orders, and in any case is prohibited by statute.

[2.20] Trade Union and Labour Relations (Consolidation) Act 1992, section 236

No court shall, whether by way of—
(a)   an order for specific performance or specific implement of a contract of employment, or
(b)   an injunction or interdict restraining a breach or threatened breach of such a contract,
compel an employee to do any work or attend at any place for the doing of any work.

The strike action itself would almost certainly constitute a breach of contract that would entitle the employer at common law to claim damages or to dismiss the employee, even without the additional breach of contract constituted by breach of any express peace obligation. Therefore it seems unlikely that employers would ever wish to enforce this aspect of any collective agreement.

2.4.5 Conclusion

Unlike most other legal systems, collective agreements in the United Kingdom are not usually legally enforceable by the parties. The purpose of this approach is to keep the courts out of the task of adjudication over claims based upon collective agreements, especially those by employers seeking to enforce a peace obligation. But this legal abstention leaves uncertain the precise significance of collective agreements for the individual contracts of employment. Whether or not a term of a collective agreement becomes incorporated into a contract depends partly on whether it has been expressly or impliedly incorporated and partly on whether the term is apt for incorporation. The latter test grants the courts considerable discretion on a fundamental question of industrial relations, that is whether or not the employer is legally bound by promises made in collective agreements to the workforce.

2.5 Authority and co-operation

2.5.1 The legal construction of hierarchy

In previous sections we have noted that the legal construction of the employment relation presumes that it contains a structure of authority. The employer obtains the authority to direct work and the employee assumes an implied obligation to obey lawful orders. Some kind of governance structure is certainly required to achieve efficient production. The employer needs to adjust the details of work according to ever-changing requirements. These detailed adjustments cannot be specified in advance by the express terms of the contract but need to be handled by a governance structure, that is an arrangement for filling in the details of the contract of employment by further directions. The common law presumed that the governance structure should be one that accorded to the employer a general discretionary power or 'prerogative' to direct labour unilaterally. It did not require joint decisions by the employer and employee, or even prior consultation about change; rather it conferred unilateral discretion upon management to direct production. In practice where a strong union is recognised by the employer, it will be necessary for the employer to negotiate significant changes through collective procedures, but, as we noted in the previous section, these collective procedures are not themselves usually regarded as legally binding. The effect of this legal structure was to create a hierarchical power relation at the heart of the legal institution of the contract of employment. Disobedience to the directions of the employer was regarded as a fundamental breach of contract, which entitled the employer to dismiss the employee summarily without any compensation.

[2.21] P. Davies and M. Freedland, *Kahn-Freund's Labour and the Law* (3rd edn., London, Stevens, 1983) 18

But the relation between an employer and an isolated employee or worker is typically a relation between a bearer or power and one who is not a bearer of power. In its inception it is an act of submission, in its operation it is a condition of subordination, however much the submission and the subordination may be concealed by that indispensable figment of the legal mind known as the 'contract of employment'. The main object of labour law has always been, and we venture to say will always be, to be a countervailing force to counteract the inequality of bargaining power which is inherent and must be inherent in the employment relationship. Most of what we call protective legislation—legislation on the employment of women, children and young persons, on safety in mines, factories and offices, on payment of wages in cash, on guarantee payments, on race and sex discrimination, on unfair dismissal, and indeed most labour legislation altogether—must be seen in this context. It is an attempt to infuse law into a relation of command and subordination.

[2.22] S. Webb and B. Webb, *Industrial Democracy* (London, Longmans, 1902) (first published 1897) 842, fn

The capitalist is very fond of declaring that labour is a commodity, and the wage contract a bargain of purchase and sale like any other. But he instinctively expects his wage-earners to render him, not only obedience, but also personal deference. If the wage contract is a bargain of purchase and sale like any other, why is the workman expected to toff his hat to his employer, and to say 'sir' to him without reciprocity . . . ?,

In the twentieth century, as the size of firms grew, the power of the employer was exercised through the ranks of management. Management became a distinct function within the enterprise, with its object to maximise the productive capacity of the business including labour. Managers developed their own 'science' of how best to improve efficiency. They held themselves out as experts in organising production, for which purpose they required the power to command and control the workforce. The most developed version of this management science in the early part of the twentieth century was a movement named Taylorism or scientific management, which involved the centralised, detailed control over every aspect of factory production. This method justified bureaucratic hierarchies, the minimisation of worker discretion, and the subordination of the worker in every detail of work to the authority of management.

This section of the chapter examines how the common law has constructed controls over the manner in which the employer may legitimately exercise its discretionary powers to manage the workforce. Using the mechanism of terms implied by law, the courts have placed constraints on the way in which managerial

---

Taylorism

Named after F.W. Taylor, an American 'industrial engineer', this dominant managerial movement in the first half of the twentieth century sought to improve the efficiency of business through superior organisation and control. The method of scientific management increased the division of labour, breaking down each job into simple tasks that could be performed by cheap, unskilled labour, with the work co-ordinated and designed by management, using techniques such as 'time and motion' studies, in order to achieve the best use of labour power. The efficiency of production was measured by a cost-accounting system, which was also used to fix standard times for work to be performed. The influence of this scientific management approach was considerable on UK industry and management thought. Its effect on the experience of work was for many employees a de-skilling of tasks to be performed, the removal of any discretion in performance of work, the intensification of work effort, and systematic, detailed surveillance of the worker and production. Essays by Taylor were later published as F.W. Taylor, *Scientific Management* (New York, Harper and Row, 1947).

---

discretionary powers may be exercised. As the quotation from Kahn-Freund above indicates, legal controls over the abuse of managerial power is a central theme of employment regulation, and therefore it is a concern that will be considered in all the subsequent chapters. At this point we are merely considering how this concern is met to some extent in the legal construction of the fundamental aspects of the basic legal institution of the contract of employment. The principal vehicle through which the courts have sought to place constraints on the abuse of managerial power is through the implied term of mutual trust and confidence.

2.5.2 Mutual trust and confidence or good faith in performance

One of the most remarkable changes in the common law of the contract of employment during the last twenty-five years has been the emergence of the term implied by law that an employer should not act in a manner calculated to destroy mutual trust and confidence. The breadth of this implied term permits employees to argue that an employer has committed a fundamental breach of contract if it can be demonstrated that the employer has abused its discretionary powers to direct the business. In practice employees usually raise this argument after they have terminated the employment relation in response to the perceived abuse of discretionary power and for the purpose of supporting a common law claim for damages for breach of contract or for bringing a statutory claim for constructive unfair dismissal. In such claims it is necessary for the employee to demonstrate a fundamental breach of contract by the employer, and breach of the implied term of mutual trust and confidence suffices for that purpose. The following case illustrates the emergence of the implied term in a series of decisions of the EAT concerning claims for constructive unfair dismissal.

[2.23] *The Post Office v Roberts* **[1980] IRLR 347 (EAT)**

A junior clerical assistant was refused a transfer to a different area. She discovered that the reason for the refusal of the transfer was that Mr O'Keefe, a senior manager, had written on her personnel record that she was unlikely to qualify for promotion, and that she was irresponsible and lacked industry and comprehension. The senior manager had no grounds for this opinion, since her immediate supervisor had indicated that she was fully acceptable in her present junior grade. The employee resigned and brought a claim for unfair dismissal, arguing that in handling her application for a transfer unfairly the employer had broken a fundamental implied term of the contract of employment that either the employer will treat an employee in a reasonable manner or that an employer will not act in a way to destroy mutual trust and confidence between the employer and employee. The EAT upheld this claim, though resting the decision on the implied term of mutual trust and confidence rather than relying on a general requirement of reasonableness, which was considered too wide and too uncertain. In the following passage, the EAT considers the scope and implications of this implied term that the employer should not act in a way to destroy mutual trust and confidence.

Talbot J:
The final point of complaint made by Mr Carr [counsel for the employer] is that the Industrial Tribunal's finding of a breach of the obligation of mutual trust and confidence is erroneous, in that the conduct relied upon was incapable in law of amounting to a repudiation. In this respect the main burden of his submission was that, for the obligation of mutual trust and confidence to be destroyed, there must be deliberate conduct or bad faith in the appraisal reports. Though there was a finding that Mr O'Keefe had failed to discharge his responsibilities it was not deliberate and it was not in bad faith. To support this submission Mr Carr cited a number of authorities: the first was *Isle of Wight Tourist Board v Coombes* [1976] IRLR 413. In that case the respondent had been a personal secretary to the appellant's director and in the course of an argument that director had spoken to another employee about her, saying that she was an 'intolerable bitch on a Monday morning'. The Employment Appeal Tribunal held that the relationship between the director and his personal secretary must be one of complete confidence and they must trust and respect each other, that in calling his secretary a 'bitch' the employer's director had shattered that relationship. Thus, they confirmed the Industrial Tribunal's decision that there had been a constructive dismissal.

We do not find in that decision any hint of the need for the conduct to be deliberate and intentional or prompted by bad faith.

The next case was *Courtaulds Northern Textiles Ltd v Andrew* [1979] IRLR 84. Again this was a case where words had been spoken in an argument. The words spoken by the assistant manager of the respondent were 'You can't do the bloody job anyway'. Again the Employment Appeal Tribunal, in this case Arnold J presiding, referred to the implied term of the contract of employment that 'the employers will not without proper reason and cause conduct themselves in a manner calculated or likely to destroy or seriously damage the relationship of confidence and trust between the parties'. That part of the headnote is borne out in the judgment which appears at paragraph 10. We will read the latter part of that dictum, where Arnold J said:

'We think that, thus phrased, the implied term (as regards "calculated") extends only to an obligation not to conduct themselves in such a manner as is intended, although not intended by itself, to destroy or seriously damage the relationship in question.'

Mr Carr stressed the verb 'intended' in that part of Arnold J's judgment. In addition, Mr Carr referred to words that appear earlier in that judgment, where having set out the facts, Arnold J said:

'Those, we think, are the facts except for one very important addition, and that is, that when Mr Sneyd said "You can't do the bloody job anyway", that was not an expression of his opinion; he thought that Mr Andrew could do the job. That is important because it removes this case altogether from the sort of cases which we suppose are very much more common, in which a criticism is made from an industrial point of view of the subordinate's performance; cases in which complaint is made that the criticism was unjustified but in which it was nevertheless a criticism in which management believed. Nothing in this case has any relevance to a consideration of that sort of case'.

Thus, Mr Carr submitted that Arnold J was drawing a distinction and pointing out the difference where there was a case in which there was a criticism in which the management did believe; the inference being Mr Carr submits, that in such a case there could not be a constructive dismissal arising from such a criticism.

Those words of Arnold J naturally we pay close attention to, but we do not think that he was there endeavouring to set out a rule that was to govern every conceivable set of circumstances. We do not think it prevents us from looking at the circumstances of this case and deciding, even though Mr O'Keefe may have believed in his criticism, whether or not there was conduct amounting to a constructive dismissal. With regard to the reference to 'intention' it is true that in that particular appeal, *Courtaulds Northern Textiles*, it was a relevant matter; but, as we shall point out later, it is not necessarily a relevant matter in every case.

The next authority was *FC Gardner Ltd v Beresford* [1978] IRLR 63. In substance, the complaint in that appeal was that there had been no increase in pay for two years. Phillips J, giving the judgment of the Employment Appeal Tribunal, referred to the obligation on an employer not to behave arbitrarily, capriciously, or inequitably in matters of remuneration. Certainly, we can see no complaint about that; that is absolutely right. But that is not this case. In the headnote (and this is borne out by the judgment) it is stated:

'On the other hand, if there was evidence to support a finding that the employers were deliberately singling the respondent out for special treatment inferior to that given to everybody else and that they were doing it arbitrarily, capriciously and inequitably, that might well lead the Industrial Tribunal to say that she had a good claim even under the new test for constructive dismissal'.

Again we fail to see why that plain and sensible dictum applied to the question of remuneration states a general principle that applies to cases of the kind with which we are dealing.

Then there was the authority of *Robinson v Crompton Parkinson Ltd* [1978] IRLR 61. In that appeal Kilner Brown J referred to this obligation of mutual trust and confidence. He said, in his judgment:

'It seems to us, although there is no direct authority to which we have been referred, that the law is perfectly plain and needs to be re-stated so that there shall be no opportunity for confusion in the future. In a contract of employment, and in conditions of employment, there has to be mutual trust and confidence between master and servant. Although most of the reported cases deal with the master seeking remedy against a servant or former servant for acting in breach of confidence or in breach of trust, that action can only be upon the basis that trust and confidence is mutual. Consequently where a man says of his employer, "I claim that you have broken your contract because you have clearly shown you have no confidence in me, and you have behaved in a way which is contrary to that mutual trust which ought to exist between master and servant," he is entitled in those circumstances, it seems to us, to say that there is conduct which amounts to a repudiation of the contract'.

In stating that principle, in our view Kilner Brown J does not set out any requirement that there should be deliberation, or intent, or bad faith.

Finally, there are very important words in a part of the judgment in *Palmanor Ltd v Cedron* [1978] IRLR 303, the words appearing in the judgment of Slynn J at page 305. It is a short quotation and reads as follows:

'It seems to us that in a case of this kind the Tribunal is required to ask itself the question whether the conduct was so unreasonable that it really went beyond the limits of the contract. We observe that in the course of the argument on behalf of the employee, it was submitted that the treatment that he was accorded was a repudiation of the contract'.

Mr Barry brought to our attention an authority on this matter, *British Aircraft Corporation Ltd v Austin* [1978] IRLR 332. In that case goggles, which were necessary for the work, had been provided for the respondent. She was unable to wear them because of her spectacles. She made complaints and they were not heeded or investigated and constructive dismissal was found. At paragraph 13 of the judgment of Phillips J, having referred to the case of *Western Excavating (ECC) Ltd v Sharp* [[5.24] below] said:

'First of all, before looking at that case, it is desirable perhaps to say that that case and *Scott v Aveling Barford Ltd* ([1978] ICR 214) are by no means in total opposition, and if employers do behave in a way which is not in accordance with good industrial practice to such an extent—and this is how it was put in that case—that the situation is intolerable or the situation is that the employee really cannot be expected to put up with it any longer, it will very often be the case, perhaps not always but certainly very often be the case, that by behaving in that way the employers have behaved in breach of contract because it must ordinarily be an implied term of the contract of employment that employers do not behave in a way which is intolerable or in a way which employees cannot be expected to put up with any longer. That is an aside, and we certainly do not wish Industrial Tribunals to guide themselves otherwise than in accordance with the judgment in *Western Excavating (ECC) Ltd v Sharp*'.

We would agree with Phillips J's statement that there may be conduct so intolerable that it amounts to a repudiation of contract. There are threads then running through the authorities whether it is the implied obligation of mutual trust and confidence, whether it is that intolerable conduct may terminate a contract, or whether it is that the conduct is so unreasonable that it goes beyond the limits of the contract. But in each case, in our view, you have to look at the conduct of the party whose behaviour is challenged and determine whether it is such that its effect, judged reasonably and sensibly, is to disable the other party from properly carrying out his or her obligations. If it is so found that that is the result, then it may be that a Tribunal could find a repudiation of contract.

Finally, therefore, we have to consider whether the conduct relied upon by the Industrial Tribunal was such that it was capable in law of amounting to repudiation by the Post Office. We do not think it helpful in this case to enter into any inquiry as to whether the Post Office's behaviour was deliberate or malicious, as there may well be cases involving such consideration. We think in this case that we should consider whether the employer's conduct was such, however it arose, as to destroy the mutual trust and confidence which must exist between them and their employees. We agree with Mr Barry that we have to look at the conduct in its entirety and not in sections, as Mr Carr invited us so to do. The Industrial Tribunal had evidence that the respondent's appraisal was that she was a capable worker. There was then the fact that Mr O'Keefe, without proper consideration (so the Industrial Tribunal found), had given her a bad report. There followed the refusal of her transfer, the reason given being that she was entitled to think meant that there were no vacancies for her job, when, in fact, it was because of Mr O'Keefe's report. Finally, after some six weeks of inquiry she discovered fully the true reason for the refusal to transfer her. In our judgment, on those facts the Industrial Tribunal were entitled to come to the conclusion that the conduct of the employer entitled the respondent to consider that the employer had broken the vital trust and confidence that must exist, and entitled her to terminate the contract. That being something which, in our view, the Industrial Tribunal on the facts of this case were entitled to find, this appeal must be dismissed.

As well as endorsing the implied term of mutual trust and confidence, the EAT approves in this decision other formulations of the idea that the employer's discretionary power should not be abused. It accepts that in matters of remuneration an employer should not act arbitrarily, capriciously, and inequitably. In another formulation, the principle is expressed as conduct by the employer that is so intolerable and unreasonable that an employee cannot be expected to put up with it any longer. The courts also refer to the idea of good faith in performance. In subsequent cases, the terminology is often used cumulatively and interchangably.

[2.24] *Transco plc v O'Brien* [2002] EWCA Civ 379, [2002] ICR 721 (CA)

Pill LJ:
In this case, for good commercial reasons the employers decided to offer their workforce (the relevant part of which was over 70 strong) a new contract on better terms. To single out an employee on capricious grounds and refuse to offer him the same terms as were offered to the rest of the workforce is, in my judgment, a breach of the implied term of trust and confidence. There are few things which would be more likely to damage seriously (to put it no higher) the relationship of trust between an employer and employee than a capricious refusal, in present circumstances, to offer the same terms to a single employee . . .

In the present case it was plainly a breach of contract to treat an employee as not being entitled to benefits resulting from his being a permanent employee when he was in fact a permanent employee. The good faith with which the erroneous belief was held does not alter the character of the failure. Had the employers assessed the applicant's status correctly he would have been offered the enhanced terms. The appeal tribunal were correct to conclude that the applicant must be placed in the position in which he would have been but for the breach of contract.

Although these different formulations of the implied term are often used, the predominant expression has become the implied term of mutual trust and confidence as a result of its endorsement in the next case, which is also known by the name of one of the other plaintiffs *Malik*.

[2.25] *Mahmoud v Bank of Credit and Commerce International S.A.* **[1998] AC 20 (HL)**

The appellants were dismissed for redundancy following the collapse of the employing bank amid allegations that the bank's business had been conducted fraudulently. Though innocent of any wrongdoing, the appellants claimed to be unable to obtain employment in the banking sector due to a stigma being attached to them. They sought a claim in damages against the liquidator of the bank for this loss known as stigma damages. The possibility of such a claim was confirmed by the House of Lords. In reaching this conclusion, the speeches described modern judicial perceptions of the nature of the employment relation and its implied terms.

Lord Steyn (with whom a majority of the Judicial Committee agreed):

The implied term of mutual trust and confidence

The applicants do not rely on a term implied in fact. They do not therefore rely on an individualised term to be implied from the particular provisions of their employment contracts considered against their specific contextual setting. Instead they rely on a standardised term implied by law, that is, on a term which is said to be an incident of all contracts of employment: *Scally v Southern Health and Social Services Board* [1992] 1 AC 294 **[[2.39]** below]. Such implied terms operate as default rules. The parties are free to exclude or modify them. But it is common ground that in the present case the particular terms of the contracts of employment of the two applicants could not affect an implied obligation of mutual trust and confidence.

The employer's primary case is based on a formulation of the implied term that has been applied at first instance and in the Court of Appeal. It imposes reciprocal duties on the employer and employee. Given that this case is concerned with alleged obligations of an employer I will concentrate on its effect on the position of employers. For convenience I will set out the term again. It is expressed to impose an obligation that the employer shall not: 'without reasonable and proper cause, conduct itself in a manner calculated and likely to destroy or seriously damage the relationship of confidence and trust between employer and employee': see *Woods v W.M. Car Services (Peterborough) Ltd.* [1981] ICR 666, 670 (Browne-Wilkinson J.) (below **[5.26]**), approved in *Lewis v Motorworld Garages Ltd.* [1986] ICR 157 CA (below **[5.25]**) and *Imperial Group Pension Trust Ltd. v Imperial Tobacco Ltd.* [1991] 1 WLR 589 HC . . .

The evolution of the term is a comparatively recent development. The obligation probably has its origin in the general duty of co-operation between contracting parties: Hepple & O'Higgins, *Employment Law*, 4th ed. (1981), pp. 134–135, paras. 291–292. The reason for this development is part of the history of the development of employment law in this century. The notion of a 'master and servant' relationship became obsolete. Lord Slynn of Hadley recently noted 'the changes which have taken place in the employer-employee relationship, with far greater duties imposed on the employer than in the past, whether by statute or by judicial decision, to care for the physical, financial and even psychological welfare of the employee:' *Spring v Guardian Assurance Plc.* [1995] 2 AC 296 HL 335B **[[2.29]** below]. A striking illustration of this change is Scally's case, to which I have already referred, where the House of Lords implied a term that all employees in a certain category had to be notified by an employer of their entitlement to certain benefits. It was the change in legal culture which made possible the evolution of the implied term of trust and confidence.

There was some debate at the hearing about the possible interaction of the implied obligation of confidence and trust with other more specific terms implied by law. It is true that the implied term adds little to the employee's implied obligations to serve his employer loyally and not to act contrary to his employer's interests. The major importance of the implied duty of trust and confidence lies in its impact on the obligations of the employer: Douglas Brodie, 'Recent cases, Commentary, The Heart of the Matter: Mutual Trust and Confidence' (1996) 25 ILJ 121. And the implied obligation as formulated is apt to cover the great diversity of situations in which a balance has to be struck between an employer's interest in managing his business as he sees fit and the employee's interest in not being unfairly and improperly exploited.

The evolution of the implied term of trust and confidence is a fact. It has not yet been endorsed by your Lordships' House. It has proved a workable principle in practice. It has not been the subject of adverse criticism in any decided cases and it has been welcomed in academic writings. I regard the emergence of the implied obligation of mutual trust and confidence as a sound development.

Given the shape of the appeal my preceding observations may appear unnecessary. But I have felt it necessary to deal briefly with the existence of the implied term for two reasons. First, the implied obligation involves a question of pure law and your Lordships' House is not bound by any agreement of the parties on it or by the acceptance of the obligation by the judge or the Court of Appeal. Secondly, in response to a question counsel for the bank said that his acceptance of the implied obligation is subject to three limitations: (1) that the conduct complained of must be conduct involving the treatment of the employee in question; (2) that the employee must be aware of such conduct while he is an employee; (3) that such conduct must be calculated to destroy or seriously damage the trust between the employer and employee.

In order to place these suggested limitations in context it seemed necessary to explain briefly the origin, nature and scope of the implied obligation. But subject to examining the merits of the suggested limitations, I am content to accept the implied obligation of trust and confidence as established.

Breach of the implied obligation

Two preliminary observations must be made. First, the sustainability of the applicants' claims must be approached as if an application to strike out was under consideration. That is how the judge and the Court of Appeal approached the matter. And the same approach must now govern. Secondly, given the existence of an obligation of trust and confidence, it is important to approach the question of a breach of that obligation correctly. Mr Douglas Brodie, of Edinburgh University, in his helpful article to which I have already referred put the matter succinctly, at pp. 121–122:

> 'In assessing whether there has been a breach, it seems clear that what is significant is the impact of the employer's behaviour on the employee rather than what the employer intended. Moreover, the impact will be assessed objectively'.

Both limbs of Mr Brodie's observations seem to me to reflect classic contract law principles and I would gratefully adopt his statement.

It is arguable that these relatively senior bank employees may be able to establish as a matter of fact that the corruption associated in the public mind, and in the minds of prospective employers, with the bank may have undermined their employment prospects. They may conceivably be able to prove that in the financial services industry they were regarded as potentially tarnished and therefore undesirable employees to recruit. In that way these particular employees may be able to sustain their assertions of fact that they have suffered financial loss. But that is not the end of the matter. Account must now be taken of the bank's counter-arguments. The bank's arguments closely mirror the three limitations on the implied obligation suggested by counsel. First, counsel for the bank submitted that the dishonest behaviour of the bank was directed at the defrauding of third parties and that therefore there could be no breach of the implied obligation. The conclusion is not warranted by the premise. The implied obligation extends to any conduct by the employer likely to destroy or seriously damage the relationship of trust and confidence between employer and employee. It may well be, as the Court of Appeal observes, that the decided cases involved instances of conduct which might be described 'as conduct involving rather more direct treatment of employees:' [1996] ICR 406, 412. So be it. But Morritt LJ held, at p. 411, that the obligation:

> 'may be broken not only by an act directed at a particular employee but also by conduct which, when viewed objectively, is likely seriously to damage the relationship of employer and employee'.

That is the correct approach. The motives of the employer cannot be determinative, or even relevant, in judging the employees' claims for damages for breach of the implied obligation. If conduct objectively considered is likely to cause serious damage to the relationship between employer and employee a breach of the implied obligation may arise. I would therefore reject the first limitation as misconceived.

That brings me to the second suggested limitation on the implied obligation namely, that the employee must have been aware of such conduct whilst he was an employee. The argument is that the implied obligation serves to protect the contract of employment. Accordingly, it is said, conduct of which an employee is not aware can never amount to a breach of the implied obligation. That is so because the reach of the implied obligation must be dictated by its purpose. At first glance this argument seemed plausible. But there is a fallacy in it. The example was put to counsel for the bank of a senior employee, who does discover that the bank has been carrying on corrupt and dishonest operations on a vast scale. The employee wishes to terminate the contract forthwith for breach of the implied obligation of trust and confidence. May he do so? Counsel for the bank says 'No.' Counsel says he will have to give notice and continue to serve his corrupt employer during the notice period or, alternatively, he must abandon his post in breach of contract. If a train of reasoning leads to an unbelievable consequence, it is in need of re-examination. Counsel's answer must be wrong: it is a classic case of a breach of the implied obligation. And the breach is of a gravity which entitles the employee to terminate his employment contract. Having arrived at this conclusion, it follows that termination is not necessarily the employee's only remedy. Subject to proof of causation and satisfying the principles of remoteness and mitigation, the employee ought on ordinary principles of contract law to be able to sue in contract for damages for financial loss caused by any damage to his employment prospects. But counsel for the bank insists that if the employee left the bank in ignorance of the dishonest and corrupt operations of the bank, and his employment prospects are then subsequently damaged, he can have no claim in law. This argument gains some support from observations of Morritt LJ. While not deciding the case on this basis he said, at p. 412:

> 'But it is inherent in conduct of the kind which we are required to assume in this case that, if it is to be successful, it is secret and hidden from most of the employees as well as the rest of the world. So long as it remains secret it can have no effect on the trust and confidence of the employee from whom it is concealed. Moreover, not only could there be no breach without knowledge, there could be no stigma damage either until the fraud was revealed. Once the employee has left his employment the subsequent revelation of the fraud can have no effect on the trust and confidence for, by definition, it has ceased anyway'.

This reasoning treats the decisive issue as being whether the relationship of trust and confidence has as a matter of fact survived until the moment of termination of the employment. It gives inadequate weight to the existence of an obligation in law. And there is nothing heterodox about allowing a claim for damages for a breach occurring during the contractual relationship where damage resulting from the breach only becomes manifest after the termination of the relationship. In truth the ignorance of an employee of a breach of the implied obligation is only relevant to the choice of remedies: obviously the employee cannot decide to terminate on a ground of which he is unaware. Moreover, if counsel's submission were right it would mean that an employer who successfully concealed dishonest and corrupt practices before termination of the relationship cannot in law commit a breach of the implied obligation whereas the dishonest and corrupt employer who is exposed during the relationship can be held liable in damages. That cannot be right. For these reasons I would therefore differ from the Court of Appeal on this point and reject counsel's second suggested limitation.

It is now necessary to examine counsel's third suggested limitation, namely that such conduct destroys or seriously damages the relationship of trust and confidence between the employer and the employee. It will be noted that this supposed 'limitation' is already part and parcel of the implied obligation of trust and confidence. This limitation raises no separate legal issue. But I understood counsel for the bank to emphasise that the agreed statement of facts which was produced at the invitation of the judge simply describes the applicants as 'employees' of the bank. He submits that, cleaning or even clerical staff of the bank could not credibly assert that their employment prospects have been damaged by their association with the bank, which carried on dishonest and corrupt operations. He said that no reasonable person would regard any stigma arising from the bank's corrupt and dishonest dealings as attaching to such employees. That may or may not be right. It is, however, a question of fact unsuitable for determination in these proceedings. In any event, the judge and the Court of Appeal were asked to decide the case on the basis that the applicants were relatively senior employees. The statement of facts and issues lodged in this case described their positions as being respectively a manager of a branch and the Head of Deposit Accounts and Customer Services at a branch. It is quite unrealistic now to ignore these facts. And it is arguable that as a matter of fact such relatively senior employees of the bank may be able to prove that there has been a breach of the implied obligation and that their employment prospects were damaged. It follows that I would also reject counsel's submissions under this heading.

This interpretation of the implied term of mutual trust and confidence undoubtedly extends it beyond the earlier cases where the issue was the unfair and disrespectful treatment of the employee. In the *Malik* case, the employer's conduct complained of concerned the purposes to which the business had been directed, and their alleged effect of damaging the subsequent employability of the former managers, rather than unfair disciplinary action. Subsequent decisions of the House of Lords have confirmed the implied term of mutual trust and confidence, though they have confined its application to the employer's performance of the contract as opposed to the employer's reasons for and manner of dismissal (5.1, below). A broad description of the implied term has been endorsed:

> The trust and confidence implied term means, in short, that an employer must treat his employees fairly. In his conduct of his business, and in his treatment of his employees, an employer must act responsibly and in good faith (Lord Nicholls, *Eastwood v Magnox Electric plc* [2004] UKHL 35, [2004] IRLR 732, para.11 [5.12 below].

In the same case Lord Steyn suggested that it might be more conducive to clarity if the courts used the terminology of an implied obligation of good faith (para.50). The terminology of good faith may be useful to stress the special obligations arising in this type of contract, and perhaps link it to comparable developments in other types of commercial contracts such as the contracts that create an occupational pension scheme (e.g. *Imperial Group Pension Trust Ltd v Imperial Tobacco Ltd* [1991] ICR 524 (HC)). But it should be remembered that deliberate misconduct is not necessary for a breach of the implied term of good faith; an honest, if perhaps careless mistake, was sufficient for liability for breach of the implied term in *Transco plc v O'Brien* (**[2.24]** above), and *Post Office v Roberts* (**[2.23]** above).

Why have the courts developed this obligation of mutual trust and confidence or good faith in the last twenty-five years? The opening remarks of Lord Steyn in *Mahmoud* above reveal that the judges regard the purpose of the implied term as to bring the common law into line with modern views about fairness in employment relations by controlling the abuse of managerial power in the workplace. The courts perceive a symmetry between an employee's duty to perform the contract in good faith, as illustrated in *British Telecommunications Plc v Ticehurst* [1992] ICR 383 (CA) (**[2.5]** above), and the employer's duty not to act in a way calculated to destroy mutual trust and confidence. This modern parity of obligations differs sharply from the older model of hierarchy and subordination, in which the employer's general discretionary power to manage the workplace was unfettered except by reference to express terms of the contract and implied duties with respect to health and safety. It is arguable that the image of the employment relationship used by the courts in the construction of the implied obligations is no longer one in which the employee simply acts as the agent of the employer in carrying out instructions faithfully, but now has become one where the employer is also considered as in some respects like an agent of the employee, that is the employer must act in good faith and use the powers conferred by the contract for proper purposes.

In the context of disputes about the exercise of managerial discretion in relation to pay, the description of the implied term or obligation is commonly framed in terms of an obligation not to act arbitrarily, capriciously, or irrationally (see *Horkulak v Cantor Fitzgerald International* **[5.11]** below). This language suggests that the implied obligations of the employment relation may have been influenced by public law standards (D. Brodie, 'Legal Coherence and the Employment Revolution' (2001) 117 LQR 604), especially when the express terms of the contract apparently confer on the employer an unlimited discretionary power (H. Collins, Discretionary Power in Contracts', in D. Campbell, H. Collins, J. Wightman (eds), *Implicit Dimensions of Contract* (Oxford, Hart, 2003) 219).

[2.26] *Mallone v BPB Industries plc* **[2002] EWCA Civ 126 [2002] IRLR 452 (CA)**

> The claimant was dismissed as managing director of an Italian subsidiary of the defendant employer. He claimed compensation for the withdrawal of all his share option entitlements as a result of a directors' resolution under a rule of the share option scheme that permitted the directors to award share options to employees whose employment had been terminated in an 'appropriate proportion' . . . 'as the directors in their absolute discretion shall determine'. The Court of Appeal found the directors' exercise of discretion a breach of contract. Even with regard to such an unfettered discretion, the directors were bound by the purposes of the scheme to provide incentives for good performance to executives to the extent that decisions about the exercise of the discretion should not be made dishonestly, for an improper motive, capriciously, arbitrarily, and that

the exercise of discretion would be invalid if the directors reached a decision that no reasonable employer could have reached on analogy with the test in *Associated Provincial Picture House ltd v Wednesbury Corporation* [1948] 1 KB 223 (CA). In this case the judge at first instance was entitled to find that the directors' decision was one that no reasonable employer could have reached, even though, of course, the decision was expected to save the employer more than £100,000.

Returning to the issue of the causes of the development of these implied terms, it seems likely also that modern statutory employment legislation, such as the law of unfair dismissal, has influenced judicial perceptions about the underlying structure of the legal composition of the employment relation. As an employer is now under a legal duty created by statute not to dismiss employees unfairly, it seems a short step to reason by analogy towards the conclusion that the employer should also treat employees fairly or in good faith during the performance of the contract. It may also be possible to detect in the evolution of the implied term of mutual trust and confidence the influence of changes in employer's perceptions of how to maximise the productivity of the workforce.

A strict and unforgiving hierarchical authority structure cannot always achieve the greatest measure of productivity from the workforce. Fear of disciplinary sanctions provides some motivation to work hard, but better productivity can often be achieved through more active co-operation between the workforce and a psychological attitude of identification with the goals of the enterprise. In order to achieve more active co-operation, management techniques have often become more sophisticated during the twentieth century than the measures adopted under the influence of Taylorism.

Hierarchies can be legitimated by the creation of an impersonal system of rules in a bureaucratic organisation. Work tasks and methods can be allocated by mechanisms of consultation with the workforce or their representatives. Payment systems can introduce incentives for hard work and co-operation by promising promotion or performance-related pay. Hierarchies can be eliminated altogether by delegating responsibility for the achievement of efficient production to the work groups themselves. All these methods and others are commonplace in modern managerial techniques for securing the active co-operation of the workforce. The different methods are often referred to as human resources management (HRM). Many of the seeds of the ideas of HRM can be discovered in conclusions drawn from an American study at the Hawthorne plant of the Western Electric Company (see Box below). The central problem addressed by HRM is that hierarchical work relations are unlikely to achieve the highest possible work effort from employees, because workers will resent their position of subordination and tend to suspect, perhaps correctly, that additional effort will not be rewarded in the long term by higher pay. The solution devised by management theorists to this problem is to soften hierarchies, to encourage a sense of team-work, and to grant employees greater autonomy in determining working methods. The following study illustrates how HRM techniques can be used by management to reduce hierarchy and to expand worker autonomy for the purpose of improving the efficiency of the business.

The Hawthorne Experiment

In one of the assembly rooms at this electric components manufacturer, the experimenters agreed a programme of changes in working conditions with the workers with a view to determining which conditions would produce greater productivity. Various changes in working conditions were introduced, one at a time: rest periods of different numbers and length, changes in the length of the working day and the week, variations in lighting, the provision of food and refreshments. Slowly, but steadily, the output of the group of workers in the test room increased. What was striking was the increase in productivity whatever changes were made, including a reversion to the original working conditions. Even stranger, the workers concerned reported that they felt less tired and that they were not working harder. A plausible explanation of this remarkable result is that the crucial dimension of the experiment was that the group of workers was consulted closely on all the changes in working conditions, many of which they suggested themselves. The experiment was written up in: F.J. Roethlisberger and W.J. Dickson, *Management and the Worker* (Harvard, Harvard University Press, 1939), but has been examined subsequently by many management theorists: *e.g.* E. Mayo, *The Social Problems of Industrial Civilization* (London, Routledge, 1949) Ch.4.).

[2.27] P. Rosenthal, S. Hill and R. Peccei, 'Checking Out Service: Evaluating Excellence, HRM and TQM in Retailing' (1997) 11 *Work, Employment & Society* 481

[This study investigated the effects of the introduction of an HRM and quality initiative in a leading supermarket store (known as 'ShopCo'). The supermarket aimed to improve its customer service by a number of training measures designed to alter the culture of the organisation and the attitude of staff. In addition, staff were given slightly enlarged discretion in their dealings with customers ('empowerment'), including making spontaneous accommodations with disgruntled customers, and management were required to adopt a more 'approachable' style with less of an attitude of 'command and control' towards staff. The research was designed to assess in the light of the evidence available from one small study the debates around such management initiatives. These debates, as the authors explain, question whether the 'empowerment' of employees in the 'pursuit of excellence' is in fact a more subtle and intensive form of subordination.]

A number of the principles expounded in contemporary management thought underpin most recent attempts to improve service quality. At the centre is the individualising philosophy of the contemporary enterprise culture, in particular the values of self-actualisation, freedom and 'respect for the individual'. This philosophy informs the 'excellence' approach to organisations, which in turn influences human resource and quality management. A second principle is that of the full utilisation of human resources as a basis for obtaining competitive advantage, through high employee satisfaction, commitment and productivity. A third is the notion of assigning more discretion and responsibility ('empowerment') which is central to all approaches. Fourth, there is the weight given to customer satisfaction achieved through continuous improvement and service excellence. Finally, there is the emphasis placed on the need to integrate individual and organisational goals through the creation of 'strong' performance-oriented corporate cultures.

Discussions of quality management and HRM have a tendency to polarise. The optimistic position is that the principles underlying the approaches are genuine, being both realisable and genuinely held by managers, and that quality management and HRM benefit both firms and employees alike. The critical stance is that quality and human resource management, and the broader ideas of enterprise and excellence, increase the subjection of employees. One view is that greater subjection results from the refinement of techniques of surveillance that permit enhanced control, while the other is that it arises out of the manipulation of meaning. New managerial fashions therefore contain a large element of sham in terms of what they claim to deliver to employees. The control approach has its roots in the labour process tradition, while some recent variants of control develop the 'panopticon' element of the Foucaultian perspective on power. Panopticonism increases the potential for management to control individuals via the deployment of techniques of individualisation and enhanced surveillance. Those concerned with the manipulation of meaning suggest that, in structuring meaning, corporations manage to influence how their employees think about and interpret 'reality'. Structuring may take place either via ideologies or discursive practices, following different theoretical perspectives, and the effect is to create norms and meanings that are congruent with corporate interests . . .

Conclusion
This investigation provides no support for the view that, if a company's objectives of improving service quality are realised, they are achieved through some combination of sham empowerment, work intensification and increased surveillance. From senior management's perspective, the programme does appear to have had a positive impact in Shopco. First, a large majority of employees strongly endorse Service Excellence, and there is a substantial level of support for the values and concepts of service quality and internalisation of the language. This endorsement has survived into the second year of the programme. Second, half of the staff say that they engage in the sort of customer-oriented *behaviours* that the programme was seeking to elicit. As 20 per cent were apparently pre-committed to customer service, the programme seems to have had a positive effect on 30 per cent of staff. This can be seen as a fairly substantial impact within a system as large as Shopco.

It is particularly significant for our argument that high levels of customer service are neither achieved through, nor associated with, disempowerment or work intensification. The discretion people have at work has increased rather than decreased and is not trivial, although this empowerment has a limited scope. The same applies with respect to freedom of expression on the job. In the interviews, people report greater opportunities for self-expression with customers. At the same time, they recognise that constraints on their freedom of action remain; but they do not see these as illegitimate or as contradicting the message of Service Excellence. Finally, there is no evidence that the attempt to improve customer service via the programme has led to a systematic intensification of work at store level. Thus, within clear limits, the optimism of the management writers and others is better supported here than the pessimism of the control school . . .

What of the role of discourse in the overall process of change within Shopco? Was the new managerial discourse of quality instrumental in (re)shaping the consciousness of employees? There seems to have been a strong initial impact. The interviews showed that many employees took on the language of Service Excellence and appeared to structure their representations of work activity in its terms. The survey indicated that systematic exposure to the new quality discourse through structured training had a significant effect on employees' attitudes towards customer service. Indeed, normative re-educative training appeared to have more of an effect than prior orientation to the quality message.

This suggests that managerial discourse did have an effect on how employees viewed certain aspects of their organisational world. It lends little support, though, to more radical arguments about hegemony and cultural homogeneity. First, there was considerable variation in how receptive people were to the message of service excellence and in the strength of their customer orientation: some employees were more resistant than others to the 'dominant' discourse. Second, there was no sign that the longer the programme lasted the more people endorsed the aspects that we were able to measure. Indeed, the qualitative evidence may suggest some decline in the language of service excellence.

Third, there was the unanticipated consequence of Service Excellence, that employees used its language and concepts to try to bring managers into line with worker expectations. The deeper implications of our evidence for the use of managerial rhetoric against its instigators are of course subject to interpretation and debate. One view would interpret this as a rational and instrumental action on the part of workers, because they know that it is less easily resisted by managers. In this account, language is calculatedly turned back on managers to the potential benefit of employees: through such action they are better able to resist peremptory treatment from supervisors or managers. Thus management has ceded some control. An alternative view might interpret our evidence as signalling the *greater* subjection of employees. Here, the 'turning back' of rhetoric would illustrate what is seen to be management's increasing ability to dictate the parameters of possible dissent. Service Excellence contributes to management's project of totalising control, through the displacing of other and more significant points of resistance from the consciousness of employees . . .

It seems possible that these modern management techniques have influenced judicial preconceptions about the basic structure of the employment relation. As managers have questioned the efficiency of strict hierarchies founded upon unquestioning obedience by a subordinate workforce, and have sought to replace them with steering mechanisms that seek to promote co-operation, it is possible that the courts have responded by recognising that co-operation based upon mutual trust and confidence better approximates to the expectations of the parties in most employment relations rather than the former pattern of submission to managerial prerogative power.

2.5.3 Employee's duty of loyalty

Although the cases discussed above establish a measure of symmetry in the obligation to perform in good faith imposed on employers and employees, an employee's obligation is also described as an obligation of loyalty or fidelity, which perhaps implies a more extensive obligation. The employee's oblgation extends further than performance of the job in good faith to include an obligation not to be disloyal to the employer. This disloyalty might occur if the employee damages the employer's business reputation or gives aid to a competitor of the employer: *Hivac Ltd v Park Royal Scientific Instruments Ltd* [1946] Ch. 169 (CA).

The obligation of loyalty or fidelity is sometimes invoked as the basis for an argument that an employee has committed a breach of contract for failure to disclose his own misconduct. The venerable authority of Lord Atkin in *Bell v Lever Bros Ltd* [1932] AC 161 (HL) stands in the way of such a contention. 'The servant owes a duty not to steal, but, having stolen, is there superadded a duty to confess that he has stolen? I am satisfied that to imply such a duty would be a departure from the well established usage of mankind and would be to create obligations entirely outside the normal contemplation of the parties concerned.' But the courts have developed ways in which to circumvent that dictum. If the employee lies to the employer as part of a cover-up, that fraudulent concealment will amount to a breach of the duty of fidelity. It has also been held that a manager may be required to disclose information about misconduct by subordinates: *Sybron Corp v Rochem Ltd* [1983] ICR 801 (CA). Where the nature of the employee's tasks requires the employee to disclose all relevant information to the employer, a failure to disclose information may also amount to a breach of the obligation of fidelity. *Bell v Lever Bros Ltd* concerned an agreement for termination of employment, and it seems unlikely that the law would require an employee at that time to confess previous misdeeds. But where the employer makes a disadvantageous business decision as a result of an employee's failure to disclose information, knowing that the omission would cause the employer loss, it seems posssible that the employee would be found to be in breach of the duty of loyalty (compare the case of a director *Item Software (UK) Ltd v Fassihi* [2004] EWCA Civ 1244, [2005] ICR 450 (CA). This additional duty of fidelity imposed upon employees does not, however, amount to the imposition of a general fiduciary duty upon employees as an implied term of the contract. Unlike directors of companies, it is unusual for employees to become subject to the onerous obligations of a trustee or a fiduciary, where no conflict of interest is permitted. Such duties may occasionally arise, as in the case where an employee receives money as an agent for the employer, in which case there is a duty to account for the money. Equally, if an employee receives a secret commission or a bribe from a customer or supplier of the employer, the employee will be liable to account to the employer for the sum (as well as facing criminal prosecution). Similarly, the employee may be held accountable for any profits made from the unauthorised use of the employer's property, as in the case of the misuse of trade secrets (2.6.5 below). In the unusual case where the employee is under a fiduciary duty, there is also a duty to disclose any conflict of interest: *Tesco Stores Ltd v Pook* [2003] EWHC 823, [2004] IRLR 618 (Ch). But in general, the obligation of loyalty does not create a fiduciary relation between employee and employer; it merely amounts to an extended aspect of the implied term of performance in good faith. As a consequence, the normal remedy for the employer beyond the self-help remedy of dismissal is a claim for compensation for breach of contract, and other equitable remedies such as a duty to account will not be available.

[2.28] *Nottingham University v Fishel* [2000] IRLR 471 (HC)

Dr Fishel was the scientific director of a clinic that provided invitro fertilisation to patients. As well as running the clinic successfully, he also undertook work privately abroad at other clinics, and occasionally he sent his junior staff to perform such work. After termination of the employment, the University claimed compensation for the value of this private work, arguing that it was performed in breach of contract in that Dr Fishel had not sought prior permission, as required under his contract of employment. Elias J. held that although Dr Fishel had broken his contract by failing to obtain prior permission, the University could only claim damages for breach of contract, since there was no fiduciary relation to account for that income either under the standard incidents of the contract of employment or the terms of this particular contractual arrangement. The University had in fact suffered no loss, because the patients would not have come to the clinic in the UK, and in fact the University may have benefited from Dr Fishel's opportunity both to improve his expertise and to publicise the reputation of the

University. However, Dr Fishel was in breach of a fiduciary duty by directing junior staff to take outside work, because this step created a potential conflict between his duty to the University to direct those employees to work for the university and his personal interest in profiting from their work. For that breach of fiduciary duty, Dr Fishel was liable to account for the profits that he made from his staff's outside work.

2.5.4 Conclusion

The last 25 years have undoubtedly witnessed a rapid evolution in the implied terms of the contract of employment with respect to the construction of the authority relation at its heart. In place of the simple command and obedience model of managerial authority, the courts have developed a standard or default model of the employment relation that modifies the duties of both parties. The employer is under a duty not to act in a way that destroys mutual trust and confidence, or to perform in good faith, a duty that can be breached by a wide variety of abuses of discretionary power. But the employee's duty of co-operation has been subtly extended by the requirement of performance in good faith, so that mere obedience to rules and orders may not always be sufficient to qualify as satisfactory performance of the work obligation. We have suggested tentatively that these developments in the implied terms that define the authority relation may have co-evolved with the introduction of new statutory rights and trends in managerial strategies for securing the most efficient production from the workforce. No doubt this evolution in the legal framework of the authority relation also reflects broader changes in society, such as reductions in the severity of social hierarchies and greater emphasis upon ideals of equality and treating individuals with dignity and respect.

These broader social attitudes towards authority relations provoke a further question. Should it be possible any longer for employers to insist upon the older command and obedience model of the authority relation in the workplace? As a matter of conventional legal doctrine, it should nearly always be possible for employers through suitably worded express terms of the contract of employment to oust implied legal constraints on the exercise of their powers to direct and control the workforce. There remains the mandatory limitation on express terms that an employer can only validly give lawful orders to employees. In addition, for some employees, especially those in the public sector, it may be possible to rely upon the Human Rights Act 1998 to insist that limits should be placed upon the express terms of the contract. But these constraints do not go so far as to prohibit an employer from expressly excluding the implied obligation not to act in a way that is likely to destroy mutual trust and confidence. To insist that such an exclusion should be invalid because it destroys the foundation or a necessary incident of the employment relation would be to revive a discredited notion in the general law of contract that contracts have fundamental terms that cannot be excluded even by express terms. Against this legal orthodoxy that always protects freedom of contract, it might be argued that courts should at least be reluctant in their interpretations of contracts of employment, which are after all much like standard form contracts imposed on a take it or leave it basis, either to permit express exclusions of obligations to perform in good faith or to countenance a substantial imbalance in the obligations owed between the parties.

2.6 Information

The regulation of the dissemination and use of information is always an important dimension of legal intervention in markets. There are three principal grounds for the legal regulation of information in connection with contracts. First, the law may be used to prevent the dissemination of false or misleading information, so that people do not enter unfair or disadvantageous contracts as a result of deception, and so that fair competition is not impeded by falsehoods. Secondly, the law may require disclosure of information, so that a market may operate more competitively and fairly on the basis of better information. Thirdly, the law may also require parties to contracts or negotiations to keep some information confidential, or at least not to use it for personal commercial advantage, in order to prevent one person exploiting the labour of another in acquiring the information or expertise. Regulation of the supply and quality of information shared between parties to contracts thus has the twin objectives of both improving the competitiveness of markets and also preventing unfair or unsatisfactory transactions. These grounds for legal intervention apply across all types of contracts, but find special forms of application in the context of the contract of employment and the labour market.

It is arguable that the labour market and employment relations present special difficulties for the parties with respect to the extent and reliability of information in comparison to most other contracts such as a sale of goods. The qualities of the worker are hard for the employer to ascertain in advance of employment, so that reliance has to be placed on formal qualifications and reputation. Equally, the employee will have difficulty in discovering all the details of a proposed job, for so much of the experience will depend on how the employer exercises managerial discretion. During the performance of the contract of employment, since it is both long-term and incomplete by design, both parties need to share information in order to achieve co-operation and co-ordination of production. To counter these difficulties of acquiring relevant information in advance, it should be expected that legal regulation will pay close attention to rules regarding disclosure of information in the formation and performance of contracts of employment.

Nevertheless, the starting-point of the legal analysis comprises an application of the general law of contract, which rarely imposes duties of disclosure of information on the parties to contracts. Prior to the formation of the contract, the common law duty is confined to the avoidance of misrepresentation, a topic we consider first. During the performance of the contract, neither party is under a general implied duty to provide information as one of the standard incidents of employment. This principle is perhaps surprising in view of the long-term nature of contracts of employment and the need to co-operate in performance. Perhaps an implied duty to perform the contract in good faith may lead to the evolution of duties to supply information during performance. Although there is no general duty to provide information, perhaps because that would prove too vague, we can identify a number of areas where statute and common law have developed limited duties of disclosure placed upon the employer: (a) information about the terms of the contract of employment; (b) information about health and safety risks; (c) information about business plans for the purposes of collective consultation and negotiation. The final topic in this section concerns legal obligations to preserve the confidentiality of information that is disclosed during the performance of the contract.

2.6.1 Dissemination of false or misleading information

The common law of misrepresentation applies to the formation of contracts of employment. If either the employer or the employee provides false information which induces the other to enter the contract, the innocent party can rescind or avoid the contract. It is also possible to claim compensatory damages for any losses caused by reliance upon the false information, where that false information was provided either intentionally or negligently. The kinds of problems that may arise in the context of employment concern false statements by the employer about the nature of the job or false statements by the employee about his or her qualifications and experience. An employer may be able to rescind a contract of employment if the employee told material lies in order to obtain a job, without this rescission amounting to dismissal for the purposes of claims for wrongful or unfair dismissal. (For the special case of concealment by an employee of former trade union activities see *Fitzpatrick v British Railways Board* [1992] ICR 221 (CA), **[8.6]** below). If an employer makes false statements about the terms of employment, it is also possible for the employee to rescind the contract, but it may be more advantageous for the employee to claim that the false statements became terms of the contract, breach of which would entitle the employee to claim compensation whilst retaining the job.

In order to obtain accurate information about potential employees, many employers require a letter of reference from a former employer or educational institution before offering employment. Potential employers seek from these references not only accurate information about the employment and education history of the applicant for a job, but also an assessment of the applicant's character, motivation and abilities. Since businesses often place heavy reliance on recommendations in order to select between candidates for jobs, applicants for jobs can be seriously disadvantaged in their job prospects by unfavourable and unfair references. No legislation governs the provision of references, except that they are required in the financial services sector. In recent years, the courts have crafted common law principles to regulate letters of recommendation in order to protect employees and perhaps potential employers against unfair and inaccurate references.

Regulation by the common law has been explored only recently, because it had been established that references could not create liability under the law of defamation unless they were deliberately false or 'malicious'. The claim in the following case, however, was based upon negligence and breach of an implied term in the contract.

[2.29] *Spring v. Guardian Assurance plc* **[1995] 2 AC 296 (HL)**

> Mr Spring worked as a sales director for a company called Corinium, which was an authorised agent for the sale of Guardian Assurance insurance policies. Following

termination of his contract, Mr Spring tried to establish himself in business selling insurance policies of other companies. He was unable to do so because under the rules of the governing statutory body at the time, LAUTRO, these insurance companies were required to obtain references regarding his honesty and competence. An official of Guardian Assurance sent unsatisfactory references based upon inaccurate information supplied by Mr Spring's former managers at Corinium. The effect of such references was to prevent Mr Spring from obtaining any work as an insurance salesman. He claimed compensation for his economic loss in being unable to obtain employment owing to his former employer's negligence in supplying an inaccurate reference. A majority of the House of Lords accepted in principle the possibility of a claim in negligence, and Lords Woolf and Slynn also permitted the claim for breach of an implied term of the contract of employment. The case was remitted to the lower court to determine the question whether the inaccurate reference had in fact caused the alleged losses.

Lord Woolf:
The claim based on negligence
  The claim here is in respect of economic loss. Before there can be a duty owed in respect of economic loss, it is now clearly established that it is important to be able to show foreseeability of that loss, coupled with the necessary degree of proximity between the parties. It is also necessary to establish that in all the circumstances it is fair, just and reasonable for a duty to be imposed in respect of the economic loss. Deferring for the moment consideration of the consequences of there being possible alternative causes of action of defamation and injurious falsehood and the related public policy considerations, there can really be no dispute that the plaintiff can establish the necessary foreseeability and proximity.
  It is clearly foreseeable that if you respond to a request for a reference by giving a reference which is inaccurate, the subject of the reference may be caused financial loss. Where the reference is required by a prospective employer, the loss will frequently result from a failure to obtain that employment. The prospect of such loss is considerably increased if the reference relates to an applicant, like the plaintiff, for a position as a company representative in an industry which is subject to a rule which is in equivalent terms to r 3.5 of the Lautro rules. That rule provides:

'(1) A person shall not be appointed as a company representative of a member unless the member has first taken reasonable steps to satisfy itself that he is of good character and of the requisite aptitude and competence, and those steps shall . . . include . . . the taking up of references relating to character and experience.

(2) A member which receives an enquiry for a reference in respect of a person whom another member or appointed representative is proposing to appoint shall make full and frank disclosure of all relevant matters which are believed to be true to the other member or the representative'.

  Judge Lever QC, at first instance, accepted the description of the reference by plaintiff's counsel as being 'the kiss of death' to the plaintiff's career in insurance. This was the inevitable consequence of the reference. The reference related to a time and was based upon events which occurred while the plaintiff was working for Corinium and was engaged in selling policies issued by Guardian. The relationship between the plaintiff and the defendants could hardly be closer. Subject to what I have to say hereafter, it also appears to be uncontroversial that if an employer, or former employer, by his failure to make proper inquiries, causes loss to an employee, it is fair, just and reasonable that he should be under an obligation to compensate that employee for the consequences. This is the position if an employer injures his employee physically by failing to exercise reasonable care for his safety and I find it impossible to justify taking a different view where an employer, by giving an inaccurate reference about his employee, deprives an employee, possibly for a considerable period, of the means of earning his livelihood. The consequences of the employer's carelessness can be as great in the long term as causing the employee a serious injury . . .

The defamation issue

There would be no purpose in extending the tort of negligence to protect the subject of an inaccurate reference if he was already adequately protected by the law of defamation. However, because of the defence of qualified privilege, before an action for defamation can succeed (or, for that matter, an action for injurious falsehood) it is necessary to establish malice. In my judgment the result of this requirement is that an action for defamation provides a wholly inadequate remedy for an employee who is caused damage by a reference which due to negligence is inaccurate. This is because it places a wholly disproportionate burden on the employee. Malice is extremely difficult to establish. This is demonstrated by the facts of this case. The plaintiff . . . was able to establish that one of his colleagues, who played a part in compiling the information on which the reference was based, had lied about interviewing him, but this was still insufficient to prove malice. Without an action for negligence the employee may, therefore, be left with no practical prospect of redress, even though the reference may have permanently prevented him from obtaining employment in his chosen vocation.

If the law provides a remedy for references which are inaccurate due to carelessness this would be beneficial. It would encourage the adoption of appropriate standards when preparing references. This would be an important advantage as frequently an employee will be ignorant that it is because of the terms of an inaccurate reference, of the contents of which he is unaware, that he is not offered fresh employment.

The availability of a remedy without having to prove malice will not open the floodgates. In cases where the employee discovers the existence of the inaccurate reference, he will have a remedy if, but only if, he can establish, instead of malice, that the reason for the inaccuracy is the default of the employer, in the sense that he has been careless. To make an employer liable for an inaccurate reference, but only if he is careless, is, I would suggest, wholly fair. It would balance the respective interests of the employer and employee. It would amount to a development of the law of negligence which accords with the principles which should control its development. It would, in addition, avoid a rather unattractive situation continuing of a recipient of a reference, but not the subject of a reference, being able to bring an action for negligence. It would also recognise that while both in negligence and defamation it is the untrue statement which causes the damage, there is a fundamental difference between the torts. An action for defamation is founded upon the inaccurate terms of the reference itself. An action for negligence is based on the lack of care of the author of the reference . . .

Public policy

It would alter the situation, if it would be contrary to some identifiable principle of public policy for there to be a liability for negligence imposed on the giver of a negligent reference. If there were to be such a principle it would be an unusual one since, unless *Hedley Byrne & Co Ltd* v. *Heller & Partners Ltd* [1964] AC 465 (HL) was wrongly decided, it would apparently apply to the negligent provider of a bad but not a good reference . . .

It is obviously in accord with public policy that references should be full and frank. It is also in accord with public policy that they should not be based upon careless investigations. In the case of references for positions of responsibility this is particularly important. That is confirmed by the Lautro rules. It has also to be accepted that some referees may be more timid in giving full and frank references if they feel there is a risk of their being found liable for negligence. However, there is already such a possible liability in respect of a negligently favourable reference, so all that needs to be considered is the possible adverse consequences of a negligently unfavourable reference. For reasons to which I have already referred I consider there is little practical likelihood of no reference at all being given nowadays. Certainly this could not happen in the case of appointments to which the Lautro rules apply.

However, the real issue is not whether there would be any adverse effect on the giving of references. Rather the issue is whether the adverse effects when balanced against the benefits which would flow from giving the subject a right of action sufficiently outweigh the benefits to justify depriving the subject of a remedy unless he can establish malice. In considering this issue it is necessary to take into account contemporary practices in the field of employment; the fact that nowadays most employment is conditional upon a reference being provided. There are also the restrictions on unfair dismissal which mean that an employee is ordinarily not capable of being dismissed except after being told of what is alleged against him and after he has been given an opportunity of giving an explanation. This is also the widespread practice, especially in the Civil Service, of having annual reports which the subject is entitled to see—which practice, apparently even in an ongoing employment situation, is not defeated by any lack of candour. There is now an openness in employment relationships which did not exist even a few years ago.

There is also the advantage, already referred to, of it being appreciated that you cannot give a reference which could cause immense harm to its subject without exercising reasonable care.

A further consideration mentioned by Cooke P in *Bell-Booth Group Ltd* v. *A-G* [1989] 3 NZLR 148 at 156 is the undesirability of infringing freedom of speech. This is a consideration as least as important to the common law as it is under the international conventions by which it is also protected. Here it is necessary to bear in mind that, as is the case with all fundamental freedoms, the protection is qualified and not absolute. Freedom of speech does not necessarily entitle the speaker to make a statement without exercising reasonable care. Freedom of speech has to be balanced against the equally well recognised freedom both at common law and under the conventions that an individual should not be deprived of the opportunity of earning his livelihood in his chosen occupation. A development of the law which does no more than protect an employee from being deprived of employment as a result of a negligent reference would fully justify any limited intrusion on freedom of speech.

When I weigh these considerations I find that public policy comes down firmly in favour of not depriving an employee of a remedy to recover the damages to which he would otherwise be entitled as a result of being a victim of a negligent reference . . .

The claim based on the breach of contract
As I indicated earlier it is possible to approach this appeal as being primarily one involving a contractual issue. This was the preferred approach of Lord Bridge of Harwich in *Scally* v. *Southern Health and Social Services Board* [1992] 1 AC 294 [[2.39] below] in a speech, with which other members of the House agreed, from which I obtained singular assistance . . .

Here, it is also possible to specify circumstances which would enable a term to be implied. The circumstances are: (i) the existence of the contract of employment or services; (ii) the fact that the contract relates to an engagement of a class where it is the normal practice to require a reference from a previous employer before employment is offered; (iii) the fact that the employee cannot be expected to enter into that class of employment except on the basis that his employer will, on the request of another prospective employer made not later than a reasonable time after the termination of a former employment, provide a full and frank reference as to the employee.

This being the nature of the engagement, it is necessary to imply a term into the contract that the employer would, during the continuance of the engagement or within a reasonable time thereafter, provide a reference at the request of a prospective employer which was based on facts revealed after making those reasonably careful inquiries which, in the circumstances, a reasonable employer would make.

In this case the plaintiff's employers were in breach of that implied term. Although the person actually writing the reference was not negligent, she delegated the task of ascertaining the facts to others, and as is the case with the employer's duty to exercise reasonable care for the safety of his employee, the employer cannot escape liability by so delegating his responsibility . . .

The principle in *Spring v Guardian Assurance* requires employers to take reasonable care in preparing accurate references, though it may be possible to disclaim liability by a suitably worded exclusion clause. The liability is based either on tort or an implied term of the contract. The decision is important because it provides employers with an incentive to take care in the preparation of references, and reduces the risk for other employers that an inaccurate reference will be supplied. Lord Woolf also suggests that the principle in *Hedley Byrne & Co Ltd v Heller & Partners Ltd* [1964] AC 465 (HL) applies to the case where a prospective employer who is provided negligently with an inaccurate reference about a potential recruit can claim compensation against the former employer who provided the reference.

The scope of liability to former employees for references has been expanded further, however, by using the implied terms of the contract. Whereas in *Spring v Guardian Assurance*, the implied term was to provide a reference prepared on the basis of reasonably careful enquiries, in the next case the implied term is extended to a requirement that the reference should avoid giving a misleading impression to potential employers, even if it is entirely accurate in its statement of facts.

[2.30] *TSB Bank Plc v Harris* [2000] IRLR 157 (EAT)

Ms Harris worked as a savings and investment advisor. Owing to steadily worsening relations with her manager, she applied for similar job with Prudential. She was interviewed and then Prudential requested a reference from TSB Bank Plc, as required under the regulations of the financial services industry set at that time by LAUTRO. TSB Bank Plc provided no general assessment as to the character or ability of the claimant, but revealed that 17 complaints had been made against her, of which 4 had been upheld and 8 were outstanding. Ms Harris had only been informed about 2 complaints, both of which she had been able to answer. Prudential declined to employ her. She resigned, and claimed constructive unfair dismissal. The employment tribunal upheld her claim on the ground that the employer had broken the implied term of mutual trust and confidence by providing a reference which, though factually accurate, gave a misleading impression about the character and ability of the claimant. Compliance with the minimum requirements set by LAUTRO was not sufficient to discharge the employer's obligation to provide a fair and reasonable reference. The fact that the employer followed its standard practice in this case, and there was evidence that this practice corresponded to an industry wide practice, did not prevent the provision of a purely factual reference from amounting to a breach of the implied term of trust and confidence if its effect was to lead potentially to the destruction of a person's career. The EAT dismissed the appeal, finding no error of law in the tribunal's decision.

Using the implied term of mutual trust and confidence, the EAT approves in this case the proposition that employers should provide a fair and reasonable reference, a duty which goes beyond the obligation to take reasonable care to avoid inaccurate statements of fact. The failure to provide a fair and reasonable reference amounts to a breach of contract that entitles the employee to claim constructive dismissal and damages. This bold regulatory move may counter one reaction of employers to the earlier decision in *Spring v. Guardian Assurance plc*, which was to confine letters of recommendation to statements of provable fact. But the extension of the duty upon employers may make them unwilling to write letters of recommendation at all, which, outside the financial services industry and in the absence of unlawful discrimination between employees, is permitted by the law. It may therefore become necessary for the courts to add a further extension to the common law implied terms, that of an obligation to supply a letter of recommendation on the request of an employee.

2.6.2 Disclosure of terms of employment

Many of the cases that we have considered so far in this chapter reveal considerable confusion about the terms of the contract of employment. Often the arrangement remains informal, relying on custom or convention to fill out the details of the parties' expectations. Where the contract is written down, difficult questions often arise regarding the incorporation of other documents such as collective agreements and staff handbooks. Much of the content of the contract of employment depends upon the terms implied by the court into the agreement. As a result, the employee may be unclear about the terms of the engagement at the outset, and disputes may arise subsequently about differing expectations and implicit understandings. There may even be doubt about which entity is the employer when there is a complicated corporate arrangement such as a group of companies.

Legal regulation has refrained from taking the step of requiring a contract of employment to be in writing. Instead, the model adopted has been to give employees the right to written information, and this right can be enforced by a claim in an employment tribunal. The four most important provisions regarding the disclosure of information about the contract concern:

(1) a statement of the principal terms and conditions of employment within two months of the commencement of employment: Employment Rights Act 1996, section 1;
(2) the requirement of itemised pay statements explaining how wages have been calculated: Employment Rights Act 1996, section 8;
(3) a written statement of reasons for dismissal: Employment Rights Act 1996, section 92;
(4) written notification of terms of the contract that permits an employer to make deductions from wages: Employment Rights Act 1996, section 13; **[2.6]** above.

The duty to supply information about the terms of employment to a new employee under (1) above seeks to combat the problem of the confusing multiple sources of employment terms. The legislation dates from the Contracts of Employment Act 1963. Its requirements for disclosure of information have been expanded several times, most recently in order to conform to the requirements of EC Directive 91/533. The stated objectives of this Directive are to clarify the contractual rights of employees, in order to avoid confusion and disputes, and to create greater transparency and competitiveness in the labour market. But the regulation provides a weak and ineffective instrument for achieving these objectives.

Since the written documents do not have to be provided in advance of the commencement of employment, the regulation fails to tackle the problem of helping the potential employee to make an informed choice about whether or not to accept an appointment. For this reason, the legislation does little to improve transparency in the labour market, though in long-term employment relations, the statement of written particulars can provide the necessary information for discussion of variations and modifications of the contract.

Nor does the legislation go far enough to reduce confusion and disputes about terms of employment. There is no requirement that the information supplied in the written particulars should provide a comprehensive description of the terms of employment. As a result of many amendments, the main items of an employment relationship must now be mentioned under domestic legislation.

[2.31] Employment Rights Act 1996, section 1

(1) Where an employee begins employment with an employer, the employer shall give to the employee a written statement of particulars of employment.

(2) The statement may (subject to section 2(4)) be given in instalments and (whether or not given in instalments) shall be given not later than two months after the beginning of the employment.

(3) The statement shall contain particulars of—

(a)   the names of the employer and employee,

(b)   the date when the employment began, and

(c)   the date on which the employee's period of continuous employment began (taking into account any employment with a previous employer which counts towards that period).

(4) The statement shall also contain particulars, as at a specified date not more than seven days before the statement (or the instalment containing them) is given, of—

(a)   the scale or rate of remuneration or the method of calculating remuneration,

(b)   the intervals at which remuneration is paid (that is, weekly, monthly or other specified intervals),

(c)   any terms and conditions relating to hours of work (including any terms and conditions relating to normal working hours),

(d)   any terms and conditions relating to any of the following—

(i)   entitlement to holidays, including public holidays, and holiday pay (the particulars given being sufficient to enable the employee's entitlement, including any entitlement to accrued holiday pay on the termination of employment, to be precisely calculated),

(ii)   incapacity for work due to sickness or injury, including any provision for sick pay, and

(iii) pensions and pension schemes,

(e)   the length of notice which the employee is obliged to give and entitled to receive to terminate his contract of employment,

(f)   the title of the job which the employee is employed to do or a brief description of the work for which he is employed,

(g)   where the employment is not intended to be permanent, the period for which it is expected to continue or, if it is for a fixed term, the date when it is to end,

(h)   either the place of work or, where the employee is required or permitted to work at various places, an indication of that and of the address of the employer,

(j)   any collective agreements which directly affect the terms and conditions of the employment including, where the employer is not a party, the persons by whom they were made, and

(k)   where the employee is required to work outside the United Kingdom for a period of more than one month—

   (i)   the period for which he is to work outside the United Kingdom,

   (ii)   the currency in which remuneration is to be paid while he is working outside the United Kingdom

   (iii)   any additional remuneration payable to him, and any benefits to be provided to or in respect of him, by reason of his being required to work outside the United Kingdom, and

   (iv)   any terms and conditions relating to his return to the United Kingdom.

(5) Subsection (4)(d)(iii) does not apply to an employee of a body or authority if—

(a)   the employee's pension rights depend on the terms of a pension scheme established under any provision contained in or having effect under any Act, and

(b)   any such provision requires the body or authority to give to a new employee information concerning the employee's pension rights or the determination of questions affecting those rights.

Although this list of items to be recorded in the written statement is extensive, there may be further unexpected but important issues of which the employee may remain in ignorance or which may remain ambiguous. It is arguable that UK legislation does not conform in this respect to the principle stated in European law.

[2.32] Directive 91/533 on an employer's obligation to inform employees of the conditions applicable to the contract of employment relationship, OJL 1991 288

Article 2

1. An employer shall be obliged to notify an employee to whom this Directive applies, hereinafter refereed to as the "employee", of the essential aspects of the contract or employment relationship.

In Case 350/99, *Lange v Georg Schunemann GmbH* [2001] IRLR 244 (ECJ), the ECJ held that Article 2(1) imposes an independent duty to supply information about 'any element which, in view of its importance, must be considered an essential element of the contract', even if that item is not specifically mentioned by the Directive. ERA 1996 section 1 transposes the detailed requirements of the Directive, but does not create a similar obligation to supply significant terms beyond those contained in the list. Even if it is not practicable to require employers to supply a comprehensive account of all the important terms of employment, perhaps they should not be permitted to rely on alleged terms of employment that have not been supplied in the written particulars.

We have observed that a fair part of the confusion surrounding terms of employment stems from the use of incorporated documents to provide details of the terms. These documents may be collective agreements, staff handbooks, occupational pension schemes, and similar documents. The legislation does not require the employer to give new employees copies of these documents, but places two constraints on satisfying the duty to supply information by merely referring to such documents. The written notification of terms can only be achieved by reference to other documents produced by the employer in respect of information about rights in relation to sickness or injury, occupational pension rights, and disciplinary and grievance procedures (ERA 1996, sections 2(2), 3(1)). Where notification is attempted by reference to other documents, the employee must have a reasonable opportunity of reading these documents in the course of employment or the documents must be made reasonably accessible in some other way (ERA 1996, section 6). The employer is also permitted to refer employees to relevant collective agreements to satisfy the requirement of written notification of any terms of employment, though again the document must be made reasonably accessible (ERA 1996, section 6). Apart from these exceptions, the employer should provide the main written particulars in one document (ERA 1996, section 2(4)).

It must be questioned whether these restrictions on supplying information by reference to accessible documents adequately serve the purpose of clarifying for employees the terms of their engagement, though it must be appreciated that more stringent requirements might force employers to incur considerable expense in producing elaborate documentation for each new recruit. The legal requirement of reasonable access to documents is surely too vague to guide employers to what is required. Examples of where employers claim compliance with this requirement by holding one copy of the document in the head office or making it available only on written request to a senior manager cast doubt on the extent to which the requirement achieves the delivery of information to employees (see P. E. Leighton and S.L. Dumville, 'From Statement to Contract—Some Effects of the Contracts of Employment Act 1972' (1977) 6 *Industrial Law Journal* 133, 147). Perhaps modern electronic storage of information together with computer terminal access could reduce the cost to employers and make all the documents properly accessible to new employees. Nevertheless, we should observe that substantial compliance with most of the legal requirement for written particulars is now achieved by most employers. Analysis of the Workplace Employment Relations Survey of 1998 reveals that in about 93 per cent of establishments with 10 or more employees, the employer does provide written details of the principal ingredients of the wage–work bargain as required by the legislation on appointment or shortly afterwards (W. Brown, S. Deakin, D. Nash and S. Oxenbridge, *The Employment Contract: From Collective Procedures to Individual Rights* (Cambridge, ESRC Centre for Business Research, Working Paper 171, 2000).

It is also not at all clear that the supply of information really assists to resolve disputes about terms of employment. The information that must be supplied by the employer has an unreliable status: it is the employer's view of the governing terms of employment. But it is always possible that the true terms reached by agreement between the parties were different, or that the employer's view of what counts as a term of the contract is incorrect, because a court will regard a particular rule in the staff handbook merely as a legally binding term rather than an aspect of the employer's discretion.

[2.33] *System Floors (U.K.) Ltd v Daniel* [1982] ICR 54 (EAT)

The employee claimed unfair dismissal. As a preliminary point, the employer argued that the employee lacked the necessary qualifying period of employment to bring a claim for unfair dismissal by about a week. As a result of a mix-up, however, the employee's original statement of written particulars had declared that his employment had commenced a week earlier, with the possible effect that he satisfied the qualifying period. The industrial tribunal held that the employer was bound by the statement, but the EAT allowed the employer's appeal, and found that the applicant failed to satisfy the necessary qualifying period.

Browne-Wilkinson J:

There is some authority as to the effect of the statutory particulars of the terms of employment. In *Turriff Construction Ltd* v. *Bryant* (1967) ITR 292 the Divisional Court had to consider for the purposes of redundancy payment what effect was to be given to the number of hours worked specified in a statutory statement. Speaking of the statutory predecessor of [ERA 1996 section 1] Lord Parker, giving the decision of the Court, said this:

'It is of course quite clear that the statement made pursuant to s.4 of the Act of 1963 is not a contract. It is not even conclusive evidence of the terms of a contract'.

Again, the Divisional Court in *Parkes Classic Confectionery Ltd* v. *Ashcroft* (1973) 8 ITR 43 overruled the decision of an Industrial Tribunal which had held that where the terms of the contract of employment had been varied, but the employer had failed to serve particulars in the terms . . . , the employer was not entitled to rely on the varied contract. The Divisional Court held that notwithstanding the failure to to serve the necessary statutory statement . . . , there was nothing in the Act to provide that a change of contractual terms should be ineffectual between the parties merely because the employer had failed to give written notice of the change.

It seems to us, therefore, that in general the status of the statutory statement is this. It provides very strong *prima facie* evidence of what were the terms of the contract between the parties, but does not constitute a written contract between the parties. Nor are the statements of the terms finally conclusive: at most, they place a heavy burden on the employer to show that the actual terms of contract are different from those which he has set out in the statutory statement.

Against that background we turn to consider the decision of the Court of Appeal in *Gascol Conversions Ltd v Mercer* [1974] ICR 420 which was the basis of the Industrial Tribunal's decision in this case. In that case there was an agreed variation in the terms on which the employees were engaged. . . . [T]he employer sent a new contract of employment to each of their men. Each man was given a copy to keep, and he was required to sign a document in these terms: 'I confirm receipt of a new contract of employment dated 25.2.72, which sets out . . . the terms and conditions of employment'. Mr Mercer signed such a document. The Court of Appeal held that in those circumstances the document constituted a binding written contract and that accordingly no evidence was admissible to show that the terms of the contract were otherwise. In our view that case does not cover the present case. In that case Mr Mercer had signed a document which he confirmed was a new contract of employment and that it set out the terms and conditions of his employment. The Court of Appeal treated that as a contract in writing, as indeed it was, having been signed by both parties. But in the case of an ordinary statutory statement served pursuant to the statutory obligation, the document is a unilateral one merely stating the employer's view of what those terms are. In the absence of an acknowledgement by the parties that the statement is itself a contract and that the terms are correct (such as that contained in the *Mercer* case), the statutory statement does not itself constitute a contract in writing.

In the present case, all that Mr Daniel did was to sign an acknowledgement that he had received the statement. In no sense did he sign it as a contract or acknowledge the accuracy of the terms in it. We therefore think that the Industrial Tribunal erred in law in treating the date of commencement mentioned in the statement as decisive because it was a contractual term. In our view the statement is no more than persuasive, though not conclusive, evidence of the date of commencement.

This approach to treating the employer's statement as merely evidence of the terms of the contract has been approved by the Court of Appeal (*Robertson v British Gas Corp.* [1983] ICR 351), and it also applies under the European Directive: Cases C–253/96 to C–258/96 *Kampelmann v Landschaftsverband Westfalen-Lippe* [1998] IRLR 333 (ECJ). Many employers now seek to satisfy the statutory requirement of supplying written particulars at the same time as establishing a written contract of employment by requiring the employee to sign a document that serves both purposes, as illustrated by *Gascol Conversions Ltd v Mercer* [1974] ICR 420 (CA) (discussed in the last extract). Although this side-effect of the legislation was probably not intended, the practice has the merit that it brings forward the time when written details are supplied and gives the employee the opportunity to discover and negotiate about particular aspects of the offer at the time of the formation of the contract. In a clarification of the legislation, section 7B ERA 1996 provides that a written contract of employment or letter of engagement containing the particulars of employment given before the employee's job commences will be regarded as satisfying the duty to supply a written statement of those particulars. There are probably other legal reasons that motivate employers to require employees to sign a written contract of employment: for example, to ensure the lawfulness of deductions from pay according to section 13 ERA 1996 (**[2.6]** above), and to overcome any problems presented by the common law rule in relation to standard form contracts that the employer should take reasonable steps to notify the employee of any unusual and onerous terms (e.g. *Peninsula Business Services Ltd v Sweeney* [2004] IRLR 49 (EAT)). To this extent, the legislation does indirectly serve the purpose of enhancing transparency and competitiveness in labour markets by inducing employers to make written offers of employment.

The national legislation applies only to employees, not the broader category of worker, though as usual with European Directives the scope is defined to include 'every paid employee having a contract or employment relationship' (Directive 91/533, Article 1(1); below p. 173). The right does not apply to an employee if his or her employment continues for less than a month (ERA 1996, section 198). Thus for temporary workers, casual workers, and freelance workers, there is a risk that the legislation may not apply, as in *Carmichael v National Power Plc* [1999] ICR 1226 (HL), unless they can establish continuity of employment for more than a month through a succession of short-term contracts of employment. This exception is presumably designed to reduce costs for employers, but again it undermines the effect of the regulation to promote transparency in the labour market. If the effect of national legislation is to exclude some employees who in fact work more or less continuously for longer than a month, it may not satisfy the principle established in the Directive of requiring an objective justification for exclusions.

[2.34] Directive 91/533 on an employer's obligation to inform employees of the conditions applicable to the contract or employment relationship, OJL 1991 288

Article 1
2. Member States may provide that this Directive shall not apply to employees having a contract or employment relationship—
   (a) with a total duration not exceeding one month, and/or with a working week not exceeding eight hours; or
   (b) of a casual and/or specific nature provided, in these cases, that its non-application is justified by objective considerations.

The accuracy or adequacy of any statement issued by an employer can be questioned in an employment tribunal by the employer or employee making a reference: ERA 1996, section 11. The tribunal may then issue the correct particulars or particulars that ought to have been given: ERA 1996, section 12. The same provisions apply to the requirement to give itemised pay statements. The job of the tribunal is not to create terms for the parties, but merely to discover what terms had been agreed expressly or by implication, if any, and ensure their accurate transposition into the statutory statement: *Eagland v British Telecommunications Plc* [1992] IRLR 323 (CA). The absence of any monetary sanction reduces the effectiveness of this legislation to promote disclosure of information about the terms of the contract, though we have noted that larger employers routinely comply with its provisions by adopting written contracts of employment. This problem has been addressed only in one peculiar set of circumstances by giving employment tribunals the power to order two weeks' pay, or if it is just and equitable, up to four weeks' pay, where the tribunal discovers in the course of other proceedings, such as claims against deductions and unfair dismissal, that the employer has not complied with sections 1 or 4 ERA 1996, and where the tribunal finds in favour of the employee in the main proceedings and yet makes no financial award (Employment Act 2002 s.38).

The legal effects of the statutory statement of particulars of employment have affected the development of the law of implied terms of the contract of employment. The list of terms that should normally be mentioned in a statutory statement of particulars provides the courts with a model that can be regarded as the normal incidents to be implied into an employment relation. This style of reasoning was used in the following case to approve the implication of a term imposing a duty on an employer to provide a grievance procedure based on the additional provisions in ERA 1996, section 3 (as amended by Employment Act 2002 s.35).

Groups of Companies and Associated Employers

Section 1 ERA 1996 requires the employer to inform the employee of the name of the employer. No doubt the identity of the employer is usually clear. But many businesses comprise groups of companies, which sometimes renders the identity of the employer obscure. The group of companies may not reflect functional divisions, but may be created for tax or liability reasons. The companies may all occupy the same premises and be owned centrally by a holding company or through interlocking share ownership. As a result, an employee may know that he or she is working for the group of companies, but remain unclear about which corporate entity is the employer. The statutory statement in this respect may of course be inaccurate. The issue may become critical for the employee, for example, when some of the companies in the group become insolvent, or some are sold, or when the employee believes that he is effectively being transferred from one company to another in the group. The starting-point of the legal analysis of the identity of the employer is that only one company in the group can be the employer, and that the law will not 'pierce the corporate veil' to hold that an employee of a subsidiary company is employed by the group of companies or the holding company. Equally, an employee of the holding company is not an employee of a subsidiary (e.g. *Michael Peters Ltd v Farnfield and Michael Peters Group Plc* [1995] IRLR 190 EAT). Employees can move between corporate entities within the group of companies, but only with notice and their consent, for such a move represents in law (though this may not always be appreciated in fact) a change of employer and the offer of a new contract of employment.

Employment law combats several potential disadvantages to employees resulting from this respect for the corporate veil by means of the concept of '**associated employer**.' Two employers are regarded as 'associated' if '(a) one is a company of which the other (directly or indirectly) has control, or (b) both are companies of which a third person (directly or indirectly) has control' (ERA 1996 s.231, TULRCA 1992, s.297). Using the concept of 'associated employer', for example, an employee retains continuity of employment for the purposes of qualifying for employment rights despite transfers between associated employers in a group of companies (ERA 1996 s.218(6)). Similarly, in calculating the total number of employees for the purpose of determining whether various statutory rights apply or fall within an exclusion for small businesses, it is usual to include associated employers in the count of employees. The courts have interpreted the term 'control' in the definition of associated employer to refer to ownership of shares. For two companies to count as associated employers, either a single legal entity has to own 51% of the shares in both companies, or a group of persons, which always acts in concert, has similar voting control by virtue of share ownership in two companies. It follows that neither common ownership by a single individual of 50% of the shares in two companies, nor actual control of two companies by the same minority shareholder suffices to satisfy the test of control (*e.g. Poparm Ltd v Weekes* [1984] IRLR 388; *South West Launderettes Ltd v Laidler* [1986] ICR 455). The use and interpretation of the concept of 'associated employer' will be examined further in particular contexts below. Here the point to be emphasised is that English law usually locates the identity of the employer as a particular corporate entity.

European law, in contrast, often describes an employer in Directives by the term 'undertaking', which refers to an economic entity rather than a particular legal form, so that an 'undertaking' might be larger or smaller than a particular corporate entity. This point becomes significant, for example, in connection with transfers of undertakings, because even though an employee's corporate employer might not be party to the sale of part of the business of the group, the employee might nevertheless be transferred if he or she works for the economic entity that is transferred (*Sunley Turriff Holdings Ltd v Thompson* [1996] IRLR 184 EAT).

[2.35] Employment Rights Act 1996, section 3

(1) A statement under section 1 shall include a note—
  (a) specifying any disciplinary rules applicable to the employee . . .
  (aa) specifying any procedure applicable to the taking of a disciplinary decision relating to the employee, or a decision to dismiss the employee . . .
  (b) specifying (by description or otherwise)—
    (i)   a person to whom the employee can apply if dissatisfied with any disciplinary decision relating to him or any decision to dismiss him, and
    (ii) a person to whom the employee can apply if dissatisfied with any redress of any grievance relating to his employment . . .

[2.36] *W.A. Goold (Pearmak) Ltd v McConnell* [1995] IRLR 516 (EAT)

The applicants claimed unfair dismissal. They had resigned in response to a persistent failure of the managing director, Mr Maloney, to deal with their grievance that, owing to changes in the business, they had suffered substantially reduced remuneration. The managing director also prevented them from approaching the chairman of the company directly. The employers had never issued a statutory statement of written particulars of employment. The question before the tribunal was whether the employer had committed a fundamental breach of contract (a constructive dismissal) by failing to deal with the grievance. The tribunal upheld the claim for unfair dismissal, and the EAT dismissed the employer's appeal.

Morison J:
It seems to us quite clear that the breach of contract identified by the industrial tribunal related to the way the employees' grievances were dealt with. Their process of reasoning was that Parliament requires employers to provide their employees with written particulars of their employment in compliance with the statutory particulars. [ERA 1996, section 3(1)] provides that the written statement required under s. 1 of the Act shall include a note specifying, by description or otherwise, to whom and in what manner the employee may apply if he is either dissatisfied with any disciplinary decision or has any other grievance, and an explanation or any further steps in the grievance procedure. It is clear, therefore, that Parliament considered that good industrial relations requires employers to provide their employees with a method of dealing with grievance in a proper and timeous fashion. This is also consistent, of course, with the codes of practice. That being so, the industrial tribunal was entitled, in our judgment, to conclude that there was an implied term in the contract of employment that the employers would reasonably and promptly afford a reasonable opportunity to their employees to obtain redress of any grievance they may have. It was in our judgement rightly conceded at the industrial tribunal that such could be a breach of contract.

Furthermore, it seems to us that the right to obtain redress against a grievance is fundamental for very obvious reasons. The working environment may well lead to employees experiencing difficulties, whether because of the physical conditions under which they are required to work, or because of a breakdown in human relationships, which can readily occur when people of different backgrounds and sensitivities are required to work together, often under pressure.

There may well be difficulties arising out of the way that authority and control is exercised—sometimes by people who themselves have insufficient experience and training to exercise such power wisely.

It is of course regrettable, in this case that the employers have failed to comply with their statutory obligations, or to appreciate the need to provide a specific mechanism whereby a genuine sense of grievance can be ventilated and redressed. Instead, the employees, in this case, were fobbed off, and Mr Maloney plainly felt his authority was threatened by the employees' wish to speak to the chairman. The provision of a sensible grievance procedure could cost nothing and may well have avoided this litigation.

Suffice it to say, we are of the view that the appeal raises no real arguable point of law.

Although this decision uses the requirement to supply written particulars to help to create an implied term in the contract, it should be treated with caution, for usually the courts argue that silence on a particular item in the written particulars cannot be rectified by the courts implying an appropriate term. For example, the statutory particulars require details about accrued holiday pay on termination of employment to be given, but a court will not infer from this requirement that it is an implied term of every contract of employment that such an entitlement arises: *Morley v Heritage Plc* [1993] IRLR 400 (CA). By virtue of ERA 1996, section 2(1), an employer is required to state in the written particulars that there are no relevant terms of employment to be supplied under section 1(3) or (4), but of course this statement may be inaccurate. Nevertheless, by recognising the possibility of the absence of terms on many crucial matters, the statute strengthens the courts' reluctance to imply terms on the basis of necessity or the standard incidents of the employment relation. Perhaps we may be witnessing a reversal of this attitude, however, as in recent decisions such as *Scally v Southern Health and Social Services Board* [1992] 1 AC 294 (HL), **[2.39]** below. In the particular example of a grievance procedure, it might be argued for instance that the refusal to listen to reasonable concerns of employees amounts to a breach of the implied term of mutual trust and confidence. The legal position with respect to grievance procedures as an implied term has now been further developed by statute (above 1.3.2.1).

It is important to remember, however, that the written particulars supplied by an employer do not necessarily contain terms of employment as opposed to information about the employer's organisational rules. The 'particulars' supplied by an employer may be characterised either way, depending on how a court construes the contract of employment.

[2.37] *Johnson v Unisys Ltd* [2001] UKHL 13, [2001] ICR 480 (HL)

The employee brought an unsuccessful claim for compensation for breach of the implied term of trust and confidence that comprised the employer's failure to follow its own disciplinary procedure (below **[5.6]**). As a subsidiary issue, the question was raised whether the description of the disciplinary procedure, which had been given to the employee in the handbook in compliance with ERA 1996 section 3, was an express term of the contract.

Lord Hoffmann:
Consistently with [ERA 1996, sections 1, 3], Mr Johnson was written a letter of engagement which stated his salary and summarised the terms and conditions of his employment, including the notice period. Apart from the statement that in the event of gross misconduct, the company could terminate his employment without notice, it made no reference to disciplinary matters. It was however accompanied by the Employee

Handbook, which the letter of engagement said 'outlines all the terms and conditions of employment'. This was divided into various sections, the first being headed 'Employment terms and conditions'. These made no reference to the disciplinary procedure, which appeared in a subsequent section under the heading 'Other procedures'. There one could find the various stages of the disciplinary procedure: formal verbal warning, written warning, final written warning, culminating in dismissal, as well as the separate procedure for summary dismissal in cases of serious misconduct.

So did the disciplinary procedures constitute express terms of the contract of employment? Perhaps for some purposes they did. But the Employee Handbook has to be construed against the relevant background and the background which fairly looms over the disciplinary procedure is Part X of the 1996 Act [the statutory claim for unfair dismissal]. The whole disciplinary procedure is designed to ensure that an employee is not unfairly dismissed. So the question is whether the provisions about disciplinary procedure which (to use a neutral phrase) applied to Mr Johnson's employment were intended to operate within the scope of the law of unfair dismissal or whether they were intended also to be actionable at common law, giving rise to claims for damages in the ordinary courts . . .

My Lords, given this background to the disciplinary procedures, I find it impossible to believe that Parliament, when it provided in section 3(1) of the 1996 Act that the statement of particulars of employment was to contain a note of any applicable disciplinary rules, or the parties themselves, intended that the inclusion of those rules should give rise to a common law action in damages which would create the means of circumventing the restrictions and limits which Parliament had imposed on compensation for unfair dismissal. The whole of the reasoning which led me to the conclusion that the courts should not imply a term which has this result also in my opinion supports the view that the disciplinary procedures do not do so either. It is I suppose possible that they may have contractual effect in determining whether the employer can dismiss summarily in the sense of not having to give four weeks' notice or payment in lieu. But I do not think that they can have been intended to qualify the employer's common law power to dismiss without cause on giving such notice, or to create contractual duties which are independently actionable.

The obligation to supply information about the principal terms of employment is a continuing one during the lifetime of the employment relation.

[2.38] Employment Rights Act 1996, section 4 (1)

If, after the material date, there is a change in any of the matter particulars of which are required by sections 1 to 3 to be included or referred to in a statement under section 1, the employer shall give to the employee a written statement containing particulars of the change.

The mere issuing of new written particulars does not of course effect a change in the terms of the contract of employment unless they have been agreed by the employee: *Jones* v. *Associated Tunnelling Co Ltd* [1981] IRLR 477 (EAT), (**[10.4]** below). Again the statute provides no penalty for failure to supply this information about changes in the terms.

Nevertheless, the common law may provide compensation for breach of contract in some circumstances where the employee can demonstrate economic loss resulting from the failure to supply information about a variation in the terms of employment.

[2.39] *Scally v Southern Health and Social Services Board* **[1992] 1 AC 294 (HL)**

Junior hospital doctors missed an opportunity to enhance their occupational pensions owing to a failure by their employer to notify them of a change in the pension scheme and the employer's subsequent refusal to waive the deadline to apply for the additional benefit. The doctors claimed compensation for the loss of this potential benefit by alleging a breach of an implied term in their contracts of employment. The claim was successful in the House of Lords.

Lord Bridge of Harwich:
Here the express terms of the contract of employment confer a valuable right on the employee which is, however, contingent upon his taking certain action . . . Where that situation is known to the employer but not to the employee, will the law imply a contractual obligation on the employer to take reasonable steps to bring the existence of the contingent right to the notice of the employee? . . .

The problem is a novel one which could not arise in the classical contractual situation in which all the contractual terms, having been agreed between the parties, must, *ex hypothesi*, have been known to both parties. But in the modern world it is increasingly common for individuals to enter into contracts, particularly contracts of employment, on complex terms which have been settled in the course of negotiations between representative bodies or organisations and many details of which the individual employee cannot be expected to know unless they are drawn to his attention. The instant case presents an example of this phenomenon arising in the context of the statutory provisions which regulate the operation of the health services in Northern Ireland . . .

The employment of doctors both in hospital appointments and in general practice being a function exercised on behalf of the department . . . by the board, it is the board who . . . have all the liabilities of employers, but the terms of the contracts of employment are determined by the department, no doubt in negotiation with representative bodies representing doctors' interests. . . .

When the Regulations of 1974 introduced the opportunity for employees in the health services to buy added years, it was intended that this should be for their benefit. They could not, however, enjoy that benefit unless they were aware of the opportunity. There are three possible views of the legal consequences arising from this situation. The first is that it could be properly be left to individual employees, knowing that they were compulsory contributors to a superannuation scheme, to make enquiries and ascertain the details of the scheme for themselves. In the light of the judge's findings, I think this view can be confidently rejected. There was no reason whatever why young doctors embarking on a career in the health services should appreciate the necessity to enquire into the details of the superannuation scheme to which they were contributors in order to be in a position to enjoy its benefits. The second view is that the law provided no means of ensuring that the intended beneficiaries of the opportunity to buy added years became aware of it, so that it would be a matter of chance whether or not, in relation to any individual employee, the relevant provision of the Regulations of 1974 achieved its intended purpose. I find this view so unattractive that I would accept it only if driven to the conclusion that there was no other legally tenable alternative.

The third view is that there was an obligation on either the employing board or the department to take reasonable steps to bring the relevant provision to the notice of employees in time to avail themselves of the opportunity to buy added years if they so decided. . . .

Will the law then imply a term in the contract of employment imposing such an obligation on the employer? The implication cannot, of course, be justified as necessary to give business efficacy to the contract of employment as a whole. I think there is force in the submission that, since the employee's entitlement to enhance his pension rights by the purchase of added years is of no effect unless he is aware of it and since he cannot be expected to become aware of it unless it is drawn to his attention, it is necessary to imply an obligation on the employer to bring it to his attention to render efficacious the very benefit which the contractual right to purchase added years was intended to confer. But this may be stretching the doctrine of implication for the sake of business efficacy beyond its proper reach. A clear distinction is drawn in the speeches of Viscount Simonds in *Lister v Romford Ice and Cold Storage Co. Ltd.* [1957] AC 555 (HL) and Lord Wilberforce in *Liverpool City Council v Irwin* [1977] AC 239 (HL) between the search for an implied term necessary to give business efficacy to a particular contract and the search, based on wider considerations, for a term which the law will imply as a necessary incident of a definable category of contractual relationship. If any implication is appropriate here, it is, I think, of this latter type. Carswell J accepted the submission that any formulation of an implied term of this kind which would be effective to sustain the plaintiffs' claims in this case must necessarily be too wide in its ambit to be acceptable as of general application. I believe however that this difficulty is surmounted if the category of contractual relationship in which the implication will arise is defined with sufficient precision. I would define it as the relationship of employer and employee where the following circumstances obtain: (1) the terms of the contract of employment have not been negotiated with the individual employee but result from negotiation with a representative body or are otherwise incorporated by reference; (2) a particular term of the contract makes available to the employee a valuable right contingent upon action being taken by him to avail himself of its benefit; (3) the employee cannot, in all the circumstances, reasonably be expected to be aware of the term unless it is drawn to his attention. I fully appreciate that the criterion to justify an implication of this kind is necessity, not reasonableness. But I take the view that it is not merely reasonable, but necessary, in the circumstances postulated, to imply an obligation on the employer to take reasonable steps to bring the term of the contract in question to the employee's attention, so that he may be in a position to enjoy its benefit. Accordingly I would hold that there was an implied term in each of the plaintiffs' contracts of employment of which the boards were in each case in breach . . .

The assessment of damages should accordingly evaluate the prospect in 1982 of a successful application to purchase added years and of the likely terms of that purchase on the footing that it was then known to the department that the failure to make application within the relevant time limit was due in each case to the board's breach of contract and not to any failure on the part of the doctor.

This general obligation of disclosure appears to be limited to supplying information about the terms of the contract where the employee could not otherwise become aware of those terms. It has not been extended to a duty to give advice about how best to exercise rights under the contract of employment, though if the employer voluntarily assumes the responsibility to give advice and to help the employee, the employer will be liable for negligence in providing that advice and assistance: *Lennon v Commisioner of Police of the Metropolis* [2004] EWCA Civ 130, [2004] IRLR 385

(CA). It may seem fair that an employee should seek his own advice about his contractual position, but in relation to complex terms such as the occupational pension scheme established by the employer (e.g. *University of Nottingham v Eyett* [1999] ICR 721 (ChD)), the case for imposing a duty to give advice has seemed more pressing, though this argument has ultimately been rejected by the courts.

[2.40] *Crossley v Faithful & Gould Holdings Ltd* **[2004] EWCA Civ 293 [2004] ICR 1615 (CA)**

> The claimant suffered a nervous breakdown and after a period of sick leave agreed to take early retirement. Under the terms of the employer's long-term disability insurance scheme, the claimant was entitled to benefits provided he remained in employment. His entitlement therefore ceased on taking retirement. Mr Crossly claimed that by failing to alert him to this consequence of taking early retirement, the employers had breached an implied term of the contract of employment. The Court of Appeal rejected the claim. There is no standard implied term in all contracts of employment that an employer will take reasonable care of an employee's well-being, nor an implied duty for an employer to give an employee financial advice in relation to benefits accruing from his employment. This case was distinguishable from *Scally v Southern Health and Social Services Board* **[2.39]** above), because, as a senior manager, the employee could reasonably have been expected to be aware of the relevant provisions of the insurance scheme and the employee also had access to advice from the insurance company.

2.6.3 Risk assessment

The safety of employees in the workplace often depends as much on the information that they may be given about the potential dangers and risks of their jobs as any practical measures to eliminate risks. For this reason, both common law and statute place obligations on the employer to disclose information to employees about risks in the workplace and how to avoid or minimise them. Under the common law, the employer is under a duty grounded in both the tort of negligence and an implied term of the contract to devise a proper system of work. As Lord Reid stated in *General Cleaning Contractors Ltd v Christmas* [1953] AC 180 (HL), 194: 'It is the duty of the employer to consider the situation, to devise a suitable system, to instruct his men what they must do and supply any implements that may be required'. This principle is replicated as one of the general statutory duties of employers, reinforced by criminal penalties.

[2.41] Health and Safety at Work Act 1974, section 2

> **(2)** [the duty of the employer extends to] (c) the provision of such information, instruction, training and supervision as is necessary to ensure, so far as is reasonably practicable, the health and safety at work of his employees.

But more recent regulation, in the hope of achieving prevention of injuries and improvements in safety, has emphasised rather more the need for the employer to carry out assessments of the risks in the workplace, and then to convey that information to the workforce. This requirement of risk assessments is central to the approach of EC law in the general 'framework' Directive, which is a statement of general principles, to be supplemented by more detailed regulations about particular types of work.

[2.42] EC Directive 89/391 measures to encourage improvements in the safety and health of workers [1989] OJ L183/1

Article 10
1. The employer shall take appropriate measures so that workers and/or their representatives in the undertaking and/or establishment receive in accordance with national laws and/or practices which may take account, *inter alia*, of the size of the undertaking and/or establishment, all the necessary information concerning—
   (a) the safety and health risks and protective and preventative measures and activities in respect of both the undertaking and/or establishment in general and each type of workstation and/or job; . . .

[2.43] Management of Health and Safety Regulations 1992, SI 1992/2051

Regulation 3 (1) Every employer shall make a suitable and sufficient assessment of—
   (a) the risks to the health and safety of his employees to which they are exposed whilst they are at work; . . .

Regulation 8 (1) Every employer shall provide his employees with comprehensible and relevant information on—
   (a) the risks to their health and safety identified by the assessment;
   (b) the preventive and protective measures. . .

Other detailed regulations, which in general create minor criminal offences, impose duties on employers to generate and to provide employees with information about particular detailed risks (e.g. Health and Safety (Display Screen Equipment) Regulations 1992). Where breach of these regulations contributes to a worker's personal injury, this breach of statutory duty will usually found a claim for compensation in tort. Employers may not yet appreciate the significance of the duty to carry out risk assessments prior to the commencement of work, since they may typically simply leave a job to be done by an experienced employee.

[2.44] *Swain v Denso Marston Ltd* [2000] ICR 1079 (CA)

Mr Swain's right hand was crushed by a heavy roller in the course of his work as a production fitter. He claimed compensation against the employer in tort, basing the action on the employer's breach of regulation 4(1)(b) of the Manual Handling Operations Regulations 1992. Under that regulation, if it is not reasonably practicable for an employer to avoid the need for employees to undertake any manual handling operations at work which involve a risk of their being injured, the employer shall 'make a suitable and sufficient assessment of all such manual handling operations to be undertaken by them, having regard to the factors which are specified in column 1 of Schedule 1 to these Regulations and considering the questions which are specified in the corresponding entry in column 2 of that Schedule'. . . The employer had instructed the plaintiff as the most experienced and expert worker in the factory to carry out the job on his own. The Court of Appeal found a breach of the Regulations because before the task had commenced the employee should have undertaken a risk assessment under the guidance of the employer's health and safety officer. The employee should have been given time to plan the task, to be given any assistance that might have been required, and to have the opportunity to contact the suppliers of the machinery to obtain detailed information about it. The claimant was awarded an agreed sum of £2040.

2.6.4 Disclosure of business plans to representatives of the workforce

The most contentious duties of disclosure of information imposed upon employers require revelations about the financial position of the business and its future plans to representatives of the workforce. This information is essential for the representatives of the workforce to carry out their functions productively. Yet employers will be reluctant to reveal these plans lest they may provoke industrial action, claims for higher wages, or give some advantage to a competitor. We consider this regulation in detail in chapter 8 in the context of the rights of recognised trade unions and other workplace representatives, and also in chapter 10 in the context of worker participation in decisions to make redundancies and sales of the business. The Information and Consultation of Employees Regulations 2004, SI No 3426, which implement the European Information and Consultation Directive 2002/14, (OJ L 80, 23.3.2002), have the potential to extend the required scope of disclosure of business plans beyond the former restricted requirement of information necessary for the purposes of collective bargaining (TULRCA 1992, section 181(2); below **[8.52]**). The new Regulations also create for the first time the possibility of a penalty being imposed upon the employer for failure to disclose information after having been ordered to do so by the CAC, as opposed to the former remedies of compensation (e.g. a protective award under TULRCA 1992, section 189) or a requirement to conform to new terms and conditions for employees imposed by an award by the CAC (TULRCA 1992, section 185; below 8.5.3).

2.6.5 Confidential information

The parties to a contract of employment usually acquire confidential information about each other. Most employers keep detailed personnel records which contain information that employees may wish to keep private. At the same time, employees learn information about the employer's business, such as the techniques employed in production and marketing. Both parties will often wish to keep this information solely between themselves, that is to keep it confidential. But there are competing policy considerations that place limits on how much information must be regarded as confidential.

2.6.5.1 Employees' obligations

Whilst at work employees may acquire skills, confidential information, trade secrets and other types of knowledge. During the currency of the employment relation, the employee owes a duty of fidelity or loyalty to his or her employer (above 2.5.3) . This implied obligation requires employees not to disclose confidential information to third parties such as rival businesses during the existence of the contract of employment.

Where the employee leaves the job and takes confidential material in breach of the duty of fidelity, a court may issue an injunction (known as a 'springboard injunction') against the employee to restrain him or her from using the information for a period of time, and issue an order to return any physical property.

[2.45] *Roger Bullivant Ltd v Ellis* **[1987] ICR 464 (CA)**

> Mr Ellis, the managing director of the company, resigned and took with him 'the black book' containing trade secrets and a card index of customers. These documents were retrieved by a seizure authorised by the court. The company then sought an injunction to prevent the use of the information, and in particular to prevent Mr Ellis from entering into or fulfilling contracts with any persons listed on the card index who had been contacted when the index was in his possession. The Court of Appeal approved the injunction on the ground that it was issued not so much to protect the company from competition as to prevent Mr Ellis from taking unfair advantage of his breach of the employee's duty of fidelity.

Apart from the special case of 'springboard injunctions', the implied obligation of fidelity in contracts of employment does not persist after the termination of the employment relation. In order to protect confidential information, the employer must either introduce express protection for the information in the contract of employment through a confidentiality clause, or try to persuade a court that the former employee has interfered with the employer's intellectual property rights. These property rights do not extend to all confidential information, but are limited to trade secrets such as secret processes, designs and recipes, and equivalent interests.

[2.46] *Faccenda Chicken Ltd v Fowler* **[1986] ICR 297 (CA)**

> The defendant resigned from his position as sales manager of the plaintiff company, and set himself up in competition by employing staff of the plaintiff. He used knowledge about how the trade worked, how prices were set, and the kinds of customers in the trade, which he had acquired in his former job. His former contract of employment did not contain any express terms regarding the use of confidential information. The company sought an injunction to prevent the defendant from using this information. The claim was unsuccessful.

Neill LJ (giving the judgment of the court):

In these two appeals it will be necessary to consider the interaction of three separate legal concepts. (1) The duty of an employee during the period of his employment to act with good faith towards his employer: this duty is sometimes called the duty of fidelity. (2) The duty of an employee not to use or disclose after his employment has ceased any confidential information which he has obtained during his employment about his employer's affairs. (3) The prima facie right of any person to use and to exploit for the purpose of earning his living all the skill, experience and knowledge which he has acquired in the course of previous periods of employment . . .

(1) Where the parties are, or have been, linked by a contract of employment, the obligations of the employee are to be determined by the contract between him and his employer . . .

(2) In the absence of any express term, the obligations of the employee in respect of the use and disclosure of information are the subject of implied terms.

(3) While the employee remains in the employment of the employer the obligations are included in the implied term which imposes a duty of good faith or fidelity on the employee. For the purposes of the present appeal it is not necessary to consider the precise limits of this implied term, but it may be noted (a) that the extent of the duty of good faith will vary according to the nature of the contract . . . (b) that the duty of good faith will be broken if an employee makes or copies a list of the customers of the employer for use after his employment ends or deliberately memorises such a list, even though, except in special circumstances, there is no restriction on an ex-employee canvassing or doing business with customers of his former employer . . .

(4) The implied term which imposes an obligation on the employee as to his conduct after the determination of the employment is more restricted in its scope than that which imposes a general duty of good faith. It is clear that the obligation not to use or disclose information may cover secret processes of manufacture such as chemical formulae . . . , or designs or special methods of construction . . ., and other information which is of a sufficiently high degree of confidentiality as to amount to a trade secret.

The obligation does not extend, however, to cover all information which is given to or acquired by the employee while in his employment, and in particular may not cover information which is only 'confidential' in the sense that an unauthorised disclosure of such information to a third party while the employment subsisted would be a clear breach of the duty of good faith. . . .

We can well appreciate that in certain circumstances information about prices can be invested with a sufficient degree of confidentiality to render that information a trade secret or its equivalent. The price put forward in a tender document is an obvious example. But there may be many other cases where the circumstances show that a price or prices are matters of great importance and highly confidential. Information about the price to be charged for a new model of a car or some other product or about the prices negotiated, for example, for various grades of oil in a highly competitive market in which it is known that prices are to be kept secret from competitors occur to us as providing possible further instances of information which is entitled to protection as having the requisite degree of confidentiality.

But in the present case the following factors appear to us to lead to the clear conclusion that neither the information about prices nor the sales information as whole had the degree of confidentiality necessary to support the plaintiff's case. We would list these factors as follows. (1) The sales information contained some material which the plaintiffs conceded was not confidential if looked at in isolation. (2) The information about the prices was not clearly severable from the rest of the sales information. (3) Neither the sales information in general, nor the information about the prices in particular, though of some value to a competitor, could reasonably be regarded as plainly secret or sensitive. (4) The sales information, including the information about prices, was necessarily acquired by the defendants in order that they could do their work. Moreover, as the judge observed in the course of his judgment, each salesman could quickly commit the whole of the sales information relating to his own area to memory. (5) The sales information was generally known among the van drivers who were employees, as were the secretaries, at quite a junior level. This was not a case where the relevant information was restricted to senior management or to confidential staff. (6) There was no evidence that the plaintiffs had ever given any express instructions that the sales information or the information about prices was to be treated as confidential. We are satisfied that, in the light of all the matters set out by the judge in his judgment, neither the sales information as a whole nor the information about prices looked at by itself fell within the class of confidential information which an employee is bound by an implied term of his contract of employment or otherwise not to use or disclose after his employment has come to an end.

Accordingly these appeals must be dismissed.

Protection of confidential information which might assist a competitor but which does not count as a trade secret or its equivalent must therefore be achieved through an express term that imposes an obligation to keep certain specified types of information secret after the expiration of the contract of employment. The same effect may be achieved by a clause that restrains the employee from trading in the same line of business for a limited period under a reasonable restraint of trade clause (see Box above p. 91). Although the issue has not been finally determined, it seems likely that an express confidentiality clause will remain effective to bind an employee even after an employer's repudiatory breach of contract: *Campbell v Frisbee* [2002] EWCA Civ 1374, [2003] ICR 141 (CA).

The employer's remedy for breach of the employee's obligation not to divulge confidential information may include an injunction to prevent use of the information and an accounting of any profits made from misuse of the confidential information. This remedy was extended marginally in its application in the following case where the information was no longer confidential.

[2.47] *Attorney General v Blake* **[2001] 1 AC 268 (HL)**

Blake had been a member of the UK intelligence service, but had acted also as a spy for the Soviet Union, for which he was convicted. He escaped from prison, wrote his memoirs, and sold them to a publisher. The Attorney General sought to prevent the payment of royalties to Blake. Under the terms of his contract of employment, Blake had agreed to an express confidentiality clause that applied after the termination of employment. The Attorney General claimed damages for breach of contract assessed by reference to the amount of royalties. Such a claim would have fallen within the existing remedies for breach of confidence if the information had been still confidential, but since the information was about 50 years old and public knowledge, it was no longer confidential, nor was there any damage or loss to the public interest. Nevertheless, the House of Lords, by a majority, permitted, exceptionally, a remedy of 'disgorgement of profits' as the measure of damages for breach of contract. A distinguishing feature of this case was thought to be the breadth of the contractual undertaking that Blake was not to divulge any information, confidential or otherwise, obtained during his service in the intelligence service, for his lifetime, and that, of course, Blake was hoping to obtain the royalties by doing the very thing that he had promised not to do. Lord Hobhouse, dissenting, asserted the orthodox view that a claim for accounting for profits could be successful only if the defendant had used the employer's proprietary rights (e.g. trade secrets) or commercial information still protected by the duty of confidence or fidelity.

2.6.5.2 *Employers' obligations*

Employers collect personal information about workers for many legitimate purposes, such as the payment of taxation, conformity to health and safety regulations, and compliance with discrimination laws. The problem that may arise is that information collected for a legitimate purpose may then be used for some inappropriate purpose, including disclosure to another person without the worker's knowledge or consent. Employees may also seek access to information held about them in order to correct inaccuracies. These problems are now addressed by the Data Protection Act 1998, which is intended to implement EC Directive 95/46 on the processing of personal data. The Data Protection Act 1998 is likely to apply to personnel files, whether kept in electronic form or otherwise, if individuals can be identified from the information. The Act is mostly directed towards personal information, but it may have some wider implications. For example, an employer who uses an automated system for evaluating employees' performance at work has to inform employees about the logic or criteria of that system. But the Act is careful in Schedule 7 to exclude the right of access to confidential employment references, to data concerned with the intentions of the employer with respect to negotiations about the terms of employment, and more generally to the business plans of the employer. In addition, an employer's misuse of personal information may infringe the right to privacy under the Human Rights Act 1998. The details of these legislative safeguards are considered in relation to workplace surveillance (**[6.5]** below).

   In addition to the protection of confidential information provided by statute, the common law may also restrict the purposes for which an employer may divulge information to third parties. An express term of the contract of employment, perhaps incorporated from a collective agreement, may require an employer to keep certain information confidential. Furthermore, it may be possible to prevent disclosure on the ground of an implied obligation of confidentiality, that is an implied duty to use information supplied by the employee only for the purpose for which it was given. This obligation would be equivalent to that owed by an employee during the course of his employment to respect confidential information about the employer. This argument was accepted in principle in pre-trial proceedings, in order to prevent an employer from disclosing information about the names and addresses of employees to a local authority, which had sought the information for the purpose of checking whether or not the employees had paid a local tax (*Dalgleish* v. *Lothian and Borders Police Board* [1991] IRLR 422 (Ct Sess, Outer House)).

2.6.6 Conclusion

Legal regulation of the supply of information in the labour market and during performance of the contract of employment provides a patchwork of measures that often appear ineffective and full of gaps. The heritage of the common law, which from its commercial law perspective permitted the parties to contracts to keep information to themselves and required each party to look after his own interests, fits uneasily onto the expectations of both employer and employee in the context of modern work relations. There the expectation is rather of disclosure of information as part of the implied duties of co-operation and performance in good faith. Although statutes have addressed some issues, there remain striking omissions. Although the employer is required to supply a written statement of the main terms and conditions of employment, there is no obligation to ensure the accuracy or comprehensiveness of this statement. Nor is the employer required to give information to employees about non-contractual rights, such as their statutory entitlements and rights to workplace representation. Legal regulation does not appear to have adjusted to the modern context of elaborate standard form contracts supplemented by extensive organisational rules and statutory regulation, in which it is extremely hard for most employees to know where they stand without the employer supplying the relevant information and advising employees about their entitlements.

2.7 The scope of employment regulation

The legal framework governing employment relations commences with the basic disposition of the common law to grant freedom of contract to the parties. This common law framework has been substantially modified by the increasing use of legislation to impose further supplementary and mandatory rules upon the parties to the employment relation. For this legislation to apply to a particular economic relation, however, it must first identify the characteristics of the economic relations that it governs. The legislation must therefore determine the scope of the application of labour law. The issue of the scope of employment regulation raises fundamental questions about the justifications for labour law.

The need to determine the field of application of regulation looks at first sight as if it poses merely a practical problem. The question is what types of contractual relation should be governed by employment regulation? The issue can be solved by describing the types of contractual relation or the types of parties to a contractual relation that will be covered by the legislation. In the case of unfair dismissal, for instance, the Employment Rights Act 1996 section 94 confers the right not to be unfairly dismissed upon employees working under a contract of employment. But this solution to the problem of determining the scope of mandatory labour law rules is incomplete in three fundamental respects.

First, the application of mandatory rules to particular kinds of contractual relations encounters the problem that the legal classification of contracts lacks precise criteria. In the case of contracts of employment, for instance, there is no convenient formula for distinguishing this economic relation from other kinds of contract through which services are supplied. Two contracts for the provision of a particular service such as carpentry may appear very similar, but the eventual legal classification may differ according to minor contrasts, such as whether the worker is paid by the day or by the job, and whether the worker supplies his or her own tools. By reference to these minor differences the worker may be classified in law as an employee or self-employed (an independent contractor), with the consequence that regulation designed to protect the interests of employees will have no application to those workers classified as self-employed.

This problem of classification of contractual relations for the purposes of social regulation is accentuated by the basic disposition of the common law to grant freedom of contract to the parties. This freedom permits a plethora of types of economic relations to be formed for the provision of work. Although standard patterns emerge in similar types of work, it is always possible for the parties to vary the legal characterisation of the relation by, for example, altering the allocation of a particular risk, such as the risk of the absence of work to be performed. Regulatory legislation often presupposes sharp and standardised conceptual contrasts between contractual types that do not exist in practice: each contractual relation is liable to be idiosyncratic in its allocation of risks, with the result that classification is a complex and indeterminate process.

Secondly, the proper scope of application of any particular mandatory legislation will always be controversial at the margins. It may be agreed, for instance, that the law of unfair dismissal should apply to employees working under a contract of employment, but should the law also apply to a person providing professional services such as a lawyer, or a skilled carpenter contracted to perform a particular job, or the franchisee of a distribution outlet? It seems to make sense to exclude these types of workers from the scope of unfair dismissal legislation, because they appear to be running independent businesses. But this legal form may in fact conceal the kind of authority structure that is typical of employment relations and that the law of unfair dismissal was expected to regulate. These workers may in practice perform services solely for one employer, be subject to detailed instructions and control from that employer, and termination of the contract for some unfounded or irrelevant reason may be as offensive and economically damaging to these workers as the dismissal of an employee. Reliance upon the contractual form of the relation between the parties therefore may not correlate with the social issue that the regulatory legislation is designed to address.

Realisation of this problem of formal classification forces us to reflect further on the exact nature of the harm that the regulation is designed to relieve, and to try to use that purpose in order to guide the scope of the application of the regulation. Once this step has been taken, however, we appreciate that employment regulation addresses a variety of social harms that appear to require different fields of application. For example, the law of unfair dismissal seems to be aimed against the abuse of the managerial power to terminate contracts for work, but the law regarding safety in the workplace seems to be equally applicable to anyone present at the workplace, whether they be employees, independent businesses or simply visitors to the site. The proper scope of application for other regulation is even less clear in other cases. Consider the example of sex discrimination: should the law seek to combat sex discrimination in cases beyond contracts of employment in contracts made by an individual to perform services, as for example where a small business with a few employees, owned and managed by a woman, is turned down for a contract on discriminatory grounds? The purposive application of employment regulation raises the difficult question of how to determine its proper scope of application whilst making satisfactory distinctions between the objectives of different pieces of regulation.

Finally, the legislation needs to consider the extent to which it should permit the parties to exclude its application by arranging their economic relation through different contractual forms. For instance, if the law of unfair dismissal is correctly limited to contracts of employment, should it be permissible for the parties to create a contract for services that avoids the legal incidents of an employment relation, thereby avoiding the application of the mandatory legislation? Should the employer of the carpenter in our earlier example be permitted to avoid the law of unfair dismissal by merely rewriting the contract to make the carpenter an independent contractor rather than an employee? By tying mandatory social legislation to particular contractual forms, an invitation is presented to employers to avoid the legislation by selecting a different contractual form. The questions posed by such a practice are whether this avoidance is undesirable, and also whether anything can be done to prevent it?

We now develop the discussion of these three issues in turn: how does the law classify contractual relations involving work? What should be the proper scope of application of labour laws? To what extent should freedom of contract be permitted to determine the scope of application of employment regulation? In answering these questions, we need to become more aware of the variety of contractual forms through which work can be performed.

2.7.1 Classification of contractual relations

The problem of determining the limits of legal obligations by reference to types of contractual relation is not unique to labour regulation. Indeed, the courts have been wrestling with the proper scope of application of common law principles and other types of legal regulation to contracts involving the performance of services for centuries. For example, tax and social security laws distinguish between work performed under a contract of employment and services supplied under other types of contract. One important difference is that employers under a contract of employment are required to deduct income tax and social security payments before payment of wages, whereas employers under other contracts for services incur no such obligation. In the common law, the liability of employers to compensate workers who have been injured has turned traditionally on the question whether or not the worker was an employee. If the worker was an employee, the employer certainly owed the employee an extensive duty of care, whereas if the worker was an independent contractor providing professional services, the employer might owe no duty of care in respect of the performance of work, because the independent contractor was supposed to take care of himself. Furthermore, if an employee caused loss to another person by a tortious act committed in the course of employment, the employer would be vicariously liable for that tort, whereas this 'enterprise liability' was not attached to the torts committed by independent contractors or to employees acting in a way that lacked a 'sufficient connection' to their duties under the contract of employment (*Lister v Hesley Hall Ltd* [2002] 1 AC 215 (HL); S. Deakin, 'Enterprise-Risk: The Juridicial Nature of the Firm Revisited' (2003) 32 *Industrial Law Journal* 97). This common law distinction between contracts of employment (contracts of service) and independent contractors (contracts for services) established a confusing body of precedents for determining which contractual relations should be regarded as contracts of employment. The next case provides a modern illustration of the operation of this distinction in the law of tort.

[2.48] *Lane v Shire Roofing Company (Oxford) Ltd* [1995] IRLR 493 (CA)

The plaintiff suffered severe head injuries in 1986 when he fell off a ladder whilst working on a roof. The plaintiff claimed compensation from the company, but the claim failed at first instance on the ground that he was a self-employed contractor, not an employee of the company, and therefore the company owed him no duty of care at common law. This reasoning was supported by the facts that the plaintiff was categorised as 'self-employed' for tax purposes, that he had traded as a one-man firm doing roofing business, that he used his own equipment, and that he worked for a fee without supervision. The defendant company, which was also a small business, avoided having many employees, but rather subcontracted particular jobs. In this particular instance, the company had agreed a fixed fee of £200 for the plaintiff to perform the job for the company's customer (the Birds at Sonning Common). The Court of Appeal allowed the appeal and awarded damages of £102,500, after a deduction of 50 per cent for the plaintiff's contributory negligence. On the question whether the plaintiff was an employee or an independent contractor, the Court made the following observations.

Henry LJ:
The next question is whether the respondents owed to the plaintiff the common law or statutory duty of an employer to his employees, or whether the appellant when doing that job was acting as an independent contractor. When it comes to the question of safety at work, there is a real public interest in recognising the employer/employee relationship when it exists, because of the responsibilities that the common law and statutes such as the Employers' Liability (Compulsory Insurance) Act 1969 place on the employer.

The judge was to find that the appellant was not an employee, but was an independent contractor. In that event the appellant would have been responsible for his own safety; the respondent would have owned him no duty of care, and would have had no responsibility (statutory or at common law) for the safety of the work done by the appellant. That was the context in which the question was asked.

We were taken through the standard authorities on this matter: *Readymix Concrete (South East) Ltd v Minister of Pensions and National Insurance* [1968] 2 QB 497; *Market Investigations Ltd v Minister of Social Security* [1969] 2 QB 173 [[2.51] below]; and *Ferguson v Dawson & Partners (Contractors) Ltd* [1976] IRLR 346, to name the principal ones. Two general remarks should be made. The overall employment background is very different today (and was, though less so, in 1986) than it had been at the time when those cases were decided. First, for a variety of reasons there are more self-employed and fewer in employment. There is a greater flexibility in employment, with more temporary and shared employment. Second, there are perceived advantages for both workman and employer in the relationship between them being that of independent contractor. From the workman's point of view, being self-employed brings him into a more benevolent and less prompt taxation regime. From the employer's point of view, the protection of employee's rights contained in the employment protection legislation of the 1970s brought certain perceived disincentives to the employer to take on full-time long-term employees. So even in 1986 there were reasons on both sides to avoid the employee label. But, as I have already said, there were, and are, good policy reasons in the safety at work field to ensure that the law properly categorises between employees and independent contractors.

That line of authority shows that there are many factors to be taken into account in answering this question, and, with different priority being given to those factors in different cases, all depends on the facts of each individual case. Certain principles relevant to this case, however, emerge.

First, the element of control will be important: who lays down what is to be done, the way in which it is to be done, the means by which it is to be done, and the time when it is done? Who provides (i.e. hires and fires) the team by which it is done, and who provides the material, plant and machinery and tools used?

But it is recognised that the control test may not be decisive—for instance, in the case of skilled employees, with discretion to decide how their work should be done. In such cases the question is broadened to whose business was it? Was the workman carrying on his own business, or was he carrying on that of his employers? The American Supreme Court, in *United States of America v Silk* (1946) 331 US 704, asks the question whether the men were employees 'as a matter of economic reality'. The answer to this question may cover much of the same ground as the control test (such as whether he provides his own equipment and hires his own helpers) but may involve looking to see where the financial risk lies, and whether and how far he has an opportunity of profiting from sound management in the performance of his task (see *Market Investigations v Minister of Social Security, supra*, at p 185).

And these questions must be asked in the context of who is responsible for the overall safety of the men doing the work in question. Mr Whittaker, [owner/manager of the company], . . . was cross-examined on these lines and he agreed that he was so responsible. Such an answer is not decisive (though it may be indicative) because ultimately the question is one of law, and he could be wrong as to where the legal responsibility lies (see *Ferguson v Dawson, supra*, at 1219G) . . .

The judge's reasons for finding that the appellant was an independent contractor, not an employee, were these:

'The defendant company (which was really Mr Whittaker's company) had only been in operation for six months and it would obviously be of advantage to him to be able to enter into contracts with other people for specific works without having a continuous payroll for those parts. I consider it important that the plaintiff himself had his own genuine roofing business, so that he was a roofing specialist, and he had the benefit of 714 certificates so that he could pay his own tax and was paid gross. He continued with that system while he was working on contracts for the defendant company. I note that the plaintiff was obviously capable of working without supervision and that Mr Whittaker relied upon him to do so, although it seems that Mr Whittaker was subsequently rather disappointed with the quality of the plaintiff's work and subsequently thought that the plaintiff had more experience with clay tiles than the artificial slates which he was using on the final contract. There was no guarantee given by Mr Whittaker of continuing work for the defendant, no provision for notice or dismissal and, as pointed out by Mr Matthews, that would have been unnecessary if this was genuine sub-contracting work, because each job had to be taken on its own and there was no guarantee that the plaintiff would be employed thereafter, though both the plaintiff and Mr Whittaker were obviously anticipating that further jobs would arise which Mr Whittaker could give to the plaintiff. In all the circumstances, therefore, I find that the plaintiff was an independent contractor throughout the time that he was working for the defendant company and in particular, of course, on the contract in question at the Birds's'.

Each of those four reasons given by the judge would apply equally to the work being done under a short-term single job contract of employment. All of them concentrate on what Mr Whittaker wanted, and not on whose business it was. Mr Matthews, for the respondents, rightly distinguishes between a *Ferguson v Dawson* situation, where an employer engages men on 'the lump' to do labouring work (where the men are clearly employees, whatever their tax status may be), and when a specialist sub-contractor is employed to perform some part of a general building contract. That team or individual clearly will be an independent contractor. He submits that the appellant in this case falls somewhere in between. With that I would agree, but would put this case substantially nearer 'the lump' than the specialist sub-contractor. Though the degree of control that Mr Whittaker would use would depend on the need he felt to supervise and direct the appellant (who was just someone answering the advertisement) the question 'Whose business was it?' in relation to the Sonning Common job could only in my judgment be answered by saying that it was the respondents' business and not the appellant's. In my judgment, therefore, they owed the duties of employers to the appellant. Consequently, for my part I would find that the first ground of appeal against the judge's judgment succeeds . . .

The origin of this common law distinction between employees and independent contractors in the law of tort explains why such emphasis is placed upon such factors as control and the allocation of risks of profit. If the alleged employer has no control over how the work is performed, it is hard to see how an employer can fairly be held responsible either for the worker's negligence under the principles of vicarious liability or for any self-inflicted injuries to the worker. The relevance of the allocation of risk to the question of liability in tort is that through the doctrine of vicarious liability the pattern has been set of holding enterprises responsible for the risks that they create during productive activities. But one capital unit such as a firm is not responsible for the risks created by another enterprise, an independent contractor. These factors devised for drawing the limits to liability in tort make sense in that context, though as the *Lane* case illustrates, their application in particular instances such as services provided by skilled craftsmen provokes considerable difficulty.

This traditional common law distinction between employees and independent contractors appears to create the type of sharp conceptual contrast required for determining the application of labour regulation. Many employment rights have been tied to the existence of a contract of employment. These rights include statutory minimum notice periods, the right to a written statement of terms and conditions, maternity rights, unfair dismissal, redundancy payments, statutory sick pay, protection from action short of dismissal for being a member of a trade union, and rights in the event of insolvency and the sale of the business. The flaw in this approach to determining the scope of regulation by reference to the classification of the contract lies in the flexibility granted by the common law to create specially tailored contractual relations. By using this flexibility creatively, an employer can obtain equivalent services, with better control over work, but without using a contract of employment, or, more precisely, without using a contractual form that a court might identify as constituting a contract of employment.

The principal technique for achieving this goal of efficient acquisition of labour power without using a contract of employment is to transfer as many business risks as possible onto the worker. The types of risks that are shifted are that the employee will not work diligently or carefully, the chance that unforeseen contingencies will hamper or obstruct performance of the job, and the likelihood of a shortage of work. By transferring all or most of these risks onto the worker, by for example using a piecework payment system or offering casual employment only when the employer has a requirement for work to be done, the employer not only gains protection against the possible adverse consequence of the materialisation of these risks, but also is likely to reduce the chance that the worker will be regarded as an employee at all. The reason for this legal effect is that the allocation of business risks has traditionally been regarded as one of the decisive criteria for distinguishing between employees and independent contractors. This emphasis upon the significance of risk allocation was stated most clearly in the following much cited passage.

[2.49] *Market Investigations v Minister of Social Security* **[1969] 2 QB 173 (HC)**

Cooke J:
The observations of Lord Wright, of Denning LJ, and of the judges of the Supreme Court in the USA suggest that the fundamental test to be applied is this: 'Is the person who has engaged himself to perform these services performing them as a person in business on his own account?' If the answer to that question is 'yes', then the contract is a contract for services. If the answer is 'no' then the contract is a contract of service. No exhaustive list has been compiled and perhaps no exhaustive list can be compiled of considerations which are relevant in determining that question, nor can strict rules be laid down as to the relative weight which the various considerations should carry in particular cases. The most that can be said is that control will no doubt always have to be considered, although it can no longer be regarded as the sole determining factor; and that factors, which may be of importance, are such matters as whether the man performing the services provides his own equipment, whether he hires his own helpers, what degree of financial risk he takes, what degree of responsibility for investment and management he has, and whether and how far he has an opportunity of profiting from sound management in the performance of his task'.

The effect of the significance attached to risk allocation in determining the classification of contracts involving the performance of services is that the more risks that a worker agrees to bear under the common law doctrine of freedom of contract, the less likely it is that he or she will be classified as an employee, with the consequence that he or she will be excluded from many employment protection rights. For example, where the terms of the contract provide that the worker will supply a substitute worker whenever he or she is unable to perform the work personally, this allocation of the risk of sickness or injury to the worker is usually regarded as inconsistent with a contract of employment. This practice of undertaking to provide a substitute worker is common among lorry drivers. As a consequence of assuming the risk of illness or absence, the drivers are classified as independent contractors: *Express & Echo Publications Ltd v Tanton* [1999] ICR 693 (CA); *Ready Mixed Concrete (South East) Ltd v Minister of Pensions and National Insurance* [1968] 2 QB 49. But the employee's ability to appoint a substitute worker to perform the work will not prevent a finding of a contract of employment, if the employer reserves the power to approve the substitute and substitution is only permitted when the employee is unable to perform the work personally through illness or some other reason foreseen in the contract: *Byrne Bros (Formwork) Ltd v Baird* [2002] ICR 667 (EAT). In the following case, the workers assumed the risk of the unavailability of work by working as 'casuals'. Their acceptance of this risk of partial unemployment led the court to conclude that they were not employees, with the consequence that the workers could not receive the protection afforded by the law of unfair dismissal to the right to belong to a trade union.

[2.50] *O'Kelly v Trusthouse Forte* [1984] QB 90 (CA)

Some waiters at a hotel, who were also stewards of their union, claimed unfair dismissal and interim relief against dismissal (under ERA 1996 section 128] on the ground that the reason for dismissal was their membership of a trade union. Due to the fluctuating demand for banquets and private functions, the employer had a small number of permanent staff plus a pool of casual waiters, who regularly supplied services when called upon, and who were paid at a set rate for each job. Some of these 'regulars', including the applicants, worked for no other employer, and in practice worked almost every week of the year for between 30–40 hours per week on average. The waiters worked under the supervision of the hotel's management, were paid weekly on the company's computer payroll, and had tax and social security deducted as employees. Although the casual waiters were not legally obliged to perform any job, if they refused they would be dropped or suspended from the list of those regularly asked to work. The letters of 'dismissal' were statements that the applicants would not be asked to work again. The industrial tribunal rejected the claim for unfair dismissal on the ground that the applicants were not employees under contracts of employment and therefore had no statutory right. The tribunal reached this conclusion by considering a number of factors, but placed great weight on the lack of 'mutuality of obligation', that is the absence of a duty on the employer to supply work and on the employee to work when requested, together with the presumed intention of the parties based upon the custom of the trade to regard casuals as independent contractors. The tribunal rejected the waiters' claim that they worked under contracts of employment either in the form of an 'umbrella contract' which persisted all the time, or under separate contracts of employment each time that they worked at a function. On appeal, the EAT reversed the decision, but the Court of Appeal restored the decision of the tribunal.

Sir John Donaldson MR:
In the instant appeal the industrial tribunal directed itself to 'consider all aspects of the relationship, no single factor being in itself decisive and each of which may vary in weight and direction, and having given such balance to the factors as seems appropriate, to determine whether the person was carrying on business on his own account.' This is wholly correct as a matter of law and it is not for this court or for the appeal tribunal to re-weigh the facts.

The industrial tribunal then concluded that there was no contract of employment extending over a series of engagements. This conclusion was based upon an evaluation of the large number of factors set out in their reasons, but it is clear that the majority attached great importance to the fact that, as they saw it, there was no mutuality of obligation and that in the industry casual workers were not regarded as working under any overall contract of employment.

The appeal tribunal refused to interfere with this conclusion and in my judgment they were right to do so. So far as mutuality is concerned, the 'arrangement,' to use a neutral term, could have been that the company promised to offer work to the regular casuals and, in exchange, the regular casuals undertook to accept and perform such work as was offered. This would have constituted a contract. But what happened in fact could equally well be attributed to market forces. Which represented the true view could only be determined by the tribunal which heard the witnesses and evaluated the facts. Again, although how the industry and its casual workers regarded their status is not directly material, any generally accepted view would be part of the contractual matrix and so indirectly material, although in no way decisive. This again was a matter for the industrial tribunal.

Although I, like the appeal tribunal, am content to accept the industrial tribunal's conclusion that there was no overall or umbrella contract, I think that there is a shorter answer. It is that giving the applicants' evidence its fullest possible weight, all that could emerge was an umbrella or master contract for, not of, employment. It would be a contract to offer and accept individual contracts of employment and, as such, outside the scope of the unfair dismissal provisions.

This leaves the question of whether the applicants entered into individual contracts of employment on each occasion when they worked for the company and it is here that the appeal tribunal and the industrial tribunal parted company. The appeal tribunal dealt with this aspect of the matter by saying:

> 'For whatever reason, the industrial tribunal have not dealt with the point, nor have they weighed the factors bearing on the question: 'was each contract for services?' in the same careful way in which they weighed those factors when looking at the nature of an overall contract of employment. In our judgment, the mere assertion by the industrial tribunal that it was a succession of contracts for services entered into by independent contractors cannot stand as good in law in the absence of any reason for that conclusion. We must therefore consider the point and reach our own decision on it'.

This, in my judgment, does less than justice to the decision of the industrial tribunal. It had weighed the relevant factors governing the relationship between the parties with great care in the course of determining whether any umbrella contract was one of employment or for the provision of services. It had rejected the umbrella contract on the grounds that there was no contract at all, but it had also concluded:

> 'the applicants were in business on their own account as independent contractors supplying services and are not qualified for interim relief because they were not employees who worked under a contract of employment'.

This, unless erroneous in law, was wholly sufficient reason for holding that the individual contracts, which clearly existed, were contracts for the provision of services. If and in so far as the appeal tribunal was criticising the industrial tribunal for failing to say so, it should be pointed out that there was only one question which it had to decide, namely, whether the applicants were employees who worked under a contract of employment. It answered this question in the negative as a matter for decision under the heading 'Decision.' The purpose of what followed under the heading 'Reasons' was to explain this decision. Those reasons, by explaining that there was no umbrella contract and that the applicants were independent contractors, disposed in different ways of the two different forms of contract of employment which had been suggested in argument. The fact that the argument was primarily about the umbrella contract does not persuade me that the status of the individual contracts was not carefully considered, particularly as Ms Gill, who appeared for the applicants, says that she argued in the alternative for a succession of individual contracts of employment. Furthermore, in the light of the industrial tribunal's finding of lack of mutuality in relation to the umbrella contract the only point of considering 'service v. services' was in relation to the individual contracts. . . .

In pursuance of this declared intention to reach its own decision, the appeal tribunal reviewed and re-evaluated the various factors, concluding that there was a series of ad hoc contracts of employment. In so doing, in my judgment it quite clearly usurped the function of the industrial tribunal. This was not a case in which no reasonable tribunal could have reached the conclusion reached by the industrial tribunal and no reasonable tribunal could have failed to reach that reached by the appeal tribunal. The industrial tribunal's decision may have been surprising, but it was certainly not 'perverse' in the legal or any other sense.

The appeal tribunal justified its own conclusion by saying:

'Standing back and looking at the matter in the round, what we have to ask is whether these applicants can be said to have been carrying on business on their own account. We can well understand that casuals who have their services to sell, and sell them in the market to whoever needs them for the time being, can be said to be in business on their own account in the marketing or selling of their services; but we find it difficult to reach that conclusion in a situation where the services are, in fact, being offered to one person only against a background arrangement (albeit not contractual) which requires the services to be offered to one person only and which involves a repetition of those contracts (albeit under no obligation to do so) as is shown by the weekly pay packet, the holiday pay and other matters of that kind. In our judgment, each of these individual contracts is a contract of employment, not a contract for services'.

This must involve a misdirection on a question of law or every independent contractor who is content or able only to attract one client would be held to work under a contract of employment. Indeed, I could as well point out that what distinguishes the applicants' contracts from those of waiters who admittedly work under contracts of employment is that the applicants were employed to wait at a given function and were not available to the company for general deployment as waiters during their hours of work. But if I did so, I too should be usurping the functions of the industrial tribunal.

I can detect no error of law on the part of the industrial tribunal and I would therefore allow the appeal and dismiss the cross-appeal, thereby restoring the decision of the industrial tribunal.

The reasoning in *O'Kelly* placed considerable weight on the evidence of customs in the trade to discover the intentions of the parties. This evidence highlighted the widespread practice of employers in the catering industry of failing either to issue written particulars of employment or to give any notice of dismissal. The waiters were seeking to contest these practices as abuses and breaches of statutory entitlements. The tribunal used these practices, however, to justify the conclusion that no employment relations had been formed. It seems that the more that employers ignore statutory entitlements for employees, the more likely it is that a tribunal will accept that there was no employment relation from which statutory rights arose.

In so far as the decision in *O'Kelly* rejects the idea of umbrella contracts of employment, it can be supported. Unless the framework agreement contains obligations on the employer to supply work and on the employee to work when required, there may be no 'consideration' or 'mutuality of obligation' to support any kind of contract at all. This view of the position of casual workers was confirmed in *Carmichael v National Power Plc* [1999] ICR 1226 (HL), where tour guides used by an employer as required and when they were available were found not to have any long-term contract at all. Even if such a binding 'requirements contract' can be discovered, this arrangement may not be a contract of employment in itself, but rather as Sir John Donaldson MR suggested in *O'Kelly*, a form of option contract. In some umbrella contracts both parties may undertake some obligations, thereby establishing consideration, but unless those obligations include an obligation to provide work and for the employee to do the work personally when offered, the contract will not be regarded as a contract of employment (e.g. *Mingeley v Pennock and Ivory [2004] EWCA Civ 328* (**[2.59]** below)). It is possible, however, that a court might infer an obligation on the employer to provide work on a regular basis and on the employee to accept it, based upon the course of dealing between the parties and any express or implied undertakings of the parties, thus creating the possibility of a long-term contract of employment.

[2.51] *Nethermere (St. Neots) Ltd v. Gardiner* **[1984] ICR 612 (CA)**

The applicants had worked for several years, though not every week, at home sewing boys' trousers for the company. There were no fixed hours of work, payment was by reference to the piece, and the applicants were not obliged to accept any fixed amount of work. They claimed unfair dismissal when the company dispensed with their services following a dispute. The industrial tribunal decided that the applicants were employees for the purpose of bringing a claim for unfair dismissal. The Court of Appeal, by a majority, upheld this decision, finding that the tribunal had not misdirected itself in law. The Court approved of the tribunal's finding of an 'umbrella contract' of employment, because there was evidence from the dealings between the company and the workers that there was in fact a mutual obligation to offer work and to accept it, though the quantities and timing were flexible. For example, employees who would be unable to undertake work in a particular week would notify the company in advance, and the company ensured that the work was evenly distributed among their eleven homeworkers unless they requested otherwise.

The most unsatisfactory aspect of *O'Kelly* v. *Trust House Forte Plc* was the surprising conclusion of the industrial tribunal that when the waiters worked at each banquet they were not working under short-term contracts of employment. Later decisions have tended to discover such short-term contracts of employment for casual workers. In *Carmichael* v. *National Power Plc* [1999] ICR 1226 (HL), though unnecessary for the decision in that case, Lord Hoffmann suggested that probably the casual 'as required' tour guides worked under short-term contracts of employment when they actually performed the service. Similarly, in *McMeechan v Secretary of State for Employment* [1997] ICR 549 (CA) (**[2.64]** below) a temporary agency worker was found to have a contract of employment with the agency when the worker actually performed work by way of an assignment to a client. Even so, Lord Donaldson was correct in *O'Kelly* to point out that the mere fact that someone only performs work for a single client, that is he is in practice a 'dependent entrepreneur', does not in itself prevent that worker from being regarded as an independent contractor as opposed to an employee.

2.7.2 Flexibility and atypical workers

As Henry LJ observed in the *Lane* case, the problem of determining the application of regulation and legal obligations to particular kinds of economic relations such as the contract of employment has been exacerbated since the 1980s by changes in the way in which employers seek to acquire labour that have been described loosely as a search for flexibility. Instead of employers acquiring labour power through standard, full-time, contracts of employment, located within an internal labour market, there has been a willingness to consider other kinds of flexible working relations. From a historical perspective, we should note that all the different kinds of contracts for the performance of work have been used extensively in the past. Some early contractual forms, such an internal contracting with a gang of workers (see box below, p. 169), have become less common, whereas others, such as external contracting or out-sourcing, as in the case of the homeworkers in *Nethermere (St Neots) Ltd v Gardiner*, above, have increased.

What seems to be new is the extent to which the model that became dominant in the first half of the twentieth century, the full-time contract of employment, has declined as a proportion of the workforce to about 50 per cent. Non-standard forms of work may be classified in a number of ways, by reference to hours, location, pay-ment systems, legal incidents of the relation, and so forth. A particular worker may be non-standard in several respects: part-time, working at home, payment for tasks completed, using a particular classification for tax purposes.

The largest group of non-standard workers, representing about 25% of the workforce, is part-time employees. This category can be defined by reference to upper limits of hours of work, such as 18 hours or 12 hours per week, or by reference to their level of earnings below a certain threshold such as the income tax threshold. For current labour law purposes, however, the definition of part-time work is simply less than full-time employees in the same establishment or undertaking. Part-time work is often an important strategy for workers to manage the balance between earning a wage and caring for dependants, so we will consider the detailed regulation of part-time work in Chapter 4 in the context of the work/life balance. Here we should note that the growth in part-time work was almost certainly driven by the need for employers to obtain flexibility in the number of workers available at particular times rather than the preferences of workers for shorter hours.

One way to account for the proliferation of all types of non-standard work is to understand that in part it is an effect of a particular management strategy, which is known as the development of the flexible firm.

[2.52] J. Atkinson 'Flexibility or Fragmentation? The UK Labour Market in the Eighties' (1987) 12 *Labour and Society* 87 (footnotes omitted)

Employers' flexibility priorities

So far as British employers are concerned there appear to be three broad approaches to internal labour market flexibility.

1. *Numerical flexibility:* Numerical flexibility is the ability of firms to adjust the number of workers or the level of worked hours, in line with changes in the level of demand for them. It is therefore concerned with employers' ability to adjust employment levels to workload, period by period. As that workload fluctuates (i.e. the use of additional workers) or by changing the distribution of worked time (i.e. the use of existing workers). The main determinants of how they do this appear to be (*a*) the scale, frequency and predictability of these workload fluctuations; (*b*) the legal, administrative and labour market possibilities for securing additional workers who will not enjoy continuity of employment; and (*c*) the nature of the jobs in question.

Of course, firms have always required numerical flexibility to some extent, but undoubtedly the pressures on employers to achieve it have intensified recently; output fluctuations have become larger, more frequent and/or more unpredictable, and companies have become less able to bear the short-term costs of not being numerically flexible. In addition, the opportunities to pursue numerical flexibility have also increased. Legal deregulation has somewhat increased the potential for using additional short term and/or part time and/or contract workers, but in the United Kingdom legislation has never been a serious constraint in this regard. More important has been an increase in the supply of labour likely to accept the jobs so produced, attendant on increasing unemployment and rising female participation rates.

2. *Functional flexibility:* Just as numerical flexibility is concerned with how employers adjust the numbers of people employed or the hours they work to changing workload levels, so functional flexibility is concerned with how they adjust the deployment of those people and the contents of their jobs to meet the changing tasks generated by that workload. Functional flexibility is the ability of firms to reorganise jobs, so that the jobholder can deploy his or her skills across a broader range of tasks. Such a redeployment may be sequential (e.g. redeployment out of a redundant job) or involve the simultaneous use of old and new skills; it may be permanent or temporary; it may involve working up into a higher skilled job, working down into a less skilled job or shifting between functions.

The need for functional flexibility has also been increasing. The dominant pressures leading employers towards increasing their workforces' functional flexibility seem therefore to be technological and organisational. Job boundaries are being blurred by technological change and this is accelerating. At the same time, reducing headcount increases pressure to spread a smaller workforce over a given number of tasks.

3. *Distancing:* Distancing represents the displacement of employment contracts by commercial contracts, as exemplified by sub-contracting. It is really an alternative to flexibility, rather than another form of flexibility. Thus, rather than organise its own workforce flexibly to meet peaks in workload, a company may simply contract out those peaks to another individual or organisation. Similarly, if it finds that another firm can achieve functional flexibility more readily than itself, it may opt to buy in that capacity rather than keep it in-house. Distancing strategies are increasing too, as competitive pressures lead United Kingdom firms to specialise in areas of comparative advantage, leaving other areas to those whose comparative advantage they are. In addition, cost-cutting programmes lead to distancing if outsiders are able to achieve economies of scale, exert monopsony buying power, achieve greater workforce flexibility, pay lower wages, etc. . . .

From what has gone before, it should be clear that while United Kingdom firms demonstrate implicitly many of these characteristics within their internal labour market, it is only a small minority who have explicitly and consciously divided up their workforce in this way. Most simply demonstrate tendencies in this direction. But for the labour market as a whole this is sufficient to produce a substantial growth of secondary/peripheral forms of employment in virtually every sector. For the United Kingdom this is not in doubt; all the available evidence, on part-timers, self-employment, casual and temporary work, subcontracting and agency employment point to substantial growth since 1979. . . .

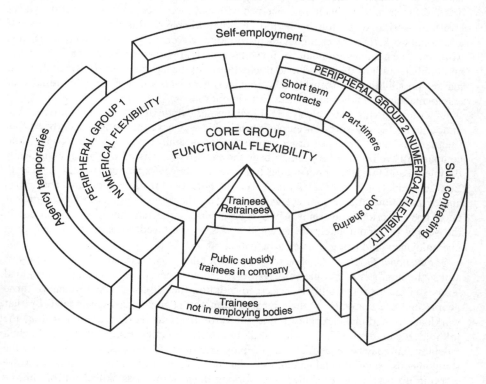

Figure 2.1 *The flexible firm*

The facts of *O'Kelly v Trust House Forte Plc* (above [2.50]) and *Nethermere (St. Neots) Ltd v Gardiner* (above [2.51]) illustrate this model of the flexible firm in operation. The employers have a core staff, but obtain numerical and functional flexibility by being able to draw upon a pool of regular casual workers with a variety of specialised skills.

Although the extent to which employers adopted this model of the flexible firm as a coherent and sustained managerial strategy has been contested, (e.g. L. Hunter, A. McGregor, J. MacInnes and A. Sproul, 'The "Flexible Firm": Strategy and Segmentation' (1993) 31 *British Journal of Industrial Relations* 385) there can be little doubt that during the 1980s there was a considerable increase in non-standard forms of work. In other words, instead of the vast majority of the workforce being employed under contracts for full-time work of indefinite duration, the pattern changed with the rise of part-time work, self-employment, temporary work and casual work. It is also true, however, that variations of the flexible firm have been common since the inception of the industrial revolution: see box on Internal Contracting. Owing to the underlying commitment of the common law to freedom of contract, the legal system placed no brake on this transformation of work relations. The crucial legal question was rather whether or not these non-standard forms of work were covered by employment protection regulation. These workers might be excluded on a number of grounds: that they were not employees, that they lacked continuity of employment sufficient to satisfy a qualifying period for a particular right, that the hours of work were too short to satisfy a condition of entitlement, or that the rate of pay was too low to qualify for an entitlement. There was a widespread suspicion that part of the employer's reason for the use of non-standard work relations was precisely for the purpose of the avoidance of employment protection legislation, thereby saving costs for the employer.

Detailed studies of the use of atypical forms of employment reveal a more complex picture, with the avoidance of regulatory social policy usually a very minor consideration. A typical reason of employers for using part-time work was simply to achieve longer operating times, such as shop opening hours, without having to pay overtime rates of pay, and to be able to respond quickly to fluctuations in demand. The use of outsourcing from independent contractors might also reflect the need to

---

Internal Contracting

Under this contractual arrangement, which was used extensively in factories and transport in the nineteenth century, the employer arranges with the leader of a group of workers a fixed price for a job to be performed, leaving the issue of the distribution of the wages to the leader. Workers often disliked this system, because the leader could determine wages in a discretionary way. From the employer's perspective, however, the system could be efficient because the level of wages was depressed by competition between groups for the work, and the arrangement also compelled co-operation between the workers. From a legal perspective it is not at all clear who is the employer of the worker, the main employer or the leader of the group, and whether the worker's contract is a contract of employment. Although trade unions managed to abolish this system of contractual relations in most industries, it still occurs today in some sectors. In *New Century Cleaning Co Ltd v Church* [2000] IRLR 27 CA, the company operated a business of cleaning windows in large buildings by hiring a team of workers with a leader to perform a particular job for a fixed price, leaving it to the leader to inform the employer what proportion of the price should be awarded to each worker as wages. The legal question in this case was whether the employer had imposed an unlawful deduction from wages when it reduced its price for all jobs by 10%. A majority of the Court held that there had been no deduction from wages, since the wages of each worker did not depend upon a fixed proportion of the total price, and therefore the level of remuneration had not been fixed by any contract of employment with the employer. Sedley LJ, dissenting, argued that in industrial reality all the workers had suffered a 10% wage cut, and that to focus upon the terms of the contract was to ignore the purpose of the legislation to protect workers against unilateral wage cuts by employers. Mark Freedland argues persuasively that the correct question should have been whether an implied term of the contract of employment with the company limited its discretion to vary unilaterally the price for jobs: 'Deductions, Red Herrings, and the Wage-Work Bargain' (1999) 28 *Industrial Law Journal* 255.

Homeworkers

Many people work at home or work from home for part of the week, and the number is rising, perhaps reaching as many as 2 million or 10% of the UK workforce. In the past, homeworkers have typically been low-paid, casual workers, being paid by the piece, with contested status as employees, as in *Nethermere (St. Neots) Ltd v Gardiner* ([2.51] above). With the advent of telecommunications, including computers and the Internet, however, it has become possible for many types of service work to be performed from home. These 'teleworkers' may perform basic clerical tasks, such as data inputting, though they may also be skilled workers (as in the example of copy editors), professionals, including lawyers, or highly paid consultants. These skilled workers often only work from home for part of the time. These developments of the 'Information Age' suggest that the sharp distinction between home and workplace created by the industrial revolution will be effaced to some extent. These working arrangements can prove attractive to workers because they may offer flexible hours, the avoidance of commuting, the accommodation of a disability, and more autonomy in work. Employers may save on office and equipment costs, and may be able to recruit better skilled workers. There are dangers for workers in such jobs, however, such as the hidden costs of supplying office space at home (e.g. heating, insurance), stress arising from combining work and child care simultaneously, and exclusion from information and opportunities such as training and advancement in a career structure. These different types of homeworker engender similar problems for legal regulation as other types of atypical workers, such as whether they are employees, but they present a crucial additional problem that it is extremely difficult to monitor compliance with labour standards. For example, how can an employer or an inspector monitor the hours of work to ensure that rest breaks are taken? Similarly, both the inspectors of health and safety and the employer will have difficulty in ensuring that workstations comply with standards that protect workers against repetitive strain injuries. In principle, these legal standards apply equally to homeworkers, but in practice it seems unlikely that effective monitoring and enforcement mechanisms will be developed. Some specific legislation applies to homeworkers. For example, there is a specific extension to the National Minimum Wage Act 1998, so that by section 35 its provisions apply to homeworkers, even if they do not satisfy the statutory definition of a 'worker' because they may employ others such as family and neighbours to perform some of the work. This result is achieved by including homeworkers who undertake to perform work 'whether personally or otherwise'.

---

be able to increase or reduce production capacity quickly, but also might be a way of acquiring specialist skills and to permit management to concentrate its attention on the core business. For example, in a survey asking why 14 publishers had changed from employing editorial assistants under contracts of employment to the use of 'freelance', independent, self-employed, contractors to perform the same task, the most common reason for the change was to match more precisely the availability of labour power with demand ('numerical flexibility'), or, to put the point another way, to transfer the risk of unemployment due to lack of demand onto the provider of the service rather than the employer (Celia and John Stanworth, 'Managing an Externalised Workforce: Free-lance Labour-use in the UK Book Publishing Industry' (1997) 28 *Industrial Relations Journal* 43). Avoidance of social regulation does not appear to have been a significant consideration.

The selection of atypical work forms by workers may represent a choice for certain types of flexibility, such as control over hours of work, or may fulfil a desire to avoid the subordinate position of becoming an employee in favour being one's own boss as a self-employed worker. As demonstrated by the following study, which involved structured interviews with individuals in non-standard jobs such as agency work, fixed term contracts, and casual work, many people take this kind of work because it is the only type available.

[2.53] B. Burchell, S. Deakin and S. Honey, *The Employment Status of Individuals in Non-standard Employment*, Employment Relations Research Series No. 6 URN/99/770 (London, Department of Trade and Industry, 1999) paragraph 7.5

> Some respondents saw the advantages and disadvantages of particular forms of work in terms of trade-offs between flexibility and security, suggesting that they exercised a degree of choice in weighing up which form of work to adopt. In numerous cases, however, the choice of non-standard work was seen as influenced and constrained by external pressures, the most important of which were family commitments, retraining costs, age and disability discrimination, and the lack of availability of alternative work. In particular, for those with family obligations, it was a matter of necessity to find employment which offered them the opportunity to arrange their work around domestic commitments. Those returning to employment after a period of unemployment or after family commitments chose non-standard work because of the costs of acquiring or re-acquiring skills of the kind needed for a more stable and permanent position. There was a perception that it was easier for older workers to get employment with an agency than with an employer looking for a longer-term commitment.

2.7.3 Proper scope of regulation

The use of freedom of contract to create many non-standard forms of work concentrates attention on the fundamental question at stake, namely what is the appropriate scope of regulation in the labour market? Is there an appropriate single field of application for all labour regulation, such as contracts involving the performance of services, or must the scope of regulation be determined according to the purposes of each policy embodied in each particular piece of legislation? There is a reluctance to admit the possibility that no single field of application exists, because that admission undermines the coherence of labour law as a subject, for its unity is often thought to depend upon its link to a particular social phenomenon: contracts for the performance of work. Given the variety of types of regulation and their different purposes, is it possible to determine a single appropriate field of application for all labour regulation?

The current legislation makes a series of distinctions that describe concentric circles of application of regulation.

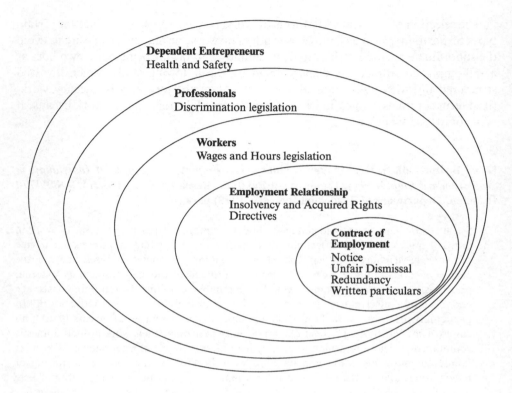

Figure 2.2

2.7.3.1 Employees

The smallest circle is defined by employees working under a contract of employment. Employment regulations normally apply to all contracts of employment, which usually include contracts of apprenticeship as well.

[2.54] Employment Rights Act, 1996 section 230

> **(1)** In this Act 'employee' means an individual who has entered into or works under (or, where the employment has ceased, worked under) a contract of employment.
> **(2)** In this Act 'contract of employment' means a contract of service or apprenticeship, whether express or implied, and (if it is express) whether oral or in writing.

Within that circle, however, there may be further exclusions based upon such factors as hours of work and length of service. For example, the law of unfair dismissal applies only to employees who have completed one year's continuous service for an employer, and the right to claim a redundancy payment applies only after two years of service (below 5.3). Notice that the statute makes no serious attempt to define a contract of employment. A contract of employment, we are told, is a contract of service, but we need to remember that a contract of service is, of course, a contract of employment. The meaning of contract of employment depends upon the common law test, which, as we observed in *Lane v Shire Roofing Company (Oxford) Ltd* (**[2.48]** above), merely considers an indeterminate list of factors including, principally, (a) the obligation to pay wages in return for a promise to perform personally work, (b) a degree of control exercised by the employer over the performance of work, (c) the extent to which the employee is integrated into the organisation, and (d) the allocation of risks onto the worker.

2.7.3.2 Employment relationship

The next circle is fixed by the use of the phrase 'contract of employment or employment relationship' in many European directives, as for example in Article 1 Directive 91/533 on the employer's obligation to inform employees of the conditions applicable to the contract of employment (above **[2.34]**). The reason for adopting this looser description of protected contracts is that the sharp contrast between contracts of employment and other contracts for services is not common in other European jurisdictions. The implication of this phrase for the law in the UK appears to be that some contractual relations, though not fitting exactly within the definition of a contract of employment, should nevertheless be included within the scope of the regulation required by the Directive. The term 'employment relationship' is, however, never defined, and furthermore the ECJ has always insisted that the precise interpretation of such concepts must be a matter for national law. This view is strengthened by the directives themselves, which frequently include the statement such as: 'This Directive shall be without prejudice to national law as regards the definition of contract of employment or employment relationship' (Acquired Rights Directive 77/187, Article 2.2, as amended). The scope of application of many directives thus turns on the meaning of the concept of 'employment relationship' in UK law, though no such concept has hitherto existed in English law. It seems possible, for instance, that persons holding a 'public office', such as judges, who would not be regarded as working under a contract of employment under UK law, might be classified as having an 'employment relationship' suitable for the acquisition of rights under EC law (e.g. *Percival-Price* v. *Department of Economic Development* [2000] IRLR 380 (NICA)). It also seems that an 'employment relationship' does not necessarily require the existence of a contractual relation.

[2.55] *Governing Body of Clifton Middle School v Askew* **[2000] ICR 286 (CA)**

> A local authority reorganised its school system by closing 'first' and 'middle' schools and creating 'primary' schools. Teachers at the schools had contracts of employment with the local authority, but were managed for all practical purposes by the governing body of each school. The applicant was dismissed for redundancy by the governing body and local authority of a middle school, but was not offered a new job by the new governing body and the local authority at the primary school which replaced it on the same site. The applicant claimed that he had been unfairly dismissed, a claim which depended in part on whether there had been a 'transfer of an undertaking' within the meaning of the Acquired Rights Directive 77/187. The local authority argued that it was the employer in both the old middle school and the new primary school, so that there had been no transfer of an

undertaking from one employer to another. The employee argued that for practical purposes the governing bodies managed the schools and determined dismissals, so that there had been a transfer between the different governing bodies, and that although the applicant did not have a contract of employment with the governing body, he did have an 'employment relationship' within the meaning of the Directive. A majority of the Court of Appeal rejected the employee's appeal against the decision of the EAT that had rejected his claim for unfair dismissal. On the question of the meaning of 'employment relationship', the Court of Appeal expressed differing views. Peter Gibson LJ held that an 'employment relationship' must comprise a contractual relation of some kind, though not necessarily one that fitted into the category of contract of employment. Ward LJ held that an 'employment relationship' required the existence of legal rights and obligations capable of being transferred, though these rights and obligations might be found in a source other than a contract. Chadwick LJ agreed with the latter view, but unlike Ward LJ, found that such a source existed for this case in a special statutory instrument (Education (Modification of Enactments Relating to Employment) Order 1989, SI 1989/901, Articles 3 and 4) under which the governing body of a school was deemed to be a teacher's 'employer' as well as the local authority for the purposes of claims of unfair dismissal . Chadwick LJ was thus in a minority in finding that an employment relationship had been established in this case.

One possible implication of the absence of the need for a contract is that 'employment relation' might include volunteers, who, as unpaid workers, may not have any contractual relation owing to the absence of consideration.

2.7.3.3 Worker

In the next circle, recent legislation such as the National Minimum Wage Act 1998 and the Working Time Regulations 1998 adopts the term 'worker' to describe a combination of employees under contracts of employment and self-employed contractors

---

Volunteers

Governments encourage voluntary work for charities and other voluntary organisations both to develop citizens' sense of community and in some cases to provide work experience as a route back into paid employment. Do these volunteers fall within the scope of any labour law? Volunteers will not have a contract unless they are paid or receive some other consideration for their work. For this purpose, pay does not include recoupment of expenses incurred, provided the expenses paid do not conceal a hidden system of wages. The absence of a contract excludes volunteers from the statutory definitions of employee, worker, professional, though not necessarily the European concept of employment relation. To reinforce that result, s.44 of the National Minimum Wage Act 1998 expressly excludes from its coverage volunteers who merely receive expenses, benefits in kind such as meals and accommodation, or monetary payments for the purpose of subsistence. Although it makes sense to exclude most volunteers from the national minimum wage, it is less satisfactory that other labour laws such as discrimination and working time rules do not apply to them. It is surely not unreasonable to expect voluntary organisations to comply with the legal standards regarding equality of opportunity, respect for the dignity of individuals, and all health and safety measures. See: D. Morris, 'Volunteering and Employment Status' (1999) 29 *Industrial Law Journal* 249.

who perform work personally other than on the basis of conducting a profession or a business undertaking.

[2.56] Employment Rights Act 1996, section 230

> (3) In this Act 'worker' . . . means an individual who has entered into or works under (or, where the employment has ceased, worked under)—
>
> (a) a contract of employment; or
>
> (b) any other contract, whether express or implied and (if it is express) whether oral or in writing, whereby the individual undertakes to do or perform personally any work or services for another party to the contract whose status is not by virtue of the contract that of a client or customer of any profession or business undertaking carried on by the individual; . . .

There is no statutory definition of the concepts of 'profession' or 'business undertaking'. With respect to the notion of 'profession', in the context of a claim brought by freelance wildlife cameramen and women under the statutory trade union recognition procedure (8.4.2 below), which applies only to a similar concept of 'worker' (Trade Union and Labour Relations (Consolidation) Act 1992 section 296(1)), it was held that although the existence of a regulatory body is probably a sufficient condition for a person to count as a 'professional', it is not necessary condition, so that other factors such as skills and academic qualifications might be sufficient to exclude a person as a professional: *R v Central Arbitration Committee* [2003] EWHC 1375 Admin [2003] IRLR 460 (QB) (8.4.2 below). With respect to the phrase 'business undertaking', this phrase cannot be understood simply as the common law concept of 'independent contractor', for that interpretation would deprive the concept in (b) of any meaning. The type of independent contractors to be included as 'workers' should be self-employed individuals who for the most part only enter contracts to perform work personally for a single employer, and whose degree of dependence or subordination is essentially the same as that of employees. Under this interpretation there would be a good chance that casual workers such as the waiters in *O'Kelly* would be covered during their particular engagements at banquets. The concept of worker has been held to include bricklayers contracted personally to perform particular jobs on building sites though clearly in the capacity of independent contractors rather than employees: *Redrow Homes (Yorkshire) Ltd v Wright* [2004] EWCA Civ 469, [2004] IRLR 720 (CA). But a sub-postmaster who provides his own premises and can employ staff to perform the work has been held to be carrying on a business undertaking: *Commissioners of Inland Revenue v. Post Office Ltd* [2003] IRLR 199 (EAT). It has been estimated that the definition of worker extends employment protection laws to a further 5 per cent of the workforce (B. Burchell, S. Deakin and S. Honey, *The Employment Status of Individuals in Non-standard Employment*, Employment Relations Research Series No. 6 URN/99/770 (London, Department of Trade and Industry, 1999) paragraph 8.2).

As well as this UK statutory definition of 'worker', the scope of some European Community law applies also to the concept of 'worker'. But confusingly, this EC concept of worker has its own meaning and does not defer to national interpretations of the concept.

[2.57] Case C–256/01 *Allonby v Accrington and Rossendale College* **[2004] ICR 1328 (ECJ).**

The college failed to renew the contracts of fixed term part-time lecturers, most of whom were women, and instead engaged them through an employment agency with which the lecturers were registered as self-employed independent contractors. Under these new arrangements the lecturers' income fell, and they lost some fringe benefits including an occupational pension scheme. In a claim for equal pay in comparison with a retained full-time permanent male employee, the Court of Appeal referred certain questions to the ECJ regarding the scope of European equal pay law as determined by Article 141 of the European Community Treaty. The ECJ held that Article 141 applied to 'workers', which had a Community meaning. A worker was a person who, for a certain period of time, performs services for and under the direction of another person in return for remuneration. Thus a person who was formally classified as self-employed or an independent contractor under national law could be a 'worker' withing the EC law governing equal pay if her independence disguised the reality of a relation of subordination. Although this interpretation of 'worker' enabled the claim to be brought, the ECJ also decided that the comparison with a full-time male employee of the College could not be made for the purposes of equal pay law, because the part-time lecturers were now paid by a different 'employer', the employment agency.

This EC concept of 'worker' seems in fact to be closely similar to the next and wider circle of coverage of labour laws.

2.7.3.4 Professional

A wider circle of coverage drops the exclusion of professionals and independent businesses from statutory rights.

[2.58] Sex Discrimination Act 1975, section 82(1)

In this Act, unless the context otherwise requires—
. . . 'employment' means employment under a contract of service or of apprenticeship or a contract personally to execute any work or labour . . .

This statutory formula is generally applicable to anti-discrimination legislation including equal pay law. The requirement that the contract should be one containing an obligation to perform work, a requirement that is common to the legal definition of 'worker' above, has been interpreted to mean that the contract should be of a kind in which the employee undertakes to perform work and the employer promises to provide work.

[2.59] *Mingely v Pennock and Ivory (trading as Amber Cars)* **[2004] EWCA Civ 328, [2004] ICR 727 (CA)**

Mr Mingely, who is of black African origin, worked as a minicab driver. Under his oral contract with Amber Cars, he paid the firm £75 per week and in return he was given a computer system for his car that allocated calls to drivers from customers of Amber Cars. Mr Mingely was entirely free to determine his hours of work, if any, and kept the fares paid by customers for himself. While working, however, Mr Mingely was required to have a city licence and to wear the firm's uniform. As a preliminary issue in a claim for race discrimination, the question arose as to the nature of his contract with Amber Cars and whether it was a contract personally to perform work, as required under section 78 of the Race Relations Act 1976. The Court of Appeal concluded that as there was no obligation on Mr Mingely to perform any work at all, his contract was beyond the reach of section 78. The Court also doubted, however, that Parliament could have intended such a result.

In addition, the courts have imposed a further gloss on the statute, which insists that the dominant purpose of the contract should be that it is an undertaking to perform work personally. The contrast is with a contract where the undertaking is merely to ensure that the work is performed by managing the performance of the service by others.

[2.60] *Mirror Group Newspapers* v. *Gunning* [1986] ICR 145 (CA)

The applicant's father had held a distributorship for newspapers, which involved the purchase of newspapers in bulk, and then the resale and delivery of newspapers to about 90 retail outlets by means of employing about eight people using rented vans. The father's work involved direct supervision of the collection of the newspapers and their loading onto the vans. On her father's retirement, the applicant applied for the distributorship, where she had been employed by her father, but the defendant refused the application and instead gave the work to two other businesses in the area. The applicant brought a claim

---

Training Contracts

Many workers undertake as their first experience of working life a contract for training under which they expect to be taught a trade or profession. If the contract comprises an apprenticeship under which the apprentice agrees to work under the instruction of the employer in return for training in a particular skill, the arrangement is usually included within the statutory concept of a contract of employment. But not every training contract involves a duty to perform work; it may rather permit the individual to attend a workplace, to observe practice, and develop skills. Such a trainee may or may not be paid some remuneration. These training contracts may fall outside the scope of labour law regulation altogether.

Edmonds v Lawson QC [2000] IRLR 391 CA.

A pupil barrister sought to claim the minimum wage. The claimant held a 12-month unpaid pupillage in the defendant's chambers. It is necessary to complete such a pupillage in order to qualify as an advocate. The pupil master is under a duty to provide adequate tuition and experience. The pupil is not under a duty to work, but rather to be conscientious in receiving instruction. The Court of Appeal held that the pupillage represented a contract, but it was not a contract of employment or an apprenticeship, because the pupil was not under an obligation to work for the pupil master. Nor was the pupil a 'worker' under the National Minimum Wage Act 1998, because she did not undertake to perform any work.

for sex discrimination. A preliminary question was whether the legislation applied to the distributorship agreement. Recall that discrimination legislation applies to the category of 'professional' above, so the question was whether the contract satisfied the requirement under section 82(1) of the Sex Discrimination Act 1975 that it was 'a contract of employment or . . . a contract personally to execute any work or labour'. Reversing the industrial tribunal and the EAT, the Court of Appeal found that the distributorship did not satisfy that requirement.

Balcombe LJ:

Before us Mr Michael Beloff QC, for Mrs Gunning, submitted in his skeleton argument that the word 'any' in the phrase 'a contract personally to execute any work or labour' refers to the amount or quantity, and not to the kind of work or labour to be performed, so that any obligation personally to execute work or labour, however limited in amount the work or labour might be, was sufficient to bring the contract containing that obligation within the statutory definition. Mr Alexander Irvine QC, for Mirror Group Newspapers, referred us to the case of *Ready Mixed Concrete (South East) Ltd v Minister of Pensions and National Insurance* [1968] 2 QB 497, and the distinction there drawn by Mr Justice McKenna, between a contract of service and a contract for services. He submitted, with justification as it seems to me, that the purpose of extending the definition of employment beyond that of employment under a contract of service or apprenticeship, to include employment under a contract personally to execute any work or labour, was so as to embrace within the definition work done by an independent contractor under a contract for services which, while clearly within the mischief which the Act was intended to remedy, would not otherwise qualify. He explained the use of the word 'any' in the phrase 'contract personally to execute any work or labour' as referring to the kind of work or labour, by reference to the legislative history of the phrase. In the Industrial Relations Act 1971 a distinction was drawn between 'employee' meaning an individual who had entered into or worked under a contract of employment, and 'worker', which included a person who worked (a) under a contract of employment, or (b) under any other contract whereby he undertook to perform personally any work or services for another party to the contract who was not a professional client of his—see s.167(1) of the 1971 Act. In the 1975 Act it was not appropriate to exclude from those entitled to the protection of the Act those persons who rendered professional services, and accordingly the word 'any' was inserted to make it clear that in this case the categories of work or labour concerned were not limited as in the 1971 Act.

While I accept Mr Irvine's submissions as set out above, I cannot accept his primary submission that the phrase 'contract personally to execute any work or labour' contemplates only a contract whose sole purpose is that the party contracting to provide services under the contract performs personally the work or labour which forms the subject matter of the contract. As was suggested during the course of argument, this would exclude from the definition a contract with a sculptor, where it was contemplated that some of the menial work might be carried out by persons other than the contracting party, a contract with a one-man builder, who might be expected to sub-contract some of the specialist work, or even a contract with a plumber, who might be expected to have his mate with him on all occasions.

However, I do accept Mr Irvine's alternative submission that the phrase in its context contemplates a contract whose dominant purpose is that the party contracting to provide services under the contract performs personally the work or labour which forms the subject matter of the contract. In the course of oral argument before us, Mr Beloff conceded that a single obligation to provide personal services in a contract is not of itself sufficient to bring the contract within the phrase; you have to look at the contract as a whole to see the extent to which that obligation colours the contract, which goes a long way towards accepting the 'dominant purpose' test. In my judgment, you have to look at the agreement as a whole, and provided that there is some obligation by one contracting party personally to execute any work or labour, you then have to decide whether that is the dominant purpose of the contract, or whether the contract is properly to be regarded in essence as a contract for the personal execution of work or labour, which seems to me to be the same thing in other words.

This dominant purpose test permits the inclusion of some contracts for work even though some of the work will be performed by others. This test was applied in *Kelly v Northern Ireland Housing Executive* [1998] ICR 828 (HL) to an application by a partner in a firm of solicitors for inclusion on a panel of solicitors, members of which would be given work by a public authority, when it was alleged that the application had been rejected on grounds of religious belief and/or political opinion contrary to The Fair Employment (Northern Ireland) Act 1976. Although a solicitor is likely to delegate some of the tasks to an assistant or a secretary, it was sufficient to satisfy the statutory formula that a particular partner in the firm would be legally responsible to ensure that the work was carried out satisfactorily.

2.7.3.5 Dependent entrepreneur

The widest circle for legal regulation of employment can be created by the inclusion of small businesses working for a single customer or dependent entrepreneurs. To qualify as a dependent entrepreneur, the worker will be performing services as an independent contractor, either personally or by managing the work of others, though in practice this independent contractor will be economically dependent on a single customer or client. Many of the cases considered in this section concern dependent entrepreneurs, who though formally in business on their own account, in practice are economically dependent and accept a degree of subordination to a single client or customer. This economic dependence and subordination are so similar to ordinary employment relations that in many instances the courts will stretch the boundaries of the legal categories to include these workers within the relevant protective law. The roofer in *Lane v Shire Roofing Company (Oxford) Ltd* (**[2.48]** above) was a dependent entrepreneur in this sense, but was classified as an employee for the purpose of a claim for compensation in tort; similarly, the bricklayers in *Redrow Homes (Yorkshire) Ltd v Wright* [2004] EWCA Civ 469, [2004] IRLR 720 (CA) were classified as 'workers'. Yet the waiters in *O'Kelly v Trusthouse Forte* (**[2.50]** above), were dependent entrepreneurs in this sense, and so too was the applicant for a distributorship in *Mirror Newspapers v Gunning* (**[2.60]** above), yet the former were not classified as employees, and the latter did not satisfy the requirement of a contract personally to execute work. This category of dependent entrepreneur thus lies at the fringes of the other legal classifications of contracts appropriate for labour law regulation, and provides the crucial testing ground for the proper scope of employment laws.

The sole protective legislation that clearly applies to dependent entrepreneurs concerns health and safety in the workplace. The Health and Safety at Work Act 1974 applies to independent contractors in two ways. Under section 3(1) the employer is required to 'conduct his undertaking in such a way as to ensure, so far as is reasonably practicable, that persons not in his employment . . . are not exposed to risks to health and safety'. This creates a duty towards independent contractors and their employees, provided that the work of the contractor can be regarded as the main employer's method for the 'conduct of the undertaking' (e.g. *R v Associated Octel Ltd* [1996] 1 WLR 1543 (HL)). Alternatively, the independent contractor may be protected by section 4 of the 1974 Act, which imposes a duty on the controller of premises to take such measures as it is reasonably practicable to ensure that the premises are safe.

The circles in Fig. 2.2 mark the principal boundaries for the scope of employment regulation, though each piece of legislation must be examined carefully with respect to its exclusions and inclusions. Do the circles describe an intelligible pattern? It may be possible to argue that when the legal regulation is primarily directed at the possible misuse of managerial authority, the legislation is confined to contracts of employment, because those contracts contain the implied terms of the requirement of obedience and performance in good faith. When the legislation is directed primarily at the operation of the labour market, however, as in the case of wages and hours regulation and laws against discrimination, the scope is broader because it is recognised that the market for performance of work extends beyond traditional contracts of employment. But this pattern behind the legislation is certainly not followed consistently. For example, the regulation in ERA 1996, section 1([2.32] above), which is designed to improve transparency in labour markets by compelling employers to disclose the terms of employment in writing, is confined to contracts of employment. Furthermore, we must doubt whether the singling out of the contract of employment as the unique site where the risk of abuse of managerial power is present relies upon a satisfactory analysis of the construction of power relations in the labour market.

Consider the implications (for the application of employment protection legislation) of the following study of how contracts for the service of doorstep milk delivery were altered from contracts of employment to franchises. Notice how the employer achieves better control over performance of work and more effective disciplinary power by abandoning the contractual form of employment. Despite the continuing presence of an authority structure, the new economic relation of a franchise only fits into the outer circle of a dependent entrepreneur. As a result, the milkmen may not be covered by any labour law rights except, perhaps, safety laws, and possibly, with the assistance of the dominant purpose test, anti-discrimination laws.

[2.61] Julia O'Connell Davidson, 'What do Franchisors Do? Control and Commercialisation in Milk Distribution' (1994) 8 *Work, Employment & Society* 23

[This study of three dairies sought to understand why dairies had decided to stop employing milkmen to make doorstep deliveries, but instead to organise distribution through franchises of rounds. The dairies operated in the context of a declining demand for milk and competition for doorstep deliveries from lower prices in supermarkets.]

The Limitations of the Retail System
To begin with, managers in dairies that now operate franchises claim that the retail round system generated excessively high overheads in terms of clerical support and relief roundspeople. They further argue that it exacerbated problems of absenteeism and

labour turnover. Absenteeism has always been a major problem for dairies, not just because of the early start time, but also because bad weather makes milk delivery w ork particularly gruelling. One manager estimated that on rainy days around 12% of direct employees would simply fail to turn up, and that in severe weather the figure was even higher. Dairies also experienced a fairly high level of labour turnover, especially amongst new recruits. Being a roundsperson is hard physical work, in poor conditions; it is isolating and the hours are unsocial. Many people would therefore accept a job, undergo training and then leave after a short period, making turnover an expensive problem for the dairy.

The retail system is also held to generate problems of labour control. The nature of milk delivery work precludes direct supervision of the workforce. Each milk roundsperson works over a large geographical area and the employer is hardly likely to employ a supervisor to accompany every employee on his or her round. The employer thus faces two particular problems of labour control. Since roundspeople cannot be surveilled as they undertake their routine tasks, the employer must find alternative ways of preventing theft and/or substitution of goods on the one hand, and of controlling the pace and intensity of working on the other. The first problem has typically been resolved through the use of highly bureaucratic systems which monitor the allocation and issue of goods to roundspeople. A line manager at one family-owned dairy which still operates the retail system claimed that, 'every time on the float, every delivery is recorded . . . There is no way that goods can just go missing. We can check every payment . . . against the items that have been issued to him'.

Controlling the pace and intensity of working is more problematic. Direct supervision is not a viable option, and because rounds vary both from each other, and on a day to day basis (the volume of work associated with each individual round fluctuates according to whether customers cancel milk, order extra items, etcetera), it is extremely difficult for the employer to devise a payment system which encourages optimal effort. To pay an hourly rate when direct supervision is impossible might encourage employees to perform their tasks more slowly, and a simple piece rate would disadvantage those employees whose rounds cover a larger geographical area and who therefore have to travel relatively long distances between drops. A bonus system based on pre-targeted times would also be difficult to implement, since the length of time involved in delivering milk and collecting money varies according to the geographical spread, population density and even socio-economic composition of customers. Equally important is the fact that many dairies were well unionised and bonus systems were opposed by the unions. As one personnel manager remarked, 'the TGWU and USDAW always pushed for a solid basic wage. They did not like the bonus to be that big a proportion of the take home pay'. . . .

Directly employed roundspeople not only exercise discretion over the pacing of work, but also a great deal of control over the size of their rounds, and therefore over the amount of labour power they supply in exchange for the wage. This is because it is fairly easy for roundspeople to lose calls or custom. They can, for example, appear rather less than willing when a prospective customer enquires about their services; they can allow debts to build up until there is little chance of a customer being able to pay; they can point out the price difference between goods supplied by the dairy and those purchased at the supermarket. As a manager put it, 'If they didn't want the call, they would find a way to lose it'. Although many directly employed roundspeople put a good deal of effort into building up their rounds, others (known as 'flyers' or 'runners') preferred to keep their rounds as small as possible and their working hours to the minimum. Indeed, for those roundspeople with dependants and large mortgages, this often made better financial sense, since more money could be earned from a second job than from the commissions that came from a larger round.

Managers in dairies which now operate franchise systems further claim that the retail system failed to provide workers with a great enough incentive to control debt. Directly employed roundspeople were responsible for collecting payment from customers, and the dairy's cash flow depended directly upon the degree of zeal with which workers undertook this task. However, collecting money is an arduous and time consuming activity and managers found it difficult to devise effective ways of encouraging roundspeople to control debts under the job and finish system. . . .

Franchised Milk Rounds

WHAT DO FRANCHISORS DO?

'the right to use the franchisor's trade mark, [and] also [to] operate under specific guidelines covering all aspects of the business, including a marketing strategy and plan, operating manuals and standards, accounting and finance procedures . . . even the colour of the uniforms worn' [A. Felstead, The Social Organization of the Franchise: A Case of Controlled Self-Employment (1991) 5 *Work, Employment and Society* 37, at p. 40].

In the dairy industry, these rights are typically bought by the franchisee with a one-off payment, and after this he or she is entitled to a fixed margin on every pint of milk and all goods sold under the dairy's trade mark. Franchisees must also put up a returnable bond which is effectively a deposit on the milk supplied by the dairy. Taking the bond and the fee together, the franchisee's initial outlay can be anything between £1,500 and £8,000. Prospective franchisees are told that this investment will allow them to benefit from the goodwill owned by the franchisor as well as from the franchisor's expertise in running the business. It is the round itself which is franchised, so that the franchisee is buying the right to serve an established customer base in a clearly defined geographical area and he or she is generally assured assistance with legal, accountancy, sales promotion and advertising matters. The arrangement between franchisor and franchisee is drawn together in the franchise contract. The following section draws principally upon the franchise contract used in one of the dairies investigated for this study, which will be referred to as 'Midlands Dairy', to outline the contractual rights and obligations of franchisees.

The Franchise Contract

Franchisees enter into a two year contract with Midlands Dairy which formally guarantees him or her an entitlement to serve a particular delivery area. The contract also formally commits the dairy to providing advice and the 'benefits of the dairy's knowledge and experience' in connection with any problems encountered in running the franchise. However, for the most part the dairy's obligation to support the franchisee's business is rather cautiously worded. It undertakes, for example, 'to use all *reasonable endeavours* to supply sufficient Milk and Dairy Products to the Franchise Operator (*subject to availability*)' [emphasis added], and to make a milk delivery vehicle available to the franchisee (for a fee) except when anything 'beyond the reasonable control of the dairy' prevents it from so doing. No such reticence is apparent when the contract turns to the franchisee's obligations. The franchisee is formally obliged to 'maintain goodwill'. He or she must undertake to provide a 'regular and efficient' service to the existing customers in the franchise area; to buy milk and goods from the dairy alone; to use his '*best*' (rather than reasonable) endeavours '*at all times*' to promote and increase the dairy's milk trade and reputation in the franchise area. There is also a clause which allows the dairy to send out a relief roundsperson to deliver milk on the franchisee's round should the franchisee fail to arrive for work, and to charge the franchisee for this service. A senior manager explained the rationale behind this clause as follows;

'My job at the end of the day is to make sure that everyone who wants Midlands Dairy milk gets it. So we will never see a round standing in the depot, even if the depot manager has to take that round out himself. But, we charge the franchisee quite a bit for that service, as much as we need to prohibit him from absenteeism'.

As well as imposing these rather diffuse obligations, the contract imposes some very specific controls over how franchisees must organise their work. The dairy specifies the type of roundsbook that the franchisee must use and the franchisee is obliged to keep the book 'properly, correctly and up to date'. The contract obliges the franchisee to wear the dairy uniform and to ensure that any employee or assistance does likewise. A time period within which debts must be collected is specified, the franchisee is obliged to take part in promotional activities when requested to do so by the dairy, to return empty bottles and crates in a good and clean condition, and to make extra deliveries within their area should the dairy require them to do so 'on such terms as the dairy may *reasonably* specify'. The contract also forbids certain activities. The franchisee is not allowed to obtain milk or goods from any supplier other than the dairy or to sell any product without the agreement of the dairy. Franchisees cannot terminate the contract except by giving six months written notice to the dairy, and after the contract is terminated, they may not retail or distribute milk or dairy products in the franchise area for one year, whether as a sole trader or as an employee of another dairy.

Finally, the contract includes a clause referring to compensation for increased and decreased milk sales, and this is typical of franchise contracts in the dairy industry (see National Dairymen's Association 1992). When a round is franchised, it is franchised as an area with a specified number of customers and a specified gallonage of milk to be delivered. The compensation clause states that if the franchisee manages to expand the customer base and increase the gallonage delivered on the round, then, on termination or renewal of the contract, the dairy 'shall pay compensation to the Franchise Operator based on the average goodwill value per weekly gallon obtaining in respect of the excess'. If, on the other hand, customers and gallonage have been lost, the contract states that the franchisee must pay compensation to the dairy. Given that franchising is being introduced in the context of a steady fall in milk sales, this clause clearly disbenefits the franchisee.

Franchising and Labour Costs
When dairies replace retail rounds with franchise operations, the overheads associated with direct labour are immediately and dramatically reduced. As franchisors, these firms are not responsible for making national insurance or pension contributions and, unlike employers, franchisors have no obligation to provide workers with sickness or holiday pay. Instead, it is the franchisee who must pay for such luxuries. Since franchisees are contractually bound to deliver milk regularly, they must either find someone to take their round when they fall sick or want a holiday, or else pay the franchisor for supplying a relief worker. Many dairies now operate 'Holiday Relief Schemes', where the franchisee pays a sum to the dairy each week in order to save up for an annual holiday.

These very obvious financial benefits are not always offset by costs in terms of losing the skill and knowledge of experienced roundspeople, for the vast majority of franchisees are recruited from the ranks of those who were previously direct employees of the dairy. Furthermore, as a personnel manager in a dairy which has used franchising for some seven years now explains, even when inexperienced labour is recruited, franchising is cheaper since the cost of training is borne by the franchisee.

This dairy makes franchisees pay a £4,000 'start up fee', in return for which they receive four weeks' training prior to starting their round. At Midlands Dairy no charge is made for training, but franchisees are made to carry the cost of labour turnover. A senior manager commented:

> 'New recruits have to pay £1,000 for the training, and if they take on the franchise, we credit that £1,000 to their bond . . . but if they don't take on the franchise, then I'm afraid that costs them £750, because I've had to put someone on to train them, I had to delay the benefit from franchising that round'.

As well as savings in terms of employment costs and those arising from recruitment, training and labour turnover, franchising allows dairies to reduce overheads associated with clerical and administrative work. Under the retail system, roundspeople collected cash from their customers and brought it in to cashiers, who then had to count, sort and bank the money. With the franchise system, franchisees are billed weekly for the milk and goods they take out, and they pay this bill by cheque. This vastly reduces and simplifies the dairy's clerical activities. Finally, the franchise system cuts labour costs by reducing the number of relief roundspeople that need to be employed. Sickness and absenteeism is extremely rare amongst franchisees simply because, as one depot manager put it, 'If they go sick now, (a) they don't get paid and (b) they have to pay us to find somebody to do their round'. This has facilitated quite savage cuts to direct labour levels. In one Midlands Dairy depot, for example, the number of relief workers was reduced by 60% after the shift to franchised operations.

Franchising and Labour Control
Management rhetoric about franchising emphasises the autonomy of the franchisee—'he' is running 'his' own business; franchisor and franchisee are now 'partners' with a shared interest in expanding output. The role of management has changed. Management is no longer about driving or cajoling workers to increase their effort levels, it is simply about 'supporting' unfettered entrepreneurs. Yet when asked whether the franchisees' 'autonomy' reduces managerial control over the process of milk distribution, they reply that the contract is designed in such a way as to ensure, perhaps even extend, their control.

The contract is seen as an effective substitute for what would once have been a job description and allows management to closely prescribe the day to day activities of the franchisee just as it would have controlled the activities of direct employees. Managerial control is also extended by franchising in two main ways. First, the contract commits the franchisee to delivering a fixed gallonage of milk, which effectively binds the roundsperson to maintaining a certain level of output, or else pay compensation to the franchisor for lost gallonage. Managers believe that this clause gives them control over how much effort the worker puts into acquiring and retaining customers, something which previous systems of labour control had failed to secure. Second, franchising increases the pressure on workers to collect debt, another area over which management previously found it hard to exercise effective control. Since franchisees have to pay the franchisor for milk on a weekly basis, it is the individual franchisee rather than the dairy that carries the cost of uncollected debts. This provides the franchisee with an incentive to work hard to collect all the money owed each week, and should he or she fail to do so, it is not a problem for the dairy—at least, not in the short term. . . .

Rewards Without Headaches? The Experience of Franchisees . . .
Though management laid great emphasis on the increased autonomy that would accompany their new self-employed status, effectively these workers were buying back their old jobs. None of those interviewed for this study felt that they 'owned their own business'. Management's description of franchising as a 'partnership' is equally

misleading, for the two parties involved enjoy very different levels of power and control. It is the franchisor that sets depot charges and vehicle charges, the franchisor that controls what franchisees sell and how much they charge for it, the franchisor that controls the size of the round and thereby controls who the franchisee can and cannot sell to.

Not only are the two 'partners' unequally matched but, further, roundspeople point out that the franchisor is less than fully committed to protecting the commercial interests of franchisees. Though the franchisee is tied to a single supplier, the franchisor is under no similar constraint. The dairy sells milk not just to its own franchisees, but also to its franchisees' competitors—supermarkets, small shops and independent milk roundspeople (referred to as 'pirates' by the roundspeople). More extraordinary still, in the light of management's rhetoric about partnership, symbiosis and co-operation, the dairy sells milk to the franchisees on *less* favourable terms than it sells to their competitors. . . .

Franchising has also had profound and extremely negative effects upon workers' daily lives. This is partly because many of the existing retail rounds were too small in terms of gallonage to offer even the potential for an adequate income to a franchisee. In order to make rounds viable as franchises is was therefore necessary to increase their size quite considerably, which in turn means that the workload of a franchisee, in terms of deliveries alone, is greater than that of a retail roundsperson. Franchising has also involved job enlargement in the sense that their self employed status forces them to undertake administrative activities that were previously performed by clerical staff. On top of this, franchisees must now spend far longer on collecting money than they did as direct employees. This is because they are obliged to pay the dairy for milk weekly, so that any shortfall between monies collected and the dairy's bill is borne by the franchisee. Indeed, some workers identify this as the most important feature of franchising:

'I think they introduced franchising because the whole depot was carrying too much debt , . . there was thousands of pounds on the books that wasn't collected or couldn't be collected in . . . They're passing on the risk with franchising, it ain't their problem any more.' . . .

The actual number of hours worked by each franchisee varies according to the nature of the round and estimates range from 40 to 80 hours per week. Even taken at face value (and the estimates made by self-employed individuals as to the number of hours they work are notoriously unreliable), these estimates suggest that franchisees work more hours than they did as direct employees, especially when the fact that they no longer have holidays or rest days is taken into account. What are the financial rewards for working so many hours? A few franchisees claim to be taking home more money than they did as direct employees but the majority estimate that their income is roughly the same or even reduced. Furthermore, many franchisees are dependent on the labour of their wives and/or children to sustain their income. In this sense, franchising has wrought changes to the sexual division of labour in the milk industry, which has, in the past, relied almost exclusively on the labour of male workers to deliver milk and collect money. Although Midlands Dairy has no female franchisees, women are now involved in collecting money, book keeping and to a lesser extent, deliveries. One franchisee explained:

'I don't pay anyone else to help . . . it's not worth it. Me wife, she comes out with me on Friday from 9 a.m. till about 2 p.m. to help with the collecting, then she normally comes out from about 3.30 a.m. Saturday to about 4 o'clock in the afternoon to help with the delivery and the collecting, because my round is fairly big and without the two of us doing it, it wouldn't be possible'.

The puzzle that this example of a 'dependent entrepreneur' presents for employment regulation is whether the purposes of regulation should lead to the conclusion that the relationship should be covered, even though in form it is a contract between two businesses. If, for example, the income achieved by a milkman was less than the national minimum wage in view of the hours actually worked on a round, should the milkman be able to claim an increase? Similarly, if the hours worked each week exceeded the statutory limit of 48, should the regulation apply to invalidate the contract? Could the franchisee milkman even claim compensation for unfair dismissal if the franchise were terminated without warning or for unfounded reasons, or should such action simply be regarded as the termination of contract between two businesses? There is much to be said for cutting through the contractual form of the relation in order to fulfil the purposes of employment regulation by applying these statutes to the position of the franchisee milkman. His or her degree of economic dependence and subordination to the dairy seems to be equivalent to or even more intense than the position of the former employee milkmen. There are certainly occasions when the courts cut through the form of a contract that has the appearance of a transaction between two businesses in order to find an employment relation: e.g. *Young & Woods Ltd* v. *West* [1980] IRLR 201 (CA) ([5.36] below). A particularly striking example occurred in the next case, where the worker had formed a limited company through which to supply his services.

[2.62] *Catamaran Cruisers Ltd v Williams* **[1994] IRLR 386 (EAT)**

> The case concerned a claim for unfair dismissal in the context of a business restructuring (considered **[10.23]** below). A preliminary issue was whether Mr Williams was an employee. At the suggestion of the employer, Catamaran Cruisers, he had formed a limited company (Unicorn Enterprises) with his mother through which he provided his personal services to the employer. The employer paid Unicorn Enterprises a fee and did not deduct income tax or national insurance contributions, though at one point it offered Mr Williams 'holiday pay' and 'sick pay'. Under the normal principles of company law, Unicorn Enterprises represents a separate legal entity. Mr Williams, if he was the employee of any company, should have been the employee of Unicorn Enterprises (as well as a director and major shareholder: see *Bottrill v Secretary of State for Trade and Industry* [1999] IRLR 326 (CA)). Any contract entered into by Catamaran Cruisers was plainly with Unicorn Enterprises, not directly with Mr Williams, so logically not only did Mr Williams not have a contract of employment with Catamaran Cruisers, he probably had no contractual relation at all. Notwithstanding this logical problem, the tribunal, whose decision was upheld by the EAT, found that Mr Williams had on the special facts of this case a contract of employment with Catamaran Cruisers.

In effect, the tribunal 'pierced the corporate veil'. The use of such personal service companies for the purpose of obtaining the more favourable tax position accorded to independent businesses has recently been discouraged for 'disguised employees' by the Finance Act 2000 section 60 and the Social Security Contributions (Intermediaries) Regulations 2000, SI 727.

It is sometimes suggested that the boundary of labour law should be fixed by the requirement that the work should be performed personally, as opposed to contracts that permit or expect the contractor to employ others or to use substitutes. The courts have not always acknowledged that boundary. The homeworker who used family and neighbours to perform some of the work was regarded as an employee in *Nethermere (St. Neots) Ltd v Gardiner* (**[2.51]** above). The dominant purpose test used in applying the statutory formula of 'an undertaking to perform personally work' enables some small employers, such as the partner in a firm of solicitors, to fall within the scope of anti-discrimination legislation: *Kelly v Northern Ireland Housing Executive* [1998] ICR 828 (HL). As we have seen in the example of the franchisee milkmen, the ability to use substitutes and to employ assistants may not indicate any reduction in the degree of economic dependence and subordination experienced by the worker. For this reason, this proposed boundary to the scope of labour law has been criticised.

[2.63] P. Davies and M. Freedland, 'Employees, Workers, and the Autonomy of Labour Law' in H. Collins, P. Davies and R. Rideout (eds.), *Legal Regulation of the Employment Relation* (London, Kluwer, 2000) 267, 282–4

> There are three reasons which one might advance for not accepting the obligation of personal service as a sine qua non for the application of labour law. The first and most obvious is that it is a boundary which is open to manipulation by the contracting parties, and in particular by the employer. The employee might be given, for example, a contractual freedom to provide substitute labour which is in fact a fanciful freedom because the employee has only a limited capability to take advantage of it . . .
>
> Second, it is far from clear that the freedom not to do the work personally is a fully reliable indicator of non-dependent work relationships. It is significant that both German and British law in their definitions of 'homework' embrace situations where the homeworkers employs assistants in the homework business . . .
>
> [O]ur final submission is that some problems in commercial law may be best solved by the application of techniques drawn from labour law; and this constitutes out third reason for not excluding labour law *in limine* from this type of contract . . .
>
> Space permits but one example of this approach. We refer to EC Directive 86/653/EEC on self-employed commercial agents . . . The definition of a self-employed commercial agent is in terms of the agent's function, i.e. to negotiate the sale or purchase of goods on behalf of or in the name of a principal. There is no requirement that this service be rendered personally and indeed the agent may be a corporate body . . . What the Directive does is adapt labour law techniques to solve a commercial law problem . . . From labour law it takes the ideas of mandatory notice periods for the termination of the agency contract and also the notion of compulsory payments by the principal to the agent upon termination . . .

Perhaps the most troublesome instance of dependent entrepreneurs for the proper scope of labour regulation concerns temporary agency workers. In this triangular relation, the worker asks an agency to find temporary work with its clients for the worker. If the worker accepts a placement, the agency pays the worker an agreed rate, and in return, the worker undertakes to comply with the rules of the agency. If the agency finds such a placement, it enters into a contract with the client for fees for its service. There is no express contractual relation between the worker and client, though whilst on an assignment the worker will be performing work personally for

the client and under the control of the client. For the application of labour regulation, the question arises as to the nature of the express contract between the worker
and the agency: is it a contract of employment, or some kind of contract to perform
personally work or services, or some other species of contract that falls outside the
scope of labour law? The terms of the contract for the placement with a client usually
describe the position of the worker as an independent contractor or self-employed,
but the label attached by the parties to the contract will not determine the court's
assessment of the correct classification in the light of the whole agreement and its
factual matrix.

[2.64] *McMeechan v Secretary of State for Employment* [1997] ICR 549 (CA)

Under the legislation governing insolvency, now contained in ERA 1996 section 182
(below 10.4.1), an employee of a company that goes into insolvent liquidation may claim
unpaid wages from the Secretary of State for Employment. Mr McMeechan had been a
temporary worker registered with an employment agency, Noel Employment Ltd, and had
fulfilled a series of engagements arranged by the agency. There was no written contract
to govern the relation between the parties in general, but for each assignment Mr
McMeechan was issued with a job description and a written statement of terms and
conditions. When the employment agency went into insolvent liquidation, Mr McMeechan
was not paid his wages for his last job for a client working as a catering assistant for four
days. He claimed the £105 from the Secretary of State, who disputed the claim on the
ground that Mr McMeecham was not an employee as required by the statute (then EPCA
1978, section 122). The Court of Appeal upheld the claim for wages on the ground that
during the four days of work under the job sheet Mr McMeecham was an employee of the
employment agency.

Waite LJ:
The job sheet . . . was headed with the name of the contractor [the agency] and began with
a series of boxes in which the temporary worker was required to enter his or her name and
payroll number, the end date of the week concerned, the nature of the booking, the place
of booking, the invoice address, the client account and order number, the person to whom
the worker was to report, and the starting day and time. The relevant boxes had been
completed by the applicant on the copy job sheet he produced to the industrial tribunal by
inserting 15 January 1993 as the week ending date and 12 January as the starting date. The
nature and place of booking were described respectively as general catering assistant and
Sutcliffe Catering (Swindon) . . .
Below that were set out the following conditions:

'Conditions of Service (Temporary Self-Employed Workers)
(1) You will provide your services to the contractor as a self- employed worker and not
under a contract of service. (2) You will provide your services commencing on the date
shown on the timesheet until the end of the same week or such earlier date as the hirer
(referred to below as 'the client') may determine. (3) The contractor agrees to offer you
the opportunity to work on a self-employed basis where there is a suitable assignment
with a client but the contractor reserves the right to offer each assignment to such
temporary worker ('temporary') as it may elect in cases where that stated above
assignment is suitable for one of several temporaries. (4) The contractor shall pay your
wages calculated at the rate stated above payable weekly in arrears subject to

deductions for the purposes of National Insurance, PAYE or any other purpose required by law. An overtime premium will be paid provided this is agreed in writing by the client. (5) You are under no obligation to accept any offer made under paragraph (3) but if you do so you are required to fulfil the normal common law duties which an employee would owe to an employer as far as they are applicable. In addition, you will at all times when services are to be performed for a client comply with the following conditions. You will: (a) not engage in any conduct detrimental to the interests of the contractor; (b) upon being supplied to the client by the contractor not contract with any other contractor, consultant or agency for the purpose of the supply of your temporary services of what ever nature to the client unless a period of 13 weeks has elapsed since the time that you ceased to be supplied to the client by the contractor; (c) be present during the times, or for the total number of hours, during each day and/or seek as are required by the contractor or the client; (d) provide to the client faithful service of a standard such as would be required under a contract of employment; (e) take all reasonable steps to safeguard your own safety and the safety of any other person who may be affected by your actions at work; (f) comply with any disciplinary rules or obligations in force at the premises where services are performed to the extent that they are reasonably applicable; (g) comply with all reasonable instructions and requests within the scope of the agreed services made either by the contractor or the client; and (h) keep confidential all information which may come to your notice whilst working for the client and keep secret all and any of the client's affairs of which you may gain knowledge. (6) The contractor is not obliged to provide and you are not required to serve any particular number of hours during any day or week. In the event of your declining to accept any offer of work or failing to attend work for any reason for any period, this contract shall terminate. (7) You are not entitled to payment from the contractor for holidays (including statutory holidays) or absence due to sickness or injury. The contractor provides no pension rights. (8) The contractor shall be responsible for making all statutory deductions relating to earnings related insurance and income tax under Schedule E in accordance with the Finance (No 2) Act 1975 and transmitting these to the Inland Revenue. (9) You acknowledge and confirm that the nature of temporary work is such that there may be periods between assignments when no work is available. (10) The contractor may instruct you to end an assignment with a client at any time on summary notice to that effect, without specifying any reasons. (11) Following a decision by the contractor that your services are no longer required on a self-employed basis you shall have the right to request a review of the decision by the relevant branch manager. (12) If you have any grievance connected with the offered assignment or relations with client or any employee of the client, you shall have the right to present the grievance to the manager of the branch of the contractor through which you are offered work. If no conclusion satisfactory to you is reached at this stage you may present the grievance for ultimate decision to the area manager. (13) The qualifying days for statutory sick pay shall be Monday to Friday or the days in the week when you would be available for work and when a suitable assignment had been offered but in any event shall not exceed Monday to Friday inclusive. (14) You are required to inform the contractor by no later than 10 am on the first qualifying day of sickness so that the contractor can make arrangements to provide alternative workers to the client' . . .

This appeal involves a familiar but elusive question: what marks the difference between a contract of service and a contract for services? . . .

Temporary or casual workers pose a particular problem of their own, in that in their case there will frequently be two engagements, to use a neutral term, which the tribunal may be called upon to analyse. There is the general engagement, on the one hand, under which sporadic tasks are performed by the one party at the behest of the other and the specific engagement on the other hand which begins and ends with the performance of any one task. Each engagement is capable, according to its context, of giving rise to a contract of employment. That was acknowledged by this court in *Nethermere (St Neots) Ltd v Gardiner* [1984] ICR 612 and accepted by the majority in *O'Kelly's* case ...

Lord Meston's fundamental submission that no claim to single-stint employee status as between the temporary worker and the contractor is maintainable in law has already been stated. I would reject it for the following reasons.

(1) In a case like the present where the money claimed is related to a single stint served for one individual client, it is logical to relate the claim to employment status to the particular job of work in respect of which payment is being sought. I note that the editors of *Harvey on Industrial Relations and Employment Law* appear to take a similar view, where they suggest, at paragraph A53:

> 'the better view is not whether the casual worker is obliged to turn up for, or do, the work but rather if he turns up for, and does the work, whether he does so under a contract of service or for services'.

(2) There is nothing inherently repugnant, whether to good relations in the workplace or in law, about a state of affairs under which, in an employment agency case, the status of employee of the agency is allocated to a temporary worker in respect of each assignment actually worked, notwithstanding that the same worker may not be entitled to employee status under his general terms of engagement. In *O'Kelly v Trusthouse Forte Plc* the industrial tribunal reached, fortuitously, a decision that both the general and the specific engagement failed to give rise to a contract of service. The importance of the case, however, is that the tribunal did give independent consideration to both heads of engagement, and was held to have been right to do so ...

(3) The force of (2) is not lost in cases where, following what appears to be a common though potentially confusing practice, the agency and the temporary worker have committed themselves to standard terms and conditions which are intended to apply both to the general engagement and to the individual stints worked under it. The only result of that fusion is that the same conditions will have to be interpreted from a different perspective, according to whether they are being considered in the context of the general engagement or in the context of a single assignment. That does not make the task of the tribunals any easier, and is liable to lead to the unsatisfactory consequence that the same condition may need to be given a different significance in the one context from that accorded to it in the other. Those disadvantages do not, however, supply any valid reason for denying the temporary worker or the contractor the right to have the issue of contractual status judged separately in the two contexts ...

The issue is whether the individual assignment worked by the applicant for Sutcliffe Caterers for a period of four days during January 1992, in respect of which he claims his unpaid remuneration, did or did not amount to a contract of service in its own right. That is a question which, though it remains essentially one of fact and degree (*O'Kelly v Trusthouse Forte Plc* [1983] ICR 728, 762 and *Lee Ting Sang v Chung Chi-Keung* [1990] ICR 409 (PC)), is one which largely falls to be determined on the interpretation of the conditions.

Those must, however, be construed according to the context afforded by a specific, as opposed to a general, engagement. That requires them to be interpreted, in my judgment, as follows.

(1) The importation of common law duties by the latter part of condition 5 favours the

inference of a contract of service, because, even though the notional importation of a master servant relationship is expressed to apply in the first instance only as between the temporary worker and the client, the sub-paragraphs of the condition contain a number of instances where there is a duality of duty owed both to the client and to the contractor . . .

(2) The conditions (3, 6, 9 and the first sentence of 5) excluding mutuality of obligation are irrelevant in this context. That is not to say that in the different context of a general engagement they would be without effect. They might there turn out to be of crucial, even decisive, importance. In the circumstances of a specific engagement, however, there is nothing on which they can operate. When it comes to considering the terms of an individual, self-contained engagement the fact that the parties are not obliged in future to offer, or to accept, another engagement with the same, or a different, client must be neither here nor there.

(3) Weighing the conditions in the way that the law requires, there is to be set on the one side (contract for services) the express statement that the worker is to be regarded as self-employed and not to be working under a contract of service and the liberty reserved to the worker of being able to work on a self-employed basis for a particular client. On the other side (contract of service) are to be set the reservation of a power of dismissal for misconduct; the power of the contractor to bring any assignment to an end; the provision of a review procedure if such termination takes place; the establishment of a grievance procedure; the importation referred to in (1) above and the stipulation of an hourly pay rate, which is subject to deductions for unsatisfactory time keeping, work, attitude or misconduct.

(4) When those indications are set against each other and the specific engagement is looked at as a whole in all its terms, the general impression which emerges is that the engagement involved in this single assignment gave rise, despite the label put on it by the parties, to a contract of service between the temporary worker and the contractor.

In this decision, despite the express statement in the contract between the agency and the worker that he was to be regarded as self-employed, the court was able to rely on other inconsistent terms of the contract that imposed obligations of employment to reach the conclusion that the worker was an employee of the agency. The difficulty with this conclusion is, of course, that the worker actually performs the work for and is under the control of another party, namely the client of agency. Should the worker be regarded as an employee of the client for whom the work is actually performed, or of the agency that pays his wages, or neither on the ground that in none of the triangular relations can we discover the normal pattern of employment that one party agrees to pay wages in return for performance of work by the other?

[2.65] *Dacas v Brook Street Bureau (UK) Ltd* **[2004] EWCA Civ 217 [2004] ICR 1437 (CA)**

A claimant for unfair dismissal had worked for about five years under a placement provided by an employment agency as a cleaner in a hostel called West Drive run by Wandsworth Borough Council, the client of the agency. Following a complaint about alleged misconduct on the part of the claimant made by the Council, the agency told her that it would no longer be finding work for her and she ceased working at the hostel. The employment tribunal concluded that she had been employed neither by the Council nor the agency, and that accordingly she had no right to bring a claim for unfair dismissal against either party. The claimant successfully appealed to the EAT against that decision with respect to the finding that the agency was not her employer. On further appeal by the agency, the Court of Appeal allowed the appeal, holding that the employment tribunal had correctly concluded that the worker's contract with the agency could not be classified as a contract of employment because the agency was under no obligation to provide work, the applicant was under no obligation to accept work, and the agency did not exercise day-to-day control over her work. The Court of Appeal also heard argument on the issue of whether the Council was her employer instead, though since that point had not been raised in the appeal, the issue was only relevant in so far as a possible contract of employment with the Council might negative a finding of a contract of employment with the agency. A majority of the Court of Appeal (Mummery, Sedley LJJ, with Munby J dissenting) expressed the view that the employment tribunal should have considered the possibility that despite the absence of an express contract between the client (or end-user) and the worker, an implied contract of employment had arisen as a result of the conduct of the parties.

Mummery LJ:

The statutory definition of a contract of employment as a 'contract of service' expressly includes an 'implied' contract . . . As already indicated, the overall situation under consideration is shaped by the triangular format used for the organisation of work: the applicant, the employment agency and the end-user are all involved. Each participant in the triangular situation may have an express contract with either one of, or with each of, the other two parties.

The critical point is that, although the construction of the contractual documents is important, it is not necessarily determinative of the contract of service questions, as contractual documents do not always cover all the contractual territory or exhaust all the contractual possibilities . . . The totality of the triangular arrangements may lead to the necessary inference of a contract between such parties, when they have not actually entered into an express contract, either written or oral, with one another . . .

If the applicant has a contract of service in a triangular situation of this kind, it may be with (a) the end-user, the contract usually being an implied one, or (b) the employment agency, depending on the construction of the express contract between the applicant and the agency and on other admissible evidence or, though this is more problematical, (c) more than one entity exercising the functions of an employer, namely the employment agency and the end-user jointly (see M. Freedland, *The Personal Employment Contract* (Oxford, OUP, 2003) pp. 42-43.) . . .

I approach the question posed by this kind of case on the basis that the outcome, which would accord with practical reality and common sense, would be that, if it is legally and factually permissible to do so, the applicant has a contract, which is not a contract of service, with the employment agency, and that the applicant works under an implied contract, which is a contract of service, with the end-user and is therefore an employee of the end-user with a right not to be unfairly dismissed. The objective fact and degree of control over the work done by Mrs Dacas at West Drive over the years is crucial. The council in fact exercised the relevant control over her work and over her. As for mutuality of obligation, (a) the council was under an obligation to pay for the work that she did for it and she received payment in respect of such work from Brook Street, and (b) Mrs Dacas, while at West Drive was under an obligation to do what she was told and to attend punctually at stated times. As for dismissal, it was the council which was entitled to take and in fact took the iniative in bringing to an end work done by her at West Drive. But for the council's action she would have continued to work there as previously. It is true that the obligations and the power to dismiss were not contained in an express contract between Mrs Dacas and the council. The fact that the obligations were contained in express contracts made between Mrs Dacas and Brook Street and between Brook Street and the council does not prevent them from being read across the triangular arrangements into an implied contract and taking effect as implied mutual obligations as between Mrs Dacas and the council.

This suggestion that there may be an implied contract of employment between the client and the worker, though plausible because of the element of personal service and control by the client, has to overcome the central difficulty that the client is not in fact under an express contractual obligation to pay the worker, but on the contrary only has an express contractual relation with the agency to pay its fees. It was for this reason that Munby J doubted that any implied contract of employment, or indeed any contract at all, could be found between the client and the worker. Despite the attractions of Mummery LJ's proposed analysis for workers, it must also be recognised that clients use the services of employment agencies both to achieve flexibility in manpower and to avoid the obligations of employment law. Thus the economic rationale of these business arrangements is precisely to enable employers to contract out of many statutory protections for their employees. The alternative approach, as illustrated in *McMeecham v Secretary of State for Employment* (**[2.64]** above), is to strive to characterise the relation between the agency and the worker as a contract of employment. This approach has the advantage that the employment agency is required to assume the normal obligations of employers as part of their business, and those costs can be passed on to clients through an increase in fees. In contrast to these rival analyses under UK law, the approach of the ECJ to the concept of 'worker' under the equal pay principle is remarkably free from concern about the details of the contractual arrangements. In Case C–256/01 *Allonby v Accrington & Rossendale College* [above **2.57**] the part-time lecturers supplied as independent contractors by an employment agency were regarded as 'workers' for the purpose of bringing a claim for equal pay. The ECJ stressed that even if the lecturers were not under any obligation to undertake an assignment offered by the agency, if in practice they were subordinate to the client by being directed in the performance of work, they should be included in the scope of the concept of worker.

Employment agencies (described in law as 'employment businesses') of the kind considered in the above cases, together with recruitment businesses or 'headhunters' (known technically as 'employment agencies') are already subject to extensive regulation (Employment Agencies Act 1973, as amended by Employment Relations Act 1999 s.31; Conduct of Employment Agencies and Employment Businesses Regulations 2003, SI 2003/3319). This regulation primarily addresses the major abuses of 'labour trafficking', such as the requirement for workers to pay a proportion of their income to the person who arranges a job for them, though undoubtedly this still happens to illegal migrant workers and prostitutes. There is power to make delegated legislation on the way in which and the terms on which services may be provided by persons carrying on such agencies and businesses (Employment Agencies Act 1973, s, 5(1)(eb)). But this power has been used primarily to require employment businesses and agencies to be transparent in the terms on which they deal, and it does not restrict the freedom of the employment business to determine that the worker will be regarded as an independent contractor. The tax legislation, however, requires these workers to be treated as employees (Income and Corporation Tax Act 1988, section 134; Social Security (Categorisation of Earners) Regulations 1978, SI 1978/1689). The National Minimum Wage Act 1998, section 34 also deems agency workers to be included within its scope regardless of the precise contractual arrangements. Proposals for a European Directive on temporary agency workers have failed to achieve political agreement: L. Zappala, 'The Temporary Agency Workers' Directive: An Impossible Political Agreement? (2003) 32 *Industrial Law Journal* 310. In these proposals the European Commission both seeks to reduce restrictions in national laws on the use of temporary agency workers and at the same time to enact a non-discrimination principle, under which employers would be required to offer agency workers terms and conditions that are at least as favourable as those of directly employed permanent employees. This non-discrimination principle is likely to be rejected by employers precisely because they seek the flexibility of temporary agency workers to escape the constraints of the normal terms and conditions of their contracts of employment and the associated statutory employment rights.

2.7.4 Limits to flexibility

One conclusion that can be drawn from the attempts by the law to determine the scope of employment regulation is that the flexibility accorded to employers by the underlying principle of freedom of contract ensures that whatever boundary is selected by regulation, it will always be possible to find instances that fall outside the boundary yet arguably within the intended purpose of the legislation. In order to increase the flexibility of determining the scope of labour regulation and to counter the problem of idiosyncratic arrangements forged through the use of freedom of contract, the minister now has new delegated powers to make ad hoc inclusions of particular categories of workers.

[2.66] Employment Relations Act 1999, section 21

> **(1)** This section applies to any right conferred on an individual against an employer (however defined) under or by virtue of any of the following—
> (a)   the Trade Union and Labour Relations (Consolidation) Act 1992;
> (b)   the Employment Rights Act 1996;
> (c)   this Act;
> (d)   any instrument made under section 29(2) of the European Communities Act 1972.
> **(2)** The Secretary of State may by order make provision which has the effect of conferring any such right on individuals who are of a specified description. . . .

A similar power to extend the coverage of the legislation has been adopted in other statutes (e.g. National Minimum Wage Act 1998, section 41).

When should these powers be exercised? The preceding argument suggested that one approach should be to examine the purpose of the regulation and then determine whether the worker should be included within the scope of the regulation because the worker requires that protection against freedom of contract. Another approach is to insist that there should be a strong presumption in favour of the inclusion of a broader category than contracts of employment. It would also be possible to adopt a rebuttable statutory presumption that someone performing work is a worker (or an employee) for the purposes of statutory regulation. From an economic perspective, it might be argued that the special problems addressed by labour law are all associated with the worker's position of economic dependence: the worker has in fact only one purchaser of his or her labour power. This economic approach suggests that the boundaries of most labour regulation should be set where there is in practice a single purchaser of the worker's labour power, regardless of the form of the contract through which these services are acquired.

As we noted at the beginning of this chapter, the contract of employment as a legal concept also became a foundation for the tax system and the social security system, which together enabled the social guarantees known as the Welfare State to operate. If the model of dependent entrepreneur becomes a standard type of work relation, the coverage of the social guarantees will have to be altered so that they can provide income security and other forms of social protection to this group. But the problem remains for labour law and welfare law of how to describe a broad range of work relations through legal concepts that include all those workers who should receive employment protection rights and social protection (and exclude everyone else). No single legal concept can achieve this goal, because some legal rights, such as protection of health and safety and equality laws, should apply regardless of the form or even presence, of a contractual relation. But those rights that might be described as employment protection rights, which have as their focus the relation of subordination between the owner of the means of production and the worker, clearly cannot any longer be restricted to the traditional standard pattern of the contract of employment. To solve this problem there are apparently only three options:

- Develop a new legal concept, which avoids reference to contractual forms, and instead focuses on a criterion such as economic dependence owing to the presence of a sole purchaser in fact of labour power;
- Approach the problem on an *ad hoc* basis for each group of workers in respect of each piece of legislation, which is the method adopted in section 21 of the Employment Relations Act 1999; or
- Constrain the choice of the parties with respect to the forms of contract available for the performance of work. We consider this last option in conclusion.

It would be legally possible to place restraints on freedom of contract by requiring employers to adopt particular forms of employment relation or to prohibit certain forms. Once the number of permissible contractual forms of work relations is limited, it becomes possible to determine the scope of regulation with precision.

Such interference with freedom of contract carries its own dangers. By reducing the flexibility accorded to employers to devise efficient methods for the acquisition of labour power, employers may decide that they can no longer offer work of any kind (an unemployment effect), or that they should cut wage costs to compensate for the inflexibility that reduces the competitiveness of business. In the example of casual workers, if an employer were forced to offer contracts of employment guaranteeing some minimum hours of work, these fixed overheads might force the employer to reduce staff, reduce wages, or increase its prices and lose business. In the case of milk delivery, if the dairy were prevented from using the franchise system, it might conclude that it could no longer operate milk delivery at a profit and give up the line of business altogether. These possible outcomes are, of course, entirely speculative, but they illustrate the potential dangers of prohibitions against certain contractual forms of work relationship. Nor should we ignore the possibility that workers may have a strong preference for certain types of work relations. A worker who places a strong value on independence and the chance to earn a higher income may prefer the risks associated with self-employment, whereas another worker may prefer employment because it offers relative security of earnings and work.

Despite the obvious consequence of the exclusion of swathes of the nation's workforce from many employment protection laws from which they might benefit, for the most part governments have been persuaded by these economic reasons for rejecting control over contractual forms. Regulation has rather sought to accommodate itself to the variety of contractual forms, and the courts have generally accepted the power of the parties to fix their own terms without question. They have not perceived any illegitimacy in the various forms of atypical work, even when they so clearly, as in the *O'Kelly* and *McMeechan* cases, are designed to avoid the application of employment protection rights. In particular, the courts have not used the general prohibition against contracting out of the statutory rights in section 203 ERA 1996 ([**5.30**] below) to challenge the employer's use of non-standard forms of employment.

The general legal disposition to grant freedom of contract will constantly throw up examples of work relations that are hard to fit into the established legal categories which determine the scope of labour law such as the concept of employee or worker. Changing economic conditions may lead to the widespread adoption of contractual forms that, owing to allocation of the risks of the wage/work bargain onto the worker, appear to make the workers dependent entrepreneurs, which is a contractual form that usually falls outside the scope of labour law. For the present, the legislation seeks to address this problem by granting the minister the discretion in the Employment Relations Act 1999 s.21 ([**2.66**] above) to include particular groups of workers within particular pieces of regulation. In the longer term, however, this solution of ministerial discretion may prove unsatisfactory, because we can anticipate that the loopholes created by the fertility of freedom of contract will be closed, if at all, only long after the crucial events have occurred. What may be required is rather a general test for the application of labour laws, which emphasises the factual presence of economic dependence rather than the contractual allocation of risks. Economic dependence should be understood in this context as being comprised of reliance upon the other party as the principal supplier of work and the main source of income. The concept of 'worker', which has been adopted in legislation during the 1990s, is a useful step in that direction, but its exclusion of professional workers and independent businesses may be drawn too widely, because it may exclude types of dependent entrepreneurs who deserve statutory employment rights.

2.8 Public sector workers and public law

Most legal systems have traditionally drawn a distinction between private sector employees and employees of the State. The latter are often not even described as employees or workers. Other terms are applied instead, such as 'officials', 'office-holders', 'officers' and 'constables'. The terminology reveals that the legal status of public sector workers may not be defined by an ordinary contract of employment, or indeed any contract at all. The origin of this special category of public sector workers lie in their position as representatives and agents of sovereign power. This position created both special privileges and onerous obligations and disabilities. In particular, the ordinary private law of contract and labour law regulation were often inapplicable to these 'office-holders'. Instead, the rights of the parties were largely determined by public law.

The expansion of the role of the State during the twentieth century, however, so that it encompasses large areas of administration and management of the economy, both centrally and locally, makes these ancient categories appear antiquated and inappropriate. Why, it might be asked, should a teacher, a nurse, a chairman of an employment tribunal or a prison officer not be regarded in law like other employees? Special rules might be appropriate for ministers of the government, such as dismissal at the Queen's pleasure, or for judges, for whom perhaps dismissal should not be possible at all, or only in cases of grave dereliction of duty. Apart from these special categories, should there continue to be a fundamental distinction drawn in law between the public and private sectors, under which public sector workers are excluded from the rights and protections afforded by labour law to private sector workers? The following essay makes the case for regarding the State as a special kind of employer.

[2.67] G.S. Morris and Sandra Fredman, 'Is There a Public/Private Labour Law Divide?' (1993) 14 *Comparative Labor Law Journal* 115 (footnotes omitted)

The distinctive characteristics of State employment stem from two related factors. The first is the dual role of the State as employer and as government, which in a democratic system means that it is accountable to the legislature for its actions. The second is the source of revenue for the services the State provides. Unlike private sector employers, which derive their revenue primarily from profit and are generally dependent upon maintaining a competitive position in the market in order to survive, the State derives its revenue predominantly from taxation. The State is, therefore, subject largely to political and macroeconomic, rather than market-led, constraints in making its decisions. . . .

The effect of the differences between State and non-State employment spans a wide range of contexts. Firstly, in relation to the provision of public services, questions as to the number of workers required to provide an 'adequate' service, the level at which they should be paid, and their conditions of employment are political, and not commercial, judgments. . . .

Secondly, the difference between State and non-State employment can be seen in the context of industrial relations, where the government may override commercial considerations in favour of political goals. . . .

During a civil service strike in Britain in 1981, for example, the amount of lost revenue resulting from the refusal of inland revenue officers to collect taxes far outweighed the cost of the unions' claim. Few private sector employers could afford to make tactical decisions of this sort.

Thirdly, governments are able to introduce or invoke legislation to mitigate the impact of industrial disruption, an option not open to employers in the private sector. . . .

The distinctive position of the State as employer is also reflected in the methods of determining terms and conditions of employment and in dispute settlement procedures. With regard to the former, the ultimate accountability of government to Parliament has meant that a measure of unilateral decision making is always retained in the hands of the State. This is manifested in more extreme forms in some countries than in others, but is always evident. The strongest form is found in countries where the fact that expenditure on public service pay, like other government expenses, must be approved by Parliament has been taken to imply that the determination of pay and conditions of public employees belongs only to the sovereign power of Parliament. . . .

In relation to dispute settlement procedures, the sovereign employer concept has also proved important. Historically, in many systems, the very idea of disputes was regarded as a challenge to the existence of State authority, and procedures were therefore not developed to deal with them. . . .

Even where arbitration has been permitted, it may still remain open to the legislature to override an arbitral award. In England, the 1925 Civil Service Arbitration Agreement provided that the Government would give effect to the awards of the arbitral body '[s]ubject to the over-riding authority of Parliament,' such qualification being inserted 'to preserve the constitutional supremacy of Parliament and the possibility of a Government defeat there'. . . .

Later agreements with civil service unions expressly preserved the right of government itself to override the award; however, the government recently completely terminated arbitration agreements within the civil service. . . .

It is clear that the dual nature of the State as employer and as sovereign, coupled with the source of public service funding, means that although industrial relations practices and procedures in the State and non-State sectors may appear to be identical, in reality, fundamental differences between the two will always exist. . . .

Although these arguments seem powerful enough to justify the separate treatment of public sector workers, they assume that the State is not run on commercial lines. It was precisely this assumption that was challenged by the movement known as 'New Public Management'. This movement argued that public services could be delivered more cheaply and effectively by emulating or adopting the private market system. Public services could be reorganised so that market or 'quasi-market' relations would govern the links between units. In other words, contractual relations would be formed both between organisational units, and within those units between the public agency and the workers. Moreover, once reorganised in this way, public services could be privatised, that is contracted out to private sector organisations. This outsourcing could save substantial costs, particularly labour costs, and might also improve efficiency. The special features of the State as employer still remain pertinent, but this 'contractualisation' of public service provision diminishes their significance substantially. Furthermore, the boundaries of the realm of the public sector become unclear, because private employers become vested with the task of the provision of public services.

From these trends in government administration, that is the expansion of the role of the State into most sectors of the economy followed by the process of the 'contractualisation' or 'marketisation' of administration, we can detect three significant developments in the legal regulation of the position of public sector workers. First, the position of most public sector workers became approximated to the position of private sector workers both by the construction of ordinary contracts of employment and by the application of the private sector labour laws to public sector workers. Secondly, the courts responded to these developments by the withdrawal of public law as a tool for regulating public sector employment relations. Thirdly, most recently, the law has had to address the new question of the extent to which special rules should apply to those sectors of private business that are supplying public services.

2.8.1 The approximation of public and private sectors

It is now accepted that for the bulk of public sector workers, such as employees of the National Health Service, teachers and civil servants, their rights and obligations are defined like those of private sector workers by their contracts of employment and the employment rights legislation. To avoid doubt on this question, employment rights legislation has been extended expressly to most categories of state employees including civil servants, prison officers, and the armed forces, but with some permitted exceptions on grounds of national security (ERA 1996, sections 191–93; TULRCA 1992, sections 272–76). The principal excluded category that remains is the police force; officers probably lack contracts of employment and are excluded from statutory rights: ERA 1996, section 200.

There remain a few public sector workers, however, whose position is more complicated, because the employment relation is perhaps created without a contract of employment. This legal result can occur when by statute or prerogative power the relevant public authority has the power to appoint a person to an office. These office-holders may not have a contractual relationship at all, so their rights and obligations will be fixed by the enabling powers of the appointing authority. The question whether a contract exists in such cases depends first on whether the public authority has the power to enter into such a contract, and secondly on whether it in fact did. It was established in *R v Lord Chancellor's Department, ex parte Nangle* [1991] ICR 743 (CA) that a central government civil servant might well have a contract of employment, though ultimately this depended on the intention of the parties. In the absence of a contractual relation, office-holders will not be able to use the ordinary courts and tribunals in order to assert any legal entitlements, but will have to use the distinctive procedures of public law known as CPR part 54 (formerly Order 53).

These rare cases of office-holders aside, most public sector workers have contracts of employment and the normal bundle of statutory rights. But some special rules still apply to some groups of public sector workers. Some public sector workers have been subject traditionally to two statutory disabilities: their exclusion from the right to strike and restrictions on their right to participate in political activities. The reasons given for the prohibition on strike action by some public sector workers are to protect law and order (as in the case of the police and prison officers), to preserve national security (as in the case of the armed services and spies) and, more controversially, to ensure the supply of essential services. The problem with the last justification is, of course, that arguably all public sector workers are engaged in the provision of essential services. In the UK, restrictive legislation that imposes criminal sanctions against industrial action has generally been confined to the police, prison officers, and the armed services (e.g. Police Act 1996, section 91; Incitement to Mutiny Act 1797). For other public sector workers performing essential services, the State can use emergency powers to replace strikers, and it often uses civil actions for injunctions to prevent industrial action that does not comply with the ordinary rules described in Chapter 9. The other major restriction on public sector workers, the limitation on the ordinary civil liberty to participate in political activities can be justified as necessary in order to preserve the appearance of the political neutrality of the police, the armed forces and civil servants in the implementation of government policy. These workers can, of course, vote, but are restricted in their right to stand for election and to give public support for a political party.

As a democratically accountable body, which must set high standards of integrity and transparency in all its operations, the State is subjected to much more detailed investigations, accounting procedures and public scrutiny than private employers. These requirements may indirectly afford employees of the State with some additional rights and benefits. In the central civil service, for instance, disappointed applicants for posts can complain to Civil Service Commissioners against any failure to comply with a code of practice on recruitment, which requires appointment solely on the basis of merit. A controversial area in this respect is whether the State should be permitted to insert confidentiality clauses into contracts of employment that might have the effect of preventing public sector workers from revealing mismanagement and wrongdoing.

2.8.2 The retreat of public law

The exclusion of office-holders from contractual rights and labour law regulation may not always prove to their disadvantage. The standards of public law may give better entitlements, particularly with respect to the fairness of procedures and limits on the abuse of power, and may afford powerful remedies such as avoiding a decision of a public authority entirely. For example, in *Ridge v Baldwin* [1964] AC 40 (HL), a chief constable of a police authority was regarded as an office-holder, who could succeed in having a dismissal decision quashed on the ground of a breach of natural justice (or fair procedure). Due to the attractiveness of these public law standards and remedies, other public sector workers attempted to use the public law procedure of judicial review in order to protect their interests. In general, however, these actions will fail now on the ground that most public sector employees have access to the normal avenues for the pursuit of contractual claims and statutory rights. Public law remedies will only be available to public sector workers under limited conditions.

[2.68] *McClaren v The Home Office* [1990] IRLR 338 (CA)

A prison officer, Mr McClaren, commenced an action for breach of contract when the Governor of the prison varied the shifts. He had refused to work the new shifts and had been suspended without pay. The old shifts had been agreed between the Governor and the union, the Prison Officers' Association, under a policy known as 'Fresh Start'. Mr McClaren sought a declaration that his contract had incorporated the old Fresh Start agreement, which could not be varied without his consent. The Home Office had succeeded at first instance in having the claim struck out on the ground that no contractual claim could exist, because prison officers did not have a contract of employment. The Court of Appeal allowed the appeal on the ground that the Home Office did have the power to enter contractual agreements, so Mr McClaren would be permitted to try to establish that a contract had been made and that it contained terms which restricted the Governor's power to alter shifts.

Woolf LJ:
There are two issues on this appeal:
1. Is a plaintiff required to bring his claim against the Home Office by way of judicial review?
2. If he is not required to bring his proceedings by way of judicial review has he a reasonable cause of action or was his claim correctly struck out as being clearly unsustainable?

The first issue
In resolving this issue the following principles have to be borne in mind:
   1. In relation to his personal claims against an employer, an employee of a public body is normally in exactly the same situation as other employees. If he has a cause of action and he wishes to assert or establish his rights in relation to his employment he can bring proceedings for damages, a declaration or an injunction (except in relation to the Crown) in the High Court or the County Court in the ordinary way. The fact that a person is employed by the Crown may limit his rights against the Crown but otherwise his position is very much the same as any other employee. However, he may, instead of having an ordinary master and servant relationship with the Crown, hold office under the Crown and may have been appointed to that office as a result of the Crown exercising a prerogative power or, as in this case, a statutory power. If he holds such an appointment then it will almost invariably be terminable at will and may be subject to other limitations but whatever rights the employee has will be enforceable normally by an ordinary action. Not only will it not be necessary for him to seek relief by way of judicial review, it will normally be inappropriate for him to do so (see *Kodeeswaran v The Attorney-General of Ceylon* [1970] AC 1111; *R v East Berkshire Health Authority ex parte Walsh* [1984] IRLR 278 and *ex parte Noble* [1990] IRLR 332).
   2. There can however be situations where an employee of a public body can seek judicial review and obtain a remedy which would not be available to an employee in the private sector. This will arise where there exists some disciplinary or other body established under the prerogative or by statute to which the employer or the employee is entitled or required to refer disputes affecting their relationship. The procedure of judicial review can then be appropriate because it has always been part of the role of the court in public law proceedings to supervise inferior tribunals and the court in reviewing disciplinary proceedings is performing a similar role. As long as the 'tribunal' or other body has a sufficient public law element, which it almost invariably will have if the employer is the Crown, and it is not domestic or wholly informal its proceedings and

determination can be an appropriate subject for judicial review. An example is provided here by the decision of the Divisional Court in *R v The Civil Service Appeal Board, ex parte Bruce* [1988] 3 AER 686. If there had not been available the more effective alternative remedy before an industrial tribunal, the Divisional Court would have regarded the decision of the Civil Service Appeal Board in that case as reviewable upon judicial review. The decision of this Court which has just been given in *ex parte Attard* is another example of the same situation. There what was being considered by this Court were the powers of a prison governor in connection with disciplinary proceedings in respect of prison officers. The prison governor's disciplinary powers in relation to prisoners are reviewable only on judicial review (see *Leech v The Deputy Governor of Parkhurst Prison* [1988] AC 533) and they can be also reviewed on judicial review where they affect a prison officer on the application of that officer.

3. In addition if an employee of the Crown or other public body is adversely affected by a decision of general application by his employer, but he contends that that decision is flawed on what I loosely describe as *Wednesbury* grounds, he can be entitled to challenge that decision by way of judicial review. Within this category comes the case of *R v Secretary of State for Foreign and Commonwealth Affairs ex parte The Council of Civil Service Union* [1985] IRLR 28. In the House of Lords there was no dispute as to whether the case was appropriately brought by way of judicial review. The House of Lords assumed that it was and I would respectfully suggest that they were right to do so. The decision under challenge was one affecting employees at GCHQ generally. The action which was being challenged was the instruction by the Minister for the Civil Service in the interests of national security to vary the terms and conditions of service of the staff so that they would no longer be permitted to belong to trade unions. Although the decision affected individual members of the staff, it was a decision which was taken as a matter of policy, not in relation to a particular member of staff, but in relation to staff in general and so it could be the subject of judicial review.

4. There can be situations where although there are disciplinary procedures which are applicable they are of a purely domestic nature and therefore, albeit that their decisions might affect the public, the process of judicial review will not be available. However this does not mean that a particular employee who is adversely affected by those disciplinary proceedings will not have a remedy. The existence of the disciplinary proceedings may be highly material to indicate that the category of employee concerned, unlike an ordinary employee, is not limited to a claim for damages but can in the appropriate circumstances in an ordinary action seek a declaration or an injunction to ensure that the proceedings are conducted fairly. (As to dismissal see *Ridge v Baldwin* [1960] AC 40, per Lord Reid at p.65 and *Law v National Greyhound Racing Club Ltd* [1983] 1 WLR 1302 and *R v BBC ex parte Lavelle* [1982] IRLR 404.)

In giving his judgment in this case, Hoffmann J was of the view that there was no 'arguable distinction between the facts of this case and those of Mr Bruce (referring to the case cited above)'. I disagree. In this case, unlike the *Bruce* case which falls within the second category, Mr McLaren is not making any complaint about disciplinary proceedings. He is seeking declarations as to the terms of his employment and a sum which he alleges is due for services rendered. If those claims have any merit they fall within the first category set out above. They are private law claims which require private rights to support them. Mr Tabachnik firmly disavowed any suggestion that any public law claim is being advanced by Mr McLaren. Whether or not he is an employee of the Crown or has a contract of service, or holds an office under the Crown, he is entitled to bring private law proceedings if he has reasonable grounds for contending that his private law rights have been infringed. As his claim is pleaded and advanced by Mr Tabachnik, it is entirely unsuited to judicial review. Unlike continental jurisdictions in which there is a

Conseil d'État, claims of the kind which are made by Mr McLaren have to be brought by ordinary civil proceedings unless they are subsidiary to other public law claims, in which case it may be possible for them now to be disposed of in the same proceedings on an application for judicial review. The first issue must therefore be resolved in favour of the appellant.

The second issue

. . . There is now a considerable number of dicta which indicate that it is possible for a servant of the Crown to have contractual rights. . . . In the *Bruce* case itself Roch J recognised that there could be terms of the appointment of a civil servant which could have legal effect. If there are such terms then they would give rise to private rights. In the case of prison officers they would result from the exercise by the Home Office of their statutory powers which are incidental to their statutory power to appoint prison officers but even if they were derived from the prerogative, this would not alter the nature of the rights created, only the source of the authority for creating the rights.

Once it is conceded, as in my view it has to be, that there is at least an arguable case for contending that the relationship between prison officers and the Home Office could have a contractual element, then (subject to it not affecting the power of the Crown to dismiss) the extent and the effect of the contractual element is a matter to be determined after evidence and full argument at the hearing.

Although the task with which the plaintiff is faced, as Dillon LJ has pointed out, is the difficult one of establishing that Fresh Start is incorporated into his terms of service, even in the absence of any express agreement to this effect, the task is by no means impossible. It is to be borne in mind that Fresh Start has been incorporated de facto into the plaintiff's terms of service and the issue at the trial will be limited to ascertaining whether it has been incorporated de jure as well.

Outside the special category of office-holders without contractual rights, this judgment makes clear that the possibility of a claim for judicial review depends upon the nature of the decision that has been taken. Woolf LJ identifies two categories of decision where a claim for judicial review might succeed. The first category comprises the legality of decisions of domestic tribunals constituted under statutory powers. The decision of a tribunal may be quashed, for instance, because the tribunal has acted outside its powers (illegality or *ultra vires*) or because it has failed to provide a fair hearing or to give reasons for a decision (procedural impropriety or breach of natural justice). The second category is the claim to impugn the rationality of the decision of a public authority on the ground that no reasonable body could have reached such a decision. Although public sector employees are more likely to wish to challenge such decisions, in principle a claim for judicial review might be available for private sector workers who wish to challenge a decision of a public body that adversely affects them. In *R v Secretary of State for Employment, ex parte Equal Opportunities Commission* [1994] IRLR 176 (HL), for instance, the EOC obtained a declaration under the public law procedure that UK legislation on the entitlements of both public and private part-time workers to redundancy payments were incompatible with the European Equal Treatment Directive. Examples of challenges mounted against decisions of public authorities that affect employees include decisions to vary terms and conditions of employment (*R v Hertfordshire County Council, ex parte NUPE* [1985] IRLR 258 (CA)), and decisions to make redundancies (*R v Liverpool City Council, ex parte Ferguson The Times*, 20 November 1985, noted G.S. Morris, (1986) 15 ILJ 194).

Examples of permitted claims by workers under public law procedures and principles are unlikely to be frequent. Most disputes between public sector workers and their employer can be classified by the court as a contractual dispute, to be governed by the private law of contract and statutory employment rights, without any public law issue being raised at all. Alternatively, many modern statutes conferring employment rights expressly extend many of those rights to special status workers in the public sector, such as officers of the Crown (ERA 1996 s. 191), members of the armed forces (ERA 1996 s.192), and Parliamentary staff (ERA 1996 ss. 194-5). Furthermore, even when workers have established their right to use a public law procedure in order to challenge the decision of a public authority, the courts retain a discretion to refuse to grant a remedy on the ground that another forum or process would be more appropriate. In particular, where the legal issues could be adequately explored by the employee bringing a claim for a contractual right or a statutory employment right before a court or a tribunal, a court is likely to exercise its discretion to deny a public law remedy.

[2.69] *R v East Berkshire Health Authority, ex parte Walsh* [1984] ICR 743 (CA)

A senior nursing officer was dismissed for misconduct by a district nursing officer (Miss Cooper). The terms of employment were fixed by a statutory procedure for reaching collective agreements within the National Health Service known as the Whitely Council agreement. The dismissed employee sought judicial review of the dismissal with a view to having it declared void on the grounds that the district nursing officer had no power to dismiss (*ultra vires*) and that the procedure followed prior to dismissal was unfair (a breach of the rules of natural justice). The Court of Appeal stopped the proceedings on the ground that the application was a misuse of the procedure for judicial review.

Sir John Donaldson MR:
I now return to the main issue, namely whether the applicant's complaints give rise to any right to judicial review. They all relate to his employment by the health authority and the purported termination of his employment and of his contract of employment. Essentially they fall into two distinct categories. The first relates to Miss Cooper's power to act on behalf of the authority in dismissing him. The second relates to the extent to which there was any departure from the rules of natural justice in the procedures which led up to that dismissal. Both fall well within the jurisdiction of an industrial tribunal. The first goes to whether or not the applicant was dismissed at all within the meaning of section 55 of the Employment Protection (Consolidation) Act 1978. The second goes to whether the dismissal, if such there was, was unfair. Furthermore, both are issues which not uncommonly arise when the employer is a company or individual, as contrasted with a statutory authority. However, this only goes to the exercise of the court's discretion, whether or not to give leave to apply for and whether or not to grant judicial review. As the authority seek to have the proceedings dismissed in limine, if they are to succeed they can only do so on the basis that, accepting all the applicant's complaints as valid, the remedy of judicial review is nevertheless wholly inappropriate and the continuance of the application for judicial review would involve a misuse—the term 'abuse' has offensive overtones—of the procedure of the court under R.S.C., Ord. 53. . . .

In *Ridge v Baldwin* [1964] AC 40 (HL), Lord Reid classified dismissals under three heads in terms of the right to be heard. They were (a) dismissal by a master, (b) dismissal from an office held during pleasure, and (c) dismissal from an office where there must be something against a man to warrant his dismissal. He held that in case (b) there was no right to be heard and that in case (c) there was always a right to be heard. Dealing with master and servant cases (case (a) above) he said, at p. 65:

> 'The law regarding master and servant is not in doubt. There cannot be specific performance of a contract of service, and the master can terminate the contract with his servant any any time and for any reason or for none. But if he does so in a manner not warranted by the contract he must pay damages for breach of contract. So the question in a pure case of master and servant does not at all depend on whether the master has heard the servant in his own defence: it depends on whether the facts emerging at the trial prove breach of contract. But this kind of case can resemble dismissal from an office where the body employing the man is under some statutory or other restriction as to the kind of contract which it can make with its servants, or the grounds on which it can dismiss them'.

In *Ridge v Baldwin* the power of dismissal was conferred by statute: section 191(4) of the Municipal Corporations Act 1882 (45 & 46 Vict. c.50). In *Malloch v Aberdeen Corporation* [1971] WLR 1578 (HL) again it was statutory: section 3 of the Public Schools (Scotland) Teachers Act 1882 (45 & 46 Vict. c.18). As Lord Wilberforce said, at pp. 1595–1596, it is the existence of these statutory provisions which injects the element of public law necessary in this context to attract the remedies of administrative law. Employment by a public authority does not per se inject any element of public law. Nor does the fact that the employee is in a 'higher grade' or is an 'officer.' This only makes it more likely that there will be special statutory restrictions upon dismissal or other underpinning of his employment: see *per* Lord Reid in *Malloch v Aberdeen Corporation*, at p. 1582. It will be this underpinning and not the seniority which injects the element of public law. Still less can I find any warrant for equating public law with the interest of the public. If the public through Parliament gives effect to that interest by means of statutory provisions, that is quite different, but the interest of the public per se is not sufficient.

I have therefore to consider whether and to what extent the applicant's complaints involve an element of public law sufficient to attract public law remedies, whether in the form of certiorari or a declaration. That he had the benefit of the general employment legislation is clear, but it was not contended that this was sufficient to attract administrative law remedies. What is relied upon are statutory restrictions upon the freedom of the authority to employ senior and other nursing officers on what terms it thought fit. This restriction is contained in the National Health Service (Remuneration and Conditions of Service) Regulations 1974 (S.I. 1974 No. 296), which provides by regulation 3(2):

> 'where conditions of service, other than conditions with respect to remuneration, of any class of officers have been the subject of negotiations by a negotiating body and have been approved by the Secretary of State after considering the result of those negotiations, the conditions of service of any officer belonging to that class shall include the conditions so approved'.

The conditions of service of, inter alios, senior nursing officers were the subject of negotiations by a negotiating body, namely the Whitley Council for the Health Service (Great Britain) and the resulting agreement was approved by the Secretary of State. It follows, as I think, that if the applicant's conditions of service had differed from those approved conditions, he would have had an administrative law remedy by way of judicial review enabling him to require the authority to amend the terms of service contained in his contract of employment. But that is not the position. His notification of employment dated 12 May 1975, which is a memorandum of his contract of employment, expressly adopted the Whitley Council agreement on conditions of service.

When analysed, the applicant's complaint is different. It is that *under* those conditions of service Miss Cooper had no right to dismiss him and that *under* those conditions he was entitled to a bundle of rights which can be collectively classified as 'natural justice.' Thus he says, and I have to assume for present purposes that he is correct, that under section XXXIV of the Whitley Council's agreement on conditions of service, his position as a senior nursing officer is such that his employment can only be terminated by a decision of the full employing authority and that this power of dismissal cannot be delegated to any officer or committee of officers. I do not think that he relies upon any express provision of those conditions when claiming the right to natural justice, but if he has such a right, apart from the wider right not to be unfairly dismissed which includes the right to natural justice, it clearly arises out of those conditions and is implicit in them.

The ordinary employer is free to act in breach of his contracts of employment and if he does so his employee will acquire certain private law rights and remedies in damages for wrongful dismissal, compensation for unfair dismissal, an order for reinstatement or re-engagement and so on. Parliament can underpin the position of public authority employees by directly restricting the freedom of the public authority to dismiss, thus giving the employee 'public law' rights and at least making him a potential candidate for administrative law remedies. Alternatively it can require the authority to contract with its employees on specified terms with a view to the employee acquiring 'private law' rights under the terms of the contract of employment. If the authority fails or refuses to thus create 'private law' rights for the employee, the employee will have 'public law' rights to compel compliance, the remedy being mandamus requiring the authority so to contract or a declaration that the employee has those rights. If, however, the authority gives the employee the required contractual protection, a breach of that contract is not a matter of 'public law' and gives rise to no administrative law remedies. . . .

I therefore conclude that there is no 'public law' element in the applicant's complaints which could give rise to any entitlement to administrative law remedies. I confess that I am not sorry to have been led to this conclusion, since a contrary conclusion would have enabled *all* National Health Service employees to whom the Whitley Council agreement on conditions of service apply to seek judicial review. Whilst it is true that the judge seems to have thought that this right would be confined to senior employees, I see no grounds for any such restriction in principle. The most that can be said is that only senior employees could complain of having been dismissed in the exercise of delegated authority, because it is only senior employees who are protected from such dismissal. *All* employees would however have other rights based upon the fact that Parliament had intervened to specify and, on this view, protect those conditions of service as a matter of 'public law'.

In my judgment, this is not therefore a case for judicial review.

How convincing is the reasoning in this case? Would it be possible to question whether any dismissal had taken place at all through an action for breach of contract? That seems extremely doubtful, since a dismissal in breach of contract is regarded by private law as a repudiation of the contract, not an action with no legal effects at all (below 5.1.2). Would it have been possible to assert that the employer was in breach of an implied term of 'natural justice' in the contract of employment? This might be possible, though not in exactly those terms or with the same strict safeguards, for a misuse of a contractual disciplinary procedure might amount to a breach of the implied term of trust and confidence. What is evident in this decision, however, is a determination to exclude most disputes between the State and its employees from public law procedures and standards.

One reason why the courts may have been so reluctant to permit public law procedures to be used to benefit public sector workers was a belief that the standards of public law might give these workers superior rights to those of workers in the private sector, and therefore might overly restrict the power of management in the public sector. Although some doubt has been cast on the difference between public law standards and those established through the private law of contract and statutory employment rights, there is a strong case for thinking that public law standards, especially those concerned with fair procedures or natural justice, set more rigorous standards for employers. Public law requires the procedure to be fair and unbiased unless the departure from this standard creates no risk of unfairness and no possible perception of unfairness: *R v Chief Constable of Thames Valley Police, ex parte Cotton* [1990] IRLR 344 (CA). Under the law of unfair dismissal, however, deviations from these standards are permitted on the looser grounds of practicability and reasonableness (below 5.4.3). The public law standard also strongly resists the argument that a fair procedure would not have altered the outcome and would therefore have been futile: *Chief Constable of North Wales Police v Evans* [1982] 1 WLR 1155, 1160–1, 1174–5 (HL); *Malloch v Aberdeen Corporation* [1971] 1 WLR 1578 (HL); whereas the law of unfair dismissal permits the reduction or elimination of procedures on grounds of reasonableness including the futility of the exercise: *Polkey v A.E. Dayton Services Ltd* [1988] ICR 142 (HL), ([5.52] below). Furthermore, public law holds out the possibility that a decision to dismiss a worker may be quashed, with the effect that the worker retains his or her job, whereas contractual and statutory remedies for dismissal seldom provide reinstatement as a remedy. The philosophical difference of approach between private law and public law is considered in the following passage.

[2.70] Mark Freedland, 'Status and Contract in the Law of Public Employment' (1991) 20 *Industrial Law Journal* 72

> The theory I am putting forward suggests that, in the context at least of a contrast with public law status, the contractual approach to the employment relationship concentrates on the substantive and specific aspects of the relations; by contrast, the approach in terms of public law status concentrates on the procedural and diffuse aspects of the relationship. The contractual approach presents the relationship in terms of a mutually conditional agreement to employ and remunerate on the one hand and to work on the other. The mutual conditions will tend to be defined in specific substantive terms; thus the employer's obligation to employ is limited or limitable in point of time, and usually conditional upon the employee's not committing serious misconduct. On this approach, if the employee does commit serious misconduct, the employer's obligation to employ is negated; the employee has no expectation which was violated by his dismissal. The public law status approach, on the other hand, envisages the employer and the employee or office-holder as bound by more diffuse and procedural obligations; the employee must proceed according to the dictates of commitment, and the employer must proceed according to those of fairness. On this approach, the justice of a dismissal will depend on the interplay between these two sets of essentially procedural expectations, rather than upon a set of facts which exists independently of those expectations.

2.8.3 Government by contract

Our discussion so far has assumed that a clear distinction can be drawn between public sector workers employed by the State and private sector workers. The distinction is based upon the legal status of the employer: if the employer is a public authority, created by either statute or prerogative power, any employee must be a public sector worker. As a result of privatisation measures and the development of strategies for delivering public services through contractual arrangements with the private sector through outsourcing, however, many of these workers who provide essential public services are not longer employed by the State. These developments are likely to intensify as a result of competition policy within the EU. All public and private undertakings that are entrusted with the operation of services of general economic interest are subject to the principles of the Treaty of the European Community that guarantee free access to markets and control monopolies, which has the effect that many public services must become open to competition from other potential providers. The question for labour law is whether any special rights and obligations traditionally applied to workers employed by the State should also be extended to those workers who are performing public service jobs but in the private sector. In the following passage this group of workers are described as the 'public-service sector'.

[2.71] Mark Freedland, 'Law, Public Services, and Citizenship—New Domains, New Regimes?' in Mark Freedland and Silvana Sciarra (eds), *Public Services and Citizenship in European Law: Public and Labour Law Perspectives* (Oxford, Oxford University Press, 1998) (footnotes omitted)

We are witnessing, in the law and practice of European countries, quite a rapid evolution of a third sector which we might call the public-service sector, which we have to distinguish from, on the one hand, the state sector and, on the other hand, the wholly private sector. In this third sector, ideas about citizenship (both at State level and at European Community level) are particularly significant and influential, especially in the way that they inform the shape and application of public law and labour law. . . .

But we should not be deceived, by the high-sounding references to notions of public service and of citizenship, into thinking that this is a sector in which there is a particular consensus as to values and policies which should determine the shape of the legal regime. On the contrary, by identifying this third sector, we actually concentrate attention upon a set of conflicts and tensions which occur, certainly, in the other sectors, but which are experienced especially acutely in this sector. . . .

For the purposes of our argument, then, we offer the following working definition of the third, public-service, sector. It is the sector of the economy in which services or activities, recognized as public in the sense that the State is seen as ultimately responsible for the provision of them, are nevertheless not provided by the State itself but by institutions which are intermediate between the market and the State. These institutions are, on the one hand, too independent of the State to be regarded as part of the State, but are, on the other hand, too closely and distinctively associated with the goals, activities, and responsibilities of the State to be thought of as simply part of the private sector of the political economy. . . .

It is important, for this purpose, to realize that the existence of this distinctive third intermediate sector is not asserted as a matter of existing political, economic, or legal theory. In fact, the point will be made that the assertion of the distinctness of the public-service sector cuts across and challenges much conventional legal analysis, which is of an essentially binary character, insisting on a straightforward dichotomy between the public and the private sectors, between the realms of public and of private law. . . .

If, as we shall hope to argue, it is thus possible to construct a useful tripartite theoretical model from these practical realities, it is at the same time also important to acknowledge the limitations of that model. Above all, it is essential to acknowledge that the intermediate public-service sector, which is of course the critical and novel feature of our model, is nevertheless not homogeneous in character. Indeed, that is evident from the variety of the arrangements to which we have referred. That is to say, the secondary responsibility of the State which is the distinguishing feature of this sector will be embodied in various different kinds of regulatory arrangements, such as the institution of a regulator, or on the other hand a process of enforcement of compliance with extra-commercial standards in contracts, or even the use of a 'golden share' in an otherwise purely commercial company. . . .

It has been argued earlier that when governments engaged on neo-liberal projects of privatization transfer activities from the purely public sector into the public-service sector, there nevertheless remains in place a significant secondary relationship between the citizen and the State in relation to that activity. In the context of labour law, however, we find that such transfers result in a much more complete severance of relationships between the employee and the State. In particular, the interposition of the public-service provider between the employee and the State operates to exclude the perception that the employee is a functionary of the State with a resulting special set of expectations about security of employment and the protection of a high standard of terms and conditions of employment. That is one of the main reasons why transfers of activities from the pure public sector to the public-service sector are often so controversial, especially in labour law systems where the public-sector regime is very distinct, and very strongly ring-fenced from the private sector. . . .

At least as a broad generalization, we can say that, both in principle and practice, the goals, objectives, or tasks of executive government and its institutions tend to be more diverse and diffuse, a more complex bundle of political, social, and economic factors than the corresponding goals, objectives, or tasks of public-service providers.

That is not to say that the goals, objectives, or tasks of public-service providers are in themselves simple or uni-directional ones. They are normally not simple, if only because we may regard it as one of the features which distinguish the public-service sector from the private sector that in the public-service sector, governments will have acquired or retained the power to some degree to shape and determine those goals, objectives, or tasks. Nevertheless, it is normally the case that the very rationale for the transfer of an activity from the purely public sector into the public-service sector is to ensure that there will be a unit of delivery of the service in question whose goals, tasks, and objectives will be more clearly and tightly defined than would be the case if that activity were being conducted directly by one of the institutions of executive government. . . .

The public-service provider constitutes, and is created or chosen because it constitutes, the best vehicle for this kind of new public management and this kind of flexibilization of employment. That is to say, it can be endowed with tightly defined (yet controllable) goals, objectives, and task definitions; and the legal and contractual norms of employment within that institution can be made flexible by reference to those controllable goals, objectives, and task definitions, as regards both tenure of employment (especially by means of fixed-term contracts of employment or contracts of employment the duration of which is task-defined) and terms and conditions of employment (especially by means of performance-related remuneration, where the criteria of assessment can be tied to the immediate objectives of the public-service provider). . . .

We saw in an earlier section that one of the most significant attributes of the intermediate public-service sector was the way in which it provided fertile ground for the establishment and growth of a market or consumerist conception of citizenship. The importance of that in relation to public law was, we saw, considerable; in relation to labour law, especially that of the traditional public sector, it is positively transformative. We shall seek to show that this is true in more than one dimension of labour law.

One such dimension is that of the flexibilization of employment in the public-service sector, as described in the previous section. In relation to the public-service sector, it proves to be especially attractive, and perhaps effective, for governments, when demanding and requiring efficiency, and in particular flexibility of employment in pursuit of efficiency, to do so in the name of the market citizen or the consumer citizen. One could almost say that they sometimes create the consumer citizen precisely in order to perform this task, to fulfil this disciplinary role. . . .

Once it is accepted that employment by the State is no longer a significant boundary in determining whether or not special rights and obligations should be attached to a particular employment relation, it becomes difficult to defend the use of this boundary by the law. For instance, the regulations governing prison officers should normally be the same, regardless of whether the employer is the State or a private company entrusted with the management of a prison. The issue becomes rather whether special rules should apply to a particular employment relation in view of the type of work involved. If restrictions are imposed on such workers, such as limitations on industrial action for prison officers, the question that should be posed is whether these restrictions can be justified independently on grounds such as public order, or whether the restrictions really derive from an earlier era when it was assumed that most public sector employees were subject to special disabilities.

[2.72] Gillian S. Morris, 'Employment in Public Services: The Case for Special Treatment' (2000) 20 *Oxford Journal of Legal Studies* 167, 180–1 (footnotes omitted)

At one time many systems imposed restrictions on public employees, such as prohibiting industrial action, purely because of their status as such rather than because of the deleterious consequences which that action may produce. In the contemporary environment to impose restrictions on public employees on this basis is anachronistic. Not only does it risk the imposition of unnecessary restrictions; equally seriously, it may result in a failure to extend appropriate restrictions to workers in the private sector who perform identical task to their private sector counterparts. For this reason it is important that even those restrictions which it may be thought appropriate to apply across the public sector as a whole, such as those relating to hospitality, should be justified by reference to functional and not status-based criteria. As a corollary of this, where restrictions are confined to public sector groups, such as those governing the political activities of local government workers, this should raise serious doubts as to the justification for their continuation, or non-extension to the private sector, as the case may be.

Our conclusion about public sector workers is that, as a general principle, labour law should not treat them as a special category. In so far as special considerations such as national security and public order can justify restrictions and disabilities for particular workers, those rules must be guided by the type of work performed rather than the nature of the employer. Public sector workers may differ in their entitlements, however, because government action must always be legitimate, accountable and transparent. The Human Rights Act 1998 has potential importance in this respect, because section 7 may enable public sector employees to challenge the actions of their employer more directly and effectively for violations of human rights than the indirect routes available to private sector employees (below, chapter 6).

2.9 The adequacy of the contractual framework for employment

This chapter has explored the implications of the legal categorisation of the employment relation as a contract. The major implication is that the ordinary principles of contract law apply to the employment relation. In particular, the principle of the freedom of the parties to choose the terms of their arrangement creates a baseline for all legal intervention in employment relations. The principal advantage of this framework is the flexibility that it accords to the parties to select efficient relations of production. But we have observed that the contractual framework is not without its drawbacks.

The contractual discourse established by the common law always seeks to ground the legal rights and obligations in the agreement of the parties. This priority accorded to the agreement places obstacles in the way of attempts to impose mandatory standards. Any statutory protection needs to be supplemented with an express statutory prohibition against the parties agreeing by contract to modify or waive statutory rights, for otherwise the employer may slip such an exclusion into a standard form contract of employment. Furthermore, freedom of contract provides employers with the opportunity to use their bargaining power to create an organisational structure that establishes a strict authority relation over employees and permits managerial action that takes scant notice of any interests of employees. An employee's bargaining disadvantage can be explained as arising from three sources.

[2.73] M. W. Reder, 'On Labor's Bargaining Disadvantage' in C. Kerr and P.D. Staudohar, *Labor Economics and Industrial Relations* (Cambridge, Mass., Harvard University Press, 1994) 237, 250–1

The notion of employee bargaining disadvantage has (at least) three variants:

1. Typically, the worker is poorer than his employer and consequently [more] risk averse. Hence, in the absence of an employment relation, the typical worker accepts a lower average wage than he could obtain under similar conditions if he were wealthier and (therefore) less risk averse.

2. Most employers find it efficient to set terms of compensation such that their

employees would rather tolerate occasional pressure for increased exertion and occasional worsening of working conditions than quit. Bargaining disadvantage consists of being induced to tolerate a situation in which working conditions will vary in response to changes in the employer's 'needs', but not in response to the worker's. . .

3. Employee bargaining disadvantage arises from the fact that the transaction cost for the employer of negotiating terms of employment with an individual worker exceeds the cost of letting him quit or refuse an offer of employment. That is, the worker is given a take-it-or-leave-it offer even though he and the employer, jointly, could find acceptable contract terms that would cost no more (except for the cost of negotiation). Hence employment terms are set by the employer, with the worker having no opportunity to negotiate; this is perceived as a bargaining disadvantage.

The courts have shown themselves to be adept in recent years at manipulating the implied terms of the contract of employment in order to provide some protection for employees against abuse of managerial power, as in the development of the implied duty imposed upon the employer not to destroy the trust and confidence at the root of the employment relation. Nevertheless, the courts must always approach this task with one hand tied behind their backs, for according to orthodox contract law they cannot manipulate implied terms in such a way as to contradict directly and openly the express contractual agreement established by the employer. One should question, though, whether or not this orthodox position should be maintained at least in the context of certain fundamental implied terms in employment relations such as the obligation of mutual trust and confidence or the obligation to operate a safe system of work (an issue explored further in *Johnstone v Bloomsbury Health Authority* [1992] QB 333 (CA), **[10.8]** below).

A second drawback to the contractual framework for the legal analysis of employment relations concerns the assumption of the common law that the initial agreement fixes the rights and obligations of the parties. This assumption runs directly contrary to the expectations of the parties to many employment relations, which, in the context of a long-term relation, are to envisage a constant process of adjustment. These adjustments are likely to occur either as a result of the exercise of managerial discretion or by collective agreement or simply by custom and practice. There is a stark 'contrast between the lawyer's static model of the formation of terms and the evolutionary character of actual practice' (P. Davies and M. Freedland, *Labour Law* (2nd edn., London, Weidenfeld, 1984) 299). The legal analysis insists rather rigidly that the adjustment required by an employer (or an employee) either involves an alteration in the terms of employment, in which case it can only be achieved by agreement of the parties to the contract, or is merely an exercise of managerial discretion permitted by the contract, in which case the adjustment can be implemented unilaterally. In practice, however, the expectations of the parties about adjustments are usually more subtle: the employer expects to be permitted to alter working conditions when necessary, but the workforce expects such changes to be implemented reasonably, following consultation, and in a spirit of co-operation. As we shall see when we examine this issue of the variation of contracts more deeply in chapter 10, to some extent the courts can express these expectations by means of implied terms. But these implied terms do not fully articulate the expectation of co-operation, and they can be restricted by contrary express terms.

A third weakness of the contractual framework for the legal analysis of employ-ment relations concerns the application of a legal model that envisages two parties to an agreement to the organisational context of employment. In the wings of the stage set by the contract of employment often stands the trade union, which may negotiate many of the vital elements of the contract, yet which appears to have no legal status at all with respect to the contract of employment. The union is not usually the agent of the employee, and the collective agreements reached may or may not have any legal application depending on how the individual contract of employment incorpo-rates the collective agreement. When there is a strong recognised union in the workplace, the legal emphasis upon individual consent to the contractual agreement may only remotely correspond with the perceptions of the participants in the organi-sation. At a deeper level, the contractual framework has difficulty in expressing the relations between workers in the organisation. Although all employees have a con-tract with the employing entity, the relations between each other, especially those between managers and subordinates, are constituted and regulated by the bureau-cratic rules of the organisation rather than any direct contracts between members of the organisation. When a manager dismisses a worker, for instance, there is no legal relation between them directly; rather the manager's authority depends upon the rules governing his or her contract of employment and the power to act as an agent for the employer, and the worker's obligations depend upon the content of the worker's contract of employment. Everyday work relations between manger and worker therefore exist in a strange legal vacuum filled in by reference to contracts with a third party, the employing organisation.

These weaknesses of the contractual framework of the legal analysis have led to suggestions that it ought to be replaced or supplemented by some other framework of legal analysis. One suggestion is that the power relation within the organisation represented by managerial discretion, works rules, and the power to redirect labour, should be likened to other kinds of power relations such as those between State and citizen. This analogy indicates that principles rather like those found in public law might be adapted to provide a set of mandatory regulations for the employment rela-tion. These rules might insist that power should be exercised according to fair procedures, only by persons who have been granted such powers, and according to principles that respect the fundamental rights of individuals. 'Once managerial power is likened to governmental power, old questions concerning the absence of democ-racy and respect for civil liberties in the workplace begin to press upon us with renewed intensity' (H. Collins, 'Market Power, Bureaucratic Power, and the Contract of Employment' (1986) 15 *Industrial Law Journal* 1, 14).

There are hints in the cases from time to time that such public law analogies do influence the direction of judicial decisions, though the legal argument is usually expressed in familiar contractual terms. For example, in a contract of employment that contains a detailed disciplinary procedure involving hearings and appeals, the court may imply a term that the procedures should be conducted fairly in accordance with standards equivalent to the principles of natural justice: *R v BBC, ex parte Lavelle* [1983] ICR 99 (HC). One of the broadest statements of this kind occurred in a case involving the dismissal of an official of a trade union.

[2.74] *Stevenson v United Road Transport Union* **[1977] ICR 893, 902 (CA)**

Buckley LJ:
Where one party has a discretionary power to terminate the tenure or enjoyment by another of an employment or an office or a post or a privilege, is that power conditional upon the party invested with the power being first satisfied upon a particular point which involves investigating some matter upon which the other party ought in fairness to be hear or to be allowed to give his explanation or put his case? If the answer to that question is 'Yes', then unless, before the power purports to have been exercised, the condition has been satisfied after the other party has been given a fair opportunity of being heard or of giving his explanation or putting his case, the power will not have been well exercised.

Such statements are merely hints that at times the courts draw on other legal categories such as public law in order to assist them in seeking to express adequately their regulation of employment relations through the device of implied terms.

The legal framework for analysing the employment relation as a contract also provokes many difficulties for devising effective regulation. A central problem that has been addressed in this chapter is that freedom of contract permits the parties to devise contractual arrangements that escape the province of regulation in so far as that regulation is tied to particular contract types. But more generally, the contractual framework of employment directs the courts towards particular styles of interpretation of all regulatory legislation. We have noticed, for instance in *The Post Office v Roberts* (**[2.23]** above), on the crucial question whether an employer's conduct justifies an employee's resignation for the purposes of making a claim for unfair dismissal, the courts determine the outcome according to whether the employer has broken a fundamental term of the contract. Yet the law of unfair dismissal can be likened to a review of the proper exercise of bureaucratic power, with the implication that not contractual entitlements but rather the rationality and fairness of the exercise of power should be the primary issue. The contractual approach to interpretation of regulatory legislation obstructs the opportunity to construct more appropriate standards that reflect the expectations of the parties more fully.

Despite these reservations about the legal construction of the employment relation as a contract, there is no doubt that this traditional analysis provides the legal foundation of employment law. In order to give effect to the special features of the employment relation, they have to be expressed in law as terms of contracts or as modifications of terms by regulation. The task for labour lawyers becomes one of exploring the capacity of the private law of contract to describe and enforce the complex institutional features of the employment relation, whilst at the same time giving effect to the written and implicit expectations and conventions in the workplace.

[2.75] M. Freedland, 'The Role of the Contract of Employment in Modern Labour Law' in L. Betten (ed.), *The Employment Contract in Transforming Labour Relations* **(Deventer, Kluwer, 1995) 17, 24–6**

It helps to clarify this argument if we distinguish between two levels at which contracting or norm-making takes place within work relationships. At the first level, we are concerned with the exchange of services for remuneration . . . At the second level, we are concerned with the creation of obligations concerned with the security of expectations. For the worker, these are expectations about security of income, security of employment, and regard for health, safety and well being. For the employer, these are expectations about how the work will affect the relations of the employer's goals either positively by making and implementing commitments going beyond the rendering of particular services, or negatively by refraining from competition. The contract of employment/contract for services dichotomy encourages the view that these two levels are separable, with the contract for services operating only at the first level and the contract of employment operating mainly at the second level. Employment arrangements need to be recognised as operating in a more fluid and complex way between the two levels . . .

It is at the second, relational, level of contracting that most of the concerns which labour law has developed for social values comes into play. The shift to short fixed-term or task-defined contracting threatens to move the contracting process towards the first level, leaving the relational issues to be resolved, if at all, by other parts of the common law -tort of negligence, fiduciary law—or by statute law—e.g. pensions law. So the role of contract law is in danger of being re-defined not just in terms of an enhanced or re-asserted freedom of contract, but in terms of a rudimentary conception of contractual employment relationships—a conception in which collective and associative considerations are marginalised . . .

It is worth observing, finally, in respect of the contract of employment, that the continuity of the legal institution masks, at least for lawyers, some profound changes in the social significance of the employment relation. The legal institution of the contract of employment formed the linchpin in the scheme of the Welfare State to provide economic security for the population. This economic security was achieved by contract of employment of indefinite duration, devised and protected through collective bargaining, which was subsequently supplemented by legal regulation such as laws governing dismissals, combined with a social security system that taxed employers and employees through National Insurance contributions in order to provide economic security through welfare payments in the event of unemployment or retirement. The growth of atypical work, especially part-time work and dependent entrepreneurs, and the revival of managerial strategies of numerical flexibility through the flexible firm remove the contractual promise of job security and at the same time have the tendency to exclude workers from the protection of the social security system by virtue of their low wages that place them below the threshold of National Insurance or by reclassifying them as independent contractors, which takes them outside the protection against unemployment. The promise of economic security offered by the Welfare State thus becomes attenuated for a growing segment of the workforce. In order to re-establish economic security, though now in a different form, legal regulation needs to consider other strategies, such as the enhancement of the 'employability' of workers through improvements to their education and skills, the promotion of entrepreneurship through assistance to small businesses, and the reconfiguration of the economic security provided by the Welfare State so that it affords protection to those whose participation in work does not take the form of a permanent full-time job.

FURTHER READING

B. Barrett, 'The Impact of Safety Legislation on the Contract of Employment' in H. Collins, P. Davies and R. Rideout (eds.), *Legal Regulation of the Employment Relation* (London, Kluwer, 2000) 247.

D. Brodie, 'Beyond Exchange: the New Contract of Employment' (1998) 27 *Industrial Law Journal* 79.

H. Collins, 'Independent Contractors and the Challenge of Vertical Disintegration to Employment Protection Laws' (1990) 10 *Oxford Journal of Legal Studies* 353.

P. Davies and M. Freedland, 'The Impact of Public Law on Labour Law 1972–1997' (1997) 26 *Industrial Law Journal* 311.

— and —, 'Employees, Workers, and the Autonomy of Labour Law' in H. Collins, P. Davies and R. Rideout (eds.), *Legal Regulation of the Employment Relation* (London, Kluwer, 2000) 267.

— and —, 'Changing Perspectives Upon the Employment Relationship in British Labour Law', in C. Barnard, S. Deakin and G.S. Morris (eds), *The Future of Labour Law* (Oxford, Hart, 2004) 129.

S. Deakin, 'The Changing Concept of the "Employer" in Labour Law' (2001) 30 *Industrial Law Journal* 72.

— —'The Many Futures of the Contract of Employment' in J. Conaghan, M. Fischel and K. Klare (eds.), *Globalisation and Transforming Labour Law* (Oxford, Oxford University Press, 2001).

S. Fredman, 'Women at Work: The Broken Promise of Flexicurity' (2004) 33 *Industrial Law Journal* 299.

M. Freedland, *The Personal Employment Contract* (Oxford, Oxford University Press Press, 2003).

J. Freedman, *Employed or Self-Employed? Tax Classification of Workers and the Changing Labour Market* (London, Institute for Fiscal Studies, 2001).

B.A. Hepple, 'Restructuring Employment Rights' (1986) 15 *Industrial Law Journal* 69.

The Honorable Mr Justice Lindsay, 'The Implied Term of Trust and Confidence' (2001) 30 *Industrial Law Journal* 1.

G. S. Morris, 'The Future of the Public/Private Labour Law Divide', in C. Barnard, S. Deakin and G.S. Morris (eds), *The Future of Labour Law* (Oxford, Hart, 2004) 159.

A. Stewart, Redefining Employment? Meeting the Challenge of Contract and Agency Labour' (2002) 15 *Australian Journal of Labour Law* 235.

K. Stone, 'The New Psychological Contract' (2001) 48 *UCLA Law Review* 519.

A. Supiot, *Beyond Employment: Changes in Work and the Future of Labour Law in Europe* (Oxford, Oxford University Press, 2001).

Equality

3.1 Introduction

This chapter is concerned with British anti-discrimination law, namely the Equal Pay Act 1970 (EqPA), the Sex Discrimination Act 1975 (SDA), the Race Relations Act 1976 (RRA) the Disability Discrimination Act 1995 (DDA), the Employment Equality (Sexual Orientation) Regulations 2003 and the Employment Equality (Religion or Belief) Regulations 2003 (SORs and RBRs respectively). Significant changes have been made in the last few years to accommodate Council Directives 2000/34/EC and 2000/78/EC (the Race and Employment Equality Directives) which were adopted by the EU under Article 13 of the EC Treaty and which came into force in July and December 2003 respectively. These changes will be commented upon throughout the text.

The RRA prohibits discrimination on 'racial grounds' in employment, education, housing, the provision of goods, services and facilities and, by virtue of its recent amendment, discrimination by public authorities. It also imposes positive obligations on such authorities to promote equality of opportunity on grounds of race. The SDA similarly prohibits discrimination on grounds of sex in employment, education, etc, but does not as yet prohibit all discrimination by public authorities or impose any positive obligations on them (although the Equality Bill 2005 proposes amendment to the SDA to this effect). The SDA also prohibits employment-related discrimination against married persons and direct (but not indirect) employment-related discrimination in connection with gender reassignment and the EqPA deals with sex discrimination in the contractual terms of employment (such discrimination being excluded from the provisions of the SDA). The DDA, whose coverage is similar to that of the SDA, prohibits discrimination against the 'disabled'. The Disability Discrimination Act 2005 amends the DDA to regulate discrimination by public authorities and impose positive obligations along similar lines to the RRA. The SORs and the RBRs regulate discrimination on grounds of sexual orientation and religion in the context (only) of employment and third level education, though the Equality Bill 2005 proposes the prohibition of discrimination on grounds of religion or belief in access to goods, facilities and services.

The scope of the various Acts is mentioned only in order to place in context their employment-related provisions which are the focus of this chapter. The various pieces of anti-discrimination legislation do not form a coherent code. Sex discrimination has been subject to regulation throughout the UK since 1975. But disability discrimination remained largely unregulated until 1996 and the RRA was not extended to cover Northern Ireland until 1997. Discrimination on grounds of religious belief and political opinion has, since 1976, been prohibited in Northern Ireland, but remained lawful in Great Britain until December 2003 (when the RBRs were implemented) except to the extent (see 3.2.4 below) that it contravened the RRA's prohibitions on race discrimination or other employment legislation (such as the unfair dismissal provisions of the Employment Rights Act 1996). Some discrimination on grounds of gender reassignment is prohibited (this as a result of the ECJ's decision in Case 13/94, *P v S & Cornwall* **[3.1]** below and, more recently, the Gender Recognition Act 2004). But sexual orientation discrimination remains outside the scope of the SDA (subject to any developments under the Human Rights Act 1998, discussed in chapter 6). Leaving aside the interpretive obligations imposed by the HRA, discrimination against Jews and Sikhs is regulated by the RRA, discrimination against Rastafarians is not, and discrimination against Muslims may or may not be so regulated depending on the precise ethnicity of those concerned. This is no longer hugely problematic in the employment context, because of the implementation of the RBRs. But these Regulations do not, as yet, extend beyond employment and third level education so the problem of uneven coverage remains. At present age discrimination is not regulated as such. But such discrimination may amount to indirect sex discrimination (see, for example, *Price v Civil Service* [1978] ICR 27) and age-related legislation broadly along the lines of the RBRs and SORs will have to be in place by December 2006 to comply with the Employment Equality Directive. In December 2004 the Secretary of State for Trade and Industry announced that employers would still be able to enforce retirement ages subject to a right to request deferral along the lines of the right to request flexible working (see further chapter 4).

Just as the substantive provisions of the various legislative measures differ, so, too, do their enforcement mechanisms. Whereas individual actions under the RRA, SDA and DDA are subject to broadly similar procedural rules, remedies and 'collective' enforcement (i.e., enforcement by the commissions established under the various Acts) differ to some extent. The Commission for Racial Equality, the Equal Opportunities Commission and the Disability Rights Commission (CRE, EOC and DRC) are charged, respectively, with supervisory obligations in connection with the RRA, the SDA and EqPA and the DDA. But while the former two commissions were established almost simultaneously with the Acts to which their responsibilities relate, the DRC came into existence only in 1999. Further, whereas the sex, race and disability discrimination provisions are separately administered in Great Britain, Northern Ireland has since 1999 boasted a single Equality Commission which absorbed the roles of the former NIEOC and CRE for Northern Ireland (itself only established in 1997) as well as the Fair Employment Commission (previously responsible for policing the prohibition, then unique to Northern Ireland, on religious and political discrimination). The ECNI also absorbed responsibility for the DDA which, unique among the discrimination legislation, applies to Northern Ireland (the SDA and RRA being transposed by means of Orders in Council and the Equal Pay (Northern Ireland) Act

1970 and Northern Ireland SORs mirroring the terms of the British legislation). The various British equality commissions are likely to be replaced in the medium term with a single Commission for Equality and Human Rights. Consultations are ongoing about the replacement of Northern Ireland's various different statutory regimes with a single Equality Act and, after years of resistance to thorough-going overhaul of British discrimination law, the government announced in August 2004 that one of the first tasks for the CEHR would be to devise single equality legislation.

The enforcement powers of the various equality commissions also differ as between the discrimination regimes. All four commissions are entitled to carry out 'formal investigations', further discussed below. But the legal restrictions to which those investigations are subject are more draconian in the case of the CRE and the EOC than they are for the DRC, and the ECNI must, at present, comply with different procedural requirements depending on whether its enforcement actions relate to discrimination on grounds of sex, race, disability, religious belief or political opinion. The lack of consistency, indeed of coherence, between the various anti-discrimination regimes, renders more complicated an area of law which is already complex. Much of this complexity stems from the interplay between domestic and EU law. The latter applied, until recently, mainly to discrimination on grounds of sex but its influence in this area has affected concepts, such as that of justification, which are common to the discrimination regimes and recent years have seen the implementation of Council Directive 2000/43 (the Racial Equality Directive) and the Employment Equality Directive, which extend the influence of EU law into discrimination on grounds of race orethnic or national origin, sexual orientation, religion or belief, disability and (from December 2006) age.

Neither the SDA nor the EqPA can be considered in isolation from Council Directive 76/207 (the Equal Treatment Directive), Council Directive 75/117 (the Equal Pay Directive) and Article 141 of the Treaty Establishing the European Community (TEC). Article 141 may be relied upon in the face of inconsistent national provisions in order to claim equal pay, 'pay' being very broadly defined as 'the ordinary basic or minimum wage or salary and any other consideration, whether in cash or in kind, which the worker receives, directly or indirectly, in respect of his employment from his employer'. This has been interpreted to include most aspects of pensions; gratuitous as well as contractual travel concessions; contractual and statutory redundancy pay; sick pay; maternity pay; paid leave and over-time pay in respect of attendance at trade union training etc; rules governing the accrual of seniority, where seniority is directly related to pay; unfair dismissal compensation and periodic unemployment payments made by the employer. The Equal Treatment Directive regulates non pay-related sex discrimination. It may be relied upon directly only vis-à-vis the state (though for the indirect effect of the Directive see *Webb v EMO (No 2)*, section 3.3.1.2 below). Amendments to this Directive take effect in October 2005 with the implementation of Council Directive 2002/73/EC which, broadly speaking, modernises the Equal Treatment Directive in line with the Employment Equality Directive. The implications of the Directive 2002/73/EC are considered where relevant below.

The EAT's decision in *Bossa v Nordstress* [1998] IRLR 284 drew attention to Article 39 TEC, which prohibits discrimination on grounds of nationality between citizens of the EU and Norway, Liechtenstein and Iceland (these three countries comprising, with EU Member States, the European Economic Area). Article 39 is frequently overlooked in the UK context because it is, in general, less comprehensive than the RRA, applying only to EEA nationals and to discrimination on the basis of nationality (as distinct, for example, from race, ethnic or national origins or colour). The European influence on discrimination law does not stem exclusively from the UK's membership of the EU. In addition, the Council of Europe's Convention on Human Rights (ECHR), to which the UK is a signatory, is of significance in this area. The Convention, incorporated into domestic law in the UK by the HRA, does not contain a free-standing prohibition on discrimination. But it does (Article 14) provide the right to be free from discrimination in the exercise of the rights and freedoms established by the Convention. Protocol 12 further provides a freestanding right not to be discriminated against but it has not been (and is unlikely in the forseeable future to be) ratified by the UK. Article 14 and the other Convention provisions are considered further in chapter 6 and, where relevant to anti-discrimination law, below.

3.2 Prohibited grounds of discrimination

3.2.1 'Sex'

The SDA regulates discrimination on grounds of sex (whether against men or women) and discrimination (in the employment field alone) against married persons. The Act was amended in 1999 to provide some protection from discrimination in connection with gender reassignment but does not prohibit discrimination in connection with sexual orientation.

The 1999 amendment of the SDA was made necessary by the decision of the ECJ in *P v S & Cornwall.*

[3.1] Case 13/94 *P v S & Cornwall County Council* [1996] ECR I–2143 (ECJ)

The applicant was dismissed after she began to undergo male-to-female gender-reassignment. A tribunal referred to the ECJ the question whether the dismissal breached the Equal Treatment Directive, having formed the view that it was lawful under the SDA. The ECJ ruled that it did.

Judgment:
The principle of equal treatment 'for men and women' to which the Directive refers in its title, preamble and provisions means, as Articles 2(1) and 3(1) in particular indicate, that there should be 'no discrimination whatsoever on grounds of sex' . . .

[T]he Directive is simply the expression, in the relevant field, of the principle of equality, which is one of the fundamental principles of Community law.

Moreover, as the Court has repeatedly held, the right not to be discriminated against on grounds of sex is one of the fundamental human rights whose observance the Court has a duty to ensure . . .

Accordingly, the scope of the Directive cannot be confined simply to discrimination based on the fact that a person is one or other sex. In view of its purpose and the nature of the rights which it seeks to safeguard, the scope of the Directive is also such as to apply to discrimination arising, as in this case, from the gender reassignment of the person concerned.

Such discrimination is based, essentially, if not exclusively, on the sex of the person concerned. Where a person is dismissed on the ground that he or she intends to undergo, or has undergone, gender reassignment, he or she is treated unfavourably by comparison with persons of the sex to which he or she was deemed to belong before undergoing gender reassignment.

To tolerate such discrimination would be tantamount, as regards such a person, to a failure to respect the dignity and freedom to which he or she is entitled, and which the Court has a duty to safeguard.

The SDA now provides that, in respect of the employment and training provisions (and those covering barristers and advocates):

[3.2] Sex Discrimination Act 1975, section 2A

S. 2A(1) A person ("A") discriminates against another person ("B") . . . if he treats B less favourably than he treats or would treat other persons, and does so on the ground that B intends to undergo, is undergoing or has undergone gender reassignment.

The EqPA does not apply in relation to gender reassignment, section 2(3) SDA as amended providing instead that contractual discrimination connected with gender reassignment shall be dealt with under the SDA. Protection vests as soon as the person declares an intention to undergo gender reassignment. It will be noted, however, that section 2A prohibits only direct discrimination whereas *indirect* as well as *direct* discrimination is generally prohibited by the Act (see section 3.5 below). Further, the SDA provides as follows:

[3.3] Sex Discrimination Act 1975, section 2A

S.2A(3) . . . B is treated less favourably than others under . . . arrangements [made in relation to absence] if, in the application of the arrangements to any absence due to B undergoing gender reassignment—
(a) he is treated less favourably than he would be if the absence was due to sickness or injury, or
(b) he is treated less favourably than he would be if the absence was due to some other cause and, having regard to the circumstances of the case, it is reasonable for him to be treated no less favourably.

This approach has been rejected by the ECJ in relation to pregnancy-related sex discrimination. It may be the case that, bound by the interpretative obligations imposed by EU law and the HRA, the domestic courts ought to interpret the SDA, even absent its further amendment, so as to prohibit indirect discrimination on grounds of gender reassignment. The prohibition on discrimination is subject to the normal genuine occupational qualifications and to a number of 'supplementary GOQs'. These are further discussed at section 3.7 below.

3.2.2 'Sexual orientation'

The SORs regulate employment-related discrimination on grounds of sexual orientation (defined by Regulation 2(1) as 'a sexual orientation towards— (a) persons of the same sex; (b) persons of the opposite sex; or (c) persons of the same sex and of the opposite sex'.

Discrimination outside the field of employment remains largely unregulated, subject to interpretive developments flowing from the HRA (see further chapter 6). It has been argued for some time, however, that the SDA is capable of interpretation to prohibit discrimination connected with sexual orientation.

[3.4] D Pannick, 'Homosexuals, Transsexuals and the Law' [1983] *Public Law* **279, pp. 281–84 (footnotes omitted)**

> Adverse treatment of an individual by reason of his or her sexual preferences may constitute sex discrimination notwithstanding that sex discrimination can only be established by comparing the treatment of the complainant with the treatment of a person of the opposite sex . . .
>
> The simplest case is where the employer refuses to employ male homosexuals but is willing to employ lesbians. A male homosexual who is refused employment by reason of his sexual preferences can establish direct discrimination contrary to the [SDA]: he has been less favourably treated by reason of his sex than a woman whose 'relevant circumstances . . . are the same, or not materially different,' the comparison required by section 5(3). The Employment Appeal Tribunal has emphasised that 'in deciding whether the circumstances of the two cases are the same, or not materially different, one must put out of the picture any circumstances which necessarily follow from the fact that one is comparing the case of a man and of a woman' . . .
>
> A claim of direct sex discrimination can also be formulated if the defendant adversely treats homosexuals of each sex because of their sexual preferences. The less favourable treatment of the complainant on the ground of his or her sex compared with a person of the other sex might, again, be established. Suppose the employer dismisses a male homosexual from employment because he has a rule that he will employ neither men or women who have sexual preferences for persons of their own sex. The complainant can argue that this is sex discrimination because if two employees—one male, and one female—are romantically or sexually attached to the same actual or hypothetical male non-employee, the employer treats the male employee less favourably on the ground of his sex than he treats the female employee . . . The California Supreme Court, in deciding a case under the state Fair Employment Practices Act (which prohibits discrimination on the ground of 'sex') rejected a similar analysis. While recognising that 'as a semantic argument, the contention may have some appeal,' the court concluded that the legislation did not contemplate discrimination against homosexuals [*Gay Law Student Association v Pacific Telephone and Telegraph Co.* 19 FEP Cases 1419 (1979)]. In *DeSantis v Pacific Telephone and Telegraph Co. Inc.* [608 F2d 327 (1979)], the US Court of Appeals considered the argument that discrimination against homosexuals breached Title VII

because 'if a male employee prefers males as sexual partners, he will be treated differently from a female who prefers male partners . . . [T]he employer thus uses different employment criteria for men and women.' The court firmly rejected the 'appellants' efforts to "bootstrap" Title VII protection for homosexuals . . . [W]e note that whether dealing with men or women the employer is using the same criterion: it will not hire or promote a person who prefers sexual partners of the same sex. Thus this policy does not involve different decisional criteria for the sexes'.

The judgment of the US Court of Appeals in *DeSantis* emphasises that one's conclusion on the validity of this claim of sex discrimination depends on the classification of the problem and the precise comparison one adopts with regard to the treatment of a man and a woman. Should one conclude that if a male employee is adversely treated for his sexual relationship with a third party X (a male) when a female employee is not so treated for her sexual relationship with the same X, such a disparity in treatment is by reason of the sex of the employee? Or should one conclude that the comparison is false as one of the employees is a homosexual and the other is not. This difficult issue will be determined by an English court or tribunal pursuant to section 5(3) of the 1975 Act. In making the comparison between the treatment of the male employee and the female employee, we are dealing with cases which are 'such that the relevant circumstances in the one case are the same, or not materially different, in the other'? The problem is that the 1975 Act provides no criteria of 'relevance.' The Employment Appeal Tribunal held in *Grieg v Community Industry* [[1974] ILR 256] that section 5(3) is 'principally although not exclusively talking about . . . the personal qualifications of the person involved as compared with some other person.' It is arguable that, on this criterion, the private sexual preferences of the complainant are not 'relevant circumstances' unless the employer can establish that the sexual preferences of his staff are material to their ability to perform the job. This argument is strengthened by the fact that section 5(3) applies an objective test and does not provide for the comparison to be made by reference to those circumstances that the employer deems relevant.

The homosexual who suffers a detriment by reason of his sexual orientation can, by comparing his treatment with the more favourable treatment of the person of the sex opposite to his, show that he has been less favourably treated on the ground of his sex . . . In the case of sexual preferences, the sex of the complainant (and the sexual stereotypes which the employer associates with that sex) is very much in the foreground as the activating cause of the less favourable treatment of which complaint is made. The employer who has said that a sexual relationship with Mr. X is conduct permissible in a female employee but conduct impermissible in a male employee has clearly differentiated in treatment of male and female employees. The differentiation is on the ground of sex: women may have relationships with Mr. X and retain their jobs: if men have such relationships they will be sacked. The employer may well believe that he has good reason for differentiating between men and women in this respect. But, subject to the express exceptions contained in the 1975 Act, it is no defence for the employer to say that 'what was done was done with good motives or was done, even objectively, in the best interests of the person concerned or in the best interests of the business with which the case is concerned.' That the employer has an ulterior motive for differentiating in his treatment of men and women cannot abrogate the conclusion that such differentiation is on the ground of sex.

In *R v Ministry of Defence, ex parte Smith* [1996] QB 517 the Court of Appeal rejected the argument that discrimination on grounds of sexual orientation amounted to sex discrimination. The claim was brought under the Equal Treatment Directive which was directly enforceable by the applicants (see also *Smith v Gardner*

Merchant [1999] ICR 134). And in Case 249/96, *Grant v South-West Trains* [1998] ECR I–0621 the ECJ refused to interpret the Equal Treatment Directive to prohibit sexual orientation discrimination. But just as domestic legislation cannot be interpreted absent consideration of the relevant EU provisions, so UK and EU law are influenced by the European Convention on Human Rights which provides that:

[3.5] European Convention on Human Rights, Article 8

> 1   Everyone has the right to respect for his private and family life, his home and his correspondence.
> 2   There shall be no interference by a public authority with the exercise of this right except such as is in accordance with the law and is necessary in a democratic society in the interests of national security, public safety or the economic well-being of the country, for the prevention of disorder or crime, for the protection of health or morals, or for the protection of the rights and freedoms of others.

The application of this provision to workplace sexual orientation discrimination was established by the European Court of Human Rights in 1999 in a pair of cases (*Lustig-Prean & Beckett v UK* (1999) 29 EHRR 548 and *Smith & Grady v UK* 29 EHRR 493) which arose from the UK's ban on gays in the military. In *Macdonald v Ministry of Defence, Pearce v Governing Body of Mayfield School* [2003] ICR 937 the House of Lords ruled that the SDA did not regulate discrimination on grounds of sexual orientation, confirming the earlier decision of the Court of Appeal in *Smith v Gardner Merchant*. It is important to note, however, that the decision of their Lordships was made on the basis that the HRA 1998 did not apply as the discrimination at issue pre-dated the implementation of that Act in October 2000. It is possible, given the very robust approach to interpretation adopted by the House of Lords in HRA cases (see, most recently, *Ghaidan v Godin-Mendoza* [2004] 2 AC 557) that the SDA may yet be interpreted to regulate sexual orientation discrimination. Meanwhile the SORs apply in the employment context.

3.2.3 'Race'

Section 1 RRA prohibits direct discrimination on 'racial grounds', and defines indirect discrimination in terms of the applicant's 'racial group'.

[3.6] Race Relations Act 1976, section 3

> S.3(1) In this Act, unless the context otherwise requires—
>   'racial grounds' means any of the following grounds, namely colour, race, nationality or ethnic or national origins;
>   'racial group' means a group of persons defined by reference to colour, race, nationality or ethnic or national origins, and references to a person's racial group refer to any racial group into which he falls.

(2) The fact that a racial group comprises two or more distinct racial groups does not prevent it from constituting a particular racial group for the purposes of this Act.

While the SDA prohibits only less favourable treatment of a person 'on the grounds of her [his] sex', the RRA defines as unlawful discrimination less favourable treatment 'on racial grounds'.

[3.7] *Weathersfield Ltd t/a Van & Truck Rentals v Sargent* **[1999] ICR 425 (CA)**

> A white woman claimed that she had been the victim of race discrimination after she resigned in circumstances where she had been ordered unlawfully to discriminate against potential customers on racial grounds. The Court of Appeal, finding that she had been constructively dismissed, accepted that the dismissal had been 'on racial grounds'.

Most of the cases brought under the RRA concern discrimination on grounds of race, colour and ethnic origins. But the Act's prohibitions extend to discrimination on the basis of nationality and 'national origins'. Discrimination against (say) Irish people would be caught within the prohibition on nationality discrimination. And, as the EAT confirmed in *Northern Joint Police Board v Power* [1997] IRLR 610, the prohibition on discrimination on grounds of national origin is breached by discrimination as between English and Scottish people (equally between Northern Irish and Welsh). A similar decision was reached by the Scottish Court of Session in *BBC Scotland v Souster* [2001] IRLR 150.

The Race Equality Directive, which has resulted in significant amendments to the RRA (in particular, in the employment context, in relation to the definition of indirect discrimination and the burden of proof—see sections 3.5 and 3.10 below), applies to discrimination on grounds of 'racial or ethnic origin' and explicitly does not apply to discrimination in grounds of nationality. The approach taken in the UK was to apply the required amendments to discrimination on grounds of 'race' and 'ethnic or national origin' while leaving the original provisions of the RRA intact as they apply to discrimination on grounds of 'colour' and 'nationality'. This will no doubt create difficulties as to the distinction between discrimination on grounds, for example, of 'race' and 'colour', 'nationality' and 'national origins'.

Prior to the recent amendments to the RRA, the main area of contention under the RRA concerned the width of 'ethnic origins'. The leading decision is that of the House of Lords in *Mandla*:

[3.8] *Mandla v Dowell Lee* **[1983] 2 AC 548 (HL)**

> A Sikh boy was refused admission to a private school because he wore a turban. One of the questions which arose for decision by the House of Lords concerned whether, as a Sikh, the boy was a member of a 'racial group' within s 3(1) such that the application of a 'no Turban' rule could amount to indirect discrimination against him. According to the evidence before the Court, Sikhs were racially indistinguishable from other Punjabis, with whom they shared a common language. They were originally a religious community founded towards the end of the fifteenth century in the Punjab area of India, but were no

longer purely a religious group, rather a separate community with distinctive customs.

Both the County Court and the Court of Appeal ([[1983] QB 1) ruled that Sikhs did not constitute a 'racial group'. The House of Lords allowed the applicant's appeal. Having ruled that Sikhs could not be defined 'by reference to colour, race, nationality or national origins', Lords Fraser and Templeman (with both of whose speeches Lords Edmund-Davies, Roskill and Brandon agreed) went on to consider whether they could, nevertheless, be regarded as an 'ethnic group'. Lord Fraser pointed out that ' "ethnic". . . is used nowadays in an extended sense to include other characteristics which may be commonly thought of as being associated with common racial origin'.

Lord Fraser:

[A]n ethnic group in the sense of the [RRA] . . . must . . . regard itself, and be regarded by others, as a distinct community by virtue of certain characteristics. Some of these characteristics are essential others are not essential but one or more of them will commonly be found and will help to distinguish the group from the surrounding community. The conditions which appear to me to be essential are these: (1) a long shared history, of which the group is conscious as distinguishing it from other groups, and the memory of which it keeps alive (2) a cultural tradition of its own, including family and social customs and manners, often but not necessarily associated with religious observance. In addition to those two essential characteristics the following characteristics are, in my opinion, relevant: (3) either a common geographical origin, or descent from a small number of common ancestors (4) a common language, not necessarily peculiar to the group (5) a common literature peculiar to the group (6) a common religion different from that of neighbouring groups or from the general community surrounding it (7) being a minority or being an oppressed or a dominant group within a larger community, for example a conquered people (say, the inhabitants of England shortly after the Norman conquest) and their conquerors might both be ethnic groups.

A group defined by reference to enough of these characteristics would be capable of including converts, for example, persons who marry into the group, and of excluding apostates. Provided a person who joins the group feels himself or herself to be a member of it, and is accepted by other members, then he is, for the purpose of the [RRA], a member. That appears to be consistent with the words at the end of sub-s (1) of s 3: 'references to a person's racial group refer to any racial group into which he falls.' In my opinion, it is possible for a person to fall into a particular racial group either by birth or by adherence, and it makes no difference, so far as the [RRA] is concerned, by which route he finds his way into the group . . .

The result is, in my opinion, that Sikhs are a group defined by a reference to ethnic origins for the purpose of the [RRA], although they are not biologically distinguishable from the other peoples living in the Punjab.

Lord Templeman:

[Having pointed out that the RRA did not prohibit discrimination on grounds of religion] a group of persons defined by reference to ethnic origins must possess some of the characteristics of a race, namely group descent, a group of geographical origin and a group history. The evidence shows that the Sikhs satisfy these tests. They are more than a religious sect, they are almost a race and almost a nation. As a race, the Sikhs share a common colour, and a common physique based on common ancestors from that part of the Punjab which is centred on Amritsar. They fail to qualify as a separate race because in racial origin prior to the inception of Sikhism they cannot be distinguished from other inhabitants of the Punjab. As a nation the Sikhs defeated the Moghuls, and established a kingdom in the Punjab which they lost as a result of the first and second Sikh wars they fail to qualify as a separate nation or as a separate nationality because their kingdom never achieved a sufficient degree of recognition or permanence. The Sikhs qualify as a group defined by ethnic origins because they constitute a separate and distinct community derived from the racial characteristics I have mentioned. They also justify the conditions enumerated by my noble and learned friend Lord Fraser. The Sikh community has accepted converts who do not comply with those conditions. Some persons who have the same ethnic origins as the Sikhs have ceased to be members of the Sikh community. But the Sikhs remain a group of persons forming a community recognisable by ethnic origins within the meaning of the [RRA].

The significance of *Mandla* is that it adopts a relatively wide approach to 'ethnic' by de-coupling it to some extent from issues of race. But the decision is not wide enough to apply the protection of the RRA to all religious discrimination.

3.2.4 'Religion and Belief'

The EAT accepted in *Seide v Gillette* [1980] IRLR 427 that Jews could be defined as a racial group by reference to race or ethnic origin (and in *CRE v Dutton* [1989] QB 783 (EAT), that 'gipsies', as distinct from 'travellers', also qualified). But in *Dawkins v Department of the Environment* [1993] ICR 517 (CA), Rastafarians were denied protection against religious discrimination on the ground that they lacked a sufficiently long 'shared history' to satisfy the test set out by Lord Fraser in Mandla. And discrimination against Muslims has proved particularly difficult to bring within the framework of the RRA.

[3.9] B Hepple QC and T Choudhury, *Tackling Religious Discrimination; Practical Implications for Policy-Makers and Legislators* (London, Home Office, 2001) Home Office Research Study 221, p 12 (footnotes omitted)

Actions taken by an employer causing detriment to Muslims as a class, such as refusal to allow time off work for religious holidays, might be held to constitute indirect racial discrimination against those from an ethnic or national background that it predominantly Muslim. This does not help Muslims who come from a country where Muslims are in a minority. The limitation of using indirect race discrimination to tackle religious discrimination is highlighted in the decision of the tribunal in *Safouane & Bouterfas* (1996). In that case two Muslim complainants were dismissed for doing prayers during their breaks. The tribunal held that the acts did not constitute indirect race discrimination because the applicants belonged to the same North African ethnic Arab minority as the respondents and they had a good record for employing staff from a diversity of backgrounds . . .

Religious discrimination may contravene the unfair dismissal provisions of the ERA if it takes the form of a dismissal, whether actual or constructive. But much interference with workers' manifested religious and other beliefs remained unregulated by domestic law prior to the implementation in December 2003 of the RBRs. These Regulations are further considered below. It should be noted, however, that they do not as yet apply beyond the area of employment (and third level education) so

Muslims and those of a number of other faiths remain significantly unprotected from discrimination in relation to housing, access to goods and services, etc. The Equality Bill 2005 proposes the prohibition of discrimination on grounds of religion or belief in access to goods, facilities and services.

Prior to the implementation of legislation dealing specifically with discrimination on grounds of religion attempts were made to rely on Article 9 of the ECHR, which protects freedom of religion and belief. These attempts were unsuccessful, however, in part because of the very unsympathetic approach of the European Commission on Human Rights to arguments that Article 9 required the religious needs of workers to be accommodated by employers (see, in particular, *Ahmad v UK* (1982) 4 EHRR 126 (Commission) and *Stedman v UK* (1997) 23 EHRR CD (Commission)).

[3.10] K.D. Ewing, 'The Human Rights Act and Labour Law' (1998) 27 Industrial Law Journal 275, pp 288–9 (footnotes omitted)

> In *Ahmad* the Commission held that there had been no violation of the applicant's article 9 right to freedom of religion, partly because the content of the right could 'as regards the modality of a particular manifestation, be influenced by the situation of the person claiming that freedom', including any employment contract to which he or she was a party. And in *Stedman v United Kingdom*, where the applicant was dismissed by her employer 'for refusing on religious grounds to accept a contract which meant that she would have to work on Sundays', the Commission concluded that the applicant had been dismissed 'for failing to agree to work certain hours rather than for her religious belief as such and was free to resign and did in effect resign from her employment'.

The RBRs form part of the transposition in Great Britain of the Employment Equality Directive's prohibition of discrimination on grounds of 'religion or belief'. The Directive does not define 'religion or belief', though it is clear from the preparatory documents that the expression was not intended to be interpreted narrowly, and the inclusion of 'belief' has the effect of extending protection beyond religious views. Article 9 of the ECHR, which protects 'belief' as well as 'religion', applies (*McFeely v UK* [1981] 3 EHRR 161 (Commission)) not to 'mere opinions or deeply held feelings' but only to 'spiritual or philosophical convictions which have an identifiable formal content'. The RBRs define 'religion or belief' (Regulation 2(1)) as 'any religion, religious belief, or similar philosophical belief'.

[3.11] DTI, Explanatory Notes for the Employment Equality (Sexual Orientation) Regulations and the Employment Equality (Religion and Belief) Regulations

> 10.   It will be for the courts and tribunals to determine, in accordance with the Directive's requirements, whether a religion or belief falls within this definition.
> 11.   The reference to 'religion' is a broad one, and is in line with the freedom of religion guaranteed by Article 9. It includes those religions widely recognized in this country such as Christianity, Islam, Hinduism, Judaism, Buddhism, Sikhism, Rastafarianism, Baha'is, Zoroastrians and Jains. Equally, branches or sects within a religion can be considered as a religion or religious belief, such as Catholics or Protestants within the Christian church,

for example. The European Court of Human Rights has recognized other collective religions inclusing Druidism, the Church of Scientology as the Divine Light Zentrum. The main limitation on what constitutes a 'religion' for the purposes of Article 9 is that it must have a clear structure and belief system . . Even if a belief does not constitute a religion for these purposes, it may constitute a 'similar philosophical belief' (see below).

12.   The reference to 'similar philosophical belief' does not include any philosophical or political belief unless it is similar to a religious belief. This does not mean that a belief must include a faith in God/Gods or worship of a God/Gods to be 'similar' to a religious belief. It means that the belief in question should be a profound belief affecting a person's way of life, or perception of the world. Effectively, that belief should occupy a place in the person's life parallel to that filled by the God/Gods of those holding a particular religious belief. As with a religious belief, a similar philosophical belief must attain a certain level of cogency, seriousness, cohesion and importance, be worthy of respect in a democratic society, and not incompatible with human dignity . . . Examples of beliefs which generally meet this description are atheism and humanism; examples of beliefs which generally do not are support for a political party, support for a football team.

14.   References to 'religious belief' and 'similar philosophical belief' include references to a person's belief structure involving the absence of particular beliefs, because these are two sides of the same coin. This is in line with Article 9 ECHR . . . For example, if a Christian employer refuses an individual a job, because he is not a Christian, regardless of whether he is Muslim, Hindu, atheist (etc), that would be direct discrimination on grounds of the individual's religious belief, which can be described as 'non-Christian'. It is not necessary to identify the individual as an atheist or a Hindu for the purposes of the Regulations in such circumstances if he can be identified as a 'non-Christian'. The same is true of persons who might describe themselves as 'unconcerned' by religious beliefs, or 'unsure' of them.

15.   The definition of 'religion or belief' does not include the 'manifestation' of, or conduct based on or expressing a religion or belief (see also the distinction made in Article 9 ECHR). For example, a person may wear certain clothing, or pray at certain times in accordance with the tenets of her religion, or she may express views, and say or do other things reflecting her beliefs. In such a case it would not in itself constitute direct discrimination on grounds of religion or belief under the Regulations . . . if a person suffers a disadvantage because she has said or done something in this way. It would only be direct discrimination if a person with different beliefs (or no beliefs) was treated more favourably in similar circumstances. However, if an employer does set down requirements about (for example) clothing or breaks for prayers, these may constitute indirect discrimination . . . under the Regulations unless they are justified . . .

The assertion that the RBRs protect those who have no religious beliefs has been challenged, Michael Rubenstein arguing ('Is lack of belief protected?' (2004) 128 *Equal Opportunities Review*) that although 'the government *intended* to protect non-believers against discrimination on grounds of their absence of belief . . . it is difficult to reconcile' this with the DTI's statement (in the guidance above) that 'the phrase "similar philosophical belief" does not include any philosophical or political belief unless it is similar to a religious belief . . . be a profound belief affecting a person's way of life or perception of the world [and] . . . occupy a place in the person's life parallel to that filled by the god/gods of those holding a particular religious belief'. The Equality Bill 2005 proposes the amendment of the RBRs to provide (proposed new Regulation 2(1)(d)) that 'a reference to belief includes a reference to lack of belief'.

3.2.5 'Disability'

Save in respect of victimisation, the DDA's prohibitions on discrimination apply only in relation to those it defines as 'disabled'. The definition of disability adopted by the Act is a *medical* and *functional* one, rather than the *social* definition preferred by many disability campaigners. The significance of this will become apparent below. It is for the complainant to establish that s/he has a disability.

[3.12] Disability Discrimination Act 1995, section 1 and Schedule 1

S1(1) Subject to the provisions of Schedule 1, a person has a disability for the purposes of this Act if he has a physical or mental impairment which has a substantial and long-term adverse effect on his ability to carry out normal day-to-day activities.

(2) In this Act 'disabled person' means a person who has a disability.

S2(1) The [employment-related and various other] provisions of this [Act] apply in relation to a person who has had a disability as they apply in relation to a person who has that disability.

SCHEDULE 1

Para 1(1) "Mental impairment" includes an impairment resulting from or consisting of a mental illness only if the illness is a clinically well-recognised illness . . .

Para 2(1) The effect of an impairment is a long-term effect if—
   (a) it has lasted at least 12 months;
   (b) the period for which it lasts is likely to be at least 12 months; or
   (c) it is likely to last for the rest of the life of the person affected.

(2) Where an impairment ceases to have a substantial adverse effect on a person's ability to carry out normal day-to-day activities, it is to be treated as continuing to have that effect if that effect is likely to recur . . .

Para 3(1) An impairment which consists of a severe disfigurement is to be treated as having a substantial adverse effect on the ability of the person concerned to carry out normal day-to-day activities . . .

Para 4(1) An impairment is to be taken to affect the ability of the person concerned to carry out normal day-to-day activities only if it affects one of the following—
   (a) mobility;
   (b) manual dexterity;
   (c) physical co-ordination;
   (d) continence;
   (e) ability to lift, carry or otherwise move everyday objects;
   (f) speech, hearing or eyesight;
   (g) memory or ability to concentrate, learn or understand; or
   (h) perception of the risk of physical danger . . .

Para 6(1) An impairment which would be likely to have a substantial adverse effect on the ability of the person concerned to carry out normal day-to-day activities, but for the fact that measures are being taken to treat or correct it, is to be treated as having that effect . . .
   (3) Sub-paragraph (1) does not apply—

(a) in relation to the impairment of a person's sight, to the extent that the impairment is, in his case, correctable by spectacles or contact lenses or in such other ways as may be prescribed . . .

Para 8(1) Where—
  (a) a person has a progressive condition (such as cancer, multiple sclerosis or muscular dystrophy or infection by the human immunodeficiency virus),
  (b) as a result of that condition, he has an impairment which has (or had) an effect on his ability to carry out normal day-to-day activities, but
  (c) that effect is not (or was not) a substantial adverse effect,

he shall be taken to have an impairment which has such a substantial adverse effect if the condition is likely to result in his having such an impairment . . .

The Act is supplemented by the Disability Discrimination (Meaning of Disability) Regulations 1996 (SI 1996 No 1455) which provide further restrictions on the meaning of disability (and the question whether, for the purposes of S1 DDA, an impairment is to be treated as having a 'substantial adverse effect' on a person's ability to carry out day-to-day activities). Regulation 3 provides that, save in the case of medically prescribed drugs, 'addiction to alcohol, nicotine or any other substance is to be treated as not amounting to an impairment for the purposes of the Act'. Regulation 4 excludes from the definition of 'impairment' exhibitionism, voyeurism and the tendency to set fires, to steal, or to engage in physical or sexual abuse of others. It also excludes hay fever save in cases where it aggravates the effect of another condition. Regulation 5 provides that tatoos (save where they have been removed) and non-medical piercings shall not be regarded as having a substantial adverse effect on the ability to carry out normal day-to-day activities.

The Act does not protect against discrimination on grounds of *perceived* disability (where, for example, someone is dismissed because he is wrongly believed to be suffering from terminal cancer) or from discrimination on grounds of a medical condition (such as HIV) which does not in fact impair the functional abilities of the sufferer. The Disability Discrimination Act 2005 brings within the definition of 'disabled' anyone with 'cancer, HIV infection or multiple sclerosis' subject to the power of the Secretary of State to make regulations excluding from the definition certain types of cancer. The Act does not, however, alter the position as regards perceived disability so the person sacked because he is wrongly suspected of being HIV positive would remain unprotected by the DDA, as would someone refused a job because her employer wrongly assumes that a condition (such as, for example, controlled diabetes) will impact on her attendance record. The recommendation by the Joint Parliamentary Committee on the draft Disability Discrimination Bill that the DDA be amended to protect those associated with a disabled person or who are perceived to be disabled was rejected but the government did accept the committee's proposal for the scrapping of the-then requirement that mental illness be 'clinically well recognised'.

Para 6 of Schedule 1 DDA provides that, save in the case of glasses or contact lenses, the effects of medical treatment are to be discounted in determining whether an impairment has a substantial adverse effect on the ability of the person concerned to carry out normal day-to-day activities. In *Abadeh v British Telecommunications* [2001] ICR 156 the EAT distinguished between continuing and concluded medical treatment ruling that, in the latter case, the 'deduced effect' provisions had no application and the claimant had to be assessed as he or she presented. The EAT further distinguished between continuing medical treatment which has resulted in a permanent improvement, and that which has not. As in the case of concluded medical treatment, continuing treatment whose impact is permanent (or, more precisely, which was permanent at the time of the discrimination) ought not to be disregarded for the purposes of determining whether the claimant is 'disabled' for the purposes of the DDA. Tribunals ought, however, to bear in mind that a claimant who is discriminated against on the basis that he or she has been disabled in the past is also protected by the DDA.

The Secretary of State has issued guidance about the matters relevant to (a) whether an impairment has a 'substantial adverse effect on a person's ability to carry out normal day-to-day activities' and (b) whether such an impairment has a 'long-term effect'. The Guidance on Matters to be Taken into Account in Determining Questions Relating to the Definition of Disability states (Part II, para A1) that 'a substantial effect is one which is more than "minor" or "trivial"', and provides that tribunals ought to have regard, in deciding whether an impairment has such an effect, to:

- the time taken to carry out an activity;
- the way in which an activity is carried out;
- the cumulative effects of an impairment (ie, less than substantial adverse effects on multiple matters listed in Schedule 1, para 4, may together amount to a substantial adverse effect on ability to carry out 'normal day-to-day activities';
- the effects of behaviour (ie, whether reasonable coping strategies would prevent the disability having a substantial adverse effect though (A 9) 'If a disabled person is advised by a medical practitioner to behave in a certain way in order to reduce the impact of the disability, that might count as treatment to be disregarded' (section 6(1));
- the effects of environment.'

The Guidance must be taken into account, where it appears relevant, by any tribunal or court and its relevance to the question whether an applicant is disabled within the Act. In *Goodwin v Patent Office*, however, the EAT suggested that its relevance was confined to 'marginal' cases and was critical of tribunals which used it as 'an extra hurdle' over which applicants in 'clear cases' must jump.

[3.13] *Goodwin v Patent Office* [1999] ICR 302 (EAT)

The applicant, who had been diagnosed as suffering from paranoid schizophrenia, was dismissed partly because of bizarre behaviour consistent with that diagnosis. A tribunal rejected his DDA claim, ruling that his condition, as a result of which he experienced auditory hallucinations which impaired his concentration, did not have a substantial adverse effect on his normal day-to-day activities sufficient to amount to a 'disability'. The tribunal considered the question whether he was disabled without reference to the guidance and concluded that, because he could 'perform his domestic activities without the need for assistance, [could] get to work efficiently and . . . carry out his work to a satisfactory standard', his illness did not *substantially* affect his ability to carry out normal day-to-day activities. The EAT allowed his appeal, ruling (*per* Morison J) that the tribunal had misdirected tself as by failing to look 'at the effect which the applicant's disability had on his abilities', moving rather 'from the finding that the applicant was able to cope at home to the conclusion that, therefore, he fell outwith the provisions of the Act'. The EAT declared it 'most surprising that any tribunal should conclude that a person admittedly diagnosed as suffering from paranoid schizophrenia and who had been dismissed partly because of what one might call bizarre behaviour, consistent with that diagnosis, fell outside the definition in s 1 of the Act'. The appeal tribunal went on to lay down guidance for tribunals determining the question of disability.

Morison J:

> Section 1(1) defines the circumstances in which a person has a disability within the meaning of the Act. The words of the section require a tribunal to look at the evidence by reference to four different conditions . . . [1] Does the applicant have an impairment which is either mental or physical? . . . [2] Does the impairment: affect the applicant's ability to carry out normal day-to-day activities in one of the respects set out in para 4(1) of Schedule 1 to the Act, and does it have an adverse effect? . . . [3] Is the adverse condition (upon the applicant's ability) substantial? . . . [4] Is the adverse condition (upon the applicant's ability) long-term?
>
> Frequently, there will be a complete overlap between conditions (3) and (4), but it will be as well to bear all four of them in mind. Tribunals may find it helpful to address each of the questions but at the same time be aware of the risk that disaggregation should not take one's eye off the whole picture . . .

Morison J went on to discuss each of these conditions, expressing the view that the question whether a condition had an adverse impact on the applicant's ability to carry out normal day-to-day activities 'may be the most difficult of the four conditions to judge', given the adjustments frequently made by disabled people:

> Thus a person whose capacity to communicate through normal speech was obviously impaired might well choose, more or less voluntarily, to live on their own. If one asked such a person whether they managed to carry on their daily lives without undue problems, the answer might well be 'yes', yet their ability to lead a 'normal' life had obviously been impaired. Such a person would be unable to communicate through speech and the ability to communicate through speech is obviously a capacity which is needed for carrying out normal day-to-day activities, whether at work or at home. If asked whether they could use the telephone, or ask for directions or which bus to take, the answer would be 'no'. Those might be regarded as day-to-day activities contemplated by the legislation, and that person's ability to carry them out would clearly be regarded as adversely affected. Furthermore, disabled persons are likely, habitually, to 'play down' the effect that their disabilities have on their daily lives . . . It will be borne in mind that the effect of a disability on a person's ability to conduct his daily life might have a cumulative effect, in the sense that more than one of the capacities had been impaired . . .
>
> On the assumption that the impairment and adverse effect conditions have been fulfilled, the tribunal must consider whether the adverse effect is substantial . . .

The question whether an impairment has a 'substantial' effect is one for the tribunal, rather than a medical expert, and should be determined in marginal cases having regard to the Secretary of State's guidance. In *Vicary v BT* a tribunal had ruled that a woman who was unable to prepare vegetables, cut meat or roast potatoes or carry a meal on a tray did not suffer from any impairment which *substantially* impaired her ability to carry out her normal day to day activities. The EAT allowed Ms Vicary's appeal.

[3.14] *Vicary v British Telecommunications plc* [1999] IRLR 680 (EAT)

Morison J:

. . . the Employment Tribunal has not considered the interpretation of the word 'substantial'. It seems to us clear that they must have approached the case on the basis that 'substantial' means more than what the word means in this context . . . Paragraph 6 of annex 1 of the Code of Practice issued by the Secretary of State for Education and Employment . . . 'A substantial adverse effect is something which is more than a minor or trivial effect. The requirement that an effect must be substantial reflects the general understanding of disability as a limitation going beyond the normal differences in ability which might exist among people.' . . .

[I]n this case there was in fact no need for the Employment Tribunal to refer to the guidance once they had properly understood the meaning of the word 'substantial'. Having concluded that the ability of the Applicant to do the activities specified [above] was impaired, the Tribunal inevitably should have concluded that the Applicant was a person suffering from a disability within the meaning of the Act. Instead, the Employment Tribunal appears to have used the guidance in a somewhat literal fashion so as to arrive at the surprising conclusion that the Applicant was not substantially impaired in her ability to carry out normal day-to-day activities . . .

It is clear that an ability to prepare vegetables, cut up meat and carry a meal on a tray would all be regarded as examples of normal day-to-day activities. An inability to carry out those functions would, in our view, obviously be regarded as a substantial impairment of an ability to carry out normal day-to-day activities . . .

The fact that a person is able to mitigate the effects of their disability does not mean that they are not disabled within the meaning of the Act. It seems to us obvious that it would be a substantial impairment on a normal day-to-day activity if the Applicant could not use a hand-held bag or carry washing, other than in small quantities, or unload her shopping trolley other than in small quantities . . .

. . . we should wish to add for the consideration of the Employment Tribunals in the future that a relatively small proportion of the disabled community are what one might describe as visibly disabled, that is people in wheelchairs or carrying white sticks or other aids. It is important, therefore, that when they are approaching the question as to whether someone suffers from a disability, they should not have in their minds a stereotypical image of a person in a wheelchair or moving around with considerable difficulty. Such persons may well have a physical impairment within the meaning of the Act and are thus to be treated as disabled, but it of course does not follow that other persons who are not in such a condition are inherently less likely to have a physical or mental impairment of a sort which satisfies the terms of the legislation.

In *Leonard v Southern Derbyshire Chamber of Commerce* [2001] IRLR 19 the EAT emphasised that tribunals ought not to balance what a claimant could against what she could not do for the purposes of determining whether her condition substantially impaired her ability to carry out normal day-to-day activities. In that case the Claimant, who was clinically depressed, was able to eat and drink and catch a ball, but could not negotiate pavement edges safely. The EAT ruled that the tribunal had erred in balancing the former abilities against the latter disability as her ability to catch a ball did not assist the Claimant in negotiating pavements. The tribunal ought to concentrate on what a claimant cannot do or can do only with difficulty.

3.3 Direct discrimination

Discrimination is categorised by most of the legislative provisions here under consideration as 'direct' or 'indirect', or as occurring by way of 'victimisation' further discussed below. That categorisation will be adopted here. But it should be recognised that the dividing line between direct and indirect discrimination is not entirely clear. Philosophers may argue about the moral distinctions between the concepts of direct and indirect discrimination, and the relationship between them and different notions of justice (see, for example, A Morris, 'On the Normative Foundations of Indirect Discrimination Law: Understanding the Competing Models of Discrimination Law as Aristotelian Forms of Justice' (1995) 15 *Oxford Journal of Legal Studies* 199, and J Gardner, 'Discrimination as Injustice' (1996) 16 *Oxford Journal of Legal Studies* 353). The most significant distinction from the point of view of employment lawyers is that indirect discrimination is, but direct discrimination is not, subject to a general justification defence. Even direct race discrimination is lawful where it falls within one of the specific exceptions established by the RRA (the same is true in relation to sex, religion, etc.). But indirect discrimination may, in addition, be justified in general terms (see further section 3.5.4 below).

3.3.1 Direct discrimination

There are two approaches to direct discrimination. That under the RBRs and the SORs (Regulation 3) is materially identical to that taken by the RRA, the relevant section of which is reproduced below. The DDA and SDA, also reproduced below, take a different line. In addition, the DDA utilises a wider form of discrimination (disability-related discrimination) which is considered further at [3.23] below. The EqPA does not use the term 'discrimination', whether direct or indirect. But, as we shall see below (section 3.10.2), the absence of discrimination is central to whether or not a pay difference is lawful.

[3.15] Race Relations Act 1976, section 1

S.1 A person discriminates against another in any circumstances relevant for the purposes of any provision of this Act if—

(a) *on racial grounds* he treats that other less favourably than he treats or would treat other persons [our emphasis] . . .

[3.16] Sex Discrimination Act 1975, section 1

S.1 A person discriminates against a woman in any circumstances relevant for the purposes of any provision of this Act if—
(a) *on the grounds of her sex* he treats her less favourably than he treats or would treat a man [our emphasis] . . .

[3.17] Disability Discrimination Act 1995, section 3(5)

S.3(5) A person directly discriminates against a disabled person if, *on the ground of the disabled person's disability*, he treats the disabled person less favourably than he treats or would treat a person not having that particular disability whose relevant circumstances, including his abilities, are the same as, or not materially different from, those of the disabled person [our emphasis].

The RBRs and SORs are materially identical to the RRA and, like it, capture discrimination against A on the grounds of *another person's* race, sexual orientation, etc. (see *Weathersfield v Sargeant* **[3.7]**) whereas the SDA and the DDA apply only in relation to discrimination on the ground of the claimant's *own* sex or disability. Section 3A(5) DDA incorporates within its text the comparator provision found in sections 5(3) and 3(4) of the SDA and RRA respectively and considered at 3.3.1.2 below.

The SDA, RRA, DDA and SORs and RBRs all proscribe less favourable treatment on the prohibited grounds. But they do not require (by contrast with the position under the EqPA) that the complainant point to an actual person who has been more favourably treated. The ability to point to an actual instance of differential treatment will ease the burden of proof (of which more below), but a claim can be made out under the SDA, RRA, DDA, SORs or RBRs on the basis of a hypothetical comparator alone.

3.3.1.1 Intention, motivation and discrimination

Direct discrimination is defined in terms of less favourable treatment on the grounds of sex, race, etc. In a number of early SDA cases, respondents attempted to argue that treatment which, although less favourable in respect of one group than another, was motivated benignly, did not amount to unlawful discrimination. In other cases, respondents have sought to argue that the disputed treatment, although different, was no less favourable to one group than another. Both of these arguments were employed, unsuccessfully, by the respondents in the following case.

[3.18] *R v Birmingham City Council ex parte Equal Opportunities Commission* **[1989] AC 1155 (HL)**

The EOC brought an action for judicial review against the Council in its capacity as local education authority on the grounds that it provided only 360 grammar school places for girls in comparison with 540 for boys. The EOC won a declaration at first instance that the Council was in breach of the SDA, which declaration was upheld by the Court of Appeal. The Council appealed to the House of Lords, arguing that the EOC had failed to show (a) that selective education was better than non-selective education, proof of which, the council argued, was necessary to establish 'less favourable treatment' of girls; and (b) that the Council had intended or been motivated to discriminate against girls. The House of Lords dismissed the Council's appeal.

Lord Goff (for the Court):
. . . it is not, in my opinion, necessary for the commission to show that selective education is 'better' than non-selective education. It is enough that, by denying the girls the same opportunity as the boys, the council is depriving them of a choice which (as the facts show) is valued by them, or at least by their parents, and which (even though others may take a different view) is a choice obviously valued, on reasonable grounds, by many others . . . As to the second point, it is, in my opinion, contrary to the terms of the statute. There is discrimination under the statute if there is less favourable treatment on the ground of sex, in other words if the relevant girl or girls would have received the same treatment as the boys but for their sex. The intention or motive of the defendant to discriminate, though it may be relevant so far as remedies are concerned . . . is not a necessary condition to liability . . . if [it were] it would be a good defence for an employer to show that he discriminated against women not because he intended to do so but (for example) because of customer preference, or to save money, or even to avoid controversy.

The approach taken by the House of Lords in *EOC v Birmingham* in respect of motive was reiterated the following year in *James v Eastleigh* and, more recently, applied by that court in *Nagarajan v London Regional Transport* [1999] ICR 877 (**[3.32]** below) to discrimination by way of victimisation.

[3.19] *James v Eastleigh Borough Council* **[1990] 2 AC 751 (HL)**

Mr James complained of direct discrimination after he was charged entrance to the local swimming pool on the grounds that, both he and his wife being aged between 60 and 65, she but not he had reached state pensionable age upon which free entrance depended. The case was argued as one of direct discrimination on the assumption that, if the discrimination at issue were accepted as indirect, the Council would succeed in a justification plea.

Lord Goff:
In the Court of Appeal in the present case, Sir Nicolas Browne-Wilkinson V-C approached the matter as follows. Referring to section 1(1)(a) of the [SDA] . . . he said . . .

'In the case of direct discrimination "a person discriminates against a man . . . if on the ground of his sex he treats him less favourably . . . " Those words indicate that one is looking, not to the causative link between the defendant's behaviour and the detriment to the plaintiff, but to the reason why the defendant treated the plaintiff less favourably. The relevant question is "Did the defendant act on the ground of sex?" not "Did the less favourable treatment result from the defendant's actions?" Thus, if the overt basis for affording less favourable treatment was sex (eg an employer saying 'no women employees') that is direct discrimination. If the overt reason does not in terms relate to sex (e g in selection for redundancy, part-time employees are the first to go) that is not on the face of it direct discrimination since sex does not come into the overt reason given for the action. If, but only if, it is shown that the overt reason is not the true reason but there is a covert reason why the employer adopted those criteria (e g to get rid of his female employees) will it be direct discrimination. In such a case the true reason for the policy is the desire to treat women less favourably than men the employer is therefore acting on that ground'.

On this approach, a defendant will only have committed an action of direct discrimination if either his overt or his covert reason for his action is the sex of the complainant. So the question whether or not there has been direct discrimination can only be answered by asking why the defendant acted as he did. Sir Nicolas Browne-Wilkinson V-C, however, went on to state that the defendant's intention or motive may be relevant for the purpose of ascertaining the defendant's reason for his behaviour. I will return to the use of these three words, intention, motive and reason, at a later stage.

In reaching this conclusion, Sir Nicolas Browne-Wilkinson V-C was infiuenced primarily by the wording of the subsection. He considered that the words 'on the ground of sex' referred, in this context, not to the causative link between the defendant's behaviour and detriment to the complainant, but to the reason why the defendant treated the complainant less favourably . . .

As a matter of impression, it seems to me that, without doing any violence to the words used in [section 1(1)(a)] . . . it can properly be said that, by applying to the plaintiff a gender-based criterion, unfavourable to men . . . they [sic] did on the ground of sex treat him less favourably than it treated women of the same age, and in particular his wife. In other words, I do not read the words 'on the ground of sex' as necessarily referring only to the reason why the defendant acted as he did, but as embracing cases in which a gender-based criterion is the basis on which the complainant has been selected for the relevant treatment. Of course, there may be cases where the defendant's reason for his action may bring the case within the subsection, as when the defendant is motivated by an animus against persons of the complainant's sex, or otherwise selects the complainant for the relevant treatment because of his or her sex. But it does not follow that the words 'on the ground of sex' refer only to cases where the defendant's reason for his action is the sex of the complainant and, in my opinion, the application by the defendant to the complainant of a gender-based criterion which favours the opposite sex is just as much a case of unfavourable treatment on the ground of sex. Such a conclusion seems to me to be consistent with the policy of the Act, which is the active promotion of equal treatment of men and women. Indeed, the present case is no different from one in which the defendant adopts a criterion which favours widows as against widowers, on the basis that the former are likely to be less well off, or indeed, as my noble and learned friend Lord Bridge has pointed out, a criterion which favours women between the ages of 60 and 65, as against men between the same ages, on the same basis. It is plain to me that, in those cases, a man in either category who was so treated could properly say that he was treated less favourably on the ground of sex, and that the fact that the defendant had so treated him for a benign motive (to help women in the same category, because they are likely to be less well off) was irrelevant . . .

I am reluctant to have to conclude that those who are concerned with the day-to-day administration of legislation such as the [SDA], who are mainly those who sit on industrial tribunals, should have to grapple with such elusive concepts as [intention, motive, reason and purpose]. However, taking the case of direct discrimination under s 1(1)(a) of the Act, I incline to the opinion that, if it were necessary to identify the requisite intention of the defendant, that intention is simply an intention to perform the relevant act of less favourable treatment. Whether or not the treatment is less favourable in the relevant sense, i e on the ground of sex, may derive either from the application of a gender-based criterion to the complainant, or from selection by the defendant of the complainant because of his or her sex but, in either event, it is not saved from constituting unlawful discrimination by the fact that the defendant acted from a benign motive. However, in the majority of cases, I doubt if it is necessary to focus on the intention or motive of the defendant in this way. This is because, as I see it, cases of direct discrimination under s 1(1)(a) can be considered by asking the simple question: would the complainant have received the same treatment from the defendant but for his or her sex? This simple test possesses the double virtue that, on the one hand, it embraces both the case where the treatment derives from the application of a gender-based criterion, and the case where it derives from the selection of the complainant because of his or her sex and on the other hand it avoids, in most cases at least, complicated questions relating to concepts such as intention, motive, reason or purpose, and the danger of confusion arising from the misuse of those elusive terms. I have to stress, however, that the 'but for' test is not appropriate for cases of indirect discrimination under s 1(1)(b), because there may be indirect discrimination against persons of one sex under that subsection, although a (proportionately smaller) group of persons of the opposite sex is adversely affected in the same way.

The House of Lords once again embraced the 'but for' test in *Nagarajan* in the face of the attempt made by Lord Browne-Wilkinson, then the senior Law Lord, to consign it to history. Their Lordships there ruled that the test for victimisation was materially identical, so far as is relevant here, to that for direct discrimination. This was called into a question a few months later in *Chief Constable of West Yorkshire Police* v *Khan* [2001] ICR 1065, further considered at **[3.34]** below. In *Shamoon* v *Chief Constable of the Royal Ulster Constabulary (Northern Ireland)* [2003] ICR 337, which is extracted at **[3.22]** below, the House of Lords appeared to emphasise the need for scrutiny of the reasons for less favourable treatment, perhaps at the expense of the 'but for' test. And in the *ex parte European Roma Rights Centre* case the Court of Appeal ([2004] QB 811) appeared to turn its back on *James* and its progeny, ruling that the application of more rigorous scrutiny to Romas than to non-Romas seeking to enter the UK from Prague did not amount to direct discrimination under the RRA. Romas were 400 times more likely than others to be refused entry to the UK. The House of Lords overturned, Lord Steyn remarking that 'there is in law a single issue: why did the immigration officers treat Roma less favourably than non-Roma? In my view the only realistic answer is that they did so because the persons concerned were Roma. They discriminated on the grounds of race. The motive for such discrimination is irrelevant' (citing *Nagarajan*).

[3.20] *European Roma Rights Centre v Immigration Officer at Prague Airport* **[2005] 2 WLR 1**

Baroness Hale *(with whom their Lordships agreed):*
The Roma were being treated more sceptically than the non-Roma. There was a good reason for this. How did the immigration officers know to treat them more sceptically? Because they were Roma. That is acting on racial grounds. If a person acts on racial grounds, the reason why he does so is irrelevant [citing *Nagarajan*]. The law reports are full

of examples of obviously discriminatory treatment which was in no way motivated by racism or sexism and often brought about by pressures beyond the discriminators' control: the council which sacked a black road sweeper to whom the union objected in order to avoid industrial action . . . the council which for historical reasons provided fewer selective school places for girls than for boys [citing *ex p EOC*]. But it goes further than this. The person may be acting on belief or assumptions about members of the sex or racial group involved which are often true and which if true would provide a good reason for the less favourable treatment in question. But 'what may be true of a group may not be true of a significant number of individuals within that group [citing Hartmann J in *Equal Opportunities Commission v Director of Education* [2001] 2 HKLRD 690, High Court of Hong Kong]. The object of the legislation is to ensure that each person is treated as an individual and not assumed to be like other members of the group. As Laws LJ observed dissenting, below:

> 'The mistake that might arise in relation to stereotyping would be a supposition that the stereotype is only vicious if it is *untrue*. But that cannot be right. If it were, it would imply that direct discrimination can be justified . . . '

As we have seen, the legislation draws a clear distinction between direct and indirect discrimination and makes no reference at all to justification in relation to direct discrimination. Nor, strictly, does it allow indirect discrimination to be justified. It accepts that a requirement or condition may be justified *independently* of its discriminatory effect.

3.3.1.2 The comparator problem

Useful as the 'but for' test has proved to discrimination complainants, it does not provide a comprehensive answer to the question whether direct discrimination has occurred in any particular case. Where a woman is subjected to detriment for a reason connected with pregnancy, the application of the 'but for' test provides contradictory answers depending on how it is considered. (The question has been a significant one because of the shortcomings, now largely overcome, of the statutory protection accorded specifically to pregnant woman.) On the one hand, it is true to say that, 'but for' the fact that she was a woman, she would not have been pregnant and would not, therefore, have been dismissed. On the other hand, her pregnancy can be regarded as a 'sex plus' state. Being pregnant is not one and the same thing as being a woman, any more than having testicular cancer is one and the same thing as being a man.

It could be argued that discrimination on the basis of a 'sex plus' factor should not be regarded as discrimination on grounds of sex. This was the approach taken by the US Supreme Court in *Geduldig v Aiello*, in which that court ruled, by a majority, that pregnancy discrimination was not sex discrimination.

[3.21] *Geduldig v Aiello* **417 US 484 (1974)**

Justice Stewart (for the majority):
While it is true that only women can become pregnant, it does not follow that every legislative classification concerning pregnancy is a sex-based classification. [Dealing with medical insurance programme which excluded pregnancy coverage] . . . The programme

divides potential recipients into two groups--pregnant women and nonpregnant persons. While the first group is exclusively female, the second includes members of both sexes.

The decision in *Geduldig* notwithstanding, the English courts have recognised that treatment based on pregnancy was treatment 'by reason of' sex. But the question of whether less favourable treatment connected with pregnancy amounts to sex *discrimination* has been bedevilled by the SDA's 'comparator' requirement.

Section 5(3) SDA provides that 'A comparison of the cases of persons of different sex . . . under section 1(1) . . . must be such that the relevant circumstances in the one case are the same, or not materially different, in the other'. Section 3(4) RRA and Regulation 3(2) of each the SORs and the RBRs are in similar terns, and we saw above that section 3A(5) DDA incorporates a similar test into the definition of direct discrimination itself. In order to determine whether a complainant has been 'less favourably treated' on the relevant grounds it is necessary to compare her treatment with than of a person of a different sex, race, sexual orientation etc. in the same 'relevant circumstances'.

In *Webb v EMO*, a woman claimed that her pregnancy-related dismissal breached the SDA (the case preceded the blanket protection against such dismissals now afforded by the ERA 1996, see chapter 4). Her claim was rejected by the tribunal, the EAT and the Court of Appeal on the grounds that a sick man (whom the courts took to be the appropriate comparator for the purposes of section 5(3) SDA) would have been similarly treated. The House of Lords referred to the ECJ the question whether, as a matter of EC law, less favourable treatment connected with pregnancy had to be regarded as sex discrimination. The ECJ had already ruled, in Case 177/88, *Dekker* v *Stichting Vormingscentrum Voor Jonge Volwassen (VJV-Centrum) Plus* [1990] ECR I–3941, that pregnancy discrimination should be regarded as sex discrimination without any requirement for a male comparator. Lord Keith, for the House of Lords (*Webb* v *EMO Air Cargo (UK) Ltd* [1993] ICR 175) insisted that 'The relevant circumstance for purposes of the comparison required by section 5(3) to be made is expected unavailability at the material time', though the 'precise reason for the unavailability is not a relevant circumstance, and in particular it is not relevant that the reason is a condition which is capable of affecting only women or, for that matter, only men'. The ECJ, on a reference from the House of Lords, ruled (Case 32/93 [1994] ECR I–3567) that pregnancy-related dismissal amounted to sex discrimination without need for consideration of any 'comparable' man and on the case's return the House of Lords (*Webb* v *EMO (No 2)* [1995] ICR 1021) accepted (*per* Lord Keith) that 'in a case where a woman is engaged for an indefinite period, the fact that the reason why she will be temporarily unavailable for work at a time when to her knowledge her services will be particularly required is pregnancy is a circumstance relevant to her case, being a circumstance which could not be present in the case of the hypothetical man'.

Lord Keith expressed the view in *Webb* that a different approach might apply to a case in which a woman was 'denied employment for a fixed period in the future during the whole of which her pregnancy would make her unavailable for work', or 'where after engagement for such a period the discovery of her pregnancy leads to cancellation of the engagement'. This position is no longer tenable as a result of the decision of the ECJ in Case 438/99, *Jiménez Melgar v Ayuntamiento de Los Barrios*

[2001] ECR I–06915 that the Equal Treatment Directive was breached by a failure to renew a pregnant woman's fixed term contract. In Case 109/00 *Tele Danmark* [2001] ECR I–06693 the ECJ rejected the argument that the employee was at fault for failing to notify the employer of her pregnancy. And a similar approach was taken in Case 109/00 *Busch v Klinikum Neustadt* [2003] ECR I–020341, in which the ECJ ruled that a woman was entitled to shorten her maternity leave and return to work while pregnant again (this in order to avail herself of maternity leave in relation to the second pregnancy). She could not be required to inform the employer of the fact of her second pregnancy (in order that the employer could refuse to permit her early return to work). According to the ECJ, the fact that the Claimant would be unable to carry out all her job functions on her return—or, indeed, that she returned solely to qualify for enhanced payment in respect of the second maternity leave—could not justify any exception to the prohibition under the Equal Treatment Directive of pregnancy-related discrimination. Women are also protected (*Brown v Rentokil Ltd* Case 394/96, [1998] ECR I–04185) from dismissal/ detriment in connection with any period of sickness during the period of pregnancy or maternity leave. (The ECJ caselaw is read into the SDA which is at present silent as to the definition of pregnancy discrimination as sex discrimination, but it is proposed that the Act will be amended expressly to cover pregnancy and maternity discrimination from October 2005, as part of the implementation of Council Directive 2002/78/EC (the Equal Treatment Amendment Directive).

In *Shamoon* the House of Lords recognised the problems generated by the comparator approach. The case involved a complaint under the Sex Discrimination (Northern Ireland) Order 1976, which is materially identical to the SDA. The Claimant was a chief inspector whose appraisal duties were removed from her after a number of complaints had been made against her in connection with her conduct of appraisals. Her claim was upheld by a tribunal but dismissed by Northern Ireland's Court of Appeal (to which claims from tribunals go directly) on the basis that her chosen comparators—two male chief inspectors—were not similarly situated (this because no complaints had been made against them in connection with their performance of appraisals).

The House of Lords agreed that the actual comparators relied upon by the Claimant were inappropriate and that the tribunal had given no reasons to justify the finding of sex discrimination. Their Lordships did, however, make some interesting observations about the question of comparators.

[3.22] *Shamoon v Chief Constable of the Royal Ulster Constabulary (Northern Ireland)* [2003] ICR 337 (HL)

> *Lord Hope:*
>
> the choice of comparator requires that a judgment must be made as to which of the differences between any two individuals are relevant and which are irrelevant. The choice of characteristics may itself be determinative of the outcome . . . This suggests that care must be taken not to approach this issue in a way that will defeat the purpose of the legislation, which is to eliminate discrimination against women on the ground of their sex in all the areas with which it deals.

Lord Nicholls, with whom Lord Rodger agreed on this point, noted that the general practice of tribunals was to ask, first, 'whether the claimant received less favourable treatment than the appropriate comparator' (the 'less favourable treatment' issue), and to treat this question effectively as a 'threshold which the claimant must cross before the tribunal is called upon to decide' the second question – 'whether the less favourable treatment was on the relevant proscribed ground' (the "reason why" issue)'. He accepted that this practice could be 'convenient and helpful' but stressed that there was 'essentially a single question: did the claimant, on the proscribed ground, receive less favourable treatment than others [received or would have received]?' The 'sequential analysis' could 'give rise to needless problems', 'especially where the identity of the relevant comparator is a matter of dispute. Sometimes the less favourable treatment issue cannot be resolved without, at the same time, deciding the reason why issue. The two issues are intertwined.'

In the instant case Lord Nicholls pointed out that it was not possible to answer whether the Claimant's chosen comparators were appropriate without addressing the question why she had been relieved of her appraisal duties: if the reason was connected with the complaints against her the comparators were not appropriate. But the action taken against her may have had nothing to do with the complaints, in which case the comparison she advocated would have entailed 'comparing like with like, because in that event the difference between her and her two male colleagues would be an immaterial difference'. Equally, the question whether the Claimant was less favourably treated than a hypothetical comparator:

> is incapable of being answered without . . . identifying the ground on which she was treated as she was. Was it grounds of sex? If yes, then she was treated less favourably than a male chief inspector in her position would have been treated. If not, not. Thus, on this footing also, the less favourable treatment issue is incapable of being decided without deciding the reason why issue. And the decision on the reason why issue will also provide the answer to the less favourable treatment issue.

On the basis of this analysis Lord Nicholls concluded that tribunals:

> may sometimes be able to avoid arid and confusing disputes about the identification of the appropriate comparator by concentrating primarily on why the claimant was treated as she was. Was it on the proscribed ground which is the foundation of the application? That will call for an examination of all the facts of the case. Or was it for some other reason? If the latter, the application fails. If the former, there will be usually be no difficulty in deciding whether the treatment, afforded to the claimant on the proscribed ground, was less favourable than was or would have been afforded to others.

Lord Nicholls' approach fits well with the domestic model of direct discrimination which permits claimants to establish discrimination in relation to a *hypothetical* comparator. Once it has been established that the treatment complained of was *by reason of* a protected ground, the comparator question is largely a formality save in cases in which the discriminator alleges that *differential* treatment was not *less favourable* (as, perhaps, if single-sex toilet facilities were to be challenged). But Lord Nicholls' approach does not solve all the problems to which the analysis of discrimination gives rise. Indeed it is perhaps precisely because of the difficulties associated with determining the reasons for differential treatment that a comparator-driven approach can appear attractive. The House of Lords' embracing of the 'but-for' test in *James* v *Eastleigh* was intended to avoid unnecessary confusion as to intention, motive, etc. It operates in practice by emphasising what Lord Nicholls referred to in *Shamoon* as the 'less favourable treatment' question over the 'reason why' question. In order to determine whether a claimant would have been treated more favourably 'but for' her sex the question required by section 5(3) SDA is whether a similarly situated man was or would have been treated more favourably than she was. But as their Lordships generally recognised in *Shamoon*, the answer to this may depend on the characteristics assigned to the 'similarly situated' man or other relevant comparator.

Particular examples of this arise in the context of pregnancy dismissals and discrimination against gay men and lesbians. In the case of pregnancy the question is whether the similarly situated man require a similar period of absence from work? Or—because pregnancy can only happen to women—must that which is inevitably connected with it be excluded from the 'relevant circumstances' under section 5(3) SDA? In the case of discrimination against gay men and lesbians the question is whether the similarly situated woman or man respectively is one who (a) would or does have sexual relationships with men (where the claimant is a gay man) or women (where the claimant is a lesbian) or (b) one who has or would have sexual relationships with members of their own sex? In either of these cases the difficulties are not alleviated whether (as in *James*) an objective 'but for' test is adopted or whether (as suggested by Lord Nicholls in *Shamoon*) the 'reason why' test is brought to the fore. If the former then all hangs on the choice of comparator. If the latter the question is whether discrimination connected with pregnancy, on the one hand, and discrimination against gay men and lesbians, on the other, is discrimination which ought in principle to be recognised as *sex* discrimination.

The approach adopted by the House of Lords in *James* was liberal and purposive in defining direct discrimination widely without requiring malign motivation on the part of the discriminator. But the *James* approach does not do away with the need to ask questions about reasons for discrimination and whether they are properly categorised as coming within the protected grounds or not. It is clear from the decision in *James* that differential treatment which is based on criteria which themselves directly discriminate between men and woman will directly discriminate on grounds of sex. Equally, differential treatment which is based on criteria which themselves directly discriminate on racial grounds will directly discriminate on racial grounds. It follows from this that, if a woman were dismissed *solely because* she was pregnant she should be regarded as having been discriminated against on grounds of sex. There is in principle no need in such a case to identify a comparator but, to the extent that one is required by 5(3) SDA, he must simply be a man if the dicta in *James* is to be given effect. A man in the same relevant circumstances—whatever those circumstances were—could not possibly be pregnant and would not therefore have been sacked.

But once the reason put forward for the dismissal of a pregnant woman is something other than the fact of pregnancy *itself* (as, for example, where the employer points to the period of required leave or the flouting of moral standards by an unrepentant single pregnant woman) the picture is muddied. The question which arises under the 'reason why' approach is whether these reasons are reasons of sex. That which arises under the 'less favourable treatment' approach is whether the comparator should in the first example need a comparable period of leave and whether, in the second, he should be someone similarly morally tarnished in the eyes of the discriminator or whether, on the other hand, the same approach is required as would be applied if the reason for the dismissal was the fact of pregnancy *itself*. This is certainly desirable and—in the absence of other adequate legal protection from pregnancy-related discrimination—crucial if women are to be permitted even the most minimal claim to an even playing field at work. It is also required by EU law and will, as was mentioned above, soon become explicit on the face of the SDA. But the fact that this answer has been supplied in the pregnancy context for reasons which are extraneous to the model of discrimination adopted by the SDA does not supply a principled answer which necessarily ought to be applied in other circumstances.

The complications associated with sections 5(3) SDA and its equivalents were avoided by the DDA's prohibition of 'disability-related discrimination', which contains no equivalent provision. Leaving aside the possibility of justification and the duty of reasonable accommodation (at 3.6.1 and 3.6.2 below), section 3A(1)DDA defines as 'discrimination' less favourable treatment 'for a reason which relates to the disabled person's disability', rather than (in the case of direct discrimination) less favourable treatment *on grounds of* disability, sexual orientation, religion, etc.). Such less favourable treatment, as long as it does not amount to direct discrimination under the DDA, is unlawful only if (section 3A(1)(b)) the discriminator 'cannot show that the treatment in question is justified'.

The difference between 'disability-related' discrimination and 'direct discrimination' became apparent in the following decision.

[3.23] *Clark v TDG Ltd (tla Novacold)* [1999] ICR 951 (CA)

The applicant was dismissed because of a period of disability-related absence from work. An employment tribunal rejected his DDA claim, ruling that the treatment accorded to him had to be compared to that which a non-disabled employee who was absent for a similar period of time had or would have received. (This, the reader will recognise, is the approach taken, pre-*Webb (No 2)*, by the UK courts to pregnancy dismissal.) The tribunal took the view that such an employee would also have been dismissed. Mr Clark's appeal to the EAT was dismissed, that court taking the same approach to the meaning of discrimination under the DDA as had the tribunal. He appealed successfully to the Court of Appeal.

Having pointed out that the differences between the RRA and SDA, on the one hand, and the DDA, on the other, were such that the interpretation of the latter 'is not facilitated by familiarity' with the former, Mummery LJ pointed out that discriminatory treatment under the DDA was unlawful only where it was not justified (see further section 3.6.1 below). He relied both on statements made by the Minister for Social Security and Disabled People during the second reading of the Bill and upon the Code of Practice on Rights of Access to lay down, *inter alia*, the following principles:

Mummery LJ *(for the Court):*
Treatment is less favourable if the reason for it does not or would not apply to others.In deciding whether that reason does not or would not apply to others, it is not appropriate to make a comparison of the cases in the same way as in the [SDA] and the [RRA]. It is simply a case of identifying others to whom the reason for the treatment does not or would not apply. The test of less favourable treatment is based on the reason for the treatment of the disabled person and not on the fact of his disability. It does not turn on a like-for-like comparison of the treatment of the disabled person and of others in similar circumstances . . .

The dismissal in *Clark* was connected with the claimant's disability-related absence and was, accordingly, dismissal for a reason related to disability and, subject to the possibility of justification, unlawful discrimination under the DDA. More recently, in *Edwards* v *Mid Suffolk District Council* [2001] ICR 616, the EAT ruled that a claimant who suffered from chronic anxiety disorder, and who was dismissed as a result of his inability to work with his assistant, had been subject to disability-related discrimination. A tribunal had found that the dismissal resulted from the claimant's 'deliberate, selfish, consistent and obdurate' refusal to work with a personal assistant assigned to him and that he was 'using his mental illness as a stick with which to beat the employer'. The EAT allowed Mr Edwards' appeal on the basis that the tribunal had erred in law by failing to make a finding on the impact of the claimant's disability on his behaviour and ability to carry out his work, and remitted the case to a differently constituted employment tribunal.

It follows from the decision in *Clark* that employers can discriminate contrary to the DDA although ignorant of a worker's disability.

[3.24] *London Borough of Hammersmith & Fulham v Farnsworth* **[2000] IRLR 691 (EAT)**

> Ms Farnsworth's job application was rejected after the doctor to which the employer referred her for 'medical clearance' reported, on the basis of her history of depression, that her future attendance could be affected if her health problems recurred. The applicant complained that she had been discriminated against on the grounds of her disability (section.2 of the Act extending its protections to past as well as existing disabilities). A tribunal found in her favour on the basis that the Council knew of the applicant's disability (the tribunal imputing the doctor's knowledge to the council on the basis that the former had been acting as the latter's agent). In any event, the council had been 'put on notice that; the applicant had an illness and ought to have 'inquired as to its nature and why Dr Cooper considered that her attendance at work would be affected'.
>
> *Charles J:*
> Whether the reason the Borough withdrew its offer of employment was because the persons who made the decision on its behalf (apart from Dr Cooper) thought that [the applicant] would have poor attendance or considered that she did not have a satisfactory medical reference, in our judgment the effect of the decision in the Clark case is that at the 's 5(1)(a) stage' of the statutory test their knowledge of Ms Farnsworth's disability is irrelevant.
>
> It follows that if such knowledge is relevant it is relevant at the . . . 'justification stage' of the statutory test [section 3.6.1 below]

3.3.1.3 *'Less favourable treatment'—harassment and appearance rules*

We have considered the difficulties experienced by the English courts in selecting the appropriate comparator (real or hypothetical) against whose treatment that of the discrimination complainant can be compared. In dealing with the other problematic areas: harassment and clothing and appearance rules, the courts have struggled with the requirement that the complainant have been treated *less favourably* than that comparator. We saw (**[3.18]** above) the robust approach taken by the House of Lords in *EOC v Birmingham* to the respondent's claim that, although different, the treatment it accorded to female pupils was no less favourable than that afforded to boys: their Lordships ruled that the denial of a choice sufficed to establish less favourable treatment. In *Strathclyde Regional Council v Porcelli* the Court of Session adopted a similarly robust approach to the argument that sexual harassment consisting of specifically sexualised treatment (there sexual assault) was no less favourable than other forms of hostile treatment which might have been accorded to a man. Treatment (whether specifically sexualised or not) would be 'less favourable' if it was designed to keep a workplace white or male (or, for that matter, black, Asian or female), the appropriate comparator being a white person or a man (or a black or Asian person or a woman) who, not being perceived as 'other', would not have been subject to hostilities. But the argument put forward by the employers in this case was that the reason the plaintiff had been treated as she was was sex-neutral. This being the case, a claim of discrimination could only succeed if the treatment itself could be regarded as less favourable on grounds of sex.

[3.25] *Strathclyde Regional Council v Porcelli* [1986] ICR 564 (IH)

A woman laboratory technician who was driven from her job by sustained verbal and physical harassment of a sexual nature, claimed that she had been subject to sex discrimination contrary to the SDA. A tribunal rejected her claim, ruling that the harassment was motivated by her aggressors' dislike of her, and that a man who was so disliked by them would have been treated equally badly. Accordingly, she had not been discriminated against contrary to the SDA. The EAT allowed an appeal, a decision upheld by the Court of Session (Inner House).

Lord President Emslie:
S1(1)(a) is concerned with 'treatment' and not with the motive or objective of the person responsible for it. Although in some cases it will be obvious that there is a sex related purpose in the mind of a person who indulges in unwanted and objectionable sexual overtures to a woman or exposes her to offensive sexual jokes or observations that is not this case. But it does not follow that because the campaign pursued against Mrs Porcelli as a whole had no sex related motive or objective, the treatment of Mrs Porcelli by Coles, which was of the nature of 'sexual harassment' is not to be regarded as having been 'on the ground of her sex' within the meaning of s 1(1)(a). In my opinion this particular part of the campaign was plainly adopted against Mrs Porcelli because she was a woman. *It was a particular kind of weapon, based upon the sex of the victim, which . . . would not have been used against an equally disliked man* [our emphasis].
The . . . Tribunal . . . fail[ed] to notice that a material part of the campaign against Mrs Porcelli consisted of 'sexual harassment', a particularly degrading and unacceptable form of treatment which it must be taken to have been the intention of Parliament to restrain. From their reasons it is to be understood that they were satisfied that this form of treatment—sexual harassment in any form—would not have figured in a campaign by Coles and Reid directed against a man. In this situation the treatment of Mrs Porcelli fell to be seen as very different in a material respect from that which would have been inflicted on a male colleague, regardless of equality of overall unpleasantness . . .

Lord Grieve:
In order to decide whether there ha[s] been a breach of s 1(1)(a) consideration . . . ha[s] to be given . . . to the weapons used against the complainer. If any could be identified as what

I called 'a sexual sword', and it was clear that the wound it inflicted was more than a mere scratch, the conclusion must be that the sword had been unsheathed and used because the victim was a woman. In such a circumstance there would have been a breach of s 1(1)(a).

The potential difficulty in *Porcelli* lay in the claim that, the applicant's treatment being motivated by (allegedly non-sex-related) dislike, the harassment she suffered was not less favourable to her than the treatment which would have been accorded to an equally disliked man. In a case in which it is claimed that harassment results from unrequited sexual attraction or, as discussed above, from a desire to retain the homogeneity of a workplace or job, there would be no room for the argument put forward in *Porcelli*.

The Court of Sessions in *Porcelli* did accept that the use of a sexual (or, it may be assumed, a racial) 'sword' rendered 'harassing' treatment less favourable than otherwise comparable treatment not involving the use of such a sword. But that Court stopped short of defining sexual harassment as sex discrimination *per se*. A claim of discrimination will succeed only if the 'weapon' used would not have been used on a person of the opposite sex/ a different racial group, etc. The problems caused by this requirement came to the fore in *Stewart v Cleveland Guest (Engineering) Ltd* [1996] ICR 535, in which the EAT ruled that a woman who resigned in connection with her subjection to 'pin-ups' had not been subject to discrimination, as 'the display of these pictures was not necessarily aimed at women, or a woman, in the way that direct touching or sexually suggestive remarks can be said to be aimed at the individual woman [but] . . . was neutral' and 'A man might well [have found it] . . . as offensive as the applicant did.' In *British Telecommunications Plc v Williams* [1997] IRLR 668, Morison J expressed the view that any 'gender specific' conduct amounting to sexual harassment would of necessity amount to sex discrimination: 'there is no necessity to look for a male comparator. Indeed, it would be no defence to a complaint of sexual harassment that a person of the other sex would have been similarly so treated'. But this approach was to prove short-lived. In *Smith v Gardner Merchant Ltd* [1999] ICR 134 the Court of Appeal disapproved of Morrison J's approach in the *Williams* case and in *Pearce v Governing Body of Mayfield School* the House of Lords cast doubt even on the more conservative *Porcelli*.

[3.26] *Pearce v The Governing Body of Mayfield Secondary School* [2003] ICR 937 (HL)

The Claimant was a lesbian school teacher who had been subject to sex-specific taunting such as 'lesbian', 'dyke', 'lesbian shit', 'lemon', 'lezzie' or 'lez'. It was argued on her behalf that such taunting should be regarded as amounting to sex discrimination within *Porcelli*. The EAT and the Court of Appeal rejected this argument and the House of Lords rejected her appeal.

Lord Nicholls:

Sexual harassment is only prohibited by the [SDA] if the claimant can show she was harassed because she was a woman. Section 1(1)(a) requires the employment tribunal to compare the way the alleged discriminator treats the woman with the way he treats or would treat a man. In any case where discrimination is established, this exercise must involve comparing two forms of treatment which are different, whether in kind or in degree. It also involves the tribunal in evaluating the differences and deciding which form of treatment is less favourable.

The suggestion in some cases that if the form of the harassment is sexual or gender-specific, such as verbal abuse in explicitly sexual terms, that of itself constitutes less favourable treatment on the ground of sex, could not be reconciled with the language or the scheme of the statute. The fact that harassment is gender-specific in form cannot be regarded as of itself establishing conclusively that the reason for the harassment is gender-based, 'on the ground of her sex'. It will be evidence, whose weight will depend on the circumstances, that the reason for the harassment was the sex of the victim, although in some circumstances, the inference may readily be drawn that the reason for the harassment was gender-based, as where a male employee subjects a female colleague to persistent, unwanted sexual overtures. In such a case, the male employee's treatment of the woman is compared with his treatment of men, even though the comparison may be self-evident. However, the observation of Lord Brand in *Strathclyde Regional Council v Porcelli* that if a form of unfavourable treatment is meted out to a woman to which a man would not have been vulnerable, she has been discriminated against, and the observation of Lord Grieve in the same case that treatment meted out to a woman on the ground of her sex would fall to be regarded as less favourable treatment simply because it was sexually oriented, could not be approved insofar as they were suggesting that it was not relevant whether the claimant was treated less favourably than a man where the harassment is sexually oriented. Similarly, Morison J read too much into *Porcelli* when he said in *British Telecommunications plc v Williams* that it would be no defence to a complaint of sexual harassment that a person of the other sex would have been similarly so treated.

In the case of Ms Pearce, the natural inference to be drawn from the homophobic terms of abuse was that the reason for this treatment was her sexual orientation, even though the form which the abuse took was specific to her gender. The issue under s.1(1)(a) cannot turn on a minute examination of the precise terms of the abuse. Ms Pearce had not put forward any evidence that a male homosexual teacher would have been treated differently. Therefore, she did not establish that the harassment was on the ground of her sex.

Lord Hope (having cited the second paragraph of Lord Emslie's, extracted above at [3.24]):

. . . In my opinion Morison J read too much into *Porcelli* when he said in *British Telecommunications plc v Williams* that it would be no defence to a complaint of sexual harassment that a person of the other sex would have been similarly so treated. It was precisely because the tribunal's reasons showed that they were satisfied that sexual harassment in any form would not have been used in a campaign which Coles and Reid directed against a man that Lord President Emslie felt able to say that if they had asked themselves whether Mrs Porcelli had been treated less favourably than a man they would have been bound to answer the question in the affirmative. In so far as Lord Grieve and Lord Brand may be taken to have been suggesting that this was not a relevant question where the harassment is sexually orientated, I would disapprove of their observations . . .

There is no escape, then, from the need to resort to a comparison. The words 'less favourable treatment' in s.1(1)(a) render this inevitable. It may be that the conduct complained of is so specific to the claimant's gender that there is no need to do more than to ask the question, to which the answer may well be, as Ward LJ put it in *Smith v Gardner Merchant Ltd*, *res ipsa loquitur* . . . But that conclusion may be more easily drawn in cases of sexual harassment which do not involve any homophobic element than in cases such as those of Mr Macdonald and Ms Pearce where the context for the abuse is the abuser's belief that the victim is a homosexual. This is because those who abuse homosexuals tend to pick on them not because of their gender but because they are homosexual. The form which the abuse takes may well be specific to the gender of the person who is being abused, but this is because the terminology which is used to describe homosexuals and the acts which they can perform with each other tend to vary according to the gender of those who are involved in this relationship. That is not to exclude the possibility that an abuser may treat a woman who is a homosexual less favourably than he would treat a male homosexual. That may indeed happen, and an employment tribunal must always be alert to this possibility. But whether this is so will be a question of fact in each case.

Lord Rodger went further, disapproving of the approach taken by Lord Emslie in the *Porcelli* case (as distinct from its subsequent application in the *BT* case. According to his Lordship, *Porcelli* had involved a 'widening' of the concept of sexual harassment from the 'classic cases' in which conduct has a sexual motivation to cases 'where the motivation of the harasser was not sexual', and the decision though 'influential . . . is not satisfactory':

Lord Rodger's views did not command majority support. But the approach of the House of Lords is no ringing endorsement of the principle for which *Porcelli* has come to stand, and highlights the inadequacy of the 'make do and mend' approach which UK lawyers, lacking any tailored harassment prohibition upon which to rely, have been forced to adopt. This development is perhaps of limited significance given the legislative definition of harassment as discrimination in the context of sexual orientation, religion or belief and race (race, ethnic or national origins). The SDA must be amended to incorporate an express definition of sexual harassment as sex discrimination by October 2005, but the old provisions continue to govern harassment on grounds of nationality or colour (save to the effect that such harassment also amounts to harassment on grounds of 'race, ethnic or national origin'), non employment-related harassment connected with disability and (in Northern Ireland) religion and belief and, most likely, sexual harassment outside the employment field. It is a matter of serious concern that the jurisprudence of the domestic courts does not fully recognise harassment as a form of discrimination.

The EAT recognised in *Driskel v Peninsula* that superficially comparable treatment of men and women could amount to the less favourable treatment of one sex than another. (The facts of the case are set out at **[3.77]** below.)

[3.27] *Driskel v Peninsula Business Services Ltd* [2000] IRLR 151 (EAT)

Holland J:

a tribunal should not lose sight of the significance [in determining whether discrimination occurred] of the sex of not just the complainant but also that of the alleged discriminator. Sexual badinage of a heterosexual male by another such cannot be completely equated with like badinage by him of a woman. Prima facie the treatment is not equal: in the latter circumstance it is the sex of the alleged discriminator that potentially adds a material element absent as between two heterosexual men . . . the tribunal seriously misdirected itself in putting any weight on [the discriminator's] sexual vulgarity towards male employees for the reasons already set out in this judgment, that is, that being heterosexual that which he said to men was vulgar without being intimidatory.

In *Brumfitt v Ministry of Defence* [2005] IRLR 4, by contrast, a woman subjected to offensive and obscene remarks by a military training instructor had her complaint of sexual harassment dismissed by an employment tribunal which found (i) that she found the language to which she had been exposed 'offensive and humiliating to her as a woman', (ii) that women would be more likely to be offended by the conduct than men but (iii) that the claimant had not been subjected to sex *discrimination* because, the language having been used to men and women alike, she had not been subjected to it *because* of her sex. The EAT dismissed her appeal, Judge Birtles ruling for the appeal tribunal that the use of offensive words of a sexual nature by a man to a woman was not discriminatory (presumably regardless of its effect) 'unless it can be shown or inferred that this was less favourable treatment than the man would have meted out to another man in a comparable situation.' As the IRLR commentary pointed out: 'What is missing from the analysis . . . is recognition that identical treatment of women and men can amount to less favourable treatment of women than men where it is regarded differently by a woman than a man . . . On the reasoning in *Brumfitt*, a woman whose male supervisor persistently patted her bottom would have no remedy under sex discrimination law as it now stands, so long as the supervisor took care to pat a man's bottom as well'. The commentary contrasts the decision of the EAT in *Moonsar v Fiveways Express Transport Ltd* [2005] IRLR 9 in which the appeal tribunal, Judge Ansell presiding, accepted that a woman's exposure to pornographic images could amount to sex discrimination even where men were similarly so exposed.

The Racial and Employment Equality Directives both expressly define harassment as forms of discrimination, thus obviating the requirement for a comparator. 'Harassment' is defined for the purposes of the Directives as 'unwanted conduct' which 'relates to' a regulated ground and which 'takes place with the purpose or effect of violating the dignity of a person and of creating an intimidating, hostile, degrading, humiliating or offensive environment'. A similar approach is taken by the amended Equal Treatment Directive which comes into force in October 2005, and which regulates both 'harassment' (defined as in the Employment and Race Equality Directives) and 'sexual harassment' ('any form of unwanted verbal, non-verbal or physical conduct of a sexual nature occurs, with the purpose or effect of violating the dignity of a person, in particular when creating an intimidating, hostile, degrading, humiliating or offensive environment'). The RRA, to which the SORs and RBRs (Regulation 5) are materially identical, now provides as follows:

[3.28] Race Relations Act 1976, section 3A

> S.3A(1) A person subjects another to harassment . . . where, on grounds of race or ethnic or national origins, he engages in unwanted conduct which has the purpose or effect of—
> (a) violating that other person's dignity, or
> (b) creating an intimidating, hostile, degrading, humiliating or offensive environment for him.
> (2) Conduct shall be regarded as having the effect specified in paragraph (a) or (b) of subsection (1) only if, having regard to all the circumstances, including in particular the perception of that other person, it should reasonably be considered as having that effect.

This approach is wider than that required by the Race Equality Directive in that it provides (a) and (b) as *alternative* rather than *cumulative* requirements, this as a result of arguments put that to require *both* (a) and (b) would amount to a regression in domestic law. It will be noted that harassment on grounds of colour or nationality will be unlawful only where it amounts to discrimination under the original provisions of the RRA, or where it *also* amounts to harassment (within the new definition) 'on grounds of race or ethnic or national origins'. This formulation: the replacement of 'relates to' with 'on grounds of', appears to narrow the Directive's definition of harassment and may be inadequate by way of transposition, this because it carries the danger of incorporating into the new definition of harassment the approach taken by the House of Lords in *Pearce*. Thus, for example, the abuse to which Ms Pearce was subjected was 'related to' her sexual orientation (consisting as it did in part of lesbian-specific abuse). But could it have been said to be 'on grounds of' her sexual orientation, if a gay man would have been similarly treated? It might well be argued that such abuse would still be 'on grounds of' sexual orientation if a heterosexual would not have been similarly treated (that is, subjected to *sexual-orientation-*specific abuse). On the other hand, their Lordships in *Pearce* did not accept that subjection to *sex*-specific abuse was sexual harassment.

The formulation 'relates to' is adopted in the DDA (s.3B) but it is to be regretted that the government did not elsewhere adopt the wording of the directive, a failing repeated in the draft Employment Equality (Sex Discrimination) Regulations 2005 by which the government propose to implement the amendments required to bring domestic law into compliance with the Equal Treatment Amendment Directive. Thus proposed new s.4A(1) and (3) SDA define 'harassment' on grounds of sex and on grounds of gender reassignment in terms which are materially identical to s.3A(1) RRA (above), save that they also provide that 'sexual harassment' occurs (s.4A(1)(b)) where someone engages in unwanted etc. 'verbal, non-verbal or physical conduct of a sexual nature' and that harassment occurs (s.4A(1)(c)) where 'on the ground of her rejection of or submission to unwanted conduct of a kind mentioned in paragraph (a) or (b), he treats her less favourably than he would treat her had she not rejected, or submitted to, the conduct'. Whether this is sufficient to comply with the directive remains to be seen.

The argument has also been made that the objective test provided by section 3A(2) RRA (and replicated across the existing and proposed legislative provisions) is inconsistent with the directives which do not provide for any objective test and, although they do permit 'the concept of harassment [to] be defined in accordance with the national laws and practice of the Member States', do not permit 'regression' (i.e., reduction in protection). It has been argued that the objective test now enshrined in legislation is more difficult to satisfy than the test established, for example, in *Driskel* (see [3.27] above). Again it remains to be seen whether successful challenges will be mounted on this basis.

The question of whether sex (or race) specific treatment is 'less favourable' has not been confined to harassment claims. In *EOC v Birmingham* the House of Lords rejected an argument based on the comparability of grammar and comprehensive schooling to the effect that, while the disputed treatment varied by sex, it was not 'less favourable' to the girls affected by it than it was or would have been to boys. By contrast, it is characteristic of sex discrimination challenges to clothing and appearance rules that this argument has succeeded. Such rules are common, and frequently apply different restrictions to male and female employees. The approach of the courts was established in the *Schmidt v Austicks* case.

[3.29] *Schmidt v Austicks Bookshops* [1978] ICR 85 (EAT)

A woman dismissed for refusing to comply with her employer's clothing and appearance rules claimed sex discrimination. Women employees were forbidden to wear trousers and required to wear overalls while serving customers while male employees were prohibited only from wearing tee shirts at work and were not required to don overalls. The EAT upheld a tribunal's rejection of the complaint. Having ruled that the requirement to wear an overall could not amount to an actionable 'detriment' within section 6(2) SDA (this aspect of the decision is further considered below) The EAT went on to consider whether the applicant's dismissal for refusal to wear a skirt was discriminatory.

Phillips J:

. . . the evidence showed that although there was less scope for positive rules [i.e., 'no skirts'] in the case of the men, in that the choice of wearing apparel was more limited, there were restrictions in their case, too. For example, they were not allowed to wear [tee] shirts; and it is quite certain, on a reasonable examination of the evidence, that they would not have been allowed to wear, had they sought to do so, any out-of-the-way clothing. And so they were subjected to restrictions, too, albeit different ones—because, as we have already said, the restrictions to which the women were subjected were not appropriate to the men. Experience shows that under the [SDA] a lot depends on how one phrases or formulates the matter of which complaint is made. Here it has been formulated in the terms of skirts and overalls. As has been pointed out, in another case it might be in terms of ear-rings for men, long hair, all sorts of possibilities. But it seems to us that the realistic and better way of formulating it is to say that there were in force rules restricting wearing apparel and governing appearance which applied to men and also applied to women, although obviously, women and men being different, the rules in the two cases were not the same. We should be prepared to accept . . . an alternative contention . . . 'that in any event, in so far as a comparison is possible, the employers treated both female and male staff alike in that both sexes were restricted in the choice of clothing for wear whilst at work and were both informed that a certain garment should not be worn during working hours'.

It seems to us, if there are to be other cases on these lines, that an approach of that sort is a better approach and more likely to lead to a sensible result, than an approach which examines the situation point by point and garment by garment . . .

an employer is entitled to a large measure of discretion in controlling the image of his establishment, including the appearance of staff, and especially so when, as a result of their duties, they come into contact with the public.

The *Schmidt* approach entails (1) accepting that a 'sex appropriate dress code' can be a 'relevant circumstance' within section 5(3) of the SDA, and (2) finding discrimination only if the terms of the code, as they govern employees of the claimant's sex, are significantly less favourable than those which govern employees of the opposite sex. This approach is problematic for a number of reasons, not least because the courts appear blind to the social significance of dress. In *Schmidt* the EAT took the view that requiring women, but not men, to wear overalls could not be regarded as detrimental to women, despite the messages about women's position within the organisational hierarchy that this must have conveyed. A similar failure of imagination afflicted the Court of Appeal in *Burrett v West Birmingham Health Authority* (3 March 1994, unreported) in which the Court of Appeal rejected a discrimination challenge to a uniform code requiring female (but not male) nurses to wear starched linen caps which served no practical purpose and which Ms Burrett, likening them as she did to chambermaids' hats, found demeaning and undignified. A tribunal, the EAT ([1994] IRLR 7) and the Court of Appeal all took the view that she had been treated no less favourably than her male colleagues. Evans LJ, for the Court of Appeal, accepted that the application of a demeaning requirement could found a claim of less favourable treatment but did not accept that the Claimant's views were reasonable despite the fact that a ballot of staff had shown opposition to the wearing of caps by women (this after a different ballot had supported the cap) and the evidence of the director of nursing services that hats 'served no useful purpose', that they 'stereotype[d] nurses' and perpetuated the 'traditional view that nurse is handmaid to doctor' and that nursing was 'not considered a profession'. Evans LJ took the view that the evidence of the director of nursing services did 'not give any support for the conclusion . . . that the feeling which the applicant undoubtedly had, that this particular part of the uniform was demeaning for her to wear, was reasonably based and broadly shared', this being the test he set out as determinative of the issue.

More recently again, the *Schmidt* approach was applied by the Court of Appeal in *Smith v Safeway plc* [1995] ICR 868, a case in which a male delicatessan assistant challenged a rule that men had to have short hair, women being allowed to wear long hair tied off their faces. EAT ([1995] IRLR 472) had, by a majority, distinguished *Schmidt* on the basis that the appearance rule, unlike the uniform rule in *Schmidt*, impacted on employees outside as well as inside the workplace. According to Phillips LJ, (with whom Peter Gibson and Leggatt LJJ concurred): 'while this may be a relevant consideration when applying the appropriate test, it does not affect the test itself. Appearance depends in part on ephemera: clothes, rings and jewellery worn; but it depends also on more permanent characteristics: tattoos, hairstyle, hair colouring and hair length. The approach adopted in *Schmidt* can in my judgment properly be applied to both types of characteristic'.

Counsel for the employee in *Smith* sought to rely on the decision in *Rewcastle v Safeway* 22482/89 IT, in which a tribunal questioned 'whether a policy which is designed to mirror "conventional" differences between the sexes can be reconciled with the underlying rationale of the sex discrimination legislation which is to challenge traditional assumptions about sexes, not only as to their roles in society and the tasks they perform, but also as to their appearance and dress'. This argument received very short shrift, Phillips LJ declaring that he was 'unaware of any justification for those last few words' and that any dress code 'is likely to operate unfavourably with regard to one or other of the sexes unless it applies a [conventional] standard: . . . Can there be any doubt that a code which required all employees to have 18-inch hair, earrings and lipstick would treat men unfavourably by requiring them to adopt an appearance at odds with conventional standards?'.

[3.30] P. Skidmore, 'Sex, Gender and Comparators in Employment Discrimination Law' (1997) 26 *Industrial Law Journal* 51, pp 54–56 (footnotes omitted)

Safeway . . . argued in line with the decision in *Schmidt* that Smith had not suffered less favourable treatment and that different treatment of men and women could be non-discriminatory. Phillips LJ accepted this by placing an unacceptable gloss on 'less favourable treatment' (as had been done in *Schmidt*). He chose firstly to look at the dress code as a whole, rather than item by item, and assumed secondly that any overall package which reinforces conventional gender stereotypes (or as he put it 'a conventional standard of appearance') does not give rise to less favourable treatment. . . . This gloss on 'less favourable treatment' cannot be justified. A restriction on hair length which applies to men and not to women is less favourable treatment of men. In the light of *James*, this should be the full extent of the analysis. All the surrounding factors are totally irrelevant. Thus Peter Gibson LJ's discussion of the employer's motives or rationale should have had no place in this judgment. He also suggests that it is a matter of fact and degree whether the employee has been subjected to less favourable treatment. This seems to be allowing the tribunal too great a degree of discretion . . . . For a man to lose his job for having long hair when a woman with hair of the same length would not have done so, should on any interpretation constitute less favourable treatment . . . .

A number of cases decided post *Smith* v *Safeway* suggested that the tide might have turned. In *Owen* v *Professional Golf Association* (2000), for example, an employment tribunal decided that an instruction to a female employee to go home and change from a smart trouser suit into a skirt discriminated on grounds of sex. Female Eurostar guards persuaded their employer to allow them to wear trousers at work after a dispute. And the EOC won a settlement in a well-publicised case involving a challenge brought by a school girl to a uniform requirement that girls wore skirts rather than trousers. But the orthodox approach was recently restated by the EAT.

[3.31] *Department for Work and Pensions* v *Thompson* [2004] IRLR 248 (EAT)

The case concerned a challenge to a dress code imposed on Jobcentre Plus staff which required all staff to dress 'in a professional and businesslike way' but which stipulated that men were required to wear a collar and tie while women had 'to dress appropriately and to a similar standard'. The Claimant, an administrative assistant whose job did not involve public contact, refused to wear a collar and tie and received a formal warning. An employment tribunal ruled that the dress code breached the SDA, this on the basis that women had greater choice than their male colleagues as to what they could wear. The EAT overruled, applying the classic *Schmidt* approach.

Keith J:
It is unquestionably the case that the requirement on male members of staff to wear a collar and tie meant that female members of staff had a far greater choice in what they could wear than men. But the employment tribunal acknowledged Jobcentre Plus's right to introduce and enforce a dress code whose aim was to achieve a uniform level of smartness on the part of all its staff. Thus, in the context of the overarching requirement for its staff to dress in a professional and businesslike way, the question for the employment tribunal was whether, applying contemporary standards of conventional dresswear, the level of smartness which Jobcentre Plus required of all its staff could only

be achieved for men by requiring them to wear a collar and tie. The level of smartness which Jobcentre Plus thought appropriate for women can be seen from the photographs of Mr Thompson's five women colleagues. If, for example, a level of smartness for men which equates to dressing in a professional and businesslike way which is appropriate for an undertaking like Jobcentre Plus can be achieved by men dressing otherwise than in a collar and tie, then the lack of flexibility in the dress code introduced by Jobcentre Plus would suggest that male members of staff are being treated less favourably than female members of staff because it would not have been necessary to restrict men's choice of what to wear in order to achieve the standard of smartness required. The issue is not resolved by asking whether the requirement on men to wear a collar and tie meant that a higher level of smartness was being required of men rather than women. It is resolved by asking whether an equivalent level of smartness to that required of the female members of staff could only be achieved, in the case of men, by requiring them to wear a collar and tie . . .

It is not for the Employment Appeal Tribunal to decide whether men have to wear a collar and tie in order to achieve the level of smartness which Jobcentre Plus required of both sexes. That is for the employment tribunal to decide. Mr Thompson's case will therefore have to be remitted to the employment tribunal for that issue to be addressed.

Dress codes have been challenged under the RRA on the basis that they discriminate indirectly on grounds of race by failing to make accommodation to wearers' (generally religiously based) cultural needs. Obvious examples would include codes requiring women to have uncovered hair, or prohibiting them from wearing trousers. The issue of dress codes and religious/ race discrimination will be touched on again below. But it is worth noting here that the implementation of the HRA may provide workers with additional tools by which to challenge restrictions on their physical appearance. The Convention rights are considered in chapter 6. Here it is sufficient to note that Articles 8, 9, 10 and 14 may well provide a basis for legal challenge, though we see there that the obligation on employers to accommodate workers' religious and other needs appears to be scant. But where the accommodation would consist merely of permitting a Muslim woman to wear trousers instead of a skirt, or a Rastafarian man to wear his hair in dreadlocks, and where the employee challenged rule interferes significantly with the workers' religious or other freedom, a different approach might be taken. This might also be the case where a rule, such as that upheld by the Court of Appeal in *Smith v Safeways*, has implications outside the workplace.

3.4 Victimisation

Many who complain of discrimination find that they are subject to further disadvantage as a result of so doing. Between 1980 and 1984, one third of those applicants who succeeded in bringing equal pay or sex discrimination claims experienced difficulty in finding subsequent employment. All of them attributed this difficulty in part at least to their claim (A. Leonard, *Pyrrhic Victories: Winning Sex Discrimination and Equal Pay Cases in the Industrial Tribunals, 1980—1984* (London: HMSO, 1987). See also J. Gregory, *Trial by Ordeal: A Study of People Who Lost Sex Discrimination Cases in the Industrial Tribunals in 1985 & 1986* (London: HMSO, 1989)).

The RRA defines, as discrimination, less favourable treatment by reason that the person has:

[3.31] Race Relations Act 1976, section 2

S.3(1) . . . (a) brought proceedings against the discriminator or any other person under this Act; or

(b) given evidence or information in connection with proceedings brought by any person against the discriminator or any other person under this Act; or

(c) otherwise done anything under or by reference to this Act in relation to the discriminator or any other person; or

(d) alleged that the discriminator or any other person has committed an act which (whether or not the allegation so states) would amount to a contravention of this Act,

or by reason that the discriminator knows that the person victimised intends to do any of those things, or suspects that the person victimised has done, or intends to do, any of them.

(2) Subsection (1) does not apply to treatment of a person by reason of any allegation made by him if the allegation was false and not made in good faith.

The SDA, DDA, RBRs and SORs are in materially identical terms (sections 4 and 55 and Regulation 4 respectively).

The victimisation provisions had an unhappy early history, decisions such as those of the EAT in *Kirby* v *Manpower Services Commission* [1995] ICR 48 and the Court of Appeal in *Aziz* v *Trinity Street Taxis Ltd* [1989] 1 QB 463 requiring, in effect, that claimants establish that they had been less favourably treated specifically by reason that the action taken by them had been in connection with the relevant discrimination legislation. An employer who could suggest that the treatment complained of was motivated, however unreasonably, by the complainant's actions themselves, rather than the relationship between those actions and the relevant discrimination provisions, could escape liability for victimization. This approach altered with the decisions of the House of Lords in *Nagarajan* v *London Regional Transport* and in *Chief Constable of West Yorkshire Police* v *Khan*. In *Nagarajan* their Lordships overruled the Court of Appeal's decision ([1998] IRLR 73) to the effect that a victimisation complainant must prove that the less favourable treatment was *consciously* influenced by the claimant's commission of a protected act. A tribunal had found an interview panel's assessment of the claimant, who had taken action under the RRA against the organisation on previous occasions, inexplicable and so, given the knowledge of the interviewing panel members of the background, had felt bound to draw an inference of victimisation. Both the EAT and the Court of Appeal disagreed, Peter Gibson LJ for the latter requiring 'conscious motivation' on the part of the alleged discriminator. The House of Lords reinstated the tribunal's decision.

[3.33] *Nagarajan v London Regional Transport* [2000] AC 501 (HL)

Mr Nagarajan, who had previously been employed by London Underground, had during that time made a race discrimination claim against the company. The claim had been settled and he had left their employment. He subsequently applied for a job and, his application having been rejected, claimed that he had been victimised in connection with his previous complaint. A tribunal ruled in his favour on the grounds that his assessment by the interview panel was inexplicable unless at least subconsciously motivated by the panel's knowledge of the previous complaint. The tribunal's inference of victimisation was overruled by the EAT and the Court of Appeal.

Lord Steyn (with whom Lords Hutton and Hobhouse agreed, Lord Nicholls concurring):
Quite sensibly in section 1(1)(a) cases the tribunal simply has to pose the question: Why did the defendant treat the employee less favourably? It does not have to consider whether a defendant was consciously motivated in his unequal treatment of an employee. That is a straightforward way of carrying out its task in a section 1(1)(a) case. Common sense suggests that the tribunal should also perform its functions in a section 2(1) case by asking the equally straightforward question: Did the defendant treat the employee less favourably because of his knowledge of a protected act? Given that it is unnecessary in section 1(1)(a) cases to distinguish between conscious and subconscious motivation, there is no sensible reason for requiring it in section 2(1) cases . . .

Lord Steyn's assertion that the motivation of the discriminator is as irrelevant to a victimisation claim as it is to a claim of direct discrimination has been called into question by the subsequent decision of the House of Lords in the *Khan* case.

[3.34] *Chief Constable of West Yorkshire Police v Khan* [2001] ICR 1065 (HL)

The case concerned a victimisation complaint brought by a police officer who, while a race discrimination claim against his employer was pending, applied for a job in another force. His race discrimination claim was made in connection with his non-promotion (this because of criticisms of his communication and leadership skills). A request for a reference in respect of Sergeant Khan was met with a refusal on the basis that, because the Claimant had an outstanding tribunal application against the Chief Constable, the latter was 'unable to comment any further for fear of prejudicing his own case before the tribunal'. A request for Sergeant Khan's most recent staff appraisals was also refused.

Sergeant Khan's victimisation complaint was accepted by a tribunal (which dismissed his race discrimination claim), and the Chief Constable's appeal rejected by the EAT and the Court of Appeal. The House of Lords, however, overruled the tribunal's decision. Having accepted that the Claimant had been treated less favourably than someone who had not made the discrimination claim, their Lordships ruled that the treatment was not 'by reason that' he had brought proceedings against his employer.

Lord Nicholls (with whom Lords Hutton, Hoffman and Scott agreed, Lord Mackay concurring):

Victimisation occurs when, in any circumstances relevant for the purposes of any provision of the Act, a person is treated less favourably than others because he has done one of the protected acts . . . The statute is to be regarded as calling for a simple comparison between the treatment afforded to the complainant who has done a protected act and the treatment which was or would be afforded to other employees who have not done the protected act.

Applying this approach, Sergeant Khan was treated less favourably than other employees. Ordinarily West Yorkshire provides references for members of the force who are seeking new employment . . .

Contrary to views sometimes stated, the third ingredient ('by reason that') does not raise a question of causation as that expression is usually understood. Causation is a slippery word, but normally it is used to describe a legal exercise. From the many events leading up to the crucial happening, the court selects one or more of them which the law regards as causative of the happening. Sometimes the court may look for the 'operative' cause, or the 'effective' cause. Sometimes it may apply a 'but for' approach. For the reasons I sought to explain in *Nagarajan v London Regional Transport*, a causation exercise of this type is not required either by s.1(1)(a) or s.2. The phrases 'on racial grounds' and 'by reason that' denote a different exercise: why did the alleged discriminator act as he did? What, consciously or unconsciously, was his reason? Unlike causation, this is a subjective test. Causation is a legal conclusion. The reason why a person acted as he did is a question of fact . . .

Employers, acting honestly and reasonably, ought to be able to take steps to preserve their position in pending discrimination proceedings without laying themselves open to a charge of victimisation. This accords with the spirit and purpose of the Act. Moreover, the statute accommodates this approach without any straining of language. An employer who conducts himself in this way is not doing so because of the fact that the complainant has brought discrimination proceedings. He is doing so because, currently and temporarily, he needs to take steps to preserve his position in the outstanding proceedings . . .

This is a difficult distinction to draw, though perhaps helpful is Lord Hoffman's observation that: 'A test which is likely in most cases to give the right answer is to ask whether the employer would have refused the request if the litigation had been concluded, whatever the outcome. If the answer is no, it will usually follow that the reason for refusal was the existence of the proceedings and not the fact that the employee had commenced them'.

Lord Nicholls, above, refused to categorise the 'by reason that' question as one of causation and suggested that the test applicable to direct discrimination and victimisation were the same. Lord Hoffman's approach was somewhat different. His Lordship remarked that: 'Of course, in one sense the fact that [Sergeant Khan] had brought proceedings was a cause of his being treated less favourably. If he had not brought proceedings, he would have been given a reference'. He went on to distinguish the 'by reason that' test applicable in victimisation claims with the 'but for' test which applied in direct discrimination cases.

Lord Hoffman:

There are parallels between the purposes of ss.1 and 2 [RRA] (and between the corresponding sections 1 and 4 [SDA]): see *Nagarajan*. But the causal questions which they raise are not identical. As Mr Hand QC, who appeared for Mr Khan, readily accepted, one cannot simply say that Mr Khan would not have been treated less favourably if he had not brought proceedings. It does not follow that his bringing proceedings was a reason (conscious or subconscious) why he was treated less favourably. In *Nagarajan*'s case Lord Steyn said that s.2:

'contemplates that the discriminator had knowledge of the protected act and that such knowledge caused or influenced the discriminator to treat the victimised person less favourably than he would treat other persons . . . But . . . it does not require the tribunal to distinguish between conscious and subconscious motivation.'

This is not at all the same thing as saying that, but for the protected act, he would not have been treated in the way he was . . . once proceedings have been commenced, a new relationship is created between the parties. They are not only employer and employee but also adversaries in litigation. The existence of that adversarial relationship may reasonably cause the employer to behave in a way which treats the employee less favourably than someone who had not commenced such proceedings. But the treatment need not be, consciously or unconsciously, a response to the commencement of proceedings. It may simply be a reasonable response to the need to protect the employer's interests as a party to the litigation. It is true that an employee who had not commenced proceedings would not have been treated in the same way. Under s.1, one would have needed to go no further. Under s.2, however, the commencement of proceedings must be a reason for the treatment . . .

The other issue raised in the House of Lord's decision in *Khan* concerned the question what constitutes the 'protected act' *but for* the performance of which the victimised person would not have suffered less favourable treatment. In the previous edition of this book I posed the question whether it was (A) the act of bringing legal proceedings, giving evidence in connection with such proceedings, otherwise doing anything 'under or by reference to' legislation or alleging that the discriminator or another has contravened legislation?; or (B) bringing legal proceedings *under the relevant anti-discrimination legislation*, giving evidence in connection with proceedings *under the relevant anti-discrimination legislation*, otherwise doing anything 'under or by reference to' *the relevant anti-discrimination legislation* or alleging that the discriminator or another has contravened *the relevant anti-discrimination legislation*? The Court of Appeal in *Aziz* demanded a connection between the specific legislation in connection with which the victimised person acted and the motivation of the discriminator. It was clear from the decision in *Nagarajan* that this *motivation* does not have to be established. It might still have been the case that the relevant question was whether the less favourable treatment was 'by reason that' the claimant acted under the *particular* anti-discrimination legislation.

The Respondent in the *Khan* case had argued that the proper comparator for Sergeant Khan was someone who had brought proceedings under different legislation, an argument rejected by the EAT, and by the Court of Appeal in *Brown v TNT Worldwide (UK) Ltd* [2001] ICR 182. Lord Hoffman, who alone of their Lordships expressly addressed this question, stated that: 'if the fact that the employee had commenced proceedings under the Act was a real reason why he received less favourable treatment, it is no answer that the employer would have behaved in the same way to an employee who had done some non-protected act, such as commencing proceedings otherwise than under the Act'.

As a result of the decisions of the House of Lords in *Nagarajan* and *Khan* claimants and others engaged in actual or prospective litigation will be protected by the discrimination provisions in cases in which they are less favourably treated than those who have not taken steps to enforce their or others' rights, so long as the less favourable treatment was 'by reason that' the person victimised took such steps. It will be no defence to a discriminator that s/he would have meted out the same treatment to someone who took similar steps under other legal provisions. An employer may, however, take steps to safeguard his or her legal position where proceedings are outstanding, so long as the steps are taken because of the fact that the proceedings are extant rather than because they have been brought. No breach of the victimisation provisions will occur even if these steps involve treating a person less favourably than one who is not involved with proceedings.

The decisions in *Nagarajan* and in *Khan* have done much to ease the path of victimisation complainants. But one very significant problem remains.

[3.35] *Waters v Commissioner of Police of the Metropolis* [1997] ICR 1073 (CA)

The applicant claimed that she had been raped outside work by a colleague. Having complained about this incident to her employers she was subjected to a catalogue of appalling treatment at the hands of her colleagues and superiors. A tribunal dismissed her victimisation claim on the ground that, the alleged rape not constituting actionable discrimination within the SDA (this aspect of the decision is considered further below), her complaint about it was not a 'protected act' within section 4 SDA. Both the EAT and the Court of Appeal upheld the tribunal's decision.

Waite LJ:
Mr Allen [for the applicant] relies on: (1) The need . . . to construe discrimination legislation purposively in accordance with its objects and (so far as possible) those of the equal treatment Directive. (2) The breadth of language employed by s 4 itself . . . (3) The genus of complaint with which the section is concerned. Any complaint requiring protection from future victimisation is likely, in the nature of things, to have been made spontaneously at a moment of stress or crisis, and without time or opportunity for legal advice. It would be an unreal and unduly restrictive intention, therefore, to attribute to Parliament that every complaint should, as a condition of protection from future victimisation, spell out the relevant allegation in language so unequivocal as to leave no room for doubt in the mind of the employer that the complaint is founded upon discrimination on the ground of sex.

With those considerations in mind, the intention properly to be attributed to Parliament is, Mr Allen submits the following:

'Section 4(1)(d) has to be construed in such a way as to treat as protected acts any allegations which, objectively considered, are aimed at claiming (ie provide the basis for development of a claim for) protection under the equality legislation (Sex Discrimination or Equal Pay Act)' . . .

That submission fails, in my judgment, for this reason. True it is that the legislation must be construed in a sense favourable to its important public purpose. But there is another principle involved—also essential to that same purpose. Charges of race or sex discrimination are hurtful and damaging and not always easy to refute. In justice, therefore, to those against whom they are brought, it is vital that discrimination (including victimisation) should be defined in language sufficiently precise to enable people to know where they stand before the law. Precision of language is also necessary to prevent the valuable purpose of combating discrimination from becoming frustrated or brought into disrepute through the use of language which encourages unscrupulous or vexatious recourse to the machinery provided by the Discrimination Acts. The interpretation proposed by Mr Allen would involve an imprecision of language leaving employers in a state of uncertainty as to how they should respond to a particular complaint, and would place the machinery of the Acts at serious risk of abuse. It is better, and safer, to give the words of the subsection their clear and literal meaning. The allegation relied on need not state explicitly that an act of discrimination has occurred—that is clear from the words in brackets in s 4(1)(d). All that is required is that the allegation relied on should have asserted facts capable of amounting in law to an act of discrimination by an employer within the terms of s 6(2)(b). The facts alleged by the complaint in this case were incapable in law of amounting to an act of discrimination by the Commissioner because they were not done by him, and they cannot (because the alleged perpetrator was not acting in the course of his employment) be treated as done by him for the purposes of s 4(1).

The SDA aspects of the *Waters* decision were not appealed, but the House of Lords allowed the applicant's appeal against the dismissal by the High Court and Court of Appeal of her civil action for negligence in respect of the alleged harassment, unfair treatment and victimisation by her police colleagues after her rape complaint. The High Court had struck out this claim, the Court of Appeal agreeing that the Commissioner was not under any personal duty of care to PC Waters equivalent to that of an employer. Nor, given that Court's finding that police officers were under no duty of care to each other, was the Commissioner vicariously liable for any torts committed by other police officers against the applicant. On appeal, the House of Lords accepted that it was 'clear, or at the least arguable' (*per* Lord Slynn, with whom the others agreed) that 'duties analogous to those owed to an employee are owed to officers in the police service'. Much of the decision in *Waters* was concerned with the particular position of the police, and with the public policy arguments involved in imposing liability in these circumstances. But it is very clear from the decision that, in the case of normal employment, an employer could be liable in tort for harm resulting from 'victimisation' falling outside the statutory definition.

We saw, above, the concern expressed by Waite LJ that 'discrimination (including victimisation) should be defined in language sufficiently precise to enable people to know where they stand before the law' (this apparently to permit the lawful victimisation of those whose claims fell outwith the technical requirements of the discrimination legislation). In the House of Lords a somewhat different anxiety was expressed:

[3.36] *Waters v Commissioner of Police of the Metropolis* [2000] ICR 1064 (HL)

Lord Hutton:
if the plaintiff succeeds at the trial in proving in whole or in substantial part the truth of her allegation that she was subjected to serious and prolonged victimisation and harassment which caused her psychiatric harm because she had made an allegation of a serious offence against a fellow officer and that the Commissioner through his senior officers was guilty of negligence in failing to take adequate steps to protect her against such treatment, such proof would reveal a serious state of affairs in the Metropolitan Police. If such a state of affairs exists I consider that it is in the public interest that it should be brought to light so that steps can be taken to seek to ensure that it does not continue, because if officers (and particularly women officers who complain of a sexual offence committed against them by a male colleague) are treated as the plaintiff alleges, citizens will be discouraged from joining the police, or from continuing to serve in the police after they have joined, with consequent harm to the interests of the community. In my opinion this is a consideration which carries significant weight when placed in the scales against the argument that the continuance of the action will place unreasonable and disproportionate burdens on the police and distract them from their primary task of combating crime.

3.5 Indirect discrimination

'Indirect discrimination' is concerned with the application of facially neutral rules, practices etc. which serve *in practice* to disadvantage groups of people defined by reference to a protected characteristic such as race, religion or belief, etc. This type of discrimination has undergone significant change in recent years as a result of EU developments which have simplified the test to be applied in the majority of employment-related cases. The original definition of indirect discrimination utilised by the SDA and RRA is considered below (the DDA does not employ the concept at all). The original definition now applies, however, only to sex discrimination (or, in Northern Ireland, discrimination on grounds of religion or political opinon) outside the employment context (and so outside the scope of this book) and to discrimination on grounds of colour or nationality (to the extent that such discrimination is not *also* discrimination on grounds of 'race, ethnic or national origin'). For this reason we will start with the new definitions of indirect discrimination, and will confine discussion of the old approach mainly to where it throws light on the advantages associated with the new approach.

The RRA, to which Regulation 3(1)(b) of each the SORs and the RBRs are materially identical, provide as follows:

[3.37] Race Relations Act 1976, section 1(1A)

S.1(1A) A person . . . discriminates against another if . . . he applies to that other a provision, criterion or practice which he applies or would apply equally to persons not of the same race or ethnic or national origins as that other, but—
(a) which puts or would put persons of the same race or ethnic or national origins as that other at a particular disadvantage when compared with other persons,
(b) which puts that other at that disadvantage, and
(c) which he cannot show to be a proportionate means of achieving a legitimate aim.

The SDA is materially similar insofar as it applies to employment:

[3.38] Sex Discrimination Act 1975, section 1(2)

S.1(2) . . . a person discriminates against a woman if . . .
(b) he applies to her a provision, criterion or practice which he applies or would apply equally to a man, but
   (i) which is such that it would be to the detriment of a considerably larger proportion of women than of men, and
   (ii) which he cannot show to be justifiable irrespective of the sex of the person to whom it is applied, and
   (iii) which is to her detriment.

The SDA's employment-related test for indirect discrimination is the result of the Act's amendment in 2001 to comply with the Burden of Proof Directive. Prior to that point the test was materially identical to section 1(1) RRA (below). The old test still applies other than in relation to employment (broadly defined). The government proposes to amend the SDA to be materially identical to section 1(1A) RRA in transposing the Equal Treatment Amendment Directive.

The amendments to the RRA and the implementation of the SORs and RBRs occurred too recently (July and December 2003 respectively) to permit anything to be said about the operation in practice of these definitions. Some light can be shed on them by pointing out the changes which have been made from the original definition of indirect discrimination. Section 1(1) RRA, which continues to apply to discrimination related to colour or nationality (as distinct from 'race, ethnic or national origin') provides as follows:

[3.39] Race Relations Act 1976, section 1(1)

> S.1(1) A person discriminates against a another in any circumstances relevant for the purposes of any provision of this Act if . . .
> (b) he applies to that other a requirement or condition which he applies or would apply equally to persons not of the same racial group as that other but
> (i) which is such that the proportion of persons of the same racial group as that other who can comply with it is considerably smaller than the proportion of persons not of that racial group who can comply with it and
> (ii) which he cannot show to be justifiable irrespective of the colour, race, nationality or ethnic or national origins of the person to whom it is applied and
> (iii) which is to the detriment of that other because he cannot comply with it.

The new definitions replace the term 'requirement or condition', which had been very narrowly interpreted by the Court of Appeal in *Perera* and *Jones* (see section 3.5.1 below) with the deliberately broad 'provision, criterion or practice'. They also replace the demand that this requirement or condition be 'such that the proportion of persons' of the claimant's group who can comply with it 'is considerably smaller than the proportion of persons not of that . . . group who can comply with it' with one that the provision, criterion or practice 'is such that it would be to the detriment of a considerably larger proportion of women than of men' (the SDA) or (in the case of the RRA and the RBRs and SORs) 'puts or would put persons' of the claimant's group 'at a particular disadvantage when compared with other persons'. The requirement that the claimant in an indirect discrimination claim suffers detriment *because of his or her inability to comply* with the impugned requirement or condition has been replaced by a requirement (in the case of the SDA) that the provision, criterion or practice is to the claimant's detriment or (in the case of the RRA, the SORs and RBRs) that s/he is 'put at' the particular disadvantage referred to in the previous paragraph by the provision, criterion or practice. The test for justification has not changed from the original to the amended definition of indirect discrimination in the SDA (in both cases the burden is on the discriminator to justify the impugned requirement, etc., 'irrespective of' the sex, race, etc., of the person to whom it is applied). The RRA and the SORs and RBRs, by contrast, place the obligation on the discriminator to show that the application of the impugned provision, criterion or practice is a 'proportionate means of achieving a legitimate aim'. It is highly questionable, however, whether the rubric adopted by section 1(1A)(c) RRA and its equivalents is adequate to transpose the European definition of justification which is couched in terms of 'appropriate and necessary' means of achieving 'legitimate aims'.

The definition and prohibition of 'indirect' discrimination was intended to reflect the concept of 'disparate impact' discrimination recognised in the United States in the following case.

[3.40] *Griggs v Duke Power Co* (1971) 401 US 424

The black applicants claimed that the employer's requirement, in respect of particular jobs, of a high school diploma or success in an IQ test, discriminated against them on grounds of race contrary to Title VII of the Civil Rights Act 1964. A disproportionate number of black workers were excluded from these jobs by the requirement. The lower courts had found that the employer's previous practice of race discrimination had ended, and that there was no evidence that the requirements had been adopted in order to discriminate on racial grounds. The Supreme Court found in favour of the applicants.

Chief Justice Burger *(for the Court):*
The objective of Congress in the enactment of Title VII is plain from the language of the statute. It was to achieve equality of employment opportunities and remove barriers that have operated in the past to favor an identifiable group of white employees over other employees. Under the Act, practices, procedures, or tests neutral on their face, and even neutral in terms of intent, cannot be maintained if they operate to 'freeze' the status quo of prior discriminatory employment practices . . .

the Act does not command that any person be hired simply because he was formerly the subject of discrimination, or because he is a member of a minority group. Discriminatory preference for any group, minority or majority, is precisely and only what Congress has proscribed. What is required by Congress is the removal of artificial, arbitrary, and unnecessary barriers to employment when the barriers operate invidiously to discriminate on the basis of racial or other impermissible classification.

Congress has now provided that tests or criteria for employment or promotion may not provide equality of opportunity merely in the sense of the fabled offer of milk to the stork and the fox. On the contrary, Congress has now required that the posture and condition of the job-seeker be taken into account. It has—to resort again to the fable—provided that the vessel in which the milk is proffered be one all seekers can use. The Act proscribes not only overt discrimination but also practices that are fair in form, but discriminatory in operation. The touchstone is business necessity. If an employment practice which operates to exclude Negroes cannot be shown to be related to job performance, the practice is prohibited.

The concept of indirect (disparate impact) discrimination is relatively straightforward. But the tests originally established under the SDA and RRA are numerous and complex. In *Kidd* v *DRG* [1985] ICR 405 Waite J, then President of the EAT, stated that '[t]he concept of indirect discrimination was one which clearly needed to be framed from the outset with the maximum flexibility if it was fully to encompass the mischief at which the anti-discrimination laws are directed'. But, as it has been interpreted by the UK courts the original test for indirect discrimination is far from flexible, as will become evident in the succeeding sections.

3.5.1 'Provision, criterion or practice'

The 'provision, criterion or practice' step has replaced the 'requirement or condition' originally required in order to establish indirect discrimination. Early decisions had applied the 'requirement or condition' provision flexibly. In *Clarke v Eley (IMI) Kynoch Ltd* [1983] ICR 165, for example, Browne-Wilkinson J in the EAT relied on *Griggs* in ruling that it 'is not right to give these words a narrow construction' and that the fact that the legislation was intended to 'eliminate those practices which had a disproportionate impact on women or ethnic minorities and were not justifiable for other reasons', although it 'cannot be used to give the words any wider meaning than they naturally bear . . . is in our view a powerful argument against giving the words a narrower meaning thereby excluding cases which fall within the mischief which the Act was meant to deal with'. In *Perera v The Civil Service Commission* [1983] ICR 428, however, the Court of Appeal adopted a narrow and restrictive reading of the 'requirement or condition' provision, ruling that it applied only to factors which were 'absolute bars'. Thus, as Geoffrey Mead pointed out ('Intentions, Conditions and Pools of Comparison' (1989) 18 *Industrial Law Journal* 59): 'if an advertisement states that applicants for the job of a cleaner should either have lived in the area for 20 years or have a degree of law, then although the first criterion might have a detrimental effect on certain racial groups, who might be new to the area, the fact that they could get the job if they had a law degree means that they have not been indirectly discriminated against'.

The *Perera* approach was much criticised but was applied by the Court of Appeal in *Meer v Tower Hamlets* [1988] IRLR 399 and approved by that Court in *Jones v University of Manchester* [1993] ICR 474 (an SDA case). It does not, however, apply in cases (now the majority of employment discrimination cases) in which the new test for indirect discrimination is applicable. It is generally understood that the 'provision, criterion or practice' will not pose any difficulties for claimants as long as they can show that something done by the employer has the effect (albeit not the intention) of disadvantaging them in the way set out in the other aspects of the indirect discrimination test.

3.5.2 The collective disadvantage test

Under the old test, indirect discrimination claimants had to establish that the requirement of condition applied was such that a 'considerably smaller proportion' of their sex or racial group, etc., than of others, could comply with it. The new test asks whether the provision, criterion or practice 'is such that it would be to the detriment of a considerably larger proportion of women than of men' (the SDA) or (in the case of the RRA and the RBRs and SORs) 'puts or would put persons' of the claimant's group 'at a particular disadvantage when compared with other persons'. Under the old test, the questions which arose for consideration were : (1) how to measure the relative proportions of the claimant's group and of others who could comply, and (2) what was meant by 'a considerably smaller proportion'. Under the new test the first limb is significantly altered. Under the SDA the questions are: (1) how to measure the proportions of men and women to whom the provision, criterion or practice would be to the detriment, and (2) what is meant by 'a considerably larger proportion'. Under the RRA and the SORs and RBRs, the sole question is how to determine whether the provision, criterion or practice 'puts or would put persons' of the claimant's group 'at a particular disadvantage when compared with other persons'. The same is likely to be true of the SDA from October 2005.

Under the old approach to indirect discrimination tribunals used to devise an appropriate 'pool for comparison', ie, a description of those workers who (leaving aside the disputed requirement or condition) were in the same 'relevant circumstances' as the applicant (see section 5(3) and 3(4) of the SDA and RRA respectively). The proportions of the claimant's sex or race-based group and of others who could comply with the requirement or condition were determined by comparing those of the claimant's group and of others who are within this pool and who could comply. Questions which arose included whether, and to what extent, pools should be geographically restricted or, in some cases, confined to those working for the employer. In *Kidd v DRG* the EAT tried to limit appeals on the question of pools by characterising the selection of the pool as a question of fact for the tribunal subject to the availability of appeal in 'exceptional cases where it can be shown that good sense has not prevailed, and the tribunal has chosen to make the proportionate comparison within an area of society so irrationally inappropriate as to put it outside the range of selection for any reasonable tribunal'.

Courts did not always, but sometimes did, require elaborate statistical proof of disparate impact (in *Kidd* itself, for example, the EAT refused to accept that married women were considerably less likely than their single counterparts to work full-time). The classification of the choice of pool as a question of fact for the tribunal could present real difficulties for claimants in cases in which they came armed with the statistics to demonstrate disparate impact in relation to one pool, only to have the tribunal select a different pool and dismiss the claim for lack of evidence. The *Kidd* approach gradually gave way to a recognition that the choice of pool is both crucial to the outcome of an indirect discrimination claim and susceptible to a correct answer. It became apparent reasonably early on that the higher courts would overturn the choice of pool if it was not such that the 'relevant circumstances' of those (both of and not of the claimant's relevant group) within it were 'the same or not materially different'. In *University of Manchester v Jones*, for example, the Court of Appeal ruled that tribunals had erred in artificially restricting the category of people included in the pool. The case was brought by a 44 year old woman who was turned down for a job limited to graduates aged 27–35. The woman had taken her degree as a mature student and she claimed that the age limit discriminated against women who had obtained their degrees as mature students. The tribunal selected, as the pool for comparison, men and women who had obtained degrees at the age of 25 or over. Of these, the proportion of women aged under 35 was smaller than the proportion of male students under that age. The tribunal's finding in favour of Ms Jones was overturned on appeal and the EAT's decision upheld by the Court of Appeal.

In *Allonby & Accrington & Rossendale College* [2001] ICR 1189 the Court of Appeal (*per* Sedley LJ) sounded a 'strong note of caution' about the approach taken in *Kidd*: 'once the impugned requirement or condition has been defined there is likely to be only one pool which serves to test its effect. I would prefer to characterise the identification of the pool as a matter neither of discretion nor of fact-finding but of logic . . . Logic may on occasion be capable of producing more than one outcome, especially if two or more conditions or requirements are in issue. But the choice of pool is not at large'. And in *Rutherford v Town Circle* and *Rutherford v Town Circle (No.2)* the EAT and (in the latter) the Court of Appeal found that a tribunal had erred in its selection of a pool for comparison. The Claimant, who was made redundant at 67, was prevented from claiming unfair dismissal or a statutory redundancy payment by sections 109 and 156 ERA 1996, which provide that employees who have reached age 65 do not have the right either not to be unfairly dismissed or to receive redundancy payments. He argued that the upper age limit breached Article 141 TEC because it was indirectly discriminatory against men, 7.6% of whom were economically active after age 65 by comparison with only 3.4% of women. The EAT ([2002] ICR 123) allowed the employer's appeal against a tribunal's finding in his favour and remitted the case to another tribunal which reached the same conclusion. The EAT again allowed an appeal ([2003] IRLR 858), a decision upheld by the Court of Appeal. On the issue of the appropriate pool for comparison the Court ruled as follows.

[3.41] *Rutherford v Towncircle Ltd* [2005] ICR 119 (CA)

Mummery LJ (for the Court):

. . . In the assessment of the disparate adverse impact of the upper age limit on male and female employees a great deal turns on how the relevant pool is defined: whether it is by reference to the entire workforce or only by reference to part and, if so, what part. The assessment differs significantly according to how the tribunal defines the pool within which the disparate impact is to be assessed. Should it be defined, as the applicants contend, only by reference to those who are or might be adversely affected (disadvantaged) by the upper age limit, because they are, or might be, unable to comply with the requirement of being under 65 at the relevant time? Or should it be defined, as the Secretary of State contends, by reference to a wider pool embracing all employees in the work force to whom the age limit applies, including all those who are not adversely affected (i.e. advantaged) by the upper age limit, because they are able to comply with the requirement of being under the age of 65 at the relevant time? . . .

the correct pool depends on the proper understanding and application of the legal principles laid down by the ECJ and the House of Lords in *R v Secretary of State for Employment ex parte Seymour-Smith* [[2000] ICR 244] . . . in general, the relevant statistical comparison involves (a) taking as the pool 'the workforce' (i.e. the entire workforce) to whom the age limit is applicable, not taking just a small section of the workforce, confined to those who are adversely affected by being over 65 or within 10 years of the age of 65; (b) ascertaining the proportion of men in the workforce who are under the age of 65 and are advantaged by being able to meet the requirement, and the proportion of men who are excluded from the right and are therefore disadvantaged by being unable to meet the requirement; (c) ascertaining the proportion of women in the workforce who are under the age of 65 and are therefore advantaged by being able to meet the requirement, and the proportion of women who are excluded from the right and are therefore disadvantaged by being unable to meet the requirement; (d) comparing the results for men with the results for women in order to see whether the percentage (not the numbers) of men in the workforce who are advantaged is considerably smaller than the percentage of women who are advantaged . . .

In my judgment, the employment tribunal erred in law, as it failed to adopt the approach to disparate adverse impact laid down in *Seymour-Smith*. It should have taken the statistics for the entire workforce, to which the unfair dismissal and redundancy pay requirement of being under 65 applied. It should then have primarily compared the respective proportions of men and women who could satisfy that requirement. It should not have defined and distorted the relevant pool by excluding the 'figures' relied on by the Secretary of State as not relevant for it to consider and by referring only to those who were disadvantaged by the disputed upper age limit requirement. In brief, the employment tribunal erred in regarding as irrelevant to its consideration the figures relied on by the Secretary of State relating to those in the workforce who could comply with the age requirement. If the correct approach is taken, the statistics in evidence clearly establish that the difference in the working population between the proportion of men aged under 65 who can comply and the proportion of women aged under 65 who can comply is very small indeed. The disparities are certainly not 'considerable' in the sense required by *Seymour-Smith*.

Instead, and in error, the employment tribunal treated the statistics concerning the advantaged group as irrelevant to its consideration of the disparate adverse impact point. It appears from paragraph 16 of the extended reasons that the tribunal focused on and made comparisons by reference to very small pools of persons who were disadvantaged by being unable to satisfy the requirement of the right or were approaching the age when they would be disadvantaged. In concentrating exclusively on the statistics for those who cannot comply and on the older members of the workforce, for whom it was thought that retirement has 'a real meaning', instead of on the entire workforce and primarily on those in it who can comply with the requirement, the tribunal reduced the size of the pool and thereby departed from the approach laid down in *Seymour Smith* and in the line of Court of Appeal cases leading up to *Seymour Smith*: see, for example, *University of Manchester v Jones* and *London Underground v Edwards (No 2)* [1999] ICR 494.

The adoption of the SDA's test for indirect discrimination in 2001 ([3.38]) does not appear to alter the application of collective disadvantage test in any significant way. The question asked of those in the pool is different admittedly: instead of the focus being on those *unable to comply* it is simply on the relative proportions of those to whom the provision, criterion or practice *operates to the detriment of*. The shift from 'can comply' is considered below. The question is, however, likely to be resolved in practice (prior to the amendment of the SDA to comply with the amended Equal Treatment Directive in October 2005) by reference to a pool for comparison. The same is not true, however, in the case of race, sexual orientation or religion or belief discrimination (or, from October 2005, sex discrimination). Here the question is whether the provision, criterion or practice in dispute 'puts or would put persons' of the claimant's group 'at a *particular disadvantage* when compared with other persons'. This does require some element of comparison, but is not at all clear that it requires recourse to any *pool* for comparison. The European Commission made it clear in the Explanatory Memorandum to the Racial Equality Directive that the definition of indirect discrimination therein was intentionally chosen to avoid the need for statistical proof. And in the absence of any such need it is difficult to ascertain the purpose of any comparative pool (as distinct from evidence of some sort about actual or expected disparate impact).

Turning to the second question raised under the old test for collective disadvantage, tribunals originally had to ascertain whether the proportion of the allegedly disadvantaged group which was able to comply with the disputed requirement or condition was 'considerably smaller' than the proportion of others who could so comply. Under the SDA tribunals now have to determine whether the proportion of women disadvantaged by the provision, criterion or practice at issue is considerably *larger.*

In *Rutherford v Towncircle Ltd*, the EAT set out guidelines for the determination of the question whether the proportion of (there) men who were disadvantaged by the disputed provision (there the upper age limit on unfair dismissal and redundancy claims) was 'considerably larger' than that of women. Note that the claim was brought under Article 141 TEC and that the relevant question was whether a considerably larger proportion of men could comply with the disputed provision, rather than (as in the unamended SDA) a considerably smaller proportion of women could comply. But as Linsday J pointed out: 'The apparent clarity of that provision is not . . . reflected in the language used in the cases, either domestic or in the European Court of Justice'. On appeal (in *Rutherford (No.2)*) to the Court of Appeal, Mummery LJ ruled as follows:

[3.42] *Rutherford v Towncircle Ltd* **[2005] ICR 119 (CA)**

Mummery LJ (for the Court):
The primary focus is on the proportions of men and women who can comply with the requirement of the disputed rule. Only if the statistical comparison establishes a considerable disparity of impact, must the court then consider whether the disparity is objectively justifiable.

While leaving open the question whether the proportions in the disadvantaged group, as well as in the advantaged group, should be considered, Lord Nicholls [in *Seymour-Smith*] did not suggest that it was correct to consider only the proportions in the disadvantaged group, as was done by the employment tribunal in this case. Indeed, as was pointed out in the Divisional Court in *Seymour Smith* . . . concentration on the proportions of men and women in the workforce, who are disadvantaged because they cannot comply with a disputed requirement, can produce seriously misleading results, as in the simple case of a requirement with which 99.5% of men can comply and 99% of women can comply. If the focus is then shifted to the proportions of men and women who cannot comply (i.e. 1% of women and 0.5% of men), the result would be that twice as many women as men cannot comply with the requirement. That would not be a sound or sensible basis for holding that the disputed requirement, with which the vast majority of both men and women can comply, had a disparate adverse impact on women . . .

The IRLR commentary was critical of this approach, pointing out that:

[3.43] IRLR 'Highlights', November 2004

. . . there appears to be no rule of European law that the primary focus is on the advantaged group. In the seven ECJ decisions reported in IRLR which have looked at this issue since *Seymour-Smith*, six of them have focused on the proportions of women and men disadvantaged by the requirement being challenged. Thus, in *Lewen* [2000] IRLR 67, the ECJ said: "According to settled case law, indirect discrimination arises where a national measure . . . works to the disadvantage of far more women than men." In *JämO*

[2000] IRLR 421, it asked, is there "a substantially higher proportion of women than men in the disadvantaged group"? In *Steinicke*, it referred to "significantly more women than men . . . are excluded". In *Krüger* [1999] IRLR 808, it said that the criterion was whether the rule "actually affects a considerably higher percentage of women than men". In *Jørgensen* [2000] IRLR 726, the formulation was "once it is established that a measure adversely affects a much higher percentage of women than men, or vice versa, that measure will be presumed to constitute indirect discrimination on grounds of sex". Most recently, *Allonby* [2004] IRLR 224, the ECJ noted that "among the teachers who . . . fulfil all the conditions except that of being employed under a contract of employment . . . there is a much higher percentage of women than men". This focus on those who are adversely affected makes sense from a policy standpoint. The purpose of indirect discrimination is to protect those who are disadvantaged, so that is where the primary focus should normally be. The effect of focusing on the advantaged group, as was done by the Court of Appeal in *Rutherford*, is to dilute the impact of the requirement on the excluded group (if the whole of the workforce is taken into account) or to ignore it altogether (if only those under age 65 are considered). A pool for comparison must be a relevant pool. It is difficult to see the logic in deciding whether the exclusion of those aged 65 and over from unfair dismissal and redundancy rights is indirectly sex discriminatory on the basis that it does not impact either men or women aged 25, 35 or 45. In his classic opinion in the *Enderby* case, Advocate General Lenz emphasised that "The purpose of a conceptual scheme is to comprehend methods by which women are placed at a disadvantage in their working lives and not to create additional obstacles to claims being made before the courts in respect of sex-related pay discrimination. For this reason, a formalistic approach should not be adopted when categorising actual instances where women are placed at a disadvantage at work." These principles should be applied equally where men are placed at a disadvantage.

It is unlikely, in light of the *Rutherford* case, that the shift from the question whether a significantly smaller proportion of women can comply with a disputed requirement to the question whether a significantly larger proportion of women would have had any significant impact on the outcome of sex discrimination claims. That shift will be overtaken, in any event, when the SDA is amended to give effect to the amended Equal Treatment Directive. It is unclear as yet the extent to which the approach developed under the old and intermediate approaches to indirect discrimination will be carried over into the new test for indirect discrimination, which requires only that the claimant establish that the disputed provision, criterion or practice 'would put [her] at a particular disadvantage' by comparison with others.

3.5.3 The individual disadvantage test

The modified versions of the indirect discrimination test ask only whether the provision, criterion or practice is to the claimant's detriment (in the case of the SDA) or whether (under the RRA and SORs and RBRs) whether s/he is 'put at' a particular disadvantage by it. The old test required, rather, that the claimant established that s/he suffered detriment *because of his or her inability to comply* with the impugned requirement or condition. It is arguable that the inclusion of any individual disadvantage test in the new definitions of indirect discrimination is incompatible with EU law: the Burden of Proof Directive (which resulted in the amendment of the SDA's definition of indirect discrimination) provides that such discrimination occurs 'where an apparently neutral provision, criterion or practice disadvantages a substantially higher proportion of the members of one sex unless that provision, criterion or practice is appropriate and necessary and can be justified by objective factors unrelated to sex', while the Race Equality and Employment Equality Directives define it as occurring 'where an apparently neutral provision, criterion or practice would put persons [of a group identified by reference to a protected factor] at a particular disadvantage compared with other persons unless that provision, criterion or practice is objectively justified by a legitimate aim and the means of achieving that aim are appropriate and necessary'. No reference is made by either of these definitions to the need for an individual claimant to establish detriment. But the new domestic tests (which the government proposes to replicate in the SDA from October 2005 do provide a lower standard than the original by doing away with the requirement that the claimant establish his or her inability to comply with the requirement or condition at issue.

The domestic courts had, for the most part, taken a liberal approach to the question whether a claimant could comply. In *Price v Civil Service Commission* [1978] ICR 27, for example, the EAT accepted that the applicant, a 35 year old woman, could not comply with a requirement to be aged between 17½ and 28. Phillips J accepted that all women could be regarded as capable of complying in theory with the age bar: women were 'not obliged to marry, or to have children, or to mind children; [they] may find somebody to look after them, and as a last resort [they] may put them into care'. But such a construction of the test for indirect discrimination was in his view 'wholly out of sympathy with the spirit and intent' of the SDA and in determining whether women could comply with disputed requirements or conditions tribunals could 'take into account the current usual behaviour of women in this respect, as observed in practice, putting on one side behaviour and responses which are unusual or extreme'.

In *Mandla v Dowell Lee* the House of Lords addressed the question whether the claimant, a Sikh boy, could comply with a requirement not to wear a turban to school. According to Lord Fraser, with whom the others agreed, while it was 'obvious that Sikhs, like anyone else, "can" refrain from wearing a turban, if "can" is construed literally', the word 'can' had to be understood in this context . . . not as meaning "can physically", so as to indicate a theoretical possibility, but as meaning "can in practice" or 'can consistently with the customs and cultural conditions of the racial group'.

Mandla and *Price* were progressive decisions which avoided placing unnecessary hurdles in the path of discrimination claimants. But in other cases, such as *Clymo v Wandsworth London Borough Council* [1989] ICR 250 (discussed by Jeremy Lewis at (1989) 18 *Industrial Law Journal* 244) the courts have taken a less generous approach, in particular in relation to claims by women that they could not comply with conditions concerning working hours. These decisions are perhaps relatively rare, but the removal of the 'cannot comply' provision is nevertheless to be welcomed. A woman who wishes to work reduced hours in order to accommodate her caring responsibilities will suffer a detriment if she is not permitted to do so (where, for example, this means that she has to buy in expensive childcare), whether or not she could work full-time. And an observant Muslim who is denied adequate facilities for purification before prayer will suffer a detriment even if it is possible, though inconvenient, to comply with the religious requirements. What w ill be interesting is to see how tribunals handle the question whether 'detriment' or 'disadvantage' will be satisfied in a case in which the claimant can point to no economic loss, but rather to a denial of choice.

3.5.4 Justification

The starting point for the justification of indirect discrimination is the decision of the Court of Appeal in *Hampson*.

[3.44] *Hampson v Department of Education and Science* **[1989] ICR 179 (CA)**

The plaintiff, a Hong Kong Chinese teacher, completed Hong Kong's two-year teacher-training programme, taught for a number of years and then pursued a further one-year training course. Her application for recognition as a UK teacher was rejected by the Secretary of State for Employment on the grounds that her teaching qualification was not 'comparable' to a UK qualification, not having consisted of a three consecutive year course. Ms Hampson complained of race discrimination, arguing that the three consecutive year rule imposed by the Secretary of State indirectly discriminated against her as a Hong Kong Chinese person. The EAT and the Court of Appeal ruled against her on the ground that the Secretary of State's act was protected under section 41 RRA. But Balcombe LJ, dissenting in the Court of Appeal, set out the current test for justification.

Balcombe LJ:
In *Ojutiku v Manpower Services* [[1982] ICR 661] this court was concerned with the meaning of 'justifiable' where it appears in s 1(1)(b)(ii) of the [RRA] and of course that decision is binding on us insofar as it decides that meaning. However, I regret that I do not find, in two of the judgments in *Ojutiku*, any clear decision as to that meaning. The first judgment was that of Lord Justice Eveleigh. He dealt with the question in the following passage . . .

' . . . I myself would not accept that it is essential, or at least that it is always essential, for the employer to prove that the requirement is necessary for the good of his business. It may well be that in a particular case that is the argument which is advanced by the employer; it does not follow that that is what the statute demands. I am very hesitant to suggest another expression for that which is used in the statute, for fear that it will be picked up and quoted in other cases and built upon thereafter, with the result that at the end of the day there is a danger of us all departing far from the meaning of the word in the statute. For myself, it would be enough simply to ask myself: is it justifiable? But if I have to give some explanation of my understanding of that word, I would turn to a dictionary definition which says "to adduce adequate grounds for"; and it seems to me that if a person produces reasons for doing something, which would be acceptable to right-thinking people as sound and tolerable reasons for so doing, then he has justified his conduct.'

With all due respect to [Eveleigh LJ, and to Kerr LJ who concurred on similar grounds] . . . I derive little help from [their] judgments. 'Justifiable' and 'justify' are words which connote a value judgment, as is evident from the dictionary definition cited by Lord Justice Eveleigh: 'to produce adequate grounds for', but neither Lord Justice indicates what test should be applied. Lord Justice Kerr says it applies a lower standard than 'necessary', but does not indicate how much lower. It was, however, accepted by Mr Carlisle, and rightly so, that whatever test is to be applied it is an objective one: it is not sufficient for the employer to establish that he considered his reasons adequate.

However, I do derive considerable assistance from the judgment of Lord Justice Stephenson. At p 423 he referred to:

'. . . the comments, which I regard as sound, made by Lord McDonald, giving the judgment of [EAT] given by Phillips J in *Steel v Union of Post Office Workers* [[1978] ICR 181] . . . What Phillips J there said is valuable as rejecting justification by convenience and requiring the party applying the discriminatory condition to prove it to be justifiable in all the circumstances on balancing its discriminatory effect against the discriminator's need for it. But that need is what is reasonably needed by the party who applies the condition . . .'

In my judgment 'justifiable' requires an objective balance between the discriminatory effect of the condition and the reasonable needs of the party who applies the condition. This construction is supported by the recent decision of the House of Lords in *Rainey v Greater Glasgow Health Board* . . . [[3.87] below, in which the House of Lords applied] the decision of the European Court in *Bilka-Kaufhaus GmbH v Weber von Hartz* . . . [[3.47] below, to the effect that, in order to justify indirect sex discrimination] the employer had to show a real need on the part of the undertaking, objectively justified, although that need was not confined to economic grounds; it might, for instance, include administrative efficiency in a concern not engaged in commerce or business. Clearly it may, as in the present case, be possible to justify by reference to grounds other than economic or administrative efficiency . . .

I can find no significant difference between the test adopted by Lord Justice Stephenson in *Ojutiku* and that adopted by the House of Lords in *Rainey*. Since neither Lords Justices Eveleigh nor Kerr in *Ojutiku* indicated what they considered the test to be—although Lord Justice Kerr said what it was not—I am content to adopt Lord Justice Stephenson's test as I have expressed it above, which I consider to be consistent with *Rainey*. It is obviously desirable that the tests of justifiability applied in all these closely related fields [i.e., under the SDA, the RRA and the EqPA] should be consistent with each other.

Balcombe LJ, dissenting in *Hampson*, would have referred back to the tribunal the question of justification in that case. The test he suggested was widely adopted before being approved by the House of Lords in *Webb* v *EMO* [1993] ICR 175 in which that Court, the Court of Appeal and the EAT were unanimous that the dismissal of Ms Webb was justified under that test. (These decisions predated that of the House of Lords in *Webb* v *EMO (No 2)* [1995] ICR 1021 in which it ruled that the applicant's pregnancy-related dismissal was directly discriminatory on grounds of sex and not, therefore, open to justification.) The application of the *Hampson* test in a number of cases is considered below, one of the most common contexts in which it is argued concerning employers' refusals to adapt working hours to accommodate (women) workers' family responsibilities. Men faced with such refusals cannot rely on the SDA save by establishing direct discrimination in the differential treatment of men and women with such responsibilities. But women can argue that they, as women, are less able to comply with requirements to work full-time, extended hours, inflexibly, or flexibly according to the employer's needs, all of these being difficult to reconcile with caring responsibilities (such as those for children or elderly dependants) which, contrary to the view of the EAT in *Kidd* (section 3. 5.2 above), remain disproportionately the lot of women.

[3.45] *London Underground Ltd v Edwards (No 2)* [1997] IRLR 157 (EAT)

Ms Edwards, a lone parent, had been forced to resign from her job as an underground train driver when her employers imposed a new shift system which made it impossible for her to organise child care. A tribunal ruled that the employers had failed to justify the imposition of the system on Ms Edwards on the grounds that they 'could . . . easily, without losing the objectives of their plan and reorganisation, have accommodated the applicant who was a long-serving employee . . . *They did not address themselves to these issues*' (our emphasis). The EAT dismissed the employers' appeal.

Morison J:

There was evidence to justify the conclusion that London Underground could—and, we would add, should—have accommodated Ms Edwards's personal requirements. She had been working for them for nearly ten years. Her family demands were of a temporary nature . . . there was good evidence that London Underground could have made arrangements which would not have been damaging to their business plans but which would have accommodated the reasonable demands of their employees. It may be that London Underground would have wished to implement the single parent link but gave in to pressure from their predominantly male workforce.

We would wish to add three observations. In the first place, employers should recognise the need to take a reasonably flexible attitude to accommodating the particular needs of their employees. In a case such as this, had it been obvious that London Underground could have accommodated Ms Edwards's needs, without any difficulty or expense, there might have been a case for alleging direct discrimination. Changing the roster in a way which they must have appreciated would cause her a detriment might have justifiably led to an inference that they had treated her less well than they would have treated male train operators who had been in a similar position. In other words, the more clear it is that the employers unreasonably failed to show flexibility in their employment practices, the more willing the tribunal should be to make a finding of unlawful discrimination . . .

Second, in many cases, an employer will be able, readily, to justify a roster system, even if people with childcare responsibilities could not sensibly be accommodated within it. But the lesson from this case is that employers should carefully consider the impact which a new roster might have on a section of their workforce . . .

Third, nothing we have said in this judgment should be construed as favouring positive discrimination.

In *London Underground* the employers failed to take a reasonable step which they had themselves identified (and which, as the EAT pointed out, would have involved no 'difficulty or expense') in order to reduce the impact of the disputed requirement on the applicant. It would be difficult to argue that such a failure was justified. But the test of justification is not difficult to satisfy.

[3.46] *Jones v University of Manchester* [1993] ICR 474

Here the Court of Appeal considered whether the disparate impact of the upper age limit on men and women could be justified under the *Hampson* test. The University had argued that the age limit was justified (a) because careers advisers should not be 'not too far removed in age from the students' and (b) because it was necessary to achieve a better spread in the ages of advisers in the department whose staff were presently aged 62, 63, 54, 47, 45 and 42. A tribunal had ruled against the university on the issue of justification, its decision being overruled by the EAT on the basis that the tribunal had 'effectively dismissed the matters relied upon by [the university] once it was demonstrated that they were not essential'. The Court of Appeal upheld the EAT's decision:

Ralph Gibson LJ:
The [tribunal] is required to determine the discriminatory effect of the requirement. That seems to me to require the [tribunal] to ascertain both the quantitative effect, ie how many men and women will or are likely to suffer in consequence of the discriminatory effect; and, also, what is the qualitative effect of the requirement upon those affected by it, ie how much damage or disappointment may it do or cause and how lasting or final is that damage?

I therefore do not agree that it is improper in the balancing exercise to take into account the particular hardships which have lain in the way of the particular applicant, provided that proper attention is paid to the question of how typical they are of any other men and women adversely affected by the requirement. That, I think, is what the [tribunal] did . . .

Nevertheless, in my judgment, the [tribunal] did misdirect itself in carrying out the balancing exercise. As against the reasonable needs of the University, the [tribunal] must set the discriminatory effect of the application by the University of the requirement to Miss Jones and any others excluded by it. If, contrary to my view, the [tribunal] was entitled to hold as it did that the application of the requirement to Miss Jones was indirectly discriminatory . . . yet in carrying out the balancing exercise it was necessary, in my judgment, for the [tribunal] to keep in mind the process by which their conclusion was made out and, in particular, that the women in that small section of the total number of graduates represents a small proportion of the total of eligible women graduates . . .

For the reasons I have already stated, I consider that the [tribunal] was entitled to assess as it did the effect upon 'women like Miss Jones' of the impact of such a requirement when, after finally getting their degrees, they are excluded from suitable employment by an age bar. I share the [tribunal's] view of the nature of such an obstacle upon mature women graduates generally. It is, however, clear that the [tribunal], in carrying out the balancing exercise, was putting into the scale their assessment of the impact of such a requirement upon the 'thousands of women enrolled as mature students in English universities who will not obtain their degree until they are aged 30 or more and that many of them will come up against the obstacle of gaining the type of employment for which those qualifications make them suitable if such a requirement or condition as the one applied by the [University] to [Miss Jones] in this case is imposed'. Thus, in my judgment, the [tribunal] was placing in the balance the discriminatory effect of this requirement if permitted to be applied by employers. That was not right. This is not a case concerned with the potential effect of age requirements generally or of a university seeking to justify an age limit for general or normal recruitment of a particular class of employee. It was claiming to justify the imposition of an age requirement on this occasion of recruiting a replacement to fill one permanent post, enlarged to two permanent posts in the circumstances described, for a department which has, in addition, to the director and his deputy, seven careers advisers. The discriminatory impact is not to be measured for this purpose with reference to the impact upon the thousands of women mentioned by the [tribunal]. The indirect discrimination as established to the satisfaction of the [tribunal] was upon a small section of the total relevant number and with reference to the selection upon one occasion of two recruits to the careers advisory department of the University. There was thus, in my judgment, misdirection by the [tribunal] in the conduct by them of the balancing exercise in their consideration of the issue of justification.

Sir David Croom-Johnson and Evans LJ concurred.

It was noted, above, that the *Hampson* test for justification claims to incorporate the ECJ's approach to the justification of indirect sex discrimination into UK law. *Hampson* was a race discrimination case but, as Balcombe LJ pointed out in that case, section 1(1)(b)(ii) SDA 'is identical, *mutatis mutandis*, to section 1(1)(b)(ii) [RRA]'. Accordingly, he applied the same approach to justification under the RRA as he would have applied under the SDA and as the House of Lords had applied in [*Rainey* **[3.87]** below] to the EqPA. This approach, in Balcombe LJ's view, was consistent with that adopted by the ECJ in *Bilka-Kaufhaus*.

[3.47] Case 170/84 *Bilka-Kaufhaus GmbH v Weber von Hartz* [1986] ECR 1607 (ECJ)

The applicant alleged a breach of Article 141 (then Article 119) on the grounds that, as a part-time worker, she had been refused pension payments under a contractual scheme wholly funded by her employer and supplementary to the German state pension. One issue which arose for consideration was whether such pension payments were 'pay' within Article 141. This aspect of the decision is further considered below. Here we are concerned with the question whether, consistent with Article 141, part-timers could be paid less than full-timers where this practice impacted disadvantageously upon women.

Judgment:
Mrs Weber . . . asserted that the requirement of a minimum period of full-time employment for the payment of an occupational pension placed women workers at a disadvantage, since they were more likely than their male colleagues to take part-time work so as to be able to care for their family and children.

Bilka on the other hand, argued that . . . there were objectively justified economic grounds for its decision to exclude part-time employees from the occupational pension scheme. It emphasized in that regard that in comparison with the employment of part-time workers the employment of full-time workers entails lower ancillary costs and permits the use of staff throughout opening hours. Relying on statistics concerning the group to which it belongs, Bilka stated that up to 1980 81.3% of all occupational pensions were paid to women, although only 72% of employees were women. Those figures, it said, showed that the scheme in question does not entail discrimination on the basis of sex . . .

if . . . it should be found that a much lower proportion of women than of men work full time, the exclusion of part-time workers from the occupational pension scheme would be contrary to Article [141] of the Treaty where, taking into account the difficulties encountered by women workers in working full-time that measure could not be explained by factors which exclude any discrimination on grounds of sex.

However, if the undertaking is able to show that its pay practice may be explained by objectively justified factors unrelated to any discrimination on grounds of sex there is no breach of article [141] . . .

It is for the national court, which has sole jurisdiction to make findings of fact, to determine whether and to what extent the grounds put forward by an employer to explain the adoption of a pay practice which applies independently of a worker's sex but in fact affects more women than men may be regarded as objectively justified economic grounds. If the national court finds that the measures chosen by Bilka correspond to a real need on the part of the undertaking, are appropriate with a view to achieving the objectives pursued and are necessary to that end, the fact that the measures affect a far greater number of women than men is not sufficient to show that they constitute an infringement of article [141].

The ECJ jurisprudence did not come to a standstill with the decision in *Bilka*, that Court further developing the test for justification through the decisions in the *Rinner-Kühn*, *Danfoss* and *Nimz* cases.

Case 171/88 *Rinner-Kühn* v *FWW Spezial-Gebaudereinigung GmbH* [1989] ECR 2743 was brought by a part-time worker who challenged her employer's refusal to pay her sick-pay. National law required (and provided for the reimbursement to the employer of) such payment only for those working more than 10 hours a week. Having decided that sick pay was 'pay' within Article 141 and that its denial to part-timers amounted, *prima facie*, to indirect discrimination against women, the ECJ went on to dismiss the German government's proferred justification for the discrimination (that those working less than 10 hours a week were not as integrated in, or as dependent on, the undertaking employing them as other workers). The ECJ accepted that the question of justification was one for the national court to determine, but declared that 'generalizations about certain categories of workers . . . do not enable criteria which are both objective and unrelated to any discrimination on grounds of sex to be identified'.

The Claimant in Case 109/88 *Handels-og Kontorfunktionaerernes Forbund I Danmark* v *Dansk Arbejdsgiverforening (acting for Danfoss)* [1989] ECR 3199 challenged, *inter alia*, a practice whereby individual pay was set according to factors including adaptability, training and seniority, reliance on these factors serving to disadvantage women by comparison with men. The ECJ ruled that the reward of adaptability to variable hours and varying places of work, or of training, was justifiable (where it disadvantaged women) only to the extent that at it was 'of importance for the performance of specific tasks entrusted to the employee'. In this, the *Danfoss* case, the ECJ was prepared to accept that the reward of seniority, even where it operated so as to disadvantage women: 'length of service goes hand in hand with experience and since experience generally enables the employee to perform his duties better, the employer is free to reward it without having to establish the importance it has in the performance of specific tasks entrusted to the employee'. This approach was rapidly revised in Case 184/89 *Nimz* v *Freie und Hansestadt Hamburg* [1991] ECR I–297, in which the challenge related precisely to the reward of service where this served to disadvantage part-time workers and, accordingly, women. The employers claimed that full-time employees acquired the abilities and skills relating to their particular job more quickly than others, and ought accordingly to be paid more. According to the Court: 'such considerations, in so far as they are no more than generalizations about certain categories of workers, do not make it possible to identify criteria which are both objective and unrelated to any discrimination on grounds of sex. Although experience goes hand in hand with length of service, and experience enables the worker in principle to improve performance of the tasks allotted to him, the objectivity of such a criterion depends on all the circumstances in a particular case, and in particular on the relationship between the nature of the work performed and the experience gained from the performance of that work upon completion of a certain number of working hours'. (*Cf* the decisions of the EAT and the Court of

Appeal in *Health & Safety Executive v Cadman* [2004] ICR 378 and [2004] IRLR 971.)

Bilka-Kaufhaus concerned discrimination by employers. In cases where the discrimination is practised by the state against categories of persons (such as part-time workers), 'somewhat broader considerations apply' and the ECJ accepted in *Rinner-Kühn* that such discrimination may be justifiable where they 'meet a necessary aim of [a Member State's] social policy and that they are suitable and requisite for attaining that aim'. The test is still a proportionality one, but it appears easier to satisfy. More recently, however, in Case 226/98 *Jørgensen v Foreningen af Speciallæger, Sygesikringens Forhandlingsudvalg* [2000] ECR I–02447, the ECJ ruled that 'budgetary considerations cannot in themselves justify discrimination on grounds of sex'. This approach, the ECJ explains, is necessary to avoid the varying application of the principle of equal treatment with the public finances of individual Member States. This approach was applied again in Case 77/02 *Steinicke v Bundesanstalt für Arbeit* [2003] ECR I–09027 and in *Kutz-Bauer* in which the ECJ ruled that a scheme which encouraged part-time work by those not yet entitled to a state pension (which was provided to the majority of women at 60, and the majority of men at 65) breached the Equal Treatment Directive.

[3.48] Case 187/00 *Kutz-Bauer v Freie und Hansestadt Hamburg* [2003] ECR I–02741

Judgment:

The German Government submits that one of the aims pursued by a scheme such as the one at issue in the main proceedings is to combat unemployment by offering the maximum incentives for workers who are not yet eligible to retire to do so and thus making posts available. To allow a worker who has already acquired entitlement to a retirement pension at the full rate to benefit from the scheme of part-time work for older employees implies, first, that a post which the scheme intends to allocate to an unemployed person would continue to be occupied and, second, that the social security scheme would bear the additional costs, which would divert certain resources from other objectives.

As regards the argument which the German Government derives from the encouragement of recruitment, it is for the Member States to choose the measures capable of achieving the aims which they pursue in employment matters. The Court has recognised that the Member States have a broad margin of discretion in exercising that power . . .

Furthermore, as the Court stated at paragraph 71 of its judgment in *Seymour-Smith and Perez*, it cannot be disputed that the encouragement of recruitment constitutes a legitimate aim of social policy [but] . . . mere generalisations concerning the capacity of a specific measure to encourage recruitment are not enough to show that the aim of the disputed provisions is unrelated to any discrimination based on sex or to provide evidence on the basis of which it could reasonably be considered that the means chosen are or could be suitable for achieving that aim.

As regards the German Government's argument concerning the additional burden associated with allowing female workers to take advantage of the scheme at issue in the main proceedings even where they have acquired entitlement to a retirement pension at the full rate, the Court observes that although budgetary considerations may underlie a Member State's choice of social policy and influence the nature or scope of the social protection measures which it wishes to adopt, they do not in themselves constitute an aim pursued by that policy and cannot therefore justify discrimination against one of the sexes . . .

Nor can the City of Hamburg, whether as a public authority or as an employer, justify discrimination arising from a scheme of part-time work for older employees solely because avoidance of such discrimination would involve increased costs . . .

It is therefore for the City of Hamburg to prove to the national court that the difference in treatment arising from the scheme of part-time work for older employees at issue in the main proceedings is justified by objective reasons unrelated to any discrimination on grounds of sex.

The test for objective justification, developed through *Bilka-Kaufhaus* and subsequent cases, requires that employers demonstrate that the factors upon which pay depends are relevant to the actual job done by the worker, where those factors impact differently as between men and women. (The question is not—Case 4/02 and 5/02, *Schönheit v Stadt Frankfurt am Main* [2003] ECR I–12575—what reason was put forward by the employer at the time of the adoption of the disputed practice, rather what the reasons are for it now.) Further, the justifiability of determining pay in line with such disparately impacting factors will depend on questions of proportionality. And where an employer's pay practices lack transparency, a demonstration by the applicant of disparities between the average pay levels of men and women within particular grades will be sufficient to raise a (rebuttable) presumption of discrimination.

The ECJ cases extracted above were reached under Article 141 TEC, which provides a directly effective right to equality in pay (broadly defined). National legislation distinguishes between non-contractual provisions (including those which would qualify as 'pay' under Article 141), which are governed by the SDA, and contractual provisions (whether related to 'pay' under Article 141 or not) which are governed by the EqPA, discussed in more detail below (section 3.10).

The EqPA, like the SDA and the RRA, prohibits unjustified indirect discrimination as well as direct discrimination. It does so by providing that unequal contractual conditions in respect of comparable work done by a man and a woman are lawful only to the extent that they are (a) not the result of direct discrimination and (b), if the result of indirect discrimination, that they are objectively justified. The structure of the EqPA and its regulation of indirect discrimination in pay and contractual conditions, are further considered below. Here it is sufficient to reiterate the acceptance by the House of Lords in *Rainey* and the Court of Appeal in *Hampson* that the test established by the ECJ in *Bilka-Kaufhaus* was applicable to the EqPA, the SDA and the RRA. The *Bilka-Kaufhaus* test as it has developed through *Rinner-Kühn, Danfoss* and *Nimz* is certainly applicable in relation to sex-related pay discrimination, whether that discrimination is challenged under the EqPA or (as in Case 12/81 *Garland v British Rail*, [1982] ECR 0359), the SDA. Bearing in mind the dicta in *Rainey* and in *Hampson*, it ought also to be applied to the SDA more broadly and to the RRA.

[3.49] *Allonby v Accrington and Rossingdale College* **[2001] ICR 1189 (CA)**

Here the Court of Appeal attempted to reconcile the decisions in *Bilka-Kaufhaus* and in *Hampson*. The employers had dismissed (predominantly female) part-time staff and re-employed them through an intermediate agency at an estimated saving of £13,000 in total to the college, but with costs to the staff in terms of loss of benefits including sick pay and reductions in hourly pay. A tribunal decided that any indirect sex discrimination was justified: 'any decision taken for sound business reasons would inevitably affect one group more than another group'. The EAT agreed but the Court of Appeal did not. The Claimant had appealed on the question of justification, arguing that less discriminatory measures were available to the college and so that its action was disproportionate and therefore unjustified and that, further, the action taken by the college was itself based on discrimination and so incapable of justification.

Sedley LJ:

The House of Lords in *Barry v Midland Bank plc* [1999] ICRR 859 endorsed the decision in this court, where Peter Gibson LJ had said:

'[In *Bilka-Kaufhaus* . . . the European Court of Justice] held that the employer could exclude part-time workers from the pension scheme on the ground that it sought to employ as few part-time workers as possible only where it was found that "the means chosen for achieving that objective correspond to a real need on the part of the undertaking, are appropriate with a view to achieving the objective in question and are necessary to that end.

In our judgment it would be wrong to extrapolate from those words written in that context that an employer can never justify indirect discrimination in a redundancy payment scheme unless the form of the scheme is shown to be necessary as the only possible scheme. One must first consider whether the objective of the scheme is legitimate. If so, then one goes on to consider whether the means used are appropriate to achieve that objective and are reasonably necessary for that end.'

That approach, as Peter Gibson LJ went on to point out, has the support of the House of Lords in *Rainey v Greater Glasgow Health Board* ... and in *Webb v EMO* ... where the judgment of Balcombe LJ in *Hampson v Department of Education and Science* ... was expressly approved. Balcombe LJ said: 'In my judgment, "justifiable" requires an objective balance between the discriminatory effect of the condition and the reasonable needs of the party who applies the condition.'

In *Barry*, in their Lordships' House, Lord Nicholls amplified this:

'More recently, in *Enderby v Frenchay Health Authority* ... the Court of Justice drew attention to the need for national courts to apply the principle of proportionality when they have to apply Community law. In other words, the ground relied upon as justification must be of sufficient importance for the national court to regard this as overriding the disparate impact of the difference in treatment, either in whole or in part. The more serious the disparate impact on women or men, as the case may be, the more cogent must be the objective justification. There seem to be no particular criteria to which the national court should have regard when assessing the weight of the justification relied on.'

There is further authority, on which Ms Gill [for the Claimant] relies, for the proposition that where the employer's objective is itself discriminatory, it can never justify discriminatory means [citing *ex parte EOC* and *ex parte Seymour-Smith*].

In my judgment, the employment tribunal has failed to apply the scrutiny which the law requires when a discriminatory condition is said to be justifiable. Moreover, such reasons as it gives do not stand up in law.

The major error, which by itself vitiates the decision, is that nowhere, either in terms or in substance, did the tribunal seek to weigh the justification against its discriminatory effect. On the contrary, by accepting that 'any decision taken for sound business reasons would inevitably affect one group more than another group', it . . . disabled itself from making the comparison.

Secondly, the tribunal accepted uncritically the college's reasons for the dismissals. They did not, for example, ask the obvious question why departments could not be prevented from overspending on part-time hourly-paid teachers without dismissing them. They did not consider other fairly obvious measures short of dismissal which had been canvassed and which could well have matched the anticipated saving of £13,000 a year. In consequence, they made no attempt to evaluate objectively whether the dismissals were reasonably necessary – a test which, while of course not demanding indispensability, requires proof of a real need.

In this situation it is not enough that the tribunal should have posed, as they did, the statutory question 'whether the decision taken by the college was justifiable irrespective of the sex of the person or persons to whom it applied'. In what are extended reasons running to 15 closely typed pages, there has to be some evidence that the tribunal understood the process by which a now formidable body of authority requires the task of answering the question to be carried out, and some evidence that it has in fact carried it out. Once a finding of a condition having a disparate and adverse impact on women had been made, what was required was at the minimum a critical evaluation of whether the college's reasons demonstrated a real need to dismiss the applicant; if there was such a need, consideration of the seriousness of the disparate impact of the dismissal on women including the applicant; and an evaluation of whether the former were sufficient to outweigh the latter. There is no sign of this process in the tribunal's extended reasons. In particular, there is no recognition that if the aim of dismissal was itself discriminatory (as the applicant contended it was, since it was to deny part-time workers, a predominantly female group, benefits which Parliament had legislated to give them) it could never afford justification.

It is conceivable that the tribunal misunderstood Lord Nicholls's remark, at the end of the passage quoted above, that 'There seem to be no particular criteria to which the national court should have regard when assessing the weight of the justification relied upon.' Lord Nicholls was not saying that the question was at large or the answer one of first impression: he was saying that, in the exercise which he had spelt out, no single factor or group of factors was of special weight.

I would therefore allow the appeal on this ground. This court is not in a position to say that the outcome of a proper approach will inevitably be in the appellant's favour, and I would therefore remit the case for a further hearing on this issue and that of proportionate impact considered above.

[3.50] M Connolly, 'Discrimination Law: Justification, Alternative Measures and Defences Based on Sex' (2001) 30 *Industrial Law Journal* 311, 313-18 (footnotes omitted)

Sedley LJ's reconciliation of *Bilka* and *Hampson* could be interpreted in two ways. First, *Bilka* and *Hampson* were two stages of a compound definition of justification. We decide first if there was a 'real need' (*Bilka*) and second, if its discriminatory effect outweighed the College's needs (*Hampson*). This is an unlikely interpretation though. Sedley LJ quoted Lord Nicholls in *Barry v Midland Bank* . . . 'The more serious the disparate impact on women . . . the more cogent must be the objective justification.' This said Sedley LJ, 'amplified' the *Hampson* test. Although Sedley LJ failed to mention that Lord Nicholls was discussing the Community Law principle of proportionality (*Hampson* was not cited in *Barry*), we must assume that, Sedley LJ (and Lord Nicholls) were equating the

Hampson 'objective balance' test with the principle of proportionality. This undermines the theory that Sedley LJ was crafting a two-stage test. This is because the principle of proportionality is inherent in the *Bilka* test, which demands that a measure must be 'suitable' and 'necessary' to achieve the goal. Proportionality, or *Hampson*, cannot work as a separate test. An employer who has shown that a practice was suitable and necessary, has at the same time shown that it was proportionate. It would be absurd to ask again, was it suitable and necessary? And in cases where an employer had failed to show that a practice was suitable and necessary, a separate question of proportionality would be pointless.

So we must accept the second interpretation, that *Hampson* merely reflects parts (b) and (c) of the *Bilka* test. This is the neatest integration yet of the *Bilka* and *Hampson* 'tests'. Hitherto, British courts have done no more than treat the tests as expressing the same thing in different language . . .

However, Sedley LJ's assimilation of *Bilka*—or more precisely proportionality—and *Hampson* is not perfect. The obvious difference is in the language. The word 'necessary' appears nowhere in the *Hampson* test. But there is a difference in substance as well. Asking if a practice is suitable and necessary is different from asking whether it is outweighed by its discriminatory effect. This becomes clear where, as Ms Allonby argued, there exists an alternative. Under *Hampson* the existence of a less discriminatory alternative practice achieving the same goal is merely an ingredient in the 'balance' test; under *Bilka* it will always defeat a justification defence . . .

Case law history also demonstrates that the British judiciary understood that there was a lower standard of justification than *Bilka*. In the early years of the British legislation, tribunals (influenced by US case law, upon which our legislation was based), spoke of 'necessity'. For example, in *Steel v Union of Post Office Workers* . . . Phillips J, President of the EAT said . . . that the practice must be *inter alia* 'genuine and necessary'.

In 1982, however, the Court of Appeal in *Ojutiku v Manpower Services Commission* . . . contrasted the word 'necessary' with the statutory word 'justified'; Kerr LJ stated . . . that 'justifiable . . . clearly applies a lower standard than . . . necessary'. Eveleigh LJ considered . . . it to mean 'something . . . acceptable to right-thinking people as sound and tolerable'. Balcombe LJ in *Hampson* retrieved the situation somewhat with his 'objective justification' test. However, he did not restore the standard to the pre-*Ojutiku* position. Otherwise he would have simply used the word 'necessary'. Obvious support for a lower standard lies in the legislative history. The RRA and SDA use the term 'justified' rather than 'necessary'. In Parliament, the Government resisted amendments to the Sex Discrimination Bill that would have replaced 'justifiable' with 'necessary'. Lord Harris stated that where a body offered reduced fares for pensioners, the policy might be justifiable, but not necessary (362 HL Deb, 14 July 1975, cols 10116-17).

Meanwhile, the ECJ was developing its jurisprudence on indirect discrimination. The *Bilka* test expressly demanded that any measure should be 'necessary' to achieve the goal. The existence of a less discriminatory alternative will defeat a defence of justification. However, under *Hampson*, the mere existence of a less discriminatory alternative is not enough to defeat a defence. As *Enderby* . . . illustrates, if the discriminatory effect of the disputed measure is 'outweighed' by the employer's needs, then the defence will succeed, no matter haw many less discriminatory alternatives exist. This approach slowly permeated the British cases until the Court of Appeal in *Hampson* felt compelled to reconcile it with the British position . . .

None of this is to say that British courts will refuse to consider alternatives in the justification debate. Sedley's LJ judgement was not as clear-cut as that. Indeed the Court of Appeal remitted *Allonby's* case for reconsideration because, among other things, the tribunal had not considered the 'obvious' alternatives open to the College. Of course, asking a tribunal to 'consider' an alternative in the 'balance' test is different from ruling that the mere existence of an alternative will defeat the justification defence. Sedley LJ's judgement further departs from *Bilka* with his attendant comments. He noted . . . that the tribunal had failed 'to evaluate . . . whether the dismissals were reasonably necessary-a test which, while of course not demanding indispensability, requires proof of a real need'. Here Sedley LJ has diluted *Bilka* by qualifying 'necessary' with 'reasonably necessary' and not indispensable. He spoke only of obvious alternatives. This is the language of compromise. One can only conclude that he intended a broad-brush approach. Tribunals should only consider 'fairly obvious' alternatives. This deepens the impression (eg given in *Ojutiku* and *Hampson*) that the English courts will apply *Bilka* in form only, whilst actually subjecting employers to the lower *Hampson* standard of justification.

Finally, this does not mean that the difference between *Hampson* and *Bilka* is merely a matter of degree. It is a fundamental difference. The compromise in the *Hampson* test upsets the theory of indirect discrimination. Where a practice having a disparate impact is shown to be absolutely necessary to achieve a genuine non-discriminatory goal, then the cause of the disparate impact lies elsewhere. No action lies against the employer. The cause(s) of any disparate impact can only be identified if the courts impose a strict test of necessity. A lesser standard gives employers leeway to discriminate and blurs the causes of a disparate impact. As *Enderby's* case illustrates, 'excess' disparate impact amounts to discrimination. Further, a strict test of necessity forces employers to eliminate discriminatory employment practices, which by their nature, are inefficiencies. The irony is that as many men as women, and far more whites than non-whites, would benefit from that . . .

This case was remitted because the tribunal failed to apply any sort of objective test of justification. The tribunal's failure to consider an alternative was evidence of this and no more. The Court of Appeal did not recommend that the justification defence necessarily should fail because there was a 'fairly obvious' alternative. This reveals that the Court of Appeal did not apply the *Bilka* standard, only the lower *Hampson* one.

Allonby follows a series of cases in our senior courts (eg *Hampson*, *Barry*, *Webb*) where a 'balance' test has been equated with the principle of proportionality, first set out in Bilka. Clearly *Hampson* does not reflect fully the proportionality principle, which means no more than necessary. The effect of this is notable where there exists a less discriminatory alternative able to achieve the employer's goal. Under *Bilka*, the mere existence of one will defeat a justification defence; *Enderby* illustrates that. But according to *Allonby*, only 'obvious' alternatives qualify to be balanced against the 'reasonable' and 'not indispensable' needs of the employer. This less onerous test upsets the theory of indirect discrimination by sanctioning a certain amount of discrimination and blurring its cause(s). It also weakens the attack on business inefficiencies that benefits all.

As the law stands, the existence of less discriminatory alternative practice achieving the same goal will, under EU legislation and in the United States, defeat a defence of justification. However, under domestic legislation an alternative practice is merely an ingredient in a 'balance' test. Where the claimant can identify an alternative practice they would be well advised to bring their claim under EU legislation, where possible.

Concern has been expressed above that the articulation of justification in the RRA as amended (as well as in the SORs, the RBRs and the proposed amendments to the SDA) has made the test easier to satisfy by failing to require (by contrast with the directives) that the means used are *necessary* to any legitimate aim pursued by an employer. A further potential problem lies in the fact that under the new definitions that there is no requirement to establish justification *irrespective* of the race, etc., of the person to whom the provision, criterion or practice applied. It remains to be seen whether this is the case in practice, though one advantage of the amended test is that it may leave room for the justification of indirectly discriminatory practices which are intended to ameliorate, rather than designed (wittingly or otherwise) to perpetuate the disadvantage experienced by certain groups defined by race, religion or belief or sexual orientation.

3.6 The DDA

3.6.1 Justification under the DDA

The DDA provides for a justification defence to disability-related discrimination, except where that discrimination also amounts to direct disability discrimination [3.16]. The 2004 amendments to the DDA were significant in limiting the justification defence both by introducing the concept of direct discrimination (incapable of being justified) and by removing the defence of justification in relation to failures to make reasonable adjustments. The duty to make reasonable adjustments is detailed at 3.6.2 below. First, however, we will consider the justification defence as it operates under the DDA.

Section 3A(3) DDA provides that less favourable treatment is justified 'if, but only if, the reason for it is both material to the circumstances of the particular case and substantial', section 3A(4) providing that 'treatment of a disabled person cannot be justified under subsection (3) if it amounts to direct discrimination falling within subsection [section 3A(5)'. The DRC's new Code of Practice on Employment suggests that direct disability discrimination will occur, *inter alia*, where 'less favourable treatment occurs because of the employer's generalised, or stereotypical, assumptions about the disability or its effects', providing examples of a blind woman not short-listed for a job involving computers because the employer wrongly assumes that blind people cannot use them, of a severely disfigured man denied a job as a shop assistant because the employer is concerned that other employees would be uncomfortable working alongside him, of a job description which states that anyone with a history of mental illness would not be suitable for the post. Where disability-related discrimination outside the category of direct discrimination is concerned, the most noteworthy thing about the justification test is the ease with which it can be satisfied.

[3.51] *Post Office v Jones* **[2001] ICR 805 (CA)**

The claimant had been removed from driving duties after he became insulin dependent as a result of diabetes. A tribunal took the view that the discrimination, which was conceded by the employer, was unjustified, this on the grounds that a correct appraisal of the Claimant's medical condition would have led the Post Office to conclude that he was fit to continue driving duties. The EAT overruled on the grounds that the employers were entitled to prefer their medical evidence to that put forward by the Claimant. The employee's appeal was dismissed, the Court of Appeal ruling that the tribunal was not entitled to find against the employer on the justification issue on the basis that the medical evidence relied upon was incorrect. The Court ruled that the DDA confined tribunals to considering whether the reason given for less favourable treatment could properly be described as material to the circumstances of the particular case and substantial. The tribunal was entitled to investigate facts and to assess the employer's decision by determining whether there was evidence on the basis of which a decision could properly be taken. So, for example, if the employer had not carried out any risk assessment, or had made a decision other than on the basis of appropriate medical evidence, or had acted irrationally, the tribunal could find the treatment unjustified.

Pill LJ:

. . . The 1995 Act is plainly intended to create rights for the disabled and to protect their position as employees, but those intentions must be considered in the context of the employer's duties to employees generally and to the general public. I cannot accept, in a case such as the present, involving an assessment of risk, that Parliament intended in the wording adopted to confer on employment tribunals a general power and duty to decide whether the employer's assessment of risk is correct. The issue is a different one from whether a person has a disability, within the meaning of s.1 of the Act, which is to be determined by the employment tribunal . . .

Upon a consideration of the wording of s.5(3) [now section 3A(3)] in context, I conclude that the employment tribunal are confined to considering whether the reason given for the less favourable treatment can properly be described as both material to the circumstances of the particular case and substantial. The less favourable treatment in the present case is the limit upon the hours of driving. The reason given for it is the risk arising from longer periods of driving. The respondent obtained what are admitted to be suitably qualified and expert medical opinions. Upon the basis of those opinions, the respondent decided that the risk was such as to require the less favourable treatment. In order to rely on s.5(3) it is not enough for the employer to assert that his conduct was reasonable in a general way; he has to establish that the reason given satisfies the statutory criteria. The respondent asserts in this case that the risk arising from the presence of diabetes is material to the circumstance of the particular case and is substantial. Where a properly conducted risk assessment provides a reason which is on its face both material and substantial, and is not irrational, the tribunal cannot substitute its own appraisal. The employment tribunal must consider whether the reason meets the statutory criteria; it does not have the more general power to make its own appraisal of the medical evidence and conclude that the evidence from admittedly competent medical witnesses was incorrect or make its own risk assessment.

The present problem will typically arise when a risk assessment is involved. I am not doubting that the employment tribunal is permitted to investigate facts, for example as to the time-keeping record of the disabled person or as to his rate of productivity, matters which would arise upon some of the illustrations given in the Code of Practice. Consideration of the statutory criteria may also involve an assessment of the employer's decision to the extent of considering whether there was evidence on the basis of which a decision could properly be taken. Thus if no risk assessment was made or a decision was taken otherwise than on the basis of appropriate medical evidence, or was an irrational decision as being beyond the range of responses open to a reasonable decision-maker (a test approved by Sir Thomas Bingham MR in a different context in *R v Ministry of Defence ex parte Smith*, the employment tribunal could hold the reason insufficient and the treatment unjustified.

The tribunal cannot, however, in my judgment, conclude that the reason is not material or substantial because the suitably qualified and competently expressed medical opinion, on the basis of which the employer's decision was made, was thought by them to be inferior to a different medical opinion expressed to them. Moreover, a reason may be material and substantial within the meaning of the section even if the employment tribunal would have come to a different decision as to the extent of the risk. An investigation of the facts by the tribunal will often be required, but it cannot go to the extent of disagreeing with a risk assessment which is properly conducted, based on the properly formed opinion of suitably qualified doctors and produces an answer which is not irrational. This constraint limits the power of tribunals to provide relief to disabled employees, but in my view it follows from the wording of the section, which requires consideration of the reason given by the employer, and recognises the importance of the employer's responsibility for working practices.

Arden LJ:

An example may help throw light on the function of the word 'material' in s.5(3). Suppose that it is shown that diabetes (of either type) leads to diminished night-time vision and the employer of an employee with diabetes prohibits that employee from doing night-time shifts for the reason that he has diabetes. In this example there would be a material connection between the employer's reason and the circumstances of the particular case. Miss Tether [for the Claimant] sought to argue that materiality also involved correctness. However, in my judgment, if the employer in the example last given believed that diabetes diminished night-time vision but was entirely wrong in that belief, the requirement for materiality in the example which I have given would still be met. However, there would be difficulty in the employer meeting the second requirement of substantiality, to which I now turn.

The second requirement in s.5(3) is that the reason should be 'substantial'. This means, in my judgment, that the reason which the employer adopted as his ground for discrimination must carry real weight and thus be of substance. However, the word 'substantial' does not mean that the employer must necessarily have reached the best conclusion that could be reached in the light of all known medical science. Employers are not obliged to search for the Holy Grail. It is sufficient if their conclusion is one which on a critical examination is found to have substance. Thus a reason which on analysis is meretricious would not be a 'substantial' reason. It would fail to meet the test in s.5(3).

A tribunal faced with a claim of justification may well find it helpful to proceed by asking the following questions:

What was the employee's disability?

What was the discrimination by the employer in respect of the employee's disability?

What was the employer's reason for treating the employee in this way?

Is there a sufficient connection between the employer's reason for discrimination and the circumstances of the particular case (including those of the employer)?

Is that reason on examination a substantial reason?

The first three of those questions involve pure questions of fact. The fourth and fifth questions, however, involve questions of judgment. The latter questions may involve hearing expert evidence, but the employment tribunal should not conduct an enquiry into what is the best course of action to take in all the circumstances of the case. Nor are the tribunal required to be persuaded themselves. They are not entitled to find that the employer's reason for the discrimination was not justified simply because they take the view that some conclusion, other than that to which the employer came, would have been preferable. Nor can they conclude that justification has not been shown simply because they entertain doubts as to the correctness of the employer's conclusion. If credible arguments exist to support the employer's decision, the employment tribunal may not hold that the reason for the discrimination is not 'substantial'. If, however, the employer's reason is outside the band of responses which a reasonable employer might have adopted, the reason would not be substantial. (This test was applied by the Court of Appeal in the different context of unfair dismissal in *Post Office v Foley* [2000] IRLR 827.) In short, so far as the second limb of s.5(3) of the 1995 Act is concerned, justification is shown provided that the employer's reason is supportable.

Statute can provide different levels of protection for employees in different situations depending on the meaning of the language which Parliament has used. The scale ranges from 'de novo', or complete retrial of the issue which the employer had to decide at one end of the scale – which is the test which the employment tribunal applied in this case – to absolute deference to the employer's decision provided he acts in good faith, at the other end of the scale. There are many intermediate points on this scale. The test in this case of sufficient connection and supportable grounds represents one of these intermediate points.

The fact that the true construction of a particular statutory provision indicates that the protection given to an employee in one respect is not the maximum protection that could have been conferred or as great as the protection conferred in other areas of statute law is not of itself a reason for rejecting that construction. The right level is a matter for Parliament. It may be that in the case of disability discrimination Parliament had in mind that an employer has to balance the interests of the employee with a disability with those of fellow employees and indeed also of members of the public. Accordingly, I reject Miss Tether's submission that it would be surprising if the criteria for review under s.5(3) [DDA] were less rigorous than, for instance, under the [RRA] or [SDA].

[3.52] J Davies, 'A Cuckoo In The Nest? A "Range Of Reasonable Responses", Justification and The Disability Discrimination Act 1995' (2003) 32 *Industrial Law Journal* 164, 170-71 (footnotes omitted)

On Pill LJ's reasoning, the quality of the investigative process will be a crucial factor in determining the reasonableness of the resulting response. In stipulating that only decisions based on 'proper' risk assessments or 'properly formed' opinion of 'suitably qualified' medical experts are capable of falling within a range of reasonable responses, Pill LJ effectively establishes a lower boundary of the range as applied within the DDA. 'Proper' investigation acts as the gatekeeper to the range of reasonable responses. Only once this threshold has been crossed, may an otherwise discriminatory decision fall within the range and so be justified.

A standard of 'proper' investigation, if rigorously applied by employment tribunals, offers a basis for objective assessment of employers' reasons for their discriminatory decisions. However, objectivity is likely to be undermined both by the realities of tribunal adjudication, and by application of the range of reasonable responses test to employers' decisions. On a practical level, what are 'proper' investigations? How are tribunals to identify them? Do they have the expertise to do so? In attempting to find a workable way forward, Pill LJ's reasoning creates new complexities of adjudication for tribunals . . .

Although neither of the other two judges in Jones considers explicitly the subtle distinctions in Pill LJ's reasoning between the investigative process and decisions, Kay LJ endorses 'entirely' the reasoning and conclusions of his colleague, while Arden LJ agrees with both the other judgements. On her analysis, however, 'proper' risk assessment or medical evidence is relevant only to whether a reason is substantial, not to whether it is material.

Pill LJ's approach is clearly fuelled by the need, on the facts of *Jones*, to balance employers' protective duties to meet health and safety requirements with Parliament's intention to create equality of employment opportunity for disabled persons. The range of reasonable responses formula offered the neat solution of an apparently objective test of employers' decisions. However, the test has a chequered history even in its home environment . . .

Jones imposes a very low threshold for the justification of discrimination. There are, however, two very important provisos. In the first place, section 3A(6) DDA (extracted above) provides that an employer cannot justify less favourable treatment unless, in a case in which a duty to adjust applied, the less favourable treatment would have been justified even if the employer had complied with the duty. Secondly, the *Jones* test does not apply in relation to the justification of a failure to make reasonable adjustments.

An example of the application of section 3A(6) DDA is provided by the Code of Practice on Employment which suggests that: '[if] an employee who uses a wheelchair is not promoted, solely because the work station for the higher post is inaccessible to wheelchairs—though it could readily be made so by rearrangement of the furniture . . . [t]he refusal of promotion would . . . not be justified'. Section 3A(6) was successfully relied on appeal by the claimant in *Paul* v *National Probation Service* [2004] IRLR 190. Mr Paul, who suffered from a chronic depressive illness, was rejected for a position with the respondents because of the assessment of the employer's occupational health adviser that the job would be unduly stressful for him given his medical history. The adviser reached this conclusion without having discussed the claimant's case with his consultant psychiatrist, relying instead on a medical report from his GP (who did not know the claimant well and had not been involved in the treatment of his depression). The GP's report did not, further, deal with the claimant's fitness for the position sought or his ability to deal with stress. An employment tribunal dismissed the claimant's DDA challenge on the ground that the discrimination involved in denying him the position was justified within the DDA, applying the Court of Appeal's decision in *Jones* v *Post Office*. The EAT overruled, in part on the basis that the tribunal had not considered the employers' duty to adjust. The occupational health adviser's assessments, which were part of the employers' appointment arrangements, placed the claimant at a substantial disadvantage, and reasonable steps might have included the obtaining of specialist advice from the claimant's consultant, discussions with the claimant himself, a reference back to the occupational health adviser and possible adjustments to the job itself.

Secondly, the *Jones* test does not apply in relation to the justification of a failure to make reasonable adjustments. We saw, above, that the justification defence has been removed in cases in which *employers* fail to comply with duties to make reasonable adjustments in line with the DDA. It remains available outside the employment context. But much of its sting has been removed by the decision of the Court of Appeal in *Collins* v *Royal National Theatre Board Ltd* [2004] IRLR 395 in which the Court ruled that a failure to make reasonable adjustments could not be justified by reference to factors which had already been taken into account in deciding whether an adjustment was reasonable. The decision appears to signal a retreat on the part of the Court from the very permissive approach in *Jones*.

3.6.2 Duties of reasonable accommodation

The DDA does not expressly prohibit indirect discrimination. Its perceived failure to regulate this type of discrimination formed one of the most significant grounds for criticism of the Act. But the duty of reasonable adjustment provided for by the Act (immediately below), together with its prohibition on 'disability-related discrimination' [3.23] go a long way towards regulating what would otherwise be dealt with as indirect discrimination. Here we consider the duty to adjust and then the question whether the concept of indirect discrimination should, in addition, be introduced into the DDA.

Prior to its amendment in October 2004 the duty to make reasonable adjustments was set out in section 6(1) DDA and was relatively limited (applying only in relation to 'any arrangements made by or on behalf of an employer' and 'any physical feature of premises occupied by an employer', which 'place[d] the disabled person concerned at a substantial disadvantage in comparison with persons who are not disabled'. Difficulties arose as to whether the duty to adjust arose in relation to the provision of personal assistance (*Kenny* v *Hampshire Constabulary* [1999] ICR 27), dismissal (*Clark* v *Novacold* [1999] ICR 951) and the essential functions of a person's job (*Archibald* v *Fife Council (Scotland)* [2004] ICR 954). It is no longer necessary to consider these cases, as section 6 DDA (which originally set out the duty to adjust as it related to employment) has been replaced (as of October 2004) by section 4A DDA which provides as follows:

[3.53] Disability Discrimination Act 1995, section 4A

> S.4A(1) Where—
> (a) a provision, criterion or practice applied by or on behalf of an employer, or
> (b) any physical feature of premises occupied by the employer
> places the disabled person concerned at a substantial disadvantage in comparison with persons who are not disabled, it is the duty of the employer to take such steps as it is reasonable, in all the circumstances of the case, for him to have to take in order to prevent the provision, criterion or practice, or feature, having that effect.
>
> (3) Nothing in this section imposes any duty on an employer in relation to a disabled person if the employer does not know, and could not reasonably be expected to know—
> (a) in the case of an applicant or potential applicant, that the disabled person concerned is, or may be, an applicant for the employment; or
> (b) in any case, that that person has a disability and is likely to be affected in the way mentioned in subsection (1).

Section 3A(2) DDA provides that a failure to comply with the duty imposed by section 4A amounts to discrimination, the previously available justification defence having been removed in this context in October 2004. Section 18B DDA sets out factors to which tribunals are required to have regard in determining whether any particular step would have been reasonable for an employer to take. These include, *inter alia*, 'the extent to which taking the step would prevent the effect in relation to which the duty is imposed', questions of practicability, costs and disruption, the availability to the employer of resources and outside assistance. Among the examples of the steps provided by section 18B(2) are the making of adjustments to premises, transfer of the disabled employee and/or reallocation of some of his or duties, changes to hours or place of work, the provision of time-off, mentoring, special equipment, assistance from (for example) a reader or interpreter, etc. The Code of Practice on Employment and Occupation provides concrete examples of the types of steps which might be required of employers, suggesting (for example) that 'making adjustments to premises' might include: 'widening a doorway, providing a ramp or moving furniture for a wheelchair user; relocating light switches, door handles or shelves for someone who has difficulty in reaching; providing appropriate contrast in décor to help the safe mobility of a visually impaired person'.

An employer will not fail to comply with the duty to adjust in a case in which it does not know (and ought not to have known) of the employee's disability (*Callaghan v Glasgow CC* [2001] IRLR 724, EAT). But once the employer does have knowledge (actual or constructive) it is for the employer rather than the disabled worker to determine any reasonable steps which might be taken. This is not to say that the employee cannot make suggestions, or that s/he ought not to be consulted (quite the contrary). But in *Cosgrove v Caesar & Howie* [2001] IRLR 653 the EAT ruled that a tribunal had erred in law in finding against the Claimant because 'neither [she] nor her medical witness were able to state what adjustments the respondents could have made to improve her situation and to facilitate an eventual return'. According to Lindsay J (P): 'the duty to make adjustments . . . is upon the employer' and the fact that neither the Claimant nor her GP could think of any useful adjustment did not entitle the tribunal in that case to leap to the conclusion that no useful adjustment could have been made. And in *Mid Staffordshire General Hospital NHS Trust v Cambridge* [2003] IRLR 566 the EAT ruled that the duty to make reasonable adjustments included a preliminary duty on employers to put themselves in a position to determine suitable adjustments which might be made by making enquiries as to what is required to eliminate a disabled person's disadvantage.

The failure of the DDA to prohibit indirect discrimination in terms appears to be consistent with the Employment Equality Directive which provides that:

[3.54] Council Directive 2000/78/ EC (the Employment Equality Directive), Article 2(b)

Article 2(b) . . . indirect discrimination shall be taken to occur where an apparently neutral provision, criterion or practice would put persons having a particular religion or belief, a particular disability, a particular age, or a particular sexual orientation at a particular disadvantage compared with other persons unless:
(i)   that provision, criterion or practice is objectively justified by a legitimate aim and the means of achieving that aim are appropriate and necessary, *or* [our emphasis]
(ii) as regards persons with a particular disability, the employer or any person or organisation to whom this Directive applies, is obliged, under national legislation, to

> take appropriate measures in line with the principles contained in Article 5 in order
> to eliminate disadvantages entailed by such provision, criterion or practice.

The DDA was amended to ensure, in the employment context, that a duty to adjust would apply in every case in which 'an apparently neutral provision, criterion or practice would put persons having a particular . . . disability . . . at a particular disadvantage compared with other persons'. It is possible, however, that the UK approach is flawed inasmuch as the duty to adjust applies only where the disabled person is placed at a '*substantial* disadvantage in comparison with persons who are not disabled' (section 4A(1)) and requires an employer to take only '*such steps as it is reasonable*, in all the circumstances of the case, for him to have to take in order to prevent the provision, criterion or practice, or feature, having that effect' (our emphasis). The Directive uses the term 'particular' rather than 'substantial' and disapplies the prohibition on indirect discrimination only in cases in which 'as regards persons with a particular disability, *the employer . . . is obliged*, under national legislation, *to take appropriate measures* in line with the principles contained in Article 5 in order to eliminate disadvantages entailed by such provision, criterion or practice' (our emphasis).

[3.55] Council Directive 2000/78/ EC (the Employment Equality Directive), Article 5

> In order to guarantee compliance with the principle of equal treatment in relation to persons with disabilities, reasonable accommodation shall be provided. This means that employers shall take appropriate measures, where needed in a particular case, to enable a person with a disability to have access to, participate in, or advance in employment, or to undergo training, unless such measures would impose a disproportionate burden on the employer. This burden shall not be disproportionate when it is sufficiently remedied by measures existing within the framework of the disability policy of the Member State concerned.

It is arguable that, in a case in which no steps could reasonably be taken under the DDA, the Directive requires indirect discrimination to be prohibited in the sense that the operation of the provision, criterion, or practice or the existence of the feature of the premises would have to be justified in order to comply with the Directive.

3.7 Exceptions

The various legislative provisions contain a number of exceptions to their prohibitions on discrimination. These are too numerous and scattered to discuss here, but examples include sections 4 and 10 RRA, which partly disapply the prohibition on discrimination on grounds of colour and nationality (but not 'race or ethnic or national origin') in the case of households and small partnerships respectively and section 74 of the Act which permits Ministers to restrict public sector employment 'to persons of particular birth, nationality, descent or residence'; sections 17–19 SDA which permit some (albeit limited) discrimination in respect of police and prison officers and discrimination in the appointment of ministers of religion; section 64(7) DDA which provides that the Act has no application to the armed forces (though a wide variety of other exceptions, such as those relating to fire-fighters, prison officers and the police, were swept away in October 2004 when the reach of the Act was extended to reflect that of the RRA and SDA by covering discrimination against barristers, advocates and office holders, *inter alia*, and discrimination by qualifying bodies). There are also varying geographical limitations on the scope of the various legislative provisions. More important exceptions include those relating to national security, typical of which is section 42 RRA, and acts done under statutory authority (section 41 RRA, sections 51 and 51A SDA, section 59 DDA). Constraints of space preclude discussion of these provisions which are considered in detail in A McColgan, *Discrimination: Text, Cases and Materials* 2nd edn (Oxford, Hart, 2005). What will be discussed here, with one exception, are the genuine occupational qualification and genuine occupational requirement defences established under the various discrimination provisions.

Before we turn to the GOQ/GOR defences it is perhaps appropriate to mention one very significant exception in the SORs, Regulation 25 of which provides that that they do not 'render unlawful anything which prevents or restricts access to a benefit by reference to marital status'. The provision rests not on any article of the Employment Equality Directive but rather on Recital 22 of the Preamble to the Directive which provides that the measure 'is without prejudice to national laws on marital status and the benefits dependent thereon'. The effect of Regulation 25 is to exclude from the scope of the Regulations discrimination in relation to, for example, surviving spouses' pensions, although they will prohibit discrimination between same sex and opposite sex *unmarried* couples. This provision was unsuccessfully challenged in a judicial review claim brought against the government by a number of trade unions. Insofar as relevant here, however, the Claimants argued that the Regulations were *ultra vires* the European Communities Act 1972 (under which they were passed) because they were incompatible with the obligations imposed by the Directive. Richards J ruled that the legislative intention behind the Directive was clear from Recital 22 of the Preamble, and that Regulation 25 did not interfere with Article 8 ECHR or breach the non-discrimination guarantee laid down by Article 14 of the Convention.

Turning to the the original, GOQ defences, sections 7 and 5 of the SDA and RRA respectively set out a number of situations in which discrimination is expressly permitted. Section 7(1) SDA provides (section 5(1) RRA being in equivalent terms) that, in relation to appointments to particular jobs and promotions into particular jobs, the prohibition on sex discrimination does not apply where 'being a man [or a woman] is a genuine occupational qualification for the job'.

[3.56] Sex Discrimination Act 1975, section 7

S.7(2) Being a man [or a woman] is a genuine occupational qualification for a job only where—

(a) the essential nature of the job calls for a man for reasons of physiology (excluding physical strength or stamina) or, in dramatic performances or other entertainment, for reasons of authenticity, so that the essential nature of the job would be materially different if carried out by a woman; or

(b) the job needs to be held by a man to preserve decency or privacy because—

   (i) it is likely to involve physical contact with men in circumstances where they might reasonably object to its being carried out by a woman, or

   (ii) the holder of the job is likely to do his work in circumstances where men might reasonably object to the presence of a woman because they are in a state of undress or are using sanitary facilities; or

(ba) the job is likely to involve the holder of the job doing his work, or living, in a private home and needs to be held by a man because objection might reasonably be taken to allowing to a woman—

   (i) the degree of physical or social contact with a person living in the home, or

   (ii) the knowledge of intimate details of such a person's life, which is likely, because of the nature or circumstances of the job or of the home, to be allowed to, or available to, the holder of the job; or]

(c) the nature or location of the establishment makes it impracticable for the holder of the job to live elsewhere than in premises provided by the employer, and—

   (i) the only such premises which are available for persons holding that kind of job are lived in, or normally lived in, by men and are not equipped with separate sleeping accommodation for women and sanitary facilities which could be used by women in privacy from men, and

   (ii) it is not reasonable to expect the employer either to equip those premises with such accommodation and facilities or to provide other premises for women; or

(d) the nature of the establishment, or of the part of it within which the work is done, requires the job to be held by a man because—

   (i) it is, or is part of, a hospital, prison or other establishment for persons requiring special care, supervision or attention, and

   (ii) those persons are all men (disregarding any woman whose presence is exceptional), and

   (iii) it is reasonable, having regard to the essential character of the establishment or that part, that the job should not be held by a woman; or

(e) the holder of the job provides individuals with personal services promoting their welfare or education, or similar personal services, and those services can most effectively be provided by a man, or

(g) the job needs to be held by a man because it is likely to involve the performance of duties outside the United Kingdom in a country whose laws or customs are such that the duties could not, or could not effectively, be performed by a woman, or

(h) the job is one of two to be held by a married couple.

(3) Subsection (2) applies where some only of the duties of the job fall within paragraph (a), (b), (c) or (d) as well as where all of them do.

(4) Paragraph (a), (b), (c), (d) (e) . . . or (g) of subsection (2) does not apply in relation to the filling of a vacancy at a time when the employer already has male employees—

   (a) who are capable of carrying out the duties falling within the paragraph, and

   (b) whom it would be reasonable to employ on those duties; and

   (c) whose numbers are sufficient to meet the employer's likely requirements in respect of those duties without undue inconvenience.

The operation of section 7(4) is illustrated by the following decision.

[3.57] *Etam plc v Rowan* [1989] IRLR 150 (EAT)

Mr Rowan applied, unsuccessfully for a job in a woman's wear shop. He was refused employment because the job involved changing room duties, the employers arguing that section 7(2)(b) SDA applied. His claim of sex discrimination was accepted by a tribunal, the employer's GOQ defence being rejected on the basis that there were 15 other sales staff in the shop at any given time who could between them undertake the changing room duties without undue inconvenience. The employers appealed, unsuccessfully, to the EAT. Despite the fact that a considerable proportion of a sales assistant's time might ordinarily be spent on changing room duties, the tribunal was entitled to find against the employers on the basis that the unsuccessful applicant 'would have been able to adequately carry out the bulk of the job of sales assistant, and such parts as he could not carry out could easily have been done by other sales assistants without causing any inconvenience or difficulty for the appellants'.

Section 7A SDA provides that discrimination in connection with gender reassignment is not unlawful under that Act if being *either* a man *or* a woman would be a GOQ for the job *and* the employer can show (section 7A(b)) 'that the treatment is reasonable in view of the circumstances described in the relevant [GOQ] and any other relevant circumstances'. Section 7B goes on to provide a number of additional GOQs applicable exclusively in connection with gender reassignment where:

[3.58] Sex Discrimination Act 1975, section 7B

S.7B(2)
(a) the job involves the holder of the job being liable to be called upon to perform intimate physical searches pursuant to statutory powers;
(b) the job is likely to involve the holder of the job doing his work, or living, in a private home and needs to be held otherwise than by a person who is undergoing or has undergone gender reassignment, because objection might reasonably be taken to allowing to such a person—
  (i) the degree of physical or social contact with a person living in the home, or
  (ii) the knowledge of intimate details of such a person's life, which is likely, because of the nature or circumstances of the job or of the home, to be allowed to, or available to, the holder of the job;
(c) the nature or location of the establishment makes it impracticable for the holder of the job to live elsewhere than in premises provided by the employer, and—
  (i) the only such premises which are available for persons holding that kind of job are such that reasonable objection could be taken, for the purpose of preserving decency and privacy, to the holder of the job sharing accommodation and facilities with either sex whilst undergoing gender reassignment, and
  (ii) it is not reasonable to expect the employer either to equip those premises withsuiable accommodation or to make alternative arrangements; or
(d) the holder of the job provides vulnerable individuals with personal services promoting their welfare, or similar personal services, and in the reasonable view of

the employer those services cannot be effectively provided by a person whilst that person is undergoing gender reassignment.

(3) Subsection (2) does not apply in relation to discrimination against a person whose gender has become the acquired gender under the Gender Recognition Act 2004.

All GOQs apply in relation to dismissal as well as recruitment in the case of gender reassignment (by contrast with their application in the case of sex). This is necessary to cover gender reassignments which take place after recruitment. It should be noted here that, once a person has acquired a new gender under the Gender Recognition Act 2004, they are to be considered as being of that new gender for all employment-related purposes and at that stage only the normal GOQs would be applicable to them (i.e., if a man reassigns to become a woman, she will be subject to any GOQs applicable to *women*, not to men).

The RRA provides both a GOQ defence, which is applicable to discrimination on grounds of nationality and colour (which does not amount to discrimination on grounds of 'race, ethnic or national origin') and a GOR defence which is applicable to discrimination on grounds of 'race, ethnic or national origin'. The GOQ defence is similar in form to that set out in the SDA, though the circumstances in which the defence operates is considerably narrower, section 5 providing that 'being of a particular racial group is a genuine occupational qualification for the job' where:

[3.59] Race Relations Act 1976, section 5(2)

S.5(2)
   (a)   the job involves participation in a dramatic performance or other entertainment in a capacity for which a person of that racial group is required for reasons of authenticity; or
   (b)   the job involves participation as an artist's or photographic model in the production of a work of art, visual image or sequence of visual images for which a person of that racial group is required for reasons of authenticity; or
   (c)   the job involves working in a place where food or drink is (for payment or not) provided to and consumed by members of the public or a section of the public in a particular setting for which, in that job, a person of that racial group is required for reasons of authenticity; or
   (d)   the holder of the job provides persons of that racial group with personal services promoting their welfare, and those services can most effectively be provided by a person of that racial group.

Section 5(3) & (4) are materially the same as section 7(3) & (4) SDA, reproduced above. The operation of the GOQ defence has been criticised in relation both to the SDA and the RRA. David Pannick, for example, suggested (*Sex Discrimination Law*, Oxford, OUP, 1985) that the provision 'more often furthers the objectives of those who opposed the 1975 Act than the objectives of those who supported the legislation'. He was critical of its attempt to deal with 'three separate types of cases, those of physical, functional, and social differences between the sexes'. Whereas physical differences made some jobs impossible of performance by persons of one or other sex, Pannick suggested that the recognition of 'functional' differences by provisions such as subsections 7(2)(d) and (e) was 'hard to reconcile with the fundamental premiss of the 1975 Act that one should consider persons as individuals irrespective of the qualities commonly possessed by or associated with their sex' and 'inconsistent with the principle that sex is not a GOQ merely because of customer preference'. He warned, further, that section 7(2)(a) might permit a men's club to employ (women-only) topless waiting staff, though generally speaking serving alcohol would not be a job whose 'essential nature' would be 'materially different if carried out by a man', and was generally critical of the social differences recognized by the defence, pointing out the vagueness of the 'criterion of reasonableness in section 7(2)(c)(ii)' and pointing out, as Baroness Seear had done in Parliament, that 'in other European countries "it is far more common for men and women to share certain premises and conveniences" (for example, train couchettes)':

[3.60] D. Pannick, Sex Discrimination Law (Oxford, OUP, 1985)

> The question under section 7(2)(c)(ii) is whether it is reasonable to expect the employer to provide separate sleeping accommodation and private sanitary facilities for each sex, not whether it is reasonable to refuse to employ women because there are no such facilities provided. Section 7(2)(c) adopts a very conservative approach to this question, allowing employers to refuse jobs to women even if women are prepared to share facilities with men, and even if those men are prepared to share the facilities with the women. It is not a precondition for the applicability of section 7(2)(c), as it is for the applicability of section 7(2)(b), that relevant men (or women) 'might reasonably object' to the employment of members of the other sex. Section 7(2)(c) needs amendment to include such a precondition . . .

Pannick went on to question the need for section 7(2)(d) in cases in which ss.7(2)(b), 7(2)(c) or 7(2)(e) did not apply, to point out the distasteful nature of enshrining (by section 7(2)(g)) in domestic law 'the prejudices of other countries' and to question the rationale of section 7(2)(h) which, it appears, is intended to permit 'an employer, taking on a married couple for two jobs, to specify which job should be done by which spouse'. These provisions do not appear to have been much relied upon.

Turning to consider the compatibility of the SDA's GOQ defence with the Equal Treatment Directive, Article 2(2) of that Directive provides that the general prohibition on sex discrimination 'shall be without prejudice to the right of Member States to exempt from its field of application those occupational activities and, where appropriate, the training leading thereto, for which, by reason of their nature or the context in which they are carried out, the sex of the worker constitutes a determining factor'. Article 2(3) also permits 'provisions regarding the protection of women, particularly as regards pregnancy and maternity', while Article 9(2) requires that Member States 'periodically assess the occupational activities referred to in Article 2(2) in order to decide, in the light of social developments, whether there is justification for maintaining the exclusions concerned'.

Articles 2(2) and 2(3) have been considered by the ECJ on a number of occasions, generally in cases concerning restrictions on women in the armed services (though see Case 165/82 *Commission of the European Communities v UK* [1984] ECR 3431, in which the ECJ permitted discrimination in access to midwifery). These decisions have been less than radical, that Court accepting in *Johnston v Royal Ulster Constabulary* that it was not necessarily inconsistent with the Directive to prohibit women from carrying firearms despite the very serious implications for their employment in the service (Ms Johnston had been made redundant in pursuit of a policy of not renewing the fixed term contracts of women full-time reservists on the basis that a significant proportion of general police duties required the carrying of firearms). The RUC purported to justify the ban on the grounds 'that [1] if women were armed they might become a more frequent target for assassination and [2] their fire-arms could fall into the hands of their assailants, that [3] the public would not welcome the carrying of fire-arms by women, which would conflict too much with the ideal of an unarmed police force, and that [4] armed policewomen would be less effective in police work in the social field with families and children in which the services of policewomen are particularly appreciated'.

It will be noted that the reasons 1 and 2 appear to apply equally as between men and women, unless women are more vulnerable than men to (1) assassination and (2) losing their weapons. The Respondents did not seek to explain why armed women constitute a greater departure from the ideal of an unarmed police than do armed men, while the question of public opinion simply incorporated discriminatory views into the analysis. Finally, the argument that unarmed policewomen were rendered more able to function in a social work capacity itself rested on sex discrimination in the allocation of this type of work. But the ECJ did not rule against the UK, instead leaving it for the referring court (an industrial tribunal) to determine whether Article 2(2) applied 'having regard to the specific duties which [the claimant] is required to carry out'.

[3.61] Case 222/84 *Johnston v Chief Constable of the Royal Ulster Constabulary* [1986] 5 ECR 1651 (ECJ)

Judgment:

Article 2(2) . . . being a derogation from an individual right laid down in the directive, must be interpreted strictly. However, it must be recognized that the context in which the occupational activity of members of an armed police force are carried out is determined by the environment in which that activity is carried out. In this regard, the possibility cannot be excluded that in a situation characterized by serious internal disturbances the carrying of fire-arms by policewomen might create additional risks of their being assassinated and might therefore be contrary to the requirements of public safety.

In such circumstances, the context of certain policing activities may be such that the sex of police officers constitutes a determining factor for carrying them out. If that is so, a member state may therefore restrict such tasks, and the training leading thereto, to men. In such a case, as is clear from article 9(2) of the directive, the member states have a duty to assess periodically the activities concerned in order to decide whether, in the light of social developments, the derogation from the general scheme of the directive may still be maintained.

It must also be borne in mind that, in determining the scope of any derogation from an individual right such as the equal treatment of men and women provided for by the directive, the principle of proportionality, one of the general principles of law underlying the community legal order, must be observed. That principle requires that derogations remain within the limits of what is appropriate and necessary for achieving the aim in view and requires the principle of equal treatment to be reconciled as far as possible with the requirements of public safety which constitute the decisive factor as regards the context of the activity in question . . .

. . . it is for the national court to say whether the reasons on which the Chief Constable based his decision are in fact well founded and justify the specific measure taken in Mrs Johnston's case. It is also for the national court to ensure that the principle of proportionality is observed and to determine whether the refusal to renew Mrs Johnston's contract could not be avoided by allocating to women duties which, without jeopardising the aims pursued, can be performed without fire-arms.

The tribunal ruled in favour of Mrs Johnston and others, the ruling resulting in the payment of over a million pounds (the highest settlement at that time) by the RUC and, in 1994, in the arming of women in that police service. But in Case 273/97 *Sirdar v The Army Board & Secretary of State for Defence* [1999] ECR I–7403 the ECJ again refused to prohibit the differential treatment of women in the armed services. There the claimant had been refused a position in the marines with the effect that she was made redundant from her original army position as a chef. Women were not permitted to serve in any capacity in the marines because of the principle applied in that regiment of 'interoperability', i.e., that all marines must be capable of fighting in a commando unit coupled with the ban on women engaging in active combat service in the British forces. The ECJ confirmed that the armed services were, in principle, subject to the provisions of the Equal Treatment Directive and, as in *Johnston*, ruled that Article 2(2) had to be read narrowly and subject to Article 9(2) of the Directive. But 'depending on the circumstances, national authorities have a certain degree of discretion when adopting measures which they consider to be necessary in order to guarantee public security in a Member State' and the unique nature of the Marines as 'the 'point of the arrow head' was such that 'the competent authorities were entitled, in the exercise of their discretion as to whether to maintain the exclusion in question in the light of social developments, and without abusing the principle of proportionality, to come to the view that the specific conditions for deployment of the assault units of which the Royal Marines are composed, and in particular the rule of interoperability to which they are subject, justified their composition remaining exclusively male'.

The EOC called on the government 'to urgently review all of the remaining exclusions of women to determine whether they comply with the ECJ's test (i.e., whether they had the purpose of guaranteeing public security and were appropriate and necessary to achieve that aim'. The Ministry of Defence paid Ms Sirdar £2000 'as a token of its regret' for the distress caused her and confirmed its commitment to 'equal opportunities so far as is consistent with the operational combat effectiveness of the Armed Forces' although its subsequent review resulted in a decision to maintain the status quo (*Women in the Armed Forces* (May 2002)). Subsequently, in Case 285/98 *Kreil v Germany* [2000] ECR I–0069, the ECJ ruled that Germany's complete ban on women in military service (other than non-armed positions in the medical and military-music services) was not saved by Article 2(2). The Equal Treatment Amendment Directive replaces Article 2(3) with a provision materially identical to the GOR to be found in the Racial and Employment Equality Directives. Somewhat surprisingly, the draft Employment Equality (Sex Discrimination) Regulations 2005 do not propose any amendment to the SDA's GOQ defence, save to insert a requirement of proportionality in s.7B(2)(a) **[3.58]**.

The GOQ provided by the RRA has also come in for criticism, the CRE arguing (in *Reform of the Race Relations Act 1976*, 1998) that 'The current criterion of 'authenticity' is too wide [in that it] enables the unjustifiable underrepresentation of ethnic minorities in theatre, opera, cinema, television drama etc to continue indefinitely' and that 'the criterion of racial 'authenticity' should not be relevant to future employment patterns in the catering industry in Britain'. The Commission argued that the 'authenticity' exception should 'be restricted to cases in which the employer could demonstrate that being of a particular racial group was an essential, defining feature of the job', a formulation which would have enabled people to be selected on racial grounds in order to test for race discrimination. For all of the criticism, however, it appears that the GOQ defences have been relatively rarely relied upon. In addition to the SDA cases mentioned above there are a couple of appellate decisions under the RRA both of which will be briefly considered. *Lambeth* v *CRE*, deals with the boundaries of section 5(2)(d), but could equally be applied to section 7(2)(e) SDA. It has been regarded as one of the most significant decisions on the scope of the GOQ defences, but is of limited importance now given that the GOQ defence no longer applies to discrimination on grounds of 'race, ethnic or national origin' and it is difficult to envisage how colour or nationality falling outside these categories could impact on a person's ability to provide personal services promoting welfare to persons of a group defined by colour or nationality as the case may be. The equivalent provision continues to apply under the SDA although this Act's GOQ defence ought to be replaced by a GOR defence by October 2005 in order to comply with the amended Equal Treatment Directive. *Tottenham Green v Marshall* concerns the question how important the duties in respect of which the GOQ is pleaded must be to the overall nature of the job in order that the GOQ might apply. Again, it is strictly relevant now only to the GOQ defences which are of limited application.

[3.62] *Lambeth London Borough Council v Commission for Racial Equality* [1990] ICR 768 (CA)

The CRE challenged advertisements which stipulated African-Caribbean or Asian applicants for jobs in the Council's housing department. Blacks and Asians together comprised over 50% of Council tenants and the advertisement was prompted by the Council's policy of making the housing benefits system 'more sensitive to the needs and experiences of black [and Asian] people'. In pursuit of this aim the Council had reserved two positions in the housing benefits section for African-Caribbean/Asian workers. A tribunal ruled that, the jobs being of a managerial or administrative nature involving limited contact with the public, they did not involve 'personal services' and the Council, accordingly, had failed to make out the section 5(2)(d) defence. The tribunal further ruled that the racial groups of the post holder and the recipient of his services were not sufficiently identified so as to establish that the holder and the recipient were of the same racial group. Both the EAT ([1989] ICR 641) and the Court of Appeal rejected the Council's appeal.

Balcombe LJ:
The posts advertised were that of group manager and assistant head of housing benefits

in the local authority's housing benefits department . . . the posts advertised were within the private sector department. The head of that department has an assistant head and, apart from the payments and control group, has three group managers, who in turn control team leaders and housing benefit officers, who are those officers spread through the borough and who are the first point of contact for the members of the public . . .

The services provided by the local authority's housing benefits department undoubtedly promote the welfare of the recipients to those benefits, but the rest of the phrase is qualified by the word 'personal.' 'Personal' is defined by the Oxford English Dictionary as 'Of, pertaining to, concerning or affecting the individual or self (as opposed, variously, to other persons, the general community, etc . . .); individual; private; one's own.' The use of the word 'personal' indicates that the identity of the giver and the recipient of the services is important. I agree with the appeal tribunal . . . when they say that the Act appears to contemplate direct contact between the giver and the recipient—mainly face-to-face or where there could be susceptibility in personal, physical contact. Where language or a knowledge and understanding of cultural and religious background are of importance, then those services may be most effectively provided by a person of a particular racial group . . .

the decision in any particular case whether the holder of a particular job provides persons of a particular group with personal services promoting their welfare is a question of mixed law and fact, and that unless the industrial tribunal have come to a decision which is wrong in law, neither the appeal tribunal nor this court can interfere. The industrial tribunal held that the holders of the jobs advertised, being managerial positions, did not provide personal services promoting the welfare of persons of a particular racial group. I can find no error of law in that decision. On this ground alone I would dismiss this appeal . . .

Mann LJ concurred on the basis that the question was one of fact for the tribunal to decide, its conclusion being susceptible to interference by the higher court only if 'irrational'. Mustill LJ agreed with both speeches.

[3.63] *Tottenham Green Under Fives' Centre v Marshall (No 2)* **[1991] ICR 320 (EAT)**

The claimant, a white man, claimed that the centre's refusal to interview him was unlawful under the RRA. The Centre, which attempted to maintain racial diversity among both children and staff, had advertised for an African-Caribbean worker to replace one of the two workers of that racial group who was leaving (the Centre had 84% African-Caribbean children, five of the seven staff were white). It argued that the post was covered by section 5(2)(d) RRA ('the holder of the job provides persons of that racial group with personal services promoting their welfare, and those services can most effectively be provided by a person of that racial group'). The centre argued, in particular, that an African-Caribbean worker would be more effective at maintaining the cultural background link for the children of African-Caribbean background; dealing with the parents and discussing those matters with them; reading and speaking, where necessary, in dialect; and generally looking after their skin and health, including plaiting their hair. A tribunal ruled in Mr Marshall's favour on the ground that reading and speaking in patois was the only factor in respect of which a non-African-Caribbean worker could not be equally as effective, and that this was the 'least emphasised' of the centre's justifications, 'in the nature of a desirable extra and no more'. The EAT allowed the centre's appeal, ruling that the tribunal were not entitled to disregard a factor relied upon in relation to a GOQ defence unless it was either so trivial as properly to be regrded as *de minimis* or was 'a sham or smokescreen'. Neither was relevant in this case and the tribunal had not been entitled to exclude the operation of the GOQ on the ground that the disputed duty was 'relatively unimportant but not trivial'.

The implementation of the new Race Equality Directive has resulted in the amendment of the RRA which now provides a GOR (but not a GOQ) defence to discrimination on grounds of 'race, ethnic or national origins'. The draft Race Relations Act 1976 (Amendment) Regulations had proposed the amendment of s.5 RRA to apply to 'racial discrimination other than that which is referred to in section 4A', that is, discrimination on grounds of colour or nationality, but *not* discrimination on grounds of 'race or ethnic or national origins'. The RRA as amended, however, does not contain that provision, s.5 instead providing that it applies 'in cases where section 4A does not apply' and the explanatory notes describing section 4A as 'a new exception (from the discrimination in employment provisions)'. On its ordinary reading this appears to suggest that discrimination on grounds of 'race or ethnic or national origins' is subject both to the GOR defence provided by s.4A and also (where the discrimination at issue does not fall within s.4A) to the GOQ defence provided by s.5. If this is the case, the UK is almost certainly in breach of the principle of non-regression given that protection provided in relation to discrimination on grounds covered by the Racial Equality Directive has actually been subject to more, rather than fewer, exceptions.

[3.64] Race Relations Act 1976, section 4A

S.4A(1) In relation to discrimination on grounds of race or ethnic or national origins—
  (a) section 4(1)(a) or (c) does not apply to any employment; and
  (b) section 4(2)(b) does not apply to promotion or transfer to, or training for, any employment; and
  (c) section 4(2)(c) does not apply to dismissal from any employment;
where subsection (2) applies.

(2) This subsection applies where, having regard to the nature of the employment or the context in which it is carried out—
  (a) being of a particular race or of particular ethnic or national origins is a genuine and determining occupational requirement;
  (b) it is proportionate to apply that requirement in the particular case; and
  (c) either—
      (i) the person to whom that requirement is applied does not meet it, or
      (ii) the employer is not satisfied, and in all the circumstances it is reasonable for him not to be satisfied, that that person meets it.

The new GOR defence, consisting as it does of a principled test rather than a list of situations in which race discrimination is permitted, meets some of the criticisms made by the CRE in 1998 of the GOQ. But it also raises some interesting questions. Article 6(2) of the Racial Equality Directive provides that 'The implementation of this Directive shall under no circumstances constitute grounds for a reduction in the level of protection against discrimination already afforded by Member States in the fields covered by this Directive'. In some respects the new GOR is narrower than the old GOQ inasmuch as it applies only where race is a 'genuine and determining occupational requirement', and where its application in a particular case is *proportionate*. On the other hand, the GOR covers dismissal as well as refusal to appoint or promote whereas the GOQ did not; and GOR permits the defence of discrimination in situations falling outside the list contained in section 5 RRA. It also applies where the context in which a job is carried out, rather than the job itself, requires someone to be of a particular ethnic, racial or national origin. The CRE draft Code of Practice on Employment suggests (para. 2.38 b) that this would cover 'the post of a manager of a sexual health clinic for Pakistani women as well as the post of a counsellor'. To the extent that this is accurate it suggests a reduction (however desirable) in the protection from discrimination from the test established in the *Lambeth* case. Finally the GOR applies where 'the employer is not satisfied, and in all the circumstances it is reasonable for him not to be satisfied, that' the person to whom the GOR is applied does not meet it, as well as where this is actually the case. It remains to be seen whether the GOR will be subject to successful challenge on the grounds that it breaches Article 6(2) of the Racial Equality Directive.

The DDA contains no GOQ or GOR, direct discrimination being defined (as we saw above [3.17]) so as to capture only those cases in which a disabled person's 'relevant circumstances, including his abilities, are the same as, or not materially different from' those of the comparator. The SORs and RBRs both contain GOR defences based on the Employment Equality Directive which provides.

[3.65] Council Directive 2000/78/ EC (the Employment Equality Directive), Article 4

1 . . . Member States may provide that a difference of treatment which is based on a characteristic related to any of the grounds referred to in Article 1 shall not constitute discrimination where, by reason of the nature of the particular occupational activities concerned or of the context in which they are carried out, such a characteristic constitutes a genuine and determining occupational requirement, provided that the objective is legitimate and the requirement is proportionate.

2. Member States may maintain national legislation in force at the date of adoption of this Directive or provide for future legislation incorporating national practices existing at the date of adoption of this Directive pursuant to which, in the case of occupational activities within churches and other public or private organisations the ethos of which is based on religion or belief, a difference of treatment based on a person's religion or belief shall not constitute discrimination where, by reason of the nature of these activities or of the context in which they are carried out, a person's religion or belief constitute a genuine, legitimate and justified occupational requirement, having regard to the organisation's ethos. This difference of treatment shall be implemented taking account of Member States' constitutional provisions and principles, as well as the general principles of Community law, and should not justify discrimination on another ground.

Provided that its provisions are otherwise complied with, this Directive shall thus not prejudice the right of churches and other public or private organisations, the ethos of which is based on religion or belief, acting in conformity with national constitutions and laws, to require individuals working for them to act in good faith and with loyalty to the organisation's ethos.

Article 4(1) is transposed into domestic law by Regulation 7(1) of each of the RBRs and the SORs which provides that the prohibitions on discrimination in relation to recruitment, arrangements and offers of employment, promotion or transfer to, or training for, any employment; and dismissal from any employment shall not apply where:

[3.66] Employment Equality (Sexual Orientation) Regulations, Employment Equality (Religion and Belief) Regulations, Regulation 7

> Reg. 7(2) . . . having regard to the nature of the employment or the context in which it is carried out—
> (a) being of a particular religion or belief [sexual orientation] is a genuine and determining occupational requirement;
> (b) it is proportionate to apply that requirement in the particular case; and
> (c) either –
>   (i)   the person to whom that requirement is applied does not meet it, or
>   (ii) the employer is not satisfied, and in all the circumstances it is reasonable for him not to be satisfied, that that person meets it.

The SORs provide that Regulation 7(2) applies 'whether or not the employment is for purposes of an organised religion', the RBRs 'whether or not the employer has an ethos based on religion or belief'. This difference between otherwise materially identical provisions relates to the additional (and different) GORs provided by the Regulations. The RBRs provide (Regulation 7(3)) that the prohibition on discrimination on grounds of religion or belief shall not apply:

[3.67] Employment Equality (Religion and Belief) Regulations, Regulation 7

> Reg. 7(3) . . . where an employer has an ethos based on religion or belief and, having regard to that ethos and to the nature of the employment or the context in which it is carried out—
> (a) being of a particular religion or belief is a genuine occupational requirement for the job;
> (b) it is proportionate to apply that requirement in the particular case; and
> (c) either –
>   (i)   the person to whom that requirement is applied does not meet it, or
>   (ii) the employer is not satisfied, and in all the circumstances it is reasonable for him not to be satisfied, that that person meets it.

The SORs similarly provide (Regulation 7(3)) that the prohibition on discrimination on grounds of sexual orientation shall not apply:

[3.68] Employment Equality (Sexual Orientation) Regulations, Regulation 7

> Reg. 7(3) where—
> (a) the employment is for purposes of an organised religion;

(b) the employer applies a requirement related to sexual orientation—
   (i) so as to comply with the doctrines of the religion, or
   (ii) because of the nature of the employment and the context in which it is carried out, so as to avoid conflicting with the strongly held religious convictions of a significant number of the religion's followers; and
(c) either –
   (i) the person to whom that requirement is applied does not meet it, or
   (ii) the employer is not satisfied, and in all the circumstances it is reasonable for him not to be satisfied, that that person meets it.

The additional GORs provided by Regulations 7(3) of the RB and, more particularly, the SORs, have proved controversial. The DTI's Explanatory Notes to the Regulations suggest that Regulation 7(3) of the RBRs goes further than Regulation 7(2) inasmuch as an employer whose organisation has *an ethos based on religion or belief* 'is not required to show that religion or belief is a determining (i.e. decisive) factor in selection for the post in question. However, the employer must still show that the religion or belief is a requirement, and not just one of many relevant factors'. The Notes go on to provide an example of a Christian hospice which, it is suggested:

[3.69] DTI, Explanatory Notes for the Employment Equality (Sexual Orientation) Regulations and the Employment Equality (Religion and Belief) Regulations

> could probably show that it was a requirement for its chief executive to adhere to that faith, because of the leadership which a chief executive must give in relation to maintaining and developing the religious ethos . . . On the other hand, it would not be a GOR for a shop assistant to be of a particular faith in order to work in a bookshop with a religious ethos, if for all practical purposes the nature and context of the job are the same as for a shop assistant in any other bookshop. The fact that the employer or customers may prefer a person of the same faith is not relevant to whether or not a GOR applies to the job.

Turning to the additional GOR set out by Regulation 7(3) of the SORs, this caused a great deal of controversy as it was inserted at the last minute by the government and was not consulted on (though it is widely thought to have been the result of pressure from organised religious groups). The DTI's notes stress that the provision 'applies to a limited range of employment', although they go on to state that the provision covers 'staff working for an organised religion . . . in a local body or place of worship such as a church, temple, or mosque, or in a body which coordinates the work of such bodies or places of worship throughout the country [and] . . . this may include: a General Secretary, official spokesperson, typists, support staff, cleaners'. The notes go on to point out that Regulation 7(3) does not apply merely because an organisation 'has some form of religious ethos' but only to 'employment . . . for purposes of the religion', but points out that Regulation 7(3) 'refers to the employer applying "*a requirement related to sexual orientation*", rather than to the situation [Regulation 7(2)] where "*being of a particular sexual orientation*" is a requirement (emphasis in original). In this respect, Regulation 7(3) is slightly broader. For example, a requirement not to engage in sex with a same-sex partner would be a requirement related to sexual orientation, which would be covered by Regulation 7(3) but not Regulation 7(2)'.

Various aspects of the SORs were challenged in a judicial review brought by a number of trade unions shortly after their implementation.

[3.70] *Amicus v Secretary of State for Trade & Industry* **[2004] EWHC 860 (Admin), [2004] IRLR 430 (HC)**

The High Court upheld the legality of applying the GORs in cases in which employers were not *satisfied* that a person met the requirement, as well as where the person did not do so as a matter of fact. Perhaps of more importance, the Court (*per* Richards J) adopted a very narrow approach to Regulation 7(3). Noting that the provision was intended to form part of the implementation of Article 4(1) of the Directive, rather than of Article 4(2) (on which Regulation 7(3) of the RBRs is based) the Court rejected the argument put for the applicants that the provision would permit a church's refusal to employ a gay cleaner 'in a building in which he is liable to handle religious artefacts, to avoid offending the strongly-held religious convictions of a significant number of adherents', or a Catholic Order's dismissal of a science teacher for having a lesbian relationship, or a religious shop's refusal to employ a lesbian shop assistant where the shop was engaged in 'selling scriptural books and tracts on behalf of an organisation formed for the purpose of upholding and promoting a fundamentalist interpretation of the Bible . . . since her sexual orientation conflicts with the strongly held religious convictions of a significant number of Christians and/or of that particular organisation', or the refusal of an Islamic institute 'to employ as a librarian a man appearing to the employer to be homosexual, reasoning that his sexual orientation will conflict with the strongly held religious convictions of a significant number of Muslims'.

Counsel for the Secretary of State suggested that none of these examples would fall within Regulation 7(3) and Richards J regarded it as 'clear from the Parliamentary material that the exception was intended to be very narrow; and . . . is, on its proper construction, very narrow. It has to be construed strictly since it is a derogation from the principle of equal treatment; and it has to be construed purposively so as to ensure, so far as possible, compatibility with the Directive. When its terms are considered in the light of those interpretative principles, they can be seen to afford an exception only in very limited circumstances'. In particular, he emphasised its application only to employment 'for purposes of an organised religion' and suggested that 'employment as a teacher in a faith school is likely to be "for purposes of a religious organisation" [under the RBRs] but not "for purposes of an organised religion"' [under the SORs]. In addition, the employer had to apply the requirement 'so as to comply with the doctrines of the religion', a test which Richards J took to be objective rather than subjective, as was the test in Regulation 7(3)(b)(ii).

3.8 'Positive' discrimination

It is clear from the foregoing that direct discrimination otherwise covered by the SDA, RRA, SORs or RBRs can be justified where it falls within a GOQ or GOR defence. In addition, the prohibitions on employment are not without exceptions such as those mentioned at section 3.7 above. But it is important to emphasise that domestic employment discrimination law does not permit any general justification defence in respect of direct discrimination. It follows that, as a general rule, 'positive' discrimination is not permitted except under the DDA whose protections apply, save in the case of victimisation, only to 'disabled' persons. (The position differs for the purposes of EU law which permits, but does not require, a more generous measure of positive discrimination—see A McColgan, *Discrimination: Text, Cases and Materials* 2nd edn, (Oxford, Hart, 2005), chapter 3).

The SDA, RRA, SORs and RBRs all provide some limited scope for positive action. Section 48 SDA permits employers to provide single sex training, and to encourage female or male applications, in respect of jobs in which, over the previous year, that sex has been significantly under-represented. Section 38 RRA is in similar terms and Regulations 26(1) of each the SORs and the RBRs also permit the encouragement of applications from persons of a particular sexual orientation or religion or belief respectively. Section 47 SDA, section 37 RRA and Regulation 26 (2) of each the SORs and the RBRs permit targeted training by persons other than employers along lines similar to those provided by sections 48 and 38 SDA and RRA respectively and Regulation 26(1). In addition, section 47(3) of the SDA permits training to be targeted at those 'in special need of training by reason of the period for which they have been discharging domestic or family responsibilities to the exclusion of regular full time employment'. Although gender-neutral in form, this provision permits indirect discrimination in favour of women. All the anti-discrimination provisions also permit some limited positive action by non-employers such as, *inter alia*, trade unions (sections 49 and 35 SDA and RRA respectively and Regulation 26(3) of each the SORs and the RBRs).

One significant difference between the RRA and the SDA, on the one hand, and the SORs and the RBRs, on the other, is that the latter make targeted training, advertising etc. lawful where the action 'reasonably appears to the organisation . . . to prevent[] or compensate[] for disadvantages linked to sexual orientation [religion or belief] suffered by those of that sexual orientation [religion or belief]' who are doing or likely to take on the relevant work, or are holding or likely to hold the relevant posts, whereas the SDA and RRA require statistical under-representation evidence of which is likely to pose significantly greater difficulties in the context of sexual orientation and religion or belief.

The scope for positive discrimination is considerably wider under EU law (which, however, *permits*, rather than *requires* it).

[3.71] Council Directive 76/207/EEC (the Equal Treatment Directive), Article 2(4):

> This Directive shall be without prejudice to measures to promote equal opportunity for men and women, in particular by removing existing inequalities which affect women's opportunities in the [employment context].

In Case 450/93 *Kalanke v Freie Hansestadt Bremen* [1996] ECR I–03051 the ECJ ruled that an automatic preference accorded to the under-represented sex in a 'tie-break' situation breached the Equal Treatment Directive. This decision proved tremendously unpopular and in Case C–409/95 *Marschall v Land Nordrhein-Westfalen* [1997] ECR I–06363 the Court softened its approach, permitting such schemes so long as there was full consideration of the individual qualities of the candidate of the over-represented sex. In Case C–158/97 *Badeck v Hessen* [2000] ECR I–01875 the ECJ accepted the legality of a range of public sector positive discrimination measures including:

- binding targets for increasing the proportion of women in areas of the public sector in which they were under-represented;
- the retention of more than half of all positions arising during the two year duration of each positive action plan to women, save in exceptional cases;
- the requirement that women be promoted at least in proportion to their relative position in the lower rung of employment;
- the requirement that the proportion of women had to be protected in the event of redundancies;
- the operation of particular measures in academic jobs including requirements that the appointment of women had to correspond at least with the proportion of women graduates, higher graduates or students in the discipline (the latter in the case of academic assistants without degrees);
- the establishment of quotas for public sector training positions in occupations in which women were under-represented;
- in sectors in which women were under-represented, the requirement that at least as many women as men (or all the women applicants) were to be interviewed as long as they satisfied the minimum conditions for the position;
- where targets were not fulfilled in respect of each two-year plan, the requirement that every further appointment or promotion of a man in a sector in which women were under represented was to require the approval of the body which had approved the advancement plan or, in some cases, the provincial government.

Shortly after the decision in *Badeck* Article 141 TEC came into force. It appears to embrace a more generous approach to positive discrimination.

[3.72] Treaty Establishing the European Community, Article 141

> (4) With a view to ensuring full equality in practice between men and women in working life, the principle of equal treatment shall not prevent any Member State from maintaining or adopting measures providing for specific advantages to make it easier for the under-represented sex to pursue a vocational activity or to prevent or compensate for disadvantages in professional careers.

Article 141(4), which applies only to sex discrimination, is echoed by the Racial Equality Directive and the Employment Equality Directive. But in Case C–407/98 [2000] ECR I–05539 *Abrahamsson & Anderson v Fogelqvist* the ECJ ruled that Swedish regulations whereby universities which were recruiting to academic jobs in which women were under-represented were required to grant preference to a candidate from the under-represented sex would have breached that provision had it been in force. The regulations, which provided that the less qualified candidate was not to be appointed 'where the difference between the candidates' qualification is so great that such application would give rise to a breach of the requirement of objectivity in the making of appointments', had been adopted following the failure of earlier regulations which permitted (but did not require) positive action significantly to affect the under-representation of women in the academic sphere. The ECJ ruled that the scheme breached Article 2(1) and (4) of the Equal Treatment Directive, and that it would have done so even if applied only in relation to a predetermined number of posts or to posts created as part of a specific programme of a particular higher educational institution allowing the application of positive discrimination measures. Having reiterated the *Marschall* holding that the Equal Treatment Directive was consistent with the granting of preference to a candidate of the under-represented sex where qualifications were equal and candidatures were subjected to an objective assessment taking account of the specific personal situations of all the candidates, the Court went on to rule that:

> even though Article 141(4) EC allows the Member States to maintain or adopt measures providing for special advantages intended to prevent or compensate for disadvantages in professional careers in order to ensure full equality between men and women in professional life, it cannot be inferred from this that it allows a selection method of the kind at issue in the main proceedings which appears, on any view, to be disproportionate to the aim pursued.

The decision in *Abrahammson* has not gone uncriticised.

[3.73] D Caruso, "Limits of the Classic Method: Positive Action in the European Union After the New Equality Directives" 44 (2003) *Harvard International Law Journal*, 331, 343–44 (footnotes omitted)

The Commission welcomed the *Abrahamsson* decision. Interestingly, on its official Web site, the Commission advertised the case as one that "upheld Swedish measures to combat female under-representation in employment". This is only partly true. The Court did confirm the permissibility of positive discrimination in favour of women, and explained that gender may operate as a tie-breaker once a tie is established, thereby rejecting with unprecedented clarity the logic of *Kalanke*. However, *Abrahamsson* significantly curtailed the scope of the Swedish regulation in question. The administrators of the University interpreted it to mean that, because the principle of objective assessment was not violated – the female candidate was certainly worthy of the academic post – the requirement of par qualifications could be mildly relaxed. Quite the contrary, after *Abrahamsson*, the formalistic threshold of equal qualifications must be unquestionably met. The female candidate must be just as good as her male competitor. It is only at that point that, rather than tossing a coin, the University deans can use gender as a basis for their final decision.

The case reveals a serious clash of attitude between the ECJ and a member state on affirmative action. In the view of the Swedish establishment, the *Marschall* prerequisite of par qualifications is clearly inadequate to address representational deficiencies in the academic community. Yet, it continues to control the supranational legitimacy of positive action policies

For all of the criticisms which may be levelled at the ECJ's approach to positive discrimination, the test established in *Marschall*, *Badeck* and *Abrahamsson* is far more permissive than that which prevails under domestic law.

3.9 Prohibited discrimination

None of the legislation under discussion prohibits discrimination in all of the forms outlined above in every social or economic context, although the SDA, RRA and DDA extend beyond the employment context to regulate discrimination in the provision of goods, services, etc. This is beyond the scope of this chapter. As far as employment-related discrimination is concerned, the position is governed by sections 4, 6, and 4 of the RRA, SDA and DDA and Regulation 6 of each the SORs and the RBRs. The RRA provides that:

[3.74] Race Relations Act 1976, section 4

s.4(1) It is unlawful for a person, in relation to employment by him at an establishment in Great Britain, to discriminate against another—
(a) in the arrangements he makes for the purpose of determining who should be offered the employment; or
(b) in the terms on which he offers that employment; or
(c) by refusing or deliberately omitting to offer him that employment.

(2) It is unlawful for a person, in the case of a person employed by him at an establishment in Great Britain, to discriminate against that employee—
(a) in the terms of the employment which he affords him; or
(b) in the way he affords him access to opportunities for promotion, transfer or training, or to any other benefits, facilities or services, or by refusing or
(c) deliberately omitting to afford him access to them; or
(d) by dismissing him, or subjecting him to any other detriment.

Section 6 SDA is materially identical except that it contains no equivalent of section 4(2)(a), contractual terms being covered instead by the Equal Pay Act 1970 (see further section 3.10 below). Section 4 DDA is drafted in similar terms to section 4 of the RRA as are Regulation 6 of each the SORs and the RBRs. All the statutory provisions provide (sections 27 A RRA, 16A DDA and 20A SDA, and Regulation 21 of the SORs and the RBRs) that protection from employment-related discrimination [and, in the case of the Regulations and the RRA, 'harassment'] continues after the termination of the relationship 'where the discrimination or harassment arises out of and is closely connected to that relationship'. These provisions were inserted into the RRA, SDA and DDA to achieve compliance with the express terms of the Employment Equality and Race Equality Directives and the ECJ's interpretation of the SDA (Case 185/97 *Coote v Granada Hospitality Ltd* [1998] ECR 1–5199). The extension of the RRA applies only in relation to discrimination on grounds of 'race or ethnic or national origin', but the statutory amendments are consistent with the House of Lords decision in *Relaxion Group v Rhys-Harper* [2003] ICR 867 in which their Lordships ruled that such discrimination was in any event covered by the SDA, DDA and RRA in their original forms.

The category of workers protected against discrimination is wider than those generally afforded employment-related protection. Not only does protection extend to agency and contract workers, barristers, partners and office holders, but 'employment' is defined as 'employment under a contract of service or of apprenticeship' or a contract 'personally to execute any work or labour' (SDA and RRA or (DDA, SORs and RBRs) 'personally to do any work'. These definitions extend beyond the category of workers generally protected by the Employment Rights Act 1996, although only to cover those the 'dominant purpose' of whose contract with the alleged discriminator 'is that the party contracting to provide services under the contract performs personally the work or labour which forms the subject matter of the contract' (*Mirror Group Newspapers Ltd v Gunning* [1986] ICR 145).

Both the CRE and the EOC, in their 1998 reform proposals, called for the extension of the Acts to volunteers. The government has indicated its intention to draw up a code of practice with respect to volunteers but no steps have yet been taken and the new Regulations do not apply to volunteers.

Most incidents of discrimination in employment will come within the relevant legislative provisions. It is clear, for example, that discriminatory dismissals (actual or constructive) will be covered (these may, in addition, also be challenged under the ERA 1996). So, too, will discriminatory refusals to employ, discriminatory interviewing and other recruitment arrangements. The difficulties which arise in the application of sections 4 and 6 tend to relate to the 'catch-all' provision 'any other detriment' set out in sections 4(2)(c), 6(2)(c)(b) and 4(2)(d) of the RRA, SDA and DDA respectively and Regulation 6 SORs and RBRs.

A number of early cases were characterised by a willingness on the part of the courts to dismiss 'detriment' claims as 'de minimis' (*Peake v Automotive Products Ltd* [1978] QB 233 (CA); *Ministry of Defence v Jeremiah* [1980] QB 87; *cf Gill & Coote v El Vino Ltd* [1983] 1 All ER 398 (CA)). More recently, in *Staffordshire County Council v Black* [1995] IRLR 234, the EAT rejected the claim that a factory check on all black workers entering the building amounted to a 'detriment' under the RRA. The EAT did not accept that the applicant had been 'put under a disadvantage' by the check, which had been imposed in order to prevent entry by one particular black man. And in *Clymo v Wandsworth*, the EAT ruled that a woman refused permission to return to work on a job-share basis had not been subjected to any detriment.

[3.75] *Clymo v Wandsworth London Borough Council* **[1989] ICR 250 (EAT)**

> *Wood J:*
> it seems to us that the word 'detriment' as used in this subsection . . . must be some unpleasantness or burden or less favourable treatment arising out of or in the course of that employment. It cannot amount to a failure to provide some advantage so long as such an advantage is not offered to others in the same grade of employment, ie to other branch librarians. Thus for instance it would not be a detriment to the applicant if the local authority failed to offer her the perk of a company car or the right to work overtime which it had not offered to others in the same grade.
>
> In the present case job sharing was not an option for branch librarians and thus the applicant was no worse off than other branch librarians. She resigned—left of her own accord—and this does not seem to us to be a 'detriment' caused by anyone but herself

Difficulties have arisen also in relation to sexual harassment claims. In *Porcelli* the Court of Sessions took the view that, in order to amount to actionable harassment, treatment which was accepted as being 'on the grounds of sex' (**[3.25]**) had to involve 'dismissal or other disciplinary action by the employer, or some action by the employee such as leaving the employment on the basis of constructive dismissal [as there], or seeking transfer to another plant'. This understanding was soon to change.

[3.76] *De Souza v The Automobile Association* **[1986] ICR 514 (CA)**

> A black employee claimed race discrimination by way of racial harassment after she heard herself being referred to in racially derogatory terms by her manager. The Court of Appeal recognised that the harassment itself could amount to 'detriment' for the purposes of the RRA (and, by analogy, the SDA or DDA) in a case where 'the putative reasonable employee could justifiably complain about his or her working conditions or environment . . . whether or not these were so bad as to be able to amount to constructive dismissal, or even if the employee was prepared to work on and put up with the harassment'.

The Court of Appeal in *De Souza* did not accept that the applicant had been subjected to a 'detriment' on the facts, May LJ for the Court ruling that the act complained of was insufficient to permit a 'reasonable worker' to conclude that 'he [or she] had thereby been disadvantaged in the circumstances in which he had thereafter to work' (also that Ms de Souza could not 'properly be said to have been 'treated' less favourably by whomsoever used the [derogatory term] . . . unless he intended her to overhear the conversation in which it was used, or knew or ought reasonably to have anticipated that the person he was talking to would pass the insult on or that the appellant would become aware of it in some other way'). These aspects of the decision have been criticised, but the ruling did open the door to judicial recognition of harassment as actionable discrimination.

[3.77] *Driskel v Peninsula Business Services Ltd,* **[2000] IRLR 151 (EAT)**

The applicant complained of sex discrimination after an incident in which, having subjected her to a series of sexual remarks, her manager advised her to wear a short skirt and a transparent blouse during a promotion interview with him. A tribunal dismissed her claim on the basis that she had not objected at the time to the earlier remarks which, accordingly, the manager could not have known were offensive to her; and that the interview-related comments, though 'tasteless and inappropriate', were 'intended as flippant, could not reasonably have been taken seriously, and [were] not taken seriously by Mrs Driskel when the words were spoken'. The EAT allowed the applicant's appeal:

Holland J:
[having cited the EAT's earlier decision in *Reed and Bull Information Systems Ltd v Stedman* [1999] IRLR 299 to the effect that] 'It is particularly important in cases of alleged sexual harassment that the fact-finding tribunal should not carve up the case into a series of specific incidents and try [to] measure the harm or detriment in relation to each.' Sexual harassment is helpfully categorised in *Reed and Bull* . . .

'It seems to us important at the outset that "sexual harassment" is not defined by statute. It is a colloquial expression which describes one form of discrimination in the workplace made unlawful by s 6 of the [SDA]. Because it is not a precise or defined phrase, its use, without regard to s 6, can lead to confusion. Under s 6 it is unlawful to subject a person to a "detriment" on the grounds of their sex. Sexual harassment is a shorthand for describing a type of detriment. The word detriment is not further defined and its scope is to be defined by the fact-finding tribunal on a common-sense basis by reference to the facts of each particular case. The question in each case is whether the alleged victim has been subjected to a detriment and, second, was it on the grounds of sex'.

(1) The finding of less favourable treatment leading to 'detriment' is one of fact and degree so that a single act may legitimately found a complaint . . .

(2) The ultimate judgment, sexual discrimination or no, reflects an objective assessment by the tribunal of all the facts. That said, amongst the factors to be considered are the applicant's subjective perception of that which is the subject of complaint and the understanding, motive and intention of the alleged discriminator. Thus, the act complained of may be so obviously detrimental, that is, disadvantageous (see *Insitu [Cleaning Co Ltd v Heads* [1995] IRLR 4]) to the applicant as a woman by intimidating her on undermining her dignity at work, that the lack of any contemporaneous complaint by her is of little or no significance. By contrast she may complain of one or more matters which if taken individually may not objectively signify much, if anything, in terms of detriment. Then a contemporaneous indication of sensitivity on her part becomes obviously material as does the evidence of the alleged discriminator as to his perception. That which in isolation may not amount to discriminatory detriment may become such if persisted in notwithstanding objection, vocal or apparent . . . By contrast the facts may simply disclose hypersensitivity on the part of the applicant to conduct which was reasonably not perceived by the alleged discriminator as being to her detriment—no finding of discrimination can then follow . . .

In *Shamoon v Chief Constable of the Royal Ulster Constabulary* [2001] ICR 337 Northern Ireland's Court of Appeal ruled that a claimant would establish a 'detriment' under Northern Ireland's equivalent of the SDA only where she suffered some 'physical or economic consequence' (relying on the decision of the EAT in *Lord Chancellor v Coker* [2002] ICR 321). It ruled that the Claimant there, who had been stripped of her staff appraisal function, had not suffered a detriment according to this test. The House of Lords, which rejected Ms Shamoon's appeal on other grounds, ruled that the Court of Appeal had erred in its approach to detriment. According to their Lordships ([2003] ICR 337) a 'detriment' would be established in relation to employment, by reason of the act or acts complained of, a reasonable worker would or might take the view that she had thereby been disadvantaged in the circumstances in which she had thereafter to work. An unjustified sense of grievance cannot amount to 'detriment', but it was not necessary for the claimant to establish that she had suffered some physical or economic consequence. In the instant case the House of Lords accepted that a reasonable employee in Ms Shamoon's position might well feel that she was demeaned in the eyes of those over whom she was in a position of authority when her appraisal duties were removed.

More recently, in *Thomas v Robinson* [2003] IRLR 7, the EAT ruled that an employment tribunal has erred in law by finding that a black African-Caribbean woman had been discriminated against contrary to the RRA by a racially-insensitive remark made to her by a work colleague, without expressly considering whether she suffered any detriment as a result of the remark. The EAT accepted that she had been less favourably treated by virtue of the remark but went on (*per* Judge Reid) to state that she had in addition to show that the employer 'subjected [her] to any other detriment'. According to the EAT, 'harassment' involved two elements: 'The first is the targeting of the person being harassed. The second is the causing of distress to the target.' The appeal tribunal accepted that the latter element would 'in very many cases . . . be extremely easy for the employee to establish, but this does not entitle the tribunal to assume [it] . . . nor to decide that proof of the language created an irrebuttable presumption of detriment.'

The new SORs and RBRs and the RRA as amended define 'harassment' as set out at 3.3.1.3 above, a materially identical definition having been adopted also by the amended Equal Treatment Directive. The incorporation of these or similar definitions within domestic legislation would do away with the requirement, which proved fatal in *de Souza*, that the complainant have been 'subjected to' detriment, the question instead being whether the overheard comments amounted to 'conduct related to ethnic or racial origin', and whether they had the prohibited effect. They would also avoid the need for an express finding of 'detriment', although it is possible that analogous disputes could arise regarding whether the treatment complained of amounted to 'harassment' defined as above. (On the facts of *Stewart v Wadman Carpenter*, for example, an employer could dispute the reasonableness of a complainant's perception of her exposure to 'pin-ups' as 'creating an intimidating, hostile, offensive or disturbing environment'.)

The final issue which arises, in particular, in cases involving allegations of 'harassment', but which is not confined to them (see, for example, the decision of the Court of Appeal in *Martins v Marks & Spencers plc* [1998] ICR 1005), involves the need for a link to be established between the offending conduct and the employer. This may be done by way either of vicarious or direct liability. Sections 41, 32 and 58 of the SDA, RRA and DDA respectively and Regulation 22 of each the RBRs and the SORs impose vicarious liability upon employers for '[a]nything done by a person in the course of his employment . . . whether or not it was done with the employer's knowledge or approval', subject to a 'due diligence' defence whereby employers can escape liability (sections 41(3), 32(3), and 58(5) and Regulation 22(3) SORs and RBRs) by proving that they 'took such steps as were reasonably practicable to prevent the employee from doing that act, or from doing in the course of his employment acts of that description' (see *Canniffe v East Riding of Yorkshire Council* [2000] IRLR 555 on the scope of this defence). Alternatively, the employer might incur direct or personal liability for the detriment, in a case in which s/he was him or herself the harasser, or where s/he subjected the harassed employee to a detriment by failing to deal with past harassment about which the employer had knowledge and other harassment over which s/he had control.

[3.78] *Jones v Tower Boot Co Ltd* [1997] ICR 254 (CA)

The Claimant, who was of mixed race, was subjected to severe racial harassment by his colleagues. He had been branded with a hot screwdriver, whipped, had metal bolts thrown at his head. He had also had a notice stuck on his back which read 'Chipmonks are go', and been the victim of repeated racist name-calling. A tribunal found his employers vicariously liable for the harassment, which ruling was overturned by the EAT on the ground that the harassers' actions were not done in the course of their employment. In reaching this conclusion the EAT had applied the test set out by the Court of Appeal in *Irving v The Post Office* [1987] IRLR 289 in which that Court, applying the common law test of vicarious liability, restricted an employers' vicarious liability under the RRA (and, by analogy, the SDA) to 'acts actually authorised by him [and] . . . acts which he has not authorised, provided they are so connected with acts which he has authorised that they may rightly be regarded as modes—although improper modes—of doing them'. The Court of Appeal reinstated the tribunal's decision, ruling that the statutory test for vicarious liability was wider than that applicable at common law.

Waite LJ:
A purposive construction . . . requires s 32 of the [RRA] (and the corresponding s 41 of the [SDA]) to be given a broad interpretation. It would be inconsistent with that requirement to allow the notion of the 'course of employment' to be construed in any sense more limited than the natural meaning of those everyday words would allow . . .

the anomaly which would result . . . from adopting any other interpretation . . . will be that the more heinous the act of discrimination, the less likely it will be that the employer would be liable . . . [This would] cut[] across the whole legislative scheme and underlying policy of s32 (and its counterpart in sex discrimination), which is to deter racial and sexual harassment in the workplace through a widening of the net of responsibility beyond the guilty employees themselves, by making all employers additionally liable for such harassment, and then supplying them with the reasonable steps defence under s32(3) which will exonerate the conscientious employer who has used his best endeavours to prevent such harassment, and will encourage all employers who have not yet undertaken such endeavours to take the steps necessary to make the same defence available in their own workplace.

Even where vicarious liability cannot be established, employers may be directly liable for workplace harassment. *Burton and Rhule v De Vere Hotels* [1997] ICR 1 involved a race discrimination claim brought by two black waitresses after they had been exposed to racist jokes made by Bernard Manning, and associated racial and sexual abuse, at a police function at which they served. Their employers could not be held vicariously liable for the abuse they suffered as their harassers were neither employed by it nor acting under its authorisation. The EAT ruled that (1) 'An employer subjects an employee to the detriment of racial harassment if he causes or permits the racial harassment to occur in circumstances in which he can control whether it happens or not' and (2) where the treatment to which the employer had permitted the employees to be subject was race specific, there was no need for the Claimants to prove that the employers treated them less favourably than they did or would treat employees of a different racial group. The decision in *Burton* was relied upon in a number of cases in which employers were pinned with direct liability for harassment which they culpably failed to control. But in *Pearce v Mayfield School* the House of Lords ruled that it had been wrongly decided in two respects. First, race-specific treatment did not necessarily amount to less favourable treatment on grounds of race ([3.26]). Secondly, the employer would only have been liable for treating the waitresses less favourably on racial grounds if its failure to protect them from the treatment they received was itself connected with their race. The employment tribunal had found that this was not the case and the EAT, accordingly, was not entitled to find that the employer had discriminated on grounds of race.

[3.79] *Pearce v Governing Body of Mayfield School* [2003] ICR 937 (HL)

Lord Nicholls:

Viewed in the broadest terms, the *Burton* decision has much to commend it. There is, surely, everything to be said in favour of a conclusion which requires employers to take reasonable steps to protect employees from racial or sexual abuse by third parties. But is a failure to do so 'discrimination' by the employer? Where the *Burton* decision is, indeed, vulnerable is that it treats an employer's inadvertent failure to take such steps as discrimination even though the failure had nothing to do with the sex or race of the employees . . . the harassment in *Burton* was committed by third parties for whose conduct the employer was not vicariously responsible. Despite this, [the EAT] seems to have proceeded on the basis that the racial harassment of the waitresses by the speaker and some of the guests constituted discrimination on the part of the employer, and that the only issue left outstanding on the appeal, if the discrimination claim were to succeed, was whether the employers had by active or passive conduct subjected the waitresses to racial harassment by the speaker and the offending guests. This cannot be right. In order to succeed the two Caribbean waitresses had to prove discrimination by their employer.
Smith J said . . .

'The [employment] tribunal should ask themselves whether the event in question was something which was sufficiently under the control of the employer that he could, *by the application of good employment practice*, have prevented the harassment or reduced the extent of it. If such is their finding, then the employer has subjected the employee to the harassment" [emphasis added]'.

This decision, I have to say, seems to have proceeded on altogether the wrong footing. 'Subjecting' an employee to 'detriment' is one of the circumstances in which it is unlawful for an employer to 'discriminate' against an employee: section 4(2)(c) of the Race Relations Act 1976. Thus section 4(2)(c) is not satisfied unless the conduct constituted 'discrimination' . . . The hotel's failure to plan ahead properly may have fallen short of the standards required by good employment practice, but it was not racial discrimination . . .

Had the factual position been otherwise, and had the employer permitted exposure of the black waitresses to racist remarks by a third party when it would not have treated white employees similarly in a corresponding situation, this would have been a case of racial discrimination. This conclusion would follow from the difference in treatment afforded to black waitresses on the one hand and the treatment which would have been afforded to white waitresses on the other hand . . .

Lords Hobhouse and Rodger agreed with Lord Nicholls on *Burton* and Lord Hope's remarks on the issue echoed those of Lord Nicholls. Lord Scott agreed that *Burton* was wrongly decided because it overlooked the need to establish discrimination by the employer.

The decision of the House of Lords in *Pearce* overruled *Burton*, but does not do away with the concept of direct liability. An employer will be liable for any action which amounts to less favourable treatment of a worker and which is on a protected ground. Thus, for example, had the manager in *Burton* exhibited less concern for the Claimants there than he would have for white waitresses or waiters subjected to equally offensive treatment, he (and through him the hotel) would have been liable for discriminating against them.

3.10 Sex discrimination in pay and contractual terms—the EqPA

We saw above that, whereas the RRA and DDA regulate discrimination in terms and conditions of employment including pay, this type of sex discrimination is covered by the EqPA, rather than the SDA. The EqPA operates by way of a strict comparator requirement, providing that women are entitled to benefit from the same contractual terms (including pay) as suitable male comparators, unless the employer can establish that the difference in pay (or other contractual term) 'is genuinely due to a material difference (other than the difference of sex) between her case and his' (section 1(3)).

The approach of the EqPA relieves the applicant from having to prove that the disputed difference in pay or other contractual terms is the result of sex discrimination (the burden passing to the employer to defend a difference between the woman and a suitable comparator—*cf* the approach of the Part-time Workers Regulations, discussed in chapter 4). But this advantage comes at a heavy price. No claim is possible under the EqPA by reference to a hypothetical comparator (at least until the implementation of the amended Equal Treatment Directive, see further 3.10.2 below). And, as we shall see immediately below, the question of with whom an equal pay complainant can establish a comparison has a narrow answer indeed.

3.10.1 Selecting a comparator

The mechanism adopted by the EqPA consists of the individualistic 'equality clause' whereby a woman is entitled to have her contractual terms amended to match those of a male comparator in any of three circumstances. In all cases the comparator be employed by the same or an associated employer, and must be 'in the same employment' as the equal pay applicant (see further 3.10.3 below). He must, in addition, be employed on 'like work', 'work rated as equivalent' or 'work of equal value' to hers.

Turning first to the requirement that the equal pay claimant and her comparator be employed by the same or an associated employer, section 1(6)(c) provides that 'two employers are to be treated as associated if one is a company of which the other (directly or indirectly) has control or if both are companies of which a third person (directly or indirectly) has control'. This narrow test has been challenged on a number of occasions as inconsistent with the directly effective Article 141 (formerly Article 119) TEC.

[3.80] *Scullard v Knowles* **& Southern Regional Council for Education & Training [1996] ICR 399 (EAT)**

> The applicant, who wished to claim equal pay with a man whose employer was not 'associated' with her own under section 1(6) EqPA, sought to rely on Article 141 TEC. (In Case 43/75 *Defrenne* (No 2) [1976] ECR 455, the ECJ had ruled that Article 141 required equal pay 'for equal work which is carried out in the same establishment or service, whether private or public.' Both Ms Scullard and her chosen comparator were employed by Regional Advisory Councils which were independent *inter se* and of the Secretary of State for Employment, but which were funded by the Department of Employment.

> *Mummery J (P):*
> . . . [Section]1(6) . . . excludes, for example, employees of different employers who, though not companies, are all under the direct or indirect control of a third party and have common terms and conditions of employment. The crucial point is that the class of comparators defined in s 1(6) is more restricted than that available on the application of Article [141], as interpreted by the European Court of Justice. Article [141] is not, for example, confined to employment in undertakings which have a particular legal form, such as a limited company . . .
> In *Defrenne* no distinction is drawn between work carried out in the same establishment or service of limited companies and of other employers, whether incorporated or not . . .
> The crucial question for the purposes of Article [141] is, therefore, whether Mrs Scullard and the male unit managers of the other councils were employed 'in the same establishment or service'. The tribunal did not ask or answer that question. To the extent that that is a wider class of comparators than is contained in s 1(6) of the [EqPA], s 1(6), which is confined to 'associated employers', is displaced and must yield to the paramount force of Article [141] . . .

Article 141 has also been successfully relied upon to require consideration of a comparator who preceded (*Macarthys Ltd v Smith (No 2)* [1981] QB 180 (CA)) and one who succeeded (*Diocese of Hallam Trustees v Connaughton* [1996] ICR 860 (EAT)) the applicant in employment. In *South Ayrshire Council v Morton* [2002] ICR 956 the

Court of Sessions ruled that an employment tribunal had been entitled to permit a teacher employed by one local authority to compare herself with a man similarly so employed by another such authority. But the claimants in *Lawrence v Regent Office Care Ltd* posed a much more radical challenge to women's underpayment. They, like the women in *Ratcliffe*, below, had been employed by North Yorkshire County Council as 'dinner ladies'. Their jobs, like those of many other women in the public sector, had been contracted out as a result of CCT. Some were transferred on the assumption that TUPE applied, others on the assumption that it did not. All ended up working on less favourable terms and conditions than they had previously enjoyed, and on less favourable terms than men (retained in the public sector) working in jobs which had previously been rated as equivalent to theirs (see further below). Their equal pay claims, which relied on those men as comparators, were dismissed both by the tribunal and by the EAT, the latter rejecting the argument that Article 141 permitted comparison with men who were employed by a different employer. The Court of Appeal ([2000] IRLR 608) referred to the ECJ the question whether Article 141 required that they be permitted to make the comparison they sought. The ECJ ruled (Case 320/00 [2002] ECR I–07325) that, although the scope of Article 141 was not limited to cases in which men and women worked for the same employer, it could not be relied upon to challenge pay differences in a case such as this in which the pay differences at issue could not be attributed to a single source, since there was no body which was responsible for the inequality and which could restore equal treatment.

The ECJ was again asked to consider the scope of Article 141 in the *Allonby* case.

[3.81] Case 256/01 *Allonby v Accrington & Rossendale College* [2004] ECR I–00873 (ECJ)

The claim [also considered above at [3.48]] was brought by a part-time hourly lecturer whose job had been contracted out by her employers who wished to avoid the implications of the Part-time Workers Regulations (see chapter 4). She, with all her part-time colleagues, was made redundant and advised to supply her services on a self-employed basis through Education Learning Services. This had the effect of reducing her hourly income and various benefits including sick pay and career structure, and of denying her access to her former employer's pension scheme which was open only to employees of the college. The claimant cited as her comparator a male full-time lecturer at the college. The Court of Appeal ([2001] ICR 1189, [3.49]) referred to the ECJ the questions (1) whether, under Article 141, she could compare herself with an employee of the college in the circumstances and (2) whether Article 141 had direct effect so as to entitle her to claim access to the pension scheme either (i) by comparing herself with a man still employed by the college or (ii) by showing statistically that a considerably smaller proportion of female than of male teachers who were otherwise eligible to join the scheme could comply with the requirement of being employed under a contract of employment. The ECJ ruled, on the same basis as it had in *Lawrence*, that she could not make an equal pay claim using the comparator employed by the college. But it went on to rule that . . .

Judgment:
According to Article 2 EC, the Community is to have as its task to promote, among other things, equality between men and women. Article 141(1) EC constitutes a specific expression of the principle of equality for men and women, which forms part of the

fundamental principles protected by the Community legal order . . . As the Court held in *Defrenne (No.2)*, cited above . . . the principle of equal pay forms part of the foundations of the Community.

Accordingly, the term worker used in Article 141(1) EC cannot be defined by reference to the legislation of the Member States but has a Community meaning. Moreover, it cannot be interpreted restrictively.

For the purposes of that provision, there must be considered as a worker a person who, for a certain period of time, performs services for and under the direction of another person in return for which he receives remuneration . . .

Provided that a person is a worker within the meaning of Article 141(1) EC, the nature of his legal relationship with the other party to the employment relationship is of no consequence in regard to the application of that article . . .

In the case of teachers who are, vis-à-vis an intermediary undertaking, under an obligation to undertake an assignment at a college, it is necessary in particular to consider the extent of any limitation on their freedom to choose their timetable, and the place and content of their work. The fact that no obligation is imposed on them to accept an assignment is of no consequence in that context . . .

When it is necessary to consider whether a set of rules conforms with the requirements of Article 141(1) EC, it is in principle the scope of those rules which determines the category of persons who may be included in the comparison.

Thus, in the case of company pension schemes which are limited to the undertaking in question, the Court has held that a worker cannot rely on Article 119 of the EC Treaty . . . in order to claim pay to which he could be entitled if he belonged to the other sex in the absence, now or in the past, in the undertaking concerned of workers of the other sex who perform or performed comparable work . . . On the other hand, in the case of national legislation, in case 171/88 *Rinner-Kühn* . . . the Court based its reasoning on statistics for the numbers of male and female workers at national level.

In order to show that the requirement of being employed under a contract of employment as a precondition for membership of the TSS – a condition deriving from State rules – constitutes a breach of the principle of equal pay for men and women in the form of indirect discrimination against women, a female worker may rely on statistics showing that, among the teachers who are workers within the meaning of Article 141(1) EC and fulfil all the conditions for membership of the pension scheme except that of being employed under a contract of employment as defined by national law, there is a much higher percentage of women than of men.

If that is the case, the difference of treatment concerning membership of the pension scheme at issue must be objectively justified. In that regard, no justification can be inferred from the formal classification of a self-employed person under national law.

In view of the foregoing considerations, the answer to the first part of part (b) of the second question must be that, in the absence of any objective justification, the requirement, imposed by State legislation, of being employed under a contract of employment as a precondition for membership of a pension scheme for teachers is not applicable where it is shown that, among the teachers who are workers within the meaning of Article 141(1) EC and fulfil all the other conditions for membership, a much lower percentage of women than of men is able to fulfil that condition. The formal classification of a self-employed person under national law does not change the fact that a person must be classified as a worker within the meaning of that article if his independence is merely notional . . .

As far as ELS is concerned, the national court seeks to ascertain in essence whether the applicability of Article 141(1) EC vis-à-vis an undertaking is subject to the condition that the worker concerned can be compared with a worker of the other sex who is or has been employed by the same employer and has received higher pay for equal work or for work of equal value and that a woman cannot therefore invoke statistics in order to claim, on the basis of that provision, eligibility for membership of a pension scheme set up under State legislation.

In that connection it must be held that a woman may rely on statistics to show that a clause in State legislation is contrary to Article 141(1) EC because it discriminates against female workers. Where that provision is not applicable, the consequences are binding not only on the public authorities or social agencies but also on the employer concerned . . .

The answer to the second part of part (b) of the second question must therefore be that Article 141(1) EC must be interpreted as meaning that, where State legislation is at issue, the applicability of that provision vis-à-vis an undertaking is not subject to the condition that the worker concerned can be compared with a worker of the other sex who is or has been employed by the same employer and who has received higher pay for equal work or work of equal value.

The amended Equal Treatment Directive, which will come into force in October 2005, will make very significant changes in the context of equal pay.

[3.82] Council Directive 76/207/EEC (the Equal Treatment Directive) as amended by Council Directive 2000/73/EC

Article 2
1. For the purposes of the following provisions, the principle of equal treatment shall mean that there shall be no discrimination whatsoever on grounds of sex either directly or indirectly by reference in particular to marital or family status.
2. For the purposes of this Directive, the following definitions shall apply:
—direct discrimination: where one person is treated less favourably on grounds of sex than another is, has been or would be treated in a comparable situation,
—indirect discrimination: where an apparently neutral provision, criterion or practice would put persons of one sex at a particular disadvantage compared with persons of the other sex, unless that provision, criterion or practice is objectively justified by a legitimate aim, and the means of achieving that aim are appropriate and necessary . . .

Article 3
1. Application of the principle of equal treatment means that there shall be no direct or indirect discrimination on the grounds of sex in the public or private sectors, including public bodies, in relation to . . .
(c) employment and working conditions, including dismissals, as well as pay as provided for in Directive 75/117/EEC . . .

What this means is that, for the first time, discrimination in relation to pay is covered by the Equal Treatment Directive whose prohibitions on discrimination do not require recourse to an actual comparator. The generally comparator-driven approach adopted by Article 141 and the Equal Pay Directive (as well as the EqPA) may continue to prove useful where such a comparator does exist, in which case the claimant is relieved of the burden of proving that any pay disparity is sex-related (though the employer may defend the claim by demonstrating that it is not). But where there is no such comparator, the amended Equal Treatment Directive appears to permit pay-related sex discrimination to be challenged in like manner as any other form of employment-related sex discrimination. This view is not apparently shared by the government, however, the draft employment Equality (Sex Discrimination) Regulations not proposing any amendment of the EqPA's comparator requirement.

Returning to the provisions of the EqPA itself, and subject to any amendments made in order to achieve compliance with the amended Equal Treatment Directive, the Act restricts comparators not only to those men employed 'by the same employer' but also to those 'in the same employment' as the applicant. This is, in turn, defined by section 1(6) to include not only employment 'in the same establishment' but also employment 'at establishments in Great Britain . . . at which common terms and conditions of employment are observed either generally or for employees of the relevant classes'.

[3.83] *British Coal Corp v Smith* [1996] ICR 515 (HL)

The case involved an equal pay claim made by female canteen and clerical workers using, as their comparators, surface mineworkers. The Court of Appeal ([1994] ICR 810) had ruled that the tribunal should not have let the cases proceed to the appointment of an independent expert, 'common terms and conditions' under section 1(6) requiring, in that court's view, that the woman and their comparators, if employed at different establishments, had to be employed on 'the same', as distinct from 'broadly similar' or 'essentially similar', terms and conditions. (Although clerical workers shared the same terms nationwide, surface mineworkers were governed by a national agreement in respect of which local variations had been agreed in respect of concessionary fuel and incentive bonuses (entitlement to each being established at national level) and canteen workers' terms and conditions were governed by national agreements which entitled them to identical incentive bonuses to those received, in each particular workplace, by surface workers while they were not entitled to concessionary coal.)

Lord Slynn of Hadley (with whom the others agreed):
. . . Your Lordships have been referred to a number of dictionary definitions of 'common' but I do not think that they help. The real question is what the legislation was seeking to achieve. Was it seeking to exclude a woman's claim unless, subject to *de minimis* exceptions, there was complete identity of terms and conditions for the comparator at his establishment and those which applied or would apply to a similar male worker at her establishment? Or was the legislation seeking to establish that the terms and conditions of the relevant class were sufficiently similar for a fair comparison to be made, subject always to the employers' right to establish a 'material difference' defence under s.1(3) of the EqPA? [discussed below] . . .

The purpose of requiring common terms and conditions was to avoid it being said simply 'a gardener does work of equal value to mine and my comparator at another establishment is a gardener'. It was necessary for the applicant to go further and to show that gardeners at other establishments and at her establishment were or would be employed on broadly similar terms. It was necessary, but it was also sufficient. Whether any differences between the woman and the man selected as the comparator were justified would depend on the next stage of the examination under s 1(3). I do not consider that the s 1(3) inquiry, where the onus is on the employer, was intended to be excluded unless the terms and conditions of the men at the relevant establishments were common in the sense of identical. This seems to me to be far too restrictive a test . . .

The fact that an equal pay applicant's chosen comparator is employed by the same or an associated employer (or, if Article 141 is relied upon, that he is 'in the same establishment or service'); and that he is 'in the same employment' as her, do not of course entitle her to equal pay with him. A claim under the EqPA turns upon whether she can establish, in addition, that she and her comparator are employed on 'like work', 'work rated as equivalent' or 'work of equal value'.

- 'Like work' is (section 1(4)) 'work . . . of the same or a broadly similar nature . . . the differences (if any) . . . not [being] of practical importance in relation to terms and condition of employment'.
- 'Work rated as equivalent' is (section 1(5)) work which has 'been given an equal value, in terms of the demand made on a worker under various headings (for instance effort, skill, decision), on a study undertaken with a view to evaluating in those terms the jobs to be done by all or any of the employees in an undertaking or group of undertakings, or would have been given an equal value but for the evaluation being made on a system setting different values for men and women on the same demand under any heading'. There is no obligation on an employer to undertake any job evaluation scheme.
- 'Work of equal value' is (section 1(2)(c)) assessed 'in terms of the demands made on [the workers] (for instance under such headings as effort, skill and decision).

In the case of a like work or work rated as equivalent claim, the tribunal first assesses whether the woman's job and that of her comparator are comparable under section 1(5) or 1(6) respectively before considering any GMF defence put forward by the employer (this is further discussed below). The procedure for equal value claims is complex and has been subject to significant recent change (in particular by the Employment Tribunals (Constitution and Rules of Procedure) (Amendment) Regulations 2004). Under the new regime a tribunal has to hold an initial hearing to determine whether the claimant's job and that of her comparator have been rated as unequal by a job evaluation scheme and, if so, whether there are reasonable grounds for determining that the scheme can be shown to be discriminatory on grounds of sex or otherwise unsuitable. Assuming the claim is not blocked by a valid JES, the tribunal has to decide whether to appoint an independent expert or to determine the question of value itself. Tribunals can no longer dismiss a claim without determining the question of value on the grounds that there are 'no reasonable grounds for determining that the work is of equal value'.

3.10.2 Sex discrimination in pay: the EqPA and the genuine material factor defence

[3.84] Equal Pay Act, section 1(3)

s.1(3) An equality clause shall not operate in relation to a variation between the woman's contract and the man's contract if the employer proves that the variation is genuinely due to a material factor which is not the difference of sex and that factor—

(a) in the case of an equality clause falling within subsection (2)(a) or (b) above, must be a material difference between the woman's case and the man's; and

(b) in the case of an equality clause falling within subsection (2)(c) above, may be such a material difference.

There is no practical difference between the defences established under section 1(3)(a) and 1(3)(b), the House of Lords in *Rainey*, below, having overruled the Court of Appeal decision in *Clay Cross v Fletcher* that, in order to qualify as a 'material differ- ence' under section 1(3)(a), the factor relied upon by the employer had to be 'personal' to the workers concerned: that is, relating to (*per* Lord Denning MR) 'much longer length of service . . . superior skill or qualifications . . . bigger output or productivity . . . or [placement] . . . owing to down-grading, in a protected pay categ- ory, vividly described as "red circl[ing]"; or to other circumstances personal to [the worker] in doing his job'. Lord Denning had refused, in *Clay Cross*, to countenance that 'extrinsic forces' such as 'market forces' could amount to a GMF.

[3.85] *Clay Cross (Quarry Services) Ltd v Fletcher* [1979] ICR 47 (CA)

Ms Fletcher was one of three clerks who was paid £35 a week. When one of her colleagues left, the replacement man (the only suitable candidate) was recruited on £43 per week to match his previous salary, and the disparity thus created was maintained after a subsequent pay increase. Ms Fletcher's succeeded in an equal pay claim, the EAT overruling the tribunal on the ground that the employer had established a GMF (i.e., the man's previous salary). The Court of Appeal reinstated the tribunal's decision.

Lord Denning MR:
An employer cannot avoid his obligations under the [EqPA] by saying: 'I paid him more because he asked for more', or 'I paid her less because she was willing to come for less'. If any such excuse were permitted, the Act would be a dead letter. Those are the very reasons why there was unequal pay before the statute. They were the very circumstances in which the statute was intended to operate.

   Nor can the employer avoid his obligations by giving the reasons why he submitted to the extrinsic forces. As for instance by saying: 'He asked for that sum because it was what he was getting in his previous job', or 'He was the only applicant for the job, so I had no option'. In such cases the employer may beat his breast, and say: 'I did not pay him more because he was a man. I paid it because he was the only suitable person who applied for the job. Man or woman made no difference to me.' Those are reasons personal to the employer. If any such reasons were permitted as an excuse, the door would be wide open. Every employer who wished to avoid the statute would walk straight through it.

   Lawton LJ agreed, Browne LJ concurring. The House of Lords in *Rainey* disagreed.

[3.86] *Rainey v Greater Glasgow Health Board* [1987] 1 AC 224 (HL)

A woman prosthetist claimed equal pay with a male colleague who, although having comparable qualifications and experience, was paid almost 40% more. Male prosthetists had been recruited 'indirectly' (i.e., from private practice) by the Board which had established a prosthetic fitting service, this service previously having been provided by private contractors. In order to attract employees from the private sector, the Board had offered to recruit them on the terms and conditions upon which they had been employed in the private sector. The claimant, in common with all the other female prosthetists, had been recruited 'directly' and placed on what was considered the 'appropriate' NHS scale.

No arrangements were made to phase out the pay disparities between directly recruited staff and those originally from the private sector.

Lord Keith (*for the Court*):

[Having cited the words of Lord Denning, above, in *Clay Cross*, and of Lawton LJ, which were in a similar vein] In my opinion these statements are unduly restrictive of the proper interpretation of section 1(3). The difference must be 'material,' which I would construe as meaning 'significant and relevant,' and it must be between 'her case and his.' Consideration of a person's case must necessarily involve consideration of all the circumstances of that case. These may well go beyond . . . the personal qualities by way of skill, experience or training which the individual brings to the job. Some circumstances may on examination prove to be not significant or not relevant, but others may do so, though not relating to the personal qualities of the employee. In particular, where there is no question of intentional sex discrimination whether direct or indirect (and there is none here) a difference which is connected with economic factors affecting the efficient carrying on of the employer's business or other activity may well be relevant . . .

In *Bilka-Kaufhaus* [3.47] . . . the European Court . . . made it clear that it was not sufficient for the employers merely to show absence of any intention to discriminate, saying . . . :

'It is for the national court, which has sole jurisdiction to make findings of fact, to determine whether and to what extent the grounds put forward by an employer to explain the adoption of a pay practice which applies independently of a worker's sex but in fact affects more women than men may be regarded as objectively justified economic grounds. If the national court finds that the measures chosen by Bilka correspond to a real need on the part of the undertaking, are appropriate with a view to achieving the objectives pursued and are necessary to that end, the fact that the measures affect a far greater number of women than men is not sufficient to show that they constitute an infringement of Article [141] . . . '

I consider that read as a whole the ruling of the European Court would not exclude objectively justified grounds which are other than economic, such as administrative efficiency in a concern not engaged in commerce or business. The decision of the European Court on Article [141] must be accepted as authoritative . . .

The position in 1980 was that all National Health Service employees were paid on the Whitley Council scale, and that the Whitley Council negotiating machinery applied to them. The prosthetic service was intended to be a branch of the [NHS]. It is therefore easy to see that from the administrative point of view it would have been highly anomalous and inconvenient if prosthetists alone, over the whole tract of future time for which the prosthetic service would endure, were to have been subject to a different salary scale and different negotiating machinery . . . Accordingly, there were sound objectively justified administrative reasons, in my view, for placing prosthetists in general, men and women alike, on the Whitley Council scale and subjecting them to its negotiating machinery. There is no suggestion that it was unreasonable to place them on the particular point on the Whitley Council scale which was in fact selected, ascertained by reference to the position of medical physics technicians and entirely regardless of sex. It is in any event the fact that the general scale of remuneration for prosthetists was laid down accordingly by the Secretary of State. It was not a question of the appellant being paid less than the norm but of [her comparator] being paid more. He was paid more because of the necessity to attract him and other privately employed prosthetists into forming the nucleus of the new service . . .

Counsel for the appellant put forward an argument based on section 1(1)(b) of the [SDA] . . . This provision has the effect of prohibiting indirect discrimination between women and men. In my opinion it does not, for present purposes, add anything to section 1(3) of the [EqPA], since, upon the view which I have taken as to the proper construction of the latter, a difference which demonstrated unjustified indirect discrimination would not discharge the onus placed on the employer. Further, there would not appear to be any material distinction in principle between the need to demonstrate objectively justified grounds of difference for purposes of section 1(3) and the need to justify a requirement or condition under section 1(1)(b)(ii) of the [SDA].

The decision in *Rainey* is authority for the propositions (1) that indirect, as well as direct, pay discrimination is (subject to the possibility of justification) contrary to the EqPA and (2) that the interpretation by the ECJ of Article 141's prohibition on pay-related discrimination (direct or indirect) must be read into section 1(3) of the EqPA. This being the case, the developments which have occurred in the ECJ juris-prudence subsequent to *Bilka* (namely, the decisions in *Rinner-Kühn*, *Danfoss* and *Nimz* (p 278 above) must be read into section 1(3). An employer must not merely demonstrate that a factor put forward under section 1(3) is not one which discrimi-nates directly between men and women workers (different 'male' and 'female' rates, for example, or the application of a discriminatory 'merit' pay scheme, as in *Danfoss*). In addition, to the extent that the reward of any factor impacts disparately upon men and women employees, reliance upon the factor may be justified only to the extent (*Danfoss*, *Nimz*) that 'it is of importance for the performance of specific tasks entrusted to the employee'.

Since the decision in *Rainey*, the House of Lords have considered the GMF defence on a number of occasions and the ECJ has delivered judgment on its proper interpretation. The theme which has linked these decisions (all of which are extracted below) concerns the relationship between the GMF defence and the question of dis-crimination. Thus, in *Enderby v Frenchay* [3.87], the question was whether the applicant had to prove indirect discrimination in pay or whether the employer had to disprove it; in *Ratcliffe v North Yorkshire* whether a tribunal had erred in finding that the GMF put forward by the employer was not 'not the difference of sex'; in *Strath-clyde v Wallace* and in *Glasgow v Marshall* (respectively, [3.89] and [3.90] below) whether employers had to justify reliance upon non-discriminatory pay-related fac-tors. The answers to these questions are, in theory, clear. But the law is complicated by an excess of enthusiasm on the part of the courts for declaring that pay-related factors are not discriminatory. In *Rainey*, for example, Lord Keith declared it an 'ac-cident' that the lower-paid prosthetist in this case was a woman and her comparator a man. But the fact that every prosthetist recruited from the (higher paying) private sector was male might have been taken to indicate discrimination within the private sector. If this was the case, the retention of the enhanced rates payable to private sector prosthetists, coupled with the payment of lower rates to directly recruited staff, at least raised a requirement of objective justification. This justification, in turn, would have had to be made out taking into account its discriminatory impact, an impact ignored by the House of Lords because of its characterisation of the male/female gap as an 'accident'.

[3.87] Case 127/92 *Enderby v Frenchay Health Authority* [1993] ECR I–5535 (ECJ)

A senior speech therapist claimed equal pay with senior hospital pharmacists and clinical psychologists who earned up to 40% more than her. A industrial tribunal ruled that the difference in pay was the result of the different bargaining structures and their history, which were (individually considered) non-discriminatory, and from the structures within the three professions which were also (individually considered) non-discriminatory. The EAT ([1991] ICR 382) dismissed Dr Enderby's appeal and the Court of Appeal referred to the ECJ the question whether the employer's reliance on the separate negotiating structures was objectively justifiable within Article 141. It also asked the ECJ to rule on whether, 'if the employer could establish that serious shortages in one of the comparator professions explained part, but not all, of the difference in pay, the whole or only part of that difference should be regarded as justified'.

Judgment:
It is normally for the person alleging facts in support of a claim to adduce proof of such facts. Thus, in principle, the burden of proving the existence of sex discrimination as to pay lies with the worker who, believing himself to be the victim of such discrimination, brings legal proceedings against his employer with a view to removing the discrimination.

However, it is clear from the case law of the Court that the onus may shift when that is necessary to avoid depriving workers who appear to be the victims of discrimination of any effective means of enforcing the principle of equal pay. Accordingly, when a measure distinguishing between employees on the basis of their hours of work has in practice an adverse impact on substantially more members of one or other sex, that measure must be regarded as contrary to the objective pursued by Article [141] of the Treaty, unless the employer shows that it is based on objectively justified factors unrelated to any discrimination on grounds of sex [citing *Bilka* and *Nimz*]. Similarly, where an undertaking applies a system of pay which is wholly lacking in transparency, it is for the employer to prove that his practice in the matter of wages is not discriminatory, if a female worker establishes, in relation to a relatively large number of employees, that the average pay for women is less than that for men [citing *Danfoss*] . . .

[I]f the pay of speech therapists is significantly lower than that of pharmacists and if the former are almost exclusively women while the latter are predominantly men, there is a *prima facie* case of sex discrimination, at least where the two jobs in question are of equal value and the statistics describing that situation are valid . . .

The fact that the rates of pay at issue are decided by collective bargaining processes conducted separately for each of the two professional groups concerned, without any discriminatory effect within each group, does not preclude a finding of *prima facie* discrimination where the results of those processes show that two groups with the same employer and the same trade union are treated differently. If the employer could rely on the absence of discrimination within each of the collective bargaining processes taken separately as sufficient justification for the difference in pay, he could, as the German Government pointed out, easily circumvent the principle of equal pay by using separate bargaining processes . . .

If . . . the national court has been able to determine precisely what proportion of the increase in pay is attributable to market forces, it must necessarily accept that the pay differential is objectively justified to the extent of that proportion. When national authorities have to apply Community law, they must apply the principle of proportionality.

If that is not the case, it is for the national court to assess whether the role of market forces in determining the rate of pay was sufficiently significant to provide objective justification for part of all of the difference.

The significance of *Enderby* lay in the ECJ's recognition that a *prima facie* case of discrimination could be established simply by a variation in pay between two comparable jobs, and that mere explanation of that pay difference by reference to an apparently gender-neutral (but actually disparately-impacting) factor did not suffice to justify reliance upon that factor. This ought not to have required confirmation in a

British case, the EqPA placing the onus firmly upon the employer to show that the pay-related factor was 'not the difference of sex'. But the lower courts had, in the *Enderby* litigation, required the applicant to prove that the difference in pay was due to an indirectly discriminatory pay practice, the test for indirect discrimination having been imported from the SDA.

[3.88] *Ratcliffe v North Yorkshire County Council* [1995] ICR 833 (HL)

The applicants were 'dinner ladies' who, their jobs having been rated as being of equivalent value to those of various male employees, had their rates of pay cut in an attempt to keep the provision of school meals 'in-house'. The council was obliged to set up Direct Service Organisations to compete commercially with outside providers, and could use those DSOs to provide services only where they were successful in tendering against outside organisations. The DSO employing the 'dinner ladies' had taken the view that costs had to be reduced by 25% in order to compete, a decision which had not been necessary in the case of those DSOs employing the woman's comparators. The Council argued that the variation in pay was 'genuinely due' to compulsory competitive tendering, this being a material factor 'not the difference of sex' within section 1(3). The tribunal ruled against the employer:

> [The DSO manager] . . . perceived that it was necessary to [reduce the dinner ladies' terms] in order to be able to compete in the open market, that is to say due to his perception of market forces in a market which is virtually exclusively female doing work which is convenient to that female workforce and which, but for the particular hours and times of work, that workforce would not be able to do . . . It was clear to [him] that it was a workforce that would, by and large, continue to do the work, even at a reduced rate of pay, when the alternative was no work or ceasing to have the advantages of remaining a county council employee and becoming an employee of a commercial catering organisation doing the same work for less favourable terms in any event. It is clear that both the DSO and the employees were over the proverbial 'barrel' due to the fact that competitors only employed women and, because of that, employed them on less favourable terms than the council did previously . . . That may well have been a material factor but it was certainly a material factor due to the difference of sex arising out of the general perception in the United Kingdom, and certainly in North Yorkshire, that a woman should stay at home to look after the children and if she wants to work it must fit in with that domestic duty and a lack of facilities to enable her, easily, to do otherwise' . . .

The EAT allowed the employer's appeal, and the Court of Appeal ([1994] ICR 810) rejected the women's appeal on the ground that the applicants had failed to prove that the 'market forces' relied on in this instance were indirectly discriminatory. The House of Lords allowed the women's appeal.

Lord Slynn of Hadley *(for their Lordships):*
The relevant question under the [EqPA] is whether equal treatment has been accorded for men and women employed on like work or for men and women employed on work rated as equivalent . . . In the present case . . . the women were found to be engaged on work rated as equivalent to work done by men. That is sufficient for the women to be entitled to a declaration by the industrial tribunal in their favour unless s 1(3) of the [EqPA], as set out previously, is satisfied.

This was the question for the industrial tribunal to consider. By a majority they were satisfied that the employers had failed to show that the variation between the appellants' contracts and those of their male comparators was due to a material factor which was not the difference of sex.

In my opinion it is impossible to say that they were not entitled on the evidence to come to that conclusion. It is obvious that the employers reduced the appellants' wages in order to obtain the area contracts and that to obtain the area contracts they had to compete with CCG who, the tribunal found, employed only women and 'because of that, employed them on less favourable terms than the Council did previously under the [National Joint Council] agreement' . . . The fact, if it be a fact, that CCG [the external competitor] discriminated against women in respect of pay and that the DSO had to pay no more than CCG in order to be competitive does not, however, conclude the issue. The basic question is whether the DSO paid women less than men for work rated as equivalent. The reason they did so is certainly that they had to compete with CCG. The fact, however, is that they did pay women less than men engaged on work rated as equivalent. The industrial tribunal found and was entitled to find that the employers had not shown that this was genuinely due to a material difference other than the difference of sex.

The women could not have found other suitable work and were obliged to take the wages offered if they were to continue with this work. The fact that two men were employed on the same work at the same rate of pay does not detract from the conclusion that there was discrimination between the women involved and their male comparators. It means no more than that the two men were underpaid compared with other men doing jobs rated as equivalent . . .

The fact that they paid women less than their male comparators because they were women constitutes direct discrimination and *ex hypothesi* cannot be shown to be justified on grounds 'irrespective of the sex of the person' concerned . . .

It was clear in *Ratcliffe* that the factor relied upon by the employer was one which operated to the disadvantage of women. If such a factor is directly discriminatory (as the House of Lords accepted here was the case) the employer cannot justify reliance upon it and the GMF defence fails. If it is indirectly discriminatory it will amount to a GMF only to the extent that it is justified in line with the test developed in *Bilka-Kaufhaus*, *Rinner-Kühn*, *Danfoss* and *Nimz*, etc. If the factor is neither directly nor indirectly discriminatory, the employer does not have to justify reliance upon it.

[3.89] *Strathclyde Regional Council v Wallace* [1998] ICR 205 (HL)

The applicants, who were teachers, claimed equal pay with male principal teachers with whom they were doing the same work while 'acting up' without pay or appointment. A tribunal found in favour of the women, ruling at the same time that none of the factors relied upon by the employer were discriminatory (most of the 'acting up' teachers were men), and that the employers had failed to justify their reliance on these grounds. The EAT overruled the tribunal, and the women appealed unsuccessfully as far as the House of Lords.

Lord Browne-Wilkinson *(for the Court)*:

. . . The selection by the appellants in this case of male principal teachers as comparators was purely the result of a tactical selection by these appellants: there are male and female principal teachers employed by the respondents without discrimination. Therefore the objective sought by the appellants is to achieve equal pay for like work regardless of sex, not to eliminate any inequalities due to sex discrimination. There is no such discrimination in the present case. To my mind it would be very surprising if a differential pay structure which had no disparate effect or impact as between the sexes should prove to be unlawful under the [EqPA] . . .

To establish a sub-s (3) defence, the employer has to prove that the disparity in pay is due to a factor 'which is not the difference of sex', ie is not sexually discriminatory . . . Indirect discrimination can be 'justified' if it is shown that the measures adopted by the employers which cause the adverse impact on women 'correspond to a real need on the part of the [employers], are appropriate with a view to achieving the objectives pursued and are necessary to that end' [citing *Rainey*].

The cases establish that the [EqPA] has to be construed so far as possible to work harmoniously both with the [SDA] and Art [141]. All three sources of law are part of a code dealing with unlawful sex discrimination . . . the words 'not the difference of sex' where they appear in s 1(3) of the [EqPA] must be construed so as to accord with the SDA and art [141], ie an employer will not be able to demonstrate that a factor is 'not the difference of sex' if the factor relied upon is sexually discriminatory whether directly or indirectly. Further, a sexually discriminatory practice will not be fatal to a sub-s (3) defence if the employer can 'justify' it applying the test in the *Bilka-Kaufhaus* case . . .

There is no question of the employer having to 'justify' (in the *Bilka* sense) all disparities of pay. Provided that there is no element of sexual discrimination, the employer establishes a sub-s (3) defence by identifying the factors which he alleges have caused the disparity, proving that those factors are genuine and proving further that they were causally relevant to the disparity in pay complained of . . .

The apparent willingness of the courts to accept that pay-related factors are not discriminatory has been remarked upon (Lord Keith's acceptance in *Rainey* that the composition by sex of the directly and indirectly recruited prosthetists was an 'accident'; their Lordship's failure, in *Wallace*, to compare the composition by sex of the 'acting-up' teachers and the headteachers). But the principle embraced by the House of Lords in *Wallace* is correct given the EqPA's prohibition, not of all unjustified pay differentials between comparable jobs, rather of those differentials which an employer has failed to prove 'genuinely due to a material factor which is not the difference of sex'. What is problematic, however, is the tendency of the courts to overlook section 1(3)'s requirement that the pay-related factor on which the employer seeks to rely must be 'material'. It appeared, on the facts in *Wallace*, that this requirement was satisfied. But Lord Browne-Wilkinson's failure to advert to that fact, in stressing that only discriminatory factors require to be justified, was unfortunate.

A similar approach was taken by their Lordships in *Glasgow City Council v Marshall* in which the claimants, instructors in special schools, claimed equal pay with teachers also employed in the special schools. The teachers' qualifications were higher but the work undertaken by the applicants and their comparators was found by an industrial tribunal to be 'like'. The tribunal rejected the employer's GMF defence—that teachers' and instructors' pay was determined differently (by statutory procedure and national collective bargaining respectively), ruling that the employers had not justified the difference. The House of Lords disagreed, ruling that the employer did not have to justify any difference which was unrelated to sex (as here).

[3.90] *Glasgow City Council v Marshall* **[2000] ICR 196 (HL)**

Lord Nicholls (for the Court):
The scheme of the [EqPA] is that a rebuttable presumption of sex discrimination arises

once the gender-based comparison shows that a woman, doing like work or work rated as equivalent or work of equal value to that of a man, is being paid or treated less favourably than the man. The variation between her contract and the man's contract is presumed to be due to the difference of sex. The burden passes to the employer to show that the explanation for the variation is not tainted with sex. In order to discharge this burden the employer must satisfy the tribunal on several matters. First, that the proffered explanation, or reason, is genuine, and not a sham or pretence. Second, that the less favourable treatment is due to this reason. The factor relied upon must be the cause of the disparity. In this regard, and in this sense, the factor must be a 'material' factor, that is, a significant and relevant factor. Third, that the reason is not 'the difference of sex'. This phrase is apt to embrace any form of sex discrimination, whether direct or indirect. Fourth, that the factor relied upon is or, in a case within section 1(2)(c), may be a 'material' difference, that is, a significant and relevant difference, between the woman's case and the man's case.

When section 1 is thus analysed, it is apparent that an employer who satisfies the third of these requirements is under no obligation to prove a 'good' reason for the pay disparity. In order to fulfil the third requirement he must prove the absence of sex discrimination, direct or indirect. If there is any evidence of sex discrimination, such as evidence that the difference in pay has a disparately adverse impact on women, the employer will be called upon to satisfy the tribunal that the difference in pay is objectively justifiable. But if the employer proves the absence of sex discrimination he is not obliged to justify the pay disparity.

In Case 381/99 *Brunnhofer v Bank der Österreichischen Postsparkasse AG* [2001] ECR I–04961 the ECJ ruled that, once an applicant had established that she was paid less than a man performing the same work or work of equal value, the burden passed to the employer to justify the difference in pay. The significance of the decision was considered by the EAT in *Parliamentary Commissioner for Administration v Fernandez* [2004] ICR 123. An employment tribunal had found against the employer on the basis that the factor upon which it relied in relation to a disputed pay difference, although neither directly nor indirectly discriminatory, was nevertheless not justifiable. The EAT overruled the decision on the basis that no justification was required in the absence of discrimination and that the decision in *Brunnhofer* should not be taken to have laid down any requirement to the contrary. In *Ministry of Defence v Armstrong* [2004] IRLR 672, however, a differently constituted EAT upheld a tribunal ruling that the employer had not made out the section 1(3) defence in a case in which the employer had sought to explain the difference in pay by reference to different arrangements for pay determination applicable to the claimant and comparator groups. According to Mrs Justice Cox, for the EAT, the concept of indirect discrimination under the Equal Pay Act was broader than that provided for by the SDA and 'the fundamental question' under the EqPA was simply 'whether there is a causative link between the applicant's sex and the fact that she is paid less than the true value of her job as reflected in the pay of her named comparator'. If the cause of the pay difference was tainted by sex-related factors, the GMF defence failed.

3.11 Procedural and related issues

3.11.1 Proving discrimination

The first point to be made here is perhaps the most fundamental, and it applies to all the anti-discrimination legislation as well as to employment-related cases in general. As Brian Doyle put it ('Disabled Workers' Rights, the Disability Discrimination Act and the UN Standard Rules' (1996) 25 *Industrial Law Journal* 1): 'Although tribunals will be subject to the *physical* accessibility requirements of the [DDA], this does not mean that there is *legal* access in practice. In particular, legal aid does not extend to the tribunals'.

Doyle contrasted the position of DDA claimants (at the time denied a Commission) with that of claimants under the RRA and the SDA, who could apply to the CRE and the EOC, respectively, for financial and other assistance. The National Disability Council (a purely advisory body established under the DDA) has been replaced by a Disability Rights Commission along the lines of the EOC and the CRE. But this should not be regarded as answering Doyle's point. A Parliamentary answer by Lord Sainsbury for the DTI on 4th June 2004 indicated that the EOC, CRE and DRC had between them spent only £1.67 million in 2003–4 on funding discrimination cases, down from £1.81 million in 2002-3 (expenditure on such assistance accounted for 4.5%, 2.3% and 5.7% of the Commission's respective budgets in 2003–4). Planned expenditure is to drop to £1.51 million in 2004–5 (3.1%, 2% and 5.5% of the Commissions' budgets).

The burden of proof in discrimination claims, as in other employment-related actions, is on the claimant. The domestic courts have recognized the difficulties associated with proving discrimination—in particular, the fact that direct evidence of such discrimination is only rarely available. It is one thing to demonstrate that a claimant has been treated less favourably than someone of a different sex, racial group, etc., and to demonstrate that s/he has suffered a detriment thereby. But only in the rarest cases will a discriminator admit that the less favourable treatment was 'by reason of' the claimant's sex, race, etc.: that s/he would not have been so treated 'but for' the protected reason. Courts and tribunals have, therefore, to *infer* unlawful discrimination from primary facts (i.e., to conclude that the reason for proven less favourable treatment was a prohibited one). Such inference might also be necessary in a case which turns on a hypothetical, rather than an actual, comparator, in order to establish the very fact of less favourable treatment.

The leading authority for a number of years was the decision of the Court of Appeal in *King v The Great Britain-China Centre*, as affirmed by the House of Lords in *Glasgow City Council v Zafar*. Below we consider recent legislative amendments to the burden of proof, but the *King/Zafar* approach is still binding in relation to the SDA and DDA as they apply outside the employment sphere, and to the RRA as it applies to discrimination on grounds of colour and nationality.

The *King* case was brought by a woman of Chinese origin who claimed that she had been subject to race discrimination in a job application. Her claim succeeded at tribunal, a majority finding that the employers 'had failed to demonstrate that the applicant had not been treated unfavourably [in not being shortlisted], or that such unfavourable treatment was not because of her race'. The EAT allowed the employers' appeal, ruling that the tribunal had incorrectly placed the burden of proof on them. The Court of Appeal, however, reinstated the tribunal's decision, Neill LJ summarising the existing authorities as follows:

[3.91] *King v The Great Britain-China Centre* **[1992] ICR 516 (CA)**

Neill LJ (for the Court):

(1) It is for the applicant who complains of racial discrimination to make out his or her case. Thus if the applicant does not prove the case on the balance of probabilities he or she will fail.

(2) It is important to bear in mind that it is unusual to find direct evidence of racial discrimination. Few employers will be prepared to admit such discrimination even to themselves. In some cases the discrimination will not be ill-intentioned but merely based on an assumption 'he or she would not have fitted in'.

(3) The outcome of the case will therefore usually depend on what inferences it is proper to draw from the primary facts found by the Tribunal. These inferences can include, in appropriate cases, any inferences that it is just and equitable to draw in accordance with s 65(2)(b) of the [RRA] from an evasive or equivocal reply to a questionnaire.

(4) Though there will be some cases where, for example, the non-selection of the applicant for a post or for promotion is clearly not on racial grounds, a finding of discrimination and a finding of a difference in race will often point to the possibility of racial discrimination. In such circumstances the Tribunal will look to the employer for an explanation. If no explanation is then put forward or if the Tribunal considers the explanation to be inadequate or unsatisfactory it will be legitimate for the Tribunal to infer that the discrimination was on racial grounds. This is not a matter of law but, as May LJ put it in [*North West Thames Regional Health Authority v Noone* [1988] ICR 813], 'almost common sense'.

(5) It is unnecessary and unhelpful to introduce the concept of a shifting evidential burden of proof. At the conclusion of all the evidence the Tribunal should make findings as to the primary facts and draw such inferences as they consider proper from those facts. They should then reach a conclusion on the balance of probabilities, bearing in mind both the difficulties which face a person who complains of unlawful discrimination and the fact that it is for the complainant to prove his or her case.

In *Glasgow City Council v Zafar* the House of Lords ruled that a tribunal which considered itself *bound* to infer unlawful discrimination from a finding of less favourable treatment, coupled with an unsatisfactory explanation from an employer, would err as a matter of law. Their Lordships also warned against inferring *less favourable* (i.e., *prima facie* discriminatory) treatment from *bad* treatment. The *Zafar* approach encouraged employers to run the so-called 'bastard' defence: 'yes I treated the applicant badly/unfairly/unreasonably/appallingly. But I would have treated someone of a different sex/race/other protected factor equally badly'.

Recognition of the problems experienced more generally by those attempting to prove discrimination resulted at the European level in the adoption in 1997 of the Burden of Proof Directive which provides (Article 4(1)) that:

> Member States shall take such measures as are necessary, in accordance with their national judicial systems, to ensure that, when persons who consider themselves wronged because the principle of equal treatment has not been applied to them establish, before a court or other competent authority, facts from which it may be presumed that there has been direct or indirect discrimination, *it shall be for the respondent to prove that there has been no breach of the principle of equal treatment* [our emphasis]'.

At the time, European legislation only applied to sex discrimination and so the Burden of Proof Regulations amended only the SDA (and then only in its application to 'employment', broadly defined).

[3.92] Sex Discrimination Act 1975, section 63A(2)

> s.63A(2) Where, on the hearing of the complaint, the complainant proves facts from which the tribunal could, apart from this section, conclude in the absence of an adequate explanation that the respondent—
> (a)   has committed an act of discrimination against the complainant which is unlawful by virtue of Part 2 [the employment-related provisions] . . .
> the tribunal shall uphold the complaint unless the respondent proves that he did not commit, or, as the case may be, is not to be treated as having committed, that act.

Section 66A makes similar provision for claims brought in the county or sheriff court in relation to discrimination against barristers or pupil barristers or in relation to vocational training (these being regarded as employment-related for the purposes of EU law). The CRE called, in 1998, for primary legislation to bring the RRA into line with the Burden of Proof Directive. This did not, in the event, happen until 2003 when it was required as part of the implementation of the Racial Equality Directive which, with the Employment Equality Directive, applies the same rule to the proof of discrimination on grounds of racial and national origin, sexual orientation, religion and belief, disability and age as the Burden of Proof Directive does to discrimination on grounds of sex. The RRA has, accordingly, been amended in its application to discrimination on grounds of racial, ethnic and national origin (but neither colour nor nationality) and provides that, where it is alleged that a respondent has committed an act of discrimination or harassment, on grounds of race or ethnic or national origins:

[3.93] Race Relations Act 1976, sections 54A and 57ZA

> (2) Where, on the hearing of the complaint, the complainant proves facts from which the tribunal [or county court] could, apart from this section, conclude in the absence of an adequate explanation that the respondent—
> (a) has committed such an act of discrimination or harassment against the complainant . . .

the tribunal [or county court] shall uphold the complaint unless the respondent proves that he did not commit or, as the case may be, is not to be treated as having committed, that act.

The SORs and RBRs (Regulation 29) are materially identical as is section 17A DDA (which applies only in relation to employment, broadly defined). The *King/Zafar* approach is applicable to non-employment related discrimination under that Act, under the SDA and under Northern Ireland's Fair Employment and Treatment Order (which regulates discrimination on grounds of religion and political belief), as well as to discrimination on grounds of nationality and colour under the RRA. The SORs and RBRs and the amendments to the RRA have been in place for a very short time. But questions of proof have quickly proven a fruitful source of litigation under those provisions as under the amended SDA.

In *Barton* v *Investec Henderson Crosthwaite Securities Ltd* [2003] ICR 1205 the EAT considered the application of the burden of proof in the SDA post amendment. The case concerned allegations both under the EqPA and the SDA by an analyst who had been paid less and granted less favourable non-contractual bonuses than a male comparator. The EAT ruled (*per* Judge Ansell) that, once the applicant proved 'facts from which the tribunal could conclude, in the absence of an adequate explanation, that the respondents have committed an act of discrimination against the applicant' the burden of proof passed to the respondent 'to prove that he did not commit' the act of discrimination: 'That requires a tribunal to assess not merely whether the respondent has proved an explanation for the facts from which such inferences can be drawn, but further that it is adequate to discharge the burden of proof on the balance of probabilities that sex was not any part of the reasons for the treatment in question. Since the facts necessary to prove an explanation would normally be in the possession of the respondent, a tribunal would normally expect cogent evidence to discharge that burden of proof'. Dispute subsequently broke out about what was required by way of a *prima facie* case before the burden of proof shifts. In *Igen Ltd v Wong* [2005] IRLR 258 the Court of Appeal endorsed the approach taken by the EAT in *Barton* and ruled that a tribunal had been entitled to draw an inference of discrimination, in the absence of a satisfactory explanation by the employer, from unreasonable conduct on the part of the employer.

3.11.2 Time limits

A further significant difficulty which discrimination complainants frequently encounter relates to the time limits imposed by legislation.

[3.94] Sex Discrimination Act 1975, section 76

S.76 (1) An [employment] tribunal shall not consider a complaint . . . unless it is presented to the tribunal before the end of the period of three months beginning when the act complained of was done . . .

(5) [(6) RRA] A court or tribunal may nevertheless consider any such complaint . . . which

is out of time if, in all the circumstances of the case, it considers that it is just and equitable to do so.

Section 68 RRA is materially identical as is Regulation 34 of both the SORs and the RBRs and schedule 3, para 3 DDA. Tribunals remain free to disapply time limits if they regard it as just and equitable so to do (SDA section 76(5) and equivalents). This discretion is much wider than that afforded under the Employment Rights Act 1996, section 111(2) of which provides that a tribunal 'shall not consider' a claim made out-of-time unless made 'within such further period as the tribunal considers reasonable in a case where it is satisfied that it was not reasonably practicable' for the complaint to be presented in time.

The discretion accorded to tribunals in this context is broad. In *London Borough of Southwark v Afolabi* [2003] ICR 800 the Court of Appeal ruled that a tribunal had not erred in hearing a race discrimination complaint which concerned the terms of the Claimant's appointment to a position some nine years before. It was not until shortly prior to the issue of the complaint that the Claimant had seen his personnel file which revealed that the employer's refusal to appoint him to the position he had originally sought (as distinct from the more junior one in which he was taken on) was made notwithstanding very high ratings he had received at his interview. The tribunal ruled that it was just and equitable to consider his complaint, there having been no reason for him to inspect his personal file before he did, and Mr Afolabi having brought his claim within three months of seeing the file. The EAT and the Court of Appeal upheld the tribunal's exercise of discretion.

Under the EqPA, the time-limit is six, rather than three, months (section 2(4)), and generally runs from the termination of the employment contract to which the claim relates. Tribunals have no discretion to extend this period, although the EqPA makes special provision for when time begins to run in cases in which the applicant was misled as to pay or where she was operating under a disability (new section 2ZA EqPA).

3.11.3 Remedies

Sections 65 and 56 respectively of the SDA and the RRA provide that remedies may consist of:

(a) an order declaring the rights of the complainant and the respondent in relation to the act to which the complaint relates;

(b) an order requiring the respondent to pay to the complainant compensation . . .

(c) a recommendation that the respondent take within a specified period action appearing to the tribunal to be practicable for the purpose of obviating or reducing the adverse effect on the complainant of any act of discrimination to which the complaint relates.

Section 8 DDA is in similar terms, save that 'practicable' in (c) is substituted by the words 'reasonable, in all the circumstances of the case'.

In 1998 the CRE criticised the individualistic focus of section 56(c) RRA and proposed that it be widened to allow tribunals to make recommendations 'regarding the future conduct of the respondent to prevent further acts of discrimination', including recommendations 'regarding any of the respondent's practices or procedures which have been at issue and future treatment of the applicant by the respondent . . . whether or not she or he remains in employment' (*Reform of the Race Relations Act 1976*, p. 299 above). In the same year the EOC criticised the narrow range of remedies available and called for powers to be given to tribunals to order 'reinstatement, re-engagement, appointment, or promotion as appropriate' as well as 'action needed to end the discrimination [against] the person bringing the complaint *and anyone else who might be affected*. The Fair Employment and Treatment Order (FETO) permits a recommendation 'that the respondent take . . . action . . . for the purpose of obviating or reducing the adverse effect on a person *other than the complainant* of any unlawful discrimination to which the complaint relates'.

Declarations and recommendations are fairly rare under the SDA and RRA, being issued in the late 1980s in only around 3% of cases (C. McCrudden, D. Smith and C. Brown, *Racial Justice at Work* (London, Policy Studies Institute, 1991). By far the most common remedy in both race and sex discrimination cases (though still only awarded in a minority of successful cases) is the award of compensation which, since the early 1990s, has been subject to no maximum figure. Some very substantial awards have been made in recognition of the pecuniary loss (including loss of pension rights) suffered by the victims of discrimination, in particular by the many women forced to leave the armed services when they became pregnant. Levels of compensation have increased gradually since the mid 1990s and a few cases have generated huge awards (see further below). By 2003 just 7% and 5% of awards in sex and race discrimination employment cases were of less than £1,000 and just over 21% (almost 33% of race cases) were of £10,000 or more. And, whereas average payouts in 1995 were £3,617 and £5,032 in sex and race respectively, and median payments £3,000 in each, by 2003 the average figures for sex and race respectively were £7,960 and £12,225, although median figures were a more modest £5,677 and £5,100 respectively (the *Equal Opportunities Review* regularly publishes guides to compensation awards). In 2003, average and median awards in employment disability cases ran at at £15,634 and £5,310 respectively while in 2003 just under 8% of awards in disability cases were for £1,000 or less and almost 34% for £10,000 or more. The first successful claim under the SORs resulted in the award in January 2005 of £35,345 to a gay man constructively dismissed from his £54,000 managerial post as a result of sustained verbal taunting (*Observer* 30 January, 2005, reporting *Whitfield v Cleanaway*) while the first reported tribunal award under the RBRs was of £10,000 to a Muslim sacked for taking leave to make a pilgrimage to Mecca (Times online, 15 January 2005, reporting *Khan v NIC Hygiene*).

A significant proportion of discrimination compensation typically consists of an award for injury to feelings (this being the largest factor, typically, in harassment claims) and accounting for 39% of the total awarded in 2003, 48% of that in sex and race cases). Only rarely will such compensation not be awarded. Typically, race discrimination claims attach the largest awards for injury to feelings (in recent years, pregnancy claims have attracted the lowest awards in respect of injury to feelings of sex discrimination cases). In *Vento v Chief Constable of West Yorkshire Police (No.2)* the Court of Appeal laid down guidelines for injury to feelings awards, suggesting that:

[3.95] *Vento v Chief Constable of West Yorkshire Police (No.2)* [2003] ICR 318 (CA)

Mummery LJ (for the Court):
(i) The top band should normally be between £15,000 and £25,000. Sums in this range should be awarded in the most serious cases, such as where there has been a lengthy campaign of discriminatory harassment on the ground of sex or race. This case falls within that band. Only in the most exceptional case should an award of compensation for injury to feelings exceed £25,000.
(ii) The middle band of between £5,000 and £15,000 should be used for serious cases, which do not merit an award in the highest band.
(iii) Awards of between £500 and £5,000 are appropriate for less serious cases, such as where the act of discrimination is an isolated or one-off occurrence. In general, awards of less than £500 are to be avoided altogether, as they risk being regarded as so low as not to be a proper recognition of injury to feelings.

In *Scott v Commissioners of Inland Revenue* [2004] ICR 1410 the Court of Appeal ruled that aggravated damages were a separate element from damages for injury to feelings and ought to be awarded to mark injury resulting from high-handed, malicious, insulting or oppressive behaviour by the respondent. And in *Gibbons v South West Water Services Ltd* [1993] 2 WLR 507 the Court of Appeal ruled that exemplary damages were available in respect only of those torts, whether statutory or common law, which existed prior to the decision of the House of Lords in *Rookes v Barnard* [1964] AC 1129. On this view, such damages were not available in respect of sex or race discrimination. But in *Kuddus v Chief Constable of Leicester Constabulary* [2002] 2 AC 122, the House of Lords held that the availability of exemplary damages depended on the conduct of the public authority rather than the cause of action sued upon, and that such damages were available in that case on a complaint of misfeasance in public office notwithstanding the fact that the tort had not been accepted as a cause of action before 1964. In *Virgo Fidelis Senior School v Boyle* the EAT considered whether exemplary damages were available under the public interest disclosure provisions of the ERA.

[3.96] *Virgo Fidelis Senior School v Boyle* [2004] ICR 1210 (CA)

Ansell J:
we would venture to suggest that once the cause of action test no longer exists and the *Rookes v Barnard* test becomes fact sensitive rather than cause of action sensitive we see no reason why in principle exemplary damages could not be awarded, provided that the other conditions are made out. Clearly in the majority of cases aggravated damages would be sufficient to mark the employer's conduct.

Section 2(5) EqPA originally restricted equal pay awards to a period of not more than two years prior to the date of the claim. This 'back-stop' was successfully challenged in Case 326/96, *Levez v Jennings (Harlow Pools) Ltd* [1998] ECR I-7835 and subsequently disapplied by the EAT (*Levez v Jennings (Harlow Pools) Ltd, Hicking v Basford Group Ltd (No 2)* [2000] ICR 58). Sections 2(5) and 2ZB EqPA now provide that damages may be backdated to (in England and Wales) six years prior to the point of claim (or, in a concealment or disability case – see 3.11.2 above, six years prior to the discovery (constructive or otherwise) or the removal of the disability respectively). In Scotland the general limit is five years with special provision also being made (sections 2(5) and 2ZC) for cases of fraud and disability.

3.12 Conclusion

In this chapter we have attempted to clarify and bring sense to the maze of provisions which make up UK anti-discrimination law. What will be clear to the reader at this point, however, is that task is a difficult one. There is a singular lack of coherence and principle in the current law and there seems as yet to be little political will to change this. The government did, in December 2003, appear to give way to a rising chorus of demands for the introduction of a single equality Act. It remains to be seen, however, whether any such legislation would simply gather the existing mess into a single framework document (no doubt accompanied by myriad secondary provisions), or whether it would attempt to iron out some of the many contradictions and confusions indicated above.

FURTHER READING

M Connolly, 'Discrimination Law: Justification, Alternative Measures and Defences Based on Sex' (2001) 30 *Industrial Law Journal* 311

J Davies, 'A Cuckoo In The Nest? A "Range Of Reasonable Responses", Justification and the Disability Discrimination Act 1995' (2003) 32 *Industrial Law Journal* 164

L Dickens, 'Gender, Race and Employment Equality in Britain: Inadequate Strategies and the Role of Industrial Relations Actors' (1997) 28 *Industrial Relations Journal* 282.

B Hepple QC and T Choudhury, *Tackling Religious Discrimination; Practical Implications for Policy-Makers and Legislators* (London, Home Office, 2001) Home Office Research Study 221

A McColgan, *Discrimination Law: Text, Cases and Materials* 2nd ed (Oxford, Hart, 2005).

A McColgan, 'Equality and Discrimination', in K D Ewing and J Hendy (eds), *A Charter of Workers Rights* (London, Institute of Employment Rights, 2002)

A McColgan, *Equality and Diversity* (ed) (London, Institute of Employment Rights, 2003) and chapters 1, 7 and 8 therein

S Poulter, 'Muslim Headscarves in School: Contrasting Approaches in England and France' (1997) 17 *Oxford Journal of Legal Studies* 43.

P Skidmore, 'Sex, Gender and Comparators in Employment Discrimination Law' (1997) 26 *Industrial Law Journal* 51

M Wynn, 'Pregnancy discrimination: equality, protection or reconciliationfi' (1999) 62 *Modern Law Review* 435.

Protecting the Work/Life Balance?

4.1 Introduction

Increasing concern about the 'long hours culture' and escalating demands for 'flexibility' on the part of workers, together with recent debates about working time regulation and parental leave and changes to maternity leave, have focused public and political attention on the question how workers are to combine paid work with their domestic, caring and other, generally unremunerated, responsibilities. This problem is particularly acute for parents of young children, but it affects a considerable number of those with caring responsibilities for elderly and/or disabled dependants and, more generally, all those who wish to pursue life outside the workplace.

The traditional response to the 'work/life balance' involved the gendered division of paid and unpaid work between parents. The prevalence of this model should not be overstated: it gained prominence with the movement of remunerative labour out of the home with the industrial revolution and reached a peak, in the public imagination at any rate, in Victorian England. Then it was largely confined to the middle classes, Victorian sensibilities about the proper role of women in the domestic sphere accommodating widespread paid labour amongst women of the lower orders. Challenged to some degree during the World Wars, the 'traditional' model experienced another peak in the 1950s. The last 50 years have witnessed the movement of women, in particular the mothers of young children, into paid work. Coupled with the more recent decline in trade unionism and the apparently inexorably increasing demands by employers for (hours-related) 'commitment' on the part of workers, this movement has focused attention on the conflicting pressures experienced by workers in general, parents and other carers in particular.

A typical pattern of work/life 'balance' currently consists, for white families, of a full-time male worker (labouring, as we shall see, for increasingly long hours) and a woman working short part-time hours. This may be contrasted with the position elsewhere: while the Netherlands and Scandinavian countries exhibit levels of part-time working comparable with those in the UK (and significantly higher than those elsewhere in Europe), part-time jobs there tend to involve longer hours, and full-time jobs considerably shorter hours, than is the case in the UK. (Equally, and in contrast to the position in the UK, part-time jobs in the Netherlands and Scandinavia tend to be comparable, in terms of hourly rates and other conditions of work, with full-time jobs.) The gendered model of work which currently prevails in the UK is not without significant social cost. British men work the longest hours in the EU and, as we shall see below, are often denied the opportunity to participate fully in family life as a result. According to the Institute for Policy Studies, 'Working Long Hours: a Review of the Evidence' (2003), 11% of all workers, but a third of men in households containing children, worked in excess of 50 hours per week. And in October 2003 the *Equal Opportunities Review* reported that over 50% of fathers worked more than 40 hours a week, 30% more than 48%. Many men are not even able to share a family meal each day. This has obvious costs both to men and to children, not least in the event of family breakdown. And the 'long hours' culture serves to exclude women with children from many of the high-status jobs in which that culture is most prevalent: few mothers feel able to work the 50 or 60+ hours that are demanded by some such jobs, though the *Equal Opportunities Review* reported in October 2002 that 13% of women (up from 6% in 2000) worked more than 60 hours per week. The 2002 *Equal Opportunities Review* report suggested that no less than 86% of employees were stressed by their current worklife balance, while in 2003 the Mental Health Foundation reported research which showed that a poor work-life balance damages mental health.

The near-50% of British women workers who work part-time are, for the most part, segregated into low-paid jobs in predominantly female, predominantly part-time workplaces and sectors. The lifetime cost to women of the typical pattern of work is high—in 1992 H Joshi and H Davies estimated that a period of time out of the paid labour force, followed by a period of part-time working, cost a typical working mother as much as 57.4% of what she would otherwise have earned between age 25 and retirement (*Childcare and Mothers' Lifetime Earnings: Some European Contrasts*, London, Centre for Economic Policy Research, 1992). Women who work part time do not generally, even if they return to full-time work, regain their former labour market positions. And the increasingly common breakdown of marriage and other relationships condemns many women to impoverished lone-parenthood and, eventually, old-age.

[4.1] Cabinet Office Briefing, *Women's Incomes Over the Lifetime* (2000)

> Income sharing within families can be an important component of women's lifetime incomes . . . [But m]any women lose out financially on divorce. If Mrs Mid-skill with two children get divorced, her income loss is £169, 000 where her marriage is short (seven years) and £127, 000 for a long marriage (17 years) . . .
>
> The notable differences in women's lifetime earnings are reflected in their individual income in retirement . . .
>
> Mrs Low-skill's small lifetime earnings lead to a small individual retirement income . . . Low-skilled mothers lose 42% of their earnings-related pension if they have two children (84% if they have four). For Mrs Mid-skill, comparable losses of pension are 21% if they have two children (69% with four).

This chapter considers the statutory provisions, not including sex and other discrimination legislation, which impact most significantly on the work/life balance. Some such legislation is intended directly to affect this balance: the Parental Leave Directive and Regulations are aimed at allowing parents to balance the demands of work and family life, while the Part-time Workers Directive and Regulations attempt to improve the position of those who work part-time. Rights to maternity leave are essential if women are to retain their jobs after childbirth and to have access to some (however inadequate) income during the period immediately around childbirth. And minimum wage regulation is necessary to counter the 'poverty trap' which excludes many on social security from paid work, and to reduce the necessity for the very low paid to work excessive hours. The EU Working Time Directive, on which the domestic Working Time Regulations are based, will also be considered, though it is interesting to note the UK Government's recent reluctance (discussed further below at 4.5.8) to see this as an instrument of work-life balance rather than a bare health and safety measure.

4.2 Part-time workers

It was noted, above, that the typical white female response to the 'work/life balance', at least in the case of those having young children, involves part-time work. Over six and a half million people, more than 25% of all workers and half of women workers, work part-time. Part-time working has increased radically over the past few decades. Whereas, in 1951, only 4% of all workers (12% of women) worked part-time, by 1984 this had risen to 21% (45% of women workers) and by 1996 to 25% (the proportion of women workers having stabilised at around 45%). Two thirds of employed mothers work part-time, this for reasons including men's long working hours and the shortage and expense of formal child care. Women's share of full-time employment has remained relatively stable at around 25% since the 1960s while men account for less than 20% of part-time workers and tend to work part-time at the start and end of their working lives, if at all.

Long working hours impose costs on male workers in terms of their exclusion from family life. Part-time working imposes costs on women in terms of the denial of access to high-quality jobs and their segregation into poorly paid occupations and workplaces. The lifetime costs to women, and their implications for poverty in old age, have been noted above.

[4.2] EOC, Memorandum to the House of Commons Select Committee on Education and Employment, *Part-Time Working* Vol II, (Second Report 1998–99, HC 346-II), Executive Summary

> The British workforce appears to have a more divergent pattern of working than other
> European countries. The long hours worked by men employed full-time in Britain

contrast with the relatively shorter working hours of female part-time workers. Women working part-time in the UK tend to work shorter hours than their European counterparts. Taking full-time and part-time work together, the average working hours of British women was 30.7 per week compared with an EU average of 32.8 hours per week. British women average the second shortest hours per working week in Europe—only Dutch women work on average shorter hours. In contrast male full-time workers in the UK work a longer working week on average than in any other European country (43.6 hours per week compared with an EC average of 40.1 hours per week). Men's long working hours appear to be related to parenthood: fathers in Britain work on average hours longer per week than men without children.

It is probable that these working patterns are connected: women's opportunity for working is constrained by the relatively long hours worked by their partners. Other European countries also make better provision for childcare and provide better maternity rights, giving women greater opportunities to return to full-time work or to work relatively long hours.

Whereas in Britain part-time work is concentrated in lower level service jobs, this is not the case in other EC countries, where part-time workers are found more extensively in professional occupations. Part-time working is used more widely in Europe as a way of retaining women within their current occupations when they have had children. It is also used more frequently than in Britain as a strategy for worksharing, to reduce unemployment levels.

The availability of part-time work is frequently held out as beneficial to workers, particularly to women with childcare and other domestic responsibilities. But it is not an unmitigated blessing.

[4.3] EOC, Memorandum to the House of Commons Select Committee on Education and Employment, *Part-Time Working* Vol II, (Second Report 1998–99, HC 346-II)

4. For many years part-time workers have been regarded as peripheral workers, of lesser importance and less committed to their work than full-time staff. This perception, together with many employers' desire to employ part-time staff as a means of containing costs, has influenced the pay and terms and conditions of employment for part-time staff. Many part-time workers . . . are employed on less favourable terms than full-time employees, with less security of employment and few opportunities for career development and promotion . . .

32. The hourly pay of part-time workers is consistently lower on average than the hourly pay of full-time staff . . . [in winter 1996–97] part-time average hourly earnings were only 66 % of average full-time hourly earnings . . .

33. . . . A part-time employee is up to three times more likely to be low paid than their full-time counterpart . . .

35. The low average hourly pay of part-time workers is attributable to a combination of factors. These . . . include:

> —occupational segregation and the concentration of part-time workers in the lowest paid occupations within a workplace
> —the exclusion of some groups of part-time workers from the main payment structure . . .
> —the payment by some employers of a lower basic rate of pay to part-time workers than their full-time counterparts . . . Unequal treatment for part-timers in relation to profit sharing and performance pay is not uncommon

—the lack of access of part-time workers to overtime pay and other unsocial hours payments. Overtime pay can be an important source of income, particularly in manual work, but most part-time staff will not be paid overtime rates until their additional hours worked exceed the standard working week . . .

. . . part-time workers are more likely than full-time workers to be in employment where no pension scheme is offered—54 % of male part-timers and 42 % of female part-timers work for employers who do not have a pension scheme, compared with only a quarter of full-time men and women. . . . even where pension schemes are available, part-time workers are far less likely to be a member of the scheme than their full-time colleagues. Just 21 % of the male part-timers and 44 % of female part-timers whose employer has a scheme are members of the scheme. The corresponding figures for full-time staff is 78 % of male and 72 % of female full-timers . . .

43. Until recently, many occupational pension schemes expressly excluded part-time workers from scheme membership. For example, a 1993 pensions survey showed that only 51% of companies with occupational pension schemes admitted all part-time employees to their schemes, and 17% refused admission to any part-time staff . . . However, another reason for the low pension scheme membership of part-time workers is that they are often reluctant to join and pay contributions, despite efforts from pension fund managers to encourage take-up . . .

45. Relatively little part-time work is available in managerial and professional employment. For those who want to reduce their working hours for family reasons, or who are contemplating returning to part-time work after a break from employment, the choices may be limited. Many . . . have to accept a diminution of professional status and pay in order to secure the hours and patterns of work which will fit in with their family responsibilities . . . . once in part-time work career prospects may be poor. One aspect is the shortage of part-time posts in more senior positions; another is that part-time staff may be assumed to be uninterested in career progression and are overlooked for promotion even if they are willing to resume full-time working; a further problem may be lack of investment in training for part-time workers . . .

48. Even where training is provided, there can be logistical difficulties which make access to training more difficult for part-time workers, for example because of their family responsibilities or because training is held at times when they are not due to be in work . . .

[4.4] A Manning and B Petrongolo, 'The Part-time Pay Penalty' (LSE and Women and Equality Unit, 2004)

- In 2003 women working part-time in the UK earned, on average, 22% less than women working full-time – this is the part-time pay penalty. The part-time pay penalty has increased over the past 30 years with most of the rise occurring prior to the mid-1990s.
- This average pay differential between part-time and full-time working women cannot be used as an estimate of the pay penalty that would be suffered by a given woman moving from full-time to part-time work because women working part-time and women working full-time are very different in their characteristics and do very different jobs . . . the part-time penalty for identical women doing the same job is estimated to be about 10% if one does not take account of differences in the occupations of FT and PT working women and 3% if one does.
- The pay differential between full-time and part-time working women within occupation is very small and the occupational segregation of part-time and full-time working women can explain most of the part-time pay penalty.

- The aggregate part-time pay penalty has risen over time but almost all of this rise can be explained by a rising contribution of occupational segregation. Women working part-time have failed to match the occupational up-grades made by women who work full-time.
- Women who move from full-time to part-time work are much more likely to change employer and/or occupation when making this transition than are women who maintain their hours status.
- Women moving from full-time to part-time work, on average, make a downward occupational move, evidence that many women working part-time are not making full use of their skills and experience. This downward occupational mobility is less marked for those women who move from full-time to part-time work without changing their employer . . .
- Women working part-time in the other EU countries have similar problems to the UK but the UK has the highest part-time pay penalty and one of the worst problems in enabling women to move between full-time and part-time work without occupational demotions . . .
- The most effective way to reduce the part-time pay penalty would be to strengthen the ability for women to move between full-time and part-time work without losing their current job.

[4.5] Colette Fagan, Memorandum to the House of Commons Select Committee on Education and Employment, *Part-Time Working* Vol II, (Second Report 1998–99, HC 346-II),

14. . . . . . . the average hourly pay of women part-timers relative to men in full-time jobs has not improved since the late 1970s, in contrast to the relative gains made by women in full-time jobs . . . On average, women part-timers receive 58 % of the hourly pay rate for men in full-time jobs, while the ratio for women in full-time jobs relative to their male counterparts has risen from 72% in 1978 to 80% in 1996. This indicates a growing inequality in wage conditions between women full-timers and part-timers alongside the persistence of gender wage inequalities. Furthermore, it should be noted that the NES [New Earnings Survey] under-estimates the differentials between part-timers and full-timers, for the NES excludes many of the lowest paid part-timers . . .

17. In recent years, pay level for many part-timers have been forced downwards in some parts of the economy by the abolition of the wage councils and by the introduction of compulsory competitive tendering in many areas of the public sector. Part-timers have also been used to reduce the premia costs of using full-timers to provide extended or unsocial operating hours. For example the liberalisation of shop opening hours has been accompanied by the increased use of part-time week-end workers and a dismantling of Sunday premia payments in many sectors . . .

19. Another important factor which has contributed to the expansion of marginal (short hour, low paid) part-time work in Britain is the organisation of the social security contributory system. Both the employer and the employee are exempt from paying social security contributions when the wage falls below the lower earnings threshold, and even when the threshold is crossed there is favourable treatment of low earners. This is equivalent to 12–15 hours per week on the basis of average hourly pay for part-timers, a coincidence which has persisted over time . . . Official estimates in 1989–90 were that 2.5 million employees had earnings which fell below the LEL, of which 95 % were part-time employees and seven out of eight were women . . . Most other EU member states do not provide this subsidy to employers of low wage part-time workers.

In 1998 the EOC reported (Low Pay and the National Insurance System, extracted immediately below) that 0.6 million men and 2 million women (5.5 and 19% of male and female employees respectively) earned below the LEL. 93% of these worked part-time and almost 33% of part-time women workers earned below the LEL. It also reported that some employers set hours and rates of pay in order to ensure that part-time employees remained below the LEL. The exclusion of many part-time workers from the National Insurance scheme has serious repercussions.

[4.6] EOC, *Low Pay and the National Insurance System* (1998), Summary, pp 1–2

Employees who do not pay sufficient NICs [National Insurance contributions] do not acquire rights to contributory benefits, including the contributory element of Jobseeker's Allowance . . . Incapacity Benefit and State pension. In addition, eligibility for Statutory Sick Pay and Statutory Maternity Pay is dependent on average earnings being at or above the LEL [Lower Earnings Limit]. The potential long-term effects on pension entitlement are of particular concern, since the vast majority [93% and 98% respectively] of those earning below the LEL do not have personal pensions or access to an occupational pension so they may be forced to rely on Income Support in retirement . . .

Most [70% of] men who earn below the LEL are aged under 25. They are usually single, work part-time (often in casual jobs) and are often still in the education system or on a government training scheme. Very few men remain in low paid jobs over an extended period of time and so there is only a limited impact on their pension entitlement . . .

However, whereas very few men aged 25–54 earn below the LEL, one in seven women in this age group do so. Very importantly, a significant number of women remain in low paid jobs for an extended period. Thus, while the main effect on earning below the LEL for most men is a loss of eligibility for short-term contributory benefits, the impact on women is much greater, since both short-term and long-term benefits are affected.

[4.7] EOC, *Lower Earnings Limit in Practice* (1999), Summary, pp 1, 7

The LEL was introduced at a time when a married woman was expected to rely upon her husband's earnings and upon the benefit elements deriving from his NI contributions. People who worked for only a few hours each week, or only now and then, were not seen as part of the labour force and were not generally assumed to be reliant upon waged work.

Changes have been made to the NI system, but they have not kept pace with changes in the household division of labour and the structure of the workforce, in particular the huge expansion of part-time working.

Women's earnings from part-time employment are often a crucial component of household and individual budgets and the failure of low-earning employees to build up their entitlement to benefits can often have a devastating effect as their circumstances change.

Changing cultural and economic trends—especially the reduction in marriage rates and the increase in divorce rates—make it important for women to be capable of financial independence in both the short-term and the long-term, since fewer women than in the past can, or want to, depend on the support of a male partner . . .

. . . many low paid employees . . . experience a considerable degree of fluctuation in weekly pay . . . above and below the LEL [which] mean that, due to the strict rules governing benefit entitlement, low paid workers often pay National Insurance contributions from which they are unlikely to benefit: the 'lost contributions'. An assessment of lifetime contributions, rather than the current situation where the calculation of pension entitlement is based on qualifying years, would be a fairer alternative.

The EOC's 1999 report (extracted immediately above) recommended that any threshold for determining entry into the NI system 'should be set so low as to include the vast majority of part-time and low-paid workers' and that '[e]ntitlement to benefits which cover specified risks, such as unemployment, sickness, incapacity and retirement, should not be withheld from employees merely on the basis of the low level of their earnings'. The Welfare Reform and Pensions Act 1999 did make some changes to the system by raising the NI payment threshold for employee contributions to the level of the income tax threshold by April 2001 (it stood at £94 per week as of April 2005) while providing that those earning at least the LEL (£82 per week as of April 2005), would retain their entitlement to contributory benefits, and by granting Maternity Allowance (discussed below) to those earning at least £30 a week rather than, as was previously the case, the LEL. But it left unchanged the exclusion from the contributory element of Jobseeker's Allowance, Incapacity Benefit and State pension of those earning less than the LEL.

In March 2004 the *Equal Opportunities Review* estimated that that 0.5 million men and 1.4 million women earned less than the LEL threshold. These workers may contribute to 'stakeholder pensions'. But there is no obligation on their employers to facilitate access to such pensions, much less to contribute to them. And it remains the case that workers who (as is common for women) dip into and out of employment may well pay NI contributions for years, but fail to build up sufficient years of contributions (10) to be eligible for even a partial state pension. An estimated 100,000 such workers, the large majority of them women, effectively subsidise those (predominantly male) workers whose working lives are less interrupted. Half a million women in 2003 had no entitlement to a state pension and only 13% of women had full state pensions (Age Concern and the Fawcett Society, 'One in Four' (2003)). And whereas married men enjoy an average income of £104 from occupational pensions, married women have only £17 per week.

Full-time women workers currently in employment and aged between 25 and 34 are marginally more likely than full-time men to be members of occupational schemes (70% as against 68%). But only 44% of part-time women workers of the same age are members of occupational schemes (Age Concern and the Fawcett Society, 'Simplicity, Security and Choice' (2003)), only 7% of Pakistani women and 27% and 14% respectively of full-time and part-time women workers in unskilled manual occupations. This picture is likely to get worse rather than better. *Social Trends* predicts that 14% of women pensioners will be divorced by 2021 and, although pension sharing on divorce was introduced in December 2003, only 1300 pension sharing orders have been granted since then in 300,000 divorce settlements.

4.2.1 The Part-Time Workers Directive

The Directive on part-time work marked the culmination of almost twenty years' efforts to regulate 'atypical' work at the European level. It eventually adopted under the Social Chapter, the UK having vetoed attempts to pass it under Article 118 (now

137). The social partners concluded an agreement on part-time work in accordance with the procedure established by the Social Chapter, the agreement being adopted as Directive 96/34/EC.

The Directive prohibits discrimination against part-time workers in employment-related (as distinct from social-security) matters, save where such discrimination is justified on objective grounds. The segregated nature of part-time work was mentioned above, but remains largely untouched by the Directive which merely exhorts employers:

- 'to give consideration' to requests to transfer into part-time work and *vice versa*;
- to provide information to workers' representatives about part-time work and about suitable vacancies to workers interested in transferring; and
- to facilitate the development of part-time work across the enterprise and of part-time workers' access to vocational training.

Member States and the Social Partners are further instructed to 'identify and review' and, where appropriate, eliminate legal and administrative hurdles to part-time work, subject to:

- the principle of non-discrimination;
- the aims of the Directive (removing discrimination against part-time workers, improving the quality of part-time work, facilitating the development of part-time work on a voluntary basis and contributing to the flexible organisation of working time in a manner which takes into account the needs of employers and workers); and
- the rule that the Directive's implementation shall not be valid grounds for a general reduction in the protection of part-time workers.

Workers are not, however, to be penalised in connection with a refusal to transfer from full-time to part-time work or vice versa, except according to law and for reasons which 'arise from the operational requirements of the establishment concerned'. This would cover, for example, hours reductions to avoid job losses in a redundancy situation.

[4.8] M Jeffrey, 'Not Really Going to Work? Of the Directive on Part-Time Work, 'Atypical Work' and Attempts to Regulate it' (1998) 27 *Industrial Law Journal* 193, pp 198–202 (footnotes omitted)

> [I]t seems to have been assumed that the encouragement of part-time work, together with a general requirement of non-discrimination, would automatically lead to a balance being set between the—often conflicting—wishes of employers and workers. However a requirement that employers should not treat part-time workers any worse than full-time workers, and a request that employers think about facilitating transfers between full-time and part-time work are not the same as a requirement that employers take workers' interests into account when setting the working hours of part-time workers. This aim of the Directive turns out to be little more than a pious hope, combined with the uncritical repetition of an unsubstantiated argument about 'atypical work' more usually put forward in order to support calls for 'de-regulation' and 'flexibility' . . .

[C]ertain clauses in the Agreement—and thus now the Directive—are closely based upon the clauses of [ILO Convention No 175 of 1994 on establishing minimum standards in part-time work and the supplementary Recommendation 182]. Nonetheless, the Directive is significantly weaker than both the supplementary standards of the Recommendation and the basic standards of the Convention itself. The ILO requirements are more precise than those of the Directive; they are wider in scope (social security systems are expressly included); and they admit fewer—and more tightly-controlled—exceptions . . .

The scope of the proposals for European level legislation was significantly weakened in 1994, when the German Presidency of the Union made a concerted effort to come up with a new draft directive which would overcome all the objections of the various Member States; not least—but not only—the opposition of the British Conservative government. It was only then that a general principle of non-discrimination was introduced to replace . . . specific requirements, that the scope was narrowed and social security dropped, and that a wide range of express exceptions was countenanced; eventually, the scope of the proposals [which had originally covered 'atypical' work more generally] was limited to part-time work only. The resulting proposal was reluctantly accepted by the Commission as representing . . . ' . . . the minimum of the minimum, below which nothing is conceivable in social protection' . . .

When this attempt failed and the Commission decided to make use of the new procedures under the Protocol and Agreement on Social Policy [thus excluding the British veto], it stressed that the German proposal would not be taken as the starting point for the negotiations between the Social Partners . . . [but] just three years later, the Commission was prepared to accept an agreement between the social Partners . . . which appears to offer even less than the 'minimum of the minimum' proposal of 1994 . . .

Both the Commission and the [European Trade Union Confederation] seem to have decided that it was more important for the Social Dialogue to appear successful in advance of the Council meeting [on the form which European social policy making should take] than it was to reach an agreement which was—according to their previously stated standards—satisfactory in substance . . .

The Part-time Workers Directive was not binding on the UK, given its adoption under the-then Social Chapter of the Treaty. But the Labour Government signed up to the Directive in agreeing the incorporation of the Chapter as part of the treaty and, in 2000, adopted the Part-time Workers Regulations (PtWRs 2000, SI 2000 No 1551).

4.2.2 The Part-time Workers Regulations 2000

[4.9] Part-time Workers Regulations, Regulation 5

Reg 5 (1) A part-time worker has the right not to be treated by his employer less favourably than the employer treats a comparable full-time worker—
  (a) as regards the terms of his contract; or
  (b) by being subjected to any other detriment by any act, or deliberate failure to act, of his employer.

(2) The right conferred by paragraph (1) applies only if—

(a) the treatment is on the ground that the worker is a part-time worker, and

(b) the treatment is not justified on objective grounds.

(3) In determining whether a part-time worker has been treated less favourably than a comparable full-time worker the pro rata principle shall be applied unless it is inappropriate.

(4) A part-time worker paid at a lower rate for overtime worked by him in a period than a comparable full-time worker is or would be paid for overtime worked by him in the same period shall not, for that reason, be regarded as treated less favourably than the comparable full-time worker where, or to the extent that, the total number of hours worked by the part-time worker in the period, including overtime, does not exceed the number of hours the comparable full-time worker is required to work in the period, disregarding absences from work and overtime.

The accompanying guidance ('Part-time workers: the law and best practice, a detailed guide for employers and part-timers') suggests that equality of treatment should extend to basic hourly rates and (subject to Regulation 5(4)) overtime, as well as to contractual sick and maternity pay; access to occupational pension schemes, selection for redundancy; leave and career breaks (on a *pro rata* basis where appropriate); reorganisation of hours; promotion and training, the latter 'to be structured wherever possible to be at the most convenient times for the majority of staff including part-timers'.

The PtWRs 2000 apply to workers 'paid wholly or in part by reference to the time [they] work' (and not, therefore, to piece workers), and define part-time and full-time workers according to the custom and practice of the employer. The Regulations, in their draft form, referred to 'employees' rather than to 'workers', but the DTI relented in the face of threatened legal action by, *inter alia*, the TUC which claimed that they were insufficient to comply with the requirements of the Directive. Criticism directed by the TUC and others against other provisions of the draft Regulations was less effective.

Perhaps the most controversial aspect of the PtWRs is their restriction of the right not to be discriminated against to cases in which the part-time worker has an actual comparator (*cf* the discrimination provisions considered in chapter 3).

[4.10] Part-time Workers Regulations, Regulation 2

Reg 2(4) A full-time worker is a comparable full-time worker in relation to a part-time worker if, at the time when the treatment that is alleged to be less favourable to the part-time worker takes place—

(a) both workers are—

    (i) employed by the same employer under the same type of contract, and

    (ii) engaged in the same or broadly similar work having regard, where relevant, to whether they have a similar level of qualification, skills and experience; and

(b) the full-time worker works or is based at the same establishment as the part-time worker or, where there is no full-time worker working or based at that establishment who satisfies the requirements of sub-paragraph (a), works or is based at a different establishment and satisfies those requirements.

A claim made under the Equal Pay Act 1970 requires that the claimant establish a difference in treatment between her and a man engaged in broadly the same work, in work of equal value or in work which the employer has accepted as equivalent (see 3.10.1 above). The comparator required by the PtWRs 2000 is, as can be seen from Regulation 2, much narrower. Not only must the full-time comparator be engaged in essentially the same work in the same establishment (or at a related establishment if there is no comparator at that establishment), but the comparator must also be engaged under the same type of contract as the claimant.

[4.11] Part-time Workers Regulations, Regulation 2

Reg 2(3) For the purposes of paragraphs (1), (2) and (4), the following shall be regarded as being employed under different types of contract—
  (a) employees employed under a contract that is not a contract of apprenticeship;
  (b) employees employed under a contract of apprenticeship;
  (c) workers who are not employees;
  (d) any other description of worker that it is reasonable for the employer to treat differently from other workers on the ground that workers of that description have a different type of contract.

[4.12] *Matthews v Kent & Medway Towns Fire Authority* [2005] ICR 84

This case concerned a claim by retained part-time firefighters for equal treatment vis-à-vis full-time firefighters whose terms and conditions were more favourable. An employment tribunal ruled that the claimants were not employed on the 'same type of contract' as full-time firefighters for the purposes of Regulation 2, taking the view that the full-time firefighters fell within 2(3)(a) and the retained firefighters within 2(3)(d). It also ruled that the retained and full-time firefighters did not do the 'same or broadly similar work' within Regulation 4(a)(ii), this on the basis that the latter not only responded to emergencies but also engaged in educational, preventive and administrative tasks. The tribunal's finding was upheld by the EAT but the Court of Appeal, although it dismissed the retained firefighters' appeal, ruled that the tribunal and the EAT had erred in finding that the retained firefighters were not employed under the 'same type of contract' as their full-time firefighter comparators. The categories established by Regulation 2(3)(a) – (d) above were mutually exclusive with the effect there that the employer could not argue that (part-time) 'retained' firefighters were employed on different contracts from their full time colleagues, given that both fell within (a). The claim failed, however, on the basis that full-time and 'retained' firefighters did not do the 'same or broadly similar work', the Court of Appeal accepting that the tribunal had been entitled to reach this finding given the fact that full-timers carried out educational, preventive and administrative tasks as well as firefighting and responding to other emergencies (the firefighters have been granted leave to appeal to the House of Lords).

The only cases in which a claim may be made without reference to an actual full-time comparator are outlined in Regulations 3 and 4.

[4.13] Part-time Workers Regulations, Regulations 3 and 4

Reg 3 (1) This Regulation applies to a worker who—

(a) was identifiable as a full-time worker in accordance with Regulation 2(1); and

(b) following a termination or variation of his contract, continues to work under a new or varied contract, whether of the same type or not, that requires him to work for a number of weekly hours that is lower than the number he was required to work immediately before the termination or variation.

(2) Notwithstanding Regulation 2(4), Regulation 5 shall apply to a worker to whom this Regulation applies as if he were a part-time worker and as if there were a comparable full-time worker employed under the terms that applied to him immediately before the variation or termination.

(3) The fact that this Regulation applies to a worker does not affect any right he may have under these Regulations by virtue of Regulation 2(4).

Reg 4 (1) This Regulation applies to a worker who—

(a) was identifiable as a full-time worker in accordance with Regulation 2(1) immediately before a period of absence (whether the absence followed a termination of the worker's contract or not);

(b) returns to work for the same employer within a period of less than twelve months beginning with the day on which the period of absence started;

(c) returns to the same job or to a job at the same level under a contract, whether it is a different contract or a varied contract and regardless of whether it is of the same type, under which he is required to work for a number of weekly hours that is lower than the number he was required to work immediately before the period of absence.

(2) Notwithstanding Regulation 2(4), Regulation 5 shall apply to a worker to whom this Regulation applies ('the returning worker') as if he were a part-time worker and as if there were a comparable full-time worker employed under-

(a) the contract under which the returning worker was employed immediately before the period of absence; or

(b) where it is shown that, had the returning worker continued to work under the contract mentioned in sub-paragraph (a) a variation would have been made to its term during the period of absence, the contract mentioned in that sub-paragraph including that variation.

(3) The fact that this Regulation applies to a worker does not affect any right he may have under these Regulations by virtue of Regulation 2(4).

The guidance which accompanies the PtWRs 2000 ('Part-time Workers: the Law and Best Practice') states that differential treatment will be objectively justified for the purposes of the Regulations where 'it is necessary and appropriate to achieve a legitimate business objective' (note the objective justification test for indirect sex discrimination, discussed at 3.5.4 above). The guidance suggests that pay differentials might be justified where 'workers are shown to have a different level of performance measured by a fair and consistent appraisal system' and that, while participation in share option and profit sharing schemes should, in general, be open to part-timers (benefits to be distributed *pro rata*), the exclusion of part-timers from the former could be justified 'where the value of the share options was so small that the potential

benefit to the part-timer of the options was less than the likely cost of realising them'. It also suggests that where, as in the case of health insurance, pro-rating is not possible, this might be a ground on which the denial of the benefit to part-timers could be justified.

4.2.3 Impact of the Regulations

The Government's own Regulatory Impact Assessment estimated that the PtWRs 2000 would benefit only around 7% of the UK's part-time workers, all but 17% being excluded for want of an appropriate comparator. It was pointed out above that the comparator requirement sits uncomfortably in the body of UK anti-discrimination law. The EqPA 1970 does require an actual (if more broadly defined) comparator, but that Act presumes discrimination, absence of proof to the contrary, once such a comparator is identified. The PtWRs 2000, by contrast, demand *both* that a suitable comparator is put forward and *also* that the claimant prove that she was treated less favourably than the comparator on the ground that she worked part-time. It is true that the Regulations (Regulation 8(6)) provide that 'it is for the employer to identify the ground for the less favourable treatment or detriment'. But the burden of proof on the issue of discrimination remains with the applicant, the employer being under no obligation to provide evidence to support the asserted reason for the less favourable treatment.

The Part-time Workers Directive provides a right for part-timers, subject to the possibilities of objective justification, to be treated no less favourably than full-time workers 'in the same establishment having the same type of employment contract or relationship, who [are] engaged in the same or a similar work/occupation, due regard being given to other considerations which may include seniority and qualification/skills.' But the Directive provides, where no such comparator is available, that 'comparison shall be made by reference to the applicable collective agreement or, where there is no applicable collective agreement, in accordance with national law, collective agreements or practice.' 'National law and practice' could be taken to require that a hypothetical comparator be available in this context. This approach might suggest that the UK's transposition of the comparator requirement breaches the Part-time Workers Directive.

The Second Report of the House of Commons Education and Employment Sub-Committee, 1998–1999, warned that 'if the Directive on Part-time Work is transposed in its basic form it will be no more effective, and in some areas less effective than existing legislation'. The Sub-Committee was particularly concerned about the Directive's comparator-driven approach in view of the strongly segregated nature of part-time work. It recommended that:

[4.14] House of Commons Select Committees on Education and Employment, *Part-Time Working* Vol I, (Second Report 1998–99, HC 346-I), p 139

> the definition of a comparator should be a full-time worker with the same employer or in the same service engaged in like work or work of equal value and in such cases where no such comparator exists, but where a primary fact gave cause for the Tribunal to draw an

inference that there had been unlawful discrimination, the use of a hypothetical comparator should be acceptable.

The disadvantage suffered by part-time workers was set out above. The then Secretary of State for Trade and Industry, Stephen Byers, declared that the PtWRs 2000 would 'ensure that part-timers are no longer discriminated against'. But this claim is sustainable only to the extent that 'discrimination' is understood as the unjustifiable differential treatment of otherwise identical workers on the grounds that one works full-time and the other part-time. As then Employment Minister Ian McCartney testified, when questioned by the Education and Employment Sub-Committee, what the DTI meant by 'discrimination' was 'the specific area of, for example, where part-time workers work alongside full-time workers in the same establishment. There is generally little or no evidence in pay, for example, that discrimination takes place'. (HC 346-II,Qu 217). The Minister went on, however, to acknowledge that 'it is absolutely true that in general in the workplace part-time workers suffer in terms of lower levels of pay, something like only two-thirds of the average.'

The PtWRs 2000 do nothing to challenge the major part of the disadvantage associated with part-time work. They do not require that jobs are opened up to part-time working, not even (as the Employment Sub-committee's Second Report recommended) that women be entitled to return to their jobs part-time after maternity leave. Further, they do not appear to protect against dismissal connected with a refusal to transfer between part-time and full-time work. Although the 'detriment' from which workers are protected under Regulation 5(1)(b) presumably covers 'dismissal', a dismissal for refusing to transfer to full-time work will breach the Regulation only where it is 'on the ground that the worker is a part-time worker' and it is less favourable treatment than that accorded to an actual full-time comparator. Such a dismissal might, of course, be unfair within the Employment Rights Act 1996 (it might also, if the part-time worker is female, amount to indirect sex discrimination). But the unfair dismissal provisions of that Act apply only to employees with at least one year's qualifying service. And we saw in chapter 3 above the difficulties associated with challenging indirect discrimination under the SDA. It is strongly arguable, therefore, that the PtWRs 2000 are not sufficient to comply with Article 5(2) of the Directive which provides that: 'A worker's refusal to transfer from full-time to part-time work or vice-versa should not in itself constitute a valid reason for termination of employment, without prejudice to termination in accordance with national law, collective agreements and practice, for other reasons such as arise from the operational requirements of the establishment concerned'.

The PtWRs 2000 do provide some additional protection to a number of part-timers, in particular those who retain the same employer during a move to part-time work. They also provide significant additional protection to male part-time workers, freed as they are from the requirement to prove that they were less favourably treated than a woman part-timer would have been. (The first appellate decision reached under the Regulations, *Matthews v Kent & Medway*, concerned a claim by male retained firefighters.) But they do little to address the real problems associated with part-time work: that it is provided, by and large, in low paying workplaces and low paying jobs, women frequently being denied the opportunity to continue in their previous roles on changing to part-time work. We shall see, below, that some progress has been made with the the recent introduction of the right to request changes to the hours or other organisation of work. But much discrimination against part-time workers will continue to be challenged, if at all, under the SDA and EqPA, the inadequacies of which (discussed in chapter 3) led to the need for specific legislation dealing with part-time workers.

4.3 Time-off rights

In addition to entitlements provided by the Working Time Regulations (see 4.5.1 below) to daily and weekly rest and to paid holidays, statute provides employees with a variety of rights to time off (paid and unpaid) in connection with trade-union duties and activities, impending redundancy, public duties and the performance of duties by employees who have undertaken service as trustees of occupational pension schemes, and employee representatives (for example, in connection with the WTRs 1998). Given the focus of this chapter, discussion is limited for the most part to maternity, paternity, adoptive and parental leave rights. These are important not only to the immediate needs of workers (more precisely, employees) facing impending parenthood but, as we shall see below, have significant implications for the allocation of paid work and caring responsibilities between parents in general, men and women in particular. For the sake of completeness, the broader issues surrounding pregnancy, maternity and parental leave will also be addressed. The question of pregnancy discrimination as sex discrimination is considered at 3.3.1.2 above.

4.3.1 Maternity rights

The ERA 1996 provides that an employee (no protection is afforded, other than by the SDA 1975, to non-'employed' workers) who is dismissed shall be regarded . . . as unfairly dismissed if (section 99) 'the reason or principal reason for the dismissal is of a prescribed kind'. The Maternity and Parental leave, etc. Regulations 1999 (SI 1999 No 3312, MPLRs 1999) list the 'prescribed' reasons to include:

[4.15] Maternity and Parental leave, etc. Regulations 1999, Regulation 20(3)

> Reg. 20(3)(a) the pregnancy of the employee;
> (b) the fact that the employee has given birth to a child;
> (c) the application of a relevant requirement, or a relevant recommendation, as defined by section 66(2) of the 1996 Act [suspension on medical grounds];
> (d) the fact that she took, sought to take or availed herself of the benefits of, ordinary maternity leave;
> (e) the fact that she took or sought to take—

      (i)   additional maternity leave . . .
(ee) the fact that she failed to return after a period of ordinary or additional maternity
      leave in a case where-
      (ii) the employer did not notify her, in accordance with Regulation 7(6) and (7) or
          otherwise, of the date on which the period in question would end, and she
          reasonably believed that that period had not ended, or
      (iii) the employer gave her less than 28 days' notice of the date on which the period in
          question would end, and it was not reasonably practicable for her to return on
          that date.

Section 99 also applies (Regulation 20) where 'the reason or principal reason for the
dismissal is that the employee is redundant, and either Regulation 10 [which requires
that women on maternity leave be offered any available suitable alternative
employment in the event of redundancy] has not been complied with', or the
selection for redundancy was wholly or principally on one of the grounds listed
above. Dismissal for redundancy, whether or not in breach of these special rules, will
bring maternity leave to an end and terminate the employment relationship, although
the employee remains entitled to any notice period and, subject to the normal rules,
to a redundancy payment.

    Section 99 ERA does not, however, apply where:

[4.16] Maternity and Parental leave, etc. Regulations 1999, Regulation 20(6), 20(7)

Reg. 20(6)(a) [in the case of a woman returning from additional maternity leave]
immediately before the end of her additional maternity leave period (or, if it ends by
reason of dismissal, immediately before the dismissal) the number of employees employed
by her employer, added to the number employed by any associated employer of his, did
not exceed five, and
    (b) it is not reasonably practicable for the employer (who may be the same employer or
a successor of his) to permit her to return to a job which is both suitable for her and
appropriate for her to do in the circumstances or for an associated employer to offer her a
job of that kind;

or

Reg. 20(7)(a) [in the case of a woman on either ordinary or additional maternity leave] it is
not reasonably practicable for a reason other than redundancy for the employer (who may
be the same employer or a successor of his) to permit her to return to a job which is both
suitable for her and appropriate for her to do in the circumstances;
(b) an associated employer offers her a job of that kind, and
(c) she accepts or unreasonably refuses that offer.

The implementation in the UK of Council Directive 2000/73/EC (the amended Equal
Treatment Directive) will result in the removal of this small employer exemption.

4.3.1.1 Statutory maternity leave

The right to statutory maternity leave has changed considerably over the past few years. Originally available only to women with two years' qualifying service, a reluctant Conservative government was forced by Directive 92/85/ EC (the Pregnant Workers' Directive) to extend the right to all women. The same Directive required the removal of the then-standard two-year qualifying period for pregnancy-related unfair dismissal claims. Implementation of the Directive occurred in a minimalist fashion, universal maternity leave being restricted to a 14-week period while those women with at least two years' qualifying service were entitled to additional leave on satisfaction of procedural requirements of mind-numbing complexity. Such were the horrors of these requiremets that Lord Justice Ward once protested (in *Halfpenny v IGE Medical Systems Ltd* [1997] ICR 1007) that 'It is surely not too much to ask of the legislature that those who grapple with this topic should not have to have a wet towel around their heads as the single most important aid to the understanding of their rights'.

The maternity leave provisions were extended and simplified by the Employment Relations Act 1999 (which replaced the former ss 71–80 ERA 1996), and the MPLRs 1999 and more recently by the Maternity and Parental Leave (Amendment) Regulations 2002 (SI 2002 No 2789) which extended (paid) ordinary maternity leave (OML) to 26 weeks and (unpaid) additional maternity leave (AML) to a further 26 weeks. Employees may enjoy more favourable contractual terms. Where this is the case (Regulation 21 MPLRs 1999) they are entitled to enjoy whichever of the contractual or statutory provisions is more favourable in any given respect, though not to exercise them separately.

All women are now entitled to 26 weeks' OML in respect of childbirth (Regulation 7). Those who have 26 weeks' qualifying employment at the beginning of the fourteenth week before the expected week of childbirth (EWC) are entitled to an additional 26 week AML period. (The Chancellor of the Exchequer announced in December 2004 the government's intention to increase the paid portion of maternity leave to nine months from April 2007 and thereafter to twelve months.) Women may choose the date on which maternity leave begins, although this date may not be more than 11 weeks prior to the beginning of the EWC. Maternity leave will also be triggered automatically by absence from work 'wholly or partly because of pregnancy' in the four weeks prior to the beginning of the EWC (Regulation 6). Maternity leave is compulsory for two weeks after the birth (ERA 1996 section 72 and MPLRs 1999, Regulation 8—this is extended to four weeks for factory workers and longer where statutorily required). All women are entitled, on production of appropriate evidence, to reasonable paid time off for ante-natal care (ERA 1996, sections 55 and 56). The DTI's *Maternity Rights: A Guide for Employers and Employees* suggests that this includes 'relaxation classes and parentcraft classes as long as these are advised by a registered medical practitioner, midwife or registered health visitor'. Expectant fathers have no such time-off rights, though the DTI has recently suggested that employers give consideration to requests from individuals to accompany their partners to some ante-natal appointments ('Fathers-to-be and ante-natal appointments: a good practice guide', 2004).

In order to qualify for maternity leave the employee must notify the employer of her pregnancy, the EWC and the date on which she intends her maternity leave to begin 'no later than the end of the fifteenth week before her expected week of childbirth, or, if that is not reasonably practicable, as soon as is reasonably practicable' (MPLRs 1999, Regulation 4). This notice requirement does not apply in a case where maternity leave is triggered by the birth itself, in which case notice must be given 'as soon as is reasonably practicable' of the absence or the birth. Notice must be given in writing, and medical evidence of the pregnancy supplied, if the employer so requests.

[4.17] J Mair, 'Maternity Leave: Improved and Simplified?' (2000) 63 *Modern Law Review* **877, pp 880–881 (footnotes omitted).**

> The previous legal provisions made it clear that the woman had neither the right to ordinary maternity leave nor the right to return to work unless she satisfied the notice requirements. In the DTI Consultation which preceded the publication of the draft Regulations, it was recognised that '[o]ccasionally things go wrong and an employee does not give the correct notice for starting or returning from maternity leave'. While recognising the need for rules to deal with this situation it was suggested that the current rules which might result in the loss of the right to leave were unduly harsh. The government proposed that failure to give the required notice of the commencement of maternity leave should result in the leave being delayed. The Equal Opportunities Commission, in their response to the DTI, while welcoming the move towards reducing the harsh consequences of failure to comply with the notice requirements, highlighted the practical difficulties of delaying leave where an employee needs to commence maternity leave due to health reasons. They recommended that a woman who commenced leave without proper notice should be treated as on unauthorised leave and dealt with according to the employer's normal disciplinary process. In the end, this proposal has not been included in the final Regulations. Sections 71 to 73 of the amended Employment Rights Act 1996 provide that an employee may be absent during ordinary, compulsory and additional maternity leave provided that she satisfies prescribed conditions. These conditions have now been set out in Regulation 4 of the Maternity and Parental Leave Regulations which states that an employee is entitled to ordinary maternity leave provided that she gives the requisite notice. Both additional maternity leave (reg 5) and compulsory maternity leave (reg 8) are dependent on entitlement to ordinary maternity leave. While the requirements to give notice have been simplified, it appears that the harsh consequences of failure to comply with the requirements have not been lessened. This criticism of the existing provisions has not been addressed and to this extent the Regulations have failed to fulfil the expectations raised by *Fairness at Work* and the DTI's consultation document.

4.3.1.2 Rights during maternity leave

During the period of 'ordinary maternity leave' employees are entitled to retain many of their terms and conditions of employment.

[4.18] Employment Rights Act 1996, section 71(4)

> S71(4) Subject to section 74, an employee who exercises her right under subsection (1)[OML]—
>
> (a) is entitled, for such purposes and to such extent as may be prescribed, to the benefit of the terms and conditions of employment which would have applied if she had not been absent,
> (b) is bound, for such purposes and to such extent as may be prescribed, by any obligations arising under those terms and conditions (except in so far as they are inconsistent with subsection (1)), and
> (c) is entitled to return from leave to a job of a prescribed kind.

The 'terms and conditions' referred to in s.71(4)(a) are contractual and non-contractual, but do not include those governing 'remuneration', narrowly defined (by Regulation 9) as 'sums payable to an employee by way of wages or salary' for the purposes of section 71. Thus, as the DTI guidance points out:

[4.19] DTI, *Maternity Rights*: *Detailed Guidance for Employers and Employees*, pp 25-27

> if . . . holiday entitlement would normally accrue while the employee was at work, it must continue to accrue while she is on maternity leave . . . Further examples of contractual terms and conditions which women should continue to benefit from during maternity leave are participation in share schemes; reimbursement of professional subscriptions; the use of a company car or mobile phone (unless provided for business use only) and other perks such as health club membership. An employee resuming work after ordinary maternity leave is entitled to benefit from any general improvements which may have been introduced for her grade or class of work while she has been away . . . The . . . ordinary maternity leave period . . . counts towards [the employee's] period of continuous employment for the purposes of entitlement to other statutory rights . . . It also accounts [sic] for assessing seniority, pension rights and other personal length-of-service payments, such as pay increments under her contract of employment.

Contractual claims arising out of maternity leave have to be pursued through the civil courts (rather than the employment tribunals) unless they are outstanding on termination (including termination by way of constructive dismissal). The same is true of contractual claims arising in relation to AML, the position of those on on such leave being less favourable than that of those on OML.

[4.20] Employment Rights Act 1996, section 73(4)

> S.73(4) Subject to section 74, an employee who exercises her right . . . [to AML]—
>
> (a) is entitled, for such purposes and to such extent as may be prescribed, to the benefit of the terms and conditions of employment [contractual or otherwise, but not including those governing 'remuneration', narrowly defined] which would have applied if she had not been absent,

(b) is bound, for such purposes and to such extent as may be prescribed, by obligations arising under those terms and conditions (except in so far as they are inconsistent with subsection (1)) . . .

[4.21] The Maternity and Parental Leave etc. Regulations 1999, Regulation 17

Reg 17 An employee who takes additional maternity leave or parental leave—
(a) is entitled, during the period of leave, to the benefit of her employer's implied obligation to her of trust and confidence and any terms and conditions of her employment relating to—
   (i)   notice of the termination of the employment contract by her employer;
   (ii) compensation in the event of redundancy, or
   (iii) disciplinary or grievance procedures;
(b) is bound, during that period, by her implied obligation to her employer of good faith and any terms and conditions of her employment relating to—
   (i)   notice of the termination of the employment contract by her;
   (ii) the disclosure of confidential information;
   (iii) the acceptance of gifts or other benefits, or
   (iv) the employee's participation in any other business.

[4.22] DTI, *Maternity Rights: Detailed Guidance for Employers and Employees*, pp 29–32

The continuation of any other terms and conditions is a matter for negotiation and agreement . . . An employee resuming work after additional maternity leave is entitled to benefit from any general improvements to the rate of pay (or other terms and conditions) which may have been introduced for her grade or class of work while she has been away . . . . The . . . additional maternity leave period . . . counts towards [the employee's] period of continuous employment for the purposes of entitlement to other statutory rights . . . Unlike the period of ordinary maternity leave, the additional maternity leave period is not required to be counted for the purpose of assessing seniority, pension rights and other payments based on an individual's length of service—such as pay increases linked to length of service, (unless the employee's contract of employment provides [otherwise]) . . . In these circumstances the period of employment before the start of additional maternity leave will be 'joined up' with the period of employment on her return to work as if they were continuous.

It is clear from the above that women are not entitled to normal pay during maternity leave, in the absence of contractual provision to the contrary. We saw (section 3.3.1.2 above) that discrimination on grounds of pregnancy is equated, for the purposes of EU law, to discrimination on grounds of sex. So, for example, the ECJ ruled in Case 32/93 *Webb v EMO Air Cargo (UK) Ltd* [1994] ECR I–3567 that the dismissal of a pregnant woman because of her anticipated need for time-off work breached the Equal Treatment Directive, as did the refusal to employ a woman who would, during the period of her pregnancy, be legally prohibited from working in the relevant position (Case 207/98 *Mahlburg v Land Mecklenburg-Vorpommern* [2000] ECR I–00549).

In Case 342/93 *Gillespie v Northern Health and Social Services Boards* [1996] ECR I–047, the Court accepted that maternity pay was 'pay' for the purposes of Article 141 of the Treaty etablishing the Europeam Community. Thus, it might be assumed, discrimination on grounds of pregnancy (including: *Webb*, *Mahlburg*, discrimination based on a woman's pregnancy-related absence) should breach Article 141. But all attempts to argue that Article 141 requires the continuation of normal pay during maternity leave have failed (see, for example, *Gillespie* and *Boyle v EOC*, **[4.24]** below). Rather than demanding the continuation of full pay during (at least) the minimum period of leave (this on the grounds that maternity pay is 'pay' within Article 141 TEC and the same provision prohibits sex discrimination: i.e., the penalisation of women absent for the unique and protected reason of maternity), the ECJ has chosen instead to rely on the Pregnant Worker's Directive to read down pregnant women's pay-related rights.

[4.23] Council Directive 92/85/EEC (the Pregnant Workers Directive), Article 11

In order to guarantee workers within the meaning of Article 2 the exercise of their health and safety protection rights as recognized in this Article, it shall be provided that [during periods of maternity leave required by the Directive] . . .

2. The following must be ensured . . .
(b) maintenance of a payment to, and/or entitlement to an adequate allowance for, workers . . .

3. The allowance referred to in point 2 (b) shall be deemed adequate if it guarantees income at least equivalent to that which the worker concerned would receive in the event of a break in her activities on grounds connected with her state of health, subject to any ceiling laid down under national legislation;

4. Member States may make entitlement to pay or the allowance referred to in points 1 and 2 (b) conditional upon the worker concerned fulfilling the conditions of eligibilty for such benefits laid down under national legislation . . .

These conditions may under no circumstances provide for periods of previous employment in excess of 12 months immediately prior to the presumed date of confinement.

The sick pay to which, by virtue of Article 11(3), maternity pay or allowance must be equivalent is, according to the ECJ in *Boyle v. EOC*, statutory sick pay rather than that to which the worker would have been entitled under her contract. The European Commission had argued that the contractual rate of sick pay should be used by way of comparison. The ECJ disagreed:

[4.24] Case 411/96 *Boyle v EOC* [1998] ECR I–6401 (ECJ)

Judgment:
The concept of pay used in art 11 of that directive, like the definition in . . . Art [141] of

the Treaty, encompasses the consideration paid directly or indirectly by the employer during the worker's maternity leave in respect of her employment (see *Gillespie* [above] . . .). By contrast, the concept of allowance to which that provision also refers includes all income received by the worker during her maternity leave which is not paid to her by her employer pursuant to the employment relationship.

According to Art 11(3) of Directive 92/85, the allowance—

'shall be deemed adequate if it guarantees income at least equivalent to that which the worker concerned would receive in the event of a break in her activities on grounds connected with her state of health, subject to any ceiling laid down under national legislation.'

This is intended to ensure that, during her maternity leave, the worker receives an income at least equivalent to the sickness allowance provided for by national social security legislation in the event of a break in her activities on health grounds.

However, although Art 11(2)(b) and (3) requires the female worker to receive, during the period of maternity leave referred to in Art 8, income at least equivalent to the sickness allowance provided for under national social security legislation in the event of a break in her activities on health grounds, it is not intended to guarantee her any higher income which the employer may have undertaken to pay her, under the employment contract, should she be on sick leave . . .

[4.25] M Wynn, 'Pregnancy Discrimination: Equality, Protection or Reconciliation?' (1999) 62 *Modern Law Review* 435, pp 442–444 (footnotes omitted)

Despite the injunction in Article 2 of Directive 92/85/EC that the protection of the health and safety of such workers should not jeopardise equal treatment, the Court of Justice has firmly rejected the possibility of any equality comparison between women on maternity leave and other workers on the basis that such women are in a special position, but are not actually at work; thus the usual obligations deriving from the contract of employment do not arise. Furthermore, the delineation of women on maternity leave as dependent mothers as opposed to productive workers has allowed the Court to by-pass notions of equality and locate the problem in the realm of social protection where economic justifications are more likely to gain recognition. Protected status has thus resulted in a regime which has penal consequences for women in that entitlement to adequate income and immunity from dismissal during maternity leave without the need for inappropriate male comparisons has been substituted for substantive equality . . . .

The result of *Boyle and Gillespie* is that women on maternity leave are left without effective recourse where employers exploit the modicum of protection provided by Directive 92/85/EC. Financial detriments will continue to be incurred by women who choose to combine work and childbearing and employers will not be penalised for minimising their costs as long as the threshold of adequacy of income is not undermined. These cases indicate that the limits of maternity protection are determined by the European Court's perception of national autonomy in matters of social welfare. The result of balancing competing interests on the social plane is that the cost of applying the principle of equal treatment militates against the vindication of individual rights. As Advocate General Iglesias noted in *Gillespie*, to give full protection to pregnant mothers 'would threaten to upset the balance of the entire social welfare system'.

By contrast with these decisions on maternity rights, recent cases concerning pregnant workers indicate that a more favourable regime applies to the pregnant woman *qua* worker. In *Thibault* [Case 136/95, [1998] ECR 1– 2011], the Court of Justice stated that pregnancy and maternity require substantive, not merely formal rights. Here it was the woman's capacity as a worker which the Court emphasised as the factor which triggered the operation of discrimination law, as pregnancy itself could not act as the cause for any adverse treatment in working conditions. Thus the deprival of the right to an annual performance assessment as a result of absence on maternity leave was regarded as unfavourable treatment. Notably, *Gillespie* was referred to in order to support the conclusion that the taking of maternity leave should not deprive a woman of any benefits from pay rises due to her as a worker.

The bifurcation in the Court's jurisprudence on pregnancy and maternity rights has received more specific confirmation in *Hoj Pedersen* [Case 66/96, [1998] ECR 1–7327]. The applicants were deprived of full pay when they became unfit for work because of pregnancy-related illness before the beginning of their maternity leave. According to Danish national legislation, pregnancy-related incapacity for work entitled the worker to half pay, whereas incapacity for other illness resulted in full benefits. The Court of Justice held that it was contrary to Article [141] TEC and Directive 75/117/EEC to withhold full pay from a pregnant woman who became unfit for work before the commencement of maternity leave by reason of a pathological condition connected with pregnancy.

The importance of this case lies in the explicit comparison made between pregnancy and maternity rights. Advocate General Colomer had made clear in *Boyle* that there is no basis for comparison between a woman on maternity leave and a man on sick leave because the man's contractual obligations are only suspended for so long as he undergoes treatment for a sickness, whereas maternity leave is a special 'block' period granted to protect specific pregnancy and maternity needs ie to protect the biological condition of pregnancy and the relationship between mother and child. This distinction was developed in *Pedersen* where the Advocate General rejected the view that unfitness for work caused by pregnancy before maternity leave began amounted to 'pre-maternity' leave. He stated that maternity leave differs from pregnancy-related sickness absence in a number of respects: first, maternity leave has a finite duration; secondly, entitlement is not linked to illness; thirdly, a woman is released from all employment obligations including work. This reasoning focuses on differences in employment rights: whereas pregnant workers must prove unfitness for work in order to be released from employment obligations, workers on maternity leave acquire rights independently of any such obligations. The dichotomy between maternity leave as social protection and pregnancy unfitness as worker incapacity allows the 'sick-male comparison' to operate only in cases of pregnancy. Gender specific rights attaching to maternity leave are diluted because they are welfare rights; pregnancy rights as equal rights emphasise the point of similarity with men and are thus conditioned by factors shaping the rights of male workers.

Returning to the UK's statutory provisions concerning payment during maternity leave, women who are employed and have have been continuously employed for 26 weeks during the fifteenth week before the EWC, who earn in excess of the LEL (£82 per week as of April 2005), and who provide proper notification to their employers (Social Security Contributions and Benefits Act 1992, section 164(4) as amended) are entitled to 90% of salary for six weeks followed by the 'lower rate' (£102.80 per week as of April 2005 or, where this is lower, 90% of their average weekly earnings, for a further 20 weeks. Employers are reimbursed 92% of the statutory maternity pay (SMP) (104.5% in the case of very small employers—Maternity Allowance and Statutory Maternity Pay Regulations 1994 (SI 1994/1230), as amended).

Women who do not qualify for statutory maternity pay SMP may qualify for Maternity Allowance at a similar rate to the lower rate of SMP or may be entitled to Incapacity Benefit, Income Support or Tax Credits, and are also entitled to a one-off Sure Start Maternity Grant which, having been frozen for a decade at £100, was raised in 2000 to £300 and in 2002 to £500. During paid maternity leave, whether ordinary or additional and whether paid by virtue of statute or contract, an employee is entitled to full occupational pension contributions from her employer. Her contributions, if any, should be based on her actual payment during leave. Employers' pension contributions do not have to be maintained during unpaid *additional* leave, unless the rules of the pension scheme provide otherwise (section 71 ERA 1999). A woman whose OML is unpaid (because, for example, she has not fulfilled the notice requirements upon which SMP depends) remains entitled to her employer's contributions.

4.3.1.3 Return from maternity leave

A woman who wishes to return to work prior to the expiry of the 26 week or longer period of leave to which she is entitled must give 28 days' notice. No notice is required if she intends to return at the end of the full period of leave (whether OML or AML) available to her, the end date of which leave should have been notified to her by her employer (Regulation 7(6), 7(7)) within 28 days of her notification of intention to take maternity leave.

On return from ordinary (26 week) maternity leave, a woman is entitled (Regulation 18, and subject to Regulation 20(7), [4.16] above) to 'the job in which she was employed before her absence'. Weaker provisions apply after additional leave, the right being to return (again, except in the case of redundancy) either to 'the job in which she was employed before her absence' or, 'if it is not reasonably practicable for the employer to permit her to return to that job, to another job which is both suitable for her and appropriate for her to do in the circumstances' (see also Regulation 20(6), [4.16] above).

We saw above that sections 71 and 73 ERA 1996 now provide for the continuation of certain contractual terms during ordinary and additional maternity leave respectively. It follows that the contract of employment is regarded as subsisting throughout maternity leave and that, by contrast with the situation prior to 1999, failure on the part of the woman to comply with the notice requirements governing return does not strip her of protection from dismissal. Although any such dismissal will not be automatically unfair by virtue of s 99 ERA 1996, she will nevertheless be able to challenge it (either under the normal unfair dismissal rules or—section 3.3.1.2 above, under the SDA 1975).

Sections 71(7) and 73(7) ERA 1996 permit the Secretary of State to make regulations in relation to return from ordinary and additional maternity leave respectively about '(a) seniority, pension rights and similar rights and (b) terms and conditions of employment on return'.

[4.26] Maternity and Parental Leave, etc. Regulations, Regulation 18A

> Reg 18A (5) An employee's right to return [from OML or AML] is a right to return—
> (a) with her seniority, pension rights and similar rights—
>   (i) in a case where the employee is returning from additional maternity leave, or consecutive periods of statutory leave which included a period of additional maternity leave or additional adoption leave, as they would have been if the period or periods of her employment prior to her additional maternity leave or (as the case may be) additional adoption leave were continuous with the period of employment following it;
>   (ii) in any other case, as they would have been if she had not been absent, and
> (b) on terms and conditions not less favourable than those which would have applied if she had not been absent.
>
> (3) The provisions in paragraph (1)(a)(ii) and (b) for an employee to be treated as if she had not been absent refer to her absence—
> (a) if her return is from an isolated period of statutory leave, since the beginning of that period;
> (b) if her return is from consecutive periods of statutory leave, since the beginning of the first such period.

There is no express statutory right for women to return to work part-time or on flexible or reduced hours after the birth of a child, although the refusal to alter working hours in these circumstances may (see chapter 3) be unlawful sex discrimination and (see further section 4.3.6 below) returning mothers, together with other parents of young children, are entitled to request changes to their hours or other organisational aspects of work.

4.3.2 Adoptive leave

Sections 75A and 75B ERA 1996, introduced by the Employment Act 2002, provide for ordinary and additional adoptive leave. Supplemented by the Paternity and Adoption Leave Regulations 2002 (SI 2002 No 2788) and the Paternity and Adoption Leave (Amendment) Regulations 2004 (SI 2004 No 923), they provide a child's 'adopter' (sole adoptive parent or, where the child is adopted by a couple, the parent undertaking primary responsibility for the purposes of the Regulations) with a period of leave equivalent to maternity leave (Regulations 15 and 20). As with maternity leave, the employee may select whichever is individually more favourable of statutory and contractual entitlements (Regulation 30) but may not enjoy them separately. The same qualifying periods apply (calculated at the point at which the adopter is notified of the child's placement) and ordinary leave may start at the expected date of placement or up to fourteen days before, providing that the adopter has given the employer notice no later than seven days after being notified of the placement (Regulation 17, or, if this was not reasonable practicable, notified the employer as soon as reasonably practicable). Provisions governing terms and conditions applicable during leave and the right to return are also materially identical to those governing maternity leave as are those governing detriment, unfair dismissal and redundancy (Regulations 28, 29). Special provision is made (Regulation 22) for the non-placement or death of a child. The Social Security Contributions and Benefits Act 1992 has been amended and regulations passed thereunder (the Statutory Paternity Pay and Statutory Adoption Pay (General) Regulations 2002 (SI 2002 No 2822)) to provide for statutory adoption leave pay which is set at the same rate as the lower rate of maternity pay (i.e., there is no entitlement to a higher rate for the first six weeks) and is subject to similar notice requirements (the date of notice being fixed from the notification of the placement rather than the EWC). No entitlement to adoptive leave or pay arises other than in relation to new placements (eg. a person adopting their partner's children by a former partner is not entitled to leave or pay).

4.3.3 Paternity leave

Sections 80A and 80B ERA 1996, introduced by the Employment Act 2002, provide for paternity leave in the case of natural births and adoptions (in the latter case to the partner, male or female, of the child's 'adopter'). The leave, which is for a period of up to two (consecutive) weeks, is paid at the same rate as the lower rate of statutory maternity pay (£106 at April 2004) and is subject to notice requirements (Regulations 6, 10) and to a requirement for 26 weeks' qualifying service at (generally) the expected date of birth or notification of adoption (Regulations 4, 6). As with maternity leave, the employee may select whichever is individually more favourable of statutory and contractual entitlements (Regulation 30) but may not enjoy them separately. Like adoptive leave, paternity leave is governed by the PALRs 2002 as amended and the rate of pay applicable by the Social Security Contributions and Benefits Act 1992 and the Statutory Paternity Pay and Statutory Adoption Pay (General) Regulations 2002 (SI 2002 No 2822). Paternity leave has to be taken 'for the purposes of caring for a child or supporting the child's mother' or 'adopter' (Regulations 4, 8) and must be taken during the period starting with the date of birth or adoption and ending 56 days after that date or the date of the EWC in the case of an early birth (Regulation 5). Regulation 12 provides that employees are entitled to the benefit of, and remain bound by, all the terms of conditions of employment (except those relating to pay) during the period of paternity leave and Regulation 13 provides that the right to return after a period of paternity leave not additional to a period of more than four weeks' parental leave (see further section 4.3.4 below) is a right to return to the job in which the person was employed before his absence. Regulation 14 provides that the right to return is a right to return with seniority, pension rights and similar rights as if the employee had not been absent, unless the paternity leave was coupled with an extended period of parental leave, and on terms and conditions not less favourable than those which would have applied if he had not been absent. Provisions governing detriment, redundancy and dismissal are materially identical to those which apply to ordinary maternity and adoptive leave (Regulations 28, 29).

4.3.4 Parental leave

4.3.4.1 Introduction

Maternity leave is a crucial factor in permitting women to combine childbearing with paid work but, even at its lengthiest, does not permit the long-term reconciliation of working and family life. We saw above that part-time working is one of the most significant ways in which workers, the vast majority of them women, attempt to juggle work with childcare and other domestic and caring responsibilities. Below we consider the contribution to this balancing act which parental leave (additional to maternity leave) might play. Before doing so, however, it is useful to consider the role which non-parental childcare plays. It is clear from the following extracts that the provision of high-quality, affordable childcare in the UK is woefully inadequate. As Wilkinson and Briscoe point out (**[4.28]** below), however, even vastly increased provision would not alleviate the need for measures to permit parents personally to parent their children. It is in this context that the introduction in the UK of a right to parental leave is of particular significance.

[4.27] DfEE, DSS and Minister for Women, *Meeting the Childcare Challenge* **(1998, Cm 3959), paras 1.11–1.24**

> For too long, the UK has lagged behind in developing good quality, affordable and accessible childcare. The approach taken by previous Governments to the formal childcare sector has been to leave it almost exclusively to the market. But this has failed to meet the needs of many children and parents as society has changed. The voluntary sector has been expected, with little Government support, to fill gaps in services for parents caring for their own children and informal carers. As a result we are all losing out—children, parents, employers and society as a whole. Childcare in the UK today has three key problems:
>
> - the quality of childcare can be variable;
> - the cost of care is high and out of the reach of many parents; and
> - in some areas there are not enough childcare places and parents' access to them is hampered by poor information.
>
> Good quality childcare does not come cheap. The Daycare Trust has estimated that the typical weekly cost of a full-time childminding place for a child under five years old varies from £50 to £120 and that the cost of a full-time place at a private day nursery for the same child ranges from £70 to £180. Even when a child starts school and no longer needs full-time childcare, parents can be faced with typical costs of £15 to £30 a week for an after school club and £50 to £80 a week for a holiday playscheme. This means that a family on average income with two children could pay out as much as one third of it on childcare.
>
> For families on low or moderate incomes, especially lone parent families dependent on one income, the cost of childcare can be so high that they cannot afford to work. Others have to use a substantial proportion of their disposable family income on childcare.
>
> There is a shortage of childcare places across the country and parents' access to those places can be hampered by poor information about what is available. There may be particular problems in rural areas or inner cities. There are only 830,000 registered

childcare places for the 5.1 million children aged under eight in England. Provision is also patchy: Walsall has 66 day nursery places per 10,000 children under eight while Calderdale has 1,186; Hertfordshire has 160 childminder places per 10,000 children under eight compared with 1,060 in Oxfordshire.

There is clear evidence of unmet demand for childcare. Four out of five non-working mothers say they would work if they had the childcare of their choice, and one in seven mothers who do not have a job but want one see childcare as a barrier to finding work.

Not only is there an overall shortage of places, but children's and families' particular needs may not be met. Parents of children with special educational needs or disabilities have difficulty finding appropriate care and so do parents with unusual working hours.

The Green Paper went on to set out the Government's plans to increase the quality, affordability and accessibility of childcare. Much of the increased provision, however, takes the form of nursery places for four and, eventually, three year olds. Such places may or may not be beneficial to children. But, typically consisting as they do of a few hours' attendance in the morning or afternoon, they do not meet the childcare needs of working parents. In 2004 the Daycare Trust put the typical cost of a full-time nursery place for a child under two at £134 a week, almost £7000 a year; a rise of nearly 5% since 2003.

- In some parts of the country, particularly London and the South East the cost of a nursery place is much higher—typically £168 a week in Inner London or over £8750 a year. The highest cost identified in our 2004 survey was £338 a week, over £17,600 a year.
- The typical cost of a full-time place with a childminder for a child under two is £121 a week— over £6,300 a year.
- pre-school and playgroups cost £3 to £5 a session but you may be asked to pay for a block booking of around half a term in advance.
- The typical cost for an after school club is £35 for 15 hours a week.
- Nannies cost anything from £150 to £400 a week, depending on whether they live in or out. Families are also responsible for paying their tax and national insurance.
- The typical weekly cost of a place for a child in a summer play scheme is £73.71 a week (up from £67.70 a week in 2003).
- The highest cost of a summer play scheme identified in the Daycare Trust's 2004 survey is £200 a week, or £1200 for the six-week summer holiday period. Some parents pay additional costs for trips out and visits.
- British parents—mainly mothers—pay around 75 per cent of the cost of childcare—far more than in most OECD countries.
- The current average award through the childcare element of the Working Tax Credit is £49.83 a week. There is no extra help for parents with three or more children

Figures released by the Trust in January 2005 showed that the costs of childcare had continued to rise inexorably, the average annual cost of a nursery place in Inner London having exceeded £10,000. The previous month the Chancellor had, in his pre-budget statement, announced significant increases in the childcare component of Working Tax Credits (to £170 per week for one child, £300 for two or more), from April 2005 (subject to a maximum payment of 70% of childcare cost, rising to 80% from April 2006), with a weekly 'return to work' bonus of £40 for lone parents in the first year. But even on the Chancellor's own calculations, a dual income family earning a combined £34,000 would still pay 75% of their total childcare costs after the increases (by comparison with 85% at present. Perhaps more useful will be the pledges of 15 hour a week nursery provision (for 38 weeks annually) for all three and four year olds by 2010 and of out of school placements for all children aged up to 14 by the same year.

[4.28] H Wilkinson & I Briscoe, *Parental Leave: The Price of Family Values* (London, Demos, 1996)

> British policy itself has been laissez-faire; direct public subsidy is minimal, and there are only marginal tax breaks for childcare, despite popular demand. Parenting has been treated implicitly as the concern of the individuals and family not of the state, whose role is simply to regulate the private sector and to lay down minimum conditions for the care of the nation's children.
>
> *Background to parental leave: drivers of change*
> Some would like this approach to continue, keeping government and public policy as far away from the family as possible. But this view is rapidly becoming untenable as the old economic base for parenting continues to unravel.
>
> *Dual earning and the rise of the working mother*
> Over the last few decades women have entered the workforce in unprecedented numbers. Joint breadwinning is now the norm and the proportion of dual earning couples has risen from 43% in 1973 to 60% in 1992. Nearly half of married and cohabiting women with pre-school age children, are working today compared with just a quarter 15 years ago . . .
>
> *The home is becoming more important to men*
> Whilst women are becoming more attached to their work, men are becoming more involved at home. From the mid 1970s to the mid 1980s time spent on routine housework actually doubled (from a low base) whilst for married women of the same period there was a consistent decline [in time] spent in housework. The father's role is also changing. According to one study in Avon there have been substantial changes across the generations. In the 1950s just 5% of fathers were present at the birth of their child. In the 1990s attendance is almost 97% (many under pressure from their partners!) and other research has suggested that men have more of an emotional need and desire to be involved than in the past. Other surveys have shown that time spent looking after children or playing with them has more than doubled for full-time employed fathers during the same period.
>
> *Yet women still do most of the parenting*
> Over the last few decades, the overall trend in relationships and family life has been away from fixed gender roles to a much greater degree of flexibility. But this process has not been painless nor is it complete. Women's entry into the workforce has been inherently destabilising because their move out of the home has not been matched by men's preparedness to share childcare at home on the scale needed nor to accept joint responsibility. The two trends described above may be converging, but there is still a wide gap—a gap which has become one of the main causes of tensions in relationships. In our own study, 69.3% of 25–34 year old women with children take full responsibility for childcare compared to less than 3% of men and 65% of women look after their children if they are ill compared to just 11% of their spouses.

The main advantages to complementing childcare with parental leave are these:

- First, that it is in the interests of children. There is now abundant evidence that direct parental care—*if voluntary and desired*—is better in the early years of child-rearing than other more standardized forms of childcare provision.
- Second, childcare often tends to be of poor quality, especially if it is not supported by public policy. In such cases it is far harder to guarantee quality care than if parents are encouraged to stay at home.
- Third, even where there is state supported childcare, there is a strong case for giving parents choice, not least because this allows them to regulate the quality of childcare. The introduction of parental leave in Denmark for example has been associated with a reduction in public childcare and in Sweden parental leave is now so much part of the culture that few babies under one year old are in childcare. In our own qualitative research we have found that many parents would like to be able to mix professional childcare and greater parental care.
- Fourth, parental leave can help raise the birthrate. As we shall see this has been an important argument in some countries, and could again become significant for the UK. A fifth of women born since the 1960s are expected to remain childless throughout their lives. Given that the average size of families is also falling there is the very real prospect that there will be an inadequate population of taxpayers and workers to sustain a growing population of the elderly and infirm. Parental leave policies have been successful elsewhere in raising the birthrate.
- Fifth, parental leave strengthens women's rights. Paid parental leave, like subsidised childcare, can reduce material inequality between men and women. For example, Norway has not subsidised childcare as much as Sweden or France, but the existence of generous parental leave means that it has no greater material inequality between men and women. By acting as an extension of maternity rights, parental leave also helps the significant minority of women who currently opt out of the labour market and lose their right to return because they want to spend longer parenting than the current maternity provisions allow. A 1991 study in Britain found that over a quarter of mothers would like to see improved maternity rights.

British debate about family policy has sometimes assumed that there is a conflict between policies to promote women's equality and policies to boost the family. The former depended on encouraging women into jobs, while the latter depended on encouraging them to stay at home. Instead, the evidence from the most successful schemes abroad suggests that there is no inherent conflict between women's equality and initiatives to boost the family. In Norway for example women's position has been greatly strengthened not by extensive childcare but rather by ensuring generous paid leave—and leave to look after sick children. Sweden, whose parental leave scheme is the most generous in Europe, also has the second highest birth rate. In both countries equality has advanced in tandem with pro-natalism.

- Sixth, parental leave is in fathers' interests. Unlike childcare it makes it easier for men to choose to play an active role in fathering, without jeopardising their career. It makes it easier to realise the goal of shared and equal parenthood, and so also indirectly benefits women many of whom want fathers to have the right to take time off when a child is born. In our own focus group work the majority of men in their twenties and thirties believed that they should qualify for some form of paternity or parental leave, if only for a few weeks.

- Finally, parental leave, like other policy initiatives for *parenting* (as distinct from policies to enhance women's labour force participation), has a symbolic importance. It visibly puts a value on parenting. This is important because the material base of many families has been eroded in recent years and the number of families with dependent children below the poverty line has increased dramatically. In our discussion groups, many said that work was dominating their lives too much and that they wanted to be able to live a simpler life. A significant minority of women in our discussion groups (mostly full-time mothers) felt under-valued and were resentful that society as a whole did not appear to value parenting. Our survey also found that 67% of working women under 35 agreed that 'a woman who chooses to look after the home and children is just as emancipated as a woman with a career', a figure which rises to 74% for those women not in work. This sentiment appears to be spreading beyond traditionalists. Indeed it could be interpreted more as an evolution of feminism than as a reaction to it.

4.3.4.2 The parental leave provisions

The right to parental leave was eventually introduced in Britain by the MPLRs 1999. The Regulations are intended to implement Council Directive 96/34 (the Parental Leave Directive), which was adopted under the social dialogue procedures then set out in the Social Protocol (now within the Treaty itself). The Directive provides for the implementation of the agreement, annexed thereto, between the social partners. The agreement in turn sets out 'minimum requirements on parental leave and time off from work on grounds of force majeure (4.3.5), as an important means of reconciling work and family life and promoting equal opportunities and treatment between men and women'. The preamble to the Directive provides that 'management and labour are best placed to find solutions that correspond to the needs of both employers and workers and must therefore have conferred on them a special role in the implementation and application of the present agreement'. Accordingly, the Directive sets out minimum standards and provides considerable room for decision-making by management and labour. So, for example, the Directive permits Member States or management and labour to determine the maximum age of a child in respect of whom parental leave may be taken (subject to a maximum age of eight). It also provides that:

[4.29] The Parental Leave Directive, clause 2

2 (3) The conditions of access and detailed rules for applying parental leave shall be defined by law and/ or collective agreement in the Member States, as long as the minimum requirements of this agreement are respected. Member States and/or management and labour may, in particular:
  (a) decide whether parental leave is granted on a full-time or part-time basis, in a piecemeal way or in the form of a time-credit system;
  (b) make entitlement to parental leave subject to a period of work qualification and/or a length of service qualification which shall not exceed one year;
  (c) adjust conditions of access and detailed rules for applying parental leave to the special circumstances of adoption;
  (d) establish notice periods to be given by the worker to the employer when exercising the right to parental leave, specifying the beginning and the end of the period of leave;

(e) define the circumstances in which an employer, following consultation in accordance with national law, collective agreements and practices, is allowed to postpone the granting of parental leave for justifiable reasons related to the operation of the undertaking (e.g. where work is of a seasonal nature, where a replacement cannot be found within the notice period, where a significant proportion of the workforce applies for parental leave at the same time, where a specific function is of strategic importance). Any problem arising from the application of this provision should be dealt with in accordance with national law, collective agreements and practices;

(f) in addition to (e), authorize special arrangements to meet the operational and organizational requirements of small undertakings.

The core right to parental leave is as follows:

[4.30] Maternity and Parental Leave, etc. Regulations 1999, Regulations 13–15

Reg 13 (1) An employee who—
(a) has been continuously employed for a period of not less than a year; and
(b) has, or expects to have, responsibility for a child,
is entitled, in accordance with these Regulations, to be absent from work on parental leave for the purpose of caring for that child.

Reg 14 (1) An employee is entitled to thirteen weeks' leave in respect of any individual child.

Reg 15 An employee may not exercise any entitlement to parental leave in respect of a child—
(a) except in the cases referred to in paragraphs (b) to (d), after the date of the child's fifth birthday;
(b) in a case where the child is entitled to a disability living allowance, after the date of the child's eighteenth birthday;
(c) in a case where the child was placed with the employee for adoption by him (other than a case where paragraph (b) applies), after—
(i) the fifth anniversary of the date on which the placement began, or
(ii) the date of the child's eighteenth birthday,
whichever is the earlier . . .

Leave may also be taken after the child's fifth birthday when the delay is due to postponement (see below) by the employer. The right to parental leave does not, at present, include any right to payment.

The Regulations reflect the Parental Leave Directive inasmuch as their detailed provisions on parental leave are by way of a default position, the primary method by which the Regulations are intended to be implemented being through collective or 'workforce agreements'. The provisions concerning the definition of such agreements, and the mechanisms for electing workforce representatives, are materially identical to those in Schedule 1 of the Working Time Regulations 1998, reproduced at [4.61] below. Where workforce or collective agreements on parental leave are in place, they will provide the detail concerning notice requirements, timing and duration of parental leave. Schedule 2 of the MPLRs 1999 provide the default provisions applicable to any employee:

[4.31] Maternity and Parental Leave, etc. Regulations 1999, Regulation 16

Reg 16 . . . whose contract of employment does not include a provision which
(a) confers an entitlement to absence from work for the purpose of caring for a child, and
(b) incorporates or operates by reference to all or part of a collective agreement or workforce agreement.

Schedule 2 imposes requirements in terms of evidence of parenthood and notice periods (at least 21 days save in cases of birth or adoption, in which cases 21 days' notice of the expected birth or adoption date respectively: Schedule 2, paras 1–5). It also provides (paras 7 and 8) that leave may be taken in blocks of no less than one week at a time, except in the case of children in receipt of disability living allowance, and that no more than four weeks may be taken 'in respect of any individual child during a particular year'. An employer may (para 6) postpone leave, save at the time of birth or adoption, if /he or she 'considers that the operation of his business would be unduly disrupted if the employee took leave during the period identified in his notice' and providing that he or she offers alternative leave within six months, as a date 'determined by the employer after consulting the employee'. Notice of postponement must be in writing and with reasons and be given within seven days.

Workers on parental leave are subject to similar provisions as those applying to women on additional maternity leave ([4.20] above)—that is, they are contractually entitled and bound in the same manner and to the same extent (Regulation 17). Those who take parental leave in a block no longer than four weeks are entitled to return to the same job, those who take longer leave to return to the same job 'or, if it is not reasonably practicable for the employer to permit . . . return to that job, to another job which is both suitable for [the employee] and appropriate for her to do in the circumstances' (Regulation 18(1) and (2)) (note also the application of Regulation 20(7), [4.16] above). Terms and conditions on return must be no less favourable than they would have been had the employee not been absent, and (Regulation 18A(1)) with 'seniority, pension rights and similar rights . . . as they would have been if she had not been absent' unless the absence included a period of additional maternity or adoptive leave in which case 'as they would have been if the period or periods of her employment prior to her additional . . . leave were continuous with the period of employment following it'.

[4.32] Maternity and Parental Leave, etc. Regulations 1999, Regulation 19

Reg 19(1) An employee is entitled under section 47C of the [ERA] 1996 not to be subjected to any detriment by any act, or any deliberate failure to act, by her employer done for any of the reasons specified in paragraph (2).

(2) The reasons referred to in paragraph (1) are that the employee . . .

(e) took or sought to take . . .
    (ii) parental leave, or
(f) declined to sign a workforce agreement for the purpose of these Regulations, or

(g) being—
    (i)   a representative of members of the workforce for the purposes of Schedule 1, or
    (ii) a candidate in an election in which any person elected will, on being elected, become such a representative,
performed (or proposed to perform) any functions or activities as such a representative or candidate.

(4) Paragraph (1) does not apply in a case where the detriment in question amounts to dismissal within the meaning of Part X of the 1996 Act.

(7) For the purposes of paragraph (6), in the absence of evidence establishing the contrary an employer shall be taken to decide on a failure to act—
(a) when he does an act inconsistent with doing the failed act, or
(b) if he has done no such inconsistent act, when the period expires within which he might reasonably have been expected to do the failed act if it were to be done.

Reg 20(1)An employee who is dismissed is entitled under section 99 of the 1996 Act to be regarded for the purposes of Part X of that Act as unfairly dismissed if—
(a) the reason or principal reason for the dismissal is of a kind specified in paragraph (3) . . .

(2) An employee who is dismissed shall also be regarded for the purposes of Part X of the 1996 Act as unfairly dismissed if—
(a) the reason (or, if more than one, the principal reason) for the dismissal is that the employee was redundant;
(b) it is shown that the circumstances constituting the redundancy applied equally to one or more employees in the same undertaking who held positions similar to that held by the employee and who have not been dismissed by the employer, and
(c) it is shown that the reason (or, if more than one, the principal reason) for which the employee was selected for dismissal was a reason of a kind specified in paragraph (3).

Regulation 20(3) is in identical terms to Regulation 19(2) (above). No qualifying period applies in respect of these types of unfair detriment or dismissal, nor does the upper age limit for unfair dismissal apply (again, however, note the application of Regulation 20(7), **[4.16]** above).

4.3.4.3 Evaluating parental leave

The MPLRs 1999 have been widely criticised. It will be noted that they apply only to 'employees' rather than to workers (the same is true of maternity, adoptive and paternity rights). While the CBI was largely mollified by the lack of provision for payment and the restrictions as to maximum periods of leave, the TUC has been critical of aspects including employers' powers to postpone leave and the adoption of the five-year, rather than eight-year, cut-off.

[4.33] A McColgan, 'Family Friendly Frolics: The Maternity and Parental Leave, etc. Regulations 1999' (2000) *Industrial Law Journal* 125, pp 139–142 (footnotes omitted)

. . . the aspect of the 1999 Regulations which has provoked most censure is their failure to provide for payment in respect of parental leave. The House of Commons Select Committee on Social Security, in its report on the social security implications of parental leave, while drawing attention to and commending the Government's decision to allow the low paid to claim benefits during parental leave, concluded:

> We . . . are concerned that take-up [of parental leave] will be very low unless there is an element of payment. We recommend that the Government should introduce a flat-rate method of payment for those taking parental leave. Such a method of payment would be relatively inexpensive and could form the basis for more generous provision in the future.

In making this recommendation the Committee reflected the concerns of many of those who gave evidence to it. It remarked on the consensus to the effect that 'the payment of leave in some form would increase the take-up of the new entitlement'; 'the experience of other countries—and the conclusions of successive reviews of the subject— suggest that there is a strong case for parental leave being paid, if it is to be widely used and provide parents with a genuine choice'; 'if unpaid, leave is unlikely to be taken up in sufficient quantities to make a real difference to people's lives and is highly unlikely to be taken up by single parents, the low-paid or fathers'. The Low Pay Unit warned that only if parental leave was to be paid would the low-paid benefit from it, and the NSPCC argued that 'Rights for parents are worthless if you can't afford to claim them. The government's current plans will discriminate against the poor. They will only allow the well-off to take advantage of unpaid parental leave.' . . .

The firm evidence is that uptake of leave turns on whether it is paid or not. Submissions from Professor Peter Moss to the Committee pointed out that the UK was one of only six EU Member States in which parental leave was unpaid (the others being Greece, Ireland, Netherlands, Portugal and Spain). In those Member States in which parental leave was earnings-related, take-up by women was high though, with the exception only of Sweden, few fathers took such leave. Moss concluded that 'payment is a necessary but not sufficient condition for high take-up by fathers'. And according to the *Equal Opportunities Review* (1996) volume 66, p.22:

> The number of parents taking parental leave in countries where no benefit is available, such as Greece, Portugal, Spain and the Netherlands, is believed to be correspondingly low, even though there are no precise figures available . . . In Germany, where flat-rate payments are available, the vast majority of mothers take parental leave, although men account for only 1% of all leave-takers . . . In Denmark, where an additional entitlement to leave was introduced in 1992, take-up . . . was initially low, due mainly to the fall in income that this would cause . . .

Take-up rates of parental leave are highest in countries paying earnings-related benefit, such as Finland, Norway and Sweden. In Finland, virtually all mothers take parental leave, although fathers account for only 2% of takers . . . Sweden is unusual in that, in addition to nearly all mothers taking leave, a high percentage of fathers—around 50%—also take up their option to parental leave. This may be due to the fact that leave arrangements are very flexible, with parents being able to take short or long periods of full- or part-time leave. In addition, the law stipulates that at least one month of earnings-related leave must be taken by either parent.

The aims of the parental leave directive are to promote (a) the balancing of work and family life, (b) equal opportunities for men and women, (c) women's participation in the workforce and (d) the assumption of a more equal share of family responsibilities by men. The Government is also vocal in its commitment to the elimination of sex discrimination and the promotion of equality between men and women, not least in relation to family life. All the evidence is, however, that failing to pay parental leave will have the effect that it will be taken almost exclusively by women. This, in turn, will increase the incentives for prospective employers to discriminate against women of child-bearing age and against the mothers of young children . . .

It is no secret that British men work the longest hours in the EU, employed fathers working an average of no less than 47 hours a week and men with children under 12 working longer hours than those without children. The working time directive was intended to address this problem but its implementation in the UK has left particularly problematic gaps, individual employees being permitted to opt out and many managers not being subject to its provisions of the Working Time Regulations. Particularly in these circumstances, the low take-up of parental leave by fathers which is widely anticipated is a matter for concern. The detachment of working fathers from the domestic scene has implications not only for women's aspirations to equality, but also for the relationships which develop between fathers and children. These are vitally important, most especially given that early bonding promotes continued contact between fathers and children in the (ever-more likely) event of family breakdown . . .

Given the clear indications in the consultation documents which preceded the 1999 Regulations that parental leave would be unpaid, the TUC lobbied hard for the leave to be available 'in principle, flexibly, in months, weeks or shorter periods or on a reduced hours basis, subject to objective justification by employers in small chunks'. The availability of such flexible leave is seen as particularly important in encouraging its uptake by men, experience from EU Member States suggesting that men are far more likely to take leave where, as in Sweden, very flexible arrangements apply . . .

These arguments, too, were rejected, the Regulations providing that leave may be taken in minimum one-week blocks under the default arrangements.

4.3.5 Emergency leave

Before leaving the issue of parental leave the matter of 'emergency leave' should be mentioned. Until 1999, workers had no statutory entitlement to take time off work to deal with illness suffered by children or other dependents. This left many—particularly the mothers of dependent children, forced to resort to subterfuge when their presence was required at home. The dilemma facing parents and other workers was recognised in the Parental Leave Directive.

[4.34] The Framework Agreement on Parental Leave concluded by UNICE, CEEP and the ETUC and annexed to the Parental Leave Directive, Clause 3

3(1)   Member States and/or management and labour shall take the necessary measures to entitle workers to time off from work, in accordance with national legislation, collective agreements and/or practice, on grounds of force majeure for urgent family reasons in cases of sickness or accident making the immediate presence of the worker indispensable.

(2)   Member States and/or management and labour may specify the conditions of access and detailed rules for applying clause 3.1 and limit this entitlement to a certain amount of time per year and/or per case.

Clause 3 was given effect to by an amendment to the Employment Rights Act 1996.

[4.35] Employment Rights Act, section 57A

S57A(1) An employee is entitled to be permitted by his employer to take a reasonable amount of time off during the employee's working hours in order to take action which is necessary—

(a)   to provide assistance on an occasion when a dependant falls ill, gives birth or is injured or assaulted,

(b)   to make arrangements for the provision of care for a dependant who is ill or injured,

(c)   in consequence of the death of a dependant,

(d)   because of the unexpected disruption or termination of arrangements for the care of a dependant, or

(e)   to deal with an incident which involves a child of the employee and which occurs unexpectedly in a period during which an educational establishment which the child attends is responsible for him'.

'Emergency leave' is available only to employees, but no qualifying period of employment is imposed. Section 57A(2) ERA 1996 provides that the employee must inform the employer as to the reason for absence 'as soon as reasonably practicable', and, save where no notice could practically be given, of the likely period of absence. No absolute limits are imposed on the amount of time-off permitted annually or in relation to a single emergency, the Government having pointed out that:

[4.36] *Fairness at Work,* Cm 3968 (1998)

5.28. Legislation already provides rights to reasonable time off for specified reasons, for example to arrange training if the employee is being made redundant, or to carry out public duties. Industrial tribunals also take into account the needs of the business in deciding whether an employer has reasonably refused time off.

The thinking behind section 57A was explained by Lord Sainsbury for the Government in the House of Lords debates on the legislation.

The statutory right will be limited to urgent cases of real need . . . We have now set out clearly on the face of the Bill the circumstances in which leave can be taken . . . We intend the right to apply where a dependant becomes sick or has an accident, or is assaulted, including where the victim is distressed rather than physically injured.

We have not set a limit on the amount of time which employees can take off. This right is to help people deal with emergencies. A limit would not make sense and could be seen as a minimum, which employees might well consider an entitlement to be added to their annual leave. In all cases, the right will be limited to the amount of time which is reasonable in the circumstances of a particular case. For example, if a child falls ill with chickenpox the leave must be sufficient to enable the employee to cope with the crisis—to deal with the immediate care of the child and to make alternative longer-term care arrangements. The right will not enable a mother to take a fortnight off while her child is in quarantine. In most cases, whatever the problem, one or two days will be the most that are needed to deal with the immediate issues and sort out longer-term arrangements if necessary (HL Debs, 8 July 1999, cols 1084-5).

[4.37] *Qua v John Ford Morrison Solicitors* **[2003] ICR 482**

The Claimant challenged her dismissal in connection with 17 days' absence connected with her young son's medical problems. The employment tribunal dismissed her complaint on grounds that she had failed to comply with her obligation under section 57A(2) to tell her employer, 'as soon as reasonably practicable', 'for how long she expected to be absent'. The EAT allowed her appeal, ruling that section 57A does not require the employee to provide the employer with daily updates on her likely return to work but, rather, to tell her employer about the reason for her absence and, except where she was unable to do so before she returned to work, how long she expected to be absent. The provision did not impose a continuing obligation on the employee to update the employer as to her situation. The tribunal had erred in dismissing the claim on the basis of non-compliance with section 57A(2) without making clear findings as to the extent to which, if at all, she had complied with the subsection and in suggesting that she was under a duty to report to her employer on a daily basis. Furthermore, the tribunal erred in law in directing themselves that the disruption caused to the employer's business by the employee's time off was relevant to the question of whether a reasonable amount of time was taken. The tribunal should not take into account the disruption or inconvenience caused to the employer's business by the employee's absence in determining what amount of absence was 'reasonable' under section 57A.

Cox J:
A tribunal asked to determine this issue should ask themselves the following questions:
(1) Did the applicant take time off or seek to take time off from work during her working hours? If so, on how many occasions and when?
(2) If so, on each of those occasions did the applicant (a) as soon as reasonably practicable inform her employer of the reason for her absence; and (b) inform him how long she expected to be absent; (c) if not, were the circumstances such that she could not inform him of the reason until after she had returned to work?
If on the facts the tribunal find that the applicant had not complied with the requirements of section 57A(2), then the right to take time off work under subsection (1) does not apply. The absences would be unauthorised and the dismissal would not be automatically unfair. Ordinary unfair dismissal might arise for consideration however, if the employee has the requisite length of service.
(3) If the applicant had complied with these requirements then the following questions arise:
(a) Did she take or seek to take time off work in order to take action which was necessary to deal with one or more of the five situations listed at paragraphs (a) to (e) of subsection (1)?
(b) If so, was the amount of time off taken or sought to be taken reasonable in the circumstances?
(4) If the applicant satisfied questions (3)(a) and (b), was the reason or principal reason for her dismissal that she had taken/sought to take that time off work?
If the tribunal answers that final question in the affirmative, then the applicant is entitled to a finding of automatic unfair dismissal

The EAT made the point in *Qua* that section 57A did not entitle employees to provide care other than on an emergency basis.

> Whilst we recognise that no limit has been set on the number of times when an employee can exercise this right, an employee is not in our view entitled to unlimited amounts of time off work under this section even if in each case s/he complies with the notice requirements in s. 57A(2) and takes a reasonable amount of time off on each occasion. Logically this could result in an employee being entitled, regularly, to take a day or more off each week whenever the medical condition causes the child to become unwell; and we do not regard this as being what the legislation is intended to provide. The legislation contemplates a reasonable period of time off to enable an employee to deal with a child who has fallen ill unexpectedly and thus the section is dealing with something unforeseen. Once it is known that the particular child is suffering from an underlying medical condition, which is likely to cause him to suffer regular relapses, such a situation no longer falls within the scope of subsection (1)(a) or indeed within s.57A at all. An employee would, in such circumstances, be permitted to reasonable time off work in order to make longer-term arrangements for care, as is provided by subsection (1)(b). Where the line is to be drawn seems to us to be a matter which will always fall to be decided on the facts of each case. A parent who has been permitted time off to deal with a child who has fallen ill with chickenpox might, for example, subsequently be permitted to further time off if unexpected complications arise requiring immediate action. The key to this is in our view, foreseeability and it will inevitably be a question of fact and degree in each situation.

The enactment of a right to emergency leave is to be welcomed, as is the introduction of statutory rights to parental and paternity leave and the improvements to maternity leave effected by the ERA 1999. But, returning to the theme developed by Wilkinson and Briscoe (**[4.28]** above), it is clear that the 1999 Act and the accompanying Regulations do not provide parents with the opportunity to take significant periods of time out of the workforce in order to care for their children. Even if greater periods of leave were permitted, its unpaid nature would mean that, in practice, women rather than men would take advantage of it. On the one hand, to the extent that such leave entitled women to return to their own jobs after a longer period of leave than is possible at present, it would be of benefit to those who currently lose their labour market position by taking extended time out. On the other hand, the expectation that women would take longer periods of leave in connection with maternity would provide an additional incentive for employers to discriminate against them. As is clear from the extract below, such discrimination, and the denial of parental and maternity rights, is already a significant problem.

[4.38] NACAB, *Birth Rights*, paras 1.13–1.24, 2.12, 3.16–3.18

> . . . of the some 700,000 men and women who seek employment-related advice from a CAB every year, tens of thousands do so in relation to the birth, adoption or care of a child. Some of these enquiries relate to the new right to parental leave or the non-existent right to *paid* paternity leave, whilst others involve an employer's refusal to countenance a reduction or variation in the worker's hours following childbirth. But the overwhelming majority involve a basic denial of statutory maternity or parental rights—and principally pregnancy-related dismissal or detrimental treatment.

Typically—but by no means exclusively—the workers in question are low-skilled, and low-paid. They have no written contract of employment, are non-unionised, and are thus extremely vulnerable to exploitation. Many work in residential care and nursing homes; cleaning companies; bars, hotels and restaurants; hairdressers; small professional firms; the retail trade; and light industry . . . .

In short, many of the aggrieved workers who seek employment advice from CABx earn their living in what one commentator has described as the 'Bleak House' of the labour market. Vulnerable and low-paid, they work for employers who feel, perhaps understandably, that it is simply not worth the time to learn the detail of dauntingly complex (and frequently changing) employment law, or who simply lack the means to implement the policies necessary for compliance without damaging their business.

Such workers are and will remain a significant feature of the UK labour market. Public policy is littered with rhetoric about the knowledge-driven economy, the globalised market place, and 'internet-enabled flexible working'. But we cannot get our furniture moved by ISDN or our hair cut by email, and care for the elderly cannot be delivered by a WAP 'phone.

It is also true that there are some employers who *deliberately* set out to mislead workers about their rights and entitlements, and to flout their legal obligations to their workforce. More than a decade ago, a NACAB report concluded that many workers 'tolerate very poor working conditions because they are fearful of losing their jobs and the subsequent consequences of unemployment' and that 'some employers clearly flout their obligations under the law'. Whilst such exploitative employers are undoubtedly a small minority, they remain all too numerous today . . . .

Some workers are simply not aware of their legal entitlements. Others *are* aware of their rights but have no idea how to go about enforcing them, or are anxious about doing so—not least because of the dauntingly adversarial nature of the employment tribunal system (see below). And, of course, pregnant women and new parents are particularly vulnerable and may well have other priorities at such a demanding and stressful time of their lives.

Moreover, even when advised of their rights, many aggrieved workers are reluctant to approach their employer for fear of suffering victimisation and, ultimately, of losing their jobs—despite the potential protection offered by the legal prohibition on unfair dismissal and detrimental treatment. For, even if a dismissed worker is subsequently able to bring a successful claim of unfair dismissal before an employment tribunal, the resultant financial compensation is likely to be small—hundreds rather than thousands of pounds. And of course he or she would still be out of a job . . . .

In any case, many aggrieved workers—whether dismissed or still in their job—are daunted by the idea of taking their case to an employment tribunal. The reasons for this have been well documented by NACAB and others in recent years, and include: perceptions about the low probability of winning the case; the likely (small) value of any tribunal award plus the difficulties in enforcing it; and apprehension about the hearing process and the (sometimes aggressive) tactics used by lawyers at tribunal hearings.

Such concerns are compounded by the lack of Legal Services Commission funding (formerly known as legal aid) to cover legal representation at the tribunal hearing, and are particularly understandable in the case of pregnant women and new parents. As the Maternity Alliance has noted, 'new parents feel vulnerable, tired and poor and are not in a position to fight a rearguard action over a lost job'—or even over a denied entitlement.

With the growth in the use of 'casual', temporary and agency-provided labour, an increasing number of working men and women are not legally defined as 'workers' rather than 'employees', and thus lose out on a range of basic employment rights—including the rights to maternity and parental leave, and to time off for ante-natal care. The

Government has stated that 'in a modern economy, we need a flexible labour market'. But in our view that flexibility must not come at the cost of denying a growing number of (generally low paid) workers their basic minimum rights.

A woman who takes *additional* maternity leave has the right to return to the original job, except that where it is not reasonably practicable for a woman's employer to take her back in her original job after additional maternity leave, she must be offered a job which is suitable and appropriate for her in the circumstances, and with terms and conditions that are no less favourable than those of her original job at the date of her return . . . .

Again, however, the evidence from CABx indicates that many employers do not comply with these statutory provisions, and that many women find themselves returning to very different jobs—or to very different terms and conditions—after taking maternity leave . . .

At its worst, such unlawful action by the employer can leave the worker with no job at all . . .

4.3.6 The right to request 'flexible working'

At **[4.4]** above we quoted the conclusion drawn by DTI-funded research that 'The most effective way to reduce the part-time pay penalty would be to strengthen the ability for women to move between full-time and part-time work without losing their current job'. The Government has not provided a right to work part-time. But the Employment Act 2002 did provide a right to request flexible working. Section 80F ERA 1996, inserted by the 2002 Act, now provides that an employee may apply to have his or her terms relating to hours, timing and/or place of work (permanently) varied in order to care for a child under the age of six (eighteen if the child is disabled, and the government announced, in June 2004, its intention to extend this right to carers of elderly or disabled relatives.) An employer who receives an application in the appropriate form must consider it in accordance with a procedure which requires a meeting between employer and employee, the provision of reasons for the employer's decision and of an appeal. But the employer may reject a request for flexible working on grounds of (1) cost (2) 'detrimental effect on ability to meet customer demand'; (3) 'inability to re-organise work among existing staff" or (4) 'to recruit additional staff'; (5) 'detrimental impact on quality' or (6) 'performance'; (7) "insufficiency of work during the periods the employee proposes to work'; or (8) 'planned structural changes' (the Secretary of State may add additional grounds). An employee whose request is refused may complain to an employment tribunal that the appropriate procedure was not followed or that the employer's refusal was based on 'incorrect facts'. But the tribunal will not scrutinise whether, in the absence of factual mistakes, an employer's refusal of a request for contractual change is justified on the grounds given by the employer and the remedy is limited to eight weeks' pay at a maximum £270 per week.

It would be easy to be scathing about the new rights created by the 2002 Act which entitles employees to request flexible working (and not to be subject to detriment for so doing), rather than to work flexibly. But it appears that many employers who are required at least to go through the motions of giving such requests serious consideration actually find that they can be accommodated without undue strain. So, for example, whereas the *Equal Opportunities Review* reported in 2000 (May/June) that

54% of those who asked for changes to their working patterns in order to improve their work-life balances had their requests refused or unacceptable alternatives offered them, in April 2004 a survey by the Office for National Statistics found that no less than 80% of those requesting changes to their patterns of work under the EA 2002 had had their requests granted. The second work-life balance survey, carried out in 2003 for the DTI, found that there was little employee resistance to flexible working by parents. Contrary to the oft-cited suggestion that other employees (in particular childless women) are aggrieved by the special needs of working parents, the survey found that 85% of employees agreed that employers should make a special effort to accommodate the particular needs of parents of young and disabled children. It also reported that one in six parents had approached their employers about flexible working, and that:

[4.39] MORI, Second Work-Life Balance Survey: Results from the Employees' Survey (DTI Employment Series No. 27)

- . . . [t]hese requests were most likely to be made by women, mothers, parents whose youngest child was under two years old and those in services and sales, and least likely by older employees (45+) and full-time workers.
- Nearly three in ten employees who made a request to change how they regularly work (29 per cent) wanted to reduce their hours (including working part-time). A further 23 per cent wanted to change *when* they worked including the number of days they worked (such as a compressed working week or changing shifts). One in eight wanted to work flexi-time, and less than 10 per cent wanted to work longer hours (nine per cent) or take some form of time off (eight per cent).
- Nearly half (48 per cent) of requests were dealt with by a line manager or supervisor rather than by the managing director (21 per cent), the head of department (14 per cent) or the personnel department (12 per cent). Just over a quarter of employees who made a request (27 per cent) put their request in writing, whereas three-quarters had a meeting to discuss the request (with their employer or line manager/ supervisor).
- Of those employees who made a request to change the way they regularly work, over three quarters (77 per cent) said their request had been agreed. Agreement to such requests did not vary significantly by the size of the establishment that the employee worked in, an employee's occupation or their length of service, or by whether they were a parent.

The Executive Summary for the results of the survey of employers concluded that the results 'support the business case for the provision of work-life balance practices. Despite some concerns about staff shortages, the majority of employers that provided flexible working practices and leave arrangements found them to be cost effective, with a positive impact on labour turnover, motivation and commitment and employee relations'. The results of the second work-life balance survey were echoed by those of another survey carried out for the DTI between September 2003 and February 2004.

[4.40] T Palmer, Results of the first flexible working employee survey (DTI Employment Series, April 2004), pp 1–2 & 6–10

Summary of results

- Just over half (52 per cent) of all employees were aware of the right to request flexible working introduced on 6 April 2003. This is a marked improvement in the awareness rate of 41 per cent immediately prior to the new employment rights. Female employees were somewhat more aware of the new right than males (55 versus 49 per cent).
- Around one in eight (13 per cent) of all employees reported requesting to work flexibly since April 2003, most commonly requesting to work part-time (38 per cent) or flexitime (25 per cent). Female employees were more likely to request to work flexibly than male employees (16 and 10 per cent respectively). A greater percentage of female employees requested to work part-time than their male colleagues (41 per cent versus 31 per cent).
- Meeting childcare needs was the most common reason given by employees for requesting to work flexibly (43 per cent), particularly women (58 per cent). It was a less frequent reason for men (17 per cent), ranking equally with having more free time (17 per cent).
- The large majority (86 per cent) of flexible working requests made since April 2003 were either fully or partly accepted by employers. This is a marked improvement on the employer acceptance rate of 77 per cent immediately prior to the new employment rights. Only 11 per cent of flexible working requests made since April 2003 were declined. This represents a near halving of the rate of refusal by employers compared with the previous two years, suggesting the new employment rights have significantly increased employers' willingness to consider seriously employee requests.
- Fifty-eight per cent of both employees with children under six and employees with children under sixteen reported awareness of the right to request flexible working compared to 50 per cent of employees without dependent children.
- Almost one quarter (24 per cent) of employees with children under six and one fifth (20 per cent) of employees with children under sixteen requested to work flexibly since the introduction of the new law. This compares to only one in ten (10 per cent) employees without dependent children who had requested flexible working since April 2003.
- Amongst working parents with children under six, almost two-fifths of women employees reported requesting to work flexibly since April 2003 (37 per cent). This was nearly four times as high as requests by male employees with children under six (10 per cent).
- Since April 2003, 14 per cent of employees reported taking time off to fulfil caring responsibilities, most commonly caring for dependent children. Employees with children under six and sixteen were more likely to report taking time off to fulfil caring responsibilities than employees without dependent children (41, 31 and 6 per cent respectively). Similar percentages of male and female employees reported taking time off to fulfil caring responsibilities (13 and 15 per cent respectively) . . .

Working flexibly

- A much higher percentage, 37 per cent, of female employees with children under six requested flexible working since April 2003 compared with only 10 per cent of their male counterparts. Female employees with children under sixteen were also considerably more likely to request to work flexibly than their male counterparts (27 and 11 per cent respectively). Male and female employees without dependent children were the least likely to request flexible working, with 10 per cent of both groups requesting to work flexibly since April 2003 . . .

- The flexible working employee survey found that 38 per cent of employees who reported requesting flexible working requested to change to part-time working arrangements since the introduction of the new employment law on 6 April 2003. Additionally, of those employees who requested flexible working: 25 per cent requested flexi-time, 13 per cent requested reduced hours for a limited period, 10 per cent requested to work from home on a regular basis and 8 per cent requested a compressed working week.

- Of those employees who requested to work flexibly: female employees were more likely to request to work part-time than male employees (41 per cent versus 31 per cent). Thirty per cent of male employees and 23 per cent of female employees requested to work flexi-time. Twelve per cent of female employees requested to work reduced hours for a limited period and 17 per cent of male employees requested to work from home on a regular basis . . .

- . . . by far the most common reason given by employees for requesting flexible working was to meet childcare needs (43 per cent).

- Thirteen per cent of employees reported requesting to work flexibly to make their life easier, 11 per cent wanted to spend more time with their family and similarly 11 per cent wanted more free time. Seven per cent of employees reported requesting to work flexibly to fit in with travel arrangements and 7 per cent needed to meet the caring needs of relatives or friends. Six per cent of employees reported requesting to work flexibly due to health problems.

- Though 58 per cent of women employees said they had requested to work flexibly to meet childcare needs, it was a much less frequently given reason by male employees, ranking equally with having more free time (both 17 per cent). Female employees also cited making life easier (12 per cent) and spending more time with their family (10 per cent) as reasons for requesting flexible working . . .

- Eighty-two per cent of employees with children under sixteen and 98 per cent with of employees with children under six who reported requesting to work flexibly did so for childcare reasons. Employees without dependent children reported free time (19 per cent) and making their life easier (18 per cent) as reasons for requesting to work flexibly . . .

- The large majority (86 per cent) of flexible working requests made since April 2003 were either fully or partly accepted by employers. This is a marked improvement on the employer acceptance rate of 77 per cent immediately prior to the new employment right.

- Seventy-seven per cent of flexible working requests were fully accepted by employers and a further 9 per cent were either partly accepted or a compromise arrangement was reached.

- Respondents stated that only 11 per cent of flexible working requests made since April 2003 were declined. This represents a near halving of the rate of refusal by employers since the introduction of the new employment right, suggesting they have significantly increased employers' willingness seriously to consider employee requests.

- Female employees reported that a slightly higher percentage of requests were fully accepted (78 per cent) than for male employees (75 per cent). Nine per cent of requests made by female employees were partly accepted or compromised on and 10 per cent were declined.

• Similar percentages of flexible working requests made by employees with children under six, employees with children under sixteen and employees without dependent children were accepted (77, 77 and 78 per cent respectively).

A note of caution was, however, struck by Liz Kendall (director of the Maternity Alliance) in the following article:

[4.41] *The Guardian*, **5 April 2004**

The Maternity Alliance has conducted a detailed survey of parents' experiences of flexible work. We found that while two-thirds of parents had their request agreed or reached a compromise, a quarter of these have accepted worse conditions, such as a cut in their salary or job status.

And only a quarter say their new arrangement is going well in practice. The most common problem is increased workloads. A typical example is a woman who asked to work four extended days a week instead of five. Her employer agreed, but said she had to take a cut in pay and holiday entitlement. She had to check her emails when she wasn't in the office and take on new areas of work. As a result, she ended up going back to full-time work.

A quarter of parents have had their request for flexible work refused, often for reasons disallowed by the law. Some employers fail to give reasons for their refusal. Others say they 'don't do part-time work' or 'don't want to open the floodgates' to requests from other staff. Its not just employees of small businesses who experience these problems—similar cases can be found in high-street chains, hospitals and local councils. Few parents are willing to challenge decisions because they're worried about losing their jobs or harming future career prospects. While many parents suffer in silence, others feel there is no option but to give up work.

Why is the law failing to deliver for many parents? Lack of awareness is partly to blame. A quarter of parents don't know they have a 'right' to request flexible work and almost half say their employers don't know or don't follow the correct procedure when considering requests.

The law also lacks 'bite'. Employers can refuse requests for a range of reasons open to broad interpretation. And employers' reasons for refusal cannot be challenged by tribunals: parents can only challenge on the grounds their employer failed to follow the correct procedure for considering a request. Parents who mount a challenge and win only receive a maximum of £270 compensation a week for eight weeks.

Other factors also prevent the shift towards flexible work. The long-hours work culture is still rife in Britain, despite the lack of evidence that this makes us more economically productive. It is overwhelmingly women who are seeking flexible work.

This is partly because many fathers don't know that the law also applies to them, but also because women still do the lion's share of caring. Fathers are becoming more involved in bringing up their children, but until they demand flexible work in similar numbers to mothers, many employers will continue to ignore or downplay the issue . . .

A new right to work fewer hours when children are less than one year old would help many parents at a crucial stage in their child's development. Introducing a code of practice for employers to assess employees' requests for flexible work; giving parents the right to challenge a refusal; and raising compensation levels, would all help ensure flexible work becomes a reality for more parents.

Liz Kendall challenges the level of success of requests for flexible working suggested by the Government's data. Her concerns chime with the *Equal Opportunities Review* October 2003 headline 'Slow-progress on work–life balance'. The article reported evidence of 'pockets of resistance to flexible working and a narrow approach among many employers, prompting calls for an end to the long-hours culture and the extension of the legal right to request flexible working to include all workers'. A recent report by the TUC similarly reports problems experienced by parents requesting flexible work and, alarmingly, a very narrow approach on the part of tribunals to the application of the Regulations. Kendall makes the point that the existence of a right to work flexibly can serve further to entrench gendered working arrangements. This is particularly true of gender-specific leave such as maternity leave (now twelve months long and non-transferable between parents). But even where entitlement to family-related leave and work-related flexibility is equal between parents, men are radically less likely to take advantage of (particularly unpaid) leave than are women. Jane Pillinger warned that:

[4.42] *Equal Opportunities Review* **107, July 2002**

> Across Europe, some experiments in making working time more flexible have had the consequence of legitimising women's exit from the labour market, and therefore further undermining their position within it. For example, working time experiments in Finnish municipalities and health services, to introduce a six-hour day, part-time work, part-time benefits and work rotation—the bulk of which have been taken up by women—have had this negative consequence associated with them. Parental leave schemes in Sweden have had such a low take-up from fathers that a father's month is now included in the 12-month leave entitlement for parents [i.e., it can be transferred to the mother rather than simply lost].

Pillinger reports that, as a result of the problems of take-up associated with parental leave: 'in a growing number of countries, the collective reduction and reorganisation of working time has become strategically more important to achieving equality and the sharing of work and family life'. The regulation of working time in the UK forms the subject matter of section 4.5 below.

4.4 Minimum wage regulation

Rights such as those provided by the WTRs 1998 and the MPLRs 1999 cannot be considered in the abstract: unless working people are provided with some measure of guaranteed minimum income, they will not be in a position to exercise any real control over the balance between their lives inside and outside the workplace. It is for this reason that the National Minimum Wage Act 1998 is included in this chapter.

The Social Charter 1961 provides a right to a fair remuneration, framed by Article 4 in terms of 'remuneration such as will give them and their families a decent standard of living', a level which has been set by the Committee of Independent Experts at 60 per cent of the national average wage in the relevant country (see K.D. Ewing, 'Social Rights and Human Rights: Britain and the Social Charter—The Conservative Legacy' [2000] *European Human Rights Law Review* 91, p.98). But before the implementation of the National Minimum Wage Act, Britain was relatively isolated in Europe in lacking any comprehensive minimum wage protection (at however low a level). The importance of minimum wage protection had been recognised at the start of the twentieth century by none other than Winston Churchill MP, later to become Conservative Prime Minister.

[4.43] Winston Churchill MP, 155 HC Debs (24 April 1906) col 1888

> It is a national evil that any class of Her Majesty's subjects should receive less than a living wage in return for their utmost exertions . . . where you have what we call sweated trades, you have no organisation, no parity of bargaining, the good employer is undercut by the bad and the bad by the worst; the worker, whose whole livelihood depends upon the industry, is undersold by the worker who only takes up the trade as a second string . . . where these conditions prevail you have not a condition of progress, but a condition of progressive degeneration.

Churchill was speaking during the debates on the Trade Boards Act 1909, which established wage-fixing mechanisms for the 'sweated industries' (those providing wages 'barely sufficient to sustain existence, . . . hours of labour . . . such as to make the lives of the worker periods of almost ceaseless toil . . . sanitary conditions . . . injurious to the health of the persons employed and . . . dangerous to the public'—Select Committee on the Sweating System, 5th Report (1890)). The Trade Boards, later re-named Wages Councils, were eventually abolished in 1993. According to the Department of Employment's 1988 Consultation Document on Wages Councils, wage regulation was inflationary and inflexible and led to knock-on effects throughout industry. At the time, Wages Council rates were set at between 34% and 43% of the full-time male average hourly rate. But the 1988 document interpreted the clustering of up to a third of those workers covered by Wages Councils on or around the minimum rates as:

> evidence that council minima continue to be above the levels required to fill jobs . . . most workers in Wages Council trades are part-time, many of them contributing a second income to the home . . . It has become increasingly clear that Wages Councils' decisions continue to prevent employers from developing pay structures wholly in accordance with the best interests of their businesses.

Agricultural Wages Boards remained. Although the UK Government denounced ILO Convention No 26, which required minimum wage-fixing machinery, in 1985, to pave the way to removal of the Wages Councils, it had missed the opportunity in 1983 to denounce Convention No 99 which obliges signatories to establish minimum wage regulation in the agricultural sphere.

4.4.1 Introduction of the national minimum wage

Within four years of Wages Councils' death rattle, the Labour Party had taken office on a pledge to establish a national minimum wage. Economists are divided as to the wisdom of minimum wage regulation, the analysis which underpinned the abolition of Wages Councils being disputed by those such as Wilkinson and Deakin, extracted below, who point to the social costs of poverty wages.

[4.44] F Wilkinson and S Deakin, *Labour Standards—Essential to Economic and Social Progress* (London, IER, 1996) (footnotes omitted)

> The availability of under-valued labour has important negative influences on productive efficiency by providing a means by which firms can compensate for organisational and other managerial inefficiencies, delay the scrapping of obsolete capital equipment and engage in destructive price competition. The absence of wage discipline means that technologically and managerially backward firms can survive and this helps prevent more progressive firms from expanding their share of the market. The overall effect is a lower average level of productivity and the slow rate of introduction of new techniques and products.
>
> Price competition based on wage cutting also fosters obsolete product structures. Competition based on the development of new, and the modification of existing, products has the effect of continuously shifting product market boundaries. Failures by firms to respond traps them in declining market niches and although they may remain viable by cutting labour costs and capturing a larger share of a reduced demand this can only be a short term expedient. The long term depends on being competitive in terms of quality and not simply price, and this requires an emphasis on research and development, product design and innovation. But this is discouraged by low wage competition and its continuous downward pressure on profit margins, which rules out long term considerations and encourages cost paring which threatens quality standards . . .
>
> Orthodox economics argues that low pay reflects low levels of productivity. However, when low pay and poor working conditions result from the undervaluation of labour the direction of causation runs in precisely the opposite direction. Sweat shop conditions and the hard driving associated with the absence of effective employment rights or shop floor representation are directly detrimental to the health and general wellbeing of workers, and hence to worker productivity in the long term . . . .
>
> Productive efficiency is best served by worker cooperation. But low pay, poor con-ditions, harash supervisory regimes and unemployment threats are far from the best way of achieving this objective. It is now widely recognised that high trust work organisation is necessary to secure worker cooperation in technical development, product enhancement and continuous quality control. Worker involvement is the key to such development but this can be expected to require evidence of a long term commitment by employers to their work force and the assurance that workers' interests will not be summarily sacrificed to those of other stakeholders in the firm. Fair wages and job security are best secured by offering to workers rights equal to those of other stakeholders; guarantees of standards and effective representation.
>
> The undervaluation of labour leads to its dissipation because of the inverse relationship between poor pay and working conditions and training. The orthodox economic explanation for low pay is that it results from lack of training and that higher pay will further discourage employers from training. But experience shows that low paying

employers are the least likely to train; they are in the business of exploiting rather than creating human capital. Secondly, jobs with poor terms and conditions of employment are unlikely to be afforded high social status whatever their skill level and this will help discourage individuals from acquiring the necessary entry qualifications by undertaking education and training.

Inequality in income distribution resulting from the undervaluation of labour has a detrimental effect on both the level and structure of consumer demand. The surplus of income generated by labour undervaluation in the lower segments of the labour market is transferred to higher income receivers with higher propensities to save, thereby reducing the level of aggregate demand. A more even distribution generated by labour standards will itself therefore increase employment. In addition, the distribution of income has important implications for the composition of consumption are related growth processes. Greater income equality will contribute to improved labour quality by encouraging healthier diets and help improve the environment by allowing a wider range of households to afford more expensive, environmentally-friendly consumption patterns. Moreover, the broad consumer base resulting from a more even distribution of income can be expected to encourage product and process development and by providing a larger home market for high value added goods give the platform for exports in growing markets with higher margins.

Labour market deregulation and the consequent relative decline in wages at the bottom end of the labour market has important negative consequences on government finances. Since 1979, rising unemployment and decline in the relative earnings of the low paid has counteracted reductions in benefit levels, so that total social security spending has been rising. In April 1989 there were 285,000 claims for family credit at a monthly cost of around £7 million. By January 1994 the number of claims had risen to 521,000 at a monthly cost of £24 million (annual expenditure on family credit in 1993–94 was over £1 billion) and this can be expected to grow sharply. Wage subsidisation encourages employers to pay lower wages and the means tested family credit discourages workers from pressing for or seeking out higher wages by imposing a high marginal tax rate on any increases they secure.

There are further costs to the policy of promoting 'non-standard' forms of work. The proliferation of part-time work at low rates of pay and self-employment means that the tax base is being eroded. In construction, which saw a considerable increase in self-employment in the 1980s which was encouraged by government, both (lawful) tax avoidance and (illegal) tax evasion have become widespread. The resulting loss to government revenues has been estimated at between £2 and £4 billion annually. The tax regme for construction has also contributed to a policy of cut-throat competition over labour costs which is undermining training and leading to skills shortages . . .

The weight of empirical evidence is that far from being of little worth the work of the low paid is generally substantially undervalued. Moreover, the wage structure is sufficiently flexible to allow this source of chronic economic inefficiency to be countered by means of a legal minimum wage without significant unemployment or inflationary consequences. From this starting point the case for statutory minimum wage embraces economic and social arguments. In the interests of social justice, equality and a civilised society there should be some minimum acceptable reward for effort expended in wage labour. The problems of a shortage of jobs productive enough to provide this minimum reward cannot be solved by low wages but only by effective aggregate demand, and an industrial and labour market policy designed to generate economic growth. Minimum wage protection will contribute to this by exerting economic pressure on employers to improve management, technology and products and by encouraging them to make better use of their workers by improved trained and personnel policy.

A statutory minimum wage also has an important part to play in reforms of the social security system and policies to increase labour market participation.

Finally, a legal minimum wage is an important complement to effective wage determination by restricting the undercutting of agreed rates and by obliging firms to pay careful attention to evaluating jobs and making the best use of their workforce. Equal pay and equal value legislation has demonstrated that employers respond to statutory pressure by negotiating new terms and conditions of employment particularly under pressure from trade unions. The generalisation of this compulsion by the introduction and progressive raising of a minimum wage would provide trade unions with wide opportunities to participate in the enforcement process and in negotiating job evaluation, training and other schemes to smooth the introduction of more equitable payment systems.

Many of the arguments made by Deakin and Wilkinson were also advanced by the Low Pay Commission (LPC) which was appointed by the new Labour Government in July 1997 in order to advise as to the appropriate rate for the new NMW. The Commission also pointed out the vulnerability to low wages of particular groups.

[4.45] The National Minimum Wage, *First Report of the Low Pay Commission* (June 1998), paras 3.7–3.10

Some groups of workers are more likely to be low paid than others. These include . . . women, young people, ethnic minorities, people with disabilities, part-time workers, lone parents, temporary and seasonal workers and homeworkers . . . Many sectors in which low pay prevails—such as cleaning, hospitality and social care—are those where female workers have traditionally been in the majority. In the social care sector, for example . . . 90 per cent of staff in residential and nursing homes are women. But . . . certain types of working patterns in which female workers predominate—such as part-time work and homeworking—can significantly influence the level of pay. Many jobs with those working patterns exist in the lowest-paying sectors, which creates further downward pressure on women's pay.

It could be argued that the existence or otherwise of minimum wage regulation is of secondary importance to the question whether, social security being taken into account, reasonable minimum incomes are guaranteed. There may be an element of truth in this so far as individual workers are concerned—issues of human dignity aside, an income is an income. But subsidising low pay means subsidising low-paying employers, giving rise to the problems discussed by Wilkinson and Deakin, above. Wage subsidies also carry some of the 'poverty trap' problems associated with out-of-work benefits. Nevertheless it is important, particularly when we come to consider the relationship between the NMW and working time regulation, to see the former in a broader context which includes redistributive benefits such as the Working Tax Credits.

The minimum wage was set in April 1999 (its introduction) at £3.60 per hour (£4.85 from October 2004). A rate of £3.00 per hour (£4.10 from October 2004) was set for those aged 18–21, no minimum rate being applied to those aged under 18 until 1 October 2004 since when it has been set at £3.00 per hour.

4.4.2 The National Minimum Wage

On 18th June 1998 Margaret Beckett, then President of the Board of Trade, declared that:

> Introducing the minimum wage at the levels I have announced today will help some 2 million workers escape from poverty pay without adverse effects on jobs or inflation. These will include: 1.4 million women; over 1.3 million part-time workers; some 200,000 young people; around 110,000 homeworkers; approximately 175,000 lone parents who work; and some 130,000 ethnic minority workers.

Section 1(2) of the NMWA provides that the NMW applies in respect of any 'worker' who 'work[s], or ordinarily works, in the United Kingdom under his contract'. Members of the armed forces are excluded from the NMW by section 37, share fishermen, unpaid volunteers, residential members of religious communities (except independent schools and providers of further and higher education) and prisoners by sections 43–45. But section 54(3)(b) defines 'worker' widely to include apprentices (though not those under 19 or under 26 and in their first 12 months of training and see *Edmonds v Lawson* [2000] ICR 567), and those contracted 'to do or perform personally any work or services for another party to the contract whose status is not by virtue of the contract that of a client or customer of any profession or business undertaking carried on by the individual'. Section 34 expressly applies the NMW to 'agency workers' 'as if there were a worker's contract . . . between the agency worker' whichever of the agent or the principal either (a) is responsible for paying the worker or (b) actually does so, and section 35 to home workers. Section 35 expressly includes 'homeworkers' as 'workers' and section 41 permits the Secretary of State to designate others as 'workers'.

Much of the detail of the national minimum wage is supplied by the National Minimum Wage Regulations 1999 (NMWRs 1999 SI 1999, No 584), which were drawn up by the Secretary of State after the report of the Low Pay Commission. The Regulations exclude from the coverage of the Act au pairs, family members engaged in family businesses and those engaged in specified training (see Regulation 12). They also permit payment of a lower rate to adults in the first 26 weeks of employment which includes at least 26 days' 'accredited training' (Regulation 13).

Regulation 8 defines as 'pay' 'payments paid by the employer to the worker in his capacity as a worker before any deductions are made, excluding' payments made by way of advances, pension, 'allowance or gratuity in connection with the worker's retirement or as compensation for loss of office', tribunal award, redundancy payment or 'payment by way of an award under a suggestions scheme'. Regulation 9 provides that 'pay' does not include 'any benefit in kind provided to the worker, whether or not a monetary value is attached to the benefit', save that a maximum of £3.75 per day (October 2004) may be deducted for living accommodation), and that it does not include 'any voucher, stamp or similar document capable of being exchanged for money, goods or services (or for any combination of those things) provided by the employer to the worker'.

[4.46] B Simpson 'A Milestone in the Legal Regulation of Pay: The National Minimum Wage Act 1998', (1999) 28 *Industrial Law Journal* **1, pp 14–15 (footnotes omitted)**

From this, what might be called 'gross' amount, any one or more of a number of 'reductions' may be required under Regulations 20–24 and in appropriate cases it may be subject to a deduction in respect of the provision of accommodation under Regulation 25.

The 'reductions' in order to exclude overtime premiums (20(1)(c)), allowances (20(1)(d)) and tips or gratuities not paid through the payroll (20(1)(e)) follow the LPC recommendations. Allowances are defined in Regulation 6(1) as payments attributable to a particular aspect of working arrangements including unpleasant or dangerous conditions, unsocial hours, working in a particular area, tasks or responsibilities additional to those ordinarily involved, being available for work when no work is provided—which could cover guarantee pay in some circumstances—or being on call. Where they are consolidated into standard pay, however, they fall outside the definition of allowance and therefore they do count towards meeting the obligation to pay the NMW. The NMW legislation thus provides a significant incentive to employers to consolidate such payments into basic pay, at least for low paid workers, where they are able to do so. The position in respect of tips or gratuities may also be a cause for some concern. Tips paid directly to the worker, even if pooled by workers and redistributed in accordance with an agreed formula, may be taxable as emoluments but it is hard to see how they could be taken into account for NMW purposes in any meaningful way, let alone the social justification for doing so. Their exclusion from pay for NMW purposes is therefore easily understandable. The inclusion of tips and gratuities distributed through the payroll is more controversial. It is not immediately obvious why an employer's labour costs should be reduced simply because its clients or customers choose a particular way of expressing their appreciation for services provided by the workforce.

Regulation 20(1)(b) provides for reduction of payments received during a PRP [pay reference period] in respect of time in the PRP when the worker was absent from work. This covers sick pay, holiday pay and, in some circumstances, guarantee pay. It reflects an important general principle underlying the NMW legislation. This is that the law seeks to guarantee a minimum level of pay for workers only in respect of times when they are working. As is explained below, the provisions of the regulations in relation to the times at which a worker is deemed to be working for NMW purposes basically exclude times when the worker is absent from work. For those workers who qualify, statutory sick pay provides a minimum guarantee of income during sickness—at well below the NMW rate in most cases. While Regulation 13 of the Working Time Regulations provides an entitlement to [four] weeks paid holiday . . . the failure to provide any link between this and the NMW has resulted in an apparent lacuna in the government's social policy. While it can be readily appreciated that the NMW legislation is primarily concerned with the reward workers receive for work actually done, it is generally accepted that paid holiday is earned over the working year. To the extent that this is so, a provision that holiday pay for the period of the statutory minimum entitlement should be at least equivalent to the worker's NMW entitlement for normal working would appear to be both appropriate and desirable.

Hourly wages are averaged over a 'pay reference period' (according to Regulation 10, either one month or such shorter period by reference to which the worker is paid). In the case of 'salaried hours workers' (see further below), the hours in any pay reference period are calculated by dividing the annual number of contractual hours by the number of pay reference periods in the year (Regulation 21), appropriate adjustment being made in respect of any absence from work.

Contractual payment systems are not always based upon time, but may be linked to output or performance of tasks. Specific provisions are made in respect of 'time work', 'salaried hours work', 'output work' and 'unmeasured work':

- 'Time work' is defined as work paid wholly by reference to time but also that paid in part on this basis but also in accordance with output (Regulation 3). In determining the rate of pay, the hours worked in relation to 'time work' are the hours so worked (Regulation 20).
- 'Output work' is work measured wholly by reference to output (whether measured in terms of production, for example, or completed transactions, Regulation 24). The rate of pay for such work may be calculated in relation to the hours actually worked (Regulation 24) or (Regulation 25) where the worker does not have any 'normal, minimum or maximum working hours', 'the employer does not in practice determine or control the hours worked by the worker in relation to the subject piece or the subject task', and the employer has determined the 'mean hourly output rate' and has notified the employee in advance of the fact that the rate will be calculated. In order to utilise a 'mean hourly output rate' the employer has to test or to estimate the average speed of workers (the latter – Regulation 26A – by making fair adjustments to the tested rate of workers performing reasonably similar tasks in similar circumstances, or the same task in different working circumstances. The piece rate must be set at a level to ensure that the average worker earns at least the NMW (from April 2005, 120% of the NMW). The 'mean hourly output rate' approach replaces the previous 'fair estimate' system (scrapped in October 2004) which allowed workers to be paid as little as 80% of the NMW. The DTI estimated in January 2004 ('Partial Regulatory Impact Assessment: Proposal to introduce fair piece rates for output workers, including homeworkers') that non-compliance with the provisions then in place directly cost workers (most of them homeworkers) around £250 million a year: an average annual underpayment of £2550 per affected worker).
- Both 'time work' and 'unmeasured work' are defined so as to exclude 'salaried hours work' which is, in turn, defined (Regulation 4) as work in respect of which wages are paid in equal installments (or, if unequal, in installments which are equal in respect of each three month period), regardless of any fluctuation in hours worked. Such work may include that in respect of which performance bonuses (Regulation 2(1)) may be paid from time to time. Provision is made for unpaid absences and for cases in which basic hours are exceeded (though if additional hours are paid for these are counted as time work).
- 'Unmeasured work' is defined (Regulation 6) as 'any other work that is not time work, salaried hours work or output work including, in particular, work in respect of which there are no specified hours and the worker is required to work when needed or when work is available. Regulation 27 provides that 'the unmeasured work worked by a worker in a pay reference period shall be the total of the number of hours spent by him during the pay reference period in carrying out the contractual duties required of him under his contract to do such work', except where (Regulation 28) there is a prior written agreement 'determining the average daily number of hours the worker is likely to spend in carrying out the duties required of him' (the employer having to prove that this average was realistic), in which case (Regulation 29) the working hours are treated as being those estimated hours.

Hours of work do not include time spent travelling to and from work, though other travelling done for the purposes of work is included (NMWRs 1999, Regulations 7 and 15–18). So, too, is time spent engaged in or travelling to training other than at the place of work where that training is 'wholly or mainly in connection with . . . work' and has been approved by the employer (Regulation 19); and 'time when a worker is [awake and] available at or near a place of work, other than his home, for the purpose of doing . . . work and is required to be available for such work' (Regulation 15). The latter ensures that 'zero hours' workers are be entitled to payment when 'clocked-off' during quiet periods during which they were, nevertheless, required to remain at or near work.

[4.47] *British Nursing Association v Inland Revenue (National Minimum Wage Compliance Team)* **[2002] IRLR 480 (CA)**

In this case the Court of Appeal ruled that time spent by workers at home overnight during which they answered telephone queries but were otherwise free to perform other activities such as read or watch television counted in its entirety as working time for the purposes of entitlement to the NMW. According to the Court, which upheld the decision of an employment tribunal and of the EAT, the workers were 'working' when waiting to answer calls just as they would have been had they been in the employer's own premises during the day. It would, the Court took the view, make a 'mockery' of the NMW if it were to find that workers were only working when they were actually dealing with phone calls. The employers had attempted to rely on the then Regulation 15(1) of the 1999 Regulations which provided that 'time work includes time when a worker is available at or near a place of work, other than his home, for the purpose of doing time work, and is required to be available for such work except that, in relation to a worker who by arrangement sleeps at or near a place of work, time during the hours he is permitted to sleep shall only be treated as being time work when the worker is awake for the purpose of working.' The employers argued that the Regulations drew a distinction between work at the employer's workplace and activities carried on at the worker's own home, was misconceived. But the Court ruled that Regulation 15(1) applied only to 'on call' time spent at home and not to time spent, as here, actually working.

[4.48] *Scottbridge Construction Ltd v Wright* **[2003] IRLR 21 (IH)**

In this case Court of Session ruled that section15(1) did not apply in the case of a night watchman who was required to work seven nights a week between 5pm and 7am for a weekly wage of £210, this despite the fact that he was permitted to sleep during his shifts (and could in fact have done so for an average of all but four hours per shift).

Lord President Cullen *(for the Court):*
The terms on which the respondent was engaged . . . make it clear that in return for remuneration at the rate of £210 per week the respondent was required to attend at their premises between 5 pm and 7 am seven days per week as a nightwatchman. The work which was paid for under his contract by reference to the time for which he worked was . . . his attendance as a nightwatchman for the whole of those hours. The fact that the activities of a nightwatchman were not spelt out in the letter is neither here nor there. More importantly the fact that the respondent had little or nothing to do during certain hours when he was permitted to sleep does not take away from the fact that he was

throughout in attendance as a nightwatchman and required at any time to answer the telephone or to deal with alarms. The employment tribunal, in our view, confused their estimate of the hours during which the respondent was generally active with an overall consideration of what was required of him as a nightwatchman at any time. Thus we do not accept as conclusive the decision of the employment tribunal as to the period which was relevant for the purposes of the national minimum wage. On the facts before it, the whole 14 hours' period fell to be regarded as 'time work' for the purposes of the Regulations.

The decisions in the *BNA* case and in *Scottbridge* can be contrasted with that of the Court of Appeal in *Walton v Independent Living Organisation Ltd* [2003] ICR 688 in which it upheld a tribunal decision that a care worker required to remain on her client's premises for 24 hours a day and paid £31.40 a day was not entitled to the NMW on the basis of a 24 hour day. Her employing agency had, in connection with a visit from the NMW compliance team, estimated that the tasks she completed for her client absorbed an average 6 hours 50 minutes a day (an assessment with which Ms Walton agreed). According to the Court of Appeal, the tribunal had been entitled to regard Ms Walton's working hours as 'unmeasured' and to treat the agreed 6 hour 50 minute estimate as an agreement for the purposes of Regulation 28 (this despite the fact that her pay was expressed as being on a daily basis). This being the case, the claimant was paid £4.60 an hour, a sum in excess of the NMW rate then in force. The Court of Appeal distinguished the *BNA* and *Scottbridge* cases on the basis that, in both, it had been agreed that the workers were employed on time work, the dispute being as to whether they worked the whole of their shifts.

Regulation 15(1) now defines as 'time work' time:

[4.49] National Minimum Wage Regulations 1999, Regulation 15

Reg 15(1) . . . when a worker is available at or near a place of work for the purpose of doing time work and is required to be available for such work except where—
(a) the worker's home is at or near the place of work; and
(b) the time is time the worker is entitled to spend at home.

(1A) In relation to a worker who by arrangement sleeps at or near a place of work and is provided with suitable facilities for sleeping, time during the hours he is permitted to use those facilities for the purpose of sleeping shall only be treated as being time work when the worker is awake for the purpose of working.

Similar provision is made by Regulation 16 in relation to salaried hours work.

[4.50] B Simpson 'A Milestone in the Legal Regulation of Pay: The National Minimum Wage Act 1998', (1999) 28 *Industrial Law Journal* 1, pp 17–18 (footnotes omitted)

subject to these provisions on travelling and training, times when a worker is absent from work are excluded from time work (3(3)). It may be noted that times when absent from work also appear to be excluded from the 'hours' spent on output work or non-hours work that are counted for NMW purposes by Regulations 13(1) and 16 respectively. In any event, in a provision redolent with difficulties but which on past evidence is likely to be construed against the worker in all circumstances, Regulation 2(2) provides that 'time when the worker is engaged in industrial action' is excluded from all definitions and is to be treated as time when the worker is absent from work. Finally, in what appears to be a provision motivated by a miserly attitude which is wholly inconsistent with the policy behind a statutory NMW, Regulation 3(4) provides that where a worker is *entitled* to a rest break, the period of the break shall be treated as time absent from work. Regulation 12 of the Working Time Regulations 1998 provides that all adult workers who work more than six hours a day are entitled to a rest break of at least 20 minutes, subject to the provisions of any applicable collective agreement or 'workforce agreement'. Workers who are paid at the full NMW rate from April 1999 will therefore, it appears, forfeit £1.20 for their entitlement to a 20 minute break whether or not they take it, an astonishing provision which is arguably inconsistent with the health and safety underpinning of the Working Time Regulations.

4.4.3 Enforcement of the National Minimum Wage

The NMW may be enforced both individually and administratively. Section 17 of the NMWA 1998 provides workers with a contractual right to any shortfall between their wages and the NMW. This right may be enforced either by way of a contractual claim or a claim under section13 ERA 1996 in respect of an unauthorised deduction from wages (see chapter 2). The NMWA 1998, section 18 permits such claims even by those who are not generally entitled to protection under the ERA 1996. In either case section 28 NMWA 1998 imposes on the employer the burden of proving that the worker does not qualify for the NMW, alternatively that the appropriate NMW rate was paid.

Proposals in the draft NMW Regulations that employers be required to issue national minimum wage statements together with or as part of the itemised pay statements to which workers are entitled were absent from the final Regulations. But the Regulations do require that employers keep records in respect of those workers covered by the NMW 'sufficient to establish that he is remunerating the worker at a rate at least equal to the national minimum wage' (Regulation 38). Workers may (NMWA 1998, section 10) 'inspect . . . examine . . . and copy' those records if (and only if) they 'believe on reasonable grounds that [they are] or may be being, or ha[ve] or may have been, remunerated for any pay reference period . . . at a rate which is less than the national minimum wage'. Workers may chose to be accompanied 'by such other person as the worker may think fit' for the purposes of the inspection, the right to inspect turning on the provision by the worker to the employer of a 'production notice . . . requesting the production of any relevant records relating to such period as may be described in the notice'. The production notice must state, where relevant, the worker's intention to be accompanied (NMWA 1998, section 10(6)).

Failure by an employer to permit inspection can be challenged (NMWA 1998, section 11) before an employment tribunal, the remedy consisting of a declaration and a maximum payment of 80 times the hourly NMW then in force. The complaint must be made within the normal three month period of failure to produce or, '[w]here the employment tribunal is satisfied that it was not reasonably practicable' for a complaint to be made in time, 'within such further period as the tribunal considers reasonable'.

Sections 25 and 23 respectively provide workers with the right not to be subject to dismissal or to other detriment (by act or deliberate omission) 'on the ground that' action was taken by or on behalf of the worker in order to 'enforc[e], or otherwise secur[e] the benefit of' the NMW; or that the employer was prosecuted for any offence connected with the NMW (of which more, below), or that 'the worker qualifies, or will or might qualify' for the NMW or a particular rate thereof. These sections are in similar terms to new sections 45A and 101A ERA 1996, extracted at **[4.62]**. Section 104A applies to selection for redundancy as well as to dismissal and, as in the case of other automatically unfair reasons for dismissal, neither a qualifying period nor an upper age limit applies in relation to the protection.

Turning to the administrative enforcement of the NMW, NMW compliance officers (appointed by the Inland Revenue on behalf of the Secretary of State) are empowered (NMWA 1998, section 14) to inspect, examine and copy employers' records and to compel evidence from individuals. (Agricultural wages inspectors enforce the NMW where it applies in the agricultural sector, as well as enforcing the agricultural minimum wage.) If compliance officers find a failure to comply with the NMW they may serve an enforcement notice requiring the employer thereafter to comply with the NMW and to make retrospective payments (section 19). Such notices may be appealed to an employment tribunal within four weeks' of service, the tribunal having powers of amendment or rescission. Failure to comply with a notice may result in the issue by the officer of a penalty notice requiring payment to the state of a sum equal to twice the hourly rate of NMW per affected worker per day in respect of which the penalty applies (NMWA 1998, section 21). These notices, too, may be appealed to an employment tribunal. In addition, compliance officers are given the power (NMWA 1998, section 20) to complain, on behalf of any workers in respect of whom an enforcement notice is not complied with, of an unlawful deduction from wages under the ERA 1996, or to commence proceedings for breach of contract.

4.4.4 Impact of the National Minimum Wage

[4.51] NACAB, *The Impact of the National Minimum Wage on CAB Clients* (1999), paras 3.4, 5.1–6.16

> The bulk of the research material illustrates failure to pay and refusal to employ those entitled to the minimum wage. The following themes emerge:
>
> - refusal to pay minimum wage entitlements
> - incorrect information given to employees by employers about entitlement
> - dismissal in order to avoid payment
> - unilateral variation in terms and conditions in order to compensate for additional wage costs consequent on the payment of the minimum wage
> - reduction in wage levels paid prior to the minimum wage
> - reduction in other employment benefits and conditions in place prior to the minimum wage.

Most queries made by CAB users during the period of the survey related to non-compliance by employers in implementing the minimum wage requirements:

- non-payment of the minimum wage (58%)
- dismissal to avoid paying the minimum wage (10%)
- reduced hours of work in order to meet minimum wage levels (13%) . . .

Some people were unsure whether or not they were being paid the minimum wage (34%). More than a third of these (39%) were unsure due to inadequate information provided on their pay slip.

For those employees not being paid the minimum wage, the main reason noted was that their employer had either refused to pay or had said they were not entitled (27%). Another factor that led to non-payment was being required to work extra unpaid hours (4%). There were also other reasons noted but not specified (27%).

Of those who had been dismissed, the main reason given was that the employer said they were unable to afford paying the minimum wage (44%). A fifth (22%) had been dismissed because they had challenged their employer over failure to pay the minimum wage . . . .

. . . In the main, the themes that emerge [from case studies supplied by CABx] are consistent with those reflected in the survey. However, there are some exceptions and additions:

- bureau evidence forms point to substantial use of dismissal to avoid payment—at least 20% of reported cases involved actual dismissal compared to 10% in the survey; there is widespread evidence of unilateral variation in terms and conditions of employment, including reduced hours;
- non-payment of the minimum wage is compounded by other breaches of statutory duties;
- there is evidence of actual wage loss consequent on the introduction of the minimum wage . . . .

Many employees report a general reduction in their terms and conditions of employment in order to compensate employers for additional costs due to the minimum wage. In some cases this has led to no increase in their pay as a result of minimum wage implementation. In other cases it has led to an actual reduction in pay and conditions in place prior to the minimum wage . . . .

The main changes in terms and conditions reported by CABx are:

- pay cuts to minimum wage levels
- abolition of benefits in cash and kind
- reduction in hours worked and requirement to work unpaid hours
- reduction in holiday entitlement and pay
- contrived self-employed status.

Some employers have reduced additional payments and benefits to employees in order to finance their legal obligations. In many cases, CABx report the withdrawal of payments in kind, overtime and other special rates of pay, and tips. It is not clear from some of these cases whether this has made employees worse off than before the minimum wage.

The situation in catering is particularly complex. Tips are part of pay for the purpose of minimum wage calculations provided they are pooled and paid through the payroll. In any other situation tips should be paid in addition to the minimum wage. Some employers are clearly well informed about this detail of the legislation. In the cases below, from the information provided, it is not clear whether the employers are acting illegally or not. However, in neither case will employees benefit from the implementation of the minimum wage by their employer.

> Restaurant customers are being encouraged to pay tips on credit cards. These tips are then used to top up wages to minimum wage and any tips over this amount are not distributed to staff. Reduction in income as a result of reduced tips for staff. (CAB Western Region)

> Client is a waitress and has been told that the tips she now receives will be used to make up her wages to the minimum wage. This means that the employer is not having to pay any more and the client anticipates that she will be no better off. This situation appears to defeat the object of the minimum wage. (CAB Southern Region)

Unilateral reduction in working hours in order to meet minimum wage requirements is one of the most common actions taken by employers to minimise additional costs. In many cases reported by CABx employees are expected to do the same work in less time for the same pay, or to work unpaid hours in order to cover the workload. Either way, the employee does not gain from the implementation of the minimum wage . . .

There is some evidence of health and safety risks arising, to workers and to the workplace, as a result of pressure placed on workers to maintain productivity levels on reduced hours . . .

Many CABx provided examples where employees have lost entitlement to pre-minimum wage arrangements for holiday pay. This was a very common problem reported by bureaux and highlights, again, the link between different statutory employment rights and the complexities in enforcement of minimum wage rights through other employment rights . . .

Some employers are telling staff that they are now self-employed. In most cases reported by CABx this is clearly being used in order to avoid paying the minimum wage . . .

Many of the people contacting bureaux did not want to take any enforcement action for fear of its consequences, despite information about their entitlements . . .

In a few cases it was evident that reprisals taken by employers against employees extend to taking advice about the minimum wage. This places considerable pressure on employees wishing to inform themselves about their rights . . .

It is clear from CAB evidence forms that many employees are only happy to take enforcement action once they have left or been dismissed from their job . . .

There is some evidence about the readiness of employees to use the minimum wage Enforcement Agency. Again, employees are hesitant to make use of the Agency whilst still in work. Some CABx note difficulties in getting through to the Agency by phone . . .

There is little evidence available, as yet, about the work and effectiveness of the Enforcement Agency. However, the case below shows the dilemma for employees and those working on their behalf to enforce statutory rights; in particular, the need to protect the interests of the employee against reprisals. These are familiar dilemmas for advice agencies who, acting only with the permission of their client, are used to tactical advocacy in difficult circumstances. The role of the Agency is different, in that they do not ultimately take their instruction from employees but must act on any statutory breach uncovered. This may lead to some conflict of interest between employee and Agency. The experience of the advice sector may have some useful lessons to share with the Enforcement Agency about the balance between protecting the interests of the employee and getting a good result.

The NACAB evidence on non-compliance with the NMW is qualitative rather than quantitative. But in January 2001 the TUC revealed the estimated extent of non-compliance:

[4.52] TUC Press release, 26 January 2001, 'TUC Says 170,000 Are Still Earning Less Than the Minimum Wage'

Government figures show since the minimum wage was introduced almost two years ago, the Inland Revenue has made over 7,000 visits to employers suspected of not paying the legal minimum rate, has issued almost 250 enforcement notices, and recovered £2.25 million in unpaid wages . . .

The TUC figures on the numbers of people who are being paid hourly rates less than the legal minimum are based on government figures which suggest that 300,000 people are not getting the adult rate. The TUC estimates that some 130,000 employees are probably not earning £3.70 an hour for legitimate reasons (perhaps because they are on accredited training courses and are getting the £3.20 training rate or are being paid less an hour because they receive free or subsidised accommodation). This leaves 170,000 who should be getting the minimum wage but who are not.

[4.53] TUC Press release, 11 November 2004, 'TUC Calls for Increase to National Minimum Wage'

- The minimum wage has increased from £3.60 in 1999 to £4.85 in 2004, 50 per cent faster than the growth in average earnings across the whole economy.
- Despite employer protestations, this rapid rise has had no detrimental effects. In fact, the number of jobs in the low paying sectors as a whole have increased by 4.9 per cent since the minimum wage was introduced, adding an extra 260,000 jobs to the UK economy. (The low paying sectors are retail, hospitality, social care, cleaning, textiles and footwear, security and hairdressing.)
- Profits and investment levels are also healthy. Clearly there is more 'headroom' for the minimum wage than employers would like to admit.
- Despite the rapid increases since 1999, the minimum wage has never benefited as many people as the Low Pay Commission hoped. Had the LPC known that they would undershoot their target coverage they would probably have set a higher rate. Therefore there is room for a bold increase.

4.5 The regulation of working time

Jane Pillinger's warning about the potential of 'family friendly' working policies further to undermine women's position in the labour market was extracted at **[4.42]** above, as was her report of the increasing emphasis given in a number of countries to 'the collective reduction and reorganisation of working time' as a strategy to promote equality and 'the sharing of work and family life'. In 1993 the European Council of Ministers adopted Council Directive 93/104/EC, the Working Time Directive. The Directive was bitterly opposed by the then Conservative British Government which mounted an unsuccessful legal challenge against it (Case 84/94 *UK v Council* [1996] ECR I–5755). The Working Time Regulations were introduced by the new Labour Government in 1998, almost two years after the deadline for implementation of the

Directive had passed. The DTI's consultation paper welcomed the Directive as 'an important addition to health and safety protections for workers' and 'an important part of the Government's project to create a flexible labour market underpinned by minimum standards'. But it also contained indications of another strand of thinking which was to achieve greater prominence in subsequent years:

[4.54] *Measures to Implement Provisions of the EC Directives on the Organisation of Working Time and the Protection of Young People at Work—Public Consultation*, paras 8 and 11

> The Government favours maximum flexibility in implementation but does not believe that this should be at the expense of fair minimum standards and the proper protection of workers from risks of excess working time leading to stress, fatigue and risks to health and safety.
>
> The Government also recognises there is a balance to be struck between effective protection and placing unnecessary regulatory burdens on business. The Government's approach to the draft Regulations has been to maximise flexibility wherever possible as to the particular arrangements that should apply in the workplace. The Government believes that it is best that employers and workers come to sensible arrangements appropriate to their particular working situation. For this reason, the Government has taken advantage of the derogations provided by the Directives where it believes there is a case for doing so.

'Flexibility' has become an ever more popular catch phrase, appearing to offer benefits to workers as well as to employers. But the question which ought not to be ignored is: 'Whose flexibility? We shall see throughout this chapter that employers' demands for 'flexibility', particularly in connection with working time, can exert heavy costs indeed on their workforces.

4.5.1 The Working Time Regulations 1998 (SI 1998 No 1833) – an introduction

The Working Time Regulations (WTRs 1998) came into force on 1st October 1998. They provide as follows:

[4.55] Working Time Regulations 1998, Regulation 4

> Reg 4(1) Unless his employer has first obtained the worker's agreement in writing to perform such work, a worker's working time, including overtime, in any reference period [see box below] which is applicable in his case shall not exceed an average of 48 hours for each seven days.
>
> (2) An employer shall take all reasonable steps, in keeping with the need to protect the health and safety of workers, to ensure that the limit specified in paragraph (1) is complied with in the case of each worker employed by him in relation to whom it applies.

Regulation 6 provides that night work shall not generally exceed 8 hours in any 24 and Regulation 7 imposes obligations on employers to provide free health assessments to night workers and, where possible, to transfer them to day work when their health requires. Regulations 8, 10, 11 and 12 impose obligations on employers to provide rest breaks and daily and weekly rest periods and Regulations 13 and 16 provide a minimum annual entitlement of four weeks' paid holiday. Given the focus of this chapter on the work-life balance the concentration will be on those provisions dealing with maximum working hours and holidays, rather than rest-breaks and the regulation of night work.

4.5.1.1 Coverage

The provisions of the WTRs 1998 apply to 'workers'. Undefined by the Working Time Directive, 'workers' are broadly defined by the Regulations to cover all but the genuinely self-employed. A worker is:

[4.56] Working Time Regulations 1998, Regulation 2

> Reg 2 . . . an individual who has entered into or works under . . . a contract of employment; or any other contract, whether express or implied and (if it is express) whether oral or in writing, whereby the individual undertakes to do or perform personally any work or services for another party to the contract whose status is not by virtue of the contract that of a client or customer of any profession or business undertaking carried on by the individual.

The WTRs 1998 also provide (Regulation 36)) that agency workers not otherwise within the definition above are to be treated as 'workers' as long as the agency worker 'is not a party to a contract under which he undertakes to do the work for another party to the contract whose status is, by virtue of the contract, that of a client or customer of any profession or business undertaking carried on by the individual'. Where this is not the case, they are to be treated as employed, for the purposes of the WTRs 1998, by whoever is responsible for paying them (or actually pays them). Crown employees and House of Commons and House of Lords staff are covered, though the Crown cannot be criminally liable for breaches of the Regulations, and the application of the Regulations to the armed forces and the police is somewhat modified (see below).

However broad the definition of 'worker', many were excluded from the protection of the WTRs 1998 prior to their amendment in 2003. Regulation 18 in its original form entirely excluded workers in the air, rail, road, sea, inland waterway and lake transport and sea fishing industries (whether or not they were themselves engaged in transport etc: Case 133/01 *Bowden v Tuffnells Parcels Express Ltd* [2001] ECR I–07031) from the protections of the Directive. It also excluded those concerned in other work at sea and doctors in training, The exclusion of junior doctors from the protection of the Regulations ended in July 2004 though their maximum weekly hours of work are set at 58 until 31 July 2007 and 56 between then and 31 July 2009. Regulation 18 continues to exclude from all or most of the WTRs provisions those workers who are now covered by sector-specific directives or regulations (notably *mobile* seafarers, fishermen, inland waterways workers, civil aviation and some road transport workers). *Non-mobile* workers in the previously excluded sectors have been brought within the scope of the Working Time Directive (now, in its amended form, Directive 2003/88/EC).

The WTRs 1998 contain numerous qualifications in relation to restrictions on night work and the periods of rest they prescribe. Regulation 21, for example, provides that workers whose places of work and residence are very far removed, who are engaged in security and surveillance activities requiring a permanent presence or whose work requires continuity of service or production, etc., may be denied normal weekly, daily and in-work rests as long as they are provided with compensatory rest periods, while Regulation 22 makes special provision for shift workers. The weekly hours of such workers (and of junior doctors) are also calculated over 26 rather than 17 weeks and domestic workers are excluded from entitlement except in respect of annual leave and rest periods (Regulation 19). Mobile workers who do fall within the provisions of the WTRs 1998 are excluded from the normal limits on night work and entitlement to weekly, daily and in-work breaks (Regulation 24A) although they are entitled to 'adequate rest' except in the case of *force majeure*.

Regulation 18(2)(b) provides that restrictions on maximum weekly hours, night work, rest periods and holiday entitlement 'do not apply where characteristics peculiar to certain specified services such as the armed forces or the police, or to certain specific activities in the civil protection services, inevitably conflict with the provisions of these Regulations'. The provision, which echoes Article 2(2) of the earlier Directive 89/391/ EEC which was incorporated into Article 1(3) of the Working Time Directive, has not gone uncriticised. Pitt and Fairhurst (*Blackstone's Guide to Working Time* (London, Blackstone, 1998), p 32) pointed out that Article 2(2) 'would seem to suggest that the Member State's implementing legislation should actually specify which services have characteristics conflicting with the legislation' rather than, as Regulation 18(2) does, leaving the question open. As Pitt and Fairhurst go on to point out, however: 'the exclusion operates only in so far as there is an inevitable conflict between the Regulations and the operational demands of the services', a question on the final analysis for decision by the courts.

[4.57] Case 308/98 *Sindicato de Médicos de Asistencia Pública (Simap) v Conselleria de Sanidad y Consumo de la Generalidad Valenciana* [2000] ECR 1–7963

The case involved a challenge to the Spanish legislation transposing the Working Time Directive. The Spanish legislation applied only to private sector workers. The question raised was whether the Spanish doctors were engaged in work whose 'characteristics peculiar to certain specific public service activities, such as the armed forces or the police, or to certain specific activities in the civil protection services inevitably conflict[ed] with' the Directive.

Judgment:
Since doctors in primary care teams perform their activities in a context which links them to the public sector, it is necessary to consider whether such activities come within the scope of the exclusion mentioned in [Art 1(3)].

It is important to note, first, that it is clear both from the object of the basic Directive, namely to encourage improvement in the safety and health of workers at work, and from the wording of Article 2(1) thereof, that it must necessarily be broad in scope.

It follows that the exceptions to the scope of the basic Directive, including that provided for in Article [1(3)], must be interpreted restrictively.

In addition, Article [1(3)] of the basic Directive refers to certain specific public service activities intended to uphold public order and security, which are essential for the proper functioning of society.

It is clear that, under normal circumstances, the activity of primary [health] care teams cannot be assimilated to such activities.

[4.58] Cases 397/01–403/01 *Pfeiffer v Deutsches Kreuz, Kreisverband Waldshut eV*, [2004]

In this case, which concerned emergency workers employed by the German Red Cross, the ECJ took a narrow approach to Article 1(3), ruling that the exclusion:

Judgment:
    . . . was adopted purely for the purpose of ensuring the proper operation of services essential for the protection of public health, safety and order in cases, such as catastrophy, the gravity and scale of which are exceptional and a characteristic of which is the fact that, by their nature, they do not lend themselves to planning as regards the working time of teams of emergency workers . . .

However, the civil protection service in the strict sense thus defined, at which the provision is aimed, can be clearly distinguished from the activities of emergency workers tending the injured and sick which are at issue in the main proceedings.

Even if a service such as the one with which the national court is concerned must deal with events which, by definiiton, are unforseeable, the activities which it entails in normal conditions and which correspond moreover to the duties specifically assigned to a service of that kind are none the less capable of being organised in advance, including, in so far as they are concerned, the working hours of its staff.

The service thus exhibits no characteristic which inevitably conflicts with the application of the Community rules on the protection of the health and safety of workers and therefore is not covered by the exclusion in [Article 1(3)].

4.5.2 Annual leave

The entitlement to paid annual leave is governed by Regulations 13 and 16 which are intended to give effect to Article 7 of the Directive.

[4.59] Council Directive 2003/88/EC (the Working Time Directive), Article 7.1

7(1) Member States shall take the measures necessary to ensure that every worker is entitled to paid annual leave of at least four weeks in accordance with the conditions for entitlement to, and granting of, such leave laid down by national legislation and/or practice.

Regulation 13(7) originally provided that no annual leave entitlement accrued until a worker had been employed continuously for 13 weeks. But in the *BECTU* case the ECJ ruled that this was incompatible with the Directive.

[4.60] Case 173/99 *R v Secretary of State for Trade and Industry ex parte BECTU* [2001] ECR I–04881

Judgment:

As regards, first, the purpose of Directive 93/104, it is clear both from Article 118a of the Treaty, which is its legal basis, and from the first, fourth, seventh and eighth recitals in its preamble as well as the wording of Article 1(1) itself, that its purpose is to lay down minimum requirements intended to improve the living and working conditions of workers through approximation of national provisions concerning, in particular, the duration of working time.

According to those same provisions, such harmonisation at Community level in relation to the organisation of working time is intended to guarantee better protection of the health and safety of workers by ensuring that they are entitled to minimum rest periods and adequate breaks.

In that context, the fourth recital in the preamble to the directive refers to the Community Charter of the Fundamental Social Rights of Workers adopted at the meeting of the European Council held at Strasbourg on 9 December 1989 which declared, in point 8 and the first subparagraph of point 19, that every worker in the European Community must enjoy satisfactory health and safety conditions in his working environment and that he is entitled, in particular, to paid annual leave, the duration of which must be progressively harmonised in accordance with national practices.

As regards, second, the system established by Directive 93/104, whilst Article 15 allows in general terms the application or introduction of national provisions more favourable to the protection of the safety and health of workers, the directive makes it clear, on the other hand, in Article 17, that only certain of its provisions, which are exhaustively listed, may be the subject of derogations introduced by the Member States or the two sides of industry. Moreover, the implementation of such derogations is subject to the condition that the general principles of protection of the health and safety of workers are complied with or that the workers concerned are afforded equivalent periods of compensatory rest or else appropriate protection.

Now it is clear that Article 7 is not one of the provisions from which Directive 93/104 expressly allows derogations . . .

It follows that the entitlement of every worker to paid annual leave must be regarded as a particularly important principle of Community social law from which there can be no derogations and whose implementation by the competent national authorities must be confined within the limits expressly laid down by Directive 93/104.

It is significant in that connection that the directive also embodies the rule that a worker must normally be entitled to actual rest, with a view to ensuring effective protection of his health and safety, since it is only where the employment relationship is terminated that Article 7(2) allows an allowance to be paid in lieu of paid annual leave.

In addition, Directive 93/104 defines its scope broadly in that, as is clear from Article 1(3), it applies to all sectors of activity, whether private or public, within the meaning of Article 2 of Directive 89/391, with the exception of certain specific sectors which are expressly listed.

Furthermore, Directive 93/104 draws no distinction between workers employed under a contract of indefinite duration and those employed under a fixed-term contract. On the contrary, as regards more specifically the provisions concerning minimum rest periods contained in Section II of that directive, they refer in most cases to every worker, as indeed does Article 7(1) in relation to entitlement to paid annual leave.

It follows that, with regard to both the objective of Directive 93/104 and to its scheme, paid annual leave of a minimum duration of three weeks during the transitional period provided for in Article 18(1)(b)(ii) and four weeks after the expiry of that period constitutes a social right directly conferred by that directive on every worker as the minimum requirement necessary to ensure protection of his health and safety.

Legislation of a Member State, such as that at issue in the main proceedings, which imposes a precondition for entitlement to paid annual leave which has the effect of preventing certain workers from any such entitlement not only negates an individual right expressly granted by Directive 93/104 but is also contrary to its objective.

By applying such rules, workers whose employment relationship comes to an end before completion of the minimum period of 13 weeks' uninterrupted work for the same employer are deprived of any entitlement to paid annual leave and likewise receive no allowance in lieu even though they have in fact worked for a certain period and, under Directive 93/104, minimum rest periods are essential for the protection of their health and safety.

National rules of that kind are also manifestly incompatible with the scheme of Directive 93/104 which, in contrast to its treatment of other matters, makes no provision for any possible derogation regarding entitlement to paid annual leave and therefore, a fortiori, prevents a Member State from unilaterally restricting that entitlement which is conferred on all workers by that directive. Article 17 makes the derogations for which it provides subject to an obligation on Member States to grant compensatory rest periods or other appropriate protection. Given that no such condition is laid down in relation to the right to paid annual leave, it is all the more clear that Directive 93/104 was not intended to authorise Member States to derogate from that right.

Furthermore, rules of the kind at issue in the main proceedings are liable to give rise to abuse because employers might be tempted to evade the obligation to grant the paid annual leave to which every worker is entitled by more frequent resort to short-term employment relationships.

Consequently, Directive 93/104 must be interpreted as precluding Member States from unilaterally limiting the entitlement to paid annual leave conferred on all workers by applying a precondition for such entitlement which has the effect of preventing certain workers from benefiting from it.

Regulation 15A WTRs 1998 now provides that workers accrue entitlement to holiday at the rate of one twelfth of time worked on the first day of each month during their first year of employment. Workers who take less than their entitlement during the course of a year are entitled, on termination, to pay in lieu (Regulation 14), though employers are not entitled to recoup payment in respect of holiday taken in excess of entitlement in the absence of a collective or workforce agreement to that effect (Regulation 14(4): *Hill v Chapell* [2003] IRLR 19).

The WTRs 1998 contain specific provisions relating to 'young workers' (aged under 18 but not of compulsory school age) who are subject to more rigorous restrictions on night work and maximum daily hours. In *Addison t/a Brayton News* v *Ashby* [2003] ICR 667 the EAT ruled that a 15 year old paper boy was not entitled to paid holiday as children as defined by the Children and Young Persons Act 1933 (which imposes restrictions on the employment of those of compulsory school age) did not qualify as 'workers' for the purposes of the Regulations.

One of the other problems which has arisen under the Regulations has concerned payment for holiday periods and, in particular, whether employers could 'roll-up' holiday pay into hourly rates and require workers effectively to save for their periods of leave. In *Caulfield v Marshalls Clay Products* and *Clarke v Frank Staddon Ltd* [2004] ICR 1502 the Court of Appeal ruled that this practice did not contravene the WTRs 1998, but referred to the ECJ a question on its compatibility with the Directive because of the decision of the Court of Session in *MPB Structures Ltd v Munro* [2004] ICR 430 that the latter required payment for annual leave at the time the leave was taken.

4.5.3 The operation of the Regulations

Trade unions, where they are recognised, have a significant role in the operation of the WTRs which permit the determination of a number of matters by collective agreement (or, where there is no recognised union, 'workforce agreement'). These matters include the reference periods by which average weekly hours and night work may be calculated, the duration of daily and weekly rest periods and entitlement to in-work breaks for adult workers, the identification of hazardous or heavy night work, the start dates for weekly rest and annual leave and the notice provisions governing the latter, as well as provisions permitting the claw-back of excess annual leave on termination of employment.

The concept of 'workforce agreements' was novel at the introduction of the WTRs 1998 but has subsequently been utilised in relation to parental leave, discussed at 4.3.4.2 above.

[4.61] Working Time Regulations 1998, Schedule 1

1. An agreement is a workforce agreement for the purposes of these Regulations if the following conditions are satisfied—
(a) the agreement is in writing;
(b) it has effect for a specified period not exceeding five years;
(c) it applies either—
　(i) to all of the relevant members of the workforce, or
　(ii) to all of the relevant members of the workforce who belong to a particular group;
(d) the agreement is signed—
　(i) in the case of an agreement of the kind referred to in sub-paragraph (c)(i), by the representatives of the workforce, and in the case of an agreement of the kind referred to in sub-paragraph (c)(ii) by the representatives of the group to which the agreement applies (excluding, in either case, any representative not a relevant member of the workforce on the date on which the agreement was first made available for signature), or
　(ii) if the employer employed 20 or fewer workers on the date referred to in sub-paragraph (d)(i), either by the appropriate representatives in accordance with that sub-paragraph or by the majority of the workers employed by him;

(e)   before the agreement was made available for signature, the employer provided all the workers to whom it was intended to apply on the date on which it came into effect with copies of the text of the agreement and such guidance as those workers might reasonably require in order to understand it fully.

2. For the purposes of this Schedule—
"a particular group" is a group of the relevant members of a workforce who undertake a particular function, work at a particular workplace or belong to a particular department or unit within their employer's business;
   "relevant members of the workforce" are all of the workers employed by a particular employer, excluding any worker whose terms and conditions of employment are provided for, wholly or in part, in a collective agreement;
   "representatives of the workforce" are workers duly elected to represent the relevant members of the workforce, "representatives of the group" are workers duly elected to represent the members of a particular group, and representatives are "duly elected" if the election at which they were elected satisfied the requirements of paragraph 3 of this Schedule.

3. The requirements concerning elections referred to in paragraph 2 are that—
(a)   the number of representatives to be elected is determined by the employer;
(b)   the candidates for election as representatives of the workforce are relevant members of the workforce, and the candidates for election as representatives of a group are members of the group;
(c)   no worker who is eligible to be a candidate is unreasonably excluded from standing for election;
(d)   all the relevant members of the workforce are entitled to vote for representatives of the workforce, and all the members of a particular group are entitled to vote for representatives of the group;
(e)   the workers entitled to vote may vote for as many candidates as there are representatives to be elected;
(f)   the election is conducted so as to secure that—
   (i)   so far as is reasonably practicable, those voting do so in secret, and
   (ii)   the votes given at the election are fairly and accurately counted.

Sections 45A, 101A and 105(4A) ERA 1996 also prohibit detriment and dismissal on the ground that the worker (in the case of an unfair dismissal claim, on the ground or principal ground that the employee):

[4.62] Employment Rights Act 1996, sections 45A-(1)/101A

(c)   failed to sign a workforce agreement for the purposes of those Regulations, or to enter into, or agree to vary or extend, any other agreement with his employer which is provided for in those Regulations,
(d)   being—
   (i)   a representative of members of the workforce for the purposes of Schedule 1 to those Regulations, or
   (ii)   a candidate in an election in which any person elected will, on being elected, be such a representative,
   performed (or proposed to perform) any functions or activities as such a representative or candidate.

Schedule 1, paragraph 2 defines the 'relevant members of the workforce', on behalf of whom workforce agreements may be reached, to exclude 'any worker whose terms and conditions of employment are provided for, wholly or in part, in a collective agreement. This accords a degree of primacy to collective agreement. But the WTRs 1998 fall well short of requiring that any collective opt-out be negotiated with union representatives even when a recognition agreement is in place.

An as-yet unpublished report by Barnard, Deakin and Hobbs to the European Commission (*The Use and Necessity of Article 18.1(1)(b) of the Working Time Directive in the UK*, Final Report, December 2002) suggested that workforce agreements were little used. The authors suggested that this was because of the complexity of the procedures set out in the WTRs 1998 and the 'counter-cultural' nature of such agreements to the UK in which employers were loath to negotiate on working hours lest it encouraged workforce expectations about negotiation on other issues.

4.5.4 Working time

[4.63] Working Time Regulations 1998, Regulation 2(1)

Reg 2(1) . . . 'working time', in relation to a worker, means—
(a) any period during which he is working, at his employer's disposal and carrying out his activity or duties,
(b) any period during which he is receiving relevant training, and
(c) any additional period which is to be treated as working time for the purpose of these Regulations under a relevant agreement.

The DTI guidance (*Your Guide to the Working Time Regulations*) provides that working time includes working lunches, travel undertaken as part of (but not to and from) work and job-related training, but that it does not include rest breaks during which no work is performed, time spent travelling outside normal working time or on non-job-related evening classes or day-release courses. From the start, the position of 'on-call' workers was uncertain. The DTI's public consultation paper on the (then) proposed Regulations suggested that:

> given the general nature of the definition there is scope for difference of views as to whether it is satisfied or not . . . Many service sector jobs require workers to be at their place of work waiting until required to serve a customer (e.g.. shop assistant or a waiter): this is often an inevitable aspect of their job and they are likely to consider themselves to be working during such time. However, if a worker is 'on call' but otherwise free to pursue their time as their own, it would appear that they are less likely to be working until 'called' to work. Similarly, it is not clear whether a lunch break, which was part of a worker's contractual hours, was working time or not . . . In cases of dispute, it would ultimately be for the courts to decide. However, workers (or their representatives) and employers may well conclude that they want to take steps to avoid such uncertainties (*Measures to Implement Provisions of the EC Directives on the Organisation of Working Time and the Protection of Young People at Work—Public Consultation* (1998), para 26).

In the *SIMAP* case the ECJ ruled that time spent by doctors 'on-call', that is, time during which they were 'obliged to respond to requests for home visits and urgent requests', was 'working time' for the purposes of the Directive. According to the Court:

[4.64] Case 308/98 *Sindicato de Médicos de Asistencia Pública (Simap) v Conselleria de Sanidad y Consumo de la Generalidad Valenciana* [2000] ECR 1–7963

Judgment:

. . . [the] Directive defines working time as any period during which the worker is working, at the employer's disposal and carrying out his activity or duties, in accordance with national laws and/or practice. Moreover, in the scheme of the Directive, it is placed in opposition to rest periods, the two being mutually exclusive.

In the main proceedings, the characteristic features of working time are present in the case of time spent on call by doctors in primary care teams where their presence at the health centre is required. It is not disputed that during periods of duty on call under those rules, the first two conditions are fulfilled. Moreover, even if the activity actually performed varies according to the circumstances, the fact that such doctors are obliged to be present and available at the workplace with a view to providing their professional services means that they are carrying out their duties in that instance.

That interpretation is also in conformity with the objective of Directive 93/104, which is to ensure the safety and health of workers by granting them minimum periods of rest and adequate breaks . . . It is clear, as the Advocate General emphasises in point 35 of his Opinion, that to exclude duty on call from working time if physical presence is required would seriously undermine that objective.

As the Advocate General also states in point 37 of his Opinion, the situation is different where doctors in primary care teams are on call by being contactable at all times without having to be at the health centre. Even if they are at the disposal of their employer, in that it must be possible to contact them, in that situation doctors may manage their time with fewer constraints and pursue their own interests. In those circumstances, only time linked to the actual provision of primary care services must be regarded as working time within the meaning of Directive 93/ 104.

The question of 'on call' hours came before the ECJ again in the Case 151/02 *Landeshauptstadt Kiel v Jaeger* [2003] ECR I–08389 which involved a doctor who, during his on-call periods (which took place between normal shifts), stayed at his place of work (a hospital) which provided him with a room where he could sleep when his services were not required. The relevant collective agreement provided that the average time spent working during on-call periods (which ranged from 16 hours mid-week to 25 hours on a Saturday) should not exceed 49% of the on-call period. The claimant argued that all the time he spent on-call should be regarded as 'working time' for the purposes of the Directive, his employers that only the periods he actually spent working should so count (as was the case under domestic law). The ECJ agreed, ruling that all time during which the claimant was required to be physically present at the hospital must be regarded as 'working time' for the purposes of the Directive even if he was permitted to sleep. The other aspect of this case concerned the entitlement of staff to rest periods after periods of work, and the impact of the decision was to provoke enormous concern amongst Member States as to how their health services, in particular, could be organised if doctors' 'on-call' time both counted towards the maximum weekly hours and generated entitlement to rest periods immediately thereafter. This problem threatened to become particularly acute with the extension, from August 2004, of the Working Time Directive to junior doctors. The Select Committee on the European Union, in its 9th report of 2003-4 (HC 42 ix), recorded the 'unanimous evidence' of Government and the medical profession that compliance with the Directive would prove impossible in the wake of the *SIMAP* and *Jaeger* cases, and the Government's response to the Commission's Communication on re-examination of the Directive stated that, in order to comply with the 56 hour limit on junior doctors, they were currently on 72 hour contracts to include on-call time. The TUC also expressed grave concern at the threat that many other Member States would follow the UK in adopting individual opt-outs from the maximum hourly week (a practice which has recently been adopted in specific sectors such as hotels and catering and health by Luxembourg, Spain, France and Germany and more generally, on their accession to the EC in 2004, by Cyprus and Malta).

The Working Time Directive (Article 18) provided for a re-examination of the individual opt out (discussed below) by the Council of Ministers by November 2003 'on the basis of a Commission proposal accompanied by an appraisal report'. The recommendations made in respect of the individual opt-out are considered below, but the Commission took the opportunity to propose a number of other modifications of the Directive among which was the inclusion of the new definitions of 'on-call time' and 'inactive part of on-call time' into Article 2 of the Directive.

[4.65] Proposal for a Directive of the European Parliament and of the Council amending Directive 2003/88/EC concerning certain aspects of the organisation of working time COM/2004/0607 final, Explanatory Memorandum

> . . . the interpretation of certain provisions of the Directive by the European Court of Justice . . . had a profound impact on the concept of 'working time' and, consequently, on essential provisions of the Directive. The Commission therefore considered that it was necessary and convenient to analyse the effects of this case law, in particular of the rulings in the *SIMAP* and *Jaeger* cases . . .
>
> These two new definitions aim to introduce a concept into the Directive which is not strictly speaking a third category of time, but a mixed category incorporating, in different proportions, the two concepts of 'working time' and of 'rest period'. The proposed notion of 'on call time' covers situations in which the worker must stay at the workplace . . . As a result of the insertion of the two new definitions, this Article aims to define the arrangement applicable to on-call time and more specifically to the inactive part of on-call time. It is clearly established that the inactive part of on-call time is not considered 'working time', unless otherwise stipulated by national law or, in conformity with national law and/or practice, by collective agreement or agreement between the two sides of industry. As regards the periods during which the worker carries out his activities or duties, they must be regarded entirely as working time within the meaning of the Directive.

4.5.5 Exceptions to the 48 hour week

We noted, above, the significance of working time regulation to the work/life balance. If the WTRs 1998 are effectively to insulate individuals' out-of-work time from encroachment by employment-related demands, the exceptions and derogations therein would have to be limited indeed. We shall see, however, that many workers are denied protection from excessive working hours, this in large part because of the individual 'opt-out' provisions discussed immediately below and, in addition, as a result of Regulation 20 (see 4.5.6).

[4.66] Council Directive 2003/88/EC (the Working Time Directive), Article 22 (originally Article 18(b) Council Directive 93/104/EC)

22(1) A Member State shall have the option not to apply Article 6 [maximum weekly hours], while respecting the general principles of the protection of the safety and health of workers, and provided it takes the necessary measures to ensure that:

(a) no employer requires a worker to work more than 48 hours over a seven-day period . . . unless he has first obtained the worker's agreement to perform such work,

(b) no worker is subjected to any detriment by his employer because he is not willing to give his agreement to perform such work,

(c) the employer keeps up-to-date records of all workers who carry out such work,

(d) *the records are placed at the disposal of the competent authorities, which may, for reasons connected with the safety and/or health of workers, prohibit or restrict the possibility of exceeding the maximum weekly working hours* [our emphasis],

(e) the employer provides the competent authorities at their request with information on cases in which agreement has been given by workers to perform work exceeding 48 hours over a period of seven days . . .

Regulation 4 is reproduced at **[4.52]** above. It will be noted that the 48 hour maximum week applies only (Regulation 4(1)) 'Unless his employer has first obtained the worker's agreement in writing to perform . . . work' in excess of the maximum. Regulation 5 then provides that:

[4.67] Working Time Regulations 1998, as amended by the Working Time Regulations 1999, Regulation 5

Reg 5(2) An agreement for the purposes of Regulation 4—

(a) may either relate to a specified period or apply indefinitely; and

(b) subject to any provision in the agreement for a different period of notice, shall be terminable by the worker by giving not less than seven days' notice to his employer in writing.

(3) Where an agreement for the purposes of paragraph (1) makes provision for the termination of the agreement after a period of notice, the notice period provided for shall not exceed three months.

The individual opt-out is based on the Directive which provides (at present) that 'a Member State shall have the option not to apply' the 48 hour maximum 'while respecting the general principles of the protection of the safety and health of workers, and provided it takes the necessary measures to ensure that:

[4.68] Council Directive 2003/88/EC (the Working Time Directive), Article 18(1)(b)(i)

—no employer requires a worker to work more than 48 hours over a seven-day period . . . unless he has first obtained the worker's agreement to perform such work,

—no worker is subjected to any detriment by his employer because he is not willing to give his agreement to perform such work,

—the employer keeps up-to-date records of all workers who carry out such work,

—the records are placed at the disposal of the competent authorities, which may, for reasons connected with the safety and/or health of workers, prohibit or restrict the possibility of exceeding the maximum weekly working hours,

—the employer provides the competent authorities at their request with information on cases in which agreement has been given by workers to perform work exceeding 48 hours over a period of seven days . . . '

Pfeiffer v Deutsches Kreuz (**[4.58]** above) concerned the question whether emergency workers employed by the German Red Cross could be required, consistent with the Working Time Directive, to work 49 hours per week under a collective agreement. There, as in the *SIMAP* case, the ECJ ruled that the exception created by Article 18(1)(b)(i) required the consent of the individual worker, which consent could not be given on his or her behalf by means of a collective agreement:

[4.69] *Pfeiffer v Deutsches Kreuz, Kreisverband Waldshut eV* Cases 397/01–403/01 [2004] ECR I–00000

Judgment:
Directive 93/104 . . . seeks to guarantee the effective protection of the safety and health of workers by ensuring that they actually have the benefit of, inter alia, an upper limit on weekly working time and minimum rest periods. Any derogation from those minimum requirements must therefore be accompanied by all the safeguards necessary to ensure that, if the worker concerned is encouraged to relinquish a social right which has been directly conferred on him by the directive, he must do so freely and with full knowledge of all the facts. Those requirements are all the more important given that the worker must be regarded as the weaker party to the employment contract and it is therefore necessary to prevent the employer being in a position to disregard the intentions of the other party to the contract or to impose on that party a restriction of his rights without him having expressly given his consent in that regard . . .

It follows that, for a derogation from the maximum period of weekly working time . . . to be valid, the worker's consent must be given not only individually but also expressly and freely.

Those conditions are not met where the worker's employment contract merely refers to a collective agreement authorising an extension of maximum weekly working time. It is by no means certain that, when he entered into such a contract, the worker concerned knew of the restriction of the rights conferred on him by Directive 93/104

The review of Article 18(1)(b)(i) by the European Commission has been mentioned above and will be returned to below. Until recently the UK was the only Member State to take advantage of it. Further, the 1999 amendments to the WTRs 1998 made the approach to the opt-out more aggressive by (a) bringing the opt-out provision into the text of Regulation 4 itself in such a way as to open the possibility of 'mini-agreements' in respect of particular pieces of work which take the employee over the 48 hour limit (Regulation 4 had originally imposed the limit 'subject to Regulation 5' which in turn provided that the limit 'shall not apply in relation to a worker who has agreed with his employer in writing that it should not apply in his case'); and (b) replacing detailed record keeping requirements previously imposed in respect of 'opted-out' workers. The Explanatory Note to the WTRs 1999 states that the new requirement that employers simply maintain a list of such workers, without record of the hours they work: 'reflect[s] terms which appear in the Directive, to keep up to date records of such workers.' The European Commission, however, made clear in 2003 its view that the UK approach was inadequate to comply with the Directive, stating that Article 22.1(d) and (e):

[4.70] COM (2003) 843 final, Communication from the Commission concerning the re-exam of Directive 93/104/EC concerning certain aspects of the organization of working time

> . . . clearly show that the intention of the Community legislature was that the employer should keep a record of the hours actually worked by workers who had signed an opt-out agreement. This clearly derives from the text of [Article 22.1(d)], which provides for compulsory records 'of all workers who carry out such work' (i.e. who work more than 48 hours during the reference period applicable) and not of workers who have signed a declaration. In order to know which workers 'carry out such work', it is of course necessary to keep records of the number of hours actually worked.
>
> This derives also from the aim underlying [Article 22.1(d)]. The aim is that the competent authorities may prohibit or restrict the possibility of working more than 48 hours in order to protect the health and safety of workers. Clearly it is only possible to take a reasoned decision to prohibit or restrict the option of working more than 48 hours if one has access to the records of hours actually worked by the persons who signed the opt-out agreement . . .
>
> These provisions of national law have moreover led to a paradoxical situation where there may be records on hours actually worked by workers subject to the 48-hour limit but not for those who have opted to work longer hours, who are significantly more exposed to risks to their health and safety.
>
> There is also the additional problem that it is impossible to monitor compliance with other provisions of the Directive. How can compliance regarding the daily rest period (Article 3), breaks (Article 4) or weekly rest period (Article 5) be monitored if there are no records of the time actually worked by these workers? In fact, the way the Directive is transposed into national law, it could in practice prevent the workers in question from benefiting from certain rights laid down in the Directive, which was evidently not the intention of the Community legislature.

The individual opt-out provisions of the WTRs 1998 have been the subject of much criticism. The TUC has been particularly critical of the provision, consistently calling for its removal both on the basis that individuals should not, as a matter of principle, be permitted to opt out of health and safety provisions, and also on the basis that many cases of opting out are not truly voluntary. The WTRs 1998 do not prevent employers from requiring workers to sign opt-out agreements as a condition of recruitment. And although workers remain free in theory to opt back in at any time by giving notice, it is probable that many workers are deterred by fear of the consequences of so doing. Case studies collated by the TUC from Citizens' Advice Bureaux suggests that the opt-out has proved problematic and Neathy and Armstrong's DTI-commissioned research showed a significant use of opt-outs by employers.

[4.71] TUC, 'Working Time Directive Review 2003: the use and abuse of the "opt-out" in the UK'

The principal problem has been that our Government allows all UK workers to opt-out of the 48-hour average weekly working time limit.

The result of these opt-outs has been that the number of long-hours workers was only reduced by 3% when the directive was applied in the UK. Just under four million UK workers still work more than 48 hours per week, whilst more than half a million work in excess of 60 hours per week. To make matters worse, many workers are still being pressured to work more than 48 hours per week by their employers. Although this practice is actually illegal under UK law, the enforcement regime in the UK is far too weak to be able to protect the rights of these workers. The overwhelming response to the directive by UK long-hours employers has been to ensure that their employees have opted-out, to check that they pay four weeks annual leave (which in UK law may include all of our eight public holidays), and to ignore the other five provisions. In fact, a substantial minority of employers think that the opt-out absolves them from all the provisions of the directive except for the obligation to pay four weeks annual leave.

Our findings are consistent with the conclusions of an earlier study of the strategies used to implement the UK Working Time Regulations by 416 companies with long hours workers. This study [D Goss and D Adam-Smith, 'Pragmatism and Compliance: Employer Responses to the Working Time Regulations' (2001) 32.3 *Industrial Relations Journal* p. 195] found that 13% took action to reduce hours, 81% sought individual opt-outs and 6% simply ignored the law . . .

The TUC has consistently argued that there can be no case for allowing workers to opt-out of health and safety law. If workers undermine their own health by working excessive hours then the cost is born by the health service, the welfare system and their families. If they work when they are dangerously fatigued then they may put the health and safety of other people at risk. Clearly a worker's legitimate right to choose how long they work for must be tempered by a strong duty not to harm themselves or others.

In reality, the effect of allowing people to opt out of a safety law is similar to the effect of repealing the law. One might just as easily argue that it is acceptable to break the speed limits on the roads when one is in a hurry to get to meeting, or that it is acceptable to remove the guard from a lathe so that one can work faster when the job must be completed quickly. In fact, these are just the sort of arguments that some employers have used against the introduction of every safety law that has ever been enacted. These arguments are completely invalid, and must be rejected if health and safety are to be properly protected . . .

The LFS show that most long hours workers (68%) are unhappy with their working hours, and that one quarter of them (24%) are unhappy enough to say that they would be willing to take a pay cut in order to be able to work fewer hours. These findings suggest that employers have used a strong element of compulsion in order to maintain excessive hours working . . .

The TUC also commissions regular opinion polls on work issues. Our September 2003 poll found that:

- Two thirds of those who work more than 48 hours have not been asked to opt out of the WTR.
- Of those who have signed an opt-out one in four were not given a choice about opting out.

Pressure to opt-out comes in a number of ways. The most commonly reported method is that the opt-out is entrenched in the bureaucracy of employment. In simple terms, when a worker accepts a new job, they will often receive the opt-out form along with their starting details, with a request that the opt-out form should be filled in and returned to the employer. Workers in this situation often feel that they have no choice but to comply with the employer's demand.

The report of the European Commission prepared by Barnard et al on the use of the opt-out in the UK found similar practices in 2 of its 13 cases studies. In other cases, the pressure to opt-out is less subtle. Sometimes employers simply resort to old-fashioned bullying to make workers work long hours. Another case in the Barnard report concerned a financial services institution that had simply ignored the UK Working Time Regulations (1998) and made the opt-out compulsory. A Government study of 20 firms [Neathy and Armstrong, [4.79]] found a case of a utility company where the opt-out was effectively compulsory. This company put the opt-out in the staff handbook. A member of the workforce said that 'people had the feeling that this is the way that it is going to be, so there was no option'. However, a follow up study found that things were getting worse. A second firm from the sample, an engineering company, had now made the opt-out compulsory for new recruits to the night shift [citing F Neathy, 'Implementation of the Working Time Regulations: follow up study' DTI, 2003] . . .

Barnard *et al* cited evidence of concern on the part of employees about unspoken threats to job security if they were to stand on the 48 hour week, of 'internal professional pressure' such as a sense of commitment to overstretched colleagues and (from trade unions and the HSE) of some direct coercion from employers. The report mentioned the widespread use by employers of the opt-out as a standard term of employment.

The European Commission, making its second proposal for amendments to the Working Time Directive ([4.65] above) recorded that there was 'some evidence that the opt-out was being misapplied in the UK . . . employees are often asked to sign the opt-out agreement at the same time as the contract of employment. This can put them under pressure to agree to opt out and undermines their freedom of choice'. The Commission proposed that the individual opt-out be retained but the restrictions on its use tightened: the opt-out could not be signed at the same time as the contract of employment or during probation, it would have to be in writing, would lapse after 12 months (though it would be renewable) and would not permit work in excess of 65 hours per week. The proposed amendments to the Directive would also clarify employers' obligations to record the number of hours actually worked by opted-out workers and provide that the individual opt-out could only apply if it has both been expressly allowed under a collective agreement or an agreement between the social partners, as well as being agreed to buy the individual, although in the absence of a recognised union or relevant collective agreement the individual alone could agree, and would permit the extension by legislation as well as workforce agreement of the reference period by which average weekly hours can be calculated to 52 weeks.

4.5.6 Excluded workers and working time

The next very major limitation on the 48 hour week is found in Regulation 20.

[4.72] Working Time Regulations 1998, Regulation 20

Regulations 4(1) and (2), 6(1), (2) and (7), 10(1), 11(1) and (2) and 12(1) [which impose maximum weekly hours, restrictions on hours of night work and entitlement to daily and weekly rest periods and in work rest breaks] do not apply in relation to a worker where, on account of the specific characteristics of the activity in which [they are] engaged, the duration of . . . working time is not measured or predetermined or can be determined by the worker himself, as may be the case for—
(a) managing executives or other persons with autonomous decision-taking powers;
(b) family workers; or
(c) workers officiating at religious ceremonies in churches and religious communities.

(2) Where part of the working time of a worker is measured or predetermined or cannot be determined by the worker himself but the specific characteristics of the activity are such that, without being required to do so by the employer, the worker may also do work the duration of which is not measured or predetermined or can be determined by the worker himself, Regulations 4(1) and (2) and 6(1), (2) and (7) [restrictions on weekly hours and hours of night work] shall apply only to so much of his work as is measured or predetermined or cannot be determined by the worker himself.

Regulation 20(1) is taken almost directly from Article 17 of the Working Time Directive which provides that, in the case of these workers and '[w]ith due regard to the general principles of the protection of the safety and health of workers' Member States may derogate from those provisions of the Directive.

Early research commissioned by the DTI found that the utilisation of Regulation 20(1) by employers was restricted by uncertainty as to its scope, only half of the 20 organisations surveyed having taken advantage of it (Neathy and Arrowsmith). In those organisations having a recognised trade union presence, the DTI research found that little or no use of the unmeasured time derogation was made or planned. The 1998 Regulations were subsequently amended, however, to include new Regulation 20(2), also extracted above.

[4.73] DTI, _Your Guide to the Working Time Regulations_, section 8.4

Any time spent on such additional work will not count as working time towards the weekly working time or night work limits. Simply put, additional hours which the worker chooses to do without being required to by his employer do not count as working time; therefore, this exception is restricted to those that have the capacity to chose how long they work. The key factor for this exception is worker choice without detriment . . . This exception does not apply to: working time which is hourly paid; prescribed hours of work; situations where the worker works under close supervision; any time where a worker is expressly required to work, for example attendance of meetings; any time a worker is implicitly required to work, for example because of the loading or requirements of the job or because of possible detriment if the worker refuses.

Regulation 20(2) was a response to the hostility shown by business towards the 1998 Regulations, an article by then Director-General of the CBI, Adair Turner, for example (*Guardian*, 28 September 1999), complaining that the Regulations in their original form were 'an unreasonable restriction on freedom of choice'. He suggested that policy advisers to the Prime Minister might have to 'declare themselves unable to give advice if their hours threatened to exceed the decreed limit', that staff might find themselves forbidden to attend conferences for fear they might exceed their permitted hours, and that the Regulations created problems for managers who flipped through paperwork on the train or 'while keeping an eye on the children, or the television'. Turner went on to declare the Regulations 'restrictive of individual freedom because [they] tell[] adults how to run their lives'. The truth was, of course, that those who wished to work in excess of 48 hours a week were free to opt-out of the provisions and that the beauty of Regulation 20 from the business point of view is precisely that its application does *not* turn on the agreement of the worker.

The trade union movement was fundamentally opposed to any weakening of the Regulations, then General Secretary John Monks warning that trade unions and the government were 'heading for their sharpest clash since Tony Blair came to power' (*Guardian*, 10 September 1999) and the TUC making what were described by the *Independent* (16 September 1999) as 'uncharacteristically forceful' submissions to the DTI.

[4.74] TUC, *Briefing on the Government's Proposed Amendments to the Working Time Regulations 1998*

It is clear from Article 17 of the Directive [upon which Regulation 20 is based] that this provision is supposed to be applied in the limited cases where workers genuinely control their own working time. That is why the Directive and the Regulations use the example of 'managing executives with autonomous decision taking powers'. Indeed, the Supplementary Guidance produced by the DTI in June 1999 reaffirmed the Government's interpretation that this derogation was only intended to apply to genuinely 'autonomous' workers.

The proposed amendment to Regulation 20 is a significant step away from this position. It will have the effect of removing virtually all salaried workers doing unpaid voluntary overtime from the scope of the Regulations. This group of workers have witnessed the greatest increase in their average working hours over the last decade and have the greatest difficulty in reconciling work and family life . . .

[4.75] TUC, *Six Days a Week, A Report on the Working Time Regulations—their Implementation and the Impact of the Government's Proposed Amendments*

If workers have hours of work fixed by their contracts of employment but work voluntarily beyond their contractual hours, those additional hours will not count towards the 48 hour limit on the maximum working week. The effect of this [is] to leave salaried workers working unpaid overtime with no legal protection against pressure from employers to work very long hours . . .

So, for example, if a worker has hours of work specified in their contract and works additional hours without being 'required' to do so by their employer, then the additional hours will not count towards the calculation of the 48 hour limit. This means that a salaried worker (not paid overtime) who works late in order to finish a task, meet a deadline or deal with the sheer pressure of work, would not have these extra hours counted as 'working time' for the purposes of the Regulations. The extra hours would be categorised as 'unmeasured', and therefore outside the scope of the Regulations. This would remove all salaried workers doing unpaid overtime from the protection of the Regulations—and would deprive them of the right not to work more than 48 hours per week.

Most of the workers who would be affected by this amendment fall into the categories of managers, professionals and associate professionals. These groups make up 35% of UK employees. Thus the amendment would exclude over o.1e in three employees from any protection against long working hours . . . managers and professionals work the longest hours in the UK. These workers and their families desperately need the protection of the Regulations . . .

[The] so-called 'individual opt-out' is scheduled to be removed from the Working Time Directive in 2003. As a matter of principle, the EU member states have agreed that persistently working more than an average of more than 48 hours poses risks to health and safety . . . The net effect of the Government's proposed amendments will be that, after 2003, salaried workers in the UK will be the only people in the whole of the EU who can lawfully work more than an average of 48 hours a week.

A campaign to encourage companies to end the long-hours culture, enabling people to see more of their family, will be launched by the Government in the autumn. Ministers believe that encouraging employers to adopt more family-friendly working practices will reduce marital breakdown, help children's educational and emotional development, and increase business productivity . . . Ministers want the initiative to embrace fathers and those workers who have care responsibilities for elderly or disabled relatives.

This campaign is a very positive initiative that seeks to address the damage of the long hours culture on family relationships. But the proposed amendment to the WTR will blunt this campaign by removing legal protection against long working hours from the employees who most need it. Government critics are likely to take advantage of this apparent inconsistency . . . workers are generally unhappy with their current hours of work, and large numbers would like to reduce their working hours. This is strongest amongst the best paid [graph using British Household Panel Survey statistics shows 9% of women and 11% of men at the lowest quintile of earnings, rising through 41% and 31% respectively in the middle quintile to 57% and 43% of women and men in the highest quintile of earnings wish to work fewer hours] . . .

The Government itself has recognised that the long hours culture in the UK poses a threat to family relationships and in particular reduces the time that parents are able to spend with their children. The Working Time Regulations have provided an opportunity for employers and employees, trade unions to negotiate a reorganisation of working time which is beneficial to both employers and employees and provide some protection for workers against long hours working. The amendments would take away this protection for a very large section of the British workforce—and ensure that, after 2003, salaried workers in the UK would be the only people who could lawfully work more than an average 48 hour week . . .

The Government has a clear commitment to promote employment that is family-friendly and enables parents to strike a better balance between work, leisure and their caring responsibilities . . .

The government headed off threatened revolt by the trade unions at the Labour Party conference by promising that legally enforceable guidance to accompany the Regulations would clarify the application of Regulation 20 only to senior managers and executives, rather than the nine million workers the TUC otherwise claimed would be affected by the new Regulation 20(2) (*Guardian*, 13 September 1999). But the TUC castigated the draft guidance which was eventually produced in January 2000 as 'lamentable' (The *Times*, 25 January 2000), claiming that it was 'legally wrong and designed to deprive workers of their rights'. Some amendments were made to the draft guidance criticised by the TUC. But it is far from clear that the new guidance issued by the DTI restricts the application of the 'unmeasured working time' to senior staff. Certainly, Regulation 20 is silent as to status. And while the guidance provides that the 'exception is restricted to those that have the capacity to chose how long they work' and does not apply to hourly-paid work or required, closely supervised work or time in which a worker is expressly or implicitly required to work, the examples used in the guidance leave open as many questions as they answer:

[4.76] DTI, *Your Guide to the Working Time Regulations*, section 8

Worker C's contract specifies that she is to work 42 hours a week, but she regularly works longer because the volume of work is greater than could be done in the time. The nature of her job means that *C works to deadlines and has to complete her work*. She cannot control the volume of the work. The extra hours do not fall within the scope of this exception because she is required to do the work.

Worker D's contract also requires a working week of 42 hours, but the volume of work coming to him is greater than someone could reasonably be expected to do in that time. However, *he has discretion and a clear choice over how much work is done, how his work is done* and how to meet his objectives, for example he can prioritise his tasks and so, if he chose to, he could limit his working week. Therefore, to the extent that he can limit them, the time worked beyond that required by his contract falls within the scope of this exception.

Worker E, whose contract requires a working week of 40 hours, works in an environment where colleagues habitually do a 12-hour day even though the work does not always necessitate such hours. Worker E works the long hours because *she is lead [sic] to believe that her employer considers it unacceptable to work shorter hours*. Therefore, the time does not fall within the scope of this exception because she is required by her employer to work the extra time.

Worker F has a managerial or professional role *which allows him to decide how and when he works, chooses what is done, establishes priorities and determines the time and effort that are devoted to tasks*. Time worked above F's contracted hours will fall within the scope of this exception because he can determine the volume of his work . . .

Worker H is a well paid sales representative who *chooses to work beyond the hours necessary to meet her targets for reasons of personal motivation*, for example additional commission. These additional hours will fall within the scope of the exception because H determines the volume of her work [our emphasis throughout].

In one sense these examples are clear, stressing the voluntary nature of the additional hours within the exception. On the other hand, the underlined sections are replete with uncertainties. C, we are told, 'works to deadlines and has to complete her work', the volume of which she cannot control. But can it truly be the case that D has 'a clear choice over how much work is done'? What happens to the work that D does not do? And how might D clearly be distinguished from E, who 'is lead [sic] to believe that her employer considers it unacceptable to work shorter hours'. If shorter hours insisted upon by D have the effect that work remains undone, might there not be an implicit understand that longer hours are required? Equally, if H works long hours because of her understanding that this will assist her chances of promotion, does this count as (mere) 'wishes to gain promotion, does this count as (mere) 'personal motivation' taking those hours outside the WTRs 1998 as amended? Perhaps most problematic is professional F. Professional jobs, of their nature, are task-, rather than time-defined. What professional can truly say that she is free to cap her hours as she chooses, as distinct from being 'free' to work 'in her own time'?

In February 2004 the European Commission started proceedings against the UK in the ECJ in connection with Regulation 20(2). A report on the proceedings by the European Industrial Relations Observatory on-line makes the point, however, that 'the significance of a ruling by the ECJ against the UK's provisions on partly unmeasured working time will remain limited for as long as the UK can continue to allow employees to opt out of the 48-hour ceiling on weekly working hours altogether'.

4.5.7 Enforcement of the Working Time Regulations

Employers are obliged to keep records to show that the 48 hour maximum is complied with, although these do not have to be in any particular form and the obligation may be satisfied by records, such as payroll, kept for other purposes. The DTI's guidance expressly states that employers 'do not have to keep a running total of how much time workers work on average each week . . . need only make occasional checks of workers who do standard hours and who are unlikely to reach the average 48-hour limit [but] . . . . should monitor the hours of workers who appear to be close to the working time limit—and make sure they do not work too many hours'. Employers are also required to keep records of health assessments carried out on night workers, but not of rest breaks, days off or annual leave. Records must be retained for two years. The WTRs 1998 required that employers keep a record of all 'opted-out' workers), together with the hours worked by them in every reference period. The Working Time Regulations 1999, as we saw above, replaced this requirement with an obligation to 'keep up-to-date records' of opted-out workers.

Enforcement is carried out by the Health and Safety Executive and the environmental health departments of local authorities in respect of working time limits, breach of the limits on weekly hours, time limits and other protections for night workers and record requirements amounting to criminal offences. The enforcement of other aspects of the WTRs 1998 is through the normal employment tribunal route, jurisdiction being provided in respect of refusals to permit daily, weekly and in-rest breaks and annual leave and of failure to pay the latter. Complaints are subject to a three-month time which may be extended (Regulation 38(2)(b)) similarly to that which applies in unfair dismissal cases. Tribunals may award declarations and/or such compensation as is 'just and equitable', the latter to include any pay withheld in respect of annual leave.

The WTRs 1998 do not expressly provide any individual rights of enforcement in connection with the 48 hour maximum week (save in cases of dismissal or detriment as at [4.53] above). But an alternative mechanism has been carved out of the contract of employment itself.

[4.77] *Barber v RJB Mining (UK) Ltd* [1999] ICR 679 (HC)

The applicants were pit deputies who challenged their employers' insistence that they work in excess of 48 hours per week, having refused to opt out of the Working Time Regulations. The applicants, who had worked in excess of 48 hours in each of the 17 weeks since the Regulations came into force, sought a declaration of their rights under Regulation 4 and enforcement of those rights by means of injunctions. They argued that the Regulations incorporated into their contracts of employment an enforceable right to work no more than 48 hours a week. The employers argued that Regulation 4 did not confer any freestanding right upon workers but, read with 4(2) ([4.55] above), merely required employers to take all reasonable steps to ensure that the 48 hour limit was complied with. This obligation could be enforced by workers only if they were subject to detriment or dismissal for refusing to work in excess of the limit. Gage J ruled, however, that 'Parliament intended that all contracts of employment should be read so as to provide that an employee should work no more than an average of 48 hours in any week during the reference period' and that the 'qualified obligation' imposed on employers by Regulation 4(2) (see [4.55] above) did not interfere with the 'clear and precise terms' of Regulation 4(1). He went on to declare that the claimants' rights under Regulation 4(1) had been breached, this having the effect that they could 'if they so choose . . . refuse to continue working until the average working hours come within the specified limit'. He resisted their application for injunctions to prevent the employer requiring them to work 'until such time as the average working time falls within the specified limit' and prohibiting the employer from subjecting them to any detriment:

Gage J:
Any detriment which may be caused to the plaintiffs can be the subject of a complaint to an employment tribunal under s 45A of the 1996 Act. So far as the other form of injunction sought, in my opinion, on that matter, the background to this dispute ['the fact that these proceedings must be seen against the background of negotiations and as a tactical manoeuvre in the union's dispute with the defendant'] is important. To grant an injunction would be to force the defendant to take action which would be detrimental to its business and to other employees. The benefit to the plaintiffs would be to enable them to stop working for a maximum of five weeks in one case and minimum of two weeks in another case. The effect of injunction would be disproportionate to the benefit to the plaintiffs. That is not to say that as a result of my finding in this case the plaintiffs are not entitled to exercise their right not to work. It seems to me, however, that it is better that

that matter is left to the individual choice of each plaintiff and negotiations between them, Nacods and the defendant.

The shortcoming of the *Barber* approach is that tribunals have jurisdiction over contractual complaints only where they arise out of or are outstanding on termination of the employment relationship. Barnard *et al* report a degree of confusion in the employment tribunals, some having proven willing to award damages for flouting of the 48 hour week while others have declined jurisdiction. In any event, where tribunals have awarded compensation it has been very low indeed (one award of £100 and another of £177 is mentioned).

Workers who attempt to enforce their employment rights, whether statutory or contractual, are always vulnerable to victimisation by their employers. The ERA 1996 makes some provision for this, prohibiting employers from dismissing employees or subjecting them (or, in some cases, 'workers') to 'detriment' in connection with their exercise of various statutory rights. The WTRs 1998 amend the ERA 1996 to provide protection to workers exercising their rights under the Regulations in respect of 'detriment' (section 45A ERA 1996), dismissal (including constructive dismissal, section 101A ERA 1996) and selection for redundancy (section 105(4) ERA 1996).Neither the qualifying period of employment nor the upper age limit for unfair dismissal applies in these cases. The Barnard report suggests that prosecutions by the HSE under the WTRs were all but unheard of (it cites a single prosecution and notes the lack of resources afforded to the HSE, as well as practical failings by the Executive) and that very few cases had been brought in the employment tribunals. Those cases which the authors did track down tended to include working time matters only as additions to another central complaint (for example of dismissal on unrelated grounds).

4.5.8 Impact of the Working Time Regulations

The CBI's hostility to the regulation of working time has been mentioned above. The findings of independent research commissioned by the DTI (F Neathy and J Arrowsmith, *Implementation of the Working Time Regulations*, [4.79] below) suggested that the impact of the Regulations was not as significant as business had feared. Neathy and Arrowsmith reported in 2001 that 'Ten of the 20 case study organisations indicated that the WTR had had marginal or no impact when assessed against a range of criteria', smaller organisations having experienced least impact as (not surprisingly) did those which 'made extensive use of individual opt-outs, derogations and collective flexibilities'. More recently, a follow-up report by Neathy into 15 of the organisations visited in 2000 ('Implementation of the Working Time Regulations: follow-up study' (2003, DTI)) found (p 9) that 'In most cases the WTR were not seen as a major business issue [although] the interviews produced some evidence of working time reduction arising from the Regulations and examples were given of operational benefits including more efficient ways of working and the positive impact on worker flexibility and efficiency of reduced working hours. Where a negative impact was cited it was most commonly in relation to increased labour costs, however only one company identified substantial costs which were directly associated with the WTR'. The Barnard report suggested that the Directive had had little impact on the organisation of working time in the UK, citing research by the TUC, the DTI and the DfEE, although it did note a small annual reduction between 1998 and 2001 in the number of those working in excess of 48 hours a week. Working hours have fallen in the UK since the introduction of the WTRs. But as the TUC pointed out in a press release criticising the Government's submisisons to the European Commission's review of the Directive ('Government evidence on long hours is "riddled with errors"', 17th May 2004) this reduction 'has been so slow that it will take the UK another 40 years to reach the EU average'. In 2003 the TUC expressed the view that 'only the paid annual leave entitlements in the directive have had any effect in the UK so far, and that even the application of this provision has been seriously flawed and must be strengthened.

[4.78] TUC, 'Working Time Directive Review 2003: the use and abuse of the "opt-out" in the UK'

The combined effect of the so-called 'individual opt-out' and the UK's weak enforcement regime has been that the Working Time Directive has so far failed to protect UK workers . . . The sad result of this omission is that the UK still has an entrenched long hours culture with an incidence of long hours working that is twice the EU average, UK full-time workers work the longest hours in the EU, and our workers suffer from a high incidence of all of the ailments that are associated with working excessive hours, such as heart problems, stress and depression . . .

In 2002 the TUC undertook a major review of the data on long hours in the UK using the official Labour Force Survey . . . The main findings on long hours were that:

- Nearly 4 million people in the UK work more than 48 hours per week (17% of employees), 1.5 million work more than 55 hours per week and 0.6 million work more than 60 hours per week;
- The numbers working long hours had grown by over 20% between 1992 and 1998. The growth in the number of people working long hours was halted by the transposition of the directive into UK law, but was not reversed;
- 80% of long hours workers are male/ 20% female;
- 2.25 million long hours workers are in managerial or professional occupations
- 1.07 million long hours workers are in the skilled trades or are 'operatives'
- When asked why they work extra hours, 46% said that they needed to generate overtime pay, whilst a further 34% said that they needed extra time to cope with unmanageable workloads.
- There is an enormous mismatch between the number of hours that people want to work and their actual hours. 10 million workers want fewer hours, whilst 2 million (mostly part-time) workers want more hours. Taken together, 1 in 2 UK employees are dissatisfied with their hours . . .

The TUC has also used LFS data to quantify the problem. We calculate that 1.6 million UK workers working more than 48 hours are in receipt of some overtime pay, whilst the remaining 2.4 million do not get any extra pay at all for the extra contribution that they make.

When measured against the relative salaries, the value of the unpaid overtime worked by UK workers is £23 billion pounds per annum. The amount of unpaid overtime worked has risen rapidly in recent years. Some employers are quick to complain about 'the burden of regulation' that stems from increased workers rights, but are perfectly happy to encourage their employees to work for nothing.

Workers will never be able to use employment rights that they do not know that they have. An opinion poll commissioned by the TUC found low awareness of the 48-hour limit amongst UK workers. Only 1 in 3 knew that there was a legal right not to work more than 48 hours. This reflects the minimal impact that the WTD has had on long hours in the UK so far . . .

The TUC report also drew attention to problems with the implementation of the right to paid holiday.

Article seven of the Working Time Directive grants all workers the right to four weeks paid annual leave. This provision has had the biggest impact in the UK and has led to an increase in the holiday entitlements of some five million workers.

However, there are some serious flaws in the UK's implementation of the annual leave provisions that should be rectified. There are three main problems:

- public holidays can be counted as part of the four weeks leave entitlement;
- the UK's weak enforcement regime allows some employers to ignore the law. Their chances of getting caught are slim;
- because the paid annual leave provisions are merely entitlements, many workers are bullied out of their holidays, or are simply given too much work to do to allow them to take all their leave . . .

The bank holidays loophole affects 4.9% of all full-time employees. The TUC's analysis of the Labour Force Survey data suggests that 865,000 full-time employees working a five-day weak are being paid between 12.0 and 19.5 days annual leave per year. Their employers are either using the bank holidays loophole to incorporate some of the 8 public holidays into annual leave or simply breaking the law. It is likely that the non-compliance problem is worse amongst part-time employees.

One study of the implementation of the Working Time Directive in the UK found that 28% of employers were not complying with the paid annual leave entitlements . . . The TUC believes that non-compliance is still widespread.

There is also evidence that even when the bank holidays are counted, a substantial number of employees are not able to take four weeks leave. The LFS shows that 426,000 full-time employees are taking less than 12 days paid annual leave per year. This represents 2.4% of all full-time employees.

Our labour market intelligence suggests that a considerable number of employers include the correct paid annual leave in workers' contracts, but then act in ways that make it impossible for workers to take all their leave. A common tactic is to repeatedly deny requests for leave on the grounds of 'pressures of work'. In the end, the leave year expires and the entitlement is simply lost. In other cases, managers fail to ensure that heavy workloads and lack of 'cover' do not combine to deny workers their leave rights.

The Commission's Communication concerning certain aspects of the organization of working time (see [4.70] above) listed as one of the four criteria for working time review 'to make it easier to reconcile work and family life' (the others were a high level of health and safety, more flexibility for Member States and firms in the management of working time and the avoidance of unreasonable constraints upon small and medium sized enterprises). The UK Government's response to the Communication attributed the decline in working hours since 1997 to the Working Time

Directive, together with national measures to promote work/life balance. But it stated the view that workers' in the UK wanted freedom to choose longer, as well as shorter, working hours and suggested that the imposition of an inflexible 48 hour week would encourage employers to increase the working hours of those currently working under this threshold and thus make the worklife balance more difficult for them. In a section on work/life balance the UK Government went on to state the view that the Directive 'is designed to protect the health and safety of workers, and it is therefore not a suitable vehicle for measures aimed at producing improvements in more general working conditions'.

4.6 Conclusion

The theme of this chapter has been the work/life balance. We have seen that a significant number of recent legislative developments have gone some way towards supporting the reconciliation of working and family life. But we have also seen that, particularly in the case of workers with dependent children, the balance is far from easy. For the most part, and despite the introduction of rights to parental and emergency family leave, dual income households with children are likely to continue to operate on the basis of a gendered division between full-time and part-time paid work. Attention has been drawn throughout the chapter to the social and economic costs of this division.

The final issue which will be addressed, albeit briefly, concerns the future development of work patterns and their implications for the work/life balance.

[4.79] F Neathy and J Arrowsmith, *Implementation of the Working Time Regulations* pp 3–4

Pressures for working time flexibility

Increasing competition in the private sector and a scarcity of resources and increasing 'marketisation' in the public sector have produced significant pressures to introduce greater and more cost-effective flexibility in working hours, as well as in many cases to an extension of operating times. In manufacturing, changes n production processes such as cellular teamworking and 'just-in-time' production have combined with the need to respond to the fluctuating volume and design stipulations of customers to place an increasing emphasis on the flexibility of labour scheduling . . . . At the same time, increasing capital intensity provides greater pressures to more effectively amortise capital investments in order to reduce marginal costs . . . . As a result, employers have simultaneously had to find ways to vary their labour inputs, through overtime, variable shift or annualised hours working, and to extend operational time by making additional changes to shift working arrangements.

Intensifying competition in private services has also had far-reaching implications for working time arrangements. In food retailing, for example, key developments have been the arrival of the discounters in the early 1990s and the deregulation of opening hours. In such a labour intensive industry, where union organisation tends to be low, managements have focused both on redistributing total labour hours to cover extended opening, through increased part-time working and the creation of new shifts, and on reducing labour costs, through the removal of hours premia and allowances. All of this has been facilitated by developments in new technologies such as EPOS (automatic scanning at the point of sale) and integrated staff scheduling systems, which have enabled companies to match working time more closely to the highly variable but generally predictable patterns of demand . . . . Similar trends can be found in financial services and the privatised utilities (gas, electricity, water and telephones), where increased competition following deregulation, coupled with the introduction of new technology, has been the stimulus to change . . . .

In the public sector, it is budgetary flexibility resulting from tightening controls over public spending, together with the introduction of greater managerialism and market testing, that have been important catalysts for change, particularly in the NHS and local government . . . . Between them, these sectors employ a total workforce of over three million people with labour costs accounting for some 70 per cent of total costs. Working time flexibility was a direct concern of the 1997 national harmonisation deal for local government staff . . . . The agreement allowed decentralisation to local level of arrangements for determining any premium rates for weekend, overtime and shift working. It also introduced the facility to average the newly reduced standard working hours over periods other than a week to meet varying demand for services.

In the NHS, working time flexibility has long been a prime concern due to the need to reconcile permanent opening with variable levels of demand. Also of increasing importance is the need to make working time arrangements more acceptable to the workforce owing to recruitment and retention problems associated with relatively low pay, demanding work and the high proportion of 'unsocial hours' . . . . In addition, the response of local managers to a regime of tight cash limits and highly centralised pay settlements for groups such as nurses has been a major driver of change. In effect, they have had little option but to focus on the variables in labour costs under their control, if they are to live within their budgets, which means the numbers of workers employed and the hours that they work.

The trend towards longer full-time hours has already been mentioned. Neathy and Arrowsmith also draw attention to a trend from fixed towards variable hours, and from permanent to temporary working. Concerns about these types of flexibility are raised by the following extract which also considers other forms of 'flexibility':

[4.80] NACAB, *Flexibility Abused: A CAB Evidence Report On Employment Conditions in the Labour Market* **pp 1, 4–5**

Summary and recommendations
. . . Flexibility can mean that employers can manage their workforce to meet fluctuating demands for labour in the short term, and can adapt to technological and other organisational change in the longer term. Employees may have the opportunity to balance work with other commitments, in circumstances which can otherwise exclude them from the world of work altogether.

But for many, flexibility also means withdrawal from the responsibilities associated with the employment relationship. From this perspective, basic employment standards such as protection from unfair dismissal and decent rates of pay are seen as constraints on flexibility, and so as damaging to the health of the economy.

[The report identifies] two broad categories [of flexible working]. The first general grouping comprises contractual arrangements whereby employers provide more flexible terms of employment: variable hours contracts; temporary work; and part-time work . . .

Chapter 1
In recent times, the virtues of flexibility in the UK's labour market have come to seem incontrovertible. International bodies such as the Organisation for Economic Co-operation and Development and the World Economic Forum have acknowledged the importance of flexibility in their generally favourable assessments of the UK's economic performance. For the previous Conservative administration, labour market flexibility was a key factor in guaranteeing the UK's economic well-being. Employers are increasingly favouring flexible working arrangements, and employees are looking to employers to facilitate greater flexibility, particularly in relation to working time. As the above quotation illustrates, the current Labour Government is also party to this broad consensus.

What is far less straightforward, and open to much debate, is what we actually mean by labour market flexibility. When the various statements on the issue are examined in detail, the one thing which becomes clear is that flexibility means different—even conflicting—things to different people. For some, flexibility is about adaptability and employability, which in turn requires mutual respect for the interests of employers and workers. For others, flexibility is synonymous with deregulation, so the main feature of flexibility is the refusal to accept responsibilities for the workforce, and the absence of employment rights.

There can surely be no dispute about the advantages of an approach where employers and workers acknowledge each other's interests, and work together to promote those interests. Flexible working hours which enable employees to combine child care with continued employment, and also enable employers to meet fluctuating levels of demand for labour, are just one obvious example of such mutually beneficial flexibility. Nor is there any doubt that some employers pursue this kind of flexible working through a genuine commitment to the well-being of their workforce, recognising that investing in the workforce is an important element in improving competitiveness and attaining economic success.

All forms of 'flexibility' mentioned above have repercussions for the balance between work and family life. On the one hand, the deterioration of terms and conditions associated with the contracting-out of 'peripheral' work functions undermines workers' ability to earn reasonable wages, and drives those with children out of work or into reliance on 'in work' benefits. On the other hand, the demand for 'flexible' working hours, 'flexibility' defined according to employers', rather than workers', needs, renders the work/life reconciliation problematic at best, impossible for many.

[4.81] NACAB, *Flexibility Abused* pp 1–2, 26–8, 35–8

The second broad category of flexible working arrangements are those whereby the 'employer' withdraws from the employment relationship altogether. The report considers three options available to employers who wish to pursue this approach. One is to use 'self-employed' workers, which—from CAB clients' perspective—often means the imposition of self-employed status on workers who were previously regarded as employees. As a result, the workers lose many of the rights and benefits enjoyed by the employed workforce, often in circumstances which suggest that they should really be treated as having employee status. The use of agency workers offers the same potential advantages to employers in terms of minimising their obligations, and creates comparable problems in terms of inferior working conditions and uncertain employment status for workers. These problems are compounded by the poor standards of organisation displayed by some agencies.

A third way in which employers can avoid the responsibilities associated with the employer/employee relationship is to contract out or 'outsource' discrete functions, such as cleaning or security. CAB evidence of the 'contract culture', including the consequences of Compulsory Competitive Tendering, shows how this leads to deteriorating terms and conditions for the workers whose jobs are contracted out. Reports from CABx also provide a worrying insight into the wider practices of some contracting companies . . . .

The level of self-employment within the British labour market has increased significantly in recent years. Labour Force Survey statistics show that in Spring 1979 there were 1,769,000 self-employed workers; by Winter 1996/7, the figure had risen to 3,277,000—an increase of about 85%.

. . . there are potential advantages for workers who adopt self-employed status. These include the possibility of greater autonomy in determining the nature and quantity of their work, and a more immediate share in the success of the enterprise in which they are involved. The down side, however, is considerable. By definition, self-employed workers will be excluded from many of the statutory and contractual rights and benefits enjoyed by employees. This covers specific benefits like paid holidays and pension rights, along with the underlying insecurity which comes from the loss of protection against unfair dismissal and other legal provisions.

For the fortunate among the workforce, this will come down to a straightforward trade-off between the security and benefits associated with employee status, and the potential for greater self-determination enjoyed by some of the self-employed. For many, however, the reality is rather different. Employers, keen to reduce their legal obligations, simply give workers the 'choice' between self-employed status and loss of work altogether . . . .

. . . One of the potential consequences of confusion over employment status is that no tax or National Insurance is paid on behalf of the worker concerned. As a result, the worker will lose out on entitlement to contributory benefits (see the previous chapter for a discussion of the importance of National Insurance contributions and contributory benefits). Failure to pay tax and National Insurance contributions is also illegal, which may mean that the employment contract will be 'tainted with illegality', which in turn means that the employee may not qualify for statutory rights such as protection against unfair dismissal and redundancy payments—unless they can convince a tribunal that they were not in any way at fault. There is also the important consideration that employers who fail to pay tax and National Insurance contributions are defrauding the Government of lawful revenue . . . .

In theory, the conditions of employment of many ['contracted-out'] workers should be protected by the Transfer of Undertakings (Protection of Employment) Regulations of 1981—known as the TUPE regulations. TUPE is intended to protect the employment rights of employees when a business is transferred from one employer to another. The principal aspects of this protection are twofold: contracts of employment are transferred from one employer to the next, so that employees should not be dismissed purely as a result of the transfer; and employees who are transferred therefore have the contractual right to keep the same terms and conditions of employment.

In practice, however, CAB clients frequently find that their terms and conditions of employment deteriorate when their work is contracted out, or when the contract is passed from one contractor to another. This is predictable enough, since the contractors will often have won the contract by putting in the lowest bid, and one of the main ways of achieving this will be to reduce labour costs. As a result, employees will frequently have changes in their terms and conditions imposed upon them unilaterally when their work is first contracted out—and may well experience further problems when the initial contract comes up for renewal . . .

These concerns about the wider organisational functioning of the enterprises using contracted labour are compounded by evidence of the other problematic employment practices identified elsewhere in this report—such as enforced (and questionable) self-employment, and the use of zero hours contracts. The combined result can be employees who experience the utmost insecurity of employment, together with falling standards for vulnerable users of the essential public services.

FURTHER READING

D Goss and D Adam-Smith, 'Pragmatism and Compliance: Employer Responses to the Working Time Regulations' (2001) 32.3 *Industrial Relations Journal* p 195

M Jeffrey, 'Not Really Going to Work? Of the Directive on Part-Time Work, "Atypical Work" and Attempts to Regulate it' (1998) 27 *Industrial Law Journal* 193.

J Mair, 'Maternity Leave: Improved and Simplified?' (2000) 63 *Modern Law Review* 877.

A McColgan, 'Family Friendly Frolics: The Maternity and Parental Leave, etc. Regulations 1999' (2000) *Industrial Law Journal* 125;

A McColgan, 'The 'family friendly' Employment Relations Act?', in KD Ewing (ed), *Assessing the Employment Relations Act* (London, Institute of Employment Rights, 2001)

——, 'Missing the Point?: The Part-time Workers Regulations 2000' (2000) *Industrial Law Journal* 260.

F Neathy and J Arrowsmith, *Implementation of the Working Time Regulations*, Employment Relations Research Series Report No 11 (London, Department of Trade and Industry. (2001)

F Neathy, 'Implementation of the Working Time Regulations: follow up study' (London, DTI, 2003)

B Simpson 'A Milestone in the Legal Regulation of Pay: The National Minimum Wage Act 1998', (1999) 28 *Industrial Law Journal* 1

B Simpson, *Building on the National Minimum Wage* (London, IER, 2001).

F Wilkinson and S Deakin, *Labour Standards—Essential to Economic and Social Progress* (London, IER, 1996).

M Wynn, 'Pregnancy Discrimination: Equality, Protection or Reconciliation?' (1999) 62 *Modern Law Review* 435.

5

Dismissal

The potential significance of a termination of the contract of employment differs for the parties. When the employee terminates the contract by resignation, the employer usually needs to find a replacement. This task imposes search and recruitment costs upon the employer. Training costs for the replacement employee may also be incurred. When the employer terminates the contract, however, the employee loses his or her main source of income and may forfeit long-term opportunities to augment income through work experience, seniority and promotion. In addition, in so far as work provides an opportunity to create social relations, bonds of friendship, and to establish a position of status in the community, the loss of a job can inflict psychic damage on the employee. The stakes on termination of employment are therefore usually uneven between the parties: the employer needs to replace labour power, the employee is threatened with social exclusion.

The power to dismiss an employee is nevertheless an important dimension of the employer's ability to direct the workforce towards productive tasks. In order to co-ordinate production and to discourage actions that impede the objectives of the business, an employer needs the power to discipline the workforce. The most powerful sanction in support of this necessary disciplinary power is the ability to dismiss employees in circumstances where their continued employment threatens the economic success of the enterprise. Although the threat of dismissal may not be carried out very often, its presence in the background provides employers with the necessary power to issue instructions that will normally be obeyed. The legal question that arises is not whether the employer should have the power to dismiss employees, but whether this power should be exercised according to legally mandated constraints on the procedures and substantive grounds for dismissal. These legal constraints on the termination of employment by an employer may be constructed either by the terms of the contract itself or by mandatory legal rules, such as statutory protection against unfair dismissal. The task for any legally mandated standards is to strike a balance between the interest of the employer in preserving the credibility of the sanction of dismissal and the interest of the employee in receiving protection against misuse of this power.

The interests of employers and employees with respect to the termination of contracts of employment are not completely opposed. Employees have a long-term interest in the efficient management of the business, so that a disciplinary power exercised in order to exclude incompetent, absent or disruptive employees serves the interests of employees as well as the owners of the business. Equally, employers share an interest with employees that the power to dismiss employees should be exercised for its proper purposes and not abused, for the dismissal of competent and reliable workers imposes costs on the business. These costs include unnecessary recruitment and training expenses, but more significantly the misuse of disciplinary power may undermine the confidence of employees that the employer will treat them with respect, which in turn may lead to a withdrawal of co-operation. An employer has an interest in earning a reputation for fair treatment, in order to encourage commitment and co-operation on the part of employees.

Nevertheless, the exercise of disciplinary power does provoke a conflict of interest. Because employees have more at stake in relation to dismissals, they would prefer the employer to adopt more elaborate and costly procedures that are designed to investigate the facts carefully and to weigh the appropriate disciplinary sanction. Employees also prefer less permissive and discretionary justifications or substantive standards for dismissal than those normally selected by an employer, so that they can be clear in advance about the content of the rules for which disciplinary sanctions will be imposed. Furthermore, employees may insist upon a stricter requirement of proportionality than the employer, for the employer may wish to enhance the general deterrent effect of disciplinary measures, whereas the employee will be concerned to emphasise the merits of the particular case. In the development and interpretation of the relevant legal standards, therefore, the legal system has to determine where the balance between these conflicting interests should lie.

As well as being an aspect of the disciplinary power of the employer, the power to terminate the contract of employment is an important dimension of the employer's ability to adjust labour supply and costs in the light of changing business conditions. More than a million people lose their jobs involuntarily each year, but about 80 per cent of these dismissals will be for economic rather than disciplinary reasons (DTI estimate based on the Labour Force Surveys in *The Unfair Dismissal and Statement of Reasons for Dismissal Order 1999—regulatory impact statement*, paragraph 41). The reduction of the size of the workforce in response to reduced demand for the product permits employers to preserve or enhance the solvency or profitability of the company. In many instances, therefore, reductions in the size of the workforce will be a necessary measure to protect the economic interests of the remaining employees and the investors in the company. Although the action of termination of employment by the employer remains the same in these instances of economic dismissals as in those concerning disciplinary dismissals, the potential justifications for legal intervention are quite different. In economic dismissals the issues concern, first, the extent to which the law may seek to place brakes on reductions in the workforce by either mandatory procedures or substantive criteria, and, secondly, the extent to which the employer may be required to pay financial compensation to the employees or the social security system, in order to reduce the costs of the dismissals to the employees or the taxpayer. We consider the legal regulation of economic dismissals in Chapter 10, which addresses more broadly the topic of restructuring the business.

This chapter examines the legal regulation of disciplinary dismissals. The need for legal regulation of the employer's power of dismissal has been a cornerstone of international conventions regarding employment, as in Article 30 of the Charter of

Fundamental Rights of the European Union 2000 (above [1.2]) and the following convention (signed, but not ratified, by the UK).

[5.1] ILO Convention No. 158 concerning Termination of Employment at the Initiative of the Employer (1985)

Article 4
The employment of a worker shall not be terminated unless there is a valid reason for such termination connected with the capacity or conduct of the worker or based on the operational requirements of the undertakings, establishment or service.

Article 7
The employment of a worker shall not be terminated for reasons related to the worker's conduct or performance before he is provided an opportunity to defend himself against the allegations made, unless the employer cannot reasonably be expected to provide this opportunity.

Article 8
1. A worker who considers that his employment has been unjustifiably terminated shall be entitled to appeal against that termination to an impartial body, such as a court, labour tribunal, arbitration committee or arbitrator.

In the UK, there are two systems of legal regulation to be considered: the common law rules governing the termination of employment and the statutory right to claim unfair dismissal, which was introduced in 1971. The statutory rules do not pre-empt the common law, so that in principle a dismissed employee may advance both claims before an employment tribunal. The employee's choice between the regimes depends upon detailed consideration of the qualifying conditions for the claim, the divergent standards, and the available remedies. Although the statutory regime is more advantageous for the majority of workers, better paid employees who benefit from elaborate contractual arrangements have often discovered that the common law promises a superior remedy.

Many interesting questions of principle and technique emerge in the consideration of disciplinary dismissals.

- Does the law strike a fair balance between the interests of employers and employees in determining the justice of disciplinary dismissals? This question can be divided into an examination of the fairness of the required procedure and the adequacy of the substantive grounds that may justify a disciplinary dismissal.
- To what extent should the parties be permitted to set their own standards of justice for disciplinary dismissals through their contractual arrangements?
- How can legal regulation establish workable standards and yet prove sensitive to the variety of contexts in which disciplinary dismissals occur?
- How can legal regulation be effective in ensuring compliance with its standards?

5.1 The common law of wrongful dismissal

During the nineteenth century, English courts began to apply the ordinary private law of contract to the employment relation. This scheme of legal regulation emphasised the importance of the terms of the contract in setting the standards governing disciplinary dismissals. In principle, the parties were free to regulate the conditions under which dismissal could take place, and breach of those conditions would result in an award of damages for breach of contract. In practice, of course, for most workers these terms afforded no protection at all against the employer's misuse of disciplinary power. A casual oral agreement at the time of hiring would be supplemented by implied terms based upon the customs of the workshop and the default rules provided by the common law. Under these terms, the employer enjoyed a general power to terminate the contract for disciplinary reasons, because any kind of misconduct or incompetence was likely to amount to a breach of the implied terms.

Nevertheless, the common law could enforce respect for any terms agreed explicitly or implicitly between the parties that placed limits upon the employer's power to dismiss a worker. This potential of the common law became important in the second half of the twentieth century when, as a result of the increasing effectiveness of collective bargaining to determine the terms of contracts of employment, the extensive self-regulation of employment issues by public authorities, and the increasing formalisation of the contract of employment in the private sector, the terms of the contract of employment began to contain both procedural and substantive restrictions on the power of the employer to terminate the contract for disciplinary reasons. Under the ordinary law of contract, the courts were bound to enforce these restrictions, thereby protecting employees against disciplinary dismissals in breach of the terms of the contract.

The vital question then became what remedies might be afforded to employees in order to protect their contractual rights. For most breaches of contract, the ordinary remedy offered by the courts is an award of damages. One crucial question became how such compensation should be calculated? If employees might obtain substantial compensation, the benefits afforded by the terms of the contract would become serious constraints upon the employer's disciplinary power. If the compensation remained low, however, the standards set by the contract of employment would become ineffective, for employers might decide that it would be more efficient to breach the terms. In some instances, however, courts may be prepared to offer injunctive relief against breach of contract. A second crucial question became whether employees might be able to obtain an order forbidding the employer from breaching the terms of the contract with the ultimate threat of contempt of court. Such a remedy would greatly enhance the benefits promised by the terms of the contract, for in effect it would prevent employers from breaching the contract whenever it seemed efficient to do so.

When the statutory right to claim unfair dismissal was introduced in 1971, it was widely believed that the common law offered scant protection for employees against unjust disciplinary action. It was assumed, first, that the terms of employment would continue to be set primarily by the employer, so that they would grant few protective rights to employees. A second assumption was that the measure of compensatory damages afforded by the common law was too meagre to provide any substantial deterrent to an employer's breach of contract. Thirdly, it was believed that injunctive relief was unavailable to enforce the terms of contracts of employment. With hindsight, we have learned that none of these assumptions was wholly accurate. Although the common law does not guarantee protection to workers against unfair disciplinary dismissals, under certain conditions it can offer employees safeguards superior to the statutory regime. This fresh understanding of the protection afforded by the common law will be examined by a consideration of the measure of compensation and the conditions for the availability of injunctive relief.

5.1.1 Compensation for wrongful dismissal

To claim damages under the ordinary law of contract, a dismissed employee must prove that the employer has breached a term of the contract causing loss. There is no general claim for damages against an employer simply for terminating the contract. Where the contract provides expressly or by implication that the employer can terminate it for any reason without following any particular procedural steps, so that the contract is 'terminable at will', dismissal may not involve breach of any term of the contract, and therefore no liability will arise. But such contracts are rare in the United Kingdom. In practice, contracts of employment usually contain terms that specify procedures to be followed prior to dismissal, and sometimes include substantive criteria that must be satisfied prior to lawful termination of the contract. Our examination of the measure of compensation for breach of the terms of the contract by termination of employment, which is known as a claim for wrongful dismissal, is divided into a consideration of the principal types of terms that are likely to broken.

- Implied procedural terms (the duty to give reasonable notice);
- Express procedural terms;
- Express substantive conditions for termination;
- Fringe benefits and collateral undertakings;
- Implied substantive terms limiting the power of dismissal.

5.1.1.1 Implied procedural terms

5.1.1.1.1 Presumption of reasonable notice. Contracts of employment may have a fixed or indefinite duration. Under contracts for an indefinite duration, either the express terms of the contract fix a period of notice prior to termination, or the common law implies a term of reasonable notice. It is common these days for contracts to determine explicitly the required period of notice. In the absence of an express term, however, since the late nineteenth century the courts have implied a term requiring both parties to give reasonable notice. This rule of reasonable notice prior to termination probably served the joint interest of employer and employee, for the employer wanted to be able to adjust labour costs more rapidly than in the old agricultural practice of yearly hirings, and employees wanted to be able to leave lawfully in order to avoid criminal penalties under the Master and Servant Act 1824 (J Feinman, 'The Development of the Employment at Will Rule' (1976) 20 *American Journal of Legal History* 118). The modern legal presumption is that contracts of indefinite duration may be terminated by either party on giving reasonable notice.

This implied term permits notice of termination for any substantive reason, but requires an employer to give reasonable notice of termination or to pay damages for breach of that obligation. The determination of the period of reasonable notice depends upon all the circumstances of the case. If any clear custom can be established, that custom determines the period of notice. Otherwise two factors predominate in the common law's determination of a period of reasonable notice. The period between payment of wages under the contract provides a starting point (*Nokes v Doncaster Collieries Ltd* [1940] AC 1014 (HL)), but, secondly, this period is likely to be extended for high status employees such as managers and professionals. The effect of the presumption of a requirement of notice is to create a thin measure of job security at common law. Although an employer remains free to dismiss employees for any substantive reason, the dismissal can occur lawfully only after an employer follows the procedure of giving warning or notice.

5.1.1.1.2 Statutory minimum notice.   The idea that notice periods provide a degree of security of employment was used by the Contracts of Employment Act 1963 to link seniority rights to statutory minimum periods of notice for the sake of enhancing job security. The current form of the legislation provides employees with a minimum period of notice based upon periods of service.

[5.2] Employment Rights Act 1996 (ERA), section 86

86 (1) The notice required to be given by an employer to terminate the contract of employment of a person who has been continuously employed for one month or more—
(a) is not less than one week's notice if his period of continuous employment is less than two years,
(b) is not less than one week's notice for each year of continuous employment if his period of continuous employment is two years or more but less than twelve years, and
(c) is not less than twelve weeks' notice if his period of continuous employment is twelve years or more.

(2) The notice required to be given by an employee who has been continuously employed for one month or more to terminate his contract of employment is not less than one week.

(3) Any provision for shorter notice in any contract of employment with a person who has been continuously employed for one month or more has effect subject to subsections (1) and (2); but this section does not prevent either party from waiving his right to notice on any occasion or from accepting a payment in lieu of notice.

(4) Any contract of employment of a person who has been continuously employed for three months or more which is a contract for a term certain of one month or less shall have effect as if it were for an indefinite period; and, accordingly, subsections (1) and (2) apply to the contract.

The effect of this legislation was to increase substantially the minimum notice period for low status employees paid on a weekly basis who had several years of continuous service for a particular employer, for whom otherwise the common law was likely to imply a period of reasonable notice of one week. The statute does not prevent an employer from terminating a contract with immediate effect, but it does give the employee a right to compensation at common law for breach of the notice provision. The clumsy phasing in subsection (3) is intended to provide that the seniority entitlement to a minimum period cannot be excluded in the express terms of the contract. On termination of the contract of employment by the employer, however, the employee may agree to relinquish the statutory right to notice with or without compensation. An employee rarely has any incentive either to waive the right to notice or to relinquish compensation for breach of that right, so courts should be suspicious of assertions of such agreements. An alleged waiver was upheld in *Baldwin v British Coal Corporation* [1995] IRLR 139 (HC), however, because by agreeing to waive the right to receive £3,000 for a notice entitlement of 12 weeks, the employee qualified for a government payment of £5,000 conferred by a special statutory scheme to compensate miners for redundancies.

These statutory rights to a minimum period of notice on the basis of continuous employment of one month or more apply equally to contracts for the performance of a particular task or for a fixed term. At common law, it was difficult to assert that the contract could be terminated on reasonable notice under an implied term when the contract expressly specified a fixed duration such as three months or a year. But it is possible to have both a fixed term contract and express provision for earlier notice. ERA 1996, section 86(4) prevents exclusion of the statutory entitlement to notice by the technique of a succession of one month (or shorter) fixed term contracts. For example, in *Brown v Chief Adjudication Officer* [1997] ICR 266 (CA), a care worker was employed on a daily basis every week for about nine months. It was held that she was entitled to the statutory right to a week's notice, even though at common law her contract terminated at the end of each day as a fixed term contract. These statutory provisions for a right to a minimum period of notice apparently do not apply when the contract of employment is frustrated (below 5.2.3).

5.1.1.1.3 Dismissal without notice.   An employer may decide to breach these contractual and statutory notice provisions by summarily dismissing the employee, that is, dismissing the employee peremptorily without warning, or on shorter notice than required under the statute or by the contractual terms, or by failing to pay the employee all or part of the wages due during the notice period. In response to any of these actions, the employee may bring a claim for breach of contract. In addition, a shortfall in payment of wages will be recoverable as an unauthorised deduction under ERA 1996, section 13 (above **[2.8]**. The breach of contract provides the basis for a claim for damages, but the available damages are usually fairly meagre.

The quantification of damages for breach of the notice provision commences with the upper limit of the wages and other types of remuneration that might be claimed under the contract during the required notice period. It is assumed that the employer will take advantage of any contractual provision that permits an abatement of wages by, for example, declining to award a discretionary bonus. The statute provides detailed rules on the calculation of the wages due during the notice period, though these rules do not apply if the notice due under the contract exceeds by one week or more the statutory minimum: ERA 1996 section 87(4). The general rule for the calculation of wages due during the statutory notice period is that the employee is entitled to wages for 'normal working hours' provided the employee is ready and willing to work, subject to special provisions for sickness, pregnancy and holidays: ERA 1996, section 88 (for an application of these provisions, see *Notcutt v Universal Equipment Co (London) Ltd* [1986] ICR 414 (CA), **[5.28]** below). In the absence of 'normal working hours', as in the case of piecework or casual workers, a week's pay is calculated by reference to the average hours and average hourly pay over a 12-week period: ERA 1996, sections 89, 221–24, 226, 234. This upper limit is then subject to numerous reductions designed to ensure that the employee is no better off than if he had worked out the notice period. The gross wages are reduced by the amount of normal deductions such as tax: *British Transport Commission v Gourley* [1956] AC 185 (HL). The compensation is also reduced by any social security benefits received by the employee as a result of being made unemployed. The employee also falls under the normal duty to mitigate loss, so that compensation will be reduced if the court believes that by taking reasonable steps the employee could have obtained fresh employment to reduce his losses resulting from dismissal. Although these reductions of compensation apply to the normal common law method for awarding the net loss as compensatory damages for breach of contract, the effect can be in many instances to remove much of the support for job security intended by the provisions for statutory minimum periods of notice. Because the claim for wages during a notice period that has not been worked is not regarded as an action for debt but merely one for damages, if an employee obtains another job immediately (or should reasonably have done so), the employer may not have to pay any compensation for breach of the statutory right to a minimum period of notice.

Damages for wrongful dismissal in breach of the implied notice provision will therefore not usually afford an employee a substantial measure of compensation. The provisions for statutory minimum periods of notice have also been criticized as failing to conform to the European Social Charter Article 4 by not providing sufficient notice of termination of employment for workers with less than three years' service (Council of Europe, Committee of Experts, Conclusions XIV-2, vol 2 (1998), p. 774). It is only when the required notice period of a highly paid employee extends over many months and the employee cannot reasonably mitigate his or her loss that the measure of compensation may function to deter dismissal and protect job security.

5.1.1.1.4 Justified summary dismissal.   Employers may defend themselves against a claim for damages for wrongful dismissal in breach of any notice requirement by arguing that the summary dismissal was justified in the circumstances. If the defence succeeds, the employee is not entitled to any compensation for breach of the notice provision. To establish the defence of justification, the employer must prove a serious breach of contract by the employee.

There are two possible legal bases for this defence. On one view, the defence relies upon an implied exclusion clause in every notice provision which states that the employee forfeits the right to notice by breaching any fundamental term of the contract. On another view, the defence operates as part of the rules governing repudiatory breach of contract: by committing a serious breach of contract the employee in effect indicates a repudiation of the contract, and the employer's action

Payment in lieu of notice

It is common for employers to pay 'wages in lieu of notice' on making a summary dismissal or a dismissal on short notice. The legal implications of such payments can turn on subtle distinctions, which nevertheless may have important practical consequences. The underlying issue is whether the payment of wages somehow turns the summary dismissal in breach of the notice provision into a lawful termination with notice. If the employer has not breached the contract, some terms such as restraint of competition clauses may still be valid. In addition, if the employer has not paid the wages in full, the missing amount can be claimed as a deduction from 'wages' under ERA 1996 s.13 (above [2.6]). The question of whether a summary dismissal combined with full payment of wages for the notice period is a breach of contract may also affect the calculation of the effective date of termination for the purpose of bringing a statutory claim for unfair dismissal under ERA 1996 s.97 (below, [5.42]). That underlying issue is connected to the question whether the payment made by the employer is really for the wages due, or in fact for the liability in damages arising from the employer's breach of contract. If the payment is analysed as one of damages for breach of the notice provision, the legal consequence is that the employee is under a duty to mitigate loss by seeking alternative employment, so that the employer should in principle be entitled to recover any excess of the payment made above the actual losses of the dismissed employee. In addition, the employee cannot recover any shortfall in the payment of damages under ERA 1996 s.13, which only applies to 'wages', but must bring a claim for wrongful dismissal. To explore these possible legal implications and ramifications, each case must be considered carefully, both with respect to the terms of the contract and to the intentions of the parties when the payment is accepted. Four typical situations may be distinguished.

(1) A proposed payment by the employer acknowledges its breach of contract and purports to settle a potential claim for damages. If the employer fails to pay the sum of money agreed by way of settlement, the sum should not be regarded as either wages or damages, but should be recoverable as a debt under the settlement.

(2) Another possibility is that the contract is terminated by agreement, thereby avoiding breach of contract, with a supplementary agreement to pay a sum of money calculated by reference to wages payable during the statutory or contractual notice period. Again, this supplementary agreement should be legally enforceable as an agreed sum without a duty to mitigate, and should not be regarded as 'wages'.

(3) A third possibility is that the employer is purporting to exercise a power conferred by the contract to terminate a contract summarily, the consideration for which in the original contract of employment might be a provision for a 'golden parachute' of a fixed sum of money, perhaps equivalent to a contractual period of notice. Again this payment is not wages, and there is no duty to mitigate loss: *Abrahams v Performing Rights Society* [1995] IRLR 486 CA.

(4) A fourth possible analysis is that the employer terminates the contract unilaterally by wrongful dismissal, and gives the employee a sum of money in anticipation of a claim for damages which can be set-off against any eventual claim. This sum of money does not represent wages, and the employee is under a duty to mitigate loss: *Cerberus Software Ltd v Rowley* [2001] IRLR 160 CA.

Lord Browne-Wilkinson suggested in *Delaney v Staples* [1992] ICR 483 HL, in the context of a dispute about the meaning of 'wages' under ERA 1996 s.13, that category (4) was the most common case, and that therefore section 13 would not be applicable. But it seems equally possible that most cases of payment in lieu represent an agreed termination under category (2) above, the consideration for which is the promise of a lump sum payment, which may not be taxable, and which leaves the employee unencumbered by the duty to mitigate loss in seeking alternative employment. In the first three cases, the agreed sum need not be fixed by reference to wages and the notice period. Under ERA 1996 s.86(3) the employer and employee may enter an agreement to terminate the contract without notice, and for the agreement to fix an agreed level of compensation, which may be greater or lesser than the potential liability for damages for breach of the notice provision contained in the contract. In *Gothard v Mirror Group Newspapers Ltd* [1988] ICR 729 CA, for instance, the Court of Appeal interpreted a settlement involving early retirement which included 'a payment in lieu . . . for any unworked notice' as promising gross pay rather than net pay after tax.

of dismissal is merely an acceptance of that repudiation. The former view probably explains the origins of the defence, for the courts applied this limitation to their imposition of the notice requirement in the nineteenth century. In this model of the employment relation, the notice provision was conditional on the employee's conformity to fundamental implied terms of the contract, such as the requirements of obedience, loyalty and the preservation of trust and confidence. But in modern cases, the question of justification is usually discussed in the language of repudiatory breach of contract. The court seeks evidence of a breach of contract by the employee that exhibits an intention no longer to be bound by the contract. The following case illustrates the difference between these two approaches to the issue of justification of summary dismissal.

[5.3] *Laws v London Chronicle (Indicator Newspapers) Ltd* [1959] 1 WLR 698 (CA)

The employee disobeyed an order not to leave the room and was dismissed without notice. The plaintiff had left the room because a fierce argument had developed between her immediate superior and the managing director of the company, and in so doing had followed the instruction of her immediate superior and had ignored the order of the managing director. The action of disobedience to a lawful instruction given by the managing director was certainly a breach of one of the fundamental implied terms of the contract of employment. Yet it was also plain on the facts that the employee had no intention of repudiating the contract of employment, that is indicating an intention no longer to be bound by the contract. The Court of Appeal held that summary dismissal was not justified, relying on the analysis of repudiatory breach rather than the implied condition attached to the requirement of notice.

Lord Evershed MR:
Since a contract of service is but an example of contracts in general, so that the general law of contract will be applicable, it follows that the question must be—if summary dismissal is claimed to be justifiable—whether the conduct complained of is such as to show the servant to have disregarded the essential conditions of the contract of service. It is, no doubt, therefore, generally true that wilful disobedience of an order will justify summary dismissal, since wilful disobedience of a lawful and reasonable order shows a disregard—a complete disregard—of a condition essential to the contract of service, namely, the condition that the servant must obey the proper orders of the master, and that unless he does so the relationship is, so to speak, struck at fundamentally . . .

One act of disobedience or misconduct can justify dismissal only if it is of a nature which goes to show (in effect) that the servant is repudiating the contract, or one of its essential conditions; and for that reason, therefore, I think that you find in the passages I have read that the disobedience must at least have the quality that it is 'wilful': it does (in other words) connote a deliberate flouting of the essential contractual conditions . . .

Thus an employee's breach of a fundamental term of the contract does not warrant summary dismissal unless in the circumstances of the case the breach can be construed as conduct that is calculated to destroy the employment relation. An employee's absence from work or failure to comply with an instruction therefore does not justify termination without notice unless these breaches of contract evidence a repudiation of the contractual relation in its entirety. The difficult question becomes what interpretation to place upon a serious breach of contract. The dominant approach asks whether in all the circumstances of the case the breach of contract reasonably destroyed the employer's trust and confidence in the employee. Depending on the gravity of the employee's misconduct, an isolated breach may therefore constitute repudiatory conduct. For example a repudiation was found to justify summary dismissal in *Denco Ltd v Joinson* [1991] IRLR 63, where an unauthorised employee used a password in order to obtain computer access to information to which he was not entitled. The following case illustrates how the assessment of whether there was a repudiatory breach by the employee depends upon minute inspection of the circumstances in order to assess whether the employer reasonably believed that the misconduct had destroyed mutual trust and confidence.

[5.4] *Wilson v Racher* **[1974] ICR 428 (CA)**

The plaintiff was summarily dismissed from his position as head gardener after the defendant employer had made numerous complaints which resulted in an argument and the use of obscene language. The defendant appealed against the first instance judge's finding of wrongful dismissal.

Edmund Davies LJ (with whom Cairns and James LJJ agreed):
There is no rule of thumb to determine what misconduct on the part of the servant justifies summary termination of his contract. For the purpose of the present case, the test is whether the plaintiff's conduct was insulting and insubordinate to such a degree as to be incompatible with the continuance of the relation of master and servant: *per* Hill J. in *Edwards v Levy* (1860) 2 F. & F. 94, 95. The application of such a test will, of course, lead to varying results according to the nature of the employment and all the circumstances of the case. Reported decisions provide useful, but only general guides, each case turning upon its own facts. Many of the decisions which are customarily cited in these cases date from the last century and may be wholly out of accord with current social conditions. What would today be regarded as almost an attitude of Czar-serf, which is to be found in some of the older cases where a dismissed employee failed to recover damages, would, I venture to think, be decided differently today. We have by now come to realise that a contract of service imposes upon the parties a duty of mutual respect . . . .

It was after luncheon that the defendant and his wife and three young children were in the garden when the plaintiff passed and greeted them. The defendant asked where he was going, and the plaintiff replied that he was going to the garden shed to get his boots. Thereafter the defendant showered the plaintiff with questions. He shouted at him, and he was very aggressive. He accused the plaintiff of leaving this work prematurely on the Friday afternoon. The plaintiff explained that he had stopped cutting the hedge only because it would have been dangerous to continue, whereupon the defendant said, 'I am not bothered about you, Wilson, that's your lookout'. Though there was some reference to the ladder, the defendant did not make clear what his complaint was. But when the defendant accused the plaintiff of shirking his work on the Friday afternoon, there is no doubt that the plaintiff used most regrettable language, and it is part of my unpleasant duty to repeat it so as to make clear what happened. The plaintiff said: 'If you remember it was pissing with rain on Friday. Do you expect me to get fucking wet?' The judge, who found that Mrs Racher and the children did not hear those words, said:

> 'The plaintiff had a clear conscience, and he did reply somewhat robustly when he expressed the state of the weather. I think he felt under a certain amount of grievance at that remark'.

According to the judge, 'The defendant then moved to what he thought was stronger ground', thereby obviously referring to his determination to get rid of the plaintiff. The judge dealt with an allegation about a line of string having been left in the garden by the plaintiff, and commented:

> 'A more trivial complaint it would be difficult to imagine . . . It was an extremely trivial ground of complaint, if indeed justified at all. I think it is clear from this and other evidence that [the defendant] sets very high standards and this seems to me to be an absurdly high standard of tidiness. The defendant's second barrel is very odd and illustrates that the defendant was determined to get the plaintiff on something'.

There was a dispute as to whether the string belonged to the plaintiff or to the defendant, and there was a complaint about leaving other things lying about. The judge accepted that the plaintiff moved away in an attempt to avoid any further altercation. But he was called back, and was then bombarded with questions. The defendant was going at him, and this was, indeed, confirmed to some extent by the evidence of the defendant himself. Finally, the plaintiff told the defendant, 'Get stuffed,' and 'Go and shit yourself' . . . .

In those circumstances, would it be just to say that the plaintiff's use of this extremely bad language on this solitary occasion made impossible the continuance of the master and servant relationship, and showed that the plaintiff was indeed resolved to follow a line of conduct which made the continuation of that relationship impossible? The judge thought the answer to that question was clear, and I cannot say that he was manifestly wrong. On the contrary, it seems to me that the parties could have made up their differences. The plaintiff apologised to Mrs Racher. There are no grounds for thinking that if the defendant had given him a warning that such language would not be tolerated, and further, if he had manifested recognition that he himself had acted provocatively, the damage done might well have been repaired and some degree of harmony restored. Perhaps there was such instinctive antipathy between the two men that the defendant would, nevertheless, have been glad to get rid of the plaintiff when October 23, 1972, arrived.

In my judgment, in the light of the findings of fact the judge arrived at a just decision. That is not to say that language such as that employed by the plaintiff is to be tolerated. On the contrary, it requires very special circumstances to entitle a servant who expresses his feelings in such a grossly improper way to succeed in an action for wrongful dismissal. But there were special circumstances here, and they were of the defendant's own creation. The plaintiff, probably lacking the educational advantages of the defendant, and finding himself in a frustrating situation despite efforts to escape from it, fell into the error of explosively using this language. To say that he ought to be kicked out because on this solitary occasion he fell into such grave error would, in my judgment, be wrong. I am not persuaded that the judge was in error in holding that that was unfair dismissal, that it was wrongful dismissal, and that the plaintiff was entitled to the damages awarded. I would therefore be for dismissing the appeal.

5.1.1.1.5 Other implied procedural terms.   Does the common law recognise, in addition to the implied term to give reasonable notice, any other implied obligations to follow a fair procedure when conducting disciplinary dismissals? We have already noted that there have been moments in public law cases (e.g. *R v BBC, ex parte Lavelle* [1983] ICR 99 (HC)), and sometimes further afield (*Stevenson v United Road Transport Union* [1977] ICR 893 (CA), above **[2.73]**), when the courts have almost suggested that contracts of employment include an implied term that is analogous to the principles of natural justice in public law. But they have always held back from asserting as a general rule the presence of an implied term that grants an employee the right to an impartial and fair disciplinary procedure.

[5.5] *Malloch v Aberdeen Corporation* [1971] 1 WLR 1578 (HL), at 1581

Lord Reid:

At common law a master is not bound to hear his servant before he dismisses him. He can act unreasonably or capriciously if he so chooses but the dismissal is valid. The servant has no remedy unless the dismissal is in breach of contract and then the servant's only remedy is damages for breach of contract.

The continuing validity of this statement of principle was contested in the next case. Although the House of Lords accepted that the common law might have developed a suitable implied term, such as an implied term to exercise the power of dismissal in good faith, it was held that the statutory remedy of unfair dismissal had been created by Parliament for this purpose, so that a parallel and perhaps inconsistent development in the common law was undesirable and unnecessary.

[5.6] *Johnson v Unisys Ltd* [2001] UKHL 13 [2001] ICR 480 (HL)

Mr Johnson had been summarily dismissed from his job in a multinational software service company. He won a claim for unfair dismissal on the ground that the company had not given him a fair opportunity to defend himself and had not complied with its disciplinary procedure. The tribunal awarded £11,691 in compensation, that is, the statutory maximum at that time. Mr Johnson then commenced a claim for £400,000 at common law for breach of contract and in tort. He alleged that as a result of the fact of his dismissal and the manner of his dismissal, he had suffered a mental breakdown, which had prevented him from working again. The House of Lords, Lord Steyn dissenting, struck out this claim. The disciplinary procedure in the employer's handbook was not an express term of the contract, and so could not provide the basis for a claim for damages. Nor was there an implied term that the employer would conduct a fair disciplinary procedure. The invention of such an implied term would circumvent the limits imposed by Parliament on remedies for unfair dismissal. For the same reason, the claim in tort based upon a duty of care was also rejected.

Lord Hoffman:

My Lords, the first question is whether the implied term of trust and confidence upon which Mr Johnson relies, and about which in a general way there is no real dispute, or any of the other implied terms, applies to a dismissal. At common law the contract of employment was regarded by the courts as a contract like any other. The parties were free to negotiate whatever terms they liked and no terms would be implied unless they satisfied the strict test of necessity applied to a commercial contract. Freedom of contract meant that the stronger party, usually the employer, was free to impose his terms upon the weaker. But over the last 30 years or so, the nature of the contract of employment has been transformed. It has been recognised that a person's employment is usually one of the most important things in his or her life. It gives not only a livelihood but an occupation, an identity and a sense of self-esteem. The law has changed to recognise this social reality. Most of the changes have been made by Parliament. The Employment Rights Act 1996 consolidates numerous statutes which have conferred rights upon employees. European law has made a substantial contribution. And the common law has adapted itself to the new attitudes, proceeding sometimes by analogy with statutory rights.

The contribution of the common law to the employment revolution has been by the evolution of implied terms in the contract of employment. The most far reaching is the implied term of trust and confidence. But there have been others . . .

The problem lies in extending or adapting any of these implied terms to dismissal. There are two reasons why dismissal presents special problems. The first is that any terms which the courts imply into a contract must be consistent with the express terms. Implied terms may supplement the express terms of the contract but cannot contradict them. Only Parliament may actually override what the parties have agreed. The second reason is that judges, in developing the law, must have regard to the policies expressed by Parliament in legislation. Employment law requires a balancing of the interests of employers and employees, with proper regard not only to the individual dignity and worth of the employees but also to the general economic interest. Subject to observance of fundamental human rights, the point at which this balance should be struck is a matter for democratic decision. The development of the common law by the judges plays a subsidiary role. Their traditional function is to adapt and modernise the common law. But such developments must be consistent with legislative policy as expressed in statutes. The courts may proceed in harmony with Parliament but there should be no discord.

My Lords, I shall consider first the problem posed by the express terms of the contract. In developing the implied term of trust and confidence and other similar terms applicable to the continuing employment relationship, the courts were advancing across open country. No express provision that BCCI would be entitled to conduct a fraudulent business, or that the employer in *W A Goold (Pearmak) Ltd v McConnell* [1995] IRLR 516 EAT [[2.37] above] would have no grievance procedure, stood in their way. But the employer's right to dismiss the employee is strongly defended by the terms of the contract. In the present case, Mr Johnson's contract provided: 'If you decide to leave UNISYS you are required to give the company four weeks notice; equally, the company may terminate your employment on four weeks notice . . . In the event of gross misconduct, the company may terminate your employment without notice.' . . .

My Lords, in the face of this express provision that Unisys was entitled to terminate Mr Johnson's employment on four weeks notice without any reason, I think it is very difficult to imply a term that the company should not do so except for some good cause and after giving him a reasonable opportunity to demonstrate that no such cause existed.

On the other hand, I do not say that there is nothing which, consistently with such an express term, judicial creativity could do to provide a remedy in a case like this. In *Wallace v United Grain Growers Ltd* (1997) 152 DLR (4th) 1, 44–48, McLachlin J (in a minority judgment) said that the courts could imply an obligation to exercise the power of dismissal in good faith. That did not mean that the employer could not dismiss without cause. The contract entitled him to do so. But in so doing, he should be honest with the employee and refrain from untruthful, unfair or insensitive conduct. He should recognise that an employee losing his or her job was exceptionally vulnerable and behave accordingly. For breach of this implied obligation, McLachlin J would have awarded the employee, who had been dismissed in brutal circumstances, damages for mental distress and loss of reputation and prestige.

My Lords, such an approach would in this country have to circumvent or overcome the obstacle of *Addis v Gramophone Co Ltd* [1909] AC 488 (HL), in which it was decided that an employee cannot recover damages for injured feelings, mental distress or damage to his reputation, arising out of the manner of his dismissal. Speaking for myself, I think that, if this task was one which I felt called upon to perform, I would be able to do so. In M*ahmud v Bank of Credit and Commerce International SA* [1998] AC 20 (HL), 51 Lord Steyn said that the true ratio of *Addis's* case was the damages were recoverable only for loss caused by a breach of contract, not for loss caused by the manner of its breach. As McLachlin J said in the passage I have quoted, the only loss caused by a wrongful dismissal flows from a failure to give proper notice or make payment in lieu. Therefore, if wrongful dismissal is the only cause of action, nothing can be recovered for mental distress or damage to reputation. On the other hand, if such damage is loss flowing from a breach of another implied term of the contract, *Addis's* case does not stand in the way. That is why in *Mahmud's* case itself, damages were recoverable for financial loss flowing from damage to reputation caused by a breach of the implied term of trust and confidence.

In this case, Mr Johnson says likewise that his psychiatric injury is a consequence of a breach of the implied term of trust and confidence, which required Unisys to treat him fairly in the procedures for dismissal. He says that implied term now fills the gap which Lord Shaw of Dunfermline perceived and regretted in *Addis's* case (at pp 504–505) by creating a breach of contract additional to the dismissal itself.

It may be a matter of words, but I rather doubt whether the term of trust and confidence should be pressed so far. In the way it has always been formulated, it is concerned with preserving the continuing relationship which should subsist between employer and employee. So it does not seem altogether appropriate for use in connection with the way that relationship is terminated. If one is looking for an implied term, I think a more elegant solution is McLachlin J's implication of a separate term that the power of dismissal will be exercised fairly and in good faith. But the result would be the same as that for which Mr Johnson contends by invoking the implied term of trust and confidence. As I have said, I think it would be possible to reach such a conclusion without contradicting the express term that the employer is entitled to dismiss without cause.

I must however make it clear that, although in my opinion it would be jurisprudentially possible to imply a term which gave a remedy in this case, I do not think that even if the courts were free of legislative constraint (a point to which I shall return in a moment) it would necessarily be wise to do so. It is not simply an incremental step from the duty of trust and confidence implied in *Mahmud v Bank of Credit and Commerce International SA* [1998] AC 20. The close association between the acts alleged to be in breach of the implied term and the irremovable and lawful fact of dismissal give rise to special problems . . .

Some of the potential problems can be illustrated by the facts of this case, in which Mr Johnson claims some £400,000 damages for the financial consequences of psychiatric damage. This form of damage notoriously gives rise at the best of times to extremely difficult questions of causation. But the difficulties are made greater when the expert witnesses are required to perform the task of distinguishing between the psychiatric consequences of the fact of dismissal (for which no damages are recoverable) and the unfair circumstances in which the dismissal took place, which constituted a breach of the implied term. The agreed statement of facts records that for the purposes of this appeal against a strike-out it is accepted that Mr Johnson's psychiatric illness was caused by 'the circumstances and the fact' of his dismissal. At a trial, however, it would be necessary to decide what was caused by what.

Another difficulty is the open-ended nature of liability. Mr Johnson's case is that Unisys had knowledge of his psychological fragility by reason of facts lodged in the corporate memory in 1985–87 and therefore should have foreseen when he was engaged that a failure to comply with proper disciplinary procedures on dismissal might result in injury which deprived him of the ability ever to work again. On general common law principles it seems to me that if the necessary term is implied and these facts are made out, the claim should succeed. It may be that such liability would be grossly disproportionate to the employer's degree of fault. It may be likely to inhibit the future engagement of psychologically fragile personnel. But the common law decides cases according to principle and cannot impose arbitrary limitations on liability because of the circumstances of the particular case. Only statute can lay down limiting rules based upon policy rather than principle . . .

It follows, my Lords, that if there was no relevant legislation in this area, I would regard the question of whether judges should develop the law by implying a suitable term into the contract of employment as finely balanced. But now I must consider the statutory background against which your Lordships are invited to create such a cause of action . . .

My Lords, this statutory system for dealing with unfair dismissals was set up by Parliament to deal with the recognised deficiencies of the law as it stood at the time of *Malloch v Aberdeen Corporation* ([5.5] above). The remedy adopted by Parliament was not to build upon the common law by creating a statutory implied term that the power of dismissal should be exercised fairly or in good faith, leaving the courts to give a remedy on general principles of contractual damages. Instead, it set up an entirely new system outside the ordinary courts, with tribunals staffed by a majority of lay members, applying new statutory concepts and offering statutory remedies. Many of the new rules, such as the exclusion of certain classes of employees and the limit on the amount of the compensatory award, were not based upon any principle which it would have been open to the courts to apply. They were based upon policy and represented an attempt to balance fairness to employees against the general economic interests of the community. And I should imagine that Parliament also had in mind the practical difficulties I have mentioned about causation and proportionality which would arise if the remedy was unlimited. So Parliament adopted the practical solution of giving the tribunals a very broad jurisdiction to award what they considered just and equitable but subject to a limit on the amount.

In my opinion, all the matters of which Mr Johnson complains in these proceedings were within the jurisdiction of the industrial tribunal. His most substantial complaint is of financial loss flowing from his psychiatric injury which he says was a consequence of the unfair manner of his dismissal. Such loss is a consequence of the dismissal which may form the subject-matter of a compensatory award. The only doubtful question is whether it would have been open to the tribunal to include a sum by way of compensation for his distress, damage to family life and similar matters. As the award, even reduced by 25%, exceeded the statutory maximum and had to be reduced to £11,000, the point would have been academic. But perhaps I may be allowed a comment all the same. I know that in the early days of the National Industrial Relations Court it was laid down that only financial loss could be compensated: see *Norton Tool Co Ltd v Tewson* [1973] ICR 45; *Wellman Alloys Ltd v Russell* [1973] ICR 616. It was said that the word 'loss' can only mean financial loss. But I think that is too narrow a construction. The emphasis is upon the tribunal awarding such compensation as it thinks just and equitable. So I see no reason why in an appropriate case it should not include compensation for distress, humiliation, damage to reputation in the community or to family life.

Part X of the Employment Rights Act 1996 therefore gives a remedy for exactly the conduct of which Mr Johnson complains. But Parliament had restricted that remedy to a maximum of £11,000, whereas Mr Johnson wants to claim a good deal more. The question is whether the courts should develop the common law to give a parallel remedy which is not subject to any such limit.

My Lords, I do not think that it is a proper exercise of the judicial function of the House to take such a step. Judge Ansell, to whose unreserved judgment I would pay respectful tribute, went in my opinion to the heart of the matter when he said:

> 'there is not one hint in the authorities that the . . . tens of thousands of people that appear before the tribunals can have, as it were, a possible second bite in common law and I ask myself, if this is the situation, why on earth do we have this special statutory framework? What is the point of it if it can be circumvented in this way? . . . . it would mean that effectively the statutory limit on compensation for unfair dismissal would disappear.'

I can see no answer to these questions. For the judiciary to construct a general common law remedy for unfair circumstances attending dismissal would be to go contrary to the evident intention of Parliament that there should be such a remedy but that it should be limited in application and extent.

The same reason is in my opinion fatal to the claim based upon a duty of care. It is of course true that a duty of care can exist independently of the contractual relationship. But the grounds upon which I think it would be wrong to impose an implied contractual duty would make it equally wrong to achieve the same result by the imposition of a duty of care.

This decision appears to block any possibility of the common law in the United Kingdom developing further implied terms with respect to the procedure or manner of dismissal. Lord Steyn, dissenting, argued that the statutory remedy for unfair dismissal was plainly inadequate with respect to the amount of compensation provided to employees with substantial salaries where they suffered serious loss of employment prospects due to the manner of their dismissal. In providing a remedy for less serious cases, Parliament should not be attributed with the intention of preventing the development of the common law. Nor, in Lord Steyn's opinion, did the express term of the contract that permitted dismissal by giving four weeks' notice prevent the implication of a term of good faith or fair dealing, for there was no conflict between the express right to terminate the contract and the implied term not to do so in a harsh and humiliating manner. These powerful and persuasive arguments did not, however, win the support of the other members of the Judicial Committee. There may still be a possibility of implied procedural terms, however, in a case where the disciplinary procedure is an express contractual term. A court may decide that the disciplinary procedure should be conducted fairly as a term implied in fact. We now consider the potential remedy for breach of a contractual disciplinary procedure.

5.1.1.2 Express procedural terms

A contract of employment may incorporate a disciplinary or grievance procedure in its terms. This procedure may be created by the employer or by a collective agreement. If the procedure fixes steps that must be taken prior to a dismissal, then breach of this procedure may also create a separate and additional liability in damages for breach of contract.

The measure of damages has been calculated by reference to the net wages payable during the period when the contractual disciplinary procedure would have operated. These damages are in addition to any damages for breach of the notice provision. This basis for assessment does not compensate the employee for the loss of a chance that the dismissal decision would have been reversed by the disciplinary procedure (*Janciuk v Winerite Ltd* [1998] IRLR 63 (EAT)). The decided cases may have favoured the reference to the period of the disciplinary procedure because it is a normal provision of such contractual disciplinary procedures that, pending the outcome of the procedure, the employee should be suspended on full pay. If compensation for the likely period of suspension is the basis for the award of damages, it may not be appropriate to reduce the damages by reference to the duty to mitigate loss, for the employee may reasonably claim that his or her contractual entitlement to suspension pending the outcome of the procedure implicitly removes the duty to seek alternative employment.

[5.7] *Gunton v Richmond-Upon Thames London Borough Council* [1980] ICR 755 (CA)

The plaintiff sought a declaration that the defendant council had failed to follow the contractual disciplinary procedure and claimed damages. Under the terms of the contract, the council had a power to dismiss on one month's notice, but in addition there were provisions for a disciplinary procedure. This procedure was applicable to the plaintiff's dismissal for misconduct, but had not been followed precisely. In fact, he had been dismissed without notice and given one month's wages in lieu. The Court of Appeal upheld the plaintiff's claim for damages for breach of the disciplinary procedure.

Buckley LJ:
In the present case the plaintiff has accepted the repudiation. He did so at the trial, if not earlier.

Where a servant is wrongfully dismissed, he is entitled, subject to mitigation, to damages equivalent to the wages he would have earned under the contract from the date of dismissal to the end of the contract. The date when the contract would have come to an end, however, must be ascertained on the assumption that the employer would have exercised any power he may have had to bring the contract to an end in the way most beneficial to himself; that is to say, that would have determined the contract at the earliest date at which he could properly do so; see *McGregor on Damages*, 13th ed. (1972), paras 884, 886 and 888.

If a master, who is entitled to dismiss a servant on not less than three months' notice, wrongfully purports to dismiss the servant summarily, the dismissal, being wrongful, is a nullity and the servant can recover as damages for breach of contract three months' remuneration and no more, subject to mitigation; that is to say, remuneration for the three months following the summary dismissal. If the master wrongfully purports to dismiss the servant on a month's notice and continues to employ him and pay him during that month, no breach occurs until the servant is excluded from his employment at the end of the month, in which case he would be entitled, subject to mitigation, to damages equivalent to three months' remuneration from the date of exclusion. If the master were to pay the servant one month's remuneration in lieu of notice and were to exclude him from his employment forthwith, there would be an immediate breach of the contract by the master;

the servant would be entitled to three months' remuneration by way of damages, but would have to give credit for the one month's remuneration paid in lieu of notice.

Suppose, however, that the master were to dismiss the servant summarily or on a month's notice, and the facts were such as to justify the view that the servant did not accept the master's repudiation of the contract until the end of 10 weeks from the servant's exclusion from his employment. In such a case, if I am right in supposing acceptance of a repudiation to be requisite in master and servant cases, the master would be guilty of a breach of contract continuing *de die in diem* for refusing to offer the servant employment from the date of exclusion down to the date of acceptance, and thereafter for damages on the basis of a wrongful repudiation of the contract. Could the servant properly claim damages under the second head in relation to a period of three months from the date of acceptance as well as damages under the first head in relation to the 10-week period? In my judgment, he clearly could not. This cause of action would have arisen when he was wrongfully excluded from his employment. The subsequent acceptance of the repudiation would not create a new cause of action, although it might affect the remedy available for that cause of action. The question must, I think, be for how long the servant could have insisted at the date of the commencement of his cause of action upon being continued by the master in his employment.

In the present case, in my view, the council could, on January 13, 1976, have determined the plaintiff's contract of service on February 14, 1976, without assigning any reason, or for any given reason other than a disciplinary reason. They did not, however, do so. It is common ground that the letter of January 13, 1976, purported to relate the plaintiff's dismissal to disciplinary matters. Mr Mitchell, as I understood his argument, submitted that that circumstance was not significant; the plaintiff received one month's notice, which was all that he was entitled to insist upon. As I have already indicated, I feel unable to accept that view because, in my opinion, the effect of the incorporation in the contract of the disciplinary regulations was to entitle the plaintiff not to be dismissed on disciplinary grounds until the disciplinary procedures prescribed by the regulations had been carried out. Some of the preliminary stages of those procedures never were carried out. Accordingly, in my judgment, the plaintiff was entitled at January 14, 1976, when he was excluded from his employment, to insist upon a right not to be dismissed on disciplinary grounds until the disciplinary procedures were re-commenced and carried out in due order but with reasonable expedition. Consequently, in my view, the period by reference to which the amount of damages recovered by the plaintiff in this case should be assessed is a reasonable period from January 14, 1976, for carrying out those procedures, plus one month, the plaintiff giving credit for one month's salary which he received in respect of the month ended February 14, 1976, and for anything earned in other employment during the period.

The precise basis for compensation for breach of an express procedural term remains unclear from this decision. One particular difficulty with this case is that apparently the employer had the option of dismissing on one month's notice without going through the procedure at all. On the normal principles governing the award of damages for wrongful dismissal, it is usually assumed that the employer will take advantage of any contractual provision that permits early termination of the contract in order to minimise the liability to pay damages. Despite the uncertain basis for the measure of damages, the *Gunton* case has been followed in subsequent cases by awards of compensation for the likely period of time that the disciplinary procedure would have taken (in addition to the notice period): *Boyo v London Borough of Lambeth* [1995] IRLR 50 (CA) (below **[5.17]**). Additional compensation for breach of an express contractual procedure may, however, only be available where (a) the terms of the procedure apply to the dismissal (or for some other reason the employer is estopped from denying that they apply), and (b) where under the procedure the employee is entitled to receive remuneration until the outcome has been determined. It might also be possible to argue that an employer's decision not to use an express disciplinary procedure, or to avoid the procedure by following another option provided for by the contract, may constitute a breach of the implied term of mutual trust and confidence: M Forde, 'Commentary: Re-Thinking the Notice Rule' (1998) 27 *Industrial Law Journal* 220, 230.

5.1.1.3 Express substantive conditions for termination

The express terms of the contract may limit the power of the employer to terminate the contract by reference to substantive conditions. The contract may specify that the contract can be terminated only for 'good cause', 'gross misconduct' or 'redundancy'. Such a term differs from the procedural terms considered above, because it appears to displace the ordinary implied term of notice entirely. Instead of the employer enjoying the implied power to terminate the contract on notice for any reason, the employer is entitled under the express terms of the contract only to terminate the contract (with or without notice) for specific reasons. Under the ordinary principles of the law of contract, these express terms should trump the implied notice provision. Nevertheless, it may be anticipated that the courts might be reluctant to infer an intention on the part of the employer to relinquish entirely a right to dismiss for misconduct that might justify summary dismissal or to lose the right to reduce the workforce for business reasons. These considerations did not apply, however, in the leading House of Lords decision which confirmed that express terms might confer a kind of tenure upon employees by excluding ordinary implied terms regarding dismissal.

[5.8] *McClelland v Northern Ireland General Health Services* [1957] 1 WLR 594 (HL)

> After the introduction of the National Health Service, Mrs McClelland was employed in a 'permanent' and 'pensionable' position as a senior clerk. The terms of employment provided in condition 12 that: 'The board may dismiss any officer for gross misconduct and may dismiss any officer who is proved to their satisfaction to be inefficient and unfit to merit continued employment.' After five years of satisfactory employment, the employer dismissed her with six months' notice for breach of a rule of the employers (inserted subsequent to the formation of the contract of employment) that: 'Female officers will on marriage be required to tender their resignations to the board'. By a majority of 3:2, the House of Lords upheld the employee's appeal. The construction placed by the majority on the terms and conditions was that the express powers to dismiss contained in condition 12 were exhaustive and excluded any implied power to dismiss on giving reasonable notice. The minority view was that the terms were insufficiently explicit to exclude the normal presumption that every contract of employment is terminable on reasonable notice.

The minority view probably expresses the normal approach to the construction of express substantive conditions. A court will require considerable persuasion that ordinary implied terms of notice have been excluded, either by express terms or a special statutory scheme, as in *Vine v National Dock Labour Board* [1956] AC 488 (HL). Most of the legal difficulties in these instances of substantive limits on dismissal concern the interpretation of the express terms of the contract of employment. Since contracts of employment are typically long-term, they may be modified frequently. Collective agreements may also become incorporated and serve to modify the written terms. As a consequence of this accretion of terms, the provisions of the contract may become inconsistent on their face. The task of the court is to interpret all the written terms as they would be understood in the context of the whole contract.

[5.9] *Taylor v Secretary of State for Scotland* [2000] ICR 595 (HL)

> A prison officer claimed breach of contract when the employer dismissed him in pursuance of a collective agreement with the union for making redundancies. Under the contract of employment, the employee could be retired on three months' notice once he was over the age of 55. But the contract also contained a provision that 'no one in the service should be discriminated against on the grounds of gender, race, religion, sexual preference, disability or age'. The collective agreement had accepted compulsory retirement of all officers aged over 55 in order to avoid compulsory redundancies. The House of Lords rejected the employee's claim for breach of the term against age discrimination, arguing that the term was subject to the other term that permitted the employer to compel retirement on three month's notice. Age discrimination in breach of contract would have been committed by the employer only if the employer had distinguished between employees over the age of 55 on the grounds of their age.

In these cases of substantive protection against dismissal, which in some instances may be described as giving the employee 'tenure', the question arises how to calculate the measure of compensation for dismissal in breach of the substantive conditions.

[5.10] K D Ewing, 'Job Security and the Contract of Employment' (1989) 18 *Industrial Law Journal* 217

> The proper level of damages should be wages earned from the date of unlawful dismissal to the date when the contract could lawfully have been terminated. Where there is a contractual term of the kind under discussion, this could mean that damages would be assessed from the date of termination to the date of retirement taking into account such eventualities as premature death of the employee, winding up of the company, or termination for cause.

This approach to quantification has been used in Australia, though the damages were much less than the wages due until retirement date either owing to the probability of termination for good cause under the permitted conditions of the contract (*Gregory v Philip Morris Ltd* (1988) 80 ALR 455), or owing to the duty to mitigate loss (*Wheeler v Philip Morris Ltd* (1989) 97 ALR 282).

A different analysis suggests that the employer's dismissal in breach of the substantive conditions of the contract amounts to a repudiatory breach of contract. By claiming compensation for wrongful dismissal, the employee necessarily accepts this repudiatory breach and brings the contract to an end. The claim for compensation must therefore be limited to the period until a claim is brought. Since the employee is under a duty to mitigate loss as well, the employee must take reasonable steps to seek alternative employment, and the acceptance of another job should normally be regarded also as acceptance of the employer's repudiatory breach of contract. On this view, there is no possibility of a claim for compensation of wages until the normal retirement age. Under these principles of quantification, the employee can claim net wages for the period of time until either the contract is terminated by acceptance of repudiation or the employee should reasonably be expected to have obtained alternative employment.

Although the UK courts seem likely to adopt this restrictive approach to compensation, economic analysis suggests a third way in which to formulate the measure of compensation. The limitation on the employer's power of dismissal is a valuable benefit for the employee, and it may be supposed that there is a commensurate reduction in salary to reflect this benefit of tenure. By abrogating this contractual right, the employer has demonstrated that it never intended to be bound by this limitation. The real loss of the employee has therefore been the reduction of wages during the period of employment without receiving any consideration for it. Compensation should therefore amount to the abatement of wages for the entire period of employment.

5.1.1.4 Compensation for fringe benefits and collateral undertakings

Termination of the contract may not only deprive the employee of wages but also remove many fringe benefits, such as occupational pension rights, holiday pay, other deferred payments such as bonuses, personal loans, private health care insurance, share options, and a company car. In principle, the employee is entitled to compensation for the loss of these additional benefits resulting from termination of employment. In so far as the compensatory damages are taxable, the amount of compensation will be increased so that the net amount after tax will represent the employee's actual loss flowing from wrongful dismissal (*Shove v Downs Surgical Plc* [1984] ICR 532 (QB)). Claims for these types of benefits often encounter two obstacles.

The first obstacle concerns the discretionary nature of some fringe benefits. The contract may provide that the employer has the unfettered discretion to give or to withhold the benefit. The employer can object to the award of compensation for such a discretionary fringe benefit on the ground that the benefit was not an entitlement and the employer had exercised its discretion not to award it. The employee must counter this objection by asserting that the discretion was in fact limited by express or implied terms in the contract, so that the discretion should not have been exercised to deny the benefit to the employee.

[5.11] *Horkulak v Cantor Fitzgerald International* **[2004] EWCA Civ 1287 [2005] ICR 402 (CA)**

The claimant, a dealer trading in interest rate derivatives, was appointed under a three year fixed-term contract, with a basic annual salary of £250,000, together with some guaranteed bonuses and an 'annual discretionary bonus', either to be fixed by mutual agreement, or by a 'final decision' at the 'sole discretion' of the president of the company. In the face of bullying and abusive behaviour, the claimant resigned and succeeded in a claim for wrongful dismissal and was awarded about £900,000 in damages, about half of which represented loss under the discretionary bonus scheme. The employer appealed against any award of compensation for losses under the discretionary bonus scheme. The Court of Appeal upheld this aspect of the award, though reduced the award slightly for the claimants failure to mitigate his loss. The Court held that the discretion conferred by the contract must not only be exercised honestly and in good faith but, having regard to the provision of the contract by which it is conferred, it must not be exercised arbitrarily, capriciously or unreasonably. This implied term was necessary to give genuine value, rather than nominal force, to the obligation of the party required or empowered to exercise discretion. The implied term represents a presumption that it is the reasonable expectation and the common intention of the parties that there should be a genuine and rational exercise of the discretion. Damages should be awarded on the basis of what bonus would have been awarded, if the employment had continued, and if the employer had honestly and in good faith exercised its discretion according to its customary criteria (such as performance and loyalty). The broad principle that a defendant is not liable for that which he is not contractually bound to do is not applicable in a case where there is a contractual obligation to exercise a discretion rationally.

The second obstacle is that contractual rights to fringe benefits will usually be limited in time, which places a cap on the possible measure of compensation. For some fringe benefits, the entitlement may only arise when the employee is actually performing work, as in the case of free meals or luncheon vouchers (*Mcgrath v de Soissons* (1962) 112 LJ 60). In most other instances, fringe benefits such as health care insurance and share options terminate with the expiration of the contract of employment. A claim for compensation will therefore be limited to the date when the contract has been terminated by notice or acceptance of repudiatory breach. The value of the claim can therefore turn crucially on the moment when the employer has succeeded in bringing the contract to an end: *Brompton v AOC International Ltd* [1997] IRLR 639 (CA). For occupational pensions, however, the scheme should make express provision either for the vesting of rights, which may be claimed on the employee reaching retirement age, or, in the case of short service employees, for the refund of contributions. It may be possible to argue that the employer commits a breach of an implied term such as performance in good faith or mutual trust and confidence, if the employer uses the power to terminate the contract for the purpose of avoiding liabilities to pay fringe benefits: *Adin v Seco Forex International Resources Ltd* [1997] IRLR 280 (Ct Sess, Outer House). But this argument must overcome the problem that a court usually regards contractual behaviour as reasonable and fair, if it merely exercises powers under the contract to reduce liabilities.

In the case of some fringe benefits, it may be possible to argue that the withdrawal of the benefit or the failure to supply it should give rise to compensation not only for the loss of economic value but also for the loss of expected comfort and pleasure.

Although damages for breach of contract do not usually include compensation for vexation and disappointment, where the purpose of a contractual promise was to guarantee comfort or enjoyment a court may award compensation for breach of that undertaking. If, for example, an employee was promised rent-free accommodation in a luxury home in order to induce him to accept a relocation of his employment to a foreign country, and on arrival he discovered that the house did not exist or was squalid, the employee might claim compensation not only for the loss of the value of the promised accommodation but also for the deprivation of comfort.

5.1.1.5 Implied substantive terms

The final basis for an award of compensation for wrongful dismissal might arise from a breach of an implied substantive obligation imposed upon the employer. These implied substantive obligations have already been examined in the context of the development of the implied terms of the contract of employment. Although these obligations can be extensive, as in the case of health and safety, rarely do they apply to termination of contracts of employment. Apart from the procedural provision about giving reasonable notice and possibly some further implied limitations on the manner of dismissal, the courts have not developed implied substantive limitations on the permissible reasons for dismissal.

In the United States, some jurisdictions have accepted an implied term that an employer will not exercise the power to terminate the contract in bad faith, but this application of the Uniform Commercial Code's principle that contracts should be performed in good faith has not been imitated in the United Kingdom. The decision in *Johnson v Unisys Ltd* (**[5.6]** above), rejected the implication of such an implied term on the grounds not only that it would contradict the express and implied term that the contract of employment could be terminated for any reason on giving notice, but also that such a term would conflict with the restrictions imposed by Parliament on the statutory claim for unfair dismissal. Similarly, in *Reda v Flag Ltd* [2002] IRLR 747 (PC), the Privy Council rejected an argument that an express contractual power to dismiss summarily without cause could be circumscribed by an implied term either with respect to procedure, such as reasonable notice, or substance, such as good faith or mutual trust and confidence.

Nevertheless, *Johnson v Unisys Ltd* does not preclude the possibility that an employee might claim compensation for breach of substantive implied terms during the performance of the contract. And in practice, such claims are likely to brought after termination of the contract, because at that time the employee will be more will-ing to make claims against his or her employer. In particular, an employee may seek compensation for breach by the employer during the performance of the contract of the implied term that neither party should conduct themselves in a way calculated to destroy mutual trust and confidence. Similarly, the employee may seek compensation in tort or for breach of an implied term regarding the employer's duty to care for the health and safety of the employee during the currency of the employment relation. The potential advantage of such common law claims over a claim for the statutory right of unfair dismissal is that there is no upper limit on the potential compensation payable by the employer.

In such common law claims, however, the breach of implied term by the employer may have comprised a series of actions culminating in the dismissal of the employee. The question left open after *Johnson v Unisys Ltd* was whether that decision also barred claims for breach of contract if the conduct of the employer comprised part of the circumstances leading to termination of the contract of employment. In the next case, the House of Lords decided that, in principle, if an employee had acquired a cause of action in law for breach of contract or otherwise prior to any dismissal or termination of the contract, that cause of action remained in existence even though the employee was subsequently dismissed and therefore became entitled to claim the statutory right to compensation for unfair dismissal.

[5.12] *Eastwood v Magnox Electric plc; McCabe v Cornwall County Council* [2004] UKHL 35 [2004] ICR 1064 (HL)

In the Eastwood case, the assumed facts were that a supervisor harboured a grudge against Mr Eastwood, and used his position to bring false allegations of misconduct against him. When Mr Eastwood brought an internal appeal against a finding of misconduct, another manager demanded that a fellow employee, Mr Williams, should provide a false statement against Mr Eastwood. When Mr Williams refused to do so, he was threatened with a trumped up investigation of misconduct. Mr Eastwood's internal appeal was successful, but then the managers encouraged another worker to revive and 'beef up' earlier allegation of sexual harassment against Mr Eastwood, and extend it to Mr Williams. After the internal appeal during which no witnesses were found to support the charges, both employees were dismissed. Subsequently both employees accepted a financial settlement of their claims for unfair dismissal, but they continued with their claims at common law for personal injuries in the form of psychiatric illness caused by the manager's deliberate abuse of the disciplinary process. In the McCabe case, the employee schoolteacher won a claim for unfair dismissal on the ground that the serious allegations of inappropriate behaviour towards certain female pupils had not been properly investigated prior to the dismissal. Mr McCabe then brought an action at common law for compensation for psychiatric illness caused by the employer's failure to investigate the allegations properly. In both cases the central legal issue was whether the decision in *Johnson v Unisys Ltd* barred such common law claims. Differently constituted Courts of Appeal had excluded the claims by Mr Eastwood and Mr Williams, but had permitted the claim brought by Mr McCabe to proceed. The House of Lords held that all three claims should be permitted to proceed as the assumed facts constituted causes of action which accrued before the dismissal.

Lord Nicholls (with whom the other members of the judicial committee agreed):
27. Identifying the boundary of the 'Johnson exclusion area', as it has been called, is comparatively straightforward. The statutory code provides remedies for infringement of the statutory right not to be dismissed unfairly. An employee's remedy for unfair dismissal, whether actual or constructive, is the remedy provided by statute. If before his dismissal, whether actual or constructive, an employee has acquired a cause of action at law, for breach of contract or otherwise, that cause of action remains unimpaired by his subsequent unfair dismissal and the statutory rights flowing therefrom. By definition, in law such a cause of action exists independently of the dismissal.
28. In the ordinary course, suspension apart, an employer's failure to act fairly in the steps leading to dismissal does not of itself cause the employee financial loss. The loss arises when the employee is dismissed and it arises by reason of his dismissal. Then the resultant claim for loss falls squarely within the Johnson exclusion area.

29. Exceptionally this is not so. Exceptionally, financial loss may flow directly from the employer's failure to act fairly when taking steps leading to dismissal. Financial loss flowing from suspension is an instance. Another instance is cases such as those now before the House, when an employee suffers financial loss from psychiatric or other illness caused by his pre-dismissal unfair treatment. In such cases the employee has a common law cause of action which precedes, and is independent of, his subsequent dismissal. In respect of his subsequent dismissal he may of course present a claim to an employment tribunal. If he brings proceedings both in court and before a tribunal he cannot recover any overlapping heads of loss twice over.

30. If identifying the boundary between the common law rights and remedies and the statutory rights and remedies is comparatively straightforward, the same cannot be said of the practical consequences of this unusual boundary. Particularly in cases concerning financial loss flowing from psychiatric illnesses, some of the practical consequences are far from straightforward or desirable. The first and most obvious drawback is that in such cases the division of remedial jurisdiction between the court and an employment tribunal will lead to duplication of proceedings. In practice there will be cases where the employment tribunal and the court each traverse much of the same ground in deciding the factual issues before them, with attendant waste of resources and costs.

31. Second, the existence of this boundary line means that in some cases a continuing course of conduct, typically a disciplinary process followed by dismissal, may have to be chopped artificially into separate pieces. In cases of constructive dismissal a distinction will have to be drawn between loss flowing from antecedent breaches of the trust and confidence term and loss flowing from the employee's acceptance of these breaches as a repudiation of the contract. The loss flowing from the impugned conduct taking place before actual or constructive dismissal lies outside the Johnson exclusion area, the loss flowing from the dismissal itself is within that area. In some cases this legalistic distinction may give rise to difficult questions of causation in cases such as those now before the House, where financial loss is claimed as the consequence of psychiatric illness said to have been brought on by the employer's conduct before the employee was dismissed. Judges and tribunals, faced perhaps with conflicting medical evidence, may have to decide whether the fact of dismissal was really the last straw which proved too much for the employee, or whether the onset of the illness occurred even before he was dismissed.

32. The existence of this boundary line produces other strange results. An employer may be better off dismissing an employee than suspending him. A statutory claim for unfair dismissal would be subject to the statutory cap, a common law claim for unfair suspension would not. The decision of the Court of Appeal in *Gogay v Hertfordshire County Council* [2000] IRLR 703 is an example of the latter. Likewise, the decision in Johnson's case means that an employee who is psychologically vulnerable is owed no duty of care in respect of his dismissal although, depending on the circumstances, he may be owed a duty of care in respect of his suspension.

33. It goes without saying that an inter-relation between the common law and statute having these awkward and unfortunate consequences is not satisfactory. The difficulties arise principally because of the cap on the amount of compensatory awards for unfair dismissal. Although the cap was raised substantially in 1998, at times tribunals are still precluded from awarding full compensation for a dismissed employee's financial loss. So, understandably, employees and their legal advisers are seeking to side-step the statutory limit by identifying elements in the events preceding dismissal, but leading up to dismissal, which can be used as pegs on which to hang a common law claim for breach of an employer's implied contractual obligation to act fairly. This situation merits urgent attention by the government and the legislature.

Lord Steyn:
The majority's reasoning in *Johnson* also means that, although the exercise of the power to suspend must be exercised with due regard to trust and confidence (or fairness), the more drastic power of dismissal may be exercised free of any equivalent constraint. An employee confronted with a repudiatory breach of contract by an employer who elects to treat the contract as continuing may still have a claim for breach of contract. But in practice an employee may often not have much choice but to accept the repudiation. If the employee accepts the repudiation, the claim becomes one of unfair dismissal and the *Johnson* exclusion zone comes into play. In constructive dismissal cases the employee's response to the employer's breach will dictate whether there can be common law liability. The more outrageous the breach the less likely it is tht the employee can affirm the contract: Lizzie Barmes, 'The Continuing Conceptual Crisis in the Common Law of the Contract of Employment' (2004) 67(3) MLR 435, at 451.

This decision reveals the confused state of the common law after the pragmatic decision in *Johnson v Unisys Ltd* to prevent claims for wrongful dismissal from circumventing the qualifications and limits placed on the statutory right to claim unfair dismissal. Especially in those cases where the employee has suffered substantial economic losses resulting from psychiatric illness caused by the employer's conduct leading up to the dismissal, the common law now has to attempt to draw what may prove to be an illusory distinction between, on the one hand, misconduct by the employer during the course of employment, and on the other, misconduct by the employer as part of the process of dismissal. To attempt to apply such a distinction to cases where the employer's misconduct consists of abuse of the internal disciplinary process that may lead to dismissal is surely impracticable and unpredictable. Even if the distinction can be drawn, there remains the difficult issue of determining what losses were caused by the breach of an implied term during performance of the contract as distinct from those losses caused by the dismissal.

In those cases that avoid the Johnson exclusion zone and succeed in a claim for a breach of an implied term during performance of the contract, the question becomes how will the courts assess the measure of damages? Unlike an ordinary claim for wrongful dismissal, where the measure of damages is confined to the loss of wages during the notice period, the assessment for breach of an implied term during performance of the contract should attempt to quantify the losses caused by that breach. The courts have decided that any economic losses caused by the employer's breach are recoverable. In *Mahmoud v Bank of Credit and Commerce International SA* [1998] AC 20 (HL), (above **[2.28]**), the leading decision on the implied term of trust and confidence, the final issue was whether employees could be awarded compensation for the financial loss they had suffered by being unable to obtain employment after their employer's bank had collapsed amid allegation of mismangement and corruption. The House of Lords approved in principle an award of 'stigma damages' or compensation for damage to reputation causing economic loss in the form that the employees could not obtain employment owing to their linkage to the fraudulent bank. Similarly, if in breach of contract an employer negligently writes an inaccurate and damaging reference for an employee, which harms his job prospects, in principle the employee should be able to recover compensation for the economic losses caused by the damage to reputation: *Spring v Guardian Assurance plc* [1994] ICR 596 (HL) (above **[2.30]**). This claim for the economic loss resulting from damage to reputation faces great obstacles in practice, however, because the employee will have to prove the causal link between the stigma and his failure to obtain employment. In effect the employee will have to bring evidence from prospective employers that his or her job application was rejected owing to the cloud of suspicion caused by the employer's misconduct or negligent reference, and that this cause of rejection was more weighty than other considerations such as qualifications and experience (e.g. *Bank of Credit and Commerce International SA v Ali* [1999] IRLR 508 (ChD)).

In contrast to the broad acceptance of claims for economic loss resulting from the employer's breach of implied terms of the contract, claims for compensation for anxiety, frustration, and disappointment have been rejected. In *French v Barclays Bank Plc* [1998] IRLR 652 (CA) **[2.13]**, a bank employee was required to relocate and move house. Being unable to sell his house immediately, the employee took advantage of the employer's scheme for an interest free bridging loan. After a period of time, however, the employer withdrew this facility on short notice, which plunged the employee into sever financial difficulties. The employee was awarded damages for his economic losses resulting from the employer's breach of the implied term of trust and confidence. But his claim for an award of compensation for the stress and anxiety caused by the breach of contract was rejected. Under the general principles of the common law of contract, the only circumstances in which recovery for such items may be possible is where it is accepted that an object of the contract was to provide pleasure, relaxation, peace of mind or freedom from molestation: *Farley v Skinner* [2001] UKHL 49, [2002] 2 AC 732. Although a contract of employment is unlikely to have such an object, it might be possible to maintain such a claim in an unusual case, as in the example discussed above of the fringe benefit where the employer promises luxury accommodation as part of the emoluments of a job.

Although these principles prevent claims for compensation for distress and anxiety caused by the employer's breach of implied terms, it is possible to seek compensation for a recognised psychiatric illness caused by the employer's breach of its duty of care with respect to the health and safety of employees. To establish such a claim, which can be regarded as either a breach of an implied term or an independent tort of negligence, it is necessary to establish that the employer has failed to perform its duty of care, and that this breach caused the psychiatric illness of the employee.

[5.13] *Waters v Commissioner of Police for the Metropolis* [2000] IRLR 720 (HL)

A woman police officer alleged that she had been sexually assaulted by a male police officer when they were off duty. After inquiries, no action was taken against the man. The woman further alleged that after she had made her complaint, she had been harassed, treated unfairly, and victimised by other police officers, to such an extent that she had suffered mental illness. The House of Lords held that a claim in tort for breach of the employer's personal duty of care should not be struck out as disclosing no cause of action in these circumstances. The employer might be in breach of its duty of care either if the employer knew that employees were committing acts against another employee that might cause her physical or mental harm, or if the employer could foresee that such acts might happen, and if the employer failed to take reasonable steps to protect her against such victimisation or harassment.

It seems that a breach of the employer's duty of care may be discovered in conduct that is in breach of the implied term not to act in a way which seriously damages the relationship of trust and confidence. In *Gogay v Hertfordshire County Council* [2000] IRLR 703 (CA), the employee successfully claimed that an unjustified suspension from work amounted to a breach of the implied term of trust and confidence. The court approved a claim for general damages for an identifiable psychiatric illness that resulted from the suspension. This claim, it should be noted, was framed as a breach of the implied term of trust and confidence, and not as a breach of the duty of care, though perhaps a better analysis would be that the conduct that amounted to bad faith also constituted a breach of the employer's duty of care.

Many claims for compensation for psychiatric illness are based on an argument that it was caused by the employer's management of the undertaking which caused excessive stress to be placed on employees. In response to such claims, the courts have insisted that there is no breach of duty by merely a result of the fact that work is hard and stressful. Where, however, the employer knows, or ought reasonably to know, that the stress is particuarly affecting an individual employee, who as a result may foreseeably suffer psychiatric illness such as depression, the employer's duty of care requires the employer to take reasonable steps to reduce the stress. If the employee simply puts up with the pressure without complaint, the employer's duty to take special measures will not be triggered.

[5.14] *Hatton v Sutherland [2002] EWCA Civ 76, [2002] ICR 613 (CA)*

In four consolidated appeals concerning claims brought by employees against employers for psychiatric illness caused by stress arising from work, the court summarised the relevant principles.

Hale LJ:
(1) There are no special control mechanisms applying to claims for psychatric (or physical) illness or injury arising from the stress of doing the work the employee is required to do . . .

(2) The threshold question is whether this kind of harm to this particular employee was reasonably foreseeable . . .

(3) Foreseeability depends upon what the employer knows (or ought reasonably to know) about the individual employee. Because of the nature of of mental disorder, it is harder to foresee than physical injury, but may be easier to foresee in a known individual than in the population at large. An employer is usually entitled to assume that the employee can withstand the normal pressures of the job unless he knows of some particular problem or vulnerability . . .

(4) The test is the same whatever the employment . . .

(5) Factors likely to be relevant in answering the threshold question include: (a) the nature and extent of the work done by the employee . . . (b) signs from the employee of impending harm to health . . .

(6) The employer is generally entitled to take what he is told by his employee at face value, unless he has good reason to think to the contrary.

(7) To trigger a duty to take steps, the indications of impending harm to health arising from stress at work must be plain enough for any reasonable employer to realise that he should do something about it . . .

(8) The employer is only in breach of duty if he has failed to take the steps which are reasonable in the circumstances, bearing in mind the magnitude of the the risk of harm occurring, the gravity of the harm which may occur, the costs and practicability of preventing it, and the justifications for running the risk . . .

(9) The size and scope of the employer's operation, its resources and the demands it faces are relevant in deciding what is reasonable . . .

(10) An employer can only reasonably be expected to take steps which are likely to do some good . . .

(11) An employer who offers a confidential advice service, with referral to appropriate counselling or treatment services, is unlikely to be found in breach of duty . . .

(12) If the only reasonable and effective step would have been to dismiss or demote the employee, the employer will not be in breach of duty in allowing a willing employee to continue in the job . . .

(13) In all cases, therefore, it is necessary to identify the steps which the employer both could and should have taken before finding him in breach of his duty of care . . .

(14) The claimant must show that that breach of duty has caused or materially contributed to the harm suffered. It is not enough to show that occupational stress has caused the harm . . .

[5.15] *Barber v Somerset County Council [2004] UKHL 13, [2004] ICR 457 (HL).*

One of the cases in the consolidate appeals heard in *Sutherland v Hatton* was further appealed to the House of Lords, because the employee's successful claim had been overturned by the Court of Appeal when applying those principles. Mr Barber was a mathematics teacher in a school. As a consequences of cuts in resources, he had to take on additional work in order to maintain his salary, and he was working up to 70 hours per week, including sometimes at weekends. During a summer term he was off work for three weeks with a medical note explaining that he was suffering from stress and depression. On his return to school, the head teacher and deputies were not sympathetic and no steps were taken to remedy the situation. At the beginning of the next term, his workload had further increased, and he went to see his doctor, but before the doctor took action, Mr Barber had a breakdown at work, and never returned to work. The House of Lords allowed the claimant's appeal, and restored the original judgment for damages for £72,547. The Judical Committee approved the general guidance provided by Hale LJ, but disagreed in this particular case on the issue of whether the employer had been in breach of the duty of care. The employer had broken the duty of care by failing to take any steps after the employee had been off work for three weeks for anxiety and depression in the summer term. The duty to take reasonable steps was a continuing one, which existed in the autumn term as well, when the managers of the school should have enquired into the claimant's mental health and when they could have taken steps to reduce his workload.

It is hard to summarise this rapidly evolving area of the common law. The *Johnson* case rules out claims for compensation at common law for breach of implied terms or a duty of care in connection with a dismissal, but it seems likely in many cases that the employer's conduct prior to the dismissal may provide the grounds for similar claims. The courts will award compensation for economic loss attributable to breaches of contract or negligence in the employer's performance of the contract. Although the courts will not award compensation for stress, anxiety, and distress caused by the employer's breach of contract, if the employee suffers a identifiable psychiatric illness resulting from a breach of the employer's duty of care, that can form the basis for a substantial claim for general damages. In effect, the scope of the *Johnson* decision has been narrowly confined, thereby allowing the common law once again to develop according to basic principles.

5.1.2 Injunctions and declarations

At the same time as the more elaborate express and implied terms of the contract of employment have afforded some employees the chance to obtain substantial damages for breach of contract, these express terms that limit an employer's disciplinary powers create the chance for an employee to seek an injunction against a dismissal. This claim seeks a declaration from a court that a proposed dismissal is in breach of the express terms of the contract, and, if this claim is successful, the employee asserts an additional claim that the court should issue an injunction that forbids the employer from committing the breach of contract. At the time of the enactment of the statutory right to claim unfair dismissal, it was doubted that any such claim might be successful, except in the special case of public officials holding an office under statute. Yet this view immediately turned out to be a misconception of the capacity of private law to respond to claims to job security based upon express terms of the contract.

Nevertheless, a claim for an injunction against a dismissal at common law encounters substantial hurdles. First, the employee must demonstrate that the proposed dismissal breaches an express term of the contract. There is often ample scope for argument about the proper construction of the terms, which can be resolved by a declaration by the court.

[5.16] *Jones v Gwent County Council* [1992] IRLR 521 (HC)

> Following a claim for sex discrimination against her employer, a college lecturer was accused of 'gross misconduct'. The employer's disciplinary procedure was then used twice in order to prove that the charge was justified, but on both occasions the disciplinary committee rejected the allegation. Notwithstanding this outcome of the contractual disciplinary procedure, the employer dismissed the employee with notice. In an action before the High Court for a declaration and an injunction, the court exercised its power to determine a question of law at any stage of the proceedings to declare that the letter of dismissal was not 'valid and effective'. The contract specified that dismissal on the ground of 'gross misconduct' could only occur after the allegation had been upheld by the disciplinary committee. The dismissal after the allegation had been rejected could not constitute an exercise of the disciplinary power conferred by the contract of employment.

The effect of the declaration is to confirm that the employer is in breach of contract and that the contract has not been terminated according to its provisions.

The second hurdle in applications for injunctions is that the employee must establish that the contract has not already been terminated by dismissal or some other mechanism, for otherwise there remains no contract for the court to enforce. As a practical matter, therefore, the employee needs to act swiftly before the contract has been terminated by means of an application for an interlocutory or pre-trial injunction pending a full trial. A court will issue such an injunction if it finds that there is a serious issue to be tried and the balance of convenience favours an order.

The serious issue test raises a third hurdle, for there cannot be a serious issue unless the employee has some prospect of success. A court will issue a permanent injunction at trial only if it is persuaded both that damages would not be an adequate remedy and that an injunction would not compel the employer to continue to employ a person in whom the employer had lost trust and confidence. The same principles are usually applied to pre-trial injunctions.

The final hurdle in the way of injunctions is the question of the balance of convenience. The employee needs to show that his legal position will be harmed without the injunction and that the proposed order does not impose a serious disadvantage on the employer. The adverse effect on the employee focuses on the possible deprivation of employment by the employer's termination of the contract. The potential disadvantage to the employer concerns the continuing presence of the employee at the workplace, which might cause disruption to working arrangements. This last problem can be avoided by drafting the terms of the order so that the employee does not attend work or agrees to comply with the employer's instructions.

Here we focus on the two most difficult legal issues: (i) the effect of a dismissal in breach of contract on the continuation of the contract (the second hurdle); and (ii) the criteria of the inadequacy of damages and the presence of trust and confidence (the third hurdle).

5.1.2.1 Termination of the employment relation

The legal effect on the existence of a contract of employment of a dismissal in breach of contract, either by way of a breach of an express term in the contract or by an unjustified summary dismissal, remains controversial. Three opposing views attract considerable support in the cases.

- The unilateral view holds that the employer's dismissal, notwithstanding any breach of contract, is effective to terminate the contract of employment. This is believed to be a special rule for the contract of employment.
- The elective theory holds that the normal principles of contract law apply to the contract of employment, so that the employer's dismissal constitutes a repudiatory breach of contract that does not bring the contract to an end until the employee accepts the repudiation.
- The partial survival theory suggests a modification to the unilateral theory in that some terms of the contract may survive the termination of the main employment relation, rather like an arbitration clause or a liquidated damages clause survives the termination of a commercial contract. On this view, contractual disciplinary procedures and restraint of competition clauses may survive the termination of the main employment relation by a dismissal.

In the absence of clear authority from the House of Lords on this issue, the weight of authority in the Court of Appeal, especially the majority view in *Gunton v Richmond-Upon-Thames London Borough Council* [1980] ICR 755 (CA) (above [5.7]), supports the elective theory and the application of ordinary contractual principles. The success of applications for injunctions, as in *Hill v CA Parsons & Co Ltd* [1972] Ch 305 (CA), below [5.20], despite a summary dismissal, also implies the application of an elective theory. Nevertheless, the next case reveals that the issue remains surrounded in controversy. The Court of Appeal feels bound by authority to follow the elective theory, whilst strongly disapproving of it in favour of either the unilateral view or the partial survival theory.

[5.17] *Boyo v London Borough of Lambeth* [1994] ICR 727 (CA)

Mr Boyo worked for the council as an accountant. The police brought charges against him for fraud at work, and the council suspended and then dismissed him. The contract of employment provided for a period of one month's notice. In addition, the contract incorporated disciplinary rules and procedures. These rules provided that an employee would be dismissed with or without notice if an allegation of gross misconduct was substantiated after investigation and due consideration. The council did not follow the disciplinary procedure, because the council was concerned that the procedure would interfere with the pending criminal prosecution. Instead, the council decided to dismiss the plaintiff, originally claiming 'frustration' of the contract, but subsequently conceding that this had been a wrongful dismissal. The court of first instance awarded the plaintiff compensation calculated by reference to six months' wages, which comprised one month for the period of notice and five months for the period during which the disciplinary procedure for gross misconduct would have operated. Both parties appealed. The employee claimed damages for loss of salary up to the date of trial, which he asserted was the date when he accepted the repudiatory breach of contract. The council claimed that its liability should be limited to the notice period or alternatively to when the employee commenced proceedings for dismissal. The Court of Appeal, dismissing the appeal and cross-appeal, held that although the employer's wrongful repudiation of the contract did not unilaterally terminate the contract of employment, the employer's liability to pay compensation was limited to the time at which the employer could have lawfully terminated the contract unilaterally. This period was the notice period plus the time which the disciplinary procedure would reasonably have taken.

Ralph Gibson LJ felt bound to follow *Gunton v Richmond-upon-Thames London Borough Council* [1980] ICR 755 (CA), and to apply the principle that a repudiatory breach by the employer terminated the contract of employment only when accepted by the employee. He preferred, however, the view that repudiation brought the contract to an end, with some exceptions of the kind envisaged by the partial survival theory. He applied the rule for the measure of damages that the maximum amount was the period for which the employer would be liable for wages if the employer had terminated the contract lawfully by giving notice and following the disciplinary procedure.

Staughton LJ:
The principal conclusions of Judge James in this case were as follows:

(1) The Council's letter of 29 October 1991 was a repudiation of the contract of employment.

(2) Unilateral termination by the council was ineffective until accepted by Mr Boyo.

(3) It was accepted by Mr Boyo being ready for trial and obtaining a hearing date. (This occurred on some day between May and December 1992.)

(4) Nevertheless Mr Boyo could not recover his salary up to that date, or for any period after October 1991, since he had not done any work.

(5) He could recover damages for a period starting at the end of October 1991.

(6) That period should be the sum of one month (the minimum notice required) and the time that disciplinary procedures could be expected to take.

(7) Disciplinary procedures would have taken five months.

I agree with the judge's conclusions on points (1) and (7). As to point (1), the council's letter of 29 October 1991 was a forthright repudiation of the contract of employment. It said in so many words that Mr Boyo would no longer be employed, and no longer paid. The excuse given (frustration) could not be supported, as is now accepted.

On point (7), I can readily accept the judge's conclusion . . .

I now turn to points (2) and (6) of the judge's reasoning. In my opinion:

(a)   those points are established by the authority of this Court (through a majority) in *Gunton v London Borough of Richmond-upon-Thames* [1980] ICR 755; and

(b)   the judge was obliged to follow that decision, as we are; but

(c)   I would otherwise have reached the opposite conclusions.

Not only are we bound to follow the majority view in *Gunton's* case, Miss Williams for the council disclaims any wish for us to depart from it. Perhaps the council take the view that, for good or ill, the claim of Mr Boyo should be finally determined in this court; and have no desire to achieve immortality as the defendant who took the point to the House of Lords. What is more, the monetary result which the judge reached was much nearer to the sum which I would have reached if *Gunton's* case had not been binding upon us, than that which Mr Boyo contends for.

Unconstrained by authority, my conclusions on points (2) and (6) would have been as follows:

(2) A direct repudiation, whether by employer or employee, determines a contract of employment. Such a contract is in that respect in a class of its own. An employee cannot be compelled to do work if he declines to do so, nor be restrained from working for anybody else. So the employer too should not be compelled to treat the contract as still in existence against his will.

(3) I see no ground for treating something as acceptance of repudiation in an employment case, if it would not be an acceptance in the general law of contract. It must demonstrate to the guilty party that the contract is accepted as at an end. Mr Boyo was not doing that when he pursued his claim for arrears of salary.

(4) Although there is powerful authority to the contrary, I do not accept that an employee has no right to salary if he has done no work. Interestingly enough, it seems that Lambeth Council pays its employees on the 15th of the month, although only half their work has then been done.

(5) If, as *Gunton's* case and Judge James held, a contract of employment is not terminated by repudiation, I would have awarded Mr Boyo his salary up to the date of trial. However, I consider (as stated in point (2) above) that it is terminated; so I would agree that Mr Boyo is entitled only to damages calculated at 1 November 1991.

(6) Those damages, in accordance with ordinary law, should be assessed on the basis that the council would otherwise have brought Mr Boyo's employment to an end as soon as they lawfully could. For the period thus ascertained, Mr Boyo should be awarded a sum equal to his salary less what he earns, or should have earned, elsewhere in mitigation. I rather think that, in agreement with Shaw LJ and for the reasons which he gave, I would have taken that period as one month, and not included the time which would have been taken by disciplinary proceedings. But the point is not easy. As it is, *Gunton's* case decides that the disciplinary period should be included.

There remains the point that disciplinary action would or might have been postponed until after the completion of criminal proceedings. Like Ralph Gibson LJ, I would not on that ground increase the total period of six months for which damages are awarded. In the first place, the allowance of a period for disciplinary proceedings is artificial, notional, hypothetical: on the facts admitted or proved Mr Boyo was guilty of no misconduct and no crime; so proceedings, whether disciplinary or criminal, can with hindsight be assumed to have ended as soon as they were begun. Secondly, I only allow a five-month period for disciplinary proceedings because *Gunton's* case says that I must. It requires no more than that.

It is unusual, and perhaps improper, for this Court to be so critical of a decision by which we are bound. But we have been somewhat critical of the administrative council in this case. It is only fair to confess that the law cannot stand in a white sheet, and in this area is distinctly lacking in rhyme and reason. I would dismiss the appeal and the cross-appeal.

Sir Francis Purchas:

I agree that we are bound, as was the judge, by the *rationes decidendi* in the majority judgments in *Gunton v London Borough of Richmond-upon-Thames* [1980] ICR 755. In the particular circumstances of this case, I should have reached very much the same conclusion in any event. Starting from the principle that contracts for the provision of personal services, whether in the normal master and servant sense or for the provision of professional expertise in the context of personal employment, should normally be subject to the ordinary rules of contract, it is clearly desirable that exceptions should be limited as strictly as possible so long as the result accords with convenience and common sense. The central question which arises in this appeal is whether an exception should be recognised in cases of wrongful dismissal of the employee by the employer.

Immediately it should be noted that there is already in existence an important exception well embedded in the common law, namely that the courts will not grant a decree of specific performance in the case of contracts for personal service. If the courts were to recognise for the purposes of permitting an employee whose contract of service has been wrongfully repudiated by the employer to sue in debt for the wages which he would have earned more or less ad infinitum, this would be little different to achieving a decree of specific employment by the back door without the obligation of having to provide the service. With respect to the approach of Lord Aylmerton in the case of *Rigby v Ferodo Ltd* [1988] ICR 29 (HL), I would not find it necessary to rely on a fiction of assent by the wronged employee in order to dispense with the contract to pay wages. I would prefer to rely on an exception in those cases where the employer, by unequivocal unilateral action, repudiates his obligations under the contract in a manner in which his decision is brought to the attention of the servant, then the exception should apply and it would not be open to the employee to reject the repudiation. His duty to mitigate his loss would involve of necessity the immediate recognition of the employer's repudiation. In this I would respectively not merely not follow that, but also agree with the judgment of Buckley LJ in *Gunton*'s case. In other circumstances this would involve interfering with the order of the judge below; but as has already been explained by Ralph Gibson LJ, the council do not rely on this argument on this appeal because of a concession already made.

Apart from this, for the reasons given in the judgment of Ralph Gibson LJ, I would dismiss the cross-appeal and also dismiss the appeal.

This controversy in the Court of Appeal reveals that, although the elective theory is believed to be binding on that court, it is regarded as unsatisfactory. The principal argument for the rival unilateral theory, that is applying a special rule to contracts of employment which permits the employer's dismissal in breach of contract to terminate the employment relation, seems, however, to be questionable. One reason for the unilateral theory relies on the general absence of specific performance for contracts of employment to suggest that dismissal is effective to terminate the employment. But this argument overlooks the point that in practice specific performance will not be available in most commercial contracts where damages will be an adequate remedy. Furthermore, the reasoning is suspiciously circular. The argument runs that unilateral termination is effective because specific performance is unavailable and that specific performance is unavailable because the termination has been effective.

A more substantial concern voiced by the judges concerns the possibility that the employee will not accept the employer's repudiation of the contract, and claim damages for an indefinite period. If it were assumed that the employer's summary dismissal could only terminate the contract of employment with the consent of the employee under the ordinary law of contract, it might be argued that the employee could in principle refuse to accept the dismissal and claim his wages indefinitely as a debt with no duty to mitigate loss.

[5.18] *Saunders* v *Earnest Neale Ltd* [1974] ICR 565 (NIRC)

Sir John Donaldson:
Why should not the servant sue for wages if it is the act of the employer which has prevented his performing the condition precedent of rendering services? And if he can sue in debt for his wages, no duty to mitigate would arise and there would be no practical necessity to accept a wrongful dismissal as terminating the contract of employment, provided that the employer is solvent and the servant is sure that the dismissal was wrongful.

The view that this outcome is contrary to 'convenience and common sense' is repeated frequently with increasing alarm.

[5.19] *Boyo* v *London Borough of Lambeth* [1995] IRLR 50 (CA)

Sir Francis Purchas:
If the courts were to recognise for the purposes of permitting an employee whose contract of service has been wrongfully repudiated by the employer to sue in debt for the wages which he would have earned more or less ad infinitum, this would be little different to achieving a decree of specific employment [[sic] ?performance] by the back door without the obligation of having to provide the service.

But in fact this possibility cannot arise. The employee cannot bring a claim in debt unless work has been performed. The work cannot usually be performed without the co-operation of the employer. The employee's claim must therefore be for damages for breach of a term of the contract. The principal term that has been broken is the express or implied notice provision, together with any further contractual procedural requirements. The employee cannot claim compensation under these headings without conceding that the employment relation has been terminated, for the gist of his claim must be that the compensation is due for termination without the correct procedure. In any event, an employer could terminate the contract lawfully by giving proper notice. As in *Boyo* v *London Borough of Lambeth* itself, this period of time for lawful unilateral termination is used to fix the maximum period of damages, for the court assumes that the employer would take any lawful steps required to minimise the extent of damages. Thus there is no possibility of the indefinite claim for wages, so this reason for favouring the unilateral view lacks any foundation.

The alleged reasons for deviating from ordinary contract law principles with respect to the termination of employment appear to be unfounded. Under these principles, a contract must always be terminated by consent (except in the anomalous case of frustration, below p 5.2.3). The consent may be contained in the contract itself or may be the result of a post-breach agreement. The consent in the contract takes the form of the notice provision and disciplinary procedures. The legal analysis of a notice provision is that by agreement the parties consent to unilateral termination of the employment relation provided that the requisite period and procedural steps have been followed. When those terms are broken, the employer commits a repudiatory breach of contract, which the employee accepts by bringing an action for compensation. The compensation is measured by the wages during the notice period (and any required period of suspension), subject of course to the duty to mitigate loss. When the employer does not conform to the notice provision, the dismissal amounts to a repudiatory breach of contract, which must be accepted by the employee before the contract is terminated. This acceptance of the employer's repudiatory breach will usually be discovered in the employee's action of commencing a claim for damages wrongful dismissal. Acceptance might also be inferred when an employee asks for a tax statement for the purpose of taking another full-time job, though in *Brompton* v *International Ltd* [1997] IRLR 639 (CA), the majority of the court, perhaps unconvincingly, held that in the special circumstances of the case those actions did not, exceptionally, amount to acceptance of repudiation. But an action for a declaration and an injunction against dismissal should not be construed as an acceptance of the employer's repudiatory breach. Any delay in acceptance of repudiation does not augment the employee's damages, for the damages will be confined to breach of the notice provision and other contractual terms, and the employee will not be able to continue to claim wages.

There is, therefore, no good reason for grafting onto the law a special rule for contracts of employment that avoids the principle that termination of contracts can be effected only by consent. We agree with Templeman LJ, who, in *London Transport Executive* v *Clarke* [1981] ICR 355 (CA), where the obverse position was contended, that is, it was alleged unsuccessfully that the employee had terminated the contract unilaterally (i.e. dismissed himself), observed about the idea that the contract of employment was exceptional in relation to termination: 'In my view any such exception is contrary to principle, unsupported by authority binding on this court and undesirable in practice'. If the elective view is correct, it opens the door to the possibility for injunctions against repudiatory dismissals in breach of contract. Assuming that the contract is still in existence after a summary dismissal, however, the dismissed employee still needs to overcome the standard objections to the granting of an injunction against dismissal, to which we now turn.

5.1.2.2 *Inadequacy of damages and trust and confidence*

The two principal criteria for exercising the discretion to grant specific relief in contracts of employment—the requirement of trust and confidence and that damages should be an inadequate remedy—have been subject to close examination since the decision in *Hill* v *C.A. Parson & Co. Ltd* [1972] Ch. 302 (CA), which occurred at exactly the same time as the statutory right to claim unfair dismissal was being enacted. The Court of Appeal recognised that these principles did not present a complete bar to injunctive relief. It was possible, despite a dismissal, that an employer, especially if a large organisation, might retain trust and confidence in the employee. Furthermore, doubts were expressed about the adequacy of damages for wrongful dismissal in many instances.

[5.20] *Hill v CA Parsons & Co Ltd* [1972] Ch. 305 (CA)

Sachs LJ:

The plaintiff in this action is claiming an injunction to restrain the defendants from implementing a notice given by them on July 30 to determine his contract with effect from August 31 this year.

That short notice was one which the defendants were manifestly not entitled to give and their letter thus constituted an unlawful repudiation of the contract under which the plaintiff was serving them. That repudiation has never been accepted—on the contrary the whole purpose of the writ issued on August 13 was to keep the contract alive.

By August of this year the plaintiff, aged 63, with qualifications of Chartered Engineer and Fellow of the Institution of Mechanical Engineers, had served the company loyally for no less than 35 years. He had attained a highly responsible and pensionable post with a salary of £3,000 per annum and belonged to the trade union referred to as UKAPE. There is not the slightest suggestion but that he had at all material times the full confidence of his employers in his work: they sought to dismiss him solely because he would not join a trade union referred to as DATA which he sincerely felt he could not conscientiously join for reasons given in his affidavit. Appropriate notice for a man holding such a high grade appointment has been conceded by the defendants to be either three or six months: and on the material so far before us it seems that it could not be less than the latter period. According to uncontradicted evidence a man of his age has in essence no material chances of obtaining fresh employment once he has been dismissed by his regular employer. Damages for wrongful dismissal, however, would at common law be limited to amounts equivalent to such salary and pension rights as are lost to a plaintiff during the further period he would have served if given a valid notice.

The terms of the contract under which he was serving—and those under which he had served for so many years—did not oblige him to join any trade union whatsoever. Accordingly, until the defendants sought to dismiss him for not complying with a non-existent term of his contract he had every prospect of continuing to serve them till he reached the normal retiring age and thus earning increments in salary and pension rights. It follows that, as in so many cases, the damages recoverable under the common law rule are in practice by no means adequate to compensate this particular plaintiff for the loss he would really suffer—a point to which I will return.

The defendants contend that the courts are powerless to prevent the plaintiff suffering an obvious injustice, and the question is whether the submissions made in that behalf are correct.

[Sachs LJ then considered the probable effects of the Industrial Relations Act 1971 on the plaintiff's position. The Act was due to come into force during the period of notice, and was likely to give the plaintiff the right to reinstatement or superior compensation under the new law of unfair dismissal.]

Against the background of the above facts I now turn to the points raised in the helpful submissions of counsel. *In limine* comes the primary contention advanced for the defendants that a wrongful repudiation of a contract of service terminates that contract irrespective of whether or not the other party elects to accept it. It was urged that in this respect contracts of service are an exception to the general rule. This is a question which has now been fully argued before me twice this year with the aid of a considerable range of authorities—first in the *Decro-Wall International SA v Practitioners in Marketing Ltd* case [1971] 1 WLR 361(CA), and now in the instant case . . . .

But having now heard the matter so well argued again it is only right to say that I feel reinforced in the view, of which I am now convinced, that the defendants' primary contention is wrong.

It does not seem necessary in support of that view to add to the reasons given by Lord Denning M.R. and those already stated by me in the *Decro-Wall* case. Nor do I propose to rehearse those exceptional but possible ancillary or terminal clauses which might be found in contracts of service, which were canvassed in argument before us, and of which it could properly be said that damages would not afford an adequate remedy for a breach. Suffice it to emphasise two points. First, in so far as the defendants' contention rests on the basis that in cases relating to contracts of service declarations as to the subsistence of the contract or decrees for specific performance—which, as was pointed out in the next cited case, may well in certain instances amount in practice to the same thing—are never granted (a question to which I will return) it seems apposite to quote the words of Lord Morris of Borth-y-Gest in *Francis v Kuala Lumpur Councillors* [1962] 1 WLR 1411, 1417:

'In their Lordships' view, when there has been a purported termination of a contract of service a declaration to the effect that the contract of service still subsists will rarely be made. This is a consequence of the general principle of law that the courts will not grant specific performance of contracts of service. Special circumstances will be required before such a declaration is made and its making will normally be in the discretion of the court'.

I read that quotation as a recognition that in rare cases such declarations or decrees have been and may be granted, and thus stating the law with exactitude.

Secondly, contracts of service cannot be looked at in isolation. They are not the only category in which the successful performance of the contract depends on mutual co-operation or mutual confidence.

Accordingly, in my judgment the plaintiff is bound to establish at trial that the defendants' primary contention is wrong; that their repudiation of the relevant contract did not in this case terminate that contract in the absence of it being accepted; and that this contract will continue to subsist until the end of the period of any proper notice that the plaintiff may be given by the defendant company. Consequently he will in all probability be found entitled to relief in the shape of such injunctions or declarations as may be appropriate at the date judgment comes to be given . . . . .The real question is whether the court has power to grant and in its discretion should grant the particular remedy which is claimed by way of interlocutory relief in aid of maintaining the status quo ante till trial.

At one stage, it seemed that a challenge was being offered to the jurisdiction of the courts to grant an order of the nature sought by the plaintiff: but that suggestion was not pursued—it was bound to fail. Thus in essence the defendants' submission became one that in relation to contracts of service the practice that no such order should be made was so settled that it had by now become an inXexible rule of law which brooked no exceptions. In this behalf the previously mentioned general statements of law in a number of judgments were again relied upon—but the same answer applies as in the case of the primary contention that the contract itself could not subsist after the expiry of an unlawfully short notice. On an examination of the authorities the position in my judgment is that stated by Lord Denning M.R.: there is no such inflexibility.

It thus becomes relevant first to consider whether an order in the instant case would contravene the main grounds upon which it would be refused in the vast majority of master and servant cases. Foremost amongst the grounds given in Fry on *Specific*

Performance, 6th ed. (1921), p. 50 is that it is wrong to enforce a contract which needs personal confidence as between the parties when such confidence may not exist. Here such confidence does exist. Another ground is that common law damages normally provide an adequate remedy. Here they do not. It is well recognised that such cases can in practice arise as regards contracts of employment—hence the new 'compensation' provisions in the Industrial Relations Act 1971, which undoubtedly envisage that account should be taken of factors such as the employee's 'legitimate expectations for the future in [his] employment' (see the *Report of the Royal Commission on Trades Unions and Employers' Associations 1965–1968*, Cmnd. 3623, para. 553). For an instance of recognition that such damages can be inadequate, see the judgment of Jenkins L.J. in the *Vine* case [1956] 1 QB 658, 676. A further ground is often the difficulty of reinstatement when the plaintiff's post has been filled. That difficulty does not exist here.

Next one comes to the other previously mentioned factors introduced by the provisions of the Industrial Relations Act 1971 to which Brightman J. was not referred—and which in this particular case produce such an unusual situation.

Looking at the aggregate of the matters just recited it appears to me that this is indeed an exceptional case and that relief should be granted unless there is some good counter argument. For the defendants it was suggested that an order of the court, if made as claimed, would endanger industrial peace as between the defendant company and its employees. I decline to assume that either DATA as an entity or its individual members would in the highly unusual circumstances act in some way that would be unreasonable and incidentally detrimental to their long term interests—far less that they would seek to interfere with an order of the court.

Finally it was urged that any order made would run contrary to the policy or trend of previous practice. At the risk of reiterating views expressed in my judgments on other subject-matters, it seems appropriate to repeat that in matters of practice and discretion it is essential for the courts to take account of any important change in that climate of general opinion which is so hard to define but yet so plainly manifests itself from generation to generation. In that behalf account must, *inter alia*, be taken of the trend of the views of the legislature expressed on behalf of the community in its enactments and also of the trend of judicial decisions.

Over the last two decades there has been a marked trend towards shielding the employee, where practicable, from undue hardships he may suffer at the hands of those who may have power over his livelihood—employers and trade unions. So far has this now progressed and such is the security granted to an employee under the Industrial Relations Act 1971 that some have suggested that he may now be said to acquire something akin to a property in his employment. It surely is then for the courts to review and where appropriate to modify, if that becomes necessary, their rules of practice in relation to the exercise of a discretion such as we have today to consider—so that its practice conforms to the realities of the day.

It follows that in my judgment there exists no good reason against regarding the instant case as being one in which an order should be made as proposed: so I too would allow the appeal and make that order.

Since that decision in *Hill v CA Parsons*, in suitable cases, especially those seeking to enforce a disciplinary procedure, it has become accepted that a court may issue a pre-trial injunction against breach of the terms of the contract of employment. The following case illustrates the modern application of the principles.

[5.21] *Irani v Southampton and South West Hampshire Health Authority* **[1985] ICR 590 (ChD)**

The claimant, Mr. Irani, a part-time ophthalmologist, was dismissed by the employer following a quarrel with a full-time senior colleague, Mr Walker. The employer decided that the differences between the employees were such that they could no longer work together, and in the absence of alternative employment, the junior part-timer would have to go. Mr Irani brought an action for a declaration that the employer had failed to follow the disciplinary procedure contained in section 33 of the 'blue book' incorporated into his contract of employment and for an injunction restraining the defendants from implementing their decision to terminate the employment with notice without following the contractual procedure. The claimant then successfully sought an interlocutory injunction pending trial, giving an undertaking not to attend the relevant hospitals.

Warner J:

So the only question now is whether I should grant the interlocutory injunction sought by Mr Harwood-Stevenson on behalf of Mr Irani. I start with this, that Mr Clifford concedes that there is a triable issue as to whether, in the circumstances of this case and on a proper construction of the contract, the defendant failed to carry out some procedure that the contract required . . . .On the basis of that concession, Mr Harwood-Stevenson said that there were three reasons why damages would not be an adequate remedy for Mr Irani and why therefore I should grant an interlocutory injunction.

The first was that, if I did not grant an interlocutory injunction, it would be arguable, indeed eminently arguable, at the trial, that the judge could not grant a final injunction in the terms sought because the fact that the notice dated 8 June 1984 had taken effect, and that therefore Mr Irani's employment with the defendant authority was undoubtedly at an end, would mean that section 33 could no longer be operated in his case.

The second reason that Mr Harwood-Stevenson gave was that, if Mr Irani lost his appointment with the defendant authority, he would become unemployable in the National Health Service. In that respect he is supported by the evidence of Mr Coley who is the industrial relations officer of the British Medial Association for the Wessex region . . . . That is uncontradicted by any evidence on behalf of the defendant authority. Its evidence on this point is confined to saying that the authority itself would of course state to a prospective employer that it had no complaint about Mr Irani's conduct or about his professional competence. It would explain that he had been dismissed simply because of incompatibility with the consultant with whom he worked. But it is admitted on behalf of the defendant authority that it could not control what Mr Walker said in a telephone conversation with a colleague.

The third reason put forward by Mr Harwood-Stevenson why damages here would not be adequate remedy was that Mr Irani would thereby lose any right he has to use the facilities of the Lymington Hospital, which is a National Health hospital, to treat his private patients. There is a dispute as to whether in fact Mr Irani has any right to use those facilities for his private patients. But it appears to me to be a dispute of a kind such that it could only be resolved by a trial judge . . . .

I mentioned that Mr Clifford seeks to distinguish *Hill* v *C A Parsons & Co Ltd* [1972] Ch. 305 on the ground that it was a very exceptional case indeed. I find it helpful in that respect to refer to the judgment of *Megarry J* in *Chappell v Times Newspapers Ltd* [1975] ICR 145 (ChD), where he deals with the reasons why *Hill* v *C A Parsons & Co Ltd* [1972] Ch 305 was such an exceptional case. He says, at p 159:

'There were three main grounds for this decision. First, there was still complete confidence between employer and employee: the defendant did not want to terminate the plaintiff's employment but had been coerced by the union. Second, the Industrial Relations Act 1971 was expected to come into force shortly: it had been passed but the relevant parts had not been brought into operation. As soon as the Act was in force, one probable result would be that the closed shop would no longer be enforceable and the plaintiff would be free to remain a member of the union of his choice. He would also obtain the rights conferred by the Act to compensation for unfair dismissal if he was then dismissed. Third, in the circumstances of the case damages would not be an adequate remedy'.

I will take those three reasons *seriatim* and, in relation to each, compare the situation. First:

'complete confidence between employer and employee: the defendant did not want to terminate the plaintiff's employment but had been coerced by the union'.

I have already mentioned the fact that the defendant authority here makes no complaint as to or criticism of Mr Irani's conduct or professional competence . . . . I think the true position here is that the defendant authority would be willing to continue to employ Mr Irani were it not for the fact that they are convinced that his and Mr Walker's continued employment are incompatible . . . [I]t remains the fact that the defendant authority has perfect faith in the honesty, integrity and loyalty of Mr Irani.

Turning to Megarry J's second reason for the decision in the *Parsons* case, it seems to me that there is a comparable reason here. In the *Parsons* case, Mr Hill was seeking the protection of the Industrial Relations Act 1971. Here Mr Irani is seeking the protection of section 33 of the blue book to which he is entitled is the circumstances are appropriate.

Thirdly, as Mr Harwood-Stevenson has pointed out, this is a case—and I anticipate now on what I shall have to say in a moment about some subsidiary submissions of Mr Clifford—where damages would not be an adequate remedy.

If I were to decline to grant the injunction sought by Mr Harwood-Stevenson, I would in effect be holding that, without doubt, an authority in the position of the defendant is entitled to snap its fingers at the rights of its employees under the blue book. Indeed, that is what Mr Clifford invited me to hold. He invites me to hold that, despite the existence in the blue book of sections 33 and 40, a health authority is entitled to dismiss a medical practitioner summarily and to say that, if and insofar as his rights under those sections are infringed, his remedy lies in damages only . . . In his subsidiary, he took issue with Mr Harwood-Stevenson on the latter's grounds for saying that in this case damages would not be an adequate remedy. As to the point made by Mr Harwood-Stevenson on the basis of Mr Coley's evidence that, if dismissed by the defendant, Mr Irani will never again be able to secure employment in the National Health Service, Mr Clifford said that if, at the trial, Mr Irani could show that he was entitled to the benefit of section 33 and that, as a result of the action of the defendant authority, he never could again obtain employment within the National Health Service, damages could be assessed. Similarly, he said that if Mr Irani could show at the trial that he was indeed entitled to treat private patients in the Lymington hospital and that, because of the action of the defendant authority, he had been deprived of that right, again damages could be assessed.

I do not myself find those submissions very convincing, any more than I find convincing Mr Clifford's further submission that Mr Irani ought to put to the test his ability to obtain employment elsewhere in the National Health Service. (Mr Clifford pointed out in that connection that Mr Irani also works in London). Mr Clifford conceded, however that, whatever might be the answers to those points, he had no answer, if he was wrong—as I have held—in his primary submission, to the point made by Mr

Harwood-Stevenson that, if no injunction issued now, it was very possible that at the trial it would be too late for Mr Irani to rely on section 33 because he would by then have ceased to be an employee of the defendant authority.

I accordingly propose to grant the injunction sought by Mr Harwood-Stevenson.

This decision suggests that employees have a good chance of success in obtaining interlocutory injunctions against dismissals in breach of express contractual procedures, provided that the employee makes suitable undertakings to avoid any deleterious effects to the employer's operations. If the employee can demonstrate a serious question to be tried that the employer has broken the disciplinary procedure, the balance of convenience usually favours the interlocutory injunction. The same reasoning can be applied to a procedure for selection for redundancy: the employer can be held by injunction to a contractual agreement to operate a particular procedure, for despite the inconvenience to the employer of having to conform to the agreement, the balance of convenience favours the employee who is about to lose his job (see *Anderson v Pringle of Scotland Ltd* [1988] IRLR 64 (Ct of Sess, Outer House)).

The traditional objections to permanent injunctions seem to have little force. The employee can meet the point about the breakdown of trust and confidence by demonstrating, as in *Irani* (and also *Powell v Brent London Borough Council* [1988] ICR 176 (CA)), that there had been no breakdown between employer and employee. Alternatively, the employee can meet the objection based upon a breakdown of trust and confidence by confining the claim to an order for the contractual disciplinary procedure to be carried out without continuing performance of work. In *Jones v Gwent CC*, ([5.16] above), the court issued an injunction forbidding the employer to take any further action in respect of its purported dismissal, and a further injunction pending full trial of the matter restraining the employer from dismissing the employee without following the proper procedure. With respect to the adequacy of damages, there is a recognition by the courts that damages for wrongful dismissal are not generous and that they may fail to compensate for many types of remote losses. In *Irani*'s case, the claimant was concerned about effective exclusion from employment in the National Health Service, the major employer in his profession. In *Robb v London Borough of Hammersmith and Fulham* [1991] IRLR 72 (QB), damages were held to be an inadequate remedy because they would not compensate the plaintiff for the manner of his dismissal and his deprivation of the opportunity to ventilate his case and justify himself under the contractual disciplinary procedure.

5.1.3 The revival of the common law

Our examination of the common law of wrongful dismissal has revealed that many of the assumptions which led to the introduction of a statutory right to claim unfair dismissal proved to be only partially true. Compensation for wrongful dismissal is not necessarily derisory. Substantial damages may be awarded either where the employee is entitled to a lengthy notice period, is protected by either a disciplinary procedure or substantive constraints on the discretion to dismiss, or where dismissal causes the loss of valuable fringe benefits. The success of claims for interlocutory injunctions also reveals that in some instances the common law has the capacity to protect the employee's expectations of job security based upon the terms of the contract of employment.

For the most part, these changes in the common law position did not require the introduction of new principles of law, but merely the application of the ordinary law of contract. The crucial change was rather in the content of the contract of employment, which became in the second half of the twentieth century a more elaborate transaction better suited to the development of internal labour markets. Once the employer's undertakings designed to secure improved co-operation from the workforce had been rendered explicit in staff handbooks and incorporated as terms into the contract of employment, the law of contract could be used to prevent the employer from reneging on those undertakings. The effectiveness of the common law in controlling the abuse of disciplinary power always remains contingent on the content of the standards agreed between the parties in the contract of employment. Once these standards offer precise procedural or substantive protections for job security, however, the common law has the capacity to forge remedies of compensation or specific relief to deter opportunist breaches of those standards.

As a practical matter, however, a common law claim has in the past been perceived as more complex and expensive than the pursuit of a claim for unfair dismissal before an employment tribunal. The employee had to commence proceedings in the ordinary courts, often being restricted to the High Court in view of the magnitude of the claim or the remedy sought. To some extent this procedural obstacle has been reduced by the grant of jurisdiction to employment tribunals to hear claims for damages or any other sum arising from a breach of contract or is outstanding on the termination of the employee's employment. But their jurisdiction does not include claims for specific relief, nor does it include claims for breaches of contractual terms relating to intellectual property rights and covenants in restraint of trade. Nor does the jurisdiction extend to claims for personal injuries, which includes claims for psychiatric illness caused by the employer's conduct. Employment tribunals are also limited in the amount of compensation they can award with respect to these common law claims for breach of contract to £25,000. (Employment Tribunals Act 1996; Employment Tribunals Extension of Jurisdiction (England and Wales) Order 1994). By adding the common law claim to a claim for unfair dismissal, however, a dismissed employee can use one set of legal proceedings in order to recover all potential heads of compensation.

The noticeable absence in this development in the common law has been the forging of implied substantive or further procedural limits upon the power to dismiss employees. In other countries, the general principles of contract law have been the source of implied limitations. We have noted already that in the USA, for instance, many states have recognised an implied term not to terminate a contract in bad faith, a principle of commercial contracts, which has been applied to dismissals. Another principle recognised by many states is that it may constitute a tort to dismiss someone for reasons contrary to public policy. In civil law jurisdictions, it is possible to use a similar good faith principle and also to prevent 'abuse of rights', such as the arbitrary or opportunist use of the legal right to dismiss an employee. The outstanding question is whether English common law is poised to develop such a principle, perhaps in this case using the implied term of mutual trust and confidence, or one of good faith. A crucial difficulty will be to reconcile such a principle with the accepted doctrine that an employer is entitled, subject to express terms of the contract, to terminate the contract for any reason provided due notice is given. In *Johnson v Unisys Ltd* (**[5.6]** above), the House of Lords apparently blocked the possibility of the evolution of the common law towards a principle of fairness in termination of contracts. Yet that decision has been strongly criticised both on the ground that it creates the need for the untenable distinctions drawn in *Eastwood v Magnox Electric plc* (**[5.12]** above), and that the decision was made on the false assumption that the statutory claim for unfair dismissal covered all the grounds of the complaint against the employer including the possibility of claiming damages for losses caused by psychiatric illness and damages for the shock and humiliation caused by the unfair manner of dismissal. Unless Parliament intervenes to broaden the possible grounds for compensation in claims for unfair dismissal and to remove the upper limit on compensation, the common law courts will face constant pressure to reconsider or qualify the decision in *Johnson v Unisys Ltd*, so that employees may receive adequate compensation for all their losses flowing from the employer's fundamental breach of contract.

5.2 Statutory concept of dismissal

The statutory claim for unfair dismissal was introduced in 1971. The details of the legal rights now consolidated in the Employment Rights Act 1996 have been altered frequently, but the structure and core principles have remained constant. The general objective of the legislation is to provide mandatory standards to control the employer's exercise of the discretionary power of dismissal. These standards are described by a general concept of fairness, which has to be interpreted and applied to particular cases by an employment tribunal. The standards are mandatory, so that in principle they cannot be excluded by contrary agreement. The enforcement mechanism is usually a claim for compensation brought by the dismissed employee. The statutory claim therefore imitates the common law to the extent that it envisages that employees will enforce the standards, but differs because the standards are not fixed by the contractual agreement but rather by the tribunal's interpretation of the law. Since its inception, the law of unfair dismissal has provided the bulk of litigation in the field of employment relations. Nearly every statutory provision has been subjected to close inspection and rival interpretations. As an introduction to the study of this topic, we consider some key legal issues.

A first group of issues goes to the jurisdiction of the tribunals. We focus attention on the concept of dismissal, the ability of employees to contract out of statutory rights, and the statutory exclusions from the rights. These jurisdictional issues are important because they fix the limits of mandatory regulation and determine the scope for flexibility in standards. The second main topic is the interpretation placed on the general concept of fairness by the tribunals. Here the principal question is how far these interpretations have articulated a coherent and justifiable limitation on the employer's power to dismiss workers. The third topic examines the remedies provided to employees under the legislation with a view to an assessment of whether these remedies are adequate to achieve efficient levels of compliance with the standards.

For the purpose of bringing a statutory claim for unfair dismissal or redundancy, the employee must demonstrate that a dismissal has occurred. This concept of dismissal has a statutory definition, which differs from the common law's notion of termination of the contract of employment.

[5.22] Employment Rights Act 1996, section 95

95 **(1)** For the purposes of this Part an employee is dismissed by his employer if (and, subject to subsection (2) and section 96, only if)—
  (a) the contract under which he is employed is terminated by the employer (whether with or without notice),
  (b) he is employed under a limited-term contract and that contract terminates by virtue of the limiting event without being renewed under the same contract, or
  (c) the employee terminates the contract under which he is employed (with or without notice) in circumstances in which he is entitled to terminate it without notice by reason of the employer's conduct.

The objective of this statutory definition is to exclude claims for compensation in certain cases of termination of employment. The principal exclusion is intended to comprise the case where the employee resigns voluntarily. In order to achieve this objective, the statute includes as part of the concept of dismissal not only the case where the employer initiates termination either by notice or summary dismissal, but also the two additional situations of the expiry of a limited-term contract and forced resignation (known as constructive dismissal: below 5.2.2.). A limited-term contract is one not intended to be permanent and provision is made in the contract for it to terminate at the expiration of a period of time (a fixed-term contract), or on the completion of the performance of a specific task, or on the occurrence of an event when that event happens: ERA 1996 section 235(2A)(2B). This expanded concept of dismissal is also required in order to block possible attempts by the employer to avoid the legislation. If the expiry of fixed-term contracts did not count as dismissals, employers could place all employees on short fixed-term contracts and simply permit them to expire without renewal if the employer wanted to effect a dismissal. Similarly, if constructive dismissal were not included within the statutory definition, employers could avoid a statutory claim by refraining from outright dismissal, and instead making the employment relation intolerable through actions such as reducing wages, increasing hours, and augmenting responsibilities, thereby compelling the employee to resign.

We now consider in greater detail the contrast between dismissal and resignation, and the concept of constructive dismissal. The section concludes with an evaluation of the application of the doctrine of frustration to contracts of employment.

5.2.1 Dismissal or resignation?

The statute defines the principal example of dismissal to include termination of the contract initiated by the employer either with notice or summarily. This definition departs from the elective theory of termination, for it holds that the contract may be terminated unilaterally by summary dismissal, whether or not the summary dismissal was justified. The crucial question under this first limb of the statutory definition is whether the employer initiated the dismissal or whether the employee in fact resigned. On its face, the statute poses a question of fact and causation. The issue is whose actions initiated the termination of the contract, or simply 'Who really terminated the contract of employment?': *Martin v MBS Fastenings (Glynwed) Distribution Ltd* [1983] IRLR 198, 201 (CA). Although the courts have emphasised that this issue is primarily a question of fact for the tribunal, this stance is misleading. The issue slides into broader issues of attribution of responsibility, which ask who should be held responsible for termination.

This broadening of the enquiry occurs for three reasons. First, there are no formalities which require dismissals or resignations to be carried out in a particular way such as in writing. An employee can request a written statement of the employer's reasons for dismissal: ERA 1996, section 92, and the employer's failure to comply can result in an award of compensation equal to two weeks' pay: ERA 1996, section 93. But no formality is required to effect the dismissal itself. Under the ordinary law of termination of contracts, termination can be initiated by both express statements and conduct which is held to evince an intention no longer to be bound by the contract. The interpretation of this evidence provides the opportunity for tribunals to expand the scope of the enquiry towards the dimension of responsibility. The approach applies an objective test to words and conduct, having regard to all the circumstances, so that the employee's actual intention is not decisive. The test is 'whether a reasonable employer or employee might have understood the words to be tantamount to dismissal or resignation': *J & J Stern v Simpson* [1983] IRLR 52, 53 (CA).

Secondly, the ordinary law looks for a precise moment for the initiation of the termination, a repudiatory breach of contract, but in the repetitive contact required by the employment relation there is rarely a single moment in which it is absolutely clear that one party has initiated termination. Instead, we find a breakdown of relations over a period of time and ambiguous statements indicating that the employment relation is likely to end. Indeed, careful and considerate personnel management, when confronted with a disciplinary issue, is likely to produce initially cautious statements such as: 'It may be in your best interests to resign rather than face a disciplinary enquiry': *Martin v MBS Fastenings (Glynwed) Distribution Ltd* [1983] IRLR 198 (CA). There have been suggestions that unambiguous statements of dismissal or resignation should be always interpreted as initiating termination of employment, but in fact tribunals must always consider the context of the statements in order to judge their intended meaning, their reception, and whether it would be reasonable for the other party to act on them. Even apparently clear statements, such as 'I am resigning' (*Sothern v Franks Charlesly & Co* [1981] IRLR 278 (CA)), must be viewed in context in order to comprehend whether they should be regarded as an assumption of responsibility for commencing the termination of the contract.

Thirdly, the personal relations often involved in employment relations sometimes cause dismissals and resignations to take place in the context of heated disagreements and abusive language. The language may be explicit on such occasions, such as 'Go, get out, get out' (*J & J Stern v Simpson* [1983] IRLR 52 (CA)), but whether this statement really amounts to a dismissal may have to be established by reference to subsequent conduct and the general context of the statement. Tribunals are reluctant to conclude that statements uttered in the heat of the moment should be treated at face value, even though in a commercial context such statements would inevitably indicate repudiation of the contract. Tribunals have gone so far as to suggest that good personnel relations management should require employers 'not to accept resignations made in the heat of the moment too readily, but to check clearly that that is the true intention of the employee and to inquire when matters are clearer and calmer'. But these remarks of an employment tribunal were rejected on appeal in the following case on the ground that they could not be reconciled with the legal test for initiating termination by repudiation.

[5.23] *Kwik-Fit (GB) Ltd v Lineham* [1992] ICR 183 (EAT)

The claimant had succeeded before an Employment Tribunal in a claim for unfair dismissal, but the employers appealed on the ground that he had not been dismissed. Mr Lineham was manager of a depot, where he sometimes worked unpaid very late. He was responsible for security and locking up. One night on the way home from the pub he stopped at the depot to use the toilet. His employers learned of this late night entry and issued him with a final written warning in front of other staff. Being angry, upset and humiliated, there was a further altercation, and Mr Lineham threw his keys down on the counter and drove off. The following day he telephoned the company, asked for his wages, and told the employer's manager, Mr Kattner, that he was going to a tribunal.

Wood J:

Let us first look at the problem from the approach of sound management. As we have said, the industrial members take the view that the way in which this Industrial Tribunal have expressed themselves puts too high a burden upon employers. If words of resignation are unambiguous then prima facie an employer is entitled to treat them as such, but in the field of employment, personalities constitute an important consideration. Words may be spoken or actions expressed in temper or in the heat of the moment or under extreme pressure ('being jostled into a decision') and indeed the intellectual make-up of an employee may be relevant . . . These we refer to as 'special circumstances'. Where 'special circumstances' arise it may be unreasonable for an employer to assume a resignation and to accept it forthwith. A reasonable period of time should be allowed to lapse and if circumstances arise during that period which put the employer on notice that further enquiry is desirable to see whether the resignation was really intended and can properly be assumed, then such enquiry is ignored at the employer's risk. He runs the risk that ultimately evidence may be forthcoming which indicates that in the 'special circumstances' the intention to resign was not the correct interpretation when the facts are judged objectively.

How then is that approach to be reconciled in law? This is not a purely commercial context. In the sphere of industrial relations these special circumstances may arise due to those conflicts of personalities or individual characteristics. A resignation by an employee is a repudiation of the contract of employment, a fundamental breach. It should be accepted by the employer within a reasonable time (see *Western Excavating (ECC) v Sharp* [1978] IRLR 27 CA, per Lord Denning at p 29, 15; see also *London Transport Executive v Clarke* [1981] IRLR 166(CA)). In many cases the acceptance will be by inference. Thus where words or actions are prima facie unambiguous, an employer is entitled to accept the repudiation at its face value at once, unless these special circumstances exist, in which case he should allow a reasonable time to elapse during which facts may arise which cast doubt upon that prima facie interpretation of the unambiguous words or action. If he does not investigate these facts, a Tribunal may hold him disentitled to assume that the words or actions did amount to a resignation, although—to paraphrase the words of May LJ—Tribunals should not be astute so to find.

One then asks, what is that reasonable period of time? It may be very short—*Martin v MBS Fastenings (Glynwed) Distribution Ltd* [1983] IRLR 198 (CA). It may be over a weekend—*Barclay v City of Glasgow District Council* [1983] IRLR 313. The test is objective and one of reasonableness. It is only likely to be relatively short, a day or two, and it will almost certainly be the conduct of the employee which becomes relevant, but not necessarily so.

How then should this approach to the law be applied in the present case? Unless there are sufficient findings of fact upon which we can decide that if the Tribunal had directed itself as we think it should, the result would have been the same, it is our duty to remit this matter for a further hearing.

We have no notes of evidence. The only finding of fact, which was common ground, from the telephone conversation between the applicant and Mr Kattner on 17 October, was that the applicant was going to take Kwik-Fit to an Industrial Tribunal for unfair dismissal. Thereafter Mr Kattner was sufficiently dissatisfied with the situation to make further enquiries. Thirdly, in the subsequent telephone conversation, there was talk of an appeal and the repeated declaration by the applicant of an intent to go to an Industrial Tribunal. Although there had been mention of an appeal, there is no finding about this. The Industrial Tribunal say:

> ' . . . It is not in issue that on that occasion Mr Kattner raised the question of the applicant's right to appeal against the decision. It is not clear precisely what he was appealing against, the written warning or the dismissal or what, but the applicant was not interested, saying that he would sooner let the Industrial Tribunal decide the matter. The applicant told us in evidence that he did not think that it was worth appealing'.

It is therefore possible for us to accept that this Tribunal found first that on 17 October, there was mention of dismissal and going to the Industrial Tribunal; secondly, that there was an offer of an appeal which was rejected and the intention of going to an Industrial Tribunal repeated. By its decision, the Tribunal clearly felt that these facts required further enquiry before Kwik-Fit was entitled to assume that the actions of 16 October could properly be assumed to amount to a resignation and that in fact it was not the correct assumption. It was, of course, open to them to find that the applicant had simply refused to discuss the matter further or give any explanation, but the Tribunal did not so find. Having seen and heard the witnesses, the Tribunal found as it did in the latter part of paragraph 14 of the decision.

Not without considerable hesitation, we are prepared to accept that on the present findings of fact and upon the proper direction of law as we have understood it, this Industrial Tribunal would have reached the same conclusion, namely that the applicant had been unfairly dismissed in that Kwik-Fit was not entitled to assume in all the circumstances that what occurred on 16 October was in fact a resignation.

We are content that that should be so, because in the circumstances of this case and on the basis of the evidence available to us, the industrial members—and I agree with them—take the view that this applicant was dealt with unfairly.

Appeal dismissed.

This reasoning reveals how the courts try to reconcile the ordinary law of termination of contracts with the special continuing and personal nature of contracts of employment. In so doing, the decision strays into issues of the allocation of responsibility for the termination of employment. In other words, the crucial factor at the end of the reasoning appears to be that Mr Lineham deserved to win his claim, because he had been dealt with unfairly, and that therefore the EAT was prepared to uphold the tribunal's decision in the teeth of the facts supporting the employer's contention that the employee had unambiguously quit.

5.2.2 Constructive dismissal

The way in which the interpretation and application of the statutory concept of dismissal become embroiled in issues of responsibility becomes even more apparent in the context of constructive dismissal under the third limb of the statutory definition. On the facts of these cases of constructive dismissal, it is plain that the employee initiated the termination of employment by resignation. The question before the tribunal is whether in the circumstances of the case the employee was entitled to resign in response to the employer's conduct, with the consequence that the resignation can be deemed to have been a dismissal for the purposes of a statutory claim under ERA 1996, section 95(1)(c).

[5.24] *Western Excavating (ECC) Ltd v Sharp* **[1978] ICR 221 (CA)**

Mr Sharp was suspended without pay for five days for absence without permission. This loss of income placed him in difficult financial circumstances. The employer's welfare officer refused either to grant him a loan or to take holiday pay unless a holiday was in fact taken. The employee decided to leave, so that he could collect his holiday pay immediately. He claimed unfair dismissal. The principal question was whether the employee could claim to have been constructively dismissed.

Lord Denning MR:
Mr. Sharp was only employed by the China-Clay Co. for 20 months. He left of his own accord. Yet he has been awarded £658 as compensation for unfair dismissal. There seems something wrong about that award. What is it? . . .

The industrial tribunal were divided in opinion. Two of them thought the employee had been unfairly dismissed and that he should be awarded £658. They said that the company 'ought to have leant over backwards' to help him and that the company's conduct 'justified the employee in terminating his employment in order to obtain his accrued holiday pay, and so to meet his commitments.' The third member disagreed. He thought that the employee ought to have talked to the welfare officer again.

[ERA 1996, section 95(1)(c)] has given rise to a vast body of case law as to what comes within it. It is spoken of as 'constructive dismissal.' It has given rise to a problem upon which there has been a diversity of views among chairmen of industrial tribunals and among the judges of the Employment Appeal Tribunal . . . It is with diffidence that we approach the task. The rival tests are as follows.

The contract test
On the one hand, it is said that the words of [ERA 1996, section 95(1)(c)] express a legal concept which is already well settled in the books on contract under the rubric 'discharge by breach.' If the employer is guilty of conduct which is a significant breach going to the root of the contract of employment, or which shows that the employer no longer intends to be bound by one or more of the essential terms of the contract, then the employee is entitled to treat himself as discharged from any further performance. If he does so, then he terminates the contract by reason of the employer's conduct. He is constructively dismissed. The employee is entitled in those circumstances to leave at the instant without giving any notice at all or, alternatively, he may give notice and say he is leaving at the end of the notice. But the conduct must in either case be sufficiently serious to entitle him to leave at once. Moreover, he must make up his mind soon after the conduct of which he complains: for, if he continues for any length of time without leaving, he will lose his right to treat himself as discharged. He will be regarded as having elected to affirm the contract.

The unreasonableness test
On the other hand, it is said that the words of [ERA 1996, section 95(1)(c)] do not express any settled legal concept. They introduce a new concept into contracts of employment. It is that the employer must act reasonably in his treatment of his employees. If he conducts himself or his affairs so unreasonably that the employee cannot fairly be expected to put up with it any longer, the employee is justified in leaving. He can go, with or without giving notice, and claim compensation for unfair dismissal.

Those who adopt the unreasonableness test for dismissal say quite frankly that it is the same as the 'unreasonableness' test for fairness. That was the view taken by Megaw L.J. in *Turner v London Transport Executive* [1977] ICR 952, 964 (CA). He said:

'So far as (c) is concerned, in my judgment, the wording of this subparagraph is not a wording which involves, or implies, the same concept as the common law concept of fundamental breach of a contract resulting in its unilateral repudiation and acceptance of that unilateral repudiation by the innocent party. The employer's "conduct" here is employer's conduct to be adjudged by the industrial tribunal by the criteria which they regard as right and fair in respect of a case in which the issue is whether or not there has been "unfair" dismissal'.

The result
In my opinion, the contract test is the right test. My reasons are as follows. (i) The statute itself draws a distinction between 'dismissal' in [ERA, section 95(1)(c)] and 'unfairness' in [ERA, section 98(4)]. If Parliament intended that same test to apply, it would have said so. (ii) 'Dismissal' in [ERA, section 95(1)] goes back to 'dismissal' in the Redundancy Payments Act 1965. Its interpretation should not be influenced by [ERA, section 98(4)] which was introduced first in 1971 in the Industrial Relations Act 1971. (iii) [ERA, section 95(1)(c)] uses words which have a legal connotation, especially the words 'entitled' and 'without notice.' If a non-legal connotation were intended, it would have added 'justified in leaving at once' or some such non-legal phrase. (iv) [ERA, section 95(1)(a) and (c)] deal with different situations. [ERA, section 95(1)(a)] deals with cases where the employer himself terminates the contract by dismissing the man with or without notice. That is, when the employer says to the man: 'You must go.' [ERA s. 95(1)(c)] deals with the cases where the employee himself terminates the contract by saying: 'I can't stand it any longer. I want my cards.' (v) The new test of 'unreasonable conduct' of the employer is too

indefinite by far. It has led to acute difference of opinion between the members of tribunals. Often there are majority opinions. It has led to findings of 'constructive dismissal' on the most whimsical grounds. The Employment Appeal Tribunal tells us so. It is better to have the contract test of the common law. It is more certain: as it can well be understood by intelligent laymen under the direction of a legal chairman. (vi) I would adopt the reasoning of the considered judgment of the Employment Appeal Tribunal *in Wetherall (Bond St. W1) Ltd. v Lynn* [1978] ICR 205, 211:

> 'Parliament might well have said, in relation to whether the employer's conduct had been reasonable having regard to equity and the substantial merits of the case, but it neither laid down that special statutory criterion or any other. So, in our judgment, the answer can only be, entitled according to law, and it is to the law of contract that you have to look'.

(vii) The test of unreasonableness gives no effect to the words 'without notice.' They impose a legal test which no test of 'unreasonableness' can do.

Conclusion

The present case is a good illustration of a 'whimsical decision.' Applying the test of 'unreasonable conduct', the industrial tribunal decided by a majority of two to one in favour of the employee. All three members of the Employment Appeal Tribunal would have decided in favour of the employers, but felt that it was a matter of fact on which they could not reverse the industrial tribunal. So counting heads, it was four to two in favour of the employers, but yet the case was decided against them—because of the test of 'unreasonable conduct'.

If the contract test had been applied, the result would have been plain, There was no dismissal, constructive or otherwise, by the employers. The employers were not in breach at all. Nor had they repudiated the contract at all. The employee left of his own accord without anything wrong done by the employers. His claim should have been rejected. The decision against the employers was most unjust to them. I would allow the appeal, accordingly.

The effect of the adoption of the contract test is that tribunals must establish whether the employer was in breach of a fundamental term of the contract. This enquiry is similar to the issues posed at common law in cases of justified summary dismissal, but here the tribunal tackles the obverse situation. Instead of the question being whether the employee has broken a fundamental term of the contract of employment, the issue is whether the employer has broken a fundamental term.

The employer may commit a fundamental breach of contract by breaking either an express or an implied term of the contract. For express terms, the term must represent a fundamental or basic obligation established by the contract, such as the obligation to pay contractually agreed wages or to employ the employee in a particular job. For implied terms as well, the obligation must be one which is regarded as essential to the contract. In this context, the implied term that the employer should not do anything likely to destroy the relationship of trust and confidence became the key implied obligation that governed the boundaries of constructive dismissal. A breach of this term may be constituted either by a single event or a series of relatively minor instances of harsh or unfair treatment.

[5.25] *Lewis v Motorworld Garages Ltd* **[1986] ICR 157, 167, (CA)**

Neill LJ:
[I]t is now established that the repudiatory conduct may consist of a series of acts or incidents, some of them perhaps quite trivial, which cumulatively amount to a repudiatory breach of the implied term of the contract of employment that the employer will not, without reasonable and proper cause, conduct himself in a manner calculated or likely to destroy or seriously damage the relationship of confidence and trust between employer and employee . . .

The courts were attracted to this formulation of a general implied term, because it represents a mirror image of the employee's obligation to preserve trust and confidence. The decision in *The Post Office v Roberts* [1980] IRLR 347 (EAT) (above **[2.27]**) describes how the tribunals used this implied term to regulate harsh exercises of management discretion. But the test itself provides little guidance to tribunals on how to determine cases of alleged constructive dismissal that do not involve a breach of an express term of the contract. That rather undermines the supposed certainty of the contractual approach, which it was suggested would avoid 'whimsical decisions'.

[5.26] *Woods v WM Car Services (Peterborough) Ltd* **[1982] ICR 693 (CA)**

The employer had purchased a garage business and retained the existing staff, including the appellant, who was described as 'Chief Secretary and Accounts Clerk'. The new owners thought that she was paid too much. They tried to persuade her to accept less money or to work longer hours, but withdrew the suggestion when she objected strongly and went to solicitors. As part of a general reorganisation of the business, the new owners then suggested further changes to her duties and job title. The employee rejected all these changes. Realising that the employers were going to insist upon changes, on advice from her solicitor, she resigned and claimed constructive dismissal. The relations had become extremely acrimonious and as Lord Denning MR observed, 'All trust and confidence was lost on both sides' (696). The tribunal decided, however, that there had not been a constructive dismissal.

Lord Denning MR:
The appeal
Mrs Woods appealed to the appeal tribunal. The appeal lies only on a question of law: see [Employment Tribunals Act 1996, section 21]. Again the incidents were canvassed in detail. Left to themselves, the appeal tribunal would have reversed the industrial tribunal. But they felt bound by a recent decision in this court (*Pedersen v Camden London Borough Council (Note)* [1981] ICR 674(CA)) to dismiss the appeal: see [1981] ICR 666 (EAT). They said they would like guidance. So they gave leave to appeal to this court.

A useful parallel
Over the weekend I have found a useful parallel. It is in the cases in the old days about wrongful dismissal. Often enough a servant was employed for a time and was dismissed by his employer at a moment's notice. He was given 'the sack' (old parlance) meaning the bag in which he kept his tools. He brought an action for wrongful dismissal. The master pleaded in defence simply that 'the plaintiff misconducted himself in the said service' giving particulars of the misconduct: see *Bullen & Leake's Precedents of Pleadings*. 3rd ed. (1868), p. 650. This plea was based on the simple proposition that it was the duty of the servant to give good and faithful service: and that he had been guilty of misconduct of so

serious a kind that it justified his dismissal. In modern terminology, he had been guilty of a repudiatory breach. The judges refused to lay down any general rule as to what causes would justify the dismissal of a servant. They left it to the jury: often with a hint as to what they thought the result should be, as Pollock CB did in *Horton v McMurtry* (1860) 5 H&N 667, 678:

'Gentlemen, I believe it is for you to decide whether this was a proper ground of dismissal—but if it be a matter of law . . . my opinion is that it is a good ground of dismissal'.

The jury found for the defendant.

Once the jury had decided the matter, that was the end of it. It was for the jury to decide the nature and extent of the misconduct and whether it justified dismissal or not. Their decision would not be interfered with by the Court of Appeal, so long as there was evidence to support it . . .

Our modern cases

Now under modern legislation we have the converse case. It is the duty of the employer to be good and considerate to his servants. Sometimes it is formulated as an implied term not to do anything likely to destroy the relationship of confidence between them: see *Courtaulds Northern Textiles Ltd v Andrew* [1979] IRLR 84(EAT). But I prefer to look at it in this way: the employer must be good and considerate to his servants. Just as a servant must be good and faithful, so an employer must be good and considerate. Just as in the old days an employee could be guilty of misconduct justifying his dismissal, so in modern times and employer can be guilty of misconduct justifying the employee in leaving at once without notice. In each case it depends on whether the misconduct amounted to a repudiatory breach as defined in *Western Excavating (ECC) Ltd v Sharp* [1978] ICR 221(CA).

The circumstances are so infinitely various that there can be, and is, no rule of law saying what circumstances justify and what do not. It is a question of fact for the tribunal of fact—in this case the industrial tribunal. Once they come to their decision, the appeal tribunal should not interfere with it. Thus when the manager told a man: 'You can't do the bloody job anyway', that would ordinarily not be sufficient to justify the man in leaving at once. It would be on a par with the trenchant criticism which goes on every day. But if the manager used those words dishonestly and maliciously—with no belief in their truth—in order to get rid of him, then it might be sufficient; because it would evince an intention no longer to be bound by the contract. At any rate an industrial tribunal so held in *Courtaulds Northern Textiles Ltd v Andrew* [1979] IRLR 84 and the appeal tribunal did not interfere with it.

In our present case the appeal tribunal have presented to us a problem similar to that which faced the Privy Council (in the converse case) in *Clouston & Co Ltd v Corry* [1906] AC 122. The facts are not in dispute. The question is whether on those facts the conduct of the employers was such as to justify the employee in leaving at once without notice. The industrial tribunal found all the facts and then stated their conclusion in this way:

'It is clear to us, as we said earlier in this decision, that relations between the applicant and Mr King on behalf of the respondents, had become strained but we are not satisfied that the applicant has shown us that the employers had been guilty of conduct which entitled her to terminate her contract. Our unanimous decision therefore is that she was not dismissed by the respondents'.

The appeal tribunal disagreed with this conclusion. They made it clear that, if it were open to them, they would have reversed the decision of the industrial tribunal. They said [1981] ICR 666, 674:

'They have reached a conclusion which, although we do not agree with it, cannot be termed impossible or perverse in the sense that no reasonable man could have reached that conclusion. If this is the right approach (and it is a point on which we would value further guidance from the Court of Appeal) it seems to us inescapable that we have no jurisdiction to alter the industrial tribunal's decision even though we consider it to be wrong'.

Conclusion
In the result I think that the appeal tribunal in these cases of constructive dismissal should only interfere with the decision of the industrial tribunal if it is shown that (i) the industrial tribunal misdirected itself in law, or (ii) the decision was such that no reasonable industrial tribunal could reach it. The appeal tribunal ought not to interfere merely because it thinks that upon those facts it would not or might not itself have reached the same conclusion, for to do that would be for the appeal tribunal to usurp what is the sole function of the tribunal of fact.

Applying this principle, I am clearly of opinion that the appeal tribunal had no jurisdiction to interfere with the decision of the industrial tribunal. They were quite right to dismiss the appeal. I would dismiss the appeal also.

I hope that this may lead to the shortening of the hearings before the industrial tribunals and the length of their reasons. At any rate it should reduce the number of appeals to the appeal tribunal.

[*The other members of the Court of Appeal agreed with these principles.*]
Watkins LJ:
The obdurate refusal of the employee to accept conditions very properly and sensibly being sought to be imposed upon her was unreasonable. Employers must not, in my opinion, be put in a position where, through wrongful refusal of their employees to accept change, they are prevented from introducing improved business methods in furtherance of seeking success for their enterprise.

It becomes plain in this reasoning that the issue whether there has been a constructive dismissal is not confined to a narrow enquiry about breach of contract. The broader question of who was responsible for the termination of the employment is crucial in determining whether the employer has broken the implied term of preserving the relation of trust and confidence. In the *Woods* case, the employers had made a series of suggestions for variation of the contract, including effective demotion and reduced pay, which pattern might normally indicate an intentional destruction of the relationship of trust and confidence. Yet the Court of Appeal was unwilling to interfere with the finding of the tribunal against constructive dismissal, no doubt because it viewed the conduct of the employee in objecting to all changes as unreasonable. Questions of fault and responsibility therefore creep in under the guise of determining whether or not the employer breached the implied term of trust and confidence.

The *Woods* case is also important for affirming that the question whether the employer has committed a fundamental breach of contract is largely a question of fact for the tribunal, which cannot be overturned on appeal. Again, this approach fits uneasily with the alleged virtues of the contractual approach advocated in *Western Excavating v Sharp*, where certainty could be achieved by treating the issue as the legal question whether there had been a fundamental breach of contract. By limiting review to the question whether the tribunal had posed the right question, that is, whether the employer had broken the implied term of trust and confidence, the Court of Appeal again releases the opportunity for uncertainty and 'whimsical decision'. Nevertheless, once it is appreciated that constructive dismissal cases in fact raise broader questions of fault and the allocation of responsibility for termination of the contract, it is appropriate that the original tribunal, with the benefit of all the evidence before it, should have the dominant role in determining the outcome.

Despite this sensible restriction on the power of appeal courts to review findings of constructive dismissal, the courts can intervene where they disagree with the outcome of a tribunal by asserting that no reasonable tribunal could have reached the same conclusion. Furthermore, the question whether or not the employer's conduct amounts to a breach of the implied term of trust and confidence is plainly a matter of degree. By insisting that this issue must be judged objectively, the appeal courts can intervene by asserting that the facts before the tribunal did not establish the requisite degree of breach of the implied term of trust and confidence to amount to a repudiatory breach of contract or constructive dismissal.

5.2.3 Frustration

In the common law of long-term commercial contracts, an event which renders performance of the contract impossible or unlawful, for which the contract makes no provision, may be held to have frustrated the contract. Frustration terminates the contract without the choice or consent of the parties. In order to avoid a finding of dismissal, employers have sometimes argued that an event such as the illness or imprisonment of the employee has frustrated the contract of employment. If the tribunal agrees that the contract of employment has been frustrated, the apparent dismissal by the employer will be of no effect, and the contract will have been terminated without any action by either party. As a consequence, the employer is under no duty to give notice or compensation for lack of notice, nor can the employee bring any claim for unfair dismissal or a redundancy payment. The use of the doctrine of frustration is therefore plainly an instrumental gambit used by employers to avoid having to justify the decision to dismiss the employee. Although the courts have frequently applied the doctrine of frustration to the contract of employment, these decisions may be criticised on the grounds both that they fail to conform to the common law principles, and that they represent an unsatisfactory interpretation of the statutory concept of dismissal.

With regard to the principles of the common law, the doctrine of frustration can apply only where the parties have failed to make any provision for the event in the contract. In contracts of employment, however, the parties have almost invariably made suitable provision by creating the unilateral power to terminate the contract on giving reasonable notice. For this reason, the doctrine of frustration should apply to contracts of employment only when they are for a fixed term, with a substantial period of time yet to expire, and do not contain either expressly or by implication a power to terminate by giving notice.

[5.27] *Harman v Flexible Lamps Ltd* **[1980] IRLR 418 (EAT)**

Ms Harman was employed as a quality control inspector. In 1978 she was off sick for a total of 13 weeks. In 1979, she was again away ill for two and half months before May, when the employer dismissed her with one week's notice. The tribunal held that the contract of employment had been frustrated, or alternatively that she had been dismissed fairly. The EAT dismissed the appeal against the finding of a fair dismissal, but allowed an appeal against the finding that the contract had been frustrated.

Bristow J:
In our judgment, the circumstances of this case are a very long way indeed from any situation in which a contract of employment is discharged by operation of law because the basis of the contract has been destroyed by supervening ill health on the part of the employee. This contract was in any case terminable at a week's notice, and once the employer decided that the ill health of Miss Harman made it necessary to replace her, nothing was easier than to give her notice determining her job and to employ and train a replacement. In the employment field the concept of discharge by operation of law, that is frustration, is normally only in play where the contract of employment is for a long term which cannot be determined by notice. Where the contract is terminable by notice, there is really no need to consider the question of frustration and if it were the law that, in circumstances such as are before us in this case, an employer was in a position to say 'this contract has been frustrated', then that would be a very convenient way in which to avoid the provisions of the [ERA 1996]. In our judgment, that is not the law in these sort of circumstances.

The application of the doctrine of frustration to the contract of employment also represents an unsatisfactory interpretation of the statutory concept of dismissal. The purpose of this statutory requirement is to exclude claims when the employee has resigned without cause. In none of the cases involving frustration has the employee resigned, but instead the employer has plainly initiated the termination, albeit claiming subsequently that these actions were of no significance due to the prior frustrating event. The employer's objective is to avoid scrutiny of the fairness of the decision to dismiss the employee by a tribunal. In *Harman v Flexible Lamps Ltd*, for instance, the employer's advisors were probably concerned that the tribunal might find the dismissal unfair because the employer had not fully investigated the reasons for absence and had dismissed the employee precipitately without prior warning. In the end these concerns proved unwarranted, and the EAT was not prepared to find the tribunal's decision perverse. An event which might be regarded as frustrating the contract is therefore likely to provide a substantial ground for a fair dismissal, but it obstructs the purpose of the unfair dismissal legislation to prevent a tribunal from considering the substantive merits of the case by treating the employee's absence as equivalent to a resignation.

Despite these criticisms of the application of the doctrine of frustration to claims for unfair dismissal, the Court of Appeal has insisted that the doctrine of frustration can apply to a contract of employment terminable on notice.

[5.28] *Notcutt v Universal Equipment Co (London) Ltd* [1986] ICR 414 (CA)

The employee suffered a heart attack and a doctor's report concluded that it was unlikely that the employee would ever work again. The employers then gave the statutory minimum period of 12 weeks' notice, but made no payment of wages on the ground that under the contract of employment the employee was not entitled to sick pay. The employee brought a claim under what is now ERA 1996 sections 88(1)(b) or 89(3), which provides that if an employee is incapable of work because of sickness the employer must pay the normal wages during the period of notice. The employer resisted this claim by arguing that the employee's heart attack had frustrated the contract of employment, and that therefore the giving of notice of dismissal had been otiose, and so no payment was due. The Court of Appeal upheld this argument.

Dillon LJ:

The employee took advice, and a law centre on his behalf claimed that he was entitled to sick pay under [ERA 1996 s. 89(3)] while absent from work during the period of his notice. This took the employers by surprise. Their first reaction was to suggest that the employee might wish to be re-engaged, presumably without pay unless he unexpectedly became fit to work. This was not accepted. The employers then suggested that the notice of termination was really a sham, designed to enable the employee to obtain extra social security benefits when his contract of employment had in truth been determined without notice by mutual consent at 25 or 26 July 1984; this however the judge rejected on the facts. The employers also contended, however, that the contract of employment had been frustrated by the employee's illness before the purported notice of termination of 26 July. That argument, of frustration, the judge accepted. He accordingly dismissed the action, in which the employee claimed payment of his sick pay under [ERA 1996, section 89(3)] during the period of that notice, and it is against that decision that the employee now appeals.

I have found it impossible to discern from the wording of the Act . . . why Parliament should have required an employer to pay sick pay to an employee who is off work because of sickness or injury while under notice of termination of his contract, although the employer is under no such obligation while the employee is not under notice. Possibly it may have been thought that a good employer who, even if not obliged to, would pay sick pay to a man off sick would not be willing to do so if the man was under notice. Even this speculation, however, is difficult to fit in with [ERA 1996, section 87(4)], which does not apply in this particular case. Whatever the reason, however, it is clear that the Act has imposed such an obligation on employers. The obligation is incorporated into the contract of employment. Both counsel are therefore agreed that if the employee's contract was terminated by the notice of 26 July, he is entitled to the moneys which he has claimed. Conversely both counsel are equally agreed that if the employee's contract of employment had been frustrated before the notice of 26 July was given, that notice was of no effect and the employee cannot make any claim . . .

The arguments of Mr Allen for the employee were first, and generally, that the doctrine of frustration can have no application to a periodic contract of employment because there is no need for it—the contract can always be terminated by short or relatively short notice. And secondly that in the circumstances of the present case there was no frustration as absence for sickness, injury or incapacity was envisaged by the contract and also by [ERA 1996, section 89(3)] . . .

In the present case, the argument of frustration is of course unashamedly put forward to avoid the provisions of the Act; in that it has succeeded in the court below. Notwithstanding the views expressed by Bristow J [in *Harman v Flexible Lamps Ltd*, [5.27] above] however there have been several cases in the National Industrial Relations Court and the Employment Appeal Tribunal in which those courts have considered that a contract of employment which is terminable by relatively short notice is in law capable of being terminated, without notice, by frustration as a result of the illness of the employee, and those courts have endeavoured to list by way of guideline the factors of which account should be taken in considering whether a particular such contract has been so frustrated . . .

In this court in *Hare v Murphy Brothers Ltd.* [1974] ICR 603 (CA), Lord Denning MR held that a contract of employment of a workman was frustrated when the man was sentenced to imprisonment for 12 months. In reaching that conclusion Lord Denning MR considered by way of analogy that if the man had been grievously injured in a road accident and incapacitated for eight months his contract of employment would be frustrated. However, though the man's contract was presumably determinable on short notice, no argument was founded on this; the discussion seems to have been over whether the contract was terminated by frustration or by repudiatory breach on the part of the man in committing the offence for which he was imprisoned.

For my part, as a periodic contract of employment determinable by short, or relatively short, notice may none the less be intended in many cases by both parties to last for many years and as the power of the employer to terminate the contract by notice is subject to the provisions for the protection of employees against unfair dismissal now in the [ERA 1996], I can see no reason in principle why such a periodic contract of employment should not, in appropriate circumstances, be held to have been terminated without notice by frustration according to the accepted and long established doctrine of frustration in our law of contract. The mere fact that the contract can be terminated by the employer by relatively short notice cannot of itself render the doctrine of frustration inevitably inapplicable. Accordingly the words of Bristow J [above] must be taken as no more than a warning that the court must look carefully at any submission that a periodic contract of employment has been discharged by frustration if that submission is put forward to avoid the provisions of the Act. If Bristow J. intended to go further than that I cannot agree with him.

The principles that govern the doctrine of frustration are conveniently to be found in the speeches of Lord Reid and Lord Radcliffe in *Davis Contractors Ltd. v Fareham Urban District Council* [1956] AC 696(HL). Lord Reid said, at p. 721:

'In my view, the proper approach to this case is to take . . . all facts which throw light on the nature of the contract, or which can properly be held to be extrinsic evidence relevant to assist in its construction and then, as a matter of law, to construe the contract and to determine whether the ultimate situation . . . is or is not within the scope of the contract so construed'.

Lord Radcliffe, in a much quoted passage, said, at pp. 728–729:

'So perhaps it would be simpler to say at the outset that frustration occurs whenever the law recognises that without default of either party a contractual obligation has become incapable of being performed because the circumstances in which performance is called for would render it a thing radically different from that which was undertaken by the contract. *Non haec in foedera veni.* It was not this that I promised to do. There is, however, no uncertainty as to the materials upon which the court must proceed.'

The data for decision are, on the one hand, the terms and construction of the contract, read in the light of the then existing circumstances, and on the other hand the events which have occurred (*Denny, Mott & Dickson Ltd. v James B. Fraser & Co. Ltd.* [1944] AC 265(HL), 274–275 per Lord Wright). In the nature of things there is often no room for any elaborate inquiry. The court must act upon a general impression of what its rule requires.

It is for that reason that special importance is necessarily attached to the occurrence of any unexpected event that, as it were, changes the face of things. But, even so, it is not hardship or inconvenience or material loss itself which calls the principle of frustration into play. There must be as well such a change in the significance of the obligation that the think undertaken would, if performed, be a different thing from that contracted for'. . . .

The employee's contract provided that the employers were not bound to pay him while he was absent from work because of sickness, injury or incapacity. The contract thus envisaged the possibility that he might be away from work because of sickness, injury or incapacity. But as a matter of construction of the contract I cannot hold that the reference to injury would cover an injury which totally disabled him from performing his work under the contract, e.g. if the operation of the milling machine requires the use of his right hand and he lost his right arm, or was rendered quadriplegic in an accident away from work which was not his fault and had nothing to do with his employers. In such a case his accident would have caused his contract of employment to be frustrated as a matter of law. Again, if sickness or incapacity are considered rather than injury, the result would be the same if, e.g., he had a stroke which left his right side permanently paralysed.

On the actual facts of the present case, the effect of his coronary could not initially be assessed. But when more than six months later the doctor made his report, both parties appreciated, on the judge's findings, that he was not going to work again. He was totally incapacitated from performing the contract. That was a situation which, in my judgment, was outside the scope of the contract properly construed. To put it another way, the coronary which left him unable to work again was an unexpected occurrence which made his performance of his contractual obligation—to work—impossible and brought about such a change in the significance of the mutual obligations that the contract, if performed, would be a different thing from that contracted for.

In these circumstances I am unable to accept the arguments for the employee. The judge approached the case on a correct basis and I agree with his conclusion. Accordingly, though I feel much sympathy with the employee in that his working life has been cut short by illness or incapacity, I would dismiss this appeal.

This decision reaffirms the application of frustration to contracts of employment, and dismisses abruptly the argument that its application permits employers to avoid their statutory obligations. Although the doctrine of frustration is drawn from general contract law, it rarely operates in commercial contexts, because the parties usually make express provision for unlikely risks. In employment, however, not only are risks such as illness that will render performance by the employee impossible more frequent occurrences, but also the contracts will probably be drafted unilaterally by the employer, who has no incentive to exclude the operation of the doctrine of frustration.

5.3 Contracting out of statutory rights

The extent to which the employee may contract out of statutory rights to claim unfair dismissal and redundancy on termination of employment raises the crucial problem of reconciling the demands of flexibility in labour markets with the need to safeguard the interests of employees in job security. The policy of supporting flexibility suggests that employers and employees should be free to adopt arrangements for termination of employment that suit the needs of the business and therefore enhance its competitiveness. Short-term contracts or contracts to perform particular tasks may appear to be the only way in which an employer can acquire the labour power required for a particular job, for the employer may be uncertain about future needs for workers, both in the sense of the amount of labour and the skills required. Similarly, the employer may believe that continued employment must depend upon high levels of performance, so that any drop in standards must lead to termination of the contract. On the other hand, the employee's interest in job security should not be ignored. The law of unfair dismissal is designed to prevent unreasonable disciplinary action, not to prevent termination of employment altogether. To permit employees to contract out of the statutory rights, therefore, seems to provide employers with broader powers than they require for the purposes of flexibility. To put the point bluntly, the employer wishes to acquire the right to act unreasonably in terminating employment. Even in the context of redundancy, where many would argue that the argument for supporting the employer's need for flexibility is stronger, the ability to contract out of the statutory right to compensation is not essential, for the right does not prevent dismissal, but merely fixes a minimum level of compensation. If the employee were permitted to contract out of this right to a redundancy payment without compensation, this agreement would merely reduce the cost to the employer of adopting flexible hiring practices.

At first sight, the legislation adopts the stance that the right to claim unfair dismissal is mandatory, and therefore not subject to contractual exclusion. The statutory provisions commence with a bold declaration of the right.

[5.29] Employment Rights Act 1996, section 94

(1) An employee has the right not to be unfairly dismissed by his employer.

This impression of the mandatory quality of the right is reinforced by a further statutory outlawing of agreements to oust the right.

[5.30] Employment Rights Act 1996, section 203

(1) Any provision in an agreement (whether a contract of employment or not) is void in so far as it purports—
   (a) to exclude or limit the operation of any provision of this Act, or
   (b) to preclude a person from bringing any proceedings under this Act before an employment tribunal.

Yet when we examine the details of the legislation and the application of these provisions, it becomes clear that employers can manipulate the contractual arrangements in order to exclude the right to claim unfair dismissal. The statutory right always remains contingent upon the contractual arrangements, and since the employer usually determines those arrangements, there is considerable scope to exclude the right in order to obtain not only flexibility but also unfettered disciplinary power. In this section we examine a number of ways in which employers may use contracts to avoid controls over dismissals, but we shall also notice that the courts have sometimes blocked the most transparent devices.

5.3.1 Agreed termination and compromise agreements

The statutory concept of dismissal can be manipulated to exclude jurisdiction by avoiding dismissal through an agreed termination of the contract of employment. The courts have accepted that in addition to dismissal and resignation, a third way of bringing a contract of employment to an end consists of an agreement that terminates the contract. In cases of agreed termination, the employee's claim is blocked because there has been no dismissal. Employees are likely to be induced to agree to termination of employment by a proposed financial settlement or the fear that they may be dismissed and then experience great difficulty in obtaining compensation and another job. The danger presented by such agreements is that employees will in effect be contracting out of their statutory rights on dismissal, but there are no safeguards to alert them to the possible loss of superior entitlements. The courts have sometimes resisted this possibility.

[5.31] *Lees v Arthur Greaves (Lees) Ltd* **[1974] ICR 501 (CA), at 505**

> **Lord Denning MR:**
> If the employment is terminated by agreement, then he gets no compensation. So the tribunal and the court should not find an agreement unless it proved that he really did agree with full knowledge of the implications which it held for him.

This presumption has not been followed, however, with the consequence that employees can lose statutory claims on termination of employment, even though this implication of their agreement has not been explained.

[5.32] *Birch v University of Liverpool* **[1985] ICR 470 (CA)**

> The employer, faced by cuts in government funding, invited staff to take advantage of an early retirement scheme which was intended to reduce the workforce by 300 posts. The employee applied for early retirement. The university chose between the applicants and the claimant's application was approved. The university then formally requested the claimant's retirement on a particular date. The employee subsequently claimed a redundancy payment, but was defeated on the preliminary point that he had not been dismissed. The fact that the employer had reserved the power to determine who should be permitted to take early retirement did not prevent the case from being one of agreed termination. Nor was the absence of information for the employee that he would lose his redundancy payment fatal to the employer's defence.

We have noted already that the statutory concept of dismissal makes provision for one type of agreed termination. Under the second limb of the statutory definition of dismissal in ERA 1996, section 95 (above **[5.22]**), the expiration of a limited-term contract is deemed to be a dismissal. Without this provision, the expiry of a fixed-term would be regarded as another instance of an agreed termination without any dismissal by the employer. In order to extend the definition of dismissal and prevent evasion of the statutory right, the Court of Appeal in *Dixon v BBC* [1979] ICR 281 held that the expiration of a fixed-term contract would count as a dismissal even when the contract contained a provision for termination by notice as well. In response to the EC Directive 99/70 on fixed-term work (Annex Clause 3), through its concept of limited-term contracts, section 95 now also extends its protection to contracts for the performance of a specific task and contracts that terminate on the occurrence (or non-occurrence) of a specific event. This extension reverses earlier court decisions where it had been accepted in principle that when the contract terminated because the particular task for which employment had been given had been completed, there was an agreed termination or 'discharge by performance', and not a dismissal: e.g. *Wiltshire County Council v NATFHE* [1980] ICR 455 (CA). As a result, employers can no longer evade the statutory right to claim unfair dismissal by framing the contract as one intended to be impermanent and by fixing its duration by reference to the completion of tasks or the occurrence of events.

Some instances of agreed termination may be attacked indirectly as attempts to contract out of the mandatory regulation contrary to ERA 1996, section 203(1) **[5.29]** above. This provision does not, however, prevent either settlements of legal proceedings under the supervision of an ACAS conciliation officer (ERA 1996, section 203 (2)(e)), or compromise agreements that satisfy various conditions, including that the employee received independent legal advice.

[5.33] Employment Rights Act 1996, section 203

> **203 (3)** . . . the conditions regulating compromise agreements under this Act are that—
> (a) the agreement must be in writing,
> (b) the agreement must relate to the particular proceedings,
> (c) the employee or worker must have received advice from a relevant independent adviser as to the terms and effect of the proposed agreement and, in particular, its effect on his ability to pursue his rights before an employment tribunal,
> (d) there must be in force, when the adviser gives the advice, a contract of insurance, or an indemnity provided for members of a professional body, covering the risk of a claim by the employee or worker in respect of loss arising in consequence of the advice,
> (e) the agreement must identify the adviser, and
> (f) the agreement must state that the conditions regulating compromise agreements under this Act are satisfied.
> **(3A)** A person is a relevant independent adviser for the purposes of subsection (3)(c)—
> (a) if he is a qualified lawyer,
> (b) if he is an officer, official, employee or member of an independent trade union who has been certified in writing by the trade union as competent to give advice and as authorised to do so on behalf of the trade union,
> (c) if he works at an advice centre (whether as an employee or a volunteer) and has

been certified in writing by the centre as competent to give advice and as authorised to do so on behalf of the centre, or

(d) if he is a person of a description specified in an order made by the Secretary of State.

(An order under 3A(d) extends the role of independent adviser to a Legal Executive employed and under the supervision of a solicitor: SI 2004/54).

A simple agreement to terminate a contract, perhaps with a financial inducement, does not fall within those provisions governing valid comprise agreements. Thus the sole ground for challenging such an agreement is that it purports to exclude the right to claim unfair dismissal, even though on its face the agreement merely brings the contract to a close. The question becomes how far ERA 1996, section 203 may encompass and invalidate such agreements.

[5.34] *Igbo v Johnson, Matthey Chemicals Ltd* [1986] ICR 505 (CA)

The applicant had asked for three extra days of holiday to be tacked on to her regular entitlement. This request had been granted, but she had been asked to sign a document which stated that if she failed to return on the agreed date 'your contract of employment will automatically terminate on that date'. Owing to illness, the employee failed to return to work, but informed the manager and sent in a medical certificate. The employer nevertheless informed her that her contract of employment was terminated in accordance with the document that she had signed.

Parker LJ:

It is, we think, important to dispose at the outset of any idea that the termination of a contract of employment by agreement by itself prevents an employee being dismissed for the purposes of the [ERA 1996]. Every fixed term contract is terminated by consensual agreement on its expiry date, yet non-renewal constitutes dismissal under section [95(1)(b)]. Every contract which is subject to termination on notice terminates by agreement if the employer gives proper notice, yet such termination constitutes dismissal under section [95(1)(a)]. Hence, if on 18 August 1983 the applicant and the employers had agreed that her contract should end on 28 September without more, she would have had a contract for a fixed term and non-renewal on that date would have constituted dismissal. Furthermore it is to be noted that, by virtue of section [95(2)], an employee under a valid notice, who gives notice to leave before the expiry of the notice is nevertheless taken to have been dismissed. This can, as it seems to us, only be due to the fact that the employee is in such circumstances treated by the Act as being not genuinely willing to leave. He will have departed voluntarily before he need have done but he will only have done so because he was under notice.

If the employers' contention is correct, it must follow that the whole object of the Act can be easily defeated by the inclusion of a term in a contract of employment that if the employee is late for work on the first Monday in any month, or indeed on any day, no matter for what reason, the contract shall automatically terminate. Could it be said that such a provision did not limit the operation of sections [94 and 95]? In our judgment it could not. Such a provision would vitally limit the operation of section [94(1)], for the right not to be unfairly dismissed would become subject to the condition that the employee was on time for work on the first Monday in each month, or every day, as the case might be.

Where, as in the present case, such a provision is introduced by way of amendment to an existing contract, its limiting effect upon the operation of sections [94 and 95] is even clearer. Until, on 19 August 1983, the applicant signed the holiday agreement she was entitled to the full benefit of those sections. Her failure to report for work on 28 September would not have affected their operation at all, although it would no doubt have been relevant to any question whether a termination of her employment on 28 September was fair or unfair. Had she received notice on 28 September that her employment was terminated she would plainly have been 'dismissed' within the meaning of section [95(1)(a)].

Having signed the holiday agreement her position was, however, if the automatic termination provision is valid, radically changed. Up to 27 September the operation of sections [94 and 95] was not affected, but their continued operation thereafter became subject to the condition that she reported for work on 28 September. In such circumstances it is impossible to avoid the conclusion that the provision for automatic termination had the effect, if valid, of limiting the operation of the sections. It was therefore void by virtue of section [203] . . . We add that, in substance, the effect of the automatic termination provision is the same as if it had said in terms 'in the event of failure to return to work on 28 September, termination of the employee's employment on that ground shall not constitute dismissal under section 55', or 'shall not give rise to any claim for unfair dismissal.' Any such provision would without doubt have been void as limiting the operation of the sections. We can see no ground for saying that a provision has the like effect does not limit such operation.

The scope of this decision with respect to agreed terminations remains unclear. If the test is whether an agreement in effect deprives the employee of statutory rights, even though it does not do so expressly, any agreement which terminates employment by consent has this effect if it excludes a dismissal, and therefore all such agreements should be void. But this implication has not been accepted in subsequent decisions.

[5.35] *Logan Salton v Durham County Council* [1989] IRLR 99 (EAT)

The employee had been informed that he was shortly to face disciplinary proceedings following a recommendation of summary dismissal by his manager. He had been fruitlessly trying to press various grievances including a return to a previous posting. He concluded that the disciplinary proceedings were likely to have an unfavourable outcome and that he would be best advised to seek a settlement. His trade union official was of the same opinion, and at the employee's request the official negotiated a financial settlement with the employer that terminated the employment. The employee immediately claimed unfair dismissal. The EAT heard an appeal against the tribunal's finding that there had been no dismissal. The EAT held that the agreement had not been the product of duress and that the agreed termination negatived a finding of dismissal. The EAT distinguished the case from *Igbo v Johnson, Matthey Chemical Ltd.*

Wood J:
It seems to us that the facts of the present case are distinguishable from *Igbo*:
1. The agreement of February 1987 was not a contract of employment, it was a contract separate from the applicant's contract of employment which was entered into:
    (a) willingly
    (b) without duress and after proper advice,
    (c) for good consideration.

2. It was not a variation of an existing contract.

3. The termination of the period of employment did not depend upon the happening of a future event—which may have been envisaged—nor upon the possible happening of events which were not envisaged and which, if they had been envisaged, might well have caused the employee not to agree with the proposed term or terms—eg, the events referred to by Parker LJ in *Igbo* that an employee might be knocked down by a car within mere feet of the factory gate when he was about to enter at the proper time.

In our judgment, and particularly in the judgment of the lay members, in the resolution of industrial disputes it is in the best interests of all concerned that a contract made without duress, for good consideration, preferably after proper and sufficient advice, and which has the effect of terminating a contract of employment by mutual agreement (whether at once or on some future date) should be effective between the contracting parties, in which cases there will probably not have been a dismissal within [s. 95].

This decision affirms the possibility of agreed terminations that exclude the right to claim unfair dismissal. The crucial justification for this possibility is to preserve the ability of the parties to reach a settlement without the intervention of the legal process. But this decision also suggests limits on the validity of termination agreements. It might be possible to challenge an agreed termination on the ground that the employee gave up legal rights for no consideration, or that the terms of the agreement contained a broader exclusion of rights than the employee had expected, or that the employer exerted pressure amounting to economic duress in order to induce the employee to agree to terminate the contract. The decision also hints that the presence of independent advice might be necessary for an agreement to constitute a valid exclusion of statutory rights.

We noted above that ERA 1996, section 203(3) determines that 'compromise agreements' are valid only if they are in writing and the employee receives independent advice from a lawyer. If an effective compromise agreement requires these safeguards, it can be argued that the protection of independent legal advice is even more important for agreements which terminate employment, but do not expressly point out to the employee that one consequence will be the loss of all statutory rights on dismissal. A better view would be to hold all such terminations by agreement to be invalid under ERA 1996, section 203(1), unless they comply with the statutory provisions for compromise agreements conducted with independent legal advice. These statutory safeguards for compromise agreements were introduced after these decisions in *Igbo* and *Logan Salter*. It might be argued that the statute is now intended to provide a comprehensive regulatory system for settlements that introduces safeguards against unwitting contracting out of statutory rights by agreed termination. Under the present law, however, the more covert the employer's technique for exclusion of statutory rights on dismissal, the less the protection appears to be afforded to the employee.

5.3.2 Employment

The statutory right in ERA 1996, section 94 is available only to employees, as defined in ERA 1996, section 230 (**[2.54]** above). We have already observed in chapter 2 that this restricted ambit of protection implicitly adopts the common law's traditional distinction between contracts of employment and contracts for services provided by independent contractors. We suggested that the formula adopted in other employment protection legislation of extending protection to all 'workers', that is individuals who perform work personally under a contract except where that are conducting a profession or a business undertaking, would be a preferable definition of the scope for most rights in the ERA 1996 including unfair dismissal and redundancy. In this context of examining the potential to contract out of statutory rights, we need to recall the potential use of the terms of the agreement to allocate individuals who perform services into the category of employee or independent contractor. At bottom the difference between employees and independent contractors consists in no more than the different pattern of the allocation of risks in the contract. By defining through the contract the status of the worker as an 'independent contractor', the contract can effectively exclude the application of the right to claim unfair dismissal.

It therefore becomes crucial to know when a court will cut through sham agreements in order to reclassify workers as employees despite contrary express terms in the contract. In the following case, the Court of Appeal adopts an aggressive approach to the construction of the contract in order to provide appropriate coverage for the law of unfair dismissal. It is also worth considering whether the problem would have been solved by the alternative of extending protection to all 'workers'.

[5.36] *Young & Woods Ltd. v West* [1980] IRLR 201 (CA)

Mr West claimed unfair dismissal, even though for tax reasons he had agreed to a contract which described him as self-employed. The Court of Appeal upheld the decision that Mr West was an employee for the purposes of the law of unfair dismissal, since in fact he was treated as an employee in all respects except for deduction of taxation from wages.

Ackner LJ:
It is by now well settled that the label which the parties choose to use to describe their relationship cannot alter or decide their true relationship; but, in deciding what that relationship is, the expression by them of their true intention is relevant, but not conclusive. Its importance may vary according to the facts of the case . . . *Massey v Crown Life Insurance Co* [1978] ICR 590(CA) . . . is a good indication of circumstances in which the parties' expression of their true intention may become decisive. It became decisive for this reason. As the Master of the Rolls pointed out in giving his judgment, the situation of Mr Massey was ambiguous. In giving his judgment at pages 594 to 595 the Master of the Rolls said:

'. . . if the parties' relationship is ambiguous and is capable of being one or the other, then the parties can remove that ambiguity, by the very agreement itself which they make with one another . . . It seems to me on the authorities that, when it is a situation which is in doubt or which is ambiguous, so that it can be brought under one relationship or the other, it is open to the parties by agreement to stipulate what the legal situation between them shall be'.

Almost at the end of his judgment, in fact in the penultimate paragraph, he said:

'Having made his bed as being self-employed, he must lie on it. He is not under a contract of service'.

This was interpreted by Mr Clifford [counsel for the employers] as meaning that there was some species of estoppel which debarred a person having, so to speak, opted or elected from resiling from the situation. I do not read the judgment of the learned Master of the Rolls in that way at all. As I read his judgment he was saying: 'In this case there was ambiguity. The parties were able, if they were so minded, to resolve that ambiguity. They did in fact resolve it by their agreement, and, having done so, then the worker has made his bed and he must lie on the bed he has thus made.'

It is suggested, again by Mr Clifford, that it would be contrary to public policy to allow him to resile from his agreement . . . Public policy is a dangerous argument to mount in this type of case where it just happens that the merits are on the side of the appellant. As the majority judgment of the Employment Appeal Tribunal pointed out:

'. . . individual labelling of the relationship would strike at the root of the protection afforded to an employed person by the Employment Protection legislation'.

It would not only strike at that protection, but also at the protection afforded by other acts such as the Factory Acts and other analogous legislation.

It has been strongly urged by Mr Clifford that it would be quite wrong for the respondent to have his cake and eat it. I see no reason to assume what this unpalatable situation will result from our decision. The Inland Revenue, as I understand it, have a duty to collect taxes. It follows from our decision that the respondent was wrongly assessed under Schedule D. He should have been assessed under Schedule E. He has thus obtained since 1975 or thereabouts fiscal advantages worth some £500 per annum to which he was not entitled. I am not prepared to assume that the Inland Revenue will fail to exercise its statutory duties and take the appropriate recovery action. It may well be that this will prove for the respondent, Mr West, to be a hollow, indeed an expensive, victory. This is, however, one of the hostages which is so frequently given to fortune when a person decides to go back on his bargain in order to obtain, what he believes to be, a fortuitous advantage at the expense of the other contracting party.

This decision represents a fairly isolated, yet nevertheless remarkable, willingness to cut through the form of the contractual relation in order to prevent indirect methods for contracting out of the statutory right to claim dismissal. Whether or not employers consciously adopt forms of contractual agreement that avoid the category of employee for the purpose of escaping from the regulation is unclear. Surveys of employers do not reveal such a conscious policy.

[5.37] S Evans, J Goodman and L Hargreave, *Unfair Dismissal Law and Employment Practice in the 1980s* (London, Department of Employment, Research paper No. 53, 1985) 24.

The main reason for these shifts in employment form [referring to subcontracting, temporary, and casual workers], however, were weak and uncertain product-market demand and freer labour market opportunities. There was very limited evidence of firms turning to these casual forms of employment to avoid the constraints imposed by unfair dismissal laws.

The irrelevance of unfair dismissal law to employers' labour use strategies is also confirmed by the evidence presented in chapter 2 (above 2.7.2).

5.3.3 Temporary and probationary employees

5.3.3.1 Qualifying period

[5.38] Employment Rights Act 1996, section 108

> **(1)** Section 94 does not apply to the dismissal of an employee unless he has been continuously employed for a period of not less than one year ending with the effective date of termination.

Ever since the inception of the right to claim unfair dismissal, the right has been limited to workers with a qualifying period of continuous service. The current requirement of one year excludes both employees during their first year of service under a contract of indefinite duration and temporary workers hired for a period of less than a year if the contract is not renewed.

Several exceptions to this qualifying period of one year are contained in ERA 1996, section 108(3). The purpose of these exceptions is to protect social and legal rights that are guaranteed elsewhere in labour law. Dismissals involving breach of such rights, such as dismissals for membership of a trade union, dismissals on prohibited grounds of discrimination, or for pregnancy, are usually automatically unfair (below 5.4.1.4). This protection of social rights is strengthened by the elimination of any qualifying period. Employees who lack the requisite qualifying period for a claim for unfair dismissal often try to fit the facts of their cases into the categories of automatically unfair dismissal or discrimination law, in order to prevent their claims for unfair dismissal from being excluded by a tribunal. Apart from these special instances where the qualifying period does not preclude a claim, the statutory qualifying period creates a space for employers to exercise their disciplinary power of dismissal unfettered by regulation and oversight.

Given the difficulty of acquiring adequate information about the employee's capability and motivation, employers inevitably find that some hirings have been mistaken, and for this reason wish to insist upon a probationary period with the right to terminate the contract. But if the mistake is genuine and the employee is clearly unsuitable, the employer should have no difficulty in defending a claim for unfair dismissal. The real advantages to the employer of the statutory qualifying period are therefore the avoidance of the expense of defending claims for unfair dismissal, which would commonly amount to £5,000 in terms of management time expended and legal fees (B Hayward, M Peters, N Rousseau, K Seeds, *Findings from the Survey of Employment Tribunal Applications 2003*, Employment Relations Research Series No 33 (DTI, 2004) p. 117), and the power to effect dismissals without good reasons. This assessment provokes the question whether any qualifying period is justifiable. The selection of a qualifying period of one year in 1999 (replacing the former two-year period and extending coverage by about 2.8 million workers) was justified by the Government on the ground that it achieved the optimal balance between fairness, security and flexibility. It was argued against the abolition of a qualifying period that it might cause undesirable reactions from employers: more intensive screening of applicants, thus reinforcing the disadvantage of workers with a weak employment record; increased use of temporary workers; and reduction of the numbers employed (DTI, *The Unfair Dismissal and Statement of Reasons for Dismissal (variation of qualifying period) Order 1999—Regulatory Impact Assessment*, paragraph 8). Although the first point that a qualifying period may help the long-term unemployed to obtain a job may be valid, the second argument seems implausible, because the abolition of a qualifying period would remove the exclusion of temporary workers from the legislation so there would be no advantage to employers in preferring temporary workers. On the third point, the law of unfair dismissal has never been demonstrated to have any unemployment effects.

Surveys of employers cast considerable doubt on whether the statutory qualifying period has much influence on their attitudes to probationary periods. Very few employers adopt an open recruitment policy and subsequently 'weed out' unsatisfactory employees after a short period of time. This policy is usually inefficient if the employee requires any training. Most employers do have probation periods, but they are fixed at much less than the statutory level, and have not been affected by legislative changes to the period from one year to two years, and back to one. The most common period for probation is about 10–12 weeks, though with longer periods for jobs requiring higher skills and in larger firms.

[5.39] S Evans, J Goodman and L Hargreave, *Unfair Dismissal Law and Employment Practice in the 1980s* (London, Department of Employment, Research paper No. 53, 1985) 34

> The adoption of the statutory qualifying period as the duration of the in-house probationary period was another option which failed to find much support, although a very few firms did use this means of fixing a period. In the great majority, probation was shorter than the exclusion period, and its general length was determined by a variety of factors concerning the ability of management to evaluate fully the type of employee concerned. The type and complexity of the employee's skills were very significant to this decision; but the need for managements to indicate an employee's formal inclusion into the firm's establishment was a factor which acted to reduce the overall level of probationary period lengths. The most recent changes in the legislation were of very little influence in this area.

Since the qualifying period does not seem to play a significant role in the practice of personnel management, it is worth considering what might happen if it were abolished or drastically shortened. One possible effect is that employers would have to become clearer about what they mean by a 'probationary employee'. They could no longer treat probationary employees as short fixed-term employees who can be dismissed with impunity. Instead employers would have to give probationary employees adequate supervision, training, and support, so that if the employee still proved inadequate in performance the job, the employer would be able to defend itself successfully against any possible claim for unfair dismissal: *Post Office v Mughal* [1977] ICR 763 (EAT). Another possible effect of the abolition of the qualifying period might be that employees would be more willing to risk changing their employer. This increase in flexibility in labour markets should be attractive to governments, because by changing jobs employees can acquire new skills, establish wider networks, and improve their employability, thereby contributing more generally to competitiveness in the economy.

The qualifying period of one year thus apparently has few benefits for either employers or employees. The exceptions granted for claims based upon discrimination and other social rights reveal that behind the qualifying period lurks the view that the right to claim unfair dismissal is not as important a social right as many others. That view may have reflected public attitudes in the past, but it may be out of date today in view of the inclusion of the right to claim unfair dismissal in many international declarations of social rights, including Article 30 of the Charter of Fundamental Rights of the European Union (above **[1.2]**).

5.3.3.2 *Temporary cessation of work*

The most significant impact of the qualifying period is the way it may exclude from protection against unfair dismissal a large number of temporary, seasonal and casual workers. Provided that each contract lasts for less than a year and is not shortly renewed, these temporary workers will apparently lack the necessary continuity of employment for the purposes of establishing the year's qualifying period. Detailed statutory provisions contained in ERA 1996, Part XIV, sections 210–19 determine the calculation of the qualifying period of continuous employment and the effect of breaks in employment on continuity for this purpose. The most pertinent provisions for temporary workers are:

[5.40] Employment Rights Act 1996, section 212

> **(1)** Any week during the whole or part of which an employee's relations with his employer are governed by a contract of employment counts in computing the employee's period of employment.
>
> **(3)** Subject to subsection (4), any week (not within subsection (1)) during the whole or part of which an employee is—
>> (a) incapable of work in consequence of sickness or injury,
>> (b) absent from work on account of a temporary cessation of work, or
>> (c) absent from work in circumstances such that, by arrangement or custom, he is regarded as continuing in the employment of his employer for any purpose,
> counts in computing the employee's period of employment.

Under subsection (1), a week can count towards the computation of the qualifying period of employment provided that during at least some of the week there was a contract of employment. Hence casual workers who have no regular hours, but who are employed as required by the employer and subject to their own availability, may establish continuity each week provided that they perform some work under a contract of employment. These weeks can then be added together to amount to the year's qualifying period. Employers may challenge this approach by arguing that the short contractual relation each week is not properly classified as one of employment but rather as an independent contractor.

The effect of subsection (3)(b) is that, even though a temporary employee is dismissed, thereby terminating the contract of employment and removing the case from subsection (1), or a casual worker fails to perform any work during a week, if the period before the employee is rehired can be described as 'temporary cessation of work', continuity of employment is preserved, the period of absence counts towards the calculation of the qualifying period. The interpretation placed on this provision by the courts has served to obstruct the possibility of contractual evasion of statutory rights on dismissal by employers hiring workers for a succession of temporary contracts for periods of less than one year. The House of Lords decided in *Fitzgerald v Hall Russell & Co Ltd* [1970] AC 984 that breaks between periods of employment could be examined with the benefit of hindsight in order to determine whether or not they were merely 'temporary'. Even though the employer cannot be sure whether or not he will require the services of a dismissed temporary worker or a casual worker again in the near future, if the break between periods of work can be described as 'temporary', the periods of employment (and unemployment) can be added together to constitute the necessary qualifying period. This reasoning was applied to a succession of fixed term contracts in the next case.

[5.41] *Ford v Warwickshire County Council* [1983] ICR 273 (HL)

A teacher was employed for eight successive academic years on fixed-term contracts from September to July with a break during the annual summer holidays. The question was whether for the purpose of establishing continuing of employment for eight years, the annual summer holidays could be regarded as 'temporary cessations of work'. The House of Lords allowed the employee's appeal, holding that continuity of employment was established.

Lord Diplock:

My Lords, I am quite unable to be persuaded that [ERA 1996, section 212(3)(b)] is not applicable to cases where a contract of employment for a fixed term has expired and upon expiry has not been renewed by the employer, in exactly the same way as it is applicable to contracts of employment of indefinite duration which are terminated by the employer by notice. One looks to see what was the reason for the employer's failure to renew the contract on the expiry of its fixed term and asks oneself the question: was that reason 'a temporary cessation of work,' within the meaning of that phrase in [ERA 1996, section 212(3)(b)]?

There are many employments, of which teaching is one of the largest and most obvious, in which it is perfectly possible to predict with accuracy the periods in which the educational institution at which a teacher who is employed to conduct courses in particular subjects will have no work available for that teacher to do, i.e. during the three annual school holidays or during vacations at universities and other institutions of further education. As the evidence in the instant case discloses, it is a common practice to employ part-time teachers of courses at institutions of further education under successive fixed term contracts the length of which is fixed according to the duration of the particular course and expires at the end of it. In the interval between successive courses which may coincide with the end of one academic year at an institution of further education and the beginning of the next but may be considerably longer, there is no work available at the institution for the teacher to do, and he remains without any contract of employment until the course is resumed, when he again becomes employed under a fresh fixed term contract . . .

From the fact that there is no work available for the employee to do for the employer during the whole of the interval between the end of one fixed term contract of employment and the beginning of the next, and that this was the reason for his non-employment during that interval, it does not necessarily follow that the interval constitutes a 'temporary cessation of work.' In harmony with what this House held in Fitzgerald's case [1970] AC 984, [ERA 1996, section 212(3)(b)] in cases of employment under a succession of fixed term contracts of employment with intervals in between, requires one to look back from the date of the expiry of the fixed term contract in respect of the non-renewal of which the employee's claim is made over the whole period during which the employee has been intermittently employed by the same employer, in order to see whether the interval between one fixed term contract and the fixed term contract that next preceded it was short in duration relative to the combined duration of those two fixed term contracts during which work had continued; for the whole scheme of the Act appears to me to show that it is in the sense of 'transient,' i.e. lasting only for a relatively short time, that the word 'temporary' is used in [ERA 1996, section 212(3)(b)]. So, the continuity of employment for the purposes of the Act in relation to unfair dismissal and redundancy payments is not broken unless and until, looking backwards from the date of the expiry of the fixed term contract on which the employee's claim is based, there is to be found between one fixed term contract and its immediate predecessor an interval that cannot be characterised as short relatively to the combined duration of the two fixed term contracts. Whether it can be so characterised is a question of fact and degree and so is for decision by an industrial tribunal rather than by the Employment Appeal Tribunal or an appellate court of law.

In the instant case, however, it is conceded by the council that each of the intervals between Mrs. Ford's successive fixed term contracts could properly be characterised as 'temporary.' I would therefore allow the appeal and remit Mrs. Ford's claims to the industrial tribunal to decide such other matters, if any, as may remain in dispute between her and the council.

My Lords, as I indicated at the outset, the length of successive fixed term contracts on which part-time lecturers are employed and the intervals between them vary considerably with the particular course that the part-time lecturer is engaged to teach; so it by no means follows that a similar concession would be made or would be appropriate in each of their cases. It also follows from what I have said that successive periods of seasonal employment of other kinds under fixed term contracts, such as employment in agriculture during harvest-time or in hotel work during the summer season will only qualify as continuous employment if the length of the period between two successive seasonal contracts is so short in comparison with the length of the season during which the employee is employed as properly to be regarded by the industrial tribunal as no more than a temporary cessation of work in the sense that I have indicated.

Through this expansive interpretation of the statutory concept of a temporary cessation of work, temporary, casual, and seasonal workers, employed on a succession of short-term contracts, may be able to establish the requisite continuity of employment for the qualifying period. Employers can avoid this consequence, however, by ensuring that that the breaks between hirings of a particular employee are kept substantial in comparison to the periods of actual employment. If the pattern of employment on a succession of short fixed-term contracts continues for as long as four years, the Fixed-Term Employees (Prevention of Less Favourable Treatment) Regulations 2002 SI 2002/2034 provide in Regulation 8 that the term of the contract that limits its duration shall be of no effect, and the employee will be regarded as a permanent employee, unless the employer can justify the use of fixed-term contracts on 'objective grounds'.

5.3.3.3 Effective date of termination

During the first year of employment, an employer remains free from any legal restraint regarding dismissal unless the reason for dismissal is an automatically unfair one (below 5.4.1.4). The statutory qualifying period creates an incentive for employers to consider carefully whether or not they wish to retain an employee as the deadline of one year approaches. If an employer decides to dismiss the employee, the 'effective date of termination' of the employment must fall within the deadline.

[5.42] Employment Rights Act 1996, section 97

> **97 (1)** Subject to the following provisions of this section, in this Part 'the effective date of termination'—
>> (a) in relation to an employee whose contract of employment is terminated by notice, whether given by his employer or by the employee, means the date on which the notice expires,
>> (b) in relation to an employee whose contract of employment is terminated without notice, means the date on which the termination takes effect, and
>> (c) in relation to an employee who is employed under a limited-term contract which terminates by virtue of the limiting event without being renewed under the same contract, means the date on which the termination takes effect.
>
> **(2)** Where—
>> (a) the contract of employment is terminated by the employer, and
>> (b) the notice required by section 86 to be given by an employer would, if duly given on the material date, expires on a date later than the effective date of termination (as defined by subsection (1)),
>
> for the purposes of sections 108(1), 119(1) and 227(3) the later date is the effective date of termination.

This statutory provision is astonishingly unhelpful as a guide to employers. Having created a special statutory concept of the effective date of termination, it fails to define the concept except in the two straightforward cases of the expiry of notice and the completion of a fixed term. As a result, the provision has generated considerable litigation, particularly where employers believe that they have dismissed employees just before the end of the qualifying period. The courts have filled in the gaps in the statutory concept. In the case of summary dismissal, without notice, the effective date of termination is regarded as the day of the summary dismissal: *Stapp v Shaftesbury Society* [1982] IRLR 326 (CA). If the employer gives shorter notice than is required under the contract, the effective date of termination is the expiration of the short notice: *TBA Industrial Products v Morland* [1982] IRLR 331 (EAT). Both of these rules are subject, however, to ERA 1996 s.97(2) which extends the effective date of termination to the expiration of the statutory minimum notice period (that is, one week for probationary employees). In both cases also the effective date of termination cannot be earlier than the date on which dismissal is communicated to the employee: *McMaster v Manchester Airport Plc* [1998] IRLR 112 (EAT). Nor can the effective date of termination be antedated by agreement between the parties: *Fitzgerald v University of Kent at Canterbury* [2004] EWCA Civ 143, [2004] IRLR 300 (CA). When a contractual right to a disciplinary and appeal procedure applies, the effective date of termination depends on the terms of that procedure. If under the procedure the employee is suspended until the final outcome is known, the effective date of termination is fixed by the communication of the final approval of the decision to dismiss: *Drage v Governors of Greenford High School* [2000] IRLR 314 (CA). If the procedure provides instead that the dismissal is effective, though the employee may be reinstated by a domestic appeal, the effective date of termination is set by the initial dismissal: *J Sainsbury Ltd v Savage* [1980] IRLR 109 (CA). What renders these cases hard for the tribunals to decide is the vagueness of the contractual procedures with respect to legal implications of dismissal with a right to an appeal.

Under these rules, therefore, an employer who wishes to dismiss before the deadline of the qualifying period must either give due notice that expires before the completion of the qualifying period or summarily dismiss the employee more than a week before the end of the qualifying period. A summary dismissal, however, leaves the employer vulnerable to a claim for wrongful dismissal at common law. But the courts have decided that damages for wrongful dismissal cannot include compensation for the loss of the chance to claim unfair dismissal by completing the qualifying period even where a contractual notice period, which is longer than the statutory minimum notice, would have completed the necessary year of employment: *Harper v Virgin Net Ltd* [2004] EWCA Civ 271, [2004] IRLR 390 (CA).

5.3.4 Retirement

Prior to the advent of age discrimination legislation in 2006, section 109 ERA 1996 excludes employees over the employer's normal retiring age or, in the absence of a normal retiring age, employees aged sixty-five or above, from bringing a claim for unfair dismissal. In effect, by setting a normal retirement age below sixty-five, an employer can exclude claims for unfair dismissal from even younger workers. The concept of a normal retirement age is usually understood to be the age fixed by the contract of employment, though if some other age is used by the employer in practice for a particular group of employees, that age will be regarded as the normal retiring age. The presumption that the contract fixes the normal retiring age can then be rebutted and replaced with the age when the employer typically terminates contracts of employment (e.g. *Waite v Government Communications Headq*uarters [1983] ICR 653 (HL)). To avoid the strong presumption that the contractual arrangements determine the normal retiring age, however, employees of large employers may have to present complex statistical evidence concerning the employer's actual practice: eg *Brooks v British Telecommunications Plc* [1991] IRLR 4 (EAT). Alternatively, the employer can decline to fix a normal retiring age, with the effect that all employees aged sixty-five or above are excluded completely from the law of unfair dismissal. This provision maintains unattractive age discrimination in the law of unfair dismissal (and redundancy payments: ERA 1996, section 156(1)). About three-quarters of a million workers, or 7.5 per cent of the UK workforce, are above the state retirement age of 65, and most of them are therefore excluded from the social right against unjust dismissal.

It will be necessary to bring this legislation into conformity with the age-related provisions of EC Directive 2000/78 (the Employment Equality Directive). Following a consultation exercise, (DTI, *Equality and Diversity: Age Matters (2003)*), the UK government announced on 14/12/2004 that it proposes to keep the age of 65 as the 'default retirement age'. Employers may agree an older retirement age with their employees. Employers may also have a younger retirement age, but only if that lower age can be objectively justified. An employer might be able to justify such a requirement on safety grounds, such as a need for airline pilots to be below a certain age, though any such requirement would probably have to be supported by evidence of its necessity. The government also proposes that when the employee reaches the 'default retirement age' of 65 or the lower objectively justified contractual retirement age, the employee should have the right to request to be permitted to carry on working. An employer would be required to consider such a request seriously, and to provide adequate reasons for rejecting the request. Detailed regulations to implement these proposals will be produced in 2005.

5.3.5 The arbitration alternative

The Employment Rights (Dispute Resolution) Act 1998 enabled ACAS to create an arbitration scheme for unfair dismissal cases as an alternative to proceedings before an employment tribunal. By written agreement, the parties to the dispute may refer the claim to a panel of arbitrators supplied, but not employed, by ACAS. The written agreement must either be a settlement negotiated by an ACAS conciliation officer (below 5.5.4) or a valid compromise agreement (above 5. 3.1)) (ERA 1996, section 203(5)). The result of the arbitration will be binding on the parties, without the possibility of review by the EAT, though it is possible to challenge a decision under the Arbitration Act 1996, for serious irregularity such as exceeding jurisdiction or powers. An arbitrator may award the remedy of either reinstatement or compensation.

The stated purpose of the arbitration scheme is to reduce the number of cases going to employment tribunals. Whether or not this aim will be achieved must be doubtful, because it is unclear what employees have to gain from using this form of alternative dispute resolution. Employers may welcome the prospect of a private hearing but, unless employees also prefer confidentiality, they should be concerned that the legal rights and procedural safeguards of the tribunal system will not be available to them. Employers may also be reluctant to consent to arbitration, because it precludes them from subsequently raising jurisdictional issues, such as whether the worker was an employee, or satisfied the qualifying period, or whether the employee was dismissed. The arbitration scheme attracted only 7 claims for unfair dismissal in the period 2003/2004 (ACAS, Annual Report, 2003/4), a drop in the ocean of the close to 50,000 tribunal claims for unfair dismissal launched annually.

In our present context, however, there exists a question of principle of whether the parties should be permitted to contract out of the statutory regime governing dismissals. The arbitration proceedings are intended to be relatively informal, fast, and inexpensive in comparison to a tribunal hearing. The arbitrator is instructed not to decide the case according the legal standard of fairness, but should 'have regard to general principles of fairness and good conduct in employment relations . . . instead of applying legal tests or rules' : ACAS Arbitration Scheme (Great Britain) Order 2004 SI 2004/753 Sched. Para. 12. But the arbitrator must comply with European Community law (including UK law implenting EC Directives), the Human Rights Act 1998, and the rules governing automatically unfair dismissals. It is important to notice that an arbitration agreement in this scheme does not simply change the forum, but more significantly it alters the standard to be applied. In effect, an arbitration agreement involves contracting out of many of the legal standards created by the statutory right to unfair dismissal.

Now we shall see in the next section that the statutory standard of fairness is not without its critics, but at least the standard is transparent, and therefore open to criticisms and refinements. An 'industrial relations approach' based on vague standards such as fairness and good conduct, conducted in private, clearly augments the discretion of the decision-maker with respect to the standards to be applied and renders it more or less impervious to inspection and criticism. The arbitrators will no doubt pay close attention to the fairness of the procedures followed by the employer, as do the tribunals, for it is widely recognised that procedures which are perceived to be fair are the key to harmonious industrial relations. But in other cases, where the substance of the dispute is whether dismissal was too harsh a penalty, one wonders whether the 'industrial relations approach' will tend to prefer collective interests in restoring business as usual over the interests of the individual employee in receiving compensation for harsh treatment and vindicating his or her reputation.

5.3.6 Conclusion

Although the right to claim unfair dismissal is conventionally regarded as a mandatory right, this section has demonstrated that it is possible for employers to use agreements and particular forms of the contract of employment in order to exclude its application. To some extent this position may be justified on the ground of granting employers flexibility in managing their workforce requirements. Temporary workers can be hired to meet unexpected demand or seasonal work, without incurring the cost of having to comply with the law governing dismissal. Probationary employees can be tried out without the risk of incurring liability to pay compensation for unfair dismissal. Yet the power of employers to avoid the application of the legislation extends far beyond these arguments for granting flexibility in order to promote employment opportunities. The exclusion of older workers by the adoption of a low normal retirement age is perhaps the most striking opportunity to avoid the statutory rights without any possible justification based upon the need for flexibility.

Yet it would be wrong to suppose that it should always be impermissible to contract out of the statute. What is important rather is that contractual agreements with that effect are based upon full disclosure of information and a voluntary agreement. The employee needs to understand the consequences of the agreement upon the statutory entitlements, and the employee must be free from economic pressure when consenting to the proposal. These conditions should usually be met by a collective agreement with an independent trade union. Section 110 ERA 1996 permits collectively agreed schemes for unfair dismissal to exclude the legislation, but its restrictive

Economic Analysis of Unfair Dismissal Law

The question of whether employees should be given a mandatory right to claim unfair dismissal has been examined extensively from the perspective of neo-classical economics. This form of analysis commences with the assumption that usually contractual agreements represent an efficient transaction. The observation that most contracts do not contain a term that protects an employee against unfair dismissal is explained as an efficient market outcome. To some extent the worker prefers other benefits such as higher wages to protection of job security. In addition, it is argued that few employers will exercise disciplinary power unjustly, partly because a misuse of power will lead valued employees to quit, and partly because of the costs of searching for and training a new employee. These arguments suggest that a mandatory right to claim unfair dismissal is both unnecessary and inefficient (e.g. R Epstein, 'In Defense of the Contract at Will' (1984) 57 *University of Chicago Law Review* 947; J L Harrison, 'The "New" Terminable-at-Will Employment Contract: An Interest and Cost Incidence Analysis' (1984) 69 *Iowa Law Review* 327).

But these neo-classical economic arguments can also be turned around in favour of a mandatory right to claim unfair dismissal. First, it may be argued that new employees lack reliable information about how disciplinary power is exercised by the employer and tend to discount the risk of unjust disciplinary practices, so that they fail to bargain for the optimal level of protection against unjust dismissal (eg. G Mundlak, 'Information-forcing and cooperation-inducing rules: rethinking the building blocks of labour law', in G De Geest, J Siegers, R Van den Bergh, *Law and Economics and the Labour Market* (Cheltenham, Elgar, 1999) 55). Second, where the employee joins an internal labour market, it is likely that most of the rewards for hard work will be reaped after a long period of service through promotion and salary based upon seniority. At that later point, the employee is especially vulnerable to a cost-saving dismissal, which is a form of opportunism by employers that may require legal regulation in order to support the credibility of commitments made by employers when instituting internal labour market systems (e.g. Note, 'Employer Opportunism and the Need for a Just-Cause Standard' (1989) 103 *Harvard Law Review* 510). Third, it must be doubted under many labour market conditions that valued employees will penalise the employer's misuse of disciplinary power by quitting for another job.

These rebuttals of the neo-classical criticism of a mandatory unfair dismissal law do not necessarily justify such a statute, however, because of the difficulty of enacting a law that intervenes precisely when, and only when, the efficiency arguments based upon asymmetry of information, opportunism in internal labour markets, and the absence of the deterrence of quits apply in the particular circumstances of the case. Economic analysis therefore provides indeterminate support for a mandatory law of unfair dismissal, and other kinds of arguments, such as those based upon respect for the dignity and autonomy of workers, are required in order to make the case complete.

conditions are such that has been used only once (this in the electrical contracting industry). In effect the collectively agreed scheme had to duplicate most of the statutory provisions relating to dismissal, including those concerned with discrimination. Recent amendments are designed to introduce greater discretion for the parties to collective agreements to devise their own schemes (Employment Rights Dispute Resolution Act 1998, section 12). This ability to contract out of the legislation through collective agreement might be further extended, for it promises the possibility of local agreements designed to reconcile the employer's interests in flexibility with the employees' interest in job security in ways tailored to meet the particular circumstances of the undertaking. This opportunity has been taken in legislation derived from EC law, as for example with respect to the right of fixed-term employees to become permanent after four years of continuous service, where through collective agreement or workforce agreement the employer and representatives of the workforce may agree a different period of time or a different trigger for the creation of permanent status: Fixed Term Employees (Prevention of Less Favourable Treatment) Regulations 2002, SI 2002/2034, Regulation 8(5).

With respect to provisions in contracts made by individuals, however, we need to be much more cautious in supposing that an agreement which effectively excludes the operation of the law of unfair dismissal was based upon full information and reached without economic pressure. The test for the validity of compromise agreements, which is that the agreement was reached only after independent legal advice, should perhaps be regarded as a minimum safeguard for employees in whatever form the contract devises the exclusion.

5.4 Fairness of dismissal

The standard of fairness at the heart of the statutory right regulates the employer's exercise of disciplinary power. In determining the content of this standard, the law decides how closely managerial decisions will be scrutinised by tribunals, and determines how and when the disciplinary power of dismissal can be exercised justifiably. The statute provides only a loose framework to guide this enquiry.

[5.43] Employment Rights Act 1996, section 98

(1) In determining for the purposes of this Part whether the dismissal of an employee is fair or unfair, it is for the employer to show—
  (a) the reason (or, if more than one, the principal reason) for the dismissal, and
  (b) that it is either a reason falling within subsection (2) or some other substantial reason of a kind such as to justify the dismissal of an employee holding the position which the employee held.
(2) A reason falls within this subsection if it—
  (a) relates to the capability or qualifications of the employee for performing work of the kind which he was employed by the employer to do,
  (b) relates to the conduct of the employee,
  (c) is that the employee was redundant, or
  (d) is that the employee could not continue to work in the position which he held without contravention (either on his part or on that of his employer) of a duty or restriction imposed by or under an enactment.
(3) In subsection (2)(a)—
  (a) 'capability', in relation to an employee, means his capability assessed by reference to skill, aptitude, heal or any other physical or mental quality, and

(b) 'qualifications', in relation to an employee, means any degree, diploma or other academic, technical or professional qualification relevant to the position which he held.

(4) Where the employer has fulfilled the requirements of subsection (1), the determination of the question whether the dismissal is fair or unfair (having regard to the reason shown by the employer)—

(a) depends on whether in the circumstances (including the size and administrative resources of the employer's undertaking) the employer acted reasonably or unreasonably in treating it as a sufficient reason for dismissing the employee, and

(b) shall be determined in accordance with equity and the substantial merits of the case.

5.4.1 The structure of the fairness enquiry

The legislation establishes a framework for the tribunal's decision that defines three steps for the fairness enquiry to follow:

(1) The employer has to give the reason or principal reason for the dismissal;
(2) The employer has to show that the reason relied on for dismissal was a substantial reason, such as incapability or misconduct, which might justify a dismissal;
(3) The tribunal has to consider whether dismissal for that reason was reasonable or unreasonable in accordance with equity and the substantial merits of the case.

The principal purpose of this framework is to compel the employer to fix the reason for dismissal, so that the tribunal can assess its merits. Out of the frequently muddled allegations and suspicions that characterise the breakdown of many employment relations, the law requires the construction of what may be a rather artificial rational basis for the decision to dismiss, so that the tribunal can assess its fairness by reference to the open textured standard of reasonableness.

5.4.1.1 *Principal reason for dismissal*

The first step in this structure prevents the employer from shifting the ground for dismissal as the case proceeds. In particular, the reason for the dismissal must be one that the employer relied upon at the time of dismissal, and cannot be a reason based upon facts discovered subsequent to termination of employment. In *W Devis & Sons Ltd v Atkins* [1977] ICR 672 (HL) for instance, the employer was not permitted to justify the dismissal by reference to dishonest conduct of the employee that was discovered only after the date of the dismissal. For this purpose, the time of the dismissal appears to be the same as the statutory concept of the effective date of termination; in the case of summary dismissal the reason is fixed immediately (*West Midlands Co-operative Society Ltd v Tipton* [1986] ICR 192 (HL)), but in cases of termination by notice, the reason may be affected by events during the notice period (*Alboni v Ind Coope Retail Ltd* [1998] IRLR 131 (CA)).

In addition, the requirement to fix the reason for dismissal prevents the employer from leaving the reason obscure or indeterminate, for then the tribunal will decide that the employer has failed to provide a reason at all and that therefore the dismissal must be unfair.

[5.44] *Smith v Glasgow City District Council* **[1987] ICR 796 (HL)**

> The employee was dismissed for unsatisfactory performance relating to three separate complaints. The industrial tribunal found that the second complaint was unfounded, but held the dismissal to be fair. The Court of Session permitted the employee's appeal, and the House of Lords dismissed the employer's appeal. The dismissal was unfair because either (1) the employer had failed to establish the principal reason for dismissal by not distinguishing between the three complaints against the employee, or (2) the employer had relied upon the second complaint as part of the principal reason for dismissal, and this reason had been found by the tribunal to be neither established in fact nor believed to be true on reasonable grounds.

The ambition of fixing the reason for the dismissal at a particular time implicitly emphasises the importance of the rationality of the decision to dismiss: the dismissal must be for a clear reason based on facts and beliefs held at the time. This model of rationality fits uneasily on the common factual pattern of dismissals, where the employer has a mixture of reasons, not all of which may be mentioned at the time of dismissal. The courts therefore permit the employer to reformulate the real reason for the dismissal as one other than the reason given to the employee at the time of the dismissal if it was probably the real reason for dismissal: *Abernethy v Mott, Hay and Anderson* [1974] ICR 323 (CA). The ambition to fix the reason for dismissal has an extraordinary air of unreality about it in cases of constructive dismissal. How can the employer provide a reason for dismissal when the employer has not decided to dismiss the employee at all? The approach adopted by the courts is to require the employer to show the reasons for his conduct that entitled the employee to terminate the contract: *Delabole Slate Ltd v Berriman* [1985] IRLR 305 (CA).

5.4.1.2 Substantial reason

The second step in the structure of the fairness enquiry places no constraint upon the types of reasons for dismissal that an employer may put forward, though an employer will be advised to give a reason which may justify the dismissal, that is a substantial reason. The statute illustrates the notion of substantial reasons with the examples of capability, qualifications and misconduct, but a substantial reason does not have to be a reason of the same kind or nature as those reasons: *RS Components Ltd v Irwin* [1973] ICR 535 (NIRC). In particular, the type of reason presented need not be confined to allegations of fault or breach of contract by the employee, but can refer to general business considerations, such as the need to reduce staff or to respond to pressure from a major customer. If an economic reason for dismissal is put forward, the case may be considered as one of redundancy. The boundaries between redundancy and other substantial reasons are considered in Chapter 10. The mere expiry of a fixed term contract is not, however, in itself regarded as a substantial reason; the employer must provide a reason for failure to renew the contract, such as the completion of the temporary work or project: *North Yorkshire County Council v Fay* [1985] IRLR 247 (CA).

5.4.1.3 Test of fairness

At the third stage of the fairness enquiry, the legislation implicitly divides dismissals into three broad categories:

(1) *Disciplinary dismissals*: the general or default category, that is governed by ERA 1996, section 98(4), where the employer asserts that it was reasonable to dismiss the employee for the substantial reason proffered as the principal reason for dismissal.

(2) *Economic dismissals*: special provisions concerning redundancy, transfers of undertakings, and insolvency regulate the rights of employees on dismissal. In this context, the economic or business reason for dismissal is usually regarded as a sufficient reason for dismissal. The employer usually concedes the requirement to pay a lesser measure of compensation (a redundancy payment), but the employee can challenge the fairness of the process that led to his or her selection for redundancy. The regulation of the fairness of economic dismissals is considered separately in Chapter 10.

(3) *Automatically unfair dismissals*. This third category identifies rights of employees, which, if effectively violated by a dismissal, justify the conclusion that the employee was necessarily unfairly dismissed.

Having considered briefly the range of automatically unfair dismissals, we focus our attention on the exercise of the tribunal's discretion in the application of the standard of reasonableness to the general category of disciplinary dismissals. The interpretation placed upon ERA 1996, section 98(4) is significant for it determines how far tribunals supervise the exercise of disciplinary power by employer and the extent to which tribunals insist upon precise standards of fairness. As in the common law jurisdiction over wrongful dismissals, the standard of reasonableness comprises both substantive and procedural criteria.

5.4.1.4 Automatically unfair dismissals

The automatic unfairness of the dismissal serves as a signal to employers that they should not consider dismissal on such grounds. The automatic unfairness of dismissals applies in three kinds of cases: to protect an employee's individual civil liberties and social rights, to provide guarantees for workers who take on representative roles on behalf of the workforce, and to protect workers against victimisation if they assert their legal rights against their employer (see Box below). Some grounds for dismissal are, perhaps surprisingly, not included expressly in this category of automatic unfairness, such as dismissal on grounds prohibited by anti-discrimination legislation, though undoubtedly once such reasons are established a tribunal will immediately conclude that such an unlawful dismissal was also unfair.

Most of these special provisions are considered in subsequent chapters. It should also be recalled that the qualifying period of one year for claims for unfair dismissal does not apply in these cases of automatically unfair dismissal. Nor does the upper age limit for claims for dismissal apply in these cases: ERA 1996, section 109(2). Three broader points are worth making here.

First, the selection of categories of automatic unfairness reveals decisions about which interests of employees or workers are regarded as inalienable social rights. This pattern of thinking has not been traditional in English law, so it is not surprising that historically the reason these particular instances have been selected as categories of automatic unfairness has often been in response to decisions of the European Court of Human Rights or the European Court of Justice. We may anticipate, therefore, an expansion of this category of automatic unfairness as the implications of the Human Rights Act 1998 are brought home and as the EC reinforces the Charter of Fundamental Rights of the European Union, now contained in the proposed EU constitution, with specific legislation.

The second general observation is that the method of enforcement of employment rights selected in the UK has been to grant individuals claims for compensation. We have noted that this is a relatively ineffective method for securing labour standards. One fundamental defect is of course that most employees will be reluctant to launch a legal action against their employer. The victimisation provisions, which protect the employee's right to pursue individual employment rights, are a weak, and probably ineffectual, attempt to remove one powerful reason employees might not wish to enforce their rights. A general principle is emerging that whatever legal rights are granted to an employee, there is a parallel protection against victimisation for the enforcement of those rights, though the principle has not been applied to all individual employment rights. One must doubt, however, whether the certain success of a claim for unfair dismissal, if the victimisation occurs and the employee can prove it, provides adequate reassurance for employees.

The third general observation is that automatic unfairness does not necessarily augment the amount of compensation payable to the employee. The sanction against the employer for violating basic social rights or interfering with their enforcement is normally no greater than an ordinary unfair dismissal for poorly justified disciplinary reasons. It is perhaps surprising that there is no room for a general principle permitting an award of aggravated damages here, though such awards are permitted in discrimination claims.

5.4.2 The range or band of reasonable responses test

How far do tribunals supervise management's disciplinary practices? The legislation empowers the tribunal to determine whether the employer's reason for the dismissal was fair or unfair. Yet the tribunals have refrained from the imposition of detailed standards upon employers. Instead, tribunals have respected the autonomy of managerial disciplinary decisions by recognising a discretion within which the employer can act without detailed supervision.

Automatically Unfair Dismissals

Examples of the three kinds of automatically unfair dismissals are:

Social Rights

Dismissal for the reason that the employee is taking leave for family reasons including pregnancy, maternity, adoption, parental, paternity, and emergency leave: ERA 1996 s. 99.

Dismissal of certain shop workers and betting workers for refusing Sunday work: ERA 1996 s.101

Dismissal in connection with trade union membership and activities: TULRCA 1992 ss.152, 153

Dismissal in connection with recognition claims: TULRCA 1992, Sched. A1 paras. 161,162.

Dismissal in connection with a transfer of an undertaking: Transfer of Undertakings (Protection of Employment) Regulations 1981 Reg.8(1)

Dismissal for refusals to work under conditions of serious and imminent danger: ERA 1996 s. 100(1)(d)(e).

Dismissal for refusing to work in breach of the Working Time Regulations 1998: ERA 1996 s. 101A

Dismissal for making a protected disclosure: ERA 1996 s. 103A

Dismissal for taking protected industrial action: TULRCA 1992 s. 238A

Protection of Worker Representatives

Dismissal in connection with representation on health and safety issues: ERA 1996 s.100.

Dismissal for performing functions as trustee of occupational pension scheme: ERA 1996 s.102

Dismissal for performing functions of representing workers in connection with redundancies or transfers of undertakings: ERA 1996 s.103.

Dismissal for performing function of representative for the purposes of the Working Time Regulations 1998 Sched. 1: ERA 1996 s. 101A (1) (d).

Dismissal for performing function of representative in a European Works Council: Transnational Information and Consultation of Employees Regulations 1999 SI 3323, Reg. 28.

Victimisation

Dismissal for assertion of statutory rights enforceable in employment tribunals, including the right to a minimum wage, a working tax credit, the right to ask for flexible working: ERA 1996 ss.104, 104A, 104B, 104C.

Selection for redundancy on the above victimisation grounds: ERA 1996 s.105.

Dismissal for assertion of the right of a part-time worker not to be treated less favourably: Part-time Workers (Prevention of Less Favourable Treatment) Regs 2000, Reg. 7

Dismissal for assertion of the right of fixed-term employees not to be subjected to less favourable treatment: Fixed-Term Employees (Prevention of Less Favourable Treatment) Regs 2002, Reg. 6.

[5.45] *Iceland Frozen Foods Ltd v Jones* **[1983] ICR 17 (EAT)**

Browne-Wilkinson J:

We consider that the authorities establish that in law the correct approach for the industrial tribunal to adopt in answer the question posed by [ERA, section 98(4)] is as follows: (1) the starting point should always be the words of section [98(4)] themselves; (2) in applying the section an industrial tribunal must consider the reasonableness of the employer's conduct, not simply whether they (the members of the industrial tribunal) consider the dismissal to be fair; (3) in judging the reasonableness of the employer's conduct an industrial tribunal must not substitute its decision as to what was the right course to adopt for that of the employer; (4) in many, though not all, cases there is a band of reasonable responses to the employee's conduct within which one employer might reasonably take one view, another quite reasonably take another; (5) the function of the industrial tribunal, as an industrial jury, is to determine whether in the particular circumstances of each case the decision to dismiss the employee fell within the band of reasonable responses which a reasonable employer might have adopted. If the dismissal falls within the band the dismissal is fair: if the dismissal falls outside the band it is unfair.

The range or band of reasonable responses test suggests that tribunals must respect management's disciplinary decisions provided that the dismissal was within the scope of a reasonable exercise of discretion. Tribunals therefore refrain from acting like an appeal body against every decision to dismiss an employee. Their intervention is limited to instances of patent abuse of managerial power. This interpretation of ERA 1996, section 98(4) limits the degree of state supervision of managerial discretion. Tribunals respect the autonomy of management's power to govern the business by setting boundaries for the justifiable exercise of power, but not exercising that power themselves. The reason for this abstention may lie in part in the fear of encouraging dismissed employees to flood the tribunals with claims against every dismissal. The explanation may also lie in a reluctance to become involved in detailed managerial decisions, where the tribunal may lack adequate information and expertise to make better decisions. The approach may also reflect a perception of the proper division between public and private power: the state, as represented by the tribunals, should not intervene in private market relations except for compelling reasons of public interest. This view implicitly downgrades the public interest in the fairness of disciplinary decisions. This abstention is also reminiscent of the stance of the common law of wrongful dismissal. The common law refused to judge the substantive grounds for dismissal unless there was a breach of the agreement. The range of reasonable responses test establishes a similar abnegation, though with the new exception of the obscure boundary of unreasonableness. Whatever the explanation, there can be no doubt that the range of reasonable responses test draws the sharpest teeth from the legislation. For this reason, the range of reasonable responses test has been subjected to considerable criticism.

Under the range of reasonable responses test, the tribunals set outer limits to the exercise of management's disciplinary power. The question is how do the tribunals fix the limits of reasonableness. The answer in *Iceland Frozen Foods Ltd v Jones* is rather uninformative: the limits of the band of reasonableness are fixed by reference to the standards of a reasonable employer. But how does a tribunal ascertain the content of those standards? There is plainly a danger that the tribunal may assume that all employers act reasonably. If so, the standard of reasonableness will merely reflect the practices of employers. This 'standard-reflecting' approach, where the limits of reasonableness are fixed by the ordinary practices of employers, threatens to lead to the conclusion that, no matter how irrational, harsh or arbitrary a dismissal may appear to the tribunal, provided that other employers would have acted in the same way, the dismissal must have been reasonable. To escape this problem of a 'standard-reflecting' approach to fixing the boundaries of reasonableness, the tribunals need to impose their own standards. These standards are often described as 'objective', but where do these standards originate if not the subjective opinions of the members of the tribunal?

[5.46] *Williams v Compair Maxam Ltd* [1982] ICR 156 (EAT)

Browne-Wilkinson J:

The Industrial Tribunal is an industrial jury which brings to its task a knowledge of industrial relations both from the view point of the employer and the employee. Matters of good industrial relations practice are not proved before an Industrial Tribunal as they would be proved before an ordinary court; the lay members are taken to know them. The lay members of the Industrial Tribunal bring to their task their expertise in a field where conventions and practices are of the greatest importance.

The standards adopted by tribunals are described as objective, because they are supposed to exist already in the conventional practices of industrial relations. Such standards are not necessarily written down, but are supposed to be common knowledge among persons experienced in industrial relations. These conventions are presumably the result of explicit and implicit negotiations between employers and employees over a long period of time. In exercising disciplinary powers, the employer is reluctant to incite resentment or anger on the part of the workforce, for such reactions are likely to damage the co-operation on which efficient production depends. The employer therefore confines the exercise of disciplinary power to those instances when the employer believes dismissal will accrue, on balance, to the efficiency of the business by deterring misconduct and poor work, without damaging good working relations. This point of balance represents the product of an implicit negotiation between the employer and the employees, marking the limits to which disciplinary power can be exercised without inducing disruptive reactions from the employees. The conventions which evolve from this implicit negotiation provide the objective standard for the tribunal's decision.

Yet the conventional standard is not necessarily endorsed by the tribunal. The objective standard is held up as 'good' industrial practice. It is not every convention that can satisfy this standard. The tribunals must reflect upon those conventions and adopt only those which they regard as representing good industrial practice. In this way, the reliance upon conventional standards is not merely standard-reflecting, but does entail the imposition of some normative standards devised by the tribunal itself. Good industrial practice is an interpretation of conventions.

[5.47] H Collins, *Justice in Dismissal* (Oxford, Oxford University Press, 1992) 78

The members of the Industrial Tribunal draw upon their experience of the standards of employers, but then interpret that experience to set the boundary of the range of reasonable responses. The boundary line draws upon conventional practices, but represents an interpretation of those practices, viewing them in the light which the members of the tribunal regard as most fair and reasonable. The approach is neither wholly conventional nor normative, neither merely standard-reflecting nor standard-imposing. The tribunal adopts an interpretative approach itself, taking its own view of industrial practice viewed in its best light. Because this fairness standard is an interpretation of practice, not just a description of conventional standards, it therefore becomes susceptible to an interpretation itself.

At first sight, the standard of 'good industrial practice' offers employees considerable protection against arbitrary and unreasonable disciplinary action. But this provisional judgment must be questioned for two reasons. In the first place, it should be noticed that the conventions on which the tribunal draws have as their origin the implicit negotiation between employer and employees. These conventions therefore reflect the bargaining power between the parties. If in the past employers have enjoyed sufficient bargaining power to insist upon a harsh disciplinary policy, interpretations of these conventions are likely to uphold and reinforce standards that pay scant respect to the employees' interests in job security. Secondly, it must be recalled that the standard of 'good industrial practice' sets only the boundaries to reasonable behaviour, so that employers can operate a severe disciplinary policy provided that they do not step outside the spectrum of conventions recognised by the standard of 'good industrial relations practice'.

The former point can be illustrated by reference to employers' disciplinary rules. In order to avoid doubt and disputes, many larger employers promulgate the standards of their disciplinary policy in a written document such as works rules or a staff handbook. This document therefore represents the employer's view of where the balance should be struck in order to maximise the efficiency benefits of discipline. If the employer follows these rules, is there any likelihood that the dismissal might be found by a tribunal to be unfair?

[5.48] *Hadjioannou v Coral Casinos Ltd* [1981] IRLR 352 (EAT)

The applicant was suspended and then dismissed from his position as a blackjack inspector at one of the employer's gambling clubs. The reason for dismissal was breach of Rule 13 of the company's Rules that stated: 'Staff are not permitted to socialise with any members of the clubs or their guests on the premises and should not do so off the premises without the knowledge and consent of the management'. Mr Hadjioannou had broken this rule by having business conversations with one punter. He had also borrowed money from another customer, a lady X, and there was a suggestion that the interest of lady X in the appellant went beyond mere business matters. He acknowledged breach of the rule, but argued that other employees had broken the rule and had not been dismissed. The tribunal received evidence of disparity in treatment in that another employee who had broken the rule had been permitted to resign, and another employee had been given a warning and had been transferred. By a majority, the tribunal held the dismissal to be fair. The EAT dismissed the appeal.

Waterhouse J:

In resisting the appeal, counsel for the respondents, Mr. Tabachnik, has submitted that an argument by a dismissed employee based upon disparity can only be relevant in limited circumstances . . . Firstly, it may be relevant if there is evidence that employees have been led by an employer to believe that certain categories of conduct will either be overlooked, or at least will be not dealt with by the sanction of dismissal. Secondly, there may be cases in which evidence about decisions made in relation to other cases supports an inference that the purported reason stated by the employers is not the real or genuine reason for a dismissal . . . Thirdly, Mr Tabachnick concedes that evidence as to decisions made by an employer in truly parallel circumstances may be sufficient to support an argument, in a particular case, that it was not reasonable on the part of the employer to visit the particular employee's conduct with the penalty of dismissal and that some lesser penalty would have been appropriate in the circumstances. We accept that analysis by counsel . . .

As for the other points raised in the notice of appeal, they are very closely linked with the alleged disparity. The Industrial Tribunal considered fully the submission that it was appropriate that publicity should have been given to the staff about any tightening up of the rules before the tightening was implemented. However, the Industrial Tribunal came to the conclusion that, in the particular circumstances of this case, it was reasonable for the management to apply the rule by dismissing the appellant on the basis of his proved conduct, having regard to the employer's view of the gravity of that conduct . . .

What is most striking about this decision is the absence of any evaluation of the merits of the employer's disciplinary rule. It is assumed that the rule must state the appropriate substantive standard for disciplinary matters. There is no examination, for instance, of the question whether other employers in the same line of business apply a similar disciplinary rule, which might demonstrate the importance of the rule to the success of the employer's business. The employer's view of the gravity of the rule suffices to justify dismissal for breach of the rule. The sole line of attack available to the employee appears to be a reliance on inconsistency in management's application of the disciplinary rule. This requirement of consistency is sometimes attributed to the notion of equity in the statutory formulation.

[5.49] *Post Office v Fennell* [1981] IRLR 221 (CA)

The word 'equity in the phrase 'having regard to equity and the substantial merits of the case' in [ERA, section 98(4)] comprehends the concept that employees who behave in much the same way should have meted out to them much the same punishment.

Even when the tribunal considers evidence of inconsistent management application of the disciplinary rule, there is strong deference to management's appreciation of the differences between particular cases and respect for the employer's exercise of discretion whether or not to use the ultimate sanction of dismissal. It may be possible sometimes to challenge an employer's consistent application of a harsh disciplinary rule, but only where the employee's breach of the rule was venial and the employer had given an impression that the rule might be relaxed: *Ladbroke Racing Ltd v Arnott* [1983] IRLR 154 (Ct.Sess.). This endorsement of employers' disciplinary rules, that is deference to the employer's view of the convention governing good industrial practice at the particular workplace, reveals how the standard imposed by the tribunals is unlikely to require disapproval of dismissal decisions in many instances.

The 'range of reasonable responses test' accentuates this weakness in the control of managerial disciplinary power under the standard of 'good industrial relations practice'. Nowhere does this become more apparent than in the absence of a principle of proportionality with respect to the harshness of the punishment of dismissal in the circumstances.

[5.50] *British Leyland UK Ltd v Swift* [1981] IRLR 91 (CA)

After 18 years' service, an employee was dismissed when a car's tax disc belonging to the employer was discovered on the employee's personal vehicle. He was subsequently convicted of a criminal offence. The tribunal held that the employer had abundant evidence to support the view that the applicant had been guilty of gross misconduct, but it found the dismissal unfair on the ground that the dismissal was too severe a penalty for a relatively minor offence after many years of satisfactory service. The Court of Appeal allowed the employer's appeal.

Lord Denning MR:
The first question that arises is whether the Industrial Tribunal applied the wrong test. We have had considerable argument about it. They said: ' . . . a reasonable employer would, in our opinion, have considered that a lesser penalty was appropriate'. I do not think that that is the right test. The correct test is: Was it reasonable for the employers to dismiss him? If no reasonable employer would have dismissed him, then the dismissal was unfair. But if a reasonable employer might reasonably have dismissed him, then the dismissal was fair. It must be remembered that in all these cases there is a band of reasonableness, within which one employer might reasonably take one view: another quite reasonably take a different view. One would quite reasonably dismiss the man. The other would quite reasonably keep him on. Both views may be quite reasonable. If it was quite reasonable to dismiss him, then the dismissal must be upheld as fair, even though some other employers may not have dismissed him.

But there is a further point. It is whether the Industrial Tribunal took into account all relevant considerations. It seems to me that they failed to take into account the conduct of Mr Swift after the offence was discovered . . . Mr Swift did not 'come clean' when he was found out. He put forward a wholly untruthful account. That seems to me to be a most relevant consideration for the employers to take into account in deciding whether it was reasonable to dismiss him or not . . . . [The tribunal refer to the criminal offence] almost as if he had paid the penalty and ought not to be penalised for it any more. If a man is convicted and fined, it is a ground for dismissing him, not for keeping him on . . . .

I am not prepared to say that no reasonable employer would have dismissed him in the circumstances. On the contrary, it seems to me that many a reasonable employer in the circumstances would have thought it right to dismiss him. I would therefore allow the appeal and hold that the dismissal was fair and not unfair.

Although it must be correct that if tribunals are not to substitute their own judgments as to the fairness of a dismissal, they must refrain from precise calibrations of the proportionality of the punishment, Lord Denning's interpretation of the range of reasonable responses test effectively denies any test of proportionality at all. The tribunal had taken the view that under the conventions of good industrial relations practice, this lengthy period of satisfactory service should have reduced the sanction imposed by the employer. But the Court of Appeal tells them that they have committed an error of law: the range of reasonable responses test does not permit the enforcement of the tribunal's interpretation of the convention; the employer can act upon its own interpretation provided the tribunal accepts that other employers share that view of the convention. The Court has also subsequently made it clear that in determining the reasonableness of the severity of the sanction the employer can look beyond the facts of the particular case in order to use a severe disciplinary sanction as a deterrent to others: *British Railways Board v Jackson* [1994] IRLR 235 (CA).

The range of reasonable responses test of fairness has these two principal effects. First, it minimises judicial supervision of the exercise of managerial disciplinary power. In order to avoid detailed review of every borderline case of unfairness, the test tends towards the other extreme of permitting intervention only when the employer has acted wholly unreasonably or perversely. Secondly, the test prevents the application of the principle of proportionality of punishment. The outcome of this interpretation of the law is that tribunals frequently reach the paradoxical conclusion that a dismissal was 'harsh but fair'. The courts have been aware of the danger that this judicial interpretation of the fairness test might deprive employees of any significant protection for job security: eg *Haddon v Van Den Bergh Foods Ltd* [1999] ICR 1150 (EAT). The purpose of the statement of principles in *Iceland Frozen Foods Ltd v Jones* was to prevent the use of a test of perversity or extreme unreasonableness, which would confine cases of unfair dismissal to instances where the employer had acted irrationally or capriciously. Yet in practice it is hard to discern how the range of reasonable responses test of fairness differs from the minimal protection afforded to job security by a requirement that the employer should not have acted irrationally or capriciously.

Nevertheless, the Court of Appeal has reaffirmed the applicability of the range or band of reasonable responses test, accepting that as a consequence some disciplinary dismissals can be harsh but fair.

[5.51] *Post Office v Foley*; *HSBC v Madden* [2000] ICR 1283 (CA)

The Court considered two expedited appeals involving dismissal for suspected misconduct for the purpose of removing any doubt that the principles in *Iceland Frozen Foods Ltd v Jones* were still binding. We focus on the *Madden* case, where the employment tribunal had found an unfair dismissal of a bank employee owing to a lack of sufficient investigation of suspected fraud.

Mummery LJ:
Since Employment Tribunals throughout Great Britain decide thousands of unfair dismissal cases every month, it is crucial that uncertainty about the law to be applied by them should be dispelled as soon as possible.

In my judgment, the Employment Tribunals should continue to apply the law enacted in section 98(1), (2) and (4) of the Employment Rights Act 1996 (the 1996 Act), giving to those provisions the same interpretation as was placed for many years by this court and the Employment Appeal Tribunal on the equivalent provisions in section 57(1), (2) and (3) of the Employment Protection (Consolidation) Act 1978 (the 1978 Act).

This means that for all practical purposes:

(1) The band or range of reasonable responses approach to the issue of the reasonableness or unreasonableness of a dismissal, as expounded by Browne-Wilkinson J

in *Iceland Frozen Foods Ltd v Jones* [1983] ICR 17 at 24F–25D and as approved and applied by this court (see *Gilham v Kent County Council (No 2)* [1985] ICR 233; *Neale v Hereford & Worcester County Council* [1986] ICR 471; *Campion v Hamworthy Engineering Ltd* [1987] ICR 966; and *Morgan v Electrolux* [1991] ICR 369), remains binding on this court, as well as on the Employment Tribunals and the Employment Appeal Tribunal. The disapproval of that approach in *Haddon v Van Den Bergh Foods Ltd* [1999] ICR 1150 (EAT) on the basis that (a) the expression was a mantra which led Employment Tribunals into applying what amounts to a perversity test of reasonableness, instead of the statutory test of reasonableness as it stands, and that (b) it prevented members of Employment Tribunals from approaching the issue of reasonableness by reference to their own judgment of what they would have done had they been the employers, is an unwarranted departure from binding authority . . .

Unless and until the statutory provisions are differently interpreted by the House of Lords or are amended by an Act of Parliament, that is the law which should continue to be applied to claims for unfair dismissal. In so holding I am aware that there is a body of informed opinion which is critical of this interpretation of the 1996 Act . . .

A reminder of the fundamental constitutional difference between the interpretation of legislation, which is a judicial function, and the enactment and amendment of legislation, which is a parliamentary function, is required in view of the number of occasions on which reference was made in the submissions to a judicial gloss on the legislation. As Lord Nicholls said in *Inco Europe Ltd v First Choice Distribution* [2000] 1 WLR 586 at 592E–F:

'The courts are ever mindful that their constitutional role in this field is interpretative. They must abstain from any course which might have the appearance of judicial legislation. A statute is expressed in language approved and enacted by the legislature'.

In this case the interpretation placed by the tribunals and courts, including this court, on the provisions of the 1978 Act . . . has not led Parliament to amend the relevant provisions, even though Parliament has from time to time made other amendments to the law of unfair dismissal, since those authoritative rulings on interpretation were first made. So those rulings, which have been followed almost every day in almost every Employment Tribunal and on appeals for nearly 20 years, remain binding.

They should be applied to the two cases under appeal with the result that both appeals should be allowed and both claims for unfair dismissal fail . . .

Mr John Madden was employed by the Midland Bank (now HSBC Bank plc) from September 1986. He was a lending officer (grade 4) at the date when he was summarily dismissed on 24th October 1997 for a reason relating to his conduct. He presented a complaint of unfair dismissal to the Employment Tribunal on 21st January 1998. The tribunal unanimously held that he was unfairly dismissed for the reasons set out in the Extended Reasons sent to the parties on 17th July 1998. The Employment Appeal Tribunal dismissed the appeal on 7th March 2000.

The Employment Tribunal held that a sufficient investigation into the alleged misconduct of Mr Madden was not carried out in all the circumstances before the decision was made to dismiss him, that more inquiries and investigations should have been made and that the decision to dismiss was not taken on reasonable grounds and was therefore unfair.

The Facts
The conclusions of the tribunal were based on the following findings of fact.

(1) Mr Madden was regarded as a good and trustworthy employee at the Enfield Town branch of the Bank. In June 1996 he was transferred from that branch to the Palmers Green branch, but continued to work one Saturday in four at Enfield Town. He had an unblemished record.

(2) In June and July 1997 three customers of the Bank had their debit cards misappropriated when they were despatched for collection by them at their branches. The cards were used to obtain goods by deception. Two of the customers, Mr Wood and Mr Clark, expected to collect their cards at the Enfield Town branch and the third, Mr Porter, expected to collect his card at the Palmer's Green branch.

(3) In July 1997 a bank employee made unauthorised inquiries through the Bank's internal Nixdorf computer system about the status of each of the three customers' accounts to which the debit cards related. The inquiries coincided with the fraudulent use of the cards.

(4) Mr Madden was in the relevant branches when the cards might have been misappropriated and he was the only member of the staff who was at the respective branches when all three inquiries were made by accessing the internal Nixdorf computer.

(5) On 1st September 1997 Mr Madden was arrested. He was later released without charge. He was suspended on full pay pending further investigations.

(6) On 7th October an investigation report was made by Mr C J Murphy, an investigating officer with Midland Security. He reported that the evidence indicated that Mr Madden may have had an involvement in the thefts, although he consistently denied taking the cards or making unauthorised computer inquiries on the customers' accounts.

(7) On 24th October 1997 a disciplinary hearing was held by the area manager, Mr Brian Fielder. Mr Madden was represented by a BIFU official. At the end of the hearing he was summarily dismissed on the ground that the Bank had a reasonable belief that he had been involved in the misappropriation of the cards which had been used fraudulently and that trust had irretrievably broken down.

(8) Mr Madden exercised his right of appeal, but did not proceed with it. His appeal was dismissed in his absence.

The Legal Position

In my judgment there was an error of law in the Extended Reasons given by the Employment Tribunal for concluding that Mr Madden was unfairly dismissed. The Employment Appeal Tribunal ought to have allowed the appeal and dismissed Mr Madden's claim.

In view of the earlier discussion of the relevant statutory provisions and case law the legal position can be briefly stated as follows:

(1) Reason for Dismissal

Why did the Bank dismiss Mr Madden?

There was no dispute that the reason for the dismissal of Mr Madden related to his conduct within the meaning of section 98(2)(b) of the 1996 Act, i.e. the Bank's reasonable belief that he had been involved in the misappropriation of the three debit cards which were subsequently used fraudulently and that that led to an irretrievable breakdown in trust between the Bank and Mr Madden.

(2) Reasonableness of the Dismissal

In the circumstances did the Bank act reasonably or unreasonably in treating that reason as a sufficient reason for dismissing Mr Madden?

In holding that the dismissal of Mr Madden for that reason was unreasonable the Employment Tribunal erred in law. It did not correctly apply the law as laid down in the authorities . . .

It impermissibly substituted itself as employer in place of the Bank in assessing the quality and weight of the evidence before Mr Fielder, principally in the form of the investigating officer's report. Instead it should have asked whether, by the standards of the reasonable employer, the Bank had established reasonable grounds for its belief that Mr Madden was guilty of misconduct and whether the Bank's investigation into the matter was reasonable in the circumstances.

The extent of the tribunal's substitution of itself as employer in place of the Bank, rather than taking a view of the matter from the standpoint of the reasonable employer, is evident from the tenor of the views expressed by the tribunal on the quality and weight of the available evidence against Mr Madden. I refer to the tribunal's cumulative critical comments on the Bank's internal investigation by Mr Murphy, on the disciplinary hearing by Mr Fielder and on the probative value of the material on which Mr Fielder based the summary dismissal: that there was no clear culprit for the misappropriation of the cards; that there was no firm evidence of the precise dates on which the cards were taken; that there was no direct evidence that Mr Madden had accessed the Nixdorf system; that there was no investigation of the personal or financial affairs of other members of the staff; that no account was taken of the nature of the goods bought with the stolen cards; that Mr Fielder failed to take account of the fact that a man in Mr Madden's financial and career position would not have jeopardised all for such a relatively paltry theft; that the facts of the case should have produced more than reasonable doubt in Mr Fielder's mind; that the investigators had closed their minds to any possibility other than the guilt of Mr Madden; that Mr Fielder came to a hasty conclusion that Mr Madden was probably guilty and was content to accept the report of the investigators too readily and uncritically; and that Mr Fielder's decision to dismiss Mr Madden, who had a stainless record of 11 years service, would effectively ruin his career and was not taken on reasonable grounds.

In my judgment no reasonable tribunal, properly applying the approach in *Burchell* [below p 529] and *Iceland Foods* to the facts, could have concluded either (a) that the Bank had failed to conduct such investigation into the matter as was reasonable in all the circumstances or (b) that dismissal for that reason was outside the range of reasonable responses.

Instead of determining whether the Bank had made reasonable investigations into the matter and whether it had acted within the range of responses of a reasonable employer, the tribunal in effect decided that, had it been the employer, it would not have been satisfied by the evidence that Mr Madden was involved in the misappropriation of the debit cards or their fraudulent use and would not have dismissed him. The tribunal focused on the insufficiency of the evidence to prove to its satisfaction that Mr Madden was guilty of misconduct rather than on whether the Bank's investigation into his alleged misconduct was a reasonable investigation.

This case illustrates the dangers of encouraging an approach to unfair dismissal cases which leads an Employment Tribunal to substitute itself for the employer or to act as if it were conducting a rehearing of, or an appeal against, the merits of the employer's decision to dismiss. The employer, not the tribunal, is the proper person to conduct the investigation into the alleged misconduct. The function of the tribunal is to decide whether that investigation is reasonable in the circumstances and whether the decision to dismiss, in the light of the results of that investigation, is a reasonable response.

Does this decision illustrate the problem that the test of the range of reasonable responses tends to lead to a test of perversity? The employment tribunal had made a series of criticisms of the investigation of the suspected fraud and the adequacy of the evidence on which the employer had acted. The bank had not found anyone other than Mr Madden who had had a clear opportunity to commit the crime and this fact alone had been enough for the dismissal. The employment tribunal concluded that this step was not reasonable in the circumstances. In so doing, the tribunal had undoubtedly used its own judgment in setting the limits of reasonable behaviour for the employer. It was this use of judgement, that is the exercise of the power of the industrial jury to set standards, which the Court of Appeal castigates for misapplying the statutory test of reasonableness. Yet the Court of Appeal's approach must also involve the same step in the reasoning: it must set an objective standard of reasonableness by which to assess the employer's conduct. It also had to determine whether the bank's investigation was reasonable in the circumstances, and whether the decision to dismiss was reasonable in the light of the investigation. The difference in outcome can be explained only by the broad range of reasonableness applied by the Court of Appeal. Whereas the employment tribunal had decided that the internal investigation was flawed in various respects and that therefore the bank had not acted reasonably in dismissing the employee in the circumstances, the Court of Appeal is effectively asking itself whether no reasonable employer would have dismissed the employee and concludes that the grounds for suspicion against the employee were sufficient for the decision to dismiss to be a rational one. The bank had not acted perversely, irrationally or arbitrarily, and thus in the view of the Court of Appeal the dismissal satisfied the range of reasonable responses test.

The range or band of reasonable responses test and the principles stated in *Iceland Frozen Foods Ltd v Jones* are now only open to reconsideration at the level of the House of Lords. The lower courts have been unable to formulate a test of reasonableness that distinguishes clearly between, on the one hand, a test of perversity or irrationality under which dismissals would be found to be unfair only if no reasonable employer would have dismissed in the circumstances of the case and, on the other hand, a test of reasonableness under which a tribunal may set a more balanced standard of fairness, taking into account the interests of employees in job security, without at the same time substituting the tribunal's subjective view of the merits for that of the employer. To solve this problem of setting determinate legal limits to a broad discretionary power in the context of administrative law, the courts increasingly turn to a test of proportionality as a more appropriate and searching test of the reasonableness of executive decisions. A test of proportionality investigates whether the decision-maker is pursuing a legitimate objective and, if so, asks whether the means that were adopted were necessary and proportionate to achieving that objective. Under this test, a court scrutinises closely the means chosen in order to ensure that they did not unnecessarily or disproportionately interfere with the rights of an individual. In the context of dismissal, we could apply this approach by analogy so that the question for the tribunals would be first whether the employer was exercising the disciplinary power for a legitimate purpose such as ensuring the efficiency of production, and secondly whether the disciplinary sanction of dismissal was a necessary and proportionate means for achieving that goal in the circumstances of the case.

5.4.3 Procedural fairness

Despite the courts' evident reluctance to supervise disciplinary dismissals closely, in one respect they have been particularly assertive in setting normative standards. Courts and tribunals have insisted in their interpretation of ERA 1996 s.98(4) and as part of the conventions of 'good industrial practice' that employers should follow reasonable procedural steps prior to making a dismissal. These required procedural steps have not been formulated as preciserules, but according to the circumstances of the case the tribunal may insist that standards of fairness require, for example, the employer to give the opportunity to explain alleged misconduct, or to improve performance, before any dismissal takes place. A claim that an employer operated an unfair procedure prior to dismissal is by far the most likely ground for a successful application for unfair dismissal.

This willingness of tribunals and judges to impose procedural standards may have several explanations. Procedural requirements may be perceived by the courts as posing a lesser degree of interference with managerial discretion than substantive standards. A fair procedure can be presented as a necessary ingredient of any rational personnel policy, because it ensures both that dismissals occur only when dismissal lies in the employer's economic interest, and that potential damage to co-operation from the remaining workforce owing to resentment against harsh discipline is minimised. Another explanation may simply be that in addressing questions of procedural fairness the courts are dealing with familiar principles of 'natural justice' or 'due process', which can be applied by analogy to public law standards. The willingness to set procedural standards was reinforced by the promulgation of a detailed Code of Practice by ACAS, which articulated standards of good industrial practice with respect to disciplinary procedures. Tribunals are expected to take into account the advice from ACAS on best practice with respect to disciplinary procedures in determining whether or not the employer acted reasonably, though non-compliance with the Code does not necessarily lead to a finding of unfairness.

5.4.3.1 General fairness standard. An employer's breach of fair procedural standards can therefore render a dismissal unfair in itself under ERA 1996 s.98(4), though the eventual measure of compensation may be reduced substantially for contributory fault on the part of the employee. But these fair procedural standards are not fixed legal requirements. Ultimately, procedural standards also depend upon the application of the range of reasonable responses test, so that a tribunal may conclude that in all the circumstances an employer acted reasonably even though the procedure was perfunctory.

↳ *dutiful; mechanical .*

[5.52] *Polkey v A.E. Dayton Services Ltd* [1988] ICR 142 (HL)

> After four years of employment as a van driver, the appellant had been summoned to the manager's office and told out of the blue that he was dismissed immediately for redundancy. The tribunal described the employer's conduct as a 'heartless disregard of the provisions of the code of practice', though it also found that the employer's need to make redundancies was an urgent necessity. Mr. Polkey appealed against the tribunal's decision that the dismissal was fair because it was inevitable owing to the employer's business needs. The House of Lords allowed the appeal and remitted the case to be heard by another tribunal.

> **Lord Bridge:**
> Employers contesting a claim of unfair dismissal will commonly advance as their reason for dismissal one of the reasons specifically recognised as valid by [ERA 1996 section 98(2)(a)(b)(c)]. These, put shortly, are: (a) that the employee could not do his job properly; (b) that he had been guilty of misconduct; (c) that he was redundant. But an employer

having prima facie grounds to dismiss for one of these reasons will in the great majority of cases not act reasonably in treating the reason as a sufficient reason for dismissal unless and until he has taken the steps, conveniently classified in most of the authorities as 'procedural,' which are necessary in the circumstances of the case to justify that course of action. Thus, in the case of incapacity, the employer will normally not act reasonably unless he gives the employee fair warning and an opportunity to mend his ways and show that he can do the job; in the case of misconduct, the employer will normally not act reasonably unless he investigates the complaint of misconduct fully and fairly and hears whatever the employee wishes to say in his defence or in explanation or mitigation; in the case of redundancy, the employer will normally not act reasonably unless he warns and consults any employees affected or their representative, adopts a fair basis on which to select for redundancy and takes such steps as may be reasonable to avoid or minimise redundancy by redeployment within his own organisation. If an employer has failed to take the appropriate procedural steps in any particular case, the one question the industrial tribunal is not permitted to ask in applying the test of reasonableness posed by section [98(4)] is the hypothetical question whether it would have made any difference to the outcome if the appropriate procedural steps had been taken. On the true construction of section [98(4)] this question is simply irrelevant. It is quite a different matter if the tribunal is able to conclude that the employer himself, at the time of dismissal, acted reasonably in taking the view that, in the exceptional circumstances of the particular case, the procedural steps normally appropriate would have been futile, could not have altered the decision to dismiss and therefore could be dispensed with. In such a case the test of reasonableness under section [98(4)] may be satisfied . . . .

If it is held that taking the appropriate steps which the employer failed to take before dismissing the employee would not have affected the outcome, this will often lead to the result that the employee, though unfairly dismissed, will recover no compensation or, in the case of redundancy, no compensation in excess of his redundancy payment. Thus *in Earl v Slater Wheeler (Airlyne) Ltd.* [1973] 1 WLR 51 the employee was held to have been unfairly dismissed, but nevertheless lost his appeal to the National Industrial Relations Court because his misconduct disentitled him to any award of compensation, which was at that time the only effective remedy . . . . An industrial tribunal may conclude, as in the instant case that the appropriate procedural steps would not have avoided the employee's dismissal as redundant. But if, as your Lordships now hold, that conclusion does not defeat his claim of unfair dismissal, the industrial tribunal, apart from any question of compensation, will also have to consider whether to make any order [for reinstatement or re-engagement under ERA 1996 section 113]. In a case where an industrial tribunal held that dismissal on the ground of redundancy would have been inevitable at the time when it took place even if the appropriate procedural steps had been taken, I do not, as at present advised, think this would necessarily preclude a discretionary order for re-engagement on suitable terms, if the altered circumstances considered by the tribunal at the date of the hearing were thought to justify it.

This decision insists that the fact that a fair procedure would not have altered the employer's decision to dismiss does not itself render the dismissal fair. The point is that at the time of the dismissal the employer had failed to act reasonably by carrying out adequate procedural steps such as an investigation and a hearing which a reasonable employer would have concluded were necessary, so that at that moment it was unreasonable to dismiss the employee. Parliament has, however, rejected this logical point, and reversed this aspect of the *Polkey* decision.

Dismissal on Suspicion of Misconduct

In many instances of possible misconduct, the employer cannot be sure whether the employee suspected of misconduct has in fact committed the disciplinary offence. Money or stock may be missing and circumstantial evidence may point to the guilt of a particular employee, but the employee protests her innocence and no strong evidence of guilt can be discovered. How should the employer deal with this case? Should the law require proof of misconduct 'beyond reasonable doubt', or should the employer be permitted to dismiss fairly on the basis of suspicion alone given that the suspicion no doubt leads to a breakdown in trust and confidence? The correct approach was established in the following case, and has since been confirmed by *Post Office v Foley* [2000] ICR 1283 CA (above **[5.51]**).

British Home Stores Ltd v Burchell [1978] IRLR 379 EAT

Arnold J

What the tribunal has to decide every time is, broadly expressed, whether the employer who discharged the employee on the ground of misconduct in question (usually, though not necessarily, dishonest conduct) entertained a reasonable suspicion amounting to a belief in the guilt of the employee of that misconduct at that time. That is really stating shortly and compendiously what is fact more than one element. First of all, there must be established by the employer the fact of that belief: that the employer did believe it. Secondly, that the employer had in his mind reasonable grounds upon which to sustain that belief. And thirdly, we think, that the employer, at the stage at which he formed that belief on those grounds, at any rate at the final stage at which he formed that belief on those grounds, had carried out as much investigation into the matter as was reasonable in the circumstances.

Subsequent decisions have approved this test, though they have explained that the range of reasonable responses applies to the tests of reasonableness at the second and third stages of the approach in *British Homes Stores Ltd v Burchell*. It is therefore wrong for a tribunal to hold that an employer acted unfairly on the ground that the tribunal did not itself think that the employer had reasonable grounds for suspicion, or that the employer's investigation was inadequate. These issues must be regarded objectively by reference to the range of reasonable employers: *Sainsbury plc v Hitt* [2002] EWCA Civ 1588, [2003] ICR 111 (CA).

[5.53] Employment Rights Act 1996 section 98A

(2) ...failure by an employer to follow a procedure in relation to the dismissal of an employee shall not be regarded for the purposes of section 98(4)(a) as by itself making the employer's action unreasonable if he shows that he would have decided to dismiss the employee if he had followed the procedure.

The width of this exception to the requirement of procedural fairness set by ERA 1996 s.98(4) should not be underestimated. In most disciplinary dismissals, an employer may be able to argue plausibly that, even if the employee had been given a fair hearing, the dismissal would have gone ahead anyway.

Even without this provision, it is important to notice that the standards of procedural fairness are influenced by the requirements of substantive fairness, so that when the employer has a compelling ground for dismissal, such as grave misconduct or an urgent need to make redundancies, the employer may act within the range of reasonable responses in relaxing or ignoring procedural standards of fairness. It follows that where an employer fails to comply with a contractual disciplinary procedure, this breach of contract will not necessarily result in a finding of unfairness under section 98(4) ERA 1996. Although normally the employer's failure to comply with its own disciplinary code, by for example denying the employee a right of appeal, will result in a finding of unfair dismissal for a failure to follow a fair procedure (*West Midlands Co-operative Society v Tipton* [1986] ICR 192 (HL)), the employer may be able to persuade the tribunal that in the circumstances, such as grave misconduct, the breach of contract was within the range of reasonable responses.

5.4.3.2 Statutory minimum disciplinary procedure. The Employment Act 2002 reformed this procedural aspect of the test of fairness for unfair dismissal by introducing mandatory minimum procedural standards for disciplinary dismissals. The reform provides fairly precise procedural standards applicable to all employers in all situations, so that the uncertainties generated by the vague standard of reasonableness can be avoided. The objective of the reform was to reduce the number of unfair dismissal claims brought by employees by compelling employers to follow fair disciplinary procedures. The anticipated reduction in claims would result from employers being more careful with respect to dismissals, thereby eliminating hasty and unreasonable dismissals, and from making it much harder for employees to impugn the fairness of the procedure, assuming that employers had complied with the statute. Failure by an employer to comply with the statutory minimum disciplinary procedure results in an automatic finding of unfair dismissal.

[5.54] Employment Rights Act 1996 section 98A

> 98A An employee who is dismissed shall be regarded for the purposes of this Part as unfairly dismissed if—
> (a)   one of the procedures set out in Part 1 of Schedule 2 to the Employment Act 2002 (dismissal and disciplinary procedures) applies in relation to the dismissal,
> (b)   the procedure has not been completed, and
> (c)   the non-completion of the procedure is wholly or mainly attributable to failure by the employer to comply with its requirements.

If an employer complies with the minimum statutory procedure, an employee may still argue that the procedure adopted was unreasonable in the circumstances under section 98(4) ERA 1996. For example, if the employer ignored a contractual or internal disciplinary procedure, the employee could argue that, notwithstanding the employer's conformity to the statutory minimum, the disciplinary procedure was unreasonable in all the circumstances. Employers can contest that conclusion by arguing under section 98A(2) ERA 1996 ([5.53] above) that any more elaborate procedure would have been futile. Since employers can usually make the plausible argument that a more elaborate procedure would have made no difference to their decision to dismiss, a possible effect of this legislation may be for employers to abandon their own internal disciplinary procedures insofar as they exceed the statutory minimum requirements. In short, the minimum standard may in practice also become a maximum.

The government presented the statutory minimum disciplinary procedure as a simple 'three step' procedure—a written warning of dismissal, a hearing, and the right to an appeal. But in fact the statutory procedural requirements are far more elaborate:

- without unreasonable delay, the employer must send to the employee a written statement describing the employee's alleged conduct or characteristics, or other circumstances, which are causing the employer to contemplate dismissing the employee, and invite the employee to a meeting.
- Prior to the meeting the employer must inform the employee of the evidence that provides the grounds for the proposed dismissal and give the employee a reasonable opportunity to consider his response to that information.
- The timing and location of the meeting must be reasonable and held without unreasonable delay.
- The employee must take all reasonable steps to attend the meeting.
- No dismissal should take place prior to the meeting.
- The meeting must allow both employer and employee to explain their cases.
- The employee can choose to be accompanied by either a colleague or a trade union representative.
- After the meeting the employer must inform the employee of the decision and notify the employee of a right to appeal against the decision.
- If the employee wishes to appeal the decision, the employee must notify the employer.
- The employer should then hold a further meeting, at a reasonable time and place, and without undue delay, and the employee should take all reasonable steps to attend.
- At an appeal meeting the employer should, as far as reasonably practicable, be represented by a more senior manager than the representatives who attended the first meeting.
- At the appeal meeting, both employer and employee must be permitted to explain their cases, and the employee can be represented by either a colleague or a trade union representative.
- After the appeal meeting the employer must inform the employee of its final decision.

Although the employer is normally required to follow this minimum procedure, the legislation provides some important exceptions.

5.4.3.3 Modified procedure.   Regulations permit the employer to carry out a summary dismissal without a prior hearing under certain conditions, though the employer is still required to offer the employee an appeal process as described in the last six bullet points above.

[5.55] Employment Act 2002 (Dispute Resolution) Regulations 2004 (SI 2004/752) Regulation 3

> (2) . . . the modified dismissal procedure applies in relation to a dismissal where—
> (a) the employer dismissed the employee by reason of his conduct without notice,
> (b) the dismissal occurred at the time the employer became aware of the conduct or immediately thereafter,
> (c) the employer was entitled, in the circumstances, to dismiss the employee by reason of his conduct without notice or any payment in lieu of notice, and
> (d) it was reasonable for the employer, in the circumstances, to dismiss the employee before enquiring into the circumstances in which the conduct took place . . .

The right to use this modified procedure is therefore contingent on two conditions. First, under (c), the dismissal must be made in circumstances where under the common law of wrongful dismissal the employer would have been able to make a justified summary dismissal (5.1.1.1.4, above). Second, in addition under (d), it seems that the employer must also be able to claim that the circumstances were such that under the general test of fairness of ERA 1996 s.98(4), as interpreted in *Polkey* (**[5.52]** above), it was reasonable for the employer to conclude that it was unnecessary and futile to hold a hearing prior to dismissal. Satisfaction of both these conditions may prove difficult for employers except in cases of especially grave misconduct where the employee is caught red-handed. Even so, this support for the continuation of the managerial practice of summary dismissals may undermine the aims of the legislation, because instead of holding a hearing prior to any dismissals, employers may decide to risk a summary dismissal in the hope of satisfying the conditions for the modified procedure, thereby not going through the hearing process which the government reasonably expects would weed out most precipitate and unfair dismissals before they happen. An alternative that would have enabled employers to act swiftly to exclude a particular employee from the workplace might have been to grant a general power to employers to suspend employees, with or without pay, prior to the first hearing.

5.4.3.4 Collective disputes.   Under Regulation 4, an employer is not required to follow any statutory disciplinary procedure in the context of many collective disputes with the workforce. This exclusion applies in particular to dismissal of employees taking industrial action, and dismissals for economic reasons such as sudden business closure or mass dismissals for redundancy where the collective consultation and information procedures apply (below **[10.62]**). The existence of these exclusions can be explained on the ground that it would be better in such cases for the employer to follow a collective procedure with a recognised trade union to resolve the dispute, but it should be noted that the exclusions apply even if the employer is not engaged in collective negotiations at all.

5.4.3.5 Exceptional circumstances.   The statutory disciplinary procedures do not apply (or do not have to be completed in full) in the following circumstances:

[5.56] Regulation 11(3) Employment Act 2002 (Dispute Resolution) Regulations 2004

(a) the party has reasonable grounds to believe that commencing the procedure or complying with the subsequent requirement would result in a significant threat to himself, his property, and other person or the property of any other person;

(b) the party has been subjected to harassment and has reasonable grounds to believe that commencing the procedure or complying with the subsequent requirement would result in his being subjected to further harassment; or

(c) it is not practicable for the party to commence the procedure or comply with the subsequent requirement within a reasonable period.

The exceptional circumstance in (c) is potentially broad. An employer might find all kinds of plausible excuses for deferring the holding of a disciplinary hearing or an appeal.

5.4.3.6 Remedies for breach of the statutory minimum procedure. The employer's failure to comply with the statutory procedure where it is required results in an automatic finding of unfair dismissal. The tribunal is then instructed to increase the level of compensation awarded to the dismissed employee, unless there are exceptional circumstances such as those described above. The tribunal must increase any award it makes to the employee by 10 per cent and may, if it considers it just and equitable in all the circumstances to do so, increase it by a further amount, but not so as to make a total increase of more than 50 per cent: Employment Act 2002 section 31(3). Equally, however, if the non-completion of the statutory procedure is wholly or mainly attributable to the employee, as for example where the employee refuses to attend a hearing or an appeal, the tribunal may reduce the award of compensation by the same amounts: Employment Act 2002 section 31(3).

This statutory reform of procedural fairness in relation to disciplinary dismissals goes a long way towards reducing the uncertainty of the previous legal framework and to providing strong incentives for all employers to adopt internal disciplinary procedures that afford workers a fair hearing prior to dismissal. The statutory procedures have been criticised, however, by Professors Hepple and Morris as 'so rudimentary in nature that they afford little protection to employees': B Hepple QC and G S Morris, 'The Employment Act 2002 and the Crisis of Individual Employment Rights' (2002) 31 ILJ 245, 355. That criticism seems a little harsh when one looks at all the stages and requirements described above. Nevertheless, in its effort to keep the procedure simple and clear, the government may have omitted some vital elements of fairness in disciplinary procedures, such as a requirement for an employer to carry out a careful investigation of the facts prior to the hearing and for the employer to consider whether some lesser penalty than dismissal would be appropriate. If the employer merely conforms to the statutory procedure, it is possible for a tribunal to find the dismissal unfair on procedural grounds under the general test of fairness of ERA 1996 section 98(4). But we have observed that this additional protection has been substantially undermined by the resurrection of the futility rule in ERA 1996 section 98A(2). Furthermore, the preservation of the employer's power of summary dismissal, that is the right to dismiss for grave misconduct prior to any hearing at all, may prove a wide and unsatisfactory exception to the full mandatory statutory procedure.

5.4.4 Substantive fairness

The range of reasonable responses test of fairness grants employers considerable discretion in determining whether or not to carry out a dismissal for a particular reason. Although misconduct and lack of capability to perform the job provide the most common grounds for disciplinary dismissals, the employer can put forward any substantial reason it chooses for the dismissal, and then it is left to the discretion of the tribunal to determine whether or not it was reasonable to dismiss for this reason. This discretion is limited in particular instances, as we have noted, by the special protection afforded to certain civil liberties and social rights by the application of the rule of automatic unfairness (above 5.4.1.4). The question to be considered here is whether the tribunals have developed under the range of reasonable responses test further standards that protect employees against unfair grounds for dismissal. In particular, have the tribunals provided adequate protection to the interests of employees in preserving their liberty, dignity, and privacy? The following decision has often been criticised for both failing to insist that the employer should have a rational ground for dismissal and failing to respect the privacy of the individual.

[5.56] *Saunders v Scottish National Camps Association Ltd* **[1980] IRLR 174 (EAT)**

> The appellant was employed as a maintenance handyman at a camp visited by children for physical and mental training. The appellant was dismissed and was given a written reason for dismissal: 'the reason is that information was received that you indulge in homosexuality. At a camp accommodating large numbers of school children and teenagers it is totally unsuitable to employ any person with such tendencies'. The tribunal regarded this reason as a substantial reason which could potentially justify a dismissal. The tribunal heard evidence from a psychiatrist that in his opinion heterosexuals were as likely to interfere with children as homosexuals, though the psychiatrist did acknowledge the existence of a considerable body of opinion to the contrary that lacked any scientific basis. In applying the test of reasonableness, however, the tribunal found that a considerable proportion of employers would take the view that the employment of a homosexual should be restricted, particularly when required to work in proximity and contact with children. This view was accepted as evidence of the opinion of reasonable employers, so the tribunal held the dismissal to be fair, because it fell within the range of reasonable responses. The EAT and the Court of Session [1981] IRLR 277 upheld this application of the range of reasonable responses test as disclosing no error of law.
>
> *Lord McDonald:*
> This is one of the cases where . . . the area of decision is indeterminate, and, provided the employer has approached the matter fairly and properly, and has directed himself properly, he cannot be faulted for doing what, in his judgment, is just and proper . . . Some employers faced with this problem might have decided not to dismiss; others, like the respondents, would have felt that in the interest of the young persons for whom they were responsible to parents it was the only safe course. Neither could be said to have acted unreasonably.

This decision can be criticised as violating principles of rationality and privacy. A principle of rationality would require the employer to demonstrate harm, or the risk of harm, to the business, caused by the continued employment of the worker, and that it would be better for the business to replace the employee. This principle would have required a finding of fact that the employee posed a risk of abuse to children or that the customers of the camp had become reluctant to send their children there. A principle of privacy would insist that the employee's sexual preferences outside work were not a basis for disciplinary action unless they caused harm to the business. In *Saunders* there was no evidence that the employee's homosexuality had caused any harm to the business whatsoever. Similar issues were raised in the next case, though here the competing right of the employee concerned freedom of expression.

[5.57] *Boychuck v Symons Holdings Ltd* [1977] IRLR 395 (EAT)

> The employer objected to badges worn by the employee, particularly one declaring 'lesbians ignite', which led the employer to dismiss the employee when she refused to take the badge off. The EAT insisted that the employer should bring evidence that that the badges might cause offence to other employees and customers before the dismissal could be regarded as fair. This requirement reflects the influence of a principle of rationality, because the presence of 'offence' might constitute harm to the business. On rather slender evidence of such offence, or the risk of offence, however, the dismissal was upheld as fair. This weighing of the evidence might have been different if the tribunal had placed more emphasis on the interest of the employee in freedom of expression.

Many of the cases which have been criticised for failing to give sufficient weight to the principles of rationality and privacy have concerned criminal offences outside working hours. Some offences committed outside working hours could justify dismissal under the rationality and privacy principles, such as a conviction for reckless driving if the employee works as a van driver. But many offences seem wholly unconnected to job performance and do not present any harm or threat of harm to the business. The decision to dismiss represents an act of moral condemnation rather than a business decision. The question is whether employers should be permitted to use their economic power to impose a sanction on the employee for conduct of which the employer disapproves in addition to any state sanction meted out by the criminal justice system.

It seems possible, however, that the Human Rights Act 1998 (see Chapter 6) may induce the tribunals to place greater weight in their determinations of reasonableness on the interests of employees in freedom of expression and privacy. In *X v Y* [2004] EWCA Civ 662, [2004] ICR 1634 (CA) 9 (**[6.8]** below) the Court of Appeal accepted that the reasonableness test in ERA 1996 s.98(4) must be interpreted, so far as possible, to bring it into conformity with the Convention rights protected by the Human Rights Act 1998. It follows that it would not normally be fair for an employer to dismiss an employee for a reason that amounted to an unjustified interference with an employee's private life or freedom of expression. But the Convention rights protected by the Human Rights Act have a narrow compass, and may not provide much additional protection for employees against extensive use of disciplinary powers by employers. For example, although the right to privacy protects individuals against intrusions into their private sexual behaviour, it does not normally extend to sexual acts committed in public. Thus on facts similar to those in *Saunders*, the Court of

Appeal decided in *X v Y* that because the homosexual act had occurred in a public toilet the right to privacy did not apply at all. Furthermore, even where a tribunal finds that the reason for the dismissal did intrude on a Convention right, it is possible to argue that the interference was justifiable in the circumstances. In the case of *Boychuck,* for instance, where freedom of expression was arguably at stake, the employer could have argued that the interference was justifable in order to protect the rights of other employees and customers not to be offended, or to prevent economic harm to the business. The question for the tribunal is whether the dismissal was a proportionate response in the sense that the employer was pursuing a legitimate purpose and dismissal was necessary and appropriate to achieve that purpose. In *Pay v Lancashire Probation Service* [2004] ICR 187 (EAT), the employers satisfied this test of justification in the circumstance that they had dismissed a probation officer who worked with sex offenders and their victims because of his activities outside working hours in the entertainment industry involving bondage and sado-masochistic practices. The EAT held that although the dismissal interfered with the employee's freedom of expression, the dismissal was justified by the legitimate considerations about adverse publicity which might rebound upon the Probation Service if they continued to employ him. Assuming that this fairly low threshold for satisfying the test of proportionality in justifying interferences with Convention rights is followed by the courts, it seems unlikely that the Human Rights Act 1998 will make a significant difference to the manner in which the tribunals interpret the test of reasonableness. In particular, the law may still fail to protect the interest of the employee in resisting disciplinary action for conduct and behaviour outside working hours and in protecting freedom of expression both inside and outside the workplace.

It is also possible under restricted circumstances that the Nice Charter of Fundamental Rights of the European Union (above **[1.2]**), which is due to be incorporated into the proposed European Constitution, may have an impact on judicial interpretation of the substantive grounds for dismissal. Although these Charter Rights are not directly enforceable, the principles must be respected by all European Union institutions, including the European Court of Justice. It seems likely that the Court will be willing to consider whether national measures that implement EC law derogate unjustifiably from the Charter Rights: (J Hunt, 'Fair and Just Working Conditions' in T K Harvey and J Kenner (eds) *Economic and Social Rights under the EU Charter of Fundamental Rights—A Legal Perspective* (Oxford, Hart, 2003) Chapter 3). Although the European Union has not regulated the general field of dismissal law, several Directives have required the amendment of national legislation on unfair dismissal. These amendments have usually taken the form of a provision that a dismissal is automatically unfair if the reason for the dismissal was one prohibited by the underlying Directive. This automatic unfairness applies, for instance, to dismissals in response to leave taken for family reasons (eg pregnancy, maternity, parental) (ERA 1996 section 99), dismissals in response to the activities of health and safety representatives (ERA 1996 section 100), and dismissals in response to claims by employees that the employer had contravened the Working Time Regulations 1998 (ERA 1996 section 101A). The proper scope of these rules governing automatic unfairness depends ulitmately on the interpretation of European law, and for this purpose the Charter Rights may become relevant as a means of clarifying the exact scope to be accorded to the protection afforded by a Directive.

5.5 Remedies for unfair dismissal

5.5.1 Compliance and corrective justice

The sanctions for unfair dismissal may have two principal aims. One objective is to try to ensure that employers generally comply with the standard of fairness established by the legislation. In other words, the legislation should deter or prevent unfair dismissals. The other objective should be that an employee who has been subjected to an unfair dismissal should be properly compensated. The simultaneous pursuit of these two aims may not always prove compatible, and the pursuit of both may have to be qualified by the costs involved.

The normal outcome of a successful claim for dismissal is the award of a modest amount of compensation to the employee. Survey evidence from 2003 found the median award by tribunals for unfair dismissal was £4,231, with more than a third of successful applicants receiving less than £2000 (B Hayward, M Peters, N Rousseau, K Seeds, *Findings from the Survey of Employment Tribunal Applications 2003*, DTI Employment Relations Research Series No.33 (August 2004) p.147). This result serves neither aim very satisfactorily. The sum of money provides only a minor deterrent to the employer against breach of standards, so that in many cases the employer may conclude that it will be cheaper and more convenient to dismiss the employee and pay compensation than to comply with the law. The cost to the employer is further reduced because the expenses of dealing with a claim may be deducted from taxable profits as a business expense. Nor does the award of compensation appear to reflect all the employee's losses, especially once these include intangible expectations of security and enhanced income through long service and promotion.

An enhanced measure of compensation would redress these faults. It would supply the necessary incentive for compliance and provide full compensation for the employee. But it may be objected that heavy financial penalties for dismissal would deter employers from making even justified or fair dismissals, because the standard is too vague to provide a reliable guide for employers to use in a practical way.

Reinstatement provides a solution to this dilemma. A reinstatement reverses the dismissal, thereby ensuring compliance with the standard, without imposing major costs upon the employer. At the same time it prevents the employee's long-term losses from arising. But this remedy appears unattractive to the parties concerned: the dismissal and its surrounding events will probably have led to a loss of trust and confidence on both sides, to such an extent that neither party wishes to continue the relationship. Reinstatement therefore appears to be a solution that usually no-one wants.

The achievement of high levels of compliance with the legislation probably requires a rather different regulatory strategy. The required standards need to become part of the employer's normal operational procedures. For this purpose, the standards need to become more specific, established by Codes of Practice and similar normative guides. The employer must then be given an incentive to adopt those standards by gaining protection against claims for compensation or reinstatement, provided that the employer has genuinely complied with the detailed standards. The difficulty with this strategy is of course to agree a set of standards applicable to the wide range of different kinds of undertakings. A possible model is that each employer should be required to agree a detailed disciplinary code with a recognised trade union, a workplace council, or a labour inspector.

In the absence of such a more sophisticated regulatory strategy, the current legislation imitates a private law model of requiring the employee to bring a claim before a tribunal for reinstatement or compensation. Reinstatement is rarely awarded, so in practice the remedy lies in the modest award of compensation. In the following sections we assess whether this remedial strategy serves either of the aims for sanctions for unfair dismissal at all well.

5.5.2 Reinstatement

The primacy of the reinstatement remedy is emphasised in the legislation.

[5.58] Employment Rights Act 1996 section 112

112 (2) The tribunal shall—
   (a) explain to the complainant what orders may be made under section 113 and in what circumstances they may be made, and
   (b) ask him whether he wishes the tribunal to make such an order.
   (3) If the complainant expresses such a wish, the tribunal may make an order under section 113.
   (4) If no order is made under section 113, the tribunal shall make an award of compensation . . .

[5.59] Employment Rights Act 1996 section 113

113 An order under this section may be—
(a) an order for reinstatement . . .
(b) an order for re-engagement . . .

This procedure requires the employment tribunal to consider reinstatement or re-engagement at the request of the employee, but then gives it a discretion.

[5.60] Employment Rights Act 1996 section 116

116 (1) In exercising its discretion under section 113 the tribunal shall first consider whether to make an order for reinstatement and in so doing shall take into account—
(a) whether the complainant wishes to be reinstated,
(b) whether it is practicable for the employer to comply with an order for reinstatement, and
(c) where the complainant caused or contribute to some extent to the dismissal, whether it would be just to order his reinstatement.

Similar provisions apply to an order for re-engagement, which is an order for the employee to be re-employed on such terms as the tribunal may decide in employment comparable to that from which he was dismissed or other suitable employment: ERA 1996 section 115, 116(3).

These criteria for the exercise of discretion severely limit the scope for reinstatement and re-engagement. The tribunal is forbidden to override the wishes of the employee. By the time the case reaches the tribunal, it is likely that either the employee will have found another job and no longer wants reinstatement, or that the relations between the parties will have become acerbic, so that the employee believes that the breakdown of trust and confidence will prevent a workable and satisfactory restoration of the employment relation. In one survey, at the commencement of proceedings 75 per cent of claimants wanted reinstatement, but only 20 per cent continued to desire it after winning the case: P Lewis, 'An Analysis of Why Legislation has Failed to Provide Employment Protection for Unfairly Dismissed Workers' (1981) 19 *British Journal of Industrial Relations* 316. Later surveys suggest that a smaller percentage of employees put reinstatement as their preferred remedy on their original claim form: L Dickens et al., *Dismissed*, (Oxford, Blackwell, 1985) 116. The tribunal is also instructed to withdraw the remedy of reinstatement when the employee is to some extent at fault, if it would be just to do so. Since in most instances of disciplinary dismissals the employee is not wholly blameless, the provision has the potential to rule out reinstatement in the majority of cases. The third criterion for the exercise of discretion asks whether reinstatement is practicable. This criterion runs the risk that in effect it will give employers a veto over reinstatement. Employers can always argue that owing to a break down of trust and confidence, if not before the dismissal then certainly afterwards during acrimonious legal proceedings, it is not practicable to expect the necessary degree of co-operation for the employment relation to be restored properly. Although the courts are sensitive to this danger of giving the employer a veto over reinstatement, given their view that the employment relation depends upon co-operation, which relies on trust and confidence, the employer's assertion that there has been a breakdown of trust and confidence does strongly imply that reinstatement is impracticable.

In the unusual case where the tribunal orders reinstatement, the employer must comply or face a claim for compensation by the employee in addition to the normal compensation for unfair dismissal. This sanction is a type of punitive damages known as the additional award. This additional award may not present a strong measure of deterrence against disobedience to the order for reinstatement for two reasons. First, the level set for this additional award is not less than twenty-six and not more than fifty-two weeks' pay: ERA 1996 section 117(3). For low-paid employees this sum of money may not suffice to induce employers to comply with the order for reinstatement. Unlike the common law power of holding an employer to be in contempt of court and subject to unlimited fines for breach of an injunction, the employer can decide whether it prefers to comply with the order or pay the fixed measure of compensation instead. Second, the employer can avoid any sanction for disobedience to the order if the employer satisfies the tribunal that it was not practicable to comply with the order: ERA 1996 section 117(4)(a). This second insertion of the requirement that reinstatement should be practicable again presents the danger that the employer has a veto over the remedy. In determining this question, the statute merely provides the guidance that the fact that the employer has engaged a permanent replacement should be regarded as irrelevant, unless the employer shows that it was not practicable to arrange for the work to be done without engaging a permanent replacement: ERA 1996 section 117(7).

The following case illustrates the two tests of practicability in operation. It raises the question of whether the employer's business decision that it would not be efficient to reinstate the employee in effect determines the outcome of the case.

[5.61] *Port of London Authority v Payne* [1994] IRLR 9 CA

The employers had derecognised the union, changed terms of employment, and made a large number of dockers redundant. Among those dismissed, seventeen shop stewards succeeded in claims for unfair dismissal because they had been selected for redundancy on the ground of their trade union activities. The Industrial Tribunal ordered re-engagement for 12 claimants, making a finding at this first stage that re-engagement was practicable, but the employers failed to comply with the orders. In defence to a claim for an additional award, the employers argued that compliance with the order was not practicable on the grounds that there were no vacancies, and that it would be too disruptive and expensive to ask the remaining workforce if any wished to take voluntary redundancy in order to create suitable vacancies. The Industrial Tribunal rejected the employer's defence at this second stage. On appeal to the Court of Appeal, the court upheld the tribunal's initial decision to order reinstatement, but overturned the rejection of the employer's defence to the claim for an additional award.

Neill LJ:

It is quite true that at stage 1, that is before an order for re-engagement is made, the Industrial Tribunal must make a determination on the evidence before it whether it is practicable for the employer to comply with an order for re-engagement . . . But the determination that is made at stage 1 is a provisional determination or assessment. It is not a final determination in the sense that it creates an estoppel or limits an employer at stage 2 so that he can only rely on facts which have occurred after the order for re-engagement was made.

The conclusion that the determination at stage 1 is provisional accords with common sense and is supported by several authorities of the Employment Appeal Tribunal . . . In addition, our attention was drawn to . . . the guidance given by Wood J himself in *Rao v Civil Aviation Authority* [1992] IRLR 203 where he gave the following summary at 207:

'We extract from these cases the following principles:
(a)   Orders for reinstatement or re-engagement under [ERA 1996 section 113] are primary remedies for unfair dismissal.
(b)   Such orders are discretionary: see [ERA 1996 sections 113, 116].
(c)   The only fetter on that wide discretion is that a Tribunal must "take into account" the considerations set out respectively in [ERA 1996 sections 116(1) and (3)].
(d)   In both subsections the word "practicable" is used. It is not "possible"; is not "capable". At that stage an Industrial Tribunal is not required to reach a conclusion on practicability—whether it is or it is not practicable; that need only be decided if the provisions of [ERA 1996 section 117] become relevant, but the Act specifically requires that the Industrial Tribunal shall take into account practicability for the employer to comply with the order. An Industrial Tribunal must use its experience and common sense, looking at what has happened in the past and what can reasonably be anticipated

for the future, always maintaining a fair balance, that which is, in all the circumstances, fair, just, and reasonable between the parties.

(e) It is always unwise to seek to defines rules for different factual situations, but factors which have influenced decisions in the past are: the fact that the atmosphere in the factory is poisoned . . . the fact that the employee has displayed her distrust and lack of confidence in her employers and would not be a satisfactory employee on reinstatement . . . a change in policy which reinstatement would undermine . . . insufficient employment for the employee . . . and possibly where parties are in close relationships at work . . . '

The final conclusion as to practicability is made when the employer finds whether he can comply with the order within the period prescribed for reinstatement or re-engagement. At this second stage the burden of proof rests firmly on the employer.

[Neill LJ concluded that the Industrial Tribunal had correctly applied these principles in ordering re-engagement. He then considered the employer's appeal against the additional award for failure to comply with the order.]

It seems clear that the industrial Tribunal reached its conclusion on the practicability issue by the following process of reasoning:

(1) Mr Hills [a manager of PLA] knew that some members of the workforce might wish to apply for severance [i.e. voluntary redundancy] . . . .

(2) No efforts were made by Mr Hills to enquire whether anyone wished to apply for severance.

(3) The Tribunal did not accept the explanations that to make enquiries of the workforce was too unsettling and too expensive.

(4) Mr Hills had considered the 12 applicants as a group. Having decided that it was quite impossible to find places for them all he did not consider whether he could find places for any of them.

(5) As the PLA had not demonstrated that it was not practicable to comply with any of the re-engagement orders it had not satisfied the Tribunal on the balance of probabilities that it was not practicable to comply with the re-engagement orders as a whole . . . .

I have found this to be a very difficult part of the case. On the one hand it is necessary to bear in mind that the issue of practicability was a question of fact for the Industrial Tribunal to decide. An appellate court must therefore be very careful before it interferes with such a finding. But the test is practicability not possibility. The Industrial Tribunal, though it should carefully scrutinise the reasons advanced by the employer, should give due weight to the commercial judgment of the management unless of course the witnesses are to be disbelieved. The standard must not be set too high. The employer cannot be expected to explore every possible avenue which ingenuity might suggest. The employer does not have to show that reinstatement or re-engagement was impossible. It is a matter of what is practicable in the circumstances of the employer's business at the relevant time.

In the end I have come to the conclusion that the Industrial Tribunal misdirected itself as to the standard to be applied . . . I can well understand why the orders for re-engagement were made in the first place but it seems to me that once the matter was looked at again and in greater detail at the practicability hearing the case for the PLA was made out.

Despite the emphasis in the legislation upon reinstatement or re-engagement being the primary remedy for unfair dismissal, the remedy is rarely effective. The official statistics reveal that orders are made at most in 5 per cent of successful claims and 1 per cent of claims that proceed to a full tribunal hearing. This figure must be reduced, however, to take into account the cases reversed on appeal and those where the employer declines to comply with the order. On the other hand, these statistics do not reveal the number of cases where reinstatement is agreed as part of a settlement. ACAS reports that about 3 per cent of the cases settled through its conciliation process are resolved on the basis of the applicant being re-employed (ACAS, *Annual Report 1999/2000* (London: 2000) 33).

There is a tendency to blame the tribunals for a failure to apply the remedies of reinstatement and re-engagement. Yet the statute lays down guidelines for the exercise of discretion that prevent tribunals from making such orders. The tribunal must comply with the employee's wishes, and by the end of the tribunal hearing few employees still seek reinstatement. In the remaining instances, the test of whether the order was practicable emphasises the employer's business judgement rather than whether it might be fair or just to the employee to order reinstatement. The effect of that emphasis upon business judgement, as we saw in *Payne*, is that the employer's strong opposition can justify a refusal to make an order.

Can the legal procedures be reformed to increase the incidence of reinstatement? In order to overcome the problem that by the end of the hearing most employees no longer seek reinstatement, a tribunal might be empowered to order reinstatement as a form of interim relief. The tribunals have this power in cases where it appears to the tribunal that applicant is likely to succeed in his claim that the reason for dismissal is one which relates to trade union membership or activities, or relates to the employee's position as a health and safety representative or a trustee of the pension fund, that is some of the grounds for automatically unfair dismissals: ERA 1996 sections 128–29. But the employer can prevent reinstatement and merely continue to pay the employee's wages until the full hearing: ERA 1996 sections 129(9), 130. This power to order interim relief might be extended to all cases of unfair dismissal with a view to increasing the chances of a final reinstatement order, but it seems unlikely that employers would comply if they had the option of merely paying wages, and many employers would object to any payment at all, if they believed that the dismissal was justified. The procedure would also place a heavy and perhaps impracticable task on the tribunal to estimate the likelihood of success of a case before it had properly heard the evidence. Arbitration has also been presented as a possible procedure for enhancing the opportunity for reinstatement. But the technique of arbitration will not overcome the problem that at the time of the hearing most employees no longer seek reinstatement unless it occurs extremely quickly and avoids the antagonism of litigation. In any case, the delays associated with legal proceedings are only one factor in the absence of reinstatement as the normal remedy for unfair dismissal. Even where a settlement is achieved quickly through conciliation, it is clear that compensation is usually preferred by both parties as a solution to the dispute. The employer prefers to pay cash rather than reverse the disciplinary decision, and the employee usually believes that his best interests in the long term lie in seeking alternative employment.

Despite the primacy accorded to reinstatement in the procedures of the tribunals, the legislation in fact does not provide significant support for the remedy. It carefully avoids forcing employers to take back employees. As Lord Donaldson MR has observed, an order for reinstatment is 'wholly unenforceable': *O'Laire v Jackal International Ltd* [1990] IRLR 70, 73 (CA). It may therefore be a mistake to regard the objective of the legislation as one of protecting job security in the sense of protecting the employee's position in holding onto his job. The regulatory aim of the legislation may be rather one of improving the fairness of employer's disciplinary practices. For this purpose, a financial remedy suffices, provided that it is set sufficiently high that it becomes cost-effective for employers to alter their disciplinary practices in order to avoid the financial penalty. Indeed, a remedy of reinstatement may have much less impact upon employer's disciplinary practices, because reinstatement is usually cheap for employers, so that they can afford to ignore the regulation. Substantial financial compensation as the remedy for unfair dismissal should therefore be a much better regulatory strategy for enhancing job security. The level of compensation has, however, been kept rather low, so that the remedy has not provided sufficient incentive to comply with the objectives of the legislation.

Against these arguments for suggesting that substantial compensation may increase compliance, it must be recognised that it is hard for tribunals to provide compensation for all the expectations arising in an employment relation. The employee may have expectations of promotions and wage increases in the internal labour market of the firm, or the employee may enjoy this particular kind of work and be unable to find a similar satisfying vocation with another employer. A remedy of reinstatement can protect an employee against these losses completely, whereas an award of compensation will not capture these losses except to the extent that the employee can demonstrate that a wage increase was imminent (*York Trailer Ltd v Sparkes* [1973] ICR 518 NIRC), or that the wages in a subsequent job are lower because the employee cannot use his or her particular skills and experience. It should also be recognised that a dismissed employee is likely to find it harder to obtain work than one who is currently in employment. Although tribunals can award 'stigma damages' as part of the compensation for unfair dismissal, if the manner of dismissal impedes the employee from obtaining fresh employment (*Norton Tool Co Ltd v Tewson* [1972] ICR 501 NIRC, below **[5.63]**), reinstatement may be a more effective remedy for damage to reputation.

5.5.3 Compensation

The normal remedy for unfair dismissal comprises financial compensation in two parts: the basic award and the compensatory award. The basic award (which is the same as a redundancy payment) is calculated mathematically according to three main variables: age, years of service, and level of pay. In a simple case, an employee receives compensation amounting to a week's pay (or one and a half weeks' pay for years over 40 years old) for each year of service, up to a maximum of twenty years (ERA 1996 s. 119). There is an upper limit on a week's pay fixed at £270 (ERA 1996 s. 227). The compensatory award is, however, left to the discretion of the tribunal.

[5.62] Employment Rights Act 1996 section 123

(1) Subject to the provisions of this section and sections 124, 126, 127 and 127A(1),(3) and (4), the amount of the compensatory award shall be such amount as the tribunal considers

just and equitable in all the circumstances, having regard to the loss sustained by the complainant in consequence of the dismissal in so far as that loss is attributable to action taken by the employer.

5.5.3.1 Just and equitable award

Although the statute apparently confers on tribunals a broad discretion to award just and equitable compensation to unfairly dismissed employees, the courts moved swiftly to control the exercise of discretion by the tribunals. They insisted that the compensatory award should be calculated according to identifiable items of economic loss rather than a general award in the round. They also ruled out awards of aggravated damages to reflect any psychological suffering by the employee.

[5.63] *Norton Tool Co Ltd v Tewson* **[1972] ICR 501 NIRC**

The employee succeeded in a claim for unfair dismissal and was awarded £250 compensation. On an appeal against the measure of compensation, the National Industrial Relations Court (the forerunner of the EAT) took the opportunity to set down principles for the calculation of the compensatory award under the new jurisdiction of unfair dismissal.

Sir John Donaldson:
In our judgment, the common law rules and authorities on wrongful dismissal are irrelevant. That cause of action is quite unaffected by the Industrial Relations Act 1971 which has created an entirely new cause of action, namely, the 'unfair industrial practice' of unfair dismissal. The measure of compensation for that statutory wrong is itself the creature of statute and is to be found in the Act of 1971 and nowhere else. But we do not consider that Parliament intended the court or tribunal to dispense compensation arbitrarily. On the other hand, the amount has a discretionary element and is not to be assessed by adopting the approach of a conscientious and skilled cost accountant or actuary. Nevertheless, that discretion is to be exercised judicially and upon the basis of principle.

The court or tribunal is enjoined to assess compensation in an amount which is just and equitable in all the circumstances, and there is neither justice nor equity in a failure to act in accordance with principle. The principles to be adopted emerge from [ERA 1996 section 123]. First, the object is to compensate, and compensate fully, but not to award a bonus, save possibly in the special case of a refusal by an employer to make an offer of employment in accordance with the recommendation of the court or a tribunal. Secondly, the amount to be awarded is that which is just and equitable in all the circumstances, having regard to the loss sustained by the complainant. 'Loss' . . . does not include injury to pride or feelings. In its natural meaning the word is not to be so construed, and that this meaning is intended seems to us to be clear from the elaboration contained in [ERA 1996 section 123(2)(3)]. The discretionary element is introduced by the words 'having regard to the loss'. This does not mean that the court or tribunal can have regard to other matters, but rather that the amount of the compensation is not precisely and arithmetically related to the proved loss. Such a provision will be seen to be natural and possibly essential, when it is remembered that the claims with which the court and tribunals are concerned are more often than not presented by claimants in person and in condition of informality. It is not, therefore, to be expected that precise and detailed proof of every item of loss will be presented, although, after making due allowance for the skills of the persons presenting the claims, the statutory requirement for informality of procedure and the undesirability of burdening the parties with the expense of adducing evidence of an elaboration which is disproportionate to the sums in issue, the burden of proof lies squarely upon the complainant . . . In the present case the tribunal has not made entirely clear the principles upon which it has acted and to that extent has erred in law . . . In these circumstances, and in the light of the request of the parties to which we have already referred, we shall substitute our own award. In our judgment the employee is entitled to compensation in the sum of £375. This sum we regard as just and equitable in all the circumstances, having regard to the loss sustained by him. That loss falls to be considered under the following heads.

(a) Immediate loss of wages

The [ERA 1996 section 86] entitles a worker with more than ten years' continuous employment to not less than six [now ten] weeks' notice to terminate his employment. Good industrial practice requires the employer either to give this notice or pay six weeks' wages in lieu. The employee was given neither. In an action for damages for wrongful, as opposed to unfair, dismissal he could have claimed that six weeks' wages, but would have had to give credit for anything which he earned or could have earned during the notice period. In the event he would have had to give credit for what he earned in the last two weeks, thus reducing his claim to about four weeks' wages. But if he had been paid the wages in lieu of notice at the time of his dismissal, he would not have had to make any repayment upon obtaining further employment during the notice period. In the context of compensation for unfair dismissal we think that it is appropriate and in accordance with the intentions of Parliament that we should treat an employee as having suffered a loss in so far as he receives less than he would have received in accordance with good industrial practice. Accordingly, no deduction has been made for his earnings during the notice period.

We have no information as to whether the £25.60 per week is a gross or a take-home figure. The relevant figure is the take-home pay since this and not the gross pay is what he should have received from his employer. However, neither party took this point and we have based our assessment of this head of loss on six weeks at £25.60 per week or £153.60. The employee drew £3 unemployment benefit for a short period, but we were not asked to make any deduction for this and have not done so. Finally, we have taken no account of the extent to which the employee's income tax liability may be reduced by his period of unemployment, since we consider that the sums involved will be small and that such a calculation is inappropriate to the broad, common sense assessment of compensation which Parliament contemplated in the case of unfair dismissal of a man earning the employee's level of wages.

(b) Manner of dismissal

As the employee secured employment within four weeks of his dismissal and we have taken full account of his loss during this period, we need only consider whether the manner and circumstances of his dismissal could give rise to any risk of financial loss at a later stage by, for example, making him less acceptable to potential employers or exceptionally liable to selection for dismissal. There is no evidence of any such disability and accordingly our assessment of the compensation takes no account of the manner of his dismissal. This took place during a heated exchange of words between him and one of the directors.

(c) Future loss of wages

There is no evidence to suggest that the employee's present employment is any less secure than his former employment, and we have therefore taken no account of possible future losses due to short-time working, lay-off or unemployment, apart from loss of rights in respect of redundancy and unfair dismissal which are considered separately below.

(d) Loss of protection in respect of unfair dismissal or dismissal by reason of redundancy These losses may be more serious. So long as the employee remained in the employ of the employers he was entitled to protection in respect of unfair dismissal. He will acquire no such rights against his new employers until he has worked for them for two years [now one year] . . . Accordingly, if he is unfairly dismissed during that period, his remedy will be limited to claiming damages for wrongful dismissal, which are unlikely to exceed six weeks' wages and may be less. Furthermore, upon obtaining further employment he will be faced with starting a fresh two-year period. This process could be repeated indefinitely, so that he was never again protected in respect of unfair dismissal. Whilst it is impossible for us to quantify this loss, which must be much affected by local conditions, we think that we shall do the employee no injustice if we include £20 in our assessment on account of it.

The loss of rights under the Redundancy Payments Act 1965 [ERA 1996 Part XI] is much more serious. The employee is aged 50 and had been continuously employed for 11 years. Accordingly, if he had been dismissed on account of redundancy, he would have received about £380. In other words, he had a paid up insurance policy against dismissal by reason of redundancy which was worth this amount and would have increased in value at the rate of about £38 per annum, until it reached a maximum of perhaps £800. In his new job, the employee will receive no compensation if he is dismissed on account of redundancy within the first two years and, since he is now within 15 years of his 65th birthday, can never build up to the maximum which is based on 20 years' service. We have no evidence as to whether the employee is more or less likely to be made redundant in his new employment, but, if a redundancy situation does arise, he is clearly more likely to be selected for dismissal on the normal practice of 'last in, first out'. Nor have we any evidence as to the likelihood that if he had not been dismissed by the employers when he was, he might thereafter have been dismissed by reason of redundancy. In all the circumstances we think it just and equitable to base our award of compensation upon approximately one-half of his accrued protection in respect of redundancy; say, £200.

The arithmetical sum of these heads of compensation is £373.60, which we have rounded off at £375, which in our judgment represents compensation which is just and equitable in all the circumstances. In conclusion, we wish to emphasise that it is only because the parties so requested that we have substituted our own figure for that of the tribunal. But for that request we should have remitted the matter and, so long as the correct principles were applied and shown to have been applied, would not have interfered if they had awarded a different figure which might have been higher or lower.

This effect of this decision is to deprive the tribunal of the capacity to reflect in its award of compensation the degree of fault of the employer. '[T]he purpose of assessing compensation is not to express disapproval of industrial relations policy. It is to compensate for financial loss.': Sir John Donaldson, *Clarkson International Tools Ltd v Short* [1973] ICR 191, 196 NIRC. Under this approach, for instance, the failure of the employer to carry out a fair procedure in the case of a disciplinary dismissal contrary to ERA 1996 section 98(4) will not result necessarily in an award of compensation for the defective procedure, if either the employee suffers no economic loss from the dismissal or the employer had good substantive grounds for dismissal: *Earl v Slater & Wheeler (Airlyne) Lt*d [1972] ICR 508 NIRC. Similarly, in a case of failure to consult prior to a dismissal for redundancy, compensation will be reduced to reflect the likelihood that the dismissal would have occurred in any event (*British*

United Shoe Machinery Co Ltd v Clarke [1978] ICR 70 EAT), so that no compensation will be payable where plant closure and thus dismissal was certain (*James W Cook & Co (Wivenhoe) Ltd v Tipper* [1990] IRLR 386 CA). In sharp contrast, the tribunal is encouraged to ensure that the amount of compensation reflects the fault of the employee. 'No compensation should be awarded when in fact the employee has suffered no injustice by being dismissed': Viscount Dilhorne, *Devis & Sons Ltd v Atkins* [1977] ICR 662, 679 HL). The emphasis of the compensatory award is thus upon the employee's economic loss and fault, not the fault of the employer. As a result, the employer has little incentive to minimise deviation from standards of good industrial relations practice, and may be lucky enough to have to pay minimal compensation, if the employee suffers no financial loss by obtaining another job.

Although the above authorities insist that the just and equitable award must concentrate upon economic loss, there is no explicit statutory prohibition against awarding damages for non-economic loss such as distress and humiliation. In *Johnson v Unisys Ltd* ([5.6] above), where a claim under the common law for economic losses resulting from a mental breakdown allegedly caused by the unfair manner of the dismissal was rejected, one of the major reasons for this restriction of the common law was said to be that compensation for such injurieswere available under the statutory claim for unfair dismissal. In a passage quoted above (p 448), Lord Hoffmann insisted that: 'The emphasis is upon the tribunal awarding such compensation as it thinks just and equitable. So I see no reason why in an appropriate case it should not include compensation for distress, humiliation, damage to reputation in the community or to family life'. This view was, however, rejected subsequently.

[5.64] *Dunnachie v Kingston-upon-Hull City Council* **[2004] UKHL 36 [2004] ICR 1052 (HL).**

The employee had worked for the Council in the field of environmental health for fifteen years, when he resigned in response to bullying and harassment by his manager, and the failure of more senior managers to respond to his plight. The tribunal accepted that there had been a constructive dismissal as a result of a breach of the implied term of mutual trust and confidence. The tribunal awarded compensation for unfair dismissal up to the maximum for the compensatory award at that time of £51,700, and included in that award £10,000 for injury to feelings. The EAT disallowed that aspect of the award, but the Court of Appeal by a majority (Sedley LJ, Evans-LombeJ, Brooke LJ dissenting) restored it. The House of Lords finally rejected the award for injury to feelings.

Lord Steyn (giving the unanimous opinion):
17. It can readily be accepted that the words "loss" in varying contexts may have wider and narrower meanings. But that proposition is of no legal interest. The question before the House is the meaning of the word "loss" in section 116(1) of the [Industrial Relations Act 1971, where the 'just and equitable' award in ERA 1996 section 123(1) was originally created]. If properly construed it was restricted to economic loss, the re-enactment of the statutory formula in 1996 must bear the same meaning. It is not a case in which the ambulatory consequences of the always speaking canon of construction has any role to play. Nothing that happened since 1971 could justify giving to the statutory formula a meaning it did not originally bear.
18. In the Court of Appeal [[2004] UKHL 36] only Evans-Lombe J thought that "loss"

in section 116 could include non-economic loss: para 63. I am not persuaded by his reasoning. I agree with the statement of Brooke LJ that it is inconceivable that in this particular context Parliament intended the word to mean anything other than financial loss: para 93. It is noteworthy that Sedley LJ accepted that the "more natural meaning [of the word "loss"] in section 123 is pecuniary loss": para 34. He then proceeded to conclude that tribunals may award compensation for non-economic damage on the different basis that "in section 123(1) loss is not the defining category but a subset of the larger category of just and equitable compensation": para 32-33.

19. Counsel for the employer made a telling point about the consequence of adopting the reasoning of Evans-Lombe J on the meaning of the word "loss" in section 123. He asked: What in the language of section 123(1) would then rule out an award of aggravated or exemplary compensation by way of penalisation of the conduct of the employer? The answer is that only if the word "loss" in section 123(1) is restricted to financial loss are such awards ruled out on the face of the legislation. And nobody could seriously suggest that Parliament intended to allow such awards.

20. Sir John Donaldson in *Norton Tool* observed that the natural meaning of "loss" in section 116(1) does not include injury to feelings. He added that this view is reinforced by the elaboration in section 116(2) of the 1971 Act, now section 123(2) of the 1996 Act. It is significant that in sections 116(2) and 123(2), and indeed in the remainder of sections 116 and 123, there is no reference to non-economic loss.

21. It may be of some assistance to imagine a parliamentary draftsman, faced in 1971 with a departmental brief to prepare a bill which would make provision for compensation for financial loss as well as for a solatium for injury to feelings. Such instructions could have been given pursuant to the recommendation in 1968 of the Royal Commission that the remedy for unfair dismissal should include compensation for "injured feelings and reputation": Cmnd 3623, para 553. Is it conceivable that a parliamentary draftsman would have provided for the two radically different remedies by the rolled-up wording of section 116(1)? Intuitively, I regard it as implausible that if such a policy decision had been made the technique of providing simply for compensation for "loss" would have been adopted.

22. For all these reasons I would hold that the plain meaning of the word loss in section 123(1) excludes non-economic loss.

23. On this hypothesis I must now turn to the different ground of decision of Sedley LJ which counsel for the employee urged on the House. Counsel summarised the point as follows: The governing principle is expressed in the requirement in section 123(1) of the 1996 Act to award "such amount as the tribunal considers just and equitable in all the circumstances." In exercising its discretion, the EAT is to "have regard to" the "loss" sustained by the complainant which is attributable to the unfair dismissal, but this is not the only consideration which bears upon its determination of the compensatory award. The word loss does not limit what may be awarded under the controlling principle.

24. Sedley LJ concluded that the construction in *Norton Tool* "leaves the governing concept—compensation which is just and equitable—without a role": para 30. I would not accept this proposition. It will be recalled that in *Norton Tool* Sir John Donaldson explained that the claims with which tribunals are concerned are more often than not presented in person and informally, and that it is therefore not to be expected that precise and detailed proof of every item of loss will be presented. The phrase "just and equitable" gives the tribunal a degree of flexibility having regard to the informality of the procedures, and the fact that the maximum award is capped.

25. Sedley LJ relied on the decision of the House in *W Devis & Sons v Atkins* [1977] ICR 662. He held that *Devis* established that resultant loss is not the only element to

which regard is to be had. The leading opinion in *Devis* was given by Viscount Dilhorne. He stated that (at 679F):

"The paragraph does not, nor did section 116 of the Act of 1971, provide that regard should be had only to the loss resulting from the dismissal being unfair. Regard must be had to that but the award must be just and equitable in all the circumstances, and it cannot be just and equitable that a sum should be awarded in compensation when in fact the employee has suffered no injustice by being dismissed."

This reveals a decision to the effect that it is open to a tribunal to consider whether it is just and equitable in all the circumstances for the complainant to be awarded all or any of the loss attributable to the dismissal. It was not a ruling that a tribunal is free to award additional sums not amounting to loss.

26. In my view section 123(1) must be construed as a composite formula. The interpretation preferred by Sedley LJ splits up the formula in a way which, with great respect, is more than a little contrived. It unjustifiably relegates the criterion of loss to a subordinate role. Given the hypothesis that the legislature expressly provided for the recovery of economic loss, it fails to explain why the legislature did not also expressly provide for compensation for injury to feelings. It also fails to take full account of the context. For example, on this expansive interpretation there would as already mentioned be nothing on the face of the statute to exclude the award (subject to the cap which is now standing at £55,000) of aggravated or exemplary damages. This could not have been intended. The better view is that the provision was not intended, in the words of Brooke LJ, to provide for "palm tree" justice.

27. In his already cited note Professor Collins argued that *Norton Tool* reversed the grammar of the statute. He said that *Norton Tool* "elevated the sub-principle of causation of loss to the main principle, and then relegated the general standard of just and equitable compensation to the status of a minor limitation on the application of the principles of causation of economic loss": [(1991) 20 ILJ 201] at 202. For substantially the same reasons as I have already given I find this argument unpersuasive.

I would hold that section 123(1) does not allow for the recovery of non-pecuniary loss.

This decision confirms the earlier case-law that the compensatory award is confined to the employee's economic losses, broadly construed, caused by the dismissal. Tribunals are not permitted to award compensation for injury to feelings, affronts to dignity, distress in personal life caused by the manner or fact of dismissal, unless the employee can demonstrate that the manner of the dismissal caused additional economic loss by, for example, damage to reputation. If the manner of the dismissal causes the employee to suffer from a recognised psychiatric illness such as severe depression, the tribunal cannot award compensation for that personal injury in itself, but can increase its estimate of the economic losses flowing from the dismissal in order to take into account the probable length of time before the employee can resume paid work. A claim for psychiatric illness caused by the conduct of the employer during the performance of the contract can be brought under the common law (*Eastwood v Magnox* [2004] UKHL 35 (**[5.12]** above), but it should be remembered that *Johnson v Unisys Ltd* (above **[5.6]**) ruled out the possibility of such a claim at common law arising from the manner or the fact of dismissal itself. For the type of claim advanced in *Dunnachie*, although there would be a common law action for breach during the performance of the contract of the implied term of trust and confidence and also a claim for negligence causing personal injury, unless the claimant could establish a recognised psychiatric condition deserving of compensation, compensation for mere distress and humiliation would not be available under the principles established in *Mahmoud v BCCI* (**[2.28]** above). Thus the courts have blocked any claim, whether at common law or under statute, where the gist is to penalise the employer for harsh treatment, bullying, harassment, and affronts to dignity, whether during performance of the contract or in the manner of dismissal.

The major item of financial compensation in most claims for unfair dismissal, which differ in this respect from claims for damages for wrongful dismissal at common law, is the loss of income for the period of unemployment following dismissal. The employee is placed under a duty to mitigate loss, so that he must make reasonable efforts to secure alternative employment. If, despite such efforts, the employee fails to obtain another job, the tribunal will award compensation for the period it regards as likely to elapse before employment may be found. The tribunal has considerable discretion to make such an estimate, and these judgments may reflect the broader merits of the case. In exercising this discretion, the tribunals draw upon their knowledge of the local labour market and the characteristics of the complainant. In theory the amount of compensation awarded under this heading should on average increase during periods of high unemployment, but the difference appears to be no more than two or three extra weeks of pay (L Dickens, et al., *Dismissed*, (Oxford, Blackwell, 1985) 124), which suggests a significant degree of under-compensation in periods of high unemployment.

In many instances, however, by the time of the hearing the employee will have obtained another job. If the new job pays more, then it is conceivable that the employee will be better off than if he had not been dismissed, and should therefore receive no compensation. But the tribunals have resisted this logic, and instead have awarded compensation for loss of pay until the new permanent job was obtained: *Whelan and t/a Cheers Off Licence v Richardson* [1998] IRLR 114 EAT. In another departure from the strict logic of compensation for financial loss and the duty to mitigate, the tribunals, following *Norton Tool v Tewson*, have awarded compensation for loss of wages during the whole notice period, even when the employee has suffered reduced loss by obtaining another job immediately or shortly after dismissal: *Babcock FATA Ltd v Addison* [1987] ICR 805 CA. But in some instances where the notice period is lengthy and the dismissed employee is known to have another job lined up already, compensation for loss of wages during the notice period will be reduced to the actual period of unemployment: *Hardy v Polk (Leeds) Ltd* [2004] IRLR 420 EAT.

The employee may claim for the loss of fringe benefits such as a company car, medical insurance, share options, and an employer's occupational pension scheme. The value of these prospective benefits must be discounted to take into account the probability that the employee's job would have terminated for other reasons such as resignation or dismissal for good reasons. On the other hand, the value of these benefits such as share options may have increased since the dismissal, and the tribunal can reflect that increase in the measure of compensation (*Leonard v Strathclyde Buses Ltd* [1998] IRLR 693 Ct of Sess, Inner House).

5.5.3.2 Contributory fault

In most disciplinary dismissals, a major factor in reducing the award of compensation is contributory fault.

[5.65] Employment Rights Act 1996 section 123

> **123 (6)** Where the tribunal finds that the dismissal was to any extent caused or contributed to by any action of the complainant, it shall reduce the amount of the compensatory award by such proportion as it considers just and equitable having regard to that finding.

Some forms of alleged misconduct cannot be regarded as contributory fault. An employee's refusal to join a trade union or not to join a trade union, and a refusal to desist from taking part in trade union activities, cannot count as contributory fault: TULRCA 1992 section 155. Participation in industrial action in itself also cannot be regarded as contributory fault in those cases where a tribunal has jurisdiction due to the selective nature of the dismissals: *Crossville Wales Ltd v Tracey (No.2)* [1997] IRLR 691 HL. Aside from those limitations, however, the meaning of contributory fault in this context is broad enough to encompass not merely breach of contract but also unreasonable or foolish behaviour by the employee. This expansive interpretation of ERA 1996 section 123(6), which goes far beyond breach of contract by the employee, contrasts unfavourably with the requirement of fundamental breach of contract in the law of wrongful dismissal as a disentitlement to compensation, and seems to give employers a second bite at the cherry: reasons for dismissal that were found inadequate to justify the dismissal are resurrected to avoid paying full compensation.

[5.66] *Nelson v British Broadcasting Corporation (No. 2)* [1980] ICR 110 CA

> The BBC abolished the claimant's post, but offered him alternative employment subject to a condition providing for a report after three months on his performance in the new job. The claimant objected to the condition, refused the offer, and claimed unfair dismissal. Although the claim for unfair dismissal was successful, the tribunal reduced compensation by 60 %. The Court of Appeal rejected the employee's appeal that he was not at fault in the required sense or to such a degree as to warrant such a large reduction. The tribunal had found that the employer had acted reasonably in imposing the condition, and that the claimant had acted foolishly in refusing to comply with it even though he was contractually entitled to refuse to move altogether. The Court of Appeal declined to alter the reduction of 60 % as the tribunal had not acted perversely on the facts of the case.

> *Brandon LJ:*
> It is necessary, however, to consider what is included in the concept of culpability or blameworthiness in this connection. The concept does not, in my view, necessarily involve any conduct of the complainant amounting to a breach of contract or a tort. It includes, no doubt, conduct of that kind. But it also includes conduct which, while not amounting to a breach of contract or a tort, is nevertheless perverse or foolish, or, if I may use the colloquialism, bloody-minded. It may also include action which, though not meriting any of those more pejorative epithets, is nevertheless unreasonable in all the circumstances. I

should not, however, go so far as to say that all unreasonable conduct is necessarily culpable or blameworthy; it must depend on the degree of unreasonableness involved.

The reduction of compensation for contributory fault, even to the extent of 100 per cent, does not remove entirely the deterrent effect of a finding of unfair dismissal against the employer, for the employer will be concerned about any damage to his reputation as a fair employer, but it certainly reduces the financial incentives for an employer to comply with the standards of good industrial relations practice.

[5.67] H Collins, *Justice in Dismissal* (Oxford, Oxford University Press, 1992) 226

> By virtue of these provisions an employer can rely upon those reasons for dismissal which failed to justify the dismissal as fair in order to persuade a tribunal to reduce the measure of compensation . . . The uneven application of the principle of proportionality by the law of unfair dismissal is startling. It is extremely difficult for employees to challenge dismissals on the ground that this sanction was too severe and that some lesser penalty should have been imposed . . . Yet when the employer's interest in proportionality comes to the fore in assessments of compensation, the tribunals engage in a minute inspection of the fault of the employee in order to give the employer the benefit of any shred of justification he or she can put forward.

If the employee's misconduct was unknown to the employer at the time of the dismissal and therefore did not 'cause' the dismissal, the compensatory award may nevertheless be reduced under the general discretion of making a just and equitable award: *Devis & Sons Ltd v Atkins* [1977] ICR 662 HL. A similar provision for deduction for contributory fault applies to the basic award: ERA 1996 s.122 (2). The reduction of compensation can be as much as 100%, as in a case where the employee's misconduct was extremely grave and the only unfairness of the dismissal lay in the absence of a fair procedure (*e.g. Ladup Ltd v Barnes* [1982] ICR 107 EAT).

5.5.3.3 Upper limit

This reduction of the financial incentives for compliance by the law of contributory fault has been exacerbated in many instances by the presence of an upper limit upon compensation. The basic award is confined to a multiplier of 20 years service times a week's pay (with an upper maximum on the amount of a week's pay of £240): ERA 1996 section 119(3). The compensatory award has a blunt upper limit in ERA 1996 section 124(1), which was substantially eroded by inflation during the 1980s and 1990s, leaving it at £11,300 in 1995. The upper limit only operates if the total sum of the compensatory award minus deductions for such matters as contributory fault exceeds the limit: *Leonard v Strathclyde Buses Ltd* [1998] IRLR 693 (Ct of Sess, Inner House). The immediate effect of these upper limits was to deprive highly paid employees of most of their possible compensation, thereby creating the incentive to resort to a claim for wrongful dismissal. The original justification for an upper limit (of two years' salary) put forward by the Donovan Commission (Cmnd. 3623 para. 554) was to enable employers to take out liability insurance, though the desirability of facilitating the avoidance of the deterrent element of the law of unfair dismissal must be doubted. A more cynical explanation of the upper limit, especially as it was eroded by inflation, was that the limit ensured that it would never be prohibitively expensive for employers to make a dismissal.

The Employment Relations Act 1999 linked the upper limit to the retail price index in future, which is currently set at £55,000, an amount roughly equivalent to its original value in real terms. But proposals to abolish the upper limit on compensation entirely were dropped in the face of pressure from employers, who argued that the proposal would lead to an avalanche of new claims and would discourage settlements. These arguments seem unconvincing. The removal of an upper limit would surely make employers more cautious before dismissing highly paid employees, thereby reducing the number of dismissals and consequent claims. It is true that the upper limit assists settlements for highly paid employees, because the upper limit in effect determines the amount of compensation. But this fixed solution applies perhaps only to a hundred or so of the highest paid employees who commence an application for unfair dismissal; for the remaining thousands of settlements the upper limit is in practice irrelevant. Even so, for those employees who are denied full compensation for their losses, which is most likely to happen when a reinstatement order has be rejected by the employer and the employee seeks arrears of wages as well as compensation for a future period of unemployment, the upper limit provides a disincentive to employers to comply with the standards of the law. 'There is a degree of arbitrariness in such a cap, and anyone against whom it operates is bound to see it as unfair' (Maurice Kay LJ, *Parry v National Westminster Bank plc* [2004] EWCA Civ 1563 [2005] ICR 396, 401 (CA)).

5.5.3.4 Basic award

If the test to be applied to the remedy of compensation is whether it provides employers with sufficient financial incentives to comply with the standards of good industrial practice in disciplinary dismissals, we have noted several ways in which the compensation becomes so minimal that the incentive is significantly diminished. The way in which the discretion under the compensatory award has been exercised has been a major factor in reducing the deterrent effect upon employers. The mathematical formulation for the basic award escapes this criticism, except when it is reduced for fault, but the exact purpose of the basic award remains puzzling.

The basic award looks backwards rather than forwards, compensating the employee for seniority rather than future economic loss. Loss of particular seniority rights, such as loss of accrued statutory rights by the elimination of a qualifying period in the new job, will be compensated by the compensatory award. Thus the basic award compensates a broader notion of seniority, the idea of job security based upon length of service. In so doing, however, it engages in indirect age discrimination (by increasing the award for older employees), and almost certainly indirect sex discrimination, since women employees will not on average acquire similar lengths of service in one job owing to interruptions in paid work for family reasons. Nevertheless, the basic award may be justified as an attempt to provide compensation for the employee's expectations from employment that are hard to measure in financial terms, such as the wasted investment in firm-specific skills, job satisfaction, and the psychological distress caused by dismissal.

Social Security Benefits and Disciplinary Dismissals

Following dismissal, an employee may seek to claim social security benefits in the form of either a Jobseeker's Allowance or Income Support (a means tested assistance for those whose personal circumstances are such that they are not required to seek work as a condition of receiving the benefit). Without a job the dismissed worker may have no other means of support. Assuming that the claimant satisfies the conditions for the Jobseeker's Allowance, such as contributions of national insurance payment for a year and is actively seeking work, the claimant may still be denied the benefit or disqualified temporarily if the loss of employment was caused by misconduct or if the employee gave up his employment without just cause.

Jobseekers Act 1995 s.19

(1)   Even though the conditions for entitlement to a jobseeker's allowance are satisfied with respect to a person, the allowance shall not be payable in any of the circumstances mentioned in subsection (5) or (6) . . .

(3)   If the circumstances are any of those mentioned in subsection (6), the period for which the allowance is not to be payable shall be such period (of at least one week but not more than 26 weeks) as may be determined by the adjudication officer . . .

(6)   The circumstances referred to in subsections (1) and (3) are that the claimant—
   (a) has lost his employment as an employed earner through misconduct;
   (b) has voluntarily left such employment without just cause; . . .

These standards, which have applied to claims for contributory unemployment benefits since their inception in 1911, do not necessarily coincide with the principles of the law of unfair dismissal in determinations of whether it was fair for the employer to dismiss the employee for misconduct or for the employee to regard himself as having been constructively dismissed. The disqualifying misconduct may not be sufficiently grave to justify dismissal, and the employer's serious breach of contract may not amount to a just cause for leaving a job and claiming the allowance. It is therefore possible to be a successful claimant for unfair dismissal, but a lawfully disqualified claimant for Jobseeker's Allowance. The reason given for this strange result is that the law of unfair dismissal is concerned with the justice of the dismissal between employer and employee, whereas the social security system has to look at wider distributive considerations including the minimisation of the social costs of dismissal. In accordance with that policy, if the benefit is paid and the employee eventually wins a claim for compensation through the law of unfair dismissal, the Secretary of State can recoup the expenditure from the employer prior to the employer paying compensation to the employee to the extent that the award of compensation consists of amounts calculated as lost wages (Employment Protection (Recoupment of Jobseeker's Allowance and Income Support) Regulations 1996 SI 1996/2349). But it should be observed as well that the absence of Jobseeker's Allowance on dismissal for misconduct adds significantly to an employer's disciplinary power, because the disqualification from compulsory social insurance benefits at a time when they are likely to be needed most urgently augments the implicit sanction of economic disadvantage that provides the principal source of the employer's power over the workforce. It is also questionable whether workers, if their opinion was sought, would accept these terms of their compulsory insurance policy, instead of agreeing with Winston Churchill: 'In my judgment if a man has paid to the fund for six months he should have his benefit in all circumstances, including dismissal for personal fault even of the gravest character; two securities being the low scale of benefits, and the solid, rigid qualifying period.' (quoted in D. Lewis, 'Losing Benefits Through Misconduct: Time to Stop Punishing the Unemployed?' [1985] *Journal of Social Welfare Law* 145, 149.)

5.5.3.5 *Adjustments for non-compliance with the statutory disciplinary procedure*

The basic award and the compensatory award must be adjusted in the event of the failure by the employer or the employee to comply with the statutory disciplinary procedure. A minimum of four weeks' pay is set for the basic award unless the tribunal considers that any increase would result in injustice to the employer: ERA 1996 section 120 (1A)(1B). For the compensatory award, the tribunal must increase it by 10 per cent and may, if it considers it just and equitable in all the circumstances to do so, increase it by a further amount, but not so as to make a total increase of more than 50 per cent: Employment Act 2002 section 31(3). If the failure to complete the statutory procedure is attributable wholly or mainly to the employee, the compensatory award must be reduced to the same extent. If, therefore, the employee fails to attend a hearing or an appeal, perhaps because the employee regards such meetings as futile, the employee may lose up to 50 per cent of any compensatory award. This increase or reduction in the compensatory award must be calculated prior to any reduction on the ground of contributory fault: ERA section 124A. Thus in a case where the employer dismisses an employee for misconduct after a perfunctory disciplinary procedure, the dismissal is automatically unfair, and the tribunal must award an additional 10 per cent for the compensatory award, but the tribunal can then reduce the compensation at its discretion for contributory fault as far as 100 per cent. There is therefore a danger that in many instances the uplift in the compensatory award for breach of the statutory disciplinary procedure will prove illusory, and there will be no effective pecuniary sanction for non-compliance by the employer.

5.5.4 Conciliation and settlements

Finally, in relation to remedies for unfair dismissal, it is important to consider what happens to most claims in practice. Few cases reach a tribunal hearing, for about two thirds are either settled privately or under the auspices of a conciliation officer supplied by ACAS. Conciliation officers are neutral between the parties, but have a statutory duty to promote settlements: Employment Tribunals Act 1996, section 18(2). They are not under a duty to ensure that the conciliated settlement is fair or in accordance with legal requirements.

[5.68] L Dickens et al., *Dismissed* **(Oxford, Blackwell, 1985) 156–57**

> In this survey of applicants and employers, it was reported that:
>   Whereas less than a quarter of applicants said the conciliation officers explained the law or told them about similar cases (with a high 'don't know' proportion), two-thirds said they had pointed out the strengths and weaknesses of their cases and half said they had done the same in regard to the employer's case. More employers reported that ACAS had explained the law on dismissals, although, as with applicants, less than a quarter reported that they were told about similar cases. Most employers said that ACAS conciliation officers had pointed out the strengths and weaknesses of each side's case. About half of

all applicants (constituting 52 % of those not represented) said the conciliation officer had gone further and actually given them an opinion on whether they were likely to win or lose. Thirty-six per cent of employers (41 % of those lay-represented) reported this.

Conciliation is plainly designed to achieve a reduction of the costs of the tribunal system, in which it succeeds, but it achieves this goal only at some risk that the outcomes of the dispute will not comply with the statutory standards. For example, another survey revealed the potential bias of the pressure from conciliators to settle a claim. It found that in 13 per cent of cases where the claimant had subsequently been successful before the tribunal, the conciliation officer had encouraged the withdrawal of the claim on the ground that there was little or no chance of winning (P Lewis, 'The Role of ACAS Conciliators in Unfair Dismissal Cases' (1982) 13 *Industrial Relations Journal* 50, 54).

It is likely that the amount of compensation received by employees through a settlement will be less than the amount that would have been ordered by a tribunal. The employer will offer less, because although the employer hopes to benefit by avoiding legal costs, the employee gains by removing the risk that the claim will prove unsuccessful. Nevertheless, employees may sell themselves short in conciliated settlements. About 70 per cent of employees accept the first offer of financial compensation made by an employer, and one study calculated that the median level of compensation received through a conciliated settlement was less than half the median amount awarded by tribunals (N Tremlett and N Banerji, 'The 1992 Survey of Industrial Tribunal Applications' (1992) *Employment Gazette* 31, 38). Survey evidence from 2003 suggests an even greater disparity, with the median settlement for unfair dismissal at £1,500 compared to a median tribunal award of £4,231 (B Hayward, M Peters, N Rousseau, K Seeds, *Findings from the Survey of Employment Tribunal Applications 2003*, DTI Employment Relations Research Series No 33 (August, 2004) p.146).

[5.69] L Dickens et al, *Dismissed* (Oxford, Blackwell, 1985) 175–76

The inequality in the relationship between the individual worker and the employer is implicitly recognised by the unfair dismissal legislation itself which sought to improve the worker's position by providing a right to challenge the employer's decision to dismiss. Rather than the will of the stronger party prevailing, appeal can be made to an external standard—the concept of fairness as embodied in statute and case law. The statutory formulation of the protection against unfair dismissal is in the form of a dispute of right, the essence of which is that there is some more or less definite standard against which the alleged infringement can be judged. Adjudication on which is 'right' is being sought by unfair dismissal applicants. First, however, they are offered conciliation which has at its core not adjudication but haggling and compromise—features associated with disputes of interest where no external standards prevail, where the relative strengths of the parties are crucial and where the only 'right' solution is the one the parties agree to . . .

The existence of the right does give the individual worker some bargaining strength which would not otherwise exist in most non-unionised employments . . . The right (or the threat to exercise it) is therefore a bargaining counter for the employee. But how strong a counter is it? As noted earlier, the cost and inconvenience which the exercise of the right cause the employer in having to defend an unfair dismissal application may lead to a small 'nuisance value' sum being offered in settlement . . .

Potential cost saving through settlement is therefore 'a fact of the situation'; part of the context within which the decision to settle has to be taken. This particular fact works to the advantage of the applicant. However, there are other facts of the situation which serve to weaken the applicant's bargaining position . . . . Information about the operation of the system which may be conveyed includes: employers win two out of three cases; even if the applicant wins, re-employment is unlikely and compensation generally is not high and may be subject to deductions; chances of succeeding at tribunal are enhanced by supporting the case with documentation and witness testimony and employers are better placed to maximise their chances of success in this way; tribunals may award costs against those pursuing cases frivolously, vexatiously or unreasonably.

An applicant faced with this information, usually provided by the conciliation officer, not surprisingly is likely to be predisposed towards accepting an offer of settlement. In addition information conveyed from the employer—that legal representation will be used or costs will be asked for—may increase the reluctance to proceed to tribunal . . . .

Although ACAS, in individual conciliation as in collective, theoretically leaves the parties to assess the merits of the case themselves and to arrive at their own settlement terms, in individual conciliation the parties, particularly unrepresented applicants, do so largely on the basis of the information, advice and guidance which ACAS itself provides. Furthermore, as we have argued, the information which ACAS transmits tends to depress applicant expectations and demands. In short, the industrial tribunal system provides a context within which conciliated settlements of whatever nature will often appear preferable to a tribunal hearing. Although the marshalling and channelling of pressures inherent in the situation is again a legitimate tool for a conciliator to use, the nature of the tribunal system means this generally places the applicant at a disadvantage *vis-à-vis* the employer.

5.6 Rights and reasonableness

The law relating to dismissal is of cardinal importance to the employment relation. It sets the legal limits on the extent to which the employer can use disciplinary powers to direct and control the workforce. The law is relevant not only when the employer uses the ultimate sanction of dismissal, but also whenever the employer adopts harsh or unreasonable treatment to such an extent that the employee is entitled to resign and claim compensation for dismissal. The significance of the law relating to unfair dismissal extends also far beyond disciplinary issues. For example, one of the noted effects of the law on the conduct of personnel practice has been the intensification of selection procedures with a view to ensuring by means of better scrutiny of applicants for jobs that problems of disciplinary dismissals never arise.

[5.70] S Evans, J Goodman and L Hargreave, *Unfair Dismissal Law and Employment Practice in the 1980s* (London, Department of Employment Research Paper No. 53, 1985) 23–24

Those firms which attributed tightening up selection practices primarily to the legislation admitted, with just a few exceptions, to having inadequate work performance assessment techniques and/or supervisory resources. These problems tended to emphasize the 'risky' nature of the legislation in the minds of managements in these (mainly small) firms. Such risks had often been encountered in actual difficulties in dismissing 'problem' employees . . . Actual experience of problems in dismissing was suggested by this evidence as a crucial factor prompting the adoption by small firms of more formal and routine selection methods, and differentiating them from the majority which continued to use informal methods of assessment, together with largely subjective criteria for selection.

A central difficulty confronted by this branch of the law is to devise standards that are both workable in practice by providing clear guidance and at the same time sensitive to the variety of contexts in which disciplinary dismissals take place. Has the law achieved such a balance? The common law of wrongful dismissal approaches the problem by relying on the terms of the contract: the employer is awarded an implied power of dismissal for disobedience to lawful orders, subject only to express terms of the contract. This approach permits the employer to use a standard form contract to construct disciplinary powers with precision, though at the cost of drafting and following detailed disciplinary procedures. In contrast, the law of unfair dismissal imposes a broad standard of reasonableness, which of course permits the tribunals to examine each case in context, though the standard is obviously vague and not entirely predictable in its application. Employers thus complain that it is hard to dismiss employees because of the uncertainty surrounding the employee's legal rights. In order to make the regulation clearer and more workable in practice, what appears to be needed is a combination of these styles of regulation, that is a general standard of reasonableness, which can be supplemented and rendered more specific by agreement or self-regulation. One of the most significant responses of employers to the advent of the law of unfair dismissal has been the creation of internal disciplinary procedures. What seems so disfunctional is that even if these disciplinary procedures are agreed by employees and followed by the employer, the employee may still argue that a dismissal was unfair due to the unfairness of the disciplinary procedure. The same criticism can also be made of the reverse situation where the employer refuses to follow a contractual procedure, yet is able to claim that the dismissal was procedurally fair. The introduction of the statutory disciplinary procedures responds to these criticisms by trying to fix a clear procedural baseline for both employers and employees. Assuming that employers respond to this legislation as intended and adopt the statutory procedure as their internal disciplinary code, the uncertainty generated by the vague standards of reasonableness should be reduced, leading to fewer unfair dismissals and a reduction in claims before tribunals. To win claims for unfair dismissal where the employer has followed the statutory disciplinary procedure, employees can still argue that the procedure was nevertheless unreasonable in the circumstances, but that argument seems unlikely to succeed frequently, especially in view of the resurrection of the futility argument. Alternatively, employees may increasingly try to contest the proportionality of the sanction of dismissal in relation to the misconduct or lack of competence, but, as we have seen, the range of reasonable responses test as it is currently interpreted seems likely to thwart such arguments.

Despite these problems of ensuring effective regulation of the fairness of disciplinary dismissals, we should observe that the statutory regulation of dismissals has contributed to a profound shift in perceptions of the problem of discipline at work.

We might describe this shift in perception as a movement from collective solidarity to individualised juridification. In the 1960s, before the law of unfair dismissal was enacted and in a period of high density of union organisation, perhaps the most common response to disciplinary dismissals was collective industrial action. If the workforce perceived the dismissal to be unfair or to challenge important collective interests of the workforce, it might strike and demand the reinstatement of the dismissed worker. One of the purposes of the legislation was to provide an alternative forum for the resolution of disputes about dismissals, thereby reducing the incidence of industrial conflict. In so doing, the legislation characterises the problem as an individual dispute between an isolated employee and the particular employer rather than a collective conflict about the proper scope of managerial disciplinary powers in the workplace. The legislation thus undermines the view that discipline, as an aspect of the governance of the workplace, should be controlled jointly by agreement between capital and labour. Furthermore, the legislation transfers the dispute about the exercise of discipline into a legal forum, where arguments of rights and reasonableness provide the measurement for standards of conduct, in contrast to the negotiations through collective bargaining, where arguments of interest and power predominate. Implicit in the legal perspective is the notion that an objective standard of fairness or reasonableness exists for the assessment of disciplinary dismissals, instead of the idea that the standard of fairness represents simply a compromise of interests between capital and labour. Perhaps the most profound effect of the law of unfair dismissal has been to encourage and reinforce this alteration of perspective upon disciplinary dismissals.

FURTHER READING

S Anderman, 'The Interpretation of Protective Employment Statutes and Contracts of Employment' (2000) 29 *Industrial Law Journal* 223.

——, 'Termination of Employment: Whose Property Rights?' in C Barnard, S Deakin and G S Morris, *The Future of Labour Law* (Oxford, Hart, 2004) 101.

L Barmes, 'The Continuing Conceptual Crisis in the Common Law of the Contract of Employment' (2004) 67 *Modern Law Review* 435.

L E Blades, 'Employment at Will vs. Individual Freedom: On Limiting the Abusive Exercise of Employer Power' (1967) 67 *Columbia Law Review* 1404.

H Collins, *Justice in Dismissal: The Law of Termination of Employment* (Oxford, Oxford University Press, 1992).

—— Nine Proposals for the Reform of the Law on Unfair Dismissal (London, Institute of Employment Rights, 2004)

L Dickens, M Jones, B Weekes and M Hart, *Dismissed: A Study of Unfair Dismissal and the Industrial Tribunal System* (Oxford, Blackwell, 1985).

P Elias, 'Unravelling the Concept of Dismissal' (1978) 7 *Industrial Law Journal* 16.

R Epstein, 'In Defence of the Contract at Will' (1984) 57 *University of Chicago Law Review* 947.

K Ewing, 'Remedies for Breach of the Contract of Employment' (1993) 52 *Cambridge Law Journal* 405.

K Ewing, and A.Grubb, 'The Emergence of a New Labour Injunction?' (1987) 16 *Industrial Law Journal* 145.

M Forde, 'Commentary: Re-thinking the Notice Rule' (1998) 27 *Industrial Law Journal* 220.

M Freedland, *The Personal Employment Contract* (Oxford, Oxford University Press, 2003) Chapters 6,7,8.

M Freedland and H Collins, 'Finding the Right Direction for the "Industrial Jury" ' (2000) 29 *Industrial law Journal* 288.

W Gould, 'The Idea of the Job as Property in Contemporary America: The Legal and Collective Bargaining Framework' (1986) *Brigham Young University Law Review* 885.

B Hepple and G S Morris, 'The Employment Act 2002 and the Crisis of Individual Employment Rights' (2002) 31 *Industrial Law Journal* 245.

B Hough and A Spowart-Taylor, 'Liability, Compensation and Justice in Unfair Dismissal' (1996) 25 *Industrial Law Journal* 308.

C Kilpatrick, 'Has New Labour Reconfigured Employment Legislation?' (2003) 32 *Industrial Law Journal* 135.

P Lewis, 'An Analysis of Why Legislation has Failed to Provide Employment Protection for Unfairly Dismissed Workers' (1981) 19 *British Journal of Industrial Relations* 316.

G Pitt, 'Dismissal at Common Law: The Relevance in Britain of American Developments' (1989) 52 *Modern Law Review* 22.

M Plascencia, 'Employment at Will: The French Experience as a Basis for Reform' (1988) 9 *Comparative Labor Law Journal* 294.

M S West, 'The Case Against Reinstatement in Wrongful Discharge' (1988) *University of Illinois Law Review* 1.

Human Rights and Labour Law

Much of the material in the preceding chapters has been concerned with 'human rights'. Among the rights generally accepted as falling into this category are rights against discrimination and freedom of association, considered respectively in chapters 3, 7 and 8. Many social and economic rights, such as those concerning the reconciliation of work and family life, minimum income guarantees and prohibitions on unjustified dismissal, are protected by ILO Conventions and/or by EU or domestic legislation. This, too, has been considered in the preceding chapters. Here we consider a number of workplace issues, not elsewhere dealt with, which raise human rights-related questions. In particular, we deal with discrimination on grounds of political opinion or activism; workplace surveillance and the protection of workers' privacy interests; whistleblowing and the issues relating to freedom of expression.

Of particular significance here is the Human Rights Act 1998 (HRA 1998) by which a number of the provisions of the European Convention on Human Rights (ECHR) have been incorporated into domestic law. Some of these provisions have clear implications for employment. Most notable among these perhaps are Articles 8, 9–11 and 14 which confer, respectively, rights to respect for private and family life, to freedom of 'thought, conscience and religion', expression, and 'peaceful assembly and . . . freedom of association' and to freedom from discrimination in the 'enjoyment of the rights and freedoms set forth' in the Convention. These provisions are set out below and will be considered in this chapter. The chapter will also consider the general approach of the European Court of Human Rights (ECtHR) and the (now defunct) European Commission on Human Rights (the Commission) to the application of the Convention rights in the employment context. No attempt is made in this chapter or elsewhere in this book to cover all the areas of labour law in which the HRA 1998 might be of importance. The full implications of the Act are, at this stage, a matter for conjecture, though early indications are not particularly encouraging. The focus in this chapter will be on a limited number of areas not otherwise covered in the book in which the Act has already had, or is most likely to have, some appreciable impact.

This chapter will deal with 'human rights' as defined by the ECHR and as distinct from broader social and economic rights, whose relevance to the employment context might be more apparent. This focus is adopted because of the unique position accorded to the Convention rights by the HRA 1998. The social and economic rights recognised by the ILO Conventions and the Council of Europe's Social Charter can be directly enforced, if at all, only through the mechanisms of international law (for discussion of this see K D Ewing, 'Social Rights and Human Rights: Britain and the Social Charter—the Conservative Legacy' [2000] *European Human Rights Law Review* 91). By contrast, the HRA 1998 permits the enforcement of Convention rights directly through the domestic courts. The provisions of the Convention do not, as we shall see below, prevail over inconsistent primary legislation and may be enforced only indirectly save in the case of those employed by 'core' public authorities (see further section 6.2.1). Nevertheless, the Act secures to the Convention rights a much greater degree of protection than is available in respect of social and economic rights.

6.1 The European Convention on Human Rights

[6.1] K D Ewing, 'The Human Rights Act and Labour Law' (1998) 27 *Industrial Law Journal* 275, pp 278–79 (footnotes omitted)

The first question which the Convention presents for labour lawyers is simply this: what does it have to do with us? Unlike the Council of Europe's Social Charter—which deals with recognisable issues such as pay, working time, occupational health and safety, collective bargaining and the right to strike—the ECHR is silent on questions relating directly to the province of labour law (with the exception of course of article 11, on which more later). Yet as the case-law of the Strasbourg institutions demonstrates, the Convention nevertheless could in principle affect labour law incidentally, and not always on peripheral issues. The significance of article 6, for example, was revealed in *Süßman v v Germany* [(1997) 25 EHRR 64] where it was held to be applicable in a dispute in the Constitutional Court involving a civil servant's pension. Although the application was unsuccessful on the facts, the Court held that 'the amount of the applicant's pension entitlement was of a pecuniary nature and undeniably concerned a civil right'. Article 6 also featured prominently in *Stedman v United Kingdom* [(1997) 23 EHRR CD 168] where the Commission took the view that 'restricting access to an industrial tribunal to employees of two years' standing, pursued the legitimate aim of offering protection to those in established employment who had given a minimum of two years' service to an employer, without burdening the employer to the extent that dismissal within a two year probationary period was likely to lead to court proceedings'.

The relevance of article 8 to the workplace was revealed in the *Halford* case [discussed at **[6.36]** below] where it was held that the Assistant Chief Constable of Merseyside 'had a reasonable expectation of privacy' in respect of telephone conversations conducted on her office phones, though it by no means follows that all other employer surveillance practices will be forbidden as a result of this exceptional case. Article 9 has been raised on at least two occasions by workers who claimed in different ways that working practices violated their right to freedom of religion. In *Ahmad v United Kingdom* [(1982 4EHRR 126 (Commission)] the complainant was refused time off work with pay to attend a Mosque for Friday prayers, while in *Stedman* (to which we have already referred) the complaint related to the dismissal of a woman with less than two years' service who refused for religious and family reasons to work on Sundays. The right to freedom of expression in article 10 was successfully invoked in *Vogt v Germany* [discussed at **[6.10]** below] by a schoolteacher who was dismissed because of her membership of the Communist Party, in what appears to be a significant softening of the hard line approach adopted in Cold War decisions relating to the exclusion of communists from public service employment. The Court was influenced by the fact that the applicant was not a security risk, and that she did not use her position to seek to indoctrinate her pupils.

Ewing goes on to detail the application in the employment context of the right to freedom of association guaranteed by Article 11 remarking that 'no trade union has successfully relied upon Article 11 [which had, however] ... been used by the Court to protect individuals who suffered disadvantage because of their non-membership of a trade union'. This observation, accurate at the time of writing, was overtaken by the decision of the European Court in *Wilson and the National Union of Journalists; Palmer, Wyeth and the National Union of Rail, Maritime and Transport Workers v United Kingdom* 35 EHRR 20 (ECtHR), which is discussed at **[8.21]** below. But as chapter 8 makes clear, the approach taken by the Convention organs to trade union rights has been far from satisfactory.

Ewing considers Articles 6, 8 and 11 of the Convention which are reproduced below with Article 14 which prohibits discrimination in the application of the Convention rights.

[6.2] European Convention on Human Rights

Art 6(1) In the determination of his civil rights and obligations or of any criminal charge against him, everyone is entitled to a fair and public hearing within a reasonable time by an independent and impartial tribunal established by law. Judgment shall be pronounced publicly but the press and public may be excluded from all or part of the trial in the interests of morals, public order or national security in a democratic society, where the interests of juveniles or the protection of the private life of the parties so require, or to the extent strictly necessary in the opinion of the court in special circumstances where publicity would prejudice the interests of justice . . .

Art 8(1) Everyone has the right to respect for his private and family life, his home and his correspondence.

(2) There shall be no interference by a public authority with the exercise of this right except such as is in accordance with the law and is necessary in a democratic society in the interests of national security, public safety or the economic well-being of the country, for the prevention of disorder or crime, for the protection of health or morals, or for the protection of the rights and freedoms of others.

Art 9(1) Everyone has the right to freedom of thought, conscience and religion; this right includes freedom to change his religion or belief and freedom, either alone or in community with others and in public or private, to manifest his religion or belief, in worship, teaching, practice and observance.

    (2)   Freedom to manifest one's religion or beliefs shall be subject only to such limitations as are prescribed by law and are necessary in a democratic society in the interests of public safety, for the protection of public order, health or morals, or for the protection of the rights and freedoms of others.

Art 10(1)   Everyone has the right to freedom of expression. This right shall include freedom to hold opinions and to receive and impart information and ideas without interference by public authority and regardless of frontiers. This article shall not prevent States from requiring the licensing of broadcasting, television or cinema enterprises.

    (2)   The exercise of these freedoms, since it carries with it duties and responsibilities, may be subject to such formalities, conditions, restrictions or penalties as are prescribed by law and are necessary in a democratic society, in the interests of national security, territorial integrity or public safety, for the prevention of disorder or crime, for the protection of health or morals, for the protection of the reputation or rights of others, for preventing the disclosure of information received in confidence, or for maintaining the authority and impartiality of the judiciary.

Art 11(1)   Everyone has the right to freedom of peaceful assembly and to freedom of association with others, including the right to form and to join trade unions for the protection of his interests.

    (2)   No restrictions shall be placed on the exercise of these rights other than such as are prescribed by law and are necessary in a democratic society in the interests of national security or public safety, for the prevention of disorder or crime, for the protection of health or morals or for the protection of the rights and freedoms of others. This article shall not prevent the imposition of lawful restrictions on the exercise of these rights by members of the armed forces, of the police or of the administration of the State.

Art 14 The enjoyment of the rights and freedoms set forth in this Convention shall be secured without discrimination on any ground such as sex, race, colour, language, religion, political or other opinion, national or social origin, association with a national minority, property, birth or other status.

The Convention Articles should not be considered in isolation. The HRA 1998, which incorporates them into domestic law, provides that:

[6.3] Human Rights Act 1998, section 2(1)

S.2(1) A court or tribunal determining a question which has arisen in connection with a Convention right must take into account any—

(a)   judgment, decision, declaration or advisory opinion of the European Court of Human Rights,

(b)   opinion . . . [or]

(c)   decision of the Commission . . . or

(d)   decision of the Committee of Ministers . . .

whenever made or given, so far as, in the opinion of the court or tribunal, it is relevant to the proceedings in which that question has arisen . . .

Some of the jurisprudence of the Convention organs is considered below, after a brief outline of the scheme adopted by the HRA 1998.

6.2 Introduction to the Human Rights Act 1998

The two primary ways in which the HRA 1998 provides for the enforcement of Convention rights are by (1) imposing upon the courts an obligation to construe domestic law in conformity with those rights and (2) permitting direct actions under the Act against public authorities for breach of the rights.

Section 3 HRA provides that all legislation must be interpreted 'so far as it is possible to do so' to be compatible with Convention rights. The decision of the House of Lords in *Ghaidan v Godin-Mendoza* makes it clear that the interpretive obligation imposed by section 3 is extremely strong. The case involved a challenge to the failure of the Rent Act to provide full rights of succession to same-sex partners of tenants enjoying statutorily protected tenancies. The question for the House of Lords was whether the phrase 'person who was living with the original tenant as his or her wife or husband' could be interpreted to include same-sex partners. A mere three years before, in *Fitzpatrick v Sterling Housing Association Ltd* [2001] 1 AC 27, the House of Lords had ruled that it could not. In *Ghaidan* the House of Lords, having accepted that discrimination in this context between same-sex and opposite-sex couples breached Articles 8 and 14 of the Convention, went on to rule (Lord Millet dissenting) that section 3 HRA required the interpretation of the Rent Act that they had refused to adopt in *Fitzpatrick*.

[6.4] *Ghaidan v Godin-Mendoza* [2004] 2 AC 557

Lord Nicholls:
It is now generally accepted that the application of section 3 does not depend upon the presence of ambiguity in the legislation being interpreted. Even if, construed according to the ordinary principles of interpretation, the meaning of the legislation admits of no doubt, section 3 may nonetheless require the legislation to be given a different meaning [citing *R v A (No 2)* [2002] 1 AC 45] . . .

From this it follows that the interpretative obligation decreed by section 3 is of an unusual and far-reaching character. Section 3 may require a court to depart from the unambiguous meaning the legislation would otherwise bear. In the ordinary course the interpretation of legislation involves seeking the intention reasonably to be attributed to Parliament in using the language in question. Section 3 may require the court to depart from this legislative intention, that is, depart from the intention of the Parliament which enacted the legislation. The question of difficulty is how far, and in what circumstances, section 3 requires a court to depart from the intention of the enacting Parliament. The answer to this question depends upon the intention reasonably to be attributed to Parliament in enacting section 3.

On this the first point to be considered is how far, when enacting section 3, Parliament intended that the actual language of a statute, as distinct from the concept expressed in that language, should be determinative. Since section 3 relates to the 'interpretation' of legislation, it is natural to focus attention initially on the language used in the legislative provision being considered. But once it is accepted that section 3 may require legislation to bear a meaning which departs from the unambiguous meaning the legislation would otherwise bear, it becomes impossible to suppose Parliament intended that the operation of section 3 should depend critically upon the particular form of words adopted by the parliamentary draftsman in the statutory provision under consideration. That would make the application of section 3 something of a semantic lottery. If the draftsman chose to express the concept being enacted in one form of words, section 3 would be available to achieve Convention-compliance. If he chose a different form of words, section 3 would be impotent.

From this the conclusion which seems inescapable is that the mere fact the language under consideration is inconsistent with a Convention-compliant meaning does not of itself make a Convention-compliant interpretation under section 3 impossible. Section 3 enables language to be interpreted restrictively or expansively. But section 3 goes further than this. It is also apt to require a court to read in words which change the meaning of the enacted legislation, so as to make it Convention-compliant. In other words, the intention of Parliament in enacting section 3 was that, to an extent bounded only by what is 'possible', a court can modify the meaning, and hence the effect, of primary and secondary legislation.

Parliament, however, cannot have intended that in the discharge of this extended interpretative function the courts should adopt a meaning inconsistent with a fundamental feature of legislation. That would be to cross the constitutional boundary section 3 seeks to demarcate and preserve. Parliament has retained the right to enact legislation in terms which are not Convention-compliant. The meaning imported by application of section 3 must be compatible with the underlying thrust of the legislation being construed. Words implied must, in the phrase of my noble and learned friend Lord Rodger of Earlsferry, 'go with the grain of the legislation'. Nor can Parliament have intended that section 3 should require courts to make decisions for which they are not equipped. There may be several ways of making a provision Convention-compliant, and the choice may involve issues calling for legislative deliberation . . .

In some cases difficult problems may arise. No difficulty arises in the present case. Paragraph 2 of Schedule 1 to the Rent Act 1977 is unambiguous. But the social policy underlying the 1988 extension of security of tenure under paragraph 2 to the survivor of couples living together as husband and wife is equally applicable to the survivor of homosexual couples living together in a close and stable relationship. In this circumstance I see no reason to doubt that application of section 3 to paragraph 2 has the effect that paragraph 2 should be read and given effect to as though the survivor of such a homosexual couple were the surviving spouse of the original tenant. Reading paragraph 2 in this way would have the result that cohabiting heterosexual couples and cohabiting heterosexual couples would be treated alike for the purposes of succession as a statutory tenant. This would eliminate the discriminatory effect of paragraph 2 and would do so consistently with the social policy underlying paragraph 2. The precise form of words read in for this purpose is of no significance. It is their substantive effect which matters . . .

Lord Steyn, who agreed with Lord Nicholls and with whom Lord Rodger agreed, went further in his suggestion that the courts had to-date been too ready to issue dec-larations of incompatibility which should, in his words, be 'a measure of last resort'.

Sections 3(2)(b) and (c) provide that the interpretive power/obligation 'does not affect the validity, continuing operation or enforcement' of incompatible primary leg-islation, or of secondary legislation whose incompatibility 'primary legislation prevents [the] removal of'. The courts may strike down provisions of secondary legis-lation whose incompatibility is merely permitted, rather than required, by the primary legislation under which they have been enacted. They may also in some cir-cumstances issue 'declarations of incompatibility' in respect of incompatible primary legislation, and of secondary legislation whose incompatibility is required by primary legislation (sections 4(2)–(3)). In such cases section 10 and Schedule 2 to the HRA 1998 provide a 'fast track procedure' whereby Ministers may amend the offending provisions. Declarations of incompatibility may not be made by employment tribunals or the EAT.

The HRA 1998 imposes no express obligations upon the courts in terms of their development of the common law. But section 6(1) provides that '[i]t is unlawful for a public authority to act in a way which is incompatible with a Convention right', save as provided for by section 6(2) (reproduced at **[6.5]** below), while section 6(3)(a) defines courts and tribunals as 'public authorities' for the purposes of the HRA 1998. It follows that the courts are obliged to afford a degree of protection to Convention rights in the application of the common law. The exact degree of protection required will turn on the extent to which the rights themselves are regarded as having 'horizontal' effect, i.e., of being capable of breach by actions of individuals (and/or inaction by the state). Detailed discussion of this issue is beyond the scope of a work on labour law. But at least some of the incorporated rights relevant to employment have been accorded a degree of horizontality by the Convention organs, in the sense that Contracting States have been held responsible for interference with them by private individuals (see discussion in section 6.3 below).

[6.5] Human Rights Act 1998, section 6(2)

S.6(2) Subsection (1) does not apply to an act if—
(a) as the result of one or more provisions of primary legislation, the authority could not have acted differently; or
(b) in the case of one or more provisions of, or made under, primary legislation which cannot be read or given effect in a way which is compatible with the Convention rights, the authority was acting so as to give effect to or enforce those provisions.

Section 6(2) provides the limits to the courts' interpretive obligations, making it clear that their enforcement of incompatible primary legislation and of some incompatible provisions of secondary legislation will not involve a breach of section 6(1). But, while the meaning of section 6(2)(a) is easy to determine, the extent to which section 6(2)(b) provides wider scope for Convention-incompatible actions on the part of public authorities (including the courts) is far from clear. It permits any such actions 'to give effect to or enforce' any provisions of primary legislation 'which cannot be read or given effect in a way which is compatible with the Convention rights'. The Court of Appeal in *R (Wilkinson) v Inland Revenue Commissioners* [2003] 1 WLR 2683 rejected the argument that to read section 6(2)(b) so as to require the exercise of a power where this was necessary to avoid a conflict with the Convention would have the illegitimate effect of concerting the power into a duty. According to Lord Phillips MR, for the Court: 'if circumstances arise under which it is necessary to exercise the power in order to avoid a breach of Convention rights, we can see no basis on which the commissioners can rely upon section 6(2)(b) to justify a refusal to exercise the power'.

Section 6(1) does not only bind the courts, but also makes it unlawful for any public authority (see section 6.2.1 below) 'to act in a way which is incompatible with a Convention right', save as provided for by section 6(2). Section 7 permits the 'victims' of actions unlawful by virtue of section 6 HRA 1998 to sue directly under that Act. Those whose Convention rights are interfered with by private parties must rely instead on the interpretive obligations imposed on the courts in respect of legislation (section 3) and the common law (section 6), but will have no 'free-standing' HRA cause of action. In the earliest post HRA cases the courts demonstrated a willingness to develop common law in the light of the incorporated Articles—see *Douglas & Zeta-Jones v Hello Ltd* [2001] QB 967, and *Venables v News Group Newspapers Ltd* [2001] 2 WLR 1038. In *Wainwright v Home Office* [2004] 2 AC 406, however, the House of Lords rejected the proposition that the Act has introduced a tort of privacy in domestic law.

Section 6(2)(b) provides public authorities, including the courts, providing them with a defence to section 6 claims as discussed in the preceding paragraphs. It also permits Convention-incompatible actions by a public authority 'to give effect to or enforce' any provisions 'made under primary legislation which cannot be read or given effect in a way which is compatible with the Convention rights'. Incompatible secondary legislation is saved only (section 3(2)(c)) where its incompatibility is required by primary legislation.

6.2.1   The Human Rights Act and employment—the public/private divide

Before turning to consider those areas of employment in which the implementation of the HRA 1998 may prove of particular significance, some consideration will be given to the differential impact of the Act on those employed by 'public authorities' and on others. It has been mentioned above that those whose Convention rights are breached by public authorities may (subject to section 6(2) HRA 1998) take action directly under the Act by virtue of section 7. 'Public authority' is only partly defined by section 6 which, as we saw above, expressly includes courts and tribunals within its scope and which, further, states (section 6(3)(b)) that the term covers 'any person certain of whose functions are functions of a public nature' (it also expressly excludes from the definition 'either House of Parliament or a person exercising functions in connection with proceedings in Parliament'). But the expansive definition provided by section 6(2)(b) is constrained, in the employment context, by section 6(5): 'In relation to a particular act, a person is not a public authority by virtue only of subsection (3)(b) if the nature of the act is private'.

It is clear from the caselaw on judicial review that action taken in relation to employment is regarded, almost invariably, as 'private'. It would thus appear that only those employed by 'core' public authorities will be in a position to benefit from section 7 HRA 1998. According to the White Paper which preceded the Act, 'pure' public authorities include central and local government, the police, prisons and immigration officers (*Rights Brought Home*, Cm 3792, 1997, para 2.2). What other bodies will be covered in respect of their private as well as public acts is, as yet, unclear. In *Aston Cantlow PCC v Wallbank* [2004] 1 AC 546 the House of Lords took a narrow approach to the definition of (core) 'public authority' for the purposes of the HRA

1998, restricting it in effect to bodies exercising functions which were broadly governmental.

[6.6] G Morris, 'The Human Rights Act and the Public/ Private Divide in Employment Law' (1998) 27 *Industrial Law Journal* 293, pp 297–99, 304–05 (footnotes omitted)

One issue which will be particularly important in this area is whether a body ceases to be 'purely' public if it is empowered also to conduct activities of a commercial nature. It seems likely that a *de minimis* approach may be applied in this context; thus, the very limited powers of local authorities to supply goods or materials to other public bodies, for example, should not suffice to take them outside this category. More difficult is the position of NHS Trusts, which may make accommodation and services available to the general public for payment and thus act in competition with the private sector. Although they are empowered to do this only if it will not interfere with their duties to comply with directions given by the Secretary of State or the performance of their NHS obligations, it seems unclear that this qualification would suffice to preserve their status as 'pure' public bodies. An argument based on the fact that such activities are subsidiary to their statutory duties could also be applied to those privatised utilities which have a statutory duty to supply on demand and whose capacity to diversify their activities may be limited by the need to fulfil this duty. In considering the status of a given body, inquiry should probably focus upon its powers and duties rather than its practices, extension into which would be complex, time-consuming, and could produce differing results as between, for example, neighbouring NHS Trusts or general practitioners. Moreover, accidents of timing could result in the designation as 'pure' public authorities of organisations such as private security companies whose portfolio at the relevant time consisted only of the prison service, although they normally had a wider client base.

Bob Hepple has suggested that the distinction between the public and the private realms may be more complex than the Lord Chancellor indicated. Thus, '[I]f a recently privatised body is required to contract on special employment terms prescribed by statute, or to set up a particular machinery for consultation with employees, or to act under governmental directives, then it may be argued that this involves the exercise of functions of a public nature with the result that its employees are potential candidates for Convention rights'. It is indeed the case that, for the purposes of judicial review, the statutory underpinning of provisions governing employment may afford them the requisite 'public' element. . . . However, this article goes beyond that and argues that organisations performing public functions should be liable for employment-related acts connected with the performance of those functions in the same way as 'pure' public sector bodies, a view to which the Strasbourg jurisprudence lends support.

Article 1 of the ECHR obliges signatory states to 'secure to everyone within their jurisdiction the rights and freedoms defined in . . . [the] Convention'. A complaint that a Convention right has been violated may be brought against a state in respect of the acts of bodies for which it is deemed responsible. It is clear that, broadly speaking, these include the legislature, executive, courts, police, security forces and local government. In conceptual terms, however, the jurisprudence of the European Commission and European Court of Human Rights is surprisingly undeveloped as to the criteria which should be used to judge whether bodies such as nationalised industries have a sufficiently close relationship with the state for its responsibility to be engaged.

Although there is so little jurisprudence on the principles governing the attribution of direct state responsibility for particular bodies, the Court has emphasised that the State cannot evade its own responsibilities by contracting out its functions to private sector bodies. This was unequivocally stated in the 1993 decision of *Costello-Roberts v UK* [(1993) 19 EHRR 116]. In this case the applicant alleged that the corporal punishment inflicted on him by the headmaster of his independent school constituted a violation of Articles 3 (degrading treatment) and 8 (respect for private life) of the Convention. The nine-member Court unanimously rejected the argument that the UK was not responsible under the Convention for matters of discipline in independent schools. The majority noted that Article 2 of Protocol 1 of the Convention required the State to secure to children their right to education; that in the UK independent schools co-exist with a system of public education, the right to education being guaranteed equally to pupils in both types of schools; and endorsed the view of the applicant that 'the State cannot absolve itself from responsibility by delegating its obligations to private bodies or individuals'. The four members who issued a partially dissenting opinion (holding, unlike the majority, that Article 3 of the Convention had been breached) also 'sounded a clear message' that privatisation did not affect the scope of the protection in affirming that '[a] State can neither shift prison administration to the private sector and thereby make corporal punishment in prisons lawful, nor can it permit the setting up of a system of private schools which are run irrespective of Convention guarantees'.

In *Costello-Roberts* the Court was concerned with a service (education) which states had an obligation under the Convention to secure. In other cases, it may be more difficult to decide whether the State can properly be regarded as 'delegating *its* obligations' to the private sector, an approach which assumes a spurious consensus as to the services which states should properly provide to their citizens. However, it seems fair to assume that, at the very least, the State would be regarded as undertaking such a delegation when tasks are shared or handed over to private sector operators in areas such as the civil service (including prisons) and law enforcement agencies.

Assuming that a breach of one or more Convention Articles by a 'core' public authority is established, a free-standing breach of the HRA 1998 will be established save unless section 6(2) applies. But if the quasi breach is by a private employer ('quasi breach' because strictly speaking only the state can breach the Convention), the worker affected will not be able to rely on a 'free-standing' HRA claim. He or she may, however, use section 3 HRA 1998 to secure redress by means of interpretation of employment-related or other legislation (see *Ghaidan* **[6.4]** above). Thus, for example, where the action complained of amounts to a dismissal (express or implied), that dismissal ought to be regarded as unfair for the purposes of the ERA 1996 even if it would not have been so regarded absent consideration of the 1998 Act. This principle has been accepted by the EAT in *Pay v Lancashire Probation Service* and, more recently, by the Court of Appeal in *X v Y* (though establishing breaches of Convention rights has proved more difficult, a matter further discussed below).

[6.7] *Pay v Lancashire Probation Service* [2004] ICR 187 (EAT)

The *Pay* case was brought by a probation officer who was dismissed from a position working with sex offenders when his employers discovered that he was involved in merchandising products connected with bondage, domination and sado-masochism and that he performed shows in hedonist and fetish clubs. His claim, that the dismissal breached his Article 8 and 10 rights to privacy and freedom of expression and was therefore unfair, was rejected and his appeal to the EAT dismissed on the grounds that the activities in question were not private and that the interference with his expression was justified in line with Article 10(2) (the EAT accepting, however, that a public authority would act unreasonably for the purposes of the ERA 1996 if it violated an employee's Convention rights).

[6.8] *X v Y* [2004] ICR 1634 (CA)

The claim arose from the Claimant's dismissal from his position with a young offender's charity after it was discovered that he had been arrested and cautioned for committing a sex offence with another man in a toilet. The dismissal was said to be by reason of the Applicant's misconduct in (a) having committed a significant criminal offence and (b) having deliberately concealed it. X claimed unfair dismissal, asserting that the dismissal had been inconsistent with Articles 8 and 14 of the Convention.

An Employment Tribunal rejected X's claim and both the EAT and the Court of Appeal dismissed his appeals. According to the Court, Brooke LJ dissenting, Article 8 was not engaged. This aspect of the decision is considered further below. Mummery LJ for the Court went on to propose a framework for the analysis of unfair dismissal claims where Convention rights were at issue.

Mummery LJ:
Section 2 of the HRA requires a court or tribunal determining a question which has arisen in connection with a Convention right to take into account any judgment, decision or opinion of the relevant institutions (the European Court of Human Rights and the Commission) 'so far as, in the opinion of the court or tribunal, it is relevant to the proceedings in which the question has arisen.'

Thus, it is relevant to note that, if Article 8 can be engaged in the case of a dismissal by a private sector employer, the right to respect for private life has been interpreted by the Strasbourg institutions to cover a person's 'sexual orientation and sexual life' and the right of a person to establish relationships with others. A person's reasonable expectations of privacy may extend beyond the confines of the home and of private premises to a public space or context. As Hale LJ said in *Pearce v Mayfield School* [2002] ICR 198. 'Sexual behaviour is undoubtedly an aspect of private life, indeed a most intimate and important aspect of private life. Any interference by the state can only be justified under Article 8(2).' . . .

Further, although the essential purpose of Article 8 is to protect individual citizens against arbitrary interference by the state and by public authorities, that is not, according to decisions of the Strasbourg Court, the only possible area of application. The state may have positive obligations, which extend to securing respect for private life in the sphere of relations between individuals. There are Strasbourg authorities on the point whether the Convention is relevant only to cases involving the state and public authorities, or whether it can also be relevant to cases between private individuals, such as private sector employers and employees.

The short answer to the applicant's case was correctly given in the decisions of the tribunals below: Article 8(1) is not engaged, as the facts found by the employment tribunal do not fall within its ambit . . .

The applicant's conduct did not take place in his private life nor was it within the scope of application of the right to respect for it. It happened in a place to which the public had, and were permitted to have, access; it was a criminal offence, which is normally a matter of legitimate concern to the public; a criminal offence is not a purely private matter; and it led to a caution for the offence, which was relevant to his employment and should have been disclosed by him to his employer as a matter of legitimate concern to it. The applicant wished to keep the matter private. That does not make it part of his private life or deprive it of its public aspect.

The longer answer

A fuller explanation of the overall legal position may assist employment tribunals in other unfair dismissal cases to deal with issues of Convention rights in a more structured way than the employment tribunal did in this case. The starting point in this case, as with all private law cases, is the applicant's cause of action.

(1) The only cause of action asserted by the applicant was under s 94 of the ERA: he had a right not to be unfairly dismissed by the respondent . . . (2) The applicant did not assert any cause of action against the respondent under the HRA. He does not have an HRA cause of action. The respondent is not a public authority within s 6 of the HRA. It was not unlawful under s6 of the HRA for the respondent, as a private sector employer, to act in a way which was incompatible with article 8 . . .

The applicant invoked articles 8 and 14 of the Convention in relation to his cause of action in private law. (1) . . . article 8 is not confined in its effect to relations between individuals and the state and public authorities. It has been interpreted by the Strasbourg court as imposing a positive obligation on the state to secure the observance and enjoyment of the right between private individuals. (2) If the facts of the case fall within the ambit of article 8, the state is also under a positive obligation under article 14 to secure to private individuals the enjoyment of the right without discrimination, including discrimination on the ground of sexual orientation . . .

In the case of private employers s3 is more relevant than s6 of the HRA, which expressly applies only to the case of a public authority.

(1) Under s 3 of the HRA the employment tribunal, so far as it is possible to do so, must read and give effect to s98 and the other relevant provisions in Part X of the ERA in a way which is compatible with the Convention right in article 8 and article 14.

(2) Section 3 of the HRA applies to all primary legislation and subordinate legislation . . . Section 3 draws no distinction between legislation governing public authorities and legislation governing private individuals.

(3) The ERA applies to all claims for unfair dismissal. Section 98 of the ERA draws no distinction between an employer in the private sector and a public authority employer.

(4) In many cases it would be difficult to draw, let alone justify, a distinction between public authority and private employers. In the case of such a basic employment right there would normally be no sensible grounds for treating public and private employees differently in respect of unfair dismissal, especially in these times of widespread contracting out by public authorities to private contractors.

(5) If, for example, the applicant in this case had been an employee of the Probation Service, he could have brought an unfair dismissal claim against it and, as it is a public authority, he would also have been entitled under s6 of the HRA to rely directly on article 8, if the facts had fallen within its ambit. If the employment tribunal only had to consider article 8 and article 14 where the employer was a public authority within s 6 of the HRA, a surprising situation would have arisen in a case such as this: the applicant's unfair dismissal claim might be determined differently according to whether his employer was in the private sector, working closely with the Probation Service, or was a public authority, such as the Probation Service itself. It is unlikely that the HRA was intended to produce different results

The employment tribunal as a public authority

There is a public authority aspect to the determination of every unfair dismissal case.

(1) The employment tribunal is itself a 'public authority' within s 6(2) of the HRA.

(2) Section 6(1) makes it unlawful for the tribunal itself to act in a way which is incompatible with article 8 and article 14.

(3) Those features of s6 do not, however, give the applicant any cause of action under the HRA against a respondent which is not a public authority. In that sense the HRA does not have the same full horizontal effect as between private individuals as it has between individuals and public authorities.

(4) The effect of s6 in the case of a claim against a private employer is to reinforce the extremely strong interpretative obligation imposed on the employment tribunal by s3 of the HRA. That is especially so in a case such as this, where the Strasbourg court has held that article 8 imposes a positive obligation on the state to secure the enjoyment of that right between private individuals. Article 14 also imposes that positive obligation in cases falling within the ambit of article 8 . . .

It is advisable for employment tribunals to deal with points raised under the HRA in unfair dismissal cases between private litigants in a more structured way than was adopted in this case. The following framework of questions is suggested—

(1) Do the circumstances of the dismissal fall within the ambit of one or more of the articles of the Convention? If they do not, the Convention right is not engaged and need not be considered.

(2) If they do, does the state have a positive obligation to secure enjoyment of the relevant Convention right between private persons? If it does not, the Convention right is unlikely to affect the outcome of an unfair dismissal claim against a private employer.

(3) If it does, is the interference with the employee's Convention right by dismissal justified? If it is, proceed to (5) below.

(4) If it is not, was there a permissible reason for the dismissal under the ERA, which does not involve unjustified interference with a Convention right? If there was not, the dismissal will be unfair for the absence of a permissible reason to justify it.

(5) If there was, is the dismissal fair, tested by the provisions of s98 of the ERA, reading and giving effect to them under s3 of the HRA so as to be compatible with the Convention right?

Brooke and Dyson LJJ agreed.

That approach taken by the Court of Appeal in *X v Y* to Article 8 is highly questionable, but the decision is to be welcomed inasmuch as it imposes a section 3 framework on the unfair dismissal provisions regardless of the identity of the employer.

6.2.2 The Human Rights Act and procedural fairness

Below we turn to consider the impact of incorporation on some aspects of substantive employment law. First, however, a brief mention will be made of its impact on questions of procedure. Article 6 of the Convention, reproduced above, provides a right, *inter alia*, to 'a fair and public hearing within a reasonable time by an independent and impartial tribunal' in 'the determination of [a person's] civil rights and obligations'. In *Scanfuture UK Ltd v Secretary of State for Trade and Industry* [2001] ICR 1096 the EAT was confronted with the question whether the appointment of lay members to employment tribunals by the Secretary of State for Trade and Industry resulted in breaches of Article 6's requirement for an 'independent and impartial tribunal' in cases in which the the Secretary of State was a party to a claim. The EAT ruled that there was such a breach because the Secretary of State fixed the length of lay members' appointments, determined their re-appointment and their pay and there was a risk accordingly of improper influence or interference. But the EAT went on to state that the new system of appointment complied with Article 6 in that, although lay members are still appointed by the Secretary of State, the system now includes an element of open competition and appointments are for three year fixed periods which are automatically renewed subject to an age requirement and to seven specific grounds for non-renewal.

The IRLR predicted, in reporting *Scanfuture*, that the approach there taken by the EAT was 'likely to encourage scrutiny of analogous issues, such as the relationship between specialist employment lawyers sitting as part-time tribunal chairmen and barristers appearing before them, and whether it is appropriate for part-time EAT judges to also appear as advocates in the same court.' Within a year this had occurred, and in *Lawal v Northern Spirit Ltd* [2002] ICR 486 the EAT ruled that the fact that a QC appearing before the EAT had previously sat as a part-time EAT chair with an EAT lay member did not result in any breach of Article 6. The EAT was confident that lay members would have no difficulty in distinguishing between an individual performing judicial and advocacy roles. The Court of Appeal agreed by a majority ([2002] ICR 1507) but the House of Lords disagreed, ruling that part-time EAT judges could not, consistent with Article 6, appear as counsel before lay members with whom they had sat in their judicial capacity ([2003] ICR 856). The EAT now functions without part-time judges. Further restrictions have been imposed on the behaviour of tribunal members by the decision in *Stansbury v Datapulse Plc* [2004] ICR 523 in which the Court of Appeal ruled that the Claimant had been denied his Article 6 rights by a tribunal hearing in which one of the panel members was alleged to have been affected by alcohol and to have been asleep during part of the hearing. Perhaps alarmingly, the EAT had rejected his appeal on the basis that, even if the facts were as alleged, they were not sufficient to have denied the Claimant his Article 6 rights.

The HRA 1998 has had an impact on the conduct of hearings: in *XXX v YYY* [2004] IRLR 137 the EAT ruled that evidence should be heard in private where its admission in open court would infringe Article 8 rights to privacy (here the rights of a child captured in a video recording in a claim relating to the alleged sexual harassment of his former nanny by his father). And in *Tehrani v UK Central Council for Nursing, Midwifery and Health Visiting* [2001] IRLR 208 the Court of Session ruled that Article 6 applied to disciplinary procedures carried out by the council's Professional Conduct Committee, since these procedures could result in removal of the Claimant's name from the register of nurses and thus make it difficult for her to find work in her field involving the same duties and similar pay. The Court of Session went on to rule that the disciplinary tribunal did not have to fulfil all the requirements of Article 6 as regards independence and impartiality, as its proceedings could be considered together with those of the court to which appeals could be made. This approach is in line with that of the European Court of Human Rights to disciplinary tribunals. In *Preiss v General Dental Council* [2001] IWLR 1926, however, in which the Privy Council ruled that the GDC's disciplinary system was not compliant with Article 6 because, *inter alia*, the Council's president participated in a preliminary screening and acted as chairman of the disciplinary committee, but that the right of appeal to the Privy Council ensured overall conformity with Article 6, their Lordships went on to state, *per* Lord Cooke, that:

a disciplinary system in which a hearing satisfying Article 6(1) could be secured only by going as far as the Privy Council could not be commended. Secondly, the right is to have such a hearing within a reasonable time. Although there has been no suggestion of undue overall delay in this instance, that might not always be the case. Thirdly . . . the proceedings as a whole have to be considered in deciding whether Article 6(1) is satisfied. While again this does not apply to the instant case, there may be some risk of unpredictable circumstances where even a full Privy Council rehearing is not enough.

6.3 The application of the Convention rights to employment

Those Convention rights likely to be of most significance in the context of employment have been set out at [6.2] above and we have considered the possible operation in this context of the HRA 1998. As been noted above, a claim under or in relation to the 1998 Act requires it to be established that there has been a breach of a Convention right. Before we turn to consider the possible application of the Convention and the HRA 1998 in a number of concrete areas, it is useful to discuss in brief the general approach taken by the Convention organs in the employment context.

Articles 8, 9, 10 and 11 of the Convention will be breached where there is an interference with the substance of the relevant right and the state fails to justify the interference. The question of justification will be considered below but here we look at interference in the specific context of employment. Two main questions arise: firstly, when will disadvantages experienced in the employment context be regarded as interferences in the general sense; secondly, when will the state be held responsible for interference by a *private* employer with a person's Convention rights. We saw, above, that only public authorities can be sued directly under the HRA 1998 (and only states can be respondents to actions in the ECtHR). But the state can under some circumstances be held responsible for 'quasi breaches' by private actors, where it culpably fails to prevent the interference or to provide an adequate remedy for it.

We saw in *Ahmad* and *Stedman* ([6.1] above) the reluctance of the Convention organs to find interferences with Convention rights where employers fail to accommodate the needs of their workers (see in the domestic context also the decision of the EAT in *Copsey v WBB Devon Clays Ltd* 13 February 2004, EAT: an appeal is to be heard by the Court of Appeal in 2005). Another case in which the Convention organs have refused to find an interference with a Convention right in the employment context is extracted immediately below.

[6.9] *Kosiek v Germany* (1987) 9 EHRR 328 (ECtHR)

Rolf Kosiek, an official of the extreme right wing National Democratic Party of Germany, was dismissed from his position as a probationary academic. He had, as required by law, signed a statement to the effect that he was not a member of, and did not support the tendencies of, 'any organisation which sets out to abolish the free democratic constitutional system'. He claimed that his dismissal breached his Article 10 rights. The European Court of Human Rights rejected his claim. Pointing out that the Convention did not protect a right of access to the public sector, the Court accepted nonetheless that

Article 10 did apply in the circumstances. But it concluded that there had been no interference with the applicant's freedom of expression because the refusal to renew his contract had been because of his failure to fulfil the requirement, imposed on all German civil servants, 'that he would consistently uphold the free democratic system'. According to the Court: 'This requirement . . . cannot in itself be considered incompatible with the Convention'.

A similar decision was reached by the Count in *Glasenapp v Germany* (1987) 9 EHRR 25, there in a claim brought by a left-wing teacher also dismissed from a probationary appointment for failure to fulfil the 'personal qualifications' required for the job. More recently, however, there has been evidence of a more robust approach on the part of the Court.

[6.10] *Vogt v Germany* (1996) 21 EHRR 205 (ECtHR)

The applicant, an active member of the German Communist Party, was dismissed from her teaching post. She claimed that her Article 10 and Article 11 rights had been violated. The German Government argued, as it had in *Glasenapp* and in *Kosiek*, that her political affiliations prevented her from fulfilling the 'personal' qualifications for her position. The Court distinguished *Kosiek* and *Glasenapp* on the basis that, whereas the applicants in the earlier cases had been seeking *access* to the civil service (albeit by workers already in probationary posts), Ms Vogt had been a permanent civil servant for years prior to her dismissal which was accepted, accordingly, as having involved an interference with her Convention rights.

In *Kosiek* and in *Glasenapp* the ECtHR relied in part on the absence in the Convention of any right of access to the Civil Service, teaching jobs in Germany being within that description and the Claimants, although in fact of relatively long standing in their jobs, having at least formally 'probationary' status. *Vogt* is, however, better seen as evidence of a trend away from the very technical approach adopted in the earlier cases towards a greater willingness substantively to evaluate arguments about interferences with Convention rights. Thus, for example, in *Thlimmenos v Greece* (see box p 587) the European Court ruled that a breach of Article 9, read with Article 14, occured in a case involving a refusal of access to the profession of chartered accountancy on grounds indirectly related to the applicant's religion. Having noted that 'the right to freedom of profession [was] not . . . guaranteed by the Convention', the Court went on to accept that the 'set of facts' about which the applicant complained, ie, that he had been refused access to the profession on grounds connected with his religion, '[fell] within the ambit of' Article 9. This is not as rigorous a test to satisfy (see further the discussion of *Belgian Linguistics* and *Abdulaziz* at **[6.15]** and **[6.16]** below). But further indications of this trend are also to be found in *Smith & Grady v UK* (2000) 29 EHRR 493 and *Lustig-Prean v UK* (2000) 29 EHRR 548 in which the ECtHR ruled that the Claimants' discharge from service in pursuit of the UK's ban on gays in the military breached their Article 8 rights. These cases, like *Vogt*, involved challenges to dismissals from service. But more recently, in *Sidabras & Džiautas v Lithuania* (27 July 2004), the Court ruled that *ex ante* restrictions on the employment of former members of the KGB (the Soviet Security Service) breached Articles 8 and 14 of the Convention.

Turning to the problem of when the state can 'interfere' in the Convention rights of a private sector employee, in *Young, James & Webster v UK* (Appl. 7601/76 (1977) Yearbook XX 520) the Commission stated that 'there are Articles of the Convention which oblige the State to protect individual rights even against the action of others . . . Article 11 is such a provision as far as dismissal on the basis of union activity or as a sanction for not joining a specific trade union is concerned . . . the State is responsible under the Convention if its legal system makes such dismissal lawful'. In *X and Y v Netherlands* (1985) 8 EHRR 235, the Court accepted that Article 8 could impose on Contracting States positive obligations in respect of 'the adoption of measures designed to secure respect for private life even in the sphere of the relations of individuals between themselves'. This case, in which the Court found a violation of Article 8, related to the state's failure to provide a mechanism whereby sexual assault proceedings could be brought on behalf of a disabled child who was not competent to bring proceedings on her own account. And in *Stedman v UK* (1997) 23 EHRR CD, the Commission accepted (in the case of a private sector employee) that 'if a violation of one of [the Convention] rights is the result of non-observance of [the State's obligation under Article 1 of the Convention to 'secure to everyone within [its] jurisdiction the rights and freedoms defined in . . . [the] Convention'] in the domestic legislation, the responsibility of the State is engaged'. But the degree of positive obligation to protect Convention rights from interference by others is not as strong as the obligation on States not themselves to interfere. And a significant 'margin of appreciation' is provided to Contracting States as to the manner of protection.

The Commission accepted, in *Rommelfanger* (below), that the positive obligations imposed on Contracting States by Article 10 required some measure of protection to be afforded to private sector employees. But these obligations required only that 'a reasonable relationship' existed 'between the measures affecting freedom of expression and the nature of the employment as well as the importance of the issue for the employer'.

[6.11] *Rommelfanger v Federal Republic of Germany* (1989) DR 151 (Commission)

The applicant, a doctor, was employed in a Catholic hospital under terms and conditions which permitted his dismissal for 'breaches of loyalty or gross violations of due respect towards members of the [employing] organisation, leading persons or essential institutions of the Catholic Church, serious offences against moral principles of the Church or against State law, or other gross violations of professional duties under these guidelines'. He was dismissed for having put his name to a published letter which condemned German abortion legislation as unduly restrictive. His having signed the letter was viewed by his employers as 'a violation of the duties under his employment contract as the views expressed therein were diametrically opposed to the opinion of the Church concerning the killing of unborn human beings'. He claimed that his Article 10 rights had been violated.

Judgment:
The Commission must first determine whether in the circumstances of the case the appliant is entitled to invoke his freedom of expression under Article 10. The Government claim that he is debarred from doing so because he waived this freedom by assuming certain duties of loyalty towards the Catholic Church in his employment contract.

The Commission finds no basis for the assumption that the applicant waived his freedom of expression as such. That he accepted the status of a doctor employed by a Catholic hospital could not deprive him of the protection afforded by Article 10.

The applicant claims that there has been an indirect State interference in that the German courts failed to protect his freedom of expression against the sanction of dismissal. The Government submit that the courts were not required to protect the applicant as he had accepted limitations of his freedom of expression in his employment contract.

The Commission notes that by entering into contractual obligations vis-à-vis his employer the applicant accepted a duty of loyalty towards the Catholic Church which limited his freedom of expression to a certain extent. Similar obligations may also be agreed with other employers than the Catholic Church or its institutions. In principle, the Convention permits contractual obligations of this kind if they are freely entered into by the person concerned. A violation of such obligations normally entails the legal consequences stipulated in the contract, including dismissal. Their enforcement with the assistance of the competent State authorities does not as such constitute an 'interference by public authority' with the rights guaranteed by Article 10 para 1 of the Convention (*cf* No 11142/84, Dec. 3.12.86).

It is true that under Article 1 of the Convention the State is required to 'secure' the Convention rights to everyone within its jurisdiction. In certain cases, it may therefore be necessary for the State to take positive action with a view to effectively securing these rights.

The Commission has examined whether in the present case a similar obligation existed for the State to secure the applicant's right to freedom of expression against the measure of dismissal taken by his employer. The normal Labour Court procedure was available to the applicant and the competent courts were required to weigh the applicant's interests, including his interest in freedom of expression, against those of his employer. It is true that particular weight was finally given to the views of the Church concerning the duties of loyalty of Church employees. According to the Federal Constitutional Court this was necessary in order to safeguard the constitutional right of the Church to regulate its internal affairs. Nevertheless the Federal Constitutional Court held that there were limits to the right of the Church to impose its views on its employees. In particular the State courts were competent to ensure that no unreasonable demands of loyalty were made. The requirement to refrain from making statements on abortion in con?ict with the Church's views was not seen as an unreasonable demand because of the crucial importance of this issue for the Church. In the case of a doctor employed in a Catholic hospital it was also relevant that the Church regards the exercise of charitable functions as one of its essential tasks.

The Commission is satisfied that German law, as interpreted by the Federal Constitutional Court, takes account of the necessity to secure an employee's freedom of expression against unreasonable demands of his employer, even if they should result from a valid employment contract. If, as in the present case, the employer is an organisation based on certain convictions and value judgments which it considers as essential for the performance of its functions in society, it is in fact in line with the requirements of the Convention to give appropriate scope also to the freedom of expression of the employer. An employer of this kind would not be able to effectively exercise this freedom without imposing certain duties of loyalty on its employees. As regards employers such as the Catholic foundation which employed the applicant in its hospital, the law in any event ensures that there is a reasonable relationship between the measures affecting freedom of expression and the nature of the employment as well as the importance of the issue for the employer. In this way it protects an employee against compulsion in matters of freedom of expression which would strike at the very substance of this freedom ... The Commission considers that Article 10 of the Convention does not, in cases like the present one, impose a positive obligation on the State to provide protection beyond this standard.

It follows that there has been no State interference with the applicant's right to freedom of expression as guaranteed in Article 10 para 1 of the Convention, nor a failure to comply with positive obligations resulting from this provision. The applicant's complaint must therefore be rejected as being manifestly ill-founded within the meaning of Article 27 para. 2 of the Convention.

If the Court accepts that an interference has occurred, it proceeds to determine whether the interference was (a) prescribed by law (b) in pursuit of a legitimate aim (such as those listed in the Article at issue) and (c) 'necessary in a democratic society'. The first of these conditions may be satisfied, as in *Ahmed v UK* (below), where the interference is required or permitted by legislation or (as in *Sunday Times v UK* (1979) 2 EHRR 245, paras 46–52) the common law. In *Lustig-Prean & Beckett v UK*, the promulgated ban on gays in the armed services did satisfy this requirement (although the European Court found against the UK on the basis that the ban was disproportionate to the legitimate aim it pursued). And in *Kara v UK*, below, the Commission found that an employer's internal dress code was prescribed by law. In *Halford v UK* (1997) 24 EHRR 523 (**[6.36]** below), by contrast, the European Court ruled that the UK had failed to satisfy this condition where the applicant was subject to covert telephone surveillance. Although in a case in which the aims pursued by such covert activity were legitimate, any requirement that the target of surveillance be informed of it would frustrate such aims, the rules governing covert interference with Convention rights must 'indicate with reasonable clarity the scope and manner of exercise of the relevant discretion (*Huvig v France* (1990) 12 EHRR 528).

As to the aims which might be pursued by a refusal to employ, Articles 8(2), 10(2) and 11(2) permit interference 'for the prevention of disorder or crime' and these and Article 9(2) allow interferences 'for the protection of health and morals' and 'the rights of others', including in the case of Article 10(2) the reputations of others and the protection of 'information received in confidence'. The interference must be proportionate to the 'pressing social need' pursued.

[6.12] *Vogt v Germany* (1996) 21 EHRR 205 (ECtHR)

The Court accepted that the interference was prescribed by law and that it pursued one of the legitimate aims recognised by Article 10 (the protection of democracy), and proceeded to consider whether it was 'necessary in a democratic society'. It reiterated the 'basic principle' that exceptions to Article 10 had to be 'narrowly interpreted and the necessity for any restrictions must be convincingly established', and that the Court had to 'look at the interference complained of in the light of the case as a whole and determine whether it was "proportionate to the legitimate aim pursued" and whether the reasons adduced by the national authorities to justify it are "relevant and sufficient" '. The Court noted that Ms Vogt's membership of the DKP was known to the authorities at the date of her appointment.

Judgment:
The duty of political loyalty to which German civil servants are subject . . . entails for all civil servants the duty to dissociate themselves unequivocally from groups that attack and

cast aspersions on the State and the existing constitutional system. At the material time the German courts had held—on the basis of the DKP's own official programme—that its aims were the overthrow of the social structures and the constitutional order of the Federal Republic of Germany and the establishment of a political system similar to that of the German Democratic Republic.

The Court proceeds on the basis that a democratic State is entitled to require civil servants to be loyal to the constitutional principles on which it is founded. In this connection it takes into account Germany's experience under the Weimar Republic and during the bitter period that followed the collapse of that regime up to the adoption of the Basic Law in 1949. Germany wished to avoid a repetition of those experiences by founding its new State on the idea that it should be a 'democracy capable of defending itself'. Nor should Germany's position in the political context of the time be forgotten. These circumstances understandably lent extra weight to this underlying notion and to the corresponding duty of political loyalty imposed on civil servants.

Even so, the absolute nature of that duty as construed by the German courts is striking. It is owed equally by every civil servant, regardless of his or her function and rank. It implies that every civil servant, whatever his or her own opinion on the matter, must unambiguously renounce all groups and movements which the competent authorities hold to be inimical to the Constitution. It does not allow for distinctions between service and private life; the duty is always owed, in every context.

Another relevant consideration is that at the material time a similarly strict duty of loyalty does not seem to have been imposed in any other member State of the Council of Europe, whilst even within Germany the duty was not construed and implemented in the same manner throughout the country; a considerable number of Länder did not consider activities such as are in issue here incompatible with that duty.

However, the Court is not called upon to assess the system as such. It will accordingly concentrate on Mrs Vogt's dismissal. In this connection it notes at the outset that there are several reasons for considering dismissal of a secondary-school teacher by way of disciplinary sanction for breach of duty to be a very severe measure. This is firstly because of the effect that such a measure has on the reputation of the person concerned and secondly because secondary-school teachers dismissed in this way lose their livelihood, at least in principle, as the disciplinary court may allow them to keep part of their salary. Finally, secondary-school teachers in this situation may find it well nigh impossible to find another job as a teacher, since in Germany teaching posts outside the civil service are scarce. Consequently, they will almost certainly be deprived of the opportunity to exercise the sole profession for which they have a calling, for which they have been trained and in which they have acquired skills and experience.

A second aspect that should be noted is that Mrs Vogt was a teacher of German and French in a secondary school, a post which did not intrinsically involve any security risks. The risk lay in the possibility that, contrary to the special duties and responsibilities incumbent on teachers, she would take advantage of her position to indoctrinate or exert improper influence in another way on her pupils during lessons. Yet no criticism was levelled at her on this point. On the contrary, the applicant's work at school had been considered wholly satisfactory by her superiors and she was held in high regard by her pupils and their parents and also by her colleagues . . . the disciplinary courts recognised that she had always carried out her duties in a way that was beyond reproach . . . Indeed the authorities only suspended the applicant more than four years after instituting disciplinary proceedings . . . thereby showing that they did not consider the need to remove the pupils from her influence to be a very pressing one.

Since teachers are figures of authority to their pupils, their special duties and responsibilities to a certain extent also apply to their activities outside school. However, there is no evidence that Mrs Vogt herself, even outside her work at school, actually made anti-constitutional statements or personally adopted an anti-constitutional stance. The only criticisms retained against her concerned her active membership of the DKP, the posts she had held in that party and her candidature in the elections for the Parliament of the Land. Mrs Vogt consistently maintained her personal conviction that these activities were compatible with upholding the principles of the German constitutional order. The disciplinary courts recognised that her conviction was genuine and sincere, while considering it to be of no legal significance . . . and indeed not even the prolonged investigations lasting several years were apparently capable of yielding any instance where Mrs Vogt had actually made specific pronouncements belying her emphatic assertion that she upheld the values of the German constitutional order.

A final consideration to be borne in mind is that the DKP had not been banned by the Federal Constitutional Court and that, consequently, the applicant's activities on its behalf were entirely lawful.

In the light of all the foregoing, the Court concludes that, although the reasons put forward by the Government in order to justify their interference with Mrs Vogt's right to freedom of expression are certainly relevant, they are not sufficient to establish convincingly that it was necessary in a democratic society to dismiss her. Even allowing for a certain margin of appreciation, the conclusion must be that to dismiss Mrs Vogt by way of disciplinary sanction from her post as secondary-school teacher was disproportionate to the legitimate aim pursued. There has accordingly been a violation of Article 10.

The decision in *Vogt* is illustrative of the approach typically adopted by the ECtHR to the question whether any disputed interference is in breach of the relevant Convention Article. The question whether an interference was 'necessary in a democratic society' will turn on the relationship between the aim sought and the extent of the interference with the applicant's rights. In *Lustig-Prean & Beckett v UK* and in *Vogt* the interference was regarded as especially grave, taking into account the fact that, in each case, it consisted in dismissal and that the precise nature of the posts concerned was such that their dismissal effectively prevented the applicants from exercising their professions. But the European Court and Commission are protective of the rights and interests of employers. Lesser interferences might in either case have been regarded as proportionate to the aim sought and, thus, as 'necessary in a democratic society'.

[6.13] *X v UK* (1979) 16 DR 101 (Commission)

The applicant, a teacher, was dismissed for proselytising (he had given religious instruction during school hours, had held 'evangelical clubs' on school premises and had worn religious and anti-abortion stickers). Having failed to succeed in an unfair dismissal claim he brought an action under Article 10 of the Convention. The application was rejected by the Commission.

Judgment:
It is clear from the documents submitted by the applicant, in particular the decisions of the Industrial Tribunal and the Employment Appeal Tribunal and letters sent to the applicant by his headmaster dated 10 May 1974 and 13 November 1974 that he was dismissed because of his refusal to comply with specific instructions, not to advertise by posters or stickers on school premises his political, moral or religious beliefs.

The Commission considers that this instruction constitutes an interference with the applicant's freedom of expression. However the Commission is of the opinion that school teachers in non-denominational schools should have regard to the rights of parents so as to respect their religious and philosophical convictions in the education of their children. This requirement assumes particular importance in a non-denominational school where the governing legislation provides that parents can seek to have their children excused from attendance at religious instruction and further that any religious instruction given shall not include 'any catechism or formulary which is distinctive of any particular religious denomination' (see Education Act 1944, Sections 25 and 26).

In the present case the posters and 'stickers' objected to, reflected the applicant's strong Evangelical beliefs and his opposition to abortion. The Commission notes from the observations of the respondent Government that some of the 'stickers' worn on the applicant's lapel and on his briefcase were considered offensive to female members of staff and disturbing to children. Having regard to the particular circumstances of the case, the Commission considers that the interference with the applicant's freedom of expression is justified as being necessary in a democratic society for the protection of the rights of others within the meaning of Article 10, paragraph 2, of the Convention.

[6.14] *Kara v UK*, Appl No 36528/97, 22 October 1998 (www.echr.coe.int/eng/Judgments.htm) (Commission)

The applicant, a bisexual male transvestite, was instructed not to wear 'female' clothes at work (from time to time he had worn leggings, tights, 'halter neck' tee shirts and dresses. His appearance was regarded by his employers, Hackney Council, as contravening the Council's Code of Conduct (which required that staff should look clean, neat and appropriately dressed) and as likely to bring the Council into disrepute. The Council rejected the applicant's claim that their policy discriminated against the applicant on grounds of his religious beliefs (he described himself as a 'Berdache Shaman'—an American indigenous tradition in which certain men express themselves through dressing in conventionally female clothing) or otherwise so as to raise any 'equal opportunities' issues. Having failed to challenge his employer's actions under domestic law, the applicant claimed, *inter alia*, that his Article 8 and 14 rights had been contravened.

Judgment:
The Commission finds that constraints imposed on a person's choice of mode of dress constitute an interference with the private life as ensured by Article 8 para 1 of the Convention. . . . It is therefore necessary to examine whether this interference was justified under Article 8 para 2 . . .

The Commission recalls that the Council's restriction on the choice of mode of dress of its employees was based on its internal policy which was confirmed by the Industrial Tribunal to be lawful. Accordingly, the Commission considers that the interference was 'in accordance with the law' within the meaning of Article 8 para 2 of the Convention.

The Commission further recalls that the aim of its dress policy as stated by the Council in April 1994 was to enable it to enhance its image in its dealings with the public, the business community and representatives of Government. Accordingly, the Commission considers that the interference could be said to pursue the legitimate aim of 'the protection of the rights of others', in the sense of protecting its own proper functioning and carrying out of its duties on behalf of the public.

As to whether the interference was 'necessary in a democratic society', the Commission recalls that this phrase corresponds to the existence of a 'pressing social need' in particular, the interference must be proportionate to the legitimate aim pursued . . . The Contracting States however, have a certain margin of appreciation in assessing whether such a need exits, but this goes hand in hand with a European supervision . . .

The Commission notes that the rules as to the mode of dress at work affected the applicant during work hours on work premises and that at other times he remained at liberty to dress as he wished. The Commission considers that employers may require their employees to conform to certain dress requirements which are reasonably related to the type of work being undertaken eg. safety helmets, hygienic coverings, uniforms. This may also involve requiring employees, who come into contact with the public or other organisations to conform to a dress code which may reasonably be regarded as enhancing the employer's public image and facilitating its external contacts. While the applicant has disputed that the Council provided support for its claims that the way he dressed prejudiced its external image and the extent to which he came into contact with members of the public and the representatives of other bodies in his daily work, the Commission notes that the applicant did not deny that he had contacts outside his own office and it is satisfied that the requirements in this case, that employees dress 'appropriately' to their gender, may be reasonably regarded by the employer as necessary to safeguard their public image. Having regard to the circumstances of the case, any restrictions on the applicant's ability to dress at work in the manner which he perceives as expressing his personality and fostering personal relationships was not disproportionate.

The Commission finds that the interference in this case may be regarded as necessary in a democratic society for the aim of protecting the rights of others within the meaning of Article 8 para. 2 of the Convention. This complaint must therefore be rejected as manifestly ill-founded . . .

X v UK and *Kara* can be regarded as more favourable to employees than the decisions in *Ahmad* and *Stedman*, in the sense that the Commission was prepared at least to accept that interferences with the Convention rights had occurred. But while, in these cases, the employees were not regarded in terms as having left their Convention rights on the doorstep on their entry into the workplace, the Commission decisions illustrate how low the threshold of justification for interference with Convention rights can be in the employment context.

Even where there is no breach of a substantive Convention provision taken alone, Article 14 may be read with one or more substantive provisions to found a breach of the Convention where one might not otherwise arise.

[6.15] *Cases Relating to Certain Aspects of the Laws on the Use of Languages in Education in Belgium* (1968) 1 EHRR 252 (ECtHR)

The case involved a challenge by French speakers living in Dutch speaking regions to Belgium's insistence that their children be educated in Dutch. The applicants relied on Article 8 and Article 2 of the First Protocol to the Convention read with Article 14.

Judgment:
According to Article 14 of the Convention, the enjoyment of the rights and freedoms set forth therein shall be secured without discrimination ('*sans distinction aucune*') on the ground, *inter alia*, of language . . . .

While it is true that this guarantee has no independent existence in the sense that under the terms of Article 14 it relates solely to 'rights and freedoms set forth in the

Convention', a measure which in itself is in conformity with the requirements of the Article enshrining the right or freedom in question may however infringe this Article when read in conjunction with Article 14 for the reason that it is of a discriminatory nature . . .

In such cases there would be a violation of a guaranteed right or freedom as it is proclaimed by the relevant Article read in conjunction with Article 14. It is as though the latter formed an integral part of each of the Articles laying down rights and freedoms. No distinctions should be made in this respect according to the nature of these rights and freedoms and of their correlative obligations, and for instance as to whether the respect due to the right concerned implies positive action or mere abstention. This is, moreover, clearly shown by the very general nature of the terms employed in Article 14: 'the enjoyment of the rights and freedoms set forth in this Convention shall be secured'.

In spite of the very general wording of the French version (*'sans distinction aucune'*), Article 14 does not forbid every difference in treatment in the exercise of the rights and freedoms recognised. This version must be read in the light of the more restrictive text of the English version ('without discrimination'). In addition, and in particular, one would reach absurd results were one to give Article 14 an interpretation as wide as that which the French version seems to imply. One would, in effect, be led to judge as contrary to the Convention every one of the many legal or administrative provisions which do not secure to everyone complete equality of treatment in the enjoyment of the rights and freedoms recognised. The competent national authorities are frequently confronted with situations and problems which, on account of differences inherent therein, call for different legal solutions; moreover, certain legal inequalities tend only to correct factual inequalities. The extensive interpretation mentioned above cannot consequently be accepted.

It is important, then, to look for the criteria which enable a determination to be made as to whether or not a given difference in treatment, concerning of course the exercise of one of the rights and freedoms set forth, contravenes Article 14. On this question the Court, following the principles which may be extracted from the legal practice of a large number of democratic States, holds that the principle of equality of treatment is violated if the distinction has no objective and reasonable justification. The existence of such a justification must be assessed in relation to the aim and effects of the measure under consideration, regard being had to the principles which normally prevail in democratic societies. A difference of treatment in the exercise of a right laid down in the Convention must not only pursue a legitimate aim: Article 14 is likewise violated when it is clearly established that there is no reasonable relationship of proportionality between the means employed and the aim sought to be realised.

[6.16] *Abdulaziz, Cabales and Balkandali v United Kingdom* (1985) 7 EHRR 471 (ECtHR)

The applicants challenged immigration rules (the 1980 Rules) which discriminated on grounds of sex against (non-national) women who wished to bring their fiancés into the UK: whereas non-national men who (like the applicants) had indefinite leave to remain in the UK were entitled to bring spouses or fiancées to the UK, comparable women were not unless the woman or one of her parents had been born in the UK. The women challenged the immigration rules under Articles 8 and 14. The Court ruled that Article 8 had not been breached, the applicants remaining free to establish family life outside the UK. But it accepted that the facts 'fell within the ambit' of that provision so as to make possible an Article 14 claim and went on to find against the UK.

Judgment:

For the purposes of Article 14, a difference of treatment is discriminatory if it 'has no objective and reasonable justification', that is, if it does not pursue a 'legitimate aim' or if there is not a 'reasonable relationship of proportionality between the means employed and the aim sought to be realised' . . .

The Contracting States enjoy a certain margin of appreciation in assessing whether and to what extent differences in otherwise similar situations justify a different treatment in law . . . . but it is for the Court to give the final ruling in this respect. . . .

. . . it was not disputed that under the 1980 Rules it was easier for a man settled in the United Kingdom than for a woman so settled to obtain permission for his or her non-national spouse to enter or remain in the country for settlement. . . Argument centred on the question whether this difference had an objective and reasonable justification . . .

The Court accepts that the 1980 Rules had the aim of protecting the domestic labour market. . . . Whilst the aforesaid aim was without doubt legitimate, this does not in itself establish the legitimacy of the difference made in the 1980 Rules as to the possibility for male and female immigrants settled in the United Kingdom to obtain permission for, on the one hand, their non-national wives or fiancées and, on the other hand, their non-national husbands or fiancés to enter or remain in the country.

Although the Contracting States enjoy a certain 'margin of appreciation' in assessing whether and to what extent differences in otherwise similar situations justify a different treatment, the scope of this margin will vary according to the circumstances, the subject-matter and its background . . . .

As to the present matter, it can be said that the advancement of the equality of the sexes is today a major goal in the member States of the Council of Europe. This means that very weighty reasons would have to be advanced before a difference of treatment on the ground of sex could be regarded as compatible with the Convention.

In the Court's opinion, the Government's arguments [that immigrant men were more likely than women to seek employment] are not convincing.

It may be correct that on average there is a greater percentage of men of working age than of women of working age who are 'economically . . . Nevertheless, this does not show that similar differences in fact exist—or would but for the effect of the 1980 Rules have existed—as regards the respective impact on the United Kingdom labour market of immigrant wives and of immigrant husbands. In this connection, other factors must also be taken into account. Being 'economically active' does not always mean that one is seeking to be employed by someone else.

Moreover, although a greater number of men than of women may be inclined to seek employment, immigrant husbands were already by far outnumbered, before the introduction of the 1980 Rules, by immigrant wives . . . many of whom were also 'economically active'. Whilst a considerable proportion of those wives, in so far as they were 'economically active', were engaged in part-time work, the impact on the domestic labour market of women immigrants as compared with men ought not to be underestimated.

In any event, the Court is not convinced that the difference that may nevertheless exist between the respective impact of men and of women on the domestic labour market is sufficiently important to justify the difference of treatment, complained of by the applicants, as to the possibility for a person settled in the United Kingdom to be joined by, as the case may be, his wife or her husband.

In this context the Government stressed the importance of the effect on the immigration of husbands of the restrictions contained in the 1980 Rules, which had led, according to their estimate, to an annual reduction of 5,700. . . . in the number of husbands accepted for settlement.

Without expressing a conclusion on the correctness of the figure of 5,700, the Court notes that in point of time the claimed reduction coincided with a significant increase in unemployment in the United Kingdom and that the Government accepted that some part of the reduction was due to economic conditions rather than to the 1980 Rules themselves. . . .

In any event, for the reasons stated in paragraph 79 above, the reduction achieved does not justify the difference in treatment between men and women.

The Court accepts that the 1980 Rules also had, as the Government stated, the aim of advancing public tranquillity. However, it is not persuaded that this aim was served by the distinction drawn in those rules between husbands and wives.

There remains a more general argument advanced by the Government, namely that the United Kingdom was not in violation of Article 14. . . . by reason of the fact that it acted more generously in some respects—that is, as regards the admission of non-national wives and fiancées of men settled in the country—than the Convention required.

The Court cannot accept this argument. It would point out that Article 14 . . . . is concerned with the avoidance of discrimination in the enjoyment of the Convention rights in so far as the requirements of the Convention as to those rights can be complied with in different ways. The notion of discrimination within the meaning of Article 14 includes in general cases where a person or group is treated, without proper justification, less favourably than another, even though the more favourable treatment is not called for by the Convention.

The Court thus concludes that the applicants have been victims of discrimination on the ground of sex, in violation of Article 14 taken together with Article 8.

It follows from these decisions (and from the more recent decisions in *Mouta v Portugal* (2001) 31 EHRR 47 and in *Thlimmenos v Greece* (below) that additional justification is required in cases in which the interference with a Convention right discriminates on Article 14 grounds. Thus, for example, while a particular course of action (screening potential applicants for employment, for example, or imposing particular rules of behaviour) might be regarded either as not amounting to an

---

Prior to the decision of the ECtHR in *Thlimmenos v Greece* the application of Article 14 to indirect discrimination was unclear. The ECtHR referred, in the *Belgian Linguistics Case*, to the 'aims *and effects*' (my emphasis) of legislation. But in *Abdulaziz* the Court refused to find that an immigration rule which required that fiancés had previously met, in order that the non-patrial be permitted access to the UK, discriminated on grounds of race. Apparently overlooking the fact that the rule disproportionately disadvantaged men from the Indian sub-continent (where arranged marriages were particular common), the Court simply examined its purpose of preventing bogus marriages. In *Thlimmenos* the Court exhibited a more sophisticated approach.

Thlimmenos v Greece **(2001) 31 EHRR 14 (ECtHR)**
The applicant, a Jehovah's witness, had been convicted of a criminal offence because of his refusal, on religious grounds, to wear military uniform. His conviction was subsequently relied on to disbar him from admission as a Chartered accountant. The Greek Government argued that the rule disbarring convicted 'felons' from the profession was neutral and that Article 14 was not applicable. The Court disagreed.

Judgment:

[The applicant's] complaint . . . concerns the fact that in the application of the relevant law no distinction is made between persons convicted of offences committed exclusively because of their religious beliefs and persons convicted of other offences. In this context the Court notes that the applicant is a member of the Jehovah's Witnesses, a religious group committed to pacifism, and that there is nothing in the file to disprove the applicant's claim that he refused to wear the military uniform only because he considered that his religion prevented him from doing so. In essence, the applicant's argument amounts to saying that he is discriminated against in the exercise of his freedom of religion, as guaranteed by Article 9 of the Convention, in that he was treated like any other person convicted of a felony although his own conviction resulted from the very exercise of this freedom. Seen in this perspective, the Court accepts that the 'set of facts' complained of by the applicant – his being treated as a person convicted of a felony for the purposes of an appointment to a chartered accountant's post despite the fact that the offence for which he had been convicted was prompted by his religious beliefs – 'falls within the ambit of a Convention provision', namely Article 9.

The Court has so far considered that the right under Article 14 not to be discriminated against in the enjoyment of the rights guaranteed under the Convention is violated when States treat differently persons in analogous situations without providing an objective and reasonable justification . . . However, the Court considers that this is not the only facet of the prohibition of discrimination in Article 14. The right not to be discriminated against in the enjoyment of the rights guaranteed under the Convention is also violated when States without an objective and reasonable justification fail to treat differently persons whose situations are significantly different.

The ECtHR went on to decide, in *Thlimmenos*, that the applicant's rights under Articles 9 and 14 had been breached. Contracting States had a legitimate interest in excluding some offenders from the profession of Chartered accountancy. But the applicant had already been punished by imprisonment for his 'insubordination'. And 'unlike other convictions for serious criminal offences, a conviction for refusing on religious or philosophical grounds to wear the military uniform cannot imply any dishonesty or moral turpitude likely to undermine the offender's ability to exercise this profession'. For this reason, the Court found that his 'exclusion from the profession of chartered accountants did not pursue a legitimate aim and that, accordingly 'there existed no objective and reasonable justification for not treating the applicant differently from other persons convicted of a felony'.

interference under (say, Articles 10 and/or 11, or Article 8 respectively), or as being justified under Article 10(2) and/or 11(2), or Article 8(2), the uneven application or enforcement of such policies might be regarded as breaching Article 14 read with the relevant Convention provision. This is further considered below.

6.4 Political activities and the Human Rights Act

We turn now to consider a number of substantive aspects of employment which give rise to human rights issues, and consider the implications for these areas of domestic law of incorporation of the relevant Convention rights. The first of the specific issues for discussion relates to workers' political beliefs and activities. Employment-related interference with such beliefs and activities may take one of three forms. In the first place, civil service and some other public sector workers are subject to 'purge and positive vetting procedures' (see section 6.4 below). Secondly, some civil servants and local government workers are subject to express statutory restrictions on their political activities (section 6.4.2 below). Finally, workers not subject to formal vetting and/or restrictions may suffer employment-related discrimination because of their actual or suspected political beliefs and/or activities (see further section 6.4.3 below). Immediately below we will discuss the operation in the UK of the various types of employment-related interference with political beliefs and activities mentioned above. Thereafter we will consider the extent to which these restrictions are regulated by domestic law; the extent to which they are compatible with the ECHR (in particular, with freedom of expression and association as protected by Articles 10 and 11); and the potential impact in this context of the HRA 1998.

6.4.1 'Purge and positive vetting'

Applicants for employment in the Civil Service have for many years been subject to 'purge and positive vetting procedures'.

[6.17] K D Ewing, 'Freedom of Association' in C McCrudden and G Chambers (eds) *Individual Rights and the Law in Britain* **(Oxford, Oxford University Press, 1995), pp 245–46 (footnotes omitted)**

> [One] basis for restricting freedom of association was the perceived threat of subversion and the consequent threat to external security created by members and sympathizers of the Communist Party during the cold war. This led to the introduction of the purge and positive vetting procedures in the civil service. The purge procedure was originally introduced with communists as the main target, though it also applied to fascists. In 1985, however, it was widened to include members of any 'subversive group acknowledged as such by the Minister, whose aims are to undermine or overthrow Parliamentary democracy in the UK and Northern Ireland by political, industrial or violent means' [citing 76 HC Debs 621 (3 April 1985)]. This is a definition of quite extraordinary scope which effectively means whatever the government wants it to mean. As Fredman and Morris have pointed out, if an employee is found to be associated with such a group, he or she may be transferred from a sensitive post or, where this is not possible, dismissed. The effect is to exclude members of supporters of disapproved organizations from employment 'in all posts which are considered to be vital to the security of the State' and is invoked when the reliability of a public servant is thought to be in doubt on security grounds' [citing 177 HC Debs 159–161, written answers, 24 July 1990]. But whereas the purge procedure operates to remove individuals from sensitive work, positive vetting operates to keep them out in the first place. Under procedures revised in 1990, this seeks

to ensure that no one is employed 'in connection with work the nature of which is vital to the security of the state'. Those who may be affected include members and associates of organisations which have advocated espionage, terrorism, sabotage or action intended to undermine or overthrow Parliamentary democracy political, industrial or violent means. Positive vetting involves an investigation into the 'civil servant's character and circumstances, which includes among other matters political associations. The arrangements appear to have been designed initially to exclude from sensitive posts members and sympathizers of the Communist Party.

[6.18] HC Debs 15 December 1994 Cols 764-765W, answer by the Prime Minister John Major

Statement of HM Government's vetting policy

In the interests of national security, safeguarding Parliamentary democracy and maintaining the proper security of the Government's essential activities, it is the policy of HMG that no one should be employed in connection with work the nature of which is vital to the interests of the state who:

is, or has been involved in, or associated with any of the following activities:

—espionage,

—terrorism,

—sabotage,

—actions intended to overthrow or undermine Parliamentary democracy by political, industrial or violent means; or

is, or has recently been:

—a member of any organisation which has advocated such activities; or

—associated with any organisation, or any of its members in such a way as to raise reasonable doubts about his or reliability; or is susceptible to pressure or improper influence, for example because of current or past conduct; or

has shown dishonesty or lack of integrity which throws doubt upon their reliability; or

has demonstrated behaviour, or is subject to circumstances which may otherwise indicate unreliability.

In accordance with the above policy, Government departments and agencies will carry out a Security Check (SC) on all individuals who require long term, frequent and uncontrolled access to SECRET information or assets. A Security Check may also be applied to staff who are in a position directly or indirectly to bring about the same degree of damage as such individuals or who need access to protectively marked material originating from other countries or international organisations. In some circumstances, where it would not be possible for an individual to make reasonable progress in their career without clearance to SECRET level, it may be applied to candidates for employment whose duties do not, initially, involve such regular access.

An SC clearance will normally consist of:

a check against the National Collection of Criminal Records and relevant departmental and police records;

in accordance with the Security Service Act 1989, where it is necessary to protect national security, or to safeguard the economic well-being of the United Kingdom from threats posed by persons outside the British Islands, a check against Security Service records; and credit reference checks and where appropriate, a review of personal finances.

In some circumstances further enquiries, including an interview with the subject, may be carried out.

Individuals employed on government work who have long term, frequent and uncontrolled access to TOP SECRET information or assets, will be submitted to the level of vetting clearance known as Developed Vetting (DV). This level of clearance may also be applied to people who are in a position directly or indirectly to cause the same degree of damage as such individuals and in order to satisfy the requirements for access to protectively marked material originating from other countries and international organisations. In addition to a Security Check, a DV will involve:

an interview with the person being vetted; and references from people who are familiar with the person's character in both the home and work environment. These may be followed up by interviews. Enquiries will not necessarily be confined to to past and present employers and nominated character referees.

It is also the Government's policy that departments and agencies will carry out Counter Terrorist Checks (CTC) in the interest of national security before anyone can be:

authorised to take up posts which involve proximity to public figures at particular risk of attack by terrorist organisations, or which give access to information or material assessed to be of value to terrorists:

granted unescorted access to certain military, civil and industrial establishments assessed to be at particular risk of attack by a terrorist organisation.

The purpose of such checks is to prevent those who may have connections with terrorist organisations, or who may be vulnerable to pressure from such organisations, from gaining access to certain posts, and in some circumstances, premises, where there is a risk that they could exploit that position to further the aims of a terrorist organisation. A CTC will include a check against Security Service records. Criminal record information may also be taken into account.

Departments and agencies generally assure themselves, through the verification of identity, and written references from previous employers, that potential recruits are reliable and trustworthy. Such Basic Checks (BC) are already standard procedure for many departments and agencies. Where access needs to be granted to Government information or assets at CONFIDENTIAL level, departments, agencies and contractors engaged on government work are required to complete such checks. In some cases, at the CONFIDENTIAL level, where relevant, the Basic Check may be augmented with some of the checks normally carried out for security clearances.

McEvoy and White detail the history of vetting in Northern Ireland's public service in which, as they point out ('Security Vetting in Northern Ireland: Loyalty, Redress and Citizenship' (1998) 61 *Modern Law Review* 341) 'the fear of disloyalty and mistrust of the Catholic minority, confirmed in the minds of the majority by the periodic outbursts of Republican violence, became deeply embedded in the political and social fabric of the state. . . . Catholic/Nationalist disloyalty was viewed as axiomatic, synonymous with those who were against the British connection and wanted to withdraw from the Union, whereas Protestant Unionists were by definition loyal' (citing P Clayton, *Enemies and Passing Friends: Settler Ideologies in Twentieth Century Ulster* (London, Pluto Press, 1992), p 124). Until the end of 2003, vetting was applied to all applicants to Northern Ireland's Civil Service (not simply, as in Great Britain, to those in sensitive posts). The repercussions of this for the Catholic/ nationalist community was finally realised in 2002:

[6.19] Northern Ireland Office, Section 75 Northern Ireland Act 1998 Progress Report 1 April 2001–31 March 2002, pp 11-12

> [A]n internal review conducted in the light of the implementation of the Human Rights Act 1998, the Northern Ireland Act 1998 (including sections 75 & 76), the improving security environment and the changing political situation, into the operation of those national security vetting processes conducted in Northern Ireland . . . recognised that the way in which security vetting has operated . . . has differed from that outlined in the [Prime Minister's statement at **[6.17]** above] and has been seen to be both opaque and to have created adverse, differential impacts on Roman Catholics/Nationalists and Republicans in particular, although some Loyalists may also have felt adversely affected.

The review referred to above resulted in reform of security vetting as it applied in Northern Ireland: in December 2003 the Minister of State for the Northern Ireland Office announced that 'in future applicants for posts in the Northern Ireland Civil Service will undergo a basic check procedure, designed to ensure that they are adequately identified; and will be asked to declare any unspent criminal records. This will bring to an end the existing practice of security vetting all administrative applicants. All those staff occupying, or who are to occupy, posts in specific areas identified in the programme of reform as requiring security clearance on grounds of national security, will be required to undergo national security vetting, to the appropriate level, in accordance with stated Government policy' (HC Debs 15 Dec 2003 Column 125WS).

6.4.2 Statutory restrictions on public sector workers

'Purge and vetting' procedures serve to deny access to jobs to those whose political beliefs and/or activities are regarded as suspect by the state. The other limitation imposed on many workers relates to the political activities permitted to them while they are employed. The Civil Service Pay and Conditions Code restricts political activities by certain civil servants. 'Politically restricted' civil servants, who comprised around 20% of the total in 1995 (the date of the last available figures), are prohibited from holding office in national political parties, from expressing views on politically controversial questions, and from being candidates in or canvassing in parliamentary elections.

[6.20] Civil Service Management Code, Chapter 4

> 4.4.2 Departments and agencies must allow civil servants in industrial and non-office grades the freedom to take part in all political activities. These staff are known as the 'politically free' category . . .
> 4.4.9 Civil Servants in 'the politically restricted' category i.e. members of the Senior Civil Service and civil servants at levels immediately below the Senior Civil Service, plus members of the Fast Stream Development Programme (Administrative and European), must not take part in national political activities . . . They must seek permission to take part in local political activities . . . and must comply with any conditions laid down by their department or agency.

4.4.10 Civil servants outside the 'politically restricted' category . . . and the 'politically free' category . . . must seek permission to take part in national or local political activities . . . unless they are in a grade or area that has already been given permission to do so by means of a specific mandate from the department or agency. Where they already have permission under such a mandate, they must notify the department or agency of intended political activities prior to taking them up. They must comply with any conditions laid down by their department or agency.

4.4.11 Civil servants must not take part in any political activity when on duty, or in uniform, or on official premises.

4.4.12 Civil servants must not attend in their official capacity outside conferences or functions convened by or under the aegis of a party political organisation.

4.4.13 Civil servants not in the politically free category must not allow the expression of their personal political views to constitute so strong and so comprehensive a commitment to one political party as to inhibit or appear to inhibit loyal and effective service to Ministers of another party. They must take particular care to express comment with moderation, particularly about matters for which their own Ministers are responsible; to avoid comment altogether about matters of controversy affecting the responsibility of their own Ministers, and to avoid personal attacks.

4.4.14 They must also take every care to avoid any embarrassment to Ministers or to their department or agency which could result, inadvertently or not, from bringing themselves prominently to public notice, as civil servants, in party political controversy.

4.4.15 Civil servants who are not in the politically free category and who have not been given permission to engage in political activities must retain at all times a proper reticence in matters of political controversy so that their impartiality is beyond question.

4.4.16 Civil servants do not need permission to take part in activities organised by their trade unions. Elected trade union representatives may comment on Government policy when representing the legitimate interests of their members, but in doing so they must make it clear that they are expressing views as representatives of the union and not as civil servants.

4.4.17 Civil servants given permission to take part in local political activities must tell their department or agency if they are elected to a local authority.

4.4.18 Civil servants given permission to take part in political activities must give up those activities if they are moved to a post where permission cannot be granted.

4.4.19 Civil servants are disqualified from election to Parliament (House of Commons Disqualification Act 1975) and from election to the European Parliament (European Parliamentary Elections Act 1978). They must therefore resign from the Civil Service before standing for election in accordance with paragraphs 4.4.20 and 4.4.21.

4.4.20 Civil servants in the politically free group are not required to resign on adoption as a prospective candidate. But to prevent their election being held to be void they must submit their resignation before they give their consent to nomination in accordance with the Parliamentary Election Rules.

4.4.21 All other civil servants, including civil servants on secondment to outside organisations, must comply with the provisions of the Servants of the Crown (Parliamentary, European Parliamentary and Northern Ireland Assembly Candidature) Order 1987. They must not issue an address to electors or in any other manner publicly announce themselves or allow themselves to be publicly announced as candidates or prospective candidates for election to Parliament or the European Parliament; and they must resign from the Civil Service on their formal adoption as a Parliamentary candidate or prospective candidate in accordance with the procedures of the political party concerned. Civil servants not in the politically free group who are candidates for election must complete their last day of service before their adoption papers are completed.

The Local Government and Housing Act 1989 (the LGHA 1989) and Local Government Officers (Political Restrictions) Regulations 1990 SI 1990 No 851 (the 1990 Regulations) impose restrictions on the activities of those employed by local government. These restrictions were passed against a background of increasing politicisation of local government, concern having grown in some quarters about increasing tensions between elected members of local government and their local government officers. In 1986 the Widdicombe Committee reported that:

[6.21] *The Conduct of Local Authority Business* **(Chairman: Widdicombe), Cmnd. 9800, London, HMSO, 1986.**

6.141. The overwhelming view in the evidence we have received has been that officers (subject to very limited and closely defined exceptions) should continue to serve the council as a whole. . . . There has been equally wide agreement that the public service tradition of a permanent corps of politically impartial officers should be retained. . . .

6.180. Public service in the United Kingdom is founded on a tradition of a permanent corps of politically neutral officers serving with equal commitment whatever party may be in political control . . .

6.182. Local government in the United Kingdom has traditionally been based on the same public service tradition as central government, but this has been a matter of convention and practice.

The Committee reported that 'there have been some cases, albeit a few' where local government officers had abused the power of their offices (for example, as managers, advisers, etc.) for political ends.

The LGHA 1989 (section 2) establishes 'politically restricted posts' which encompass (category 1) the most senior post-holders in local government (heads of authorities' paid service, chief officers, deputy chief officers, monitoring officers and assistants for political groups; (category 2) officials remunerated in excess of a prescribed level and whose posts are listed for the purposes of the application of the Regulations; and (category 3) officials paid less than the prescribed level but who hold a listed post. 'Listed posts' are those whose duties involved (section 2(3)(a)) 'giving advice on a regular basis to the authority themselves, to any committee or sub-committee of the authority or to any joint committee on which the authority are represented'; or (section 2(3)(b)) 'speaking on behalf of the authority on a regular basis to journalists or broadcasters'.

The 1990 Regulations operate (Regulation 3) by means of implication into the employment contracts of those holding politically restricted posts. They prohibit such persons from standing for election to the House of Commons, the European Parliament or any local authority either as a candidate; from acting as an election agent or a canvasser in any such elections (Schedule to the Regulations, Part I, paras 1, 3 and 5 respectively). The holders of such 'politically restricted posts' are entitled to be members of political parties but may not hold any office within a political party if that would involve participating in the general management of that party or one of its branches (para 4(a)) or representing the party in dealing with others (para 4(b)). Nor (Part II, paras 6 & 7) may they speak to the public or to a section of the public or publish any written or artistic work with 'the apparent intention of affecting public support for a political party', save (para 8) to the extent necessary for the proper performance of their duties. As Ewing has remarked (**[6.17]** above) 'although such people are expressly permitted to display posters (presumably also political posters) in their homes and cars, for the most part they are free only to be in political associations but not to act in association with others by displaying that support in public or to solicit support for the organisation'.

Local authorities are obliged (LGHA 1989, section 2(2)) to draw up a list of posts falling within categories 2 and 3. Section 3 LGHA 1989 provides that local government officers within these categories are permitted to apply to an independent adjudicator to their posts removed from the list of posts to which the Regulations applied). It was estimated in the late 1990s (see *Ahmed v UK*, **[6.23]** below, paras 28–30) that some 12,000 employees fell within category 1 and a further 28,000 and 7,000 within categories 2 and 3 respectively (though over 1,000 of the 35,000 within categories 2 and 3 had successfully applied for exemption from the Regulations by the late 1990s (*Ahmed v UK*)).

The restrictions on the activities of civil servants and local government officials are not the only ones which operate in the UK. Police officers are bound by the Police Regulations 2003 which require that they 'at all times abstain from any activity which is likely to interfere with the impartial discharge of [their] duties or which is likely to give rise to the impression amongst members of the public that it may so interfere; and in particular shall not take any active part in politics' (SI 2003 No. 527, Schedule 1—police officers are also prohibited from joining trade unions—Police Act 1996, s 64). The purpose of the restrictions on police officers' political activities was considered by the House of Lords in the decision extracted immediately below.

[6.22] *Champion v Chief Constable of Gwent* [1990] 1 WLR 1 (HL)

The applicant, a police constable, was appointed to serve as a school governor on the appointments sub-committee of a local school. His Chief Constable refused him permission to serve on the sub-committee either in his own time or in duty time on the grounds that his activity was likely to give rise to the impression amongst members of the public that that activity might interfere with his impartial discharge of his duties as a police officer. The applicant appealed to the House of Lords against the refusal of his application for judicial review of the Chief Constable's decision.

Lord Griffiths (for the majority):
The applicant accepts the decision of the Chief Constable to refuse leave to attend the appointments sub-committee in duty time but challenges the power of the Chief Constable to prevent him serving on the appointments sub-committee and attending its meetings when he is off duty . . .

It is not suggested that sitting on the appointments sub-committee is likely to interfere with the impartial discharge of the applicant's police duties. And so the question is this: if members of the public get to hear that the applicant is a member of the appointments sub-committee of Caldicot Comprehensive School is it likely that they will get the impression that he may not be able to discharge his duties as a police officer impartially or, to put it in more homely language, that he will not act fairly as a policeman? . . .

The purpose of [the Regulations] is clear enough. [Their] object is to prevent a police officer doing anything which affects his impartiality or his appearance of impartiality.

Impartiality means favouring neither one side nor the other but dealing with people fairly and even-handedly. The [relevant] paragraph takes its colour from the particular prohibition on taking any active part in politics which is an overtly partisan activity in which one favours one side to the exclusion of the other. It is activities that are likely to be seen in a similar light that are aimed at, activities that identify those taking part with a particular interest or point of view in a way which will, or may be thought, make it difficult for them to deal fairly with those with whom they disagree. Exceptionally it may include activities involving controversial decisions but I would have thought that such occasions would be rare, for surely most of us are, from time to time, involved in controversial decisions without it being thought that we cannot deal fairly in other matters.

I am quite unable to take the view that sitting on an appointments sub-committee at a comprehensive school is the type of activity at which this regulation is aimed. In my view the approach of the Chief Constable is ?awed because it fails to give any weight to the use of the word 'likely' and results in the regulation being applied for a purpose for which it was never intended. This restriction is not intended to protect police officers from the occasional embarrassing decision with which they may be faced during off-duty activities; it is there to ensure both impartiality and the appearance of impartiality. There are in my view great dangers in isolating the police from the community and every encouragement should be given to police officers to play a full part in the life of the community in which they live. If very occasionally the applicant finds that possession of confidential information about a candidate prevents him attending a meeting of the appointments sub-committee, it will be for the governors to decide whether this makes him an unsuitable member of the sub-committee. If it happened more than very occasionally the governors might decide to replace the applicant on the appointments sub-committee, but this decision would be taken solely on the ground that he could not attend sufficient meetings and not on grounds of lack of impartiality. Presumably if his impartiality had been in question he would not have been elected to the sub-committee in the first place.

I would therefore allow this appeal and quash the decision of the Chief Constable.

6.4.3 Other forms of 'political' discrimination/ restrictions

The foregoing sections have been concerned with formal measures taken by the State to protect national security and the proper functioning of the democratic process. Whether such restrictions on workers' freedom of expression and association are justified in line with Articles 10 and 11 is considered below at section 6.4.4. But these forms of restriction are not the only ones which give rise to questions under the Convention.

The employment 'blacklisting' of political activists came to the fore in the late 1980s and early 1990s as a result of the activities of the 'Economic League'. The League, which was founded in 1919 to fight 'subversion in industry', was supported in 1998 by about 2000 companies including Barclays, Lloyds, and the National Westminster banks and 40 large construction companies (*Guardian*, 9 September 1998). The Ford Motor Company also used the League's services until 1991. In 1990, the League's Director-General admitted to the House of Commons Select Committee on Employment that his organisation dealt with around 200,000 annual requests from its subscribers for information on individuals. Individuals had no legal entitlement to access the information held on them.

Newspaper reports suggested that between 40,000 and 250,000 individuals were included on the organisation's 'blacklist' (held in card files to escape the provisions of the Data Protection Act 1984). The League's Director-General, Stan Hardy, told the House of Commons Select Committee on Employment in July 1990 that: 'People on whom we have records are known or avowed members of extreme organisations; innocent people have nothing to fear' (*Guardian*, 14 June 1990). This statement contrasted with that of a former director of the League who claimed, in 1988, that the organisation 'was indulging in "highly dangerous and melodramatic practices" . . . employees described simply as "troublemakers" were frequently and arbitrarily blacked by companies which passed the names to the league's registers without further inquiries [and] "[t]he league's central register is chaotic and many of the records of individuals are more fiction than fact" . . . no attempt was made to check even that names were accurate and that there was no confusion between people with similar names' (*Guardian*, 9 September 1988). And the same paper reported (2 February 1988) that information had been passed to the League about those active in the Anti-Apartheid Movement and other pressure groups, the 'blacklist' also containing information on one man who had written to a newspaper 'praising a decision by Edinburgh council to buy a portrait of Nelson Mandela'. There was also evidence that information had been passed to the League by the police. Labour MPs (including current Chancellor Gordon Brown) were included on a list drawn up by the League and information was held on doctors who had protested against hospital closures. According to the *Guardian* (13 April 1988), Oxfam, Christian Aid, the Child Poverty Action Group and the Low Pay Unit were regarded as 'suspect organisations'. So, too, was the Campaign for Nuclear Disarmament (Press Association *Newsfile*, 10 July 1990).

Trade unionists were particularly targeted by the League (until 1990 employers could lawfully refuse employment on grounds of trade union membership). Attempts to include the activities of the League within the Data Protection Act 1984 were defeated by the-then Conservative government which also defeated attempts in 1989 to ban the activities of the League and failed to implement the recommendations of the Select Committee on Employment (2nd Report 1991, *Recruitment Practices*) that job candidates rejected as 'political subversives' should have the right to see confidential files such as those supplied the Economic League. (The Committee had also recommended that a licensing regime and a Code of Practice be imposed on such organisations.) The *Mirror* newspaper bought the list of alleged subversives in 1991 and threw it open for scrutiny. The League was wound up in 1993 but its files were passed to Stan Hardy's family firm which, according to the *Guardian*, 9 September 2000:

> continued to alert businesses to individuals and organisations [Hardy] claimed were opposed to private enterprise. Through Caprim, Mr Hardy continued warning firms of those he believed could 'weaken a company's ability to manage its affairs profitably'. He condemned the Ethical Investment Research Service for 'busybodyness' in drawing investors' attention to whether firms supplied services to the defence ministry, or whether furniture firms used tropical hardwoods. His monitor warned: 'Companies need to be warned what these organisations are saying and planning. Caprim provides this information. And assesses the strength of the threat. And advises on appropriate action'.

The *Observer* reported (3 May 1994) that the service provided by Caprim 'includes tracking down left-wing militants, finding the source of leaks where companies have suffered bad publicity, and vetting potential employees. It also identified environmental activists and animal rights campaigners whose information could lead to companies being 'condemned as unethical'.

The Employment Relations Act 1999 empowered the Secretary of State (section 3) to make regulations prohibiting the compilation of lists which contain details of members of trade unions or persons who have taken part in the activities of trade unions and which are made 'with a view to being used by employers or employment agencies for the purposes of discrimination in relation to recruitment or in relation to the treatment of workers', and the use, sale or supply of such lists. No such regulations have been made. Caprim apparently continues to function (and, perhaps oddly, is listed as a corporate associate member of the Ecumenical Council for Corporate Responsibility as well as, at least as late as 2000, being active in the Institute of Directors and on the management board of a leading business school).

Domestic law provides workers with scant protection from detrimental action taken against them on account of their political activities or affiliations. Some provision is made by section 50 of the Employment Rights Act 1996 (ERA 1996) for time off in connection with 'public duties' (these include attendance at meetings by members of local authorities, police authorities, education and health authorities). Time-off rights are also provided to trade union members and officials by sections 168–173 of the Trade Union and Labour Relations (Consolidation) Act 1992 (TULR(C)A). And, to the extent that 'political' activities are trade union related, the protections discussed at section 8.2 below above may apply. Section 137 TULR(C)A prohibits discrimination in recruitment on grounds of trade union *membership*. But neither that section nor any other prohibits discrimination in connection with a worker's trade union *activities* (though see the discussion of *Fitzpatrick v British Railway Board* [1992] ICR 221 in chapter 8).

The DPA 1998 (see further section 6.5.2 below) provides some protection in respect of 'blacklisting' and surveillance of workers on account of their political activities. But only in Northern Ireland does there exist specific legislative protection from discrimination on grounds of 'political opinion'. The precursor to the Fair Employment and Treatment Order 1998, although primarily directed towards the nationalist/loyalist division of opinion, was interpreted to encompass, *inter alia*, 'left' and 'right' opinions in *McKay v Northern Ireland Public Service Alliance* [1994] NI 103, though in *Gill v Northern Ireland Council for Ethnic Minorities* [2002] IRLR 74 Northern Ireland's Court of Appeal ruled that the legislation did not extend so far as to regulate discrimination between advocates of 'anti-racist' and 'culturally sensitive' approaches to tackling race discrimination. The Fair Employment Tribunal had accepted that these were 'fundamentally disparate concepts' 'in racial awareness terms' and that they were 'political opinions' for the purposes of the FETO. The Court of Appeal disagreed, ruling, *inter alia*, that only those political opinions relating to the conduct of the government of the State or matters of public policy were protected by the FETO. Both the 'anti-racist' and the 'culturally sensitive' approach to anti-racism were concerned with advancing the interests of people from ethnic minorities and were not the type of political opinion intended by Parliament to be protected by FETO.

Elsewhere, discrimination on grounds of other political activities or beliefs may breach the ordinary employment protections where, for example, it takes the form of an express or constructive dismissal for the purposes of the ERA 1996. But the gaps in the protection afforded by that Act (in particular, its application only to employees, its qualifying periods and the laws associated with the employers' 'reasonable response' test) have been explored in chapter 5. Further, the legislation has no application in relation to refusals to employ. The Employment Equality (Religion or Belief) Regulations 2003, discussed in chapter 3, prohibit discrimination on grounds of 'belief' as well as 'religion'. But 'belief' in this context is narrowly defined and intended not to apply to political beliefs. Ironically, the context in which workers are most protected from discrimination in connection with their political beliefs is in their capacity as union members or would-be members. As we see in chapter 7, the restrictions on trade unions' freedom of association have presented significant obstacles to efforts by the movement to resist infiltration attempts by the BNP.

6.4.4 Political restrictions/discrimination and the Convention/HRA 1998

The restrictions on the activities of civil servants and the police clearly operate so as to interfere with their freedom of expression and association both by denying some individuals access to employment and by restricting the freedoms of those in employment. It is unlikely, however, that the implementation of the HRA 1998 will have any significant impact in this context.

Interference with the freedoms protected by Articles 10 and 11 may be justified *inter alia* (see **[6.2]** above) in the interests of national security and for the protection of the rights of others, Article 11 further permitting 'the imposition of lawful restrictions on the exercise of [the right to freedom of association] by members of the armed forces, of the police or of the administration of the State'. Cases such as *Kosiek* and *Glasenapp* suggest a high degree of deference to the State on the part of the Court, particularly in cases in which public sector workers have challenged refusals to appoint on grounds of their political affiliations. Bowers and Lewis remarked, in 1996, that 'until recently the case law of the . . . [European Court] suggested that the right to free expression might have only a very limited application in the workplace' ('Whistleblowing: Freedom of Expression in the Workplace' [1996] 1 EHRLR 637).

The decisions in *Vogt* (extracted above) and in *Thlimmenos* (which, like the *Kosiek* and *Glasenapp* cases) involved access to, rather than (at least in formal terms in *Kosiek* and *Glasenapp*) dismissal from, employment. Subject to any developments of the *Thlimmenos* principle the ECHR jurisprudence appears to permit wide scope for pre-employment vetting (this because of the absence from the Convention of any right of access to the 'civil service', defined to extend across public sector employment. Articles 10 and 11 of the Convention may have more significant implications, accordingly, for 'purge' than for 'vetting' procedures. Even then, it is clear from *Vogt* that the dismissal of a worker whose post, unlike hers, 'intrinsically involve[d] . . . security risks', could readily be justified on the basis of his or her political beliefs and/or activities.

The jurisprudence of the ECtHR has not been confined to cases in which workers have been dismissed or refused employment on the basis of their political beliefs and/or activities. In *Rekvényi v Hungary* (1999) 30 EHRR 519 that Court dismissed a complaint by a police officer that a Constitutional prohibitions on his membership of any political party, and on his engagement in any political activity, breached Articles 10 and 11 of the European Convention. The Court accepted that there had been an interference with the applicants' Convention rights. But having ruled that the interferences were prescribed by law, the Court had regard to Hungary's past in accepting that the depolitisation of the police was a pressing social need connected with the aims of protecting national security and public safety as well as preventing disorder. The Court further noted that a number of the other Contracting Parties to the Convention restricted political actions on the part of the police and went on to accept that, given Hungary's past, the ban was not disproportionate.

The European Court of Human Rights has also adjudicated on the compatibility of the Local Government Officers (Political Restrictions) Regulations 1990 (discussed at 6.4.2 above) with Articles 10 and 11 of the Convention. The Regulations were challenged in 1991 by four local government employees. Two were category 1 and two were category 3 employees, the latter because, as a solicitor and a Principal Valuer, they regularly gave advice to Council committees (the latter also regularly dealing with the press). The application of the Regulations had forced one of the applicants to withdraw his candidature for election to Parliament; the others to resign from office within the local Labour Party, (in two cases) to refrain from supporting and assisting Labour candidates (including their wives) for election to local government and (also in two cases), to curtail their activism on issues such as health care.

The applicants, supported by their trade union, sought judicial review of the 1990 Regulations, arguing that they were inconsistent with the government's obligations under the Convention. The application was refused on the ground, *inter alia*, that the Convention did not form part of domestic law. The Court of Appeal upheld this decision and refused leave to appeal to the House of Lords whereupon the applicants brought their complaint to the Convention organs. The Court having accepted that the restriction interfered with the applicants' freedom of expression and that it was 'prescribed by law', it went on to rule (contrary to the applicants' arguments), that the need to protect the rights of others to effective political democracy could be invoked to justify the interference even absent any 'threat to the stability of the constitutional or political order'.

[6.23] *Ahmed v UK* (1998) 29 EHRR 29 (ECtHR)

Judgment:
    . . . the local government system of the respondent State has long rested on a bond of trust between elected members and a permanent corps of local government officers who both advise them on policy and assume responsibility for the implementation of the policies adopted. That relationship of trust stems from the right of council members to expect that they are being assisted in their functions by officers who are politically neutral and whose loyalty is to the council as a whole.
    Members of the public also have a right to expect that the members whom they voted into office will discharge their mandate in accordance with the commitments they made

during an electoral campaign and that the pursuit of that mandate will not founder on the political opposition of their members' own advisers; it is also to be noted that members of the public are equally entitled to expect that in their own dealings with local government departments they will be advised by politically neutral officers who are detached from the political fray.

The aim pursued by the Regulations was to underpin that tradition and to ensure that the effectiveness of the system of local political democracy was not diminished through the corrosion of the political neutrality of certain categories of officers.

Accordingly the Court accepted that the Regulations had the legitimate aim of 'protect[ing] the rights of others, council members and the electorate alike, to effective political democracy at the local level' and went on to find that this 'pressing social need' justified the interferences with Articles 10 and 11, taking into account the fact that the officers affected by the restrictions had been carefully defined by reference to the functions they carried out, and that not all political comment or activity was restricted.

Applying the jurisprudence of the European Court of Human Rights to the political restrictions on the activities of civil servants and police officers, it is unlikely that any challenge to the restrictions on the political activities of these workers would succeed. But the neutrality as between involvement with lawful political organisations of the British purge and vetting procedures, as distinct from the restrictions on political activities of existing staff, has also been thrown into doubt over recent years. In *Blacklist* (Hogarth Press, 1988), M. Hollingsworth and R. Norton-Taylor exposed MI5 blacklisting, *inter alia*, of Jack Dromey (then national secretary of the TGWU) because of his role in industrial action and his links with the NCCL (now Liberty); of Jack Jones (a former TGWU general secretary) and Hugh (Lord) Scanlon, former president of the AUEW. According to the book, MI5 amassed some 40 volumes of material on Jones and Scanlon and made four attempts to block their appointments to top jobs under Labour governments.

In neither *Kosiek* nor *Glasenapp* did the European Court consider whether Article 14 founded a breach of the Convention when read with Article 10. (In *Vogt* the court, having found a breach of Article 10, did not consider it necessary to explore the implications of Article 14.) Additional justification is required in cases in which the interference with a Convention right discriminates on Article 14 grounds. In *Sidabras & Džiautas v Lithuania* (27 July 2004), for example, the ECtHR's ruling rested on the fact that 'the applicants were treated differently from other persons in Lithuania who had not worked for the KGB, and who as a result had no restrictions imposed on them in their choice of professional activities. In addition, in view of the Government's argument that the purpose of the Act was to regulate the employment prospects of persons on the ground of their loyalty or lack of loyalty to the State, there has also been a difference of treatment between the applicants and other persons in this respect'.

Assuming that a Convention breach could be established, those employed by a public authority (see section 6.2) could rely directly on the HRA 1998, those in the private sector on the unfair dismissal provisions of the ERA 1996 as applied by the Court of Appeal in *X v Y* **[6.8]** where the interference consists in a dismissal (including a constructive dismissal – see further chapter 5. More problematic is the situation in which interferences with Convention rights are relied upon by private sector employers to refuse access to employment. There are no legislative provisions regulating recruitment, save for the prohibitions contained in the discrimination legislation considered in chapter 3 and in TULR(C)A. The Employment Equality (Religion or Belief) Regulations (RBRs), discussed in chapter 3, prohibit employment-related discrimination on grounds of 'religion or belief'. Assuming that a refusal to employ is accepted as a 'quasi breach', i.e., that the interference is sufficiently serious to impose a positive obligation on the state (see section 6.2.1), a remedy may require inventive application of the RBRs or other legislation. Questions remain, however, as to how far the courts are obliged by the HRA 1998 to fashion a remedy from legislation not intended to remedy the wrong at issue (see the speech of Lord Caplan in the Court of Session in *MacDonald v Ministry of Defence* [2002] ICR 174). Prior to any such developments of this sort, it seems that the protections available in respect of non-recruitment other than by public authorities will be restricted to the access to information required under the terms of the Data Protection Act 1998 (see further section 6.5.2 below).

6.5 Workplace surveillance

[6.24] G Orwell, *Nineteen Eighty-Four*, cited in *Employee Privacy in the Workplace* (London, Incomes Data Services, 2001) Employment Supplement No 6, Series 2

> 'There was . . . no way of knowing whether you were being watched at any given moment . . . You had to live—did live, from habit that became instinct—in the assumption that every sound you made was overheard, and except in darkness, every movement scrutinised'.

Orwell's all-seeing state had the effect of crushing into conformity the book's central character. The novel's nightmare society may not yet have reached fruition. But the all-seeing state and, in particular, the all-seeing employer, is becoming a reality. And as the extract which follows demonstrates, even darkness does not protect from modern technologies of surveillance.

[6.25] Simon Davies, *New Techniques and Technologies of Surveillance in the Workplace* (http://www.msf-itpa.org.uk/juneconf3.shtml)

> Privacy has become one of the most important human rights issues of the modern age. At a time when computer based technology gives government and private sector organisations the ability to conduct mass surveillance of populations, privacy has become a crucial safeguard for individual rights. According to opinion polls, concern over privacy violation is now greater than at any time in recent history. Uniformally, populations throughout the world report their distress about encroachment on privacy, prompting an unprecedented number of nations to pass laws which specifically protect the privacy of their citizens . . . rapid advances in the development of powerful technology, in

conjunction with the demand for greater management efficiency, are promoting a seamless web of surveillance throughout the workplace. At the same time, inadequate laws and regulations are failing to check an expanding pattern of abuses . . .

The technology being used to monitor employees is extremely powerful, and extends to every aspect of a workers life. Miniature cameras monitor behaviour. 'Smart' ID badges track an employees movement around a building. Telephone Management Systems (TMS) analyse the pattern of telephone use and the destination of calls. Psychological tests general intelligence tests, aptitude tests, performance tests, vocational interest tests, personality tests and honesty tests—many of which are electronically assessed—raise a great many issues of privacy, control and fairness. Surveillance and monitoring have become design components of modern information systems and the modern work environment.

In the UK, employers can tap phones, read email and monitor computer screens. They can bug conversations, analyse computer and keyboard work, peer through CCTV cameras, use tracking technology to monitor personal movements, analyse urine to detect drug use, and demand the disclosure of intimate personal data. The use of this technology is often justified on the grounds of health and safety, customer relations or legal obligation. The real purpose of most surveillance, however, is for performance monitoring, personnel surveillance, or outright discrimination. Even in workplaces staffed by highly skilled information technology specialists, bosses demand the right to spy on every detail of a worker's performance. Modern networked systems can interrogate computers to determine which software in being run, how often, and in what manner. A comprehensive audit trail gives managers a profile of each user, and a panorama of how the workers are interacting with their machines . . . .

While IT companies routinely promote their technologies as a means of achieving social or workplace reform, the human rights community increasingly defines them as a means of social and political control. Surveillance technologies were defined in a 1996 report 'Big Brother Incorporated' produced by the watchdog organisation 'Privacy International' as: 'technologies which can monitor, track and assess the movements, activities and communications of individuals. These include an array of visual recording devices, bugging equipment, computer information systems and identification systems'. These innovations are used by military, police and intelligence authorities as technologies of repression. Increasingly, technologies designed for military and police purposes are finding their way onto the open market. Importantly, the time lag between military implementation and their use in the open market is shrinking rapidly.

6. STRUCTURAL ISSUES

To some extent, the problem of workplace surveillance is a child of a world-wide mania for corporate re-engineering. Over the past fifteen years, in an effort to maximise profit and efficiency, government and private sector organisations have been re-organised and delayered, abolished departments in favour of profit centres, created short term employment contracts, internal markets, and a provided a mass market for outsourcing. The result is a re-definition of the employee. As companies move to outsource their business, and as workers are put onto short term contracts, the level of surveillance intensifies . . .

Some observers have noted that these institutional and structural changes may make it more inviting for employers to monitor employee job performance electronically since there is less face-to-face monitoring possible in the new work environment.

7. VIOLATIONS OF TERRITORY (PRIVATE SPACE)

CCTV has become the most obvious facet of the emerging surveillance environment . . .

Cameras measuring 42 mm square and able to see in virtual darkness are freely available on the British market for less than £100. Tens of thousands are sold openly each year. Snooping on workers has always been a popular pastime amongst employers, but now it is an industry in its own right.

There is evidence that cameras are used for the purposes of harassment and discrimination. Following some organising activity by a local union, one US employer installed video cameras to monitor each individual workstation and worker. Although management claimed that the technology was being established solely for safety monitoring, two employees were suspended for leaving their workstations to visit the toilet without permission. According to a 1993 report of the International Labour Office, the activities of union representatives on the ?oor were also inhibited by a 'chilling effect' on workers who knew their conversations were being monitored.

The High Street is awash with technologies that can covertly detect conversations It is not illegal to sell or possess bugs in Britain, though it is technically illegal to use them for transmissions without a DTI license . . . In a 1996 report, the technology watchdog Privacy International estimated that around 200,000 bugs are sold each year in Britain. Most are simple transmitting microphones but an increasing number are capable of tapping computers and telephones, as well as recording and broadcasting visual images.

Bugs come in many shapes and sizes. They range from micro engineered transmitters the size of an office staple, to devices no bigger than a cigarette packet that are capable of transmitting video and sound signals for miles. Most equipment sells for less that three hundred pounds . . .

The use of CCTV is usually limited to environments where the workers are confined to an office. Where staff are more mobile, companies are now using a range of technologies to track geographic movements. Advances in this area now allow carrier companies to place an electronic mechanism (described as a geostationary satellite-based mobile communications system) on trucks that then sends back to a main terminal the exact position of the vehicle at all times. In this way, carrier companies can ensure that no side trips nor other deviations are taken from the prescribed route. One firm that offers this tracking service claims to have monitors in place on approximately 150,000 vehicles around the world. Wide area systems such as Trackback are in use throughout the UK.

Active badges (also known as 'electronic tags'), are used to track the movements of workers around a building or a complex. These are usually smart cards which emit a frequency that can be read and identified by receivers located in various parts of a building. Such a card (known as Radio Frequency ID cards) can be remotely read without the need for the card to make contact physically with any other machine. The movement log is integrated with electronic diaries and the telecommunication system, ensuring that the employee is never out of touch. The devices are becoming popular with IT companies such as Olivetti Research in Cambridge.

Unions in the United States say these surveillance technologies have intruded on human dignity. Workers at the Tripicana Casino in Atlantic City certainly think so. There, the management has installed a system known as Hygiene Guard, which uses an interactive network of sensors and 'smart badge' transmitters to monitor whether workers have washed their hands after visiting the toilet. Unless an employee operates the soap dispenser and stands for at least thirty seconds at a running tap, an infraction will be recorded on a computer in the Casino's management office.

8. INTRUSION INTO INFORMATION AND COMMUNICATIONS PRIVACY

Performance monitoring
An employer can monitor the level of use of a computer through monitoring the number

of keystrokes a wordprocessing employee enters in a specified period of time or the amount of time a computer is idle during the workday. Because of its high stress factor, keystroke monitoring has been linked to stress-related health problems such as carpal tunnel syndrome.

Numerous technologies are available which monitor and analyse the performance of IT workers. One . . . connects to the computer via the keyboard plug, from which it is powered, and transmits every keystroke to a receiver module, which can be located up to 150 metres away. No wires are required. The receiving module can be connected to a standard printer, which then records all key strokes. Alternatively, an optional LCD display can be used to display all characters as they are typed. Once this information is collected, it can be analysed by standard processing programmes to determine a worker's performance profile.

Another product . . . is able to provide comprehensive monitoring of all computer activity by an employee. The product, and several like it on the market, costs $55 . . .

A company spokesman told the Washington Post a surprising array of companies, organisations and individuals have bought the software since its release earlier this year. 'It's sort of like a truth meter' the spokesman said. 'It tells you exactly what's happening', adding that the software can be configured to send the manager a message whenever an employee on a company's internal network is doing something that's against the rules. 'It could be any desktop activity at all'.

Even highly skilled workers can expect to be routinely put under the microscope. It's likely that any manager who purchases network-operating software is already getting built-in eavesdropping features . . . Some . . . packages . . . allow network administrators to observe an employee's screen in real time, scan data files and e-mail, analyse keystroke performance, and even overwrite passwords . . .

Companies sometimes market such products as aids for health and safety. One . . . product, OmniTrak, provides managers with information on employees' work habits to help uncover stress, its maker says.

Product literature, though, states OmniTrak can 'objectively track and notify personnel managers of individual problems that may indicate alcohol and drug addiction or family and personal matters, as it consistently monitors work attendance patterns'.

'People with a drug or alcohol problem tend to miss repetitive Mondays or Fridays', explained Mike Bonner, president of the firm in Port Huron, Mich.

'Invasion of privacy was never the intent', said Michael Zanoni, a spokesman for product maker Magnitude Information Systems Inc. in Branchburg, N.J. 'But in order to mitigate the health risk and improve productivity, you wind up with a product that can act as Big Brother, if that's what you want to do'.

Telephone monitoring
. . . The extent of telephone monitoring in some industries is extremely high. One recent survey by the New York-based American Management Association, found that 67.3 % of all companies, up from 63.4 % two years ago, engage in some form of surveillance, including monitoring e-mail, voice-mail messages, and Internet and telephone usage, listening in on telephone conversations, and videotaping employees on the job. The survey found that for every company that monitors telephone conversations on an as-needed basis, after actions have already placed an employee under suspicion, three companies monitor conversations on a random, routine, or ongoing basis.

Companies are extensively using telephone analysis technology. Call centre workers for BT are regularly presented with a comprehensive analysis sheet, showing their performance relative to other workers. Airline reservations clerks in the US and elsewhere wear telephonic headsets that monitor the length and content of all telephone calls, as well as the duration of their toilet and lunch breaks. In one instance, telephone calls received by airline reservation agents were electronically monitored on a second-by-second basis: agents were allowed only 11 seconds between each call and 12 minutes of break time each day. One clerk observed 'It's like being connected by an umbilical cord to the computer. There is no privacy'. Other airline reservationists have complained that they are evaluated regarding how many times they use a customer's name during a call or how often they try to overcome a customer's initial objections to buying a ticket. 'Listen long enough' one reservationist claims, 'and you'll always catch an agent doing something wrong'. The level of sophistication of telephone surveillance systems can be astonishing. [One] . . . voice stress analyser, called the Truth Phone promises to analyse voices during telephone calls in order to detect possible deception . . . Voice mail systems are also subject to systematic or random monitoring by managers. Most new systems have default pass codes for administrators, and these can open all message boxes.

Email and internet monitoring
The use of email is particularly conducive to surveillance. Numerous programmes on the market are able to search for keywords that might indicate private or malicious traffic. However in recent months far more sophisticated software packages have come onto the market . . .

Employers can monitor e-mail by randomly reviewing e-mail transmissions, by specifically reviewing transmissions of certain employees, or by selecting key terms to ?ag e-mail. In the latter instance, an employer may choose to ?ag the words 'angry' or 'revenge' to identify all e-mail expressing potential hostility among employees . . .

The monitoring of website visits has also created some distress in the workplace. The programmes listed above are capable of systematically logging all internet activity, and managers can analyse these to determine 'inappropriate' activity. At first sight, such surveillance has elements in common with traditional surveillance for hard copy pornography, but there are significant dangers to workers in the realm of electronic surveillance. The use of Spam mail to advertise X rated sites results in workers entering sites that appear to be quite benign. It is only after they visit the site that the nature of the page is recognised . . .

A similar danger exists with email monitoring. Any message sent by or to an employee is centrally logged on the company server. A malicious email sent to an employee cannot simply be deleted. It remains on the system, threatening the relationship of trust between employee and management. In research for an article on email monitoring, companies contacted by *The Daily Telegraph* confirmed that employee monitoring is widespread. Barclay's confirmed that it monitors and record phone conversations. 'In our telephone banking service every call would be recorded' said a spokeswoman. 'We also monitor intranet and internet activity' . . .

VIOLATION OF BODILY (PHYSICAL) PRIVACY

Drug testing
The extent of drug testing in the UK workplace has not been clearly quantified, though it has been broadly accepted that the number of companies using these tests has risen proportionately with the decreasing costs of the tests. Dozens of companies now sell kits that can determine drug traces in all major categories. Employees in the US and Britain have claimed that these kits—available from as little as three pounds—are being used covertly to monitor employees urine. In the US, workplace drug testing is up 277 % from 1987—despite evidence that random drug testing is unfair, often inaccurate and unproven as a means of stopping drug use.

Drug testing is intrusive. It is often the case that an observer is present to ensure there is no specimen tampering. Even indirect observation can be degrading; typically, workers must remove their outer garments and urinate in a bathroom in which the water supply has been turned off . . . The lab procedure is a second invasion of privacy. Urinalysis reveals not only the presence of illegal drugs, but also the existence of many other physical and medical conditions, including genetic predisposition to disease—or pregnancy. In 1988, the Washington, D.C. Police Department admitted it used urine samples collected for drug tests to screen female employees for pregnancy—without their knowledge or consent.

Drug testing kits are freely available on the market, and are on sale through the internet . . . The tests are not infallible. A report by the Ontario Information and Privacy Commissioners Office says up to 40 % of tests are inaccurate. Sometimes drug tests fail to distinguish between legal and illegal substances. Depronil, a prescription drug used to treat Parkinson's disease, has shown up as an amphetamine on standard drug tests. Over-the-counter antiin?ammatory drugs like Ibuprofen have shown up positive on the marijuana test. Even the poppy seeds found in baked goods can produce a positive result for heroin.

A survey of 100 organisations by law firm Allen & Overy reported, in April 2001, that most conducted at least one form of the following types of surveillance (internet, email and/or CCTV surveillance, drug and/or alcohol screening, fraud prevention or stop-and-search).

[6.26] Independent Inquiry into Drug Testing at Work, *Drug testing in the workplace* (2004, Joseph Rowntree Foundation), Summary Conclusions

A MORI poll was conducted on behalf of the IIDTW in 2003. Over 200 companies were surveyed, of which 4 per cent conducted drug tests and a further 9 per cent said that they were likely to introduce tests in the next year. In addition, 78 per cent said that they would be more likely to test if they believed that drug or alcohol use was affecting performance or productivity. Overall numbers might seem comparatively low on the MORI findings, but this is highly misleading. If 4 per cent of businesses are drug testing this will affect hundreds of thousands of employees. If the 9 per cent of businesses who told MORI that they were likely to introduce testing in the next year do so, then this trebles the proportion of UK businesses testing over a 12-month period . . .

A major expansion of drug testing at work, while far from inevitable, is now a genuine possibility. The North American experience shows how rapidly drug testing at work can expand, with testing in the US developing into a multi-billion dollar industry since the 1980s. There is evidence that increasing numbers of British employers are identifying drug and alcohol use as a problem for them. There is a lack of evidence to suggest that drug and alcohol use is in fact having a serious and widespread effect on the workplace in modern Britain. There is a need for continued monitoring of trends and trajectories

Surveillance techniques such as those discussed by Davies ([6.25] above) have serious implications for employee privacy which, as he points out, 'underpins human dignity and other key values such as freedom of association and freedom of speech'. As *Employee Privacy in the Workplace* points out ([6.24] p 5), workplace and related surveillance intrudes upon the privacy of the person (by means of drug, alcohol and medical testing and body searches); privacy of personal behaviour (by the collection of information about workers' sexual preferences, religious and political activities); privacy of personal communications (by the interception of telecommunications including telephone, email and internet use); and privacy of personal data.

Rights to privacy are recognised by Article 8 of the ECHR and by other international rights instruments including the UN Declaration of Human Rights (Article 12). Article 8 contains express guarantees relating to 'private life', 'family life', 'home' and 'correspondence'. But in the UK, legal controls on workplace and related surveillance (including the use of CCTV cameras, workplace 'tracking', performance monitoring, drugs-testing, and genetic screening) are patchy. The ECJ ruled, in Case 404/92 *X v Commission of the European Communities* [1994] ECR I–4737, that a worker may not be subject to medical testing without consent (there the applicant had expressly refused to undergo HIV testing but the Commission had used the results of the routine testing to which he had consented to perform a T-cell count on the basis of which it had concluded that the applicant had AIDS). But workers are not protected from discrimination for refusing to undergo genetic, medical, or other forms of testing, save where the testing breaches the express terms (or, where carried out in bad faith, the implied terms—see *Irani v Southampton & South-West Hampshire Health Authority* [1985] ICR 590) of the employment contract. Nor is there any comprehensive legal protection from based on the results of employment-related surveillance.

Discrimination based on the results of genetic testing does not breach the DDA. Nor will discrimination based on the results of much other medical testing save where the condition is such as significantly to impair the worker's function (see section 3.2.5 above). The most egregious examples of medical or other discrimination may, if they involve dismissal, be caught by the unfair dismissal provisions of the ERA 1996 (see chapter 5). But such protection is only afforded to 'employees' with at least one year's continuous employment. Pre-employment (or promotion-related) psychometric testing could breach anti-discrimination provisions, if it was shown to discriminate either directly or indirectly and unjustifiably on one of the protected grounds (see chapter 3). If used in connection with selection for redundancy or other dismissals it could also found an unfair dismissal claim. But the difficulties associated with proof of discrimination and with challenges to redundancy selection are clear from chapters 3 and 5 above. And neither the anti-discrimination legislation nor the ERA 1996 permits comprehensive challenge to psychometric testing. The Health and Safety (Display Screen Equipment) Regulations 1992 (SI 1992/2792) ban the use of 'quantitative and qualitative' checking facilities on such equipment without the knowledge of the operator, and provide (Regulation 4) that operators' 'daily work on display screen equipment is periodically interrupted by such breaks or changes of activity as to reduce their workload at that equipment'. Stress-related keyboard injuries may incur tortious liability on the part of the employer, and some forms of surveillance might also be regarded as breaching the implied term relating to trust and confidence. But implied contractual protections will be ousted by properly drafted express terms and the remedies available in respect of contractual breaches by the employer are frequently very limited. And while disclosures to employers of confidential information relating to workers might be actionable under the law of confidence, this area of law has little impact in the context of workplace surveillance carried out by employers or their agents (as distinct from the disclosure of such information by employers to others—see *Dalgleish v Lothian & Borders Police Board* [1991] IRLR 422).

There have been a number of newspaper reports in recent years about employees dismissed for downloading pornography and 'abusing' email systems. (Among those dismissed in 1998 for downloading hardcore pornography were three Downing Street staff—*Observer*, 27 September 1998.) In one case, reported in the *Guardian* (2 December 2000), a tribunal unanimously rejected unfair dismissal claims by two men sacked for forwarding tasteless messages to colleagues not only because of the content of the messages, but also because of the amount of time wasted in the process. Significant there was the fact that the employers had a clear policy governing acceptable email content. But in other cases workers have been denied redress, even in the absence of a promulgated email policy, because they have been in employment for less than one year. According to the *Guardian*, one of six employees sacked by Cable & Wireless was dismissed because an email with the word 'fuck' was found in his in-box. The same newspaper report stated that: 'One multinational company in Germany . . . is understood to have already taken advantage of the more relaxed laws in the UK by sending all the emails sent and received by staff from its offices in Germany to London where they are monitored'. Having said this, according to a report in October 2003 (Wardhadaway solicitors, www.wardhadaway.com) there have been a number of tribunal decisions in favour of employees dismissed in connection with pornography use. One such case was brought against IBM. According to the report, the Tribunal did not accept that the employees' conduct was sufficient to warrant immediate dismissal while 'In another case a Tribunal observed that in the absence of a written policy describing the types of conduct that amounted to gross misconduct, simply using the internet for downloading pornography – what the Tribunal considered to be merely unauthorised use –would not normally justify instant dismissal'. Wardhadaway Solicitors advise that: 'Employers need to spell it out for their staff. They need to make it clear what employees can and cannot do with their computers and what they can and cannot look at online. Generic words like 'offensive' and 'objectionable' should be avoided unless they are defined with some precision'.

6.5.1 The Regulation of Investigatory Powers Act 2000

Leaving aside the patchy protection afforded against workplace and work-related surveillance (or, rather, against its employment repercussions) by the discrimination and unfair dismissal legislation, the main legislative provisions which are of significance to employment surveillance are the Regulation of Investigatory Powers Act 2000 (RIPA) and the related Telecommunications (Lawful Business Practice) (Interception of Communications) Regulations (SI 2000 No 2699, the LBP Regulations), and the Data Protection Act 1998 (DPA 1998).

RIPA is designed, according to the accompanying explanatory notes, 'to ensure that the relevant investigatory powers are used in accordance with human rights'. Prior to its passage, the interception of telephone calls and emails by the operators of private networks was largely unregulated by domestic law (see the Interception of Communications Act 1985). The decision of the ECtHR in *Halford v UK* (**[6.37]** below) made it clear that interception by an operator of a private networks (there by an employer) could breach the user's Article 8 right to privacy. RIPA extended the legal regulation of interceptions to cover private networks which are 'attached, directly or indirectly . . . to a public telecommunications system'. The 'communications' to which it applies are defined (section 81) to cover 'anything comprising speech, music, sounds, visual images or data of any description'; and signals serving either for the impartation of anything between persons, between a person and a thing or between things or for the actuation or control of any apparatus'. This appears to include, *inter alia*, e-mail messages, telephone calls, faxes, voice mail and Internet access. No criminal offence is committed by the controller of a private network (or someone authorised by him or her) who intercepts a communication in the course of its transmission by that network (section 1(6)).

[6.27] Regulation of Investigatory Powers Act 2000, section 1(3)

S.1(3) Any interception of a communication which is carried out at any place in the United Kingdom by, or with the express or implied consent of, a person having the right to control the operation or the use of a private telecommunication system shall be actionable at the suit or instance of the sender or recipient, or intended recipient, of the communication if it is without lawful authority and is either—
(a) an interception of that communication in the course of its transmission by means of that private system; or
(b) an interception of that communication in the course of its transmission, by means of a public telecommunication system, to or from apparatus comprised in that private telecommunication system.

An interception will be deemed to have taken place in the course of transmission if (section 2(7) RIPA) it occurs at 'any time when the system by means of which the communication is being, or has been, transmitted is used for storing it in a manner that enables the intended recipient to collect it or otherwise to have access to it', section 2(8) further providing that 'the cases in which any contents of a communication are to be taken to be made available to a person while being transmitted shall include any case in which any of the contents of the communication, while being transmitted, are diverted or recorded so as to be available to a person subsequently'. Thus RIPA governs interceptions of communications not only while they are in the process of transmission as that phrase is commonly understood, but also when they are stored in inboxes, or as lists of favourite web addresses, etc.

Sections 1(5), 3, 4 and 5 provide for cases in which interceptions have 'lawful authority' (where, for example, *both the sender and the recipient* of the communication have consented to the interception or where the interception is authorised by a warrant or by regulation). Most significant in the present context is the 'lawful authority' provided by para 3 of the LBP Regulations which permit businesses to *monitor or record* communications during the course of their transmission by employers' private telecommunications systems for the purposes (relevant to the current discussion) of (Regulation 3(1)(a)):

- establishing the existence of facts relevant to the business (this might include recording the substance of communications),
- ascertaining compliance with regulatory or self-regulatory practices or procedures relevant to the business,
- ascertaining or demonstrating the standards achieved or which ought to be achieved by persons using the system in the course of their duties (this might include interception and recording for the purposes of quality control);
- protecting national security;
- preventing or detecting crime;
- investigating or detecting the unauthorised use of that or any other telecommunication system (this might include checking that employees do not contravene the employer's email or internet policies); and/or
- ensuring the effective operation of the system (this might include checking for viruses).

Employers and other operators of private telecommunications systems are also permitted by Regulation 3 to monitor, *but not to record*, communications during the course of their transmission by the system for the purposes of (Regulation 3(1)(b)) ascertaining whether those communications are relevant to the business. Regulation 3(2)(c) provides that interceptions will be permitted by Regulation 3(1) 'only where the system controller has made *all reasonable efforts to inform* every person who may use the telecommunication system in question' that interceptions may occur. Further (Regulation 3(2)(a)), the interceptions authorised by Regulation 3(1) must be effected 'solely for the purpose of monitoring (or, where appropriate, recording) keeping a record of communications relevant to' the business. But any communication will be taken to be relevant to the business when, *inter alia*, it 'relates to that business , or . . . otherwise takes place in the course of carrying out that business'. It appears from this that Regulation 3 permits monitoring and recording of any communication which is not clearly private and the interception of which is not motivated by clearly non-business reasons (such as malice).

It is clear that RIPA, read with the LBP Regulations, provides little protection from workplace monitoring. The Regulations were defended by then-'e-minister' Patricia Hewitt as striking 'the right balance between protecting the privacy of individuals and enabling industry and business to get the maximum benefit from new communications technology (*Guardian*, 2 November 2000), and have been greeted with enthusiasm by the Confederation of British Industry, which 'believes that routine monitoring of email is both normal and acceptable'. Others disagree.

6.5.2 The Data Protection Act 1998

If RIPA and the accompanying Regulations were the only legislation relevant to workplace surveillance, the legal protection afforded to workers would be scant indeed. But these provisions must be read with the DPA 1998, which was passed to implement Council Directive 95/46/EC (the Data Protection Directive). The Directive is not targeted specifically at employment and subsequent attempts by the Commission to introduce such legislation have stalled. But the 1998 Act offers a number of

***The Guardian*, 2 November 2000**

But for trades unions or civil liberties organisations, the main concern is the imbalance between the rights of employers and those being monitored. 'We have been calling for the regulation of surveillance for some time now', said John Wadham, director of human rights group Liberty, 'but these regulations do not go far enough to protect people's privacy'.

Yaman Akdeniz, director of online civil liberties pressure group Cyber-Rights and Cyber-Liberties, calls the regulations 'very vague' and fears 'anything is justified under them'. Caspar Bowden, director of the Foundation for Internet Policy Research, says: 'The DTI has given bullying bosses carte blanche to pry and exploit knowledge of the private lives of employees'.

***The Guardian* 25 November 2000**

'The government has defined particular circumstances when employers can intercept electronic information, but it is hard to think of anything employers might do that is not covered by the regulations,' says TUC spokeswoman Lucy Anderson. Snooping, says the TUC, can go on 'almost without restriction and with no duty to consult or negotiate with trade unions or worker representatives'. Civil rights campaign group Liberty says: 'The whip hand is with the employer' . . .

[S]olicitor Kit Burdon of Barlow Lyde Gilbert . . . says that employees remain extremely vulnerable to employers keen to use the new regulations to get rid of them. 'An employer could use instances of alleged misuse of the e-mail system to build up a case of gross misconduct.' An employer might decide that some messages are 'harmful to the smooth running of the business that an internet user would consider inconsequential, like circulating a round robin joke'.

protections relevant to employment surveillance. In the first place, so far as the Act is most relevant to employment-related surveillance, it places restrictions on the processing of 'personal data' (see box below). 'Processing' is defined (section 1(1)) to mean obtaining, recording or holding data; carrying out any operation or set of operations on information or data, including organising, adapting, altering it, retrieving, consulting or using it, disclosing it by transmitting or disseminating it or otherwise making it available, aligning, combining, blocking, erasing or destroying it. It is clear from this definition that the DPA 1998 has implications for the collection and recording of information by means of workplace surveillance, together with its retention and use. Secondly, the Act provides individuals in respect of whom personal data are held with rights to access the data and, in some cases, to prevent or terminate its processing and to 'rectify, block, erase or destroy' personal data (see further below). It is important to note at this point, however, that none of the DPA protections apply (section 28) to personal data required for the purpose of safeguarding national security. Save for the possibility of an appeal to the Information Tribunal for a ruling that there were no reasonable grounds for the issue of a national security certificate, the issue of such a certificate by a Minister of the Crown is conclusive evidence of the fact that the personal data were required for this purpose.

The various protections afforded by the DPA 1998 are considered in more or less detail below, in each case to the extent only that they are of relevance to the legal control of workplace and related surveillance. First it is useful to outline some of the definitions adopted by the DPA.

The DPA: key definitions

'Data'

'Data' is widely defined to include (section 1 DPA 1998):

- **'automated'** information, i.e., 'information which: (a) 'is being processed by means of equipment operating automatically in response to instructions given for that purpose', or (b) 'is recorded with the intention that it should be processed by means of such equipment';
- **'manual** information, i.e., 'information which 'is recorded as part of a relevant filing system or with the intention that it should form part of a relevant filing system';
- information forming part of an **'accessible record'** held by a public authority (i.e., health or education records or records defined as 'accessible' by Schedule 12 to the Act),
- any recorded information held by a public authority which is not otherwise covered by the Act. The DPA 1998 does not apply in full to this category of data.

A 'relevant filing system', which is relevant only in the case of **manual** information held **otherwise than by a public authority**, is defined (section 1(1)) as: 'any set of information relating to individuals to the extent that, although the information is not processed by means of equipment operating automatically in response to instructions given for that purpose, the set is structured, either by reference to individuals or by reference to criteria relating to individuals, in such a way that specific information relating to a particular individual is readily accessible'. This was given a very narrow definition by the Court of Appeal in *Durant* v *Financial Services Authority* (discussed below), a decision which significantly reduces the utility of the DPA as a counter to workplace surveillance.

'Personal Data'

'Personal data' is defined (section 1(1)) as 'data' 'which relate to a living individual who can be identified from those data, or from those data and other information which is in the possession of, or is likely to come into the possession of, the data controller, and includes any expression of opinion about the individual and any indication of the intentions of the data controller or any other person in respect of the individual'. A 'data controller' is (section 1(1)) 'a person who (either alone or jointly or in common with other persons) determines the purposes for which and the manner in which any personal data are, or are to be, processed.

'Sensitive personal data'

This is defined by section 2 of the DPA as personal data relating to an individual's racial or ethnic origin; political opinions; religious or similar beliefs; membership of a trade union; physical or mental health or condition; sexual life; commission or alleged commission of any offence; or proceedings in respect of any offence committed or alleged to have been committed by him, the disposal of such proceedings or the sentence of any court in such proceedings.

Prior to the decision of the Court of Appeal in *Durant v Financial Services Authority* it was widely assumed that most employment-related records would be defined as 'manual data' for the purposes of the DPA 1998 even if they were not computerised and that, further, they would be 'personal' data' for the purposes of the Act. But in *Durant* the Court of Appeal took a narrow approach both to *personal* data and to the types of information which are covered as *manual* data by the Act. The decision in *Durant* is controversial and it is by no means certain that it is compatible with EU law. Until this question is resolved, it has generated considerable uncertainty as to the application of the DPA 1998 in the context of employment, as elsewhere.

[6.28] *Durant v Financial Services Authority* [2003] EWCA Civ 1746 (CA)

The facts in *Durant* did not concern employment but arose out of a complaint made by Mr Durant to the FSA in connection with action taken by him against Barclays Bank. He subsequently sought disclosure from the FSA of documentation. This request was rejected by the FSA and County Court and by the Court of Appeal, Auld LJ ruling (for the Court) that data were not 'personal' for the purposes of the DPA 1998 unless they were 'biographical in a significant sense' and unless they had the data subject as their 'focus', and that non-computerised data did not fall within the Act's definition of 'manual data' unless they were recorded as part of a filing system 'of sufficient sophistication to provide the same or similar ready accessibility as a computerised filing system'.

Auld LJ:
Mere mention of the data subject in a document held by a data controller does not necessarily amount to his personal data. Whether it does so in any particular instance depends on where it falls in a continuum of relevance or proximity to the data subject as distinct, say, from transactions or matters in which he may have been involved to a greater or lesser degree. It seems to me that there are two notions that may be of assistance. The first is whether the information is biographical in a significant sense, that is, going beyond the recording of the putative data subject's involvement in a matter or an event that has no personal connotations, a life event in respect of which his privacy could not be said to be compromised. The second is one of focus. The information should have the putative data subject as its focus rather than some other person with whom he may have been involved or some transaction or event in which he may have figured or have had an interest, for example, as in this case, an investigation into some other person's or body's conduct that he may have instigated. In short, it is information that affects his privacy, whether in his personal or family life, business or professional capacity . . .

It is clear from [the DPA's definitions of 'automated' and 'manual' data and 'relevant filing system'] that the intention is to provide, as near as possible, the same standard or sophistication of accessibility to personal data in manual filing systems as to computerised records . . . if the statutory scheme is to have any sensible and practical effect, it can only be in the context of filing systems that enable identification of relevant information with a minimum of time and costs, through clear referencing mechanisms within any filing system potentially containing personal data the subject of a request for information. Anything less, which, for example, requires the searcher to leaf through files to see what and whether information qualifying as personal data of the person who has made the request is to be found there, would bear no resemblance to a computerised search. And, as Mr. Sales [for the FSA] also pointed out, it could, in its length and other costs, have a disproportionate effect on the property rights of data controllers under Article 1 of the First Protocol to the ECHR, who are only allowed a limited time, 40 days, under section 7(8) and (10) of the Act to respond to requests, and are entitled to only a nominal fee in respect of doing so.

As to the 1998 Act, to constitute a 'relevant filing system' a manual filing system must: 1) relate to individuals; 2) be a 'set' or part of a 'set' of information; 3) be structured by reference to individuals or criteria relating to individuals; and 4) be structured in such a way that specific information relating to a particular individual is readily accessible. It is not enough that a filing system leads a searcher to a file containing documents mentioning the data subject. To qualify under the Directive and the Act, it requires, as Mr. Sales put it, a file to which that search leads to be so structured and/or indexed as to enable easy location within it or any sub-files of specific information about the data subject that he has requested . . .

It is plain from the constituents of the definition considered individually and together, and from the preface in it to them, 'although the information is not processed by means of equipment operating automatically in response to instructions given for that purpose', that Parliament intended to apply the Act to manual records only if they are of sufficient sophistication to provide the same or similar ready accessibility as a computerised filing system. That requires a filing system so referenced or indexed that it enables the data controller's employee responsible to identify at the outset of his search with reasonable certainty and speed the file or files in which the specific data relating to the person requesting the information is located and to locate the relevant information about him within the file or files, without having to make a manual search of them. To leave it to the searcher to leaf through files, possibly at great length and cost, and fruitlessly, to see whether it or they contain information relating to the person requesting information and whether that information is data within the Act bears, as Mr. Sales said, no resemblance to a computerised search. It cannot have been intended by Parliament - and a filing system necessitating it cannot be 'a relevant filing system' within the Act. The statutory scheme for the provision of information by a data controller can only operate with proportionality and as a matter of common-sense where those who are required to respond to requests for information have a filing system that enables them to identify in advance of searching individual files whether or not it is 'a relevant filing system' for the purpose . . .

Accordingly, I conclude, as Mr. Sales submitted, that 'a relevant filing system' for the purpose of the Act, is limited to a system:

1) in which the files forming part of it are structured or referenced in such a way as clearly to indicate at the outset of the search whether specific information capable of amounting to personal data of an individual requesting it under section 7 is held within the system and, if so, in which file or files it is held; and

2) which has, as part of its own structure or referencing mechanism, a sufficiently sophisticated and detailed means of readily indicating whether and where in an individual file or files specific criteria or information about the applicant can be readily located.

Buxton and Mummery LJJ agreed.

The Information Commissioner, formerly known as the Data Protection Commissioner, has a significant enforcement role in relation to the DPA 1998 (see further 6.5.4 below). He suggests, post-*Durant*, that 'personal data' protected by the DPA 1998 will include 'information about the medical history of an individual' or about 'an individual's tax liabilities', 'an individual's salary details, 'information comprising an individual's bank statements' or about 'individuals' spending preferences', but that it will not include 'mere reference to a person's name where the name is not associated with any other personal information', 'incidental mention in the minutes of a business meeting of an individual's attendance at that meeting in an official capacity; or where an individual's name appears on a document or e-mail indicating only that it has been sent or copied to that particular individual, the content of that document or e-mail does not amount to personal data about the individual unless there is other information about the individual within it'.

[6.29] Information Commissioner, 'The "Durant" Case and its impact on the interpretation of the Data Protection Act 1998' (2004), pp 2–5

Information that has as its focus something other than the individual will not be 'personal data'. For example, information that focuses on a property (e.g. a structural survey) is not 'personal data', nor is information about the performance of an office department or a branch of a chain of stores. While such information may include information 'about' an individual, where the focus of the information is something other than the individual, such information will not 'relate to' the individual and, therefore, is not personal data.

However, there are many circumstances where information, for example about a house or a car, could be personal data because that information is directly linked to an individual. One example would be a valuation of a house where this was being used in order to determine the assets of a particular individual in a matrimonial dispute. Another example would be the details of a car photographed by a speed camera where those details are used to direct a notice of intention to prosecute to the registered keeper of the vehicle . . .

Where manual files fall within the definition of relevant filing system, the content will either be so sub-divided as to allow the searcher to go straight to the correct category and retrieve the information requested without a manual search, or will be so indexed as to allow a searcher to go directly to the relevant page/s.

For example, a set of legal files containing files divided into sections for legal aid, pleadings, orders, correspondence by year, instructions to counsel, counsel's advice, will not be a relevant filing system because the divisions/referencing do not assist a searcher in retrieving the required personal information without the need to leaf through the file contents.

Where information is filed in a system using individuals' names as file names, the system may not qualify as a relevant filing system if the indexing/referencing/sub-division is structured otherwise than to allow the retrieval of personal data without leafing through the file. A filing system containing files about individuals, or topics about individuals, where the content of each file is structured purely in chronological order will not be a relevant filing system as the files are not appropriately structured/indexed/divided or referenced to allow the retrieval of personal data without leafing through the file.

Personnel files and other manual files using individuals' names or unique identifiers as the file names, which are sub-divided/indexed to allow retrieval of personal data without a manual search (such as, sickness, absence, contact details etc.), are likely to be held in a 'relevant filing system' for the purposes of the DPA. However, following the *Durant* judgment it is likely that very few manual files will be covered by the provisions of the DPA. Most information about individuals held in manual form does not, therefore, fall within the data protection regime.

The advice goes on to advocate the 'temp test' as a rule of thumb test to establish whether manual data falls within the DPA 1998 (at p 6):

If you employed a temporary administrative assistant (a temp), would they be able to extract specific information about an individual without any particular knowledge of your type of work or the documents you hold?' The 'temp test' assumes that the temp in question is reasonably competent, requiring only a short induction, explanation and/or operating manual on the particular filing system in question for them to be able to use it. The temp test would not apply if any in-depth knowledge of your custom and practice is required, whether of your type of work, of the documents you hold or of any unusual features of your system, before a temp is, as a matter of practice, capable of operating the system. In such cases the system would not be a relevant filing system.

Despite the narrowing effect of *Durant* the DPA 1998 continues to apply to information obtained by 'automated' means (CCTV, email interception, automatic telephone monitoring, internet monitoring etc, telephone recording). It also applies to some extent to manual personal data held by public authorities (listed in the Freedom of Information Act 2000), even where that data is not stored within a 'relevant filing system'. Public authorities are obliged to ensure that such data are accurate, up to date and accessible under section 7 DPA. Data subjects may apply for access to such personal data and for its rectification, and may claim compensation under section 13 DPA 1998 (see 6.5.4 above). Further, where issues of privacy under Article 8 of the ECnHR are at stake, section 3 HRA 1998 may well require a broader approach to 'manual information' for the purposes of the DPA 1998 than might otherwise be the case. The impact of the HRA 1998 on the DPA and RIPA is considered further at 6.5.7 below.

6.5.3 The data protection principles

The Act contains eight 'data protection principles' (DPPs) with which 'data controllers' must comply. The principles are set out below and will be discussed brie?y and only insofar as they are likely to be of relevance in the context of workplace and related surveillance.

[6.30] Data Protection Act 1998, Schedule 1, Part I

1 Personal data shall be processed fairly and lawfully and, in particular, shall not be processed unless
   (a) at least one of the conditions in Schedule 2 is met, and
   (b) in the case of sensitive personal data, at least one of the conditions in Schedule 3 is also met.

2 Personal data shall be obtained only for one or more specified and lawful purposes, and shall not be further processed in any manner incompatible with that purpose or those purposes.

3 Personal data shall be adequate, relevant and not excessive in relation to the purpose or purposes for which they are processed.

4 Personal data shall be accurate and, where necessary, kept up to date.

5 Personal data processed for any purpose or purposes shall not be kept for longer than is necessary for that purpose or those purposes.

6 Personal data shall be processed in accordance with the rights of data subjects under this Act.

7 Appropriate technical and organisational measures shall be taken against unauthorised or unlawful processing of personal data and against accidental loss or destruction of, or damage to, personal data.

8 Personal data shall not be transferred to a country or territory outside the European

Economic Area unless that country or territory ensures an adequate level of protection for the rights and freedoms of data subjects in relation to the processing of personal data.

The first DPP has most significant implications in the context of workplace surveillance and will be considered in some depth. The others will be considered more briefly and the eighth DPP not at all. Turning first to para (a) of the first DPP, the conditions set out in Schedule 2 may be satisfied (so far as they are relevant in the context of workplace surveillance), where the data subject has *consented* to the processing or where such processing is *necessary* 'for compliance with any [non-contractual] legal obligation to which the data controller is subject' or 'for the purposes of legitimate interests pursued by the data controller or by the third party or parties to whom the data are disclosed, except where the processing is unwarranted in any particular case by reason of prejudice to the rights and freedoms or legitimate interests of the data subject'.

In the case of 'sensitive personal data' (see box at p 612 above), the conditions set out in Schedule 3 may be satisfied, *inter alia*, where the data subject has given his explicit consent to the processing of the personal data, or where 'the processing is necessary . . . 'for the purpose of, or in connection with, any legal proceedings (including prospective legal proceedings)'; 'for the purpose of obtaining legal advice'; otherwise 'for the purposes of establishing, exercising or defending legal rights'; or for the purposes of exercising or performing any right or obligation which is conferred or imposed by law on the data controller in connection with employment'.

The first DPP requires not only that data processing complies with one of the conditions set out in Schedule 2 (and, where relevant, Schedule 3) but also that it be fair and lawful. Part II of Schedule 1 to the DPA 1998 provides guidance on the interpretation of the DPPs. It sets out a 'fair processing code' which provides that regard will be had, in determining whether or not information has been processed fairly, to the manner in which it was obtained. Particular regard will be had to 'whether any person from whom the data is obtained is deceived or misled as to the purpose or purposes for which the personal data are to be processed' (deception may also invalidate consent for the purposes of the first DPP). Data will be regarded as having been obtained fairly where (para 1(2)), its supply by the person from whom it was obtained was required or authorised 'by or under any enactment'. In other cases, paras 2 and 3 (the 'subject information provisions') set out conditions which must be complied with whether the data has been supplied by the data subject or by a third party. Compliance with the fair processing code, including the subject information provisions, does not itself guarantee that the data has been processed 'lawfully and fairly' (where, for example, processing takes place in breach of an obligation of confidence). But where they are satisfied, processing will be treated as having been done fairly unless there is evidence to the contrary.

Whether personal data are supplied by the data subject or by a third party, paras 2 and 3 require that the data controller 'ensures so far as practicable that the data subject has, is provided with, or has made readily available to him', information relating, *inter alia*, to 'the purpose or purposes for which the data are intended to be processed', and (para 3(d)) 'any further information which is necessary, having regard to the specific circumstances in which the data are or are to be processed, to enable processing in respect of the data subject to be fair'. Where data is received other than from the data subject, data controllers may fail to make the above information available to the data subject where (Schedule 1, Part II, para 3) its provision 'would involve a disproportionate effort', or where the recording or disclosure of the information by the data controller 'is necessary for compliance with any legal obligation to which the data controller is subject, other than an obligation imposed by contract'. These exceptions do not apply, however, where (Data Protection (Conditions under Paragraph 3 of Part II of Schedule 1) Order 2000 (SI 2000 No 185)) the data controller has received a written request for the provision of the relevant information before the data is processed.

Personal data which is processed (section 29(1)) for the purpose, *inter alia*, of (a) preventing or detecting crime or (b) apprehending or prosecuting offenders, is exempt from the fair processing code, and to the general obligation that personal data be processed fairly (although not from the conditions set out in Schedules 2 and, where relevant, 3). So, for example, if an employer uses workplace surveillance for the purpose of detecting fraud, the personal data collected thereby need not be processed fairly. However, the processing (including the collection) of such data still requires either that the subject has consented; or that it is necessary 'for the purposes of legitimate interests pursued by the data controller or by the third party or parties to whom the data are disclosed, except where the processing is unwarranted in any particular case by reason of prejudice to the rights and freedoms or legitimate interests of the data subject. The significance of this latter provision is further considered below. Data 'likely to prejudice the combat effectiveness of the armed forces' and, if the Secretary of State by order provides, data 'processed for the purposes of assessing any person's suitability for employment by or under the Crown, by a Minister of the Crown or by a Northern Ireland department (Schedule 7, para 2), is also exempt from the fair processing code, but not from the overriding obligation that data be processed fairly. The processing of any personal data is, finally, exempt from the first DPP in its entirety, where exemption is required for the purpose of safeguarding national security.

Turning to consider the second DPP, a 'specified' purpose is one (Schedule 1, Part II, para 5) which the data controller has notified to the data subject or the Information Commissioner (in which case it will appear on the Commissioner's publicly accessible Register. Para 6 provides that the question whether any disclosure of personal data is compatible with the purpose(s) for which it was obtained will depend in part on the purpose(s) 'for which the personal data are intended to be processed by any person to whom they are disclosed'. The second DPP does not apply to the disclosure by a data controller of personal data processed for the purpose of (section 29(1)) (a) preventing or detecting crime or (b) apprehending or prosecuting offenders, to the extent that compliance with the principle would be likely to prejudice the purposes mentioned in section 29(1). Exemptions are also provided (section 35) in the case of personal data whose disclosure is necessary (a) for the purpose of, or in connection with, any legal proceedings (including prospective legal proceedings), or (b) for the purpose of obtaining legal advice, or is otherwise necessary for the purposes of establishing, exercising or defending legal rights, to the extent that the principle is inconsistent with the disclosure in question. Thus, an employer may disclose to the police information gained through workplace surveillance which discloses criminal behaviour, even where the possibility of such disclosure has not been previously notifies. Again, however, the collection of such information will be compatible with the DPA only where the first DPP has been complied with (see preceding paragraph).

The same exemptions are provided to the third, fourth and fifth DPPs as to the second DPP. Nor will the fourth DPP be contravened where any inaccuracy in the personal data was contained in the information provided to the data controller by the data subject or a third party in a case where:

[6.31] Schedule 1, Part II, para 7

Para 7 (a) having regard to the purpose or purposes for which the data were obtained and further processed, the data controller has taken reasonable steps to ensure the accuracy of the data, and

(b) if the data subject has notified the data controller of the data subject's view that the data are inaccurate, the data indicate that fact.

Schedule 1, Part II, para 8, provides that the sixth DPP will be contravened only if the processor fails to supply information to the data subject as required by section 7 DPA 1998 (see 6.5.4 below), or if s/he breaches sections 10, 11, 12 or 12A DPA 1998 (these sections are discussed, insofar as they are relevant to workplace surveillance, immediately below) by failing to comply with a notice issued by the data subject.

6.5.4 Enforcement of the Data Protection Principles

The Information Commissioner must maintain a register of data controllers, such persons being obliged by the DPA 1998 to provide notification to her of, *inter alia*, the type of personal data being processed by them, the reasons for which they are being processed and the safeguards adopted in pursuit of the seventh DPP. Personal data may in general only be processed lawfully where the data controller is entered on a register maintained by the Commissioner, though those who only process information about 'qualifications, work experience or pay' or similar for the purposes of 'appointments or removals, pay, discipline, superannuation, work management or other personnel matters in relation to [their] staff' and who do not disclose such data to others except with the consent of the data subject or where necessary for the employment-related purposes are exempt from the registration requirements.

Anyone who is or believes themselves to be directly affected by any 'processing' of 'personal data' may (section 42 DPA 1998) apply to the Information Commissioner for an 'assessment' to determine whether or not it is likely that the data is being processed in compliance with the provisions of the DPA. The Commissioner may require data controllers to provide information and may (section 40 DPA 1998) serve an enforcement notice on a data controller who he is satisfied has contravened or is contravening any of the DPPs. Such a notice may require the data controller to take, or not to take, specified steps; or to refrain from processing any personal data (or 'sensitive personal data'), or to refrain from processing data for a particular purpose or in a particular manner. The DPA 1998 also provides individual rights of enforcement to 'data subjects'. Section 7 provides a right for data subjects to be informed, in response to a written request, whether a data controller is processing any personal data of which they are the subject (and, if so, what the data are, why they are being processed and to whom they are or may be disclosed. (The data controller may charge a fee, not currently exceeding £10, for this information.) Data controllers may refuse to provide information sought under section 7 where it would involve the disclosure of 'information relating to another individual who can be identified from that information' (including the identification of another person as the source of the information), unless (a) the other individual has consented to the disclosure or (b) 'it is reasonable in all the circumstances [including, *inter alia* (section 7(6)), any duty of confidentiality owed and any steps taken to seek consent], to comply with the request without the consent of the other individual'. In such cases (section 7(5)) the data controller must provide as much of the information sought as is possible without disclosing the identity of the third party.

Exemptions are provided from the section 7 right of access where (section 28) this is required for the purpose of safeguarding national security and (section 29) to data processed for the purposes of (a) the prevention or detection of crime, or (b) the apprehension or prosecution of offenders, to the extent to which the application of section 7 would be likely to prejudice either of these matters. Further, para 11 provides that the obligation to comply with a request made under section 7 does not apply 'to the extent that compliance would, by revealing evidence of the commission of any offence other than an offence under this Act, expose him to proceedings for that offence', para 11(2) providing that '[i]nformation disclosed by any person in compliance with any request or order under section 7 shall not be admissible against him in proceedings for an offence under this Act'.

Section 10(1) DPA 1998 provides individuals with a right to prevent or terminate processing (either in general or processing for a specified purpose or in a specified manner) which causes or is likely to cause 'substantial' and 'unwarranted' damage or distress to the data subject or another. The right is exercised by the provision of a notice from the data subject to the data controller, the notice having to specify the reasons for which the processing would cause or be likely to cause the damage or distress. No right to prevent or terminate processing arises under section 10 where (so far as is relevant to the current discussion) the data subject has consented to the processing, the processing is necessary 'for compliance with any legal obligation to which the data controller is subject, other than an obligation imposed by contract', or in circumstances which the Secretary of State has prescribed by order. Where a data controller receives a notice under section 10 he or she must, within 21 days, inform the data subject either as to his or her compliance or intention to comply with the notice, or with 'his reasons for regarding the . . . notice as to any extent unjustified and the extent (if any) to which he has complied or intends to comply with it'. Where a justified (or partly justified) notice has not been complied with by a data controller, a court may (section 10(4)) 'order him to take such steps for complying with the notice (or for complying with it to that extent) as the court thinks fit'.

Section 13(1) DPA 1998 provides a right to compensation to any 'individual who suffers damage by reason of any contravention by a data controller of any of the requirements of this Act', a right to compensation for distress also being provided (section 13(2)) to any 'individual who suffers distress by reason of any contravention by a data controller of any of the requirements of this Act', and who also suffers damage as a result thereof. No right to compensation arises under section 13, however, if the data controller proves that he or she has (section 13(3) taken 'such care as in all the circumstances was reasonably required to comply with the requirement concerned'.

A court may (section 14 DPA 1998), on the application of a data subject, order a data controller 'to rectify, block, erase or destroy' any inaccurate personal data relating to him or her, together with 'any other personal data in respect of which he is the data controller and which contain an expression of opinion which appears to the court to be based on the inaccurate data'. A court order for rectification, blocking, erasure or destruction of personal data may also be made (section 14(4)) if the court is satisfied (a) that a data subject would be entitled to compensation under section 13 (immediately above) and (b) 'that there is a substantial risk of further contravention in respect of those data in such circumstances'. In either case (sections 14(3) & (5)) such orders may require that the data controller notify any third parties to which the data has been disclosed of its rectification, blocking, erasure or destruction.

6.5.5 The DPA 1998 and protection against workplace surveillance

The DPA 1998 has clear implications for the regulation of workplace and related surveillance. The data 'processing' to which it applies processing' is defined (section 1(1)) to mean:

- obtaining,
- recording or
- holding data;
- carrying out any operation or set of operations on information or data, including
- organising,
- adapting,
- altering, or
- retrieving it, or
- consulting,
- using, or
- disclosing it by
- transmitting,
- disseminating, or
- otherwise making it available,
- aligning,
- combining,
- blocking,
- erasing or
- destroying it.

These protections clearly apply in respect of the collection and use of information by employers as long as the information (a) is 'personal' data for the purposes of the Act (as interpreted by the Court of Appeal in *Durant*) and (b) is covered as automated or manual data or otherwise by the Act. The first DPP is of particular importance in the context of workplace surveillance. The requirement that data be processed only where the data subject has consented to the processing or where such processing is necessary 'for compliance with any [non-contractual] legal obligation to which the data controller is subject' is of special significance. So, too, is the 'fair processing code' set out in Schedule 1, Part II, para 2 of the Act (see 6.5.3 above).

[6.32] Information Commissioner, *Data Protection Act 1998: Legal Guidance* (2001), section 3.1.5

> The Commissioner's view is that consent is not particularly easy to achieve and that data controllers should consider other conditions in Schedule 2 (and Schedule 3 if processing sensitive personal data) before looking at consent . . . Consent is not defined in the Act. The existence or validity of consent will need to be assessed in the light of the facts. To assist in understanding what may or may not amount to consent in any particular case it is helpful to refer back to the Directive. This defines 'the data subject's consent' as: 'any freely given specific and informed indication of his wishes by which the data subject signifies his agreement to personal data relating to him being processed'.
>
> The fact that the data subject must 'signify' his agreement means that there must be some active communication between the parties. A data subject may 'signify' agreement other than in writing. Data controllers cannot infer consent from non-response to a communication . . . The adequacy of any consent or purported consent must be evaluated. For example, consent obtained under duress or on the basis of misleading information will not be a valid basis for processing.
>
> Where a data subject does not signify his agreement to personal data relating to him being processed, but is given an opportunity to object to such processing, although this does not amount to consent for the purposes of the Act, it *may* provide the data controller with the basis to rely upon another Schedule 2 condition, for example, the legitimate interests condition, provided that the data subject is given the right to object before the data are obtained . . .
>
> There is a distinction in the Act between the nature of the consent required to satisfy the condition for processing and that which is required in the case of the condition for processing sensitive data. The consent must be 'explicit' in the case of sensitive data. The use of the word 'explicit' and the fact that the condition requires explicit consent 'to the processing of the personal data' suggests that the consent of the data subject should be absolutely clear. In appropriate cases it should cover the specific detail of the processing, the particular type of data to be processed (or even the specific information), the purposes of the processing and any special aspects of the processing which may affect the individual, for example, disclosures which may be made of the data.

It is clear from the extract immediately above that a generalised consent to the use of personal data ('sensitive' or otherwise) will not satisfy the requirements of the DPA 1998. Where personal data consists of performance monitoring (such as, for example, key-board usage or, in a call-centre job, telephone monitoring), its processing (including its obtaining, recording, retention, organisation, retrieval, consultation, or use) might be necessary 'for the purposes of the legitimate interests pursued by the data controller' (6.5.3 above). But this condition is not satisfied where 'the processing is unwarranted in any particular case by reason of prejudice to the rights and freedoms or legitimate interests of the data subject'. Where surveillance takes the form of 'be-havioural', rather than 'performance' monitoring (where, for example, workers are subject to CCTV or audio surveillance, where their movements are tracked, their tele-phones or email correspondence intercepted or they are subject to drugs, alcohol or medical testing), considerations of privacy (further discussed below) may override except in those cases in which employers have strong legitimate interests in surveil-lance (or, section 28, where national security issues prevail). The balance between employer interests and workers' privacy rights is further considered below.

The Information Commissioner's Code *Employment Practices Data Protection Code: Part 3: Monitoring At Work* suggests (at p 9) that sensitve personal information might include 'health information in e-mails sent by a worker to his or her manager, a personnel department or an occupational health advisor; trade union membership revealed by internet access logs which show that a worker routinely accesses a partic-ular trade union website [and] information about a worker's political opinions or religious beliefs obtained by intercepting and recording a private conversation'. The first DPP requires, in relation to the processing of such data, that one of the condi-tions set out in Schedule 3 is satisfied. Leaving aside the possibility of explicit consent by a worker, the only relevant conditions appear to be that the processing of such information is necessary (a) 'for the purposes of exercising or performing any right or obligation which is conferred by law on the data controller in connection with employment' or (b) 'for the purpose of, or in connection with, any legal proceedings (including prospective proceedings)', or 'for the purposes of establishing, exercising or defending legal rights'. Alcohol or drugs testing might be permitted under Sched-ule 3 in some cases by the employer's health and safety obligations, and CCTV monitoring where the employer had reason to believe that a criminal offence (such as theft) was being carried out in the workplace. But the obtaining of such personal data would also have to fulfil one of the conditions set out in Schedule 2 (discussed in the preceding paragraph) and otherwise to constitute 'fair and lawful' processing (see immediately below). Again, the appropriate balance to be struck between the inter-ests of employers and those of workers in this matter is considered at below.

Turning to the application of the 'fair processing code' to surveillance-related data whose processing otherwise satisfied one of the conditions set out in Schedule 2 (and, in the case of sensitive personal data, one of those in Schedule 3), such processing would still breach the first DPP if the data subject or other person who supplied it to the data controller was misled as to the purposes for which it was to be processed, unless national security (section 28) or crime prevention or detection etc. (section 29) were at issue. Such a breach might occur, for example, if medical information sup-plied for the purposes of the Working Time Regulations (section 4.5) was used to determine a workers' future employment prospects; or if urine samples taken for drug testing were used to find out whether workers were pregnant. Further, data process-ing (for example, the recording of CCTV or audio surveillance or of tracking devices, the interception of email or telephone correspondence or the collection of bodily samples for the purposes of drugs or alcohol testing) will comply with the first DPP only where workers are provided with information as to the purpose or purposes for which the data is being processed. The only surveillance-related cases in which the obligation to process personal data fairly is likely not to apply are (section 28 DPA 1998) those in which exemption is 'required for the purpose of safeguarding national security' and (section 29) where the processing is 'for the purpose of preventing or detecting crime' (as in a case in which surveillance conducted in order to detect fraud).

The likely impact of the DPA 1998 on workplace surveillance is indicated by the Information Commissioner's Code of Practice on Monitoring, mentioned above. The Code, the issue of which was very delayed, was watered down considerably from the first draft (issued October 2000) which was said by the *Independent* (11 October 2000) to have 'thrown into chaos' what that paper described as 'Government plans to allow companies to snoop on staff e-mails and phone calls' by means of the LBP Regulations.

In its final form the Code of Practice states (at p 12) that 'Monitoring is a recognised component of the employment relationship' and that most employers will make, and most workers will expect, 'some checks on the quantity and quality of work produced by their workers'. It also recognises that some monitoring has a protective function in relation to workers and that some employers (for example in the financial services sector) 'may be under legal or regulatory obligations which [they] can only realistically fulfil if [they] undertake[] monitoring'. But it warns that:

[6.33] Information Commissioner, *Employment Practices Data Protection Code: Part 3: Monitoring At Work*, p 12

> where monitoring goes beyond one individual simply watching another and involves the manual recording or any automated processing of personal information, itmust be done in a way that is both lawful and fair to workers.
>
> Monitoring may, to varying degrees, have an adverse impact on workers. It may intrude into their private lives, undermine respect for their correspondence or interfere with the relationship of mutual trust and confidence that should exist between them and their employer. The extent to which it does this may not always be immediately obvious. It is not always easy to draw a distinction between work-place and private information. For example monitoring e-mail messages from a worker to an occupational health advisor, or messages between workers and their trade union representatives, can give rise to concern.

The Code stresses the need for impact assessment to assess whether the impact of monitoring is proportional to its purposes in any given circumstances (p 16):

> An impact assessment involves:
> * identifying clearly the *purpose(s)* behind the monitoring arrangement and the benefits it is likely to deliver
> * identifying any likely *adverse impact* of the monitoring arrangement
> * considering *alternatives* to monitoring or different ways in which it might be carried out
> * taking into account the *obligations* that arise from monitoring
> * judging whether monitoring is *justified*.

It warns that monitoring can impact adversely not only on workers but also on others such as customers who might be affected by it, and warns of the implications of monitoring for 'the relationship of mutual trust and confidence that should exist between workers and their employer', 'other legitimate relationships, e.g. between trades union members and their representatives' and 'individuals with professional obligations of confidentiality or secrecy, e.g. solicitors or doctors'. Among the alternatives to monitoring it suggests are 'supervision, effective training and/or clear communication from managers', Further, where monitoring is necessary, it might be appropriate to restrict it only to 'the investigation of specific incidents or problems' and/or 'to workers about whom complaints have been received, or about whom there are other grounds to suspect of wrongdoing', or otherwise to target it 'at areas of highest risk'. The Code goes on to set out 'core principles' and 'good practice recommendations'.

[6.34] Information Commissioner, *Employment Practices Data Protection Code: Part 3: Monitoring At Work*, p 24

CORE PRINCIPLES

- It will usually be intrusive to monitor your workers.
- Workers have legitimate expectations that they can keep their personal lives private and that they are also entitled to a degree of privacy in the work environment.
- If employers wish to monitor their workers, they should be clear about the purpose and satisfied that the particular monitoring arrangement is justified by real benefits that will be delivered.
- Workers should be aware of the nature, extent and reasons for any monitoring, unless (exceptionally) covert monitoring is justified.
- In any event, workers' awareness will influence their expectations.

3.2.1 Identify who within the organisation can authorise the monitoring of workers and ensure they are aware of the employer's responsibilities under the Act . . .
3.2.2 Before monitoring, identify clearly the purpose(s) behind the monitoring and the specific benefits it is likely to bring. Determine – preferably using an impact assessment - whether the likely benefits justify any adverse impact . . .
3.2.3 If monitoring is to be used to enforce the organisation's rules and standards make sure that the rules and standards are clearly set out in a policy which also refers to the nature and extent of any associated monitoring. Ensure workers are aware of the policy.
3.2.4 Tell workers what monitoring is taking place and why, and keep them aware of this, unless covert monitoring is justified.
3.2.5 If sensitive data are collected in the course of monitoring, ensure that a sensitive data condition is satisfied.
3.2.6 Keep to a minimum those who have access to personal information obtained through monitoring. Subject them to confidentiality and security requirements and ensure that they are properly trained where the nature of the information requires this.
3.2.7 Do not use personal information collected through monitoring for purposes other than those for which the monitoring was introduced unless:
    (a) it is clearly in the individual's interest to do so; or
    (b) it reveals activity that no employer could reasonably be expected to ignore.
3.2.8 If information gathered from monitoring might have an adverse impact on workers, present them with the information and allow them to make representations before taking action.
3.2.9 Ensure that the right of access of workers to information about them which is kept for, or obtained through, monitoring is not compromised. Monitoring systems must be capable of meeting this and other data protection requirements.

The draft Code stated (at p 36) that '[i]t is difficult to see how covert monitoring of performance can ever be justified' and that '[c]overt monitoring of behaviour can only be justified in very limited circumstances . . . . where being open with employees would be likely to prejudice the prevention or detection of crime or the apprehension or prosecution of offenders'. It interpreted the first DPP and section 29 of the DPA 1998 to the effect that such covert monitoring may be used only where (p 37) 'specific criminal activity has been identified; and the need to use covert monitoring to obtain evidence of that criminal activity has been established; and an assessment has concluded that explaining the monitoring to employees would prejudice success in obtaining such evidence; and an assessment has been made of how long the monitoring should continue for'. In its final version the Code is somewhat weaker:

[6.35] Information Commissioner, *Employment Practices Data Protection Code: Part 3: Monitoring At Work*, **pp 37–38**

3.5.1 Senior management should normally authorise any covert monitoring. They should satisfy themselves that there are grounds for suspecting criminal activity or equivalent malpractice and that notifying individuals about the monitoring would prejudice its prevention or detection.

Key points and possible actions
• Covert monitoring should not normally be considered. It will be rare for covert monitoring of workers to be justified. It should therefore only be used in exceptional circumstances.

3.5.2 Ensure that any covert monitoring is strictly targeted at obtaining evidence within a set timeframe and that the covert monitoring does not continue after the investigation is complete

Key points and possible actions
• Deploy covert monitoring only as part of a specific investigation and cease once the investigation has been completed

3.5.3 Do not use covert audio or video monitoring in areas which workers would genuinely and reasonably expect to be private.

Key points and possible actions
• If embarking on covert monitoring with audio or video equipment, ensure that this is not used in places such as toilets or private offices.
• There may be exceptions to this in cases of suspicion of serious crime but there should be an intention to involve the police.

3.5.4 If a private investigator is employed to collect information on workers covertly make sure there is a contract in place that requires the private investigator to only collect information in a way that satisfies the employer's obligations under the Act.

Key points and possible actions
• Check any arrangements for employing private investigators to ensure your contracts with them impose requirements on the investigator to only collect and use information on workers in accordance with your instructions and to keep the information secure.

3.5.5 Ensure that information obtained through covert monitoring is used only for the prevention or detection of criminal activity or equivalent malpractice. Disregard and, where feasible, delete other information collected in the course of monitoring unless it reveals information that no employer could reasonably be expected to ignore.

Key points and possible actions
- In a covert monitoring exercise, limit the number of people involved in the investigation.
- Prior to the investigation, set up clear rules limiting the disclosure and access to information obtained.
- If information is revealed in the course of covert monitoring that is tangential to the original investigation, delete it from the records unless it concerns other criminal activity or equivalent malpractice.

The Code sets out detailed guidance as to the application of the general principles (above) in specific contexts (email and telephone monitoring, CCTV surveillance, vehicle tracking, etc). Medical testing is dealt with in Part 4 of the Commissioner's *Employment Practices Data Protection Code* which advises, *inter alia*, as follows:

[6.36] Information Commissioner, *Employment Practices Data Protection Code: Part 4: Information about Workers' Health,* **pp 25–32**

3.4.3 Only obtain information through a medical examination or medical testing of current workers if the testing is part of a occupational health and safety programme that workers have a free choice to participate in, or you are satisfied that it is a necessary and justified measure to:
- Prevent a significant risk to the health and safety of the worker, or others, or
- Determine a particular worker's fitness for carrying out his or her job, or
- Determine whether a worker is fit to return to work after a period of sickness absence, or when this might be the case, or
- Determine the worker's entitlement to health related benefits e.g. sick pay, or
- Prevent discrimination against workers on the grounds of disability or assess the need to make reasonable adjustments to the working environment, or
- Comply with other legal obligations . . .

3.4.4 Do not obtain a sample covertly or use an existing sample, test result or other information obtained through a medical examination for a purpose other than that for which it was originally obtained . . .

3.4.5 Permanently delete information obtained in the course of medical examination or testing that is not relevant for the purpose(s) for which the examination or testing is undertaken . . .

3.5.1 Before obtaining information through drug or alcohol testing ensure that the benefits justify any adverse impact, unless the testing is required by law.

3.5.2 Minimise the amount of personal information obtained through drug and alcohol testing . . .

3.5.3 Ensure the criteria used for selecting workers for testing are justified, properly documented, adhered to and are communicated to workers.

3.5.4 Confine the obtaining of information through random testing to those workers who are employed to work in safety critical activities.

3.5.5 Gather information through testing designed to ensure safety at work rather than to reveal the illegal use of substances in a worker's private life . . .

3.5.6 Ensure that workers are fully aware that drug or alcohol testing is taking place, and of the possible consequences of being tested.

3.5.7 Ensure that information is only obtained through drug and alcohol testing that is;

—of sufficient technical quality to support any decisions or opinions that are derived from it and,

—subject to rigorous integrity and quality control procedures and,

—conducted under the direction of, and positive test results interpreted by, a person who is suitably qualified and competent in the field of drug testing . . .

3.6.1 Do not use genetic testing in an effort to obtain information that is predictive of a worker's future general health.

3.6.2 Do not insist that a worker discloses the results of a previous genetic test.

3.6.3 Only use genetic testing to obtain information where it is clear that a worker with a particular, detectable genetic condition is likely to pose a serious safety risk to others or where it is known that a specific working environment or practice might pose specific risks to workers with particular genetic variations . . .

3.6.4 If a genetic test is used to obtain information for employment purposes ensure that it is valid and is subject to assured levels of accuracy and reliability.

6.5.6 Workplace surveillance and the European Convention

Below we will consider whether the implementation of the HRA 1998 will add to the protections provided by the DPA 1998 and other legislation in respect of workplace surveillance. The first question which arises concerns the extent to which workplace and related surveillance constitutes an interference with the protection afforded by Article 8 to workers' privacy. To the extent that such surveillance was regarded by the courts as contravening Article 8, its use by public authorities would breach section 6 of the Act unless required by legislation. Of importance to more workers is section 3 HRA which, as we saw above, requires that '[s]o far as it is possible to do so, primary legislation and subordinate legislation must be read and given effect in a way which is compatible with the Convention rights'. To the extent that Article 8 is seen as incompatible with workplace surveillance techniques, this ought to be read by the courts into RIPA, the LBP Regulations and the DPA 1998.

The first Convention case which is relevant to the application of Article 8 in this context is *Halford v UK*, in which that court rejected the UK Government's claim that surveillance which took place in the workplace could not be regarded as an interference with 'private' life.

[6.37] *Halford v UK* **(1997) 24 EHRR 523 (ECtHR)**

The applicant, one-time most senior policewoman in the UK (having held the rank of Assistant Chief Constable of Merseyside), was refused promotion to Deputy Chief Constable on a number of occasions. She eventually lodged a sex discrimination claim which resulted, she claimed, in a campaign of press leaks, telephone interception and a decision to bring disciplinary proceedings against her. The police settled her claim and she retired from service. She subsequently brought proceedings under Articles 8, 10 and 14 of the Convention, claiming that her home telephone and the telephone with which she had been provided for private use had been tapped in an attempt to obtain information to use against her in the discrimination proceedings. The complaint regarding her home telephone was determined not to have been proven, but that in respect of her work telephone succeeded before the European Court Human Rights.

Judgment:

In her application . . . to the Commission, Ms Halford complained that the interception of calls made from her office and home telephones amounted to unjustifiable interferences with her rights to respect for her private life and freedom of expression, contrary to Articles 8 and 10 of the Convention . . . that she had no effective domestic remedy in relation to the interceptions, contrary to Article 13 of the Convention . . . and that she was discriminated against on grounds of sex, contrary to Article 14 of the Convention in conjunction with Articles 8 and 10 . . .

The Government submitted that telephone calls made by Ms Halford from her workplace fell outside the protection of Article 8, because she could have had no reasonable expectation of privacy in relation to them. At the hearing before the Court, counsel for the Government expressed the view that an employer should in principle, without the prior knowledge of the employee, be able to monitor calls made by the latter on telephones provided by the employer.

In the Court's view, it is clear from its case-law that telephone calls made from business premises as well as from the home may be covered by the notions of 'private life' and 'correspondence' within the meaning of Article 8 para 1 . . .

There is no evidence of any warning having been given to Ms Halford, as a user of the internal telecommunications system operated at the Merseyside police headquarters, that calls made on that system would be liable to interception. She would, the Court considers, have had a reasonable expectation of privacy for such calls, which expectation was moreover reinforced by a number of factors. As Assistant Chief Constable she had sole use of her office where there were two telephones, one of which was specifically designated for her private use. Furthermore, she had been given the assurance, in response to a memorandum, that she could use her office telephones for the purposes of her sex-discrimination case . . .

The evidence justifies the conclusion that there was a reasonable likelihood that calls made by Ms Halford from her office were intercepted by the Merseyside police with the primary aim of gathering material to assist in the defence of the sex-discrimination proceedings brought against them . . . This interception constituted an 'interference by a public authority', within the meaning of Article 8 para 2 . . . with the exercise of Ms Halford's right to respect for her private life and correspondence.

Article 8 para 2 . . . further provides that any interference by a public authority with an individual's right to respect for private life and correspondence must be 'in accordance with the law'.

According to the Court's well-established case-law, this expression does not only necessitate compliance with domestic law, but also relates to the quality of that law, requiring it to be compatible with the rule of law. In the context of secret measures of surveillance or interception of communications by public authorities, because of the lack of public scrutiny and the risk of misuse of power, the domestic law must provide some protection to the individual against arbitrary interference with Article 8 rights . . . Thus, the domestic law must be sufficiently clear in its terms to give citizens an adequate indication as to the circumstances in and conditions on which public authorities are empowered to resort to any such secret measures . . .

In the present case, the Government accepted that if, contrary to their submission, the Court were to conclude that there had been an interference with the applicant's rights under Article 8 in relation to her office telephones, such interference was not 'in accordance with the law' since domestic law did not provide any regulation of interceptions of calls made on telecommunications systems outside the public network.

The Court notes that the [Interception of Communications Act 1985] does not apply to internal communications systems operated by public authorities, such as that at Merseyside police headquarters, and that there is no other provision in domestic law to regulate interceptions of telephone calls made on such systems . . . It cannot therefore be said that the interference was 'in accordance with the law' . . . since the domestic law did not provide adequate protection to Ms Halford against interferences by the police with her right to respect for her private life and correspondence.

It follows that there has been a violation of Article 8 in relation to the interception of calls made on Ms Halford's office telephones . . .

The lacuna identified by the Europan Court in the penultimate paragraph above has now been rectified by RIPA, although it remains to be seen whether interceptions permitted under that Act (in particular, by virtue of the LBP Regulations) are compatible with Article 8. Michael Ford (below) is critical of the decision in *Halford*, in which the finding of an interference with the applicant's Article 8 rights rested on her 'reasonable expectation of privacy' in relation to the calls on the particular facts of the case. He contrasts the decision in *Halford* with that in *Niemietz v Germany*, in which the same court took a more expansive approach to the scope of Article 8 in determining the legality of a search of a lawyer's office.

[6.38] *Niemietz v Germany* (1992) 16 EHHR 7 (ECtHR)

Judgment:
The Court does not consider it possible or necessary to attempt an exhaustive definition of 'private life'. However, it would be too restrictive to limit the notion to an 'inner circle' in which the individual may live his personal life as he chooses and to exclude therefrom entirely the outside world not encompassed within that circle. Respect for private life must also comprise to a certain degree the right to establish and develop relationships with other human beings.

There appears, furthermore, to be no reason of principle why this understanding of the notion of 'private life' should be taken to exclude activities of a professional or business nature since it is, after all, in the course of their working lives that the majority of people have a significant, if not the greatest, opportunity of developing relationships with the outside world.

[6.39] M Ford, 'Article 8 and the Right to Privacy at the Workplace', in K D Ewing (ed), *Human Rights at Work* (London, Institute of Employment Rights, 2000) pp 31 (footnotes omitted)

[T]he language of the [*Halford*] decision was perhaps more cautious than in *Niemietz*: in the absence of a warning and because of the reassurances she had been given, the Court considered that [the applicant] would 'have had a reasonable expectation of privacy' . . . The difference between the two conceptions of privacy is illustrated by how they relate to management prerogative. A conception of privacy which draws upon the right of workers to form relationships with each other ought to be resistant to attempts to remove private spaces at work. It may well require that workers are provided with locations or times when they can be sure they can be free of surveillance. But a conception based upon a reasonable expectation of privacy is, at least on its face, more easily overridden by management decisions. An employer who informs employees at his workplace that they have no right of privacy, and may be watched or listened to at any time, may argue that it has removed any prior expectation they had of privacy. Take, for example, CCTV: on the *Niemietz* conception one would expect that the employer would be under a duty to provide areas free from such surveillance; on the *Halford* conception the matter is much less clear, for it may be argued that the very presence of cameras reduces any expectation of privacy. It is significant that US case-law on the Fourth Amendment, which has drawn on a reasonable expectation test, has offered little resistance to management prerogative.

The resolution by the European Court of Human Rights of the apparent tension between the *Niemietz* and *Halford* decisions will be of great significance to the regulation of workplace surveillance under the HRA 1998 (whether the Act is used directly by applicant claiming under section 7, or indirectly by those seeking to rely on section 3's interpretive provision). If the *Niemietz* approach is preferred, the Act is capable of providing significant protections both by virtue of section 6, where public authority employers are concerned, and also by virtue of section 3. The possible application of these provisions is considered below (section 6.5.7). If, on the other hand, *Halford* is followed, the HRA 1998 may provide little additional protection, as far as the interception of workplace communications and the surveillance of workers through CCTV and the monitoring of keyboard use and internet access are concerned, to that afforded by RIPA and the DPA 1998 absent consideration of the interpretive obligation imposed by section 3 HRA 1998. Having said this, even under the *Halford* approach workers may have a 'reasonable expectation of privacy', at least in the absence of clear and express warning to the contrary, in relation to emails access to which is protected by a password, or which have been deleted. And even if *Niemietz* is preferred, surveillance by employers will still be justified where it is in pursuit of a 'pressing social need' and where it is proportionate to that end.

Halford and *Niemietz* concern the interception of workplace communications. But this is not the only type of surveillance to which Article 8 applies. It is clear from the jurisprudence of the European Court that compulsory blood and urine testing amount to 'interferences' under Article 8 (*X v Austria* (1979) 18 DR 75, *Peters v Netherlands* (1994) 77A DR 75). The decisions of the ECtHR in *Lustig-Prean & Beckett v UK* and in *Smith & Grady v UK* were mentioned above. These, too, suggest that some measure of protection against 'lifestyle' discrimination might be required by Article 8 notwithstanding the recent decision of the Court of Appeal in *X v Y* **[6.8]**. This is not to say that all such surveillance would breach Article 8. There may be circumstances in which the employer's legitimate interests (in the prevention of crime, for example, or the protection of the health and safety of employees) would justify video surveillance or alcohol testing. Where action is taken against workers on the grounds of political, trade union or related beliefs or activities discovered by workplace surveillance or otherwise, the protections afforded by Articles 10 and 11 would apply. There may also be cases where action taken against workers on the grounds of political or related beliefs or activities discovered by workplace surveillance or otherwise, could be justified in line with the employer's legitimate interests (in the case of a race equality body, or the police, prison or probation service, for example, in avoiding the recruitment or retention of BNP infiltrators). And, whether the *Halford* or the *Niemietz* test gains the ascendancy, some employers' obligations to protect staff from sexual harassment may require a degree of surveillance over the content, *inter alia*, of material downloaded by and circulated amongst staff.

[6.40] IDS, *Employee Privacy in the Workplace,* **(London, Incomes Data Services, 2001) Employment Supplement No 6, Series 2, pp 64–65**

Even if the pornography is not directly shown to a woman, it may create an embarrassing or uncomfortable work environment which in itself can lead to a finding that a woman required to work in such an environment has been discriminated against . . .

In *Morse v Future Reality Ltd* ET Case No 54571/95, for example, a woman was required to work in an open-planned office shared with several men who spent a considerable amount of their time poring over explicit pictures downloaded from the Internet. Although they never directly involved her in their activities, she nonetheless felt uncomfortable and eventually resigned. A tribunal held that the general atmosphere of obscenity in the workplace concerned was such as to cause the applicant to be discriminated against . . . The employers were liable because they had done nothing to warn the employees about their conduct and had been content to tolerate the office environment as it was. [See also *Moonsar v Fiveways Express Transport Ltd* [2005] IRLR 9, discussed in section 3.3.1.3.]

Surveillance of the content of email traffic may also be justified by the employer's interest in avoiding liability for defamatory statements by its staff. In 1998, damages of £450,000 were awarded against Norwich Union in respect of internal emails circulated by some of its employees to the effect that a rival organisation was in financial difficulties and was under investigation by the DTI. British Gas had a similar experience in 1999 to the cost of £101,000. Employers can avoid liability in respect of this type of defamation only where, *inter alia*, they took reasonable care in relation to the publication of the defamatory statement and did not know, and had no reason to believe, that their actions contributed to its publication.

[6.41] IDS *Employee Privacy in the Workplace* **(London, Incomes Data Services, 2001) Employment Supplement No 6, Series 2**

If the employer shows disregard for the activities of his employees, he is unlikely to satisfy the requirement of 'reasonable care'. The presence or absence of a clear and regulated policy on e-mail . . . usage could be crucial in this regard, since it is widely thought that the requirement of 'reasonable care' implies an obligation . . . to undertake at least some degree of monitoring. And . . . if the employer has been alerted to the possibility of an employee's e-mail being defamatory, then should he fail to take immediate steps to distance himself from the statement and remove the chance of its further dissemination he will have no defence . . .

Another problem relates to the downloading and copying of software. There is a real risk that employers may find that unlicensed software is installed on computers throughout the organisation if they do not have sufficient safeguards to prevent against such abuses.

It is clear that some types of surveillance will serve employer's legitimate interests. But, where Article 8 is engaged, interference will be justified only if prescribed by law, in pursuit of a 'pressing social need' (*Dudgeon v UK* (1982) 4 EHRR 149, *Smith & Grady v UK* and *Lustig-Prean & Beckett v UK*, above), and necessary in a democratic society. We saw that the requirement that interferences with Convention rights be 'prescribed by law' was taken to be satisfied, in *Lustig-Prean & Beckett*, by a widely publicised ban on gays in the military, and, in *Kara v UK*, by an employer's internal dress code. Where employers' surveillance policies are made clear to workers, this requirement may well be satisfied. But where, as in *Halford*, covert surveillance is employed, this condition is unlikely to be satisfied save where (*Huvig v France* (1990) 12 EHRR 528) the rules governing such surveillance 'indicate with reasonable clarity the scope and manner of exercise of the relevant discretion'.

As to the requirement for proportionality between any 'pressing social need' on the part of the employer and the means used for its pursuit, the ECtHR stressed in *Lustig-Prean & Beckett* and in *Smith & Grady*, as it had in *Dudgeon*, that when the relevant restrictions concern 'a most intimate part of an individual's private life', there must exist 'particularly serious reasons' before such interferences can satisfy the requirements of Article 8 (2) of the Convention. On the one hand, the fundamental matter of sexual orientation might be regarded as requiring especially rigorous protections. On the other hand, however, the aim to which the interference at issue in the *Lustig-Prean & Beckett* and the *Smith & Grady* cases was directed—the operational effectiveness of the armed forces and, consequently, 'the interests of national security' and 'the prevention of disorder'—attracts a considerable margin of appreciation on the part of the Contracting States (*Leander v Sweden* (1987) 9 EHRR 433).

6.5.7 Workplace surveillance and the Human Rights Act

We saw, above, that section 6 HRA 1998 makes it unlawful for public authorities to breach Convention rights save to the extent that they are required so to do by legislation. Neither RIPA nor the DPA 1998 require public authorities, as employers, to interfere with workers' privacy or with their other Convention rights. The LBP Regulations permit employers to intercept communications during the course of their transmission via private networks operated by the employer. But section 3 HRA 1998 requires the courts to interpret secondary, as well as primary legislation 'so far as it is possible to do so', to render it consistent with the relevant Convention Articles (here Article 8). The 'validity, continuing operation or enforcement' of secondary legislation is saved from the possibility of 'strike-down' only where (section 3(2)(c)) '(disregarding any possibility of revocation) primary legislation prevents removal of the incompatibility'. The LBP Regulations were issued under sections 4(2) and 78(5) RIPA which empower the Secretary of State to 'authorise any such conduct . . . as appears to him to constitute a legitimate practice reasonably required for the purpose, in connection with the carrying on of any business, of monitoring or keeping a record of—(a) communications by means of which transactions are entered into in the course of that business; or (b) other communications relating to that business or taking place in the course of its being carried on'. No requirement is imposed on the Secretary of State to issue regulations which contravene any of the Convention Articles. To the extent that the LBP Regulations are inconsistent with any such Articles, therefore, they will provide no defence under section 6(2) to public authorities. The question for the courts will be whether any particular surveillance episode contravenes any Article of the Convention.

Turning next to the application of the HRA 1998 to surveillance by employers other than 'core' public authorities (see section 6.2.1 above), the question which arises concerns the proper interpretation by the courts of the DPA 1998 and the LBP Regulations. Action may be taken by workers under RIPA itself (any defence provided to employers in respect of telecommunications interception by the LBP Regulations applying only to the extent that those Regulations are consistent with the Convention Articles) or, in an appropriate case, under the DPA 1998. If it were to be determined, in any particular case, that the interception of communications was not justified under Article 8 (bearing in mind , the diluted protection afforded by the Convention Articles in relation to private employment), such interception would amount to a statutory tort by virtue of section 1(3) RIPA. In the case of other surveillance (such as, for example, CCTV monitoring, drugs or alcohol testing, the collection of genetic or other medical data), the application of the HRA 1998 would, in the first instance, be via the interpretation of the DPA 1998. We saw above (section 6.5.2) that the DPPs limit the circumstances under which 'personal data' may be processed (this term, significantly, extending to the collection as well as the retention, disclosure, etc., of such data). The impact on the DPA 1998 of the HRA 1998 (section 3) may be felt, in particular, in the approach taken to the definitions of 'relevant filing system' post *Durant* and of the first DPP, in particular, to the questions:

- whether processing is 'lawful'; and
- whether the processing of workplace surveillance-related data 'for the purposes of legitimate interests pursued by the data controller . . . is unwarranted in any particular case by reason of prejudice to the rights and freedoms or legitimate interests of the data subject' (Schedule 2, para 6).

Taking the question of relevant filing systems first, where the processing of manual data breaches Article 8 a more generous to the application of the DPA 1998 than that adopted by the Court of Appeal in *Durant* may be required. It is unlikely that the processing of data not regarded as 'personal' by the Court of Appeal would impact on Article 8 rights. To the extent that the collection or other processing of personal data breached Article 8, section 3 HRA 1998 may be taken to require that it be regarded as unlawful for the purposes of the first DPP. The question whether interference by a private employer will in fact infringe Article 8 will turn on the degree to which that Article is accepted as imposing positive obligations on the state (see further 6.2.1 above). As far as the application of section 55 is concerned, an employer has a defence to criminal proceedings if (section 55(2)(b)) 'he acted in the reasonable belief that he had in law the right to obtain' the data'. Such a defence might be made out where (at least prior to any judicial impeachment of them), the data was obtained in reliance on the LBP Regs. Whether the defence would be made out in any other case would be a matter for the courts. Significant here, again, would be the degree of horizontality accorded to the Convention Article.

We saw, above, that the first DPP will also be breached where personal data is obtained or otherwise processed unless one of the conditions in Schedule 2 to the Act is met. In the context of workplace surveillance, those conditions likely to be of relevance are (1) that the worker has consented to the processing, or (2) that the processing was carried out 'for the purposes of legitimate interests pursued by the data controller', unless in any particular case it was 'unwarranted . . . by reason of prejudice to the rights and freedoms or legitimate interests of the data subject'. The definition of consent adopted by the Data Protection Directive is relatively narrow. Where it is not satisfied, compliance with the first DPP will turn on the balance between the employer's legitimate interests and the rights of the workers concerned. Again, the proper approach to this condition will require that the Article 8 rights of the workers are taken into account. It is of interest here to note, in connection specifically with drugs testing, the conclusions of the recent independent inquiry into this issue:

[6.42] Independent Inquiry into Drug Testing at Work, *Drug testing in the workplace* **(2004, Joseph Rowntree Foundation), Summary Conclusions**

Key findings

- The evidence on the links between drug use and accidents at work, absenteeism, low productivity and poor performance was inconclusive . . .
- There is a lack of evidence for a strong link between drug use and accidents in safety-critical industries, such as transport, engineering, quarrying and mining. Clearly, however, drug- and alcohol-induced intoxication will be a source of risk in such environments.
- However, other factors may have a greater impact on safety, productivity and performance, including bad working conditions, sleeping and health problems, excessive workloads and work-related stress.
- Evidence considered by the [Inquiry] suggests that alcohol is probably a greater cause for concern in the workplace than illicit drugs.
- There is no clear evidence that drug testing at work has a significant deterrent effect.
- Drug testing is not a measure of current intoxication and will reveal information about drug use that can have no impact on safety, productivity or performance. Someone may test positive after taking a drug days, weeks or months before.
- People are not generally required to organise their lives to maximise their productivity at work, and employers do not have a direct law enforcement function. Empowering employers to investigate private behaviour actively—in the absence of legitimate safety or performance concerns—is in conflict with liberal-democratic values.
- Drug testing services in the UK are being provided by a very disparate group of companies and individuals. Many of them are very responsible. But the picture is mixed, with evidence that some of these companies may be making what appear to be inflated claims about the extent and impact of alcohol and drug problems in the workplace and the effectiveness of their own products . . .

6.6 Whistleblowing: freedom of expression in the workplace?

The final human rights issue we deal with here concerns whistleblowing by employees. The subject has attracted considerable attention over recent years, most recently in connection with medical scandals (the deaths of heart operation babies at the Bristol Royal Infirmary, the organ-hoarding scandal at Alder Hay children's hospital and elsewhere). We saw, in chapter 2, that confidentiality is protected by implied and, frequently, express contractual terms. The implementation of the HRA 1998 is unlikely to impact significantly on the availability of injunctions to protect confidential information after the termination of employment, Article 10(2) permitting restrictions necessary to prevent the 'disclosure of information received in confidence' and the approach of the domestic courts to the type of information capable of protection, whether by express or implied term, being narrow. Different questions arise, however, concerning disclosures made by those in employment which breach express or implied terms relating to confidentiality or to fidelity. In some cases, such disclosures might be regarded as being in the 'public interest'. The same is true of disclosures made in breach of the Official Secrets Act 1989 whose terms do not permit public interest disclosures.

Prior to the implementation of the Public Interest Disclosure Act 1998 (PIDA 1998), whistleblowing employees were relatively unprotected from employer retribution. While the disclosure of criminal and other misconduct might well, in any given case, ultimately be declared to have been in the 'public interest', with the effect that no breach of confidence (express or implied) occurred, little recourse was available against employers who dismissed or otherwise acted to the detriment of whistleblowing employees. Retribution might amount to a breach of contract or, in the case of a dismissal, to a potentially unfair dismissal. But such protections as predated PIDA 1998 were wholly inadequate. Employers were not generally restricted, as a matter of contract, from dismissing for any reason, or for no reason at all. And although the dismissal of a whistleblowing employee might be unfair, external disclosure would almost certainly be regarded as misconduct by the broad range of employers, and even internal disclosure might be regarded as 'some other substantial reason' for dismissal. The 'range of reasonable responses' approach taken by tribunals to the question of fairness stacked the odds against employees, particularly when coupled with the fact that the employer's behaviour had to be assessed at the point of dismissal, rather than *ex post facto* in the light of any decision that the whistleblowing was legally justified. And even if the dismissal (actual or, in the case of detrimental treatment of an employee, constructive) was ultimately judged to have been unfair; compensation was, for the most part, limited (until the implementation of the Employment Relations Act 1999, to a maximum £12,000) and redress generally available only to those with a year's qualifying employment.

6.6.1 The Public Interest Disclosure Act

PIDA 1998 increased the protections afforded to whistleblowing employees and to other workers, very broadly defined. The Act amends the ERA 1996 to protect employees against dismissal and detriment short of dismissal on the ground of 'protected disclosures'. It provides (new section 43J ERA 1996) that 'Any provision in an agreement [between a worker and his employer] is void in so far as it purports to preclude the worker from making a protected disclosure' and makes available interim relief in respect of dismissals alleged to be by reason of protected disclosures. Compensation payable in respect of detriment or dismissal in connection with protected disclosures is unlimited and, unlike most unfair dismissal claims, can give rise to compensation for injury to feelings. In *Virgo Fidelis Senior School v Boyle* the EAT ruled that the principles applicable in discrimination cases (in particular, those set out by the Court of Appeal in *Vento v Chief Constable of West Yorkshire Police*) applied in whistle blowing cases (for the application of these principles in discrimination cases see 3.9.4).

Disclosures are 'protected' for the purposes of PIDA 1998 only if they are 'qualifying disclosures' within new section 43B ERA 1996 (below) *and* if they are made to an appropriate person. A 'qualifying disclosure' is one which 'in the reasonable belief of the worker making the disclosure, tends to show':

[6.43] Employment Rights Act 1996, section 43B

S.43B(1)(a) that a criminal offence has been committed, is being committed or is likely to be committed,

(b) that a person has failed, is failing or is likely to fail to comply with any legal obligation to which he is subject,

(c) that a miscarriage of justice has occurred, is occurring or is likely to occur,

(d) that the health or safety of any individual has been, is being or is likely to be endangered,

(e) that the environment has been, is being or is likely to be damaged, or

(f) that information tending to show any matter falling within any one of the preceding paragraphs has been, is being or is likely to be deliberately concealed.

(3) A disclosure of information is not a qualifying disclosure if the person making the disclosure commits an offence by making it.

(4) A disclosure of information in respect of which a claim to legal professional privilege (or, in Scotland, to confidentiality as between client and professional legal adviser) could be maintained in legal proceedings is not a qualifying disclosure if it is made by a person to whom the information had been disclosed in the course of obtaining legal advice.

[6.44] *Kraus v Penna plc* [2004] IRLR 260 (EAT)

Here the EAT considered the nature of 'qualifying disclosures' under PIDA 1998. The claim was brought by a human resources consultant who complained that his services to a client had been dispensed with after he advised the client that a planned redundancy programme could make the company vulnerable to unfair dismissal claims (see s. 43B(1)(b) ERA 1996). The EAT upheld a tribunal's decision to strike out his claim as misconceived, ruling (a) that the Claimant had not made any disclosure to the effect that the client 'ha[d] failed, [wa]s failing or [wa]s likely to fail to comply with any legal obligation to which he [wa]s subject', this on the ground (*per* Cox J) that 'likely' denoted 'more than a possibility, or a risk, that an employer . . . might fail to comply with a relevant legal obligation', requiring rather 'that it is probable or more probable than not that the employer will fail to comply with the relevant legal obligation'; (b) that section 43B could be breached only by a legal obligation which actually existed.

Cox J:

if the employers are under no legal obligation, as a matter of law, a worker cannot claim the protection of this legislation by claiming that he reasonably believed that they were. His belief and the reasonableness of it in our view relates to the factual information in his possession, namely what he perceives to be the facts and the basis on which he considers it reasonable to rely upon them. This can only properly be tested against the background of the legal obligation, 'to which [the employer or other person] is subject'. If there is no obligation to which they actually are subject the worker's suggestion that he reasonably believed they were cannot render the disclosure a protected one within ss.43A and B . . .

The EAT took the view that it did not have to decide whether employers were under a legal obligation not to subject workers to unfair dismissal, this because of its decision on the question of 'likely' breach. But the commentary in the IRLR was concerned with the implications of the appeal tribunal's reasoning:

[6.45] IRLR 'Highlights', April 2004

This appears to be drawing a distinction between a case where the employer is clearly under some legal obligation and the employee reasonably but mistakenly believes there was a breach, and a case where the employee reasonably but mistakenly believes that the employer was under a legal obligation which it has breached. That does not seem to be a valid distinction, at least in a case such as this one where it was beyond doubt that the employer had various legal obligations to its employees when carrying out a redundancy exercise. If the protection against victimisation for making a disclosure does not extend to both sets of circumstances, it would severely limit the scope of these provisions. In the case of an allegation of failure to comply with a legal obligation, to hold that the employer must be under a legal obligation in order for the worker to be protected means that if there is any doubt, the worker will need to take legal advice before making the disclosure.

The approach taken in *Kraus* is in one sense narrow. But Mrs Justice Cox cited with approval the EAT's earlier decision in *Parkins v Sodexho Ltd* in which the appeal tribunal had accepted that an alleged breach of contract of employment on the part of the employer amounted to a failure to comply with a legal obligation for the purposes of PIDA 1998. The Claimant had been dismissed after complaining of inadequate supervision which he alleged breached the health and safety obligations imposed on his employers by his contract of employment. A tribunal ruled that the alleged breach did not 'come . . . within the letter or spirit of the statutory provisions' but the EAT allowed his appeal on the grounds that there was no basis on which to distinguish between legal obligations arising from contract and otherwise. The decision in *Parkins* entailed a very broad approach to the provisions of what, as the IRLR commentary pointed out, is after all the Public Interest Disclosure Act.

New sections 43C–43H ERA 1996 set out the circumstances in which 'qualifying disclosures' will be protected within PIDA 1998. There are where such disclosures are made:

- in the course of obtaining legal advice (section 43D ERA 1996); or
- in good faith, to the worker's employer or to a person other than his employer, in

accordance with a procedure whose use by him is authorised by his employer (section 43C ERA 1996); or

- in good faith, where the worker reasonably believes that the relevant failure relates solely or mainly to—
  - (a) the conduct of a person other than his employer, or
  - (b) any other matter for which a person other than his employer has legal responsibility, to that other person (section 43C(1)(b) ERA 1996); or
- in good faith, to a Minister of the Crown, where the employer is (i) an individual appointed under any enactment by a Minister of the Crown, or (ii) a body any of whose members are so appointed (section 43E ERA 1996); or
- (i) in good faith, (ii) by someone who reasonably believes that the information disclosed and any allegation contained in it are substantially true and that the matter in respect of which the disclosure is made 'falls within any description of matters in respect of which that person is so prescribed', to a person prescribed by an order made by the Secretary of State (section 43F ERA 1996), or
- (i) in good faith, (ii) by someone who reasonably believes that the information disclosed and any allegation contained in it are substantially true and (iii) who does not make the disclosure for personal gain, where (iv) it is reasonable in all the circumstances of the case to make the disclosure to another person in circumstances in which the relevant failure is of an exceptionally serious nature (section 43H). Section 43H(2) ERA 1996 provides that '[i]n determining . . . whether it is reasonable for the worker to make the disclosure, regard shall be had, in particular, to the identity of the person to whom the disclosure is made; *or*
- (i) in good faith, (ii) by someone who reasonably believes that the information disclosed and any allegation contained in it are substantially true and (iii) who does not make the disclosure for personal gain, where (iv) it is reasonable in all the circumstances of the case to make the disclosure to another person in circumstances in which (section 43G):
  - (a) the worker reasonably believes that he will be subjected to a detriment by his employer if he makes a disclosure to his employer or in accordance with section 43F, *or*
  - (b) where no person is prescribed for the purposes of section 43F in relation to the relevant failure, the worker reasonably believes that it is likely that evidence relating to the relevant failure will be concealed or destroyed if he makes a disclosure to his employer, *or*
  - (c) the worker has previously made a disclosure of substantially the same information (i) to his employer, or (ii) in accordance with section 43F.

Section 43G(2) ERA 1996 provides that '[i]n determining . . . whether it is reasonable for the worker to make a disclosure other than those protected by virtue of sections 43C, 43D, 43E, 43F or 43H ERA 1996, regard shall be had, in particular, to—

- (a) the identity of the person to whom the disclosure is made,
- (b) the seriousness of the relevant failure,
- (c) whether the relevant failure is continuing or is likely to occur in the future, and
- (d) whether the disclosure is made in breach of a duty of confidentiality owed by the employer to any other person.

Further, where the disclosure has previously been made to the employer or in accordance with section 43F ERA 1996, regard shall also be had to:

(e) .... any action which the employer or the person to whom the previous disclosure ... was made has taken or might reasonably be expected to have taken as a result of the previous disclosure, and, where disclosure was made to the employer (or in accordance with a procedure authorised by the employer), and to

(f) whether in making the disclosure to the employer the worker complied with any procedure whose use by him was authorised by the employer.

These provisions are complex and require, in many cases, that a person making a disclosure comply with a number of factors in order to gain PIDA's protection.

[6.46] *Street v Derbyshire Unemployed Workers' Centre* [2004] ICR 213 (CA)

Auld LJ:
in s.43C, all that a worker who makes a disclosure to his employer or to another responsible person, or under s.43E – disclosure to a Minister of the Crown – has to do to qualify to for automatic protection is to show that his disclosure was made 'in good faith' ...

The second tier of disclosure, in which greater justification is required for protection, is that provided by s.43F – disclosure to a prescribed person – where, in addition to showing that the disclosure was made 'in good faith', the worker must show that he reasonably believed that the malpractice of which he complained falls within the description of the matters in respect of which that person is prescribed and that his complaint is 'substantially true' ...

The third tier of protection ... is that provided for in s.43G ... where the 'whistleblower' has to do much more to justify his automatic protection. In addition to showing that he made the disclosure 'in good faith' under s.43G(1)(a), he must show that it was made:

(i) in the reasonable belief that the information disclosed, and any allegation contained in it, were substantially true' (s.43G(1)(b));
(ii) it was not made for purposes of personal gain' (s.43G(1)(c));
(iii) satisfaction of *any one* of a number of specified conditions going to the worker's reasonable belief that he would suffer detriment or that evidence of the subject-matter of his complaint would be concealed (s.43G(1)(d)); and
(iv) 'in all the circumstances of the case, it was reasonable for him to make the disclosure' (s.43G(1)(e)), in the determination of which, regard must be had to a number of factors in a non-exhaustive list in s.43G(3), including the identity of the person to whom the disclosure was made, the seriousness of the failure complained of and whether it was continuing or was likely to continue.

It is plain from that summary of the relevant provisions that; (1) the conditions in s.43G(1) are cumulative, that is, that a disclosure is only a 'qualifying disclosure' if all of them are met; (2) the conditions in s.43G(2) are disjunctive, that is, it is sufficient if any one of them is met; (3) there is some overlap between them all; and (4) in making separate and cumulative provision in s.43G(1) for 'good faith' in (a), reasonable belief in the truth of the disclosure in (b) and reasonableness of the disclosure in all the circumstance in (e), the draftsman has allowed for circumstances in which the disclosure, though made with reasonable belief in its truth, would not qualify for protection because it was not made in good faith and/or reasonably.

The EAT considered the meaning of 'reasonable belief' in *Darnton v University of Surrey*. The case involved a lecturer who was dismissed after he wrote a letter to the vice-chancellor of the university in which he made a number of allegations against the head of department and the university. His claim that he reasonably believed that the allegations tended to show that a criminal offence had been committed or that the university was in breach of various legal obligations was dismissed by a tribunal on the basis that the allegations were factually incorrect. The EAT allowed his appeal, ruling that PIDA 1998 required only that it had been reasonable for him to believe that the factual basis of his allegation was true and that these facts, as understood by the worker, tended to show a relevant failure.

[6.47] *Street v Derbyshire Unemployed Workers' Centre* [2004] ICR 213 (CA)

Here the Court of Appeal went on to consider the meaning of 'good faith' and the relationship between malicious motivation and the question whether a disclosure was reasonable in the circumstances of a case. The Court rejected an appeal from a woman dismissed for gross misconduct and breach of trust in connection with allegations made by her of breach of contract of employment by a fellow worker. The Court ruled that the tribunal had been entitled to find against her on the ground that her allegations were not made in good faith, despite her belief in their truth, because they were motivated by her dislike of her fellow worker.

Auld LJ:
The tribunal clearly took the view that, although there was some overlap between the requirements of good faith and of reasonable belief in the honesty of the content of a disclosure, that of good faith did add something, namely a consideration of motive. Having taken into account the circumstances surrounding Mrs Street's allegations, including their timing and her failure to cooperate with the later investigation, it concluded that none of them had been made in good faith, but had instead been motivated by her personal antagonism towards Mr Hampton [to whom they related]. It, therefore, dismissed her claim to automatic protection under s.103A from dismissal . . .

Before moving on to the tribunal's consideration of good faith, I should say something about its favourable finding to Mrs Street on the issue of reasonableness<N>. . . It may be that [the tribunal] overlooked the fact that it was required, in the words of s.43G(1)(e), to have regard to 'all the circumstances of the case', not just those potential candidates listed in s.43G(3). It may be that it confused its enquiry as to reasonableness under those provisions with that under s.43G(1)(d) and (2) where satisfaction of any one of the conditions in s.43G(2) would suffice. It may be that it took the view that, although it had found, in considering the issue of good faith, that Mrs Street had made her attack on Mr Hampton in bad faith fuelled by her personal antagonism to him, it had to put that out of its mind when considering whether her conduct was 'in all the circumstances of the case . . . reasonable . . . ' If so, as will appear, I consider that it erred in those respects . . .

Mr. Joel Donovan, on behalf of Mrs. Street, appeared at first in his submissions to accept that the requirement of good faith in s.43G(1)(a) is distinct from that of reasonable belief in the truth of disclosure in s.43G(1)(b). The distinction that he purported to draw was that, in addition to a reasonable belief in the truth of the disclosure, for it to be made in good faith a worker must make it 'honestly' or with 'with honest intention'. But when pressed by the Court in the course of his submission as to the meaning of 'honestly' or 'with honest intention' in this context and its distinction, if any, from reasonable belief in the truth of the information disclosed, he said that they are virtually 'indivisible' in meaning. He suggested that, if motivation is relevant, it would have to be both malicious and predominant to amount to bad faith. However, he submitted that the employment tribunal, in finding that Mrs Street had believed in the truth of her allegations, accepted 'in effect' that she had acted 'honestly' or 'with honest intention' and, thereby, in good faith . . .

In his submissions, Mr Donovan drew on and adopted the written submissions to the Court of Public Concern at Work ('Public Concern'), which it made, with the permission of the Court, as an interested party. Public Concern is an independent charity and a legal advice centre established in 1993 specialising in advising both employees and employers on 'whistleblowing'. It is popularly known as 'the whistleblowing charity'. The main thrust of its submission on this appeal, for which the Court is grateful, was that it would seriously damage the purpose of the 1998 Act and the protection it provides in the public interest to 'whistleblowers' if ulterior motivation, in particular the promotion of a grudge, were to deprive a disclosure of the quality of having been made in good faith. It urged the Court to look at the general application of the Act, in particular, the protection that it provides against pre-dismissal reprisals. Its primary submission was that a disclosure made in good faith under the Act means simply one that is made honestly, that is with a view to something being done about the failure disclosed, and that where it is made with mixed motives, the good faith requirement is satisfied where it is made honestly in that sense even if accompanied by an ulterior motivation, such as a personal grudge . . .

Public Concern, in its written submission, suggested that the practical difficulty posed by any suggestion that a grudge or personal animosity or other motive is a bar to protection would be to cause a worker, considering making a disclosure in the public interest, to fear that he might lose protection and discourage him from doing so. And, as it suggested, such a state of mind is often integral to claims of this sort. That is especially so, as a claim can only be brought under the Act once the worker making it has been dismissed, and it is, therefore, easy for his employer to identify and allege . . .

On the broad point of construction by reference to the stated purpose of the 1998 Act, the reasoning of the Employment Appeal Tribunal . . . is to the point. Its purpose is not to allow persons to advance personal grudges, but to protect those 'who make certain disclosures in the public interest'; namely those specified in s.43B of the 1996 Act. And it has to be remembered that even if a worker might be deterred from making a relevant disclosure because of concern that his employer might raise against him a suggestion of bad faith in the sense of a mix of motives, including personal antagonism, or fails in his s.103A claim on that account, all is not lost. His automatic protection provided by that section is lost, but he can still maintain an 'ordinary' claim for unfair dismissal against his employer in which a mix of motives may not be fatal to his claim . . .

in my view, s.43G provides a collection of partially overlapping requirements, any one of which, if not fulfilled, will defeat a worker's right to maintain that his disclosure is 'protected' within the meaning of the Act. Whether, in the circumstances of any particular case, the claim is defeated on that account is essentially a matter for the employment tribunal to assess on a broad and common-sense basis as a matter of fact, in the light of each of requirements in paras. (1)(a)–(e) of the section. Whether it approaches the question through one or more than one of those requirements and whether or not they overlap is essentially a matter for its evaluation on the evidence before it.

In considering good faith as distinct from reasonable belief in the truth of the disclosure, it is clearly open to an employment tribunal, where satisfied as to the latter, to consider nevertheless whether the disclosure was not made in good faith because of some ulterior motive, which may or may not have involved a motivation of personal gain, and/or which, in all the circumstances of the case, may or may not have made the disclosure unreasonable. Whether the nature or degree of any ulterior motive found amounts to bad faith, or whether the motive of personal gain was of such a nature or strength as to 'make the disclosure for purposes of personal gain' or 'in all the circumstances of the case' not reasonable, is equally a matter for its assessment on a broad basis . . .

it seems more in keeping with the declared public interest purpose of this legislation, fair, and a more useful guide to employment tribunals in conducting this . . . exercise . . . to hold that they should only find that a disclosure was not made in good faith when they are of the view that the dominant or predominant purpose of making it was for some ulterior motive, not that purpose . . .

In my view, where, as here, the employment tribunal was driven on the evidence to conclude, as it did, that none of Mrs Street's disclosures 'could be regarded as made in good faith, but were instead motivated by . . . [her] personal antagonism toward Mr Hampton', it is plain, as the Employment Appeal Tribunal stated in paragraph 25 of its judgment, that it found that such personal antagonism was her dominant, if not her sole, motive. In my view, the Employment Appeal Tribunal was right not to interfere with that finding. Looked at against the broader public policy interest behind this legislation, protection of such powerfully motivated disclosures could not be said in the circumstances to serve or encourage subversion of the Act's declared overall purpose . . . of protecting those 'who make certain disclosures of information in the public interest.

Where a protected disclosure is made, section 43B ERA 1996 provides that a worker (as distinct from an employee) is entitled 'not to be subjected to any detriment by any act, or any deliberate failure to act, by his employer done on the ground that the worker has made a protected disclosure'. The 'detriment' prohibited by this section extends to 'dismissal' in the case of non-employees, other dismissals being categorised as automatically unfair (and subject to neither a qualifying period of employment nor a retirement age cut-off) under section 103A ERA 1996 (as amended by PIDA 1998). Interim relief is available and compensation, whether for detriment or dismissal in respect of protected disclosures, is not subject to limitation.

In *London Borough of Harrow v Knight* the EAT overturned a tribunal decision that the Claimant, who suffered a nervous breakdown during a lengthy investigation by his employer into allegations by him relating to breaches of environmental health regulations, had been subjected to a detriment contrary to section 47B(1) ERA 1996. The chief executive had failed to reply to letters from Mr Knight during the course of the investigation. The EAT ruled that the tribunal had failed to determine whether the detriment had been done by the employers 'on the ground that' the Claimant had made the protected disclosure, as distinct from whether the detriment was 'related to' the protected disclosure. In order to establish a claim under section 47B the Claimant had to establish that the employer had acted (consciously or unconsciously) *because of* the protected disclosure, not simply that the detriment would not have occurred *but for* the disclosure.

The implementation of PIDA 1998 has made significant improvements to the position of whistleblowers. But outside its protections remain those whose disclosures are not of the appropriate type or are to the wrong recipients. Lucy Vickers points out ('Freedom of Speech in the National Health Service' (1999) 21 *Journal of*

Social Welfare and Family Law 120) that, although in the NHS context, 'most concerns . . . . will relate to current, potential or past dangers to health and safety, if not to other listed matters . . . . general discussion of the policies adopted in running the NHS would probably not be covered'. Participation in such discussions (for example, in a televised debate) might contravene express contractual terms or, possible, implied duties of fidelity. Crucially, disclosures which breach the criminal law are not covered by PIDA 1998.

6.6.2 Whistleblowing and the European Convention

Bowers and Lewis, **[6.48]** below, discuss the justification of interference with the rights protected by Article 10 in the context of whistleblowing. The general approach taken by the ECtHR to the legality of interferences is apparent from the *Vogt* case, **[6.12]** above. In the context of Article 10, Bowers and Lewis point out that the first hurdle (that the interference must be prescribed by law) is rarely difficult to scale: '[e]ven in cases where there may have been considerable doubt as to the proper construction of the law, the European Court of Human Rights has generally been willing to accept that it is for the national authorities to interpret and apply domestic law'. As for the second hurdle (that the interference must be in pursuit of a 'legitimate aim'): '[t]here has, in fact, been no case where an infringement of Article 10 has been held to be unjustified on the basis that a legitimate aim was not pursued . . . In many cases where the restriction on freedom of expression relates to whistleblowing the restriction could be said to be aimed at protecting the rights of employers'.

Among the aims which interference with whistleblowers might pursue are the rights and the reputation of the employer (*Morissens v Belgium* (1988) 56 DR 127). The legality of the interference will generally turn on the relationship between the seriousness of the interference and the importance of the aim it is designed to pursue. Bowers and Lewis cite *Barthold v Germany* (1986) 13 EHRR 431 to the effect that an interference will only be 'necessary in a democratic society' if it it pursues a 'pressing social need' and is proportionate to that need. But 'while these general pronouncements require a particularly close scrutiny of any purported justification for interfering with the free expression of the whistleblower, the case law of the Commission and Court is considerably less reassuring'. The authors go on to identify seven factors to which particular regard is had by the Convention organs in determining whether interference with freedom of expression is justified in the whistleblowing context:

[6.48] J Bowers and J Lewis, 'Whistleblowing: Freedom of Expression in the Workplace' [1996] 1 *European Human Rights Law Review* 637, p 640 (footnotes omitted)

(1) 'the duties and responsibilities of the particular employment';
(2) the nature of the employment;
(3) 'whether the whistleblowing touches on matters of public concern';
(4) 'the manner of expression';
(5) the extent to which the accusations made by the whistleblower are well-founded;

(6) the channel of communication used by the whistleblower;
(7) 'whether the sanction is imposed by the state'.

It is clear from the authors' analysis that the incorporation of Article 10 promises little improvement, save in respect of one category of whistleblowing cases discussed below (section 6.5.3), from the position under PIDA 1998. In *Morissens v Belgium* (1988) 56 DR 127, for example, the Commission dismissed as manifestly unfounded an Article 10 claim by a schoolteacher who was dismissed after she publicly accused her employers of having discriminated against her on grounds of her sexual orientation. The Commission there took the view that Morissens 'had accepted a responsible post in the provincial education service and that she had therefore accepted certain restrictions on the exercise of her freedom of expression as being inherent in her duties'. In *Tucht v Federal Republic of Germany* (1982 Appl No 9336/81, unpublished, discussed by Bowers and Lewis at p 645) the Commission rejected an Article 10 claim by a health service employee dismissed after he copied his 'abusive and offensive' letters criticising the organisation and working of the regional public health service to the trade unions, professional associations, colleagues, political parties and the Regional Parliament. Taking into account the 'duties and responsibilities' of his employment and the employer's interests in protecting their reputation and confidential information, the Commission dismissed the claim 'without having regard to the detail of the criticisms made by the applicant and, apparently, without considering whether the criticisms were such as could provide a valuable contribution to the effective working of [the] regional [public health service' (p 645). In *Morissens* the applicant was criticised for making her allegation on television while in *Grigoriades v Greece* (1999) 27 EHRR 464, the fact that strong criticism of the military services was contained in a letter sent to the applicant's commanding officer, rather than in a more widely publicised form, contributed to a finding in his favour by the European Court of Human Rights.

6.7 Conclusion

The implementation of the HRA 1998 in the UK has not had a great deal of impact on the protections afforded to workers. Most notable perhaps in the 'no change' line-up is the decision of the Court of Appeal in *X v Y* , extracted at **[6.8]** above. It was suggested by more than one commentator that the HRA would have the effect of reversing the decision of the Court of Session in *Saunders v Scottish National Camps Association Ltd* [1981] IRLR 277, in which the 'range of reasonable responses' test was applied to find that the dismissal of a gay man from his job as a handyman at a children's camp was fair. The Court ruled that the tribunal had not erred in concluding that 'a considerable proportion of employers would take the view that the employment of a homosexual should be restricted, particularly when required to work in proximity and contact with children. Although other employers might not have decided to dismiss, the respondents could not be held to have acted unreasonably in deciding that dismissal was the only safe course'.

The decision in *X v Y* indicates that not much has changed since 1981. Having said this, the HRA gives claimants another tool in their armoury and it is not impossible, particularly in light of decisions such as that of the House of Lords in *Ghaidan* **[6.4]** that it may have some beneficial results in the long term. As against that, of course, is the scope for argument it provides for members of the BNP and the like to challenge restrictions on their operations. In sum, it is likely that human rights at work will continue to be protected more by collective action and specific statutory provisions of the kind considered in this chapter than by the 1998 Act.

FURTHER READING

J Bowers and J Lewis, 'Whistleblowing: Freedom of Expression in the Workplace' [1996] 1 *EHRLR* 637.

K D Ewing, 'The Human Rights Act and Labour Law' (1998) 27 *Industrial Law Journal* 275.

——, 'Social Rights and Human Rights: Britain and the Social Charter—the Conservative Legacy' [2000] *European Human Rights Law Review* 91.

—— (ed), *Human Rights at Work* (London, Institute of Employment Rights, 2000).

IDS, *Employee Privacy in the Workplace* (London, Incomes Data Services, 2001) Employment Supplement No.6, Series 2.

Information Commissioner, *Employment Practices Data Protection Code*, Parts 3 and 4:

S Livingstone, 'Article 14 and the Prevention of Discrimination in the European Convention on Human Rights' [1997] 1 *European Human Rights Law Review* 25

A McColgan, 'Do Privacy Rights Disappear in the Workplace?' [2003] *European Human Rights Law Review*, 120-40

——, 'Principles of Equality and Protection from Discrimination in International Human Rights Law' [2003] *European Human Rights Law Review*, 157-75

——,'Article 10 and the right to freedom of expression: workers ungagged?', in K D Ewing (ed.), *Human Rights at Work* (London, Institute of Employment Rights, 2000)

——, 'Discrimination Law and the Human Rights Act 1998' in T Campbell, K D Ewing and A Tomkins (eds) *Sceptical Approaches to Human Rights* (Oxford, OUP, 2001)

——, 'Women and the Human Rights Act' (2000) 51(3) *Northern Ireland Legal Quarterly*,

K McEvoy and C White, 'Security Vetting in Northern Ireland: Loyalty, Redress and Citizenship' (1998) 61 *Modern Law Review* 341

L Vickers, *Freedom of Speech and Employment* (Oxford, OUP, 2002)

Trade Unions and their Members

7.1 Trade unions and citizenship

Trade unions perform a crucial role in advancing rights of citizenship. Through membership of a trade union, the citizen as worker is provided with an opportunity to participate in making the rules by which he or she will be governed while at work. These rules may be made by collective bargaining to which the trade union is a party, or by legislation (such as the National Minimum Wage Act 1998) for which the union has lobbied and applied political pressure. But apart from providing an opportunity for participation in rule-making institutions, the trade union advances rights of citizenship by raising standards and widening horizons. The social rights of trade union members are likely to be more fully advanced than the social rights of other workers, and the concerns of the citizen as worker are likely to be more fully addressed where there is a trade union pressing for equality of opportunity and the protection of human rights at work, as well as for better pay and shorter working hours. In addition to these rule-making and standard-setting roles, the trade union performs other functions for the citizen at work. By assisting in the development and operation of disciplinary and grievance procedures, the trade union can help ensure that the dignity of the worker is preserved and that workers are not subjected to arbitrary or unfair treatment by their employer.

Given the pivotal role which they thus perform, it is important that trade unions generally should be open and inclusive, and that they should be conducted along democratic lines. This is essential if the individual worker's voice is to be heard and if trade unions are genuinely to be the means by which the citizen as worker may participate in decision-making institutions. It might easily be argued that organisations which fulfill a democratic purpose should themselves be organised in accordance with democratic principles, however contestable these principles may be: on which see H Morris and P Fosh, 'Measuring Trade Union Democracy: The Case of the UK Public Services Association' (2000) 38 *British Journal of Industrial Relations* 95. By the same token, it is important also that trade unions should treat their members

---

Trade Unions and Trade Union Membership

Information about trade union membership is provided annually by the Certification Officer for Trade Unions and Employers' Associations. In 2003–2004, 213 trade unions had a total membership of almost 8 million. This represents about a third of the labour force in membership of a trade union. The great bulk of trade union members (6,506,018) belonged to the 16 unions with more than 100,000 members, this representing 84% of the total. There is a growing trend towards amalgamation with the trade union movement now dominated by four large organisations: AMICUS, UNISON, T&GWU and GMB ('the big four'). In 2005, 67 trade unions with a combined membership of nearly six and half million members were affiliated to the Trades Union Congress (TUC). The TUC is the representative voice of Britain's trade unions and campaigns on behalf of working people.

---

fairly, and should not arbitrarily exclude workers from membership or deny them the benefits and services of membership without good cause. It might easily be argued that organisations which exist to promote the dignity of the citizen as worker should not themselves treat workers badly. But this is subject of course to the overriding obligation of the trade union to all of its members collectively as well as individually. As was pointed out in *Goring v British Actors Equity Association* [1987] IRLR 122 (Ch D), '[t]he essence of a trade union activity is that members are bound to act collectively to achieve the objects of the majority' (at p 125). Membership may thus have obligations as well as privileges.

Yet although there are high expectations about the way in which trade unions should be governed and administered, it is unclear how far these expectations ought to be realised by the State rather than by the members themselves. For while there is a strong case for open, democratic and accountable trade union structures, there is also a compelling case for a trade union movement which is free from interference by government. So much is recognised by ILO Convention 87, one of the most fundamental of all ILO Conventions.

[7.1] ILO Convention 87 (The Freedom of Association and Protection of the Right to Organise Convention, 1948), Article 3

1 Workers' and employers' organisations shall have the right to draw up their constitutions and rules, to elect their representatives in full freedom, to organise their administration and activities and to formulate their programmes.
2 The public authorities shall refrain from any interference which would restrict this right or impede the lawful exercise thereof.

Freedom from State interference is essential if trade unions are properly to advance the interests of their members collectively. This is not to say that there is no role for the State in supervising the activities of trade unions. Indeed although international law thus stakes a strong claim for freedom of association, the ILO supervisory authorities accept that limitations may be permissible. But trade unions should not be so burdened by regulation as to be unable most effectively to promote the interests of those they represent.

In this chapter we consider the way in which the law is used to regulate the government and administration of trade unions. The starting point is the rule-book which is enforceable in the courts as a contract between the trade union and individual members: *Goring v British Actors Equity Association* [1987] IRLR 122. As with other contracts, the express terms of the rule book may have to be supplemented by implied terms to deal with gaps in its drafting: *AB v CD* [2001] IRLR 808. The rule-book determines the lawful objects of the union, defines the composition and powers of the different organs of government, and confers rights and duties on the membership individually. The courts play an important role in the interpretation of the rule-book and consequently in regulating the powers of a trade union and its different organs of government, in terms of both the activities which may be undertaken in the name of the union and of the circumstances in which members may be disciplined or expelled. In this chapter we consider some of the themes and underlying principles which have emerged from judicial enforcement of the rule-book. But in addition to the rule-book, it is important now to address a comprehensive framework of legislation which was introduced mostly in the period from 1980 to 1993, and which has survived the election of a Labour government. This legislation deals mainly with the election of officers and the exclusion and expulsion of members, though it applies also to other questions such as a greater power of public authorities to investigate alleged financial irregularities in trade unions. As we shall see, some of this legislation goes some way beyond the boundaries set by ILO Convention 87 and other international human rights treaties. In this chapter we also consider other statutory restraints, which typically operate independently of the rule-book.

7.2 What are trade unions?

What do trade unions do? To answer this question a good starting point is the constitutions of the different trade unions: it is here that they define their aims and purposes. The objects clauses of trade unions vary to some extent, reflecting the different origins and interests of the different trade union organisations. But most have a basic core of objects, which is perhaps inevitable if each organisation is to fall within the statutory definition of a trade union (which requires the primary purposes of a trade union to be concerned with regulating relations between employers and workers: TULRCA 1992, section 1). A good example of trade union objects is provided by the following extract. It will be noted that the union in question has political objects beyond those defined by Parliament in TULRCA 1992, section 72 (on which see 7.2.2 below). Other trade unions are sometimes more colourful: the NURMTW, for example, is pledged 'to work for the supersession of the capitalist system by a socialistic order of society' while the objects of ASLEF include 'to assist in the furtherance of the Labour Movement generally towards a Socialist Society'. The privatisation of the railways must have been a particular blow to both.

[7.2] GMB Rule Book

Rule 2 Objects

The objects of this Union shall be

1 The organisation of all workers qualified for membership.
2 To regulate the relations between employees and employers, and the relations between employees and employees; and to endeavour to adjust any differences through conciliation.
3 To maintain and improve wages and conditions, and maximise employment security, including the control of the number of apprentices in each section of the trades organised; and to promote industrial democracy.
4 To reduce working hours by the regulation of overtime or other means.
5 To obtain and maintain equal pay for equal work for women, and to promote equal opportunity within the Union, the workplace and society in general, regardless of sex, race, national origin, religious beliefs, disability, age, marital status or sexual orientation.
6 To provide benefits to members in accordance with the rules of the Union.
7 To provide legal assistance in accordance with the rules of the Union.
8 To promote the training and education of members in relation to their activities on behalf of the Union, and to provide scholarships for members to educational institutions, on conditions determined by the Central Executive Council.
9 To promote or support legislation in the interests of members especially in connection with the legal rights of trade unions, industrial health, safety and welfare, social and economic welfare and environmental protection.
10 To secure the return of members to Parliament and public authorities, who will support the policies of the Union and further the interests of members through political means, providing the candidates are pledged to collective ownership, under democratic control, of the means of production, distribution and exchange.
11 To promote the social, moral and intellectual interests of the members.
12 To provide and distribute funds for the above purposes.

Although wide ranging, trade union objects clauses nevertheless tend to conceal the fact that trade unions have a number of functions. These are as follows

- A service function whereby trade unions provide a range of services to their members. These may vary from traditional 'friendly society' benefits (sickness insurance or death benefits) to the provision of legal advice and assistance;
- A workplace representation function, whereby trade unions represent members in their relations with their employer. This may take the form of individual representation in grievance or disciplinary disputes, or collective representation over pay and other working conditions;
- A regulatory function, whereby trade unions seek to regulate employment conditions. This can be done directly by collective bargaining which determines terms and conditions for a group of workers or indirectly by lobbying for legislation (such as that dealing with the minimum wage or working time);
- A political representation function, whereby trade unions seek to protect and promote the interests of their members in the political arena—whether it be local government, national government or in Europe. This may require close working relationships with political parties, legislators and governments;

• A public administration function whereby trade unions may be delegated by government with responsibility for administering or promoting public policy on behalf of the State or various State benefits in a manner which will benefit their members.

The weight and importance attached to these different functions will vary from time to time, a matter to which we return in the concluding section of this chapter.

The Legal Definition and Status of Trade Unions

A trade union is defined by TULRCA 1992, section 1 to mean:

'an organisation (whether temporary or permanent)—
(a) which consists wholly or mainly of workers of one or more descriptions and whose principal purposes include the regulation of relations between workers of that description or those descriptions and employers or employers' associations; or
(b) which consists wholly or mainly of—
(i) constituent or affiliated organisations which fulfil the conditions in paragraph (a) (or themselves consist wholly or mainly of constituent or affiliated organisations which fulfil those conditions), or
(ii) representatives of such constituent or affiliated organisations, and whose principal purposes include the regulation of relations between workers and employers or between workers and employers' associations, or the regulation of relations between its constituent or affiliated organisations.'

The question of legal status is one which has a long social, political and legal history. The position is now governed by TULRCA 1992, section 10, the marginal note to which refers to the 'quasi-corporate' status of trade unions. Section 10 provides as follows

'(1) A trade union is not a body corporate but—
(a) it is capable of making contracts;
(b) it is capable of suing and being sued in its own name, whether in proceedings relating to property or founded on contract or tort or any other cause of action; and
(c) proceedings for an offence alleged to have been committed by it or on its behalf may be brought against it in its own name.
(2) A trade union shall not be treated as if it were a body corporate except to the extent authorised by the provisions of this Part.
(3) A trade union shall not be registered—
(a) as a company under the Companies Act 1985; or
(b) under the Friendly Societies Act 1974 or the Industrial and Provident Societies Act 1965;
and any such registration of a trade union (whenever effected) is void.'

7.2.1 Trade union objects: a source of restraint

The objects clause does not simply describe what a trade union does: it also defines what it may and by implication what it may not do. If a trade union engages in activity which is not authorised expressly or impliedly by its rule-book, it may be restrained by a member in the courts. There is a considerable body of such cases which typically deal with questions such as (i) unauthorised political action by a trade union, (ii) financial support for other trade unionists involved in a trade dispute, and (iii) the indemnity of legal or other expenses incurred by members or officers of the defendant union (now unlawful by virtue of TULRCA 1992, section 15). This power of legal restraint is an important form of member protection which ensures that the union does not engage in unauthorised activities and that union funds are not used for unauthorised purposes. On the other hand, this is an equally important form of member restraint on the power of the active majority to ensure that the minority's wishes are reflected in the conduct and management of the union. So what we have is a procedure which is both a form of minority protection and a restraint on majority rule: both a safeguard for democratic procedures and a restraint upon democratic government. Part of the difficulty arises because—as with many constitutional documents—the scope and extent of the objects of a trade union are not always clear, with the result that it is left to the courts to decide what a union may or may not do in a hard case.

[7.3] *Goring v British Actors Equity Association* [1987] IRLR 122 (Ch D)

The Annual General Meeting of the union held in 1985 condemned the President of the union for working in South Africa, and demanded that the Council of the union issue an instruction to members not to work there. In March 1986 the Council held a referendum of its members in which a majority of those voting resolved that an instruction should be issued to members not to work in South Africa. In the following month the instruction was duly issued, and under the rules of the union the instruction was binding on the members. Any member who acted in breach of the instruction could be fined, suspended or expelled from the union, which in turn would make it difficult for any individual concerned to secure employment in the entertainment industry in the United Kingdom. In this case the plaintiff sought a declaration that the instruction was ultra vires the union and therefore void. The application succeeded.

Browne-Wilkinson VC:
Before referring to the rules, there are certain points of principle which, although well known, are easily lost sight of. The relationship between members of a trades union is regulated by contract. The terms of such contract are contained in the rules. If a particular decision falls within the objects of the trades union as set out in the rules, then each member is bound by his contract with the other members to give effect to that decision. If, on the other hand, the decision does not fall within the objects, there is no contractual or other legal obligation on any member to give effect to it. Alterations can be made to the rules (and therefore to the contract between the members) if, but only if, the procedures for rule changes laid down in the existing rules have been complied with. There is no right for a majority of members to change the rules otherwise than in accordance with the agreed procedure. Accordingly, although most trades unions are organised on a democratic basis (i.e. majority decisions prevail) the majority can only bind the minority if the decision is within the objects of the union to which the members have agreed.

The question therefore in this case is whether the plaintiff and others who share his views have bound themselves to accept an instruction that they shall not appear in South Africa. The objects clause of the Union has changed from time to time over the years. The current rules are contained in clause 3 under the heading 'Objects, powers and duties'. The material parts read as follows:

'A. Objects.

As a non-party political and non-sectarian Union:

    (i)   to promote, protect and further on a professional basis the art of theatre, variety, opera, dancing, films, broadcasting and similar forms of entertainment;

    (ii)   to promote, protect and further the artistic, economic, social and legal interests of its members in their professional capacity;

    (iii) to maintain the professional rights and liberties of its members individually and collectively;

    (iv) to secure by organisation and all other effective methods, unity of action to achieve the best possible terms and conditions of work in all fields in which members are engaged.

B. Powers and duties.

    (a)   To issue all necessary instructions to the members, through its elected Council, in accordance with the above objects;

    (d)   to take any lawful action the Council (as governing body) may deem advisable and desirable to promote the above objects, and protect and further the professional interests of the members;

    (n)   to co-operate with kindred organisations, societies or associations . . . but at no time to affiliate . . . to any political party or sect, or to any organisation, society or association which is itself affiliated to any political party or sect;

    (o)   to acknowledge the right of individual members to hold and express their personal political and other beliefs both in their private and professional capacities'.

The introductory words of rule 3A 'as a non-party political and non-sectarian Union' are of crucial importance in this case: I will refer to them as 'the preamble'. . . .

In my judgment, the decision of this case depends upon the proper construction of the words of the preamble. When read in conjunction with rule 3B(o) the words of the preamble in my judgment limit the express objects set out in rule 3A so as to exclude activities the purpose of which is primarily party-political or sectarian. The words of the preamble and rule 3B(o) are two sides of a coin. Rule 3B(o) makes clear the duty to respect the rights of an individual to hold and express his individual beliefs: the preamble assures that this duty to the individual member is observed by limiting the objects of the Union to those activities which are undertaken for professional purposes and do not extend to those which are party-political or sectarian purposes which might conflict with the individual views and beliefs of the individual members.

That this is the right construction is demonstrated by [Counsel for the defendant's] own example of theatre grants which are a party-political issue. If the matter is looked at purely objectively, it would not be permissible to support increased grants because that would be a party-political issue and therefore outside the ambit of the Union's legitimate activity. The only way of reconciling the words of the preamble with the specific purposes in each of the sub-rules of rule 3A is to look to the purpose for which the proposed action is to be taken. If it is to be taken for the purpose of advancing professional interests, that will be authorised. But if the purpose is to advance the cause of the party, it will not be authorised, for to take such action for such purpose would be to act as party-political union. Accordingly the purpose with which an act is done is decisive.

This construction is supported by a consideration of past amendments of the rules. Before 1979, the objects of the Union were different. A referendum was held in 1979 which approved a new objects clause in the same terms as the present clause save that the preamble read 'as a non-political and non-sectarian Union'. The referendum question was put to the members with the usual Statements For and Against. For the purposes of construction, I am not entitled to look at such Statements for the purpose of discovering the proposer's view as to the effect of the new rule. However I am entitled to look at it for the purpose of finding the mischief which it was desired to remove by the amendment to the rules. The Statement For indicated that the mischief to be eradicated were resolutions such as those proposed at an Annual General Meeting which sent 'warmest greetings to Ayatollah Khomeini' on the 'historic triumph over the Shah and his reactionary supporters in Britain' and another which 'demanded the withdrawal of British troops from Northern Ireland'.

The objects clause was amended to its present form, i.e. by substituting in the preamble the words 'non-party political' for 'non-political' by a referendum held in 1983. On that occasion, the Statement For quoted (and supported) the following words of the General Secretary of the Union:

'When dealing with matters which are of direct professional interest to our members or which relate directly to our existence as a trade union, it seems to me self-evident that we must from time to time take actions which can only be described as political. That is, if we are not to fail entirely to fulfill our obligations to our members. In the past we have always acted in this way and there is no evidence to suggest that our members wish us to behave differently in future'.

Examples of such 'political' issues were given as being entertainment tax and VAT on theatre tickets. Accordingly, the mischief aimed at by this further amendment was to ensure that the Union could take political action for professional purposes. However the Statement For made it clear that the mischief designed to be removed did not include the fact that the Union was precluded from discussing motions congratulating the Ayatollah or demanding that troops come out of Northern Ireland.

In my judgment, the history of the rule changes strongly supports the construction of the rules which I have adopted. The Union exists to promote the professional interests of its members stated in the sub-rules of rule 3A. Activities undertaken for those purposes are not to be precluded by the words of the preamble. But activities undertaken for the purpose of advancing a party-political or sectarian viewpoint are not authorised just because an ingenious mind can find ways in which they might advance the interests of the members in a remote degree.

If I am right so far, if an activity of the Union is impugned on the grounds that it is party-political or sectarian, there is no escape from having to determine the primary purpose of the activity. I accept that in some cases where the activity has been directly sanctioned by a referendum, the ascertainment of the purpose presents great difficulties. But in the present case, I have no doubt that the purpose was sectarian. The language of the 1985 AGM resolution is redolent of sectarian promotion of a boycott for the purpose of putting an end to apartheid: there is no mention of professional interests. Similarly, the Statement For (which, in this regard, I can look at to discover the purposes of those promoting the giving of the instruction) is almost exclusively directed at a general cultural boycott as opposed to the promotion of professional concerns. In the whole statement, the only reference to professional interests is the exhortation to 'support your own Afro-Asian members'. There is no suggestion in the evidence that the Council or anyone else was in favour of the instruction for the narrow, and to my mind rather remote, professional purposes relied on by the defendants in their evidence. In the absence of any evidence to the contrary, the only purpose of the instruction which has been demonstrated is to promote a general cultural boycott of South Africa (a sectarian purpose) not for the purpose of promoting the professional interests of the members. Accordingly in my judgment such instruction was not authorised by the rules and is void.

> For these reasons, in my judgment the instruction prohibiting appearance in South Africa is void as being *ultra vires* the powers of the Union.

The *Goring* case raises a number of questions about how the courts should address rule-book questions relating to trade union objects. Should they follow the formal provisions of the constitution? That is to say, should the courts accord sovereignty to the constitution? Or should they follow the wishes of the policy-making bodies of the union, in this case the AGM? That is to say, should the courts accord sovereignty to representative institutions? Or should they respect the wishes of the majority of the members voting in a referendum of the membership? That is to say, should the courts accord sovereignty to the membership? The decision in *Goring* reveals clearly a preference for the first: the fundamental principle of trade union government may thus be said to be the sovereignty of the constitution. This means that a trade union may do only those things which the constitution authorises, no matter what the members may want otherwise. If the members are to pursue new objects, the constitution will have to be changed in accordance with the procedures in the constitution itself. Although obvious parallels can be drawn with constitutional law, there is a nevertheless a balance to be struck between rigid constitutionalism and the need to encourage membership participation in trade union affairs.

The approach adopted in *Goring* is perhaps easy to understand, however much one may applaud the policy which the union introduced. It was still the case at the time the decision was reached that 'the theatrical entertainment industry is a closed shop, membership of the Union being a prerequisite of employment', with the result that 'suspension or expulsion would be a dire penalty for any member' (at p 124). Consequences of this kind place a high premium on member protection and strict adherence to the constitution. This would not be such a compelling consideration today, given that it is now unlawful to refuse someone employment because he or she is not a trade union member (TULRCA 1992, section 137, see p 730). But a commitment to constitutional sovereignty in *Goring* was perhaps all the more compelling given that only 3,320 out of a membership of 32,000 took part in the referendum, and fewer still voted in favour of the disputed policy. Although it might be argued that the courts should develop principles which are calculated to promote member participation in the affairs of the union, such a low turnout would make it difficult to persuade a court of the virtues of membership sovereignty in the event of conflict with the constitution.

7.2.2 Trade union political objects: statutory restraints

Although trade union objects are determined largely by the constitution and rules of each trade union, there are circumstances where the matter is governed also by legislation. The most prominent example of this is in relation to trade union political objects (as defined to include mainly electoral and party political objects). The position has been regulated by legislation since the Trade Union Act 1913 which was based on a political compromise to reverse the decision of the House of Lords in *Amalgamated Society of Railway Servants v Osborne* [1910] AC 87. In that case it was held that trade unions could not impose a levy on their members in order to support parliamentary representation and other political activities. The effect of the decision—which was followed in a number of other cases to restrain political action by a number of other unions—was to threaten the financing and ultimately the future of the Labour Party which had been formed in 1900 as a direct consequence of another famous House of Lords decision, and which now had 29 members of Parliament. The threat was addressed first by the introduction of a scheme for MPs' salaries in 1911, and secondly by the passing of the 1913 Act, the key requirements of which were threefold:

- a union wishing to adopt political objects had first to seek the approval of its members in a secret ballot;
- if the ballot result was favourable, the union was required to adopt political fund rules whereby political objects were to be financed from a separate political fund, to be financed in turn by a separate contribution by the members; and
- where such a fund was established, every member was to be entitled not to contribute to the fund (by contracting out) and not to suffer disability or disadvantage within the union as a result.

The political compromise of 1913 has proved to be very fragile, strongly opposed by the Conservatives at the time and periodically thereafter. Following the General Strike in 1926, the Trade Disputes and Trade Unions Act 1927 included a provision whereby trade union rules would have to provide for members to 'contract in' to rather than 'contract out' of payments to the political fund. The 1927 Act was repealed in 1946, following the election of the Attlee government. The governments of Churchill, Eden, Macmillan, Douglas-Home and Heath were content to let the matter rest, and indeed the arrangements contained in the Trade Union Act 1913 (as restored in 1946) were broadly commended by the Donovan Royal Commission in 1968 which saw no reason to change them. But the matter was revisited by the Thatcher government in 1983, though this time approaching from a rather different angle. Under the 1913 Act, a ballot once held did not have to be renewed: the Trade Union Act 1984 required trade unions to ballot their members every 10 years (see now TULRCA 1992, section 73). At a time when the support for the Labour Party amongst trade unionists was thought to be in decline and at a time when the electoral fortunes of the post-war Labour Party were at their nadir, this was a potentially fatal blow. But with one exception no trade union has had to discontinue political objects because of the outcome of a ballot, following what have now been three cycles of political fund review ballots.

7.2.2.1 Political objects

One paradoxical effect of the 1984 Act was to lead to an increase in the number of trade unions with political funds. This is because of the new definition of political objects which the 1984 Act also introduced, giving in some respects a much needed face-lift to the 1913 definition, but in the process of so doing extending the scope of political objects.

[7.4] Trade Union and Labour Relations (Consolidation) Act 1992, section 72

Political objects to which restriction applies

72 (1) The political objects to which this Chapter applies are the expenditure of money—

(a) on any contribution to the funds of, or on the payment of expenses incurred directly or indirectly by, a political party;

(b) on the provision of any service or property for use by or on behalf of any political party;

(c) in connection with the registration of electors, the candidature of any person, the selection of any candidate or the holding of any ballot by the union in connection with any election to a political office;

(d) on the maintenance of any holder of a political office;

(e) on the holding of any conference or meeting by or on behalf of a political party or of any other meeting the main purpose of which is the transaction of business in connection with a political party;

(f) on the production, publication or distribution of any literature, document, film, sound recording or advertisement the main purpose of which is to persuade people to vote for a political party or candidate or to persuade them not to vote for a political party or candidate.

(2) Where a person attends a conference or meeting as a delegate or otherwise as a participator in the proceedings, any expenditure incurred in connection with his attendance as such shall, for the purposes of subsection (1)(e), be taken to be expenditure incurred on the holding of the conference or meeting.

(3) In determining for the purposes of subsection (1) whether a trade union has incurred expenditure of a kind mentioned in that subsection, no account shall be taken of the ordinary administrative expenses of the union.

(4) In this section—

'candidate' means a candidate for election to a political office and includes a prospective candidate;

'contribution', in relation to the funds of a political party, includes any fee payable for affiliation to, or membership of, the party and any loan made to the party;

'electors' means electors at an election to a political office;

'film' includes any record, however made, of a sequence of visual images, which is capable of being used as a means of showing that sequence as a moving picture;

'local authority' means a local authority within the meaning of section 270 of the Local Government Act 1972 or section 235 of the Local Government (Scotland) Act 1973; and

'political office' means the office of member of Parliament, member of the European Parliament or member of a local authority or any position within a political party.

Subsection (1)(f) was a particular cause for concern for those unions not affiliated to the Labour Party which engaged in 'independent' electoral activity. Although this activity was not directly identified with any particular political party, it might nevertheless favour one party more than others. Several unions were beginning to engage in such activities before 1984, but now found that they were unable to do so without a political fund. It thus became necessary for trade unions to adopt political objects to engage in electoral activities even though they were not affiliated to the Labour Party.

[7.5] *Paul v NALGO* **[1987] IRLR 413 (Ch D)**

> NALGO was a large union of local government officers which was not affiliated to the Labour Party and which did not have a political fund. In January 1987, in the run up to the general election, the union launched a campaign to increase public awareness about the importance of public services and the implications of government cuts. The campaign was supported by literature, documents, posters, advertisements and other matters. The material was critical of the then Conservative government and invited people to vote and to take the union's criticisms into account. The plaintiffs were both members of the union and sought a declaration and injunction that the expenditure incurred in the campaign was unlawful on a number of grounds. These included the claim that it violated what was still the Trade Union Act 1913 (as amended in 1984) on the ground that the union had incurred expenditure in furtherance of political objects without having in place a political resolution as required by the Act. The application succeeded, the Vice Chancellor (Browne-Wilkinson) accepting that the material was covered by what is now TULRCA 1992, section 72(1)(f).

Following this decision, NALGO, as it then was, balloted to establish a political fund. The fund was strictly non-affiliated, which led to a novel compromise when NALGO amalgamated with NUPE and COHSE both of which were affiliated to the Labour Party. The new union—UNISON—has two political funds, the General Political Fund and the Affiliated Political Fund: the former is not affiliated to the Labour Party, but the latter is; non-exempt members may choose into which fund they wish to contribute. The General Political Fund is used for non-party political purposes, such as election advertising. Although there were 33 trade unions with political funds in 2004, by no means all of these were affiliated to the Labour Party. Those which are pay an annual affiliation fee to the Party and help also to meet costs incurred during an election (by contributions to the Labour Party's General Election Fund, as well as by other means). In the case of affiliated unions, these items of expenditure account for by far the greatest part, if not all, of their political expenditure. At one time affiliated trade unions accounted for almost all the income of the Labour Party. But although trade unions continue to support the Labour Party, the Party's funding has diversified so that trade unions now contribute a smaller proportion than in the past.

7.2.2.2 Political fund rules

The arrangements for political fund rules are an unusual example of state intervention in the internal affairs of trade unions, in the sense that trade unions wishing to adopt political objects must also adopt rules prescribed by the State. More recent legislation (such as that requiring ballots before strikes and in the election of executive committees and general secretaries) operates independently of the rules of the unions in question. Model political fund ballot rules and model political fund rules to comply with the requirements of the legislation are issued by the Certification Officer (CO) who took over a jurisdiction which had been performed originally by the Chief Registrar of Friendly Societies. The Certification Officer thus occupies an unusual constitutional position: he performs a curious amalgam of executive (he approves political fund rules), legislative (he drafts model rules) and judicial (he adjudicates on alleged breaches of rules) functions. The political fund rules of trade unions are thus broadly similar, though there are differences, for example in terms of how much the political contribution is in each union, and in terms of the method of its collection. Key provisions based on the requirements of TULRCA 1992, section 82, include (i) the right of members not to contribute to the fund; (ii) the right of exempt members not to be discriminated against because of their exemption; and (iii) the right of members to complain to the CO in the event of any breach of the political fund rules.

In recent years there have in fact been relatively few political fund complaints. There has been an average of two complaints annually, most of which are settled informally, and few of which are upheld. A matter which gave rise to some difficulty in the late 1970s/early 1980s was the collection of trade union subscriptions by check off. This practice led to problems in giving effect to the exemption of contracted-out members, and indeed led to the only political fund complaint to be heard by the Employment Appeal Tribunal (EAT) to whom an appeal lies from the Certification Officer (*Reeves v TGWU* [1980] ICR 728). But that matter is now resolved by legislation which effectively prohibits the practice whereby employers would deduct the full amount of general and political contributions from all union members, leaving the union to reimburse those who were paying the political levy: see p 811 below. It remains true, however, that political fund rules do not deal with all questions of discrimination on political grounds: see *Hudson v GMB* [1990] IRLR 67. A number of unions require delegates to the Labour Party Conference to be members of the Labour Party, and indeed this is required by the rules of the Party. The Labour Party also proscribes certain named organisations, such as Militant which featured in the *Hudson* case, above. It is not possible for a union to require membership of the Labour Party as a condition of being a candidate for the elections which are dealt with in section 7.4 below (TULRCA 1992, section 47), though this has been an issue in the past: see *Leigh v NUR* [1970] Ch 326.

7.3 Trade union structure and government

Trade union structure and government are determined initially by the constitution and rules of each individual union. The structure of trade unions is different, reflecting their diverse origins and perceptions about how best to achieve their goals. But it would be true to say that trade unions are generally organised formally along democratic lines, with constitutional arrangements which provide for some form of representative government of the members. Trade union constitutions will typically provide for an annual conference (though in some cases the conference may be held less frequently) which will be the policy-making forum of the union. The business of the union between conferences will normally be conducted by the executive committee of the union which, as a result of the TULRCA 1992, will now be elected directly by the members and typically will meet regularly throughout the year. But it will not normally be a full-time body, and its members will normally be employed elsewhere. The day-to-day work of the union will normally be conducted by the officers of the union, the most senior of whom will be the general secretary and the deputy general secretary, who may be accountable to the executive committee for the way in which they discharge their responsibilities for the conduct of the affairs of the union. As full-time officials, the general secretary and his or her deputy have a uniquely powerful position and an opportunity in some cases to be the directing mind of the union.

7.3.1 Constitutional constraints

As already indicated, the first point to note about trade union government is that the different organs of government will be constrained by the rules of the organisation in question. They may also be constrained by law in the sense that, whatever the rules may authorise, an organ of trade union government will not be permitted by the courts to engage in conduct which violates the general law:

[7.6] *Thomas v NUM (South Wales Area)* **[1985] ICR 886 (Ch D)**

Scott J:

First, I would agree that it must be ultra vires for a union, or indeed any company, deliberately to embark on a series of criminal acts. No objects clause could lawfully expressly authorise that to be done, and no implication to that effect would ever be read into an objects clause. Secondly, it would not, in my view, necessarily be ultra vires for a union or a company to embark on a series of acts which carried the risk that criminal offences might be committed in the course thereof. If the acts were possible to be done lawfully there is no reason why they should not be authorised under an objects clause. A fortiori, it would not be necessarily ultra vires for a union or a company to embark on a series of acts which carried the risk that torts might be committed. Indeed, I am sure that in the ordinary conduct of business a large number of companies take this sort of risk open-eyed and frequently. In the present case the union is entitled under its rules to engage in picketing. It would be ultra vires for the union to embark on a form of picketing that would be bound to involve criminal acts. It would not, in my view, be ultra vires for the union to embark on a form of picketing which was capable of involving criminal acts but not bound to do so. As to whether it would be ultra vires for the union to embark on a form of picketing which was bound to involve tortious acts I am not clear. The answer might depend upon the nature of the tort since, in the final analysis, it would, I think, be considerations of public policy on which the answer would depend. In addition, whenever a union or a company becomes exposed to tortious or criminal liability, questions may arise as to whether officers of the union or the company have been in breach of their duties of management in causing or permitting this to have happened (at p 924).

As also pointed out already, there may also be statutory constraints on what trade unions may do.

So far as the rules themselves are concerned, these may operate to restrain the different organs of government in a number of ways: a strike may be called in breach of the rules of the union; strike pay may be paid in breach of the rules of the union; subscriptions may be increased without proper authority. Apart from conduct of this kind, there may also be procedural lapses: a meeting (such as an executive committee or a conference) may be improperly called or composed, or a meeting (such as an executive committee or a conference) may be unlawfully conducted. In appropriate cases the courts clearly feel empowered to intervene to restrain action of trade union organs in breach of the rules of the union. The following case, arising from the miners' strike of 1984–5, is a good example of the existence and exercise of this power.

[7.7] *Taylor v National Union of Mineworkers (Derbyshire Area) (No 3)* **[1985] IRLR 99 (Ch D)**

The plaintiffs sought an injunction restraining the defendant trade union and its senior officers from 'using, procuring or permitting the use of' the funds of the union for the purposes of a strike called by the National Union of Mineworkers (NUM), on the ground that the strike was *ultra vires,* having been called without a national ballot. They also sought an order requiring the defendants to repay to the union money that had been used to support the strike. The plaintiffs succeeded on the first point, with Vinelott J holding that if the rules provide for strike pay during an official strike, 'it is impossible to imply consistently with that a power for officers to make a precisely similar allowance to members on 'unofficial strike' (p 107). But the court refused to make the order that the money be reimbursed to the union on the ground that strike pay had been paid in the honest belief that the union had the power to make the payments. The court was also influenced by the fact that a majority of the members of the union were on strike (apparently supporting the action) and that the defendants did not have any substantial resources.

Although the courts thus have the power to constrain conduct by union bodies which act without constitutional authority, this is a power which will be exercised only in appropriate cases. There are a number of devices employed by the courts whereby they will refrain from intervening in the domestic affairs of trade unions and other bodies. These include a principle adopted from company law, known as the rule in *Foss v Harbottle* (1843) 2 Hare 461, which prevents a trade union member from bringing an action to stop a breach of the rules of the union if the irregularity is one which could be authorised or endorsed by a majority of the members. This is in some respects a difficult issue: on the one hand the rule in *Foss v Harbottle* undermines the desire to ensure that trade unions are governed in accordance with their rules, and the principle of the rule of law in the conduct of union affairs; but on the other hand it gives effect to the equally compelling principle of autonomy in trade union government and keeps the courts out of questions of trade union government where their presence does not always inspire confidence. But for all its potential in the latter context, in practice it is the pull of the former which prevails, for it is open to question just how significant the rule in *Foss v Harbottle* really is in matters relating to trade union government.

[7.8] *Edwards v Halliwell* **[1950] 2 All ER 1064 (CA)**

The plaintiffs were members of the National Union of Vehicle Builders, the defendants its executive committee. The plaintiffs complained that union subscriptions had been increased in breach of rule 19 of the union's rules, this requiring a ballot of the members in which two thirds voted in favour of an increase. In this case an increase was authorised by a delegate meeting without a ballot being held. The plaintiffs successfully sought a declaration that the increase in subscriptions was unlawful, a decision which was upheld by the Court of Appeal.

Jenkins LJ:

The rule in *Foss v Harbottle*, as I understand it, comes to no more than this. First, the proper plaintiff in an action in respect of a wrong alleged to be done to a company or association of persons is *prima facie* the company or the association of persons itself. Secondly, where the alleged wrong is a transaction which might be made binding on the company or association and on all its members by a simple majority of the members, no individual member of the company is allowed to maintain an action in respect of that matter for the simple reason that, if a mere majority of the members of the company or association is in favour of what has been done, then *cadit quæstio*. No wrong had been done to the company or association and there is nothing in respect of which anyone can sue. If, on the other hand, a simple majority of members of the company or association is against what has been done, then there is no valid reason why the company or association itself should not sue. In my judgment, it is implicit in the rule that the matter relied on as constituting the cause of action should be a cause of action properly belonging to the general body of corporators or members of the company or association as opposed to a cause of action which some individual member can assert in his own right.

The cases falling within the general ambit of the rule are subject to certain exceptions. It has been noted in the course of argument that in cases where the act complained of is wholly *ultra vires* the company or association the rule has no application because there is no question of the transaction being confirmed by any majority. It has been further pointed out that where what has been done amounts to what is generally called in these cases a fraud on the minority and the wrongdoers are themselves in control of the company, the rule is relaxed in favour of the aggrieved minority who are allowed to bring what is known as a minority shareholders' action on behalf of themselves and all others. The reason for this is that, if they were denied that right, their grievance could never reach the court because the wrongdoers themselves, being in control, would not allow the company to sue. Those exceptions are not directly in point in this case, but they show, especially the last one, that the rule is not an inflexible rule and it will be relaxed where necessary in the interests of justice.

There is a further exception which seems to me to touch this case directly. That is the exception noted by Romer J. in *Cotter v National Union of Seamen* [[1929] 2 Ch 58]. He pointed out that the rule did not prevent an individual member from suing if the matter in respect of which he was suing was one which could validly be done or sanctioned, not by a simple majority of the members of the company of association, but only by some special majority, as, for instance, in the case of a limited company under the Companies Act, a special resolution duly passed as such. As Romer J. pointed out, the reason for that exception is clear, because otherwise, if the rule were applied in its full rigour, a company which, by its directors, had broken its own regulations by doing something without a special resolution which could only be done validly by a special resolution could assert that it alone was the proper plaintiff in any consequent action and the effect would be to allow a company acting in breach of its articles to do *de facto* by ordinary resolution that which according to its own regulations could only be done by special resolution. That exception exactly fits the present case inasmuch as here the act complained of is something which could only have been validly done, not by a simple majority, but by a two-thirds majority obtained on a ballot vote. In my judgment, therefore, the reliance on the rule in *Foss v Harbottle* [(1843) 2 Hare 461] in the present case may be regarded as misconceived on that ground alone.

I would go further. In my judgment, this is a case of a kind which is not even within the general ambit of the rule. It is not a case where what is complained of is a wrong done to the union, a matter in respect of which the cause of action would primarily and properly belong to the union. It is a case in which certain members of a trade union complain that the union, acting through the delegate meeting and the executive council in breach of the rules by which the union and every member of the union are bound, has invaded the individual rights of the complainant members, who are entitled to maintain themselves in full membership with all the rights and privileges appertaining to that status so long as they pay contributions in accordance with the tables of contributions as they stood before the purported alterations of 1943, unless and until the scale of contributions is validly altered by the prescribed majority obtained on a ballot vote. Those rights, these members claim, have been invaded. The gist of the case is that the personal and individual rights of membership of each of them have been invaded by a purported, but invalid, alteration of the tables of contributions. In those circumstances, it seems to me the rule in *Foss v Harbottle* has no application at all, for the individual members who are suing sue, not in the right of the union, but in their own right to protect from invasion their own individual rights as members.

Edwards v Halliwell thus suggests that there are a number of exceptions to the rule in *Foss v Harbottle* which make its successful application in the trade union context difficult and unusual. It is true that its relevance was restated in the litigation arising out of the miners' strike in 1984–5, on at least two occasions. Apart from the *Taylor* case above where it was held to be inapplicable, 'it was not disputed' in *Thomas v NUM (South Wales Area)* [1985] ICR 886, that the rule in *Foss v Harbottle* 'applies to trade unions' (at p 923). But it is easier to acknowledge the existence of the rule than to find an example of its successful application. Indeed since *Cotter v NUS* [1929] 2 Ch 58, it has been applied on only one occasion (*McNamee v Cooper, The Times*, 7 September 1966). More recently the High Court has shown an unwillingness to apply the rule where to do so would deny a plaintiff the right to have the affairs of his or her trade union conducted in accordance with the constitution except in the case of minor procedural lapses. In *Wise v USDAW* [1996] ICR 691, a case about the conduct of an election, Chadwick J rejected a defence based on the rule in *Foss v Harbottle*, holding robustly that the rights which the plaintiffs in that case were seeking to protect were 'rights not to have the constitutional organs of the union, and in particular the composition of a new executive council, the president and the general secretary, imposed upon them save in accordance with the rules of the union' (p 702).

7.3.2 Constitutional conflicts

As in other democratic organisations, there may from time to time be conflict between the different branches of government within a trade union. The executive committee may, for example, refuse to follow the policy directions given by conference. Or the general secretary may fail to follow instructions given by the executive committee. In these cases the courts may be called upon to resolve any dispute which arises within the organisation. The starting point in any such case will of course be the rules of the union itself. But the rules may not necessarily be conclusive, even where there is a clear breach: the court will be bound to have regard to common law principles which are engaged in cases of this kind, including again the rule in *Foss v*

Harbottle. Indeed it is in this context of conflict between two organs of government within a trade union that the only application of the rule since 1929 can be traced. But as will be seen from the following case, *McNamee v Cooper* is thought to have been wrongly decided, and was expressly repudiated by Chadwick J in *Wise v USDAW*. The priority of the courts in cases of this kind is to enforce the rules of the union, and to ensure that the wishes of the membership prevail.

[7.9] *Hodgson v NALGO* [1972] 1 WLR 130 (Ch D)

At the annual conference of NALGO in 1971 a resolution was carried opposing 'the entry of Britain into the European Economic Community (the Common Market) unless it can be shown to be in the long term interests of both Britain and the Community'. Shortly thereafter the NEC instructed the NALGO delegates to the TUC annual conference to support a motion in favour of Britain's joining the Common Market, and to vote against a motion opposing such membership. The plaintiffs in this case, all members of the Leeds branch of the union, sought an order against the union and its TUC delegation to restrain them from acting against the policy of the union as determined by its conference, which under the rules 'directed' its 'general policy'. The application was successful.

Goulding J:
This case does not fall within any of the well-known exceptions to the rule in *Foss v Harbottle*. It was urged at one time, on behalf of the plaintiffs, that what was being done was an ultra vires act, but, in my judgment, that does not hold water at all. As I said when I referred to the objects of the union, it is plain that giving instructions of any kind to delegates to the TUC to vote this way or that or to abstain from voting on the Common Market questions, is entirely within the powers of the union as such. Further, this is not one of the cases in which the individual plaintiffs can say that something in the nature of a proprietary right of theirs is being infringed, as where subscriptions are being altered, or qualifications for office are being altered, or benefits are being altered. Nothing of that kind is in question. Indeed, it is hard to imagine a matter further removed from an individual proprietary interest than the attitude of the union to proposals about the Common Market. Nor again is the case one of those in which an exception has been made from the rule on the ground that otherwise the majority might do by some informal machinery what under the rules can only be done with some special formality. Nothing of that sort arises here. . . .

   Now there was a second and an alternative ground on which it was said that the plaintiffs could escape from the difficulty raised by *Foss v Harbottle*, and that was the urgency of the matter. It is conceded that it would have been impossible after the date of the decisive meeting of the National Executive Council, namely 7th August, to go through the necessary procedure for summoning a special conference of the union. However large might have been the body of members who objected to the National Executive Council's action it would have been impossible to summon such a conference in time to ascertain its will before the meeting of the TUC. Therefore, the practical reasoning that the court should leave matters of internal decision to the proper constitutional machinery of the association really does not apply. If the directions given to delegates are left uncorrected and if the votes of the delegates should prove to be of great importance at the meeting of the TUC, it would be cold comfort to the majority of the next NALGO conference to pass a resolution saying, 'We really meant what we said last June and we did not intend to authorise the National Executive Council to alter it.' If that was their conclusion the horse would long since have left the stable and the view of the majority when expressed would be without practical effect. It is submitted, therefore, that the court ought not to allow the rule in *Foss v Harbottle* to become the possible instrument of an injustice to the majority that the majority could not afterwards correct. There does not appear to be—so far as the researches of counsel have gone—any authority on that aspect of the matter. In my view, *Foss v Harbottle* should not be applied if the result may be to deprive the majority of an opportunity of carrying out their will. In other words, if the constitutional machinery of the body cannot operate in time to be of practical effect, the court, in my view, should entertain the suit of a member or members not supported by the association itself. That, therefore, is an alternative ground on which I would decide in the plaintiffs' favour, if I am wrong in thinking that the rule in *Foss v Harbottle* does not apply to an unregistered trade union. I am conscious that in deciding in favour of the plaintiffs I am differing from a reported decision of Goff J on facts which bear a striking similarity to those of the present case. It was the case of *McNamee v Cooper* . It does not appear whether the union there in question was registered or not and it does not appear whether the other considerations on which I am relying were ever argued before the learned judge. Accordingly, I do not think that I ought to treat that decision where his Lordship rejected the claim on motion, as precluding the granting of the plaintiffs' application in the present case.

The *Hodgson* case reflects a priority attached by the court to the supremacy of conference over the executive, which might be seen as a victory for representative democracy, though it was not formally expressed in these terms. But in some subsequent cases the courts have been presented with conflicts between executive bodies and conferences in circumstances where the former sought to by-pass the latter by a direct appeal to the membership in a referendum. In these cases the courts have tended to favour the executive at the expense of conference, which may be seen as a result to be a victory for direct democracy over representative democracy. In one such case (*National Union of Mineworkers v Gormley, The Times*, 21 October 1977), the NUM agreed a productivity incentive scheme with the National Coal Board in what was said to be a violation of conference resolutions. The NEC decided to put the scheme to a ballot of the members for their approval, though there was no express authority in the rules for such a ballot. An attempt to restrain the NEC in the courts nevertheless failed. According to Lord Denning:

> The ballot was a sensible and reasonable proposal by the NEC to take the views by the democratic method of a secret ballot of all the workers affected. It was a far more satisfactory and democratic method than leaving it to the delegates of a conference who might not be truly representative in their individual capacities of the views of the various men they represented.

A similar preference for direct democracy over representative democracy is to be seen in *British Actors' Equity Association v Goring* [1978] ICR 791 (HL). Together these cases may tend to indicate in matters of trade union government a judicial preference at that time for representative democracy over executive government, and for direct democracy over representative government.

7.4 The election of trade union officers

As already pointed out earlier in this chapter, trade union government has been the subject of detailed legal controls since 1980, controls which became gradually tighter after each general election between 1979 and 1992. The Employment Act 1980 introduced a provision whereby trade unions could claim a reimbursement of the costs of holding postal ballots to a number of designated trade union elections. See *R v Certification Officer, ex parte Electrical Power Engineers' Association* [1990] ICR 682. This carrot was designed to encourage trade unions to change their practices voluntarily (R Undy and R Martin, *Ballots and Trade Union Democracy* (Oxford, Blackwell, 1983)), and was quickly followed by the stick of more coercive legislation in the form of the Trade Union Act 1984 which required trade unions to elect their principal executive committees every five years in a direct election by the members, on the background to which see *Democracy in Trade Unions* (Cmnd 8778, 1983) This meant that trade unions could no longer elect their executive committees indirectly through conference or by other means, though as first introduced the ballot could be held either at the workplace or by post. In the Employment Act 1988 the legislation was made more prescriptive in the sense that ballots were now to be held by post, and extended in the sense that it would apply not only to the principal executive committee but also to the general secretary and the president of a trade union. Further changes were made by the Trade Union Reform and Employment Rights Act 1993. Only minor changes to the law have been made since the election of a Labour government in 1997.

7.4.1 The statutory procedures

[7.10] Trade Union and Labour Relations (Consolidation) Act 1992, section 46

Duty to hold elections for certain positions

46 (1) A trade union shall secure—
(a) that every person who holds a position in the union to which this Chapter applies does so by virtue of having been elected to it at an election satisfying the requirements of this Chapter, and
(b) that no person continues to hold such a position for more than five years without being re-elected at such an election.

(2) The positions to which this Chapter applies (subject as mentioned below) are—
(a) member of the executive,
(b) any position by virtue of which a person is a member of the executive,
(c) president, and
(d) general secretary;
and the requirements referred to above are those set out in sections 47 to 52 below.

(3) In this Chapter 'member of the executive' includes any person who, under the rules or practice of the union, may attend and speak at some or all of the meetings of the executive, otherwise than for the purpose of providing the committee with factual information or with technical or professional advice with respect to matters taken into account by the executive in carrying out its functions.

(4) This Chapter does not apply to the position of president or general secretary if the holder of that position—
(a) is not, in respect of that position, either a voting member of the executive or an employee of the union,
(b) holds that position for a period which under the rules of the union cannot end more than 13 months after he took it up, and
(c) has not held either position at any time in the period of twelve months ending with the day before he took up that position.

(4A) This Chapter also does not apply to the position of president if-
(a) the holder of that position was elected or appointed to it in accordance with the rules of the union,
(b) at the time of his election or appointment as president he held a position mentioned in paragraph (a), (b) or (d) of subsection (2) by virtue of having been elected to it at a qualifying election,
(c) it is no more than five years since—
    (i)   he was elected, or re-elected, to the position mentioned in paragraph (b) which he held at the time of his election or appointment as president, or
    (ii) he was elected to another position of a kind mentioned in that paragraph at a qualifying election held after his election or appointment as president of the union, and
(d) he has, at all times since his election or appointment as president, held a position mentioned in paragraph (a), (b) or (d) of subsection (2) by virtue of having been elected to it at a qualifying election.

(5) In subsection (4) a voting member of the executive' means a person entitled in his own right to attend meetings of the executive and to vote on matters on which votes are taken by the executive (whether or not he is entitled to attend all such meetings or to vote on all such matters or in all circumstances).

(5A) In subsection (4A) "qualifying election" means an election satisfying the requirements of this Chapter.

(5B) The "requirements of this Chapter" referred to in subsections (1) and (5A) are those set out in sections 47 to 52 below.

(6) The provisions of this Chapter apply notwithstanding anything in the rules or practice of the union; and the terms and conditions on which a person is employed by the union shall be disregarded in so far as they would prevent the union from complying with the provisions of this Chapter.

Candidates

47 (1) No member of the trade union shall be unreasonably excluded from standing as a candidate.

(2) No candidate shall be required, directly or indirectly, to be a member of a political party.

(3) A member of a trade union shall not be taken to be unreasonably excluded from standing as a candidate if he is excluded on the ground that he belongs to a class of which all the members are excluded by the rules of the union.

But a rule which provides for such a class to be determined by reference to whom the union chooses to exclude shall be disregarded.

The legislation also makes detailed provisions for the issuing of election addresses (section 48), and the appointment of an independent scrutineer (section 49). All members of the union are to have an equal right to vote, though certain classes of members may be excluded (such as those who are unemployed or in arrears with their subscriptions) (section 50). Voting is to be by the marking of a ballot paper, and must be conducted on a fully postal basis (section 51). Provision is made for the counting of the votes by an independent person (section 51A). The Act may be enforced in the event of any alleged malpractice by an application either to the Certification Officer under section 55 or to the High Court under section 56. In either case an application may be made by a member of the union (provided that the applicant was also a member at the time of the contested election), or by a candidate in the election (even though he or she may no longer be a member of the union). The Certification Officer is required to make inquiries and to give the parties an opportunity to be heard, and is empowered to make a declaration and an enforcement order (section 55). An appeal lies from the CO to the EAT on a point of law 'arising in any proceedings before or arising from any decision' of the CO (section 56).

[7.11] *Ecclestone v National Union of Journalists* [1999] IRLR 166 (Ch D)

Mr Ecclestone was deputy general secretary of the NUJ, of which he had been a member for 40 years. Following a dispute with the General Secretary, the NEC passed a motion of no confidence in Mr Ecclestone and resolved to dismiss him. He decided to stand for re-election, but his candidature was not accepted on the ground that he did not have the confidence of the NEC, and therefore lacked a necessary qualification for office. Mr Ecclestone argued that his exclusion breached the rules of the union as well as TULRCA 1992, section 47 and was unlawful. His application to the High Court succeeded on both grounds.

Smith J:
The union is a democratic organisation. At grass roots level it is organised into branches known as 'chapels', which are controlled by a branch committee elected annually by branch members. The main, central administrative body of the union is the national executive council, which comprises members who represent the various sectors of the union. There are seven industrial sectors covering such areas of activity as broadcasting, freelance and newspapers and agencies. There are 12 geographical sectors covering parts of the British Isles and continental Europe. Each sector is entitled to one or more representative seats on the NEC. Members of the NEC are elected annually by the ordinary members within the sector they would represent. The NEC is the day-to-day administrative body, holding powers under the rules to carry out many functions. These functions relate to such matters as membership, finance and the organisation of elections. Under the rules the NEC is given a number of discretionary powers.

Superior in power to the NEC is the delegate meeting, which consists of voting delegates elected by branches and non-voting members, such as members of the NEC, union officials and delegates from various interest groups within the union.

The delegate meeting, which is required to meet at least once a year, so it is generally referred to as the annual delegate meeting or ADM, is the rule-making and policy-making body of the union. By rule 9(c) its decisions are final, save for decisions which are taken by the whole membership. In particular its decisions can overrule a decision of the NEC. However, as I have said, the NEC has wide powers, many of which are of a discretionary nature. In addition to its specific powers, rule 8(q) provides:

> 'The NEC shall administer the affairs of the union and shall have power in accordance with the rules to do such things on behalf of the union as may be expedient. Unless specifically prevented by these rules, the NEC shall have power to interpret the rules and to determine any question on which the rules are silent and no policy has been laid down by the ADM.'

I turn now to examine the rules which regulate who is entitled to stand for election in union ballots.

Rule 2(f) provides that membership carries certain rights, including the right to hold office in the union.

Rule 19, which is entitled 'Elections', provides at subparagraph (a) that full members and members of honour are entitled to vote and stand for office in all union elections. It is not disputed that the plaintiff is a full member of the union.

The only rules which derogate from the right to stand for office are rule 2(c) and rule 4(j). Rule 2(c) provides that no member may stand for office if he also belongs to a rival organisation which is deemed by the NEC to be contrary to the interests of the NUJ. Rule 4(j) provides that a member may not stand if he is three months or more in arrears with his union dues.

The plaintiff was not disqualified under these provisions, which I shall call 'the basic qualifications'. He contends that he is therefore prima facie entitled to stand for election.

No other rule makes any express provision as to a required qualification to stand for election. The ADM has made no rule changes in recent years to lay down any additional qualifications besides those set out above. Nor has it given any policy guidance on this topic. Nor has the NEC apparently set out any qualifications which it regards as being required for election to any of the three high offices in the union.

I have already indicated that it is rule 10(b)(i) which governs the activities of the NEC in deciding who shall be allowed to stand. I repeat the specific words of the rule:

> 'The NEC shall prepare a shortlist of applicants who have the required qualifications and submit the list to a postal ballot of the whole of the members qualified to vote. Before being considered for the shortlist, each applicant shall sign an undertaking that he accepts the terms and conditions of employment specified by the NEC.'

The plaintiff submits that the confidence of the NEC in the ability of the candidate to do the job is not, and cannot be, a required qualification. He submits that qualifications, although not limited to such things as degrees, diplomas and relevant experience, should nonetheless be construed sui generis with achievements of that kind. He submits that the confidence of one person in another, or of one body in a person, is essentially a matter of opinion. It may be a collective opinion and it may be honestly held. It may even be justified. But it is still an opinion. It cannot, in his submission, therefore be a qualification. Mr Hendy [for the union] submits that the lack of confidence of the NEC in the plaintiff is a fact and is therefore capable of being a 'required qualification'.

It seems to me that having the confidence of the NEC is an attribute, but I do not think that, without straining the language of the rule, it can possibly be described as a qualification.

Mr Hendy, as I have said, has accepted that the NEC must act rationally, fairly and in accordance with good employment practice. In my judgment, wherever a selection procedure is about to be undertaken, good employment practice requires that the selection criteria should be laid down in advance of their application. This avoids the danger that the criteria will be determined arbitrarily in order to include or exclude any particular candidates. Here consideration should have been given to what the required qualifications were to be. It seems from the documents before me that it has never been the practice of the NEC, or of the subcommittee which usually selects the shortlist, to lay down in advance the required qualifications for the job. Moreover, in my judgment good employment practice requires that the criteria adopted are capable of being objectively applied: that is, avoiding reliance on personal preferences and prejudices. Of course when a final selection of an employee is made, there may have to be an element of choice, but at the earlier stage of selecting those with required qualifications, the task is to set the required qualification and to decide who has them and who does not. It is not a question of choosing who has the most of them or the least of them.

Mr Hendy has submitted that the need for all candidates to have the confidence of the NEC is so obvious a 'required qualification' for the post of deputy general secretary that it was reasonable and within the scope of the NEC's discretion to make it an expressly required qualification, albeit that this was only done at the last minute and apparently in response to the realisation that the plaintiff was to be a candidate.

His submission is based on the premise that there must be a relationship of trust and confidence between the deputy general secretary when appointed and the NEC. Otherwise, he said, they would not be able to work together.

I can see that there may be practical difficulties if the membership were to elect a deputy general secretary which the NEC said they could not work with. But it seems to me that if the NEC is able to restrict the class of candidates with which they are prepared to work, the whole democratic process will be undermined. In any event the NEC members will be free to make known their views about the plaintiff during the election process and will be free to say that he does not have their confidence. If the electorate is persuaded by the NEC views, then they will not elect the plaintiff. If they are not persuaded and they do elect the plaintiff, then so be it. The electorate would have said that they wish the NEC to work with this man.

My conclusion is that the rules of the union as drafted do give the NEC a discretion to decide what are the required qualifications for the post in question and to decide who complies with them. To have the confidence of the NEC cannot be described as a qualification. Therefore it cannot be a required qualification. It must, in my view, have been the intention of the rule makers, the ADM, that the setting of the required qualifications and the preparation of the shortlist should be carried out fairly and in accordance with good employment practice. That Mr Hendy accepts. The actions of this NEC fell outside the scope of the discretion provided by the rules because they did not act in accordance with good employment practice. I consider that I am able to reach that conclusion without having to determine any contested issues of fact. Therefore I consider it appropriate that I should make a declaration at this stage that I find the NEC's decision to exclude the plaintiff from the shortlist was unlawful. . . .

I turn to consider the question of whether the exclusion of the plaintiff from the shortlist was also a breach of section 47 of the 1992 Act. . . .

Mr Jeans [for the plaintiff] has submitted, and I accept, that this provision is designed, first, to ensure that a person is not excluded from standing for office by the imposition of unreasonable or unfair criteria or procedures, and also to ensure that he or she is not excluded by the unfair, or unreasonable, application of criteria or procedures which are fair in themselves.

Here it seems to me that the union have sought to exclude from candidature a class of person, namely those who do not have the confidence of the NEC, which class is to be determined by reference to whom the union, in the form of the NEC, chooses to exclude. Thus it seems to me that the whole attempt to exclude by reference to that essentially subjective method falls foul of section 47(3). However, if I were wrong about that, I would in any event take the view that the application of the exclusion was so obviously unfair that I should find for the plaintiff under the statute as well as under the rules.

The NEC reached a decision that it had no confidence in the plaintiff's ability to carry out his functions as a deputy general secretary at a hearing on 24 October 1997, which was conducted in the clearest breach of the rules of natural justice. The motion of no confidence was not on the agenda before the meeting. The plaintiff was not informed that such a motion would be considered. When it was raised, the plaintiff was not informed and was not given the chance to defend himself, contrary to the clear advice of leading counsel.

There is a further disquieting aspect to those proceedings. The members had been served with a dossier of highly prejudicial material which they had read before the meeting. It is asking a great deal of persons, particularly those without a legal training, to put out of their minds prejudicial material of this kind.

The resolution to exclude the plaintiff from candidacy on 12 December was clearly closely related to the resolution of no confidence on 24 October. It is clear from the minutes of 12 December that the same material was under consideration and the same opinions were expressed, with the exception of one member who had changed sides in the interim. In my view it is clear that the opinions formed and given effect to on the 12 December were tainted by the breach of natural justice which had occurred on 24 October.

Mr Hendy accepts, as he must, that there was a breach of natural justice on 24 October, but he submits that even if the plaintiff had been given the opportunity to defend himself, the result would have been the same.

Mr Jeans makes two answers to that proposition. First he says that that is not the test which should be applied. One should not ask whether a breach of natural justice has made any difference to the result. Under the statute, if the decision to exclude the plaintiff was unfair at the time that it was taken, there is an end to the matter. Second, he says that one could not say in any event that it would have made no difference had there not been a breach of natural justice. Looking at the voting figures, he says, if the four supporters of the plaintiff had not absented themselves on 24 October, the voting would quite predictably have been 10 to seven against the plaintiff at the very worst for him. Had the plaintiff been there to defend himself, one cannot say that he would not have persuaded two more members to support him. It is right, of course, that one cannot say what would have happened had the plaintiff been able to attend and address the meeting which was about to consider the vote of no confidence against him. But I could not say with confidence that it could have made no difference. In any event, I accept Mr Jeans's first submission on this point, namely that if the decision was unfair and unreasonable at the time it was taken, it is irrelevant to the issue of breach of the statute that fairness would have made no difference to the result.

Ecclestone is unusual in the sense that it is one of the few cases under section 56 to be reported. It appears that most complaints are dealt with by the Certification Officer, who made decisions in 150 cases between 1 October 1985 (when the relevant legislation came into force) and 31 March 2004. This is an average of about eight cases a year, though the numbers have increased significantly in recent years (with 28 in 2002-2003 alone). Mr Ecclestone has made several complaints, with complaints on other matters in 2002 and 2003. In 2003 he complained about the election procedures for the president of the union (Decision D/18/03), and in a separate application about the procedures for the NEC election (Decision D/19/03). Prominent complaints include *Hill v BFAWU* (Decision D31/02) about the failure of the union to hold a ballot for general secretary since the legislation was introduced in 1985. Another is *Stokes v GMB* (Decision D/24-27/03) where a complaint was made under TULRCA 1992, s 47 about the unreasonable exclusion of the applicant from being a candidate for Deputy General Secretary. An enforcement order was made in the latter case, requiring the ballot to be re-run, though the original victor also succeeded on the second occasion as well. The EAT upheld the CO's decision following an appeal by the union.

7.4.2 The continuing role of the common law

The statutory procedures are now the primary source of regulation of trade union election procedures. But as the *Ecclestone* case reminds us, these procedures do not displace the common law altogether. Trade union elections will still be governed to some extent by the constitutions and rule-books of the unions in question, where these impose obligations or deal with matters which are additional to any obligations imposed or dealt with by the statute: see *Wise v USDAW* [1996] ICR 691, and *Douglas v GPMU* [1995] IRLR 426. It is also the case that the statutory procedures do not apply to all trade union elections, but only to those positions which are expressly governed by the legislation. Trade unions also elect members to serve at regional, district, branch and workplace level. In these cases the position will be governed by the common law rather than by statute, and the starting point will be the rule-book of the union in question. Here there are three questions for the courts to get their teeth into: the content of the rules (who may stand for election, who may vote in an election); the exercise of discretion under the rules (where the successful candidate needs to be approved by a higher authority in the union); and the conduct of the ballot under the rules (in terms of the procedures followed and applied). It is the second of these three issues which has given rise to most difficulty.

[7.12] *Breen v Amalgamated Engineering Union* **[1971] 2 QB 175 (CA)**

> The plaintiff was elected by his fellow workers as a shop steward. He had been active in the union for many years and had been a shop steward since 1954, but in 1958 had been involved in a dispute about misappropriating funds, in respect of which he was fully vindicated. But there remained a measure of resentment towards Breen on the part of Townsend, the union's district secretary. In 1965 the district committee refused to approve his appointment as shop steward, never having refused such approval in the past. This was done without notice to Breen or without giving him a hearing. When he protested against the decision, and asked why his election had been refused, the original decision was confirmed by the committee which asked Townsend to write to Breen giving the reasons. This he did in December 1965, suggesting that the refusal to accept Breen was for reasons connected with the 1958 incident, though this in fact was not the case. The district committee failed to inform Breen of the real reason once this misrepresentation came to

light at the next meeting of the committee. Breen sought to challenge the decision of the district committee to reject his election on the ground that it had been taken in breach of the rules of natural justice and was void, but his action before Cusack J failed on the ground that the rules of natural justice did not apply to the decision of the committee which in his view had an unfettered discretion under the rules. Cusack J also found that the 1958 incident played no part in the decision of the committee. Breen appealed to the Court of Appeal which by a majority (Lord Denning dissenting) upheld the first instance decision.

Lord Denning MR:

The judge held that it was not open to the courts to review the decision of the district committee: because they were not exercising a judicial or quasi-judicial function. It was entirely a matter for discretion whether Mr Breen was approved or not. It could be vitiated if it was made in bad faith, but not otherwise. And he declined to find bad faith.

In so holding, the judge was echoing views which were current some years ago. But there have been important developments in the last 22 years which have transformed the situation. It may truly now be said that we have a developed system of administrative law. These developments have been most marked in the review of decisions of statutory bodies: but they apply also to domestic bodies.

Take first statutory bodies. It is now well settled that a statutory body, which is entrusted by statute with a discretion, must act fairly. It does not matter whether its functions are described as judicial or quasi-judicial on the one hand, or as administrative on the other hand, or what you will. Still it must act fairly. It must, in a proper case, give a party a chance to be heard: see *In re H K (An Infant)* [1967] 2 QB 617, 630 by Lord Parker CJ in relation to immigration officers; and *Reg. v Gaming Board for Great Britain, ex parte Benaim and Khaida* [1970] 2 QB 417, 430 by us in relation to the gaming board. The discretion of a statutory body is never unfettered. It is a discretion which is to be exercised according to law. That means at least this: the statutory body must be guided by relevant considerations and not by irrelevant. If its decision is influenced by extraneous considerations which it ought not to have taken into account, then the decision cannot stand. No matter that the statutory body may have acted in good faith; nevertheless the decision will be set aside. That is established by *Padfield v Minister of Agriculture, Fisheries and Food* [1968] AC 997 which is a landmark in modern administrative law.

Does all this apply also to a domestic body? I think it does, at any rate when it is a body set up by one of the powerful associations which we see nowadays. Instances are readily to be found in the books, notably the Stock Exchange, the Jockey Club, the Football Association, and innumerable trade unions. All these delegate power to committees. These committees are domestic bodies which control the destinies of thousands. They have quite as much power as the statutory bodies of which I have been speaking. They can make or mar a man by their decisions. Not only by expelling him from membership, but also by refusing to admit him as a member: or, it may be, by a refusal to grant a licence or to give their approval. Often their rules are framed so as to give them a discretion. They then claim that it is an 'unfettered' discretion with which the courts have no right to interfere. They go too far. They claim too much. The Minister made the same claim in the *Padfield* case, and was roundly rebuked by the House of Lords for his impudence. So should we treat this claim by trade unions. They are not above the law, but subject to it. Their rules are said to be a contract between the members and the union. So be it. If they are a contract, then it is an implied term that the discretion should be exercised fairly. But the rules are in reality more than a contract. They are a legislative code laid down by the council of the union to be obeyed by the members. This code should be subject to control by the courts just as much as a code laid down by Parliament itself. If the rules set up a domestic body and give it a discretion, it is to be implied that that body must exercise its discretion fairly. Even though its functions are not judicial or quasi-judicial, but only administrative, still it must act fairly. Should it not do so, the courts can review its decision, just as it can review the decision of a statutory body. The courts cannot grant the prerogative writs such as certiorari and mandamus against domestic bodies, but they can grant declarations and injunctions which are the modern machinery for enforcing administrative law.

Then comes the problem: ought such a body, statutory or domestic, to give reasons for its decision or to give the person concerned a chance of being heard? Not always, but sometimes. It all depends on what is fair in the circumstances. If a man seeks a privilege to which he has no particular claim—such as an appointment to some post or other—then he can be turned away without a word. He need not be heard. No explanation need be given: see the cases cited in *Schmidt v Secretary of State for Home Affairs* [1969] 2 Ch 149, 170–171. But if he is a man whose property is at stake, or who is being deprived of his livelihood, then reasons should be given why he is being turned down, and he should be given a chance to be heard. I go further. If he is a man who has some right or interest, or some legitimate expectation, of which it would not be fair to deprive him without a hearing, or reasons given, then these should be afforded him, according as the case may demand. The giving of reasons is one of the fundamentals of good administration. Again take *Padfield's* case [1968] AC 997. The dairy farmers had no right to have their complaint referred to a committee of investigation, but they had a legitimate expectation that it would be. The House made it clear that if the Minister rejected their request without reason, the court might infer that he had no good reason: and, that if he gave a bad reason, it might vitiate his decision.

So here we have Mr Breen. He was elected by his fellow workers to be their shop steward. He was their chosen representative. He was the man whom they wished to have to put forward their views to the management, and to negotiate for them. He was the one whom they wished to tell the union about their needs. As such he was a key figure. The Royal Commission on Trade Union and Employers' Associations ((1968) Cmnd 3623) under Lord Donovan paid tribute to men such as he, p 29, para 110:

'shop stewards are rarely agitators pushing workers towards unconstitutional action . . . quite commonly they are supporters of order exercising a restraining influence on their members in conditions which promote disorder'.

Seeing that he had been elected to this office by a democratic process, he had, I think, a legitimate expectation that he would be approved by the district committee unless there were good reasons against him. If they had something against him, they ought to tell him and to give him a chance of answering it before turning him down. It seems to me intolerable that they should be able to veto his appointment in their unfettered discretion. This district committee sits in Southampton some miles away from Fawley. None of them, so far as I know, worked in the oil refinery. Who are they to say nay to him and his fellow workers without good reason and without hearing what he has to say?

Edmund Davies LJ:
I entertain substantial doubts that the judgment I am about to deliver will serve the ends of justice. That is, to say the least, a most regrettable situation for any judge, but I see no escape from it. Its effect is to turn away empty-handed from this court an appellant who, on any view, has been grossly abused. It is therefore a judgment which it gives me no satisfaction to deliver.

This case turns upon the refusal in December 1965 of the Southampton district committee of the defendant trade union to approve of the plaintiff's election by his fellow workers as a shop steward. By these proceedings he seeks a declaration that their refusal was invalid and he also claims damages from his trade union. Lord Denning MR has arrived at the conclusion that their refusal to approve his appointment was for a particular reason which was entirely erroneous and gravely prejudicial to the plaintiff. If this be right, I entertain no doubt that we should allow his appeal against the adverse judgment of Cusack J. But my difficulty is in seeing how such a conclusion is open to this court.

I do not propose to go over the painful history already described in detail by Lord Denning MR. It emerges unmistakably that the plaintiff has been pursued with venom over a period of years by Mr Townsend, the secretary of the district committee. It is not without importance that, while membership of the district committee was (in the nature of things) transient, Townsend was a permanent official and, as such, would inevitably be looked to for guidance. It was a trust which he betrayed, and the judge's stinging condemnation of his conduct seems amply justified. Examples of his hostility towards the plaintiff are not hard to find. A deplorable example of this is his conduct in relation to the vitally important incident of 1958, when it was alleged that the plaintiff had dishonestly appropriated the sum of 19s. 6d. which it was said he should have handed over in separate sums of 6s. 6d. to three shop stewards. The allegation was never established, and it was Townsend himself who at the trial said (as the judge put it) 'that the right attitude to adopt was that the plaintiff was in respect of the charge of misappropriation without a stain on his character.' Despite this concession made in the witness-box, there is no room for doubt that, although Townsend *himself* had written on July 15, 1958, a letter informing the plaintiff that the accusation was 'withdrawn,' he nevertheless persisted in the view that the plaintiff was guilty and later asserted as much both orally and in writing. Mr Townsend has, in truth, much to answer for.

But the crux of this appeal, as I see it, is what happened on December 9, 1965, when the district committee considered the suitability of the plaintiff to function as a shop steward. Cusack J. held that, as they were not then exercising judicial or quasi-judicial functions, they were not called upon to observe the rules of natural justice—whatever that phrase may comprise. I hold that he was wrong in this matter, and I respectfully adopt Lord Denning MR's powerful observations on this point. The judge said: 'It was *entirely* a matter for discretion whether the plaintiff was approved or not'. Discretion up to a point was certainly theirs, but, though wide, it was not untrammeled—it had to be fairly exercised. Nevertheless, their decision was not, in my view, bound to be based on reasons which would convince all right-thinking people. Even though mistaken, they might still arrive at an *honest* conclusion and, provided they adopted no improper methods in reaching it, the decision itself could not be attacked.

Let me illustrate what I mean. In discharging the duty placed upon them by rule 13(21), the district committee would need to consider not only the integrity and efficiency of a man appointed as shop steward, but also his capacity to co-operate, his loyalty to trade union principles, his respect for its rules, his personality, and a multitude of other considerations relevant to his fitness for the post. With great respect, I find myself unable to adopt the view expressed by the Master of the Rolls in the present case that, as the plaintiff

'had been elected to this office by a democratic process. . . . if they had something against him, they ought to tell him and to give him a chance of answering it before turning him down.'

This seems to me too wide. Certainly they should have full regard to the fact of election and should not capriciously withhold approval. But would the committee, for example, need to tell an elected candidate that in their judgment his irritability nevertheless rendered him unsuitable for the post? Or, to come to the facts of the present case, would they have to indicate to the plaintiff that their decision to withhold approval of his election was based, (at least in part) on what they regarded as his blameworthy behaviour in 1963? Townsend's letter claims that they in fact did this, but the question is whether they were obliged to tell him what they had in mind *before* coming to any conclusion.

As detailed reference has not hitherto been made to the incident which I here have in mind, let me, in fairness to the district committee, expatiate. In March 1963, the plaintiff was yet again elected as shop steward and the district committee gave its approval to his so acting. But he was soon unseated when it was discovered that he was undoubtedly in breach of the union rules. He had fallen eight weeks in arrears in payment of his union contributions and was therefore liable to have his benefits forfeited. Under rule 13(21) shop stewards' contribution cards should be examined and the convener (or examiner) should report to the district committee any who were eight weeks or more in arrear. These rules were not, it is true, observed with the same strictness in all branches and certainly not in the Hythe branch to which Breen belonged. Indeed, his own practice was to pay his subscriptions quarterly in arrear, which was contrary to the rules, but by no means uncommon. A card had to be prepared for every candidate seeking election as shop steward and it needed to conclude with a certificate, signed by the convener and stating the amount of the candidate's arrears—if any. If elected, his card was forwarded to the district committee. Following on the plaintiff's election in March 1963, the convener (a Mr. Parton) signed his card showing 'Nil' arrears, the plaintiff promising Parton that he would make up his arrears at the next branch meeting. Were this promise fulfilled, it would follow that before the card reached the district committee, the 'nil' entry would have been rendered accurate. The trial judge found that the plaintiff was well aware that his election would not be approved if the district committee learned that he was in reality still eight or more weeks in arrear. Despite his promise, the plaintiff failed to pay the arrears to Mr. Parton, who nevertheless forwarded the card to the district committee. They, believing it to be accurate, proceeded to consider the plaintiff's suitability as a shop steward and in fact approved his election. But at their next meeting the true position was discovered and they forthwith resolved that his credentials as a shop steward be withdrawn. Commenting on this episode, the trial judge said:

'It has been submitted to me on behalf of the plaintiff that he was lulled into a sense of security by the slackness in his branch in observing the rules with regard to the prompt payment of subscriptions. It has also been submitted that on other occasions shop stewards had been approved when they were more than eight weeks in arrears or when the entry on their cards with regard to arrears had simply been left blank. There is evidence to support both these contentions. But the circumstances differ from case to case, and it cannot seriously be suggested that the committee exceeded their powers in withdrawing the plaintiff's credentials. I do not think they knew about the promise made to Mr. Parton on which the plaintiff had defaulted but they were quite entitled to take the view that a shop steward should set a good example and that laxity of this kind should not be tolerated'.

The facts being unchallenged, I think those comments were entirely justified. The incident may not have been a grave one, and it certainly did not merit the discreditable attempt by Townsend to have the plaintiff suspended from work as a consequence. Nevertheless, there were features of it which the district committee were wholly entitled to bear in mind when on December 9, 1965, his name next came before them for consideration under rule 13(21). Townsend asserted that they did. If so, they were under no obligation to inform the plaintiff that they had it in mind, still less to give him an opportunity to appear and make representations regarding the incident.

[*Megaw LJ delivered a judgment concurring with Edmund Davies LJ.*]

The decision of the majority in the *Breen* case is often overshadowed by Lord Denning's dissent. But it is important to remember that the plaintiff lost, and that Lord Denning's far-reaching position was not adopted by the majority. Although the majority accepted that the courts had the power to review the exercise of discretionary decisions by bodies such as the district committee, they fell some way short of the obligations expected by Lord Denning. One case where the courts did intervene is *Shotton v Hammond* (1976) 120 Sol. Jo. 780 described as a 'rare case' where the elected shop steward was refused ratification because he declined to agree to a district committee condition that he comply with its instructions, whether lawful or not. Whatever one may think of the approach of Lord Denning in *Breen*, his emphasis on the fact that the plaintiff 'had been elected to this office by a democratic process', was at least consistent with the view which the courts had taken in the cases discussed in section 7.3 above. There it will be recalled that the pattern of cases support the view that the main concern of the courts was to favour an approach which encouraged the greatest degree of membership involvement in the decision-making process of the union. Paradoxically, this approach has not extended into the electoral processes within trade unions as the following case also reveals, though in different ways.

[7.13] *Brown v Amalgamated Union of Engineering Workers* [1976] ICR 147 (Ch D)

The plaintiff was a candidate for election to the position of divisional organiser in the union. As a result of a number of errors, not all the ballot papers were sent out, and the period of the ballot was extended by an unpublished executive committee resolution. The plaintiff was nevertheless declared elected on receiving 3,988 votes to 3,818 cast in favour of the runner-up. Following a number of complaints about the holding of the ballot, the executive committee of the union decided that it should be re-run, and on this occasion the plaintiff came second. The matter was referred to the union's final appeal court which initially decided in favour of the plaintiff and reinstated the first result. But following a protest by the other candidate, the union appeal court reconsidered the matter and upheld the other candidate's appeal and rescinded its earlier decision upholding the plaintiff's appeal. The plaintiff sought a declaration that the latter decision of the appeal court was *ultra vires*, and an injunction to restrain the union from acting on the decision. The application was successful.

Walton J:
The first question which then arises, and which has given me considerable difficulty, is the question whether the October 1972 election was not so utterly chaotic as to be completely void as an election. On this particular point no assistance is apparently to be derived from case law—at any rate no authorities were cited to me. It appears to me, however, that (save perhaps in relation to wholly exceptional facts) the crucial question which falls to be asked in this regard is whether the election was conducted substantially in accordance with the directions of the executive council, and is not simply to be answered by pointing to the fact that a considerable number of members did not receive ballot papers, or did not receive their ballot papers in time. Any postal ballot must, of its nature, be subject to the vagaries of the postal service. Similarly, the fact that no member whatsoever of one of the branches received a ballot paper is due, not to any fault in the conduct of the election, but to a mistake—a serious mistake—on the part of the secretary of that branch. True it is, that one would have hoped that any competent headquarters staff would have picked up that mistake but they did not. The fact that that mistake was made had nothing directly to

do with the conduct of the election, and hence of its overall validity. One must also keep a sense of proportion. The total electorate was over 29,000; the errors affected, so far as is known, some 600 persons. I am to some extent fortified in this conclusion by noting that Mr Waterhouse, in his extremely able address to me on behalf of the second defendant, did not really rely in this part of the case on the non- or late delivery of ballot papers, but upon the provisions of rule 2(17). He said that the terms of that sub-rule implied that all votes taken after the specified date must be counted as invalid, so that the failure by the executive council to communicate to the members that the date for voting had been extended fundamentally invalidated the whole election. I see the force of that, but it appears always to have been the practice of the executive council, doubtless in furtherance of its powers under rule 2(7), under which it exercises general control of elections, to decide all questions of late votes on their merits. It seems to me that this is what in substance happened in the present case. Doubtless the members ought to have been told of the automatic extension, and it appears that they were not so told through a mistake in the office. But against the background that the executive council had always previously decided all questions of late votes on their merits—a procedure which is not in conflict with rule 2(17), which I think merely directs what votes must be counted, not what votes may be counted—I think that this was a mere irregularity, highly regrettable but not going, as it were, to the root of the election.

The next point which then arises is, what was the power of the executive council to order a fresh ballot? It is, I think, beyond argument that if the executive council had so ordered at any time prior to the declaration of the result of the first ballot, they would have been fully justified in their decision. I think that Mr Hugh Scanlon, the well known president of the union, puts it extremely well in his affidavit sworn herein when he says:

'It has been long understood within the union, and it is submitted correctly so understood, particularly having regard to earlier rulings of the High Court in the cases mentioned below, that the powers and duties of the executive council under the rules with reference to election require and empower the executive council to take such steps as they think proper to ensure that elections are conducted fairly and in such a way as to enable the electors to exercise a free choice on the merits of the candidates for any office, and that such powers extend to the ordering of a new ballot. It is further submitted that the executive council is under the rules (in particular rules 2(7) and 15(18)) entitled to order a new ballot in one election only out of several conducted on one set of ballot forms if it judges that any known irregularities in the conduct of the postal ballot, having regard to the size of the particular majority or plurality, are likely to have affected that election only and not others carried out by means of the same postal ballot. The earlier cases in the High Court to which I referred above are those of *Scott v Smith* (unreported), 19 December 1939; *Sillars v Amalgamated Engineering Union, The Times*, March 21, 1951; *Sillars v Amalgamated Engineering Union (No. 2)* (unreported), June 7, 1951, and *Scanlon v Carron (No. 2), The Times*, July 25, 1963.'

The latter part of this paragraph is directed to the fact that there were other elections proceeding at the same time in relation to which no such fresh ballot was ordered, either because the leading candidate had such a commanding lead, or because under the rules there would, in any event, have to be a second ballot. In my judgment, Mr Scanlon has appreciated the position here with exactitude, being fully supported by the cases to which he refers.

The question still remains, however, whether the fact that the result of the election has been declared makes any difference. Mr Waterhouse says it does not, and by way of illustration he points to the lamentable present happenings in connection with the election of the president of the Oxford Union Society. The challenge to the election of the president happened, he says, only after the result of the election had been announced.

I think that this is a very good example of the wisdom of sticking close to the rule book of this union. I am unacquainted with the present rules and regulations of the Oxford Union Society but in my day, at least, they contained an express provision (rule 21) which stated that if any member not later than three clear days after any election satisfied the president that he had reasonable cause to believe that a candidate had solicited votes, a committee was to be appointed to investigate the charge, which, if proved, resulted in the candidate being ineligible for any office or committee for 12 months after the commission of the offence. Being so ineligible to be elected, his (or her) election was therefore of necessity a nullity.

This is, of course, only a more graphic way of saying that the whole matter must be resolved by reference to the relevant rules. In my judgment, the power of the executive council to order a fresh ballot, which is a power I think conferred upon them by rule 2(7), that is to say, is part of their general power of control of the election, comes to an end when the election itself comes to an end. And the election itself comes to an end when the result is declared. Down to that time, the election still continues, and fresh ballots may be ordered if the circumstances so justify. After that time, the election is over, and neither the power in rule 2(7) which has ended with the ending of the election, nor the power in rule 15(18) which, if it permitted the elected candidate to be deprived of office, would be contrary to rule 2(4), which provides that the candidate who receives a larger number of votes than the remainder combined is to be declared elected, apply.

I think that this conclusion—although I can see that it may conceivably lead to difficulties where irregularities come to the notice of the executive council long after the declaration of the result—is in accordance with common sense. There is no obligation on the executive council to declare the result within any particular time; in the present case, for very good reasons indeed, they took their time about it. They had, by the time of the declaration of the result, been fully apprised of the fact that there had been malfunctionings of the electoral machine, but they still went ahead and declared the result, because at that stage they thought that while there had been some mistakes and imperfections in the ballot, there was not enough to require or to justify the ordering of any new ballot. Thereafter, so it appears to me, unless some factors emerge which demonstrate that the whole election was a nullity—for example, that the candidate declared elected was not duly qualified, or that a sizeable slice of the votes had been cast by persons, not members of the union (or even members thereof who had no right to cast them at all) then there appears to me to be no rule under which the candidate declared elected can be deprived of his office. The rules do not provide for anything in the nature of an election petition. I think it was for this very reason that Roxburgh J, who was always meticulous in his choice of illustrations was so careful, in the first *Sillars* case, *The Times*, March 21, 1951, to indicate that the executive council, if it found evidence of irregularities or corruption:

'. . . instead of declaring the candidate elected could have postponed that declaration and decided that some action should be taken in regard to the area of corruption; or again, if the various complicated rules about the conduct of the elections had been violated, they could have postponed the declaration and directed some steps to correct that situation.'

I think that Roxburgh J meant precisely what he said, and that in his view the postponement of the declaration in such cases was, or at any rate was capable of being, essential.

I do not of course shut my eyes to the fact that this may mean that a corrupt candidate who has not committed any offences for which he is liable to be expelled from the union—and it must be borne in mind that under rule 22 there is a wide variety of possible misdemeanours justifying expulsion—may, as a result of the declaration of the poll be no longer liable to be called to account. Be that so; I think that this is a situation which is far preferable to leaving minor irregularities hanging over his head for an indefinite period. It is of the essence of any fair system for invalidating elections that any objection should be presented within fairly narrow time limits: compare section 109 of the Representation of the People Act 1949 in relation to a Parliamentary election.

This is an important case in which the court sent out powerful messages that minor procedural irregularities are not to be taken to undermine an election, even where they could have affected the result; and that a declaration of an election result is not lightly to be disturbed, even where there has been an irregularity. In this way the court is prepared to accept that, in the absence of fraud or the like, the democratic wishes of the membership may have to be discounted, in the sense that they may not be properly tested by a procedure which conceivably could be flawed from beginning to end. What can be the explanation for this apparent willingness to depart from the principle of membership sovereignty which we encountered in the cases in section 7.3 above? There are perhaps three reasons. One is the floodgates argument, with the courts perhaps reluctant to provide a forum for every contested election for every trade union position. For it is to be recalled that although the plaintiff was successful in this case, it is not a decision designed to encourage litigation by bad losers. And, secondly, there is the question of certainty in the election result, and a need to ensure against the instability caused by elections being open to challenge even after the result has been declared, affecting the validity of the decisions taken by the elected individual or the body of which he or she may be a member. A third reason was suggested by Morison J in *Douglas v GPMU* [1995] IRLR 426, where he said that

> The power to cancel an election after the result has become known and published is one which, if capable of being lawful, would require to be carefully drafted so as to avoid potential abuse of the electoral system (at p 429).

7.5 Trade union members' rights

So far our concern has been mainly with the structure of government within trade unions and the powers of the different government institutions. The question which now arises is the extent to which the members of a trade union are bound by the decisions of the governing bodies in the election of which they may have participated, or by the outcome of ballots in which they may have taken part. Do trade union members have rights, whether under the rules of the union or independently of the rules of the union, which may not be compromised by the democratic procedures of the union? As we have seen, the Trade Union Act 1913 introduced a right not to contribute to the political fund of a trade union in the case of those trade unions with political objects. More recently the Sex Discrimination Act 1975 (section 12) and the Race Relations Act 1976 (section 11) introduced rights not to be discriminated against in the provision of services and facilities by a trade union. But in the absence of more detailed legislation, this was an area where the courts took the driving seat, and there are many examples in this chapter of individuals asserting rights against the democratic structures of their union. Beginning in 1980, however, a comprehensive package of members' rights has been introduced by Parliament, and it is on three of these provisions that we concentrate in this section.

7.5.1 The right to information

A right of trade union members to have access to union financial records was first introduced in the Trade Union Act 1871. This was repealed in the 1970s, it having previously been held that the member could employ skilled agents to inspect the accounts on their behalf (*Dodd v Amalgamated Marine Workers' Union* [1924] 1 Ch 116). But in some cases the obligation found its way into trade union rule-books, and these provisions survived the repeal of the 1871 Act. In *Taylor v NUM (Derbyshire Area) (No 2)* [1985] IRLR 65 it was held that the contractual right in the rule-book was to be construed in the same way as the previous statutory right so that the union could not object to the member inspecting the books in the presence of an accountant. It would of course have been open to the union to provide expressly that the right of inspection in the rule-book was not to be construed as the plaintiffs contended, but this had not been done in this case. With the repeal of the 1871 Act, trade union members had no greater rights than members of the public to financial information about their union. Under the Trade Union and Labour Relations Act 1974, members of the public were entitled to inspect the annual return which the union was required to submit to the Certification Officer. This gave rise to expressions of concern by the then Conservative government which in *Trade Unions and their Members* (Cm 95, 1987) commented that:

> It is reasonable to assume that a union member has a greater interest in his union's affairs than members of the public. However, in a significant number of major unions, which do not contain provisions on this matter in their rule books, members may be limited to the information available from the Certification Office or on request from the union. The information required to meet statutory provisions only gives an outline of a union's financial affairs and is usually supplied by the union's head office on behalf of the whole union rather than by individual branches. In addition, because it consists of accounts which have had to be audited, it will not reflect the current state of the union's affairs [paragraph 3.24].

The position is now governed in some detail by the 1992 Act, containing measures first introduced in the Employment Act 1988.

[7.14] Trade Union and Labour Relations (Consolidation) Act 1992, sections 28–30

Duty to keep accounting records

28 (1) A trade union shall—
(a) cause to be kept proper accounting records with respect to its transactions and its assets and liabilities, and

(b) establish and maintain a satisfactory system of control of its accounting records, its cash holdings and all its receipts and remittances.

(2) Proper accounting records shall not be taken to be kept with respect to the matters mentioned in subsection (1)(a) unless there are kept such records as are necessary to give a true and fair view of the state of the affairs of the trade union and to explain its transactions.

Duty to keep records available for inspection

29 (1) A trade union shall keep available for inspection from their creation until the end of the period of six years beginning with the 1 January following the end of the period to which they relate such of the records of the union, or of any branch or section of the union, as are, or purport to be, records required to be kept by the union under section 28 . . .

(2) In section 30 (right of member to access to accounting records)—
(a) references to a union's accounting records are to any such records as are mentioned in subsection (1) above, and
(b) references to a union's accounting records for inspection are to records which the union is required by that subsection to keep available for inspection.

(3) The expiry of the period mentioned in subsection (1) above does not affect the duty of a trade union to comply with a request for access made under section 30 before the end of that period.

Right of access to accounting records

30 (1) A member of a trade union has a right to request access to any accounting records of the union which are available for inspection and relate to periods including a time when he was a member of the union.

Where there has been a failure to comply with a request made under section 30, the person who made the request may apply either to the Certification Officer or to the High Court (or Court of Session in Scotland). The Officer or the court may issue an order to ensure that the applicant is allowed to inspect the records requested, to be accompanied by an accountant when inspecting the records, or to take or be supplied with copies of or extracts from the records, as the case may be. An order of the CO is to be enforced in the same way as a court order (section 31). Trade unions are also required to provide a financial statement to members annually, this to include details of income and expenditure, as well as the salary and benefits of senior officers: TULRCA 1992, section 32A.

7.5.2 The right not to strike

Perhaps more controversial than the member's right to be supplied with information about his or her union is the right of the individual member not to strike, in the sense of not being liable to discipline or expulsion for failing to take part in a strike. This is an issue which has caused the courts difficulty from time to time in the past, leading them to thrash around unconvincingly, looking for a way of protecting the member, as in *Esterman v NALGO* [1974] ICR 625, **[7.25]** below. The issue is also addressed in the Green Paper, *Trade Unions and their Members, op cit*, where the then government claimed that:

> the right of the individual to choose to go to work despite a call to take industrial action is an essential freedom. It can often be challenged, however, by those who take a hard line view of the traditional philosophy of the trade union movement based on the concept of collective strength through solidarity [paragraph 2.10].

Concern was expressed that a trade union may:

> lead its members into action for which it has legal immunity but for which the members do not. Although it is rare for an employer to sue his workers individually, if they take industrial action they face a real possibility of being dismissed without being able to claim unfair dismissal. A tough choice therefore faces the union member called by his union to take industrial action: either to follow the union down a path which will almost certainly reduce his income and may lead to a loss of job, or to carry on working and face disciplinary action by the union [paragraph 2.11].

Although it was conceded that recent legislative changes affecting the closed shop made it less likely that expelled members would lose their jobs as a result of their expulsion from the union, still:

> trade union members have argued strongly that those who disagree with the policies and actions of their leaders none the less value their membership and do not see why dissent should lead to expulsion. Even if their present jobs are not thereby put at risk, future job prospects may still be affected particularly in those industries which operate a pre-entry closed shop agreement' [paragraph 2.15].

Some may find these concerns convincing. They gave rise to what was the Employment Act 1988, section 3, and what are now sections 64 and 65 of the TULRCA 1992. It is to be recalled that trade union members now also have a statutory right to a ballot before industrial action (TULRCA 1992, section 62). This is in addition to the duty to ballot which trade unions owe to employers as a condition of immunity from tortious liability. Trade union members thus may take part in a ballot but refuse to be bound by the outcome. Indeed if there is no obligation to accept the result, there seems little incentive to take part in the ballot in the first place. It should also be noted in assessing these arguments that the lack of protection for employees dismissed for going on strike was in breach of international law (see p 943 below), and that there is now limited protection for employees against dismissal in such circumstances. It is also the case that the pre-entry closed shop is unenforceable following measures introduced by the Employment Act 1990 (section 1) which makes it unlawful for an employer to discriminate against an applicant because he or she is or is not a member of a trade union. Anyone refused employment for non-membership of a trade union thus has a legal remedy. See pp 746–750 below.

[7.15] Trade Union and Labour Relations (Consolidation) Act 1992, sections 64–65

Right not to be unjustifiably disciplined

64 (1) An individual who is or has been a member of a trade union has the right not to be unjustifiably disciplined by the union.

(2) For this purpose an individual is 'disciplined' by a trade union if a determination is made, or purportedly made, under the rules of the union or by an official of the union or a number of persons including an official that—
(a)   he should be expelled from the union or a branch or section of the union,
(b)   he should pay a sum to the union, to a branch or section of the union or to any other person;
(c)   sums tendered by him in respect of an obligation to pay subscriptions or other sums to the union, or to a branch or section of the union, should be treated as unpaid or paid for a different purpose,
(d)   he should be deprived to any extent of, or of access to, any benefits, services or facilities which would otherwise be provided or made available to him by virtue of his membership of the union, or a branch or section of the union,
(e)   another trade union, or a branch or section of it, should be encouraged or advised not to accept him as a member, or
(f)   he should be subjected to some other detriment;
and whether an individual is 'unjustifiably disciplined' shall be determined in accordance with section 65.

(3) Where a determination made in infringement of an individual's right under this section requires the payment of a sum or the performance of an obligation, no person is entitled in any proceedings to rely on that determination for the purpose of recovering the sum or enforcing the obligation.

(4) Subject to that, the remedies for infringement of the right conferred by this section are as provided by sections 66 and 67, and not otherwise.

(5) The right not to be unjustifiably disciplined is in addition to (and not in substitution for) any right which exists apart from this section; and, subject to section 66(4), nothing in this section or sections 65 to 67 affects any remedy for infringement of any such right.

Meaning of 'unjustifiably disciplined'

65 (1) An individual is unjustifiably disciplined by a trade union if the actual or supposed conduct which constitutes the reason, or one of the reasons, for disciplining him is—
(a)   conduct to which this section applies, or
(b)   something which is believed by the union to amount to such conduct;
but subject to subsection (6) (cases of bad faith in relation to assertion of wrongdoing).

(2) This section applies to conduct which consists in—
(a)   failing to participate in or support a strike or other industrial action (whether by members of the union or by others), or indicating opposition to or a lack of support for such action;
(b)   failing to contravene, for a purpose connected with such a strike or other industrial action, a requirement imposed on him by or under a contract of employment;
(c)   asserting (whether by bringing proceedings or otherwise) that the union, any official or representative of it or a trustee of its property has contravened, or is proposing to

> contravene, a requirement which is, or is thought to be, imposed by or under the rules of the union or any other agreement or by or under any enactment (whenever passed) or any rule of law;
>
> (d) encouraging or assisting a person—
>
>   (i)   to perform an obligation imposed on him by a contract of employment, or
>
>   (ii) to make or attempt to vindicate any such assertion as is mentioned in paragraph (c);
>
> (e) contravening a requirement imposed by or in consequence of a determination which infringes the individual's or another individual's right not to be unjustifiably disciplined;
>
> (f) failing to agree, or withdrawing agreement, to the making from his wages (in accordance with arrangements between his employer and the union) of deductions representing payments to the union in respect of his membership,
>
> (g) resigning or proposing to resign from the union or from another union, becoming or proposing to become a member of another union, refusing to become a member of another union, or being a member of another union,
>
> (h) working with, or proposing to work with, individuals who are not members of the union or who are or are not members of another union,
>
> (i) working for, or proposing to work for, an employer who employs or who has employed individuals who are not members of the union or who are or are not members of another union, or
>
> (j) requiring the union to do an act which the union is, by any provision of this Act, required to do on the requisition of a member.

It will be apparent that sections 64 and 65 apply to a great deal more than the right not to strike, though they do not cover all disciplinary action. In *Medhurst v NALGO* [1990] ICR 687 it was held that the legislation did not extend to protect the applicant who had been suspended from membership for tape recording the meetings of a local executive committee. (In such cases the member will be forced back on common law remedies which may be available. See section 7.6 below.) Enforcement of TULRCA 1992, section 64 is by way of a complaint to an employment tribunal rather than the Certification Officer, with a right of appeal to the Employment Appeal Tribunal and then to the Court of Appeal. The remedy is by way of compensation, for which a separate application to an employment tribunal must be made (TULRCA 1992, sections 66, 67). The amount of compensation is such an amount as the tribunal thinks just and equitable, though it includes injury to feelings (on which see *Bradley v NALGO* [1991] ICR 359) and is subject to a statutory maximum. But although the charter for dissent is wide ranging, most of the reported cases have been concerned with strike-breakers who sought to assert their rights not to be disciplined as a result.

[7.16] *Knowles v Fire Brigades Union* [1997] ICR 595 (CA)

The appellants in this case were full time firefighters employed by Shropshire County Council who had also accepted positions as retained firefighters in their spare time. It had been accepted by the National Joint Council for Local Authorities Fire Brigades in 1977 that the engagement of full-time firefighters as retained firefighters in this way should be discontinued. Because of recruitment problems, the national employers proposed in the late 1980s that the arrangement should be reintroduced, but it was decisively rejected by the union at its annual conference in 1989, and again in 1991. In this case the appellants were full-time firefighters who were moved to a new fire station (Wellington) on a duty shift system. The station from which they were moved (Tweedale) was to be kept open but serviced by retained staff only. Although full-time firefighters (at Wellington) the appellants enrolled as retained staff at their old station (Tweedale) in clear breach of union policy that full-time firefighters should not also be engaged as retained staff. They were expelled from the union following a disciplinary hearing, and brought proceedings claiming that they had been unjustifiably disciplined contrary to TULRCA 1992, section 65(2)(a) for failing to take part in a strike or other industrial action. The issue before the industrial tribunal was whether the union's 'policy of opposing a system of whole-time firefighters being employed in addition on retained firefighting contracts' constituted 'industrial action' within the meaning of section 65(2)(a). The industrial tribunal held that it did, the EAT reversed, and the Court of Appeal upheld the EAT.

Neill LJ:

I accept that the words 'other industrial action' are not to be narrowly construed. But they have to be looked at in a context where the transition from negotiations to action may have far-reaching consequences. We are not dealing in the present case with Part V of the Act of 1992 which provides that an act done by a trade union to induce a person to take part in industrial action is not protected unless the industrial action has the support of a ballot. But it is to be noted that one of the rights conferred on trade union members by Chapter V in Part I is the right to a ballot before industrial action takes place: see section 62.

Industrial action can take many forms, but, in the absence of any statutory definition, I do not think that any attempt at a paraphrase is likely to be useful. In my judgment the question of what is industrial action for the purposes of section 65 of the Act of 1992 is a mixed question of fact and law. In large measure it is a question of fact, but the facts have to be judged in the context of the Act which plainly contemplates that industrial action is a serious step.

It is necessary to look at all the circumstances. These circumstances will include the contracts of employment of the employees and whether any breach of or departure from the terms of the contract are involved, the effect on the employer of what is done or omitted and the object which the union or the employees seek to achieve. In the present case it seems to me that the following factors are relevant.

(a) At the date when the applicants were expelled from the union the policy had been in force for over 18 months. The object to be achieved by the union's policy was to prevent a unilateral departure from the terms which had been agreed in 1977.

(b) The policy did not require full-time workers to break or to depart from the terms of their existing contracts. The policy merely required firefighters not to undertake additional work under new contracts.

(c) There is no evidence to suggest that either the county council or the union contemplated that the 'pressure' exerted by the union required the support of a ballot.

(d) There was some discussion at the hearing as to whether any of the other full-time firefighters in Shropshire had actually refused offers of retained contracts. Even in the absence of express evidence to this effect, however, it is reasonable to assume that some of the 45 other firefighters did so refuse. But their compliance with the union's policy does not seem to me on the facts of this case to amount to a clear indication that the union and its members had crossed the threshold into taking industrial action within the meaning of section 65.

(e) The evidence of Mr Bryant [an executive council member of the union], as recorded in paragraph (6) of the reasons, shows that negotiations were being continued and that, though the union were making clear that they intended to adhere to their policy, the breakdown which is almost implicit in the taking of industrial action had not occurred. As Browne-Wilkinson J said in *Midland Plastic v Till* [1983] ICR 118, 124, 'The actual taking of industrial action is the last stage and is quite distinct from the stage at which the threat of it is being used as a negotiating weapon.' One must also take account of the reaction of the lay members of the appeal tribunal in the present case to the suggestion that the mere fact that an employer may feel himself inhibited as a result of pressure applied to him means that industrial action has been taken.

In my judgment the appeal tribunal were justified in concluding that the industrial tribunal had misdirected themselves in treating pressure plus inhibition as a sufficient test of industrial action. Furthermore, I think that counsel for the union was correct in her submission that the industrial tribunal failed sufficiently to distinguish between conduct which fell short even of a threat and actual 'industrial action' within the meaning of section 65.

7.5.3 The right not to be excluded from membership

The third measure dealt with here is designed to protect the trade union member who is expelled from his or her union in order to give effect to the TUC Disputes Principles and Procedures. These are designed to stop one union poaching the members of another, and to stop one union from organising in a workplace where another is already established. Initially adopted at the annual conference of the TUC at Bridlington in 1939 (and known for some time thereafter as the Bridlington principles), the principles have been revised on a number of occasions since, most recently in 2000.

[7.17] TUC Disputes Principles and Procedures (2000)

Principle 2
It is in the interests of all affiliates and the Movement to build trade union membership, and the Movement to develop and maintain stable trade union structures. Members moving from union to union, without agreed regulation and procedure, can undermine collective bargaining structures and may even threaten the existence of trade union organisation within a particular company or group of workers. All affiliates of the TUC accept as a binding commitment to their continued affiliation to the TUC that they will not knowingly and actively seek to take into membership existing or 'recent' members of another union by making recruitment approaches, either directly or indirectly, without the agreement of that organisation'.

Notes to Principle 2 require each union to ask prospective members whether they are or have been a member of any other trade union: this is to help avoid any unauthorised transfers of members.

Where one union claims that another has acted in breach of these principles, it may make a complaint to the TUC which, if unable to conciliate a settlement, may appoint a disputes committee from a panel of leading trade unionists to investigate the matter and to make recommendations about how it should be resolved. The procedures, which are expressly stated not to be legally binding, apply only to TUC affiliated unions. Before 1993, the normal remedy where a complaint was upheld would be an order requiring the offending union to expel from membership those members who had been recruited in breach of the principles. TUC affiliated unions typically had adopted a model rule authorising, if necessary, the termination of membership after six weeks' notice of any member, to comply with a decision of the Disputes committee. The validity of the rule was upheld by the House of Lords in the following case.

[7.18] *Cheall v APEX* [1983] 2 AC 180 (HL)

The plaintiff was accepted into membership of APEX, in the knowledge that he was already a member of ACTSS. The matter was referred to a TUC Disputes Committee which instructed APEX to terminate his membership, which it did, exercising powers conferred by the model rule permitting the termination of membership to comply with a TUC Disputes Committee award. This formed rule 4 of the APEX rule-book. Cheall thereupon took legal action to restrain the expulsion but failed at first instance before Bingham J. His appeal to the Court of Appeal was successful, the court taking the view that the model rule was contrary to public policy. The House of Lords reversed the Court of Appeal.

Lord Diplock:
It was contended on Cheall's behalf that the termination of his membership was also void because the procedure which resulted in it constituted a denial to him of natural justice. He was entitled, it was suggested, not merely to be present, as he was, at the hearing of the complaint against APEX by the disputes committee, but also to make representations, written or oral, to the disputes committee explaining his reasons for wishing to switch his membership from ACTSS to APEX and the consequences that an award adverse to APEX would have upon him personally.

This contention did not find favour with any of the judges in the courts below: the only parties to the dispute that was before the disputes committee were the trade unions concerned. They, and they only, were entitled to make representations written or oral to the committee. Decisions that resolve disputes between the parties to them, whether by litigation or some other adversarial dispute-resolving process, often have consequences which affect persons who are not parties to the dispute; but the legal concept of natural justice has never been extended to give such persons as well as the parties themselves rights to be heard by the decision-making tribunal before the decision is reached. If natural justice required that Cheall should be entitled to be heard, there could be no stopping there; any other member of either union who thought he would be adversely affected by the decision, if it went one way or the other, would have a similar right to be heard. To claim that this is a requirement of 'fair play in action' (to borrow Sach LJ's description of natural justice in *Edwards v Society of Graphical and Allied Trades* [1971] Ch. 354, 382) would be little short of ludicrous.

Alternatively, though rather more mutedly, it was submitted that Cheall was entitled to be heard by the executive council of APEX before they decided to comply with the award, which was already more than one year old, by giving him notice of termination of his membership under rule 14. In his judgment Bingham J. sets out what had in fact occurred before the executive council reached its decision to act under rule 14 and Cheall's own knowledge of it. That, in the learned judge's view, made it inevitable that the only way in which APEX could fulfill its duty to act in the best interest of its members as a whole was by complying with the award of the disputes committee. His conclusion was that, in the circumstances that he recounts, there was no legal obligation on APEX to give Cheall prior notice of their decision or grant him an opportunity to be heard. 'To have done so,' said the learned judge [1982] ICR 231, 250, 'where nothing he said could affect the outcome would in my view have been cruel deception.' My Lords, I can content myself with saying: 'I agree.'

Public policy
Finally it was argued that if all the submissions with which I have already dealt failed, as in my opinion they plainly do, the Bridlington principles, which have been in operation since as long ago as 1939, are contrary to public policy, since they restrict the right of the individual to join and to remain a member of a trade union of his choice; and that any attempt to give effect to any such restriction would, upon application by the individual affected by it, be prevented by the courts.

This supposed rule of public policy has, it is claimed, always formed part of the common law of England but it has now been reinforced by the accession of the United Kingdom to the European Convention for the Protection of Human Rights and Fundamental Freedoms (1953) (Cmd. 8969). . . .

My Lords, freedom of association can only be mutual; there can be no right of an individual to associate with other individuals who are not willing to associate with him. The body of the membership of APEX, represented by its executive council and whose best interests it was the duty of the executive council to promote, were not willing to continue to accept Cheall as a fellow-member. No doubt this was because if they continued to accept him, they ran the risk of attracting the sanction of suspension or expulsion of APEX from the TUC and all the attendant disadvantages to themselves as members of APEX that such suspension or expulsion would entail. But I know of no existing rule of public policy that would prevent trade unions from entering into arrangements with one another which they consider to be in the interests of their members in promoting order in industrial relations and enhancing their members' bargaining power with their employers; nor do I think it a permissible exercise of your Lordships' judicial power to create a new rule of public policy to that effect. If this is to be done at all it must be done by Parliament.

Different considerations might apply if the effect of Cheall's expulsion from APEX were to have put his job in jeopardy, either because of the existence of a closed shop or for some other reason. But this is not the case. All that has happened is that he left a union, ACTSS, in order to join another union, APEX, which he preferred. After four years of membership he was compelled, against his will, to leave it and was given the opportunity, which he rejected, of rejoining ACTSS if he so wished.

But although the model rule thus survived the *Cheall* case (which went as far as an unsuccessful application under the European Convention on Human Rights: *Cheall v United Kingdom* (1986) 8 EHRR 44), it has since been challenged by legislation. The then government took the view that the Bridlington principles were 'another out-dated and undemocratic restriction' on employee 'freedom of choice', 'fundamentally flawed' for making no provision 'for union members to be consulted or for their wishes to be taken into account' (H C Debs, 17 November 1992, col 171). These concerns, which were trailed in the Green Paper, *Industrial Relations in the 1990s* (Cm 1602, 1991), are reflected in what is now TULRCA 1992, section 174, a measure introduced by the Trade Union Reform and Employment Rights Act 1993, section 14. Following the introduction of this measure it became necessary for the TUC to alter the Disputes Principles and Procedures, particularly in relation to the remedy which the Disputes Committee could award in the event of a breach. Because of the statutory constraints on the expulsion of members, provision is now made for the offending union to compensate the aggrieved union. See *ISTC, GMB and TGWU: MFI Manufacturing Sites*, TUC Report 2003, p 179.

[7.19] Trade Union and Labour Relations (Consolidation) Act 1992, section 174

Right not to be excluded or expelled from union

174 (1) An individual shall not be excluded or expelled from a trade union unless the exclusion or expulsion is permitted by this section.

(2) The exclusion or expulsion of an individual from a trade union is permitted by this section if (and only if)—

(a) he does not satisfy, or no longer satisfies, an enforceable membership requirement contained in the rules of the union,

(b) he does not qualify, or no longer qualifies, for membership of the union by reason of the union operating only in a particular part or particular parts of Great Britain,

(c) in the case of a union whose purpose is the regulation of relations between its members and one particular employer or a number of employers who are associated, he is not, or is no longer, employed by that employer or one of those employers, or

(d) the exclusion or expulsion is entirely attributable to *conduct of his (other than excluded conduct) and the conduct to which it is wholly or mainly attributable is not protected conduct.*

(3) A requirement in relation to membership of a union is 'enforceable' for the purposes of subsection (2)(a) if it restricts membership solely by reference to one or more of the following criteria—

(a) employment in specified trade, industry or profession,

(b) occupational description (including trade, level or category of appointment), and

(c) possession of specified trade, industrial or professional qualifications or work experience.

(4) For the purposes of subsection (2)(d) "excluded conduct", in relation to an individual, means—

(a) conduct which consists in his being or ceasing to be, or having been or ceased to be, a member of another trade union,

(b) conduct which consists in his being or ceasing to be, or having been or ceased to be, employed by a particular employer or at a particular place, or

(c) conduct to which section 65 (conduct for which an individual may not be disciplined by a union) applies or would apply if the references in that section to the trade union which is relevant for the purposes of that section were references to any trade union.

(4A) For the purposes of subsection (2)(d) "protected conduct" is conduct which consists in the individual's being or ceasing to be, or having been or ceased to be, a member of a political party.

(4B) Conduct which consists of activities undertaken by an individual as a member of a political party is not conduct falling within subsection (4A).

A complaint of unlawful exclusion or expulsion may be made to an employment tribunal (section 174(5)). Applications should normally be brought within six months beginning with the date of the exclusion or expulsion (section 175). The remedy is a declaration in the first instance which may be followed by an application for compensation to an employment tribunal. There is a minimum award of compensation of £5,900 (section 176) except in cases where

- the exclusion or expulsion is *mainly* attributable to conduct falling within section 174(4A), and
- the other conduct to which the exclusion or expulsion was attributable consisted wholly or mainly of conduct of the complainant which was contrary to (a) a rule of the union or (b) an objective of the union.

In these cases compensation may be payable, but there is no minimum award.

The material marked in the italics in **[7.19]** above and in the subsequent text represents amendments made by the Employment Relations Act 2004. As originally enacted, s 174 provided that trade unions could exclude or expel someone for a reason 'entirely attributable to his conduct' (s 174(2)(d)). But for this purpose it was expressly provided that conduct did not include being a member of a political party (s 174(4)(a)(iii)). That is to say a trade union could not lawfully exclude or expel someone because he or she was a member of a political party (even where this may have been only part of the reason for exclusion or expulsion). Anyone excluded or expelled in this way would have been entitled to recover the minimum award of compensation. Trade unions are not politically sectarian bodies, and typically this restraint would not normally give rise to any problems in practice. However, trade unions were increasingly troubled by the activities of the British National Party (BNP) and by the perceived infiltration of trade unions by BNP members and activists. The BNP policies and activities are contrary to the objects and principles of trade unionism, and some unions had taken express steps to deal with this problem. Under the rules of UNISON, for example, express powers have been taken to exclude or expel anyone who encourages or participates in the activities of fascist organisations committed to white supremacy. This issue came to a head in *Lee v ASLEF*, EAT/0625/03/RN where proceedings were brought by the applicant—a train driver— who was expelled from ASLEF after it had been discovered that he was standing as a BNP candidate in a local election. Further inquiries revealed that he was 'quite a well known activist in the BNP' and that he had stood before for the party in general elections. It was also alleged that Mr Lee had distributed anti-Islamic leaflets, and harassed a member of the Anti-Nazi League. The allegations included taking photographs, making 'throat cut' gestures, and following a woman to her home where it is alleged that he 'clocked' her house number.

The results are the rather constipated amendments to TULRCA 1992, sections 174 and 176. The effect is that a trade union may not lawfully exclude or expel someone for membership of the BNP, but may do so for taking part in the activities of the BNP. This might include standing as a candidate, campaigning in an election, speaking on or joining a public platform, distributing literature, or writing to a newspaper. Where someone is excluded or expelled mainly because of membership of a political party, the effect of the amendments to s 176 is that he or she will not be entitled to the minimum award of compensation, if it can be shown that the exclusion or expulsion was motivated in part by conduct which was contrary to the rules or policies of the union. It is not clear why the government did not simply change the law to allow trade unions to expel people because their membership of a particular political party was incompatible with membership of the union. There may have been concerns about the human rights implications of such a measure. If so, it is not clear how these concerns are assuaged by a provision that allows a trade union to exclude or expel not because of BNP membership but because of BNP activities. The latter is as likely to engage human rights as much as the former. But if there was a concern about human rights, it is a concern that may have been rather one-dimensional. Although right-wing extremists have human rights, so do trade unions and trade unionists. It is not clear how it can be said to be consistent with the Article 11 rights of trade union members that they should be compelled to associate against their wishes and against the express policy of their union with individuals who are associated with another organisation which promotes policies contrary to the policies of the union. In *RSPCA v Attorney General* [2002] 1 WLR 448, it was said by Lightman J in relation to Article 11 (in a case about whether the RSPCA could expel fox hunters): 'that freedom embraces the freedom to exclude from association those whose membership it honestly believes to be damaging to the interests of the Society'.

[7.20] Institute of Employment Rights (IER), *Submission to the Joint Committee on Human Rights (JCHR) on the Trade Union and Labour Relations (Consolidation) Act 1992, s 174* (HL102/HC 640 (2003–2004))

> 30 Although the government's amendment may be seen by some as a welcome initiative, it does not go far enough. It is strongly arguable that section 174(4)(iii) of the 1992 Act breaches the right of trade unions to freedom of association under article 11 of the ECHR for reasons considered above. It deprives the unions of the right under their rules to determine who their members will be. The amendment to s 174 introduced by the [government] eases the liability of trade unions but does not remove it. Trade unions will still be liable to individuals who have been excluded under the rules of the union in question for membership of a political party which is offensive to the union. Trade unions will also be required to accept and retain in membership individuals who are known members of the BNP. There are no other organisations in the United Kingdom – such as churches, political parties, charities, sports clubs or London clubs – which are constrained in the way that trade unions are constrained by s 174 (even after the government's amendment). The provisions prohibiting trade unions from excluding or expelling people because of their membership of a political party should be repealed. Trade unions should be free to admit and expel people in accordance with their own rules. The right to freedom of association has implications for some of the other restrictions on trade union exclusion and expulsion which are dealt with in s 174. These other provisions of s 174 also represent major restraints on trade union autonomy. They too ought to be repealed, in order to remove the risk of s 174 being declared incompatible by the courts, and the risk also of a ruling against the United Kingdom by the European Court of Human Rights.

Having regard to information supplied by the IER about 'infiltration of unions by right wing political parties', the JCHR accepted that 'it would be legitimate to allow unions to exclude from membership people who are engaged in the activities of political parties where those activities stir up hatred against people or groups on racial, national, ethnic or religious grounds' (HL 102/HC 640 (2003–2004), para 2.14). However, the Committee thought the government's amendments went too far because they 'would allow unions to expel members for participating in the activities of any political party whatever'. (*ibid*, para 2.15). The Committee was not persuaded that the government should have gone further to protect the unions' negative right of association (*ibid*, para 2.16). The Government was clearly unmoved.

7.6 Disciplinary and expulsion procedures

It is clear from the foregoing that there is now a great deal of statutory regulation of the circumstances in which trade unions may discipline or expel members. But as in the case of the arrangements for trade union elections discussed above, the legislation does not tell the whole story. There are circumstances in which a proposed disciplinary action or expulsion may not be covered by the legislation at all, for example where the member is being disciplined or expelled for non-payment of subscriptions, or because of racist or sexist language, or because of a failure or refusal to comply with union policy. In some of these cases the matter will continue to be governed wholly by common law principles. But apart from questions of substance, and the substantive grounds for discipline and expulsion, there are also procedural restraints: it is not enough that the union should have the power to discipline or expel; it must also follow the procedures set out in its constitution and rules. Indeed it is not enough that the union should follow its constitution and rules: it must also comply with the requirements of natural justice where these exceed the formal requirements of the rule-book.

7.6.1 Disciplinary powers

The first question then is whether the union has the power to discipline or expel a member. This power may be conferred expressly by the rule-book, or impliedly by the courts. In practice trade unions will normally have wide powers to discipline and expel members expressly provided in the rule-book.

[7.21] UNISON Rules, Rule I: Disciplinary Action

2 Disciplinary action may be taken against any member who:

2.1 disregards, disobeys or breaks any of the Rules or regulations of the Union applicable to her or him, or any instruction issued in accordance with the Rules;
2.2 acts in a manner prejudicial or detrimental to the Union, her/his branch, Region or Service Group;
2.3 commits
   (i)   any act of discrimination or harassment on grounds of race, gender, marital status, sexuality, gender, identity, disability, age, creed or social class; or

(ii)   any other discriminatory conduct which is prejudicial to the Aims and Objects set out in Rule B.1, B.2 and B.3;

2.4 misappropriates any money or property belonging to the Union which is under her or his control, or fails properly to account for money which was, is or should be under her or his control or defrauds the Union in any way.

It is very unusual for the courts to imply a disciplinary power where none exists, and indeed it used to be thought that 'a power to expel would not be implied; it must be found in the rules in plain and unambiguous language' (*Kelly v National Society of Operative Printers* (1915) 31 TLR 632). In one important case the court refused to imply a power in the rules of a union to enable it to expel a member in order to comply with a TUC Disputes Committee award. In *Spring v National Amalgamated Stevedores' and Dockers' Society* [1956] 1 WLR 585 it had been pressed upon Stone V-C that such a power could be implied by applying the 'officious bystander' test in *Shirlaw v Southern Foundries (1926) Ltd* [1939] 2 KB 206. But the submission was testily rejected:

> If that test were to be applied to the facts of this case and the bystander had asked the plaintiff, at the time when the plaintiff [joined the union], 'Won't you put into it some reference to the Bridlington Agreement?, I think (indeed, I have no doubt) that the plaintiff would have answered, 'What's that?'.'

It was as a result of this decision that the model rule referred to above was adopted. But although the implication of a power to discipline is rare, it is not unknown.

[7.22] *McVitae v UNISON* [1996] IRLR 33 (Ch D)

This was a case involving four NALGO shop stewards, in which it was alleged that they were guilty of intimidation and sexist conduct. A number of complaints were made: but before these could be properly investigated and proceeded with, NALGO amalgamated with COHSE and NUPE to form UNISON on 1 July 1993. Following the amalgamation, the matter was pursued and the plaintiffs were charged under UNISON Rules I 2.1, 2.2, and 2.3, in the case of three of the plaintiffs and UNISON Rules I 2.1 and 2.2, in the case of the fourth. One of the two issues before the court was whether UNISON had the power under its rules to discipline its members in relation to events which occurred before its inception. It was held that although there was no such power expressly provided in the rules, the power to discipline could nevertheless be implied. Harrison J held that it was open to the courts as a matter of principle to imply a power of this kind, and on the facts it was thought inconceivable that there should be a complete amnesty for pre-inception conduct.

7.6.2 Disciplinary procedures

As already suggested the starting point in any consideration of the procedures for the discipline and expulsion of members is the rule-book of the union in question. Rule-book procedures vary enormously, though one of the best examples (in the sense of being one of the most comprehensive) is provided by the following extract from the UNISON Rules. In addition to Rule I referred to above, which deals with disciplinary action, Schedule D deals in some detail with disciplinary procedures. A failure to comply with the procedures as laid down in the rules could be enough to render any disciplinary decision invalid and to found the basis for a challenge in the courts. The more detailed the rules, the more likely it is that there will be a procedural lapse, though it is also the case that the courts may be inclined to overlook technical breaches as opposed to breaches of substance (see *McVitae v UNISON*, [1996] IRLR 33, at p 44). It will be noted that the UNISON procedures make provision for (i) notice to be given to the respondent; (ii) an opportunity for the respondent to be represented; and (iii) an opportunity for the respondent to cross-examine the witnesses against him or her.

[7.23] UNISON Rules, Schedule D: Disciplinary Procedures

The following procedures shall be adopted for the hearing of any disciplinary charge by a Branch Disciplinary Sub-Committee, a Regional or Service Group Disciplinary Sub-Committee, or the National Executive Council or its Disciplinary Sub-Committee or any other body as decided by the National Executive Council:

1 No later than 21 days before the disciplinary hearing the member shall be sent a written notice of the charge, stating the sub-paragraph(s) of Rule I.2 under which she/he is charged and stating briefly how and when the member is said to have broken the sub-paragraph(s) concerned. At the same time the member shall be sent copies of any written material and correspondence to be considered in relation to the charge, together with the report of any investigation, and shall be told the date, time and place at which the charge against her or him is to be heard.

2 The member shall be allowed to submit, not later than 7 days prior to the hearing, any written material in support of her/his case.

3 The member shall be entitled to be represented at the hearing by another person of her/his choice (subject to the approval of the sub-committee, such approval not to be unreasonably refused).

4 The Committee hearing the charge will ensure that the charged member's rights are protected in that the provisions of Rule I and Schedule D.1 (sic) been scrupulously applied.

5 In the event that the provisions of Rule I and Schedule D.1 have not been properly applied the charge will be referred back to the body which brought the disciplinary charge.

6 At the hearing, the member shall be asked whether she/he admits or denies the charge. If she/he admits it, the Committee hearing the charge shall then consider whether and to what extent they should exercise any of the disciplinary powers conferred by the Rule.

7 If she/he denies the charge, the representative of the Branch, Regional Committee, Service Group Committee, National Executive Council or General Secretary as appropriate (who is called 'Union Representative' in this Schedule) shall state the case against the member in the presence of the member and any representative of the member, and may call witnesses. She/he will produce any documents which she/he claims support the charge.

8 The member or the member's representative shall have the opportunity to ask questions of the Union Representative and the witnesses.

9 The members of the Committee hearing the charge may ask any questions they think appropriate of the Union Representative and of any witnesses, and may question the member concerned about the charge.

10 The Union Representative shall have the opportunity to re-examine her/his witnesses on any matter about which they have been questioned by the member charged, her/his representative, and by members of the Committee hearing the charge.

11 The member or her/his representative shall put her/his case in the presence of the Union Representative, may call witnesses, and may produce any document she/he wishes that is relevant to the charge.

12 The Union Representative shall have the opportunity to ask questions of the member or the member's representative and witnesses.

13 The members of the Committee hearing the charge shall have the opportunity to ask questions of the member, or her/his representative, and witnesses.

14 The member or the member's representative shall have the opportunity to re-examine her/his witnesses on any matter about which they have been questioned by the Union Representative and/or by members of the Committee hearing the charge.

15 No written material or documents shall be submitted which do not comply with the provisions of existing rule numbers D.1, D.2, D.5 and D.9 of this Schedule.

16 No new charge may be raised at the hearing.

17 After all witnesses have been heard and documents produced, the Committee hearing the charge (i) may ask the person presenting the charge to sum up the case; and (whether she/he does so or not) (ii) must then permit the member charged, or her/his representative, to address them. The member or her/his representative shall have the right to speak last. In summing up no new matters may be introduced.

18 At any time during the procedure set out above, members of the Committee hearing the charge may seek clarification of any statement made, and may enquire of either party as to the evidence that is to be called.

19 The Committee hearing the charge has an absolute discretion to adjourn the hearing to allow either party to produce further evidence, or for any other reason.

20 The Committee hearing the charge shall then consider in private whether the charge is proved to their satisfaction, or not, on the evidence presented before them. All members of the Committee taking part in the discussion must have been present throughout the entirety of the hearing. No new matter can be raised against the member concerned. If any point of uncertainty arises, the Committee may recall both parties to clear the point. In such a case, both parties shall return notwithstanding that only one is concerned with the point giving rise to doubt.

21 If the Committee decides that the charge is not proved, they shall dismiss it.

22 If the Committee decides that the charge is proved, they shall then decide what, if any, action to take. Before determining its decision, the Committee may consider anything that the member wishes to submit in mitigation.

23 The Committee hearing the charge may inform the member of their decision orally, but it shall in any event be confirmed to the member in writing within 14 days of the conclusion of the hearing. Where the charge is found proved, the member shall be notified in writing of (a) her/his right of appeal, (b) the body to whom the appeal should be directed, and, (c) the date on which the four-week time limit for appealing expires.

24 Any penalty imposed on a member will not take effect until the expiry of the time limit within which the member can submit an appeal or, if an appeal has been submitted, until such time as the appeal has been determined.

25 No person who is a witness, or who has investigated the charge prior to its being brought, shall sit on the Committee hearing the charge or any appeal.

26 (1) If a member intends to appeal, she/he must exercise her/his right to do so by writing to the Secretary of the appropriate Committee within four weeks of her/his being notified in writing of the decision subject to the Appeal.

(2) At least three weeks' notice shall be given to the member of the date, place and time at which the appeal is to be heard

(3) A member may appeal upon any or all of the following grounds:

(a) that the provisions of Rule 1 and Schedule D were not complied with at or before the original hearing, and/or

(b) that the Committee's decision to find a charge of charges proven was unreasonable, and/or

(c) the sanction imposed by the Committee was unreasonable.

(4) Where an appeal is submitted in accordance with Schedule D26(3)(a), whether or not it is also submitted on other grounds, the Appeal Committee shall consider this ground of appeal first of all. The member or her/his representative shall present their case on this point in accordance with Schedule D.11, D.12, D.13 and D.14. The union representative shall then put forward their case on this point in the same way. The Appeal Committee shall then deliberate on this point in private. If the Appeal Committee finds that Rule 1 and Schedule D were complied with they shall dismiss this ground of appeal and proceed to hear any other grounds of appeal. If the Appeal Committee finds that Rule 1 and Schedule D were not complied with they shall refer the charge(s) back to the body which brought the disciplinary charge.

(5) Where an appeal is submitted in accordance with Schedule D26(3)(b) , whether or not it is also submitted in accordance with Schedule D26(3)(c), the appeal shall take the form of a rehearing of the charge, in accordance with the procedure set out above for the initial hearing. No material that was not before the initial hearing may be introduced, unless it is material evidence which could not reasonably have been available to either party at the time of the initial hearing. The appeal hearing shall not reopen consideration of any charge(s) which were dismissed at the initial hearing. If the Appeal Committee decides that a charge is not proved they shall dismiss that charge. If the Appeal Committee decides that one or more charges are proved, they shall then decide whether to uphold the sanction imposed at the initial hearing, or to substitute a lesser sanction.

(6) Where an appeal is submitted in accordance with Schedule D26(3)(c), the Committee shall consider anything that the member or her/his representative wishes to submit in mitigation. The Appeal Committee shall then decide whether or not to uphold the sanction imposed at the initial hearing, or to substitute a lesser sanction.

The evidence shows that not all trade union disciplinary procedures are as rigorous and detailed as these. In such cases, to adapt a dictum well known to administrative lawyers, the common law will supply the omission of the rule book. This will be done principally by the rules of natural justice, which will be readily applied even if the legal basis for their application in the context of the contract of membership is by no means clear. They will often be described as implied terms of the contract of membership, though they seem to have a mandatory quality. The scope of the rules of natural justice varies according to the circumstances of the case, but the standards are becoming gradually more demanding, and it is inevitable that their application in this context will be influenced to some extent by developments in other spheres of the law. So far as trade union cases are concerned, the courts have emphasised the following:

- the need to provide the respondent with an opportunity to state his or her case: *Radford v NATSOPA* [1972] ICR 484;
- the need to inform the respondent of the charge he or she has to meet: *Annamunthodo v Oilfield Workers' Trade Union* [1961] AC 945; *Stevenson v URTU* [1977] ICR 893;
- the right to be tried by a tribunal whose chairman did not appear to have a special reason for bias, conscious or otherwise, against the respondent: *Roebuck v National Union of Mineworkers (Yorkshire Area) (No 2)* [1978] ICR 676;
- the right to an oral hearing and to cross-examine witnesses, depending upon the nature of the case and the seriousness of the possible sanction: *Payne v Electrical Trades' Union, The Times*, 14 April 1960;
- the right of the individual to be represented in disciplinary proceedings, including legal representation: *Walker v Amalgamated Union of Engineering and Foundry Workers* 1969 SLT 150.

Perhaps the most difficult of these five principles is the third, for reasons which are touched upon in the following case.

[7.24] *Roebuck v National Union of Mineworkers (Yorkshire Area) (No 2)* **[1978] ICR 676 (Ch D)**

> The plaintiffs, who were members of the defendant union, had given evidence on behalf of the *Sheffield Star* in a libel action brought against the newspaper by Arthur Scargill, who was president of the union. Disciplinary proceedings were then brought against the plaintiffs under rule 42 of the union's rules which authorised the area executive committee to discipline a member who does any act which in the judgment of the committee was detrimental to the interests of the union. The president of the union had brought the matter to the attention of the area council of the union alleging in strong terms ('like judgment before trial') that the plaintiffs had acted in breach of rule 42, and the matter was thereafter referred by the council to the executive. Subsequent meetings of the executive chaired by the president thereafter proceeded to hear the case against the two plaintiffs. The charges were found to be established and the two men were disqualified from holding office in the union for two years. The plaintiffs successfully sought declarations that the decisions of the council and the executive committee were in breach of natural justice, and injunctions to restrain the union from acting on these decisions.

Templeman J:
Mr Roebuck and Mr O'Brien were entitled to be tried by a tribunal whose chairman did not appear to have a special reason for bias, conscious or unconscious, against them. True it is that all the members of the executive committee and the area council, in common

with all members of a domestic tribunal where the interests of their own organisation are at stake, have a general inclination to defend the union and its officers against attack from any source; this fact, every trade unionist and every member of a domestic organisation knows and accepts.

But Mr Scargill had a special position, which clearly disqualified him from taking the part in the critical meetings of the executive committee and the area committee which he did take. I say that as a question of fact and not as a question of criticism. It is a fact that Mr Scargill, as plaintiff, had clearly borne the heat and burden of the libel action. It is clear from the admissions that his cross-examination had been complicated and made difficult by the actions of Mr Roebuck and Mr O'Brien. It is clear that Mr Scargill was a witness to what had happened and to what Mr Roebuck and Mr O'Brien had said and done in the course of the libel action in the High Court. Whether or not those actions of Mr Roebuck and Mr O'Brien, before and during the High Court proceedings, were detrimental to the interests of the union, it is quite plain that they must have been gall and wormwood to Mr Scargill before, during and after the trial. Mr Scargill was a plaintiff and a witness—an important witness—in the High Court proceedings. Then he reappeared as the complainant, the pleader, the prosecutor, the advocate and the chairman in the union proceedings, which followed swiftly. It is impossible to know what would have happened if Mr Scargill had recognised his impossible position and had not acted as he did. But his presence as chairman, and his conduct (admitted conduct) undoubtedly gave the impression that the dice were loaded against Mr Roebuck and Mr O'Brien. No amount of evidence can remove that impression, or establish affirmatively that the end result was unaffected by natural resentment and prejudice in the mind of Mr Scargill for prolonging his cross-examination and jeopardising the success of the action which, true enough, affected the union, but in addition vitally affected Mr Scargill, as president of the union, and as a private individual, who had been libelled. Whether he recognised the fact or not, Mr Scargill must inevitably have appeared biased against Mr Roebuck and Mr O'Brien. The appearance of bias was inevitable; the exercise of bias, conscious or unconscious, was probable. I am content to rest my judgment on the ground that it was manifestly unfair to Mr Roebuck and Mr O'Brien that Mr. Scargill should have acted as chairman, and should have played the part which he admits to have played at the relevant meetings of the executive committee and the area council.

The authorities support this approach. Although every case turns on its own facts, I can usefully adapt the words of Dixon J in *Australian Workers' Union* v *Bowen (No. 2)* (1948) 77 CLR 601; the words which I adapt and vary slightly are at p 631; and in the present instance would read as follows:

'It is not in accordance with the principles of natural justice to have as President of the tribunal a person who has promoted the charge and supports it as the prosecutor and who is inevitably biased against the accused as a result of his participation in the controversy. . .'

Both Mr Turner-Samuels, who appeared for the union, and Mr Irvine, who appeared for Mr Roebuck and Mr O'Brien put their submissions very succinctly and fairly, and they were agreed that, for the present purposes, they cannot quarrel with the decision or dicta in *Hannam v Bradford Corporation* [1970] 1 WLR 937. Again, every case depends on its own facts; but in that case where in effect, there was an appeal from governors to a sub-committee; and on the sub-committee there were three governors who had not taken part in the original hearing by the governors, it was nevertheless held that the decision of the sub-committee could not stand, because a real likelihood of bias existed, when the three governors sat upon the staff committee, as they did not cease to be an integral part of the body whose action was being impugned.

In the present case, the fact that there was an overlap between the membership of the executive committee and the area council seems to me to be irrelevant. In this kind of domestic tribunal that must happen and is acceptable. But it is to be observed that the test is the likelihood of bias; in *Hannam v Bradford Corporation*, Cross LJ said, at p 949:

'If a reasonable person who has knowledge of the matter beyond knowledge of the relationship which subsists between some members of the tribunal and one of the parties would think that there might well be bias, then there is in his opinion a real likelihood of bias. Of course, someone else with inside knowledge of the characters of the members in question, might say: "Although things don't look very well, in fact there is no real likelihood of bias." That, however, would be beside the point, because the question is not whether the tribunal will in fact be biased, but whether a reasonable man with no inside knowledge might well think that it might be biased'.

That seems to me an answer to the plea of Mr Turner-Samuels that the trial ought to take place so that one can find out exactly what happened at the relevant meetings; what the members of the various tribunals thought; what the plaintiffs, Mr Roebuck and Mr O'Brien thought and said; and whether in fact, despite the appearance, justice, or rough justice, was done.

7.6.3 Disciplinary decisions

So much then for disciplinary powers and disciplinary procedures. What about the decisions taken under these powers and in accordance with these procedures? There are two issues here, dealt with in the seminal decision of the Court of Appeal in *Lee v Showmen's Guild of Great Britain* [1952] 2 QB 329. The first requirement is that the disciplinary body must construe the rules of the union in accordance with the law. According to Denning LJ in *Lee*, this is 'a question of law which they must answer correctly if they are to keep within their jurisdiction'. Trade union disciplinary rules generally take one of two forms, both of which are to be found in the *UNISON Disciplinary Rules* above. One category is sometimes referred to as specific disciplinary rules (discipline for a specific offence such as non-payment of contributions or sexist or racist behaviour), and the other is sometimes referred to as general disciplinary rules (discipline for unspecified offences contrary to the interests of the union, drafted in subjective terms). The first category of rules is typically construed by the courts very narrowly in favour of the member, while the subjective language of the latter will not give the union disciplinary bodies an unlimited discretion, as the following case makes clear. The approach of the court reads very much like the approach which an administrative law court would adopt in a decision involving a public authority, but without the restraint that is sometimes found in such cases.

[7.25] *Esterman v NALGO* **[1974] ICR 625 (Ch D)**

The plaintiff was a senior legal assistant employed by Islington London Borough Council. The union had been seeking an increase in the London weighting allowance, and in December 1973 had balloted its members on various forms of industrial action. Only 49 per cent had voted in favour of selective strikes on full pay, 48 per cent had voted against and 3 per cent gave no answer. In March 1974 the union reached an agreement with the employer, but this was vetoed by the government under the counter-inflation policy then in force. Thereafter the Islington branch was instructed to take selective strike action, Islington being chosen because 64 per cent of that branch had indicated a willingness to take selective strike action in the December ballot. As part of the escalation of the industrial action, the members of the branch were instructed not to volunteer their services in connection with the London borough elections to be held in May 1974, though there was no dispute between NALGO and the returning officers who were responsible for the conduct of the elections. Miss Esterman refused to comply with this instruction and was summoned to a disciplinary hearing, charged under rule 13 of the NALGO rules whereby 'any member who disregards any regulation issued by the branch, or is guilty of conduct which, in the opinion of the executive committee, renders him unfit for membership, shall be liable to expulsion'. Before the meeting was held, Miss Esterman successfully sought an interlocutory injunction to restrain her threatened expulsion until the trial of the action.

Templeman J:
In the present case I am satisfied, as far as the present evidence is concerned and without prejudice to what might come up at the trial of the action, that it is impossible to convict any member of NALGO of conduct which rendered him unfit to be a member of NALGO on the ground that the member did not comply with the instructions contained in the letter dated April 8, 1974. In brief, the evidence establishes that when the letter of April 8 was received by any member of NALGO or instructions were handed on to him, he was entitled to doubt whether the national executive council possessed power to issue the order which was contained in that letter, and he was also entitled to suspect that the national executive council might be misusing any power which they had in giving the order.

In my judgment, when the national executive council take the serious step of interfering with the right of a member to volunteer or take work of any description outside his normal employment, the national executive council are only entitled to 100 per cent and implicit obedience to that order if it is clear that they have been given power to issue the order and if it is clear that they are not abusing that power. If a member disobeys an order of the national executive council which does not satisfy those tests, then it seems to me that he cannot be found guilty on that account of conduct which renders him unfit to be a member of NALGO.

I should say at once that I have no doubt that the national executive council have acted in the utmost good faith, have only done what they have done in the firm belief that it is in the best interests of NALGO and that they are supported by all or a majority of the members of NALGO. It is agreed between counsel that we are to some extent in unknown territory. It may be some guidance to say that persons in the position of the national executive council must consider not only whether, by turning the rules upside down or inside out, they can spell out power to do what they want to do, but whether, in all the circumstances, it is right to demand from every member of the union immediate and unquestioned obedience to the order which they propose to give.

On this application, I have listened to very long and very learned argument on the interesting question of whether, on the true construction of the rules and also on the construction of the procedure for strike action, the national executive council had power to issue the order dated April 8, 1974. It is sufficient for present purposes that not only am I in some doubt now as to the answer to that question, but also that every member of NALGO who received the order could not have been clear as to whether there was power to issue that particular order. It is not clear, for example, whether NALGO had power to take industrial action against a returning officer with whom the association has no quarrel. It is not clear whether the association had power to interfere with a right of a member to employ his spare time by assisting the returning officers in an election, the holding of which had no direct relevance to the claim for London weighting allowance. Whatever the powers of the association, it is not clear whether the national executive council had power to issue the orders which they did issue in the absence of a ballot. But even if, after great deliberation, it would appear that NALGO and the national executive council in fact had the power which they claim to exercise, the special circumstances in this case are such, in my judgment, that a member could very well come to the conclusion that this was an order to which the national executive council had no right to demand his obedience and it was an order which, as a person—a loyal member of NALGO—acting in its best interests, he felt bound to disobey.

We have this background: although there was only 49 per cent support in the only ballot for selective strike action, the national executive council had already ordered the whole of the Islington branch to strike. A member could take the view that this 49 per cent might be a sufficient number to justify the national executive council in making a recommendation for a strike; it was no warrant for an order to strike with the threat in the background of expulsion for any member who had voted against the strike and thought that a strike was not in the interests of NALGO.

A member could take the view that action against the returning officers had never been submitted to a ballot and that whether or not a ballot was strictly necessary the national executive council, following the spirit as well as the letter of the instructions with regard to strikes, ought not to order, but rather—if they wished—to recommend, action against the returning officer. A member may have thought that such an order did not reasonably command obedience and that there was a possibility that it gave the appearance of coercing those who thought that action against the returning officers was not in the best interests of NALGO. He might take the view that, in all the extraordinary background of this case, he could not conscientiously accept an order given by the national executive council without a ballot or a fresh ballot against the wishes of the Minister and the secretary of the Trades Union Congress and in the existing national conditions, particularly since 100 per cent obedience to the order of the national executive council would seem to imply that 100 per cent of the members were firmly in support of the action which was being taken. A member might take the view that the national executive council order was an abuse of their powers, because, without any mandate by way of a ballot, it had the appearance, some might think, of seeking to wreck the local elections for the purpose of bringing pressure to bear on the Minister. A member might think that if the public thought that, then the reputation of NALGO might be irreparably damaged. In brief in my judgment, a member was entitled to take the view that this was an order which he might be under a positive duty to disobey. Of course, the suspicions or fears of a member that the national executive council had no power to issue the order aimed against the returning officers, or that the national executive council, even if they had the power, were misusing it and exercising it in a way objectionable to numbers of members and injurious to the reputation of NALGO, all those fears could be ill-founded. But, in my judgment, a member, faced with the order, was entitled to doubt. On the face of the order and the constitution and the rules and against all the background, there was a very large question mark hanging over the validity of the order and whether it was a proper order to issue even if there was power to do so.

Those doubts were due entirely to the insistence, as I have said no doubt bona fide and thought to be in the best interests of NALGO, but nevertheless the insistence, of the national executive council on taking a step which not only had never been put to the ballot but really was an extraordinary step to take, peremptorily ordering every member of NALGO to withdraw assistance from the local election, when what they were after dealt with London weighting allowance and they had no quarrel with the returning officers.

As at present advised, I emphatically reject the submission that it was the duty of every member blindly to obey the orders of the national executive council in the prevailing circumstances and that he could only disobey the order if he were prepared to take the risk of being expelled from NALGO. I also reject the submission that a member who disobeyed the particular order given by the national executive not to assist returning officers showed prima facie that he was unfit to be a member of NALGO. An Act of Parliament carries penalties for its breach, but it is a fallacy to assume that every democratically elected body is entitled to obedience to every order on pain of being found guilty of being unfit to be a member of an association. It must depend on the order and it must depend on the circumstances and, in my judgment, if implicit obedience is to be exacted, those who issue the order must make quite sure that they have power, that no reasonable man could be in doubt that they have power and that they are making a proper exercise of the power, and that no reasonable man could conscientiously say to himself that 'this is an order which I have no duty to obey.' In the present case, it was not so clear.

I return to the plaintiff. She deposes that before receiving the instruction not to assist the returning officer she had volunteered to do so as she had for 26 years past. When she received the instruction she decided to ignore it for three reasons. First, she did not think it right or honourable to withdraw the offer of assistance she had already made. Secondly, she thought that the object of the instruction and NALGO's campaign was to compel the employers to pay or persuade the Minister to approve an allowance beyond the permitted increases under the Counter-Inflation Act 1973 and the Pay Code. Thirdly, she thought the object of the instruction was to sabotage the election and this, she thought, was insupportable and objectionable. She read, she said, the constitution and rules of NALGO and the rules of the Islington branch and could not find power for NALGO or the branch executive to issue the instruction to her not to volunteer to assist the returning officer.

The plaintiff, as the evidence now runs, therefore questioned whether the national executive council had the requisite power and, if so, whether they were abusing that power. I am not prepared to say that her fears were fanciful. Holding the views which she did, she could not be expected blindly to obey the order and her disobedience forms no ground for the allegation that her act of disobedience demonstrated her unfitness to be a member of NALGO.

In the circumstances, I conclude that no reasonable tribunal could bona fide come to the conclusion that disobedience of this order demonstrated any unfitness to be a member of NALGO and I propose to protect the plaintiff pending trial against having to appear before the executive committee.

Apart from the approach of the court to the construction of the rule, *Esterman v NALGO* is interesting also because the court saw fit to intervene before the disciplinary committee had had a chance to deal with the matter. This is something to which we return in the following section where it will be seen that the courts have been prepared more recently to allow the disciplinary body an opportunity to get it wrong. Attending to matters immediately at hand, it will be recalled that there are two issues which have occupied the courts when examining disciplinary decisions. The second issue is not so much a question of law as a question of fact, and relates to the application of the rules to the facts of the particular case. This too is an issue raised by Denning LJ in *Lee* above, where he said that this question is essentially a matter for the domestic tribunal: the 'whole point of giving jurisdiction to a committee is so that they can determine the facts and decide what is to be done about them'. Alas, it is not so simple. For as Denning LJ also pointed out at p 345:

The two parts of the task are, however, often inextricably mixed together. The construction of the rules is so bound up with the application of the rules to the facts that no one can tell one from the other. When that happens, the question whether the committee has acted within its jurisdiction depends, in my opinion, on whether the facts adduced before them were reasonably capable of being held to be a breach of the rules. If they were, then the proper inference is that the committee correctly construed the rules and have acted within their jurisdiction. If, however, the facts were not reasonably capable of being held to be a breach and yet the committee held them to be a breach, then the only inference is that the committee have misconstrued the rules and exceeded their jurisdiction. The proposition is sometimes stated in the form that the court can interfere if there was no evidence to support the finding of the committee, but that only means that the facts were not capable of supporting the finding.

An application of this principle is to be found in the following case.

[7.26] *Radford v NATSOPA* [1972] ICR 484 (Ch D)

The plaintiff was a member of the union and was employed by Temple Press Ltd. The employer reached an agreement with the union whereby employees could leave the industry and receive a redundancy payment in excess of the statutory minimum, or be relocated to an associated employer of Temple Press, which was a member of the IPL group. The union insisted that no employee should qualify for a redundancy payment unless he left the industry altogether: he could not 'cop it and hop it', could not take the money and expect the union as an employment exchange to find alternative employment in what was a contracting industry. Following some uncertainty about his position, the plaintiff indicated that he wanted to stay in the industry (but refused work to which he had been directed by the union) while also taking legal advice about his entitlement to a statutory redundancy payment from the employer. The branch proposed to discipline the plaintiff for failing to comply with its instruction to take work at another site, and asked him to supply his correspondence with his solicitor. When the plaintiff refused to do so at a branch committee meeting to which he had been summoned, he was excluded from the union under rule 20(13) of its rule-book which provided that action taken by members against the union 'shall be declared a wilful breach of rules, and shall void the membership of the member or members so acting'. The plaintiff successfully sought a declaration that his exclusion was unlawful, an injunction restraining the union from acting on the decision, and damages for breach of contract in wrongfully excluding him.

Plowman J:
I turn now to the legal position. The first question which arises is the construction of rule 20(13) which appears at first sight to result in the automatic voidance of membership in the events specified in the clause. Unlike rule 20(9) there is no express reference to the opinion of the branch committee, or to any other subjective test. If, indeed, the clause were one for automatic forfeiture of membership without the necessity for any charge or hearing by the union, it would, in my judgment, be ultra vires and void. As Lord Denning MR said in *Edwards v Society of Graphical and Allied Trades* [1971] Ch 354, 377: 'No union can stipulate for automatic exclusion of a man without giving him the opportunity of being heard.'
It is no answer to that objection to say that in the present case the applicant was given an opportunity of being heard because the question is not how the rule was operated but what, on its true construction, it requires. But it is, I think, possible to construe the clause

in such a way as to uphold its validity. It provides that certain conduct 'shall be declared,' not 'is hereby declared,' 'a wilful breach of the rules.' And the words 'shall be declared' in my opinion point to a declaration by the appropriate organ of the union, which I take to be the branch committee. If that is so, there would be read into the clause the requirement that the member whose conduct was being called into question should be given notice to appear before the branch committee, informed in advance of the charge against him and given an opportunity of stating his case. This requirement would result either from applying [rule 20(10) (which provides for a hearing for a member charged under rule 20(1)–(9))] to the case by analogy or from applying the rules of natural justice. In the present case the applicant was held to have voided his membership without have been given any advance notice that his membership was at stake. What he was told was that the committee proposed to investigate his action of seeking legal advice. He was never charged with anything at all. That, in my judgment, is sufficient to render the branch committee's determination void.

[*Plowman J referred to* Abbot *v* Sullivan [1952] 1 KB 189 *and continued*]

I return, therefore, to rule 20(13) and will first consider what the branch committee has to find before it can decide that a member has voided his membership. Let me read part of the rule again:

'Any action against the [union] by individual members, or members acting collectively, except where redress under rule has been sought, as provided in these rules'.

The words 'except where redress under rule has been sought, as provided in these rules' refer, I think, to rule 20(11). That says: 'Any member having a complaint against the [union] or another member shall bring the matter before the branch committee.' It follows, therefore, that the relevant questions were, first, whether the applicant had a complaint against the union and, secondly, whether, not having brought it before the branch committee, he had taken any action against the union.

The committee did not regard the mere fact that the plaintiff had approached a solicitor to seek legal advice as falling within clause 13, but their view was it would do so if his action in going to a solicitor was directed, however obliquely, against the union and not just IPL, and the object of their investigation was to find out whether it was so directed. It may well be that the matter about which the applicant went to see his solicitor was not a complaint against the union or action against the union at all, and was therefore incapable of falling within clause 13, but leaving that aside, it is clear on the evidence of Mr O'Brien that the branch committee's view was that the applicant's refusal to discuss the matter meant that he had something to hide, or else he would have given the information they were seeking. And it is equally clear . . . that it was that which led them to their decision.

The question then arises whether that was an inference which they could properly draw. In my judgment, it was not. If there is evidence against a man, the fact that he refuses to answer questions may be a reason for accepting that evidence, however slight, but where there is no evidence at all his silence is no substitute for evidence. In the present case, in my judgment, there was no evidence, on which the branch committee could conclude that the applicant's conduct fell within clause 13, even assuming that the committee's own view of its meaning was right.

7.7 The adjudication of disputes

The final question arising for consideration in this chapter concerns the different procedures for dealing with disputes between trade unions and their members. We have already encountered different bodies for the resolution of disputes: the Certification Officer for political fund disputes and disputes about the statutory election procedures; the employment tribunals and the Employment Appeal Tribunal for dealing with statutory rights not to be unreasonably disciplined, or not to be unreasonably excluded or expelled from a trade union; and of course the ordinary courts with an original jurisdiction to deal with rule-book disputes, a jurisdiction shared (with the CO) to deal with disputes about the statutory election procedures; and an appellate jurisdiction in the case of the Court of Appeal (from the EAT which hears appeals from the CO and the employment tribunals). In this section we consider the role of these different bodies more fully, beginning with an examination of methods other than ordinary courts and tribunals for the resolution of disputes. In view of the doubts which the unions sometimes have about the courts in particular, it is perhaps surprising that they have not made greater use of methods of alternative dispute resolution for membership disputes.

7.7.1 The role of external review

Most trade unions now have procedures for dealing with appeals from the decisions of disciplinary bodies. UNISON Rule I, for example, provides as follows:

[7.27] UNISON Rules, Rule I: Disciplinary Action

> **9.1** A member who is dissatisfied with the decision of the branch or National Executive Council in respect of charges against her or him may exercise the following rights of appeal, whichever is appropriate:
>> **.1** from a decision of a branch to a Disciplinary Sub-Committee of the National Executive Council;
>> **.2** from a decision of the National Executive Council to the Union Appeals Committee.
>
> **9.2** The decision of the National Executive Council Disciplinary Sub-Committee or of the Union Appeals Committee as appropriate shall be final and binding upon the Union and the member concerned.
>
> **10.1** The Union Appeals Committee shall consist of three members drawn from an Appeals Panel.
>
> **10.2** Each Service Group Executive shall be entitled to nominate two members of the Service Group Executive to the Appeals Panel.
>
> **10.3** None of the three members of the Appeals Panel chosen to hear an appeal may be from the same Service Group or from the same Region as the member whose appeal is to be considered.

Typically the members of trade union appeal bodies are drawn from the ranks of the union itself. There are in fact few trade unions which provide for any external involvement in their domestic procedures, though one which does is AMICUS which provides for an appeal to an independent appeal tribunal chaired by an individual nominated by the Chair of ACAS. Perhaps the best example of external review in this country (the Public Review Board of the United Auto Workers is a good example of the phenomenon in North America) was the TUC Independent Review Committee which was established in 1976 to deal with complaints of exclusion or expulsion from a trade union in closed shop cases. But with the virtual end in practice of the closed shop following severe legal restrictions, the purpose of the Independent Review Committee has disappeared, and it no longer exists.

7.7.2 The role of the Certification Officer

As we have seen, the Certification Officer (CO) has gradually played a more prominent role in the conduct of trade union affairs. The office was first created in 1975 and provision is now made in the TULRCA 1992, by which the CO is appointed by the Secretary of State after consultation with ACAS (section 254). He has no security of tenure by statute, and there are no formal statutory qualifications: in particular there is no requirement that the CO should be a lawyer. Indeed the last incumbent did not have a legal qualification, though the present incumbent does. There have been four holders of the post since 1976. We have already encountered some of the expanding jurisdiction of the CO. Apart from issuing certificates of independence and responsibilities for political funds, he also hears complaints about alleged breaches of the statutory provisions relating to trade union elections. Otherwise the CO deals with complaints about a union's failure to maintain a register of members' names and addresses (TULRCA 1992, section 25), and trade unions must submit an annual return to the CO (TULRCA 1992, section 32), who is empowered to investigate the financial affairs of trade unions (TULRCA 1992, sections 37A–37E). As already pointed out, the CO thus performs a remarkable mélange of executive, legislative and judicial functions which would be quite out of order in a constitutional system (such as Australia and the USA) based on a strict separation of powers, as suggested by such landmarks as *Attorney General for Australia v The Queen* [1957] AC 288 (the *Boilermakers' case*). For his part, the CO sees himself as having a mixture of administrative, investigative, regulatory and quasi-judicial functions.

The jurisdiction of the Certification Officer was extended by the Employment Relations Act 1999. It has for a long time been thought desirable that internal trade union affairs should be taken from the courts and given to a less formal and more expert body. The Royal Commission on Trade Unions and Employers' Associations which reported under the chairmanship of Lord Donovan in 1968 recommended that there should be established a Review Body to hear rule book complaints (Cmnd 3623, 1968), para 176). But this recommendation was never acted upon, and the extended jurisdiction of the Certification Officer some 31 years later is the closest we have yet come to the Donovan model. According to the government the aim in extending the jurisdiction of the CO is to 'enable trade union members to secure their rights more easily and effectively' (DTI, *Fairness at Work* (Cm. 3968, 1998), para 4.31). If so, it may be mixed blessing for trade unions, and there is concern that this jurisdiction sometimes encourages frivolous complaints. It will be seen from the following extract that the extended jurisdiction of the Certification Officer will by no means exclude the courts from this general area. The member will have a choice of whether to go to the CO or the courts; in some cases the High Court will continue to have an original jurisdiction, as will the employment tribunals and the EAT in others; and the EAT and the Court of Appeal will have an appeal function even where cases are taken to the CO in the first instance.

[7.28] Annual Report of the Certification Officer 2003–2004

9.1 Individual trade union members have the right to apply to the Certification Officer if there has been a breach or threatened breach of a trade union's rules relating to any of the matters set out in section 108A(2) of the [1992] Act. The matters are:—

"(a) the appointment or election of a person to, or the removal of a person from, any office;

(b) disciplinary proceedings by the union (including expulsion);

(c) the balloting of members on any issue other than industrial action;

(d) the constitution or proceedings of any executive committee or of any decision-making meeting

(e) such other matters as may be specified in an order made by the Secretary of State."

9.2 The applicant must be a member of the union or have been a member at the time of the alleged breach or threatened breach. The Certification Officer may not consider an application if the applicant has applied to the court in respect of the same matter. Similarly once an application has been made to the Certification Officer the same matter may not be put to the court.

9.3 The Certification Officer may refuse to accept an application unless he is satisfied that the applicant has taken all reasonable steps to resolve the claim by the use of any internal complaints procedure of the union.

9.4 If the Certification Officer accepts an application he is required to make such enquiries as he things fit and, before reaching a decision on the application, provide the applicant and the trade union with an opportunity to be heard. All hearings before the Certification Officer are held in public.

9.5 The Certification Officer must give reasons for his decision in writing and, where he makes the declaration sought, is required to make an enforcement order unless he considers that to do so would be inappropriate. The enforcement order may impose on the union one or more of the following requirements—

(a) to take such steps to remedy the breach, or withdraw the threat of a breach, as may be specified in the order;

(b) to abstain from such acts as may be so specified with a view to securing that a breach or threat of the same or a similar kind does not occur in future.

Where an order imposes a requirement on the union as in (a) above, the order must specify the period within which the union must comply with the requirement of the order.

9.6 An enforcement order made by the Certification Officer may be enforced in the same way as an order of the court.

9.7 An appeal on any question of law arising in proceedings before or arising from a determination by the Certification Officer, may be made to the Employment Appeal Tribunal.

Applications and decisions

9.8 In the period 1 April 2003 to 31 March 2004 the Certification Officer received eleven applications relating to alleged breaches of union rule, two of which were determined in that period. In addition, the five applications against individual trade unions outstanding at 31 March 2003 were determined. The case of Carrigan *v* ASLEF (D/21-35/01) which had been remitted by the EAT for the Certification Officer to consider the issue of an enforcement order (see paragraph 9.10 of the Certification Officer's Annual Report 2003-2003), was also heard. At 31 March 2004 eight applications against individual trade unions remained outstanding.

9.9 The Certification Officer issued eighteen decisions during the period 1 April 2003 to 31 March 2004. No enforcement orders were issued. Of these eighteen decisions the following are noteworthy.

- **Dennison v UNISON (D/12/03).** The Certification Officer found that the suspension of the applicant's legal assistance from the union was a disciplinary penalty imposed on the applicant by her branch and was in breach of the union's disciplinary rules. The Certification Officer concluded that this was a matter within the Certification Officer's jurisdiction under section 108A(2)(b) of the 1992 Act as a matter relating to disciplinary proceedings by the union. The Certification Officer considered that it was not appropriate to make an enforcement order on the union.

- **Foster v Musicians Union (D/13-17/03).** The Certification Officer found that the union had neither breached its rules nor Article 6 of the European Convention on Human Rights in denying the applicant access to material he sought in connection with an internal disciplinary case brought against him by another member and in allegedly failing to hear the disciplinary case against him within a reasonable time. The Certification Officer rejected two other complaints on the basis that they were out of time.

- **Stokes v GMB (D/24-27/03).** The Certification Officer declared that the union had breached its rules by disqualifying the applicant from standing in the election for the post of Deputy General Secretary. An enforcement order was made requiring that the election be treated as void and that a further election be held. The Certification Officer refused to make the declarations sought in two other matters brought by the applicant relating to the same election.

- **Fradley v The Transport Salaried Staffs' Association (D/28-30/03).** At a preliminary hearing the Certification Officer dismissed the applicant's complaint as being out of time and outside the jurisdiction of the Certification Officer. Two other complaints brought by the applicant were also dismissed. In his decision, the Certification Officer commented on the extent of his jurisdiction under section 108A(2)(d) of the 1992 Act.

- **Brooks v Union of Shop Distributive and Allied Workers (D/31-34/03).** The Certification Officer refused to make the declarations sought in respect of four complaints brought by the applicant against his union. The applicant's complaints related to the attendance of full-time officials at the union's Annual Delegates Meeting and decisions taken by the union's executive council in relation to that matter.

- **Carrigan v Associated Society of Locomotive Engineers and Firemen (D/21-35/01).** This matter had been remitted to the Certification Officer by a decision of the Employment Appeal Tribunal (EAT/564/01/RN) sent to the parties on 27 February 2003 (see paragraph 9.10 of chapter 9 of the Certification Officer's Annual Report 2002-2003). The case concerned a breach by the union of its disciplinary rules and was remitted for the Certification Officer to consider whether to make an enforcement order. Following a hearing on 24 July 2003, the Certification Officer declined to make an enforcement order on the grounds that it was inappropriate to do so. On 24 October 2003 Mr Carrigan appealed to the EAT against the decision and on 23 March 2004 Mr Carrigan's appeal was struck out by the EAT.

9.10 Copies of all decisions of the Certification Officer are available free of charge from the Certification Office and decisions made since 1 August 2001 are available on the website of the Certification Office, www.certoffice.org.

9.11 In the period 1 April 2003 to 31 March 2004, a total of 563 enquiries were received.

General advice on the role of the Certification Officer	93
Appointment, election or dismissal from any office in the union	62
Disciplinary proceedings within the union	51
Balloting of union members (other than industrial action)	52
Constitution or proceedings of a union's executive committee or certain other bodies	44
Inadequate representation of members by their union	111
Union benefits or membership issues	39
Others	111
Total	563

This is an increase of 177 enquiries on the corresponding period in 2003-2003 (see para 9.12 of the 2002-2003 Annual Report).

9.12 Not all enquiries made could result in applications to the Certification Officer. For example the Certification Officer has no jurisdiction regarding the inadequate representation of members by their union or in relation to the provision of union benefits or membership.

7.7.3 The role of the courts

The increasing role of the CO does not mean that the judges will be redundant in this field. That being so, a number of issues relating to the role of the courts continue to be important. The first of these relates to *the principles of intervention* which the courts adopt and apply. Those who have read the cases in this chapter will have observed a number of different responses. It would be true to say that the courts have not adopted any settled approach to the question of trade union internal affairs: the cases tend to follow patterns which vary according to historical circumstances. In the 1960s and 1970s the courts tended to take a highly interventionist approach, championing the cause of the member and developing new forms of control over union rules, and new principles to regulate the exercise of discretionary decisions under trade union rules. These cases make nonsense of the claims sometimes made by judges about the proper role of the courts in internal union affairs:

The effect of the authorities may I think be summarised by saying that the rules of a trade union are not to be construed literally or like a statute, but so as to give them a reasonable interpretation which accords with what in the court's view they must have been intended to mean, bearing in mind their authorship, their purpose and the readership to which they are addressed.   (*Jaques v AUEW* [1987] 1 All ER 621, per Warner J)

More recent cases have—consistently with these sentiments—tended to take a much more restrained or abstentionist approach, as reflected in the following case which adopts an approach so laid back as to be scarcely believable to those familiar with the jurisprudence of a generation ago. It may be that the composition of the Bench has changed, and that the modern courts are less willing to carry out their own views of justice at the expense of principled legal reasoning. But it is difficult to escape the conclusion that the political climate is very different today from what it was a generation ago, and in particular that trade union power and influence are much less significant now than they were then. Nor is it possible to overlook the fact that legislation has largely taken the law in many of the directions that the courts were straining towards in these earlier decisions: with Parliament now in the driving seat the judges can relax and enjoy the scenery; they may even sometimes apply the brakes.

[7.29] *Hamlet v GMBATU* [1987] ICR 150 (Ch D)

The plaintiff was a candidate for a position of district delegate in the defendant union. He alleged that there had been a number of electoral irregularities and sought a declaration that he was the duly elected delegate and an injunction to restrain the other candidate in the election from being described and treated as the district delegate. The alleged irregularities were as follows:

'*(5)* the votes cast in the ballots at the Cosham and Gosport branches were void and in breach of the contract between the plaintiff and the union in that (a) in breach of rule 11(15)(h) the ballot at the Cosham branch remained open for less than one hour from 21.12 hours to 21.00 hours; (b) in breach of rules 11(15)(c) and 28(9) a number of members of the Cosham branch were permitted to vote although they were out of benefit within the meaning of rule 28(5) and (18); (c) in breach of rules 28(9), 11(15)(e), 15(1) and 16(1) at the Cosham branch the branch president and branch secretary responsible for carrying out the ballot were out of benefit within the meaning of rule 28(5) and (18); (d) in breach of rule 11(15)(c) and rule 28(9) at the Gosport branch a member Mr. White and others whom the plaintiff cannot now name voted although being retired members and hence out of benefit in accordance with rule 28 and/or retained on the books as a member for the purposes of funeral benefit within the meaning of rule 28(10) or (20); and (e) in breach of rules 11(15)(e) and 16(1) at the Gosport branch the branch secretary responsible for carrying out the ballot was not in benefit by reason of the fact that he was a retired member and hence out of benefit in accordance with rule 28. *(6)(a)* The voting result forms in respect of the Cosham and the Gosport branches of the union did not record the correct result nor were they correctly signed in that some or all of the officials of the respective branches were out of benefit and hence disentitled from conducting the election and/or from voting in them and that accordingly by reason of rule 11(15)(j) the executive council of the union had no power to count the votes recorded on the voting result forms towards the result of the election whether or not the plaintiff's objections to them were out of time. Accordingly the general council of the union had no power to reject an appeal against the purported determinations of the executive council in respect of the Cosham and Gosport branches. *(6)(b)* His appeal to the general council of the union was in any event vitiated by a breach of natural justice and/or bias or a reasonable suspicion thereof in that four members of the executive council which purported to reject the plaintiff's objections to the election were present at and took part in the hearing of the plaintiff's appeals to the general council on 21 and 22 May 1983 and that accordingly the rejection by the general council of the plaintiff's appeal was void and of no effect.'

The union moved successfully to strike out the statement of claim as disclosing no cause of action.

Harman J:

The claim advanced by Mr Langstaff for the union is that the whole of paragraph (5) fails to raise any cause of action at law by reason of the doctrine, well exemplified in the old decision, but in my judgment still current in modern days, in *Dawkins v Antrobus* (1881) 17 ChD 615. Particularly he cites the judgment of James LJ, at p 628:

'We have no right to sit as a Court of Appeal upon the decision of the members of a club duly assembled. All we have to consider is whether the notice was or was not given according to the proper rules, whether the meeting was properly convened, and whether the meeting, if properly convened, had come to the conclusion that this gentleman ought to be expelled, having before it the fact that the committee had, upon investigation of the matter, come to that conclusion, and expressed the opinion, that his conduct was such as to entitle them to call upon him to resign'.

Mr Langstaff also cited Cotton LJ, who was very much to the same effect, at p. 634: 'We are not here to sit as a Court of Appeal from the decision of the committee or of the general meeting.' That line of thought, says Mr Langstaff, is entirely applicable today. The only duty of the courts in considering questions of appeals and the internal machinery for resolving disputes in unions is to see that the machinery has been properly followed through. The decision is not one which the court has any business to go into. Indeed, Mr Langstaff submitted—and he may well be right in this—that it would not even be a proper contention, were it advanced, to say that the club or trade union in reaching its decision had taken into account matters it should not have taken into account—the administrative law rule exemplified in *Associated Provincial Picture Houses Ltd. v Wednesbury Corporation* [1948] 1 KB 223. He agreed and conceded that, if the decision was so perverse as to be described properly as a 'mere caprice,' then certainly the courts could upset it; but, unless it went to that length, the failure to take account of matters that were irrelevant was not the proper scope of a review by the courts of these sorts of decision. It was a machinery review, and perhaps a review of decisions that were wholly unreasonable, but not more than that.

In my view that is indeed the correct analysis of the law. It follows that the allegations in paragraph (5) of the statement of claim, unless they amount to an allegation that the machinery of the union was not properly followed through, cannot be heard in the court by way of appeal from that decision. The machinery is set out in the rules, which are incorporated as part of the pleading in the statement of claim and can of course be referred to as so incorporated; in particular the electoral rule, rule 11. That rule runs for several pages and provides for various requirements. The rule goes on in paragraph (17) to deal with the cross-heading 'Electoral irregularities,' and that paragraph provides: 'Any failure by any member of the society or any branch to observe any of the provisions of rule 11 shall constitute an electoral offence,' and it goes on in paragraph (18)(a) to provide that 'if any . . . member of the society alleges that any electoral offence has been committed . . . he shall make a complaint in writing to the executive council . . .' That complaint by virtue of rule 11(18)(b) must be within 28 days, although there is a discretion to receive complaints outside the time limit in the executive council. There is then a set of procedures as to how the executive council shall consider and adjudicate upon the matter and a provision in rule 11(19) that the executive council is entitled to dismiss the same, or, in rule 11(20), in its absolute discretion as to what action it may take. Rule 11(21) goes on to provide:

> 'Any person aggrieved by any decision of the executive council may under this rule appeal therefrom to the general council who may hear and decide any such appeal in whatever manner they in their absolute discretion may decide. . . .'

Those provisions are not alleged in paragraph (5) of the statement of claim not to have been gone through so far as the machinery is concerned. Paragraph (5) alleges, as I have already mentioned, various express breaches of rule 11 and rule 28 and so on. All these appear to be plainly electoral irregularities, and plainly matters requiring a complaint and an adjudication by the executive council and an appeal to the general council. It is quite clear from paragraph (4) of the statement of claim that there was what the plaintiff calls an 'objection' and what the rules call a 'complaint,' and from paragraph (6) that the executive council considered and decided to reject that objection and that the general council rejected an appeal from that decision of the executive council. There is no suggestion at any point in those allegations that the machinery was not properly followed through. Thus, if I were to permit this matter to go on, I would be encouraging a plain breach of the rule in *Dawkins v Antrobus* (1881) 17 ChD 615 and encouraging or permitting the plaintiff to attempt to have the court sit in appeal on the decision of the properly constituted body before whom, by the rules, the plaintiff had agreed the decision should be taken. It seems to me that that cannot be a matter raising a cause of action proper for litigation in these courts, or, to use the old phrase, a reasonable cause of action.

The next complaint in the proposed amendments is in paragraph (6)(a), which asserts that rule 11(15)(j) was broken. Rule 11(15)(j) is attended by some difficulty of construction. The reason is that rule 11(15)(j) starts off by providing obligations upon the branch president (who is the member appointed to assist in the management of the election) and the secretary to enter the correct result on the voting result form and to post the result form to the head office, there being a time limit upon its receipt and requirements for the completion of it. It then goes on at its very end to say that any votes recorded shall be disqualified if they are not correctly signed and 'this disqualification shall be obligatory. The executive council shall have no power, by virtue of rule 11(20) or otherwise, to waive it'.

Mr Kerr [for the plaintiff] argued that that raised a primary obligation upon the executive council (for which Mr Langstaff accepted that his client union would be directly answerable), which primary obligation, says Mr Kerr, was not a matter of electoral irregularity requiring complaint under rule 11(18) but was a free-standing and independent obligation. I have been convinced by Mr Langstaff that that is an impossible construction of paragraph (18). The paragraph is perhaps not drafted with the utmost skill; it may well be that a careful draftsman, skilled in the art, would have made the last sentence of rule 11(15)(j) to include a proviso to rule 11(20) setting out the powers of the executive council dealing with any electoral irregularity. But it has well been said that one must not construe trade union rule books as if they were statutes: one must not look at them with the eye accustomed to Income Tax Acts and strict settlements; one must consider them in a more benign and loose way of reading. It seems to me that that mode of construction is one which is entirely apt and desirable to apply to this rule.

It would be the oddest sort of result if rule 11(15)(j) created in its first three sentences electoral irregularities which were mandatory under the rules to be the subject of a complaint under rule 11(18), but in its last sentence created a different and free-standing obligation upon the executive council arising out of primarily the same facts as the undoubted electoral irregularity. Further, as Mr Langstaff observed to me, one must allow common sense to creep in, even in litigation over union rules, and how, in the name of fortune, Mr Langstaff would have liked to express it, could the executive council know that there had been an incorrect result entered upon the face of the voting form? They have, under rule 11(15)(l)(i), a duty to scrutinise the result of the election, but, if they receive a form which apparently is properly created, how are they, sitting at head office, to know that there is some voting irregularity underlying it? As it seems to me, that is a powerful reinforcement of the constructional view of the rule which I take, that the addition of the last sentence to rule 11(15)(j) is in truth a proviso to the powers of the executive council set out in rule 11(20), and is not a free-standing matter separate from all the other obligations of rule 11(15), all of which are plainly matters raising electoral irregularities within rule 11(17).

In my view the claim advanced by Mr Kerr, which at one time did seem to me to have some force, could only have force if it were taken with a very strict, wholly unrealistic (and unrelated to the true substance of that which one is construing), view of the construction of this rule book. In my view the complaints in the proposed amendments to the statement of claim that the voting result forms were not correctly signed because some persons were disentitled because out of benefit from voting in the election, must have been electoral irregularities and must have come within the ambit of complaint to the executive council followed by appeal to the general council. In fact, there was no complaint on this matter within the 28 days or at all, and, as it seems to me, that matter is irretrievably water under the bridge and cannot be dug up as a cause of action now.

Finally, there is the proposed paragraph (6)(b). That alleges that the hearing by the general council of the plaintiff's appeal was vitiated as contrary to natural justice by the fact that four members of the executive council sat upon the general council. First, in my view of the law, there is no rule of natural justice, or any justice, that a member of a body who has sat at first instance is thereby disabled from sitting upon appeal, or that, if an appeal is heard upon which such a person does sit, the appeal is in some way vitiated; that that was the law, both at equity and in the common law courts, is in my view beyond any question or doubt. *Knox v Gye* (1872) LR 5 HL 656 in the House of Lords, cited by Mr Langstaff, is a classic illustration of it, where four members of the House of Lords were sitting, two of whom had sat, one at first instance as the then Vice-Chancellor, and one on appeal as, I think, Master of the Rolls, or it may have been as Lord Chancellor upon appeal, and both had then been ennobled and were sitting in the House of Lords to try the final hearing. Nobody regarded the House of Lords as improperly constituted upon that ground. It was common-place in equity for a judge to sit upon appeal on a matter where he had been concerned below. The same applied to the common law courts. The Court in Banc regularly and habitually included the judge who had tried the matter at nisi prius, as to which a rule nisi had been obtained, which was then sought to be made absolute.

There is no sort of history of disablement of a judge, let alone of a court or tribunal from hearing a matter because one or two members have been concerned before. If a modern instance is sought on the ground that these are all very old matters and we know better than our grandfathers—a proposition I would venture to doubt in any event—one can refer to what I would call the quite modern case of *Rex v Lovegrove* [1951] 1 All ER 804 where that great judge Lord Goddard CJ laid down in plain terms the fact that the Court of Criminal Appeal, a purely statutory body constituted by the Criminal Appeal

Act 1907, was entitled to sit with Lynskey J as one of the three members, he having been the judge who had tried the offence at first instance. Lord Goddard observed in flat and clear terms that there was no rule which prevented the judge who had heard the matter sitting upon the appeal, and it was quite contrary to all rule that he should be disqualified. He said that there might be cases where it was desirable that the judge should not sit, but that was beside the point. I was told that two Commonwealth decisions—one in Canada and one in Victoria—have come to similar conclusions, and I am always glad to hear that the old learning has been followed in far distant places.

The matter, however, goes further than that. Holding, as I would, that as a matter of the rules of natural justice there is no such rule as is contended for by Mr Kerr, it goes further in the sense that the rule book here, which is the very contract sued upon, expressly provides that the general council hearing the appeal shall include the four persons who it is said sat: so they did; so they should; so the plaintiff by his contract had agreed they should. They were not, it is clear, a majority of the general council. One of the four appears to have been a mere minute taker or recorder with no voice or vote in the hearing in the general council. It is not upon that sort of proposition that I base the observations I am making. I base it upon the proposition that, where a man has expressly agreed by contract to accept a tribunal containing certain persons, he cannot thereafter come bleating to the courts complaining of a breach of natural justice when the contract is carried out exactly according to the terms as he had always known, if he had read the rule book, he was bound to accept.

In my view there is no merit in paragraph (6)(b) of the amended statement of claim either as a general proposition of law or on the particular contract here sued upon. Thus, as it seems to me, none of the matters advanced by Mr Kerr amount to a reasonable cause of action, even if, which I have not yet done, I were to allow him to amend to plead those inadmissible matters. As it seems to me, it is probably the correct procedure, but I will listen to counsel about this, to rule upon the summons for leave to amend by refusing leave to amend for the reasons I have given, that is, that the proposed amendments raised no reasonable cause of action and therefore should not clutter up the pleading, and to strike out the original pleading as it stands, which indeed Mr Kerr would concede, as it originally stood, would follow.

The second question for the courts is one of *timing*. At what stage in the proceedings should they intervene when called upon by an aggrieved member? It is clear on the one hand that the courts will not tolerate their jurisdiction being ousted. Any trade union rule which purported to have this effect would be treated as being contrary to public policy. But what about on the other hand the possibility of the courts postponing intervention to allow the internal appeal procedures to work, and to give the union an opportunity to correct any mistake? In *White v Kuzych* [1951] AC 598, it was held that where there was an express obligation of this kind, the member would be bound to exhaust internal remedies before instituting legal proceedings. A similar approach appears to have been supported by Plowman J in *Radford v NATSOPA* [1972] ICR 484, at pp 498–99 where he said:

Mr Hawser [for the union] submitted that the rules of the union provided for an appeal from the decisions of the branch committee to the executive council and ultimately to the general council of the union, and that the applicant ought to have exhausted the appeal procedure before coming to this court. Mr Turner-Samuels, for the applicant, submitted that on a true construction of the relevant rules no right of appeal existed in the present case. Let me assume, however, that Mr Turner-Samuels is wrong about this. Even so the rules are not in what I may call a *Scott v Avery* form, that is to say that they do not require recourse to the domestic tribunal to be exhausted before recourse is taken to the courts; and, accordingly, there can be no doubt that I have jurisdiction to deal with the matter, subject to a discretion to withhold it until the domestic remedies have been exhausted: see *Lawlor v Union of Post Office Workers* [1965] Ch 712; *Leigh v National Union of Railwaymen* [1970] Ch 326. In the present case the dispute is, in my opinion, one which is peculiarly appropriate for the court, depending as it does partly on construction and partly on the question of the sufficiency of evidence. I, therefore, reject Mr Hawser's submission on this point.

But where there is undue delay (of more than six months) by a union in dealing with a complaint under the rules, the courts are bound to intervene regardless of the rules of the union: TULRCA 1992, section 63. Much of the litigation which has taken place on this issue has in fact been concerned with situations where there is no provision in the rules requiring an exhaustion of internal appeals before legal action. In *Lawlor v Union of Post Office Workers* [1965] Ch 712 the court intervened because the final appeal was to the annual conference of the union, and this would take too long. We have also seen that in *Esterman v NALGO*, [1974] ICR 625, the court did not hold back. But a rather different approach is evident in the following case.

[7.30] *Longley v NUJ* [1987] IRLR 109 (CA)

The plaintiff was a member of the NUJ and a workplace representative of the union at *The Times*. Following the relocation of *The Times* from central London to Wapping, the NUJ ordered its members not to report for work there and not to cross picket lines. Only a few employees complied with the union instruction and were dismissed. The others, including the plaintiff, reported for work, and a complaint was brought against the plaintiff and other union representatives at *The Times* by a member of the union, after the NEC refused to initiate disciplinary proceedings against them. Before the matter could be heard by a complaints' committee, the plaintiff applied to the High Court for an interlocutory injunction to restrain the complaint from being heard under the union's disciplinary procedures. The application was unsuccessful, and the Court of Appeal upheld the first instance decision of Knox J.

Ralph Gibson LJ:
The learned judge held that the evidence of Mr Longley amply showed that there is a substantial issue to be tried on his allegation that he could not reasonably be held guilty of conduct detrimental to the interests of the union under the rules. I agree. Mr Longley's case is, in my judgment, on the evidence I have seen and submissions I have heard, a powerful case, but I must point out that we have not heard submissions from the defendants, for the reasons which my Lord [Nourse LJ who gave the first judgment] has explained. There is, however, no certainty that the complaints committee will reject Mr Longley's contentions, or that, if they do, the NEC will uphold their recommendations. Mr Longley has said that the ultimate penalty of expulsion will inevitably be imposed upon him. Mr Norris, the assistant general secretary of the NUJ, in his affidavit has denied this and asserted that there is no basis for the assertion that the complaints committee and the NEC had prejudged the complex issues which arise in this case. There is, I think, a real basis for Mr Longley's anxiety, but I see no reason to doubt that the members of the complaints committee and the NEC will, as Mr Norris has claimed, act responsibly and fairly.
    The rules of this union provide for the hearing and decision of complaints brought by

members or by the governing committees of the union under the rules. Participation in such proceedings by the members is an important part of the working of a voluntary society such as a trade union. The members of a union are entitled, unless there is some good reason to prevent it, to have their domestic tribunal deal with the issues which are raised for decision under their rules. I am confident that the members of this union—both those who incline to the view that the journalists working at *The Times* had no 'reasonable cause' for not complying with the instructions of the NEC and those who incline to the view that they did—would reasonably wish the present proceedings to be allowed to continue, so that the view of the complaints committee and of the NEC would be known to the members.

My Lord [Nourse LJ who gave the first judgment] has already read the passage in Mr Justice Templeman's speech in *Esterman*'s case. I agree that the court would not interfere to prevent a domestic tribunal from hearing and adjudicating a complaint unless the court was satisfied that no reasonable tribunal acting *bona fide* could uphold the complaint, and that only in the most exceptional circumstances would it be right for the court to interfere; but it does not follow—and Mr Justice Templeman of course did not suggest that it did— that it would necessarily be right for the court to prevent, by an interlocutory injunction pending the trial, the hearing of a complaint because the court is satisfied that upon the plaintiff's case the tribunal could not reasonably uphold a complaint which is made. It may well be right to leave the domestic tribunal to consider and to decide the case and to leave the plaintiff to prove his complaint after decision by the tribunal if the plaintiff then has any complaint. Legal action then would proceed upon full evidence of the material before the tribunal instead of upon evidence of what material is likely to be put before it.

Where there is no reason to doubt the intention of the tribunal's members to act fairly and responsibly in the matter, the tribunal should be left to deal with the case unless there is some good reason to protect the plaintiff from having to face the proceedings which are brought under the rules of the society to which he belongs. An example of such a reason might be that the tribunal has in the past misconstrued and misapplied the rules and is likely to do so again in a similar case. In my judgment it would not be in the interests, either of the members of such voluntary societies or of the administration of justice, if courts were required in every case to prevent any member from facing proceedings before a domestic tribunal of the society to which he belongs on all and every complaint which that tribunal, if it acts reasonably and upon a proper construction of the rules, should reject and, I would add, therefore, in very many cases probably will reject.

7.8 Conclusion

For the best part of 100 years the aim of legislation was to keep the courts out of trade union government. The Trade Union Act 1871 provided by section 4 that certain rules of a trade union were not 'directly enforceable' in the courts. True, the attempt was not very successful, as the courts found ways to defeat the intention of Parliament. But it reflected a public policy based on the principle of respect for trade union autonomy both in making and administering trade union rules. The courts were confined to a role of enforcing the rules which the unions themselves had drafted. True again, the courts did not wholly accept their role, developing techniques to prescribe or proscribe certain kinds of rule, and to constrain the operation of certain kinds of rules not otherwise unlawful. But compared to what was to come later, this intervention was marginal. So far as it is possible to draw general conclusions from the limited number of cases, and so far as it is possible to draw general conclusions from the cases without regard to their political context, two points stand out. The first is a desire on the part of the courts generally to favour a system of government which would promote membership participation over executive government, and the second is a desire on the part of the courts to create, where possible, rights for members not to be bound by democratic decisions—a kind of US-style Bill of Rights for trade unionists (but to be exercised against the governments of their trade unions).

7.8.1 The changing direction of public policy

Since 1980 the position has changed radically, with far-reaching legislation prescribing a high level of regulation not only of the way in which trade unions are governed but also of the rights and duties of trade union members: more of the former and less of the latter. In this respect public policy has comprehensively changed: trade unions are now regulated bodies, to be structured and organised on the basis of a template prescribed by the State which requires more and more resources to be devoted to internal affairs and which undermines their capacity to command the solidarity of the whole. The template is one which reflects to some extent the earlier drawings made by the courts, embracing a notion of democracy through membership participation—in the election of the executive committee and other senior offices, and in the requirement for political fund review ballots and ballots before industrial action; and embracing also a notion of membership whereby the member need not accept the contractual obligations of membership which he or she is free to accept or reject at will. This has always been true in relation to the political levy, but it was extended to include industrial action. Indeed in 1993 trade unions lost the right to exclude members except on prescribed grounds.

This is not to proclaim the virtues of a high level of trade union autonomy, or to disparage a high level of trade union regulation. Public policy is not confined to a choice between the two, with much depending on the social, economic and political problems which the law is addressing and the context in which it is set. But it is to say that the process of trade union regulation in place since 1980 is in some respects paradoxical, in the sense that it has been introduced when trade union power over workers generally and their members in particular has declined significantly. Trade union membership has declined sharply in 20 years (with current levels approaching one half of membership levels in 1980), the closed shop which sustained trade union power over trade union members has virtually vanished, and industrial action is at its lowest level since the 1870s. The paradox of regulation in these circumstances is all the greater for the fact that the nature and extent of the regulation are such as to extend beyond the boundaries of international law. The restrictions on trade union discipline, particularly of those who refuse to take part in a lawfully called strike, have been held by the ILO Committee of Experts to be in breach the freedom of association guarantees of ILO Convention 87, and by the Social Rights Committee of the Council of Europe to be in breach of the right to organise in the Social Charter of 18 October 1961 (Council of Europe, *Committee of Experts XII–1* (1992), p 115).

[7.31] ILO, International Labour Conference, 87th Session, 1999, *Report of the Committee of Experts on the Application of Conventions and Recommendations,* **Report III (Part 1A)**

Unjustifiable discipline [TULRCA 1992], (sections 64–67). The Committee recalls that the previous comments on this matter concerned the above-mentioned provisions of the 1992 Act which prevented trade unions from disciplining their members who refused to participate in lawful strikes and other industrial action or who sought to persuade fellow members to refuse to participate in such action.

In its latest report, the Government states that it strongly supports the principle that workers should be free to join the trade union of their choice as trade unions provide important services to their members. According to the Government, it therefore follows that the rights of unions to discipline and expel members need to be balanced against the rights of individuals to acquire and retain their membership. The Government adds that, under the law of the United Kingdom, individuals are almost invariably breaking their contracts under which they work when they take any form of industrial action, irrespective of whether the action is official or unofficial, or whether the action is lawfully or unlawfully organized. These workers can therefore be sued on an individual basis by employers for damages. In contrast, unions cannot be sued for damages if they organize industrial action within the law. In these circumstances, the Government considers that individuals should be free to decide whether or not to take part in lawfully organized industrial action since the potential liability is the individual's and not the union's.

The Committee must, nevertheless, once again recall that *Article 3 of Convention [87]* concerns the rights of trade unions to, inter alia, draw up their constitutions and rules and to organize their activities and to formulate their programmes, without interference by the public authorities. The free choice to join a trade union can clearly be based on a careful consideration of the provisions in such constitutions and rules. Furthermore, the Committee would recall that the prohibition of such disciplinary measures carries with it heavy financial penalties. The Committee considers unions should have the right to determine whether or not it should be possible to discipline members who refuse to comply with democratic decisions to take lawful industrial action, and that the financial penalties imposed by the legislation in this respect constitute undue interference in the right of workers' organizations to draw up their constitutions and rules freely and would therefore once again ask the Government to refrain from any such interference. As concerns the Government's argument in respect of the liability of individual workers, the Committee recalls the importance it attaches to the maintenance of the employment relationship as a normal consequence of the recognition of the right to strike.

7.8.2 The changing nature of trade unionism

There is a second and more profound change which may be at work here and which these public policy changes may both reflect and drive. This is a changing perception on the part of the State about the role and functions of trade unions in the contemporary economy. The legislation reflects not just a desire that trade unions should be responsive to the wishes of their members by means of the different statutory devices, but a desire also to change the nature of the relationship between the member and the trade union. This is a vision which sees trade unions not so much as sources of power, promoting social change by collective action; but more as sources of advice, providing services to autonomous individual actors in the labour market. Such a vision is reflected to some extent in the choice which members now have in the collective decisions in which they wish to participate, but perhaps most clearly in the views expressed by ministers when introducing what is now TULRCA 1992, section 174. According to one minister 'unions should be about attracting members and providing services for them' (Official Report, Standing Committee F, 8 December 1992, col 128), and workers should be free to move from one union where 'another union offers them better insurance deals or [because] they have a commitment to it' (*ibid*, col 124).

So what we have on this model is the trade union as a service provider, an insurance company for the workplace. This is not to suggest that this is the only role of modern trade unions. As we will see in the following chapter, trade unions also play an important part in representing workers in the workplace. There is, however, an emphasis on a partnership model of representation, in which (as we will see in chapter 9) trade unions are ill – equipped to act on behalf of their members when partnership arrangements break down. The main change in terms of the trade union function in recent years has been the decline of the regulatory role, to the extent that this function was typically performed by sectoral or industry wide collective bargaining. This role has been to some extent displaced by regulatory legislation of universal

---

Trade Unions and the Human Rights Act

Although trade unions now operate under very tight statutory restrictions, there seems no desire on the part of the Labour government to remove the restraints. The Employment Relations Act 1999 made only modest changes at the margins. Inertia on the part of government in the face of legislation which continues to breach international human rights treaties raises questions about how the Human Rights Act might be invoked by trade unions as a way of reducing some of the burden. There are questions in particular about the extent to which the restrictions on the exclusion and expulsion of members can be said to be compatible with the right to freedom of association in the European Convention on Human Rights (ECHR), and in particular whether sections 64 and 65 (on the discipline of strikebreakers) and 174 (on exclusion and expulsion generally) can be said to be compatible with the freedom of association guarantees in Article 11 (see p 730 below). Although section 174 has been amended, it is not clear whether the limited scope of the amendments do full justice to the human rights issues which are raised here. It is significant that in *Lee v ASLEF*, EAT/0625/03/RN, Burton J should say obiter that 'it would seem to us, on the authorities, that, absent a case of prejudice to livelihood, in this case the Respondent's right of negative association for the Union and its members would seem likely to override the asserted right of association of the Applicant'. In this way the courts could be called upon paradoxically to perform an unusual and uncharacteristic role: to help remove rather than impose restraints on the way in which trade unions are governed.

application and consequently of a minimum standard. In terms of the other functions of trade unions identified above, we also see—with the election of a Labour government in 1997—a growth in the government and public administration functions. The latter is in some respects the most interesting, with trade unions being enlisted by government to assist with the productivity problem in the British economy. This finds expression through partnership arrangements, but also in the involvement of trade unions in addressing the skills and learning problems in the United Kingdom. A union learning fund has been established to help trade unions meet learning needs at the workplace and a new cadre of union officers—union learning representatives—have been created with new legal rights to develop this agenda.

FURTHER READING

P Elias and K Ewing, *Trade Union Democracy, Members' Rights and the Law* (London, Mansell, 1988).

K D Ewing, 'Article 11, and the Right to Freedom of Association' in K D Ewing (ed), *Human Rights at Work* (London, Institute of Employment Rights, 2000).

—— K D Ewing, 'The Function of Trade Unions' (2005) 34 *Industrial Law Journal* 1

—— 'The Political Parties, Elections and Referendums Act 2000—Implications for Trade Unions' (2001) 30 *Industrial Law Journal* (1999).

K D Ewing (ed) *Working Life: A New Perspective on Labour Law* (London, Lawrence & Wishart, 1996), chapter 6.

J Hendy and K D Ewing, 'Trade Unions, Human Rights and the BNP, (2005) 34 *Industrial Law Journal* 197.

Institute of Employment Rights, *Submission to the Joint Committee on Human Rights on the Employment Relations Bill 2004* (www.ier.org.uk)

O Kahn Freund, 'Trade Unions, the Law and Society' (1970) 33 *Modern Law Review* 241.

E McKendrick, 'The Rights of Trade Union Members—Part I of the Employment Act 1988' (1988) 17 *Industrial Law Journal* 141.

H Morris and P Fosh, 'Measuring Trade Union Democracy: The Case of the UK Public Services Association' (2000) 38 *British Journal of Industrial Relations* 95.

B Simpson, 'Individualism versus Collectivism: An Evaluation of Section 14 of the Trade Union Reform and Employment Rights Act 1993' (1993) 22 *Industrial Law Journal* 181.

R Undy and R Martin, *Ballots and Trade Union Democracy* (Oxford, Blackwell, 1984).

R Undy, P Fosh, H Morris, P Smith and R Martin, *Managing the Unions: The Impact of Legislation on Trade Unions' Behaviour* (Oxford, Oxford University Press, 1996).

Lord Wedderburn of Charlton, *Labour Law and Freedom* (London, Lawrence & Wishart, 1995), chapter 5.

Worker Representation and Trade Union Recognition

8.1 Trade unions and collective bargaining

Trade unions perform potentially three functions at the workplace on behalf of their members (and in some cases other workers). They represent individual workers who may be in dispute with their employer: the worker may have a grievance about working conditions or may be the subject of disciplinary action by the employer. Secondly, they provide a channel for the consultation of workers collectively about a range of issues: the employer may wish to introduce new production methods or change working practices. And thirdly, they provide the means for the collective negotiation of terms and conditions of employment. By acting collectively workers can often secure better terms and conditions of employment than by acting alone. In this chapter we are concerned with the ways in which Parliament has intervened to protect workers who organise in a trade union, and to assist those workers who seek to be represented by a trade union, whether individually or collectively. We also consider the role of law in promoting the development of non union forms of worker representation.

8.1.1 Changing public policy responses

Public policy with regard to the role of trade unions and collective bargaining has changed in a number of respects over the course of the last 100 years. The State has intervened at different times and in different ways, to promote different forms of collective bargaining machinery. A good starting point is the report of the Whitley Committee in 1917 which recommended that the newly created Ministry of Labour should intervene to seek to establish industry-wide Joint Industrial Councils to conduct collective bargaining between trade unions and employers' federations. Where this proved impossible, it was proposed that a tripartite trade board should be established in the industry or sector in question under statutory authority to set wages and other conditions of employment (the employers and trade unions being represented along with a third party appointed by the Ministry). These recommendations were accepted by the government of the day, with the result that active steps were taken by the Ministry of Labour to promote joint industrial councils, and the Trade Boards Act 1918 extended the circumstances in which statutory trade boards could be created. The result was that between 1918 and 1921 an additional five million workers were covered either by a collective agreement or a trade board award.

These initiatives were not pursued by Conservative governments in the 1920s, with the result that the system established after the First World War declined and in some cases decayed for want of nourishment. In an era of high unemployment, the direction of public policy had changed, and ministers were no longer interested in using discretionary powers to promote collective bargaining. But this was not to last. Clear signs of a revival of state support for the institutions of collective bargaining are discernible from about 1934, so that by 1946 some 85 per cent of British workers were covered by a collective agreement or a trade board award. The State thus played a key role in building collective bargaining institutions: a government department was responsible for promoting the development of collective bargaining machinery; statutory machinery was introduced to establish terms and conditions of employment for sectors where collective bargaining was insufficiently established; and although collective agreements were not legally enforceable between the parties who made them, they were legalised (as the TUC referred to the process) by statutory procedures for their extension to employers who were not parties to the agreements in question, and consequently to workers who may not have been members of the union which negotiated the agreement.

This pattern of intervention was based on a model of collective bargaining conducted at sector or industry level between trade unions and employers' associations, a method of bargaining which is designed to ensure a high level of penetration. Since the report of the Donovan Royal Commission on Trade Unions and Employers' Associations (Cmnd 3623, 1968), the focus of public policy has changed quite radically in two different ways. The first is a concern not so much to promote multi-employer, industry-wide collective bargaining as to promote or facilitate collective bargaining on a single enterprise or employer basis only. The second relates to the changing tools of intervention, with specific statutory procedures being introduced for this purpose to accompany the wide discretionary powers of a government department (such as the Ministry of Labour or the Department of Employment) or a public body (such as ACAS). The Employment Protection Act 1975 gave statutory force to the Advisory Conciliation and Arbitration Service (ACAS) and conferred upon it a duty to promote or facilitate collective bargaining (a duty which was revoked in 1993 and never restored). The 1975 Act also introduced a procedure whereby a trade union could refer a recognition issue to ACAS, and empowered ACAS to make inquiries and where appropriate to recommend that the union be recognised.

The recognition procedure introduced in 1975 was repealed in 1980 by the incoming Conservative government. (Wages councils, as the trade boards had been

---

Trade Union Recognition and Collective Bargaining

If a trade union is recognised by an employer for the purposes of collective bargaining, it means that the employer bargains with the union about the terms and conditions of employment. Collective bargaining thus has a regulatory function: it determines working conditions in the employment in question. The terms of individual contracts of employment will be determined by the collective agreement for the time being in force. These terms will normally be incorporated into individual employment contracts.

---

renamed in 1945, were abolished in 1993.) But in truth the recognition legislation had been beset with problems. A number of high-profile cases in the courts exposed a number of weaknesses in the drafting, including in particular the fact that an employer could frustrate the procedure by denying ACAS access to the workforce (*Grunwick Processing Laboratories Ltd v ACAS* [1978] ICR 231). There were also difficulties encountered by virtue of the wide and largely unconstrained discretion of ACAS which enabled it to recommend recognition even though there was support from only a minority of the workers in a bargaining unit, and to refuse to make a recommendation even though there was a majority in favour in a proposed bargaining unit (*UKAPE v ACAS* [1980] ICR 201). And there was also the question of the remedy: in the event of a failure by an employer to comply with an ACAS recommendation, the remedy took the form of the unilateral arbitration of terms and conditions of employment of workers in the bargaining unit by the Central Arbitration Committee (CAC). The CAC adopted a very cautious approach to its role. These and other defects of the 1975 procedure have been instrumental in helping to shape the content of the new recognition procedure introduced by the Employment Relations Act 1999, which we consider in section 8.4 below.

But before moving on, it is perhaps appropriate at this stage to reflect on the changing functions of trade union recognition. The trade union recognition procedure introduced in 1975 was based on the idea that collective bargaining is desirable as a way of promoting the participation of workers through representative institutions in workplace decisions, a vision promoted by Kahn Freund from a legal perspective and Flanders from an industrial relations perspective. The functions of trade union recognition have now changed: not so much promoted to encourage participation as an instrument of industrial citizenship, but facilitated to encourage partnership as an instrument of economic and business efficiency.

[8.1] Department of Trade and Industry, *Fairness at Work* (Cm 95, 1998)

2.2 The best modern companies, whether large or small, have some things in common:

- they seek to harness the talents of their employees in a relationship based on fairness and through a recognition that everybody involved in the business has an interest in its success;
- they ensure that everybody understands the business so that change is readily accepted and implemented, not feared;
- they set clear objectives for employees but also encourage them to exercise their initiative and to contribute their ideas to the development of the business; and

- they develop the workforce through training and work experience to respond to and lead change.

2.3 None of this is easy for business. The pressures of global markets, hierarchical management attitudes and short-term approaches to costs and profits can all be obstacles. The values of the company have to be maintained in lean times as well as when business is good. The rewards for employees, in terms of the quality of work and job security as well as of pay, are great but so are the demands, particularly for those not used to rapid change.

2.4 But despite the difficulties, the returns from effective partnership to the business and its employees are real whether it operates in local or global markets:
- where they have an understanding of the business, employees recognise the importance of responding quickly to changing customer and market requirements;
- where they are taken seriously, employees at every level come forward with ways to help the business innovate, for example by developing new products; and
- where they are well-prepared for change, employees can help the company to introduce and operate new technologies and processes, helping to secure employment within the business.

2.5 In modern businesses relationships at work are flexible and tailored to the size and culture of the company or organisation. Sometimes, they are provided by a partnership between employers and trade unions which complements the direct relationship between employer and employee. On the other hand, some organisations achieve effective working relationships in other ways.

2.6 The Government believes that each business should choose the form of relationship that suits it best. But the freedom to choose must apply to employees as well as employers, otherwise any commitment will be hollow and will neither create trust nor underpin competitiveness. This means that employers should not deny trade union recognition where it has the clear and demonstrated support of employees.

8.1.2 Changing patterns of workplace representation

As late as 1979 it is thought that as many as 82 per cent of British workers were covered by a collective agreement or a wages council order. The coverage is now much less, with collective bargaining now extending to anywhere between 30 and 40 per cent, depending on the source. But whatever the source, it is clear that only a minority of workers are now covered by a collective agreement. There are a number of factors which explain this decline, of which the withdrawal of legal support for trade unions generally and trade union recognition in particular in the 1980s and 1990s is perhaps not among the most important. These factors include changing patterns and forms of employment, with a reduction in jobs in sectors where trade unionism was previously strong (extraction and manufacturing); and the changing ways in which collective bargaining is conducted. Unlike many European countries, there has been a change in the level at which collective bargaining takes place, with a move from sectoral or industry wide bargaining to company or enterprise wide bargaining. But the decline in the levels of collective bargaining coverage is remarkable not only in relation to the historic levels which operated in this country, but also relative to the position elsewhere in Europe, as the box on p 727 makes clear.

Collective Bargaining Density

Collective bargaining coverage in the United Kingdom is low compared to a number of our European partners. The estimates vary, though it is likely to be less than 40%. In 2001 the European Industrial Relations Observatory estimated that the coverage in Austria was 98%, Belgium 90%, Denmark 83%, France 90–95%, Netherlands 88%, Spain 81%, and Sweden 90%. Coverage in the United States is in contrast much lower than in the United Kingdom.

Accompanying this decline in collective bargaining coverage are the changes which have taken place in the ways in which workers are represented at the workplace and in the ways in which the worker's voice is heard in workplace decision-making. The public policy emphasis in Britain hitherto quite properly has been one-dimensional, designed in such a way as to give effect to the obligation in ILO Convention 98 (The Right to Organise and Collective Bargaining Convention, 1949) which by Article 4 provides that:

Measures appropriate to national conditions shall be taken, where necessary, to encourage and promote the full development and utilisation of machinery for voluntary negotiation between employers or employers' organisations and workers' organisations with a view to the regulation of terms and conditions of employment by means of collective agreements.

Developments in European law, however, have required a more flexible public policy response, to allow in prescribed cases for the representation of workers through non-union channels, particularly where collective bargaining has not been established. Acceptance of different forms of workplace representation is also to be found in the Employment Relations Act 1999 which, in permitting workers to secure the recognition of their union, acknowledges that there may be a role for other forms of workplace representation. But as the following extract makes clear, it may increasingly be the case that the workers' voice is heard directly—if at all—rather than through representative channels of any kind.

[8.2] N Millward, A Bryson and J Forth, *All Change at Work?* (London, Routledge, 2000), pp 135–37

We set out in this chapter to answer the question, 'have employees lost their voice?' The answer must be 'no'—but with important qualifications. The great majority of workplaces in 1998 had some form of communication channel between employees and managers through which employees could, at least in principle, express their views and concerns to management. This was also the case at the time of our earlier surveys in 1990 and 1984. But the nature of these channels of communication changed a great deal. There was a major shift from channels involving representatives, usually able to call upon the information and resources of independent trade unions, to channels where employees communicated directly with management, largely on occasions and on terms set by management themselves.

Comparing the results from 1998 with those of earlier surveys we saw a continuation of the widespread falls in trade union presence and aggregate membership density that had occurred during the 1980s. Membership declines in the private sector were particularly severe where there had been closed shops or very high density, but they were not confined to such circumstances. Fewer managements gave strong support to union membership, but, even where such support remained, fewer employees were members. There appeared to be a general withering of enthusiasm for union membership within continuing workplaces in both private and public sectors.

Our analysis of the extent of trade union recognition showed that it continued to be very widespread in the public sector and concentrated among large employers and workplaces in the private sector. But recognition in the private sector continued to fall in the 1990s, as it had done since 1984, reaching only 25 per cent of workplaces in 1998—only half the level of 1980. Our analysis suggested that the propensity of employers to recognize trade unions had been in decline for a very long time, since well before the change of government in 1979.

By 1998, factors that had been strongly associated with union recognition at the start of our series—manufacturing rather than services, full-time work and manual employment—had ceased to be so. But few employers actively derecognized all existing unions at workplaces that continued in existence in the 1990s. It was the persistently lower rate of recognition among new workplaces (and those that grew from being very small) that fuelled the continuing decline in the proportion of workplaces with recognition.

We found that the other main channel for collective or representative voice—functioning joint consultative committees at workplace level—had also shown a further decline in the 1990s. Among continuing workplaces there was no tendency to substitute consultative committees for trade union representation. There was an increase in workplaces with non-union representatives over the period 1980 to 1998, but in overall terms the decline in collective voice was pervasive, involving union and non-union forms alike. Between 1984 and 1998 the proportion of workplaces with some union-based employee voice fell from 66 to 42 per cent; over the same period the proportion with (more broadly defined) collective voice fell from 74 to 53 per cent. Union-only arrangements experienced the sharpest decline.

Over this same period employers and managers substantially increased their use of communication channels that provided some opportunity for employees to express their views and concerns to management directly. Periodic meetings between managers and all employees and briefing groups were both methods of 'direct participation' which were more common in 1998 than in 1984, notably in the private sector. Briefing groups grew only where there was no collective representation.

Broadly these changes were such that similar numbers of workplaces in 1998 as in 1984 had some form of employee voice mechanism. Many workplaces continued to have dual arrangements. But there had been a major shift from collective, representative, indirect and union-based voice, to direct, non-union channels.

There is thus a growing representation gap in British workplaces, with a significant decline in the role of representative institutions, whether trade union-based or otherwise. The widening of this gap has led to more subtle responses to the question of how it should be closed. One route is through legislative machinery to promote or facilitate collective bargaining, as reflected in the Employment Relations Act 1999. As we shall see, this procedure has enabled trade unions to turn the tide to some extent, though as we shall also see there are doubts about just how many workers have been brought into some kind of collective bargaining arrangements as a result of its introduction. In most cases this has arisen as a result of voluntary recognition as employers face the inevitable and rationally choose an arrangement which does not lock them into a legalistic statutory procedure. Another route to closing the representation gap is through some kind of standing works council, for union as well as non-union workplaces, as a vehicle for workers to be informed and consulted about a wide range of issues. Previously seen as a threat to established trade union organisation, an elected works council is now seen as providing an institutional forum for trade unions to establish themselves in workplaces where they are not recognised. The German experience is that most elected works council members are also trade union members, and it is thought by many that works councils could complement rather than compete with a collective bargaining strategy. For a vigorous debate on this issue from a British point of view see J Kelly, 'Works Councils: Union Advance or Marginalization?'; and R Hyman, 'Is There a Case for Statutory Works Councils in Britain?', in A McColgan (ed), *The Future of Labour Law* (London, Mansell, 1996), chapters 4 and 5 respectively. This is a matter to which we return in section 8.6 below.

8.2 Trade union membership and activities

If workers are to be represented at work by a trade union it is important that they should be free to join a trade union without fear of being penalised by an employer. Without the protection of this fundamental right there can be no trade union organisation at the workplace. It is not a surprise to learn that at common law employers were free to make it a condition of a contract that workers should not be members of a trade union, and to refuse to employ, discipline or dismiss anyone who refused or failed to comply with this condition. The right to be a member of a trade union and to take part in the activities of a trade union is, however, protected by international law, and is now protected by legislation.

[8.3] ILO Convention 98 (The Right to Organise and Collective Bargaining Convention, 1949), Article 1

1. Workers shall enjoy adequate protection against acts of anti-union discrimination in respect of their employment.
2. Such protection shall apply more particularly in respect of acts calculated to—
   (a) make the employment of a worker subject to the condition that he shall not join a union or shall relinquish trade union membership;
   (b) cause the dismissal of or otherwise prejudice a worker by reason of union membership or because of participation in union activities outside working hours or, with the consent of the employer, within working hours.

Legislation to implement this principle was a long time coming, even though the United Kingdom ratified the Convention as early as 1950. The first legislation protecting employees from acts of anti-union discrimination was the Industrial Relations Act 1971. The Act was repealed in 1974, but the Trade Union and Labour Relations

Freedom of Association and the ECHR

'1.   Everyone has the right to peaceful assembly and to freedom of association with others, including the right to form and to join trade unions for the protection of his interests.

2.   No restrictions shall be placed on the exercise of these rights other than such as are prescribed by law and necessary in a democratic society in the interests of national security or public safety, for the prevention of disorder or crime, for the protection of health or morals or the protection of the rights and freedoms of others. This article shall not prevent the imposition of lawful restrictions on the exercise of these rights by members of the armed forces, of the police or of the administration of the State.'

Act 1974 and the Employment Protection Act 1975 reintroduced protection, though in a different form. It is these latter measures—albeit amended by both Conservative and Labour administrations—which form the basis of the current legislation (Trade Union and Labour Relations (Consolidation) Act 1992, sections 137–67). The right to freedom of association (including the right of the individual to form and join a trade union for the protection of his or her interests) is protected also by Article 11 of the European Convention on Human Rights, enforceable in the domestic courts following the Human Rights Act 1998. The right to organise is protected further by Article 5 of the Council of Europe's Social Charter of 18 October 1961.

8.2.1 Access to employment

The provisions relating to discrimination at the point of hiring were not introduced until 1990. Until then employers were free not to employ someone because of trade union membership. In legislating to close this gap, it is clear that the main aim of the Employment Act 1990 was the pre-entry closed shop whereby workers could be required as a condition of employment to be members of a trade union. Nevertheless, in addressing this issue the legislation also applied to the converse situation of someone refused employment because of his or her trade union membership.

[8.4] Trade Union and Labour Relations (Consolidation) Act 1992, section 137

Refusal of Employment on grounds related to union membership

137 (1) It is unlawful to refuse a person employment—
(a)   because he is, or is not, a member of a trade union, or
(b)   because he is unwilling to accept a requirement—
   (i)   to take steps to become or cease to be, or to remain or not to become, a member of a trade union, or
   (ii)   to make payments or suffer deductions in the event of his not being a member of a trade union.

(2) A person who is thus unlawfully refused employment has a right of complaint to an employment tribunal.

Section 138 applies similar provisions to employment agencies. Remedies are dealt with in section 140, and awards of compensation may be made against third parties, such as a trade union official trying to enforce a closed shop (section 142). The substantive provisions of section 137 are, however, noticeably narrow in their application in so far as they protect rights relating to trade union membership. They apply only to the refusal of employment because of trade union membership, not also because of participation in trade union activities. Does this therefore allow the employer to continue lawfully to screen out the trade union activist?

[8.5] *Harrison v Kent County Council* [1995] ICR 434 (EAT)

The appellant had previously been employed by Kent County Council as a social worker. He left in 1991 to work in Nottingham and then had a spell in Greenwich. In 1993 he applied for a job back in Kent, but his application was unsuccessful on the ground that he had 'an unco-operative attitude and an anti-management style'. The industrial tribunal found that he had not been denied employment because of his trade union membership, but because of his trade union activities, for which there was no protection. He appealed successfully to the EAT.

Mummery J:
We are unable to accept the submission of the council that there was no error of law in the industrial tribunal's construction of section 137(1)(*a*). In our view, the tribunal erred in law for the following reasons.

(1) In construing section 137(1)(a) of the Act of 1992 the tribunal compared it to the provisions in section 146 and section 152 of the Act and concluded that, as section 137(1)(a) only referred to trade union *membership*, it was not permissible for the tribunal to have regard to past trade union *activities* in deciding whether a refusal of employment was unlawful. They had reached the conclusion, on the facts, that a major part of the reason for the council's refusal to re-employ the applicant was because of his past trade union activities. They rejected his claim because, on the construction of section 137(1)(a), trade union activities and trade union membership were two different things. Section 137(1)(a) only made it unlawful to have regard to membership of a trade union, as distinct from trade union activities. The tribunal expressed the view that, if the applicant had simply been known as a trade union member, he would have been re-employed. He was not re-employed because, in the view of the tribunal, the council had formed a view about his attitudes as manifested both 'within and without' the scope of his trade union activities. They appear to have concluded that there was nothing in section 137(1)(a) which made it unlawful to refuse employment on the ground of trade union activities.

(2) The industrial tribunal's construction of section 137(1) of the Act of 1992 takes a narrower view of the conceptual limits of membership of a trade union than is expressed by the ordinary and natural meaning of the language of the section. The fallacy in the tribunal's approach is to proceed, by analogy with section 146(1) and section 152(1), to draw a rigid distinction between, on the one hand, membership of a trade union and, on the other hand, taking part in the activities of a union. Although membership and activities are specified in separate paragraphs of section 146(1) and section 152(1), it does not follow that they are self-contained, mutually exclusive categories or concepts. Trade union membership and trade union activities overlap. In this context a divorce of the *fact* of membership and the *incidents* of membership is illusory. We agree with the comment of Dillon LJ in *Associated British Ports v Palmer* [1994] ICR 97, 101, that membership of a union means more than the bare fact that a person's name has been entered in the register

of members and that he holds a union membership card. Participation in the activities of a union is one of the ways in which membership of a union is manifested and the rights incident to it are realised. In our view, if a person is refused employment because he was or is a trade union activist or for a reason related to his union activities it is open to the industrial tribunal, under the provisions of section 137(1)(a), to conclude that he is refused employment because he is a member of the union. It will be a question of fact in each case for the tribunal to determine the reason for refusal to employ a person and whether that reason was impermissible because it related to union membership. We say nothing to deter the tribunal of fact, in an appropriate case, from being 'robust in its findings.'

(3) The construction adopted by the industrial tribunal would have a consequence inconsistent with promoting the purpose of the provision. The purpose of section 137(1)(a) of the Act of 1992 is to protect a person from being discriminated against in access to employment on grounds related to union membership. In reality, the persons most likely to be discriminated against are those who have been most active in membership. On the distinction drawn by the industrial tribunal between trade union membership and trade union activities, the more active the member, the weaker the protection. It is a construction which, in the words of Knox J in *Discount Tobacco & Confectionery Ltd. v Armitage (Note)* [1995] ICR 431, 433f, would 'emasculate the provision altogether.' We favour a purposive construction and a pragmatic approach.

It will be noted that in reaching its decision the EAT relied heavily on the Court of Appeal decision in *Associated British Ports v Palmer* [1994] ICR 97 which was concerned with the meaning of 'trade union membership' for the purposes of TULRCA 1992, section 146 (see below, p 737). This provides protection for action short of dismissal for employees for reasons related to trade union membership or activities (and now the use of trade union services). In the *Associated British Ports* case the Court of Appeal adopted a wide construction of 'trade union membership', and it is on this that the EAT in *Harrison* relied. But the House of Lords in *Palmer* (in a case conjoined with *Associated Newspapers Ltd v Wilson* (see below)) took a very different and a very narrow approach to construction. There may thus be cause to question the *Harrison* decision to the extent that it is based on an earlier Court of Appeal case which has been overruled. Any such questions may, however, be discounted in light of the European Court of Human Rights decision in *Wilson and the National Union of Journalists; Palmer, Wyeth and the National Union of Rail, Maritime and Transport Workers v United Kingdom* [2002] IRLR 128, which is considered below, but which took a robust approach to the freedom of association guarantees in Article 11 of the ECHR. As a result it is difficult to believe that the *Harrison* decision would be decided differently today by a domestic court having full regard to its duties under the Human Rights Act.

So far as access to employment is concerned, the other trick of employers relates to those workers who have evaded pre-employment screening by successfully concealing their history as trade union activists. When the worker's identity becomes known, he or she may be dismissed. But there will be no remedy under section 137 because the person in question has not been refused employment. It will be necessary here to rely on TULRCA 1992, section 152 which makes it unfair to dismiss an employee because of trade union membership (section 152(1)(a)) or activities (section 152(1)(b)). (Section 152 is considered more fully below.) The issue here is twofold: if someone conceals his or her employment history for fear of reprisal and is then dismissed, is this dismissal for reasons of trade union membership? And secondly, does the legislation apply where the employee is dismissed not because of trade union activities with his or her current employer, but because of activities with a previous employer?

[8.6] *Fitzpatrick v British Railways Board* [1992] ICR 221 (CA)

The employee applied for a job with BRB, but concealed in her application form a period of employment with Ford Motor Co which lasted only nine days before she was dismissed because of bad references. Several months after she started at BRB, an article appeared in the *Evening Standard* indicating that the appellant was a prominent trade union activist and had links with Trotskyite groups, including Socialist Action. She was then dismissed by the Board for 'untruthfulness and lack of trust'. But although the industrial tribunal concluded that the real reason for the appellant's dismissal was her trade union activities with previous employers, the application nevertheless failed. The industrial tribunal found that the dismissal was not on account of her existing trade union activities but because of her activities with these previous employers. The legislation then in force—Employment Protection (Consolidation) Act 1978, section 58 (now TULRCA 1992, section 152)—was found not to apply. The decision was upheld by the EAT but reversed by the Court of Appeal.

Woolf LJ:
In this case the employers purported to dismiss the employee on the basis of her deceit in concealing her previous trade union activities. If the industrial tribunal had accepted that it was her deceit which caused them to dismiss her, or if that was the primary reason for her dismissal, then the situation is that she would not have been able to bring herself within the language of section 58(1)(b). However, as already indicated, all three members of the industrial tribunal accepted that it was not the deceit which was the operative cause for her dismissal.

What the majority concluded was, and I read here from paragraph 27 of the decision:

'it was the [employee's] previous trade union (and possibly her political) activities, which gave her a reputation for being a disruptive force; and that was the prime reason for her dismissal.'

That paragraph, in my judgment, discloses a failure on the part of the industrial tribunal to answer the critical question. The fact that the employee had a reputation with regard to trade union activities was, as Miss Booth in her argument [for Fitzpatrick] made clear, only relevant to the employers in so far as it would have an effect on what she did while she was employed by them. Miss Booth submits, clearly with justification, that the employers did not suggest and would not in fact seek to dismiss the employee merely in order to punish her for her previous trade union activities. Miss Booth submits that what the industrial tribunal failed to do was to identify why it was that because of her previous trade union, and possibly political, activities the employers decided to dismiss the employee. If the tribunal had asked the question the answer would have been obvious. It would be that they would fear a repetition of the same conduct while employed by them.

The reason that the majority of the industrial tribunal did not address the critical question is probably because of their understanding of [*City of Birmingham District Council v Beyer* [1977] IRLR 211]. They say, having examined that decision, that so far as proposed activities are concerned it must, and I quote: 'involve some cogent and identifiable act and not some possible trouble in the future.' In other words the industrial tribunal are saying that in order to comply with the provisions of section 58(1)(b) there must have been some activity on the part of the employee to which they took exception, which was not a mere possibility but something which was sufficiently precise to be identifiable in her present employment.

In my judgment, to adopt this approach is to read into the language of section 58(1)(b) a restriction which Parliament has not identified. To limit the language, in the way which the industrial tribunal did, would prevent the actual reason for the dismissal in a case such as this from being considered by the industrial tribunal. As long as the reason which motivated the employer falls within the words 'activities that the employee . . . proposed to take part in,' there is no reason to limit the language. The purpose of the subsection, in so far as (b) is concerned, is to protect those who engage in trade union activities and I can see no reason why that should not apply irrespective of whether the precise activities can be identified.

If an employer, having learnt of an employee's previous trade union activities, decides that he wishes to dismiss that employee, that is likely to be a situation where almost inevitably the employer is dismissing the employee because he feels that the employee will indulge in industrial activities of a trade union nature in his current employment. There is no reason for a rational and reasonable employer to object to the previous activities of an employee except in so far as they will impinge upon the employee's current employment.

Persistent concerns about blacklisting of trade union activists led to the introduction of powers for regulations to be made making the practice unlawful: Employment Relations Act 1999, section 3. In the DTI *Review of the Employment Relations Act 1999* (London, 2003), however, the government made clear that it has no immediate plans to invoke these powers. Although blacklisting is said to be a covert activity which is difficult to detect, the government considered it inappropriate to introduce regulation 'where there is no evidence that a problem has existed for over a decade' (para 3.19). Although these provisions may be stillborn, it is to be noted that trade union membership information constitutes sensitive personal data for the purposes of the Data Protection Act 1998, on which see chapter 6 above.

8.2.2 Trade union membership, activities and services

Once in employment, the worker (in the case of detriment) and the employee (in the case of detriment and dismissal) will have protection against victimisation on the ground of trade union membership, participation in trade union activities, and now for making use of trade union services. The legislation has also been extended to include protection for workers or employees who are discriminated against or dismissed because they were not members of a trade union or refused to make payments to a trade union or a charity in lieu of such membership. This is considered more fully below. In none of these cases is there a qualifying period of employment before an application may be made. The protection against detriment short of dismissal is to be found in TULRCA 1992, section 146, as amended by the Employment Relations Act 1999 and the Employment Relations Act 2004.

[8.7] Trade Union and Labour Relations (Consolidation) Act 1992, section 146

Detriment related to union membership or activities

146 (1) A worker has the right not to be subjected to any detriment as an individual by any act, or any deliberate failure to act, by his employer if the act or failure takes place for the sole or main purpose of—

(a) preventing or deterring him from being or seeking to become a member of an independent trade union, or penalising him for doing so,

(b) preventing or deterring him from taking part in the activities of an independent trade union at an appropriate time, or penalising him for doing so,

(ba) preventing or deterring him from making use of trade union services at an appropriate time, or penalising him for doing so, or

(c) compelling him to be or become a member of any trade union or of a particular trade union or of one of a number of particular trade unions.

(2) In subsection (1) 'an appropriate time' means—

(a) a time outside the worker's working hours, or

(b) a time within his working hours at which, in accordance with arrangements agreed with or consent given by his employer, it is permissible for him to take part in the activities of a trade union or (as the case may be) make use of trade union services;

and for this purpose 'working hours', in relation to a worker, means any time when, in accordance with his contract of employment, he is required to be at work.

(2A) In this section—

(a) "trade union services" means services made available to the worker by an independent trade union by virtue of his membership of the union, and

(b) references to a worker's "making use" of trade union services include his consenting to the raising of a matter on his behalf by an independent trade union of which he is a member.

(2B) If an independent trade union of which a worker is a member raises a matter on his behalf (with or without his consent), penalising the worker for that is to be treated as penalising him as mentioned in subsection (1)(ba).

(2C) A worker also has the right not to be subjected to any detriment as an individual by any act, or any deliberate failure to act, by his employer if the act or failure takes place because of the worker's failure to accept an offer made in contravention of section 145A or 145B.

(2D) For the purposes of subsection (2C), not conferring a benefit that, if the offer had been accepted by the worker, would have been conferred on him under the resulting agreement shall be taken to be subjecting him to a detriment as an individual (and to be a deliberate failure to act).

(3) A worker also has the right not to be subjected to any detriment as an individual by any act, or any deliberate failure to act, by his employer if the act or failure takes place for the sole or main purpose of enforcing a requirement (whether or not imposed by his contract of employment or in writing) that, in the event of his not being a member of any trade union or of a particular trade union or of one of a number of particular trade unions, he must make one or more payments.

(4) For the purposes of subsection (3) any deduction made by an employer from the remuneration payable to a worker in respect of his employment shall, if it is attributable to his not being a member of any trade union or of a particular trade union or of one of a

number of particular trade unions, be treated as a detriment to which he has been subjected as an individual by an act of his employer taking place for the sole or main purpose of enforcing a requirement of a kind mentioned in that subsection.

(5) A worker or former worker may present a complaint to an employment tribunal on the ground that he has been subjected to a detriment by his employer in contravention of this section.

(5A) This section does not apply where—
(a)   the worker is an employee; and
(b)   the detriment in question amounts to dismissal.

For these purposes, a worker is defined to mean an individual within the meaning of TULRCA 1992, s 296, on which see chapter 2 above. 'Employer' is defined to mean '(a) in relation to a worker, the person for whom he works; and (b) in relation to a former worker, the person for whom he worked'.

Protection against dismissal is to be found in sections 152 and 153: this is in similar terms to section 146, with section 152 applying to dismissal on the ground of trade union membership and activities, again in the latter case where these take place at an appropriate time. Provision is made in sections 161–66 for interim relief, empowering the employment tribunals to make a temporary order for the continuation of the contract of employment pending the resolution of an unfair dismissal claim. Compensation for dismissal in breach of these provisions takes the form of a Basic Award (subject to a special minimum of £3,800), a Compensatory Award (subject to a maximum of £55,800), and an Additional Award (in the event of an order for reinstatement or re-engagement not being complied with). Under the Employment Act 1982, a Special Award was introduced for dismissals in breach of what is now section 152. This was in effect a punitive sum which was designed principally to protect employees dismissed because of non-membership of a trade union, but it did apply also to dismissals on account of trade union membership or activities. With the virtual extinction of the closed shop the need for such measures has disappeared, though there is a strong case for their retention for dismissals on account of trade union membership and activities. The Special Award was abolished by the Employment Relations Act 1999. The protection against dismissal in section 152 applies only to employees, though section 146(5A) suggests that a worker (but not an employee) may be able to sue under section 146 where the detriment takes the form of dismissal.

8.2.2.1   Trade union membership

The question of what constitutes trade union membership for present purposes has recently proved to be extremely controversial. Does it mean the right to protection simply for holding a union card, or does it mean more to include protection from discrimination for using the services or benefits of trade union membership? The issue has arisen in two situations in particular. The first is where the employee has been discriminated against where the employer wishes to move from collectively agreed terms and conditions of employment to personal contracts. Is the employee who is paid less because he or she insists on the former discriminated against because of his or her trade union membership? The second is where the employee seeks representation by a trade union in a disciplinary or grievance context. Is the employee who is punished for seeking such representation discriminated against or dismissed because of trade union membership?

8.2.2.1.1 The Wilson and Palmer case. TULRCA 1992, section 146 was amended by the Employment Relations Act 2004 (as was section 152) following a long running saga about its previously limited scope. Until the 2004 amendments, section 146 applied only to trade union membership and to trade union activities; it did not also apply to the use of trade union services. This gap in the statutory protection was exposed in *Associated Newspapers Ltd v Wilson* [1995] 2 AC 454 where Mr Wilson complained that his employer—the *Daily Mail*—had derecognised his union—the NUJ—and introduced personal contracts to replace the collectively agreed terms. Those employees who were prepared to enter into a personal contract were provided with a financial bonus which was denied to those employees—like Mr Wilson—who insisted on being paid under the terms of the collective agreements which had been terminated. An industrial tribunal held that Mr Wilson had been discriminated against unlawfully on the ground of his trade union membership. But the employer appealed successfully to the Employment Appeal Tribunal which held that the discrimination against Mr Wilson had not been on account of his trade union membership, a view with which the Court of Appeal disagreed following Mr Wilson's appeal. In this game of ping pong the employer then moved the case to the House of Lords which held that there had been no unlawful discrimination. There were two reasons for the Lords' decision. The first was that the protection against discriminatory treatment on the ground of trade union membership applied only to action short of dismissal: it did not also apply to omissions.

The second reason for the decision was that the conduct of the employer was in any event not for reasons of trade union membership, a term that was narrowly defined to exclude discrimination for making use of the services of a trade union. According to Lord Bridge of Harwich, to equate membership with using the 'essential' services of that union would put 'an unnecessary and imprecise gloss on the statutory language'. In so holding the House of Lords appeared to depart from an EAT decision in *Discount Tobacco & Confectioners Ltd v Armitage (Note)* [1995] ICR 431. This decision of the House of Lords did not exhaust the legal proceedings in this case, with Wilson making a complaint—this time against the British government—to the European Court of Human Rights. Together with a number of RMT members who were involved in similar litigation which had been conjoined with his in the Court of Appeal and the House of Lords, Wilson alleged that the conduct of the *Daily Mail* violated his Convention rights for which the Government was responsible. Before the case could be heard by the Strasbourg court, the newly elected Labour government brought forward amending legislation in 1999. But that legislation dealt with only one of the two grounds of the House of Lords' decision, and in any event—not being retrospective—provided little comfort to Mr Wilson and his fellow victims. The Employment Relations Act 1999 made it clear that the protection against discrimination applies to both acts and omissions, but failed to deal with the question of the scope of the protection. Even after the 1999 Act it would still be lawful for an employer to offer financial inducements to a worker to give up trade union representation and collective bargaining rights.

8.2.2.1.2 The Wilson and Palmer case and the ECHR.   While the litigation and the appeals were taking place in the domestic courts, and while the matter was pending before the Strasbourg court, the matter had been before the supervisory bodies of both the ILO and the Council of Europe's Social Charter. The law authorising the discrimination of Wilson and the RMT members was found to breach both ILO Convention 98 and the Social Charter respectively. According to the ILO Freedom of Association Committee:

> While noting from the Government's observations that collective bargaining is still an option for the employer, the Committee concludes that, given the facts available in this particular case, [the employer] has by-passed the representative organisation and entered into direct individual negotiation with its employees, in a manner contrary to the principle that collective negotiation between employers and organisations of workers should be encouraged and promoted.

The Committee concluded by calling on the Government to take steps to amend the law so that it 'ensures workers' organisations adequate protection from acts of interference on the part of the employer and so that it does not result in fact in the discouragement of collective bargaining'. (ILO Freedom of Association Committee, Case No 1852, 309th Report of the Freedom of Association Committee, Vol. LXXXI, 1998, Series B, no. 1.) In the same vein, the Social Rights Committee concluded that

> the Contracting State is obliged to take adequate legislative or other measures to guarantee the exercise of the right to organise, and in particular to protect workers' organisations from any interference on the part of employers' (see most recently Conclusions XII-2, p. 101). It also referred to its conclusion under Article 6 § 2 and its case-law to the effect that where a fundamental trade union prerogative such as the right to bargain collectively was restricted, this could amount to an infringement of the very nature of trade union freedom (see most recently Conclusions XIII-2, p. 269).
> (Council of Europe, Committee of Independent Experts, Conclusions XIII-3, 1996, p 108)

In an interesting reversal of strategy on the part of the Court, reference was made to both the ILO Conventions and the Social Charter as well as the jurisprudence relating to each: *Wilson and the National Union of Journalists; Palmer, Wyeth and the National Union of Rail, Maritime and Transport Workers v United Kingdom* [2002] IRLR 128. Unlike the cases in the 1970s, these instruments were used as aids to construction of Article 11 rather than as foreign bodies with which the latter was not to be infected. In thus using these instruments in this constructive way, the Court held that there had been a breach of Article 11, the key passage in its decision reading as follows:

> 46. The Court agrees with the Government that the essence of a voluntary system of collective bargaining is that it must be possible for a trade union which is not recognised by an employer to take steps including, if necessary, organising industrial action, with a view to persuading the employer to enter into collective bargaining with it on those issues which the union believes are important for its members' interests. Furthermore, it is of the essence of the right to join a trade union for the protection of their interests that employees should be free to instruct or permit the union to make representations to their

employer or to take action in support of their interests on their behalf. If workers are prevented from so doing, their freedom to belong to a trade union, for the protection of their interests, becomes illusory. It is the role of the State to ensure that trade union members are not prevented or restrained from using their union to represent them in attempts to regulate their relations with their employers.

47. In the present case, it was open to the employers to seek to pre-empt any protest on the part of the unions or their members against the imposition of limits on voluntary collective bargaining, by offering those employees who acquiesced in the termination of collective bargaining substantial pay rises, which were not provided to those who refused to sign contracts accepting the end of union representation. The corollary of this was that United Kingdom law permitted employers to treat less favourably employees who were not prepared to renounce a freedom that was an essential feature of union membership. Such conduct constituted a disincentive or restraint on the use by employees of union membership to protect their interests. However, as the House of Lords' judgment made clear, domestic law did not prohibit the employer from offering an inducement to employees who relinquished the right to union representation, even if the aim and outcome of the exercise was to bring an end to collective bargaining and thus substantially to reduce the authority of the union, as long as the employer did not act with the purpose of preventing or deterring the individual employee simply from being a member of a trade union.

48. Under United Kingdom law at the relevant time it was, therefore, possible for an employer effectively to undermine or frustrate a trade union's ability to strive for the protection of its members' interests. The Court notes that this aspect of domestic law has been the subject of criticism by the Social Charter's Committee of Independent Experts and the ILO's Committee on Freedom of Association (see paragraphs 32-33 and 37 above). It considers that, by permitting employers to use financial incentives to induce employees to surrender important union rights, the respondent State has failed in its positive obligation to secure the enjoyment of the rights under Article 11 of the Convention. This failure amounted to a violation of Article 11, as regards both the applicant trade unions and the individual applicants.

The decision of the Court led to two major changes to domestic law, both introduced by the Employment Relations Act 2004. The first (following paragraph 46 of the decision) was to make it clear in TULRCA 1992, s 146 that the protection for trade union membership included protection for using the services of the union. The second (following paragraphs 47 and 48 of the decision) was to bring forward a new provision (TULRCA 1992, ss 145A and 145B) to protect workers from inducements to give up their trade union membership, activities or services or to give up collective bargaining. Sections 145A and 145B are considered below.

8.2.2.2 Trade union activities

Apart from protection on the ground of trade union membership, the legislation also protects those who are subjected to a detriment or dismissal on the ground of participation in the activities of an independent trade union. TULRCA 1992, section 146 applies only if the activities are conducted at an 'appropriate time'. There are thus two issues here. One relates to the nature of the trade union activities to which the statutory protection applies. The other relates to the meaning of the phrase 'appropriate time'.

8.2.2.2.1 Activities of an independent trade union.   It has been said by the EAT that the definition applies to activities of a 'wide and varied kind' (*Dixon v West Ella Developments Ltd* [1978] ICR 856), and the case law suggests that it would apply to the recruitment of members, the formation of a union branch, and complaints about working conditions. But does it apply only to activities directed at the relationship between the employer and the union, or does it apply also to internal union matters? This is one of the issues considered in the following case, which also raises wider questions about employee free speech.

The GCHQ Case

The protection for trade union membership and activities applies to civil servants as it does to most other employees. There is, however, an exception to TULRCA, section 275, which provides that statutory rights may be excluded from some categories of Crown employees where there is in force a certificate issued by a minister of the Crown certifying that employment specified in the certificate is to be exempted on the grounds of national security. That power was exercised in 1984 in respect of staff employed at the Government Communications Headquarters. Steps were also taken under the Royal Prerogative to alter the terms and conditions of employment of staff who were no longer permitted to remain in membership of a trade union which they had been encouraged to join since 1947. Those who objected to the arrangements were given the choice of moving to new work in the civil service where they could retain their trade union membership or be sacked. A number of employees refused to accept the new terms or to be relocated, and were dismissed, and because of the certificates in force under what is now section 275 they were unable to bring unfair dismissal proceedings. Dismissal for trade union membership alone—even in the 1980s—was unusual, and all the more so when initiated by a government. The case became a great *cause célèbre*, with a big legal and political campaign waged by the trade unions for the restoration of trade unions at GCHQ. Judicial review proceedings in the domestic courts to challenge the introduction of new terms under the royal prerogative were unsuccessful: *Council of Civil Service Unions v Minister for the Civil Service* [1985] AC 374. So too was an application to Strasbourg alleging a breach of the ECHR: in the view of the European Commission of Human Rights the claim that Article 11 had been breached was defeated by the second sentence of Article 11(2) which allows for exceptions in respect of members of the armed forces, of the police or of the administration of the State. But the ILO authorities took a different approach. Both the Freedom of Association Committee and the Committee of Experts found that there had been a breach of ILO Convention 87 (The Freedom of Association and Protection of the Right to Organise Convention, 1948). This provides, by Article 2 that 'Workers and employers, without distinction whatsoever, shall have the right to establish and, subject only to the rules of the organisation concerned, to join organisations of their own choosing without previous authorisation'. Remarkably the then government refused to accept the findings of the ILO bodies. Despite repeated requests from the ILO the ban remained in place until revoked by the Labour government in 1997, in the early implementation of an election pledge. For a full account see K D Ewing, *Britain and the ILO* (2nd edn, London, Institute of Employment Rights, 1994), and G Morris, 'Freedom of Association and the Interests of the State' in K D Ewing, C A Gearty, and B A Hepple (eds) *Human Rights and Labour Law* (London, Mansell, 1994), chapter 2.

[8.8] *British Airways Engine Overhaul Ltd v Francis* **[1981] ICR 278 (EAT)**

Mrs Francis was employed by the appellants as an aircraft component worker in South Wales. She was also a shop steward for the Amalgamated Union of Engineering Workers, representing 27 women workers. The women were involved in a long-standing equal pay dispute, claiming parity with male supervisors at the workplace. They were concerned that the union was not taking their case seriously and decided to do something about it. The women met one lunchtime and resolved to secure press publicity for their campaign. A few days later the *Western Mail* carried a statement by Mrs Francis in which she was critical of the union's failure to carry out its policy of securing equal pay for women. Mrs Francis was thereafter reprimanded by her employer for acting contrary to company regulations by making statements to the 'press or otherwise' about company business. Thereupon she brought proceedings alleging a breach of the Sex Discrimination Act 1975, in the course of which the industrial tribunal referred her to the Employment Protection Act 1975, section 53 (now TULRCA 1992, section 146). The claim for breach of the Sex Discrimination Act failed, but the tribunal found a breach of section 53. The decision of the tribunal was upheld on appeal.

Slynn J:

. . . It seems to us that the evidence, when one looks at the material before the Tribunal, does fully justify their finding that Mrs Francis was engaged in the activities of an independent trade union. All the material seems to point to the fact that Mrs Francis was acting as the shop steward and she called her colleagues together as members of the union. They might, it is true, be criticising the several organs of the union for failing to carry out what Mrs Francis and her colleagues felt ought to be done. But discussion of matters with which an independent trade union is concerned, it seems to us, is quite capable of being an activity of an independent trade union within the meaning of the section. It seems here that these women were getting together, as union members, to discuss matters with which the independent trade union was concerned. It does not seem to us to be conclusive against Mrs Francis's claim that they did not do so at a meeting of some committee or at a formal meeting of the branch. They were a well defined group of the union, meeting with their shop steward, and even though the criticism which they might be making might not be acceptable to higher branches, or higher officials in the union, it seems to us that they were still engaged in their discussion, their criticism, and in their resolution, in the activities of an independent trade union. It seems to us that it really would be ignoring the reality of the issue, and the immediacy of the issue to the women at this time, to say that it was all too remote from the activities of the union, and that it ought therefore not to be treated as being incidental to the activities of a union. Accordingly, we are quite satisfied that, on this matter, the Industrial Tribunal did not err in law and that they were entitled to come to the conclusion to which they came.

The *Francis* case is important because it indicates that the protection for trade union activities is widely conceived, to cover not just the relationship between the union and the employer, but also internal union matters. But this is not to say that here are no limitations on the scope of the protection. So in *Chant v Acquaboats Ltd* [1978] ICR 643, the applicant organised a petition about health and safety matters which he had vetted by his local union office before being presented to the employer. It was held that his dismissal was not because of participation in the activities of an independent trade union: these were the activities of an individual trade unionist. It has also been said that the protection does not apply to 'wholly unreasonable, extraneous or malicious acts done in support of trade union activities' (*Lyon v St James' Press Ltd*

[1976] ICR 513). But it is difficult to find examples of cases in which applicants have failed because the tribunals or courts have disapproved of the nature of their trade union activities.

[8.9] *Bass Taverns Ltd v Burgess* [1995] IRLR 596 (CA)

Mr Burgess was a trainer of new managers who resigned after being demoted for what he had said at an induction course for new managers. He claimed that he had been constructively dismissed on the ground of his trade union activities. Mr Burgess was also a member of the National Association of Licensed House Managers and during the induction course in question had made a presentation on behalf of the union, with the consent of the company. During the course of the presentation he had some harsh words to say about the physical risks encountered by pub managers: '[y]ou will get threatened and if you get hurt it will be the union who will fight for you, not the company. At the end of the day the company is concerned with profits and this comes before everything else'. The remarks were reported to senior management, leading to the disciplinary action and the resignation. An industrial tribunal found that Mr Burgess had been unfairly dismissed for taking part in trade union activities. The EAT upheld the employer's appeal that although the dismissal was unfair it was not for trade union activities. This would affect the amount of compensation which Mr Burgess could recover. The Court of Appeal unanimously restored the industrial tribunal.

Pill LJ:

On the face of it, a consent to recruit must include a consent to underline the services which the union can provide. That may reasonably involve a submission to prospective members that in some respects the union will provide a service which the company does not. On the assumption that I am prepared to make that the life of a manager of licensed premises has its dangers and licensees are from time to time injured by members of the public, a union existing to protect the interests of licensees is entitled to claim that if such a situation arises it is the union and not the company which will fight the licensee's cause. Indeed, to bring a claim on behalf of members arising out of personal injuries is an important function of many trade unions and the service can properly be emphasised at a recruiting meeting.

In the findings of the industrial tribunal as to what the respondent said, I find nothing beyond the rhetoric and hyperbole which might be expected at a recruiting meeting for a trade union or, for that matter, some other organisation or cause. Neither dishonesty nor bad faith are suggested. While harmonious relations between a company and a union are highly desirable, a union recruiting meeting cannot realistically be limited to that object. A consent which at the same time prevents the recruiter from saying anything adverse about the employer is no real consent. Given that there was consent to use the meeting as a forum for recruitment, it cannot be regarded as an 'abuse of privilege' to make remarks to employees which are critical of the company. An industrial tribunal may be surprised at the situation which developed, but it was the employers who, at the start of their induction course, put the respondent in the position of being both trainer manager and recruiter. Having put him in that position, they cannot reasonably expect his activities in the latter role to be limited by the fact that he also was performing the role of trainer manager.

It appears to me that the industrial tribunal did base their decision on an implied term of the kind now contended for, albeit not in the same way. The company's case is not, in my judgment, improved by the present reliance upon an implied term that the recruiter should say nothing to criticise or disparage the company or upon the presence of the word 'consent' and the word 'permissible' in s[146](2)(b). One has only to consider the likely reaction if the company had attempted to make the term expressed. It is difficult to envisage any trade union official accepting a limitation upon his activities at a recruiting meeting that he should say nothing critical about his employer attempting to require such a term. It is wholly unrealistic, in my judgment, to believe that such a term can be implied in the present context. The respondent's admission that he had 'gone over the top' does not, in my judgment, provide a basis for a finding that during his speech he was not taking part in trade union activities. That is an expression sometimes used colloquially in situations when that moderation and balance normally shown in social intercourse is percieved to have been exceeded. In the circumstances of the present case, however it was not an admission that could form the basis for a conclusion that in law the contents of the speech were outside the scope of trade union activities. The Employment Appeal Tribunal correctly concluded that the industrial tribunal had fallen into error.

8.2.2.2.2 Appropriate time and the need for consent. As already pointed out, the protection in respect of trade union activities applies only where these activities take place at an 'appropriate time', as defined in TULRCA 1992, section 146(2). Reflecting the provisions of ILO Convention 98, this means that the protection applies only where the activities are undertaken outside working time, or within working time with the consent of the employer. The consent of the employer is thus not required where the trade union activities are undertaken on the employer's premises but outside working time, as for example during meal breaks or before work has started, provided that they are undertaken at a time when the employee is entitled to be on the premises. According to the House of Lords, an employee who is a member of a trade union is entitled 'to take part in the activities of his union while he is on his employer's premises but is not actually working' (*Post Office v Union of Post Office Workers* [1974] ICR 378). This would give trade union lay officials the opportunity to leaflet, hold informal meetings and recruit members. It was also pointed out that the employer must be prepared to accept that his or her normal property rights will be affected and to put up with this minor inconvenience, though not to 'incur expense or submit to substantial inconvenience' (at p 400). The EAT may have taken this further in the following case.

[8.10] *Zucker v Astrid Jewels Ltd* [1978] ICR 1088 (EAT)

The appellant had been employed by the respondent company for just over a week before she was dismissed for conducting trade union activities in 'a disruptive manner'. The case centred on the time at which these activities were conducted. Miss Zucker claimed that they had been conducted mainly during breaks, though some of the activities also took place while she was working. In neither case did she have consent from the employer. The industrial tribunal rejected the application, but the EAT upheld the appeal and remitted the case to a differently constituted tribunal. Other relevant facts appear in the judgment of the EAT.

Phillips J:
To anticipate our conclusion, we find it necessary to remit the matter to be re-heard by a differently constituted Industrial Tribunal. We do not wish to circumscribe their freedom, because they will decide the matter on the evidence which they have heard. But they will obviously guide themselves by the authority of the House of Lords in *Post Office v Union*

of Post Office Workers [[1974] AC 378]. By way of further guidance we can say that on the facts so far as they appear in this decision, there seems every reason to suppose that the circumstances of the morning tea break, at all event (the circumstances of the afternoon tea break are not so clearly stated) seem to be such that that tea break, like the lunch half-hour break, was a recognised break for a meal; and ordinarily one would have thought, therefore (though the final decision must rest with the Industrial Tribunal upon the facts as they emerge), that those breaks would be times during which the employees, albeit they were being paid, were not required to be at work and therefore were not doing whatever they did 'during working hours'. But we repeat, the final decision must be for the Industrial Tribunal.

There is another point where we think the Industrial Tribunal misdirected themselves. It may be the case that some of the activities of Miss Zucker took place, as we have already indicated, while she was working, in the course of conversation with others also working. The Industrial Tribunal will want to consider all the circumstances in relation to that. But we do not think that it is a right conclusion, from the *Post Office* case just cited, to say that activities of that kind *cannot* be activities undertaken in accordance with arrangements agreed with or consent given by the employer. It is a question for the proper conclusion to be drawn from the evidence as it turns out. But this is a matter in respect of which the Industrial Tribunal may receive some assistance from the views of the Employment Appeal Tribunal in *Marley Tile Co Ltd v Shaw* [1978] IRLR 238, the Tribunal on this point being unanimously in agreement; on one point there was a dissenting view. The unanimous view is that expressed in paragraph 13 at p 240. It was, we thought, too narrow a view to say that there could only be arrangements or consent within [section 146(2)](b) where there had been an express arrangement or express consent. We pointed out there that matters of this kind are very often dealt with, or permitted, in a quite informal way. For example if it be the case that the employees while working are permitted to converse upon anything they feel like conversing upon with fellow employees working nearby, there seems to be no reason why they should not, amongst other things, converse upon trade union activities; and if they were to do so, and if such conversation were generally allowed, to the extent that it did not interfere with the proper completion of the work or otherwise cause disruption, there seems no reason why an Industrial Tribunal, in such circumstances, could not come to the conclusion that although there was no express arrangement or express consent, there was implied consent or implied arrangements.

The consent of the employer will be required, however, where the activities are to be undertaken during working time. It will often be given formally and expressly in a facilities agreement to accredited shop stewards. But it can also arise as a matter of custom and practice, though, as was pointed out by the Court of Appeal in *The Marley Tile Co Ltd v Shaw* [1980] ICR 72, this can be very difficult to establish. What happens if the consent is refused? One answer is that if the union is recognised by the employer for the purposes of collective bargaining, a lay official of the union will be entitled by statute (TULRCA 1992, section 168) to time off with pay for trade union duties, these being industrial relations duties with his or her employer, or to undergo training in such duties. These provisions are considered in section 8.5.2 below, but it will be obvious that they provide no assistance where the union is not recognised. Yet it can hardly be said that the union official does not need time off work to attend to his or her trade union duties before the union is recognised: the work of recruitment, organising with a view to recognition, and the servicing of members (even if the union is not recognised) all require the expenditure of time. Questions also arise about the position where consent is withdrawn, a matter considered in the following case which suggests that there may be some protection for the employee.

[8.11] *Farnsworth Ltd v McCoid* [1999] ICR 1047 (CA)

Mr McCoid was a shop steward for the TGWU employed by the appellants. He complained that the employer had de-recognised him as a shop steward because 'the way he conducted himself meant that he was not suited to hold the office of shop steward'. Mr McCoid complained that the employer's action violated section 146 of TULRCA 1992 on the ground that they had taken action against him as an individual for the purpose of preventing or deterring him from taking part in the activities of an independent trade union at an appropriate time. A preliminary issue in dispute was whether the action had been taken against Mr McCoid as an individual. Both the industrial tribunal and the EAT concluded that it had, a position endorsed by the Court of Appeal.

Lord Woolf MR:
While there is a dispute as to why the employee was derecognised, what is not in dispute is that his terms of employment were not affected by that action. The only effect of the action taken by the employer is to deprive the employee of having the status and being able to perform the activities of a shop steward on behalf of his fellow employees.

The employer reads the opening words of section 146(1) so that their effect is that there has to be action short of dismissal taken against the employee as an individual by his employer, the words 'as an individual' being interpreted as meaning 'in his capacity as an employee'. The employers says it is not sufficient if the action, short of dismissal, which was taken was in a capacity which only related to his position as, here, a shop steward. That is an approach which I consider is inconsistent with the general intent of section 146(1)(b). The purpose of section 146(1)(b) is to allow an employee, who has as an individual in the claim been subject to victimisation, to put his allegation or complaint before an industrial tribunal. If the employee cannot do that, because he was only affected in his office as a shop steward, that would involve inserting into the legislation words which do not appear, namely, 'as an individual in his capacity as an employee' or such similar words to 'as an individual employee'. The addition would enable a distinction to be drawn between actions short of dismissal, in the capacity of, for example, a shop steward.

I am reinforced in that interpretation by the fact that Mr Bowers [for the employer] accepted, when making his submissions to this court, that even if (contrary to his contention) this is action taken against the employee as an individual, his clients will still have a defence if they can establish the facts on which they rely in relation to the employee's complaint. This is because the action would not have been taken against the employee for the purpose of preventing or deterring him from taking part in the activities of an independent trade union. They will have been taken for the purpose of removing somebody from the office of shop steward. Mr Bowers says that, if established, that is an answer to the complaint. If the interpretation that I have been suggesting is the correct interpretation, it will not deprive the employer of a defence on the merits. However, if the employer's interpretation is right, it will mean that an employee who is a shop steward could be victimised and would have no remedy whatsoever before an industrial tribunal as long as the action taken by the employer was limited to affecting the employee in his capacity here as the shop steward.

It could be extremely damaging to an employee to be derecognised as a shop steward. That would be a severe reflection upon his credibility. It is the intent of the Act of 1992 to provide a remedy in those circumstances. Mr Bowers says 'No, that is the type of case which it is not intended should be subject to the jurisdiction of an industrial tribunal.' He submits that this would be a dispute as to collective arrangements between a trade union and an employer. It would not be a dispute between an employee and an employer. I do not see the case in that way. I understand that the words 'as an individual' are inserted to exclude collective disputes from the ambit of section 146, but this is not such a dispute. This is a dispute where an employee is complaining about victimisation in the circumstances described in section 146(1)(b). It should go before an industrial tribunal.

8.2.2.3   The right not to be a trade union member

It will be noted that sections 137, 146 and 152 apply to protection not only on the basis of trade union membership, but on the basis also of non-membership of a trade union. So it is unlawful to refuse employment to someone because he or she is not a member of a trade union, and unlawful for an employee to be subjected to any detriment or dismissed because he or she is not a member of a trade union. These measures are designed to prohibit or render unenforceable various closed shop practices whereby employees were required to be members of a trade union as a condition of obtaining employment (the pre-entry closed shop), or within a prescribed number of days of securing employment (the post-entry closed shop). While the protection from discrimination on the ground of trade union membership and activities is covered by ILO Convention 98, there is no corresponding protection of the right not to belong, a matter on which the ILO takes a neutral position. The Council of Europe bodies now take a very different view, with the European Court of Human Rights holding that the obligation to join a trade union as a condition of employment may violate the freedom of association guarantees in Article 11 of the ECHR, and with the Social Rights Committee of the Council of Europe surprisingly taking the view in very bullish terms that closed shop practices violate the right to organise in Article 5 of the Social Charter of 18 October 1961.

The closed shop was one of the most hotly contested issues of British labour law in the post-war period. It was strongly defended by trade unions on a number of grounds. The pre-entry closed shop had a labour control function in the sense that the unions in question could control not only the quality of labour entering the market, but also the supply of labour. By restricting supply, the union could enhance the wages of its members. But the pre-entry closed shop flourished in only a few industries. The post-entry closed shop was much more common. Although it did not have a labour supply function, it did have an organisational security function which it shared with the pre-entry closed shop. This means that collective action could not be undermined by a dissident minority, particularly important in the case of a strike. Where there was a closed shop arrangement in place, those who broke the strike ran the risk of expulsion from the union and dismissal from their employment. Not unrelated to either the labour supply and organisational security functions, the closed shop also had what some might see as a fairness function. It is sometimes argued that all workers in an enterprise benefited from the activities of the union, such as the negotiation of collective agreements, so that it is only fair that all should contribute to its costs. A close analogy would be motor insurance. We all benefit from the insurance system and we are all required to contribute.

[8.12] Royal Commission on Trade Unions and Employers' Associations 1965–1968. Report (Cmnd 3623, 1968): Chairman, Lord Donovan

'The two most convincing arguments for the closed shop . . . depend upon the close link between effective collective bargaining and strong trade unions. The first is that in some industries it is difficult or impossible for a union to establish effective and stable organisation without the help of the closed shop; the second is that even where membership can be recruited and retained without its assistance there are instances where it is needed to deploy the workers' bargaining strength to the full' [paragraph 592].

But although the 'trade union arguments seem so reasonable and plausible' (C G Hanson, *Taming the Trade Unions* (London, Macmillan, 1991)), the closed shop was strongly opposed by some on overlapping grounds relating to individual liberty and economic efficiency. So far as the former is concerned, it is argued that no one should be compelled to join a trade union against his or her wishes. This is an argument which resonates with human rights lawyers, the European Court of Human Rights having held that, although the right not to associate is not expressly covered by Article 11 of the ECHR, it does not follow that it is not protected. In *Young, James and Webster v UK* (1982) 4 EHRR 38 the Court read a right not to associate in limited circumstances into Article 11, and extended this right of non-association some years later in *Sigurjonnson v Iceland* (1993) 16 EHRR 462, where it was said at p 479:

it should be recalled that the Convention is a living instrument which must be interpreted in the light of present-day conditions. Accordingly Article 11 must be viewed as encompassing a negative right of association. It is not necessary for the Court to determine in this instance whether this right is to be considered on an equal footing with the positive right.

So far as the economic arguments are concerned, these are addressed in the following extract, though the points made appear to apply to collective bargaining generally and not only to the closed shop which was simply an incident of a much larger process. Should collective bargaining also be banned?

[8.13] C G Hanson, *Taming the Trade Unions* (London, Macmillan, 1991), pp 31–32

The chief fallacy lies in the union's final argument that non-members are benefiting from collective bargaining. The truth is that collective bargaining in Britain in the twentieth century has normally gone hand-in-hand with union imposed restrictive practices which reduce rather than increase output and profitability in the companies concerned. Lower profits mean lower investment, and in the longer term real wages fall. Collective bargaining also has the effect of causing employers to consider their employees en masse instead of as individuals with different abilities and talents. They tend to deal with them second hand, through a shop steward, and problems are exacerbated rather than solved. In other words, collective bargaining, unaccompanied by regular appraisal of individual employees, is a lazy employer's way of dealing with his workforce. The closed shop adds compulsion to laziness and means that employers are less likely to get the best out of their most important asset—the people they employ.

There was no specific regulation of the closed shop until 1971, just as there was no formal regulation of the right not to suffer disadvantage because of trade union membership. The Industrial Relations Act 1971 provided that workers had the right to be or not to be trade union members without being penalised by their employers. But the right not to join was qualified in the sense that agency shop agreements were permitted, as were approved closed shop agreements in some cases. By virtue of the former a worker could be required to pay a fee to a trade union or a charity in lieu of trade union membership—a way of dealing with the free rider problem which has been found acceptable to the courts in the United States and Canada as a reasonable compromise between the interests of the trade union on the one hand and those of the individual on the other. These arrangements were swept aside by the Trade Union and Labour Relations Act 1974 (as amended in 1976), which permitted trade unions and employers to enter into union membership agreements requiring employees to be members of a specified trade union or one of a number of specified trade unions. An employee dismissed for non-membership of a trade union where a union membership agreement was in force could not bring a claim for unfair dismissal unless he or she could show genuine religious objections to trade union membership. The exclusion of unfair dismissal applied whether or not the employee had wilfully refused to join a trade union or had been expelled from the union.

It is easy to forget just how prevalent the closed shop was in the 1970s, with one study estimating that at least 23 per cent of British workers were employed in a situation where a closed shop operated. As some commentators pointed out, closed shop arrangements flourished because 'employers loved them'. For the employer the closed shop eliminated the risk of inter-union competition, enabled the employer to deal with a single representative of the workforce, and permitted the employer to rely on the union to ensure that collective agreements were obeyed. But not enough employers loved the closed shop, and the present law—as now to be found in the 1992 Act—is the culmination of a number of gradual changes introduced since 1980. Under the Employment Acts 1980 and 1982 closed shop arrangements could be continued or introduced if supported by a ballot. But the ballot threshold was very high (80 per cent of those eligible to vote or 85 per cent of those voting) and even then there were wide exemptions from the duty to belong. The 1982 Act also introduced the higher compensation awards for dismissals on account of trade union membership and activities, or non-membership of a trade union, though it is clear that the latter was the main aim of the legislation. Where the dismissal was caused by pressure from a trade union official, the trade union official could be made to pay all or part of the compensation. This is still the case, although the compensation arrangements have been simplified.

The Employment Act 1988 took the logical step of providing that it would be automatically unfair to dismiss someone because he or she was not a member of a trade union. This was followed by the Employment Act 1990 which included the provisions relating to access to employment now to be found in section 137 of the 1992 Act. The only significant change which has taken place since has been in the Employment Relations Act 1999 which abolished the special award of compensation for trade union dismissals and dismissals related to non-membership of a trade union. The present government has indicated that it is not prepared to change the existing law, and in view of the jurisprudence of the European Court of Human Rights it would be impossible even to contemplate turning the clock back as far as the 1970s. But it is important to point out that the right to non-association in Article 11 of the ECHR is not unlimited and that it is qualified by Article 11(2) which may allow some restrictions on the rights of the individual in the interests of the group as a whole. It is not clear, for example, why agency shop agreements should be prohibited, as they are currently by TULRCA, sections 146(3) and 152(3). On this basis workers could be required to contribute to the running of the union from the activities of which they benefit. One question which would arise, however, is whether the union would then have a duty fairly to represent members and non members alike, as is the case in the United States and Canada. Some of these issues are considered in the following extract.

[8.14] K Miller, 'Union Exclusivity Arrangements: A Comparative Overview' [2000] *International Journal of Comparative Labour Law and Industrial Relations* **387**

In both the United States and Canada the respective labour legislation recognises that workers also owe certain responsibilities which flow from the fact that exclusivity of representation follows upon majority support. [The National Labor Relations Act (USA)] [NLRA] recognises both the post-entry closed shop and the agency shop. [It should be remembered that NLRA section 14(b) entitles individual states to enact laws banning any form of union security in their territory.] However, the permitted form of post-entry closed shop is akin to an agency shop since it only requires employees to pay regular union dues and does not bind them to comply with other union rules. In Canada a range of union security arrangements are permitted under federal and provincial legislation. In both countries union security laws have withstood constitutional scrutiny.

In the United States, the agency shop has been challenged as a denial of freedom of speech under the First Amendment. [For earlier cases under the Railway Labor Act see *Railway Employees' Dept v Hanson,* 351 US 225 (1956) and *Machinists v Street,* 367 US 740 (1961) discussed by K Cloke, 'Mandatory Political Contributions and Union Democracy', (1981) 4 *IRLJ* 527 at 533–43.] The approach of the Supreme Court has been to recognise that compulsory union dues to support collective bargaining interfere with freedom of association. However, such fees are justified by the Government interest to avoid free riders and to preserve labour peace through collective bargaining. [*Abood v District Board of Education,* 431 US 209 (1977); *Ellis v Brotherhood of Railway, Airline and Steamship Clerks,* 466 US 429 (1984).] Accordingly, fees collected for collective bargaining purposes and for contract administration and grievance adjustment are legitimate. On the other hand, the use of fees for political or ideological purposes unrelated to collective bargaining violate First Amendment rights of freedom of association and expression.

Thus US unions and employers can require all employees in the bargaining unit to contribute dues to the union so long as that money is spent on activities germane to collective bargaining. [*Abood,* above.] Legitimate expenditure includes money used to support state and national affiliates of the local union even though those activities do not confer a direct benefit upon the objecting employees in the bargaining unit so long as the expenditure is for services that may ultimately enure to the benefit of the members of the local union. [*Lehnert v Ferris Faculty Association,* 500 US 507 (1991).] Employees who object to a union's non-collective bargaining or political activities have the right to opt-out of this portion of their dues. There are two obvious difficulties associated with this dichotomy. First, the case law indicates that it is difficult to define germane speech with ease or precision. [See the comments of Kennedy J in *Board of Regents of the*

University of Wisconsin v Southworth (Supreme Court, 22 March 2000) and *Lehnert*, above, where different Justices reached different decisions on the activities which were germane to the union's mission.] Second, the administration of the opt-out arrangements can be problematic, particularly since the union must ensure that it does not provide refunds in arrears. It has been held that such a system constitutes a temporary involuntary loan to the union to sponsor causes to which the employee has objected. [*Chicago Teachers Union v Hudson*, 475 US 292 (1986).]

In this valuable article Miller goes on to consider whether legislation permitting arrangements of this kind would be permissible in Britain in light of the ECHR and the Human Rights Act 1998. He concludes in the light of the US (and also the Canadian) jurisprudence that 'there is at least a chance that requiring non—members to contribute equivalent sums to the union would escape challenge under the Human Rights Act'.

8.2.2.4 *Trade union membership rights and financial inducements*

As we have seen, the *Wilson and Palmer* case led to a number of changes to the statutory protection relating to trade union membership and related activities. But the law has been strengthened in another respect following the decision of the European Court of Human Rights. This was done by what is now ss 145A and 145B of TULRCA, also inserted by the Employment Relations Act 2004. These latter provisions address an additional concern raised by the Strasbourg court, namely that British law then in force permitted employers to make financial inducements to give up their rights in relation to trade union representation.

[8.15] Trade Union and Labour Relations (Consolidation) Act 1992, sections 145A–145B]

Inducements relating to union membership or activities

145A (1) A worker has the right not to have an offer made to him by his employer for the sole or main purpose of inducing the worker—
(a) not to be or seek to become a member of an independent trade union,
(b) not to take part, at an appropriate time, in the activities of an independent trade union,
(c) not to make use, at an appropriate time, of trade union services, or
(d) to be or become a member of any trade union or of a particular trade union or of one of a number of particular trade unions.

(2) In subsection (1) "an appropriate time" means-
(a) a time outside the worker's working hours, or
(b) a time within his working hours at which, in accordance with arrangements agreed with or consent given by his employer, it is permissible for him to take part in the activities of a trade union or (as the case may be) make use of trade union services.

(3) In subsection (2) "working hours", in relation to a worker, means any time when, in accordance with his contract of employment (or other contract personally to do work or perform services), he is required to be at work.

(4) In subsections (1) and (2)-

(a) "trade union services" means services made available to the worker by an independent trade union by virtue of his membership of the union, and

(b) references to a worker's "making use" of trade union services include his consenting to the raising of a matter on his behalf by an independent trade union of which he is a member.

(5) A worker or former worker may present a complaint to an employment tribunal on the ground that his employer has made him an offer in contravention of this section.

Inducements relating to collective bargaining

145B(1) A worker who is a member of an independent trade union which is recognised, or seeking to be recognised, by his employer has the right not to have an offer made to him by his employer if—

(a) acceptance of the offer, together with other workers' acceptance of offers which the employer also makes to them, would have the prohibited result, and

(b) the employer's sole or main purpose in making the offers is to achieve that result.

(2) The prohibited result is that the workers' terms of employment, or any of those terms, will not (or will no longer) be determined by collective agreement negotiated by or on behalf of the union.

(3) It is immaterial for the purposes of subsection (1) whether the offers are made to the workers simultaneously.

(4) Having terms of employment determined by collective agreement shall not be regarded for the purposes of section 145A (or section 146 or 152) as making use of a trade union service.

(5) A worker or former worker may present a complaint to an employment tribunal on the ground that his employer has made him an offer in contravention of this section.

In dealing with a complaint under these latter provisions, it is for 'the employer to show what was his sole or main purpose in making the offer' or offers. It is also provided by s 145D (4) that:

In determining whether an employer's sole or main purpose in making offers was the purpose mentioned in section 145B(1), the matters taken into account must include any evidence—

(a) that when the offers were made the employer had recently changed or sought to change, or did not wish to use, arrangements agreed with the union for collective bargaining,

(b) that when the offers were made the employer did not wish to enter into arrangements proposed by the union for collective bargaining, or

(c) that the offers were made only to particular workers, and were made with the sole or main purpose of rewarding those particular workers for their high level of performance or of retaining them because of their special value to the employer.

The remedy for breach of this provision is an award of compensation. A complaint may be made by someone who has succumbed to the inducement, in which case the employer cannot enforce any agreement made by the worker, while any variation of the contract as a result of the inducement is enforceable by the worker. It remains the case, however, that the amendments made by the Employment Relations Act 2004 may not fully meet the requirements of the Strasbourg court's *Wilson and Palmer* decision, and indeed the legislation was criticised on this ground by the Joint Committee on Human Rights. There are two concerns. One is that there is no protection against an inducement when the union has been and is not now seeking recognition (that is to say after it has been derecognised). Indeed it is open to question whether *Wilson and Palmer* would be decided differently by the domestic courts today following the 2004 amendments. The other concern is that British law still does not recognise the right of the trade union to bring legal proceedings where financial inducements are made to weaken its position in the enterprise. The European Court of Human Rights recognised that financial inducements to members are calculated to undermine the authority of the union, and that such inducements constitute a breach of the union's Article 11 rights as well as the Article 11 rights of the member. It is arguable that the interest of the union may be protected to some extent—albeit indirectly—when the member takes legal action to enforce his or her rights. But there may be circumstances where the member refuses to take legal proceedings and where as a result the interests of the union cannot be protected even in this indirect may. Apart from the case of the reluctant litigant, a good example would be where the induced worker accepts the employer's seduction. The worker may have no interest in bringing legal proceedings, while the union will have no standing to do so.

8.3 Trade union representation and the right to be accompanied

One of the means by which trade unions may act on behalf of their members is by representing them in different ways at the workplace. There are two legal questions here: the first is whether the worker has the right to seek and secure such representation; and the other is whether the employer is under a duty to respond to and deal with the representative. The matter may be particularly acute for a number of reasons. There may already be a recognised trade union at the enterprise, and the worker may wish to be represented by another. Or more usually, there may not be a recognised union, and the employer may feel threatened by the presence of a trade union representative as the 'thin end of the wedge'. As we have seen, TULRCA 1992, s 146 has been amended in the light of *Wilson and Palmer v United Kingdom*, above, to make it clear that workers have the right to protection from discrimination and dismissal for making use of the services of a trade union at 'an appropriate time'. But as *Specialty Care plc v Pachela* [1996] ICR 633 indicates, this is a position to which the EAT was straining notwithstanding the House of Lords decision in *Wilson and Palmer*. Nevertheless, the clarity introduced by the amendments to ss 146 and 152 on this point is to be welcomed.

8.3.1 The right to be accompanied

Although there is thus a right to use the services of a trade union, this does not confer a duty on the part of the employer to deal with the union providing the service to the member. The worker has the right not to be discriminated against and the employee has the right not to be discriminated against or dismissed for using union services: but the employer is not required by these provisions to allow the worker or the employee to be represented in grievance or disciplinary proceedings. The *ACAS Code of Practice on Disciplinary Practice and Procedures in Employment* (1977) provided by paragraph 10 that disciplinary procedures should:

> Give individuals the right to be accompanied by a trade union representative or by a fellow employee of their choice.

But this provision (which has since been superseded) was not legally binding and could not be enforced, though it could be taken into account by a court or tribunal in unfair dismissal and other legal proceedings. A right to be accompanied by a trade union is introduced formally by the Employment Relations Act 1999, as part of a general right to be accompanied. It is to be noted that the legislation provides a right to be accompanied and not a right to be represented by a trade union official or by a colleague, though the difference between accompaniment and representation is a fine one.

[8.16] Employment Relations Act 1999, section 10

Right to be accompanied

10(1) This section applies where a worker—
(a) is required or invited by his employer to attend a disciplinary or grievance hearing, and
(b) reasonably requests to be accompanied at the hearing.

(2A) Where this section applies, the employer must permit the worker to be accompanied at the hearing by one companion who—
(a) is chosen by the worker; and
(b) is within subsection (3).

(2B) The employer must permit the worker's companion to-
(a) address the hearing in order to do any or all of the following-
     (i)   put the worker's case;
     (ii)   sum up that case;
     (iii)   respond on the worker's behalf to any view expressed at the hearing;
(b) confer with the worker during the hearing.

(2C) Subsection (2B) does not require the employer to permit the worker's companion to-
(a) answer questions on behalf of the worker;
(b) address the hearing if the worker indicates at it that he does not wish his companion to do so; or

(c)   use the powers conferred by that subsection in a way that prevents the employer from explaining his case or prevents any other person at the hearing from making his contribution to it.

(3) A person is within this subsection if he is—

(a)   employed by a trade union of which he is an official within the meaning of sections 1 and 119 of the Trade Union and Labour Relations (Consolidation) Act 1992,

(b)   an official of a trade union (within that meaning) whom the union has reasonably certified in writing as having experience of, or as having received training in, acting as a worker's companion at disciplinary or grievance hearings, or

(c)   another of the employer's workers.

(4) If—

(a)   a worker has a right under this section to be accompanied at a hearing,

(b)   his chosen companion will not be available at the time proposed for the hearing by the employer, and

(c)   the worker proposes an alternative time which satisfies subsection (5),

the employer must postpone the hearing to the time proposed by the worker.

(5) An alternative time must—

(a)   be reasonable, and

(b)   fall before the end of the period of five working days beginning with the first working day after the day proposed by the employer.

(6) An employer shall permit a worker to take time off during working hours for the purpose of accompanying another of the employer's workers in accordance with a request under subsection (1)(b).

(7) Sections 168(3) and (4), 169 and 171 to 173 of the Trade Union and Labour Relations (Consolidation) Act 1992 (time off for carrying out trade union duties) shall apply in relation to subsection (6) above as they apply in relation to section 168(1) of that Act.

8.3.2 Scope and application

It will be noticed immediately that like TULRCA 1992, section 146, these measures apply to workers rather than employees: for this purpose a worker is widely defined.

[8.17] Employment Relations Act 1999, section 13

Interpretation

13 In sections 10 to 12 and this section 'worker' means an individual who is—

(a)   a worker within the meaning of section 230(3) of the Employment Rights Act 1996,

(b)   an agency worker,

(c)   a home worker,

(d)   a person in Crown employment within the meaning of section 191 of that Act, other than a member of the naval, military, air or reserve forces of the Crown, or

(e)   employed as a relevant member of the House of Lords staff or the House of Commons staff within the meaning of section 194(6) or 195(5) of that Act.

But although TULRCA 1992, s 146 also applies to 'workers', the foregoing definition is wider in some respects than the definition used for the purposes of the latter provision. There is thus no symmetry between these two measures. A worker may complain to an employment tribunal if section 10 rights are not complied with by an employer. The tribunal may award two weeks' pay by way of compensation (section 11).

There is no question of proceedings being invalidated because the worker was denied rights under section 10. Provision is made to protect from detriment and dismissal the worker who exercises the right to be accompanied and for any companion (section 12). The right does not, however, apply to national security employees (section 15). But although the legislation thus has a wide coverage, it applies only to disciplinary or grievance hearings which the worker is 'required or invited to attend' (ERA 1999, section 10(1)(a)). There is no general obligation on an employer to have either a grievance or a disciplinary procedure, though such procedures are have been encouraged by ACAS since the publication of its first Code of Practice on Disciplinary and Grievance Procedures in 1977. The current version of the Code may be a valuable source in determining the boundaries of the suggested common law obligation on the part of employers to provide a grievance procedure, as illustrated in *W A Goold (Pearmak) Ltd v McConnell* [1995] IRLR 516 (EAT). Now, however there are also the minimum disciplinary and grievance procedures introduced by the Employment Act 2002 to encourage the settlement of disputes without the need for employees to resort to employment tribunals (s 29). These procedures are only required in relation to specified matters dealing with statutory rights. Aspects of these procedures are expressly stated to fall within the scope of the statutory right to be accompanied in the Employment Relations Act 1999 (2002 Act, Schedule 2, para 14).

8.3.3 An important qualification

Even where there are disciplinary and grievance procedures in place, the Act does not apply to them all. A most important qualification is to be found in section 13(4) which defines a disciplinary hearing, and section 13(5) which defines a grievance hearing. So far as disciplinary action is concerned, this is fairly broadly defined: a disciplinary hearing (at which the worker is entitled to be accompanied) is defined to mean a hearing which could result in: '(a) the administration of a formal warning to a worker by his employer, (b) the taking of some other action in respect of a worker by his employer, or (c) the confirmation of a warning issued or some other action taken'. According to the *ACAS Code of Practice on Disciplinary and Grievance Procedures* (2004), this would exclude 'informal discussions or counselling sessions' (paragraph 99), though it has been held that an 'informal warning' may be regarded as a formal warning if it becomes part of the employee's record: *London Underground Ltd v Ferenc–Batchelor* [2003] IRLR 252. But a meeting to inform someone that they are to be dismissed on the ground of redundancy is not a disciplinary hearing: *Heathmill Multimedia ASP Ltd v Jones* [2003] IRLR 856.

The right to be accompanied is much more narrowly defined in the context of a grievance hearing (assuming that the employer has a grievance procedure). Here section 13(5) provides that 'a grievance hearing is a hearing which concerns the performance of a duty by an employer in relation to a worker'. A 'duty' for this purpose is not defined, though it is rather presumptuously stated in the *ACAS Code of Practice* to mean 'a legal duty arising from statute or common law'. The effect of this is that the right applies only in the case of what might be referred to as conflicts of rights (grievances about existing terms and conditions of employment), not conflicts of interest (grievances about changing existing terms and conditions of employment).

[8.18] *ACAS Code of Practice on Disciplinary and Grievance Procedures* (2004)

100. For the purposes of this right, a grievance hearing is a meeting at which an employer deals with a complaint about a duty owed by them to the worker, whether the duty arises from statute or common law (for example contractual commitments)

101. For instance, an individual's request for a pay rise is unlikely to fall within the definition, unless a right to an increase is specifically provided for in the contract or the request raises an issue about equal pay. Equally, most employers will be under no legal duty to provide their workers with car parking facilities, and a grievance about such facilities would carry no right to be accompanied at a hearing by a companion. However, if a worker were disabled and needed a car to get to and from work, they probably would be entitled to a companion at a grievance hearing, as an issue might arise as to whether the employer was meeting its obligations under the Disability Discrimination Act 1995.

102. The right to be accompanied will also apply to any meetings held as part of the statutory grievance procedures. This includes any meetings after the employee has left employment.

It may be thought that in some respects the ACAS Code is too opaque and gives insufficient detail about an employer's common law obligations, which have significantly expanded in recent years. There is for example the implied contractual duty of mutual trust and confidence (on which see chapter 2 above) which may require the employer to take steps to deal with friction between fellow workers. And there is also the duty of the employer not to treat employees arbitrarily or capriciously in matters relating to pay (*F. C. Gardner Ltd v Beresford* [1978] IRLR 63), which in turn would allow a worker to be represented in a grievance hearing based on being unfairly overlooked for a wage rise or unfairly treated in the context of discretionary pay awards. Indeed it might be said generally that the Code of Practice does more to conceal than reveal the true nature of the employer's duties to employees and workers, and consequently unnecessarily fails to illuminate the circumstances in which the right to be accompanied may arise in grievance procedures.

8.3.4 The rights and responsibilities of trade unions

The focus so far has been on the rights of the worker and the responsibility of the employer. But what about the trade union in cases where the trade union is providing representative facilities? Here we find that the union has no right to insist that the employer should permit the worker to be accompanied, important because it means that the union has no standing to complain if the right is denied by the employer. It is thus for the worker to enforce his or her rights. But the worker does have the right to be represented even though the union is not recognised, and even though the union cannot invoke the new statutory recognition procedure, because for example the employer employs fewer than 21 workers. Where a union is recognised by an employer, a worker may wish to be represented by another union, to which the employer may not object. This could give rise to difficulties in practice where the recognised union objects to the presence of what it may view as a rival organisation.

There is no obligation on the part of a trade union to provide a companion, which might well be refused on a number of grounds. Apart from a reluctance to intervene where there is already a recognised union or another union actively organising at the workplace in question, the demand for such representation may stretch union resources beyond what can be dealt with. It should be borne in mind however that trade unions may have contractual duties to members which might form the basis of an obligation to provide a companion, and that they are covered by the Sex Discrimination Act 1975 and the Race Relations Act 1976 in terms of the provision of benefits and services to members. Where a union does provide a companion it must be someone experienced in or trained as acting as a worker's companion at disciplinary or grievance proceedings. But trade unions will have to be careful to ensure that an adequate standard of training has been reached before giving a certificate of competence under Employment Relations Act 1999, section 10(3)(b). Presumably trade unions will have a duty of care to workers enforceable under the law of tort to ensure that those certified are in fact properly experienced or trained. In determining the scope of that duty, paradoxically it may be of benefit to both the trade union and the companion that the worker has a right only to be accompanied, and not to be represented.

8.4 Trade union recognition and collective bargaining

We move in this Part from an examination of the organisational and representation rights of employees and workers to a consideration of the rights of trade unions to be recognised for the purposes of collective bargaining; we also consider in this Part the rights of recognised trade unions. Although this is an area of the law which has been greatly energised by the statutory recognition procedure introduced by the Employment Relations Act 1999, it is important not to lose sight of the fact that the procedure operates alongside a practice of voluntary recognition. Unlike other jurisdictions with statutory recognition procedures (or their equivalent), the voluntary route remains the principal route to recognition in the British system, and has been stimulated rather than displaced by the statutory procedures.

8.4.1 Trade union recognition: voluntary agreements

Most collective bargaining in Britain takes place without any legal obligation on either side. It occurs because employers have agreed voluntarily to recognise a trade union for the purposes of collective bargaining, and to conclude an agreement which will enable negotiations over working conditions to take place. The overwhelming majority of large employers voluntarily engage in collective bargaining which is seen to have benefits for both the employer and the workers concerned: indeed it was estimated that 84 of Britain's top 100 companies recognised trade unions, and they do so on the basis of voluntary agreements. These agreements will set out a procedure for the parties to meet on a regular basis for the negotiation of working conditions and for the settlement of any differences or disputes which may arise between them. The procedures will vary in their complexity, and in some cases machinery will be provided for dealing with different issues at different levels in the corporate structure. As already suggested most (though by no means all) collective bargaining, particularly in the private sector, is now company or enterprise rather than industry or sector based. Some modern agreements also now emphasise the importance of 'partnership', though this is a phenomenon which now may be more favoured by government and employers than by trade unions. The following is a sample recognition agreement from the Transport and General Workers Union.

[8.19] AGREEMENT BETWEEN .... (hereafter called the Company) and TRANSPORT AND GENERAL WORKERS UNION (hereafter called the Union)

OBJECTIVE

1.1 Good Industrial Relations are a joint responsibility of both parties and need the continuing co-operation of all concerned. – Management, Trade Unions and individual employees. This Agreement is designed to encourage and assist that co-operation.

1.2 This Agreement provides a system of representation and procedure through which the Parties may raise items of common concern, of either individual or collective nature.

1.3 The Parties recognise the importance of ensuring that all management and employee Relationships are based on mutual understandings and respect and that employment practices are conducted to the highest possible standards.

1.4 Both Parties are committed to ensure that equal opportunities are offered to employees or Prospective employees and that the treatment of staff will be fair and equitable in all matters of discipline and grievance.

SCOPE OF THIS AGREEMENT

2.1 This Agreement covers all employees and the Company recognises the Union as the sole Union entitled to represent the interests of the employees and negotiate on their behalf.

GENERAL PRINCIPLES

3.1 The Company believes that a Trade Union capable of representing its members with authority and responsibility is essential to the maintenance of good industrial relations.

3.2 The Company recognises the Union's responsibility to represent the interests of its members.

3.3 The Union recognises the Company's responsibility to manage its affairs in an effective and efficient manner.

3.4 The Company and the Union recognise their common interests and joint purpose in furthering the aims and objectives of the Company and in achieving reasonable solutions in all matters which concern them. Both Parties declare their common objective to maintain good industrial relations.

3.5 The Company and the Union accept that the terms of this Agreement are binding in honour upon them but do not constitute a legally enforceable Agreement.

UNION REPRESENTATION

4.1 The Company recognises the Union as the only Trade Union with which it will consult and negotiate on all matters of interest of the employees.

4.2 The Company will inform all new employees of this Agreement and will encourage them to join the Union and provide facilities for them to talk to a representative of the Union on becoming an employee. The Company will provide the Union with a list of all new employees.

4.3 Union members will elect representatives in accordance with the rules of the Union to act as their spokesperson to represent their interests. The Union agrees to inform the Company of the names of all elected representatives in writing within 5 working days of their election, and to inform the Company in a similar manner of any subsequent changes. Persons whose names have been notified to the Company shall be the sole representatives of the employees.

4.4 Facilities will be provided by the Company for elections to be held as required by Union rules.

4.5 Recognised Union representatives will be permitted to take reasonable time off during working hours to enable them to carry out Union duties.

4.6 The Company recognises that Union representatives fulfil an important role and that the discharge of their duties as Union representatives will in no way prejudice their career prospects or employment within the Company.

4.7 Subject to the agreement of the Company, recognised Union representatives will be granted special leave without loss of pay to attend training courses run by the Union or another appropriate body which are relevant to the discharge of their duties. The Company recognises the importance of such training and will allow reasonable time off, not normally exceeding ten days per year, but this may be extended by mutual agreement, for each shop steward to attend such courses.

FACILITIES

5.1 The Company will provide facilities including a notice board, secure cupboard, facilities for distribution of Union Journals, use of internal mail services by accredited shop stewards, use of internal and external telephone, photocopying and reasonable secretarial facility.

5. 2 Where possible, the Company will also provide a site or office, but if this is not possible the Company will provide facilities for Union members to meet privately with their shop steward or convenor.

UNION MEETINGS

6.1 Meetings of Union members to discuss specific issues will be held from time to time, with pay. Permission for such meetings will not be unreasonably withheld.

CHECK OFF SYSTEM

7.1 It is agreed that a check off system will operate whereby the Company will deduct Union subscriptions from the wages/salaries of Union members and pay them to the Union at (insert Union address) each month with a schedule of payment. Individual members will authorise deductions in writing, appropriate forms being provided by Union representatives.

JOINT CONSULTATION AND NEGOTIATION

8.1 The Company undertakes to consult the Union on all matters which their members have an interest, and will seek to resolve any difference by negotiation.

8.2 Detailed arrangements are shown under Procedures for the Avoidance and Resolution of Disputes/Grievance procedures (See Appendix 1)

VARIATION OR TERMINATION OF AGREEMENT

9.1 This Agreement may only be varied by the mutual agreement of both Parties. In the event of either party wishing to terminate this Agreement, the other party will be given six months notice in writing, during which period the Agreement will remain in force.

Signed on behalf of T.G.W.U.   . . . .   Date . . . .

Signed on behalf of (Company Name)   . . . .   Date . . . .

APPENDIX 1

NEGOTIATING PROCEDURE

INTENTION

This Agreement lays down the procedures by which all issues arising between the parties can be considered and resolved.

It is intended that issues will be resolved at the earliest stage possible and as speedily as possible.

Until the issue is resolved and settled whatever conditions applied prior to the grievance will apply. In the event of a failure to agree the parties will refer the matter for consultation in accordance with the following procedure.

Any matters relating to terms and conditions of employment, including changes in wages and hours of work whether initiated by claims from the Union or by proposals from the Company, will be negotiated between the Company and the Union. In the event of any failure to agree between the parties relating to such changes and conditions, it shall be referred to Stage 3 of the grievance procedure set out below.

PROCEDURE FOR THE AVOIDANCE OF DISPUTES AND RESOLUTION OF GRIEVANCES

OBJECTIVE

The aim of this procedure is to settle grievances promptly and fairly. Pending a settlement of a grievance, the same conditions that applied prior to the grievance shall continue.

PROCEDURE

STAGE 1

An employee who has a grievance must first discuss it with his/her supervisor. Such a meeting will take place within ... working days of notification. The employee may if s/he wishes be accompanied by a Union representative or colleague.

A group who have a grievance must first discuss the issue with their supervisor through their representative and such a meeting will take place within ... working days of notification.

The supervisor will make every effort to resolve the issue. If a satisfactory resolution has not been reached within ... working days from the meeting the issue will be referred to the next stage.

STAGE 2

If the grievance is not settled at Stage 1 then the Union representative/convenor/Chairperson will refer the matter to the next senior manager. The matter will be discussed at a meeting within ... working days of notification. If it is not resolved within ... working days then the matter is referred to Stage 4.

STAGE 3

If the matter is not resolved at Stage 2 then the matter will be referred to the TGWU District Officer who will raise the issue with the next level of management who will hear the stage 3 within 5 working days.

STAGE 4

If a settlement cannot then be reached, if both parties agree the issue may be referred to ACAS. Pending resolution of the matter through the procedure neither party shall engage in any unconstitutional action e.g. stoppages, lockouts etc. Until the matter is resolved and settled whatever conditions prevailed prior to the grievance will apply.

[DISCIPLINARY PROCEDURE OMITTED]

8.4.1.1 Legal status of recognition agreements

The purpose of a recognition agreement is to provide a procedure for the negotiation of terms and conditions of employment, and for the settlement of disputes which may arise between the parties. The first question for the lawyer is the legal status of these recognition agreements, the answer to which affects so much—in terms of the manner of drafting of the agreement, the personnel involved in the drafting process, and the means of enforcement. In most countries, the collective agreement—whether dealing with procedural matters such as trade union recognition and dispute resolution; or substantive matters such as terms and conditions of employment—would be a legally binding contract enforceable by either party, that is to say the employer and the trade union. Traditionally, this has not been the position in this country, where both the recognition agreement setting out the collective bargaining procedures and subsequent agreements dealing with terms and conditions of employment are not normally legally enforceable by the parties to them. The modern starting-point is the famous *Ford Motor Co* case. Quite whether the *Ford Motor Co* case should be permitted to bear the weight that it does is another matter: it has created a general presumption against the legal enforceability of collective agreements; but it is a first instance decision which was confined to its own particular facts, and it was also a decision made in interlocutory proceedings to discharge an ex parte injunction. Nevertheless it remains perhaps the fullest consideration of the question by a court in this country.

[8.20] *Ford Motor Co Ltd v AUEFW* [1969] 2 QB 302 (QBD)

A dispute arose following the negotiation of a new agreement between the Ford Motor Co and its trade unions. Some of the unions were unhappy with the agreement, and, following unofficial action at a number of plants, the dispute was declared official. The company claimed that the industrial action was in breach of earlier agreements (of 1955 and 1967) still in force, regulating the procedures for dealing with disputes between the parties. These agreements were contained in what was called the 'Blue Book'. Claiming a breach of these procedures, the company obtained an *ex parte* injunction to restrain the action. The injunction was subsequently discharged, the court giving full consideration to the general question of the legal status of collective agreements. After reviewing a wide range of legal and extra-legal authorities, Geoffrey Lane J held that 'the climate of opinion was almost unanimous to the effect that no legally enforceable contract resulted from the collective agreements' (at p 329). He continued by pointing out that '[a]greements such as these, composed largely of optimistic aspirations, presenting grave practical problems of enforcement and reached against a background of opinion adverse to enforceability, are, in my judgment, not contracts in the legal sense and are not enforceable at law. Without clear and express provisions making them amenable to legal action, they remain in the realm of undertakings binding in honour' (at pp 330–31).

The legislation now in force places the presumption against legal enforceability into statutory form. In order to overcome this presumption in TULRCA 1992, section 179 it is necessary for the collective agreement to be in writing, and to contain a provision which, however expressed, states that the parties intend the agreement to be a legally enforceable contract. The effect of section 179 is not that a collective agreement is a contract which is not legally enforceable. Rather, it is not a contract at all: *Monterosso Shipping Co Ltd. v ITF* [1982] ICR 675 (CA). Why should this be? Why should the trade unions in particular wish to preclude the legal enforceability of collective agreements? (The current legislation was introduced initially by a Labour government in 1974 and has survived the Conservative changes of the 1980s and 1990s.) One answer lies in the vulnerability of trade unions to contractual remedies if a strike were to be called in breach of a procedure laid down in a collective agreement. But in view of the statutory restraints on industrial action, this may be a less significant concern than in the past. Whatever the answer, the critical point for our present purposes is that a collective agreement whereby an employer recognises a union for collective bargaining is unlikely to be legally binding. This means that the agreement—and with it the recognition of the trade union—can be terminated at any time by the employer. At the time of writing it is known that at least one large union is contemplating a model recognition agreement which is legally binding. This model agreement also contains provisions relating to information and consultation, and it may be that the motive is to ensure that these obligations in particular are legally enforceable. But it is not easy to see what benefits there would now be for an employer in agreeing to a legally binding clause in a recognition agreement.

8.4.1.2 *Recognition agreements and the contract of employment*

Although collective agreements are not normally enforceable at the suit of either the union or the employer, the terms of a collective agreement may be incorporated into individual contracts of employment in the manner described in chapter 2 above. This means that they can be enforced by the individual worker (with the union standing behind him or her in appropriate cases). But not all terms of a collective agreement are enforceable in this way. The courts will normally distinguish between those agreements or those terms which deal with negotiating procedures, trade union facilities and dispute resolution procedures from those agreements or terms which deal with terms and conditions of employment. The courts will be prepared to accept the incorporation of the latter but not the former into individual contracts of employment. It is expressly provided by TULRCA 1992, section 180 that terms in a collective agreement restricting the right of workers to take part in a strike or other industrial action are not to be incorporated into individual contracts of employment unless certain conditions are met. Even in the absence of statutory guidance of this kind, the courts are unlikely to hold that a recognition agreement is apt to be incorporated into individual contracts of employment except in the most unusual circumstances which can barely be imagined. This means that if an employer withdraws recognition from a trade union, an individual member of the union could not sue the employer claiming that there has been a breach of the contract of employment.

[8.21] *Gallacher v Post Office* **[1970] 3 All ER 712 (Ch D)**

> The plaintiff was a member of the National Guild of Telephonists which the Post Office proposed to de-recognise as part of a restructuring of its operations, following which the Union of Post Office Workers would be given sole recognition rights. The plaintiff complained, among other things, that this was a breach of an implied term of his contract of employment, a claim based to some extent on a statement made to him orally by a Post Office training officer that he was entitled to join either the NGT or the UPW or neither. In rejecting the claim, Brightman J thought it 'altogether too far fetched to suggest that when training employees are told by their instructors that they are at liberty either to join specified unions or no union, that becomes an express term of their employment which introduces, under compulsion of necessity, the further and unspoken term that the employer will always during that contract of service continue in all circumstances to recognise the chosen trade union as a negotiating body in respect of that employee'.

It is also the case that the employer is free unilaterally to alter the recognition arrangements, without encountering any difficulties under the contract of employment. *NUM v National Coal Board* [1986] ICR 736 concerned an agreement made between the National Coal Board and the NUM in 1946 for the settlement of terms and conditions of employment, for which purpose a National Conciliation Board was established. Following the miners' strike in 1984–5 a new union was formed, the Union of Democratic Mineworkers, which was the dominant union in South Derbyshire and in Nottingham. The NCB decided to de-recognise the NUM in respect of these areas and to recognise the UDM. The NUM claimed that the 1946 agreement was legally enforceable, and also that its terms were incorporated into the contracts of employment of its members employed in the two areas where the union had been recognised. Both arguments failed. So far as the latter is concerned, Scott J said that 'the procedural provisions' of agreements such as that of 1946 'are not . . . in the least apt for contractual enforcement by individual employees. A collective agreement between an employer and a union providing machinery for collective bargaining and for resolving industrial disputes may be of very great importance to each and every worker in the industry. But it is not likely to be an agreement intended to be legally enforceable as between employer and union, and it is almost inconceivable to my mind that it could have been intended to become legally enforceable at the suit of an individual worker' (at p 733). So in practice recognition agreements are unenforceable, whether directly by the union against the employer or indirectly by means of the contract of employment.

8.4.1.3   *Recognition agreements and the transfer of undertakings*

An interesting issue relating to recognition agreements concerns the transfer of an undertaking where there is a recognised trade union to another owner or operator which may be hostile to trade unions. Can the new owner terminate a recognition agreement? The Transfer of Undertakings (Protection of Employment) Regulations 1981, SI 1981/1794 provide by Regulation 9 that:

> (1) This Regulation applies where after a relevant transfer the undertaking or part of the undertaking transferred maintains an identity distinct from the remainder of the transferee's undertaking.
> (2) Where before such a transfer an independent trade union is recognised to any extent by the transferor in respect of employees of any description who in consequence of the transfer become employees of the transferee, then, after the transfer—
> (a)   the union shall be deemed to have been recognised by the transferee to the same extent in respect of employees of that description so employed; and
> (b)   any agreement for recognition may be varied or rescinded accordingly.

This is a potentially important provision which means in principle that in some circumstances a recognition agreement will transfer with an undertaking. But in practice it is not likely to amount to very much. This is because the transferee will inherit no more than the obligations of the transferor under the agreement. So if the transferor is free to terminate an agreement because it is not legally enforceable, what is to stop the transferee from doing the same? The transferee acquires a non-binding agreement. There may be circumstances, however, where the fruits of collective bargaining from which the transferee has dis-engaged will continue to apply to the transferred employees.

[8.22] *Whent v T Cartlidge Ltd* **[1997] IRLR 153 (EAT)**

> The employment contracts of the applicant employees with Brent LBC provided that the terms and conditions of their employment would be in accordance with the National Joint Council for Local Authorities' Administrative Staff. The work in which the applicants were engaged was transferred to Cartlidge which de-recognised the union and told staff that all collective agreements would cease to apply with immediate effect. The transfer was governed by the Transfer of Undertakings Regulations, and the employees sought a declaration in the industrial tribunal that their pay was to be determined by any NJC agreement in force, including any increases; the employer argued that the rate of pay was the rate fixed when they withdrew from the NJC. The EAT decided for the employees, rejecting the point taken by the industrial tribunal in finding for the employer that it 'cannot be right that an employer is bound ad infinitum by the terms of a collective agreement negotiated by bodies other than themselves'. This was thought to be 'fallacious' for a number of reasons. One was that the employer was not bound 'ad infinitum', and was free at any time to negotiate variations of contract with individual employees or terminate their contracts on due notice and offer fresh ones. Although the latter course could give rise to proceedings for unfair dismissal, this was a matter for the employer 'to weigh commercially'.

8.4.2 Trade union recognition: the statutory procedure

The difficulty for a trade union arises where the employer refuses to recognise it for the purposes of collective bargaining, even where it has a significant membership at the workplace. It is to deal with precisely this situation that the statutory recognition procedure in the Employment Relations Act 1999 was introduced. The 1999 Act inserted a new Schedule A1 into TULRCA 1992. This is not the first time that trade union recognition has been introduced in this country, nor are we alone in adopting a procedure of this kind: earlier recognition provisions were included in the Industrial Relations Act 1971 and the Employment Protection Act 1975, while similar (though by no means identical) procedures have operated in the United States since 1935 (though worryingly the USA has the lowest level of collective bargaining coverage in the developed world). The new procedure is much more detailed than either the 1971 or 1975 procedures, and much more detailed than the comparable procedures any-where else in the world. The 1975 procedure for example was dealt with in only five sections, accounting for six pages of the statute book in total. The procedure in TULRCA 1992, Schedule A1 in contrast, ran to 172 paragraphs and no fewer than 60 dense pages, and this before it was expanded by the Employment Relations Act 2004.

There are a number of reasons for the complexity of the legislation. One is the need to remove as much discretion as possible from the statutory agency responsible for the administration of the procedure (in this case the CAC), in order to minimise the risk of judicial review. This in turn has created a need to anticipate as many

difficulties and eventualities as possible. A second is the need to deal with the anti –
union conduct of some employers, calculated by fair means or foul to stop their
workers from voting in favour of trade union recognition and the representation
which this entails But although much more detailed than its predecessors, the current
procedure is much narrower in its scope, so that a union is able to use the procedure
only to secure recognition about pay, hours and holidays. Pay for this purpose does
not now include pensions, though the Secretary of State does have the power to add
pensions by regulation. Other matters are left for voluntary agreement between the
parties; but, as we shall see, once recognised a union may have a range of consultation rights under statute, rights which apply whether recognition has been secured
voluntarily or under the statutory procedure. It is important to emphasise, however,
that the statutory procedure has been constructed in a way which will encourage the
parties at all stages to enter into a voluntary agreement and forsake the law. The aim
is to promote voluntary agreements in the shadow of the statute: on this basis the
successful use of the procedure is a sign that the parties have failed to meet the objectives of its authors.

[8.23] Department of Trade and Industry, *Fairness at Work* (Cm 95, 1998)

4.15 The Government is proposing a new system of recognition. Its starting-point is
voluntary agreement. Only where this proves impossible should another means be
invoked. Setting out the procedure will help ensure that employers, employees and trade
unions all understand clearly what will happen if they cannot agree. This should in
practice lessen the likelihood of further stages of the procedure being necessary.

4.16 The Government believes that, where a clear majority of employees wishes to be
represented by a trade union, the new procedure will enable that union to be recognised by
their employer without the disputes which have resulted from recognition claims under the
current law. A statutory procedure offers a means of settling disputes without industrial
action. The reason it is important to have clear support at a workplace is twofold. First,
without real and substantial support amongst employees, collective bargaining simply will
not work. Second, since collective bargaining has an impact on all employees, not just
those claiming union representation, it is right that it should only be granted in
circumstances where substantial support is demonstrated.

4.17 In drawing up its proposals, the Government has been determined to introduce a
procedure which will work, which will improve fairness and which will complement and
enhance competitiveness, prosperity and growth. To deter insubstantial claims, the new
procedure will rest on trade unions being able to demonstrate initially that they have
baseline support among employees before a recognition claim can proceed. The group of
employees to whom trade union recognition will apply if they choose it—the bargaining
unit—will be clearly defined to avoid disagreements. To demonstrate beyond dispute that
a vote for recognition enjoys genuine and widespread support among employees,
recognition will be awarded only where the vote in favour exceeds a minimum specified
level. Many small companies recognise trade unions already. Many do not. In many small
firms, employment relations are managed not just on an individual level, but on a
personal level. In these circumstances statutory requirements on trade union recognition
would be inappropriate. So the provisions will not apply to companies below a set
threshold. Just as employees have the right to join or not to join a trade union, employers
will have available a parallel procedure to end recognition arrangements if employee

support for them reduces significantly. And to deter unwarranted attempts to obtain recognition or derecognition, there will be a minimum time period to allow employment arrangements to demonstrate their validity.

8.4.2.1 Applications and admissibility

A request for recognition under the Act may be made to an employer only by a trade union which has a certificate of independence (TULRCA 1992, Schedule A1, paragraph 6). Certificates are issued by the Certification Officer under TULRCA 1992, section 6. An independent trade union is defined in TULRCA 1992, section 5 as meaning a trade union which '(a) is not under the domination or control of an employer or group of employers or of one or more employers' associations', or '(b) is not liable to interference by an employer or any such group or association (arising out of the provision of financial or material support or by any other means whatsoever) tending towards such control'. Otherwise, an application under the Act may be made only to an employer which (together with associated employers) employs 21 or more workers (TULRCA 1992, Schedule A1, paragraph 7).

[8.24] *R (BBC) v CAC* [2003] ICR 1542 (Admin)

> An application was made by BECTU for recognition of wildlife cameramen and -women by the BBC. The application succeeded, but the BBC successfully challenged the CAC's decision in judicial review proceedings on the ground that the CAC had misdirected itself in holding that the camera crews were not professionals. The panel had stated that before a group of workers may be said to be exercising a professional activity, that group must be subject to regulation by a body covering those engaged or seeking to be engaged in the activity in question. According to the High Court this requirement amounted to an error of law, and the matter was remitted to a different panel for re-consideration. Moses J emphasised that he was far 'from saying that the conclusion that the cameramen were workers within the meaning of [the Statute] was not open to the panel. It was a matter for them, having considered all those features which they regarded as relevant, but it was not open to them to impose the test they identified'.

Although the Act uses the more expansive 'worker' rather than the more restrictive 'employee', the threshold of 21 is nevertheless a major limitation of its scope. At the time the procedure was introduced, its effect was to exclude as many as 37 per cent of private sector workers, and as many as 90–95 per cent of private sector employers from the coverage of the scheme. It is all the more significant an exclusion for the fact that the small business sector is a growing sector of the economy. The Secretary of State has power to vary the threshold figure of 21 by statutory instrument, so that it could be increased or reduced. There is a strong case for saying that where workers are excluded from the procedure in this way, there should be some compensating equivalence. For example, workers employed in small businesses could be entitled to trade union representation on wider grounds than currently provided for in section 10 of the 1999 Act, discussed above, at pp 752–757 above.

An application for recognition must be made in the first instance by the union to the employer. The employer may agree to the request in which case the parties may

Trade Union Independence

The statutory procedure may be used only by an independent trade union. This is a concept which was introduced in its present form by the Employment Protection Act 1975, and which reflects the requirements of ILO Convention 98, article 2 (**[8.67]** below). It is designed to ensure that only bona fide trade unions enjoy various statutory benefits. These benefits are not extended to organisations which are created by employers to provide an alternative form of worker representation. The creation of such organisations has been a tactic adopted by employers throughout the world in order to discourage the activities of genuinely independent organisations of workers. They come in various forms and in various guises: staff associations, works councils, employee forums, and the like, usually funded and resourced by the employer. Denied any effective resources and without access to external sources of help, these organisations may be powerless to represent their 'members' when conflict arises in the workplace.

The question of trade union independence is now governed by TULRCA 1992, sections 5–9. As pointed out in the text a trade union may obtain a certificate of independence from the Certification Officer. The definition of independence has been considered by the courts on a number of occasions, and it was held in *Squibb UK Staff Association v Certification Officer* [1979] 2 All ER 452 that an organisation is 'liable' to interference within section 5(b) if there is a 'vulnerability to interference' rather than 'likelihood of interference'. Only organisations on a list of trade unions maintained by the Certification Officer (under TULRCA 1992, sections 2–4) may be granted a certificate of independence (section 6). A certificate of independence is conclusive evidence for all purposes that a trade union is independent (section 8), and an appeal lies to the EAT and then to the Court of Appeal (section 9). On 31 March 2004 there were 195 trade unions on the list of trade unions, and 139 trade unions with certificates of independence. There were also three trade unions on the list which had been refused a certificate of independence.

The requirement that the trade union is independent is necessary for a number of purposes other than the statutory recognition procedure. These purposes include:

* Protection against detriment or dismissal for trade union membership, activities or use of trade union services—these apply only in respect of an independent trade union (**[8.7]** above)
* Time-off for trade union duties and activities and for union learning representatives—these also apply only in respect of members of independent trade unions (**[8.42]**, **[8.46]**, **[8.48]** below)

However, the principle of discouraging non independent trade unions by providing benefits only to independent trade unions has been breached in two respects by the Employment Relations Act 1999. The right to be accompanied by a trade union official is not confined to officials of an independent trade union (**[8.16]** above). More controversially, the recognition by an employer of a non-independent trade union may operate to block an application under the statutory procedure by an independent trade union (8.6.1 below). The Staff Association set up by the government after trade unions were banned at GCHQ (see box on p 740) was refused a certificate of independence: *Government Communications Staff Federation v Certification Officer* [1993] ICR 163.

negotiate and conclude a recognition agreement. But the employer may fail to reply, the application may be rejected, or an attempt to reach an agreement (perhaps with the assistance of ACAS) may fail. At this stage an application may be made to the CAC. In order to make an application to the CAC there are a number of admissibility conditions built into the statutory scheme. The most important of these are as follows:

- An application is not admissible 'if the CAC is satisfied that there is already in force a collective agreement under which a union is (or unions are) recognised as entitled to conduct collective bargaining on behalf of any workers falling within the relevant bargaining unit' (TULRCA 1992, Schedule A1, paragraph 35(1)). It is important to note that for this purpose the union already recognised need not be an independent trade union. So while only an independent trade union may use the procedure, an existing agreement by an employer with a non—independent trade union may operate to block such an application. This is a matter to which we return at 8.6.1 below.
- An application is not admissible unless the CAC 'decides' that (a) members of the union or unions constitute at least 10 per cent of the workers in the proposed or agreed bargaining unit, and (b) a majority of the workers in the proposed or agreed bargaining unit would be likely to favour recognition of the union or unions making the application (TULRCA 1992, Schedule A1, paragraph 36). The 10 per cent requirement can be established by a membership check, comparing membership with the number of workers on the pay roll. Majority support has been established in a number of ways in the CAC decisions on whether to accept an application: majority membership, petitions, a straw poll, and statements signed by employees indicating support for collective bargaining.
- An application is not admissible if made jointly by more than one union unless the unions show that they will co-operate with each other in a manner likely to secure and maintain stable and effective collective bargaining arrangements; and that if the employer wishes they will act together in conducting collective bargaining (TULRCA 1992, Schedule A1, paragraph 37). This presumes that the unions will work together.

In addition to the foregoing admissibility requirements, an application is not admissible if made within three years of an earlier unsuccessful application by the same union in respect of the same bargaining unit. (This is even though the composition of the unit may have changed.) (TULRCA 1992, Schedule A1, paragraphs 39–41).

8.4.2.2 Trade union competition

One of the difficulties encountered with recognition procedures in the past is the competition between trade unions to represent the same group of workers. The problem of inter-union conflict is addressed by the current procedure in a number of ways. In the first place where there is already a voluntary agreement in which a trade union is recognised, another cannot use the statutory procedure to challenge the incumbent. Although there are obvious benefits with such an arrangement, it does mean—as in the *Racing Post* case—that an employer could enter into a voluntary

---

'Shabby' Conduct by Employer

In *R (NUJ) v CAC* [2005] IRLR 28 (Admin), it was held by Hodge J that 'a proper reading of para 35 means that a collective bargaining agreement can be brought into force voluntarily between an employer and a union even where the union has no significant support in the bargaining unit. Where that has happened there is nothing in Schedule A1 of the 1992 Act that allows the CAC to require the employer to enter into another recognition agreement with a union that does have majority support'. In that case the employer (Mirror Group Newspapers) had recognised a small union (BAJ) for journalists at the *Racing Post*. BAJ had only one member whereas the NUJ had a majority of the bargaining unit in membership. It was held by the CAC that the NUJ's application under the statutory procedure was inadmissible because of paragraph 35. Although accepting that the employer's treatment of the NUJ was 'shabby', Hodge J held that there were no grounds for challenging the decision of the CAC, and that the Human Rights Act did not help.

---

recognition agreement with a union which is not the union of the workers' choice and which they would have difficulty removing. See box on this page. There is no provision in the Act to enable a trade union or workers to initiate de-recognition procedures where an employer enters into a voluntary recognition agreement with an independent union in order to exclude another more appropriate or representative union.

Secondly, where applications are made under the procedure by two or more unions with a minimum of 10 per cent membership each, the CAC must refuse to accept either application. It may only accept an application where more than one is made in respect of the same group of workers if only one of the applicants has 10 per cent or more in membership (TULRCA 1992, Schedule A1, paragraph 14). There was a fear that this could enable one union—perhaps a minority union—to make a 'spoiler' application to frustrate the wishes of a dominant union. Where more than one union is represented at a workplace, it will be for the unions themselves to reach an agreement on how best to proceed. Unless they do reach an agreement, there will be a checkmate with regard to this particular group of workers. One option is for the two or more unions to reach an agreement for a joint application to be made. But in cases of intense rivalry or bitterness this may not be possible. Where both unions are affiliated to the TUC the other option is for the matter to be resolved under the TUC Disputes Principles and Procedures which are discussed also at pp 686–690 above. As well as seeking to prevent one union recruiting members from another (Principle 2), the principles are designed also to stop one union organising where another is already established (Principle 3).

[8.25] TUC Disputes Principles and Procedures (2000)

Principle 3

No union shall commence organising activities at any company or undertaking in respect of any group of workers, where another union has the majority of workers employed in membership and/or is recognised to negotiate terms and conditions, unless by arrangement with that union. Neither, in such circumstances, shall a union make approaches to an employer or respond to an employer initiative, which would have the effect of, directly or indirectly, undermining the position of the established union.

Where a union considers that another [TUC] affiliate has low levels of membership, and no agreement or a moribund agreement, within any organisation in respect of any group of workers, the union shall consult with the other affiliate, before commencing organising activities (or as soon as it is informed of the interests of another affiliate). If agreement cannot be reached, then either union should refer the matter to the TUC.

The TUC Principles are not legally enforceable (and are expressly stated not to be a contract). There is thus no legal obstacle to one union organising and recruiting in the territory of another. However, where one union claims that another has acted in breach of any of the TUC Disputes Principles, the matter may be referred to a TUC Disputes Committee for resolution. If the complaint is upheld, the respondent union may be censured, it may be required to make a compensatory settlement in favour of the complainant union, and/or it may be required to cease its organising activities. The *TUC Disputes Principles and Procedures* were revised in 2000 in order to deal with problems which may arise under the statutory procedures. One of the most important features of the initiative was the creation of a corps of officers nominated by each affiliated union in an attempt to identify and address problems as early as possible. A second feature of the revised arrangements was the commitment of the TUC to 'provide assistance' to unions applying to the CAC under the statutory procedure, in order 'to minimise any inter-union problems' and 'where appropriate' to 'facilitate joint applications'. Unions making an application to the CAC are expected to notify the TUC General Secretary at least two weeks in advance of doing so, so that the TUC may 'provide advice and assistance'. This may involve a suggestion that the union making the application to the CAC discusses the matter with another union.

8.4.2.3 The bargaining unit

Once it is established that an application has been properly made and that it is admissible, a number of opportunities are provided in the Act for the trade union and the employer to resolve the matter by agreement, and for ACAS to be involved at the request of the parties. Where this fails, the CAC will be required to consider two questions: the first concerns the bargaining unit and the second whether the union has majority support in the bargaining unit. So far as the bargaining unit is concerned, this is likely to be a cause of some difficulty in some cases, simply because bargaining units do not come tailor made. The union will propose a bargaining unit which will reflect the strength of its support, while the employer may seek a unit which will dilute the union's influence—though this could be counter-productive were the union to demonstrate majority support in the larger unit. Schedule A1 provides by paragraph 19B(2) that in determining the bargaining unit, the CAC must take into account:

(a) the need for the unit to be compatible with effective management; [and]
(b) the matters listed in sub-paragraph (3), so far as they do not conflict with that need.

So far as sub-paragraph (3) is concerned, this lists five matters for consideration, as follows:

(a)   the views of the employer and of the union (or unions);
(b)   existing national and local bargaining arrangements;
(c)   the desirability of avoiding small fragmented bargaining units within an undertaking;
(d)   the characteristics of workers falling within the proposed bargaining unit and of any other employees of the employer whom the CAC considers relevant;
(e)   the location of workers.

This gives the CAC a wide range of issues to consider, though two matters have tended to dominate. The first is that employers—as already suggested—have tried to weaken trade union strength by seeking to expand the categories of workers to be included in the proposed unit. In some cases employers may challenge a proposed bargaining unit of production workers on the ground that a 'whole company' unit of all employees may be more appropriate. The second relates to employers which may have more than one site or location, and the union may have strength in one or two but all sites or locations. In these cases the union may argue for a bargaining unit based on the sites or locations where it has support, whereas the employer may argue for a whole company multi-site unit, to include locations where the unit has no support. This was the issue in *R (Kwik-Fit)* v *CAC* [2002] ICR 1212 where the CAC accepted the union's proposed unit of all locations within the M25 London orbital road. This was successfully challenged in the High Court by the employer who argued that the unit should extend to the company at large. But the decision of Elias J was reversed by the Court of Appeal where Buxton LJ said that

> 5. Under paragraph 19(2) and (3) the CAC must decide "the appropriate bargaining unit" taking into account the matters specified, which as here relevant can be summarised as the need for the unit to be compatible with effective management; the views of the employer and of the union; the location of workers; and "'the desirability of avoiding small fragmented bargaining units within an undertaking".'

> 6. Simply reading these provisions through, it seems self-evident that the CAC's task is to start with the only proposal that it has before it, that contained in the Union's request, and to determine whether that proposal is 'appropriate.': it however being open to the CAC under paragraph 11(2)(a) determine that some other bargaining unit is appropriate.

> 7. It was complained on the part of the employer in this case that such a construction gives the union's proposal a preferable position, and upsets the industrial relations balance that ought otherwise to exist between proposals put forward by unions and proposals put forward by the employer. But, in my judgment, any such imbalance springs directly from the effect of the statutory provisions, which lay down clearly how the CAC must approach the question before it. That view is reinforced by the fact that, in the context of any particular request, the CAC of necessity can only recognize one bargaining unit. The word 'appropriate' was plainly used by the draftsman to direct the CAC's attention to whether, bearing in mind the practice set out in paragraph 19(3) and 19(4), the bargaining unit that it had wider consideration was suitable for the purpose for which it was to be used: that is, the conduct of collective bargaining in respect of a group of workers. Such a process does not exclude the consideration of bargaining units other than that proposed

by the union. They may enter the picture in two ways: as a means of testing whether the union's bargaining unit is indeed appropriate; and as an alternative bargaining unit to be inserted in the request should the union's bargaining unit be seen as inappropriate. But it should be remembered that the statutory test is set at the comparatively modest level of appropriateness, rather than of the optimum or best possible outcome. Since the CAC has only to find and can only find one bargaining unit, and has only to be satisfied that the unit that it does find is appropriate, I see no escape from the contention that, provided the CAC concludes that the union's unit is appropriate, its inquiry should stop there.

This approach would put trade unions firmly in the driving seat on bargaining unit disputes. It was strongly criticised by employers and was too permissive for the government which modified it in the Employment Relations Act 2004. The latter introduced a new paragraph 19B(4) which provides that 'in taking an employer's views into account for the purpose of deciding whether the proposed bargaining unit is appropriate, the CAC must take into account any view the employer has about any other bargaining unit that he considers would be appropriate'.

8.4.2.4 Automatic recognition and recognition ballots

Once the issue of the bargaining unit is resolved, the next main question under the procedure is the level of union support: it is only if a union has majority support that a declaration for recognition may be issued by the CAC. There are two ways by which this can be secured. The first is by the union satisfying the CAC that it has a majority of the bargaining unit in membership of the union. In that situation, the CAC must issue a declaration that the union is or unions are entitled to conduct collective bargaining on behalf of the workers constituting the bargaining unit (TULRCA 1992, Schedule A1, paragraph 22). But there are three exceptions to this, three qualifying conditions which, if satisfied, the CAC must require a ballot to be held, notwithstanding the fact that the union has majority membership (TULRCA 1992, Schedule A1, paragraph 22(4)). These are where:

- the CAC is satisfied that a ballot should be held in the interests of good industrial relations (paragraph 22(4)(a));
- the CAC has evidence, which it considers to be credible, from a significant number of the union members within the bargaining unit that they do not want the union (or unions) to conduct collective bargaining on their behalf (paragraph 22(4)(b);
- membership evidence is produced which leads the CAC to conclude that there are doubts whether a significant number of the union members within the bargaining unit want the union or unions to conduct collective bargaining on their behalf. This is designed to deal with the concern that trade unions will sign people up on cut-price deals, and the belief apparently held by some that workers join trade unions for cheap holidays, insurance and legal services rather than for the negotiation of the terms and conditions of their employment (paragraph 22(4)(c)).

These provisions were considered in *Fullarton Petitioner* [2001] IRLR 527 (OH) where speaking generally about para 22(4), Lord Johnston said that:

[34] . . . 'exceptions (b) and (c) could have a divisive effect if an employer was forced to go canvassing his workforce against the interests of the union, which would undoubtedly

antagonise the union management and might cause friction between them and its members. However . . . I am satisfied contrary to my initial reaction that exceptions (b) and (c) are workable if the employer simply generally encourages his employees by open letter, for example, to respond to the panel with their views as to collective bargaining or alternatively provide, even anonymously, evidence to the employer as to the extent of feeling about whether collective bargaining is a desirable aim of the membership. Accordingly in my opinion the employer is in a position in certain circumstances, speaking quite generally, to address the issues raised by (b) and (c), without canvassing individual workers on a personal basis, which would obviously be divisive in every respect of good industrial relations.

It is not, however, clear whether anonymous letters from workers would always constitute credible evidence for the purposes of paragraph 22(4)(b). Lord Johnston's comments were made in the context of paragraph 22(4)(b) as originally drafted. Before the 2004 amendments, this provided simply that the CAC could order a ballot—despite majority membership of the union—where a significant number of the union members in the bargaining unit inform the CAC that they do not want the union to conduct collective bargaining on their behalf. Apparently the CAC did not have to be satisfied that such evidence was credible before ordering the ballot.

[8.26] *Fullarton Petitioner* [2001] IRLR 527 (OH)

A bargaining unit consisted of hourly paid shop-floor workers, of whom 51.3% were members of the union (ISTC). The employer argued that a ballot should be held under para 24(4)(a) as being in the interests of good industrial relations in view of the slender nature of the union's majority. But although 'sensitive' to the employer's argument, it was rejected by the CAC which held that to require a ballot on that ground without further evidence that a ballot was in the interests of good industrial relations 'would impose, in effect, a threshold for recognition without a ballot higher than that stipulated by the legislators'. In judicial review proceedings, the Outer House of the Court of Session held that there were no grounds for challenging this decision, even if the court 'would have been inclined to take the view that a ballot has a stabilising influence and might well improve industrial relations rather than to cause them the deteriorate'. But the court refused to intervene, for to do so would be to substitute its views for that of the industrial jury (the CAC). That - said Lord Johnston - would be wholly inappropriate. So far as he was concerned: 'At the end of the day the decision with regard to the applicability of the exceptions lies in the discretion of the panel and it has not been demonstrated . . . that they exercised that discretion in any irrational or flawed way, even if there is room for more than one view'.

[8.27] *R (Gatwick Express) v Central Arbitration Committee* [2003] EWHC 2035 (Admin)

There were 38 workers in the bargaining unit of which 20 were union members. However, eight of these union members wrote to the company to say that they did not want the union to be recognised. The letters were in standard form, typed on company headed notepaper. Seven of the eight letters had been sent to the CAC by the company's Human Resources Department. The eighth letter, in identical terms, had apparently been sent direct to the CAC by the union member. The letters were addressed to the CAC. The CAC nevertheless held that none of the three conditions in paragraph 22(4), in particular as set out in 22(4)(b), was satisfied. According to the CAC 'there are difficulties in attesting to the validity of employee opinion when workers are required to indicate their views to their employer either by returning a pre-typed and named letter opposing recognition to the Senior Executive responsible for HR, or if they were in favour of recognition, being instructed not to return the letter'. As a result the CAC 'place[d] no evidential weight on the letters that were produced at the hearing'. The eighth letter received by the panel direct from the union member was held not to amount to a significant number so as to satisfy condition 22(4)(b). The decision was quashed by the High Court, with Judge Wilkie accepting the argument for the employer that the CACs reasoning improperly 'imported into paragraph 22(4)(b) a requirement that the CAC has to be informed direct by a worker pursuant to that paragraph and in writing'.

The second way by which a union may establish majority support is by a ballot. Under the procedure, a ballot is to be held where the CAC is not satisfied that a majority of workers in the bargaining unit are members of the union (TULRCA 1992, Schedule A1, paragraph 23), or where, as already explained, a majority of workers are members of the union but one or more of the aforementioned qualifying conditions is met (TULRCA 1992, Schedule A1, paragraph 22). Where a ballot is held the CAC must appoint a qualified independent person (QIP) to conduct the ballot (TULRCA 1992, Schedule A1, paragraph 25), the costs to be met equally by the union and the employer (TULRCA 1992, Schedule A1, paragraph 28). The ballot is to be held within 20 working days of the appointment of the QIP (which period the CAC has a discretion to extend) (TULRCA 1992, Schedule A1, paragraph 25). The ballot is to be held at the workplace, by post, or by a combination of these methods 'depending on the CAC's preference' (TULRCA 1992, Schedule A1, paragraph 25(4)). In determining how to exercise its preference, there are a number of considerations to be taken into account by the CAC, including 'costs and practicality'. A mixed ballot is to be held, however, only where there are 'special factors', including 'factors arising from the location of workers or the nature of their employment'. Where a workplace ballot is held, the CAC may require arrangements for some workers to vote by post if they are unable to vote at work (paragraph 25(6)(a)) The CAC must also inform the parties that a ballot is to be held, and the procedures to be followed (TULRCA 1992, Schedule A1, paragraph 25(9)). So far as the ballot result is concerned, there are two requirements which have to be met before the CAC may make a declaration that 'the union is (or unions are) recognised as entitled to conduct collective bargaining on behalf of the bargaining unit'. The first is that the union is or unions are supported by a majority of the workers voting, and the second is that the union is or unions are supported by at least 40 per cent of the workers constituting the bargaining unit (TULRCA 1992, Schedule A1, paragraph 29).

8.4.2.5 Recognition ballots and trade union access

If a trade union recognition application gets as far as the statutory procedure, this may indicate that it is strongly opposed by the employer. Employer opposition is a problem for trade unions given that the employer has access to the workforce from the moment they enter the premises until the time they leave. During that time the employer is free to explain to the workers why recognition of the union would not be a good idea. Although it may have support from the workforce, the union may have no comparable opportunities and indeed may be prevented by the employer from entering the premises. Yet if the union is to campaign successfully in a ballot, it needs to get its message to those workers who may be ignorant, indifferent or sceptical. It is not enough that the union should be free to communicate with workers only as they enter and leave the workplace, or that they can approach them at home after working hours. In a way unprecedented in other legal systems which have adopted similar legislation, the statutory recognition procedure now provides two opportunities for a trade union to communicate with the workforce in an enterprise where it is seeking recognition. The first of these in the sense of being earliest in the process of a statutory application was introduced by the 2004 Act and provides that a union may communicate with workers by post after an application has been accepted by the CAC. This is referred to as the 'initial period'. By virtue of Schedule A1, paragraph 19C, the union may ask the CAC to appoint an independent person 'to handle communications during the initial period between the union (or unions) and the relevant workers'.

- The relevant workers for this purpose are those within the proposed or the agreed bargaining unit.
- The employer must provide the CAC of the names and addresses of the workers in the bargaining unit, and the CAC must pass on the information to the appointed person.
- The appointed person must in turn send to the relevant workers any information supplied by the union for distribution, with the costs to be reimbursed wholly by the union.
- Where the employer fails to comply with any of these duties, the CAC may order him or her 'to take such steps to remedy the failure as the CAC considers reasonable'.
- The ultimate (and unlikely sanction) for continuing failure is that the CAC declares that the union is recognised.

The second opportunity the union has to approach the workforce directly is during the ballot period in cases where a ballot is necessary. Paragraph 26 (strengthened by the 2004 Act) imposes a number of duties on employers, of which the second is perhaps the most important for present purposes:

[8.28] Trade Union and Labour Relations (Consolidation) Act 1992, Schedule A1

26 (1) An employer who is informed by the CAC under paragraph 25(9) must comply with the following five duties.

(2) The first duty is to co-operate generally, in connection with the ballot, with the union (or unions) and the person appointed to conduct the ballot; and the second and third duties are not to prejudice the generality of this.

(3) The second duty is to give to the union(or unions) such access to the workers constituting the bargaining unit as is reasonable to enable the union (or unions) to inform the workers of the object of the ballot and to seek their support and their opinions on the issues involved.

(4) The third duty is to do the following (so far as it is reasonable to expect the employer to do so)—

(a) to give to the CAC, within the period of 10 working days starting with the day after that on which the employer is informed under paragraph 25(9), the names and home addresses of the workers constituting the bargaining unit;

(b) to give to the CAC, as soon as is reasonably practicable, the name and home address of any worker who joins the unit after the employer has complied with paragraph (a);

(c) to inform the CAC, as soon as is reasonably practicable, of any worker whose name has been given to the CAC under paragraph (a) or (b) but who ceases to be within the unit.

(4A) The fourth duty is to refrain from making any offer to any or all of the workers constituting the bargaining unit which—

(a) has or is likely to have the effect of inducing any or all of them not to attend any relevant meeting between the union (or unions) and the workers constituting the bargaining unit, and

(b) is not reasonable in the circumstances.

(4B) The fifth duty is to refrain from taking or threatening to take any action against a worker solely or mainly on the grounds that he-

(a) attended or took part in any relevant meeting between the union (or unions) and the workers constituting the bargaining unit, or

(b) indicated his intention to attend or take part in such a meeting.

(4C) A meeting is a relevant meeting in relation to a worker for the purposes of sub-paragraphs (4A) and (4B) if—

(a) it is organised in accordance with any agreement reached concerning the second duty or as a result of a step ordered to be taken under paragraph 27 to remedy a failure to comply with that duty, and

(b) it is one which the employer is, by such an agreement or order as is mentioned in paragraph (a), required to permit the worker to attend.

(4D) Without prejudice to the generality of the second duty imposed by this paragraph, an employer is to be taken to have failed to comply with that duty if-

(a) he refuses a request for a meeting between the union (or unions) and any or all of the workers constituting the bargaining unit to be held in the absence of the employer or any representative of his (other than one who has been invited to attend the meeting) and it is not reasonable in the circumstances for him to do so,

(b) he or a representative of his attends such a meeting without having been invited to do so,

(c) he seeks to record or otherwise be informed of the proceedings at any such meeting and it is not reasonable in the circumstances for him to do so, or

(d) he refuses to give an undertaking that he will not seek to record or otherwise be informed of the proceedings at any such meeting unless it is reasonable in the circumstances for him to do either of those things.

(4E) The fourth and fifth duties do not confer any rights on a worker; but that does not affect any other right which a worker may have.

(5) As soon as is reasonably practicable after the CAC receives any information under sub-paragraph (4) it must pass it on to the person appointed to conduct the ballot.

(6) If asked to do so by the union (or unions) the person appointed to conduct the ballot must send to any worker—
(a)   whose name and home address have been given under sub-paragraph (5), and
(b)   who is still within the unit (so far as the person so appointed is aware),

any information supplied by the union (or unions) to the person so appointed.

(7) The duty under sub-paragraph (6) does not apply unless the union bears (or unions bear) the cost of sending the information.

(8) Each of the powers specified in sub-paragraph (9) shall be taken to include power to issue Codes of Practice—
(a)   about reasonable access for the purposes of sub-paragraph (3), and
(b)   about the fourth duty imposed by this paragraph.

(9) The powers are—
(a)   the power of ACAS under section 199(1);
(b)   the power of the Secretary of State under section 203(1)(a)."

A Code of Practice has in fact been issued as anticipated by TULRCA 1992, Schedule A1, paragraph 26(8), and at the time of writing is in the process of being revised to take account of the amendments to the procedure introduced by the Employment Relations Act 2004. The Code deals with a number of issues, and encourages the parties to reach an access agreement to enable the union to communicate with the workforce to be balloted. But it also sets out what are in effect minimum conditions in terms of access, and seeks to give the union the opportunity (i) to conduct meetings with the workforce collectively during the balloting period, (ii) to communicate with the workforce by posters and other means (including electronic), and (iii) where appropriate, to hold surgeries at the workplace which workers would be entitled to attend for up to 15 minutes during working time. Failure on the part of the employer to comply with any of the foregoing duties is to be dealt with in accordance with paragraph 27.

[8.29] Trade Union and Labour Relations (Consolidation) Act 1992, Schedule A1

27 (1) If the CAC is satisfied that the employer has failed to fulfil any of the five duties imposed on him, and the ballot has not been held, the CAC may order the employer—
(a)   to take such steps to remedy the failure as the CAC considers reasonable and specifies in the order, and
(b)   to do so within such period as the CAC considers reasonable and specifies in the order.

(2) If the CAC is satisfied that the employer has failed to comply with an order under sub-paragraph (1), and the ballot has not been held, the CAC may issue a declaration that the union is (or unions are) recognised as entitled to conduct collective bargaining on behalf of the bargaining unit.

(3) If the CAC issues a declaration under sub-paragraph (2) it shall take steps to cancel the holding of the ballot; and if the ballot is held it shall have no effect.

There is no case in which CAC has yet been willing to impose this final sanction of ordering recognition without a ballot: nor is it clear what kind of collective bargaining would emerge should the power be used, given the likelihood of strong employer hostility, and the possibility of only a minority of workers in support of recognition.

[8.30] Department of Trade and Industry, *Draft Code of Practice: Access to Workers During Recognition and Derecognition Ballots* **(2005)**

Where will the access take place?

27 Where practicable in the circumstances, a union should be granted access to the workers at their actual workplace. However, each case will depend largely on the type of workplace concerned, and the union will need to take account of the wide variety of circumstances and operational requirements that are likely to be involved. In particular, consideration will need to be given to the employer's responsibility for health and safety and security issues. In other words, access arrangements should reflect local circumstances and each case should be examined on the facts.

28 Where they are suitable for the purpose, the employer's typical methods of communicating with his workforce should be used as a benchmark for determining how the union should communicate with members of the same workforce during the access period. If the employer follows the custom and practice of holding large workforce meetings in, for example, a meeting room or a canteen, then the employer should make the same facilities available to the union. However, in cases where the workplace is more confined, and it is therefore the employer's custom and practice to hold only small meetings at the workplace, then the union will also be limited to holding similar small meetings at that workplace. In exceptional circumstances, due to the nature of the business or severe space limitations, access may need to be restricted to meetings away from the workplace premises, and the union will need to consider finding facilities off-site at its own expense unless it agrees otherwise with the employer. In these circumstances, the employer should give all reasonable assistance to the union in notifying the workers in advance of where and when such off-site events are to take place. Where such exceptional circumstances exist, it would normally be expected that the employer would not hold similar events at the workplace.

When will the access take place?

29 The union should ensure that disruption to the business is minimised, especially for small businesses which might find it more difficult to organise cover for absent workers. The union's access to the workers should usually take place during normal working hours but at times which minimise any possible disruption to the activities of the employer. This will ensure that the union is able to communicate with as large a number of the workers as possible. Again, the arrangements should reflect the circumstances of each individual case. Consideration should be given to holding events, particularly those involving a large proportion of the workers in the bargaining unit, during rest periods or towards the end of a shift. In deciding the timing of meetings and other events, the union and the employer should be guided by the employer's custom and practice when communicating with his workforce. If, due to exceptional circumstances, access must be arranged away from the workplace, it might be practicable to arrange events in work time if they are held nearby, within easy walking distance. Otherwise, off-site events should normally occur outside work time.

The frequency and duration of union activities

30 The parties will need to establish agreed limits on the duration and frequency of the union's activities during the access period. Subject to the circumstances discussed in paragraphs 27–29 above, the employer should allow the union to hold one meeting of at least 30 minutes in duration for every 10 days of the access period, or part thereof, which all workers or a substantial proportion of them are given the opportunity to attend. In circumstances where the employer or others organise similar large-scale meetings in work time against the recognition application (or in favour of derecognition), then it would be reasonable for the union to hold additional meetings, if necessary, to ensure that in total it has the same number of large-scale meetings as the employer and his supporters.

31 Where they would be appropriate having regard to all the circumstances, union 'surgeries' could be organised at the workplace during working hours at which each worker would have the opportunity, if they wish, to meet a union representative for fifteen minutes on an individual basis or in small groups of two or three. The circumstances would include whether there was a demand from the workforce for surgeries, whether the surgeries could be arranged off-site as effectively, whether the holding of surgeries would lead to an unacceptable increase in tension at the workplace and whether the employer, line managers or others use similar one-to-one or small meetings to put across the employer's case. The union should organise surgeries in a systematic way, ensuring that workers attend meetings at pre-determined times, thereby avoiding delays before workers are seen and ensuring that they promptly return to their work stations afterwards. Wherever practicable, the union should seek to arrange surgeries during periods of down-time such as rest or meal breaks. Where surgeries do not take place, the minimum time allowed for each larger scale meeting should be 45 minutes.

32 An employer should ensure that workers who attend a meeting or a 'surgery' organised by the union with his agreement during work time, should be paid, in full, for the duration of their absence from work. The employer will not be expected to pay the worker if the meeting or surgery takes place when the worker would not otherwise have been at work, and would not have been receiving payment from the employer.

33 Where the union wishes one of the employer's workers . . .to conduct a surgery, the employer should normally give time off with pay to the worker concerned. The worker should ensure that he provides the employer with as much notice as possible, giving details about the timing and location of the surgery. Exceptionally, it may be reasonable for the employer to refuse time off. This will apply if unavoidable situations arise where there is no adequate cover for the worker's absence from the workplace and the production process, or the provision of a service cannot otherwise be maintained. Before refusing permission, the employer should discuss the matter with the union and the worker to explore alternative arrangements.

[The foregoing provisions are the same as those in the original Code of Practice published in 2000.]

8.4.2.6 *Employer resistance and worker protection*

The experience of other countries—and trade union experience in this country under the statutory procedure—suggests that employers will not always provide a smooth path for trade unions trying to negotiate statutory recognition arrangements. There are in fact three difficulties which trade unions face: the first is the problem of access to the workforce, a problem which is addressed to some extent by the Code of Practice already discussed. The second is the problem of discrimination and dismissal of workers who are campaigning to bring the union to the workplace. It is not unknown for employers to dismiss key activists, not only to eliminate the driving force behind the demand for organisation within the workplace, but also to persuade others by intimidation that a trade union presence brings risks as well as rewards to the employment security of the individuals in question. It might be thought that TULRCA 1992, sections 146 and 152 would offer protection in this situation. In *Carrington v Therm-a-Stor Ltd* [1983] ICR 208 (CA), however, it was held that the protection against dismissal for trade union membership and activities does not apply where the employee is dismissed (in that case for redundancy) in direct response to a trade union request for recognition

Although *Carrington*-type dismissals are thus not automatically unfair, two qualifications must be made. One: there will inevitably be circumstances where organising, recruiting and campaigning would be covered by the protection. Two: even though the dismissal is not automatically unfair, it may nevertheless be unfair under the general principles of unfair dismissal law for those employees who have sufficient service (now 12 months). Nevertheless, *Carrington* exposed a remarkable omission in the protection for trade union members in the workplace. So far as the statutory procedure is concerned, the Schedule directly addresses the risk of discriminatory treatment.

[8.31] Trade Union and Labour Relations (Consolidation) Act 1992, Schedule A1

Detriment

156 (1) A worker has a right not to be subjected to any detriment by any act, or any deliberate failure to act, by his employer if the act or failure takes place on any of the grounds set out in sub-paragraph (2).

(2) The grounds are that—
   (a)   the worker acted with a view to obtaining or preventing recognition of a union (or unions) by the employer under this Schedule;
   (b)   the worker indicated that he supported or did not support recognition of a union (or unions) by the employer under this Schedule;
   (c)   the worker acted with a view to securing or preventing the ending under this Schedule of bargaining arrangements;
   (d)   the worker indicated that he supported or did not support the ending under this Schedule of bargaining arrangements;
   (e)   the worker influenced or sought to influence the way in which votes were to be cast by other workers in a ballot arranged under this Schedule;
   (f)   the worker influenced or sought to influence other workers to vote or to abstain from voting in such a ballot;
   (g)   the worker voted in such a ballot;
   (h)   the worker proposed to do, failed to do, or proposed to decline to do, any of the things referred to in paragraphs (a) to (g).

(3) A ground does not fall within sub-paragraph (2) if it constitutes an unreasonable act or omission by the worker.

(4) This paragraph does not apply if the worker is an employee and the detriment amounts to dismissal within the meaning of the Employment Rights Act 1996.

(5) A worker may present a complaint to an employment tribunal on the ground that he has been subjected to a detriment in contravention of this paragraph.

(6) Apart from the remedy by way of complaint as mentioned in sub-paragraph (5), a worker has no remedy for infringement of the right conferred on him by this paragraph.

Dismissal

161 (1) For the purposes of Part X of the Employment Rights Act 1996 (unfair dismissal) the dismissal of an employee shall be regarded as unfair if the dismissal was made—
(a) for a reason set out in sub-paragraph (2), or
(b) for reasons the main one of which is one of those set out in sub-paragraph (2).

(2) The reasons are that—
(a) the employee acted with a view to obtaining or preventing recognition of a union (or unions) by the employer under this Schedule;
(b) the employee indicated that he supported or did not support recognition of a union (or unions) by the employer under this Schedule;
(c) the employee acted with a view to securing or preventing the ending under this Schedule of bargaining arrangements;
(d) the employee indicated that he supported or did not support the ending under this Schedule of bargaining arrangements;
(e) the employee influenced or sought to influence the way in which votes were to be cast by other workers in a ballot arranged under this Schedule;
(f) the employee influenced or sought to influence other workers to vote or to abstain from voting in such a ballot;
(g) the employee voted in such a ballot;
(h) the employee proposed to do, failed to do, or proposed to decline to do, any of the things referred to in paragraphs (a) to (g).

(3) A reason does not fall within sub-paragraph (2) if it constitutes an unreasonable act or omission by the employee.

Selection for redundancy

162. For the purposes of Part X of the Employment Rights Act 1996 (unfair dismissal) the dismissal of an employee shall be regarded as unfair if the reason or principal reason for the dismissal was that he was redundant but it is shown—
(a) that the circumstances constituting the redundancy applied equally to one or more other employees in the same undertaking who held positions similar to that held by him and who have not been dismissed by the employer, and
(b) that the reason (or, if more than one, the principal reason) why he was selected for dismissal was one falling within paragraph 161(2).

It will be noted that the protection against 'detriment' applies to 'workers', but that the protection against dismissal applies only to 'employees', though it appears by implication from paragraph 156(4) that a dismissed 'worker' could bring a claim under the 'detriment' provisions. It will be noted also that by virtue of the Employment Relations Act 1999, section 6, interim relief (above, p 736) is available for a dismissal in breach of TULRCA 1992, Schedule A1, paragraph 161 above.

8.4.2.7 *Employer resistance and employer campaigning*

It was suggested above that there are three potential problems to be faced by a trade union in a recognition campaign. The third is negative and hostile campaigning by the employer which has many more opportunities to convey its message to the workers than does the union. But it is not the access to a captive audience which is the problem so much as what may be said or done. The workers may be presented with threats that the business will close if the union is successful, or that key services or operations will be outsourced, or that there will be redundancies. It might be claimed by the employer that working conditions will deteriorate if he or she is required to bargain with a union; that some benefits currently provided will be withdrawn and not reinstated; or that workers will inevitably be drawn into strike or other industrial action by the union, at considerable cost to the workers involved. Conversely, the employer may introduce a pay rise just as the union has made a claim for recognition, or introduce a consultative committee for the discussion of issues affecting the workforce.

After intense lobbying by the TUC, an amendment was introduced to the statutory procedure in 2004 dealing with unfair practices. The provision is symmetrical in the sense that it applies to unfair practices by both the employer and the trade union, though in practice it is the conduct of the former that has given rise to concern. It is to be noted, however, that the scope of the measure is otherwise quite limited, both in terms of its timing and its scope of application. So far as **timing** is concerned, the provisions apply only during the ballot period, though it is possible that the new TULRCA 1992, s 145B (see pp 750–751 above) may provide some protection at an earlier stage in a recognition campaign. The Secretary of State may by order extend the period of application of the unfair practice provisions (TULRCA 1992, Schedule A1, paragraph 166B). This is important, because it is in the early stages of an organising campaign that the union will also need support to nurture a fledgling organisation at the workplace. It may be possible in these early stages of the campaign for some protection to be drawn from TULRCA 1992, section 146.

[8. 32] *Brassington v Cauldon Wholesale Ltd* **[1978] ICR 405 (EAT)**

> Workers were told by their employer that 'if the company was required to recognise the union for negotiating or other purposes he intended to close the business, dismiss the workforce and restart it under a different corporate incarnation'. The employees complained that this threat amounted to action short of dismissal contrary to what was then Employment Protection Act 1975, section 53. The complaint was upheld by the industrial tribunal, though the employees appealed against the finding relating to compensation.

So far as the **scope or content** of unfair practices are concerned, the law applies only to active aggression, such as bribes, threats or the use of undue influence. It does not apply to other more passive aggression, such as the setting up of staff associations as an anti-union strategy. Thus, paragraph 27A provides as follows:

(1) Each of the parties informed by the CAC under paragraph 25(9) must refrain from using any unfair practice.

(2) A party uses an unfair practice if, with a view to influencing the result of the ballot, the party—

(a) offers to pay money or give money's worth to a worker entitled to vote in the ballot in return for the worker's agreement to vote in a particular way or to abstain from voting,

(b) makes an outcome-specific offer to a worker entitled to vote in the ballot,

(c) coerces or attempts to coerce a worker entitled to vote in the ballot to disclose—

    (i)   whether he intends to vote or to abstain from voting in the ballot, or

    (ii) how he intends to vote, or how he has voted, in the ballot,

(d) dismisses or threatens to dismiss a worker,

(e) takes or threatens to take disciplinary action against a worker,

(f) subjects or threatens to subject a worker to any other detriment, or

(g) uses or attempts to use undue influence on a worker entitled to vote in the ballot.

(3) For the purposes of sub-paragraph (2)(b) an "outcome-specific offer" is an offer to pay money or give money's worth which—

(a) is conditional on the issuing by the CAC of a declaration that-

    (i)   the union is (or unions are) recognised as entitled to conduct collective bargaining on behalf of the bargaining unit, or

    (ii) the union is (or unions are) not entitled to be so recognised, and

(b) is not conditional on anything which is done or occurs as a result of the declaration in question.

(4) The duty imposed by this paragraph does not confer any rights on a worker; but that does not affect any other right which a worker may have.

A complaint may be made to the CAC by a trade union or an employer about an unfair practice alleged to have been committed by the other.

The applicant must show not only that the respondent used an unfair practice, but also that the unfair practice did or was likely to affect the result. Where these hurdles have been crossed, the CAC may then make orders of a kind which are now familiar: a declaration that the complaint is well founded, followed by an order that the respondent takes specified action. The CAC may also order a ballot. Where the CAC finds that the unfair practice used consisted of or included (a) the use of violence, or (b) the dismissal of a union official it is empowered to make a declaration that the union is recognised without any further formality. It is thus an important feature of this procedure that it effectively creates rights which vest in the union and which may be enforced only by the union. So threats or inducements directed to the worker will violate the right not of the worker but of the union. The worker may of course also have other rights under other statutory provisions which the same action of the employer will have violated. Apart from those already referred to above, the employer's conduct may also violate the worker or the employee's right under paragraphs 156 and 161 of the Schedule. Further details of what constitutes an unfair practice is to be found in the Access Code.

[8.33] Department of Trade and Industry, *Draft Code of Practice: Access to Workers During Recognition and Derecognition Ballots* **(2005)**

53   The statute refers to the term "money's worth" when defining an unfair offer to a worker. The term covers the making of non-cash offers to workers. Such non-cash offers usually involve the provision of goods and services, for which workers would otherwise need to pay if they procured the goods or services for themselves. Most fringe benefits - say, a better company car, subsidised health insurance or free legal services - would normally fall into this category. In addition, offers to provide additional paid holiday or other paid leave are likely to constitute "money's worth".

54   Unfair practices can involve the taking of disciplinary action against workers, where such disciplinary action has the purpose of influencing the result of the ballot. The period of ballots is relatively short and this lessens the scope for disciplinary matters to arise. However, it is worth noting that this unfair practice is not limited just to disciplinary action taken against workers entitled to vote in a ballot. It is possible that an unfair practice could be committed if, say, disciplinary action were taken against a union activist involved in the union's campaign who was not entitled to vote in the ballot. Equally, the employer is not prevented from taking any disciplinary action just because a ballot is occurring. There may be sound grounds for the employer to discipline a worker, which are totally unconnected with the ballot. Likewise, it is possible that a worker's campaigning activity—say, the use of threatening behaviour against other workers or the unauthorised use of work time for campaigning—may itself give rise to disciplinary action which would not constitute an unfair practice. When contemplating disciplinary action, the employer should in addition take note of the guidance provided in the *ACAS Code of Practice on Disciplinary and Grievance Procedures*, especially its advice on the disciplining of union officials.

55   The statutory list of unfair practices highlights actions to bribe, pressurise or exert other undue influence on workers to vote in particular ways or not to vote at all. Such conduct, especially the exertion of undue influence, can take many forms. At one extreme, undue influence may take the obvious form of actual or threatened physical violence against workers. It may also take other, and more subtle, forms of behaviour to influence the outcome of the ballot. For example, the introduction of higher pay or better conditions in the ballot period may constitute undue influence if the ballot period is not the normal time for reviewing pay or if there is not some other pressing reason unconnected with the ballot for raising pay. This Section of the Code provides guidance on those standards of behaviour which are likely to prevent undue influence or other unfair practices from occurring. Conversely, it also refers to behaviour which, if pursued, may constitute undue influence. However, given the range of possible behaviours involved, it is unrealistic for the Code to identify every circumstance which might give rise to undue influence. In any event, as Section F discusses, it is the task of the Central Arbitration Committee to judge whether an unfair practice has been committed, basing its judgment on the particular facts of a case.

8.4.2.8 The Collective Bargaining Method

An important issue for consideration for an application which gets this far relates to the potential problems which may arise if the employer refuses to comply with a CAC declaration that the union is entitled to conduct collective bargaining. Here the Act departs significantly from the approach adopted in the Employment Protection Act 1975, section 16. Under that procedure the union could complain to the CAC, which could in effect unilaterally vary the terms and conditions of employment of the workers in the bargaining unit. Under the current procedure, the parties have 30 days (from the date on which they are notified of the CAC's declaration) to agree 'a method by which they will conduct collective bargaining' (TULRCA 1992, Schedule A1, paragraph 30(1)). If no agreement is reached, either or both of the parties may apply to the CAC for assistance, in which case the CAC 'must try to help the parties to reach in the agreement period [of 20 working days from the date the CAC receives the application] an agreement on a method by which they will conduct collective bargaining' (TULRCA 1992, Schedule A1, paragraph 31(2)). If at the end of this agreement period the parties are unable to conclude an agreement, 'the CAC must specify to the parties the method by which they are to conduct collective bargaining' (TULRCA 1992, Schedule A1, paragraph 31(3)). The Trade Union Recognition (Method of Collective Bargaining) Order 2000, SI 2000/1300, sets out the method which will be adopted or imposed for this purpose.

[8.34] B Simpson, 'Trade Union Recognition and the Law, A New Approach—Parts I and II of Schedule A1 to the Trade Union and Labour Relations (Consolidation) Act 1992' (2000) 29 *Industrial Law Journal* 193 (footnotes omitted)

The 'Method' specified by the Secretary of State under paragraph 168 is a form of procedure agreement for the parties to establish a Joint Negotiating Body (JNB) comprising equal numbers of employer and union representatives (who may be full time officers or lay representatives). The JNB must deal with union proposals on pay, hours and holidays on at least an annual basis or in accordance with an agreed 'different bargaining period' (para 14). While the employer is enjoined not to vary the pay, hours or holiday of workers in the BU unless it has first discussed the proposed changes with the union in accordance with the method (para 17), that does not require the union's agreement to any change before it is made. In any event, this obligation to hold prior discussions with the union is expressly excluded in relation to workers who have agreed to direct individual negotiations with the employer. A detailed outline of the six steps in this bargaining round for proposals, counter-proposals and JNB meetings is set out. This notably circumscribes the obligation on the employer to provide information by reference to the limits on disclosure of information to recognised unions under the procedure in [TULRCA 1992,] sections 181–185. Both these provisions on information and those on facilities and time off add little, if anything, to the statutory rights which all recognised independent unions and their lay officials have under that procedure and [TULRCA 1992,] sections 168–173 respectively. What is clear from the method specified by the Secretary of State is that the legal obligation imposed on employers by a CAC declaration of recognition is an obligation to meet and talk, within a prescribed framework, about pay, hours and holidays, to observe the statutory rights of recognised unions, their officials and members, and little—if anything—else.

[Note: Paragraph references in the foregoing extract are to the specified Method set out in the Schedule to the Trade Union Recognition (Method of Collective Bargaining) Order 2000]

Of great significance in terms of being a departure from the established way of doing things, TULRCA 1992, Schedule A1, paragraph 31(4) provides that a collective bargaining method specified by the CAC under paragraph 31(3) is 'to have effect as if it were contained in a legally enforceable contract made by the parties'. The parties may, however, agree in writing that paragraph 31(4) is not to apply—in which case that agreement is also legally binding: a legally binding agreement that an otherwise legally binding method is not to be treated as a legally binding contract. The parties may also agree to vary or replace the method imposed by the CAC, in which case this too is to be treated as a legally binding contract: the drafting does not make clear whether the parties may agree that this is not to be treated as legally binding, though it would make no sense if they could not. The only remedy specified in the Act for failure to comply with a collective bargaining method imposed by the CAC is specific performance, which would have to be pursued not before the CAC but in the ordinary courts in the normal way. The Act also deals with the situation where one party fails to comply with an agreed method of carrying out collective bargaining. In that case 'the parties' (but it seems not one party alone) may apply to the CAC for assistance (TULRCA 1992, Schedule A1, paragraph 32). There are in fact few cases where the CAC has imposed a bargaining method on parties, with most bargaining orders leading to the conclusion of voluntary procedural agreements.

8.4.2.9 The question of delay

One of the main difficulties likely to arise with a statutory trade union recognition procedure is the delay which is caused in the period between the making of the application by the union and the final resolution of the application. A particular source of difficulty arises where an employer contests the application, which may lead to a long delay before the ballot is conducted. This could in turn lead to a seeping away of interest on the part of the workers in the proposed bargaining unit, in which there may have been a considerable turnover of staff in the meantime. This is a particular problem in the United States where experience has taught two lessons: one is the need for clear timetables in the procedure; the other is the need for speed in the holding of the ballot (W B Gould, *Agenda for Reform: The Future of Employment Relationships and the Law* (Cambridge, Mass., MIT Press, 1993), pp 158–62). These problems are addressed in some Canadian jurisdictions where disputes about the bargaining unit are heard after the ballot is held. In these circumstances, 'the effect of an ex post facto challenge is likely to reduce the potential for employer conduct designed to frustrate the election process' (K D Ewing (ed), *Need to be Heard at Work?* (London, Institute of Employment Rights, 1998), paragraph 7.9).

It is clear that this North American lesson has been learned by British policymakers, with a very clear timetable set out in the legislation. This is not to deny that there is nevertheless considerable scope for delay by an employer who wishes to obstruct the procedure. It is conceivable that a single application could give rise to multiple hearings before the CAC (with further delay caused by adjournments) and by judicial review proceedings. These could be on points of procedure as well as substance. However, an attempt has been made to ensure that an applications are not frustrated by delaying tactics on the part of the employer. The key steps in the statutory timetable are as follows (the paragraph references are to TULRCA 1992, Schedule A1):

- Trade union makes its request for recognition to the employer (paragraph 4)
- The parties (trade union and employer) may agree within 10 days (the first period) that the union is to be recognised, or to negotiate about the matter (paragraph 10). The parties have 20 days (the second period) from the end of the first period to reach an agreement (paragraph 10).
- If after the end of the first period the employer fails to respond or if the employer refuses the trade union's request, the matter may be referred to the CAC to decide (a) whether the proposed bargaining unit is appropriate, and (b) whether the union has sufficient support (paragraph 11).
- If the parties have tried to negotiate an agreement and no agreement is concluded by the end of the second period referred to above, here again the matter may be referred to the CAC to decide (a) the bargaining unit, and (b) whether the union has sufficient support (paragraph 12).
- On receiving an application, the CAC must decide whether it is valid and admissible within an acceptance period of 10 days. It must consider evidence supplied by the employer and the union (paragraphs 14 and 15). There is no express provision for an oral hearing.
- If the application is not withdrawn, the CAC must try to help the parties reach an agreement on the bargaining unit. It has 20 days to do so (or longer if it so specifies) from the date it gives notice of acceptance of the application (the appropriate period) (paragraph 18).
- As a result of amendments introduced by the Employment Relations Act 2004, the CAC may give notice to bring this 20 day period for agreeing the bargaining unit to a premature end if it 'concludes that there is no reasonable prospect of the parties' agreeing an appropriate bargaining unit' (para 18(3))
- As a result of amendments introduced by the Employment Relations Act 2004, the employer must send information about the bargaining unit to both the CAC and the union within 5 days of the application being accepted. The information should specify:
  (a) a list of the categories of worker in the proposed bargaining unit,
  (b) a list of the workplaces at which the workers in the proposed bargaining unit work, and
  (c) the number of workers the employer reasonably believes to be in each category at each workplace (para 18A).
- If the CAC is unable to broker an agreement about the bargaining unit during the appropriate period, it must decide whether the proposed bargaining unit is appropriate within 10 days from the end of the appropriate period, or such longer period as it may specify. If the proposed unit is not appropriate, the CAC must specify a unit which is appropriate (paragraph 19).
- If the matter proceeds beyond this point to determine whether the trade union has majority membership in the bargaining unit, there is no time limit on the CAC to decide whether a union should be automatically recognised or whether a ballot is to be held. If the union is requesting automatic recognition, there is no express provision for an oral hearing to be held before the CAC orders a ballot, should it decide to do so on any of the prescribed grounds in paragraph 22.
- If a ballot is to be held the CAC must give the parties 10 days' notice (the notification period) (which may be extended by the CAC) that the ballot is to be held

(paragraph 24). The ballot must be held within a period of 20 days (or a longer period specified by the CAC) of the appointment of the qualified independent person who is to conduct the ballot (paragraph 25). The parties must be informed of the result 'as soon as reasonably practicable' afterwards (paragraph 29).

- If the CAC issues a declaration the union is recognised, the parties have a negotiation period of 30 days (or longer with their agreement) to reach an agreement on a method by which they will conduct collective bargaining (paragraph 30). The negotiation period begins the day after the parties are notified of the declaration. The parties may call upon the CAC for assistance.
- If the parties are unable to conclude an agreement, a collective bargaining method may be imposed by the CAC. There are no time limits at this stage. But if an application is made by the union to the CAC, the proceedings may be postponed (for up to 20 days or longer by agreement) on a joint request by the parties at any time before a specified method has been imposed, to enable the parties to continue to search for an agreement (paragraph 31).

8.4.2.10 Changes in the bargaining unit and derecognition

Collective bargaining arrangements are not static. The composition of a bargaining unit may change for a number of reasons (such as those given in *Fairness at Work*, above, p 44: business restructuring, take-over, divestment, or merger of unions), and there may come a time when an employer feels that the union no longer commands the support of a majority of the workers in a bargaining unit. Provision is made for both of these eventualities in the statutory procedure. So far as the former is concerned, either party may apply to the CAC if it believes an existing unit is no longer appropriate (TULRCA 1992, Schedule A1, paragraph 66): an application will be admissible only if the CAC decides that the original unit is no longer appropriate by reason of any of the following:

(a) a change in the organisation or structure of the business carried on by the employer;

(b) a change in the activities pursued by the employer in the course of the business carried on by him;

(c) a substantial change in the number of workers employed in the original unit.

(TULRCA 1992, Schedule A1, paragraph 67).

If the CAC decides that a bargaining unit is no longer appropriate, it is empowered to decide which unit is appropriate. Having so decided, the CAC must then decide whether 'the difference between the original unit and the new unit is such that the support of the union (or unions) within the new unit needs to be assessed' (TULRCA 1992, Schedule A1, paragraph 85). If support does not need to be assessed, the CAC must issue a declaration that the union or unions is entitled to conduct collective bargaining on behalf of the new unit. If on the other hand the CAC concludes that support needs to be assessed, a ballot will have to be held.

  Turning from changing the bargaining unit to derecognition, the procedures were trailed in *Fairness at Work*, above, which stated that:

There will be a broadly similar procedure for resolving disputes where an employer seeks to derecognise a union because he believes the majority of the bargaining unit no longer supports recognition (at p 43).

These procedures are set out in Parts IV to VI of Schedule A1, and broadly speaking are essentially a mirror image of the recognition procedures. There are two key points. The first is where the number of workers employed by the employer and associated employers falls below an average of 21 in any period of 13 weeks, the employer can ask the CAC to have the union de-recognised (TULRCA 1992, Schedule A1, paragraphs 99–103). In other cases the employer may request the union to end the arrangements (TULRCA 1992, Schedule A1, paragraph 104), following which an application may be made to the CAC (TULRCA 1992, Schedule A1, paragraph 107). In order to be admissible, the CAC must decide that at least 10 per cent of the workers in the bargaining unit favour an end to the bargaining arrangements, and that a majority would be likely to favour an end to these arrangements (TULRCA 1992, Schedule A1, paragraph 110). A worker or a group of workers in a bargaining unit may also make a request to have the union de-recognised (though in this case directly to the CAC); the same admissibility criteria must be met (TULRCA 1992, Schedule A1, paragraphs 112–114). A de-recognition ballot may then be held in which at least a majority of those voting and at least 40 per cent of the workers in the bargaining unit must vote in favour of ending the collective bargaining arrangements. If they do, the CAC must issue a declaration that the bargaining arrangements are to cease (TULRCA 1992, Schedule A1, paragraph 121). A union will have a right of access to the workforce, and the Access Code will apply. Once a union has established recognition under the statutory procedure, it will thus be extremely difficult in practice for the employer to de-recognise. An employer faced with a recognition claim from a union with strong support would thus be extremely foolish not to enter into a voluntary agreement.

8.4.2.11 Operation of the statutory procedure

Given the history of trade union recognition legislation in Britain and the experience of such legislation elsewhere, there were three initial concerns with the statutory procedure introduced in 1999. These were as follows:

- To what extent would it stimulate voluntary agreements in the 'shadow of the law'? Would employers faced with demonstrated union strength strike voluntary agreements or would the statutory route become the norm?

[8.35] P Davies and M Freedland, 'The Employment Relationship in British Labour Law', in C Barnard, S Deakin and G Morris (eds), *The Future of Labour Law* (Hart Publishing, Oxford, 2004)

Despite their initial concerns about its pusillanimity, even the left wing critics of the trade union recognition legislation of the Employment Relations Act 1999 might admit that it has had more than expected success in encouraging a resurgent pattern of voluntary trade union recognition, and has halted, if not reversed the previously relentless-seeming trend of de-unionisation of the late 1980s and early 1990s

It appears to be the case that the success of the statutory procedure has been in stimulating voluntary recognition agreements.

[8.36] S Wood, S Moore and K D Ewing, 'The Impact of the Trade Union Recognition Procedure', in H Gospel and S Wood (eds), *Representing Workers* (Routledge, 2003), p 142

In terms of the government's aim that the statutory procedure should encourage voluntary resolution of disputes and be used only as a last resort, the experience of the first two years suggests that there has been some success. From the outset, the unions, coordinated by the TUC, have been concerned to ensure that the CAC procedure was not discredited or made unworkable in its first years. Its ability to act as a device that influenced voluntary discussions clearly depends on its being perceived to be working. Ensuring that the voluntary route is pursued in the first instance is a vital part of this, the implication being that the unions will not submit CAC applications as a first move in a recognition campaign prior to their having secured a base of membership. Our survey of unions revealed that unions indeed only intended to use the procedure when they gauge that the employer is unwilling to discuss a voluntary agreement and are confident that they have sufficient support to win a ballot. They were thus not over-relying upon building up membership or support once they were in the CAC process. This approach is reflected in both the low number of cases that have gone to the CAC and their proportion relative to voluntary recognition agreements.

In fact in the first two years of its operation, the direct impact of the scheme was quite limited, with only 10,567 workers covered by recognition orders made in that period. It is estimated that the proportion of workers covered by CAC orders from November 2000 to October 2001 accounted for only 7.1% of all workers covered by all voluntary recognition agreements and statutory orders in this period. But not everyone is so sanguine about the 'resurgent' impact of the legislation

[8.37] J Hendy QC, *The Future of Employment Law* (Institute of Employment Rights, 2004) (footnotes omitted)

In the three years of operation many recognition deals were agreed voluntarily without reference to the CAC (Central Arbitration Committee which handles statutory recognition claims) and some (much fewer) were imposed by the CAC. No doubt the voluntary recognition agreements were often made under the stimulus of the statutory procedure. But what is remarkable is how few recognition deals—voluntary or imposed—there were. In the years running up to the start of the statutory procedure there were on average about 85 new recognition deals a year. In the years since then there have been, in 2001: 450 deals plus 20 through the CAC; in 2002: 282 deals plus 24 through the CAC; in 2003: 137 deals plus 29 through the CAC. It is to be noted that the number of deals is small and falling but on the other hand the number of workers covered by each deal is, on average, rising. So each deal covered an average of only 195 workers in 2002; and an average of 471 in each deal in 2003. But what is really striking is the stark reality of these figures which show that only some 78,000 more workers gained recognition in 2003. It may sound a lot but, given that some 9 million workers have lost that benefit over the last 30 years, at this rate *it will take over 100 years to get back to where we were and getting on for 150 years to get back to the European average.*

• To what extent would employers resist trade union recruitment and organisation, what tactics would they employ for this purpose, and how far would the tactics of opposition be carried into the procedure itself?

On this issue concerns were expressed about the fact that there was little regulation of hostile conduct by employers (short of dismissal or discriminatory conduct directed at specific individuals). The failure rate of 33% in ballots was thought to reflect employer pressure. It was also thought to be especially significant given that the cases in question had been through the rigorous admissibility criteria in which the union had to demonstrate significant levels of support in order to have an application accepted (S Wood, S Moore and K Ewing **[8.36]**, above, p 142). Some of the tactics adopted by employers are described in the following extract.

[8.38] K D Ewing, S Moore and S Wood, *Unfair Labour Practices: Trade Union Recognition and Employer Resistance* (Institute of Employment Rights, 2003), pp 10–11 (references omitted)

As we examine how some employers make full use of the freedom which the law allows to frustrate workplace organisation, it should be emphasised that most of the strategies adopted are perfectly lawful. Only rarely will an employer stray beyond the boundaries of legality by discriminating against trade unionists because of their trade union activities. But the fact that employers are at liberty to behave in the ways that we shall describe reveals that there is a failure in some cases to meet the government's aim expressed in *Fairness at Work* that employers should not deny trade union recognition where it has the clear and demonstrated support of employees. The strategies adopted and the tactics used by employers reveal more than a vigorous attempt by employers in some cases to test the strength of worker commitment to the principle of collective bargaining. For what we find is that the law does not simply allow the employer to determine whether there is real support for the union, but also allows the employer to frustrate that free choice being exercised or free will being determined. Choice can be denied by the lawful tactic of setting up a company union or by the equally lawful tactic of the employer selecting the union. Free-will can be influenced and perhaps even undermined by saturation campaigns at a time when the union may have difficulty in getting its message to the workforce. Such campaigning can be very persuasive, and it may be accompanied by various inducements and intimidation which, although lawful, may not be consistent with the spirit of the code of practice.

Our work has revealed that 'there is variation in the extent to which employers are willing to go to prevent unionisation' but that there are four strategies adopted by hostile employers. These strategies mirror those used by some employers in Canada and the United States where a similar recognition or 'certification' regime operates. These strategies are what might be referred to as

- **Pre-emption**, where the employer seeks to pre-empt the organising activities of a trade union in one of a number of ways, such as providing other channels for worker representation, or selecting the union to represent the workers so it is in effect imposed upon them.
- **Persuasion, Coercion and Frustration**, where the employer responds to the emerging or actual presence of a union with a range of measures designed to frustrate its organising activities or recognition claim. This may involve different forms of active campaigning against the union in the workplace.
- **Shaping and Using the Legal Process**, where the employer exploits the opportunities in the legislation arising from the discretion vested in the statutory agency. This includes helping to shape the bargaining unit, or by persuading the CAC to hold a ballot if the case gets that far.
- **Legalism and Litigation**, whereby the employer sometimes with legal advice will identify and seek to exploit legal technicalities, and will use to the full the various opportunities to litigate and contest an application, both before the CAC and in judicial review proceedings.

These different strategies sometimes overlap, and several strategies may be used by the same employer. The first two strategies may begin long before an application has been made under the procedure but may continue once the application has been made. The latter two occur mainly when an application is in the system and is being contested by the employer.

Some of these concerns are addressed by the reforms introduced by the Employment Relations Act 2004. These include the restrictions on the employer's right to make financial inducements to give up union representation, the right of the union to communicate with workers before the balloting period begins, and the unfair practice provisions. But as we have seen, these changes —especially the new unfair practice provisions—fall short of what is required, both in terms of when they apply and the conduct to which they apply.

- To what extent would the courts be drawn into the operation of the procedure by judicial review, particularly in light of the contemporaneous introduction of the Human Rights Act in 2000?

This was a particularly thorny issue in light of the experience of ACAS with the statutory procedure in the 1970s. Since then we have seen the growth and development of modern administrative law, giving rise to concerns that the courts might be even more intrusive than in the past. But in fact judicial review has not yet been a problem for the CAC in the same way that it was for ACAS under the previous recognition procedure in the Employment Relations Act 1975. At the time of writing, there have been five judicial review applications in relation to CAC decisions. But although the CAC has been overturned in two of these (*BBC* **[8.24]** above, and *Gatwick Express* **[8.27]** above, it has been successful on the crucial issues affecting its jurisdiction (*Fullarton* **[8.26]**, above and *Kwik-Fit*, above, p 772). The modern judicial approach is captured by the following passage from the judgment of Moses J in *R (BBC) v CAC* **[8.24]**, above:

13.   It is clear, therefore, that the proceedings are intended to be informal, non-legalistic and conducive to good industrial relations rather than litigation. To that extent it is in marked contrast to the recognition procedure under the former Employment Protection Act 1975, in which applications became hopelessly bogged down with legal challenges. The process under Schedule A1 is designed to encourage a speedy momentum rather than delays. The intervals between each of the successive stages are specified and they are short. The CAC must decide whether to accept an application within ten working days from receipt (see paragraph 15(6)(a)). There is a discretion to extend time… reasons must be given for such an extension. Paragraphs 18 and 19 provide a period of 20 working days during which the parties have an opportunity to reach agreement in relation to the appropriate bargaining unit, after which the CAC has but 10 working days to decide an appropriate bargaining unit should there not be agreement. It is inherent within the procedure that the parties should attempt to reach agreement and only as a last resort refer to the CAC for a decision. This is quite inconsistent with a legalistic approach.

14.   These considerations reinforce the reluctance of any court to intervene and the rare occasions when it would be appropriate to do so. It is for the expert body, the panel of the CAC, to identify whether a group of individuals concerned are undertaking to work or normally working or seeking to work in the exercise of a profession, as a matter of fact, and in the context of the statutory scheme and its purpose.

15.   If authority is required in support of that proposition it can readily be found at paragraph 23 in the judgment of Elias J in *Kwik-Fit*, as endorsed by Buxton LJ at paragraph 2 of his decision in the Court of Appeal, in which he said: "I would also venture to endorse in strong terms what was said by the judge in paragraph 23 of his judgment, that the CAC was intended by Parliament to be a decision making body in a specialist area that is not suitable for the intervention of the courts. Judicial review, such as is sought in the present case, is therefore only available if the CAC has either acted irrationally or made an error of law.

It might thus be possible and appropriate for the CAC to adopt a less cautious and defensive approach in some of the cases it deals with.

8.4.2.12   *Representational versus Regulatory Bargaining Models*

As a way of promoting collective bargaining the enterprise-based model to be found in the Employment Relations Act 1999 is nevertheless not as efficient as other models, such as those found in mainland Europe where collective bargaining density is much higher than in North America. The European social model (to the extent that it is wise to generalise) is based on the principle of sectoral bargaining between trade unions and employers' associations, accompanied in some cases (though in different ways) by procedures for the extension of collective agreements to employers who are not members of the federation which concluded the agreement. So while collective bargaining coverage in the original 15 EC countries is not lower than 55 per cent with the exception of the UK, in North America it is not higher than 45 per cent and in the USA it is as low as 11 per cent. This may suggest that institutional design and the form of state support plays a large part in determining density. There is little prospect nevertheless of collective bargaining practices in Britain changing to reflect the European norm (which was once the practice here too), though there appears to be growing support among trade unions for a return to more sectoral based collective bargaining activity. The British legislation, however, is based on a diluted version of collective bargaining as a representative rather than a regulatory activity.

[8.39] K D Ewing, 'The Function of Trade Unions' (2005) 34 *Industrial Law Journal* 1 (footnotes omitted])

Although an important vehicle for the extension of collective bargaining, the whole thrust of the recognition legislation is nevertheless consistent with a representation rather than a regulatory model of trade unionism. That is to say, it is consistent with the idea of trade unions as representatives rather than regulators:

- It is based on the principle of consent, in the sense that workers must choose or elect to be represented by the trade union in pay negotiations. The need for consent to representation explains the high levels of support required in order to secure recognition under the procedure.
- It is based on the principle of *genuine* consent which means that membership of a trade union is not enough to justify the presumption that the member has joined in order to be represented rather than enjoy, say, the service benefits of membership. Hence the various devices in the legislation to enable employee consent to be tested and affirmed.
- It is based on the principle of *revocable* consent which means that it is open to a worker and an employer to enter into individual bargaining arrangements, with the worker entitled to dispense with collective representation. This applies even where a majority agree and continue to agree to trade union representation.
- It is based on the principle of *territorial* consent, which means consent within defined bargaining units. These may be quite small, confined to certain geographical parts of the enterprise, and confined to certain grades or skills within the enterprise.

A regulatory rather than a representational model of collective bargaining would require a rather different legal approach, based more on sectoral than enterprise based bargaining. As is the practice elsewhere in Europe this would mean collective agreements having sector wide application rather than being confined to the particular employers who concluded them.

8.5 Rights of recognised trade unions

The Conservative governments from 1979 to 1997 dismantled much of the collective bargaining infrastructure which they inherited from their predecessors. A few provisions nevertheless survived. These are the right of trade union members and (lay) officials to time off work for trade union duties and activities respectively (in the former case with pay), and the right of recognised trade unions to the disclosure of information. The time off provisions are underpinned by international labour law (ILO Convention 135 (The Workers' Representatives Convention, 1971)), though it is unlikely that this would have been a major impediment to their removal. Rights to time off—particularly paid time off for trade union officials—were nevertheless cut

Trade Union Recognition and Contract Compliance

There is a case for underpinning the statutory procedures by means of what are some-times referred to as contract compliance devices. Under these arrangements, a contractor can make it a condition of a contract that the other party respect the right of his or her workers to be trade union members or to recognise a trade union. Under the Fair Wages Resolution of 1946 government contractors were required as a condition of their contract to pay fair wages to their staff and to respect their rights of trade union membership (though this did not extend to include a duty to recognise a union). The Fair Wages Resolution was revoked in 1983 and a number of other similar initiatives have been discouraged or prohibited. Once actively used in this country, contract com-pliance provisions to promote trade union rights (and good employment practices generally) are closely regulated. TULRCA 1992, sections 186 and 187 provide respec-tively that a recognition requirement in a contract for goods or services is void, and that it is unlawful to refuse to deal with a supplier of goods and services because the supplier in question does not recognise a trade union or negotiate with a trade union. Similar provisions exist in relation to terms which require work to be done only by people who are or are not trade union members, and in relation to the refusal to deal with a supplier because the work is likely to be done by someone who is or is not a trade union member (TULRCA, sections 144, 145). These provisions are reinforced by local government law which prohibits local authorities form imposing a range of non commercial consider-ations in contracts with suppliers.

Although trade union recognition requirements may not be included in commercial contracts, steps are now being taken which may require employers indirectly to observe the terms of collective agreements to which they are not parties. The issue arises in the context of privatisation and outsourcing where the problem has arisen of the two tier workforce. When staff are transferred from the public to the private sector in these cir-cumstances, their terms and conditions of employment will be protected by the Transfer of Undertakings (Protection of Employment) Regulations 1981 (on which see chapter 10 below). But these regulations do not apply to new staff recruited by the contractor (or indeed to its own existing staff before the transfer) with the result that new recruits (and its own existing staff) may be paid less than the transferred staff, threatening the terms and conditions of the latter. As a result of trade union pressure the government has taken a number of steps designed to end this development. These are described as follows:

> 'The first public authority to enact a Fair Wages policy was the Greater London Authority (GLA). In 2002 the GLA introduced a fair employment clause into its contracting procedures. Private contractors working for the Greater London Authority (GLA) are now asked if they are willing to pay their staff at least the equivalent of public sector wages. The GLA has so far applied this policy to contracts for the cleaning and catering services for City Hall and new services in Trafalgar Square.

> In December 2002 the Scottish Executive signed a protocol with the STUC ensuring that in all future public private partnerships (PPPs), contract workers will receive 'fair pay' and rights over pensions, holiday and sick pay commensurate with colleagues in the public sector. The protocol has already convinced a number of Scottish councils to alter plans on staff transfers to the private sector. Councils reported increasing union involvement in discussions following the protocol.

> In February 2003 the Office of the Deputy Prime Minister introduced changes governing contracting out in all Best Value authorities including local government and police authorities. The Code of Practice on Workforce Matters in Local Authority Service Contracts obliges contractors to offer new staff 'fair and reasonable terms and conditions' which are 'no less favourable' than those of transferred employees. The Code guarantees new joiners reasonable pension provision—either membership in the Local Government Pension Scheme, a good quality employer pension scheme, or a stakeholder pension scheme with a minimum 6% employer contribution. . . .
>
> A similar Best Value Code covering local authorities and national park authorities in Wales came into force in April 2003. UNISON was part of a Joint Working Party, whose report on extending the Best Value Code to other parts of the public sector is now with the Wales Assembly Government'.
>
> > (UNISON, *Fair Wages How to End the Two Tier Workforce in Public Services and Achieve Fair Wages* (2004))
>
> UNISON is promoting fair wages legislation that would compel public sector employers 'to provide their staff—both new and transferred—with pay and conditions at least as good as those received by directly employed staff doing equivalent work'. This would help to promote the regulatory effect of collective agreements.

back in 1989 and the ACAS *Code of Practice on Time Off* was redrafted accordingly. On the other hand, new rights to time off were introduced for non-trade union-based workplace representatives, as we shall discuss in section 8.6. Additonal rights to time off—for union learning representatives—were introduced in 2002. Although the disclosure of information provisions have been largely ineffective since being introduced in their present form in 1975, it is difficult to understand why they were allowed to survive, though the Major government proposed their repeal in 1996. A general election defeat stood in the way of implementation.

8.5.1 The meaning of recognition

As we discussed in the immediately preceding section, there are two ways by which a trade union may be recognised by an employer. The first is by a voluntary agreement with the employer, and the second is by the statutory procedure. The rights and benefits to be discussed in this section apply only when the union is recognised by the employer and for this purpose recognition may have been secured by either route. Yet it may not always be clear that the union has achieved recognition, even though there may be an embryonic relationship in the making. This is likely to be an issue particularly where the union claims that it has been recognised voluntarily by the employer, but where there is no formal recognition agreement. The question whether the union is recognised or not is unlikely to arise where there is a certificate issued under the statutory procedure. And it is unlikely to arise where there is a formal agreement for voluntary recognition, unless of course the employer claims that the agreement has been terminated (unilaterally or otherwise). Recognition is defined by statute.

[8.40] Trade Union and Labour Relations (Consolidation) Act 1992, section 178

Collective agreement and collective bargaining

178(1) In this Act 'collective agreement' means any agreement or arrangement made by or on behalf of one or more trade unions and one or more employers or employers' associations and relating to one or more of the matters specified below; and 'collective bargaining' means negotiations relating to or connect with one or more of those matters.

(2) The matters referred to above are—
(a) terms and conditions of employment, or the physical conditions in which any workers are required to work;
(b) engagement or non-engagement, or termination or suspension of employment or the duties of employment, of one or more workers;
(c) allocation of work or the duties of employment between workers or groups of workers;
(d) matters of discipline;
(e) a worker's membership or non-membership of a trade union;
(f) facilities for officials of trade unions; and
(g) machinery for negotiation or consultation, and other procedures, relating to any of the above matters, including the recognition by employers or employers' associations of the right of a trade union to represent workers in such negotiation or consultation or in the carrying out of such procedures.

(3) In this Act 'recognition', in relation to a trade union, means the recognition of the union by an employer, or two or more associated employers, to any extent, for the purpose of collective bargaining; and 'recognised' and other related expressions shall be construed accordingly.

The leading cases on the meaning of recognition for this purpose are drawn from the late 1970s.

[8.41] *NUGSAT v Albury Brothers Ltd* [1979] ICR 84 (CA)

This case was concerned with whether the employer was under a duty to consult with the trade union before redundancies were implemented. The employer was a member of the British Jewellers' Association which was in turn a member of the British Wholesale Jewellers' Association that negotiated terms and conditions throughout the industry. Unknown to the employer, the union had recruited eight of its 55 employees on 5 May 1976. On 7 May the district secretary of the union wrote to the employer asking for a meeting to discuss wages at the company, alleging that they were not observing the rates set down in the national agreement between the union and the employers' federation.]

Lord Denning MR:
Coming back to the letter of May 7, 1976, Mr Shakeshaft, the district secretary, asked for a meeting to discuss the rates of pay. He did not disclose that any of the men had joined the union. Mr Albury had not had any dealings with the union before. He took the letter, and asked to see this district secretary about it. He went on May 10. The trade union secretary was busy. Mr Albury said to Mr Shakeshaft: 'What is this?'—he had the letter in his hand. The union representative said, 'I'm busy; I can't see you now.' On May 10 Mr Albury wrote to the union saying:

'We are in receipt of your letter of May 7 and further to my visit to your office today I have reviewed the trainees' rates of pay and as far as I am now aware they conform with the wages agreement of the Goldsmiths and Jewellery Trade Section (North Area) British Jewellers' Association. If at any time you would like to come and see me I shall be pleased to have a talk with you especially about trainees and perhaps you would ring my secretary, Mrs Good, to arrange a suitable appointment.'

They did arrange an appointment. They did have a meeting on May 20. They did discuss one of the young men, a man of 20, and his wages. They considered whether or not his wages came within the general scale: but they did not come to any agreement. There was a difference of opinion about it, and that was all. Before anything more transpired, the redundancy notices were given.

On that history, the question arose whether on that discussion and on those few talks and letters the employers had recognised the union for the purpose of collective bargaining. That is the one point in this case. If they had recognised them, they ought to have gone through all the statutory procedure for handling redundancies. If they had not recognised them, then they were under no such obligation.

This is a new point under a new Act. Both the industrial tribunal and the Employment Appeal Tribunal have held that there was no recognition. Only three cases have come before the appeal tribunal on it. The first one was at the end of 1976 before the Scottish tribunal—*Transport and General Workers' Union v Dyer* [1977] IRLR 93. The next one was *Joshua Wilson & Bros Ltd v Union of Shop, Distributive and Allied Workers* [1978] ICR 614. Finally *National Union of Tailors and Garment Workers v Charles Ingram & Co Ltd* [1977] ICR 530. Reading through those cases, there is general agreement and consensus of opinion in these respects: a recognition issue is a most important matter for industry; and therefore an employer is not to be held to have recognised a trade union unless the evidence is clear. Sometimes there is an actual agreement of recognition. Sometimes there is an implied agreement of recognition. But at all events there must be something sufficiently clear and distinct by conduct or otherwise so that one can say, 'They have mutually recognised one another, the trade union and the employers, for the purposes of collective bargaining'.

Then one comes to this particular case. Were those few letters and the one meeting recognition of the trade union? It is agreed by Mr Sedley [for the union] that if the employers had simply banged the door and told the union representative to go off, that would not be recognition. Is it recognition when Mr Albury goes along with the letter in his hand and is ready to discuss the wages? It seems to me that that is not sufficient. Nor is it sufficient if he starts discussing the wages of one particular man, Stephen Rickard. There must be something a great deal more than that.

The industrial tribunal (I think it was the first case they had—there was no other reported case at that time) put it quite clearly. They said:

'[This union] relies on the fact that early in May it recruited eight members of a workforce of 55 at the respondent company which hitherto had not employed union labour. Following that, there was, after correspondence, a meeting . . . at which specific reference was made to the rate of pay of one of the new recruits'—and then this is what was argued—'That, says the [union] presumably must amount to a de facto recognition by the respondent company of [this union]. We do not consider that is so'.

The appeal tribunal said likewise [1978] ICR 62, 69:

'. . . . we do not think that it can be said that the employers had recognised the union. A beginning had been made, the approach established, and if matters had continued as they had begun it might well have been that eventually a state of recognition would have been achieved; but in all the circumstances it seems to me that matters were still in the preliminary stages, and that the employers had not recognised the union by the material date'.

It seems to me that those decisions were completely correct. There was no error in point of law at all. This is not a case in which this court can or should interfere. As I said at the beginning, an act of recognition is such an important matter involving such serious consequences on both sides, both for the employers and the union, that it should not be held to be established unless the evidence is clear upon it, either by agreement or actual conduct clearly showing recognition. The conduct in this case does not come clearly up to that. I would therefore dismiss the appeal.

It was therefore held that because the union was not recognised, it had no statutory right to be consulted under the statutory procedure introduced by the Employment Protection Act 1975, section 99 (on which see below, p 823).

8.5.2 Time off for trade union duties and activities

Trade unions are first and foremost organisations of lay activists. At company or enterprise level elected lay activists (such as shop stewards) will perform an important representative function: they may be involved directly (often with the support of or supporting a full-time official of the union) in the negotiation of collective agreements, they will almost certainly be involved in the day-to-day administration of the agreement, and they will represent members who have a grievance against the employer or who may be the subject of disciplinary action by the employer. They may have other responsibilities as well, and indeed a new army of trade union officials—union learning representatives—has arrived in recent years, with responsibility to attend to the learning and skills needs of trade union members in the workplace. Much of this activity has to be done during working time and for this purpose these various lay officers of the union (who are also full-time employees of the company) will need time off work if they are to be able to perform the different duties which may be expected of them. They may also need to be trained in the performance of these duties, and may need other facilities at the workplace, such as an office, a telephone and access to notice boards and email. In many companies these needs will be met by a facilities agreement (perhaps part of the recognition agreement) whereby the company and the union agree to the facilities which the company will provide the workplace representatives of the union.

8.5.2.1 Trade union duties

An important feature of facilities agreements will be the arrangements for time off work to enable lay officials to carry out their duties. In some cases the employee in question may be paid full time to undertake union activities at the workplace. These agreements are concluded against a background of minimum standards set down in legislation, at least in so far as they relate to time off. The legislation relating to time off for trade union duties applies only to the officials of recognised trade unions, as defined above. First introduced by the Employment Protection Act 1975, the law was amended by the Employment Act 1989 to narrow the circumstances in which employers are required to permit time off *with pay*.

[8.42] Trade Union and Labour Relations (Consolidation) Act 1992, section 168

Time off for carrying out trade union duties

168 (1) An employer shall permit an employee of his who is an official of an independent trade union recognised by the employer to take time off during his working hours for the purpose of carrying out any duties of his, as such an official, concerned with—

(a) negotiations with the employer related to or connected with matters falling within section 178(2) (collective bargaining) in relation to which the trade union is recognised by the employer, or

(b) the performance on behalf of employees of the employer of functions related to or connected with matters falling within that provision which the employer has agreed may be so performed by the trade union, or

(c) receipt of information from the employer and consultation by the employer under section 188 (redundancies) or under the Transfer of Undertakings (Protection of Employment) Regulations 1981

(2) He shall also permit such an employee to take time off during his working hours for the purpose of undergoing training in aspects of industrial relations—

(a) relevant to the carrying out of such duties as are mentioned in subsection (1), and

(b) approved by the Trades Union Congress or by the independent trade union of which he is an official.

(3) The amount of time off which an employee is to be permitted to take under this section and the purposes for which, the occasions on which and any conditions subject to which time off may be so taken are those that are reasonable in all the circumstances having regard to any relevant provisions of a Code of Practice issued by ACAS.

(4) An employee may present a complaint to an employment tribunal that his employer has failed to permit him to take time off as required by this section.

The scope and content of these provisions are governed by the *ACAS Code of Practice on Time Off for Trade Union Duties and Activities*, introduced in 1977 and revised most recently in 2003. This provides details of the type of activity for which time off with pay might normally be expected to be provided as industrial relations duties (and which as a result might properly be reflected in a facilities agreement).

[8.43] *ACAS Code of Practice on Time Off for Trade Union Duties and Activities* (2003)

Examples of trade union duties

11. Subject to the recognition or other agreement, trade union officials should be allowed to take reasonable time off for duties concerned with negotiations or, where their employer has agreed, for duties concerned with other functions related to or connected with:

(a) terms and conditions of employment, or the physical conditions in which workers are required to work. Examples could include:
   - pay
   - hours of work
   - holidays and holiday pay
   - sick pay arrangements
   - pensions
   - learning and training needs
   - equal opportunities
   - notice periods
   - the working environment
   - operation of digital equipment and other machinery;

(b) engagement or non-engagement, or termination or suspension of employment or the duties of employment, of one or more workers. Examples could include:
   - recruitment and selection policies
   - human resource planning
   - redundancy and dismissal arrangements;

(c) allocation of work or the duties of employment as between workers or groups of workers. Examples could include:
   - job grading
   - job evaluation
   - job descriptions
   - flexible working practices
   - family friendly policies;

(d) matters of discipline. Examples could include:
   - disciplinary procedures
   - arrangements for representing trade union members at internal interviews
   - arrangements for appearing on behalf of trade union members, or as witnesses, before agreed outside appeal bodies or employment tribunals;

(e) trade union membership or non-membership. Examples could include:
   - representational arrangements
   - any union involvement in the induction of new workers;

(f) facilities for officials of trade unions. Examples could include any agreed arrangements for the provision of:
   - accommodation
   - equipment
   - names of new workers to the union;

(g) machinery for negotiation or consultation and other procedures. Examples could include arrangements for:
   - collective bargaining
   - grievance procedures
   - joint consultation
   - communicating with members
   - communicating with other union officials also concerned with collective bargaining with the employer.

12. The duties of an official of a recognised trade union must be connected with or related to negotiations or the performance of functions both in time and subject matter. Reasonable time off may be sought, for example, to:
   - prepare for negotiations
   - inform members of progress
   - explain outcomes to members

- prepare for meetings with the employer about matters for which the trade union has only representational rights.

An important case relating to the scope of the right to time off for industrial relations duties is the following.

[8.44] *London Ambulance Service v Charlton* [1992] ICR 773 (EAT)

The applicants were members of NUPE who had applied unsuccessfully for paid time off work for trade union duties, under what was then the Employment Protection (Consolidation) Act 1978, section 27 (now TULRCA 1992, s 168). They had applied for paid time off to attend the meetings of a union joint co-ordinating committee which had been established to monitor negotiations within each division of the negotiating machinery, to develop a common industrial relations approach to the employer, and to examine proposals from and submit proposals to the employer. The employer was willing only to permit unpaid time off. The industrial tribunal upheld the employees' claim that the activity fell within the amended statutory purposes for which paid time off should be permitted, a decision upheld by the EAT following an appeal by the employer. The EAT agreed that 'preparatory or co-ordinating meetings' were covered by EPCA 1978, section 27 as being connected with collective bargaining where they are called 'for the genuine purpose of officials discussing their approach to forthcoming negotiations or their consideration as a co-ordinating body of negotiations which have or will take place in other bodies'.

In addition to time off with pay for industrial relations duties, the 1992 Act, s 168 also makes provision for time off with pay for training in these duties. This is a matter which is also addressed by the *ACAS Code of Practice*.

[8.45] *ACAS Code of Practice on Time Off for Trade Union Duties and Activities* (2003)

19. Training should be in aspects of employment relations relevant to the duties of an official. There is no one recommended syllabus for training as an official's duties will vary according to:
- the collective bargaining arrangements at the place of work, particularly the scope of the recognition or other agreement
- the structure of the union
- the role of the official.

20. The training must also be approved by the Trades Union Congress or by the independent trade union of which the employee is an official.

21. Trade union officials are more likely to carry out their duties effectively if they possess skills and knowledge relevant to their duties. In particular, employers should be prepared to consider releasing trade union officials for initial training in basic representational skills as soon as possible after their election or appointment, bearing in mind that suitable courses may be infrequent. Reasonable time off could also be considered, for example:
- for further training particularly where the official has special responsibilities
- for training courses to develop the official's skills in representation and negotiation

- where there are proposals to change the structure and topics of negotiation about matters for which the union is recognised; or where significant changes in the organisation of work are being contemplated
- where legislative change may affect the conduct of employment relations at the place of work and may require the reconsideration of existing agreements.

8.5.2.2 *Union Learning Representatives*

The foregoing provisions relating to time off have been in place in one form or another since 1975. As already pointed out, an important addition to their ranks is the right to time off (also *with pay*) introduced for union learning representatives in 2002, as an amendment to TULRCA 1992. Union learning representatives play a part in identifying and developing the learning and skills needs of trade union members. The needs may vary greatly—from reading and writing, to letter writing, to foreign language training, to computer and IT skills. Many employers welcome this input from trade unions, as they too will benefit from a better skilled and more thoughtful workforce. Nevertheless, the right of union learning representatives to time off work applies only where the union is recognised, the government having baulked at the prospect of 'giv[ing] unions representational entitlements where their membership and organisational basis is under-developed'. It is also to be noted that the rights of union learning representatives apply only in relation to union members: there is no right to time off to attend to the needs of non-members.

[8.46] Trade Union and Labour Relations (Consolidation) Act 1992, section 168A

Time off for union learning representatives

168A (1) An employer shall permit an employee of his who is—
(a)   a member of an independent trade union recognised by the employer, and
(b)   a learning representative of the trade union,
to take time off during his working hours for any of the following purposes.

(2) The purposes are—
(a)   carrying on any of the following activities in relation to qualifying members of the trade union—
(i)   analysing learning or training needs,
(ii)   providing information and advice about learning or training matters,
(iii) arranging learning or training, and
(iv) promoting the value of learning or training,
(b)   consulting the employer about carrying on any such activities in relation to such members of the trade union,
(c)   preparing for any of the things mentioned in paragraphs (a) and (b).

(3) Subsection (1) only applies if—
(a)   the trade union has given the employer notice in writing that the employee is a learning representative of the trade union, and
(b)   the training condition is met in relation to him.

(4) The training condition is met if—

(a) the employee has undergone sufficient training to enable him to carry on the activities mentioned in subsection (2), and the trade union has given the employer notice in writing of that fact,

(b) the trade union has in the last six months given the employer notice in writing that the employee will be undergoing such training, or

(c) within six months of the trade union giving the employer notice in writing that the employee will be undergoing such training, the employee has done so, and the trade union has given the employer notice of that fact. . . .

(8) The amount of time off which an employee is to be permitted to take under this section and the purposes for which, the occasions on which and any conditions subject to which time off may be so taken are those that are reasonable in all the circumstances having regard to any relevant provision of a Code of Practice issued by ACAS or the Secretary of State.

Employees who are permitted to take time off under s 168A(1) are also permitted to take time off with pay for training as a learning representative. Little guidance is provided in the Code of Practice about the duties of union learning representatives, though it is recognised that their role and responsibilities will vary by union and by workplace (paragraph 13). There is, however, detailed provision made for the training needs of such representatives.

[8.47] *ACAS Code of Practice on Time Off for Trade Union Duties and Activities* **(2003)**

22. Employees who are members of an independent trade union recognised by the employer are entitled to reasonable paid time off to undertake the functions of a Union Learning Representative. To qualify for paid time off the member must be sufficiently trained to carry out duties as a learning representative:

• either at the time when their trade union gives notice to their employer in writing that they are a learning representative of the trade union

• or within six months of that date

23. In the latter case, the trade union is required to give the employer notice in writing that the employee will be undergoing such training and when the employee has done so to give the employer notice of that fact. It should be confirmed by the union in a letter that the training undertaken is sufficient to allow the Learning Representative to undertake their role and it is good practice for the union to give details of the training which has been completed and any previous training that has been taken into account. In the interests of good practice, the six month qualifying period during which an untrained Union Learning Representative must receive sufficient training to continue operating as a learning representative may be extended, with agreement, to take into account any significant unforeseen circumstances such as prolonged absence due to ill health, pregnancy or bereavement.

24. To satisfy this training requirement an employee will need to be able to demonstrate to their trade union that they have received sufficient training to enable them to operate competently in one or more of the following areas of activity relevant to their duties as a Union Learning Representative:

analysing learning or training needs;
- this could for example include understanding the different methods for identifying learning interests or needs, being able to effectively identify and record individual learning needs or being able to draw up a plan to meet identified learning requirements.

providing information and advice about learning or training matters;
- including, for example, the development of communication or interviewing skills
- knowledge of available opportunities, in order to be able to provide accurate information to members about learning opportunities within and outside the workplace.
- the ability to "signpost" members to other sources of advice and guidance where additional support is needed, for example, basic skills tutors or fuller depth professional career guidance.

arranging and supporting learning and training;
- for example, obtaining and providing information on learning opportunities, supporting and encouraging members to access learning opportunities and helping to develop and improve local learning opportunities.

promoting the value of learning and training;
- some examples of this activity could be, understanding the current initiatives for the development of learning and skills in the workplace, promoting the value of learning to members and within trade union networks and structures and working with employers to meet the learning and skill needs of both individuals and the organization.

25. An employee could demonstrate to their trade union that they have received sufficient training to enable them to operate competently in one or more of these areas of activity by:
- completing a training course approved by the Trades Union Congress or by the independent trade union of which the employee is a Union Learning Representative, or by
- showing that they have previously gained the relevant expertise and experience to operate effectively as a learning representative.

In the latter case previous experience and expertise gained in areas such as teaching, training, counselling, providing careers advice and guidance or human resources development, may well be relevant, as may periods of extensive on-the-job training and experience gained in shadowing an experienced Union Learning Representative.

26. Reasonable time off should also be considered for further training to help Union Learning Representatives develop their skills and competencies.

27. Although not required by law it is recognised that there would be clear advantages both to the individual and the organization if training undertaken leads to a recognised qualification standard.

8.5.2.3 Trade union activities

Time off is provided by statute not only for trade union members with trade union duties, or for union learning representatives: there is also provision for time off (*without pay*) for employees to take part in trade union activities, at the workplace or elsewhere. This provision—which has also been in force since 1975 in one form or another—is an important reflection of the nature of trade unions as organisations of lay activists who need time off work to take part in the policy-making and other activities of their union.

[8.48] Trade Union and Labour Relations (Consolidation) Act 1992, section 170

Time off for trade union activities

170(1) An employer shall permit an employee of his who is a member of an independent trade union recognised by the employer in respect of that description of employee to take time off during his working hours for the purpose of taking part in—
(a) any activities of the union, and
(b) any activities in relation to which the employee is acting as a representative of the union.

(2) The right conferred by subsection (1) does not extend to activities which themselves consist of industrial action, whether or not in contemplation or furtherance of a trade dispute.

(2A) The right conferred by subsection (1) does not extend to time off for the purpose of acting as, or having access to services provided by, a learning representative of a trade union.

(2B) An employer shall permit an employee of his who is a member of an independent trade union recognised by the employer in respect of that description of employee to take time off during his working hours for the purpose of having access to services provided by a person in his capacity as a learning representative of the trade union.

(2C) Subsection (2B) only applies if the learning representative would be entitled to time off under subsection (1) of section 168A for the purpose of carrying on in relation to the employee activities of the kind mentioned in subsection (2) of that section.

(3) The amount of time off which an employee is to be permitted to take under this section and the purposes for which, the occasions on which and any conditions subject to which time off may be so taken are those that are reasonable in all the circumstances having regard to any relevant provisions of a Code of Practice issued by ACAS.

(4) An employee may present a complaint to an employment tribunal that his employer has failed to permit him to take time off as required by this section.

(5) For the purposes of this section—

(a) a person is a learning representative of a trade union if he is appointed or elected as such in accordance with its rules, and
(b) a person who is a learning representative of a trade union acts as such if he carries on the activities mentioned in section 168A(2) in that capacity.

The scope of this provision is also governed by the *ACAS Code of Practice* which gives examples of the type of purposes for which unpaid time off should be provided.

[8.49] *ACAS Code of Practice on Time Off for Trade Union Duties and Activities* (2003)

> 29. To operate effectively and democratically, trade unions need the active participation of members. It can also be very much in employers' interests that such participation is assured. . . .

What are examples of trade union activities?

30. The activities of a trade union member can be, for example:
- attending workplace meetings to discuss and vote on the outcome of negotiations with the employer
- meeting full-time officials to discuss issues relevant to the workplace
- voting in union elections.

31. Where the member is acting as a representative of a recognised union, activities can be, for example, taking part in:
- branch, area or regional meetings of the union where the business of the union is under discussion
- meetings of official policy making bodies such as the executive committee or annual conference
- meetings with full-time officials to discuss issues relevant to the workplace.

32. There is no right to time off for trade union activities which themselves consist of industrial action.

An important case which tests the scope of this right is the following, which also raises questions about the nature and purpose of trade unions, and perhaps more importantly who should decide what these purposes should be.

[8.50] *Luce v Bexley London Borough Council* [1990] ICR 591 (EAT)

The issue in this case concerned a refusal by the employer to permit six teachers from Bexley to attend a lobby of Parliament organised by the TUC in connection with proposed legislation which affected the teaching profession. An industrial tribunal held that they were not entitled to time off under what is now TULRCA 1992, section 170, taking the view that the activities in question were not trade union activities under the section. The EAT dismissed the employees' appeals.

Wood J:

When considering complaints under sections [168] or [170] a tribunal first has to decide whether on the facts found the request falls within section [168](1)(a) or section [170](1) and (2); secondly, to apply the provisions as to reasonableness. In the present case the tribunal, as they were perfectly entitled to do, decided the first issue against the applicant and expressly declined to consider the second. It occurs to us that in these cases much of the evidence relevant to the one issue could be relevant to the other and due to that overlapping, it is preferable to decide both issues. This appeal tribunal might have decided that whether or not the proposed activity fell within section [170](2), the request was reasonably refused.

In the present case however, the tribunal decided against the applicant on the first issue and went no further. What then can we indicate which may be helpful to tribunals in approaching the phrase 'any activities of an appropriate trade union of which the employee is a member'? First, and most importantly, we are satisfied that the issue is ultimately one of degree and therefore one of fact. This must be left to the good sense and experience of the industrial tribunal which is entitled to look at all the circumstances. Secondly, although we do not consider that the phrase should be understood too restrictively, we are satisfied that it cannot have been the intention of Parliament to have included any activity of whatever nature. The whole context of the phrase is within the ambit of the employment relationship between that employee and that employer and that trade union. Quite apart from the overall considerations which we have expressed above this seems to be emphasised by the provisions of section [173(1)]. The time off is during the employee's normal working hours for which he would be contractually bound. Thus it seems to us that in a broad sense the activity should be one which is in some way linked to that employment relationship, i.e., between that employer, that employee and that trade union.

8.5.2.4 *The question of reasonableness and other facilities*

The statutory right to time off under these three different provisions is only to an amount which is 'reasonable.'The question of what is reasonable is also addressed in the ACAS Code.

[8.51] *ACAS Code of Practice on Time Off for Trade Union Duties and Activities* **(2003)**

35. The amount and frequency of time off should be reasonable in all the circumstances. Although the statutory provisions apply to all employers without exception as to size and type of business or service, trade unions should be aware of the wide variety of difficulties and operational requirements to be taken into account when seeking or agreeing arrangements for time off, for example:
• the size of the organisation and the number of workers
• the production process
• the need to maintain a service to the public
• the need for safety and security at all times.

36. Employers in turn should have in mind the difficulties for trade union officials and members in ensuring effective representation and communications with, for example:
• shift workers
• part-time workers
• home workers
• those employed at dispersed locations
• workers with particular domestic commitments.

37. For time off arrangements to work satisfactorily trade unions should:
• ensure that officials are aware of their role, responsibilities and functions
• inform management, in writing, as soon as possible of appointments or resignations of officials
• ensure that officials receive any appropriate written credentials promptly
• ensure that employers receive details of the functions of union officials where they carry out special duties or functions.

38. Employers should consider making available to officials the facilities necessary for them to perform their duties efficiently and communicate effectively with their members, colleague lay officials and full-time officers.Where resources permit the facilities could include:
• accommodation for meetings which could include provision for Union Learning Representatives and a union member(s) to meet to discuss relevant training matters
• access to a telephone and other office equipment

- the use of notice boards which could include other forms of electronic communications such as e-mail and intranet/internet
- where the volume of the official's work justifies it, the use of dedicated office space.

Requesting time off

39. Trade union officials and members requesting time off to pursue their duties or activities or to access the services of a Union Learning Representative should provide management with as much notice as possible and give details of:
- the purpose of such time off
- the intended location
- the timing and duration of time off required.

40. In addition, officials who request paid time off to undergo relevant training should:
- give at least a few weeks' notice to management of nominations for training courses
- provide a copy of the syllabus or prospectus indicating the contents of the training course.

41. When deciding whether requests for paid time off should be granted, consideration would need to be given as to their reasonableness, for example to ensure adequate cover for safety or to safeguard the production process or the provision of service. Consideration could also be given to allowing Union Learning Representatives access to a room in which they can discuss training in a confidential manner with an employee. Similarly, managers and unions should seek to agree a mutually convenient time which minimises the effect on production or services. Where workplace meetings are requested, consideration should be given to holding them, for example:
- towards the end of a shift or the working week
- before or after a meal break.

42. Employers need to consider each application for time off on its merits; they might also need to consider the reasonableness of the request in relation to agreed time off already taken or in prospect.

The *Code of Practice* also refers to 'the positive advantages for employers and trade unions in establishing agreements on time off in ways which reflect their own situations' (paragraph 43). Pay for time off under sections 168 and 168A is to be determined in accordance with TULRCA 1992, section 169. Guidance is provided by the *Code of Practice*, paragraphs 15 (trade union duties) and 28 (training). In addition to time off for officials and members, trade unions need other facilities if workplace organisation is to flourish. There may be a need for meeting rooms, a need to communicate with members, and a need to communicate with the district and national offices of the trade union. There may also be a need for privacy at the workplace, particularly where issues arise about the development of bargaining strategies or the position to be adopted in the representation of members who have a grievance or a disciplinary concern. Although facilities to meet needs of this kind will typically be included in facilities agreements, there is no direct legal obligation on the part of the employer to make any such provision. There is some reference to the need for such facilities in paragraph 38 of the *ACAS Code of Practice* which is set out above. It is perhaps possible to argue that facilities of this kind should be provided in some cases as a reasonable condition of time off, and that as a result there is an indirect legal obligation to make such facilities available. But the point does not appear to have been taken in any reported cases, and much would depend on the circumstances of individual cases.

The Check-Off

Apart from facilities of the kind discussed above, the other facility which a trade union might seek from an employer is the collection of trade union subscriptions by way of deduction from the wages of employees. Sometimes referred to as the check-off, money deducted in this way will then be passed onto the union, the employer perhaps making a small administration charge. But again a union has no right to insist on a check-off arrangement, even when it is recognised. Nevertheless such arrangements are common, as an efficient way for trade unions to collect their subscriptions, though more unions are attempting to introduce collection by direct debit from members' bank accounts. The latter combines efficient collection with protection against the threat of withdrawal of check-off facilities: the threat of withdrawal is a potent bargaining chip for employers. It is also the case that the check-off enables the employer to know the identity of union members as well as the levels of union membership in the workplace. Yet although there is no formal legal support for the collection of subscriptions by employers, the practice has not escaped attention of policy makers. The Conservative governments in particular were anxious to ensure that those where were covered by arrangements of this kind consented to have their subscriptions deducted from their wages, and renewed their consent on a regular basis.

The Employment Rights Act 1996 permits employers to deduct money from a worker's wages and pay it over to a third party (which could include a trade union), provided the worker has agreed or consented in writing (section 14(4)). The Trade Union and Labour Relations (Consolidation) Act 1992 provides further that subscriptions can be deducted from wages only if the worker has authorised the deduction in writing (section 68). The requirement that the authorisation must be renewed every three years introduced by the Trade Union Reform and Employment Rights Act 1993 has been repealed. This means that deductions can be made until such time as the worker revokes the authorisation: there is no need for periodic renewal of the authorisation. Provision is also made for the situation where the check-off operates in the case of a union which has a political fund. A trade union member exempt from paying the political levy may notify the employer of his or her exemption (or indeed that he or she has notified the union of his or her objection to paying a levy), in which case the employer 'shall ensure that no amount representing a contribution to the political fund is deducted by him from the emoluments payable to the member' (TULRCA 1992, section 86(1)). This means that the employer will have to deduct different amounts from different employees of the same union. The employer cannot refuse to operate the check-off for exempt members where he or she continues to operate it for other members of the union.

The final issue relating to trade union facilities at the workplace is the position of the trade union official, and the need to ensure that lay officials are not prejudiced in their employment because of their trade union activities. The problem in this context lies not so much in the overt discrimination against trade union activists as in the fact that, by taking themselves away from the workplace, trade union activists may suffer disadvantage when it comes to matters such as career development and promotion. A long time spent on trade union activities will be time lost in terms of professional engagement and experience. Some facilities agreements attempt to address this problem, but it can be very difficult to enforce the guarantees that the agreements provide. As we have seen there is already statutory protection against discrimination and dismissal for employees who take part in the activities of a trade union at an appropriate time (TULRCA 1992, sections 146, 152). Because facilities agreements are likely not to be legally enforceable, it is this legislation which must form the basis of any litigation by an aggrieved employee. But it is very difficult to prove that someone who has not been promoted—because of insufficient managerial experience or for lacking the requisite degree of managerial skill—is also someone who has had action taken against him or her for the purpose of deterring him or her from continuing with trade union activities: see *Department of Transport v Gallacher* [1994] ICR 967.

8.5.3 Disclosure of information

A second provision which the law makes available to recognised trade unions is access to information held by the employer which may be relevant to collective bargaining. Collective bargaining can take place effectively only if the trade union has adequate information about the economic position of the employer with whom it is dealing, if the union is to engage in an informed and measured way, and if it is to be able realistically to assess the bargaining position of the employer. There ought not to be anything controversial about employers being required to disclose information to trade unions (which may obtain access in other ways—under obligations imposed by company law and local government law, depending on the nature of the employer). Historically, employers have been required to disclose information to recognised trade unions since the Industrial Relations Act 1971 (under a statutory formula very similar to that currently in force). In other countries such as the USA and Canada the disclosure of information has long been seen as part and parcel of the employer's duty to bargain in good faith. And politically, the idea that employers disclose information to trade unions for collective bargaining purposes chimes in not only with the rhetoric about partnership in employment, but also with transparency and freedom of information generally.

8.5.3.1 The statutory obligation

The current duty of employers to disclose information to the representatives of recognised trade unions was introduced by the Employment Protection Act 1975, sections 17–21, though as we have seen the substance of the obligation has a longer pedigree. Indeed a duty to disclose was recommended by the Donovan Royal Commission in 1968, and included in the Labour government's ill-fated White Paper, *In Place of Strife*, in the following year. The 1975 legislation survives in its original form, its entire operation from 1980 to 1999 depending upon the voluntary recognition of the trade union by the employer.

[8.52] Trade Union and Labour Relations (Consolidation) Act 1992, section 181

General Duty of employers to disclose information

181(1) An employer who recognises an independent trade union shall, for the purposes of all stages of collective bargaining about matters, and in relation to descriptions of workers, in respect of which the union is recognised by him, disclose to representatives of the union, on request, the information required by this section.

In this section and sections 182 to 185 'representative', in relation to a trade union, means an official or other person authorised by the union to carry on such collective bargaining.

(2) The information to be disclosed is all information relating to the employer's undertaking which is in his possession, or that of an associated employer, and is information—

(a) without which the trade union representatives would be to a material extent impeded in carrying on collective bargaining with him, and

(b) which it would be in accordance with good industrial relations practice that he should disclose to them for the purposes of collective bargaining.

(3) A request by trade union representatives for information under this section shall, if the employer so requests, be in writing or be confirmed in writing.

(4) In determining what would be in accordance with good industrial relations practice, regard shall be had to the relevant provisions of any Code of Practice issued by ACAS, but not so as to exclude any other evidence of what that practice is.

(5) Information which an employer is required by virtue of this section to disclose to trade union representatives shall, if they so request, be disclosed or confirmed in writing.

There are a number of requirements laid down in the legislation. The first is that the union must be recognised for the purposes of collective bargaining. But what happens if the union is recognised, but has only bargaining rights on defined issues, yet consultation and representation rights on other issues? Can the union use the procedure to get access to information which relates to one of its latter roles? Or is the right to information confined to the former role only? It is this issue which forms the basis of the disagreement between the CAC and the High Court in the following case. (It is the CAC which hears complaints that an employer has failed to disclose information required by the Act: see below p 819.)

[8.53] *R v Central Arbitration Committee, ex parte BTP Tioxide Ltd* **[1981] ICR 843 (QBD)**

The union (ASTMS) was recognised by the employer on a wide range of issues. These did not include the job evaluation scheme which was expressly said to be 'non-participative', though the union had the right under the appeals procedure to make representations on behalf of members seeking re-evaluation. A dispute arose about one employee's evaluation and the union sought details of the scheme including 'the break point between grades, job descriptions and points allocated to jobs on the basis of the factors used'. The employer refused to provide the information and the union made an application under the statutory procedure. The CAC held that the union was entitled to the information, even though it did not have negotiating rights in respect of the scheme and had representational rights only. The decision was quashed by the High Court. Forbes J held that under the Act a union was entitled to the disclosure of information only in relation to those matters for which it was recognised for the purposes of collective bargaining. So if a union has negotiating rights in relation to some matters but representation rights in relation to others, it is only for the purposes of the former that the CAC may order the disclosure of information.

Where the union is appropriately recognised, the two key statutory conditions to be met before disclosure is required are that (i) the union representatives would be to a 'material extent impeded' in carrying on collective bargaining, and (ii) it would be in accordance with 'good industrial relations practice' for the employer to disclose. Some guidance on the scope of these provisions is given by the *ACAS Code of Practice* which accompanies the legislation. This particular code was revised in 1997, being first issued in 1975.

[8.54] *ACAS Code of Practice on the Disclosure of Information to Trade Unions for Collective Bargaining Purposes* **(1997)**

Providing information

9 The absence of relevant information about an employer's undertaking may to a material extent impede trade unions in collective bargaining, particularly if the information would influence the formulation, presentation or pursuance of a claim, or the conclusion of an agreement. The provision of relevant information in such circumstances would be in accordance with good industrial relations practice.

10 To determine what information will be relevant negotiators should take account of the subject-matter of the negotiations and the issues raised during them; the level at which negotiations take place (department, plant, division, or company level); the size of the company; and the type of business the company is engaged in.

11 Collective bargaining within an undertaking can range from negotiations on specific matters arising daily at the work place affecting particular sections of the workforce, to extensive periodic negotiations on terms and conditions of employment affecting the whole workforce in multiplant companies. The relevant information and the depth, detail and form in which it could be presented to negotiators will vary accordingly. Consequently, it is not possible to compile a list of items that should be disclosed in all circumstances. Some examples of information relating to the undertaking which could be relevant in certain collective bargaining situations are given below:

(i)   *Pay and benefits:* principles and structure of payment systems; job evaluation systems and grading criteria; earnings and hours analysed according to work-group, grade, plant, sex, out-workers and home-workers, department or division, giving, where appropriate, distributions and make-up of pay showing any additions to basic rate of salary; total pay bill; details of fringe benefits and non-wage labour costs.

(ii) *Conditions of service:* policies on recruitment, redeployment, redundancy, training, equal opportunity, and promotion; appraisal systems; health, welfare and safety matters.

(iii) *Manpower:* numbers employed analysed according to grade, department, location, age and sex; labour turnover; absenteeism; overtime and short-time; manning standards; planned changes in work methods, materials, equipment or organisation; available manpower plans; investment plans.

(iv) *Performance:* productivity and efficiency data; savings from increased productivity and output; return on capital invested; sales and state of order book.

(v)   *Financial:* cost structures; gross and net profits; sources of earnings; assets; liabilities; allocation of profits; details of government financial assistance; transfer prices; loans to parent or subsidiary companies and interest charged.

12 These examples are not intended to represent a check list of information that should be provided for all negotiations. Nor are they meant to be an exhaustive list of types of information as other items may be relevant in particular negotiations.

Yet notwithstanding this guidance, the statutory language has given rise to serious difficulties in practice. This is a matter to which we return below.

8.5.3.2 *Restrictions on the duty to disclose*

Predictably there are a number of restrictions on the employer's duty to disclose information.

[8.55] Trade Union and Labour Relations (Consolidation) Act 1992, section 182

182 Restrictions of general duty

(1) An employer is not required by section 181 to disclose information—

(a) the disclosure of which would be against the interests of national security, or

(b) which he could not disclose without contravening a prohibition imposed by or under an enactment, or

(c) which has been communicated to him in confidence, or which he has otherwise obtained in consequence of the confidence reposed in him by another person, or

(d) which relates specifically to an individual (unless that individual has consented to its being disclosed), or

(e) the disclosure of which would cause substantial injury to his undertaking for reasons other than its effect on collective bargaining, or

(f) obtained by him for the purpose of bringing, prosecuting or defending any legal proceedings.

In formulating the provisions of any Code of Practice relating to the disclosure of information, ACAS shall have regard to the provisions of this subsection.

(2) In the performance of his duty under section 181 an employer is not required—

(a) to produce, or allow inspection of, any document (other than a document prepared for the purpose of conveying or confirming the information) or to make a copy of or extracts from any document, or

(b) to compile or assemble any information where the compilation or assembly would involve an amount of work or expenditure out of reasonable proportion to the value of the information in the conduct of collective bargaining.

The most commonly relied on restrictions are those relating to confidential information, information relating to an individual, and claims that disclosure would cause substantial harm. The issue of confidentiality arose in the following case, which highlights the problems which arise in relation to information supplied to the employer by a third party.

[8.56] *Civil Service Union v Central Arbitration Committee* **[1980] IRLR 274 (QBD)**

The Ministry of Defence decided to move from the use of direct labour to the use of contract labour for the cleaning of a number of establishments. This would lead to redundancies, and the union was concerned to show that the cost of contract labour would not justify the change. The union asked to be supplied with information about direct cleaning costs and contract cleaning costs, and was supplied with much of what it asked for, except for the number of cleaners to be employed by the contractor and the number of hours the contractor intended to employ each cleaner. The CAC upheld the claim by the employer that the information was confidential and need not be disclosed, a view shared by the High Court which refused to quash the CAC's decision.

Forbes J:

So those are the only two matters left outstanding; the number of cleaners and the hours worked; and the case made by the department was that they were not required to disclose that information because it was given in confidence; governed therefore by s [182](1)(c); and they produced a blank form of tender document which is headed 'Contracts in Confidence', a specimen of which is supplied and is before me. A great deal of this form was filled in by the department, but two paragraphs were left to be filled in by the tenderers. The numbers of cleaners and the hours of work worked would be entered in paragraph 8, and in paragraph 9 the actual tender prices. Now it is conceded by the union that the information in paragraph 9 was confidential and therefore, under s [182], protected from disclosure. The union wanted, they said, the numbers of cleaners and the hours of work worked in order to be able to calculate the cost of contract cleaning. In other words, while acknowledging that the actual prices were confidential, they wanted sufficient information to allow them to calculate those prices. Put in that way, and that is the only way in which, to be practical, it was put, the argument seems to me to go a long way towards establishing that the information required by the union was equally confidential with the contract prices.

But Mr Weitzman [for the union] says that there is here an error on the face of the award, and I should, I think, read the appropriate paragraph. I am not going to read the whole of the award. The award starts off with the terms of reference and the background, and it sets out the submissions on behalf of the union and the submissions on behalf of the Ministry; and then, in paragraph 18, the Committee came to the view that the information requested was in fact information which fell within s [181] of the Act; and they went on (Para 19) to say this:

> 'Having decided that the requirements of s [181] of the Act were satisfied we proceeded to consider the Ministry's claims that they were prevented from giving the information required because, in the terms of s [182](1)(c), it had been communicated to them in confidence. They also prayed in aid s [182](1)(e) insofar as any breach of confidence on this occasion could seriously affect relations with contractors in other areas of defence procurement'.

I may say that no reliance has been put before me on s [182](1)(e). The matter has been dealt with purely on s[182](1)(c). In any event I do not think the argument on s [182](1)(e) really carries it any further.

The union pointed out that they were not asking either for the names of contractors or for the tender prices. They wanted only the number of cleaners to be employed and the number of hours for which they were to be employed, in respect of each of the tenders which the Ministry were likely to accept. However, they admitted that with this information they could, by relating it to local authority rates of pay, estimate the minimum cost of each tender. Indeed, this was their purpose in seeking the information.

'20. In an effort to reach a compromise, the union suggested that the information, if given, would be kept confidential to a limited number of union officials and would not, for instance, be communicated to its members. The Ministry had asked the tenderers concerned whether they would regard this procedure as meeting the need to preserve the confidence in which the information on numbers of staff and hours worked had been supplied. Some of the tenderers rejected this proposal and the Ministry therefore felt that they must maintain their objection, under s [182](1)(c), to supplying the information to the union. Although we should have been glad if such an arrangement could have been agreed between the parties, we must point out that we could not have framed our award in such a way as to have the effect required, since, as the Committee has said on previous occasions, we believe that disclosure in this limited sense is not what it is intended to provide in the Act.

'21. The Committee also hoped that the information could be provided in such a way as to ensure that it could not be related to particular contractors. But again some of the tenderers were unwilling to countenance any device of this kind. As we understood it, the main reason for their objection was that, as a matter of principle, any information given to the Ministry in confidence ought not to be given to anyone else, whatever attempts might be made to cloak it in anonymity.

'22. We had to accept the simple fact that the form on which tenders are submitted to the Ministry and which contains the information asked for by the union is headed "in confidence". With considerable reluctance we were forced to conclude that the employer is justified in claiming that for this reason alone he cannot be required to supply the information. The information specifically requested by the union relates not to the Ministry but to the contractor and his particular method of operation. Such confidentiality as exists, derives from this fact.

'23. We have considerable sympathy with the union in their present predicament. It faces an employer who proposes to make over 60 union members redundant purely on the basis of cost but then denies the union the basic information on which that decision was made. We note however that the representatives of the management from the Ministry expressed a desire to overcome the difficulties; we can only hope that further negotiation between the parties will lead to a compromise solution which is satisfactory to them both'.

Now the error of which Mr Weitzman speaks arises, he says, in paragraph 22. He says that what was required of the Committee was an interpretation of s [182](1)(c). There are, he suggests, three factors in relation to that. Three matters: (a) confidence has to be reposed in the employer by someone other than the employer; (b) the information must be of a kind which is capable of attracting confidence; and (c) the confidence did in fact exist and operate on the mind of that person other than the employer. On the true construction of paragraph 22 he suggests, the Committee decided that the mere fact that the tender forms was headed 'in confidence' was conclusive of the question whether confidence did in fact exist and operate on the mind of the contractor. In other words, they misdirected themselves by holding that the label 'in confidence' was conclusive of the nature of the transaction. This, says Mr Weitzman, is similar to a decision that the label 'licence' at the head of a document was conclusive of the question whether it was a licence or a lease.

Mr Brown [for the CAC] concedes that if this is in fact the true construction of this paragraph then there is an error of law disclosed on the face of the award. It appears therefore that the sole issue on this aspect is what is the true construction of paragraph 22.

I approach the task of determining what the Central Arbitration Committee meant to say in paragraph 22, bearing in mind that one should not subject decisions of lay Tribunals to an analysis appropriate to a section of an Act of Parliament. It is the duty of the applicant to satisfy the court that the error is apparent on the face of the award, and where, as here, the error is one of self-misdirection, the applicant must, I think, show that it is reasonably clear that the Tribunal did misdirect itself. Nor do I think it helpful to extract merely one paragraph from a much longer decision. The whole decision must be read together. It should be remembered that not only the prices but also the identity of the tenderers was accepted as confidential under s [182]. It follows that it would have been impossible to call any of the tenderers to give direct testimony about the degree of confidence reposed in the department. This therefore can only be inferred from the surrounding circumstances. The only relevant circumstances that I can see are; (a) that the document was headed 'Contracts in Confidence'; (b) that the tenderers filled in paragraphs 8 and 9; (c) that the information in paragraph 9 was accepted as being given in confidence; (d) that it was alleged however that no confidentiality attached to the information given in paragraph 8; and (e) that it was accepted that the object was to deduce from the information in paragraph 8 what was the information in paragraph 9. To these perhaps there might be added that some of the tenderers, admittedly after the event, relied on the alleged confidentiality of the information sought; matters which are referred to in paragraphs 20 and 21.

Although the Central Arbitration Committee did not spell out as I have attempted to do, the relevant circumstances (a) to (e), these circumstances are only a combination of the information on the tender form and the matters set out in paragraphs 19, 20 and 21. Faced with the task of drawing inferences, what was the Committee to do except to conclude that it was a reasonable inference that tenderers who submitted information to the Ministry on a form headed 'in confidence' were relying on the preservation of the confidentiality of that information. They correctly point out that the confidentiality serves to protect the interests not of the Ministry, but of the contractor, and it might be added the last sentence of the preceding paragraph, paragraph 21, shows that the tenderers were asserting their reliance on the confidential nature of the information and that the Committee appreciated the significance of this. I apprehend that all the Committee intended to say in paragraph 22 was that, having regard to the facts they set out in paragraphs 19, 20 and 21, the inescapable conclusion is that tenderers who submit information to the Ministry on a tender form headed 'in confidence' do so because they are relying on that label to preserve the confidentiality of the information that they give. I cannot see that this is a misdirection of law and the application should fail on that ground.

There is little guidance in the *Code of Practice* on the scope of what is now TULRCA 1992, section 182. The only specific guidance relates to section 182(1)(e)—the 'substantial injury' restriction.

[8.57] *ACAS Code of Practice on the Disclosure of Information to Trade Unions for Collective Bargaining Purposes* **(1997)**

14 Some examples of information which if disclosed in particular circumstances might cause substantial injury are: cost information on individual products; detailed analysis of proposed investment, marketing or pricing policies; and price quotas or the make-up of tender prices. Information which has to be made available publicly, for example under the Companies Acts, would not fall into this category.

15 Substantial injury may occur if, for example, certain customers would be lost to competitors, or suppliers would refuse to supply necessary materials, or the ability to raise funds to finance the company would be seriously impaired as a result of disclosing certain information. The burden of establishing a claim that disclosure of certain information would cause substantial injury lies with the employer.

8.5.3.3 A critique of the statutory provisions

The duty of the employer to disclose information is enforced by way of a complaint by a recognised trade union to the CAC (TULRCA 1992, section 183). If the complaint is upheld, the CAC may make a declaration requiring the employer to disclose specified information. In the *BTP Tioxide* case [8.53], above, it was said by Forbes J that 'these provisions only entitle the committee to deal with a complaint relating to a past failure and information already refused and do not permit a declaration of what the committee prospectively considers the employer in future cases should disclose' (at p 859). If the employer fails to comply with the declaration the matter may be referred back to the CAC by the union: the final sanction is explained by Forbes J in the *BTP Tioxide* case at p 851:

Section [185] provides the ultimate sanction. When I first encountered this section: see *Civil Service Union v Central Arbitration Committee* [1980] IRLR 274, 276, para 3, I was wholly unable to see how it could provide any worthwhile sanction and counsel in that case could not enlighten me. Mr Clarke [for the company], however, has enlightened me now, and I am profoundly grateful to him. The machinery is that after making a further complaint the union can present a claim, and this may be and, it is envisaged, would be a claim relating to remuneration, or conditions of work, or something of that kind, and the committee can, if it finds the further complaint well founded, write that claim into the relevant employees' contracts. In other words, the determination of whether the union claim should be accepted or rejected by the employer is taken out of the employer's hands and left to the arbitrament of the committee, and the committee can alter the employees' contracts so that the employer becomes legally bound to give effect, in relation to those employees, to the committee's award.

There have in fact been relatively few applications to the CAC since the legislation was introduced in 1975. According to the study below, in the 21 years between 1976 and 1997, the CAC 'handled 463 complaints, an average of 22 per year' (at p 238). There are a number of possible explanations for this low level of activity, including disappointment with the substance of the law, made even narrower by the restrictive readings of the High Court. In more recent years this has become an even less active jurisdiction. The CAC website reveals that between 2000 and 2004, only 12 (2000), 1 (2001), 2 (2002), 3 (2003) and 4 (2004) applications were made under these provisions, and of these only one went to a hearing, which the union lost on the ground that it would not be impeded in collective bargaining by the lack of the information in question. It is of course possible that in some of the applications that were withdrawn, the employer provided the information without waiting to be told to do so by the CAC.

[8.58] H Gospel and G Lockwood, 'Disclosure of Information for Collective Bargaining: The CAC Approach Revisited' (1999) 28 *Industrial Law Journal* 233

Having identified some strengths, a number of weaknesses can also be seen in the TULRCA provisions, which reduce their value and render the law unsatisfactory for any new openness in the workplace. In the first place, information need only be provided for the purposes of collective bargaining as defined by the Act and disclosure is limited to matters for which the union is recognised [see s 181(1) TULRCA]. Thus, claims for information, relating to cost and price schedules or to the decision to terminate an area of operations where the topic had not previously been an accepted bargaining subject, would fall foul of the provision [see, for example BL Cars Ltd, MG Abingdon Plant and General and Municipal Workers' Union, Amalgamated Union of Engineering Workers, Transport and General Workers' Union, Award No 80/65]. There then exist the two tests contained in section 181(2). The first test, of 'good industrial relations' practice, is vague. The CAC itself has admitted that it is hampered, in the articulation of a standard, by the weak consensus as to current practice. 'Information, which is commonly disclosed in one sector, may be regarded as a tightly guarded secret in another' [CAC, *Annual Report*, 1979, p 6, para 2.11]. Moreover, the CAC has concluded that it cannot act as a trail-blazer or standard-setter [Standard Telephone and Cables Ltd and Association of Scientific, Technical and Managerial Staffs, Award No 79/484, para 25]. However, it should be noted that in 1986 the Divisional Court held that the specialist skill and experience of the CAC enabled it to draw its own conclusions from the circumstances as to whether good industrial relations practice required the giving of the information [*R v Central Arbitration Committee ex parte BP Chemicals Ltd* 1.5.86, High Court of Justice, Queen's Bench Division, Case Co/421/86, unreported]. The second test, of material impediment, is an even bigger obstacle to a union seeking to pursue a complaint where it has managed without such information in the past. Many employers have successfully objected that there was no impediment and unions are severely disadvantaged in arguing the need for information, which they do not have. Moreover, in an early case, the Committee produced a fairly restrictive definition of material impediment: 'It might be argued that this test is a question of relevance. All relevant information prima facie makes for more open and better bargaining. But, we note the negatively expressed rule. It speaks of evidence "without which" the trade union would be impeded. This narrows considerably the test from one of relevance to one of importance' [Daily Telegraph and Institute of Journalists, Award No 78/353]. The information must be relevant and significant to the material area of collective bargaining [Civil Service Union and Central Arbitration Committee, Award No 80/73]. This seems ill suited to promoting collective bargaining. However, in BP Chemicals (Award 86/1), the CAC might be regarded as adopting a more flexible approach to 'material impediment' which could have important implications, since it was upheld on judicial review. In determining material impediment, the Committee stated in this case that: 'One should recall that the purpose of the provisions is to improve collective bargaining. If the disclosure of information would secure a more constructive and less abrasive approach, it removes an impediment to the bargaining' [BTP Tioxide and Association of Scientific, Technical and Managerial Staffs, Award No 80/107].

Another limitation of the provisions relates to the timing of disclosure. The CAC may only adjudicate upon a past failure to disclose and may not declare what information the employer should disclose in the future, even though the disclosure might help avoid a subsequent dispute between the parties [*ibid*]. In this context it has been remarked that 'the disclosure procedure cannot be used like an order of discovery in an industrial tribunal around which a case can be built' [R Rideout, 'Disclosure of Information', *Journal of the General Federation of Trade Unions*, 41(3) (1991), p 96]. Thus, the union is unable to plan its bargaining strategy in anticipation of having all relevant documents at the most appropriate time. The bargaining process would have to begin and the union suspend proceedings in order to present a claim to the CAC to obtain information which had been refused. The fact that the CAC procedure must then be exhausted before any sanction is instituted means that the matter in dispute has to be capable of being pursued over a considerable length of time. Otherwise it will mean the employer can delay disclosure of the information until its usefulness is limited or has passed. The often urgent need for the information and the laborious CAC process for obtaining it may therefore cause trade unions not to bother with the procedure.

A further weakness of the provisions is the enforcement mechanism contained in section 185, since the sanction does not force disclosure of the information or provide for a punitive element to be included in the award. To date this procedure has been used only once in the *Holokrome* case (79/451). In that instance, the union's request to the CAC did not take the form of a terms and conditions claim, but was a request for the inclusion of the contested information in the employment contracts of those covered by the reference. The Committee awarded that 'information relating to salary scales and any fixed increases for the grade of each individual employee should have effect as part of an individual's contract of employment'. However, the union was unable to secure contractual incorporation of all the information previously awarded, since parts of it were regarded as unsuitable for inclusion in the individuals' employment contracts. This is not surprising since there are undoubtedly differences between information necessary for collective bargaining and information suitable for inclusion in an individual's contract of employment. Thus, contested information, which might relate to matters between the employer and the trade union as opposed to the employer and the individual, would not be suitable for such inclusion.

A final weakness relates to the ACAS Code of Practice, with its origins in the early 1980s. On the evidence of some CAC declarations, the Code has not been of great assistance or guidance. Thus, in an one case, the CAC consulted the Code for guidance on two matters: on the general principle of 'good industrial relations' practice and on the more specific question of how bargaining units might affect the scope of disclosure. It concluded that the Code gives no clear guidance on these points [Daily Telegraph Ltd and Institute of Journalists, Award No 78/353]. In another case relating to good practice, the CAC asked: 'What is the standard of good industrial relations? It cannot be some vision which each of us have of a desirable future since that will differ infinitely according to the individual. The legislation clearly intended us to be guided by a less subjective choice than that for it is provided that we should be guided by the relevant ACAS Code of Practice. The current code is of little help in this connection' [Standard Telephones and Cables Ltd and Association of Scientific, Technical and Managerial Staffs, Award No 79/484, para 25]. Furthermore, the relationship between the Code's lists and the Act's provisions is vague and contradictory in that the Code appears to promise access to certain types of information, whereas the Act lays down specific tests to be applied.

The success of employer's defences has shown that the tests and exemptions contained in the Act are extensive and restrictive. They stifle union claims for information and provide employers with a wide range of arguments against disclosure. In what should be the lynchpin of the law on disclosure for collective bargaining, the language of the Act and weaknesses in the legal provisions have meant that the direct influence of the law has been more limited than it should otherwise have been.

8.5.4 Trade union consultation rights

In addition to rights to time off and to the disclosure of information, recognised trade unions also have certain consultation rights, which have been introduced mainly as a result of EC initiatives. These measures give rise to the slight paradox that in order to acquire statutory rights to be consulted on defined matters, a trade union must already have negotiating rights about others. The issues to which consultation rights apply are collective redundancies (introduced by the Employment Protection Act 1975, section 99, though amended on a number of occasions thereafter); the transfer of undertakings (introduced by the Transfer of Undertakings (Protection of Employment) Regulations 1981, SI 1981/1794, though also subsequently amended) (**[10.54]** below); and health and safety at work (with provisions having their origins in the Health and Safety at Work etc Act 1974). There is also a duty to consult about training—but curiously only where the trade union has been recognised under the procedures in the 1999 Act and where a collective bargaining method has been specified by the CAC (see Employment Relations Act 1999, section 5). As we shall see, with the exception of the last mentioned obligation, the employer's duty to consult is a general duty which now applies even where there is no trade union recognised for the purposes of collective bargaining, in which case the employer must consult with employee representatives or in some cases the workers directly. But where there is a recognised trade union, it enjoys a priority status in the sense that it is with the union that consultations must take place. In this section we concentrate on the redundancy consultation procedures, which arise as a result of European law.

[8.59] Council Directive 98/59/EC of 20 July 1998 on the approximation of the laws of the Member States relating to Collective Redundancies [1998] OJ 1998, L 225/16

Article 2

1. Where an employer is contemplating collective redundancies, he shall begin consultations with the workers' representatives in good time with a view to reaching an agreement.

2. These consultations shall, at least, cover ways and means of avoiding collective redundancies or reducing the number of workers affected, and of mitigating the consequences by recourse to accompanying social measures aimed, *inter alia*, at aid for redeploying or retraining workers made redundant.

   Member States may provide that the workers' representatives may call on the services of experts in accordance with national legislation and/or practice.

3. To enable workers' representatives to make constructive proposals, the employers shall in good time during the course of the consultations—
   (a)   supply them with all relevant information and
   (b)   in any event notify them in writing of—
      (i)   the reasons for the projected redundancies;
      (ii)   the number of categories of workers to be made redundant;
      (iii) the number and categories of workers normally employed;
      (iv)   the period over which the projected redundancies are to be effected;
      (v)   the criteria proposed for the selection of the workers to be made redundant in so far as national legislation and/or practice confers the power therefore upon the employer;
      (vi)   the method for calculating any redundancy payments other than those arising out of national legislation and/or practice.
   The employer shall forward to the competent public authority a copy of, at least, the elements of the written communication which are provided for in the first subparagraph, point (b), subpoints (i) to (v).

Implementing legislation is to be found in TULRCA, having first been introduced in 1975, the current Directive being an up-dated version of a measure introduced in the same year. Domestic law has had to be amended on several occasions since 1975 because of defective implementation of the Directive.

[8.60] Trade Union and Labour Relations (Consolidation) Act 1992, section 188

Duty of employer to consult representatives

188 (1) Where an employer is proposing to dismiss as redundant 20 or more employees at one establishment within a period of 90 days or less, the employer shall consult about the dismissals all the persons who are appropriate representatives of any of the employees who may be affected by the proposed dismissals or may be affected by measures taken in connection with those dismissals.

(1A) The consultation shall begin in good time and in any event—
(a) where the employer is proposing to dismiss 100 or more employees as mentioned in subsection (1), at least 90 days, and
(b) otherwise, at least 30 days,
before the first of the dismissals takes effect.

(1B) For the purposes of this section the appropriate representatives of any affected employees are—
(a) if the employees are of a description in respect of which an independent trade union is recognised by their employer, representatives of the trade union, or
(b) in any other case, whichever of the following employee representatives the employer chooses—
   (i) employee representatives appointed or elected by the affected employees otherwise than for the purposes of this section, who (having regard to the purposes for and the method by which they were appointed or elected) have authority from those employees to receive information and to be consulted about the proposed dismissals on their behalf;
   (ii) employee representatives elected by the affected employees, for the purposes of this section, in an election satisfying the requirements of section 188A(1).

(2) The consultation shall include consultation about ways of—
(a) avoiding the dismissals,
(b) reducing the numbers of employees to be dismissed, and
(c) mitigating the consequences of the dismissals,
and shall be undertaken by the employer with a view to reaching agreement with the appropriate representatives.

(3) In determining how many employees an employer is proposing to dismiss as redundant no account shall be taken of employees in respect of whose proposed dismissals consultation has already begun.

(4) For the purposes of the consultation the employer shall disclose in writing to the appropriate representatives—
(a) the reasons for his proposals,
(b) the numbers and descriptions of employees whom it is proposed to dismiss as redundant,
(c) the total number of employees of any such description employed by the employer at the establishment in question,
(d) the proposed method of selecting the employees who may be dismissed,

(e) the proposed method of carrying out the dismissals, with due regard to any agreed procedure, including the period over which the dismissals are to take effect,

(f) the proposed method of calculating the amount of any redundancy payments to be made (otherwise than in compliance with an obligation imposed by or by virtue of any enactment) to employees who may be dismissed.

(5) That information shall be given to each of the appropriate representatives by being delivered to them or sent by post to an address notified by them to the employer, or (in the case of representatives of a trade union) sent by post to the union at the address of its head or main office.

(5A) The employer shall allow the appropriate representatives access to the affected employees and shall afford to those representatives such accommodation and other facilities as may be appropriate.

(6) [repealed]

(7) If in any case there are special circumstances which render it not reasonably practicable for the employer to comply with a requirement of subsection (1A), (2) or (4), the employer shall take all such steps towards compliance with that requirement as are reasonably practicable in those circumstances. Where the decision leading to the proposed dismissals is that of a person controlling the employer (directly or indirectly), a failure on the part of that person to provide information to the employer shall not constitute special circumstances rendering it not reasonably practicable for the employer to comply with such a requirement.

(7A) Where—

(a) the employer has invited any of the affected employees to elect employee representatives, and

(b) the invitation was issued long enough before the time when the consultation is required by subsection (1A)(a) or (b) to begin to allow them to elect representatives by that time,

the employer shall be treated as complying with the requirements of this section in relation to those employees if he complies with those requirements as soon as is reasonably practicable after the election of the representatives.

(7B) If, after the employer has invited affected employees to elect representatives, the affected employees fail to do so within a reasonable time, he shall give to each affected employee the information set out in subsection (4).

(8) This section does not confer any rights on a trade union, a representative or an employee except as provided by sections 189 to 192 below.

[*For the corresponding provisions of the Transfer of Undertaking (Protection of Employment) Regulations 1981, SI 1981/1794, see below, p 1063.*]

Redundancy for this purpose is defined in section 195 to mean 'dismissal for a reason not related to the individual concerned or for a number of reasons all of which are not so related'. This is wider than the definition applicable to the law relating to unfair dismissal and redundancy payments discussed in Chapter 10.

8.5.4.1 Collective redundancy: the duty to consult

There are a number of points which arise in relation to the employer's duty to consult under section 188. The first is that the minimum consultation period now depends on the number of employees to be made redundant. Before the law was changed in 1995, employers were required to consult in respect of all redundancies, and the minimum periods then in force applied only to those involving more than a prescribed number of employees. The obligation arises only in respect of employees and not workers, though it applies to employees who may not qualify for a redundant payment, because they have insufficient service, for example. Nevertheless, the effect is to exclude many atypical workers whose dismissal will not count in determining whether 20 or 100 people are to be made redundant, and in respect of whom consultations will not have to take place. It is also the case that the obligation to consult arises only where 20 or more employees are to be dismissed at the same establishment, not by the same employer. Curiously, the term 'establishment' is not defined, and it is left to the tribunals to determine on the facts of each particular case what is an establishment for the purposes of section 188. In *Rockfon A/S v Specialarbejderforbundet I Danmark* [1996] IRLR 168 the ECJ held that:

> 'the term 'establishment' appearing in Article 1(1)(a) . . . must be understood as meaning, depending on the circumstances, the unit to which the workers made redundant are assigned to carry out their duties. It is not essential, in order for there to be an 'establishment' for the unit in question to be endowed with a management which can independently effect collective redundancies'.

Applying this finding in *MSF v Refuge Assurance plc* [2002] IRLR 324, the EAT suggested that it 'would effectively disapply s 188' in some—perhaps many—cases 'by reason of the smallness of the branches concerned and the thin spread of redundancies over a large number of them' (p 331). Apart from the foregoing, there is also the question of who is the employer, an interesting issue which affects the existence and content of the duty to consult in any particular case.

[8.61] *E. Green & Son (Castings) Ltd v ASTMS* **[1984] ICR 352 (EAT)**

> There were three employers in this case E Green & Son (Castings) Ltd, E Green & Son Ltd, and E Green & Son (Site Services) Ltd. All three operated from the same premises and were subsidiaries of the same holding company Green's Economisers Group plc. They all shared services such as accounting services, the personnel director of the holding company was responsible for all the subsidiaries, and the managing director of the holding company was responsible for a decision to make redundancies in each of these companies. It was proposed that there should be 97 redundancies in Castings, 36 in Green & Son, and 24 in Site Services. The question was whether more than 100 people were to be dismissed by the same employer at a single establishment, a crucial question which would affect the length of the minimum consultation period. The industrial tribunal concluded that there was only one establishment and appeared to conclude that the three companies constituted a single employer, but subsequently reviewed their original decision and held that there were three companies. This was a view shared by the EAT.

Nolan J:

In urging us to take the contrary view, Mr Hand developed and amplified the unions' argument that we should lift the corporate veil. First, he referred to the decision of the appeal tribunal in *National and Local Government Officers Association v National Travel (Midlands) Ltd* [1978] ICR 598. That too was a case concerning a group of companies. The parent company had decided that, owing to financial difficulties, one of the subsidiary companies would have to be merged with another. Inevitably, redundancies were likely. Subsequently, the subsidiary notified the union of the redundancies proposed. At the hearing before the appeal tribunal, the union argued that the subsidiary was bound hand and foot to the parent company, that the redundancies should be taken to have been proposed when the merger decision was made by the parent company, and that the parent company rather than the subsidiary was the employer. In their judgment, the appeal tribunal said that they were prepared to lift the corporate veil in order to see whether the union's contention could be supported. Having done so, the appeal tribunal concluded that the subsidiary was not bound hand and foot to the parent, that the proposal to dismiss did not come from the parent, and that 'certainly they were not the employers.' We do not regard that decision as providing any general authority for the lifting of the corporate veil in order to determine the identity of the employer. Once it is established that the contract of employment is genuinely made between the employee and the subsidiary company—and we do not understand that to be disputed in the present case—then it appears to us that no further inquiry is necessary.

8.5.4.2   *The meaning of consultation*

Having established that there is a duty to consult, a second question relates to when and how the consultation is to be conducted. So far as the timing is concerned, there are three major limitations or qualifications:

• The first limitation is that the legislation does not impose a duty to consult about the need for closure or restructuring that may lead to a redundancy. As explained by the EAT in *Securicor Omega Express Ltd v GMB* [2004] IRLR 9, it is a duty to consult 'in relation to the consequences of the closures, with a view to reducing, possibly even avoiding entirely, but certainly reducing, the redundancies which were consequential upon it'.

• The second limitation is that even then section 188 provides that the employer must consult where he or she is 'proposing' to dismiss. But it has been suggested that this may not meet the requirements of EC law, with Glidewell LJ pointing out in *R v British Coal Corporation, ex parte Vardy* [1993] ICR 720 at p 753:

> . . . . in the Directive consultation is to begin as soon as an employer contemplates redundancies, whereas under the Act of 1992 it only needs to begin when he proposes to dismiss as redundant an employee. The verb 'proposes' in its ordinary usage relates to a state of mind which is much more certain and further along the decision-making process than the verb 'contemplate;' in other words, the Directive envisages consultation at an early stage when the employer is first envisaging the possibility that he may have to make employees redundant. Section 188 applies when he has decided that, whether because he has to close a plant or for some other reason, it is his intention, however reluctant, to make employees redundant. . . .

These concerns were also addressed in *MSF v Refuge Assurance plc* [2002] IRLR 324 where it was also held that it is not possible to construe s 188 consistently with the Directive 'without distorting the meaning of the domestic legislation'. It would, however, be possible for a trade union to rely on and directly to enforce the Directive against an emanation of the State.

• A third limitation is that consultation must begin within the prescribed periods before the dismissals 'take effect'. It has been held that the minimum periods from which consultation must take place are to be calculated by working back from the date any notice of dismissal expires, rather than the date on which it is issued: *Middlesbrough Borough Council v TGWU* [2002] IRLR 333. However, this does not mean that consultation may begin after the employer has issued dismissal notices, even though the notice period to end the contract exceeds the minimum consultation period laid down in the statute (*E Green & Son (Castings) Ltd v ASTMS*, above).

But consultation is not just about timing: it is also about purpose and form. So far as the former is concerned, the purpose is set out in TULRCA 1992, section 188 (2); and so far as the latter is concerned there is guidance in TULRCA, section 188(4) and (5). The consultation is also to be conducted with a view to reaching an agreement, and the EAT has emphasised on a number of occasions that 'consultation must be genuine and meaningful': *Middlesbrough Borough Council v TGWU*, above. Referring to s 188(2), in this latter case, the EAT said that we 'view those three features of consultation disjunctively. Thus, an employer may genuinely consult with the unions about ways of reducing the numbers of employees to be dismissed and mitigating the consequences of the dismissals, without genuinely consulting as to the principle of whether or not to declare redundancies at all. . . . The duties under the section are mandatory. It is not open to an employer, for this purpose, to argue, as would be open to him in defending a complaint of unfair dismissal by the individual employee, that consultation would, in the circumstances, be futile or utterly useless'. Difficulty arises nevertheless about the amount of information which the employer can be expected to provide, a matter which was at issue in the following case.

[8.62] *MSF v GEC Ferranti (Defence Systems) Ltd (No 2)* [1994] IRLR 113 (EAT)

The respondent employer decided that some 800 people would be made redundant. On 13 September 1991, the union was informed of the total number of redundancies and their broad job category, but not the divisions of the company which would be affected. In a second hearing the industrial tribunal held that this was sufficient information under what is now section 188(4) to allow them to conclude that consultations began on the 13 September. The union disputed this and argued that the consultations for the purposes of the legislation could not be regarded as having begun on that day for the purposes of the 90-day minimum period, on the ground that insufficient information had been given to allow meaningful consultations to begin. The EAT agreed with the union and upheld its appeal. It is to be noted that the case was decided under the Employment Protection Act 1975, where the corresponding provisions to section 188(4) were to be found in section 99(5), though there were at the time only five rather than six items to be disclosed by the employer to the union representative.

Lord Coulsfield:
The appellants' first submission was that s 99 required that full and specific information under each of the five heads listed in subsection (5) must be provided before the consultation period can begin. In our opinion, that goes too far. The five headings in s 99(5) are not, in our view, necessarily of equal importance in every case, and cannot necessarily be treated as separate and distinct; for example, the information required under head (b) may very well overlap with that required under head (e). The appellants relied on a passage in the judgment of Slynn J in *Spillers-French (Holdings) Ltd v USDAW* [[1979] IRLR 339]. Slynn J said:

'Obviously there can be faults of different gravity. For example, one requirement of the Act is that necessary information shall be disclosed in writing. It might be that if all the information had been given orally to a trade union representative, a Tribunal would not take a very serious view of that as a failure to comply with a requirement. On the other hand, failure to give reasons at all, or failure to include one of the matters specified in s 99(5), might be more serious. A failure to consult at all, or consultation only at the last minute, might be taken to be even more serious'.

In our view, that passage does not assist the appellants in this case; it is clear that a failure to give information on one of the heads of s 99(5) *may* be a serious default, but we do not think that Slynn J intended to lay down that a failure of that kind *must* be treated as a serious default, such as to make it impossible for meaningful consultation to begin. The question is one of the whole circumstances, and primarily one for the Industrial Tribunal. The appellants' second submission was that the Industrial Tribunal had failed to deal explicitly with the evidence concerning the procedure which had been adopted, and the information which had been supplied, in connection with previous redundancies. It seems to us, however, that the relevance and significance of that material is also a matter of fact for the Industrial Tribunal to determine.

The appellants' principal argument, however, was that the Industrial Tribunal failed to apply their minds to the question whether the information supplied on 13 September satisfied the requirements of s 99(5)(b), or reached an unreasonable decision upon that question. We should say at once that we ourselves have had no hesitation in reaching the conclusion that the information supplied on that date was not adequate. The respondents' undertaking comprised six divisions. On 13 September, the respondents stated that there would be 800 redundancies, divided into the categories of manual, clerical and technical/managerial; but did not give any more precise information, and, in particular, did not say from which divisions the redundancies would be found, or in what proportions. . . We would not, of course, be entitled to interfere with the decision of the Industrial Tribunal merely because we disagreed with it, however strongly. We have, however, come to the conclusion that there are grounds which do justify us in interfering with this decision. In the circumstances of this case, in our view, there was obviously a serious question whether the information given on 13 September was sufficient to allow meaningful consultation to begin. The Industrial Tribunal do not entirely ignore that question, but they dismiss it briefly, and do not discuss the adequacy of the information at all. It appears that they took into account the fact that the employers were under an obligation to begin consultation as early as possible; but that, while true and important, is not of itself a reason for holding that the information was adequate to allow meaningful consultation. Again, the Industrial Tribunal took into account the fact that some useful discussion did take place, but while that is a relevant circumstance, it is not of itself a reason for holding the information to be adequate.

The EAT concluded in the *GEC (Ferranti)* case that the 'question whether information has been provided which is adequate to permit meaningful consultation is one which depends on the particular facts and circumstances, and, therefore, one for the Industrial Tribunal'.

So far as the form which consultation must take, this is governed by section 188(4). In what appears to be further evidence of the generally narrow scope of s 188, the EAT has given some latitude to employers in terms of complying with their procedural obligations under section 188(4). In *Securicor Omega Express Ltd v GMB* [2004] IRLR 9 (EAT), it was held that the employer is not required to provide the union with a section 188(4) notice before consultations begin. In that case union officials were called to a meeting to discuss redundancies without any further information being provided. A minute of the meeting was then sent to the union, dealing with some of the section 188(4) issues. According to the EAT, the employment tribunal was wrong to hold that in these circumstances the requirements of section 188 had not been met. The only breach arose because the minute did not provide the information required by section 188(4) (c) and (f), for which a nominal protective award of one day's pay was awarded. In seeking to do justice in accordance with its principle that 'consultation must in general be fair and meaningful', the EAT may have done so in that case at the expense of legality.

8.5.4.3 Remedies for failure to consult

The final question for consideration here relates to the enforcement of the duty to consult. What happens if the employer fails to consult, or fails to consult within the prescribed minimum times, or fails to consult in the manner prescribed by the Act? It has to be said that the sanctions are extremely weak. The Act makes provision for a complaint to be made to an employment tribunal for a protective award which has the effect of requiring the employer to continue to pay remuneration to the staff to be made redundant for a protected period (section 189). The period, which may not exceed 90 days, is 'of such length as the tribunal determines to be just and equitable in all the circumstances having regard to the seriousness of the employer's default' (section 189).

[8.63] *Susie Radin Ltd v GMB* **[2004] ICR 893**

> In *Susie Radin Ltd v GMB* [2004] ICR 893 it was held that '[t]he purpose of the award was to provide a sanction for breach by the employer of the obligations in s 188: it was not to compensate the employees for loss which they had suffered in consequence of the breach'. So a protective award may be recoverable for a failure to consult, even though the dismissals are not procedurally unfair.

Nevertheless, an employer thus cannot be compelled to consult, though in *ex parte Vardy* above the court quashed a decision by British Coal to close collieries where there was a failure to consult on the ground in that case that the union had a legitimate expectation under public law to be consulted before redundancies were made. The court then granted a declaration effectively requiring consultations to take place, giving rise to questions as to why remedies of this kind should not be available under the 1992 Act with contracts of employment continuing until consultations required by law have been held. By virtue of section 188(5) it is a defence that 'there are special circumstances which render it not reasonably practicable for the employer to comply with a requirement of subsection 1(A), (2) or (4)' of s 188, provided he or she took all such steps towards compliance' 'as are reasonably practicable in those circumstances'.

[8.64] *Clark's of Hove v Bakers' Union* [1978] ICR 1076 (CA)

On 24 October 1976 the employer terminated the employment of nearly all the workforce of 380 people and ceased trading on the same day. The company had been in financial difficulties since midsummer 1976, and had been trying to raise capital to deal with these difficulties. When it became clear that a possible source of capital was not interested in investing in the company 'it dawned upon the directors of the company that the shutters would have to be put up', and it was at that moment that a notice was posted dismissing the staff. The union complained that the company had been in breach of what was then the Employment Protection Act 1975, section 99. The employer argued that the circumstances were covered by section 99(8) (now TULRCA 1992, section 188(7)). The Court of Appeal upheld an industrial tribunal decision that the circumstances were not special.

Geoffrey Lane LJ:
Where, as here, the employers have admittedly failed to give the requisite 90 days notice the burden is clearly imposed upon them, by the statute, to show that there were special circumstances which made it not reasonably practicable for them to comply with the provisions of the Act, and also that they took steps towards compliance with the requirements, such steps as were reasonably practicable in the circumstances. There are, it is clear, these three stages: (1) were there special circumstances? If so, (2) did they render compliance with section 99 not reasonably practicable? And, if so, (3) did the employers take all such steps towards compliance with section 99 as were reasonably practicable in the circumstances?

What, then is meant by 'special circumstances'? Here we come to the crux of the case. In this aspect, also, the decision under the Road Traffic Acts appear to me to be unhelpful. The decisions are too well known to need reference. The basis of them all is probably *Whittall v Kirby* [1947] KB 194, *per* Lord Goddard CJ, at p 201:

> 'A "special reason" . . . is one . . . special to the facts of the particular case . . . special to the facts which constitute the offence, . . . A circumstance peculiar to the offender as distinguished from the offence is not a "special reason" . . .'

In so far as that means that the special circumstance must be relevant to the issue then that would apply equally here, but in these circumstances, the Employment Protection Act 1975, it seems to me that the way in which the phrase was interpreted by the industrial tribunal is correct. What they said, in effect, was this, that insolvency is, on its own, neither here nor there. It may be a special circumstance, it may not be a special circumstance. It will depend entirely on the cause of the insolvency whether the circumstances can be described as special or not. If, for example, sudden disaster strikes a company, making it necessary to close the concern, then plainly that would be a matter which was capable of being a special circumstance; and that is so whether the disaster is physical or financial. If the insolvency, however, were merely due to a gradual run-down of the company, as it was in this case, then those are facts on which the industrial tribunal can come to the conclusion that the circumstances were not special. In other words, to be special the event must be something out of the ordinary, something uncommon; and that is the meaning of the words 'special' in the context of this Act.

Accordingly it seems to me that the industrial tribunal approached the matter in precisely the correct way. They distilled the problem which they had to decide down to its essence, and they asked themselves this question: do these circumstances, which undoubtedly caused the summary dismissal and the failure to consult the union as required by section 99, amount to special circumstances; and they went on, again correctly, as it seems to me, to point out that insolvency simpliciter is neutral, it is not on its own a special circumstance. Whether it is or is not will depend upon the causes of the insolvency. They define 'special' as being something out of the ordinary run of events, such as, for example, a general trading boycott . . . Here, again, I think they were right.

Clark's of Hove was in some ways a very straightforward case, even if very distressing for all those involved. The changing nature of business ownership means that in other cases the position may not be so straightforward. Thus in some cases the employer of the redundant employees may not be the person who made the decision to close or reduce staffing levels. That decision may have been made some distance away by the managers of a parent company of which the British based company in peril is a wholly owned subsidiary. The problem in these cases is that there may be no advance notice by the parent company and no consultation before the announcement of closure and redundancy. In this situation the second sentence in s 188(7) provides that the failure of the parent company to provide information to the subsidiary cannot be excused as a special circumstance for the purposes of the first sentence of the paragraph. According to the EAT in *GMB v Beloit Walmsley Ltd* [2004] IRLR 18, '[i]t is delay in communicating that decision that is the mischief at which the special circumstances defence in s188(7) is aimed'. Quite whether the second sentence in s 188(7) will make much difference in practice is another matter.

8.5.4.4 The legislation in practice

As we have seen, there are concerns about the weakness of the sanction in the event of the employer's failure to comply with the legislation. But it does not follow from this that the procedures are wholly ineffective.

[8.65] M Hall and P Edwards, 'Reforming the Redundancy Consultation Procedure' (1999) 28 *Industrial Law Journal* 299

The scope of consultation: Much existing research suggests that managerial decision-making over redundancies is little affected by consultation. However, in the cases we looked at, where redundancy consultation was carried out via union representatives, and in the one case where consultation was via specially elected employee representatives, it appears to have been more effective than is sometimes suggested. The law requires there to be consultation about ways of avoiding the dismissals, reducing the number to be dismissed and mitigating the consequences of the dismissals. In practice, the requirement to consult 'about ways of avoiding the dismissals' was not seriously addressed because, in all eight cases, management had reviewed their operations over a period of several months and the key decisions about the basic need for redundancies had been made before the start of the consultation process. Consultation therefore focused on the process of handling job losses, not the principle, but in a number of cases nonetheless 'made a difference' in terms of influencing original managerial proposals, as the following examples show.

At one of the organisations we studied, SecurCo, where redundancies arose when two control centres were merged, the union secured some improvements to the proposed new harmonised terms and conditions, for example protecting the holiday entitlement of one group of staff, while all those selected for redundancy were offered alternative positions with the firm. At another organisation, EngCo, the union was able to defend the established principle of 'last in, first out', and also to shape the definition of how the principle actually worked. It also made some suggestions for reorganisation which were felt to have saved four or five jobs out of 65 that were under threat. Similarly, around 15 out of 80 members of staff due to lose their jobs at Urban College were retained, albeit only for a limited period. At TeleCo, where consultation was carried out via elected employee representatives, the representatives managed to persuade the company to change its initial insistence on selecting for redundancy on merit-based criteria and to allow volunteers. A range of more specific issues such as pension entitlements were also identified and resolved.

Meaningful consultation, albeit on the ways of handling redundancies and not the overall principles, thus took place in several of the organisations. The extent to which representatives could influence the process tended to reflect the context of the redundancies and the nature of managerial objectives. Consultation via union and/or employee representatives is no guarantee that effective discussion takes place but generally provides a structure or forum within which issues can be identified and discussed.

More recently, however, a number of events have shaken trade union confidence in the procedures. In 2000 and 2001 three high-profile, large scale redundancies were announced at BMW Rover, GM Vauxhall at Luton, and Corus Steel in South Wales. In all cases complaints were made that workers had not been consulted before the announcements had been made, and indeed that the workers in question heard of the company decisions in the first instance from the media. For the trade unions, the first of these events reinforced the belief based on experience that 'the remedy currently available under United Kingdom law to enforce [the Collective Redundancies] Directive is extremely weak, if not non-existent' (Trade and Industry Committee, 8th Report, *BMW and Longbridge* (HC 383, 1999–2000)), Minutes of Evidence, paragraph 142). A House of Commons Committee claimed that BMW's 'disgraceful failure to consult or even inform the workforce' may have constituted a breach of the 1975 Directive, and emphasised the importance of ensuring that the existing structure for multinational companies 'which would seem to have proved wholly ineffective on this occasion', provides real rights for workforce representatives (Trade and Industry Committee, 8th Report, *BMW and Longbridge* (HC 383, 1999–2000), paragraph 26). The government was compelled to order a review of the legislation in the light of these failings, while warning of the 'importance of striking a balance between providing minimum standards on protection of employees and maintaining the attractiveness of the UK as a destination for inward investment' (*ibid.*). The events at Longbridge, Luton and South Wales also fuelled the campaign to support the proposed EC Directive on Information and Consultation which would require employers of more than 50 employees to establish more wide-ranging information and consultation procedures.

8.6 Other forms of workplace representation

It has already been pointed out that trade unions now represent only a minority of workers, and only a minority of employers now recognise trade unions for the purposes of collective bargaining. Trade unions will no doubt hope and expect that the position will change as a result of the recognition procedure introduced by the Employment Relations Act 1999: but it is a long haul back, and the legislation will not bear the load alone. In the meantime, given that one of the purposes of trade unions is to represent workers in management decision-making, we have what in effect is a significant representation gap in British workplaces. Some suggest that this gap should be filled by mandatory works councils (or equivalent bodies) operating alongside the recognition legislation, whereby employers are required to consult (but with a view to reaching an agreement following the requirements of European law to which we have already referred) with representatives elected from the workforce as a whole. Supporters of such an initiative point to the practice of other European countries—such as Germany—where works councils have operated for some time, with wide rights of consultation about working practices, the working environment and redundancies. But in these countries, works councils operate alongside collective bargaining, which typically takes place at the sectoral or industry level, and which typically has a high level of density. The fear of some who are hesitant about works councils in the British setting is that they would operate in competition rather than in co-operation with traditional collective bargaining arrangements.

[8.66] G M Truter, *Implementing the Information and Consultation Directive in the UK: Lessons from Germany* (Institute of Employment Rights, 2003), pp 13–14 (footnotes omitted)

> Since the mechanics and outcomes of co-ordination have already been explored, this section will focus on the role that sectoral bargaining plays in sustaining social partnership in the enterprise in Germany. In this respect, sectoral bargaining can be said to have three interrelated functions. First, by giving workers 'assurances' particularly in relation to wages, the sectoral agreement fosters trust in the workplace. This in turn, allows greater co-operation in the quest for functional and temporal flexibility. Secondly, sectoral bargaining endows the co-operative venture with legitimacy. We have already seen that the union role in the functioning of works councils has a legitimizing effect in respect of works council activities. But as Hege and Dufour suggest, the real source of that legitimacy is the bargaining activity of powerful trade unions at sectoral level. What is of particular significance is the way in which that activity prevents self-interest from driving the agenda in the enterprise at the expense of collective goals (*Betriebsegoismus*). As Streeck points out, workers would not be willing 'to strike for the sectoral collective agreement if their own effective employment conditions were only decided in a second, follow-on round of bargaining, and possibly strikes, in the company.' An additional point to be made here is that through connecting the workplace with 'broader union perspectives' sectoral bargaining can assist the parties in the enterprise in realising economic and incomes policies. Finally, sectoral bargaining is said to keep the workplace

'free of fundamental conflicts' over the main distribution-related issues, thereby enhancing the 'productive and optimising effects' of co-determination.

As seen in the previous chapter, emphasis has been placed by the Commission on Co-determination on the dangers which uncontrolled decentralization would pose, not only to the stability of the collective bargaining system, but also to the functioning of works councils. In regard to the latter, the Commission states:

> 'The continued effectiveness of codetermination will depend decisively on the *maintenance of a division of tasks between codetermination and collective bargaining*. The reform of supra-plant level collective agreements in certain industries must not be achieved by methods that call into question the dual system of labour relations. In particular, the social partners at plant level must not be transferred regulatory tasks—nor should such tasks fall to them due to a failure on the part of collective bargainers—whose performance at plant level would pose a threat to trustful cooperation between the works council and management, or would bring the works council into conflict with employees' negative right of association or the trade unions' monopoly on the right to strike. Adherence to Article 77(3) of the Works Constitution Act is thus of fundamental importance.'

Works councils have a number of potential benefits which should not be overlooked. Apart from the fact that they help to bridge the representation gap, they are also bodies which are wholly inclusive. This means that a worker is eligible and entitled to take part by virtue of his or her status as a worker: there is no need also to be a member of a trade union. But there are also a number of potential drawbacks which equally should not be overlooked. The main problem of course is one of resources. A works council will depend to some extent on the employer for its financing and administration. In the event of a dispute or disagreement with the employer, the works council may not be in a position to draw on the support of an organisation external to the workplace, and may not be able to contemplate expensive legal action. It may also operate to exclude *bona fide* trade unions, by putting in place a rival to a trade union which is difficult to remove. Because of the problems associated with works councils, workers may be left with a second class form of representation, though in some cases this may be a matter of choice. The works council also provides an institutional structure within which trade unions can operate (by putting up candidates, training works council members and providing resources), thereby facilitating the process of unionisation in some cases. We conclude this chapter by addressing the way in which public policy is gradually changing to different forms of worker representation.

8.6.1 Staff associations: a rival to trade unionism

One example of this change is the legislative response to the staff association as a form of worker representation. In the 1970s the position adopted in legislation was one of outright hostility. Under the statutory recognition procedure of 1975, only an independent trade union could make a claim for recognition, and there was no question of the presence of a works council or a staff association operating to bar an application. By the same token, only independent trade unions recognised by the employer were entitled to the disclosure of information for collective bargaining purposes, the officials of only independent trade unions recognised by the employer were entitled to time off work for trade union duties, and only independent trade unions recognised by the employer were entitled to be consulted about redundancies. But the position has changed and is changing, although the legacy of the 1970s is still with us to some extent. It is true that only a trade union with a certificate of independence issued by the Certification Officer under TULRCA 1992, section 6 may make a claim under the new recognition legislation (TULRCA 1992, Schedule A1, paragraph 6). However, the new procedure is not so uncompromisingly hostile to the idea of non-union forms of representation than was the case in the past. This is despite the fact that ILO Convention 98 actively discourages non-independent trade unions.

[8.67] ILO Convention 98 (The Right to Organise and Collective Bargaining Convention, 1949), Article 2

1. Workers' and employers' organisations shall enjoy adequate protection against any acts of interference by each other or each other's agents or members in their establishment, functioning or administration.
2. In particular, acts which are designed to promote the establishment of workers' organisations under the domination of employers' organisations, or to support workers' organisations by financial or other means, with the object of placing such organisations under the control of employers or employers' organisations, shall be deemed to constitute acts of interference within the meaning of this Article'.

This changing attitude is reflected generally in paragraphs 2.4–2.6 of the White Paper, *Fairness at Work* (see above, pp 725–726), which preceded the legislation, and more particularly by the fact that a recognised staff association may block an application under the procedure. TULRCA 1992, Schedule A1, paragraph 35 (1) provides that an application is not admissible 'if the CAC is satisfied that there is already in force a collective agreement under which a union is (or unions are) recognised as entitled to conduct collective bargaining on behalf of any workers falling within the relevant bargaining unit'. For this purpose the incumbent trade union need not be independent, the legislation providing in the following cryptic terms that:

(4) In applying sub-paragraph (1) an agreement for recognition (the agreement in question) must be ignored if—
(a) the union does not have (or none of the unions has) a certificate under section 6 that it is independent,
(b) at some time there was an agreement (the old agreement) between the employer and the union under which the union (whether alone or with other unions) was recognised as entitled to conduct collective bargaining on behalf of a group of workers which was the same or substantially the same as the group covered by the agreement in question, and
(c) the old agreement ceased to have effect in the period of three years ending with the date of the agreement in question.

This means that in some (most) circumstances the presence of a works council or staff association with bargaining (not consultation) rights, could operate to prevent an application for recognition by an independent trade union. This may be so even though the works council does not have bargaining rights in respect of pay, hours or holidays, the matters in respect of which the statutory procedure applies.

[8.68] *Prison Officers' Association and Securicor Custodial Services Ltd,* CAC Case No TUR 1/5/00

> The POA sought recognition from the employer for all those employed at HMP Parc, Bridgend. 145 of the 250 employees were members of the POA. But the company argued that the application was pre-empted by paragraph 35 because it had an existing recognition agreement (dated 14 June 2000) with Custodial Services Staff Association, a non independent trade union. The CAC held that paragraph 35(4) had to be read as a whole and that its three elements were not discrete. The three elements were 'whether the Association was an independent trade union; whether there was an "old agreement" between the Company and the Association; and, whether the old agreement, if any, had ceased to have effect in the period of three years ending on 14 June 2000'. Although the union was not independent, 'there was no agreement between the Company and the Association which ceased to have effect within the period of three years ending with the date of the existing collective agreement'. Accordingly, 'the agreement of 14 June 2000 is not one that must be ignored by virtue of paragraph 35(4)', and the application was ruled inadmissible.

The only escape from this state of affairs is to knock out the non-independent union or staff association by instituting proceedings for its derecognition, under TULRCA 1992, Schedule A1, Part VI. If successful, a claim for recognition under the procedure could then be made by an independent trade union. An application for derecognition under Part VI must be made to the CAC by a worker (not an interested trade union) who must then give a copy of the application to the employer. If the application is admissible the CAC is then expected to broker an agreement between the employer, the non-independent union and the applicant. If the parties are unable to reach an agreement, the CAC will hold a ballot on the derecognition of the staff association. During the balloting period the non-independent union has a statutory right of access to the workers to be balloted (as of course does the employer): but neither the applicant nor an interested union has a similar right of access. For an application to be successful, a majority must vote in favour of de-recognition, and the majority must include at least 40 per cent of the bargaining unit. For a fuller account, see K D Ewing, 'Trade Union Recognition and Staff Associations—A Breach of International Labour Standards?' (2000) 29 *Industrial Law Journal,* 267.

[8.69] K D Ewing, S Moore and S Wood, *Unfair Labour Practices: Trade Union Recognition and Employer Resistance* (Institute of Employment Rights, 2003), pp 12–16 (references omitted)

> Employers seeking to discourage trade union membership and trade union recognition may take one of a number of pre-emptive steps. Here there are three lawful tactics that are currently visible:

- the employer may set up rival forms of organisation such as works councils or employee forums designed ostensibly to give workers a voice;
- the employer may establish its own company union to which it gives negotiating rights on a range of issues; or
- the employer may choose the union with which he or she is prepared to deal, and reach an agreement with a union that may not have the support of the workforce.

The strategy of pre-emption is well known both in this country and overseas, previously acknowledged by Bain in his study of white collar unionism. There he referred to it as the strategy of 'peaceful competition', as one of several obstacles encountered by independent trade unions. There are two problems with these forms of worker representation. The first is that they may not guarantee adequately resourced or independent representation. In one case we encountered the body in question was said by a company executive 'to have access to independent legal advice', 'at my discretion'. The second is that the imposed form of representation may not reflect the wishes of the workers who may never have been asked about how they wish to be represented in the enterprise, and the voice allowed may not be one permitted to speak loudly or for long. Moreover, it may not be a voice that is listened to.

Creating Other Channels for Worker Involvement

The statutory recognition procedure provides an extra incentive to employers to establish works councils, staff associations and other such bodies. Not only may the existence of a staff association tend to dissuade workers of the need for independent trade union representation, but the existence of such a body could protect an employer from an application under the statutory procedure. This is because the procedure cannot be used where there is a collective agreement between a trade union and an employer (TULRCA 1992, Sch A1, para 34). The trade union for this purpose need not be an independent one and the statutory definition of a trade union is such that it could apply to a works council or staff association. The body in question would however have to have been given some kind of negotiating rights for this strategy to block an application under the procedure: consultation rights would not be enough for this purpose. But a good example of this tactic in operation is *POA and Securicor Custodial Services* [TUR1/5/2000], where an application was made for recognition for prison officers at HMP Parc, Bridgend. The union had 58% membership, but the application was rejected because an existing recognition agreement was in force with the Securicor Custodial Services Staff Association, an organization set up by the company shortly before the enactment of the Employment Rights Act 1999 with the express purpose of preventing the POA achieving collective bargaining.

In our survey of CAC cases, there were formal employee representative bodies in place at the time of the CAC application in 58% of these cases; in 30 per cent of cases it is thought that these bodies were set up in response to unionisation or the Employment Relations Act 1999. Thus while in some cases the staff association or works council had been in existence for some time, in others its arrival coincided with the enactment of the Employment Relations Act 1999, and in others with an anticipated application under the procedure. In some cases the staff representatives were elected by the workers, but in others they were appointed by the management. But it appears that these bodies do not always provide the independent representation that workers wanted. So in one case which was heard by the CAC, a Staff Council had been set up in 1992. In response to a formal request for recognition from an independent trade union in July 2000 the company replied that it was not willing to agree because the Staff Council was effective. In fact the manual workers refused to recognize the staff council or the annual pay review which it discussed but did not negotiate, and did not return ballot papers in elections to it. Similarly in another case the existing Employee Forum was consultative only and representatives were effectively appointed by the company. It was dominated by employees who were opposed to the recognition of an independent trade union, and held in contempt by other members of the workforce.

The establishment of such bodies does not necessarily prevent unionisation. Indeed this tactic can backfire in the sense that a weak or transparently ineffective consultative machinery can stimulate the demand for independent representation. This may in turn lead to workers initiating or supporting a trade union recognition campaign. In one case (*AEEU and GE Caledonian, TUR1/120/2001*) the entire Works Council resigned following the union's application for recognition because of the breakdown of trust between the Works Council and the company, and the desire on the part of the Works Council members to see proper collective bargaining established. In some cases the existence of such a body provides an institutional framework for union members in a workplace to seek to influence. In fact our survey shows that where there was employee representation, in 70 per cent of these cases union representatives or members sat on these bodies, and in a number of cases the impetus for recognition came from them. So in *AEEU and GE Caledonian*, above, 8 of the 9 Works Council members were members of the union. In another case the union activists behind the recognition campaign were all members of the company's consultative body. In these cases an application under the procedure was possible only because the works council or similar body had no negotiating rights. If the employer had given the body in question such rights, no application would have been possible.

Negotiation with Non Independent Trade Unions

A variation of the foregoing tactic is for the employer to establish a consultative body or works council which is then given negotiating rights over a number of issues. The benefit to the employer of this arrangement is that not only may a functioning works council or staff association operate to discourage trade union organisation within the workplace, but it may make it virtually impossible under the statutory procedure for a union to bring an application. For this purpose the collective agreement need not include pay, hours and holidays, and it is immaterial that the trade union party to the agreement is not an independent trade union, or that it does not have a certificate of independence Where a collective agreement does exist with a non-independent trade union, the latter would have to be derecognised before an application is made under the statutory procedure. It is true that there are special provisions in the procedure to enable a non independent trade union to be derecognised, even though there is no comparable provision for the derecognition of an independent trade union which has concluded a voluntary recognition agreement. But in order to activate the procedure, the application to derecognise the non independent trade union must be made by a worker who must also give notification of the application to the employer (ibid). If the threshold conditions are met for a ballot, the non independent union then has rights of access to the workforce, rights which the workers who activated the de-recognition do not have.

The leading example of an employer which has adopted this tactic to pre-empt the union is News International, the publisher of *The Times*, the *Sunday Times*, the *Sun* and the *News of the World*. The News International Staff Association (NISA) has its origins in the mid 1980s when the company set up a Human Resources Committee at its different plants. It was at this time that the company de-recognised the existing trade unions in circumstances that are now well known The members of the Committee were appointed by the company management, though from 1989 space was provided for elected members. In 1995 the Human Resources Committee was abandoned and replaced with the Employees' Consultative Council which metamorphosed in turn to become the News

International Staff Association. Membership of NISA is granted automatically to every employee of the company, and those who do not wish to be in membership must opt out. Those who remain in membership are not required to pay any subscriptions with the result that the Association is said to be 'dependent on the employer for meeting any costs incurred in the course of [its] activities'. Appropriate administrative assistance would thus be provided by the Human Resources Manager of the company, which also undertook to meet all the reasonable costs of the association in taking legal advice, provided the advice was sought from a solicitor approved by the Director of Human Resources.

The NISA Charter was redrafted shortly after the publication of the government's White Paper, *Fairness at Work* in 1998. Under the terms of the Charter its principal purpose is the 'regulation of relations between workers and News International', and that it conducts collective bargaining with company representatives, thereby falling within the definition of a trade union as provided by TULRCA 1992, s 1. Although all staff association members are elected, NISA is not an independent trade union, having been denied a certificate of independence in May 2001. In concluding that NISA was not independent, the Certification Officer found that recent changes to its constitution and operating practices meant that it was no longer under the domination or control of the employer. Meetings of the executive were no longer coordinated, attended and minuted by members of News International Human Resources Department. But NISA still had some way to go before it could be said not to be 'liable to interference' by the employer. Weighing 'the strength of the employers, the pressures they could bring against the staff association and the facilities they could withdraw' on the one hand, against the membership base, structures and financial resources of NISA on the other, the Certification Officer found that it had not yet reached the stage where it was able to satisfy the statutory definition of independence. Its vulnerability to interference was 'not insignificant' Nevertheless it is currently impossible for an independent trade union to use the recognition procedure against the company.

8.6.2 Consulting employee representatives

Under the trade union recognition procedures, it may be said that public policy has moved to a position in which non-union forms of worker representation at the workplace are now formally accommodated. Staff associations or works councils may be tolerated rather than actively discouraged, though only if they have acquired a negotiating status. Under European law in contrast, not only are non-union forms of worker representation tolerated, they are formally required in the absence of traditional trade union structures. Under EC law, employers are required to consult with workers' representatives in the event of a redundancy or in the event of the transfer of an undertaking. Domestic legislation initially confined this as an obligation to consult only with the representatives of a recognised trade union: where there was no union recognised for the purposes of collective bargaining, the duty did not apply. The position was changed as a result of Cases 382/92, 383/92, *European Commission v United Kingdom* [1994] ICR 664, following which the legislation was amended to require employers to consult with employee representatives where there is no recognised trade union. As we have seen there are also consultation obligations in relation to health and safety. These too were expanded—in 1996.

8.6.2.1 *The priority of the recognised trade union*

There are a number of points to observe about the consultation procedures. The first is that in some but not all cases there is a priority in favour of consultation with a trade union where there is a trade union recognised for collective bargaining. This is true in the case of redundancy consultation and consultation about the transfer of undertakings, where consultation must take place with the union in respect of employees of a description in respect of whom the union is recognised. It is only where there is no recognised union (either generally or in respect of a particular group of workers) that the employer must consult employee representatives. It was not always thus: when the legislation was changed following the ECJ decision in 1994, it was open to an employer to choose to consult with either a recognised union or a representative of the employees. This same preference in favour of trade union-based consultation where there is a recognised trade union is to be found also in the consultation procedures in the field of health and safety at work. The Safety Representatives and Safety Committees Regulations 1977, SI 1977/500, provide that a recognised trade union may appoint a safety representative (Regulation 3). The Regulations impose a duty on the employer to consult safety representatives on a range of issues, and empower representatives to conduct inspections at the workplace. Safety representatives may also initiate a safety committee at the workplace. In cases where there is no recognised trade union, provision for consultation is made by the Health and Safety (Consultation with Employees) Regulations 1996, SI 1996/1513. It will be noted that they allow for consultation directly with employees individually or with their representatives.

In other cases the priority for the recognised trade union over other forms of worker representation takes a slightly different form, though it is substantially the same. This is true, for example, of the Working Time Regulations 1998, SI 1998/1833, the main features of which are considered in Chapter 4 above. Regulation 12 allows for rest breaks to be determined in accordance with a collective agreement or a workforce agreement. And by virtue of Regulation 23, a collective agreement or a workforce agreement may modify or exclude the application of Regulations 6(1)–(3) (on the length of night work), 10(1) (daily rest periods), 11(1) and (2) (weekly rest periods) and 12(1) (rest breaks). In some circumstances they may also modify Regulation 4(3) and (4) (maximum weekly working time). The following provisions suggest that if there is a trade union recognised in respect of any group of workers the employer must proceed by way of collective bargaining for the foregoing purposes. However, where a union is recognised but there is no collective agreement in force, the employer may proceed by way of a workforce agreement. Moreover, the employer may be required to proceed by way of a workforce agreement in respect of those workers in respect of whom the union is not recognised and there is no collective agreement in force.

[8.70] Working Time Regulations 1998, SI 1998/1833, Schedule 1

1. An agreement is a workforce agreement for the purposes of these Regulations if the following conditions are satisfied—
(a) the agreement is in writing;
(b) it has effect for a specified period not exceeding five years;
(c) it applies either—
  (i)   to all of the relevant members of the workforce, or
  (ii) to all of the relevant members of the workforce who belong to a particular group;
(d) the agreement is signed—
  (i)   in the case of an agreement of the kind referred to in sub-paragraph (c)(i), by the representatives of the workforce, and in the case of an agreement of the kind referred to in sub-paragraph (c)(ii) by the representatives of the group to which the agreement applies (excluding, in either case, any representative not a relevant member of the workforce on the date on which the agreement was first made available for signature), or
  (ii) if the employer employed 20 or fewer workers on the date referred to in sub-paragraph (d)(i), either by the appropriate representatives in accordance with that sub-paragraph or by the majority of the workers employed by him;
(e) before the agreement was made available for signature, the employer provided all the workers to whom it was intended to apply on the date on which it came into effect with copies of the text of the agreement and such guidance as those workers might reasonably require in order to understand it fully.

2. For the purposes of this Schedule—

'a particular group' is a group of the relevant members of a workforce who undertake a particular function, work at a particular workplace or belong to a particular department or unit within their employer's business;

'relevant members of the workforce' are all of the workers employed by a particular employer, excluding any worker whose terms and conditions of employment are provided for, wholly or in part, in a collective agreement;

'representatives of the workforce' are workers duly elected to represent the relevant members of the workforce, 'representatives of the group' are workers duly elected to represent the members of a particular group, and representatives are 'duly elected' if the election at which they were elected satisfied the requirements of paragraph 3 of this Schedule.

3. The requirements concerning elections referred to in paragraph 2 are that—
(a) the number of representatives to be elected is determined by the employer;
(b) the candidates for election as representatives of the workforce are relevant members of the workforce, and the candidates for election as representatives of a group are members of the group;
(c) no worker who is eligible to be a candidate is unreasonably excluded from standing for election;
(d) all the relevant members of the workforce are entitled to vote for representatives of the workforce, and all the members of a particular group are entitled to vote for representatives of the group;
(e) the workers entitled to vote may vote for as many candidates as there are representatives to be elected;
(f) the election is conducted so as to secure that—
  (i)   so far as is reasonably practicable, those voting do so in secret, and
  (ii) the votes given at the election are fairly and accurately counted.

These provisions of the Working Time Regulations are reflected in the Maternity and Parental Leave etc. Regulations 1999, SI 1999/3312. Under the latter regulations default provisions on parental leave in Schedule 2 of the Regulations apply unless the employee's contract of employment contains provisions on parental leave which are incorporated from a collective agreement or a workforce agreement.

8.6.2.2 *The election of employee representatives*

The second point which arises in relation to the consultation procedures relates to the myriad election procedures which are now in place to meet the different circumstances in which a duty to consult arises. Where there is a recognised trade union the duty to consult is generally with the representatives of the union: it is for the union in accordance with its procedures to determine who the representative may be, though as we have seen there may be difficulties in terms of accreditation by employers. But where there is no union, the question arises how to elect the employee representative. There is no uniformity of approach, with different procedures being used for the election of representatives for redundancies and transfers on the one hand, and safety on the other. The election of the representative to negotiate workforce agreements under both the Working Time Regulations 1998, SI 1998/1833, and the Maternity and Parental Leave etc Regulations 1999, SI 1999/3312, is different again. A striking feature of the procedures for the election of the representatives for redundancies and transfers is the degree of responsibility which is given to the employer to determine critical questions about the procedure.

[8.71] Trade Union and Labour Relations (Consolidation) Act 1992, section 188A

Election of employee representatives

188A (1) The requirements for the election of employee representatives under section 188(1B)(b)(ii) are that—

(a) the employer shall make such arrangements as are reasonably practical to ensure that the election is fair;

(b) the employer shall determine the number of representatives to be elected so that there are sufficient representatives to represent the interests of all the affected employees having regard to the number and classes of those employees;

(c) the employer shall determine whether the affected employees should be represented either by representatives of all the affected employees or by representatives of particular classes of those employees;

(d) before the election the employer shall determine the term of office as employee representatives so that it is of sufficient length to enable information to be given and consultations under section 188 to be completed;

(e) the candidates for election as employee representatives are affected employees on the date of the election;

(f) no affected employee is unreasonably excluded from standing for election;

(g) all affected employees on the date of the election are entitled to vote for employee representatives;

(h) the employees entitled to vote may vote for as many candidates as there are representatives to be elected to represent them or, if there are to be representatives for particular classes of employees, may vote for as many candidates as there are representatives to be elected to represent their particular class of employee;

(i)   the election is conducted so as to secure that—

(i)   so far as is reasonably practicable, those voting to do so in secret, and

(ii) the votes given at the election are accurately counted.

There is no public agency such as the CAC with responsibilities here, and there is no obligation for independent scrutineers as in the case of trade union internal elections. Similar provisions apply in the case of consultation for the purpose of business transfers under the Transfer of Undertakings (Protection of Employment) Regulations 1981, SI 1981/1794.

Unlike the redundancy and the business transfer procedures, in the context of health and safety the employer has no responsibility for the conduct of the election, term of office or number of representatives. The full extent of the employer's responsibility is to ensure that candidates are permitted time off with pay to attend to their functions as candidates, a duty which applies also to other workplace representatives under the other statutory provisions under consideration here. There seems to be no way of challenging the election of a safety representative, and no way the workforce can require a safety representative to stand down and submit for re-election. There is not even an obligation on the part of the employer to permit the election to be held on his or her premises or during working time. The only sanction which could bite relates to a failure to consult. But this is a criminal offence, and the legislation cannot be enforced by way of civil action. So even where the employer fails to consult there is not much that the employee representative can do about it. The only conduct for which the employer is directly accountable to the representative is in relation to a failure to allow time off work, for which proceedings can be brought in an employment tribunal. The Working Time Regulations 1998, SI 1998/1833, and the Maternity and Parental Leave etc Regulations 1999, SI 1999/3312, are more like the provisions relating to the election of representatives for redundancy and business transfer consultations, but not identical.

8.6.2.3 *Protection of employee representatives*

The third point under these procedures relates to the facilities for employee representatives and the protection that they enjoy under the law when they put themselves forward for election, when they campaign for election, and when they carry out the duties of office. The provisions relating to redundancy and business transfers provide time off to carry out the functions of a candidate for the post of representative, as well as the functions of the representative itself, and now to undergo training to perform these duties (ERA 1996, section 61). In the case of health and safety, the safety representative is also entitled to time off with pay to carry out functions as a candidate, functions as a representative, and to undergo training in the responsibilities of office. But unlike employee representatives in the case of redundancy and transfers, the employer must provide training for the health and safety representatives: Health and Safety (Consultation with Employees) Regulations 1996, SI 1996/1513. Curiously there does not appear to be any provision for time off for representatives elected to negotiate workforce agreements under the Working Time Regulations

1998, SI 1998/1833, or the Maternity and Parental Leave etc Regulations 1999, SI 1999/3312. In the case of each of the five procedures discussed here, there is statutory protection against both action short of dismissal and dismissal for carrying out the functions of a candidate or the responsibilities of office. One point to note is that the protection applies both to acts and to omissions, unlike the protection for trade union membership until the changes introduced by the Employment Relations Act 1999. For these purposes the different forms of protection are brought together under one roof, sheltering in the Employment Rights Act 1996 (sections 44, 45A and 47; and 100, 101A and 103). This is with the exception of workplace representatives under the Maternity and Parental Leave etc Regulations 1999, SI 1999/3312, who are protected from discrimination and dismissal by the Regulations themselves (Regulations 19 and 20).

In addition to time off for the representative, and protection against discrimination and dismissal, there is also the question of the facilities required by the representative to enable him or her properly to carry out the duties of office. Employee representatives are as much in need of support as are the lay officials of trade unions if they are to discharge their responsibilities properly. Facilities may take several forms. The first is training; a second is the provision of information to enable meaningful consultations to take place; a third is access to external sources of professional help, whether it be legal or financial advice; a fourth is secretarial and related facilities such as access to an office, a computer, a telephone, a notice board, a filing cabinet and the like; and a fifth is the opportunity during working hours to consult with and report to fellow employees. On most of these issues the legislation falls woefully short. Only the Health and Safety (Consultation with Employees) Regulations 1996, SI 1996/1513, require employers to ensure that representatives are provided with training, and none of the statutory provisions properly address any of the other issues referred to here. TULRCA 1992, section 188(5A) (above, p 824) provides simply that employee representatives for the purposes of redundancy consultation are to be allowed by the employer 'access to the affected employees' and 'such accommodation and other facilities as may be appropriate'. Similar provision is made in the amended Transfer of Undertakings (Protection of Employment) Regulations 1981, SI 1981/1794. It is true that the safety representative is a standing officer who may be elected for an indeterminate period, with a number of tasks to attend to, whereas the others are elected to deal with a single task. But this does not diminish the need for informed, skilful and effective representation of the employees concerned.

8.6.3 Information and Consultation Procedures

Worker representation by means other than by independent trade unions is now accepted in a number of ways. It remains the case nevertheless that all forms of worker representation have been in decline, whether independent trade union-based or not (N Millward, A Bryson and J Forth, *All Change at Work?* (London, Routledge, 2000), pp 136–37). It is also the case that the current arrangements are incoherent, irrational, and inconsistent. There seems an obvious case for building on and rationalising the many different information and consultation regimes now in play, by bringing them together in a single form, with mandatory representative bodies to exist in workplaces where there is no recognised trade union (and perhaps also where there is), with employers required to consult with these representative bodies on prescribed issues, but free to include other issues as well. An opportunity to do just that was provided by the Information and Consultation Directive, which has been implemented by the Information and Consultation Regulations. These follow on the back of the European Works Council Directive of 1994 and make provision for the creation of European Works Councils in multinational corporations operating in two or more Member States. They effectively require the creation of a standing body at European level to allow for the flow of information and consultation with workers' representatives. The details of the implementing Transnational Information and Consultation of Employees 1999, SI 1999/3323, are set out in the box on pp 858–859 below.

8.6.3.1 The Information and Consultation Directive

The Information and Consultation Directive makes provision for the introduction of information and consultation procedures at national level, though it applies only to undertakings employing more than 50 employees in any one Member State. The different objectives of the Directive are made clear by the preamble:

[8.72] Directive 2002/14/EC of the European Parliament and of the Council of 11 March 2002 establishing a general framework for informing and consulting employees in the European Community

Preamble

(6) The existence of legal frameworks at national and Community level intended to ensure that employees are involved in the affairs of the undertaking employing them and in decisions which affect them has not always prevented serious decisions affecting employees from being taken and made public without adequate procedures having been implemented beforehand to inform and consult them.

(7) There is a need to strengthen dialogue and promote mutual trust within undertakings in order to improve risk anticipation, make work organisation more flexible and facilitate employee access to training within the undertaking while maintaining security, make employees aware of adaptation needs, increase employees' availability to undertake measures and activities to increase their employability, promote employee involvement in the operation and future of the undertaking and increase its competitiveness.

(8) There is a need, in particular, to promote and enhance information and consultation on the situation and likely development of employment within the undertaking and, where the employer's evaluation suggests that employment within the undertaking may be under threat, the possible anticipatory measures envisaged, in particular in terms of employee training and skill development, with a view to offsetting the negative developments or their consequences and increasing the employability and adaptability of the employees likely to be affected.

(9) Timely information and consultation is a prerequisite for the success of the restructuring and adaptation of undertakings to the new conditions created by globalisation of the economy, particularly through the development of new forms of organisation of work. . .

(13) The existing legal frameworks for employee information and consultation at Community and national level tend to adopt an excessively *a posteriori* approach to the process of change, neglect the economic aspects of decisions taken and do not contribute either to genuine anticipation of employment developments within the undertaking or to risk prevention.

These provisions have proved to be extremely controversial and it is clear that the British government lobbied extensively to have the Directive diluted. As a result—as Truter **[8.66]** indicates at p 833—the Directive is constructed on a contradiction with a fault-line at its core. On the one hand it is seen positively as a means to address the concerns identified in the foregoing extract. But on the other hand, the preamble also reveals a concern that it may impose too big a burden on business, notwithstanding the rather modest obligations that it imposes.

[8.73] Directive 2002/14/EC of the European Parliament and of the Council of 11 March 2002 establishing a general framework for informing and consulting employees in the European Community

Preamble

(15) This Directive is without prejudice to national systems regarding the exercise of this right in practice where those entitled to exercise it are required to indicate their wishes collectively. . . .

(16) This Directive is without prejudice to those systems which provide for the direct involvement of employees, as long as they are always free to exercise the right to be informed and consulted through their representatives. . . .

(19) The purpose of this general framework is also to avoid any administrative, financial or legal constraints which would hinder the creation and development of small and medium-sized undertakings. To this end, the scope of this Directive should be restricted, according to the choice made by Member States, to undertakings with at least 50 employees or establishments employing at least 20 employees. . . .

(21) However, on a transitional basis, Member States in which there is no established statutory system of information and consultation of employees or employee representation should have the possibility of further restricting the scope of the Directive as regards the numbers of employees.

(22) A Community framework for informing and consulting employees should keep to a minimum the burden on undertakings or establishments while ensuring the effective exercise of the rights granted.

(23) The objective of this Directive is to be achieved through the establishment of a general framework comprising the principles, definitions and arrangements for information and consultation, which it will be for the Member States to comply with and adapt to their own national situation, ensuring, where appropriate, that management and labour have a leading role by allowing them to define freely, by agreement, the arrangements for informing and consulting employees which they consider to be best suited to their needs and wishes.

So although the Directive was introduced with great expectation and high hopes, more sober reflection suggests that it will neither provide a springboard for trade union organisation in unorganised workplaces nor a basis for an effective alternative to worker representation. Indeed it has been revealed that:

the ETUC, the European Trades Union Congress which represents European trade unions in Brussels . . . was startled to find that the Directive had a strong and determined enemy in the new British government. 'Britain went to war to block the Directive', is how John Monks [then general secretary of the British TUC] puts it. (F Beckett and D Hencke, *The Blairs and their Court* (Aurum Press, London, 2004), p 201)

8.6.3.2 Implementing the Directive

Having failed to block the Directive, the British government managed successfully to dilute its impact. The weaknesses of the Directive are now fully exposed by the Information and Consultation of Employees Regulations 2004, SI 3426/2004. There are in fact five concerns

- The number of employers to whom the regulations will apply
- The nature and scope of the duties which the regulations impose
- The opportunity for employers to dilute the nature of the obligations
- The lack of effective protection for workplace representatives
- The procedures for enforcement in the event of non compliance

These matters are considered more fully in K D Ewing and G M Truter, 'The Information and Consultation of Employees' Regulations: Voluntarism's Bitter Legacy' (2005) 68 *Modern Law Review* 626, on which the rest of this chapter draws. Before considering these matters, it is important to note an important strategic decision taken to implement the Directive in domestic law. As we have seen:

- it has been a feature of other worker representation arrangements—from redundancy consultation to working time arrangements—that priority should be given to the recognised trade union where one exists.
- the chosen method of implementing European obligations has been to require consultation with a recognised trade union, failing which with elected or appointed workers' representatives.

The Information and Consultation Regulations 2004 represent a sharp break with this practice by denying any priority for the recognised trade union. Rather than have a single channel for worker representation where a trade union is recognised, the Regulations anticipate the possibility of two separate channels in the same workplace.

[8.74] P Davies and C Kilpatrick, 'UK Worker Representation after Single Channel' (2004) 33 *Industrial Law Journal* 121

We develop our analysis by setting out five headline criteria which we think should have guided the UK's regulatory choices...Run together, the five criteria comprise a short paragraph which sums up our argument. Union representation is preferable to non-union representation, and should therefore be promoted. However, union promotion requires containing, and not expanding, the regulatory role of recognised unions. Especially where bargaining is concerned, UK law is in need of a 'representativity' criterion to choose between independent unions. Outside collective bargaining, UK law needs to make use of union structures which are not dependent on recognition. However, where there is no adequate union structure, elected representation is better than no representation at all. Dispensing altogether with a representative structure is never an acceptable regulatory choice…Union representation has intrinsic merits which makes it preferable to non-union representation. Workers want their representation to have a productive, cooperative, relationship with their employer, but they also place great store on their representatives being independent of their employer. Union representation can guarantee independence more effectively than any other form of worker representation. This is because, drawing on the definition of an independent union in section 5 of TULRCA 1992, independent unions are not chosen or endorsed by the employer and they are financially autonomous through members' dues. The latter also provide the union with a revenue stream which can be used to provide valuable services to members. Moreover, because UK unions are generally organised in more than one workplace, and very often in more than one firm, unions can generate comparative knowledge, accumulate skills and build up expertise. In short, unions tend to be good at representing workers because they are voluntary associations which exist primarily for that purpose.

These arrangements are perhaps all the more remarkable for the fact that they are the product of the first so-called Social Partnership agreement between the TUC and the CBI. The social partners had been asked by the government to reach an agreement about the implementation of the Directive. But although recognised trade unions have no priority under the Information and Consultation Regulations, it remains the case nevertheless that they are likely to be the key to the successful operation of the procedures, and that the most likely consequence of the regulations is that they will expand the scope of collective bargaining rather than the scope of worker representation. Partly this is because the regulations require workers to take the initiative to establish an information and consultation procedure, something which may be more likely to happen in a unionised workforce where there are already representative structures in place. And partly this is because it is possible for an employer to enter into a 'pre-existing agreement' with a union for the purposes of information and consultation. There are strong incentives for an employer to reach such an agreement, the most important of which being that the statutory enforcement procedures do not apply to such agreements. But even where there is no 'pre-existing agreement' and steps are taken to invoke the statutory procedures, it is likely that it will be a trade union in a recognised workplace that co-ordinates such an initiative and that it will be a recognised trade union which will be behind any attempts to conclude a 'negotiated agreement' under the regulations. Both 'pre-existing agreements' and 'negotiated agreements' are considered more fully below.

8.6.3.3 *The Scope of the Regulations*

The regulations apply only to undertakings employing more than 50 employees (not workers). In the British context this means that only about a third of the workforce will be covered by regulations that apply to only a small minority of companies. There are thought to be roughly some 24 million employees in the United Kingdom, of whom some 17 million are thought to work for companies employing 50 or more employees: this means that some 7 million workers will be denied coverage. There are also thought to be some 1.2 million employers in the United Kingdom, of whom only

36,500 employ 50 or more employees. Although the impact of the regulations will thus be limited, their content is such that they are designed to minimise rather than maximise their application. Thus:

- The Regulations do not apply to all employers with more than 50 employees, but only to 'undertakings' (Regulation 3), a term defined to mean 'a public or private undertaking carrying out an economic activity, whether or not operating for gain' (Regulation 2). Although this appears to be wide and generous, it is widely thought to exclude the activities of central and local government, though the government has indicated that it will introduce a code of practice to apply the substance of the Directive to these sectors. So far as an 'economic activity' is concerned, this is not a phrase which is known to British labour law, and the government seems content to leave the matter to the courts to sort out.
- The Regulations do not necessarily apply to all undertakings with more than 50 employees. This is because an employer can choose not to count certain part time employees as whole employees. By virtue of Regulation 4(2)(b) an employee working for 75 hours or less a month may be treated as a half employee. This latter provision appears to be particularly controversial, not only because there is no provision for it in the Directive, but also because it appears to cut across initiatives such as the Part Time Workers Directive which were designed to address discrimination against part time workers.

But although the regulations are to apply to public or private undertakings carrying on an economic activity with 50 or more employees, they are nevertheless to have a staged introduction (Regulation 3). They apply to relevant undertakings with at least 150 employees from 6 April 2005, to relevant undertakings with at least 100 employees from 6 April 2007, and to relevant undertakings with at least 50 employees only from 6 April 2008 (Schedule 1). But even if the employer is covered by the procedure by meeting one of these thresholds, it does not follow that a procedure will be established. A major weakness of the regulations is that (unlike the redundancy consultation procedures) there is no obligation on the part of the employer to take the initiative to establish a procedure. This reflects recital 15 of the preamble. In many cases it is thus likely that there will be no information and consultation procedure established. This is because the regulations require employers to negotiate an agreement with negotiating representatives only if a request has been made by at least 10% of the employees in the undertaking (Regulation 7). This requirement of 10% is, however, misleading in view of the fact that the request must be made by a minimum of 15 employees (Regulation 7(3)). This means that in smaller undertakings the threshold requirement is in fact much higher, and indeed may be as high as 30% in the case of an undertaking which employs 50 people. Conversely in the case of very large undertakings, if the 10% requirement would lead to more than 2,500 having to request the establishment of an information and consultation procedure, the limit is fixed at 2,500. This will affect those very large companies which employ more than 250,000 people. For the purposes of Regulation 7 a part time worker who counts as only half a person for the purposes of Regulation 4 now becomes a whole person once again.

8.6.3.4 Pre-Existing Agreements and Negotiated Agreements

Apart from the fact that the employer is not obliged to initiate a procedure (though he or she is free to do so), another concern is that it is possible to have what is referred to as a pre-existing agreement in place of a statutory information and consultation procedure. A pre-existing agreement does not mean an agreement in place before the regulations came into force as might be assumed. Rather, it means an agreement in force before an application is made by employees under Regulation 7 to set up an information and consultation procedure under the regulations. As we shall see, such an agreement may lawfully fall short of the standard information and consultation provisions in the Directive and in the regulations, raising questions about the purpose set out in recital 18 to the Preamble to the Directive. This provides that the purpose of the Directive is to 'establish minimum requirements applicable throughout the Community while not preventing Member States from laying down provisions more favourable to employees'. The proviso to the last sentence is not likely to be much of an issue in the British context. By virtue of Regulation 8, a pre-existing agreement must be in writing, it must cover all the employees in the undertaking, and it must be approved by all the employees. The agreement must also, 'set out how the employer is to give information to the employees or their representatives and to seek their views on such information.'

It is important to note that a pre-existing agreement of this kind need not require consultation as defined by the regulations, that is to say 'the exchange of views' and the 'establishment of a dialogue'. Moreover, where consultation takes place under the standard procedure, it must take place 'with a view to reaching an agreement'. A pre-existing agreement in contrast simply requires the employer to 'seek views', without so much as a duty to respond. It is true that 10% of the employees can request that a statutory information and consultation procedure is established, even where there is a pre-existing agreement. But unless 40% of the employees make the request, the employer is required to agree only after a ballot (held by the employer) in which a majority of those voting support the establishment of such a procedure. The majority must represent at least 40% of those eligible to vote (Regulation 8(6)). Complaints about ballot irregularities may be made by an employee or an employee's representative to the CAC (Regulation 10).

In still other cases the parties may make a negotiated agreement. This will arise where a valid request has been made under Regulations 7 or 8. In these circumstances the employer must make arrangements for the election or appointment of negotiating representatives and invite these representatives to enter into negotiations to reach a negotiated agreement (Regulation 14). The procedures for appointing or electing negotiating representatives must ensure that all employees are entitled to take part in the appointment or election process. The procedures must also be arranged in such a way as to ensure that all employees are represented by a representative (Regulation 14(2)). The parties have 9 months from the date of the employee request to conclude an agreement, failing which the standard procedure applies. So far as negotiated agreements are concerned, the regulations provide:

[8.75] The Information and Consultation of Employees Regulations 2004 SI 3426/2004, Regulation 16

Negotiated agreements

16.—(1) A negotiated agreement must cover all employees of the undertaking and may consist either of a single agreement or of different parts (each being approved in accordance with paragraph (4)) which, taken together, cover all the employees of the undertaking. The single agreement or each part must—

(a) set out the circumstances in which the employer must inform and consult the employees to which it relates;

(b) be in writing;

(c) be dated;

(d) be approved in accordance with paragraphs (3) to (5);

(e) be signed by or on behalf of the employer; and

(f) either—

   (i) provide for the appointment or election of information and consultation representatives to whom the employer must provide the information and whom the employer must consult in the circumstances referred to in sub-paragraph (a); or

   (ii) provide that the employer must provide information directly to the employees to which it relates and consult those employees directly in the circumstances referred to in sub-paragraph (a).

(2) Where a negotiated agreement consists of different parts they may provide differently in relation to the matters referred to in paragraph (l)(a) and (f).

(3) A negotiated agreement consisting of a single agreement shall be treated as being approved for the purpose of paragraph (l)(d) if—

(a) it has been signed by all the negotiating representatives; or

(b) it has been signed by a majority of negotiating representatives and either—

   (i) approved in writing by at least 50% of employees employed in the undertaking, or

   (ii) approved by a ballot of those employees, the arrangements for which satisfied the requirements set out in paragraph (5), in which at least 50% of the employees voting, voted in favour of approval.

(4) A part shall be treated as being approved for the purpose of paragraph (1)(d) if the part—

(a) has been signed by all the negotiating representatives involved in negotiating the part; or

(b) has been signed by a majority of those negotiating representatives and either—

   (i) approved in writing by at least 50% of employees (employed in the undertaking) to which the part relates, or

   (ii) approved by a ballot of those employees, the arrangements for which satisfied the requirements set out in paragraph (5), in which at least 50% of the employees voting, voted in favour of approving the part.

(5) The ballots referred to in paragraphs (3) and (4) must satisfy the following requirements—

(a) the employer must make such arrangements as are reasonably practicable to ensure that the ballot is fair;

(b) all employees of the undertaking or, as the case may be, to whom the part of the agreement relates, on the day on which the votes may be cast in the ballot, or if the votes may be cast on more than one day, on the first day of those days, must be given an entitlement to vote in the ballot; and

(c) the ballot must be conducted so as to secure that—

   (i)   so far as is reasonably practicable, those voting do so in secret; and

   (ii) the votes given in the ballot are accurately counted.

It will be noted again that a negotiated agreement may fall short of the standard procedure described below. Thus, the information that must be provided need not necessarily satisfy the requirements of that procedure (though equally it may go beyond what that procedure would be require). It will also be noted that although there is a duty to consult (within the definition of consultation in Regulation 2), there is no duty to consult with a view to reaching an agreement. Complaints about the appointment or election of negotiating representatives may be made to the CAC (Regulation15), as may complaints about the conduct of the ballot under Regulation 16 (Regulation 17).

8.6.3.5 *The Standard Information and Consultation Provisions*

Apart from pre-existing agreements and negotiated agreements, a third type of arrangement for which provision is made are those based on the standard procedure set out in Regulation 20. This will apply either where the parties agree that it should, or where they are unable otherwise to agree an alternative procedure. Regulation 19 provides that where the standard provisions apply, the employer must make arrangements for the holding of a ballot of its employees to elect information and consultation representatives. There should be one elected representative for every 50 employees, with a minimum of 2 and a maximum of 25 representatives. The ballot procedures are laid out in Schedule 2 to the regulations and make provision for eligibility to be a candidate (any employee) and to vote (any employee). Three key points about the procedure are that:

- It is for the employer to decide whether there should be a single constituency or a series of constituencies to 'better reflect the interests of the employees as a whole'
- It is for the employer to appoint an independent person to supervise the conduct of the ballot to ensure, among other things, that:
  —So far as reasonably practicable, those voting are able to do so in secret
  —The votes given in the ballot are fairly and accurately counted
- It is for the employer to meet the costs of the ballot (including the costs of the ballot supervisor)

Complaints about the failure to hold a ballot or about the conduct of the ballot may be made to the CAC.

[8.76] The Information and Consultation of Employees Regulations SI 3426/2004, Regulation 20

Standard information and consultation provisions

20. (1) . . . the employer must provide the information and consultation representatives with information on—

(a) the recent and probable development of the undertaking's activities and economic situation;

(b) the situation, structure and probable development of employment within the undertaking and on any anticipatory measures envisaged, in particular, where there is a threat to employment within the undertaking; and

(c) subject to paragraph (5), decisions likely to lead to substantial changes in work organisation or in contractual relations, including those referred to in-

 (i) sections 188 to 192 of the Trade Union and Labour Relations (Consolidation) Act 1992; and

 (ii) regulations 10 to 12 of the Transfer of Undertakings (Protection of Employment) Regulations 1981.

(2) The information referred to in paragraph (1) must be given at such time, in such fashion and with such content as are appropriate to enable, in particular, the information and consultation representatives to conduct an adequate study and, where necessary, to prepare for consultation.

(3) The employer must consult the information and consultation representatives on the matters referred to in paragraph (1)(b) and (c).

(4) The employer must ensure that the consultation referred to in paragraph (3) is conducted—

(a) in such a way as to ensure that the timing, method and content of the consultation are appropriate;

(b) on the basis of the information supplied by the employer to the information and consultation representatives and of any opinion which those representatives express to the employer;

(c) in such a way as to enable the information and consultation representatives to meet the employer at the relevant level of management depending on the subject under discussion and to obtain a reasoned response from the employer to any such opinion; and

(d) in relation to matters falling within paragraph (1)(c), with a view to reaching agreement on decisions within the scope of the employer's powers.

(5) The duties in this regulation to inform and consult the information and consultation representatives on decisions falling within paragraph (1)(c) cease to apply where the employer is under a duty under—

(a) section 188 of the Act referred to in paragraph (1)(c)(i) (duty of employer to consult representatives); or

(b) regulation 10 of the Regulations referred to in paragraph (1)(c)(ii) (duty to inform and consult representatives), and

he has notified the information and consultation representatives in writing that he will be complying with his duty under the legislation referred to in sub-paragraph (a) or (b), as the case may be, instead of under these Regulations. . . .

(6) Where there is an obligation in these Regulations on the employer to inform and consult his employees, a failure on the part of a person who controls the employer (either

directly or indirectly) to provide information to the employer shall not constitute a valid reason for the employer failing to inform and consult.

There are two points to note about Regulation 20. The first is that—as already indicated—it includes a higher standard in terms of information to be provided and the consultation to be undertaken than either pre-existing agreements or negotiated agreements. Thus consultation is defined as meaning the establishment of a dialogue, which must be undertaken with a view to reaching an agreement. There are thus in fact three ways in which the term consultation is used in the regulations, from the weakest form in relation to pre-existing agreements, through negotiated agreements to the highest form in relation to the standard procedure. The other point to note is that Regulation 20 deals with the interface between the regulations and the redundancy and transfer of undertaking consultation procedures. By virtue of Regulation 20(5), the former cease to apply when the latter become applicable. Unlike the former, the latter have a remedial regime in the event of non-compliance. An example of a case where both would apply is *Securicor Omega Express Ltd v GMB* [2004] IRLR 9 [8.5.4.2 above]. In that case the employer would be required to consult about the decision to close (a duty arising under the information and consultation regulations) in advance of any consultation about subsequent redundancies (a duty arising under the separate redundancy consultation procedures).

8.6.3.6 *Enforcement of the Employer's Obligation*

What happens if the employer fails to provide information or to consult as required by an information and consultation agreement? Article 8 of the Directive provides that:

> 1. Member States shall provide for appropriate measures in the event of non-compliance with this Directive by the employer or the employees' representatives. In particular, they shall ensure that adequate administrative or judicial procedures are available to enable the obligations deriving from this Directive to be enforced.
> 2. Member States shall provide for adequate sanctions to be applicable in the event of infringement of this Directive by the employer or the employees' representatives. These sanctions must be effective, proportionate and dissuasive.

In implementing this obligation the regulations provide that a complaint may be made to the CAC by appropriate employee representatives, as follows:

[8.77] The Information and Consultation of Employees Regulations SI 3426/2004, Regulations 22-24

Disputes about operation of a negotiated agreement or the standard information and consultation provisions

22. (1) Where—
(a)   a negotiated agreement has been agreed; or
(b)   the standard information and consultation provisions apply,

a complaint may be presented to the CAC by a relevant applicant who considers that the employer has failed to comply with the terms of the negotiated agreement or, as the case may be, one or more of the standard information and consultation provisions.

(2) A complaint brought under paragraph (1) must be brought within a period of 3 months commencing with the date of the alleged failure.

(3) In this regulation "failure" means an act or omission; and "relevant applicant" means—

(a) in a case where information and consultation representatives have been elected or appointed, an information and consultation representative, or

(b) in a case where no information and consultation representatives have been elected or appointed, an employee or an employees' representative.

(4) Where the CAC finds the complaint well- founded it shall make a decision to that effect and may make an order requiring the employer to take such steps as are necessary to comply with the terms of the negotiated agreement or, as the case may be, the standard information and consultation provisions.

(5) An order made under paragraph (4) shall specify—

(a) the steps which the employer is required to take; and

(b) the period within which the order must be complied with.

(6) If the CAC makes a decision under paragraph (4) the relevant applicant may, within the period of three months beginning with the day on which the decision is made, make an application to the Appeal Tribunal for a penalty notice to be issued.

(7) Where such an application is made, the Appeal Tribunal shall issue a written penalty notice to the employer requiring him to pay a penalty to the Secretary of State in respect of the failure unless satisfied, on hearing representations from the employer, that the failure resulted from a reason beyond the employer's control or that he has some other reasonable excuse for his failure.

(8) Regulation 23 shall apply in respect of a penalty notice issued under this regulation.

(9) No order of the CAC under this regulation shall have the effect of suspending or altering the effect of any act done or of any agreement made by the employer or of preventing or delaying any act or agreement which the employer proposes to do or to make.

Penalties

23. (1) A penalty notice issued under regulation 22 shall specify—

(a) the amount of the penalty which is payable;

(b) the date before which the penalty must be paid; and

(c) the failure and period to which the penalty relates.

(2) No penalty set by the Appeal Tribunal under this regulation may exceed £75,000.

(3) When setting the amount of the penalty, the Appeal Tribunal shall take into account—

(a) the gravity of the failure;

(b) the period of time over which the failure occurred;

(c) the reason for the failure;

(d) the number of employees affected by the failure; and

(e) the number of employees employed by the undertaking or, where a negotiated agreement covers employees in more than one undertaking, the number of employees covered by the agreement.

(4) The date specified under paragraph (1)(b) above must not be earlier than the end of the period within which an appeal against a decision or order made by the CAC under regulation 22 may be made.

(5) If the specified date in a penalty notice has passed and—
(a) the period during which an appeal may be made has expired without an appeal having been made; or
(b) such an appeal has been made and determined,
the Secretary of State may recover from the employer, as a civil debt due to him, any amount payable under the penalty notice which remains outstanding.

(6) The making of an appeal suspends the effect of the penalty notice.

(7) Any sums received by the Secretary of State under regulation 22 or this regulation shall be paid into the Consolidated Fund.

Exclusivity of remedy

24. The remedy for infringement of the rights conferred by these Regulations is by way of complaint to the CAC in accordance with Parts I to VI, and not otherwise.

It is to be noted that unlike the redundancy consultation procedures there is no remedy for the employee in respect of whom there has been a failure to consult, albeit that the Court of Appeal has characterised the 'remedy' as a 'sanction': *Susie Radin* **[8.63]** above. The Regulations provide at best a sanction of limited scope, but only if the union takes upon itself to pursue the employer for the imposition of a financial penalty by the CAC. But there may be little incentive for the union to incur the cost and expense of pursuing such a claim given that any penalty imposed would be paid to the Treasury rather than the union or the employees who have been affected by the failure to consult. Some may see this as a cynical way of undermining a weak enforcement regime, which raises questions about its compatibility with the requirements in the Directive that the sanctions should be 'effective, proportionate and dissuasive'.

[8.78] K D Ewing and G M Truter, 'The Information and Consultation of Employees' Regulations: Voluntarism's Bitter Legacy' (2005) 68 *Modern Law Review* 626

It must be open to question whether this is enough, and whether these provisions are sufficiently 'effective/proportionate and dissuasive'. For this purpose it is important to emphasise that the Directive uses three different words when dealing with sanctions. They each have different meanings and serve different purposes, and each has to be satisfied. *Effective* means the establishment of a regime in which employers generally comply with their obligations. This can only be judged retrospectively and only after the procedures begin to operate. But if it continues to be the case that workers are dismissed without consultation (as in recent incidents), that itself will be clear evidence that the sanctions are ineffective and may form the basis of a legal challenge to the Regulations. *Proportionate* means that the sanction must reflect the scale and gravity of the employer's failure. This may mean taking into account the size of its business and the number of employees (Regulation 23(3)). It may also mean that the sanction must have regard to the continuing needs of the enterprise and its ability to function as a going concern, or, to adopt the language of article 1.3 of the Directive, 'the interests both of the undertaking . . . and of the employees'. But it is seriously open to question whether a multi-national company with 5,000 employees in Great Britain should be subjected to a sanctions regime that appears to have been tailored to the situation of a local company employing 50 employees. It is all the more seriously open to question given the third legal requirement that the sanction should be dissuasive. This means that it should be sufficiently high to discourage companies from failing to comply with their duties. It cannot be said that this requirement will be met by a maximum civil penalty of £75,000 (but only in the most serious of cases) for a large organisation.

8.6.3.7 *The Protection of Employee Representatives*

The final issue to consider relates to the protection of employee representatives. The Directive provides by Article 7 that:

> Member States shall ensure that employees' representatives, when carrying out their functions, enjoy adequate protection and guarantees to enable them to perform properly the duties which have been assigned to them.

The corresponding provisions of the regulations are to be found in Regulations 27–34 which

- Provide a right to paid time off for negotiating representatives and information and consultation representatives. The representatives in question are entitled to 'reasonable time off' during working hours 'in order to perform his functions as such a representative' (Regulation 27). Complaints about refusal of time off or failure to pay for the time off are to be made to an employment tribunal.
- Provide protection from detriment or dismissal for an employee who is (a) an employees' representative (but not a representative under a pre-existing agreement), (b) a negotiating representative, (c) an information and consultation representative, or (d) a candidate in an election for any of these positions. The employee is protected in relation the performance of any function or activities as a representative or candidate (Regulation 30).

It might be said that this is a very minimalist interpretation of the Directive's requirements, which requires 'adequate protection and guarantees' to enable them to 'perform properly the duties of office. With this in mind, a number of points are to be noted:

- The negotiating representatives and the information and consultation representatives are entitled to time off only to enable them to perform their duties as *representatives*. This contrasts with the Employment Rights Act 1996, s 61 which deals with the right to time off of employee representatives appointed or elected for the purposes of redundancy consultation or consultation about the transfer of an undertaking. As well as time off to perform their duties as an employee representative, section 61 also allows time off for *candidates*. It is not clear why the same provision could not also apply to the Information and Consultation Regulations 2004, particularly as candidates are expressly protected from detriment and dismissal by Regulations 32 and 30 respectively. It is all the more surprising that candidates should be denied the right to time off when candidates enjoy such a right under the Transnational Information and Consultation of Employees Regulations 1999 (TICER) (Regulation 25).

- The right to time off for information and consultation representatives compares very unfavourably with the provisions in TULRCA 1992, s 168. This deals with the right of trade union officials to time off for trade union duties, defined to mean duties relating to collective bargaining. There is a difference between the two in the sense that the meaning of trade union duties is to be determined by reference to the ACAS Code of Practice 3 on Time Off for Trade Union Duties and Activities. This makes it clear that trade union duties include not only negotiations with the employer, but also, for example: preparation for negotiations, informing members of progress, and explaining outcomes to members. In the case of negotiating representatives and more likely information and consultation representatives, they may also need to consult external advisers off site and to report on these consultations to the workforce. They may also need time off to meet with other representatives in the company.

- There are concerns about the facilities to be made available to the information and consultation representatives. In particular there is no time off for training, and there is no provision for other facilities being made available. Again this contrasts unfavourably with the provisions relating to trade union officials in respect of whom provision is made in the ACAS Code of Practice. This refers to accommodation for meetings, access to office equipment, the use of notice boards, and the use of dedicated office space. It also contrasts unfavourably with the rights of employee representatives in redundancy and transfer cases. See TULRCA 1992, s 188(5A) above. There is also the question of financial resources being made available to information and consultation representatives. The silence of the Regulations compares unfavourably with TICER 1999, the Schedule to which provides that management 'shall provide the members of the European Works Council with such financial and material resources as enable them to perform their duties in an appropriate manner' (para 9(6)).

European Works Councils

The Transnational Information and Consultation of Employees Regulations, SI 1999/3323, are designed to implement the European Works Councils Directive. This provides for the establishment of European Works Council (EWCs) or agreed information and consultation procedures as an alternative. The regulations apply to UK-based transnational companies which carry on significant activities in at least one other Member State. More precisely they apply to *Community-scale undertakings* (undertakings which employ at least 1,000 employees within the Member States with at least 150 in at least two Member States); and to *Community-scale groups of undertakings* (groups of undertakings in different Member States with at least two group undertakings in different Member States; at least one group undertaking in one Member State must employ at least 150 employees; and a group undertaking in another Member State must also employ at least 150 employees (regulation 4). Where based in the UK, central management is responsible for creating the conditions necessary for a European Works Council or an information and consultation procedure (regulation 5), which may be initiated by a request by at least 100 employees or their representatives: the employees must be based in at least two undertakings in at least two Member States (regulation 9).

The constitution of the EWC or the Information and Consultation procedure is to be determined by a Special Negotiating Body (SNB) (regulation 11). This must include an employee representative from each of the Member States in which the company has an establishment and additional members based on the number of employees at the different establishments and additional members based on the number of employees in the different establishments (regulation 12). The UK members of the SNB are to be nominated by a consultative committee where one exists (regulation 15), failing which by a ballot of the UK employees (regulation 13). A consultative committee is one whose normal functions include the carrying out of an information and consultation function and which is elected by a procedure in which all employees are entitled to vote. Central management is then required to convene a meeting with the SNB with a view to concluding an agreement on the content and scope of a EWC or an information and consultation procedure (regulation 16). In seeking to negotiate an agreement, the parties are under a duty to negotiate in a spirit of co-operation with a view to reaching a written agreement on the detailed arrangements for the information and consultation of employees (regulation 17), failing which the fall back position (referred to as the 'subsidiary requirements') in the Schedule will apply (regulation 18). This makes provision for the composition of the EWC, the election of its members, and its competence.

The subsidiary requirements provide for a EWC of three to thirty members, with at least one member from each of the Member States in which the company has an establishment. Additional members are to be determined according to the number of employees in the different Member States. UK EWC members must be UK employees. Where there is a recognised union, the UK employee representatives may be appointed by union officials; otherwise they must be elected. The competence of the EWC is limited to information and consultation on matters which concern the Community-scale undertaking as a whole or the Community-scale group of undertakings as a whole, or at least two of its establishments situated in different Member States. The EWC has a right to meet with the central management once a year, to be informed and consulted about the progress of the business and its prospects. Exceptional meetings may be required to deal with 'exceptional circumstances affecting the employees' interests to a considerable extent' (such as relocations, closure or collective redundancies). Central management is to provide financial and other material resources to EWC members.

Where there is a failure on the part of central management to establish a EWC or an information and consultation procedure in accordance with an agreement under regulation 17 a complaint may be made to the EAT by a 'relevant applicant'. The same may occur where the regulation 18 procedure applies (regulations 20,21). It is a breach of statutory duty for a member of an SNB or EWC, or an information or consultation representative to disclose information which is held in confidence (regulation 23). Management is not required to disclose information if 'according to objective criteria', disclosure would 'seriously harm the functioning of, or would be prejudicial to, the undertaking or group of undertakings concerned'. Complaints about the withholding of information are to be made to the CAC (regulation 24). Provision is made for the paid time off work for representatives and candidates (regulation 25), and for the protection of representatives and candidates from detriment and dismissal on account of their performance of their duties (regulations 28-32). But save in exceptional circumstance, there is no protection against detriment or dismissal where the representative discloses information in breach of regulation 23.

8.6.3.8 *Conclusion*

The law relating to workplace representation has been radically changed since 1997, with two principal forms of representation being introduced, one relating to trade union recognition and the other to information and consultation. Both procedures are designed to achieve their objectives by stimulating voluntary agreements, and to operate outside the framework of the law. Both reflect a view about the importance of enterprise-based representation rather than the importance of regulatory collective bargaining. But as already suggested, both should nevertheless help to establish and consolidate a trade union presence in many workplaces. Although the information and consultation procedures do not expressly provide a formal union role, it is possible that such procedures will be more easily established in union rather than non- union workplaces. It is also possible that these procedures will be used by trade unions to expand the bargaining agenda to cover matters other than terms and conditions of employment. As a result there may continue to be a wide representation gap in British workplaces—between those establishments where there is a recognised union and those where there is none. If trade union recognition thus continues to be the key to workplace representation, it will be a matter of growing concern that workers employed by small businesses are cut out of both the new statutory procedures. But although these procedures will help trade unions in the workplace, we should be realistic about their impact and avoid the temptation to exaggerate. The experience of the recognition legislation shows that this is a hard struggle for trade unions and suggests that these statutory procedures will not on their own lead to a significant increase in collective bargaining coverage or workplace representation density. That will only be achieved by a new public policy which requires new sectoral collective bargaining institutions to set the terms and conditions of employment on a sector-wide basis, as is the practice elsewhere in Europe. Not only would such an initiative enhance the regulatory impact of collective bargaining, but, as Truter has persuasively argued **[8.66]**, it would also enhance the efficacy of workplace representation procedures.

FURTHER READING

B Bercusson, *European Works Councils—Extending the Trade Union Role* (London, Institute of Employment Rights, 1997).

A Bogg, 'The Political Theory of Trade Union Recognition Campaigns: Legislating for Democratic Competitiveness', (2001) 64 *Modern Law Review* 875.

— —, 'Employment Relations Act 2004: Another False Dawn for Collectivism?' (2005) 34 *Industrial Law Journal* 72.

P Davies and C Kilpatrick, 'UK Worker Representation after Single Channel' (2004) 33 *Industrial Law Journal* 121.

K D Ewing, 'The Implications of Wilson and Palmer' (2003) 32 *Industrial Law Journal* 1.

K D Ewing, S Moore and S Wood, *Unfair Labour Practices: Trade Union Recognition and Employer Resistance* (Institute of Employment Rights, 2003).

K D Ewing and G M Truter, 'The Information and Consultation of Employees' Regulations: Voluntarism's Bitter Legacy' (2005) 68 *Modern Law Review* 626.

J Hendy, *Every Worker Shall Have the Right to be Represented by a Trade Union* (London, Institute of Employment Rights, 1998).

Lord McCarthy, *Fairness at Work and Trade Union Recognition: Past Comparisons and Future Problems* (London, Institute of Employment Rights, 1999).

T Novitz, 'A Revised Role for Trade Unions as Designed by New Labour: The Representation Pyramid and 'Partnership'' (2002] 29 *Journal of Law and Society* 487.

T Novitz and P Skidmore, *Fairness at Work. A Critical Analysis of the Employment Relations Act 1999 and its Treatment of Collective Rights* (Oxford, Hart Publishing, 2001).

J O'Hara, *Worker Participation and Collective Bargaining in Britain: The Influence of European Law* (London, Institute of Employment Rights, 1996).

C W Summers, 'Unions Without Majority—A Black Hole?' (1990) 66 *Chicago-Kent Law Review* 351.

G M Truter, *Implementing the Information and Consultation Directive in the UK: Lessons from Germany* (London, Institute of Employment Rights, 2003).

P C Weiler, 'Promises to Keep: Securing Workers' Rights Self-organisation under the NLRA' (1983) 96 *Harvard Law Review* 1769.

Industrial Conflict and the Right to Strike

9.1 A fundamental right

In this chapter we consider the legal responses to workplace disputes which lead to strikes or other forms of industrial action. A strike is a withdrawal of labour by a group of workers who are in dispute with their employer, or perhaps with another party. There are many reasons why workers may feel compelled to take such action: they may be seeking to improve their terms and conditions of employment, with negotiations between the employer and their trade union having failed. Or the employer may be seeking to change existing terms and conditions of employment, with the workers fighting to hold onto what they have. There may be other reasons, such as a protest against unsafe working conditions. It is also the case that the dispute may lead to forms of action other than a strike: these include an overtime ban, working to rule, or refusing to carry out certain tasks—all designed to put pressure on the employer. Once engaged in industrial action of one of these various forms, the workers involved may seek the support of other workers. So workers employed at another establishment of the same employer may be called upon for support, if not already involved. So may workers employed by a supplier or customer of the employer in the dispute: this latter form of action is often referred to as secondary action, and a refusal of workers elsewhere to handle goods produced by or destined for a strike-bound plant is sometimes referred to as a secondary boycott, or 'blacking'. Industrial action may be called by the trade union of which the workers are members, in which case it may be referred to as official action: but if it explodes spontaneously it may be referred to as unofficial or wildcat action.

9.1.1 The function of industrial action

It is one thing to identify what we mean by a strike. But it is something again to explain its function. Industrial action is often justified principally in social and economic terms. According to Lord Wright in *Crofter Hand Woven Harris Tweed v Veitch* [1942] AC 435, 'the right to strike is an essential element in the principle of collective bargaining' (at p 463). And in the Council of Europe's Social Charter of 18 October 1961 the right to strike (recognised expressly for the first time in an international human rights treaty) appears under the rubric of the right to bargain collectively (Article 6(4)).

[9.1] European Social Charter

Article 6 – The right to bargain collectively

With a view to ensuring the effective exercise of the right to bargain collectively, the Contracting Parties undertake:

1. to promote joint consultation between workers and employers;
2. to promote, where necessary and appropriate, machinery for voluntary negotiations between employers or employers' organisations and workers' organisations, with a view to the regulation of terms and conditions of employment by means of collective agreements;
3. to promote the establishment and use of appropriate machinery for conciliation and voluntary arbitration for the settlement of labour disputes;

and recognise:

4. the right of workers and employers to collective action in cases of conflicts of interest, including the right to strike, subject to obligations that might arise out of collective agreements previously entered into.

The connection between the right to strike and collective bargaining is easy to understand. Collective bargaining would be rather empty of substance if the employer could say: 'this is my offer—take it or leave it', or if the employer could say: 'I am proposing to change the terms of the existing collective agreement—and there is nothing you can do about it, whether you agree or not'. The strike enables workers collectively to put pressure on the employer in pursuit of what they see as a just cause and a way of resisting what they see as unjust action by the employer. It would of course be possible to provide a procedure for the peaceful resolution of disputes—such as a court or an arbitral body. Proposals for bodies of this kind have been made from time to time, but there is little stomach for such institutional arrangements in Britain. It seems that neither trade unions nor employers are willing to contemplate the loss of control which bodies of this kind would entail. Nor does the emphasis on 'partnership' industrial relations eliminate a role for industrial action: new partnerships may have disputes which need to be resolved by traditional methods, the right to take part in which has been strengthened in some respects by the Employment Relations Act 1999 and the Employment Relations Act 2004 respectively.

Although predominantly a weapon in collective bargaining, in a liberal democracy the strike may have a wider function as an instrument of political protest. Indeed the strike may be said to have two important political dimensions. In the first place it is a way of enabling the *citizen as worker* to carry his or her concerns as citizen into the enterprise: the dockers who in 1919 refused to load the *Jolly George* then being supplied with armaments to help the Polish government in its campaign against Soviet Russia, the musicians in the 1950s who refused to perform in establishments which operated a colour bar, and the broadcasting technicians in 1977 who refused to broadcast the FA Cup Final to South Africa. Not all of these protests related to collective bargaining, and it is unrealistic to expect workers to leave their concerns as citizens at the entrance to the workplace. Secondly and perhaps more fundamentally, the strike is a way of enabling people to protest about government conduct: a way of enabling the *worker as citizen* to express concerns about oppressive laws in the workplace. This does not imply a right of veto of the policies of a democratically elected government: but there is a chasm which separates the activities of those who would protest and those who would obstruct. As in the General Strike in 1926, however, it is easy for governments to characterise industrial action to protest against government policy or to express sympathy with other workers as being a challenge to the authority of the government and to be a threat to democracy itself. Nevertheless this wider role of the strike as a form of political protest is to be found reflected in the jurisprudence of the supervisory bodies of the ILO, by which the right to strike is recognised as an incident of the principle of freedom of association.

[9.2] H J Laski, *Liberty in the Modern State* (Harmondsworth, Penguin Books, 1937), pp 128–31

I do not deny, of course, that both a general strike, and others of far less amplitude, inflict grave injury and hardship upon the community. But when trade unions seek for what they regard as justice, one of their most powerful sources of strength is the awakening of the slow and inert public to a sense of the position. Effectively to do this, in a real world, it must inconvenience the public; that awkward giant has no sense of its obligations until it is made uncomfortable. When it is aroused, if, for instance, trains do not run, or coal is not mined, the public begins to have interest in the position, to call for action. Without some alternative which attempts to secure attention for a just result—I know of no such alternative—the infliction of hardship on the community seems to me the sole way, even if an unfortunate way, to the end the trade unions have in view. To limit the right to strike is a form of industrial servitude. It means, ultimately, that the worker must labour on the employer's terms lest the public be inconvenienced. I can see no justice in such a denial of freedom.

Two further points it is worthwhile to make. It is sometimes agreed that while the State ought not to restrict freedom of association for industrial ends, it is justified in doing so when the strike-weapon is used for some political purpose. This, indeed, was one of the objects of the Baldwin Government in enacting the Trades Disputes Act of 1927. But I know of no formula whereby such a division of purposes can be successfully made. There is no hard and fast line between industrial action and political action. There is no hard and fast line which enables us to say, for instance, that pressure for a Factory Act is industrial action, but pressure for the ratification of the Washington Hours Convention political. Extreme cases are easy to define; but there is a vast middle ground with which the trade unions must concern themselves and this escapes definition of a kind that will not hamper the trade union in legitimate activity vital to its purpose. And there are certain types of political action by trade unions—a strike against war, for example—which I do not think they ought in the interest of the community itself, to abandon. Quite frankly, I should have liked to see a general strike proclaimed against the outbreak of war in 1914; and I conceive the power to act in that way as a necessary and wise protection of a people against a government which proposes such adventures. You cannot compartmentalize life; and where grave emergencies arise, the weapons to be utilized must be fitted to meet them. A government which knew that its declaration of war was, where it intended aggressive action, likely to involve a general strike, would be far less likely to think in belligerent terms. I do not see why such a weapon should be struck from the community's hand. I do not forget that the German Republic was saved from the Kapp Putsch by a general strike.

Nor must we forget the limits within which effective legal action is possible. *Jus est quod jussum est* is a maxim the validity of which is singularly unimpressive. When the issue in dispute seems to the trade unions so vital that only by a general strike can they defend their position adequately, they will, in those circumstances, defend their position whatever the law may be. Legal prohibition will merely exacerbate the dispute. It will transfer the discussion of the real problem at issue to a discussion of legality which serves merely to conceal it. A legal command is, after all, a mere static form of words; what gives it appropriateness is its relevance as just to the situation to which it is applied. And its relevance as just is made not by those who announce that it is to be applied, but by those who receive its application. The secret of avoiding general strikes does not lie in their prohibition but in the achievement of the conditions which render them unnecessary.

Nor is the denial of the right to declare a general strike a necessary protection of the total interest of the community. Right and wrong in these matters are matters to be defined in each particular case. A government which meets the threat of a general strike is not entitled to public support merely because it meets the threat. It is no more possible to take that view than it is to say that all governments deserve support when they confront a rebellion of their subjects. Everything depends on what the general strike is for, just as everything depends on the purpose of the rebellion; and the individual trade unionist must make up his mind about the one, just as the individual citizen must make up his mind about the other. Law in this realm is, in fact, largely futile. It could not prevent a general strike by men who saw no alternative open to them; and, in that event, it would merely intensify its rigours when it came. The limitation of liberty in this realm seems to me, therefore, neither just in its purpose nor beneficient in its results.

I do not, of course, deny that freedom of action in this field is capable of being abused. That is the nature of liberty. Any body of persons who exercise power may abuse it. It is an abuse of power when an employer dismisses his workmen because he does not like their political opinions. It is an abuse of power when the owners of halls in Boston refuse to hire them to the promoters of a meeting in memory of Sacco and Vanzetti. It was an abuse of power when British naval officers connived at the attempted internment of the Belgian socialist, M. Camille Huysmans, in England. It was, I think, an abuse of power when the Universities of Oxford and Cambridge refused to admit Nonconformists as students, or Parliament to seat Mr Bradlaugh because he was an infidel. But the trade unions are no more likely, on the historic record, to abuse their power than is Parliament itself. The latter, if it wished, has the legal competence to abolish the trade unions, to disenfranchise the working classes, to confine membership of the House of Commons to persons with an independent income. We know that Parliament is unlikely to do any of these things because omnicompetence, when gravely abused, ceases to be omnicompetent. And the same truth holds, as it seems to me, of the liberty to proclaim a general strike.

9.1.2 Legal perceptions and legal challenges

British law has tended to take a narrow view of legitimate strike action. The position of the common law, which we consider in section 9.2 of this chapter, has been unwavering, unequivocal and unmistakable. Industrial action—whatever its cause—has tended to be seen as unlawful, as violating the rights of the employer: these rights include the right to conduct his or her business without interference, and his or her rights arising from contracts with his or her employees. It is true that much of the case-law has been concerned with issues which are an affront to judicial notions of justice—strikes to enforce the closed shop (inviting judicial protection for the individual challenged by the group), and secondary action of various kinds (inviting judicial intervention to contain the dispute and to prevent its deliberate extension to innocent third parties). But this is not true of all the cases. The greatest labour law case of the twentieth century was concerned with a strike about the victimisation of a railway worker by his employer: *Taff Vale Railway Co v ASRS* [1901] AC 426, leading directly to the formation of the Labour Party and to the Trade Disputes Act 1906. Few court decisions can have had such monumental political and legal consequences. The union was nevertheless found to have committed a number of torts and in a devastating decision without precedent was held to be liable in damages.

The narrow perception of British law is of the strike as an economic tool only. To the extent that legislation protects the right to strike it is in relation to conduct which is done 'in contemplation or furtherance of a trade dispute'. This restriction seems to satisfy the British trade union movement, which has little tradition of (or taste for) industrial action for political purposes. But, as indicated, such action is by no means unknown. The point need not be laboured, for at least at the present time the prevalence of industrial action is in decline, and is now at its lowest level since the nineteenth century. Britain's strike problem is not now the high incidence of industrial action or the large number of working days lost as a result of strikes, as it was perceived to be for much of the twentieth century—giving rise to a number of anxious inquiries about how to deal with it, including the thoughtful and insightful report of the Donovan Royal Commission on Trade Unions and Employers' Associations (Cmnd 3623, 1968). On the contrary, Britain's strike problem now is that the legal controls introduced since 1980 are so tight as to make it very difficult for industrial action to be taken within the limits of the law, with the result that the United Kingdom is in breach on a number of grounds of a number of international human rights instruments, all the more paradoxical for the fact that the Court of Appeal recognised for the first time in 1996 that the right to strike is a 'fundamental human right' (*London Underground Ltd v RMT* [1996] ICR 170, at p 181).

The right of trade unions to induce workers to support industrial action by withdrawing their labour is 'a right which was first conferred by Parliament in 1906, which has been enjoyed by trade unions ever since and which is today recognised as encompassing a fundamental human right': *London Underground Ltd v NUR* [1966] ICR 170, *per* Millett LJ, at p 181.

9.1.3 The declining prevalence of strikes and industrial action

There are a number of reasons why strike activity is in decline. Most obviously, there has been a sharp decline in the number of trade union members, with membership having almost halved since 1980. Secondly, there is the great economic restructuring which has taken place since 1980, with the decline of the manufacturing and extraction industries which were often associated with worker and trade union militancy. The process of industrial restructuring itself gave rise to bitter disputes, some of which feature in the pages which follow: the steel strike of 1980, the miners' strike of 1984–5, and the News International strike of 1985–6. The expanding service sector and the growth of smaller production units have not created similar cultures, while long periods of high unemployment and job insecurity until recently are not the most propitious basis from which to fight war at work. Thirdly, there is also the question of the impact of the law, which has become an important source of restraint on trade union behaviour. Employers have indicated a willingness not only to use the courts but also to see the legal process through to a final conclusion in the sense of pursuing unions which ignored injunctions for contempt of court. Following the sequestration of the assets of a number of trade unions in the 1980s, there is no question now of trade unions disobeying the law or of the law being ineffective.

The fall in the incidence of industrial action is by no means a uniquely British experience, with trends in this country being reflected elsewhere: it is thus a largely global phenomenon, perhaps revealing the growing weakness of national trade unionism in an increasingly globalised economy. Data produced by the ILO reveal that although the British levels of industrial action are at a record low, there are countries with fewer days lost to industrial action and countries with more. It was ever thus, with the Donovan Royal Commission, above, reporting as long ago as 1968 that in terms of working days lost in relation to the numbers employed, 'the United Kingdom's recent record has been about average compared with other countries' (paragraph 363). There are doubtless several reasons for contemporary developments: reasons which are common to all countries, as well as reasons which may be peculiar to some. Countries such as Australia and Britain, which have shown such sharp falls in strike activity in recent years, are also countries which have seen the introduction of the tightest legal restrictions. But although strikes are now much less common, they do nevertheless continue to occur—albeit on a smaller scale than in the past. A number of local disputes in the 1990s attracted national attention, including the strikes by Liverpool dockers, Critchley Labels workers in Cardiff, and Magnet Joinery workers in Darlington. In more recent years we have had nationally co-ordinated action by firefighters and by civil servants. How is such action protected and regulated by law?

9.2 The basis of legal liability

Industrial action will almost invariably be unlawful as a tort at common law. The workers taking part will be acting in breach of contract, and the trade union or trade union officials will typically be committing torts in calling upon their members to take part in a strike. The origins of liability in the modern law for those organising industrial action can be traced back to 1853.

[9.3] *Lumley v Gye* **(1853) 2 E&B 216 (QBD)**

> The plaintiff was a theatre proprietor who had a contract with a Miss Wagner to perform at his theatre. Knowing of the existence of the contract, the defendant 'wrongfully and maliciously enticed and procured Miss Wagner to refuse to sing or perform at the theatre, and to depart from and abandon her contract with the plaintiff'. It was held that the conduct of the defendant was actionable, and in the course of his judgment it was said by Crompton J:
>
> > . . . . it must now be considered clear law that a person who wrongfully and maliciously, or, which is the same thing, with notice, interrupts the relation subsisting between master and servant by procuring the servant to depart from his master's service, or by harbouring and keeping him as servant after he has quitted it and during the time stipulated for as the period of service, whereby the master is injured, commits a wrongful act for which he is responsible at law (at p 224).

Although not apparently expressed with trade unions and industrial action in mind, the principle in *Lumley v Gye* (1853) 2 E&B 216 would clearly have implications for the trade union which called upon its members to take industrial action, invariably instructing them to do so in breach of their contracts of employment. But at the time of *Lumley v Gye* (1853) 2 E&B 216, civil liability for inducing breach of contract was not likely to have been a concern for the nascent trade union movement: barely legal organisations, industrial action by trade unions attracted criminal liability, from which they were not substantially freed until the Conspiracy and Protection of Property Act 1875.

9.2.1 The boundaries of liability

Although inducing breach of contract of employment was eventually to become the staple basis of liability, it was not enough on its own to arm employers and other targets of industrial action with a cause of action. Indeed, although the tort giant began to stir in the 1890s, few of the cases dealt solely or principally with liability for inducing breach of contract. It is by no means clear why this is so: it may be that cases were not reported on the ground that they did not raise novel points; or it may be that litigation was confined to what might have been considered the least defensible forms of trade union action, which in turn demanded a more imaginative response from the courts. Whatever the reason, the difficulty with inducing breach of contract as a basis of liability is that in some cases there was no contract of employment the breach of which had been induced. In such cases it was necessary to invent a different tort: conspiracy to injure.

[9.4] *Quinn v Leathem* [1901] AC 495 (HL)

The union in this case (the Belfast Journeymen Butchers' and Assistants' Association) was in dispute with the respondent meat producer (Leathem) about the fact that the latter employed non-union men. The union wanted them dismissed but Leathem refused. The union then approached a customer (Munce) of Leathem and threatened a strike at Munce's unless he refused to trade with Leathem. Munce had been accepting Leathem's beef for 20 years, though there was no written contract between the parties. None of Munce's employees had been induced to break their contracts. He nevertheless complied with the union's demand. The House of Lords held that the defendants were liable in tort to the meat producer for conspiracy to injure. The essence of the wrongdoing lay in the intention to cause harm in concert with others, for which purpose the use of unlawful means would not be necessary. So that which would be lawful if done by an individual acting alone would become unlawful if done by two or more acting together if designed to cause harm. Although the defendants were presumed to act in furtherance of what they considered to be the interests of their members, this provided no lawful excuse. According to Lord Lindley, the defendants were violating their duty to the plaintiff and his customers and employees, which was to leave them in the undisturbed enjoyment of their liberty.

Apart from developing the law of conspiracy to injure, the House of Lords in *Quinn v Leathem* [1901] AC 495 also confirmed lower court decisions asserting liability for inducing breach of contract—as it had earlier in *Taff Vale Railway Co Ltd v ASRS* [1901] AC 426, a second seminal decision of the same year in which it was also held that trade unions could be vicariously liable for the torts of their servants and agents in organising industrial action. In a third case from this era the House of Lords held further that it was no defence to an action for inducing breach of contract that the conduct of the defendants was dictated by an honest desire to promote the interests of trade union members and not to injure the employer (*South Wales Miners' Federation v Glamorgan Coal Co* [1905] AC 239). So in the context of both conspiracy and inducing breach of contract it was to prove impossible for trade unionists to provide a lawful excuse or justification for their conduct: they stood naked and unprotected at the altar of the common law. It was thus left to Parliament to respond to these developments with the Trade Disputes Act 1906, passed as one of the first measures of the landslide Liberal government, and only six years after the foundation of the Labour Party. The Act created immunities against existing torts in the context of trade disputes. Section 1 addressed civil liability for conspiracy, as follows:

An act done in pursuance of an agreement or combination by two or more persons shall, if done in contemplation or furtherance of a trade dispute, not be actionable unless the act, if done without any such agreement or combination, would be actionable. . . .

Conspiracy and Trade Union Activities—a Re-evaluation

The immunity in section 1 of the Trade Disputes Act 1906 for conspiracy was to become largely redundant following the redrawing of the boundaries of the tort by the House of Lords in *Crofter Hand Woven Harris Tweed v. Veitch* [1942] AC 435. The case concerned a dispute in the Harris Tweed Industry on the Island of Lewis in the Outer Hebrides between the TGWU and seven independent producers of tweed cloth. The union was concerned that the actions of the pursuers (it was a Scottish case) would undermine the working conditions of its members employed in the local mills. Consequently it called upon the dockers in Stornaway—also members of the TGWU—to refuse to handle all the yarn imported to the island by the pursuers, as well as the finished products produced by them. In holding that there was no actionable conspiracy in this case, the House of Lords redefined the boundaries of the tort in an important respect. According to the Lord Chancellor (Simon) at p 445:

'It is enough to say that if there is more than purpose actuating a combination, liability must depend on ascertaining the predominant purpose. If that predominant purpose is to damage another person and damage results, that is tortious conspiracy. If the predominant purpose is the lawful protection or promotion of any lawful interest of the combiners (no illegal means being employed), it is not a tortious conspiracy, even though it causes damage to another person'.

So liability (at least conspiracy without the use of unlawful means) arises only where the predominant purpose is to injure the plaintiff (or in this case the pursuer). Here there was no liability, for according to the Lord Chancellor again (at p 447):

'In the present case . . . the predominant object of the respondents in getting the embargo imposed was to benefit their trade union members by preventing undercutting and unregulated competition, and so helping to secure the economic stability of the island industry. The result they aimed at achieving was to create a better basis for collective bargaining, and thus directly to improve wage prospects. A combination with such an object is not unlawful, because the object is the legitimate promotion of the interests of the combiners, and because the damage necessarily inflicted on the appellants is not inflicted by criminal or tortious means and is not the "real purpose" of the combination'.

There has been no comparable decision admitting as wide a defence for the purposes of other torts. Conspiracy is an exception: see *TimePlan Education Group Ltd v NUT* [1997] IRLR457.

The same Act also addressed liability for inducing breach of contract and interference with business, section 3 enacting that:

An act done by a person in contemplation or furtherance of a trade dispute shall not be actionable on the ground only that it induces some other person to break a contract of employment or that it is an interference with the trade, business, or employment of some other person, or with the right of some other person to dispose of his capital or his labour as he wills.

The 1906 Act further provided by section 4 an almost complete protection for trade union funds from liability in tort, subject to a number of limited exceptions, thereby effectively overruling *Taff Vale Railway Co Ltd v ASRS* [1901] AC 426.

9.2.2 Extending the boundaries of liability

The 1906 Act was to prove an effective basis for the protection of trade union action until after the end of the Second World War. Indeed in a leading case decided during the war, the House of Lords effectively removed the need for section 1 of the 1906 Act by redefining the boundaries of the tort of conspiracy: see box on p 869. But matters were to change radically thereafter. The period from 1952 to 1969 in particular saw the emergence of new grounds of tortious liability in a period of industrial turbulence as inventive plaintiffs sought to 'get round' the immunities in the 1906 Act, in order to restrain what was typically secondary action or action to enforce the closed shop. With the demise of conspiracy, it appeared as if new causes of action had to be found to deal with the persistence of the type of conduct which caused such offence in *Quinn v Leathem* [1901] AC 495. The common law in this period was to advance along two quite different fronts, with developments coming to a spectacular climax with two decisions of the House of Lords in the mid-1960s. It has to be said, however, that the form in which the first of these decisions emerged—*Rookes v Barnard* [1964] AC 1129—came as a bolt from the blue. The question was this: could there be liability (unprotected by the 1906 Act) where the union officials did not induce their members to take strike action, but threatened the employer that they would do so? It is hard to see how a threat to do that which is not unlawful, or if unlawful protected by statute, could give rise to liability. And it is hard to see what that liability could be. But we should never underestimate the creative capacity of the legal profession, or ignore the reminder delivered to every lawyer by Lord Chancellor Halsbury in *Quinn v Leathem* [1901] AC 495 that 'the law is not always logical at all' (at p 506).

[9.5] *Rookes v Barnard* [1964] AC 1129 (HL)

Douglas Rookes was a draughtsman employed by British Overseas Airways Corporation (BOAC). He fell out with his union (the Association of Engineering and Shipbuilding Draughtsmen) and resigned. Sadly for him there was a closed shop agreement between BOAC and AESD, in consequence of which the plaintiff's colleagues resolved to strike unless he was removed from their workplace. BOAC thereupon suspended Rookes, and several months later dismissed him with one week's salary in lieu of notice. The defendants were respectively a branch chairman (Barnard), divisional organiser (Silverthorne), and shop steward (Fistal) in the union. The plaintiff sought damages alleging that he had been the victim of a tortious intimidation by defendants who had used unlawful means to induce BOAC to terminate his contract of service, the unlawful means being the threat that a strike would take place. The action succeeded before Sachs J, but he was overturned by the Court of Appeal, which was in turn reversed by the House of Lords. Despite the absence of modern authority, it was held by Lord Reid to be an unlawful intimidation for the defendants 'to use a threat to break their contracts with their employer as a weapon to make him do something which he was legally entitled to do but which they knew would cause loss to the plaintiff' (at p 1167).

9.2.2.1 Procuring breach of a commercial contract

Rookes v Barnard [1964] AC 1129—in which a new head of tortious liability was discovered— was a great landmark in the development of labour law and in defining the relationship between the courts and the trade union movement. The second decision of the House of Lords in the mid-1960s raised a rather different series of questions: what was the position if in inducing breach of a contract of employment, the defendants also intentionally procured the breach of a commercial contract—as say between the employer involved in the strike and one or more of his or her customers or suppliers? The possibility of liability to the employer (the intended target of the action) had already been accepted in principle in an important Court of Appeal decision in *D C Thomson & Co Ltd v Deakin* [1952] Ch 646. But on the facts, the ingredients of the tort were not made out. The essence of the tort is set out in the judgment of Jenkins LJ, the key parts of which are reproduced in Lord Diplock's speech in *Merkur Island Shipping Corporation v Laughton* [1983] 2 AC 570 below. Liability was established in the following case which saw a dilution of the Jenkins' principles in practice, making liability easier for plaintiffs to establish particularly in interim proceedings.

[9.6] *J & T Stratford & Son v Lindley* [1965] AC 269 (HL)

The defendants were officials of the watermen's union who had been trying unsuccessfully to be recognised by Bowker and King Ltd. In 1963 the company decided to recognise the TGWU, and did so without informing or consulting the watermen's union which was 'naturally disturbed' to have been left out. The union was not in a position whereby it could take any action against Bowker & King; but it could take action against J & T Stratford & Son which had a controlling interest in Bowker & King. An embargo was imposed on Stratford, with the result that barges which the company had hired out would not be returned. One effect of the embargo was that members of the watermen's union would not tow empty barges which were tied up at the nearest mooring, bringing the hiring business to a standstill because the barges could not be hired out again to new hirers. A second effect of the embargo was to bring the company's repair business to a standstill because the watermen would not deliver or redeliver barges of other owners which were to be or had been repaired by the company. The House of Lords found for the company.

Lord Reid

The next question is whether the principle of *Lumley v Gye* (1853) 2 E & B 216 has any application. I think that it has. The respondents acted with the intention of preventing barges out on hire from being returned to the appellants and those barges were in fact immobilised so that they could not be returned. The respondents knew that the barges were always returned promptly on the completion of the job for which they had been hired, and it must have been obvious to them that this was done under contracts between the appellants and the barge hirers. It was argued that there was no evidence that they were sufficiently aware of the terms of these contracts to know that their interference would involve breaches of these contracts. But I think that at this stage it is reasonable to infer that they did know that (pp 323–4).

9.2.2.2 Interfering with the performance of a commercial contract

An important extension of the principle of intentionally procuring breach of a commercial contract was to take place in *Torquay Hotel Co Ltd v Cousins* [1969] 2 Ch 106. The point in that case had already been anticipated by Lord Reid in *J & T Stratford & Son v Lindley* [1965] AC 269 when he reflected on the question 'whether or how the principle of *Lumley v Gye* (1853) 2 E&B 216 covers deliberate and direct interference with the execution of a [commercial] contract without that causing any breach' (at p 324). *Torquay Hotel Co Ltd v Cousins* [1969] 2 Ch 106 provided an answer (or a series of answers) to that question.

[9.7] *Torquay Hotel Co Ltd v Cousins* **[1969] 2 Ch 106 (CA)**

> The defendants imposed a fuel embargo of the plaintiff hotel company. The fuel was supplied by Esso under a contract which provided that 'neither party shall be liable for any failure to fulfil any term of this agreement if fulfilment is delayed, hindered or prevented by any circumstance whatever which is not within their immediate control, including . . . labour disputes'. How in these circumstances could there be liability for procuring breach of a commercial contract by unlawful means (inducing tanker drivers not to deliver their loads) when the commercial contract had not been broken? The answer was simple: the Court of Appeal was unprepared to permit the trade union officials to 'take advantage of the *force majeure* or exception clause in the Esso contract' (p 137). According to Lord Denning, 'If they unlawfully prevented or hindered Esso from making deliveries, as ordered by Imperial, they would be liable in damages to Imperial, notwithstanding the exception clause' (p 137). But how could liability be secured? According to Lord Denning by accepting that 'The time has come when the principle [in *Lumley v Gye* (1853) 2 E & B 216] should be further extended to cover 'deliberate and direct interference with the execution of a contract without that causing any breach' (p 138). The other members of the court decided the matter on narrower grounds, with Russell LJ holding that the exception clause did not mean that there was no breach which had been procured: in his view it was 'an exception from liability from non-performance rather than an exception from the obligation to perform' (p 143).

The principle in *Lumley v Gye* (1853) 2 E & B 216 had thus come a long way since 1853, and decisions such as *Torquay Hotel* threatened to reverse the achievements in *Crofter Hand Woven Harris Tweed v Veitch* [1942] AC 435, to say nothing of the 1906 statutory immunity which had already been extended in the Trade Disputes Act 1965 to cover liability for the new tort of intimidation introduced by the House of Lords in *Rookes v Barnard* [1964] AC 1129. (If in *Quinn v Leathem* [1901] AC 495 Munce had been persuaded to stop buying Leathem's meat because his workers refused to handle meat from Leathem, the union officials arguably would now be liable to Leathem for interference with business by unlawful means, even though there was no contract of supply between Munce and Leathem. In proceedings on this ground (in contrast to the position now in relation to conspiracy) the fact that the defendants were seeking to promote the interests of their members would be no excuse.) It is true that the courts appeared willing to accept that there could be no liability for interfering with the performance of a commercial contract by unlawful means if the means used (inducing breach of employment contracts) were protected by the statutory immunity. But the point was not conclusively resolved and uncertainty remained. It also meant that the immunity was being asked to carry a load which ultimately it could not bear. In both *J & T Stratford & Son v Lindley* [1965] AC 269 and *Torquay Hotel Co Ltd v Cousins* [1969] 2 Ch 106 it was held that there was no 'trade dispute' with the result that there was no protection for the defendant's tortious acts.

9.2.3 The expanded basis of liability

Torquay Hotel Co Ltd v Cousins was to be the high water mark in the development of tort liability for some time. The law was to be substantially recast by the short-lived Industrial Relations Act 1971. But that Act was repealed in 1974, and new immunities were introduced, based on the Trade Disputes Act 1906 but expanded to include a number of the new heads of tortious liability that had developed in the intervening years.

[9.8] Trade Union and Labour Relations Act 1974, section 13

Acts in contemplation or furtherance of trade disputes

13 (1) An act done by a person in contemplation or furtherance of a trade dispute is not actionable in tort on the ground only—
(a) that it induces another person to break a contract or interferes or induces another person to interfere with its performance, or
(b) that it consists in his threatening that a contract (whether one to which he is a party or not) will be broken or its performance interfered with, or that he will induce another person to break a contract or interfere with its performance.

(2) For the avoidance of doubt it is hereby declared that an act done by a person in contemplation or furtherance of a trade dispute is not actionable in tort on the ground only that it is an interference with the trade, business or employment of another person, or with the right of another person to dispose of his capital or his labour as he wills.

(3) For the avoidance of doubt it is hereby declared that—
(a) an act which by reason of subsection (1) or (2) above is itself not actionable;
(b) a breach of contract in contemplation or furtherance of a trade dispute;
shall not be regarded as the doing of an unlawful act or as the use of unlawful means for the purpose of establishing liability in tort.

(4) An agreement or combination by two or more persons to do or procure the doing of an act in contemplation or furtherance of a trade dispute is not actionable in tort if the act is one which if done without any such agreement or combination would not be actionable in tort.

For the next five years, there was a considerable volume of litigation. But this concentrated not on whether there was the commission of a tort for which there was no immunity, but on whether the industrial action was covered by the new expanded immunity. What we had was a concerted campaign by employers and others seeking to establish that various forms of trade union action—notably secondary action—were not protected as being done in contemplation or furtherance of a trade dispute.

In running these arguments, plaintiffs were to find a very sympathetic ear in the Court of Appeal in particular. This was to lead to a clash between the Court of Appeal and the House of Lords which led the latter on one occasion to issue a stern rebuke to the former, and to remind it of some of the basic principles of the British constitution: *Duport Steels Ltd v Sirs* [1980] ICR 161 (see below, p 894).

9.2.3.1 The wider genus of tort

But this is not to say that the development of tort liability came to a complete stand-still in 1969. The approach adopted by Lord Denning in *Torquay Hotel Co* was endorsed by the House of Lords in *Merkur Island Shipping Corporation v Laughton* [1983] 2 AC 570 where Lord Diplock said at pp 607–8:

> My Lords, your Lordships have had the dubious benefit during the course of the argument in this appeal of having been referred once more to many of those cases, spanning more than a century, that were the subject of analysis in the judgment of Jenkins LJ in *D C Thomson & Co Ltd v Deakin* [1952] Ch 646 and led to his statement of the law as to what are the essential elements in the tort of actionable interference with contractual rights by 'blacking' that is cited by the Master of the Rolls and, at rather greater length, by O'Connor LJ in their judgments in the instant case. That statement has, for 30 years now been regarded as authoritative, and for my part, I do not think that any benefit is gained by raking over once again the previous decisions. The elements of the tort as stated by Jenkins LJ, at p 697, were:
>
> > 'first, that the person charged with actionable interference knew of the existence of the contract and intended to procure its breach; secondly, that the person so charged did definitely and unequivocally persuade, induce or procure the employees concerned to break their contracts of employment with the intent I have mentioned; thirdly, that the employees so persuaded, induced or procured did in fact break their contracts of employment; and, fourthly, that breach of the contract forming the alleged subject of interference ensued as a necessary consequence of the breaches by the employees concerned of their contracts of employment.'
>
> *D C Thomson & Co Ltd v Deakin* was a case in which the only interference with contractual rights relied upon was procuring a *breach* by a third party of a contract between that third party and the plaintiff. That is why in the passage that I have picked out for citation Jenkins LJ restricts himself to that form of actionable interference with contractual rights which consists of procuring an actual breach of the contract that formed the subject matter of interference, but it is evident from the passages in his judgment which precede the passage I have cited and are themselves set out in the judgment of O'Connor LJ, that Jenkins LJ though using the expression 'breach,' was not intending to confine the tort of actionable interference with contractual rights to the procuring of such non-performance of primary obligations under a contract as would necessarily give rise to secondary obligations to make monetary compensation by way of damages. All prevention of due performance of a primary obligation under a contract was intended to be included even though no secondary obligation to make monetary compensation thereupon came into existence, because the second obligation was excluded by some *force majeure* clause.

The next logical step would be say that any interference with legal rights other than contractual rights would be actionable, whether arising under statute or in equity. These are forms of interference for which there has always been uncertain statutory protection, and for which there is now none. This stitch left hanging by the Court of Appeal in *Torquay Hotel Co Ltd v Cousins* [1969] 2 Ch 106 was picked up by the House of Lords in *Merkur Island Shipping Corporation v Laughton* [1983] 2 AC 570 where Lord Diplock addressed 'the common law tort, referred to in section 13(2) and (3) of the Act of 1974, of interfering with the trade or business of another person by doing unlawful acts'. He continued by saying at pp 609–10:

> To fall within this genus of torts the unlawful act need not involve procuring another person to break a subsisting contract. The immunity granted by section 13(2) and (3) I will call the 'genus immunity'. Where, however, the procuring of another person to break a subsisting contract is the unlawful act involved, as it is in section 13(1), this is but one species of the wider genus of tort. This I will call the 'species immunity'.

9.2.3.2 What constitutes unlawful means?

The confirmation of tortious liability on the wider ground of interference with trade, business or employment by unlawful means thus raises interesting questions about what constitutes unlawful means for the purposes of tortious liability.

[9.9] *Barretts & Baird (Wholesale) Ltd v IPCS* [1987] IRLR 3 (QBD)

A strike by Fatstock Officers employed by the Meat and Livestock Commission meant that the Commission was unable to perform certain statutory duties which it owed to abattoir owners. The owners sought an injunction to restrain the industrial action on the ground that the action interfered with their business by causing the MLC to be in breach of its statutory duties in a manner which caused loss to the plaintiffs. It was also argued that the strikers themselves were interfering with the plaintiff's business by unlawful means, the unlawful means being their breach of their contracts of employment. There were other grounds for which relief was sought, which we pass over here. Henry J accepted that the tort of interfering with trade or business by unlawful means was now 'clearly recognised'.

Henry J:
I therefore turn to consider the first category of unlawful means relied on, namely, inducing a breach of statutory duty. First, is there such a tort at all? It appears from *Meade v Haringey London Borough Council* [1979] 1 WLR 637 that where a body was in breach of a statutory duty by reason of a positive act which was ultra vires that body, then there was a remedy at the suit of a person who had suffered special damage thereby. In that case parents sued for the wrongful closure of schools by the local authority in breach of the statutory duty on the local authority to secure that sufficient schools should be available. If the breach of a statutory duty be unlawful then one would naturally expect the inducement of that breach to be unlawful. But to enable the plaintiffs to sue in tort the breach must give them a cause of action (see *Lonrho Ltd v Shell Petroleum (No 2)* [1982] AC 173) where it was held on the assumed facts that breach of a penal statute by the defendants gave the plaintiffs no cause of action in tort because on its proper construction the penal statute did not confer rights, based on civil actions, on individuals or on the public at large. So the first question here is to define the statutory duty. I have summarised the effect of the relevant legislation earlier in this judgment. The statutory duty is to provide a proper system for the inspection and certification of live and deadstock, such a

system as will enable the proper subsidies to be paid and the export of stock to be facilitated. It is in the performance of this duty that the MLC had trained and appointed 630 Fatstock Officers. The way in which that duty is performed is not laid down in the regulations but left to the discretion of the MLC. To whom is that duty owed? Originally it is owed to the producer. Of the various plaintiffs here only one is a producer. . . . Once the system which I have described is working all parties conduct their business on the basis of availability of subsidies and, in those circumstances, I regard it as eminently arguable that the duty is owed to all the plaintiffs. So arguably there is such a tort as the plaintiffs here contend for, and the plaintiffs can sue in respect of an alleged breach of that duty.

On the facts it was held that there was no breach of duty by the Commission in this case, and consequently no liability. It was also held that an individual taking industrial action in breach of contract could be committing a tort, but that an injunction would not lie to restrain it. This is because TULRA 1974, section 16 (now TULRCA, section 236) provided that no court by specific performance or injunction could restrain a breach of a contract of employment to compel an employee to work.

Liability for inducing breach of a statutory duty was confirmed by the Court of Appeal in *Associated British Ports v TGWU* [1989] ICR 557 where it was said that the inducement of a breach of a statutory duty is 'akin' to the inducement of a breach of contract, with both species of tort being 'classed as torts which involve the interference with a person's legal rights'. But it was also held that 'a breach of statutory duty cannot be relied on as unlawful means for the purposes of this tort unless it is actionable', that is to say unless the plaintiff would have a right of action in tort for breach of statutory duty against the party who is not complying with a statutory duty. Tort lawyers will be aware that not all breaches of statutory duty give rise to liability: the duty must be one which is owed by the defendant to the plaintiff. In the *Associated British Ports* case, however, the position was thought to be sufficiently unclear that an interlocutory injunction was granted to restrain the industrial action until this legal question could be resolved finally at the trial of the action. The House of Lords reversed, indicating perhaps that at the present time it is easier to assert the existence of this extended tort than it is to establish liability: but that may change. The House of Lords held that the statutory duty which had been broken in that case—in the Dock Workers (Regulation of Employment) Order 1947 (as amended)—was

---

A New Plaintiff

It is not only the base of tort liability which is continuing to expand. There are also signs that the range of potential plaintiffs may also be about to expand. In *Falconer* v. *NUR* [1986] IRLR 331—a county court decision—the question which arose was whether a rail passenger travelling from Doncaster to London and back could recover from the union damages for losses caused as a result of a rail strike which did not have the support of a ballot. It had previously been assumed that only the intended target of industrial action could sue, but not an incidental victim. As was pointed out by the judge, 'there is no case where a plaintiff—unknown to the defendant at the time the tort is alleged—has succeeded'. Undaunted the judge decided for the plaintiff on the ground that the action fell within the scope of the tort of unlawful interference with the performance of a contract, and damages of £173 were awarded. The union did not appeal, it is thought to avoid a damaging precedent being established by a higher court.

essentially a contractual obligation. As a result it was 'no more than a case of inducing other persons to break their contracts' (p 599). Liability for inducing or procuring
breach of a statutory duty is nevertheless a potentially important source of restraint,
with an unknown number of statutes imposing duties of different kinds on an
unknown number of bodies. A recent controversial example is the Fire and Rescue
Services Act 2004.

9.2.4 Statutory immunity: where are we now?

At a time when the principles of tortious liability are thus expanding, the statutory
immunity for tortious liability has contracted. The high water mark of immunity was
in the period from 1974–9 when immunity was provided in the Trade Union and
Labour Relations Act 1974 (as amended) for a number of torts where these were
committed in contemplation or furtherance of a trade dispute. Although there continues to be immunity, this has been diluted. The position is now governed by
TULRCA 1992.

[9.10] Trade Union and Labour Relations (Consolidation) Act 1992, section 219

Protection from certain tort liabilities

219 (1) An act done by a person in contemplation or furtherance of a trade dispute is not
actionable in tort on the ground only—
(a)   that it induces another person to break a contract or interferes or induces another
     person to interfere with its performance,
(b)   that it consists in his threatening that a contract (whether one to which he is a party
     or not) will be broken or its performance interfered with, or that he will induce
     another person to break a contract to interfere with its performance.
(2) An agreement or combination by two or more persons to do or procure the doing of
an act in contemplation or furtherance of a trade dispute is not actionable in tort if the
act is one which if done without any such agreement or combination would not be
actionable in tort.

Section 219 is based on section 13 of the 1974 Act (above p 875) which was amended
(principally in 1982) to remove section 13(2) and (3). Although important, the impact
of this change has not yet been devastating for the legality of industrial action. The
scope and content of section 13(2) (based on section 3(2) of the 1906 Act) was always
unclear, while the courts seem prepared (for now) to accept that conduct covered by
the immunity cannot form the basis of liability for a tort which is not protected (section 13(3)). It is also the case that section 219 has not been revised to take account of
the evolving common law, and in particular the continuing development of new species of liability since 1979. This is one of the weaknesses of an immunity as a basis of
protection for the freedom to strike: immunity can be provided only for those torts
which are known to exist at the time the immunity is enacted. In an evolving and
dynamic area of law, the immunity can quickly be outmanoeuvred by the emergence
of new grounds of liability for which there is no protection. It is for this reason (as

well as others) that a generic protection from liability based on a right to strike has obvious advantages. But again the evolution of new bases of tort liability has not yet been devastating either: new grounds for liability continue to evolve; but they have yet seriously to bite.

9.3 Trade dispute: defining the legitimate boundaries of trade union action

As we have seen the immunity from tortious liability is currently to be found in TULRCA 1992, section 219. It applies to action in contemplation or furtherance of a trade dispute, reflecting a narrow perception of the role of the strike in British law, an issue which is fully explored by some of the cases considered in this section. Not only does the fact that the immunity is restricted to trade disputes reveal a narrow perception of legitimate trade union action, the definition of a trade dispute is itself narrow and restrictive. This is particularly true following a number of amendments which were made to the definition in 1982 in particular.

[9.11] Trade Union and Labour Relations (Consolidation) Act 1992, section 244

Meaning of 'trade dispute' in Part V

244 (1) In this Part a 'trade dispute' means a dispute between workers and their employer which relates wholly or mainly to one or more of the following—
(a) terms and conditions of employment, or the physical conditions in which any workers are required to work;
(b) engagement or non-engagement, or termination or suspension of employment or the duties of employment, of one or more workers;
(c) allocation of work or the duties of employment between workers or groups of workers;
(d) matters of discipline;
(e) a worker's membership or non-membership of a trade union;
(f) facilities for officials of trade unions; and
(g) machinery for negotiation or consultation, and other procedures, relating to any of the above matters, including the recognition by employers or employers' associations of the right of a trade union to represent workers in such negotiation or consultation or in the carrying out of such procedures.

As defined, the concept of a trade dispute needs to be carefully dissected. There are a number of critical conditions: there must be (i) a dispute; (ii) it must involve proper parties; and (iii) it must relate wholly or mainly to one of the listed issues. Moreover, the conduct complained of must be done in contemplation or furtherance of the dispute. Before the amendments in 1982, the parties could be workers or a trade union and any employer (or indeed other workers or another trade union); now a dispute must be between a worker and his or her employer in order to secure immunity. Similarly, before 1982 the dispute had only to be 'connected with' one or more of the matters listed in subsection (1) in order to secure immunity; now it must be a dispute which 'relates wholly or mainly' to one or more of these matters.

9.3.1 Social and political questions

The definition of a trade dispute has historically reflected a fairly narrow view of the boundaries of legitimate trade union action: it reflects a view of the trade union as a body with exclusively or pretty much exclusively industrial aims. So the legislation refers to—and has done so since 1906—a 'trade' dispute, between employers and workers which must be concerned in some way with working conditions or workplace procedures. Industrial action to promote the wider social and political objectives of the Labour movement has always been treated with suspicion. Such action might fall at one of a number of hurdles: there may be no 'dispute' in the case of protest action; or if there is a dispute it may not be between proper parties, in the case of industrial action in furtherance of a dispute between a trade union or trade unions and the government about items in the latter's legislative programme; or if there is a dispute between proper parties, it may not be related wholly or mainly to a permitted subject-matter.

[9.12] *Express Newspapers Ltd v Keys* **[1980] IRLR 247 (QBD)**

This was an application for interlocutory relief to restrain the defendants from calling out their members to join a one day national strike as part of a TUC Day of Action to protest about the Employment Bill 1980, variously described as part of 'the anti-working class policies of this Government' and an example of 'the present reactionary attacks on the hard-won rights of the British trade union movement'. The proceedings arose out of action taken by three print unions (SOGAT, NATSOPA and NGA) and the National Union of Journalists. In the case of SOGAT members were directed to stop work on 14 May, NATSOPA members were urged to do so, NGA members were to ensure that they did not report for work, and NUJ members were encouraged to withdraw their labour and to do everything they could to bring about maximum NUJ involvement. The injunctions were granted.

Griffiths J:
. . . Each of the counsel for the defendants concedes that it is at least arguable that the defendants are inciting their members to break their contracts of employment by not working on 14 May. I go further: in my judgment it is clear beyond argument that that is precisely what they are doing. It is of course not surprising they should be so doing for they are only complying with the call of the TUC. Does the law permit them to behave in this manner? It does not. The tort of unlawful interference with another's contract is well established in our law. Unless you enjoy some statutory immunity it is unlawful to incite a person to break his contract of employment. Unions and their officers do of course have a wide immunity conferred on them by s13 of the Trade Union and Labour Relations Act 1974, as amended. They are not liable for inducing a person to break his contract of employment if they do so in contemplation or furtherance of a trade dispute; and recent

decisions of the House of Lords show how very wide is the immunity they enjoy. But there is no trade dispute in this case. This is not a call to withdraw labour arising out of an industrial dispute, it is an avowed political strike, and none of the defendants has sought to argue that they are entitled to the immunity conferred by s13.

The defendants say that they are doing no more than supporting the TUC in expressing deep frustration with the policies of the Government and of their inability to persuade the Government to alter course, and that it is their intention to make the maximum impact in the expression of their opposition to these policies. However, each of the defendants says that there is no intention to put pressure on his members in the form of disciplinary proceedings if they fail to respond to the union's call not to work on 14 May. In this sense they say the choice of their members is voluntary. Mr Williams [for the defendant] says that I have to perform a difficult balancing act between political and commercial interests and I should not interfere by way of injunction to inhibit or prevent the organisation of voluntary political protest if the commercial interest can be satisfied by an award of damages. He also draws my attention to Article 11 of the European Convention of Human Rights, which provides for the right to freedom of peaceful assembly and association with others, and he further draws my attention to those decisions such as *Ahmad v The Inner London Education Authority* [[1977] ICR 490], and *United Kingdom Association of Professional Engineers v Advisory, Conciliation and Arbitration Service* [[1979] ICR 303], which require our judges to have regard for the Convention in deciding any question to which it may be relevant. The relevance of Article 11, as I understand the argument, is that the defendants must have the right to organise assemblies and associations as part of the legitimate political protest to take place on the Day of Action, and their efforts will be reduced to chaos if I order them to withdraw the circulars which, in addition to inciting their members to break their contracts of employment, also contain directions as to where they are to assemble on the day that they break their contracts.

I propose to dispose at this point with this submission. In the *ACAS* case Lord Denning dealt with Article 11. He read the article . . .

Then Lord Denning continues:

'That article only states a basic principle of English law. The common law has always recognised that everyone has the right to freedom of association: provided always that the association does not pursue any unlawful end nor use any unlawful means and is motivated—not by a desire to injure others—but by a desire to protect the interests of its members'.

What Lord Denning has to say about association must of course equally apply to assembly. Of course the defendants are free to organise any assembly they wish provided they do so lawfully, but that right does not give them a licence to infringe the rights of others. It would not, for instance, give them a right to organise an assembly of their members to take place in someone's front garden without the permission of the owner of the property, and if they threatened to do so the court would at the suit of the owner, restrain them by injunction from committing such a trespass. By the same token, it does not make the defendants' action in inciting their members to commit a breach of contract a lawful act because they are making arrangements for them to assemble in the event of their incitement being successful.

The *Keys* case was concerned with protest action against the government: what we referred to in the introduction to this chapter as activity of the *worker as citizen*—engaging with the political process to protect rights at the workplace. So far as the legislation is concerned, this was a dispute between the government and the TUC, and even in 1980 when the immunity was at its widest, there was no protection. The following case is rather different: this dealt with what we refer to as the *citizen as worker*—concerned about a matter of political conscience which would be compromised by the performance of contractual obligations. Here too the boundaries of legitimate trade union action are revealed to have been very narrowly drawn, again at a time when the statutory protection was at its greatest.

[9.13] *BBC v Hearn* [1977] ICR 686 (CA)

The BBC sought an injunction to restrain the defendants from interfering with the broadcast of the 1977 FA Cup Final. The Association of Broadcasting Staff (ABS) had threatened to prevent its transmission to the rest of the world unless the BBC agreed not to broadcast to South Africa. Pain J held that the proposed action was protected by the statutory immunity as being in contemplation or furtherance of a trade dispute. The Court of Appeal held otherwise and an injunction was granted.

Lord Denning MR:
. . . all that was happening was that the trade union, or its officers, were saying: 'Stop this televising by the Indian Ocean satellite, stop it yourself. If you don't, we will ask our own people to stop it for you.' That is not a trade dispute. They were hoping, I suppose, that the BBC would give in; but, if they did not give in, they were going to order their members to stop the broadcast. That does not seem to me to be a trade dispute. To become a trade dispute, there would have to be something of the kind which was discussed in the course of argument before us: 'We would like you to consider putting a clause in the contract by which our members are not bound to take part in any broadcast which may be viewed in South Africa because we feel that is obnoxious to their views and to the views of a great multitude of people. We would like that clause to be put in, or a condition of that kind to be understood.' If the BBC refused to put in such a condition, or refused to negotiate about it, that might be a trade dispute. That, I think, is rather the way in which the judge approached this case. Towards the end of his judgment he said, putting it into the mouths of members through their union:

> "We wish it established as a condition of employment that we shall not be required to take part in broadcasts to South Africa so long as the South African Government pursues its policy of apartheid."

If that request had been made, and not acceded to, there might be a trade dispute as to whether that should be a condition of the employment. But the matter never reached that stage at all. It never reached the stage of there being a trade dispute. There was not a trade dispute 'in contemplation.' It was coercive interference and nothing more. If that is the right view, it means that the trade union and its officers are not exempt from the ordinary rule of law—which is that men must honour their contracts, and must not unlawfully interfere with the performance of them.

At an early stage in his submissions Mr Inskip [for the defendants] produced to us the written agreement which the BBC has with its employees. The very first clause says:

> 'You will perform to the best of your ability all the duties of this post and any other post you may subsequently hold and any other duties which may reasonably be required of you and will at all times obey all reasonable instructions given to you'.

He suggested that the instructions to televise this broadcast to the Indian Ocean satellite were unreasonable and therefore the men could disobey them. That cannot hold water for

---

The Right to Strike and Corporate Structure

A question arises about the way in which the immunity can be defeated by the manner in which companies organise themselves. The immunity can thus be made to depend on artificial considerations such as the way in which businesses are structured. This is a problem which has arisen particularly as a result of a number of the changes introduced since 1980. Under the 1974 Act a trade dispute could exist between workers and workers or between workers and an employer: for this purpose the employer need not have been the employer of the workers in question. So a trade dispute could exist between workers and any employer. The position was changed by the Employment Act 1982: this provides that a dispute may exist only between workers and their own employer, thereby restricting the scope of liability quite significantly. The impact of this change is illustrated by *Dimbleby & Sons Ltd v NUJ* [1984] ICR 386.

The facts are complex. Dimbleby newspapers were published by an associated company called Dimbleby Printers Ltd which was involved in a trade dispute with the National Graphical Association (NGA). Dimbleby newspapers then had to find an alternative printer and entered into a contract with TBF, which was an associated company of T. Bailey Forman Ltd, the publishers of the *Nottingham Evening Post*. The two companies had parallel shareholding and were controlled by the same third company. The difficulty here, however, is that the National Union of Journalists (NUJ) had been involved in a trade dispute with T. Bailey Forman Ltd since 1979. On learning of the agreement with TBF, the NUJ instructed its members at Dimbleby not to supply copy for printing by TBF, an instruction with which they complied. One of the issues in the case was whether the NUJ action at Dimbleby was in contemplation or furtherance of a trade dispute between the union and T. Bailey Forman Ltd.

The House of Lords held that it was not: Lord Diplock rejected the view that 'TBF, although a separate corporate entity from T. Bailey Forman Ltd, was nevertheless a party to the trade dispute between the NUJ and the latter company' (at p 409), though he did concede that there may be circumstances where 'even in the absence of express words stating that in specified circumstances one company, although separately incorporated, is to be treated as sharing the same legal personality of another, a purposive construction of the statute may lead inexorably to the conclusion that such must have been the intention of Parliament' (at p 410). This is a matter which has led to difficulties with the ILO, on which see below. The *Dimbleby* case also raised important questions about the restrictions on secondary action which were then in force, but which have since been displaced by more restrictive measures.

---

a moment. Nothing could be more reasonable than for the BBC to require their staff to perform their contracts, to send out this television signal so that all the viewers in Australia, Hong Kong and all the rest of the world should be able to view it. In any case a refusal to obey instructions would not make it a 'trade dispute'.

9.3.2 The right to strike and the changing public sector

An emerging issue in the case law is the extent to which the current immunity protects the right to take industrial action in order to protect job security in the context of change in the public sector. It is clear that in principle the definition is wide enough to cover many disputes about fears of job losses. But this is not universally the case, with problems arising in the context of disputes about privatisation in the 1980s and about the private finance initiative in the 1990s. The issue here is the extent to which the worker and the trade union may take action in a dispute with an employer which arises directly as a result of decisions taken in the political arena. Having failed to persuade the government of their case, how far can workers as citizens and citizens as workers take their dispute into the workplace which is where the implications of a political decision may well be felt hardest?

[9.14] *Mercury Communications v Scott-Garner* [1984] ICR 74 (CA)

The British Telecommunications Act 1981 empowered the Secretary of State for Trade and Industry to grant licences to run telecommunications systems. In 1982 he granted a licence to Mercury Communications. An agreement was subsequently struck between BT and Mercury to enable each to interconnect with the other's systems. In 1983 BT employees were instructed to secure a connection between the BT and Mercury systems, but they refused to obey, in furtherance of a union decision not to co-operate with Mercury. The union was also concerned at this time about the government's proposals to privatise BT. The Telecommunications Bill published in June 1983 proposed to abolish BT's exclusive privilege of running telecommunications systems and to transfer all its property, rights and responsibilities to a private company, the shares in which would be sold. Mercury sought an injunction to restrain the defendants from interfering by unlawful means with its contractual relations with BT. The application failed before Mervyn Davies J but was successful on appeal, where one of the key issues was whether the defendants were acting in contemplation or furtherance of a trade dispute.

Lord Donaldson MR:
The most obvious way of finding out what a particular dispute is wholly or mainly about is to inquire what the men concerned—in this case primarily those who refuse to interconnect—said to management at the time. Unfortunately we have no evidence, but it is a fair inference from what we do know that they said that the interconnection was contrary to their union's instructions. This throws one back to what the dispute between the union and BT was wholly or mainly about. That was not, of course, a relevant dispute because the union is neither an employer nor a worker in this context, but the subject matter of the dispute between BT and its employees can legitimately be taken to be the same as that between the union and BT

What the union's dispute with BT is about is the subject matter of paragraph 22 of Mr Stanley's first affidavit which I have already quoted:

> ... BT have entered into an interconnection agreement with [Mercury]. It is over this that the union are in dispute with BT ... BT ... have ... allowed a rival organisation to interconnect with its network. It is this fact which puts them at odds with my union. . . . The action which BT is taking is inconsistent with the desire of my members to retain the traditional monopoly over telecommunications facilities within BT. Once BT embarked upon a course of seeking to facilitate and implement liberalisation, they embarked upon a course which can only lead to a dispute between them and the union.

Mr. Stanley goes on to say that the *cause* of the dispute is that BT wished his members to take a step which his members regarded as putting their jobs at risk (my emphasis) and a few sentences later this suffers a further change when he states that the subject matter of the dispute is the risk to jobs.

Well; which is the subject matter—facilitating and implementing liberalisation, agreeing to interconnect, ordering interconnection or the risk to jobs? Only the latter would enable the dispute to qualify as a trade dispute. The evidence has to be looked at as a whole, but I find it impossible to conclude on the evidence at present available that the risk to jobs was a major part of what the dispute was about. I say that because I find it inconceivable that if the dispute was wholly or mainly about jobs, the union would not have approached BT asking for a guarantee of job security or a strengthening of the Job Security Agreement. Yet nothing of the sort appears to have happened and the union did not even think that this agreement was relevant to the present proceedings. On the other hand there is massive evidence that the union was waging a campaign against the political decisions to liberalise the industry and to privatise BT. In this context one has but to refer to the documentation for the Special Union Conference held in September 1983 from which we learn that

> 'The National Executive Council have set out the following objectives—(1) To seek the withdrawal of the 1983 Telecommunications Bill and the philosophy behind it. (2) Our intention is not to bring down the government but to defend the jobs and job opportunities, protect and enhance the conditions of service, pay and pensions of our members in both British Telecom and the Post Office. (3) To maintain the integrity, unity and strength of the union. (4) To prevent the breaking up of British Telecom and the Post Office. (5) To protect and enhance the services offered to the public. (6) To work for the return of a government committed to restore to public ownership without compensation any public sector industry or part thereof privatised by this government. In addition to restore the public monopoly over telecommunications and the postal service'.

Lest it be thought that all this relates to privatisation rather than liberalisation, it is right to mention that a paragraph under the heading 'Timing' is in the following terms:

> 'The timing of the union campaign against privatisation will evolve over a number of months. It will be related to: (1) Developments surrounding the Mercury interconnection issue. (2) The build-up to and the passage of the Telecommunications Bill through Parliament. (3) If the Bill is successful, the flotation of BTPLC'

The liberalisation and privatisation issues were thus interconnected as is indeed clear from much of the other documentation.

My conclusion on the evidence, provisional though it has to be, is reached without any doubt or hesitation. It is that it is most unlikely that the union will be able to establish that there was at any material time a trade dispute between B.T. and its employees.

The decision in *Mercury* reflects the importance in practice of the 1982 changes: in 'the context of an admittedly restrictive amendment to the statute', Lord Donaldson inclined to the view that 'Parliament intended a relatively restrictive meaning to be given to the phase [relating to], but this probably does not matter since the words "wholly or mainly" themselves indicate and provide a degree of restriction'. The effect is that the protection of job security may not necessarily be regarded as a legitimate trade union matter if the action is based on a challenge to the causes of that threat. There is no question that the action in the *Mercury* case would have been protected before the 1982 amendments as being connected with one of the statutory matters in what is now TULRCA 1992, section 244(1), but what was then section 29(1) of the Trade Union and Labour Relations Act 1974: see *NWL Ltd v Woods* [1979] ICR 867. Difficulties of a different but related kind are revealed in the following case, which indicates still further the extent to which the current definition of a trade dispute embraces a very narrow perception of the legitimate boundaries of trade union action. The case also shows how the amendments in the 1980s designed to deal in part with trade union opposition to privatisation (though there were other goals as well) have assumed an important restrictive role in new political circumstances. But for the workers involved the issues remain fundamentally the same.

[9.15] *University College London Hospitals NHS Trust v UNISON* [1999] ICR 204 (CA)

The employers in this case had entered into an agreement with a third party for the building of a new hospital to be financed by the private finance initiative. Some staff employed by the Trust would be employed by the new hospital. The union was concerned that this could lead to a threat to existing terms and conditions of employment, and sought to persuade the Trust to undertake that for a period of 30 years the new employer should apply the same terms and conditions applied by the Trust. When the Trust refused to agree to the union's request, industrial action followed. One of the questions was whether the action—which was supported by a ballot (as the law now required)—was in contemplation or furtherance of a trade dispute. The application succeeded before Timothy Walker J, whose decision was upheld by the Court of Appeal.

Lord Woolf MR:
I therefore turn to consider whether the more limited policy and objective of the union in this case falls within the requirements of section 244. In doing so, I note that the statutory categories of permitted purposes must be the predominant purpose. The dispute must relate wholly or mainly to those purposes. If it relates to them that is not sufficient to fulfil the statutory requirement.

Together with the objectives of obtaining a guarantee for existing employees, the union is seeking to secure the same guarantee for employees who have never been employed by the trust. As the 30-year period for which the guarantee is at present being sought progresses, there is bound to be a situation which will arise where the great majority of the employees will never have been employed by the trust. I cannot see how it is possible to apply the language of section 244(1)(a) and (5) in a way which covers the terms and conditions of employment of employees of a third party who have never been employed by the employer who is to be the subject of the strike action. This in itself is fatal to the case which the union advance on this appeal.

In addition, so far as existing employees are concerned, the strike seeks to achieve protection for them in relation to employment with the so far unidentified future employer. Recognising that this does not readily fall within the language of section 244, Mr Hendy [for the union] submits that the obtaining of the future protection does relate wholly or mainly to the existing terms and conditions of the employees of the trust because it will provide those employees with a sense of security which they would not otherwise have. He rightly submits that the terms and conditions of employment referred to can be threatened with change in the future. In addition he submits that a correct reading of subsection (5) has the effect of creating a distinction between the parties to the dispute and the subject matter of the dispute. While he accepts that the parties to the dispute must be the existing employees and the existing employer (here the trust), there is no such restriction on the subject matter of the dispute.

In support of that argument he attaches particular importance to that part of the language of subsection (5) which, so far as relevant, states: 'In this section— . . . "worker", in relation to a dispute with an employer, means—(a) a worker employed by that employer . . .' Mr. Hendy submits that the words 'in relation to a dispute with an employer' are confined to identifying the employer. He submits that the definition does not relate to the categories set out in subsection (1)(a) to (g) which are the subject matter of the dispute. He points out that there would be no purpose served by the use of the words 'in relation to a dispute with an employer' in subsection (5) if his submission was not correct. The subsection could read ' "worker" means a worker employed by that employer,' but it does not; it is confined. As to that argument, I see its force. However, in my judgment, it does not assist Mr. Hendy because, on the facts which are before the court, while it is true that a consequence of obtaining a guarantee would be to give the existing employees the additional security to which he refers, and therefore to that extent a matter which relates to their terms and conditions of employment, that is not the dispute which those employees are wholly or mainly concerned about. They are wholly or mainly concerned about the dispute with different employment; the employment with the so far unidentified new employer. For that reason, even with regard to the employees who are already employed by the trust, I consider that on the facts which are before the court, it is unlikely that the union could take advantage of the statutory immunity.

Following this decision, the union made an application to Strasbourg claiming that the restraint on its ability to organise industrial action in these circumstances amounted to a breach of its rights to freedom of association under Article 11 of the ECHR. But the application was ruled inadmissible. Although the Court held that 'the prohibition of the strike must be regarded as a restriction on the applicant's . . . freedom of association guaranteed under the first paragraph', it was also held that the restraints on the exercise of the right to strike could be justified under Article 11(2) of the Convention: *UNISON v United Kingdom* [2002] IRLR 497.

9.3.3 The Right to Strike and the House of Lords

The cases considered so far reveal the extent to which the courts have been easily impressed by employer's arguments designed to restrict the scope of the trade dispute immunity and consequently the freedom to strike. More recent decisions have shown the courts to be more resistant to these arguments and to take a more sensible approach to the circumstances in which the immunities apply. The most prominent such case is *Re P* [2003] 2 AC 663 which is all the more significant for being a decision of the House of Lords in which the Court of Appeal's decision in *BBC v Hearn* [1977] ICR 686 featured prominently. Although that decision was endorsed, it is with great difficulty and some sophistry that it can be reconciled with the approach adopted at least by Lord Hoffmann in the *P* case. The House of Lords traditionally has played a crucial role in determining the scope and content of the freedom to strike. A trilogy of cases in the first five years of the twentieth century established tortious liability for industrial action, while two decisions in the 1960s established new heads of tortious liability which was developed still further in 1983. But although it has been a major architect of common law liability for industrial action, the House of Lords has in more recent times taken a liberal view in determining the scope of the immunities. This is particularly true of several cases in 1980 where the Lords overturned more restrictive decisions of the Court of Appeal. But it should not be overlooked that these decisions coincided with the election of a Conservative government committed to changing the law on industrial relations. Can it be argued that in these cases the courts were prepared to stand back and leave the field to Parliament? Can it also be argued that they would have been less willing to do so if Labour had won the 1979 general election? We will never know. What we do know, however, is that the House of Lords is not willing to impose further constraints on today's much weakened trade unions.

[9.16] *P v NAS/UWT* [2003] ICR 386 (HL)

The appellant was a schoolboy who had been excluded from his school because of his behaviour. He appealed to the governors and was reinstated. After further incidents of disruption, the teachers complained to their union (NAS/UWT) and said that they should not be required to go on teaching P. The union then gave notice to the governors, as the teachers' employers, that they intended to ballot their members at the school over whether they should strike or take industrial action short of a strike in furtherance of their objection to having to teach P. The result of the ballot was that 26 members voted in favour of industrial action, described as not accepting 'the unreasonable direction of the head teacher, acting under the instructions of the Governing Body, made in accordance with the Teachers' Pay and Conditions Document, to teach a certain pupil'. None voted against. Paragraph 56 of the Teachers' Pay and Conditions Document says in general terms that a teacher shall carry out his professional duties 'under the reasonable direction of the head teacher'. Paragraph 57 says that he shall perform 'in accordance with any directions which may reasonably be given to him by the head teacher . . . such particular duties as may reasonably be assigned to him.' His professional duties are described in paragraph 58 and they include 'teaching . . . the pupils assigned to him' and 'maintaining good order and discipline among the pupils'. If, therefore, it was reasonable for the head teacher to direct the teachers to teach P, their industrial action in refusing to do so would have been a breach of their conditions of employment. Following the conduct of the ballot, the union wrote to all its members at the school instructing them to take industrial action from 1 December 2000. After that date the teachers refused to teach P in their classes. The head teacher arranged for him to sit in a separate room under the supervision of a supply teacher and do work which the other teachers had set for him. P then brought proceedings against the union under TULRCA 1992, section 235A (on which see p 966 below). One of the main issues in the case was whether the union was acting in contemplation or furtherance of a trade dispute within the meaning of TULRCA 1992, s 219. Both Morison J and the Court of Appeal held that the action was covered by the immunity, and the House of Lords agreed. The action was unsuccessful.

Lord Bingham:

2. Since the Trade Disputes Act 1906, trade unions and their officials have enjoyed a measure of immunity from actions against them by employers based on the tort of inducing breaches of contract by employees. But the immunity has never been, and is not now, unqualified. Under the law as it now stands, immunity is enjoyed only if the inducement is an act done in contemplation or furtherance of a trade dispute (Trade Union and Labour Relations (Consolidation) Act 1992, section 219) and only if the breach induced has the support of a properly conducted ballot (1992 Act, sections 226-234) . . .

3. The first issue turns on the definition of a trade dispute in section 244(1) of the 1992 Act as meaning (so far as relevant) "a dispute between workers and their employers which relates wholly or mainly to . . . (a) terms and conditions of employment . . .". It is plain that most disputes between employers and employees which lead to strike action or

industrial action short of a strike fall squarely within this definition however it is construed. One might instance disputes about rates of pay; ancillary benefits such as paid holidays, sick pay or pensions; working hours; overtime; rostering and shift patterns; and so on. In such situations, the employers or the employees (or their representatives) are seeking a change in some aspect of the employment relationship between them, whether strictly contractual or not, which the other party is resisting, and the action is taken to put pressure on the other party to accede. In such a case, if the ordinary processes of negotiation and collective bargaining break down, the inducement of breaches of contract (save in excepted employments, and subject to the balloting requirements) is not unlawful. So much is agreed.

4. But Mr Giffin, for the appellant P, contended that the statutory definition of trade dispute covers nothing other than a dispute about terms and conditions of employment, giving that expression the broad meaning favoured by Lord Denning MR in *British Broadcasting Corporation v Hearn* [1977] 1 WLR 1004 at 1010; [1977] ICR 685 at 692 and approved by the House in *Hadmor Productions Ltd v Hamilton* [1983] 1 AC 191 at 227, 233–234. I was for a time attracted by this argument, which was skilfully deployed and appeared to reflect the language of the statute. But I am persuaded that such a construction would be too narrow and would deny protection to genuine, employment-related disputes between employers and employees which have in the past been thought to be protected and ought in fairness to be so. Suppose, for example, an employer introduced a new machine or a new working schedule, as the employer was in principle entitled to do, but which his employees resisted on the ground that the machine was potentially dangerous or the new working schedule too onerous. There could be no doubt of the employer's duty to take reasonable care not to expose his employees to danger or to excessive stress, and it would accordingly be artificial to regard such a dispute as one about the terms and conditions of their employment, even on a broad construction of that expression. It would in truth be a dispute about the job the employees were required to do, a matter going to the very heart of the employment relationship. I would accordingly read the statutory definition as covering a genuine dispute between employees and their employer relating wholly or mainly to the job the employees are employed to do or the terms and conditions on which they are employed to do it. If this test is applied to the facts of the present case, as summarised by my noble and learned friend, it is plain that the dispute between the teaching staff and the governing body as their employers related directly to the job the teachers were required to do and were unwilling to do, which was to teach P.

Lord Hoffmann:

24. In my opinion this was plainly a dispute over terms and conditions of employment, which I regard as a composite phrase chosen to avoid arguments over whether something should properly be described as a "term" or "condition" of employment. It is sufficient that it should be one or the other. Furthermore, the use of such a composite expression shows that it was intended to be given a broad meaning: see Roskill LJ in *British Broadcasting Corporation v Hearn* [1977] 1WLR 1004, 1015.

25. In the present case, it seems to me that the dispute was about the contractual obligation of the teachers to teach P. It could be characterised as a dispute over whether there was such a contractual obligation: the union, as we have seen, contended that the head teacher's direction was unreasonable. Alternatively it could be characterised as a dispute over whether there should be such a contractual obligation. It does not seem to me profitable to try to analyse it one way or the other. The dispute arose because the head teacher said that the teachers were obliged to teach P and they said that they were not willing to do so. That seems to me a dispute which does not merely "relate to" but is about their terms and conditions of employment.

26. Mr Giffin, who appeared for P, submitted that "terms and conditions" of

"employment" meant the rules which governed the employment relationship. They need not be written out in the contract of employment. In *Hearn's* case Lord Denning MR said, at p 1010, that

> "Terms and conditions of employment may include not only the contractual terms and conditions but those terms which are understood and applied by the parties in practice, or habitually, or by common consent, without ever being incorporated into the contract."

27. But whether the rules are expressly agreed or implied from custom and practice, Mr Giffin says that they must be rules. The nature of a rule, he said, is that it is a normative statement at some level of generality. In the present case, there was a rule that teachers should comply with the directions of the headmaster. A dispute over whether they should teach P was not a dispute about the rule but about the application of the rule. It might possibly have been formulated as a dispute about terms and conditions of employment if the union had claimed that the rule should be changed to provide that "teachers should comply with the directions of the headmaster (except that they should not be required to teach P)." But the union never said that this was what they wanted.

28. My Lords, I do not think that Parliament could have intended the immunities conferred upon trade unions in industrial disputes to turn upon such fine distinctions. It is in my opinion impossible in this context to formulate a coherent distinction between a rule and the application of the rule to particular cases. A dispute about what the workers are obliged to do or how the employer is obliged to remunerate them, at any level of generality or particularity, is about terms and conditions of employment.

29. The main authority upon which Mr Giffin relied for his proposition was the actual decision of the Court of Appeal in *Hearn's* case, which was subsequently approved by this House in *Hadmor Productions Ltd v Hamilton* [1983] 1 AC 191. In Hearn's case, union members working for the BBC threatened to refuse to transmit its television signal to a satellite over the Indian Ocean during the Cup Final because the satellite broadcast would be receivable in, among many other countries, South Africa. The refusal was pursuant to a union policy of opposing apartheid and on the ground that, as Mr Peter Hain said in a letter of 22 April 1977 to the Director-General of the BBC, "the screening of the Cup Final will give considerable satisfaction to the sports loving white population." See [1977] 1 WLR 1004, 1008.

30. The Court of Appeal granted an interlocutory injunction restraining the industrial action on the ground that it was not in furtherance of a trade dispute. They gave brief unreserved judgments. Lord Denning MR said that the threat of industrial action was "coercive interference and nothing more". It had nothing to do with terms and conditions of employment. It did not become a trade dispute merely because the workers were threatening to break their contracts. The work involved in transmitting the broadcasts was not what the dispute was about. Roskill and Scarman LJJ agreed.

31. The decision was, if I may respectfully say so, correct because the dispute did not relate to anything which the workers were called upon to do. They would have had to do exactly the same things if South Africa had not been among the countries from which the satellite broadcast was receivable. Unlike the teachers in this case, who objected to having to teach P, the BBC workers had no complaint about any aspect of their work. The objection was simply that one result of their work would be to give pleasure in South Africa.

32. I can find nothing in the case which supports a distinction between a rule and a particular application of the rule. Mr Giffin relied upon the following observations of Lord Denning MR, at p 1011:

> "To become a trade dispute, there would have to be something of the kind which was discussed in the course of argument before us: 'We would like you to consider putting a clause in the contract by which our members are not bound to take part in any broadcast which may be viewed in South Africa because we feel that is obnoxious to their views and to the views of a great multitude of people. We would like that clause to be put in, or a condition of that kind to be understood.' If the BBC refused to put in such a condition, or refused to negotiate about it, that might be a trade dispute."

33. Mr Giffin says that this shows that a trade dispute must be about a rule. But in my opinion Lord Denning's remarks were intended to suggest a way in which the concept of a trade dispute might be extended to include disputes over matters which did not concern what the workers had to do or how the employer had to remunerate them. It was not intended to prevent disputes which were over such matters from being trade disputes unless they were formulated in terms of rules. In *Universe Tankships Inc of Monrovia v International Transport Workers Federation* [1983] 1 AC 366, 392 Lord Cross of Chelsea cautioned against taking Lord Denning's tentative observations too far:

> "A trade union cannot turn a dispute which in reality has no connection with terms and conditions of employment into a dispute connected with terms and conditions of employment by insisting that the employer inserts appropriate terms into the contracts of employment into which he enters."

34. The point does not seem to have surfaced in subsequent cases and your Lordships may therefore well leave it there. Mr Giffin draws attention to the fact that the scope of the protection for industrial action was narrowed after *Hearn's* case. But the only relevant change is that a trade dispute must "relate wholly or mainly" to terms and conditions of employment and must not merely be "connected" with them: *Mercury Communications Ltd v Scott-Garner* [1984] Ch 37, 75. But in my opinion the narrower requirement is entirely satisfied. To say that the dispute was related to terms and conditions of employment is, if anything, inadequate. Terms and conditions of employment are what the dispute was about. It is therefore unnecessary to say anything about the other phrases in the definition of a trade dispute on which the union placed reliance.

9.4 Restricting the boundaries of industrial action: secondary action and other restraints

One of the fundamental features of trade unionism is solidarity and the willingness to help other workers in distress. This may take many forms, both financial and practical. Help of the latter kind may involve various forms of industrial action by workers of the same union employed by another employer, or by workers of another union employed by another employer. Throughout the twentieth century, secondary action of this kind by trade unions has been a matter of great political controversy. The target of the secondary action will be a third party not directly involved in the dispute between the trade union and the employer—usually a supplier or customer of the employer involved in the dispute. The purpose of the action will normally be to put economic pressure on the employer in the dispute, in order to encourage him or

---

Trade union solidarity

Trade union rule-books will often reflect a commitment to help others, as in the following examples which describe the objects of the FBU, ASLEF and TGWU respectively to include the following

'(6) To aid and join with other trade unions or societies having objects similar to any of the objects of this Union.'

'(2) . . . the Society may aid and join with other trade or other societies or federations if societies having for their objects or one of them the promotion of the interests of workmen within the scope of any relevant statutory provisions.'

'2(j) The furtherance of, or participation, financial or otherwise, directly or indirectly, in the work or purpose of any association or federal body having for its objects the furthering of the interests of labour, trade unionism or trade unionists.'

---

her to settle on the union's terms. Good examples of secondary action from the cases we have encountered so far are *Quinn v Leathem* [1901] AC 495 where the union sought to put pressure on the plaintiff by means of his customer Munce by calling on its members at the latter to take supportive action; and *D C Thomson & Co Ltd v Deakin* [1952] Ch. 646 (referred to by Lord Diplock in *Merkur Island Shipping Corporation v Laughton* [1983] AC 2 AC 570) where NATSOPA sought to put pressure on the non-union plaintiff by disrupting its supply of paper by enlisting the support of TGWU drivers. Indeed it is a feature of many of the cases involving the development of tortious liability that they have involved secondary action of one form or another, reflecting a degree of judicial hostility to such trade union conduct, hostility which is not always thinly disguised.

9.4.1 Liability and immunity

This is not to say that secondary action has always been condemned by the courts. After all, the landmark *Crofter Hand Woven Harris Tweed v Veitch* [1942] AC 435 was a case about secondary action: a union in dispute with the independent producers calling upon dockers not to handle the supplies or finished products of the independent producers. Indeed in that case Lord Thankerton provided what was perhaps the strongest (and perhaps the only) judicial endorsement of secondary action when he said at p 460:

> In the present case the pressure was applied by means of action by the dockers, who were in no sense employees in, or directly connected with, the trade in Harris tweed; but employees in this trade were members of the same union, and the interest of the dockers and the trade employees in the union and its welfare were mutual, and I can see no ground for holding that it was not legitimate for the union to avail itself of the services of its docker members to promote the interests of the union. On the other hand, I doubt if it would be legitimate for a union to use a means of pressure with which it had no connection except that which was constituted by a money payment, for instance'.

So even here there are limits: secondary action is legitimate provided that it is taken by members of the same union as the workers in the dispute. What is not clear is whether the action by the dockers would have been as sympathetically received if it had been in support of the members of another union (as say in *D C Thomson & Co Ltd v Deakin* [1952] Ch 646). But in a sense it does not really matter: following *J & T Stratford & Son v Lindley* [1965] AC 269 and *Torquay Hotel Co Ltd v Cousins* [1969] 2 Ch 106, the foundations of liability for secondary action were to shift onto territory from which there was no escape on the basis of legitimate self-interest. It is at this point that secondary action would be protected only if it was covered by the immunity in the 1906 Act and its progeny, a matter which was to prove extremely controversial.

How then would secondary action in principle be protected by the immunity? There would not normally be a dispute between the trade union and the target of the secondary action (the customer or supplier). Traditionally, however, torts committed in the course of the secondary action would be protected as being in furtherance of the trade dispute between the trade union and the employer. The point was established in *Conway v Wade* [1909] AC 506 where Lord Loreburn said at p 512:

> I come now to the meaning of the words 'an act done in contemplation or furtherance of a trade dispute'. These words are not new in an Act of Parliament; they appear in the Conspiracy and Protection of Property Act 1875. I think they mean that either a dispute is imminent and the act is done in expectation of and with a view to it, or that the dispute is already existing and the act is done in support of one side to it. In either case the act must be genuinely done as described, and the dispute must be a real thing imminent or existing. I agree with the Master of the Rolls that the section cannot fairly be confined to

---

The General Strike of 1926

On 1 May 1926 the miners were locked out by their employers in a dispute about pay and working conditions. The government had withdrawn a subsidy from the industry and the employers proposed to cut wages. On 3 May the TUC called affiliated unions to take strike action in sympathy with the miners. The General Strike as it became known lasted for nine days and gave rise to great controversy, with the government claiming that it was a challenge to constitutional government, with the TUC seeking to coerce the government to maintain the subsidy. At a critical point of the dispute an action was heard in the High Court, brought by the only TUC affiliated union which was against the strike: the action was designed to restrain one of its dissident branches from supporting the strike contrary to the policy of the national executive committee of the union in question. The case gave rise to an important obiter dictum of Astbury J which is thought to have gone some way to persuade the TUC to call off its action. The trade union position was that the TUC action was perfectly lawful, being in furtherance of a trade dispute between the miners and their employers: it was classic sympathy action on a large scale. In *National Sailors' and Firemen's Union v. Reed* [1926] Ch 536, Astbury J disagreed, and held that the action was not in furtherance of a trade dispute. In his view, '[t]he so-called general strike called by the Trades Union Congress Council is illegal, and persons inciting or taking part in it are not protected by the Trade Disputes Act 1906. No trade dispute has been alleged or shown to exist in any of the unions affected, except in the miners' case, and no trade dispute does or can exist between the Trades Union Congress on the one hand and the Government and the nation on the other'. Action of this kind was rendered unlawful by the Trade Disputes and Trade Unions Act 1927, referred to by Laski, at p 865 above. The 1927 Act was repealed in 1946.

an act done by party to the dispute. I do not believe that was intended. A dispute may have arisen, for example, in a single colliery, of which the subject is so important to the whole industry that either employers or workmen may think a general lock-out or a general strike is necessary to gain their point. Few are parties to, but all are interested in, the dispute'.

In practice, however, the courts were reluctant to conclude that secondary action could enjoy the protection of the immunity in this way. A good example of this reluctance was *J & T Stratford & Son v Lindley* [1965] AC 269 where the union took action against the plaintiff's customers in response to a decision of an associated company to recognise a rival union. Another is the *Torquay Hotel* case, above. In these cases the courts restrained the secondary action on the ground that there was no trade dispute. As a result the immunity was cut away: if there was no trade dispute, the secondary action could not be said to have been done in contemplation or furtherance of a trade dispute.

Following the expansion of the immunities in 1974 and 1976—and the definition of a trade dispute—a new approach was adopted by some courts. Now they fastened onto the word 'furtherance', and sought to introduce a number of qualifications and restrictions, which would restrain the circumstances in which secondary action might be taken within the boundaries of the immunity. These qualifications and restrictions are considered by Lord Diplock in *Express Newspapers Ltd v MacShane* [1980] ICR 42 (see Box below) where he said at pp 57–8:

> First there is a test based on remoteness. The help given to the party to the trade dispute must be direct. 'You cannot', said Lord Denning MR in *Beaverbrook Newspapers Ltd v Keys* [1978] ICR 582, 586, 'chase consequence after consequence after consequence in a long chain and say everything that follows a trade dispute is in "furtherance" of it'. The second test, suggested by Lord Denning in the instant case, is that the act done must have some 'practical' effect in bringing pressure to bear upon the opposite side to the dispute; acts done to assist the morale of the party to the dispute whose cause is favoured are not protected. Thirdly there is the test favoured by Lawton and Brandon LJJ in the instant case: the act done must, in the view of the court, be reasonably capable of achieving the objective of the trade dispute.

At a time of great controversy the House of Lords disagreed in a strongly expressed decision, Lord Diplock observing in the process that it was not 'a legitimate approach to the construction of the sections that deal with trade disputes, to assume that Parliament did *not* intend to give to trade unions and their officers a wide discretion to exercise their own judgment as to the steps which should be taken in an endeavour to help the workers' side in any trade dispute to achieve its objectives'. According to Lord Diplock at p 57:

> Given the existence of a trade dispute . . . , this makes the test of whether an act was done 'in . . . furtherance of' it a purely subjective one. If the party who does the act honestly thinks at the time he does it that it may help one of the parties to the trade dispute to achieve their objectives and does it for that reason, he is protected by the section. I say 'may' rather than 'will' help, for it is in the nature of industrial action that success in achieving its objectives cannot be confidently predicted. Also there is nothing in the section that requires that there should be any proportionality between on the one hand the

---

Secondary Action, Statutory Immunity and the Courts

In *Express Newspapers Ltd* v. *MacShane* [1980] ICR 42, a trade dispute existed between the National Union of Journalists and the owners of local newspapers. In order to make the strike more effective, the NUJ called out on strike its members employed by the Press Association (PA). The PA supplied the local newspapers with news copy, though it also supplied the national press as well. Journalists employed by the national newspapers were instructed by the union not to handle PA copy. An injunction was granted at first instance by Lawson J to restrain the defendants from procuring the breach of employment contracts by anyone engaged by the plaintiff by instructing them to refuse to handle PA copy. The Court of Appeal dismissed the appeal, but a subsequent appeal by the defendants to the House of Lords was successful. The action of the NUJ was held to be in contemplation or furtherance of a trade dispute.

In *Duport Steels Ltd* v. *Sirs* [1980] ICR 161 a trade dispute existed between the then publicly owned British Steel and the steel workers' union, the ISTC. In order to reduce the supply of domestic steel and to put pressure on the government to find money to resolve the dispute, the union called a strike of its members who worked for private steel companies. At first instance it was held following *Express Newspapers Ltd* v. *MacShane,* above, that the secondary action was in furtherance of the trade dispute between the union and British Steel. The Court of Appeal reversed, for reasons which not even counsel for the employers felt could be rationally supported. The House of Lords restored the first instance judge, refusing to construe the phrase 'in furtherance of a trade dispute' as being 'confined to acts which are intended to have an immediate adverse trade or industrial effect on the opposite party to the trade dispute'.

---

extent to which the act is likely to, or be capable of, increasing the 'industrial muscle' of one side to the dispute, and on the other hand the damage caused to the victim of the act which, but for the section, would have been tortious.

9.4.2 Withdrawal of immunity

Since the decision of the House of Lords in *Express Newspaper Ltd v MacShane* [1980] ICR 42 and the subsequent decision in *Duport Steels Ltd v Sirs* [1980] ICR 161 the right of trade unions to organise secondary action has gradually been withdrawn by legislation. This has been done principally in two stages. The first was in the Employment Act 1980, section 17 of which was passed to 'deal with the effects of the MacShane judgment' (Cmnd 8128, 1981, paragraph 143). This limited the circumstances in which secondary action might be taken, but retained the possibility of such action being taken against the first customer or supplier of the employer in dispute. It was also possible in some circumstances to take action against an associated employer of the employer in dispute. The effect was that in the *MacShane* case (above), it would probably have been possible to have taken action against the PA, but not against the Express or other Fleet Street nationals. But for all that, the way in which the law was drafted made the position something of a lottery, and in two important and high-profile House of Lords cases secondary action was ruled unlawful as falling outside the scope of secondary action permitted by section 17. One was *Merkur Island Shipping Corporation v Laughton* [1983] 2 AC 570 and the other was

Dimbleby & Sons v NUJ [1984] ICR 386. At this stage, however, the then Conservative government appeared to accept that there may be circumstances in which secondary action might be justified. So much is indicated in the following passage from the Green Paper, *Trade Union Immunities*, which was published after the enactment of the Employment Act 1980 and in which a number of options for reforming the law on industrial action were canvassed. At this point, however, the case for a total ban on secondary action appears to have been rejected.

[9.17] Department of Employment, *Trade Union Immunities* **(Cmnd 8128, 1981)**

> **148**. The most far-reaching proposal would be to remove immunity from all secondary action. This could be achieved in a number of ways. In essence it would mean removing all immunity for inducing breaches of contract from any person who organised industrial action by employees of an employer who was not himself in dispute. There would remain immunity only for organising action by employees who were in dispute with their own employer.
>
> **149**. This would appear to be a clear restriction on immunity easily understood by all concerned and simply applied by the courts. It can be argued that it is the only limitation which would provide complete protection for those employers and employees whose companies are subjected to secondary action in support of a dispute in which they are not involved. Against this it can be argued that, in some cases, secondary action is the only means by which pressure can be brought on an employer in dispute, for example where the employer has sacked all his unionised employees; that secondary action by fellow union members is a long standing trade union practice deeply based in concepts of unity and mutual assistance; and that it could tilt the balance of power unacceptably to the benefit of employers.
>
> **150**. It has been argued that this proposal could be made less harsh if the right to sue in these circumstances were to be restored only to the employer not in dispute and were to be denied to the employer who *is* in dispute. Against this it can be said that, from the trade union official's point of view, it is immaterial whether he can be sued by the employer in dispute or not: it is the threat of being sued at all which matters. The official would still be at risk of legal action every time he organised a secondary strike or secondary blacking. Furthermore, there would always be the possibility of the employer in dispute arranging for the other employer to take legal action and promising to indemnify him against any adverse outcome.

The other limitation introduced in the 1980s which had a bearing on secondary action was the requirement to ballot before industrial action. This applied as a condition of immunity for all tortious liability: but it had a particular bearing on secondary action, as workers thought long and hard before committing themselves to someone else's cause. Workers taking secondary action (whether by blacking goods or otherwise) risked being found in breach of contract and thereby exposing themselves to a risk of penalties and sanctions such as deductions from pay, disciplinary suspensions, or even dismissal—real threats in the new industrial relations climate in the 1980s. Nevertheless these and other restrictions were felt not to go far enough by the government in 1989, and additional restrictions withdrawing immunity from all forms of secondary action were introduced by the Employment Act 1990. These new measures were trailed by a Green Paper published in 1989 in which it was said that the restrictions in the Employment Act 1980 then in force 'were framed in the light of circumstances in 1980, at a time when secondary industrial action had been much more widespread than it has been in recent years', and that it was right to ask whether the remaining immunities for secondary action were still justified. The document continued:

[9.18] Employment Department, *Removing Barriers to Employment* (Cm 655, 1989)

> **3.10.** The Government believe that the following considerations indicate that the present law needs amendment:
> —In general there is no good reason why employers who are not party to a dispute should be at risk of having industrial action organised against them;
> —Secondary action may deter employers from starting up for the first time in this country, with harmful effects on new investment and on jobs. For example, there might be a threat of secondary action being organised among workers of the new firm's customers or suppliers, with the aim of forcing the new firm to accept certain terms and conditions. This sort of threat was made when the Ford Motor Company was planning to establish a new factory at Dundee. Regardless of whether they are lawful or unlawful under the present law, there is no good reason why any threats of this kind, or the organisation of action of this kind, should enjoy immunity.
> —The law as it stands is complicated and could well be difficult for those involved to determine, in the absence of a court judgment, whether there would be immunity for organising certain secondary action. An example might be secondary action which involved a union inducing transport workers to refuse to move coal to power stations, or within power stations, in support of a dispute between British Coal and its employees. If the coal was part of a shipment including other goods from other suppliers, it might be very difficult to know whether there would be immunity for refusal to move the shipment as a whole. The same would apply if the coal was unloaded and stored with coal from other suppliers, from which it could not be distinguished, and transport workers then refused to move any part of the store of coal.

The government's position was strongly criticised by the then Opposition spokesman on employment (Tony Blair) during the parliamentary debates on what was clause 4 of the Employment Bill 1990 (Official Report, Standing Committee D, 22 February 1990, cols 171–78). In his view '[t]he abolition of sympathy action is unreasonable, unjustified and way out of line with anything that happens anywhere else'; 'it cannot be said that it is fair or even-handed', he continued, 'to allow employers to have unrestricted commercial action, but to insist that unions should act only in a private dispute'(col 177). Nevertheless the 1990 Act introduced a further restriction on secondary action, the provisions of which are now to be found in TULRCA 1992, section 224.

[9.19] Trade Union and Labour Relations (Consolidation) Act 1992, section 224

Secondary action

224 (1) An act is not protected if one of the facts relied on for the purpose of establishing liability is that there has been secondary action which is not lawful picketing.

(2) There is secondary action in relation to a trade dispute when, and only when, a person—

(a) induces another to break a contract of employment or interferes or induces another to interfere with its performance, or

(b) threatens that a contract of employment under which he or another is employed will be broken or its performance interfered with, or that he will induce another to break a contract of employment or to interfere with its performance,

and the employer under the contract of employment is not the employer party to the dispute.

(3) Lawful picketing means acts done in the course of such attendance as is declared lawful by section 220 (peaceful picketing)—

(a) by a worker employed (or, in the case of a worker not in employment, last employed) by the employer party to the dispute, or

(b) by a trade union official whose attendance is lawful by virtue of subsection (1)(b) of that section.

(4) For the purposes of this section an employer shall not be treated as party to a dispute between another employer and workers of that employer; and where more than one employer is in dispute with his workers, the dispute between each employer and his workers shall be treated as a separate dispute.

In this subsection 'worker' has the same meaning as in section 244 (meaning of 'trade dispute').

(5) An act in contemplation or furtherance of a trade dispute which is primary action in relation to that dispute may not be relied on as secondary action in relation to another trade dispute.

Primary action means such action as is mentioned in paragraph (a) or (b) of subsection (2) where the employer under the contract of employment is the employer party to the dispute.

(6) In this section 'contract of employment' includes any contract under which one person personally does work or performs services for another, and related expressions shall be construed accordingly.

Notwithstanding the Labour Party's opposition to the 1990 changes and its defence of the principle of solidarity action, the New Labour government has refused to amend the restrictions now contained in TULRCA 1992. This is despite the fact also that these restrictions violate international labour standards, on which see below.

9.4.3 International solidarity action

A variation on the above theme relates to international solidarity action—where

> **Trade Union International Solidarity**
>
> The aims and objects of UNISON include the following—
> 'To assist and support other unions, organisations, charities or individuals as deemed appropriate locally, nationally and internationally.'
> 'To participate in international trade union activities and to foster appropriate international links.'
> UNISON, Rule B4(2) and (3)

trade unions and their members take action not in support of workers in this country but in support of workers elsewhere. Trade unionism is an international movement, with British trade unions affiliated to global union federations. The best known of these to British lawyers is the International Transport Workers' Federation to which a number of British trade unions are affiliated (including ASLEF). But other international bodies include Public Services International (to which UNISON is affiliated), the International Union of Food Workers, and the International Federation of Chemical, Energy, Mine and General Workers' Union. Trade unions pursue international objectives in a number of other ways, for example by providing financial and other support to the ANC during the apartheid era in South Africa. The question here, however, is whether this international activity and this support for political and trade union movements elsewhere can take the form of industrial action by British workers. We have already encountered in this chapter a number of examples of international solidarity action, which may take a variety of forms, and which may be unlawful on one of a number of grounds. But it may be thought that the need for international solidarity action is all the more urgent in the context of globalisation and the increasing internationalisation of trade and commerce.

[9.20] Trade Union and Labour Relations (Consolidation) Act 1992, section 244

Meaning of 'trade dispute' in Part V

244 . . . (3) There is a trade dispute even though it relates to matters occurring outside the United Kingdom, so long as the person or persons whose actions in the United Kingdom are said to be in contemplation or furtherance of a trade dispute relating to matters occurring outside the United Kingdom are likely to be affected in respect of one or more of the matters specified in subsection (1) by the outcome of the dispute.

The question of international solidarity action has been prompted by threatened plant closures in 2001, which saw problems for workers at General Motors in Luton and Corus steelworks in South Wales. In the latter case the company—which also conducts operations in the Netherlands—announced some 6,000 redundancies at a number of sites in the UK. According to press reports:

Dutch steel unions . . . pledged to boycott any transfer of Corus UK's production to the Netherlands as their British counterparts began drawing up alternative plans to keep threatened plants open and prevent many of the 6,000 redundancies taking place. Leaders of the FNV union yesterday told Corus's Dutch management in Amsterdam that workers at the group's Ijmiuden plant on the North Sea coast would not undertake work previously done in Wales and other parts of the UK [*The Guardian*, 3 February 2001].

The International Transport Workers' Federation and Flags of Convenience

One example of international solidarity action is the campaign waged by the ITF against ships flying flags of convenience, that is to say ships which have been registered in countries—such as Panama and Liberia—which have poor labour standards. The aim of the ITF is to ensure that all seafarers are employed on minimum terms set down in ITF model contracts. The ITF campaign led to a great deal of litigation in this country in the late 1970s and early 1980s, one example being the *Merkur Island* case already considered. The ITF action in that case was found to be unprotected by the statutory immunity because it constituted unlawful secondary action within the terms of the Employment Act 1980, section 17. The action would now be unprotected following the 1982 amendments to the definition of a trade dispute. Before 1982 a trade dispute could be a dispute between workers or a trade union and an (any) employer. So a dispute between the ITF and a shipowner could be a trade dispute even though the seafarers in question did not ask for the ITF to intervene. Now there must be a dispute between workers and their employer which means that ITF action will be protected only if they act on behalf of workers in dispute with their own employer rather than being the party to the dispute. It is widely believed that the law was changed in this way in 1982 to spike the guns of the ITF in particular. The ITF campaign was also responsible for the introduction of the law of economic duress to the industrial relations scene: see *Universe Tankship of Monrovia* v. *ITF* [1983] 1 AC 366.

But what if the position was reversed? Would it be possible for British workers to take such action in support of workers in the Netherlands facing a closure and the transfer of their work? In order to qualify for protection, there would have to be a dispute between workers in this country and their employer. The fact that it may be said to relate to matters overseas (a plant closure) would not be a total bar to immunity if applying TULRCA 1992, section 244(3) it could be said that the workers in this country were likely to be affected in respect of one or more of the matters specified in TULRCA 1992, section 244(1) (which they ought to be able to establish on these imaginary facts). But it is quite possible that a court would take the view that there is no dispute between workers and their employer in this fictitious example, but that the industrial action in this country (which would also need the support of a ballot) is in fact in furtherance of a dispute between the Dutch unions and their employer. On that basis there is no question of the action being protected even if British workers will be affected by the outcome, and even if it does have the support of a ballot. This is because the action by the British workers would be secondary action within the meaning of section 244 and could thus be restrained by way of injunction.

It is not only solidarity action of a practical nature of this kind which would be vulnerable to challenge. The same would apply to action such as the anti-apartheid activities of the ABS in *BBC v Hearn* [1977] ICR 686. Again action of this kind could be challenged, though it is open to the unions to follow the advice tendered by the Court of Appeal in that case to request the employer to vary contracts so that the employees are not required to carry out work which is designed for—in that case—South Africa. But even here it would be open to a court to say that despite the form in which the dispute has emerged, it is not one which relates wholly or mainly to terms and conditions of employment, but is in reality a dispute about a political matter. There is the question of TULRCA 1992, section 244(3), though again it is not

---

Other Restrictions on Industrial Action

This section has concentrated on various forms of solidarity, secondary or sympathy action. There are also other circumstances where industrial action is excluded from protection.

The first of three additional circumstances is in respect of industrial action to enforce trade union membership (TULRCA 1992, section 222). So industrial action against an employer because he or she employs non-union members is not protected, nor is industrial action designed to persuade an employer to include a term in a contract for the supply of goods or services that work under the contract should be done only by union labour.

The second of the additional restrictions relates to industrial action designed to support workers who have been dismissed for taking part in unofficial industrial action (TULRCA 1992, section 223). By virtue of section 237 such workers cannot bring an action for unfair dismissal. This restriction introduced in 1990 means that they may not call on their union for help, without the union incurring the risk of liability for damages.

The third of the additional restrictions was—like the first—introduced in 1982. Industrial action to induce an employer to include a recognition requirement in a commercial contract is not protected. This is a requirement that the employer providing the goods or services recognises a trade union. Industrial action to disrupt goods or services under a contract is also unprotected if the reason for it is that the service provider does not recognise a trade union (TULRCA 1992, section 224).

---

clear how much of an issue this would be in the unlikely event that a trade dispute could be established. It is true that the dispute would relate to matters occurring outside the UK (in this example apartheid). But it is also true that the workers who are taking action in furtherance of the trade dispute (the broadcasting staff) will be affected by the outcome of the dispute in respect of one or more of the items in TULRCA 1992, section 244(1). If they succeed, their terms and conditions will be varied so as not to require them to take part in the work in dispute (the broadcast to South Africa). But in practice international solidarity action of this kind is unlikely to be protected, even if supported by a ballot.

9.5 Procedural restraints: ballots and notices

Mandatory strike ballots were introduced by the Trade Union Act 1984, making majority support in a ballot a precondition of immunity from liability in tort. The reason for mandatory ballots before industrial action were set out in the Green Paper, *Democracy in Trade Unions* (Cmnd. 8778, 1983), as follows:

> In principle the case for holding a secret ballot before a strike is called is as strong as the case for secret ballots for trade union elections. Indeed the argument is fundamentally the same in both cases: if trade unions are to serve and fairly represent the interests of their members they should ensure that any important decisions are supported by a

majority of the members voting in a secret ballot. A strike can cost an employee dearly. The result may be not only loss of pay (although that can be serious enough); it may also mean the loss of his job. As the industrial power of the unions has grown, the effects of exercising that power have become increasingly serious, not only for the strikers themselves and those at whom the strike is directly aimed, but for the community as a whole. Strikes damage economic performance, reduce living standards and destroy jobs far beyond the ambit of the parties to the dispute. In recent years it has become common for strikes to be aimed at inflicting damage on innocent third parties in the hope that the distress caused will bring about Government intervention to press the employers to yield to the unions' demands. Such strikes inflict inconvenience and hardship on the general public. Society has the right to expect that the strike weapon will be used sparingly, responsibly and democratically.   [paragraph 56]

These may strike some as strong and even compelling arguments. On the other hand there are arguments about freedom of association, whereby voluntary bodies should be free to determine their own constitutions and rules without interference by the State. It is also the case that an individual worker may leave a union if he or she does not agree with a particular decision to take industrial action, and that a trade union member may not now be penalised or expelled by his or her union for failing to take part in industrial action. This is fully considered in Chapter 7. Moreover, the duty to ballot applies regardless of the consequences of the action for the community as a whole: not all industrial action will cause major dislocation.

An interesting feature of the legislation is that, as initially enacted, responsibility for enforcement was left to employers, not trade union members and not the State. Tied to the immunity, the employer could seek an injunction to restrain action unsupported by a ballot. The legislation introduced in 1984 has, however, been amended on several occasions, most notably in 1988 and 1993. One of the important changes introduced by the Employment Act 1988 was to empower the trade union member to sue to enforce the duty to ballot before a strike, a power which still exists though there is no reported case of its having been used. The major initiative introduced by the Trade Union Reform and Employment Rights Act 1993 relates to the union's obligation to give notice of the ballot to the employer (as well as a sight of the ballot paper, notice of the ballot result, and notice of when the strike or industrial action is to commence). Other changes have concerned the move to fully postal ballots, and the need for independent scrutineers. Quite apart from the point of principle about mandatory strike ballots being imposed by the State, the complexity of the legislation has been a source of considerable difficulty for trade unions in trying to organise lawful action in accordance with the law. Ballots under the legislation are also very expensive to administer, not only because of the balloting costs themselves, but also because of the need for expensive legal advice which seems to be required by unions trying to navigate the dangerous statutory currents. The strike ballot provisions of what is now the 1992 Act have thus proved to be fertile ground for litigation. A wide range of issues has troubled the courts, some of them quite bizarre. The difficulty which has emerged is that industrial action is being challenged not because a ballot has not been held, but because the trade union has allegedly slipped up on a point of detail.

9.5.1 The statutory duty

[9.21] Trade Union and Labour Relations (Consolidation) Act 1992, section 226

Requirement of ballot before action by trade union

226 (1) An act done by a trade union to induce a person to take part, or continue to take part, in industrial action

(a)   is not protected unless the industrial action has the support of a ballot, and

(b)   where section 226A falls to be complied with in relation to the person's employer, is not protected as respects the employer unless the trade union has complied with section 226A in relation to him.

Section 226 also provides that industrial action is to be regarded as having the support of a ballot only if the different provisions of sections 226B–233 are complied with. Section 226 further provides expressly that industrial action will have the support of a ballot only if a majority voting do so in favour of the action. The legislation is complemented by a *Code of Practice on Industrial Action Ballots and Notice to Employers* (2000). The most recent edition is less open to criticism for stretching the substance of the law than its predecessors.

9.5.2 Notice to the employer

TULRCA 1992, section 226A provides that the trade union must give notice to the employer of its intention to hold the ballot (to be given at least seven days before the opening of the ballot), and a copy of the ballot paper (to be given at least three days before the opening of the ballot). Before amendments introduced by the Employment Relations Act 1999, the union was required to give notice of the names of any employees they proposed to ballot (*Blackpool and The Fylde College v NATHFE* [1994] ICR 648). The law was amended by the Employment Relations Act 1999, but these amendments proved to be just about as controversial as the measures they replaced. Indeed it was acknowledged by the Court of Appeal that the changes introduced in 1999 had in some respects made the union's task 'more onerous': *RMT v London Underground Ltd* [2001] IRLR 228. A particularly controversial feature of the 1999 amendments was the duty on the part of the union to provide 'such information in the union's possession as would help the employer to make plans and bring information to the attention of those of his employees who it is reasonable for the union to believe . . . will be entitled to vote in the ballot'. The purpose of the duty to provide information was 'to enable the employer to put his side of the argument to his workforce, for them to take into account when participating in the ballot or responding to the union's call to take action; and they are to help the employer to minimise the adverse effects of possible industrial action on his organisation, on his customers and on the general public' (HL Debs, 16 June 1999, col 299 (Lord McIntosh of Haringey)). But despite the intention, this obligation nevertheless provided a pretext for injunctions to be granted on the flimsiest grounds, and did not even require the employer in legal proceedings to identify the plans that he or she would make, or how these plans had been frustrated by the union's failure to provide information: *BT plc v CWU* [2004] IRLR 58.

Growing disquiet about the 1999 amendments led to further amendments being introduced by the Employment Relations Act 2004, with the removal of the duty to provide information to assist the employer. A trade union is nevertheless still required to provide the following information to the employer in its notice of its intention to hold an industrial action ballot:

- The total number of employees who will be balloted
- A list of the categories of employee to which those who will be balloted belong, and the number of workers in each category
- A list of the workplaces where the employees to be balloted work, and the number of such employees at each workplace

In cases where the employer operates a check-off system and deducts trade union contributions from the employees' wages on behalf of the union, the union may comply with its obligation to give notice by referring the employer to the categories of such employees who are to be balloted. It is enough that the employer should be able to deduce from the information supplied by the union (a) the total number of the affected employees, (b) the categories of employee to which the affected employees belong and the number of the affected employees in each of those categories, and (c) the workplaces at which the affected employees work and the number of them who work at each of those workplaces. But whichever of the foregoing methods is adopted, the information supplied 'must be as accurate as is reasonably practicable in the light of the information in the possession of the union at the time when it complies' with its duty. Information is in the possession of the union if it is held in the possession or under the control of an officer or employee of the union. This covers both head office and branch records, on which see *RMT v London Underground Ltd* [2001] IRLR 228. It is expressly provided that a union is not required to supply an employer with the names of the affected employees. Identical obligations arise in relation to the duty of the union to give strike notice after the ballot has been held authorising the taking of such action. These measures are considered below at pp 911–913.

9.5.3 Separate workplace ballots

Since 1988, where the strike or industrial action spreads across more than one workplace, a separate ballot must be held in each workplace. A strike may be called only at those workplaces where a majority of those voting do so in favour. The reason for this requirement was explained by the minister at the time when he said that otherwise 'it would be possible to construct an artificial constituency, the effect of which would be to ensure that one group of voters for that purpose would swamp another. In other words, one would artificially create a constituency so that if one wanted to get a certain result one could manipulate it in that way': Official Report, Standing Committee F, 14 January 1988, col. 473. In practice, however, there were wide exceptions which allowed for single and aggregate ballots in some circumstances, a point which indeed the minister was at pains to point out at some length in Standing Committee in 1988. But the legislation was extremely complex, and was amended in 1999 in an attempt to simplify the position. But it would be impossible to suggest that there is any simplicity about even the new arrangements.

[9.22] Trade Union and Labour Relations (Consolidation) Act 1992, sections 228–228A

Separate workplace ballots

228 (1) Subject to subsection (2), this section applies if the members entitled to vote in a ballot by virtue of section 227 do not all have the same workplace.

(2) This section does not apply if the union reasonably believes that all those members have the same workplace.

(3) Subject to section 228A, a separate ballot shall be held for each workplace; and entitlement to vote in each ballot shall be accorded equally to, and restricted to, members of the union who—
(a)   are entitled to vote by virtue of section 227, and
(b)   have that workplace.

(4) In this section and section 228A 'workplace' in relation to a person who is employed means—
(a)   if the person works at or from a single set of premises, those premises, and
(b)   in any other case, the premises with which the person's employment has the closest connection.

Separate workplaces: single and aggregate ballots

228A (1) Where section 228(3) would require separate ballots to be held for each workplace, a ballot may be held in place of some or all of the separate ballots if one of subsections (2) to (4) is satisfied in relation to it.

(2) This subsection is satisfied in relation to a ballot if the workplace of each member entitled to vote in the ballot is the workplace of at least one member of the union who is affected by the dispute.

(3) This subsection is satisfied in relation to a ballot if entitlement to vote is accorded to, and limited to, all the members of the union who—
(a)   according to the union's reasonable belief have an occupation of a particular kind or have any of a number of particular kinds of occupation, and
(b)   are employed by a particular employer, or by any of a number of particular employers, with whom the union is in dispute.

(4) This subsection is satisfied in relation to a ballot if entitlement to vote is accorded to, and limited to, all the members of the union who are employed by a particular employer, or by any of a number of particular employers, with whom the union is in dispute.

(5) For the purposes of subsection (2) the following are members of the union affected by a dispute—
(a)   if the dispute relates (wholly or partly) to a decision which the union reasonably believes the employer has made or will make concerning a matter specified in

subsection (1)(a), (b) or (c) of section 244 (meaning of 'trade dispute'), members whom the decision directly affects,

(b) if the dispute relates (wholly or partly) to a matter specified in subsection (1)(d) of that section, members whom the matter directly affects,

(c) if the dispute relates (wholly or partly) to a matter specified in subsection (2)(e) of that section, persons whose membership or non-membership is in dispute,

(d) if the dispute relates (wholly or partly) to a matter specified in subsection (1)(f) of that section, officials of the union who have used or would use the facilities concerned in the dispute.

The definition of workplace in section 228(4) is a response to the facts in *Inter-City West Coast Ltd v RMT* [1996] IRLR 583, where difficulty arose in determining the place of work of train crews.

9.5.4 Entitlement to vote, the voting paper and the conduct of the ballot

For the ballot to be valid, 'entitlement to vote' must be

'accorded equally to all members of the trade union who it is reasonable at the time of the ballot for the union to believe will be induced to take part, or as the case may be, to continue to take part in the industrial action in question, and to no others' (TULRCA 1992, section 227(1)).

Industrial action is not to be regarded as being supported by a ballot if any person who was a member of the trade union at the time when the ballot was held and was denied entitlement to vote in the ballot is induced by the union to take part or, as the case may be, to continue to take part in the industrial action (TULRCA 1992, section 232A). This has the effect indirectly of protecting the union which calls out members who may have joined after the industrial action started, and who as a result may not have been balloted. The issue arose before the 1999 reforms in *London Underground Ltd v NUR* [1996] ICR 170 where a number of members of one union left to join another which was engaged in a strike with their employer, which the new members were asked to join. It was held on the facts even before the 1999 reforms that the participation of the new recruits did not invalidate the ballot. Express provision is also made for some 'small accidental failures' to be disregarded where these are 'unlikely to affect the result of the ballot' (TULRCA 1992, section 232B).

[9.23] *RMT v Midland Mainline Ltd* [2001] IRLR 813 (CA)

The union balloted a number of members in a dispute about the safety duties of train crew. Notice was given to the employer under TULRCA 1992, s 226A that the union intended to hold a ballot of 'RMT members employed by your company in the grades of operational train crew'. The notice included a breakdown of the 91 members according to job category and location of work. The company contested the accuracy of the information and asked the union to supply the names and addresses of the members in question. The union refused but asked the employer to supply a list of its employees so that the union could check the list against its own records. The company refused. The union thereupon balloted 91 members, of whom 25 voted to strike and 17 voted against; the remainder did not vote. Strike notice was then given to the employer under TULRCA 199, s 234A (see below). It subsequently transpired that the union had failed to ballot 25 members who were employed by the company as operational train crew. These included 11 about whom the union had no information that they were in the relevant grades; 10 who were in arrears with their subscriptions; and 4 who were sent ballot papers to their wrong address or not sent one at all (by mistake). The employer applied successfully for an injunction to have the action restrained on the ground that the ballot violated the requirements of s 227(1) above in respect of the first of these two categories. The third category could be excused under s 232B which allows for small accidental failures to be overlooked. This decision was upheld by the Court of Appeal which addressed the question of the employer's refusal to provide information that might have enabled the union to comply with its statutory duty. According to Schiemann LJ a possible solution is for ACAS to be involved, to help ensure that membership checks are carried out on a confidential basis and that all members receive their ballot papers. Another solution might be to say that an injunction is an equitable remedy and that those who seek an injunction must have clean hands. If – as here – the employer has the information to enable the union to comply with its duty, the court in its discretion should refuse the relief sought.

Section 229 provides that the 'method of voting must be by the marking of a voting paper by the person voting'. So no hand counts and no proxies. The voting paper must contain at least one of the following questions:

- a question (however framed) which requires the person answering it to say, by answering 'Yes' or 'No', whether he or she is prepared to take part or, as the case may be, to continue to take part in a strike;
- a question (however framed) which requires the person answering it to say, by answering 'Yes' or 'No', whether he or she is prepared to take part or, as the case may be, to continue to take part in industrial action short of a strike.

The 1999 Act reversed *Connex South Eastern Ltd v RMT* [1999] IRLR 249 in the sense that overtime and call-out bans are to be treated as action short of a strike for these purposes. The voting paper must specify who is authorised to call the industrial action in the event of a vote in favour, and must contain the following statement:

> If you take part in a strike or other industrial action, you may be in breach of your contract of employment. However, if you are dismissed for taking part in strike or other industrial action which is called officially and is otherwise lawful, the dismissal will be unfair if it takes place fewer than twelve weeks after you started taking part in the action, and depending on the circumstances may be unfair if it takes place later.

The second sentence was added by the 1999 Act (and amended by the 2004 Act), and reflects the changes to unfair dismissal law introduced by that Act. Ballots are to be conducted in secret, by post (TULRCA 1992, section 230). Those voting must be allowed to do so without interference or constraint from the union, and without incurring any cost. The union may, however, campaign in favour of a 'Yes' vote (*London Borough of Newham v NALGO* [1993] IRLR 83).

9.5.5 After the ballot: calling the industrial action

After the ballot has been held, the union must inform those entitled to vote of the result (TULRCA 1992, section 231), and must also inform the employer (TULRCA 1992, section 231A). The scrutineer whom the union is required to appoint under TULRCA 1992, section 226B, must state whether or not he or she is satisfied with the way in which the ballot has been conducted, and if not to explain why (TULRCA 1992, section 231B). The requirement for a qualified person to be appointed as an independent scrutineer was introduced in 1993. The cost must be borne by the union, as must the cost of the ballot as a whole. A State scheme to help with the costs of a wide range of ballots (including strike ballots) was introduced in 1980; but this was gradually phased out in the 1990s. The only exception from the duty to provide a scrutineer is in section TULRCA 1992, section 226C which contains an exclusion for small ballots where the number to be balloted is no more than 50. Once the scrutineer is satisfied, the action must be called by a specified person (TULRCA 1992, section 233), within the period prescribed by the Act (TULRCA 1992, section 234).

[9.24] Trade Union and Labour Relations (Consolidation) Act 1992, section 234

Period after which ballot ceases to be effective

234 (1) Subject to the following provisions, a ballot ceases to be effective for the purposes of section 233(3)(b) in relation to industrial action by members of a trade union at the end of the period, beginning with the date of the ballot—
(a) of four weeks, or
(b) of such longer duration not exceeding eight weeks as is agreed between the union and the members' employer.

(2) Where for the whole or part of that period the calling or organising of industrial action is prohibited—
(a) by virtue of a court order which subsequently lapses or is discharged, recalled or set aside, or
(b) by virtue of an undertaking given to a court by any person from which he is subsequently released or by which he ceases to be bound,
the trade union may apply to the court for an order that the period during which the prohibition had effect shall not count towards the period referred to in subsection (1).

(3) The application must be made forthwith upon the prohibition ceasing to have effect—
(a) to the court by virtue of whose decision it ceases to have effect, or
(b) where an order lapses or an undertaking ceases to bind without any such decision, to the court by which the order was made or to which the undertaking was given;
and no application may be made after the end of the period of eight weeks beginning with the date of the ballot.

(4) The court shall not make an order if it appears to the court—
(a) that the result of the ballot no longer represents the views of the union members concerned, or
(b) that an event is likely to occur as a result of which those members would vote against industrial action if another ballot were to be held.

(5) No appeal lies from the decision of the court to make or refuse an order under this section.

(6) The period between the making of an application under this section and its determination does not count towards the period referred to in subsection (1).

But a ballot shall not by virtue of this subsection (together with any order of the court) be regarded as effective for the purposes of section 233(3)(b) after the end of the period of twelve weeks beginning with the date of the ballot.

As a general rule, the ballot thus provides a mandate to call the industrial action within four weeks from the date of the ballot (TULRCA 1992, section 234, below). Thereafter it ceases to be effective. But what does four weeks mean?

[9.25] *RJB Mining (UK) Ltd v NUM* [1995] IRLR 556 (CA)

A ballot closed on 10 am on 16 May 1995, and the union notified the employer that its members would be taking 24 hours' strike action as from the commencement of the day shift on Tuesday 13 June. The employers challenged the action on the ground that the four week period for the ballot expired on midnight 12 June, so that action beginning on 13 June was unprotected. For its part the union argued that the day shift on 13 June commenced at midnight, a time which straddled both the 12th and the 13th and that the action was therefore still within the protection of the ballot. The injunction was granted, and upheld by the Court of Appeal. According to Henry LJ, the union's argument was 'ingenious', but had to be rejected 'for the simple reason that while time may be seamless, days do not overlap'. The action was called for on 13 June, the ballot ceased to be effective on 12 June at the stroke of midnight, and, therefore, this industrial action was called on the wrong side of the law.

The provisions of what are now section 234(2)–(6) were first introduced in response to the events surrounding the decision in *Associated British Ports v TGWU* [1989] ICR 557 (HL) where the four week period had expired during the course of litigation which took many weeks to complete. Having successfully defended themselves, the union found that the ballot was spent. The additional ground for extending the four week period to be found in section 234(1)(b) was introduced in 1999. The measure was applauded on the Opposition benches in Standing Committee as introducing 'a welcome additional element of flexibility for unions and employers to reach agreement' (Official Report, Standing Committee E, 18 March 1999, col 476).

9.5.6 Notice of industrial action

As we have seen above, the trade union must give notice of the ballot and a sample ballot paper to the employer: the former must be supplied at least seven days before the start of the ballot; and the latter at least three days before. The employer is also to be informed of the result of the ballot, in this case, 'as soon as reasonably practicable after the holding of the ballot' (section 231A). But this is not all: an additional obligation introduced in 1993 requires the union also to give at least seven days' notice to the employer specifying when the industrial action is to start, who will be involved, and whether it will be continuous or discontinuous. In explaining the reason for this additional obligation, the responsible minister said in Standing Committee:

> Employers and the public should be protected against the damage that can be caused if unions proceed to organise industrial action without prior warning, and as soon as a ballot has been concluded. The concept of providing strike notice, albeit in the context of different institutional and legal arrangements, is familiar enough in other countries. (Official Report, Standing Committee F, 15 December 1992, col 258)

But as a rationale this is slightly disingenuous: in view of the obligation to give notice to the employer of the ballot result, there is no one who can be taken by surprise by a strike or other industrial action.

[9.26] Trade Union and Labour Relations (Consolidation) Act 1992, section 234A

Notice to employers of industrial action

234A (1) An act done by a trade union to induce a person to take part, or continue to take part, in industrial action is not protected as respects his employer unless the union has taken or takes such steps as are reasonably necessary to ensure that the employer receives within the appropriate period a relevant notice covering the act.

(2) Subsection (1) imposes a requirement in the case of an employer only if it is reasonable for the union to believe, at the latest time when steps could be taken to ensure that he receives such a notice, that he is the employer of persons who will be or have been induced to take part, or continue to take part, in the industrial action.

(3) For the purposes of this section a relevant notice is a notice in writing which—
(a) contains—
    (i)   the lists mentioned in subsection (3A) and the figures mentioned in subsection (3B), together with an explanation of how those figures were arrived at, or
    (ii) where some or all of the affected employees are employees from whose wages the employer makes deductions representing payments to the union, either those lists and figures and that explanation or the information mentioned in subsection (3C), and;
(b) states whether industrial action is intended to be continuous or discontinuous and specifies—
    (i)   where it is to be continuous, the intended date for any of the affected employees to begin to take part in the action,
    (ii) where it is to be discontinuous, the intended dates for any of the affected employees to take part in the action,

(3A) The lists referred to in subsection (3)(a) are—
(a) a list of the categories of employee to which the affected employees belong, and
(b) a list of the workplaces at which the affected employees work.

(3B) The figures referred to in subsection (3)(a) are—
(a) the total number of the affected employees,
(b) the number of the affected employees in each of the categories in the list mentioned in subsection (3A)(a), and

(c) the number of the affected employees who work at each workplace in the list mentioned in subsection (3A)(b).

(3C) The information referred to in subsection (3)(a)(ii) is such information as will enable the employer readily to deduce—
(a) the total number of the affected employees,
(b) the categories of employee to which the affected employees belong and the number of the affected employees in each of those categories, and
(c) the workplaces at which the affected employees work and the number of them who work at each of those workplaces.

(3D) The lists and figures supplied under this section, or the information mentioned in subsection (3C) that is so supplied, must be as accurate as is reasonably practicable in the light of the information in the possession of the union at the time when it complies with subsection (1).

(3E) For the purposes of subsection (3D) information is in the possession of the union if it is held, for union purposes—
(a) in a document, whether in electronic form or any other form, and
(b) in the possession or under the control of an officer or employee of the union.

(3F) Nothing in this section requires a union to supply an employer with the names of the affected employees.

(4) For the purposes of subsection (1) the appropriate period is the period—
(a) beginning with the day when the union satisfies the requirement of section 231A in relation to the ballot in respect of the industrial action, and
(b) ending with the seventh day before the day, or before the first of the days, specified in the relevant notice.

(5) For the purposes of subsection (1) a relevant notice covers an act done by the union if the person induced falls within a notified category of employee and the workplace at which he works is a notified workplace and—
(a) where he is induced to take part or continue to take part in industrial action which the union intends to be continuous, if—
  (i) the notice states that the union intends the industrial action to be continuous, and
  (ii) there is no participation by him in the industrial action before the date specified in the notice in consequence of any inducement by the union not covered by a relevant notice; and
(b) where he is induced to take part or continue to take part in industrial action which the union intends to be discontinuous, if there is no participation by him in the industrial action on a day not so specified in consequence of any inducement by the union not covered by a relevant notice.

(5B) In subsection (5)—
(a) a "notified category of employee" means—
  (i) a category of employee that is listed in the notice, or
  (ii) where the notice contains the information mentioned in subsection (3C), a category of employee that the employer (at the time he receives the notice) can readily deduce from the notice is a category of employee to which some or all of the affected employees belong, and
(b) a "notified workplace" means—
  (i) a workplace that is listed in the notice, or
  (ii) where the notice contains the information mentioned in subsection (3C), a

workplace that the employer (at the time he receives the notice) can readily deduce from the notice is the workplace at which some or all of the affected employees work.

(5C) In this section references to the "affected employees" are references to those employees of the employer who the union reasonably believes will be induced by the union, or have been so induced, to take part or continue to take part in the industrial action.

(5D) For the purposes of this section, the workplace at which an employee works is—

(a) in relation to an employee who works at or from a single set of premises, those premises, and

(b) in relation to any other employee, the premises with which his employment has the closest connection.

(6) For the purposes of this section—

(a) a union intends industrial action to be discontinuous if it intends it to take place only on some days on which there is an opportunity to take the action, and

(b) a union intends industrial action to be continuous if it intends it to be not so restricted.

(7) Subject to sub sections (7A) and (7B) where—

(a) continuous industrial action which has been authorised or endorsed by a union ceases to be so authorised or endorsed, and

(b) the industrial action has at a later date again been authorised or endorsed by the union (whether as continuous or discontinuous action),

no relevant notice covering acts done to induce persons to take part in the earlier action shall operate to cover acts done to induce persons to take part in the action authorised or endorsed at the later date and this section shall apply in relation to an act to induce a person to take part, or continue to take part, in the industrial action after that date as if the references in subsection (3)(b)(i) to the industrial action were to the industrial action taking place after that date.

(7A) Subsection (7) shall not apply where industrial action ceases to be authorised or endorsed in order to enable the union to comply with a court order or an undertaking given to a court.

(7B) Subsection (7) shall not apply where—

(a) a union agrees with an employer, before industrial action ceases to be authorised or endorsed, that it will cease to be authorised or endorsed with effect from a date specified in the agreement ('the suspension date') and that it may again be authorised or endorsed with effect from a date not earlier than a date specified in the agreement ('the resumption date'),

(b) the action ceases to be authorised or endorsed with effect from the suspension date, and

(c) the action is again authorised or endorsed with effect from a date which is not earlier than the resumption date or such later date as may be agreed between the union and the employer.

The foregoing provisions incorporate amendments made by the Employment Relations Act 2004. As with the notice of the intention to hold a ballot (discussed above), the notice of industrial action provisions previously required the union to provide information to 'help the employer to make plans'. Although this provision has been deleted, it remains open to question why trade unions should still be required to provide the amount of information that the law continues to require. There is no corresponding duty on the part of the employer to give notice to the union of the steps which he or she proposes to take in response to the dispute: yet the dispute may have arisen as a result of the unlawful or unreasonable conduct of the employer. We must resist the temptation of concluding that all strikes are acts of aggression designed to improve working conditions by beating an employer into submission and designed in the process to cause massive public disruption. On the contrary, a strike may be a purely defensive response by a workforce which is being badly treated. In these circumstances, it is far from clear why the power of the State should be enlisted to help the employer by requiring so much strike notice to allow him or her to prepare for the dispute; and why the union should not have the advantage of surprise. If legislation is to delay the right to resort to self-help remedies, there is a heavy responsibility on those who draft such legislation to ensure that there are in place alternative effective means to ensure the quick and effective restraint on employers acting unreasonably or unlawfully. This is something which British labour law historically has failed to provide.

9.5.7 A case for further reform?

The balloting rules have been in operation for some 20 years now, and have confounded the wisdom of those who thought that they would not work. It is true that there were some early teething troubles. But the presence of the contempt of court jurisdiction (on which see below) seemed enough to convince trade union leaders (said to be more cautious and risk averse than in the past) of the virtues of complying with the new law. There is evidence to suggest that 'well planned action supported by a ballot demonstrating the membership's commitment to action could significantly increase the bargaining power of the union's negotiators', but also that 'the balloting legislation probably made a minor contribution to increased moderation' (R Undy, P Fosh, H Morris, P Smith and R Martin, *Managing the Unions: The Impact of Legislation on Trade Unions' Behaviour* (Oxford, Oxford University Press, 1996)). This is not to say that the present law can be justified in its present form even after the amendments made in 1999 and 2004. Nor is it to deny that further changes may be necessary. There are many more ballots than there are strikes, not because strike ballots often lead to a vote against industrial action, but because the ballot result can itself be a means of reinforcing the strength of the union position. We have been told by one large union that at any one time it has an estimated 5–10 ballots open—somewhere between notifying the employer and announcing the result. The same union has approximately 100 ballots a year; about half result in industrial action. There are said to be great differences between these ballots in terms of their scale.

It has been said judicially that:

> Parliament's object in introducing the democratic requirement of a secret ballot is not to make life more difficult for trade unions by putting further obstacles in their way before they can call for industrial action with impunity, but to ensure that such action should have the genuine support of the members who are called upon to take part. The requirement has not been imposed for the protection of the employer or the public, but

for the protection of the union's own members. Those who are members at the date of the ballot, and whom the union intends to call on to take industrial action, are entitled to be properly consulted without pressure or intimidation.

(*London Underground Ltd v NUR* [1996] ICR 170, per Millett LJ)

If the purpose of the law is to protect the trade union member, why is the ballot a condition of the immunity from liability to an employer (or anyone else)? There is a strong case for saying that this is a matter which relates to the relationship between the union and its members, and that as such the duty to ballot should be enforced only by those to whom the duty is principally owed (the members). Since 1988 members have also had the right to restrain industrial action unsupported by a ballot: if, as in the *Midland Mainline* case (above) unballoted members do not wish to take proceedings against their union, on what rational ground should the employer be permitted to do so 'on their behalf' and in 'their' (rather than 'its' interests)?. Quite apart from who should be entitled to enforce this balloting obligation, there is also a case for a much more simplified procedure which enables trade unions to take industrial action without the constant threat of litigation and its related costs. The law as it currently stands makes nonsense of Millett LJ's claim that 'Parliament's object in introducing the democratic requirement of a secret ballot is not to make life more difficult for trade unions by putting further obstacles in their way'.

9.6 Picketing and demonstrations: reconciling conflicting freedoms

Picketing is a common feature of many trade disputes. A group of workers will assemble outside a workplace, usually for two purposes: one is to let people know that there is a dispute in place; and another will be to seek support from other workers. To this end, the pickets will seek to persuade other workers employed by their employer not to cross the picket line and to abstain from working. They may also seek to persuade workers employed by other employers (such as drivers of lorries delivering supplies) not to cross the picket line and to abstain from working. These steps will be taken in order to increase the pressure on the employer: by depriving the employer of workers and supplies, he or she may be compelled to yield to the strikers' demands. But of course, other workers may not want to stop or to abstain from working: they may disagree with the pickets' case; they may be indifferent to it; or they may be unwilling to lose pay by joining the action. They may indeed support the strike's objectives but plan to work through the strike and enjoy the benefits of any settlement afterwards. The picket line can thus quickly become a source of conflict as tensions rise and incomes (of the pickets) fall, aggravated in some cases still further by the presence of replacement workers doing the jobs once done by the strikers.

The picket line can also quickly become a source of great tension between competing liberal values: the liberty of the employer to conduct business without restraint on the one hand, and the liberty of the pickets to freedom of assembly on the other.

The way in which the courts hold the balance between these conflicting liberties has changed over time. In recent years there has been a more open acknowledgement on the part of the courts of the rights of the picket and of the civil liberties dimension to cases in which employers have sought injunctions to restrain peaceful protest. This reflects a greater willingness on the part of the courts to acknowledge and defend the right to freedom of expression and peaceful protest generally: it is possible that this is a trend which will be reinforced by the Human Rights Act 1998, with Article 10 of the European Convention on Human Rights (ECHR) including a protection for freedom of expression and Article 11 a protection for peaceful assembly (see below). Although this liberalisation of attitude is important, it is to be noted that it takes place in the context of greater statutory regulation of picketing and other forms of peaceful protest. With Parliament having taken the initiative, it is for the courts largely to police the boundaries of the law rather than set them. It is also to be noted that the liberalisation of attitude is limited to peaceful action, and that it is by no means universal.

9.6.1 Statutory protection

Protection for peaceful picketing was included in the Trade Disputes Act 1906. This provided by section 2 that:

> It shall be lawful for one or more persons, acting on their own behalf or on behalf of a trade union or of an individual employer or firm in contemplation or furtherance of a trade dispute, to attend at or near a house or place where a person resides or works or carries on business or happens to be, if they so attend merely for the purpose of peacefully obtaining or communicating information, or of peacefully persuading any person to work or abstain from working.

It will be noted that there is no restriction here as to the numbers, duration or location of the picketing. The only limit related to purpose (peaceful communication or peaceful persuasion) and circumstances (it must be in contemplation or furtherance of a trade dispute). The provisions of section 2 were substantially re-enacted in TULRA 1974, section 15, but substantially revised by the Employment Act 1980. The latter was designed to confine picketing in principle to one's own place of work. The position is now governed by section 220 of the 1992 Act.

[9.27] Trade Union and Labour Relations (Consolidation) Act 1992, section 220

Peaceful picketing

220 (1) It is lawful for a person in contemplation or furtherance of a trade dispute to attend—
(a) at or near his own place of work, or
(b) if he is an official of a trade union, at or near the place of work of a member of the union whom he is accompanying and whom he represents,
for the purpose only of peacefully obtaining or communicating information, or peacefully persuading any person to work or abstain from working.

(2) If a person works or normally works—
(a) otherwise than at any one place, or
(b) at a place the location of which is such that attendance there for a purpose mentioned in subsection (1) is impracticable,
his place of work for the purposes of that subsection shall be any premises of his employer from which he works or from which his work is administered.

(3) In the case of a worker not in employment where—
(a) his last employment was terminated in connection with a trade dispute, or
(b) the termination of his employment was one of the circumstances giving rise to a trade dispute,
in relation to that dispute his former place of work shall be treated for the purposes of subsection (1) as being his place of work.

(4) A person who is an official of a trade union by virtue only of having been elected or appointed to be a representative of some of the members of the union shall be regarded for the purposes of subsection (1) as representing only those members; but otherwise an official of a union shall be regarded for those purposes as representing all its members.

By providing lawful authority to do that which would otherwise be unlawful, section 220 provides protection from liability for a wide range of liabilities. Picketing may be unlawful for a number of reasons, attracting both criminal and civil liability. But the reach of the section 220 immunity is nevertheless unclear: although it provides authority for conduct which might otherwise constitute an unlawful watching and besetting (TULRCA 1992, section 221), an obstruction of the highway (Highways Act 1980, section 137) or a nuisance (common law), it does not appear to provide authority to obstruct a constable in the execution of his duty (see below, p 923), or to commit a trespass (on which see *British Airports Authority v Ashton* [1983] IRLR 287). It is also to be noted that the most obvious tort committed on a picket line will be inducing breach of contract, and that this is protected by TULRCA 1992, section 219 and not section 220. But immunity for inducing breach of contract or indeed the other torts mentioned in section 219 will arise only when committed in the course of picketing if the picketing is within the scope of section 220. Any economic torts committed by picketing outside section 220 have no section 219 immunity: see section 219(3).

9.6.2 The Code of Practice

The legislation is now accompanied by a *Code of Practice on Picketing* which was first issued in 1980 and revised in 1992. The Code of Practice is not legally binding as such, and indeed a substantial part of it describes the criminal and civil liabilities of pickets, noting that:

There is no legal right to picket as such, but attendance for the purpose of peaceful picketing has long been recognised to be a lawful activity. However, the law imposes certain limits on how, where and for what purpose such picketing can be undertaken. These limits help to ensure proper protection for those who may be affected by the picketing—including those who may wish to cross a picket line and go to work.

Although not legally binding, the *Code of Practice* has been approved by Parliament, and must be taken into account in legal proceedings. There are a number of respects in which the Code supplements rather than describes the current state of the law. The first of these is in relation to the number of people who may picket at any one location; the second relates to the organisation of picketing; and the third to the movement of essential supplies and services.

[9.28] DTI, *Code of Practice on Picketing* (1992)

48 Violence and disorder on the picket line is more likely to occur if there are excessive numbers of pickets. Wherever large numbers of people with strong feelings are involved there is danger that the situation will get out of control, and that those concerned will run the risk of committing an offence, with consequent arrest and prosecution, or of committing a civil wrong which exposes them, or anyone organising them, to civil proceedings.

49 This is particularly so wherever people seek by sheer weight of numbers to stop others going into work or delivering or collecting goods. In such cases, what is intended is not peaceful persuasion, but obstruction or harassment—if not intimidation. Such a situation is often described as 'mass picketing'. In fact, it is not picketing in its lawful sense of an attempt at peaceful persuasion, and may well result in a breach of the peace or other criminal offences.

50 Moreover, anyone seeking to demonstrate support for those in dispute should keep well away from any picket line so as not to create a risk of a breach of the peace or other criminal offence, being committed on that picket line. Just as with a picket itself, the numbers involved is any such demonstration should not be excessive, and the demonstration should be conducted lawfully. *Section 14 of the Public Order Act 1986 provides the police with the power to impose conditions (for example, as to numbers, location and duration) on public assemblies of 20 or more people where the assembly is likely to result in serious public disorder; or serious damage to property; or serious disruption to the life of the community; or if its purpose is to coerce.*

51 Large numbers on a picket line are also likely to give rise to fear and resentment amongst those seeking to cross that picket line, even where no criminal offence is committed. They exacerbate disputes and sour relations not only between management and employees but between the pickets and their fellow employees. Accordingly pickets and their organisers should ensure that in general the number of pickets does not exceed six at any entrance to, or exit from, a workplace; frequently a smaller number will be appropriate.

The Code also deals with the organisation of picketing (and the functions of the picket organiser) as well as essential supplies, services and operations, as already suggested. In relation to the latter it is provided that:

62 Pickets, and anyone organising a picket should take very great care to ensure that their activities do not cause distress, hardship or inconvenience to members of the public who are not involved in the dispute. Particular care should be taken to ensure that the movement of essential goods and supplies, the carrying out of essential maintenance of plant and equipment, and the provision of services essential to the life of the community are not impeded, still less prevented.

63 The following list of essential supplies and services is provided as an illustration of the kind of activity which requires special protection to comply with the recommendations in paragraph 62 above. However, the list is not intended to be comprehensive. The supplies and services which may need to be protected in accordance with these recommendations could cover different activities in different circumstances. Subject to this *caveat* 'essential supplies, services and operations' include:

- the production, packaging, marketing and/or distribution of medical and pharmaceutical products;
- the provision of supplies and services essential to health and welfare institutions, eg hospitals, old people's homes;
- the provision of heating fuel for schools, residential institutions, medical institutions and private residential accommodation;
- the production and provision of other supplies for which there is a crucial need during a crisis in the interests of public health and safety (eg chlorine, lime and other agents for water purification; industrial and medical gases; sand and salt for road gritting purposes);
- activities necessary to the maintenance of plant and machinery;
- the proper care of livestock;
- necessary safety procedures (including such procedures as are necessary to maintain plant and machinery);
- the production, packaging, marketing and/or distribution of food and animal feeding stuffs;
- the operation of essential services, such as police, fire, ambulance, medical and nursing services, air safety, coastguard and air sea rescue services, and services provided by voluntary bodies (eg Red Cross and St John's ambulances, meals on wheels, hospital car service), and mortuaries, burial and cremation services.

64 Arrangements to ensure these safeguards for essential supplies, services and operations should be agreed in advance between the pickets, or anyone organising the picket, and the employer, or employers, concerned.

Despite the legal status of the Code, some of these provisions have assumed a rather prescriptive tone. This is particularly true of the provisions regulating numbers: one early study following the changes introduced in 1980 commented that 'the suggestion that pickets should be limited to six persons rapidly entered the folk memory' (P Kahn *et al.*, *Picketing* (London, Routledge & Kegan Paul, 1983), p 90). The authors continued by claiming that both 'management and many workers . . . believe that this is a restriction in the Act itself and furthermore that it is enforceable by criminal sanctions. The police do not go out of their way to disabuse pickets of such misapprehensions'. It should be noted that the police powers referred to in paragraph 50 of the Code of Practice now apply to an assembly of two or more people: Anti-Social Behaviour Act 2003, s 57.

9.6.3 The scope of statutory protection: location and purpose

As pointed out in the *Code of Practice*, there are now limits to (i) how, (ii) where and (iii) for what purpose picketing may be conducted. So far as how is concerned, the picketing must be peaceful. So far as the *location of picketing* is concerned, it must be at or near the picket's own place of work, as defined by section 220. Note that the 1906 Act permitted picketing outside someone's home: there is now no longer protection for this. The current restriction to place of work has given rise to some difficulty in the case law.

[9.29] *Rayware Ltd v TGWU* [1989] ICR 457 (CA)

The plaintiffs carried on business on a private trading estate where they leased a site. The site was serviced by a number of private roads leading from the public highway. The premises occupied by the plaintiff company were 0.7 of a mile from the highway. In the course of a trade dispute between the plaintiffs and their employees, a picket was mounted at the gate leading to the estate, this being the nearest the pickets could get to the plaintiff's premises without committing a trespass. The plaintiffs sought an injunction to have the picketing restrained on the ground of interference with business, and succeeded at first instance. The main question in the appeal was whether the picketing was protected by what is now section 220 on the ground that it took place 'at or near' the pickets' place of work. The first instance judge had held that it did not: in his view 'Parliament intended that picketing should take place on the highway outside the employer's premises at such point that those in the factory or other premises concerned would be informed, or would know by sight or sound that picketing was taking place'. In upholding the appeal, May LJ said that the phrase 'at or near' in what is now section 220 'must be considered in a geographical sense': 'The mere fact that the plaintiffs are on a private trading estate and that other concerns also lease properties on that estate is not in my view of itself sufficient to prevent the nearest point where pickets can lawfully stand from being at or near the plaintiff's premises' (p 136). In the same vein, Nourse LJ said 'The words "at or near", not being terms of art, must be construed with a due regard for the purpose of the provision in which they are found. No experience of unlawful picketing, however grave, can obscure the clear purpose of [section 220], which, broadly speaking, is to confer on an employee or a group of employees a liberty to exert peaceful persuasion over fellow employees. It is not consistent with that purpose to construe the section so as to make it impracticable, in the conditions in which many industrial and commercial developments are now found to exist, for many groups of employees to maintain pickets at all' (p 137).

See also *News Group Newspapers Ltd v SOGAT '82 (No 2)* [1987] ICR 181.

So far as the *purpose of the picketing* is concerned, this must be confined to peaceful persuasion or the peaceful communication of information. If there is evidence of another purpose, the Act will not apply. It will often be very easy for the plaintiff or the prosecutor to show evidence of another purpose. Why are the pickets seeking to communicate information, or persuade workers not to work? Often it will be to put pressure on the employer being picketed. Does this then transform the purpose from one which is lawful to one which is not? This point is illustrated by the following case.

[9.30] *Mersey Dock & Harbour Company v Verrinder* [1982] IRLR 152 (Ch D)

Economic recession had restricted the work available for haulage contractors at Liverpool docks. Established contractors were concerned that they were being undercut by 'cowboy' operators, and in an attempt to protect its members' jobs the TGWU organised a picket of

---

Secondary picketing

Secondary picketing is a term used to describe the situation where a worker pickets outside a place of work other than his or her own. The business which is the target of secondary pickets may be a supplier to the employer engaged in the dispute. The pickets may be seeking to persuade workers employed by the secondary employer not to handle or deliver goods intended for the employer who is the party to the trade dispute. There may be other reasons for the secondary picketing. But whatever the reason, secondary picketing is not lawful under section 220 of the 1992 Act, which applies only to picketing outside one's own place of work. However, workers who picket outside their own place of work may nevertheless commit secondary action, as defined by section 224. This is because the pickets may persuade a driver employed by a supplier to their employer not to cross the picket line. The driver will then have been induced to break his or her contract of employment leading in turn to the breach of a commercial contract between the employer and the supplier. This constitutes secondary action because the pickets have induced the breach of an employment contract of someone who is not employed by a party to the trade dispute. In these limited circumstances section 224 provides that secondary action is protected by the immunity, that is to say where it occurs in the context of picketing which is protected by section 220.

---

two terminals at the port. The picketing was entirely peaceful, but it appears that it was bringing the terminal to a standstill because drivers would not cross the picket lines. An injunction was granted by Judge Fitzhugh to restrain the picketing, it being held that what is now TULRCA, section 220 did not apply. In the first place, the docks did not form part of the pickets' place of work, none of them being employed by the plaintiff company. And secondly it was held that the defendants had an improper purpose:

> 'the intention of the pickets is not merely to obtain or communicate information; it is to compel the company to ensure that at the terminals only haulage companies preferred by the defendants are employed, to the exclusion of others not acceptable to them. In other words, the intention is to force the company to take some action against shipowners who employ "cowboys" or "scalliwags". It is tantamount, in my view, to an attempt on the part of the defendants to regulate and control the container traffic to and from the company's terminals. If that is right, the conduct of the pickets is, in my view, capable of constituting a private nuisance' [p155].

See also *Tynan v Balmer* [1967] 1 QB 91.

9.6.4 Liability for picketing outside the scope of statutory protection

The cases in the previous section indicate that picketing outside the scope of the statutory protection may give rise to civil liability and be restrained by injunction. But, as *Tynan v Balmer* shows, picketing may also give rise to criminal liability. There are in fact a number of offences which may be committed. Here we deal with three provisions of particular importance, two of which arise as a result of general police powers (obstructing the highway and obstructing a police officer), the other being a reincarnation of the Conspiracy and Protection of Property Act 1875, section 7 (watching and besetting). There may also be liability under public order legislation (including the Public Order Act 1986 (as amended), on which see the important decision of the House of Lords in *DPP v Jones* [1999] 2 All ER 257) which is not covered here. Indeed in the course of a large-scale dispute such as the miners' strike of 1984–5, a wide range of offences may be committed: 9,808 people were arrested in England and Wales during that particular dispute, with another 1,483 arrested in Scotland.

[9.31] P Wallington, 'Policing the Miners' Strike' (1985) 14 *Industrial Law Journal* 145 (footnotes omitted)

> Most of the charges [were] relatively minor. This is especially noticeable in Scotland where 98 per cent of charges were of breach of the peace (678), obstructing the police (249), breach of bail conditions (53) or vandalism (30). In England and Wales the position is broadly similar—75 per cent of charges were of conduct likely or intended to cause a breach of the peace (4,314), obstructing the police (1,682), criminal damage (1,019) or obstructing the highway (640). A number of charges were also brought for offences probably unconnected with picketing activities (notably 352 of theft and 31 of burglary). However in contrast to the position in Scotland, significant numbers of serious offences were charged, including 509 of unlawful assembly and 139 of riot, as well as 21 of affray, 15 of arson, 39 of grievous bodily harm and three of murder.

9.6.4.1 Obstructing the highway

[9.32] Highways Act 1980, s 137

Penalty for wilful obstruction

137 If a person, without lawful authority or excuse, in any way wilfully obstructs the free passage along a highway he is guilty of an offence and liable to a fine not exceeding [level 3 on the standard scale].

Here TULRCA 1992, section 220 plays an important role, in providing lawful authority for conduct which would otherwise constitute a statutory offence. Simple attendance by two or more people would technically be an obstruction from which section 220 (along with the Code of Practice) offers some protection. But it must be stressed that the protection is limited as to purpose and circumstance, as the following case makes clear: if the pickets are obstructing the highway for a purpose other than the peaceful communication of information or peaceful persuasion, TULRCA 1992, section 220, offers no protection.

[9.33] *Broome v DPP* [1974] AC 587 (HL)

> The accused was a trade union official engaged in a peaceful picket during a strike by building workers. In the course of picketing he stood on the road in front of a lorry being driven by Dickinson, blocking the way. When Broome refused to move he was arrested for obstructing the highway. The question for the House of Lords was whether Broome's actions were protected by the Industrial Relations Act 1971, section 134, the provision

then in force corresponding to what is now TULRCA, section 220 (without the post-1979 restraints). The House of Lords held that Broome's conduct was not within the section because he was not attending only for the purpose of peaceful persuasion or peaceful communication of information, but for 'the further purpose, which in fact he carried out, of requiring and compelling Mr Dickinson to stop and of detaining him against his will' (Lord Morris, at pp 558–9). In an important decision, it was held that the statutory purposes do not give the pickets a right to stop and detain drivers, but only 'the right to try to persuade anyone who chooses to stop and listen'. Lord Reid could see 'no ground for implying any right to require the person whom it is sought to persuade to submit to any kind of restraint or restriction of his personal freedom. One is familiar with persons at the side of a road signalling to a driver requesting him to stop. It is then for the driver to decide whether he will stop or not. That, in my view, a picket is entitled to do. If the driver stops, the picket can talk to him but only for so long as the driver is willing to listen' (p 597).

It has been held in subsequent cases that a peaceful assembly on the highway is not necessarily unlawful, and that it may be a 'lawful user' which does not need a 'lawful excuse'. But although this is an important step forward in recognising a freedom of assembly at common law (which was taken without reference to the Human Rights Act 1998), the courts have emphasised that whether or not an assembly is lawful will depend on the circumstances of the case: *DPP v Jones* [1999] 2 All ER 257. It should not be assumed that picketing in the course of trade disputes will be treated as a 'lawful user', particularly where it falls outside the scope of TULRCA 1992, section 220. A person obstructing the highway may be arrested without a warrant: Police and Criminal Evidence Act 1984, section 24.

9.6.4.2 Obstructing a police officer

[9.34] Police Act 1996, section 89

Assaults on Constables

89 . . . (2) Any person who resists or wilfully obstructs a constable in the execution of his duty, or a person assisting a constable in the execution of his duty, shall be guilty of an offence and liable on summary conviction to imprisonment for a term not exceeding one month or a fine not exceeding level 3 on the standard scale, or to both.

This is a measure (with a long pedigree) which has a wide application in the context of public assemblies and popular protest generally, as in the well-known *Duncan v Jones* [1936] 1 KB 218 which allowed the police to require the appellant to move her soap box 75 yards down the road to stop an apprehended breach of the peace.

[9.35] *Piddington v Bates* [1961] 1 WLR 162 (QBD)

This case arose from a dispute at the Free Press Ltd in North London. There were two entrances to the premises where eight people were working. The police decided that two pickets at each entrance would be enough. Piddington then decided that he would join the pickets at one of the entrances and was duly arrested for obstructing a police officer in the execution of his duty, contrary to what was then the Prevention of Crimes Act 1885, section 2. He appealed unsuccessfully against his conviction.

Lord Parker, LCJ:

. . . It seems to me that the law is reasonably plain. First, the mere statement by a constable that he did anticipate that there might be a breach of the peace is clearly not enough. There must exist proved facts from which a constable could reasonably anticipate such a breach. Secondly, it is not enough that his contemplation is that there is a remote possibility; there must be a real possibility of a breach of the peace. Accordingly, in every case, it becomes a question of whether, on the particular facts, it can be said that there were reasonable grounds on which a constable charged with this duty reasonably anticipated that a breach of the peace might occur.

As I have said, every case must depend upon its exact facts, and the matter which influences me in this case is the matter of numbers. It is, I think, perfectly clear from the wording of the case, although it is not expressly so found, that the police knew that in these small works there were only eight people working. They found two vehicles arriving, with 18 people milling about the street, trying to form pickets at the doors. On that ground alone, coupled with a telephone call which, I should have thought, intimated some sense of urgency and apprehension, the police were fully entitled to think as reasonable men that there was a real danger of something more than mere picketing to collect or impart information or peaceably to persuade. I think that in those circumstances the prosecutor had reasonable grounds for anticipating that a breach of the peace was a real possibility. It may be, and I think this is the real criticism, that it can be said: Well, to say that only two pickets should be allowed is purely arbitrary; why two? Why not three? Where do you draw the line? I think that a police officer charged with the duty of preserving the Queen's peace must be left to take such steps as on the evidence before him he thinks are proper. I am far from saying that there should be any rule that only two pickets should be allowed at any particular door. There, one gets into an arbitrary area, but so far as this case is concerned I cannot see that there was anything wrong in the action of the prosecutor.

Finally, I would like to say that all these matters are so much matters of degree that I would hesitate, except on the clearest evidence, to interfere with the findings of magistrates who have had the advantage of hearing the whole case and observing the witnesses.

Piddington v Bates thus gives the police the power in effect to regulate the number of people who may attend a picket. Section 220 does not apply to protect the pickets. Since that decision the *Code of Practice* has been issued, proposing that no more than six pickets should attend at or near any workplace (above p 927). If, however, the police believe that fewer than six is necessary to preserve the peace, the powers of the police will override the *Code of Practice*. The powers of the police to take steps to preserve the peace are not limited to giving instructions about the numbers who may attend. The power of the police was extended in effect by *Moss v McLachlan* [1985] IRLR 76, which arose out of the miners' strike of 1984–5. It was held in that case that the police have the power to impose roadblocks at motorway exits to prevent people from travelling to picket lines where there are reasonable grounds to believe that a breach of the peace will take place. There are indications more recently of the courts being more willing to challenge the judgment of the police officer that a breach of the peace was imminent, particularly where an arrest would violate the ECHR right to freedom of expression: *Redmond-Bate v DPP*, *The Times*, 28 July 1999. But that was a case involving three women arrested for preaching outside

Wakefield Cathedral. Context is everything. Even more recent cases have upheld both *Duncan v Jones*, and *Moss v McLachlan,* despite the protection of freedom of assembly in the ECHR: *R(Laporte) v Gloucestershire Constabulary* [2004] EWCA Civ 1639.

9.6.4.3 *Watching and besetting*

[9.36] Trade Union and Labour Relations (Consolidation) Act 1992, section 241

Intimidation or annoyance by violence or otherwise

241 (1) A person commits an offence who, with a view to compelling another person to abstain from doing or to do any act which that person has a legal right to do or abstain from doing, wrongfully and without legal authority—

(a) uses violence to or intimidates that person or his wife or children, or injures his property,

(b) persistently follows that person about from place to place,

(c) hides any tools, clothes or other property owned or used by that person, or deprives him of or hinders him in the use thereof,

(d) watches or besets the house or other place where that person resides, works, carries on business or happens to be, or the approach to any such house or place, or

(e) follows that person with two or more other persons in a disorderly manner in or through any street or road.

(2) A person guilty of an offence under this section is liable on summary conviction to imprisonment for a term not exceeding six months or a fine not exceeding level 5 on the standard scale, or both.

(3) A constable may arrest without warrant anyone he reasonably suspects is committing an offence under this section.

Picketing outside the scope of TULRCA 1992, section 221 could lead to liability under the foregoing if it is 'wrongful'. The cases relating to section 221 (or the Conspiracy and Protection of Property Act 1875, section 7, which preceded it) which have been reported in recent times deal with matters such as intimidation and persistently following. In this respect, there have been a number of cases in recent years where this measure was invoked, as in the case of the Scottish tax inspectors who persistently followed a colleague by car during a dispute, and the case of the Scottish laboratory technicians who were prosecuted under section 7 for taking part in a sit in. Perhaps because of the uncertainty caused by two contradictory leading cases at the turn of the century (*J Lyons & Sons v Wilkins* [1899] 1 Ch 255 and *Ward, Lock & Co v OPAS* (1906) 22 TLR 327), there is little evidence until the miners' strike of 1984–5 of the watching and besetting provisions being used in post-war disputes. Looking again at the miners' strike of 1984–5, there is evidence of significant use of this provision, with at least 643 charges being brought, 'mainly but by no means exclusively for "watching and besetting" the homes of working miners' (Wallington, above, pp 150–51). According to Wallington:

This appears to be the first significant use of this section, certainly in recent years, and has attracted considerable comment. It does appear to be the most appropriate charge in those cases where there was neither a threat of a breach of the peace nor obstruction of the highway. However [it did not then] carry a power of arrest, and charges of besetting generally followed arrests on other grounds. The very broad offence of breach of the peace in Scots law appears to have obviated the need for besetting charges, of which there were only four in Scotland (at p 151).

It is important to note that in practice the police have a large menu of powers, but that obstruction of the highway and obstruction of a police officer are the staple diet, and indeed make anything else largely unnecessary. One of the main objects of the police will be to reduce tension and reduce numbers. These latter offences allow these goals to be achieved with a minimum of fuss. It is important also to note that most picketing takes place on the basis of co-operation between pickets and police.

9.6.5 Consumer picketing

All of the cases considered so far have focused on the picketing of workplaces where a trade dispute is in progress or at related workplaces. In recent years trade unions have widened their disputes to include the picketing of consumers in an attempt to dissuade them from buying the products of the employer with whom the union is in dispute. There are at least two possible plaintiffs who may want to stop this action, the first being proprietors of the premises being picketed, and the other being the employer whose products the union is seeking to boycott. Either way, this is not a form of picketing which is covered by the existing statutory immunity.

[9.37] *Hubbard v Pitt* [1976] 1 QB 142 (CA)

This case was concerned with the picketing of an estate agent's shop in Islington, North London. The area was being restored and renovated, drastically reducing the stock of housing available at low rents. The Islington Tenants' campaign decided to picket Prebble & Co, a prominent estate agent in the area. They held placards and distributed leaflets referring to the plaintiffs in 'opprobrious terms'. An interlocutory injunction was granted by Forbes J, and upheld on appeal, largely on procedural grounds. The case was held shortly after the House of Lords decision in *American Cyanamid Co v Ethicon Ltd* [1975] AC 396 (below at p 929) where it was held that in determining whether an interlocutory injunction should be issued in legal proceedings, it was enough for the plaintiff to establish that there is a serious question to be tried and that the balance of convenience is in favour of interim relief. Applying that test to the evidence before it, a majority upheld the trial judge's decision, despite a strong dissent by Lord Denning.

Hubbard v Pitt was thus decided on purely procedural grounds: on the ground that the defendants may have done something wrong. It is unclear whether it would be followed today. Strongly criticised at the time, it was decided before the House of Lords established in *NWL Ltd v Woods* [1979] ICR 867 (see below) that before granting an interlocutory injunction in a case where interlocutory relief is likely to settle the dispute, the court should have regard to the likelihood of the plaintiff succeeding at the trial of the action: that is to say the case should not be decided on the ground that there is a serious issue to be tried, a test which makes matters too easy for the plaintiff. The other possible plaintiff in the context of consumer picketing is the employer involved in the dispute: the party whose products the union is seeking to have boycotted by customers.

[9.38] *Middlebrook Mushrooms Ltd v TGWU* **[1993] ICR 612 (CA)**

> The plaintiff company was a mushroom grower, in dispute with the TGWU about cost-cutting proposals. 89 striking workers were dismissed by the plaintiff, whereupon the union proposed to campaign against the company by distributing leaflets outside supermarkets urging the public to boycott Middlebrook Mushrooms. The company then sought an interlocutory injunction to restrain the campaign, and succeeded before Blofeld J on the ground that the action amounted to direct interference with the employer's contracts with supermarkets. The union successfully appealed.

Picketing and the Human Rights Act

The judgment of Neill LJ in the *Middlebrook Mushrooms* case (above) contains an interesting reference to the ECHR, prompting questions about the implications of the Human Rights Act 1998 not just in the context of consumer picketing, but more generally for what remain restrictive statutory rules relating to the picketing of workplaces. An issue which the courts will have to address in the future is whether the current legislation relating to picketing is consistent with both the right to freedom of expression in Article 10 of the ECHR, and the right to freedom of assembly in Article 11. As public bodies for the purposes of the Human Rights Act 1998, it is now incumbent on the courts not to grant any remedy, interim or otherwise, which violates Convention rights. The police are also public bodies under the Act, and it is incumbent upon them too not to exercise their powers (such as the power of arrest) in a way which violates Convention rights. It has already been held by the European Court of Human Rights that the arrest and detention of peaceful protestors for breach of the peace was a violation of Article 10, though in the same case the imprisonments of an anti-hunt protestor and a campaigner against a motorway extension were held not to breach Article 10. Both had refused to be bound over to keep the peace: the former had obstructed a member of a shooting party as he lifted his gun to shoot, and the latter had chained herself to a mechanical digger (*Steel v UK* (1998) 28 EHRR 603). This is not to say that picketing (peaceful or otherwise) in this context is necessarily protected by Article 10 or 11 (particularly in the light of the qualifications in Articles 10(2) and 11(2)). But it does mean that the police and the courts may need to exercise discretionary powers more carefully than in the past. It must be open to question whether the restriction that picketing is protected only if it takes place at the picket's place of work can be justified, and indeed whether the arbitrary limit of six in the *Code of Practice* can be justified under Article 11. But care should be taken before drawing premature conclusions about the impact of the Human Rights Act. The Convention rights in Articles 10 and 11 are particularly heavily qualified, and allow restrictions to be imposed where these are prescribed by law and necessary in a democratic society for the prevention of disorder, as well as the rights of others (Article 10) or the rights and freedoms of others (Article 11).

Neill LJ:

In the present case the leaflet was directed to the customers. There was no message in the leaflets for the management of the supermarket. They were not exhorted to take any action or to desist from taking any action. In my judgment it is most important not to extend the *Lumley v Gye* (1853) 2 E & B 216 principle outside its proper limits. This category of interference is concerned with the *direct* persuasion of one of the parties to the contract to break his contract. In the present case it is an important fact that the suggested influence was exerted, if at all, through the actions or the anticipated actions of third parties who were free to make up their own minds. Though counsel for the defendants did not place any specific reliance on article 10 of the Convention for the Protection of Human Rights and Fundamental Freedoms (1953) (Cmd 8969) it is relevant to bear in mind that in all cases which involve a proposed restriction on the right of free speech the court is concerned, when exercising its discretion, to consider whether the suggested restraint is necessary. In the present case, however, one does not reach the question of the exercise of discretion. In my judgment the distribution of these leaflets in the way proposed does not fall within the *Lumley v Gye* principle at all.

9.7 Remedies and liability: injunctions, contempt and damages

The freedom of trade unions to organise and support industrial action is thus very limited. The questions for the employer may be whether, and if so how, to use the scope which the law now provides to respond to the dispute. The employer may wish to do one of a number of things: he or she may wish to have the action stopped so that production can continue uninterrupted; and/or he or she may wish to be compensated for the losses suffered as a result of the trade union's action. In addition there are sanctions which may be taken against the workforce, measures which are considered in the following section. These latter are remedies of the employer which are likely to have their roots in contract law. In this section we concentrate on the remedies which may be available mainly in tort against those who organise industrial action rather than those who participate in it.

9.7.1 Injunctions

The effect of an injunction is to have industrial action restrained. A party who feels that he or she is the victim of a legal wrong being committed by another may apply *ex parte* for interim relief to have the action restrained until the trial of the action.

[9.39] Civil Procedure Rules 1998

25.3 (1) The court may grant an interim remedy on an application made without notice if it appears to the court that there are good reasons for not giving notice.

(2) An application for an interim remedy must be supported by evidence, unless the court orders otherwise.

(3) If the applicant makes an application without giving notice, the evidence in support of the application must state the reasons why notice has not been given.

So far as granting interim relief is concerned, the landmark case is *American Cyanamid Co v Ethicon Ltd* [1975] AC 396 where Lord Diplock said that in determining whether interim relief should be granted, it is not necessary for the applicant to show a '*prima facie* case' or a 'strong *prima facie* case', but simply that 'there is a serious issue to be tried'. He continued by saying that 'unless the material available to the court at the hearing of the application for an [interim] injunction fails to disclose that the plaintiff has any real prospect of succeeding in his claim for a permanent injunction at the trial, the court should go on to consider whether the balance of convenience lies in favour of granting or refusing the interlocutory relief that is sought'. Lord Diplock continued at p 408:

As to that, the governing principle is that the court should first consider whether, if the plaintiff were to succeed at the trial in establishing his right to a permanent injunction, he would be adequately compensated by an award of damages for the loss he would have sustained as a result of the defendant's continuing to do what was sought to be enjoined between the time of the application and the time of the trial. If damages in the measure recoverable at common law would be adequate remedy and the defendant would be in a financial position to pay them, no interlocutory injunction should normally be granted, however strong the plaintiff's claim appeared to be at that stage. If, on the other hand, damages would not provide an adequate remedy for the plaintiff in the event of his succeeding at the trial, the court should then consider whether, on the contrary hypothesis that the defendant were to succeed at the trial in establishing his right to do that which was sought to be enjoined, he would be adequately compensated under the plaintiff's undertaking as to damages for the loss he would have sustained by being prevented from doing so between the time of the application and the time of the trial. If damages in the measure recoverable under such an undertaking would be an adequate remedy and the plaintiff would be in a financial position to pay them, there would be no reason upon this ground to refuse an interlocutory injunction.

It is where there is doubt as to the adequacy of the respective remedies in damages available to either party or to both, that the question of balance of convenience arises. It would be unwise to attempt even to list all the various matters which may need to be taken not consideration in deciding where the balance lies, let alone to suggest the relative weight to be attached to them. These will vary from case to case.

Where other factors appear to be evenly balanced it is a counsel of prudence to take such measures as are calculated to preserve the status quo. If the defendant is enjoined temporarily from doing something that he has not done before, the only effect of the interlocutory injunction in the event of his succeeding at the trial is to postpone the date at which he is able to embark upon a course of action which he has not previously found it necessary to undertake; whereas to interrupt him in the conduct of an established enterprise would cause much greater inconvenience to him since he would have to start again to establish it in the event of his succeeding at the trial.

This is a very low threshold for issuing an injunction, which presents problems in the context of industrial action. At the time of the decision in *American Cyanamid Co v Ethicon Ltd* [1975] AC 396 trade unions were not vicariously liable in damages for tortious acts committed in the course of a trade dispute. As a result there could be no question of an employer being compensated in damages for losses suffered during a strike, should the application ultimately succeed at the full trial. (Indeed even if damages were recoverable from the union, it is difficult to contemplate in many cases—such as large-scale national strikes—how damages would compensate.) This made it more likely that an interim injunction would be granted to restrain industrial action until the trial of the action. The difficulty, however, is that the interim injunction would effectively dispose of the matter, for the reason that, once stopped, a strike or other industrial action is very difficult to revive. Even if the trial were to take place, it could be months or even years later, by which time the dispute will have moved on, as indeed may many of the workers who were involved in the first place. So it was necessary to ensure that employers were not able to obtain interlocutory relief if their application was without substance on legal grounds, and if they were unlikely to succeed on legal grounds were the matter to come to trial. Otherwise, Parliament's intention of giving trade unions the freedom to take industrial action could in practice be frustrated by procedural law, in a manner which would undermine any simple notion of the rule of law: industrial action would be restrained not because it was unlawful, but because there was a possibility that it might be held unlawful in legal proceedings which were likely never to take place.

This is the background to what is now TULRCA 1992, section 221, containing measures which were originally to be found in the Trade Union and Labour Relations Act 1974, section 17 (as amended by the Employment Protection Act 1975).

[9.40] Trade Union and Labour Relations (Consolidation) Act 1992, section 221

Restrictions on grant of injunctions and interdicts

221 (1) Where—

(a)   an application for an injunction or interdict is made to a court in the absence of the party against whom it is sought or any representative of his, and

(b)   he claims, or in the opinion of the court would be likely to claim, that he acted in contemplation or furtherance of a trade dispute,

the court shall not grant the injunction or interdict unless satisfied that all steps which in the circumstances were reasonable have been taken with a view to securing that notice of the application and an opportunity of being heard with respect to the application have been given to him.

(2) Where—

(a)   an application for an interlocutory injunction is made to a court pending the trial of an action, and

(b)   the party against whom it is sought claims that he acted in contemplation or furtherance of a trade dispute, the court shall, in exercising its discretion whether or not to grant the injunction, have regard to the likelihood of that party's succeeding at the trial of the action in establishing any matter which would afford a defence to the action under section 219 (protection from certain tort liabilities) or section 220 (peaceful picketing).

For the position in Scotland, see K D Ewing, 'Interim Interdicts and Labour Law' (1981) 26 *Journal of the Law Society of Scotland* 422. The meaning of what is now section 221 was considered in a number of cases in the 1970s. But there was a feeling in some quarters that the Court of Appeal in particular in some of these cases was doing less than justice to the underlying purpose of the measure, or indeed to its literal provisions. The matter was addressed by the House of Lords in the following case.

[9.41] *NWL Ltd v Woods* [1979] ICR 867 (HL)

The International Transport Workers' Federation had a policy of 'blacking' ships flying a flag of convenience. The purpose of the policy was to compel the owners of the ships in question to employ crew on terms approved by the ITF, or to transfer the vessels' registration to the countries of domicile of their beneficial owners. In this case, an injunction was granted by Donaldson J to prevent the defendants from issuing instructions and or persuading stevedores, tug operators and pilots to break their contracts of employment to prevent the free passage of a ship called the *Nawala* which was docked at Redcar. The Court of Appeal discharged the injunction, and upheld another decision of Donaldson J not to grant an injunction against other defendants. The House of Lords upheld the Court of Appeal in both cases.

Lord Diplock:
My Lords, when properly understood, there is in my view nothing in the decision of this House in *American Cyanamid Co. v Ethicon Ltd.* [1975] AC 396 to suggest that in considering whether or not to grant an interlocutory injunction the judge ought not to give full weight to all the practical realities of the situation to which the injunction will apply. *American Cyanamid Co v Ethicon Ltd*, which conjoins the judge upon an application for an interlocutory injunction to direct his attention to the balance of convenience as soon as he has satisfied himself that there is a serious question to be tried, was not dealing with a case in which the grant or refusal of an injunction at that stage would, in effect, dispose of the action finally in favour of whichever party was successful in the application, because there would be nothing left on which it was in the unsuccessful party's interest to proceed to trial. By the time the trial came on the industrial dispute, if there were one, in furtherance of which the acts sought to be restrained were threatened or done, would be likely to have been settled and it would not be in the employer's interest to exacerbate relations with his workmen by continuing the proceedings against the individual defendants none of whom would be capable financially of meeting a substantial claim for damages. Nor, if an interlocutory injunction had been granted against them, would it be worthwhile for the individual defendants to take steps to obtain a final judgment in their favour, since any damages that they could claim in respect of personal pecuniary loss caused to them by the grant of the injunction and which they could recover under the employer's undertaking on damages, would be very small.

Cases of this kind are exceptional, but when they do occur they bring into the balance of convenience an important additional element. In assessing whether what is compendiously called the balance of convenience lies in granting or refusing interlocutory injunctions in actions between parties of undoubted solvency the judge is engaged in weighing the respective risks that injustice may result from his deciding one way rather than the other at a stage when the evidence is incomplete. On the one hand there is the risk that if the interlocutory injunction is refused but the plaintiff succeeds in establishing at the trial his legal right for the protection of which the injunction had been sought he may in the meantime have suffered harm and inconvenience for which an award of money can provide no adequate recompense. On the other hand there is the risk that if the interlocutory injunction is granted but the plaintiff fails at the trial, the defendant may in the meantime have suffered harm and inconvenience which is similarly irrecompensable. The nature and degree of harm and inconvenience that are likely to be sustained in these two events by the defendant and the plaintiff respectively in consequence of the grant or the refusal of the injunction are generally sufficiently disproportionate to bring down, by themselves, the balance on one side or the other; and this is what I understand to be the thrust of the decision of this House in *American Cyanamid Co. v Ethicon Ltd*. Where, however, the grant or refusal of the interlocutory injunction will have the practical effect of putting an end to the action because the harm that will have been already caused to the losing party by its grant or its refusal is complete and of a kind for which money cannot constitute any worthwhile recompense, the degree of likelihood that the plaintiff would have succeeded in establishing his right to an injunction if the action had gone to trial, is a factor to be brought into the balance by the judge in weighing the risks that injustice may result from his deciding the application one way rather than the other.

The characteristics of the type of action to which section [221] applies . . . are unique; and, whether it was strictly necessary to do so or not, it was clearly prudent of the draftsman of the section to state expressly that in considering whether or not to grant an interlocutory injunction the court should have regard to the likelihood of the defendant's succeeding in establishing that what he did or threatened was done or threatened in contemplation or furtherance of a trade dispute.

. . . Judges would, I think, be respecting the intention of Parliament in making this change in the law in 1975, if in the normal way the injunction were refused in cases where the defendant had shown that it was more likely than not that he would succeed in his defence of statutory immunity; but this does not mean that there may not be cases where the consequences to the employer or to third parties or the public and perhaps the nation itself, may be so disastrous that the injunction ought to be refused, unless there is a high degree of probability that the defence will succeed.

An important revision of these guidelines took place in *Dimbleby & Sons Ltd v NUJ* [1984] ICR 386 where Lord Diplock noted that the circumstances had been changed since the *Woods* case. Legislation in 1980 and 1982 has restricted the scope of the immunity: by virtue of the Employment Act 1980, section 17, immunity was withdrawn for certain forms of secondary action (widened in 1990 to withdraw immunity from all secondary action); and by virtue of the Employment Act 1982 trade unions could now be liable in damages for industrial action which fell outside the scope of the immunity (see below). So how should the courts proceed in the future with applications for interim injunctions? Here Lord Diplock said that what is now TULRCA 1992, section 221(2), is the test to be applied not only where the defendant is relying on the immunity, but also where 'any issue' arises 'between the plaintiff and the defendant as to whether the acts complained of were excluded from the protection of [what is now section 219] of the Act of [1992] by the provisions of section 17 of the Act of 1980' (at p 406). Presumably the same approach ought to be applied in the case of the other grounds for the exclusion of the protection introduced since 1980. This means that the courts ought to consider the likelihood of the defendant succeeding in establishing the statutory defence at the trial of the action in cases where he or she is (a) asserting the existence of a trade dispute, or (b) resisting a claim that immunity has been withdrawn—because it constitutes unlawful secondary action, or the ballot rules have not been complied with. Regarding all other issues raised by way of defence (such as a claim that the defendant's conduct was not tortious), according to Lord Diplock 'the criterion to be applied in order to make recourse to the balance of convenience necessary is the ordinary criterion laid down in *American Cyanamid Co v Ethicon Ltd* [1975] AC 396: '[i]s there a serious question to be tried'?' (at p 406). This represents a lowering of the bar set in *Woods*, and seems to be based on the assumption that it could no longer be assumed that cases will not go to trial or that the injunction will finally dispose of the matter. This is because trade unions are now liable in damages, though there are very few reported cases of damages being sought by employers. However, it continues to be relatively easy for employers to obtain interim relief even in cases where section 221 applies, as the following case reveals.

[9.42] *BT plc v CWU* [2004] IRLR 58 (QBD)

The employer proposed to introduce a productivity scheme (the SMT scheme) against the wishes of the members of the union who had rejected it. The union gave notice under TULRCA 1992, section 226A of its intention to hold a strike ballot. The notice indicated that the union intended to ballot 'all CWU engineering members employed in BT Customer Services Field Operations and in BT Northern Ireland'. The union stated that according to its information there were 14,001 members falling into these categories. It provided no other information. Following a vote in favour of industrial action, the union gave strike notice under section 234A, and when talks failed to resolve the dispute the employer sought an injunction to have the action stopped. One of the issues before the court was whether the action was in contemplation or furtherance of a trade dispute. However, Burnton J rejected the argument for the employer that there could be no trade dispute because some of those balloted were not covered by the productivity scheme and therefore could not have a dispute with the employer. The employer also argued that the notices issued by the union under sections 226A and 234A were flawed. This argument succeeded, even though it seems unlikely that the employer suffered any significant inconvenience as a result. It is to be noted that the case was decided before the amendments to sections 226A and 234A by the Employment Relations Act 2004. At that time part of the reason for giving the notice was to enable the employer 'to make plans' (see p 904 above).

Burnton J:
The first complaint relates to the identity of union members in question. In broad terms, the evidence is that 90% of those affected by the voluntary introduction of the SMT scheme are members of the union. That fact is known to both sides; indeed, it is referred to in the BT evidence. BT, while it may ascertain the membership of many (probably most and perhaps the very great majority) of the union members because they pay their dues by way of deduction from their salaries—the so-called 'check-off' system—is unable to identify all the members of the union because there are members of the union who pay their dues in other ways.

The plans referred to in s. 226A and s 234A are plans which may be made by the employer to avoid or to mitigate the consequences of industrial action proposed. It is not difficult in a case such as the present to see that the employer might, for example, wish to notify customers of the unavailability of services during the period of a strike. It might wish to organise teams of non-striking employees to carry out work having priority. It is surprising, however, that although BT asserts that they require information concerning the proposed strikers in order to make such plans, they have not identified the plans that they would make at least in evidence. It is to some extent for that reason that the relationship between s. 226(2)(c) and s. 226(3A)(a) becomes important. I ought, nonetheless, to bear in mind that these proceedings have been brought on speedily and that the failure of BT to identify the plans they would make if they had more information as to the identity of the proposed strikers should not be taken to mean that they necessarily would not have such plans if they had additional information.

The important and powerful submission made on behalf of the union in this connection is that BT have all the information as to who is to strike and the numbers involved which they need in practice. Since 90% of the workforce in question are union members (and that is an overwhelming percentage), in effect, BT know, with only minor exceptions, that all the workplace are to strike and they can make their plans accordingly. A similar point is made in relation to communications with employees who have been called out to strike.

It seems to me that the requirement in subsection (3A)(a) to provide numbers at least must be qualified by reference to the need for such numbers for some practical purpose. A number was given in this case, namely 14,001. One of the questions raised in these proceedings is whether that is a useful number. It seems to me that, under that head, BT have raised a serious issue. Although 90% of the employees are union members, it cannot be assumed that the membership of the union is uniform throughout the United Kingdom. There may be areas where the membership is considerably more than 90%, to the extent that that is possible arithmetically, and there may be areas where there is a significantly lower percentage of union members. It will, or at least arguably may, be of practical assistance to BT to have numbers broken down beyond the simple information that 14,001 is the total number concerned . . .

. . . the content of the notice complying with s. 226A must vary from case to case. All I can say is that on the evidence presently available BT have raised a serious issue that the union possesses information as to the number and category of employees beyond that which has already been communicated . . .

. . . The Act requires the court to take into account the likelihood of the defendants succeeding at the trial of the action in establishing any matter which would afford a defence to the action brought by BT, that is to say, in effect, 'the likelihood, on the basis of the findings I have made, of the notice of ballot and of strike action that have been given being held to have been insufficient for the purpose of the statute.' While that is an important consideration, it is not the only consideration, as both counsel have recognised. The balance of convenience, which in this connection involves a consideration of the losses which would be incurred on either side, must also be taken into account. The financial losses on the part of BT would be very substantial. It is not suggested that those losses, to the extent that they are quantifiable, would be recovered in due course from the union if BT establish that the strike was unlawful but no injunction is granted. On that basis, it might be thought the balance of convenience favours the grant of an injunction. The worst that will happen to the union if an injunction is granted is, assuming it does not wish to proceed to trial, that it will incur the relatively small cost of arranging a second ballot complying with the requirements of the statute. I am told the cost is some £18,500.

Against that, it is said that the likelihood is that a further ballot, if held, will have a similar result to the first. In those circumstances, BT will suffer the loss now indicated in any event. That submission involves some assessment of the likelihood of the membership voting in favour of strike action, again in circumstances in which, I would assume, the information that they would be given as to the possibility of strike action or action less than a strike action would be accurate in terms of current law.

I am of the judgment that I should assume, for present purposes, that the likelihood is that the membership should vote in favour of a strike. But I cannot take that as being a foregone conclusion. One understands that the union wishes to strike while, so to speak (as it was put), the 'iron is hot'. It seems to me, however, that that must be a minor consideration, in the scheme of things, compared with the very large sums which would be lost on the part of BT. What about the issues raised and the probability of the union succeeding? . . .

. . . I find the third head, namely the adequacy of notice, more difficult and more likely to depend on evidence as to what information could have been to BT and which would be helpful and relevant to BT for the purposes not of informing balloting members of the defendant of BT's position (since I have no doubt that they were able to and did do that) but for the purpose of their making plans. There is a significant prospect of BT succeeding under that head, although I do not put the prospect any higher.

I therefore have, on the one hand, a sensible argument on the part of BT, on the basis of my findings, plus a possibility of a substantial loss which my be incurred by them which would be avoided if an injunction were granted, while on the other hand, if I do grant an injunction, in all likelihood, the union having to defer a strike, notwithstanding the difficulties of having to defer a strike and incurring the costs of reballoting.

So far as the need to defer the strike is concerned, I am conscious of the fact that the first strike is due to take place on Monday. I am equally conscious that the other two days of strikes are to take place later. In respect of Monday, it will of course be difficult for the union to make arrangements to call off the strike. On the other hand, I imagine that, if an injunction is granted, BT itself will take steps to make the granting of the injunction known to the members.

When I weigh all these matters up as I do, I find this is a matter of some difficulty. But it seems to me that the appropriate course is indeed to grant injunctive relief rather than to refuse it. In those circumstances, there will be injunctions in terms to be discussed to restrain the holding of the strikes pending trial or further order.

9.7.2 Contempt of court

With the new restrictions on industrial action introduced in the 1980s, legal action by employers against trade unions became commonplace. Indeed the law was invoked in a number of very high-profile disputes, including the miners' strike of 1984–5 (though in this case the main proceedings were brought by union members), the News International strike of 1985–6, and the seafarers' strike of 1987–8. Legal proceedings could now be brought against trade unions on a wide range of grounds: because there was no trade dispute; because the trade union was involved in unlawful secondary action; or because the action did not have the support of a ballot, and so on. One of the issues which arose following the introduction of the new liabilities was what would happen when an injunction was issued against a trade union which refused to comply with the order. Could the unions successfully defy the law, as they had done in the 1970s with the Industrial Relations Act 1971? They were soon to find out. Failure to comply with an injunction is a contempt of court, and in the 1980s we see a number of contempt proceedings being instituted by employers: *Messenger Newspapers Group Ltd v NGA (1982)* [1984] IRLR 397; *Austin Rover v AUEW (TASS)* [1985] IRLR 162; *Express and Star Ltd v NGA* [1986] IRLR 222; and *Kent Free Press v NGA* [1987] IRLR 267. In all of these cases modest fines were imposed, except in the case of *Austin Rover* where no penalty was imposed because the court was persuaded of the union's lack of culpability. The principles governing liability for contempt are considered in the following case which arose out of the miners' strike of 1984–5.

[9.43] *Richard Read (Transport) Ltd v NUM (South Wales Area)* [1985] IRLR 67 (QBD)

The plaintiffs were hauliers who had been contracted to carry coke from Port Talbot to a number of locations. Pickets prevented the drivers from delivering their loads. The plaintiff company had obtained an interim injunction against the defendant union to restrain the pickets. But the picketing continued and there was no evidence from which an inference could be drawn that the union had revoked its instructions to its members to interfere with the plaintiff's vehicles.

Park J:
In these circumstances, by notices of motion dated 19.7.84, both plaintiffs apply to the Court, as I said, for an order that the defendant union's officials be committed to prison for their contempt in failing to comply with the terms of the interim injunctions of 17 April. The notices of motion, together with the affidavits in support, were served on the three officials of the union and on the union on 20 and 21 July. On 24 July the plaintiffs' London solicitors received from solicitors acting for the defendant union and its officials a letter dated 23 July. That letter acknowledged the receipt by the union, and by the three officials, of the notice of motion and the accompanying documents. It contained these paragraphs:

'We have seen a copy of the letter which the NUM (South Wales Area) wrote to you on 18 April last informing you that although they considered that the court proceedings were misconceived, their members had been informed of the terms of the court order dated 17.4.84 and informing you also that to the extent the order applied to the NUM (South Wales Area) they were complying with its terms. That has been and continues to be the position of the union and the three named officials.

Our clients instruct us that your clients simply do not appreciate that so long as their vehicles travel with a large number of vehicles belonging to other companies in a single convoy, it is extremely difficult to observe the terms of the court order.

We are instructed that your clients' vehicles, for many weeks past, have been travelling in convoys of anything between 50 to 130 vehicles between Port Talbot and Llanwern. There are three or four such trips a day. The convoy travels at speed, the vehicles of the various companies are bunched close together, and in these circumstances it is impossible or impractical for any person on the picket line to identify the lorries which belong to your clients and distinguish them from the remainder of the vehicles in the convoy. If your clients' vehicles were travelling in a group of their own either ahead or at the rear of the convoy and our clients were so advised of the arrangement, the position would be different as they would be clearly recognisable.

We think it right to bring this to your notice as our clients do not see how it can be said that a member of the picket line can knowingly be in breach of the Injunction Order of 17.4.84 unless he knew that the specific vehicle which would be affected by his conduct, belonged to your clients.

We are without instructions to enter an appearance, but you will no doubt disclose this letter to the Court at the hearing of your motion'.

The letter thus appears to suggest that the officials have in fact ceased to instruct or encourage the pickets to interfere with the plaintiff companies' vehicles and to abuse their drivers but that, owing to the failure of the companies in some way to distinguish their vehicles from the vehicles of other hauliers, any breaches of the injunction have been unknowingly committed. It would have been interesting to know what instructions, if any, were given to pickets in relation to the plaintiffs' vehicles. On this the letter is silent. However, neither the union nor any of the officials have put before the Court any evidence to support this unacceptable explanation, even if it be true, of the events which have been happening since 17 April.

The law, so far as it is applicable to the evidence in this case, was succinctly stated by Sir John Donaldson in *Howitt Transport Ltd v Transport and General Workers' Union* [1973] IRLR 25, where he said this:

'Before leaving this matter, the members of the Court would like to say a few general words about court orders, because some of the things that have been said today have led us to suppose that there may be a possible basis for misunderstanding. First, orders of any court must be complied with strictly in accordance with their terms. It is not sufficient, by way of an answer to an allegation that a court order has not been complied with, for the person concerned to say that he "did his best". The only exception to that proposition is where the court order itself only orders the person concerned to "do his best". But if a court order requires a certain state of affairs to be achieved, the only way in which the order can be complied with is by achieving that state of affairs'.

I am satisfied by the evidence so that I feel sure that, between the service of the interim injunction on the defendant union and its officials and 19 July, union officials have been guilty of numerous breaches of the injunctions resulting in serious interference with and disruption of the trade and business of both companies and in serious intimidation of their drivers. On the evidence, the officials appear to be completely indifferent to the consequences of the pickets' violent behaviour, although Mr Williams [a union official] has apparently admitted to a fear that someone was going to be killed. The officials are therefore in contempt of court.

The plaintiff companies say that they have no quarrel with the defendant union but they do seek the protection of the Court so that they may be permitted to carry on their business freely and without interruption, and without their drivers being put in fear of serious injury or worse. Despite all that has happened, the companies do not press me to commit to prison the union officials. It is suggested that financial penalties would be appropriate.

In view of these submissions, and with some hesitation, I have come to the conclusion that the imposition of fines is in the present circumstances the proper method of dealing with both contempts. But having regard to the manner in which the defendant union has deliberately defied the court orders, the fines have to be substantial. For the contempt in each case I fine the defendant union £25,000. The total of the fine will be £50,000 to be paid within 48 hours.

For a full account of this dimension to the miners' strike of 1984–5, see R Benedictus, 'The Use of the Law of Tort in the Miners' Dispute' (1985) 14 *Industrial Law Journal* 176.

So failure to observe an injunction could lead to a fine. But what if defiance means non-payment of the fine? Here the stakes are raised much higher, with non-payment leading to the likely sequestration of the assets of the union in question. This is a procedure governed by the Civil Procedure Rules which means that the assets of the union will be transferred to the possession of court-appointed sequestrators until the contempt is purged. It is possible for sequestrators to be appointed at the same time as the fine is imposed, without giving the union time to pay. In the *Richard Read* case, Park J drew attention to a newspaper report that the union might be seeking to avoid the payment of any fines by transferring its funds into the private bank accounts of its leaders. So he gave the plaintiffs leave to issue writs of sequestration, but also gave the union officials time to reflect on their position, the writs 'to lie in the office' for 48 hours. When the contempt is purged, the sequestrators will be discharged, the notes to the Civil Procedure Rules stating that the sequestrators will be directed 'to withdraw from possession, and to pass their final accounts, and, after retaining their costs, charges and expenses, and any payments properly made by them, to pay the balance [to the person whose property has been sequestered]'. See *News Group Newspapers v SOGAT 82* [1986] IRLR 227. The rash of cases in the 1980s revealed that sequestration was a potent weapon: union officials lose control of the assets of the union; and sequestrators run up considerable costs to be met from union funds. Resistance to court injunctions was to prove pointless, as a number of unions were to find to their cost, including the NUM, the print unions, and the seafarers. There is little talk now of defiance of the law by trade union officials, and indeed the events leading to the sequestrations of the 1980s seem far removed from the world we inhabit today. For an account of these procedures in the context of a particularly bitter dispute between News International and the print unions, see K D Ewing and B W Napier, 'The Wapping Dispute and Labour Law' (1986) 45 *Cambridge Law Journal* 285.

9.7.3 Damages

For much of the twentieth century damages as a remedy were not in practice available to employers for losses caused by a trade dispute. It is true that in *Taff Vale Railway Co Ltd v Amalgamated Society of Railway Servants* [1901] AC 426 the House of Lords held that trade unions were liable in damages for the torts of their servants and agents. But in the Trade Disputes Act 1906, Parliament gave a wide immunity from liability for specific torts for action in contemplation or furtherance of a trade dispute, and also provided by section 4 a general tort immunity for trade unions as such. So even where industrial action fell outside the scope of the immunity, there would be no trade union liability in damages. Why? The reasons are considered by the then Solicitor General (Sir William Robson) who—introducing the Trade Disputes Bill at Second Reading—argued that 'if trade unions are to be made subject to action, if they are to be put under the liabilities attaching to incorporation, they must also have the privileges of the incorporation' (H C Debs, 25 April 1906, col 1483). But under the law then in force (the Trade Union Act 1871) trade unions could not sue their members where they acted in breach of the rules of the union. It seems that there was little stomach on the government side at least for a settlement which would have as its logical corollary the prospect of trade unions being entitled to go 'to the Court of Chancery' to ask not only for damages against their members but also injunctions to restrain them from working during a strike.

The scope of the immunity was widely criticised, as giving trade unions a greater immunity from tort than the Crown. It was removed as part of the overhaul of labour law by the Conservative government's Industrial Relations Act 1971, but quickly restored with modifications in the Trade Union and Labour Relations Act 1974. Yet although there was a cogent reason (at least superficially) for the immunity in 1906, nothing as convincing was articulated in 1974. Indeed by 1974 the Trade Union Act 1871 had been repealed, enabling trade unions to sue (and to be sued by) their members. Although the Trade Union Act 1871 was always a weak justification for the immunity, it was stronger than anything put forward in 1974. This is not to say that there may not be compelling reasons for an immunity from damages, which in fact was quite fortuitous in view of the narrow interpretations of the trade dispute immunity by the courts after 1974 (see section 9.3 above). But it is to say that the case was never effectively made to convince a sceptical public. The 1974 immunity was, however, subject to qualifications. A trade union could be sued in negligence, nuisance or other breach of duty resulting in personal injury, provided that the tort was not committed in contemplation or furtherance of a trade dispute. Similarly, a trade union could be sued for any torts relating to the ownership, occupation, possession, control or use of property, again subject to the proviso of no liability where the tort was committed in contemplation or furtherance of a trade dispute.

An immunity of this kind was never likely to survive the wholesale revision of labour law which took place in the 1980s. Liability was restored by the Employment Act 1982: employers may proceed against a trade union for both injunctive relief and damages. The amount of damages which may be recovered is subject to a statutory ceiling which is based on the size of the union, though the ceiling applies to each plaintiff in an action and not to the proceedings as a whole. So in a case where there are multiple plaintiffs (as in *South Wales Miners' Federation v Glamorgan Coal Co* [1905] AC 239, above), the liability could be extensive, to say nothing of the costs, to which the ceiling does not apply. The ceiling has not been raised since 1982. Liability for losses caused by industrial action will arise of course if the action is unprotected by the immunity for whatever reason (an unprotected tort, not in contemplation or furtherance of a trade dispute, or immunity withdrawn because it constitutes secondary action or because the balloting and notice provisions have not been complied with). The reasons for the change were explained by Mr Norman Tebbit, the responsible minister who introduced the Employment Bill into the House of Commons in 1982. In the view of the then government there was 'no reason in logic or equity why trade union funds should be protected if officials of the trade unions, acting with the authority of the union, act unlawfully' (H C Debs, 8 February 1982, cols. 745–46). In some cases liability will arise only if the action has been authorised or endorsed by the rules in accordance with the following provisions.

[9.44] Trade Union and Labour Relations (Consolidation) Act 1992, sections 20–22

Liability of trade union in certain proceedings in tort

20 (1) Where proceedings in tort are brought against a trade union—

(a) on the ground that an act—

    (i) induces another person to break a contract or interferes or induces another person to interfere with its performance, or

    (ii) consists in threatening that a contract (whether one to which the union is a party or not) will be broken or its performance interfered with, or that the union will induce another person to break a contract or interfere with its performance, or

(b) in respect of an agreement or combination by two or more persons to do or to procure the doing of an act which, if it were done without any such agreement or combination, would be actionable in tort on such a ground,

then, for the purpose of determining in those proceedings whether the union is liable in respect of the act in question, that act shall be taken to have been done by the union if, but only if, it is to be taken to have been authorised or endorsed by the trade union in accordance with the following provisions.

(2) An act shall be taken to have been authorised or endorsed by a trade union if it was done, or was authorised or endorsed—

(a) by any person empowered by the rules to do, authorise or endorse acts of the kind in question, or

(b) by the principal executive committee or the president or general secretary, or

(c) by any other committee of the union or any other official of the union (whether employed by it or not).

(3) For the purposes of paragraph (c) of subsection (2)

(a) any group of persons constituted in accordance with the rules of the union is a committee of the union; and

(b) an act shall be taken to have been done, authorised or endorsed by an official if it was done, authorised or endorsed by, or by any member of, any group of persons of which he was at the material time a member, the purposes of which included organising or co-ordinating industrial action.

(4) The provisions of paragraphs (b) and (c) of subsection (2) apply notwithstanding anything in the rules of the union, or in any contract or rule of law, but subject to the provisions of section 21 (repudiation by union of certain acts).

(5) Where for the purposes of any proceedings an act is by virtue of this section taken to have been done by a trade union, nothing in this section shall affect the liability of any other person, in those or any other proceedings, in respect of that act.

(6) In proceedings arising out of an act which is by virtue of this section taken to have been done by a trade union, the power of the court to grant an injunction or interdict includes power to require the union to take such steps as the court considers appropriate for ensuring—

(a) that there is no, or no further, inducement of persons to take part or to continue to take part in industrial action, and

(b) that no person engages in any conduct after the granting of the injunction or interdict by virtue of having been induced before it was granted to take part or to continue to take part in industrial action.

The provisions of subsections (2) to (4) above apply in relation to proceedings for failure to comply with any such injunction or interdict as they apply in relation to the original proceedings.

(7) In this section 'rules', in relation to a trade union, means the written rules of the union and any other written provision forming part of the contract between a member and the other members.

Repudiation by union of certain acts

21 (1) An act shall not be taken to have been authorised or endorsed by a trade union by virtue only of paragraph (c) of section 20(2) if it was repudiated by the executive, president or general secretary as soon as reasonably practicable after coming to the knowledge of any of them.

(2) Where an act is repudiated—
(a) written notice of the repudiation must be given to the committee or official in question, without delay, and
(b) the union must do its best to give individual written notice of the fact and date of repudiation, without delay—
      (i)   to every member of the union who the union has reason to believe is taking part, or might otherwise take part, in industrial action as a result of the act, and
      (ii) to the employer of every such member.

(3) The notice given to members in accordance with paragraph (b)(i) of subsection (2) must contain the following statement—

> 'Your union has repudiated the call (or calls) for industrial action to which this notice relates and will give no support to unofficial industrial action taken in response to it (or them). If you are dismissed while taking unofficial industrial action, you will have no right to complain of unfair dismissal.'

(4) If subsection (2) or (3) is not complied with, the repudiation shall be treated as ineffective.

(5) An act shall not be treated as repudiated if at any time after the union concerned purported to repudiate it the executive, president or general secretary has behaved in a manner which is inconsistent with the purported repudiation.

(6) The executive, president or general secretary shall be treated as so behaving if, on a request made to any of them within three months of the purported repudiation by a person who
(a) is a party to a commercial contract whose performance has been or may be interfered with as a result of the act in question, and
(b) has not been given written notice by the union of the repudiation,
it is not forthwith confirmed in writing that the act has been repudiated.

(7) In this section 'commercial contract' means any contract other than—
(a) a contract of employment, or
(b) any other contract under which a person agrees personally to do work or perform services for another.

Limit on damages awarded against trade unions in actions in tort

22 (1) This section applies to any proceedings in tort brought against a trade union, except—
(a) proceedings for personal injury as a result of negligence, nuisance or breach of duty;
(b) proceedings for breach of duty in connection with the ownership, occupation, possession, control or use of property;
(c) proceedings brought by virtue of Part I of the Consumer Protection Act 1987 (product liability).

(2) In any proceedings in tort to which this section applies the amount which may be awarded against the union by way of damages shall not exceed the following limit—

Number of members of union	Maximum award of damages
Less than 5,000	£10,000
5,000 or more but less than 25,000	£50,000
25,000 or more but less than 100,000	£125,000
100,000 or more	£250,000

There are now a number of cases in which the principles to be applied in awarding damages have been considered.

[9.45] *Messenger Group Ltd v NGA* [1984] IRLR (QBD)

Following a dispute about closed shop arrangements, the company sought damages for losses caused by tortious acts of the defendants which were not protected by immunity. The action involved secondary picketing and other forms of secondary action. The question arose whether exemplary and aggravated damages are recoverable.

Caulfield J:

Now to a rather more difficult aspect of damages, in view of the fact that the plaintiff is a limited company. The plaintiff further claims both aggravated and exemplary damages. These two classes of damages are well recognised in certain torts, particularly defamation, false imprisonment and kindred torts, where the plaintiffs are human beings though the defendants are frequently but legal entities. Can the same principles be applied where the plaintiff is not human but inanimate? Can a limited company be awarded aggravated or exemplary damages in respect of the torts which I have found committed by the defendant? Secondly, can they be applied in the case of a limited company against a union?

Certainly exemplary and aggravated damages can be awarded against inanimate legal entities like limited companies, and I cannot see any reason why the same legal entities cannot be awarded aggravated and exemplary damages. Speaking of the notorious events of today—I use the word in its purest sense, in the sense everybody knows—the persons who suffer damage from unlawful tortious action in industrial strife are generally, though not invariably, limited companies. The tort of intimidation, while exercised against persons—that is employees—to be effective is exercised at the same time against an employer which is a limited company. I think the task of this Court is to decide whether on the facts of this case aggravated damages could be awarded if the plaintiff were not a limited company but a human being or a group of human beings. I conclude aggravated damages could and should be awarded if the plaintiff was an individual on the facts of this case. I think it is plain from the speeches in *Rookes v Barnard* [[1964] AC 1129], particularly that of Lord Devlin, that aggravated damages are compensatory. Lord Diplock so states in *Broome v Cassell & Co* [1972] AC 1130, and I do not think I am compelled on the authorities to evaluate aggravated damages separately from the compensatory parts. I am, however, going to do so, so that if this award is challenged in a higher Court, that Court will have the advantage of knowing for certain the extent of the award, and if I am in error, the extent of the error. It would be otherwise if I were to award one sum for compensatory damages which included, without isolating it, the element for aggravated damages.

Assuming the plaintiff was a human being, I am satisfied on the authorities that I could include in the compensatory award a sum for aggravated damages. I do conclude with ease that the defendant's intention was to close down the plaintiff's business, as I said earlier, and/or enforce a closed shop. The defendant was, on the evidence, reckless in pursuit of its intentions and acted, too, in jubilant defiance of the Court with an open arrogance. Their objects were to their knowledge unlawful and tortious. The defendant was a deliberate tortfeasor. Injured feelings of the plaintiff is only one aspect in considering aggravated damages. The more important element is where the injury to the plaintiff has been aggravated by malice or by the manner of doing the injury; that is, the insolence or arrogance by which it is accompanied. For a human being whose feelings exist, my award would have been higher, but I eliminate human feelings from my award. I see no reason why a limited company should not be awarded aggravated damages just like a human being. There is no reason why the present plaintiff should not recover. Of course, that aggravated damages can be awarded on the facts of this case is my main finding on this item, but I am not including any damages for injured feelings. I have approached the question on the manner of the doing of the injury and on the basis which I think is right, that the compensatory award which I have earlier made is not adequate. The figure I award the plaintiff for aggravated damages is the sum of £10,000, and I have approached this figure with moderation, as I shall approach the final heading of exemplary damages, to which I now turn.

I am entitled on the authority of *Rookes v Barnard* and *Drane v Evangelou* [[1978] 2 All ER 437] to award exemplary damages. Exemplary damages fall to be awarded under the second category explained by Lord Devlin in *Rookes v Barnard* and as further explained by Lord Denning in *Drane v Evangelou*, and followed by Lord Hailsham in *Cassell v Broome* and the Lords who sat with him. It is implicit, in my judgment, in the speech of Lord Devlin that exemplary damages can be awarded where the tortious conduct is intimidation. They can be awarded even in trespass, as in *Drane v Evangelou*. From *Rookes v Barnard*, certain principles have to be observed in approaching this award: The plaintiff cannot recover exemplary damages unless he is the victim of the punishable behaviour. Secondly, the award has to be moderate. And thirdly, the means of the parties have to be considered. I have adopted the approach of Lord Devlin in *Rookes v Barnard*. I am not including his words in this judgment. Mr Clegg [for the union] submits that I should not make an award of exemplary damages because in the contempt proceedings the defendant has already been punished and its contempt has been purged. I disagree. The contempt proceedings are quasi-criminal; these proceedings are not. The fines were imposed by Mr Justice Eastham because the defendant was defying and was contemptuous of the Court. The award of exemplary damages, in the words of Lord Devlin, 'can properly be awarded whenever it is necessary to teach a wrongdoer that tort does not pay'. The exemplary damages I shall award may have historically little effect on the defendant union. Even so, I award the plaintiff the sum of £25,000, so that the total award in favour of the plaintiff is £125,051.20.

In a second case—*Boxfoldia Ltd v NGA (1982)* [1988] IRLR 383 Saville J held that the limit on damages did not fetter the discretion of the court to award interest on the damages. So in addition to damages of £250,000, interest of £90,000 was awarded against the union. More recently the sum of £130,458 was awarded against a union where the action was unprotected because of notice and ballot irregularities: *Willerby Holiday Homes Ltd v UCATT* [2003] EWHC 2608 (IDS Brief 749, January 2004)

9.8 Sanctions against strikers: protected and unprotected action

The discussion so far has concentrated on steps which might be taken mainly against the trade union, principally by an employer seeking to restrain industrial action. But there are other steps which an employer might wish to take, in addition to or instead of targeting the union. These other steps involve sanctions against individual workers who are taking or who have taken part in the strike or other industrial action. As we have seen, by calling on its members to take industrial action, the union will invariably be calling on its members to take action in breach of their contracts of employment. According to Lord Templeman in *Miles v Wakefield MDC* [1987] AC 539, '[a]ny form of industrial action by a worker is a breach of contract' (p 559), though this is a view which has been disputed:

[9.46] P Elias, 'The Strike and Breach of Contract: A Reassessment', in K D Ewing, C A Gearty and B A Hepple (eds.), *Human Rights and Labour Law* (London, Mansell, 1994), chapter 11

> employees may be able to take strike action in response to a repudiatory breach by the employer in one of two ways. Either they may be able to withhold their labour until the employer is willing to perform his part of the contract; or they may be able to give notice to terminate their contracts in response to the repudiatory breach.

In view of the fact that industrial action is thus likely to constitute a breach of contract, this raises questions about the steps which the employer may lawfully take against those who are involved in such action as opposed to those who have organised it. As we saw in Chapter 2 it is unlikely that those taking part in such action will be entitled to be paid by the employer; at best they will be entitled to be paid only for work actually done where the action takes a form other than a strike. Another possibility is that the employer may wish to dismiss and replace those taking part in the strike or other industrial action in order to ensure continuity of production. Otherwise the employer may decide that the strike is the last straw and decides as a result to close the enterprise, in some cases perhaps moving to a new site and a new labour force. Historically employers have been free in principle to take such steps with little legal restraint, though whether in practice it is always possible to find a replacement labour force is another matter. So far as the common law is concerned taking part in industrial action would almost certainly constitute a breach of a fundamental term of the contract of employment which would entitle the employer summarily to dismiss the workers in question. If in doubt, it would be open to the employer to dismiss with notice.

9.8.1 Unfair dismissal: before the Employment Relations Act 1999

It might have been thought that striking employees would have been protected by the introduction of legislation on unfair dismissal. This was not the case. An employee dismissed for taking part in a strike or other industrial action (or in the course of a lock out) had no right to bring a claim for unfair dismissal unless it could be shown that the employee in question had been selectively dismissed or if the dismissed employee could show that other dismissed employees had been selectively re-engaged. In other words, the legislation provided the employer with an immunity from legal proceedings, though it was an immunity contingent upon the employer dismissing and not re-engaging all those who were on strike and who had been on strike. But even if the immunity from litigation was lost by the employer selectively dismissing a striking employee, the dismissal would not necessarily be unfair. The immunity was extended in a number of ways by the Employment Act 1982, section 9, providing most notably that an employer could selectively re-engage dismissed employees after three months: it was no longer necessary never to re-engage as a condition of retaining the immunity. Still further changes introduced by the Employment Act 1990 provided that an employee dismissed while engaged in unofficial action could not bring proceedings for unfair dismissal (even though the employee has been selectively dismissed). These provisions offered some protection for striking workers, in the sense that an employer was immune from legal proceedings (except in the case of unofficial action) only if he or she dismissed all those involved in the industrial action. But although mass dismissal might not always be possible, in truth this was a feeble form of protection. Employers in the 1980s were to take full advantage of the weaknesses of this particular approach and some appeared to feel no constraint in dismissing an entire workforce. Some of the high profile examples are to be found in the box below. These and other events exposed the defects of a system of protection for striking workers which had been introduced by a Labour government in 1974–75 (which would not have been addressed by repealing the relevant amendments of 1982 and 1990), and as such led to trade union calls for the law to be reformed to provide better protection for workers. The position appeared all the more unfair for the fact that employees could be dismissed for taking part in a strike even where the increasingly complex conditions of trade union immunity were complied with: the action could be in furtherance of a trade dispute, supported by a ballot, with proper notice given to the employer. Yet those taking part in the action could still be dismissed.

The claims of those who sought to reform the law were supported by the growing realisation that in other European countries workers were protected from dismissal for taking part in lawful strikes, and by the conclusions of international supervisory bodies (such as the Social Rights Committee of the Council of Europe, as well as the Freedom of Association Committee and the Committee of Experts of the ILO) that British law was in breach of international labour standards—notably the Council of Europe's Social Charter of 18 October 1961 and ILO Convention 87 (The Freedom of Association and Protection of the Right to Organise Convention, 1948). ILO Convention 87 does not expressly protect the right to strike, but it has been implied by the supervisory bodies from Article 3 which provides that workers' organisations 'have the right to draw up their constitutions and rules, to elect their representatives in full

Regulatory Failure in the 1980s

1. Negotiations between News International and a number of trade unions were held to consider the relocation of News International titles to Wapping in east London, and with the relocation major changes in working conditions. The unions commenced industrial action when it was clear that assurances they sought would not be given, and the company responded by dismissing some 5,500 workers and by moving its newspaper production to Wapping. Replacement labour was recruited to do the work of those on strike, the recruitment having been done with the secret assistance of the electricians' union (EETPU). The strike was a 'defensive' strike which had been called after a ballot had been held. Nevertheless the company made it clear that the strikers would not be reinstated, though it did offer an *ex gratia* compensation package to the strikers in excess of what would have been their legal due. Nevertheless this was a watershed, and set a pattern which others were to follow. If 5,500 skilled workers could be treated in this way, what price a smaller workforce of unskilled workers? See K D Ewing and B W Napier, 'The Wapping Dispute and Labour Law' (1986) 45 *Cambridge Law Journal* 285.

2. In 1988 over 2,000 seafarers were dismissed by P&O European Ferries following a strike. In December 1987 the company wrote to its employees giving three months' notice of changes to working conditions which it proposed to introduce in order to 'achieve substantial savings in labour costs'. Following the intervention of the union (in this case the National Union of Seamen), negotiations took place with the company: but these broke down and a strike ballot led to an overwhelming majority in favour of industrial action. Unsuccessful negotiations for a return to work then took place, following which the company sent letters to the strikers offering new terms. Those who did not accept the terms were dismissed and the company recommenced its operations following an extensive recruiting campaign of non-union labour. Approximately 800 of the dismissed NUS members began to drift back over the next few months while the company withdrew recognition from the union. Unfair dismissal proceedings were unsuccessfully brought by 1,025 of the 1,200 workers who had not been re-engaged: *P&O European Ferries (Dover) Ltdv. Byrne* [1989] IRLR 254. See also ILO, Official Bulletin, Vol. 74, Series B, Case No 1540 (277th Report of the Freedom of Association Committee).

3. The Timex Corporation had a factory in Dundee from which it had operated for 30 years. In 1993 a dispute emerged when the company proposed to lay off some staff because of falling orders. The union refused to accept the company's proposals and on 29 January the workers began strike action after complying with balloting and other obligations. A few weeks later the company fired the 347 people engaged in the strike and hired replacement workers, from local areas of high unemployment, at rates of pay significantly lower than those which were paid to the strikers. The replacement workers were bussed in on a daily basis, running a gauntlet of jeering pickets and demonstrators who on one occasion numbered over 5,000. Attempts to negotiate a settlement were unsuccessful, with the union and its members unwilling to countenance a permanent wage reduction of up to 27 per cent. Although the company could have continued to operate indefinitely with replacement labour, it decided to close the plant and to relocate in another country. All the remaining workers were dismissed. See K Miller and C Woolfson, 'Timex: Industrial Relations and the Use of the Law in the 1990s' (1994) 23 *Industrial Law Journal* 209.

freedom, to organise their administration and activities and to formulate their programmes'. Following a complaint arising from the dismissals in a dispute involving seafarers (see p 946), the ILO Freedom of Association Committee recommended that British law should be amended to 'give effective protection to workers who have been dismissed for having participated in a strike and in particular to enable workers who are dismissed in the course of, or at the conclusion of, a strike or other industrial action to challenge their dismissal before a judicial authority'. The ILO Committee of Experts had earlier concluded:

> it is inconsistent with the right to strike as guaranteed by [Convention 87] for an employer to be permitted to refuse to reinstate some or all of its employees at the conclusion of a strike, lock-out or other industrial action without those employees having the right to challenge the fairness of that dismissal before an independent court or tribunal.
> (ILO, International Labour Conference, 77th Session, 1989. *Report of the Committee of Experts on the Application of Conventions and Recommendations*, Report III (Part 1A))

The Committee of Experts also requested the government 'to introduce legislative protection against dismissal, and other forms of discriminatory treatment such as demotion or withdrawal of accrued rights, in connection with strikes and other industrial action'. Similar conclusions and requests by the Committee of Experts were to be made on a regular basis thereafter, and these were reinforced by the Conclusions of the Committee of Independent Experts (now called the Social Rights Committee) of the Council of Europe that British law was also in breach of the European Social Charter of 18 October 1961, Article 6: Council of Europe, Committee of Experts, *Conclusions XI–1* (1989), p 90.

9.8.2 Employment Relations Act 1999: protected industrial action

The passing of the Conservative government in 1997 has given way to a new statutory approach to the treatment of strikers dismissed for taking part in industrial action. The position of the new government was set out in *Fairness at Work* (above) in the following terms:

> The Government has no plans to change the position in relation to those dismissed for taking unofficial action. However, in relation to employees dismissed for taking part in lawfully organised official industrial action, the Government believes that the current regime is unsatisfactory and illogical. The Government believes that in general employees dismissed for taking part in lawfully organised official industrial action should have the right to complain of unfair dismissal to a tribunal. In any particular case the tribunal would not get involved in looking at the merits of the dispute; its role would be to decide whether the employer had acted fairly and reasonably taking into account all the circumstances of the case [para 4.22].

The outcome is a new section introduced into the 1992 Act by the Employment Relations Act 1999 (subsequently amended by the Employment Relations Act 2004) which provides in certain circumstances not that a tribunal may hear a case of unfair dismissal, but that in certain circumstances it is automatically unfair to dismiss an employee for taking part in a strike or other industrial action.

[9.47] Trade Union and Labour Relations (Consolidation) Act 1992, sections 238A, 238B

Participation in official industrial action

238A (1) For the purposes of this section an employee takes protected industrial action if he commits an act which, or a series of acts each of which, he is induced to commit by an act which by virtue of section 219 is not actionable in tort.

(2) An employee who is dismissed shall be regarded for the purposes of Part X of the Employment Rights Act 1996 (unfair dismissal) as unfairly dismissed if—
(a) the reason (or, if more than one, the principal reason) for the dismissal is that the employee took protected industrial action, and
(b) subsection (3), (4) or (5) applies to the dismissal.

(3) This subsection applies to a dismissal if the date of dismissal is within the protected.

(4) This subsection applies to a dismissal if—
(a) the date of dismissal is after the end of that period, and
(b) the employee had stopped taking protected industrial action before the end of that period.

(5) This subsection applies to a dismissal if—
(a) the date of dismissal is after the end of that period,
(b) the employee had not stopped taking protected industrial action before the end of that period, and
(c) the employer had not taken such procedural steps as would have been reasonable for the purposes of resolving the dispute to which the protected industrial action relates.

(6) In determining whether an employer has taken those steps regard shall be had, in particular, to—
(a) whether the employer or a union had complied with procedures established by an applicable collective or other agreement;
(b) whether the employer or a union offered or agreed to commence or resume negotiations after the start of the protected industrial action;
(c) whether the employer or a union unreasonably refused, after the start of the protected industrial action, a request that conciliation services be used;
(d) whether the employer or a union unreasonably refused, after the start of the protected industrial action, a request that mediation services be used in relation to procedures to be adopted for the purposes of resolving the dispute.
(e) where there was agreement to use either of the services mentioned in paragraphs (c) and (d), the matters specified in section 238B.

(7) In determining whether an employer has taken those steps no regard shall be had to the merits of the dispute.

(7A) For the purposes of this section "the protected period", in relation to the dismissal of an employee, is the sum of the basic period and any extension period in relation to that employee.

(7B) The basic period is twelve weeks beginning with the first day of protected industrial action.

(7C) An extension period in relation to an employee is a period equal to the number of days falling on or after the first day of protected industrial action (but before the protected period ends) during the whole or any part of which the employee is locked out by his employer.

(7D) In subsections (7B) and (7C), the "first day of protected industrial action" means the day on which the employee starts to take protected industrial action (even if on that day he is locked out by his employer).

(8) For the purposes of this section no account shall be taken of the repudiation of any act by a trade union as mentioned in section 21 in relation to anything which occurs before the end of the next working day (within the meaning of section 237) after the day on which the repudiation takes place.

(9) In this section "date of dismissal" has the meaning given by section 238(5).

Conciliation and mediation: supplementary provisions

238B (1) The matters referred to in subsection (6)(e) of section 238A are those specified in subsections (2) to (5); and references in this section to "the service provider" are to any person who provided a service mentioned in subsection (6)(c) or (d) of that section.

(2) The first matter is: whether, at meetings arranged by the service provider, the employer or, as the case may be, a union was represented by an appropriate person.

(3) The second matter is: whether the employer or a union, so far as requested to do so, co-operated in the making of arrangements for meetings to be held with the service provider.

(4) The third matter is: whether the employer or a union fulfilled any commitment given by it during the provision of the service to take particular action.

(5) The fourth matter is: whether, at meetings arranged by the service provider between the parties making use of the service, the representatives of the employer or a union answered any reasonable question put to them concerning the matter subject to conciliation or mediation.

(6) For the purposes of subsection (2) an "appropriate person" is—
(a) in relation to the employer—
   (i)   a person with the authority to settle the matter subject to conciliation or mediation on behalf of the employer, or
   (ii) a person authorised by a person of that type to make recommendations to him with regard to the settlement of that matter, and
(b) in relation to a union, a person who is responsible for handling on the union's behalf the matter subject to conciliation or mediation.

(7) For the purposes of subsection (4) regard may be had to any timetable which was agreed for the taking of the action in question or, if no timetable was agreed, to how long it was before the action was taken.

(8) In any proceedings in which regard must be had to the matters referred to in section 238A(6)(e)—
(a) notes taken by or on behalf of the service provider shall not be admissible in evidence;
(b) the service provider must refuse to give evidence as to anything communicated to him

in connection with the performance of his functions as a conciliator or mediator if, in his opinion, to give the evidence would involve his making a damaging disclosure; and

(c) the service provider may refuse to give evidence as to whether, for the purposes of subsection (5), a particular question was or was not a reasonable one.

(9) For the purposes of subsection (8)(b) a "damaging disclosure" is—

(a) a disclosure of information which is commercially sensitive, or

(b) a disclosure of information that has not previously been disclosed which relates to a position taken by a party using the conciliation or mediation service on the settlement of the matter subject to conciliation or mediation,

to which the person who communicated the information to the service provider has not consented.

9.8.2.1 A new symmetry

The new protection introduces an important symmetry between the liability of the trade union and the protection of the individual worker. Where the trade union is protected from liability in tort, the worker is protected from dismissal (for at least the first 12 weeks of the dispute). But there are nevertheless a number of interesting (not to say bizarre) consequences which flow from this. In the first place the protection of the employee applies only where the industrial action in which he or she is taking or has taken part is not actionable in tort by virtue of TULRCA 1992, section 219. This is likely to cover the large majority of cases. But it is possible nevertheless that there may be cases where the industrial action is not actionable for reasons unconnected with section 219: for example it may not be actionable because the industrial action is not tortious; a possible example being *Power Packing Casemakers v Faust* [1983] ICR 292 which concerned a voluntary overtime ban (see below). The Court of Appeal held that conduct may constitute industrial action even though it is not a breach of contract. But if it is not a breach of contract it may not be tortious even though a ballot has been held and due notice has been given to the employer.

We could thus have the paradoxical spectacle (admittedly in rare cases) of an employer arguing that the employees have no protection against dismissal because the conduct of their officials was not tortious, with the employees arguing otherwise on the ground that they will have to establish tortious liability of the union which is also protected by the immunity as a necessary condition in an application for unfair dismissal. Apart from the possibility that the industrial action may not be tortious, the protection in TULRCA 1992, section 238A may be defeated on the additional ground that the action is tortious either because it involves the commission of a tort for which there is no section 219 protection or because it involves the commission of a tort for which there is protection but the action in question falls outside the scope of the immunity (because for example it was not in contemplation or furtherance of a trade dispute). In these cases it will be in the employer's interest to argue that there is a tort but one which is unprotected, and on this occasion for the employees to argue the converse. But whatever the circumstances, one unavoidable consequence is that the employment tribunals could be drawn into the darker corners of tort law.

9.8.2.2 The limits of the statutory protection

The protection against unfair dismissal applies without the need to satisfy the normal qualifying conditions for bringing an unfair dismissal claim: in other words it is not necessary to have worked for 12 months. The protection applies from 'day one', as in the case of the protection from dismissal on the ground of trade union membership and activities. This is important in so far as it removes an otherwise possible opportunity for employers to discriminate between workers engaged in a common cause. So too is the provision which makes it clear that the protection applies to those over the normal retirement age who would normally be excluded from unfair dismissal generally. There is nevertheless one important category of workers excluded, namely those who are employed under a contract for services. The legislative protection (like the protection from dismissal on grounds of trade union membership or activities) applies only to employees (even though the title to Schedule 5 of the 1999 Act refers to 'Unfair Dismissal of Striking Workers'). There is however power vested in the Secretary of State to extend the law relating to unfair dismissal to workers other than employees. But this power has not yet been exercised.

Apart from these questions of eligibility and coverage, there are other major concerns with the protection. It is true that the protected period has been extended, by the Employment Relations Act 2004, from 8 weeks to 12 weeks. Yet there is still no guaranteed protection for the whole length of the dispute should it exceed 12 weeks. Although it is unlikely that many disputes will exceed 12 weeks, there are examples of those which do. It is also true that the procedural obligations on an employer to bring a dispute to an end have been strengthened after the 12 week period expires. Nevertheless it is not clear how extending the time limit for automatic protection addresses the claim that the legislation does not adequately meet the requirements of the international labour standards by which it was inspired, on which see T Novitz, 'International Promises and Domestic Pragmatism' (2000) 63 MLR 379. A now more pressing concern may relate to remedies, where two issues need to be addressed. In the first place, workers who are unfairly dismissed will not be entitled to be reinstated against the wishes of the employer, the only remedy lying in compensation. This limitation seems to be a rather hollow protection of the right to strike. This concern is reinforced by the experience of the Friction Dynamics workers discussed in the following extract, who succeeded in proceedings for unfair dismissal after having been dismissed for taking part in protected action during the protected period. Although they were awarded compensation, they were nevertheless unable to recover the money awarded to them by the employment tribunal after the company went into liquidation. There is a second question concerning an employer who, faced with a strike, hires replacement workers for the duration of the strike but does not dismiss the strikers. If they resign before the eight weeks are up, can they claim to have been dismissed?

[9.48] A Chamberlain, The Role of the 'Eight-Week Rule' in the Friction Dynamics Dispute, *The Lawyer*, 3 November 2003

'On 29 August, shortly before the start of this year's TUC Conference in Brighton, Sir Bill Morris, general secretary of the Transport and General Workers' Union (T&G), issued a scathing calling notice.

In it he claimed: "Government legislative failure on employment has allowed our members to be unfairly sacked whilst engaging in lawful industrial action. Despite the judgment of the industrial [sic] tribunal that the company acted unlawfully, our members are being cheated out of the compensation owed to them by an unscrupulous employer."

Morris was referring to his members at the Friction Dynamics plant in Caernarfon, who have been taking part in the longest-running current industrial dispute in the UK. It led to *Davis v Friction Dynamics* (2001), in which Morris's members successfully complained that their dismissals were automatically unfair under Section 238A of the Trade Union and Labour Relations (Consolidation) Act 1992—the so-called 'eight-week rule'. Despite this, no compensation is likely to be paid to the strikers, for on 20 August 2003 Friction Dynamics' owner placed it into voluntary liquidation. The company's business and assets have since been sold off. This is presumably what Morris meant by the Government "allowing" his members to be unfairly dismissed.

The eight-week rule was introduced in April 2000 and has two limbs. The first is that it is automatically unfair to dismiss an employee taking part in "protected industrial action" within the first eight weeks of the action. ('Protected industrial action' is action that the employee is induced to commit by their union, provided that the union's action falls within the Section 219 'golden formula': acts done in contemplation or furtherance of a trade dispute). The second limb is that a dismissal after the end of that period will be automatically unfair if the employer has not taken reasonable procedural steps to resolve the dispute.

Before the eight-week rule existed, the employer could dismiss a lawfully striking workforce with impunity under Section 238 as long as it dismissed all of the strikers and did not selectively re-engage any of them within three months. This remains on the statute book for the limited purposes of action not protected by the golden formula. Friction Dynamics was the first case to be heard under the eight-week rule, and if Morris gets his way, it could also be the last: on the first day of the TUC Conference, he proposed a motion calling on the Government to remove the "iniquitous" rule.

Briefly, the facts behind the Friction Dynamics case are these. On 30 April 2001, having followed the correct balloting and calling procedures, 86 of Morris's members at the company commenced industrial action. On 1 May 2001, company management wrote to each striker, telling them "you have . . . repudiated your contract of employment. The company . . . accepts your repudiation." Following several Acas-brokered meetings between management and T&G officials, the company wrote a further letter to each striker on 27 June 2001, just over eight weeks after the strike started, in which it purported to dismiss them with effect from the following day.

The strikers complained to the Shrewsbury Employment Tribunal that they had been unfairly dismissed on 28 June 2001 contrary to Section 238A. Because that date was more than eight weeks after the strike commenced, the complaints apparently relied on the second limb of the eight-week rule. However, the complaints were later amended to rely on the dismissals having been effected on 1 May by the letter of that date, which was within the eight-week period, thus relying on the first limb of the rule.

The case was transferred from Shrewsbury to Liverpool due to the strength of feeling running against Friction Dynamics in North Wales. After a two-week hearing in October 2002, the Liverpool Employment Tribunal decided that the strikers had been dismissed unfairly.

In the tribunal's written reasons, it stated that the dismissals had taken place on 1 May (within the eight-week period), because the words of the letter unambiguously told the strikers that their contracts of employment were terminated, and that is how management intended it to be read. It went on to state that even if the dismissal date had been 28 June (after the end of the period), Friction Dynamics had not taken reasonable steps to resolve the dispute, and therefore in either event the dismissal was automatically unfair.

The significance of the Friction Dynamics case is therefore that the complaints succeeded because of the eight-week rule, not despite it, and yet Morris still wants it to be removed from the statute book.

Friction Dynamics appealed against the tribunal's decision on the grounds that it was wrong to interpret the 1 May letter as unambiguous. However, before the company's appeal could be heard, and before the tribunal had awarded any compensation to the strikers, its owner placed it in voluntary liquidation. In the long term, this was almost inevitable in any event, because as soon as compensation for 86 unfair dismissal claims became payable (which would certainly have run well into seven figures), the company would have had no real alternative other than liquidation.

The owner allegedly subsequently bought back the assets and set up a new business under the name of Dynamex Friction. On 20 August Morris wrote to Patricia Hewitt, Secretary of State for Trade and Industry, calling for the Department of Trade and Industry (DTI) to launch an investigation into the situation, saying that he believed it was merely a tactical manoeuvre designed to avoid making the compensation payments to the dismissed strikers. That call has also since been taken up by local MPs.

Legislative changes have recently been introduced which deal with part of this problem identified by Morris - namely, that where sums owed to employees following insolvency are unsecured debts, which would include tribunal awards, those debts rank below the claims of secured creditors and preferential creditors. Previously, these included the Crown in respect of unpaid PAYE, VAT and certain other taxes.

The Enterprise Act 2002, which came into force on 15 September 2003, will in many cases now ensure that at least some funds are set aside for the benefit of unsecured creditors, including such employees. The Act provides that in respect of companies placed into formal insolvency after 15 September 2003, a prescribed part (between £5,000 and £600,000) of the company's assets, which are subject to a floating charge, will be set aside for payment to the company's unsecured creditors after the claims of preferential creditors (and certain costs) have been satisfied. Additionally, it provides that the Crown no longer ranks as a preferential creditor of such companies, but only as an unsecured creditor, thereby reducing the amount of prior ranking preferential claims.

Thus, unsecured creditors, including employees, will in future have a better prospect of recovering a proportion of the debts owed to them when a company goes into insolvency. Although this may be of little practical assistance to the Friction Dynamics strikers, they will at least have the comfort of knowing that, in future, employees in their position will be better protected'.

Addleshaw Goddard partner Andrew Chamberlain and associate Justin Beevor are members of the firm's employment group. Both acted for Friction Dynamics in responding to the unfair dismissal claims from August 2002 until the company went into liquidation.

Some of the legislative changes referred to towards the end of the foregoing article are considered in chapter 10 below.

9.8.3 Unprotected industrial action

The question which now arises is this: what happens if the industrial action falls outside the scope of section 238A? As we have seen, there are a number of reasons why industrial action may be unprotected. In these circumstances we fall back on the law

---

Unfair Dismissal and Replacement Workers

The measures protecting strikers from dismissal do not prevent an employer from hiring temporary replacements to do the work of those on strike. Any replacement workers dismissed when the dispute ends will not normally have a claim for unfair dismissal because they would not normally have 12 months' service to qualify for unfair dismissal. But although it would be premature to exaggerate any difficulties which may arise here, it remains the case that this is a matter which has caused great difficulties in the United States since the seminal decision of the Supreme Court in *NLRB v MacKay Radio and Telegraph Company*, 304 US 333 (1937). As a result it is not possible in the United States for an employer to dismiss workers for taking part in a lawful strike: but it is possible to replace strikers while the strike continues. But what happens if the strike never comes to an end? And if the employer is free to hire temporary replacements what incentive does the employer have to reach an agreement with the union to bring the strike to an end (particularly as the strikers will not—of course—be entitled to be paid or to receive other benefits while the dispute exists)?

In these circumstances the employment relationship between the employer and the striking workers may end by the workers drifting away and finding alternative employment rather than by being formally dismissed by the employer. There is perhaps a possibility in British law that the hiring by the employer of replacement workers would constitute a constructive dismissal as repudiating a fundamental term of the contract. But there are clearly difficulties in mounting such a claim: (i) would it be a breach of contract by the employer where the replacements are said by the employer to be temporary, albeit for an indefinite period?; (ii) even if it would (and it must be unlikely), would it be a breach of contract by the employer where the steps taken by the employer are defensive steps taken in response to the breach by the employees? And (iii) even if the dispute extends beyond twelve weeks would the employer not be protected by continuing to negotiate with the union, even if negotiations take the form of an unequivocal refusal to agree to any of the union's claims? In other words is it possible for the employer to defeat the protection of section 238A by replacing the strikers and holding out the possibility of reengaging any of the employees on strike on the terms and conditions in force when the dispute began?

---

in force before the Employment Relations Act 1999. The relevant provisions are now to be found in TULRCA 1992, sections 237 and 238. The effect of section 237 is that an employee has no right to complain of unfair dismissal if at the time of the dismissal he or she was taking part in an unofficial strike or unofficial industrial action. Action is unofficial if not authorised or endorsed by a trade union in accordance with TULRCA 1992, sections 20–22. In all other cases the matter will be determined by TULRCA 1992, section 238. The basic rule here is that the employer will be protected from a claim for unfair dismissal if he or she has dismissed all those taking part in the strike at the date of the claimant's dismissal. If the employer has selectively dismissed or subsequently selectively re-engaged striking employees, an unfair dismissal claim may be brought to be determined in accordance with the normal principles of unfair dismissal law. But before an applicant reaches that stage, the jurisdictional barrier has to be breached.

Unprotected Industrial Action

Industrial action may be unprotected for the purposes of section 238A for the following reasons. First, it may involve the commission of a tort for which there is no immunity. Secondly, the action may be outside the scope of the immunity because it is not in contemplation or furtherance of a trade dispute. Thirdly, the action may be in contemplation or furtherance of a trade dispute, but the immunity may have been withdrawn, for example because it constitutes unlawful secondary action or is unsupported by a ballot. Fourthly, the action may be wholly within the immunity, but may have extended beyond twelve weeks with the employer having taken all due steps to bring the dispute to an end, as anticipated by section 238A.

[9.49] Trade Union and Labour Relations (Consolidation) Act 1992, section 238

Dismissals in connection with other industrial action

238 (1) This section applies in relation to an employee who has a right to complain of unfair dismissal (the 'complainant') and who claims to have been unfairly dismissed, where at the date of the dismissal—
  (a) the employer was conducting or instituting a lock-out, or
  (b) the complainant was taking part in a strike or other industrial action.

(2) In such a case an employment tribunal shall not determine whether the dismissal was fair or unfair unless it is shown—
  (a) that one or more relevant employees of the same employer have not been dismissed, or
  (b) that a relevant employee has before the expiry of the period of three months beginning with the date of his dismissal been offered re-engagement and that the complainant has not been offered re-engagement.

(3) For this purpose 'relevant employees' means—
  (a) in relation to a lock-out, employees who were directly interested in the dispute in contemplation or furtherance of which the lock-out occurred, and
  (b) in relation to a strike or other industrial action, those employees at the establishment of the employer at or from which the complainant works who at the date of his dismissal were taking part in the action.
Nothing in section 237 (dismissal of those taking part in unofficial industrial action) affects the question who are relevant employees for the purposes of this section.

(4) An offer of re-engagement means an offer (made either by the original employer or by a successor of that employer or an associated employer) to re-engage an employee, either in the job which he held immediately before the date of dismissal or in a different job which would be reasonably suitable in his case.

(5) In this section 'date of dismissal' means—
  (a) where the employee's contract of employment was terminated by notice, the date on which the employer's notice was given, and
  (b) in any other case, the effective date of termination.

9.8.3.1 The scope of the employer's immunity

Section 238 in effect confers a conditional immunity on employers. The immunity is extremely wide in scope, and applies (i) regardless of whether the employer is at fault in provoking the strike (*Thompson v Eatons Ltd* [1976] ICR 336), (ii) regardless of whether the strike is caused by the unlawful or unreasonable conduct of the employer (*Wilkins v Cantrell and Cochrane (GB) Ltd* [1978] IRLR 483, and (iii) regardless of whether the conduct of the employees in taking industrial action involves a breach of contract on their part, as the following case makes clear.

[9.50] *Power Packing Casemakers Ltd v Faust* [1983] ICR 292 (CA)

During a dispute with the respondent company about wages, the appellant employees refused to work overtime. Overtime working was voluntary and in this case the company had asked employees to agree to overtime to help meet an urgent deadline. When threatened with dismissal unless they complied with the company's request, all but three of the company's employees agreed. The three who refused were dismissed. The Court of Appeal held that they had been dismissed while taking part in industrial action.

Stephenson LJ:

It was argued for the applicants that to constitute 'industrial action,' in the natural meaning of those words, on the part of an employee, there must be action in breach of his contract of employment. If he merely refuses to do something which he is not contractually bound to do, he cannot be taking part in industrial action. I would agree that if he refuses because he has a private commitment to visit a sick friend, or a personal preference for a football match, he is not taking industrial action. But that is not this case. If he refuses because he and others who refuse with him hope to extract an increase of wages out of his employers because their business will be disrupted if they do not grant it, that continued application of pressure is industrial action in the common sense of the words. I do not feel able to say any more about that argument of Mr. Jones that that is not the natural meaning of 'industrial action.' And when the words come at the end of the phrase 'taking part in a strike or other industrial action,' they seem to me to cover even more clearly a refusal used as a bargaining weapon, whether it is a breach of contract or not.

As the appeal tribunal said, this may be thought at first sight a somewhat startling result, a gift to employers which requires careful examination. Counsel agree that there is no authority on the question whether industrial action must involve a breach of contract, but that in all reported cases the industrial action considered has in fact involved a breach of contract. As I read *Secretary of State for Employment v ASLEF (No. 2)* [1972] ICR 19, that case is no exception, though the judgments of this court there suggest that what the employees did in the instant case may have constituted a breach of an implied contractual obligation such as the dissenting member of the industrial tribunal adumbrated. We were asked by Mr Carr, for the employers, to support the judgment of the appeal tribunal on that additional and alternative ground without a respondents' notice, and to hold, if necessary, as a point going to jurisdiction, that the employees' industrial action was a breach of contract. I express no opinion on that point, because I think the appeal can and should be decided on the grounds on which it was argued below.

The employer's immunity applies also where the dismissals take place while the employer was conducting a lock-out. Here however the position is much more difficult for the employer, for in order to retain immunity it is necessary to dismiss not only those locked out, but also those with a direct interest in the dispute in which the

> Even if a lock-out is repudiatory . . . employees would be ill-advised to resign in response; although they would have a wrongful dismissal claim, there is no protection against unfair dismissal for employees dismissed during a lock-out unless the employer discriminates between those 'directly interested' . . . This leaves the extraordinary situation that an employer can seek to impose new terms and conditions upon its workforce and then lock-out with relative impunity those who do not accept them (S Deakin and G S Morris, *Labour Law* (3rd edn, London, Butterworths, 2001) 949).

lock-out occurs, a potentially wide and unpredictable group of employees (see *Fisher v York Trailer Co Ltd* [1979] IRLR 385).

9.8.3.2 'Relevant employees'

A second major challenge for the courts relates to the requirement that in order to retain immunity, the employer must dismiss all the 'relevant employees' and not re-engage within three months a 'relevant employee' who has been dismissed. Section 238(3) defines a relevant employee to mean, in the case of a lock-out those employees 'who were directly interested in the dispute in contemplation or furtherance of which the lock-out occurred'; and in the case of a strike or other industrial action 'those employees at the establishment of the employer at or from which the complainant works who at the date of the dismissal were taking part in the action'. What this does not address is the point at which the relevant employee must be dismissed in order to enable the employer to retain his or her immunity. In the case of a strike relevant employees are those who are on strike at the date of dismissal: but the Act does not say that they have to be dismissed at the date of dismissal. This is an issue which gave rise to one of the issues before the Court of Appeal in the following case.

[9.51] *P&O European Ferries (Dover) Ltd v Byrne* **[1989] ICR 779 (CA)**

The respondent was one of 1,025 employees who were dismissed for taking part in a strike against the company about new working conditions which the company wished to introduce. The application for unfair dismissal was brought because the company had allegedly, and it seems inadvertently, not dismissed all the employees who had taken part in the strike. There were two issues for the Court of Appeal: one was whether the applicant was required to reveal to the employer the identity of the relevant employee who had not been dismissed; and the second was whether the employer could dismiss the employee on learning of his or her identity at this late stage and still retain his or her immunity from unfair dismissal proceedings. The Court responded to both questions in the affirmative.

Neill LJ:
It seems to me that there are two phrases which are of particular importance in [section 238(2)] words. One is 'shall not determine' and secondly 'unless it is shown.' It is to be remembered that the word 'determine' appears elsewhere in the Act, . . . and it seems to me that in the context of this Act the word 'determine,' at any rate prima facie, means 'reach a conclusion.' But without reaching a final decision on that phrase I, like May LJ, am particularly impressed by the use of the words 'unless it is shown'. It seems to me that,

except in special cases, where it may be that by some interlocutory process proof of a matter has been given before the hearing, the words 'unless it is shown' mean unless it is proved on the evidence and shown to the satisfaction of the tribunal. If that be the right construction of those words it seems to me inevitably to follow that the time at which the question of dismissal has to be considered must be immediately after the relevant evidence has been given. Accordingly I am unable to accept the argument that the crucial point in time is immediately before the hearing begins. It follows therefore that I reach the same conclusion as May LJ on the proper construction of section [238](2)(a).

The second question which falls for determination is whether the applicant should be required to give particulars at this stage. It is accepted both on his behalf and that of the other employees that particulars should be given at some point, but it is argued that they should not be given at this stage because of the possible consequences to Mr X and, more importantly, the possible consequences to the cases of the various applicants. In my judgment it is necessary and proper in this case that these particulars should be given to enable the employer to prepare for trial, even though the particulars may also have the effect that the employer will be able to take action which will in the result frustrate the claims which the employees make. That is a matter with which we have been much concerned in the course of this hearing, but in the light of the plain words of section [238](2), it seems to me that that is the inevitable result of the legislation as it is presently enacted.

May LJ (with whom Neill LJ agreed) had held that 'the material point in time is when the industrial tribunal either determines the substantive hearing which involves determining the jurisdiction point as well, or alternatively determines the jurisdiction point on a preliminary hearing prior to going on, or not going on, as the case may be, with the substantive hearing for compensation' (at p 786). The dismissal of the P&O seafarers was considered in 1988 by the ILO Freedom of Association Committee, which concluded that there had been a breach of ILO Convention 87.

9.9 Industrial disputes and the role of the state

The State has a number of different roles in regulating industrial conflict. In the first place, it must establish the boundaries of lawful conduct and determine the sanctions which may be imposed on those who step beyond these boundaries. But although it has a role in permitting such action, the State paradoxically also has a role in restraining it. Since the late nineteenth century, the State has been an active player in trade disputes, using its administrative and legislative power to prevent and resolve industrial disputes on the one hand, and to coerce workers back to work on the other. Historically there have been five strategies of intervention by the State, in addition to the measures which enable employers to take action to restrain industrial action: (i) the *ad hoc* intervention of ministers and others; (ii) the provision of statutory machinery for the prevention and resolution of disputes; (iii) intervention to allow production to continue during disputes; (iv) intervention to reduce the impact of disputes for third parties; and (v) penalising those who take part in disputes. These different strategies each has a long pedigree.

Redundancy and Other Statutory Rights

Although the amendments to the law relating to unfair dismissal are an important step forward, there are a number of other ways by which the statutory rights of employees may be affected by their participation in industrial action. The protection against the unauthorised deduction of wages does not apply to deductions made where the worker has taken part in a strike or other industrial action (Employment Rights Act 1996, section 14(5)); there is no right to a guaranteed payment in respect of a workless day 'if the failure to provide him with work for that day occurs in consequence of a strike, lock-out or other industrial action involving any employee of his employer or of an associated employer' (*ibid.,* section 29(3)); while all statutory rights which require a period of continuous employment may be undermined by the provision that a week does not count 'if during the week, or any part of the week, the employee takes part in a strike' (*ibid.,* section 216). But continuity is not broken either by a strike or a lock out (*ibid.*).

So far as redundancy is concerned, it is true that employees may not be selected for redundancy for participating in industrial action for which they are protected from dismissal. But as a result of the Employment Rights Act 1996, section 140 an employee may not be entitled to a redundancy payment if dismissed while taking part in a strike or other industrial action where the action is such that it would entitle the employer to terminate the contract of employment. The position is different where the strike (as defined—see below) takes place after the employer has issued redundancy notices. In this situation the employee may be required to extend the contract by the number of days lost to the strike as a condition of receiving full entitlement to a redundancy payment. If the employee refuses to agree, an employment tribunal may reduce the redundancy payment (Employment Rights Act 1996, section 143). An employee who is locked out by an employer cannot claim to have been constructively dismissed: section 136(2).

For the purposes of sections 140, 143 and 216 of the 1996 Act (but not the other measures referred to here) a strike is defined by section 235 to mean

(a) the cessation of work by a body of employed persons acting in combination, or
(b) a concerted refusal, or a refusal under a common understanding, of any number of employed persons to continue to work for an employer in consequence of a dispute, done as a means of compelling their employer or any employed person or body of employed persons, or to aid other employees in compelling their employer or any employed person or body of employed persons, to accept or not to accept terms or conditions of or affecting employment.

For the purposes of sections 136 and 216, lock out is defined to mean:

(a) the closing of a place of employment,
(b) the suspension of work, or
(c) the refusal by an employer to continue to employ any number of persons employed by him in consequence of a dispute, with a view to compelling persons employed by the employer, or to aid another employer in compelling persons employed by him, to accept terms or conditions of or affecting employment.

These definitions do not apply to unfair dismissal, and they are not relevant to the definition of a trade dispute in TULRCA. The position is thus very ad hoc and asymmetrical. For the purposes of unfair dismissal, there is now a definition of a strike as 'any concerted stoppage of work': TULRCA 1992, section 246.

9.9.1 Strategies of dispute resolution

The modern law relating to the intervention of the State in industrial disputes has its origins in the Conciliation Act 1896 and the Industrial Courts Act 1919. The system is based on the idea that the parties should seek to resolve their own differences in accordance with their own agreements, and that the State should assist where appropriate. But intervention by the State should not involve any compulsion, the 1896 Act based on the principle of voluntary conciliation, and the 1919 Act on the principle of voluntary arbitration by the Industrial Court. The 1896 and 1919 Acts remained in force until 1971 when they were repealed by the Industrial Relations Act 1971, the Industrial Court being replaced by the Industrial Arbitration Board. Conciliation was conducted by the Ministry of Labour and its successor departments for much of the twentieth century, and is now carried out by ACAS. Arbitration is now conducted by ACAS and by the Central Arbitration Committee (CAC) which is the direct descendant of the Industrial Court. Apart from specific jurisdictions which we have already encountered, the CAC has a general arbitral jurisdiction in trade disputes, exercisable with the consent of the parties to a dispute. It remains the case that trade disputes are more likely to be resolved by bodies such as ACAS than by the courts, and that trade unions are as likely to encounter the State in the form of ACAS as in the form of the High Court or the Court of Session.

Prohibiting Strikes

There are some workers in respect of whom it may be unlawful to organise industrial action. This is true of members of the armed forces and the police (inducing a police officer to withhold his or her services—contrary to the Police Act 1996, section 91). In each of these cases the restrictions may carry a criminal penalty. It is also an offence to delay or interfere with the transmission of a postal package, though not where done in contemplation or furtherance of a trade dispute: Postal Services Act 2000, sections 83–84. There are also, exceptionally, cases where workers have 'agreed' not to take part in industrial action. The clearest example of this is the Government Communications Headquarters civil servants whose freedom of association was restored in 1997 subject to a legally binding agreement on a no strike deal with the government. It is also provided in TULRCA, section 240, that it is a criminal offence for a person wilfully and maliciously to break his or her contract of employment knowing or having reasonable cause to believe that the probable consequence will be to endanger human life or cause serious bodily injury, or expose valuable property to destruction or serious injury. There is no known example of this measure (which has its origins in the Conspiracy and Protection of Property Act 1875) being used in recent times, though there are suggestions that its use was contemplated by the Attorney General to restrain by injunction industrial action by firefighters during their national pay dispute in 2002–2003. The existence of TULRCA section 240 has also been relied on by the government when called upon to justify the Civil Contingencies Act 2004, s 23(3)(b) (on which see p 965 below).

9.9.1.1 Conciliation

[9.52] Trade Union and Labour Relations (Consolidation) Act 1992, section 210

Conciliation

210 (1) Where a trade dispute exists or is apprehended ACAS may, at the request of one or more parties to the dispute or otherwise, offer the parties to the dispute its assistance with a view to bringing about a settlement.

(2) The assistance may be by way of conciliation or by other means, and may include the appointment of a person other than an officer or servant of ACAS to offer assistance to the parties to the dispute with a view to bringing about a settlement.

(3) In exercising its functions under this section ACAS shall have regard to the desirability of encouraging the parties to a dispute to use any appropriate agreed procedures for negotiation or the settlement of disputes.

It will be noted in subsection (1) that ACAS may take the initiative to intervene in disputes. It may also be noted that the definition of a trade dispute for the purposes of section 210 is based on the 1974 definition which has not been amended in the same way that the definition for the purposes of trade union immunity in tort has been amended. So the machinery for conciliation applies to trade disputes in relation to which there is no immunity: see TULRCA 1992, section 218, though in practice most disputes in which ACAS is involved are likely to fall within the trade dispute immunity definition. This means, for example, that the powers of ACAS apply to disputes between employers and workers and between workers and workers, rather than solely between employers and their own workers. It also means that a dispute need only be connected with rather than relate wholly or mainly to one or more of the statutory matters. The power to intervene in disputes relating to matters overseas is also wider than the power of the union to take action in relation to such matters without fear of liability. Some indication of how these powers are used is provided by ACAS in its Annual Reports.

[9.53] ACAS, *Annual Report 2003–04*

Collective conciliation is a process by which Acas helps employers, workers and their representatives, through further negotiations, to reach their own solutions to difficulties. This has traditionally been the main way we help the parties to resolve workplace disputes.

As the conciliation process is confidential, it is not usually revealed to those outside it, and has perhaps to some extent become shrouded in mystery. However our conciliators do not have a 'magic wand' with which to resolve disputes and the only powers they have are those of reason and persuasion. This is a voluntary process, and parties decide to use it because they want experienced 'third party' assistance to help them find a solution to the situation they find themselves in, which is usually one of deadlock. Acas conciliators use a variety of techniques—including both joint and separate discussions with the parties—to establish the issues, explore possible solutions, build trust, re-establish relationships and, hopefully, establish sufficient common ground to settle, or at least progress, the matter in dispute. . . .

. . . In terms of outcomes, although a full settlement is the ultimate objective, we still regard it as progress if we improve the situation to the extent that the parties are willing to return to direct talks. At the end of the day we aim to leave the parties in the best shape to carry on a continuing dialogue on their own.

Between April 2003 and March 2004, there were 1,245 workplace disputes in which Acas helped the parties find a solution to their differences. We were successful in helping to either resolve matters, or make progress towards this, in the overwhelming majority (92 per cent).

9.9.1.2 Arbitration and other functions

[9.54] Trade Union and Labour Relations (Consolidation) Act 1992, section 212

Arbitration

212 (1) Where a trade dispute exists or is apprehended ACAS may, at the request of one or more of the parties to the dispute and with the consent of all the parties to the dispute, refer all or any of the matters to which the dispute relates for settlement to the arbitration of—

(a) one or more persons appointed by ACAS for that purpose (not being officers or employees of ACAS), or

(b) the Central Arbitration Committee.

(2) In exercising its functions under this section ACAS shall consider the likelihood of the dispute being settled by conciliation.

(3) Where there exist appropriate agreed procedures for negotiation or the settlement of disputes, ACAS shall not refer a matter for settlement to arbitration under this section unless—

(a) those procedures have been used and have failed to result in a settlement, or

(b) there is, in ACAS's opinion, a special reason which justifies arbitration under this section as an alternative to those procedures.

(4) Where a matter is referred to arbitration under subsection (1)(a)—

(a) if more than one arbitrator is appointed, ACAS shall appoint one of them to act as chairman; and

(b) the award may be published if ACAS so decides and all the parties consent.

(5) Part I of the Arbitration Act 1996 (general provisions as to arbitration) does not apply to an arbitration under this section.

The definition of a trade dispute for the purposes of section 212 is also to be found in section 218, so that the definition for the purposes of conciliation and arbitration is the same. In addition to its conciliation and arbitration functions, ACAS is empowered to give advice to employers, workers and trade unions on a wide range of industrial relations matters (including procedures for avoiding and settling disputes) (TULRCA 1992, section 213). It may also—if it 'thinks fit'—'inquire into any question relating to industrial relations generally or to industrial relations in any particular industry or in any particular undertaking or part of an undertaking' (section 214). The 1992 Act also formally empowers the Secretary of State, 'where a trade dispute exists or is apprehended', to inquire into the causes and circumstances of the dispute, and if he thinks fit appoint a court of inquiry (section 215). Some of these powers are now used either infrequently or not as frequently as in the past. There has been no Court of Inquiry since 1977, and there is much less arbitration being conducted by the CAC than by its predecessor bodies. It is not altogether clear why this should be so, though it is possible to speculate on some of the more obvious explanations. First there are fewer trade union members and fewer trade disputes today than at any time since the Second World War. Another explanation is that at the political level the State has chosen to intervene in the industrial relations arena by the use of different tools, based on techniques of legal restraint and coercion. New powers for employers to have action stopped may have replaced other forms of dispute resolution.

[9.55] ACAS, *Annual Report 2003–04*

Acas continues to play an active role in resolving disputes through arbitration where parties are unable to agree on a resolution through conciliation.

The receipt of 69 cases, though lower that that in 2002/03, still represents a higher than average caseload compared to that of recent years.

Cases received come from business of all sizes and from a range of industries, from relatively small voluntary operations to national public and private companies. Notably, in the past year, Acas arbitration and mediation has been used effectively with the Metropolitan Police Service, Her Majesty's Prison Service and Transport for London, demonstrating Acas' continuing commitment and credibility in helping employers, unions and employees, to resolve employment relations issues in a constructive and effective way.

9.9.2 Strategies of coercion

Coercion is a strong and emotive word. It is used here to mean strategies adopted by public authorities to minimise the impact of a strike and to penalise those who take part. In this sense coercive strategies are both strategies which impact on the strikers incidentally as well as those targeted specifically at the strikers. So coercion may arise in different ways, but at base strategies of coercion are those activities of the State which are designed to persuade people back to work by actively undermining the impact of the dispute and by reducing the likelihood of a successful outcome for the strikers. Coercive strategies may be justifiable as reconciling the interests of employers, employees and others. Here we concentrate on two techniques of coercion, some of which can also be traced back to the early years of the twentieth century. But we should not overlook the fact that the most coercive strategy of recent years has been to restore the tortious liability for industrial action. The issues addressed in this section are: (i) intervention to allow production to continue during the dispute and to reduce the impact of the dispute for third parties on the one hand; and (ii) more overtly coercive devices designed to penalise those who take part in the dispute, as well as their families on the other.

9.9.2.1 Continuity of production and protection of the public

One form of intervention under this heading is to ensure that those who want to work during a strike are not prevented from doing so. This now takes two forms. The first is the removal of any possible liabilities from those who do work. So a member of a trade union who is unhappy with the call to arms is free to resign from the union without any threat to his or her job. As we saw in chapter 8, it is now unfair to dismiss someone because he or she is not a member of a trade union. A trade union or trade union official may be liable to pay some of the compensation if found to have put pressure on the employer to dismiss the individual in question. As we also saw in chapter 7, a member of a trade union who works during a strike may not be disciplined or expelled by the union for doing so. This prohibition applies even where the strike has been supported by a ballot in which the individual may have participated, despite the fact that the individual may be acting in breach of a contractual obligation to the union in behaving in this way, and despite the fact that intervention of this kind is contrary to ILO Convention 87 on Freedom of Association and the Right to Organise, as well as the Council of Europe's Social Charter of 18 October 1961.

A second form of intervention, to ensure that those who want to work during a dispute are not prevented from doing so, relates to the coordinated use of the police where necessary to ensure that workplaces are kept open, to allow access not only by workers but also by suppliers and customers. This is an issue which becomes particularly important in the context of large national disputes of a kind which have not really been seen since the miners' strike in 1984–5 when the police adopted a number of strategies to 'preserve both order and freedom of access to and from the premises picketed' (P Wallington, 'Policing the Miners' Strike' (1985) 14 *Industrial Law Journal* 145 at p 153). These strategies were said to include not only 'tactics of containment and if necessary dispersal of pickets to preserve order and access', but also the 'extensive use' of the police's 'common law preventive powers to keep pickets and their supporters away from potential troublespots'. So far as the former is concerned:

> At the pit gates, 'official' pickets were almost universally allowed by the police, though six was the maximum and in many instances the police insisted on fewer, sometimes only two. . . . Where more than the officially permitted pickets were present, it was almost universal police practice to separate the others, whom they generally classified as 'demonstrators', and to require them to stand away from the official pickets, but in some cases it was some distance away, even out of site of the colliery gates. Generally the demonstrators would be separated from the road by a police cordon, sometimes completely surrounded. The way that these groups of demonstrators were dealt with by the police also varied considerably. Striking miners in some areas complained of being routinely hemmed in or herded around, and being subjected to arbitrary police definitions of legal and illegal space. [P. Wallington, 'Policing the Miners' Strike' (1985) 14 *Industrial Law Journal* 145 at p 153].

So far as the latter strategy (keeping miners away from picket lines) is concerned, this was done mainly by the use of roadblocks which were placed on access roads to Nottinghamshire (as in *Moss v McLachlan* [1985] IRLR 76) to stop potential pickets entering the county, and at the Dartford Tunnel to stop striking Kent miners leaving the county to travel to picket lines in the north of England. Following the decision in

Moss v McLachlan, the former roadblocks were a justified use of the police preventive power, but it is seriously open to question whether the same could be said of the latter. According to Wallington, no fewer than 164,508 'presumed pickets' were turned back during the first 27 weeks of the strike in Nottinghamshire alone. He continues at p 153 (footnotes omitted):

> The use of roadblocks as such was not tested in law during the dispute, apart from an unsuccessful application for an interim injunction over the Dartford Tunnel incident which was not subsequently pursued to trial. The legal authority for setting up roadblocks is obscure, resting largely on police officers' powers to stop vehicles under the Road Traffic Act 1972. Whether these powers legalise the systematic stopping of all vehicles travelling on a particular road is open to question, and has never been directly decided. From January 1, 1986 explicit statutory powers were available under section 4 of the Police and Criminal Evidence Act 1984; 'road checks' are permissible on the authority of a superintendent, *inter alia* to establish whether vehicles contain persons intent on committing a serious arrestable offence. This appears to involve a narrower criterion than was used in Nottinghamshire, where cars were checked to see whether anyone was travelling to picket—even the sternest critic of picket line violence could hardly assert that that *necessarily* manifested an intent to commit a serious arrestable offence. However in practice it is highly unlikely that the police would regard section 4 as preventing the use of roadblocks in this way, and indeed experience during the strike appears to have convinced many senior officers of their value in averting disorder.

But the State intervenes not only to protect access to the workplace and with it the continuity of production. Also important are the steps taken to prevent the disruption in the supply of goods and services to the public. The police intervene not only to assist the employer, and to assist employees who may wish to work through the dispute, but also to assist suppliers and customers of the employer in dispute, and generally to assist the public as consumers, particularly as consumers of essential services. Formal powers for dealing with the consequences of disputes were introduced by the Emergency Powers Act 1920. This legislation was passed in the aftermath of the First World War to deal with the consequences of large-scale industrial action organised on a national basis by coal miners and transport workers in particular. Current emergency powers are now to be found in the Civil Contingencies Act 2004, which applies to a much wider range of potential emergencies than those anticipated in 1920. However, modern governments have learned to live without invoking emergency powers, and indeed the Emergency Powers Act 1920 had not been used since 1973. The fact that it was not necessary to declare a state of emergency during the miners' strike of 1984–5 or the national fire strike in 2002–2003 is an indication perhaps that emergency powers are now largely redundant in the context of industrial action, even if the 1920 Act has been invoked on 12 occasions in total. Should such powers ever be invoked, the Civil Contingencies Act 2004 provides that emergency regulations may not 'prohibit or enable the prohibition of participation in, or any activity in connection with, a strike or other industrial action' (s 23(3)(b)). The government also has the power to use troops for 'urgent work of national importance' (Emergency Powers Act 1964) without the need to make emergency regulations. This is a power which has been used during strikes, and is now perhaps more significant than formal emergency powers such as those now contained in the Civil Contingencies Act 2004.

Actions by Third Parties: Commissioner for Protection Against Unlawful Industrial Action

The TULRCA 1992, section 235A (as introduced by the Trade Union Reform and Employment Rights Act 1993) provides that a member of the public may apply to the High Court or Court of Session for an order to restrain unlawful industrial action which disrupts the supply of goods or services to the individual making the claim. The application may be made even though the applicant has no right to be supplied with the goods and services and even though he or she is not otherwise able to sue in tort. Before 1999 the applicant could apply for assistance in bringing the proceedings to the Commissioner for Protection Against Unlawful Industrial Action. The offices of the Commissioner were not heavily used: only two applications were made in 1998, both of which were withdrawn. The office was abolished, unlamented, by the Employment Relations Act 1999. The right of third party action has been retained: see *P v NASUWT* [2003] ICR 386 (HL). Should Mr Falconer be inconvenienced by a train strike again (p. 878 above), he could rely on section 235A rather than on the tort alleged to have been committed against him, which remains of uncertain scope. Proceedings may be brought under section 235A in respect of conduct which is actionable in tort 'by any one or more persons', even though the conduct is not independently actionable by the applicant. Section 235A thus allows a plaintiff to sue on someone else's tort.

9.9.2.2 Penalising strikers and their families

The most obvious example of overtly coercive tactics is the withholding of social security benefits from those who take part in a strike. Those who take part in industrial action or who are directly interested in a dispute are disqualified from both jobseekers' allowance and income support. Jobseekers allowance is both

- a contribution based benefit for unemployed claimants for up to 26 weeks who have paid sufficient national insurance contributions, and
- a means tested benefit for those who have not sufficient contributions, or who have been claiming for more than 26 weeks.

In both cases a claimant will be disqualified for benefit if he or she falls within the scope of the trade dispute disqualification.

[9.56] Jobseekers Act 1995, section 14

Trade Disputes

14 (1) Where
   (a) there is a stoppage of work which causes a person not to be employed on any day, and
   (b) the stoppage is due to a trade dispute at his place of work,
   that person is not entitled to a jobseeker's allowance for the week which includes that day unless he proves that he is not directly interested in the dispute.

(2) A person who withdraws his labour on any day in furtherance of a trade dispute, but

to whom subsection (1) does not apply, is not entitled to a jobseeker's allowance for the week which includes that day.

(3) If a person who is prevented by subsection (1) from being entitled to a jobseeker's allowance proves that during the stoppage—
(a) he became bona fide employed elsewhere;
(b) his employment was terminated by reason of redundancy within the meaning of section 139(1) of the Employment Rights Act 1996, or
(c) he bona fide resumed employment with his employer but subsequently left for a reason other than the trade dispute, subsection (1) shall be taken to have ceased to apply to him on the occurrence of the event referred to in paragraph (a), (b) or (as the case may be) the first event referred to in paragraph (c).

(4) In this section 'place of work', in relation to any person, means the premises or place at which he was employed.

(5) Where separate branches of work which are commonly carried on as separate businesses in separate premises or at separate places are in any case carried on in separate departments on the same premises or at the same place, each of those departments shall, for the purposes of subsection (4), be deemed to be separate premises or (as the case may be) a separate place.

A trade dispute for this purpose is widely defined, and is different from the definitions in TULRCA 1992. By virtue of section 35 of the Jobseekers Act 1995, a trade dispute is defined to mean 'any dispute between employers and employees, or between employees and employees, which is connected with the employment or non-employment or the terms of employment or the conditions of employment of any persons, whether employees in the employment of the employer with whom the dispute arises, or not'. This is based on the definition in place when the trade dispute disqualification was first introduced for unemployment benefit in the National Insurance Act 1911, which in turn was based on the definition of a trade dispute in the Trade Disputes Act 1906. It had been the practice to use the same definition in relation to both the trade dispute immunity and the trade dispute disqualification.

When first introduced, the trade dispute disqualification from unemployment benefit was much wider than it is now. Apart from disqualification on the ground of participation and direct interest in a trade dispute, a claimant would be disqualified also if he or she was financing the dispute, or a member of a grade or class of workers who were participating in, financing or directly interested in the dispute. Although the scope of the disqualification has been narrowed—particularly as a result of changes introduced by the Employment Protection Act 1975—it remains extremely far-reaching. It applies regardless of the merits of the dispute, and regardless of whether the claimant is on strike or locked out: it makes no difference that the dispute was caused by an employer's attempts to reduce pay or diminish working conditions, or that the strike or industrial action is lawful. The disqualification applies even though the claimant is not taking part but has a direct interest in the dispute, and even though the claimant has no control over the circumstances of the lay-off and regardless of the nature of the interest: the claimant may be opposed to the action and may be prejudiced by its outcome, yet still be disqualified for having a direct interest. And it applies for as long as the dispute lasts: unlike other disqualifications (such as dismissal for misconduct or refusing to accept the offer of employment) the disqualification does not come to an end after a fixed period (which now admittedly may be as long as 26 weeks, though it was once a maximum of six weeks). It is not surprising that the trade dispute disqualification should have given rise to a considerable volume of litigation before what is now the Social Security Commissioner. A number of these cases have been appealed to the higher courts, including the following, which is concerned with the contentious question of what constitutes a direct interest in someone else's dispute to justify disqualification.

[9.57] *Presho v Department of Health and Social Security* [1984] AC 310 (HL)

The claimant in this case was employed as a production worker in a food factory. She was a member of USDAW. A number of engineering workers at the same factory who were members of the AUEW had lodged a pay claim which had been rejected by the employer. Engineering work came to a standstill and the production workers were laid off because their machines were not maintained. The appellant applied for unemployment benefit but was refused because of the trade dispute disqualification, then to be found in the Social Security Act 1975, section 19. The insurance officer held that she was disqualified because she was directly interested in the dispute following the prevailing custom and practice at the factory whereby the outcome of the dispute with the AUEW would be applied automatically to all other workers by the employer. The decision was upheld by the local tribunal and by the Social Security Commissioner following appeals by the claimant. The Court of Appeal reversed, and the insurance officer appealed to the House of Lords which overturned the Court of Appeal and reinstated the decision of the insurance officer.

Lord Brandon:
In my view, the expression 'directly interested in the trade dispute', as used in s 19(1) of the Social Security Act 1975 as amended, must be given its ordinary and natural meaning in the context in which it occurs. That context is that of situations arising out of industrial relations, including among other possible situations that of a trade dispute causing a stoppage of work at some factory or other place of work, at which different groups of workers, belonging to different trade unions, are employed by the same employers.

Approaching the question in that way it seems to me impossible to say that a person can only be directly interested in a trade dispute if it is his own pay or conditions of work which form the subject matter of the dispute. Nor can I accept the distinction which was sought to be drawn between a person being interested in a trade dispute and his being interested in the outcome of a trade dispute. The two concepts appear to me, in the relevant context, necessarily to overlap, and indeed to amount to very much the same thing.

I would accept as a correct statement of the relevant law the exception to the broad proposition of counsel for the claimant which he felt obliged to concede, and which he said was applicable in what he metaphorically described as a 'coat-tails' situation. To put the matter more fully, I would hold that, where different groups of workers, belonging to different unions, are employed by the same employers at the same place of work and there is a trade dispute between the common employers and one of the unions to which one of the groups of workers belong, those in the other groups of workers belonging to other unions are directly, and not merely indirectly, interested in that trade dispute provided that two conditions are fulfilled. The first condition is that, whatever may be the outcome of the trade dispute, it will be applied by the common employers not only to the group of workers belonging to the one union participating in the dispute, but also to the other groups of workers belonging to the other unions concerned. The second condition is that this application of the outcome of the dispute 'across the board', as it has been aptly described, should come about automatically as a result of one or other of three things: first, a collective agreement which is legally binding; or, second, a collective agreement which is not legally binding; or, third, established industrial custom and practice at the place of work concerned.

My Lords, it is, in my opinion, a pure question of fact whether, in any particular case, the two conditions to which I have just referred are satisfied or not. It is, moreover, a question of fact of a kind which insurance officers, local tribunals and the commissioner are, by reason of their wide knowledge and experience of matters pertaining to industrial relations, exceptionally well qualified to answer. In the present case the commissioner found as a fact that these two conditions were satisfied, in that the employers would, by reason of the factual situation at the factory, by which he clearly meant the established industrial custom and practice there, apply automatically the outcome of their dispute with the AUEW to other groups of workers belonging to other unions at the same factory, including the group of workers belonging to the USDAW, of which the claimant was one. It was not, and could not with any chance of success have been, contended that there was no or insufficient evidence to support that finding of fact by the commissioner. Indeed, having read the notes of the evidence given before the local tribunal, I consider that any finding the other way would have been perverse.

It is not only jobseekers' allowance which is denied to those involved or directly interested in a trade dispute. So too is income support, the social security benefit paid to those in need who do not qualify for other benefits. Income support replaced supplementary benefit in 1988, which was introduced in 1966 to replace national assistance, which had been introduced in 1948 to replace the poor law. The present law relating to the relief of strikers can be traced back to the poor law and to a seminal decision of the Court of Appeal in *Attorney General v Merthyr Tydfil Union* [1900] 1 Ch 516, though in some respects the poor law was more generous than contemporary legislation. It was held by the Court of Appeal that the poor law authorities could not administer outdoor relief to strikers, subject to exceptional circumstances; relief could, however, be provided for the families of the strikers. This basic principle was carried forward to national assistance, supplementary benefit and now income support, the position now being governed by the Social Security Contributions and Benefits Act 1992. The basic rule until 1980 was that benefit would not be paid to meet the needs of the striker, but would be paid to meet the needs of any dependant family members. But since 1980 the amount payable to family members has been greatly reduced, following changes which were introduced in the wake of a political debate about the extent to which the State was subsidising strikers.

By virtue of the Social Security Contributions and Benefits Act 1992, section 126 a person is not entitled to income support if he or she is prevented from being entitled to a jobseekers' allowance because of the trade dispute disqualification. But the family of the striker may be eligible if they otherwise qualify for benefit, though here there are special rules which apply to limit the entitlement of family members. In the first place, all income received is taken into account in assessing the family's needs, and there is no disregard for small sums which may be made in the case of other claimants. Secondly, section 126 also includes a number of the changes introduced by the Social Security (No 2) Act 1980. An index-linked sum (£30 a week in 2005) is deducted from the income support otherwise payable, this being a sum of money

---

Social Security and Friction Dynamics

In the course of a trade dispute it is likely that some strikers and strikers' families will not receive any social security benefits. This will be the case where the striker is single or where the partner of the striker is in employment. In these cases the striker and the family will be dependent on union strike pay (which a union will be unable to continue indefinitely and which will not begin to meet lost wages), or charity. In the Friction Dynamics dispute referred to above, each striker received just £47 a week from the union—'enough to support a 55-year-old man with a working wife, savings and a small mortgage, perhaps, but not a younger man with a family'. As a result some of the strikers chose to look for work elsewhere: *The Mirror*, 12 August 2003

---

which is assumed to be paid to the striker and his or her family by the trade union. The deduction is made whether or not the claimant is a member of a trade union, whether or not the trade union pays strike pay, and whether or not the union is able to pay strike pay. Changes introduced in 1980 also provide that income tax rebates are to be deducted from any income support otherwise payable, though following changes to tax law introduced in 1981 it should be only in exceptional circumstances that such rebates are made. Tax rebates are not to be paid to anyone who is disqualified from jobseekers' allowance because of the trade dispute disqualification. This is another example of how the person engaged in a trade dispute (whether a strike or a lock-out, and regardless of how caused) is treated less favourably than other citizens, whether in terms of benefits or tax.

9.10 Conclusion

The law relating to industrial action in Britain has become extremely complex. It is unclear at the time of writing whether the current arrangements can be seen as a final settlement of an issue which has been a political battleground for at least a generation. But it is also true that the law relating to industrial action should not be the focus of any system of labour law. One of the goals of labour law as a discipline must be to create a framework of rights for both workers and trade unions which reduce the area of conflict with employers, and which encourages the parties to resolve their differences by peaceful means. It is surely a symptom of political failure (at a number of different levels) that workers are required to rely on industrial muscle alone as an instrument of social progress, and that they are required to rely on such muscle to retain the progress they make. But, as Laski points out in the extract reproduced at the beginning of this chapter, in a free enterprise economy in which employers and trade unions are ultimately serving different interests (owners and workers respectively), strikes and other forms of industrial action are inevitable if workers are not to be wholly submissive. All the more so when the legal system ultimately fails to provide effective means to prevent an employer from unilaterally changing working conditions.

The provisions considered in this chapter provide an unstable basis for what has been recognised judicially as a fundamental human right. In considering how the right to strike should be protected in a free society, there are a number of issues which need to be considered. The first of these is the form in which the law is cast. In Britain the approach has been one of immunity from common law liabilities. But is this a rational or an effective method of proceeding? Are there different forms in which the freedom to strike may be clothed? This is the issue considered in the following extract.

[9.58] K D Ewing (ed), *Working Life: A New Perspective on Labour Law* (London, Lawrence & Wishart, 1996)

8.26 Historically the freedom to strike has been protected in British law by a series of immunities from common law liabilities. This method of protection suffers, however, from a number of drawbacks and it is arguably of questionable effect. Most obviously, an immunity can only offer protection from liabilities which are known to exist at the time the legislation is passed. Yet the common law is not static, with the result that the immunities, and consequently the freedom to strike, can be seriously impaired by the emergence of new heads of liability. The immunities in the 1906 Act were undermined in 1964 by the discovery by the House of Lords of a new tort of intimidation, while the immunities in the 1974 Act were threatened by the principle of liability for procuring breach of a statutory duty, a matter of particular concern to trade unions in the public sector. There is a need for a response which is proactive rather than reactive, an approach which will seek to stop fresh controls being imposed by the common law, rather than one which simply invites such controls.

8.27 The alternative to an immunities-based protection for the freedom to strike is a rights-based approach, possibly in conjunction with an immunity, as was adopted in Australia in 1993. It is sometimes suggested by text book writers and others, however, that the way in which the freedom to strike is protected, whether by an immunity or a right, is merely a question of form. We believe this to be mistaken and to be based on a misapprehension. It is true that the right is as likely as an immunity to be undermined by a narrow interpretation by the courts. But the problem with the immunities is that they were subject to attack on two fronts: first by the emergence of new torts unprotected by the immunity and secondly by the misinterpretation of the immunity itself. The benefit of a properly drafted right is that it would overcome the first problem, clearly a benefit of substance even if the second problem remained untouched. We believe, however, that the form in which the law is drafted is relevant to the approach of the courts to its interpretation, also a matter of substance.

8.28 One of the points made time and again by the judges who indulged (gorged?) themselves in an orgy of destruction of the immunities was precisely that their action was justified because of the form of the protection adopted by Parliament. As Lord Denning pointed out by way of justification in *Express Newspapers Ltd v MacShane* [1979] ICR 210, 'Parliament granted immunities to the leaders of trade unions, it did not give them any rights'. The language of immunity thus invites a restrictive interpretation of its terms, which would not be true of a legal protection cast in the language of rights. Although it is perfectly possible that the judges would still misinterpret the legislation and misread Parliament's intention, the responsibility of the legislator is to make it more difficult for the courts to do so, and part of that process concerns the choice of means used to achieve

Parliament's goal. To the extent that the legal form may have a bearing on the integrity of the freedom, it is thus self evidently and unequivocally a matter of substance which it would be extraordinary to deny.

8.29 It is not suggested that a rights-based approach will avoid altogether the difficulties which have been encountered by the immunities, but it is likely that it would help to minimise these difficulties. It would not be possible for the courts to develop new heads of liability to circumvent the legislation: the right to strike would trump all common law liabilities whether already established or newly created. These and other considerations lead us to the firm view that the freedom to strike should be protected by a 'rights-based' system rather than one based wholly on immunities. We would also, however, propose the abolition of the principal torts by statute. These have been developed to deal specifically with trade unions, though they do have an application beyond labour law. However, the occasional reliance on these torts outside the labour law context is no justification for their retention. If the torts serve a useful purpose in other areas of the law, it would always be possible for Parliament to reintroduce the principles they embrace, but restrict their application to clearly identifiable areas of commercial or other activity.

8.30 The question arises whether it is necessary to define in legislation the meaning of the terms 'strike' or 'industrial action' for this purpose. There are examples of at least the first of these terms being defined in legislation, with the Trade Union and Labour Relations (Consolidation) Act 1992, providing in section 246 a wide definition for the purposes of that Act, a strike being defined to mean 'any concerted stoppage of work'. There are on the other hand examples of both these terms being used for other legislative purposes without the need apparently for either to be defined. The most obvious example of this is the legislation to deny jurisdiction to the industrial tribunals in the case of dismissals on the ground of participation in a strike or other industrial action, which until 1992 operated without a definition of either a strike or industrial action. Although the position is finely balanced we incline to the view that it is unnecessary in legislation to define what is meant by a strike or industrial action, which would serve only to encourage litigation on technical questions of statutory interpretation.

8.31 We are therefore proposing a new conceptual framework for the protection of the right to strike. It is no longer appropriate that the starting point of the law relating to industrial action should be based on a common law framework developed in a pre-democratic age. It is singularly appropriate that the legacy of the nineteenth century should be removed and that a fresh start should be made. It is therefore proposed that workers should have a right to strike and to engage in other forms of industrial action recognised and protected by law, within defined limits if appropriate. Those who exercise this right should not be regarded as having acted in breach of the employment relationship; they should be protected from dismissal; and those who organise industrial action should not be liable to the employer in tort or on any other ground.

Moving from form to substance, the second issue for consideration relates to the content of the right to strike. In what circumstances should the right to strike be protected by law? As paragraph 8.31 from the immediately foregoing extract suggests, there is a strong case for arguing that the right should apply to protect the trade union, the trade union official and the worker. All should enjoy equal protection when exercising a legally protected right which in the interests of effectiveness ought to be symmetrical in application. But this does not resolve our problem about the content of the right to strike. This is a matter on which views will differ widely, and on which there is no political consensus. But the basic minimum content of the right should be that set down by the supervisory bodies of the ILO and the Council of Europe. It has already been pointed out above that the right to strike is not formally protected by any ILO instrument, but it is protected by implication by ILO Convention 87 (The Freedom of Association and Protection of the Right to Organise Convention, 1948). In contrast, the right to strike is formally protected by the UN Covenant on Economic, Social and Cultural Rights (see below), the Council of Europe's Social Charter of 18 October 1961 and the Revised Social Charter of 3 May 1996. (It is now also formally recognised in the EU Charter of Fundamental Rights: see chapter 2 above.) We have also already encountered the fact that British law was in breach of both ILO and Council of Europe standards to the extent that it did not provide an opportunity for workers dismissed during a strike or other industrial action to bring proceedings for unfair dismissal. But both the ILO Committee of Experts and the Council of Europe's Social Rights Committee have found violations on other grounds as well. The following extract deals with the first main findings on the matter by the former. These have been repeated at regular intervals since, though successive British governments have paid little attention.

[9.59] ILO, International Labour Conference, 77th Session, 1989, *Report of the Committee of Experts on the Application of Conventions and Recommendations,* **Report III (Part 1A)**

The Committee has always considered that the right to strike is one of the essential means available to workers and their organisations for the promotion and protection of their economic and social interests as guaranteed by Articles 3, 8 and 10 of the Convention. It has also taken the view that restrictions relating to the objectives of a strike and to the methods used should be sufficiently reasonable as not to result in practice in an excessive limitation of the exercise of the right to strike.

The Committee notes that the common law renders virtually all forms of strikes or other industrial action unlawful as a matter of civil law. This means that workers and unions who engage in such action are liable to be sued for damages by employers (or other parties) who suffer loss as a consequence and (more importantly in practical terms) may be restrained from committing unlawful acts by means of injunctions (issued on both an interlocutory and a permanent basis). It appears to the Committee that unrestricted access to such remedies would deny workers the right to take strike or other industrial action in order to protect and to promote their economic and social interests.

It is most important, therefore, that workers and unions should have some measure of protection against civil liability. There has been legislative recognition of this imperative since 1906 in the form of a series of 'immunities' (or, more accurately, 'protections') against tort action for trade unions and their members and officials. The current version of the 'immunities' is to be found in the Trade Union and Labour Relations Act 1974 [now TULRCA 1992].

The scope of these protections has been narrowed in a number of respects since 1980. . . .

Taken together, these changes appear to make it virtually impossible for workers and unions lawfully to engage in any form of boycott activity, or 'sympathetic' action against parties not directly involved in a given dispute. The Committee has never expressed any decided view on the use of boycotts as an exercise of the right to strike. However, it appears to the Committee that where a boycott relates directly to the social and economic interests of the workers involved in either or both of the original dispute and the secondary action, and where the original dispute and the secondary action are not unlawful in themselves, then that boycott should be regarded as a legitimate exercise of the right to strike. This is clearly consistent with the approach the Committee has adopted in relation to 'sympathy strikes':

> It would appear that more frequent recourse is being had to this form of action [ie sympathy strikes] because of the structure or the concentration of industries or the distribution of work centres in different regions of the world. The Committee considers that a general prohibition of sympathy strikes could lead to abuse and that workers should be able to take such action provided the initial strike they are supporting is itself lawful. [General Survey by the Committee of Experts on the Application of Conventions and Recommendations (Geneva, 1983), paragraph 217].

Other changes to the definition of 'trade dispute' in the 1974 Act [now TULRCA 1992] also appear to impose excessive limitations upon the exercise of the right to strike: (i) the definition now requires that the subject-matter of a dispute must relate 'wholly or mainly' to one or more of the matters set out in the definition—formerly it was sufficient that there be a 'connection' between the dispute and the specified matters. This change appears to deny protection to disputes where unions and their members have 'mixed' motives (for example, where they are pursuing both 'industrial' and 'political' or 'social' objectives). The Committee also considers that it would often be very difficult for unions to determine in advance whether any given course of conduct would, or would not, be regarded as having the necessary relation to the protected purposes; (ii) the fact that the definition now refers only to disputes between workers and 'their' employer could make it impossible for unions to take effective action in situations where the 'real' employer with whom they were in dispute was able to take refuge behind one or more subsidiary companies who were technically the 'employer' of the workers concerned, but who lacked the capacity to take decisions which are capable of satisfactorily resolving the dispute; and (iii) disputes relating to matters outside the United Kingdom can now be protected only where the persons whose actions in the United Kingdom are said to be in contemplation or furtherance of a trade dispute relating to matters occurring outside the United Kingdom are likely to be affected in respect of one or more of the protected matters by the outcome of the dispute. This means that there would be no protection for industrial action which was intended to protect or to improve the terms and conditions of employment of workers outside the United Kingdom, or to register disapproval of the social or racial policies of a government with whom the United Kingdom has trading or economic links. The Committee has consistently taken the view that strikes that are purely political in character do not fall within the scope of the principles of freedom of association. However, it also considers that trade unions ought to have the possibility of recourse to protest strikes, in particular where aimed at criticising a government's economic and social policies [General Survey, paragraph 216]. The revised definition of 'trade dispute' appears to deny workers that right.

The Committee considers that the overall effect of legislative change in this area since 1980 is to withdraw protection from strikes and other forms of industrial action in circumstances where such action ought to be permissible in order to enable workers and their unions adequately to protect and to promote their economic and social interests, and to organise their activities [General Survey, paragraphs 200 and 226]. Accordingly, it would ask the government to introduce amendments which enable workers to take industrial action against their 'real' employer and which accord adequate protection of the right to engage in other legitimate forms of industrial action such as protest strikes and sympathy strikes, as guaranteed by Articles 3, 8 and 10 of the Convention.

[*Note: Article 8 provides so far as relevant that national law should not be such as to impair the guarantees provided in the Convention; and Article 10 defines the term 'organisation' which appears in Article 3 to mean any organisation of workers for furthering and defending the interests of workers.*]

Although much thus needs to be done to bring British law into line with international standards, it does not follow that international law requires that there should be an unlimited right to strike. The Observations of the Committee of Experts suggest the need to expand the definition of a trade dispute and to permit some but not necessarily all forms of secondary action. It is also the case that the ILO Committee of Experts has accepted on other occasions that restrictions on strike action may be imposed by collective agreements to which the parties may be bound, and that mandatory pre-strike ballots do not violate freedom of association principles. But there is no political support for legally binding procedure agreements in Britain, while on the other hand the difficulties associated with the complexity of the current balloting obligations and the legal costs to the unions in their operation suggest that it may be appropriate to have the matter raised again in an international forum. The ILO Committee of Experts concluded the strike balloting provisions were not in breach of Convention 87 shortly after the enactment of the Trade Union Act 1984, before the additional cumbersome provisions were added subsequently. Whatever happens in the future, there is surely a case for encouraging the positive role of the State as reflected in the conciliation and other work of ACAS. There is also a case for reviewing the circumstances in which social security benefits are withheld: the need to keep the social security authorities away from adjudicating on the merits of industrial disputes does not justify the current rules which punish both strikers and their families. But the first step is to address the gap between domestic law and international obligation, a matter considered most recently by the Parliamentary Joint Committee on Human Rights.

[9.60] Joint Committee on Human Rights, *The International Covenant on Economic, Social and Cultural Rights*, 21st Report (HL 183/HC 1188 (2003–2004)) (footnotes omitted)

The right to strike

132. The [UN Committee on Economic, Social and Cultural Rights] has repeatedly identified UK law as incompatible with the right to strike, as it is protected under Article 8 of the [International] Covenant [of Economic, Social and Cultural Rights]. Article 8 (1) (d) guarantees "the right to strike, provided that it is exercised in conformity with the laws of the particular country". This reflects similar guarantees of the right to strike, in the Conventions of the ILO, and in the European Social Charter, international instruments to which the UK is party.

136. In its concluding observations, the CESCR found, referring to its earlier concluding observations of 1997, that the failure to incorporate the right to strike in [United Kingdom] domestic law breached Article 8. Reiterating its 1997 recommendations on this point, it recommended that the right to strike should be incorporated in legislation and that strike action should no longer entail the loss of employment.

137. These conclusions are echoed in successive findings of the ILO Committee of Experts, in its reviews of UK compliance with ILO Convention 87, as well as in the

findings of the Council of Europe European Committee of Social Rights. The Institute of Employment Rights cited repeated findings by these bodies that the UK law fails to protect the right to strike.

138. The Institute of Employment Rights told us that—

If the United Kingdom is to meet minimum international standards, some radical surgery will be required to labour laws which remain the most restrictive in Europe, notwithstanding the Employment Relations Act 1999 and the enactment of the Employment Relations Bill currently before Parliament.

139. The IER argued for protection of the right to strike, either by direct incorporation of one of the international treaties, such as the ICESCR, European Social Charter, or ILO Conventions, or by legislation broadly based on one of these instruments, and a number of related legislative measures including the widening of the definition of a trade dispute under the Trade Union and Labour Relations (Consolidation) Act 1992, and the abolition of the prohibition on secondary industrial action in support of other employees, and protection against dismissal of workers for taking part in a strike.

140. The Government maintained that the current law sufficiently protects the right to strike to comply with Article 8. It noted that "the law ensures that workers are free to withhold their labour if they wish" and that trade unions are free to organise industrial action, within certain limitations. It concluded that, taken together, this legal framework was sufficient to comply with the Covenant. In particular, it disputed the CESCR's view that protection against loss of employment following strike action was necessary in order to protect the right to strike. It stated—

. . . giving protection against loss of employment is one means by which national legislatures can secure or at least assist in securing, compliance with the Covenant. But

---

The Right to Strike and the Human Rights Act

As we saw at the beginning of this chapter, the right to strike is now regarded judicially as a 'fundamental human right' (*London Underground Ltd v NUR* [1996] ICR 170). It has also been shown that the British law restricting the 'right to strike' is in breach of international human rights standards. Could these restrictions be challenged under the Human Rights Act? By Article 11, the ECHR protects the right to freedom of association, including the right to form and join trade unions for the protection of one's interests. Article 11 does not expressly include a right to strike, but it has been recognised by the European Court of Human Rights as 'one of the most important' means available to trade unions for the protection of the occupational interests of their members. But the Court has said that the duty of Member States under Article 11 is simply to permit and make possible the opportunity for trade unions to protect the occupational interests of their members, without prescribing any particular method (*Schmidt and Dahlström v Sweden* (1975) I EHRR 632). More recently, in *UNISON v United Kingdom* [2002] IRLR 497 the Strasbourg Court indicated that even if Article 11(1) did include protection for the right to strike, restrictions on the right might readily be justified by Article 11(2). But that could change if, after *Wilson and Palmer v United Kingdom* [2002] IRLR 128 the Court held that any restrictions could be justified only if consistent with ILO Convention 87 and the European Social Charter of 1961, Article 6(4). So far as domestic law is concerned, in *RMT v London Underground Ltd* [2001] IRLR 228 the Court of Appeal found that the requirements of trade unions to give ballot and strike notices to the employer did not breach Article 11. Similarly in *Willerby Holiday Homes v UCATT* [2003] EWHC 2608, it was held that the notice and ballot rules were not oppressive or disproportionate, and a challenge under Article 11 was rebuffed.

[the government] does not consider that the Covenant, which does not refer explicitly to the dismissal of strikers, makes such a protection essential in all circumstances or requires, where the protection is given, that it must be indefinite.

141. Government evidence points out that there have been very few cases of dismissal following strike action, but acknowledges that this is a possibility. Evidence from trade unions suggests that the impact of the restrictions on industrial action is significant. It cites particular cases where the weak legal protection afforded to striking employees has had serious consequences for trade union members. The Communications Workers Union stated that it has on several occasions desisted, on legal advice, from taking industrial action in cases where it would otherwise have considered such action justified and proportionate, and that it has sometimes felt obliged to repudiate strike action by members so as to avert the risk of an injunction against them, thus leaving their members unsupported against dismissal. UNISON cited cases where injunctions have been granted against it, restraining industrial action.

142. The CESCR concludes that current law places undue restrictions on the right to strike, as protected in Article 8 ICESCR. We consider that the Government should take seriously the successive findings of the authoritative international bodies overseeing treaties to which the UK has become party, and should review the existing law in the light of them.

FURTHER READING

S Auerbach, *Legislating for Conflict* (Oxford, Oxford University Press, 1990).

H Carty, 'Intentional Violation of Economic Interests: The Limits of Common Law Liability' (1988) 104 *Law Quarterly Review* 250.

P Davies and M Freedland, *Labour Legislation and Public Policy* (Oxford, Oxford University Press, 1993).

K D Ewing, 'Laws against Strikes Revisited', in C Barnard, S Deakin and G Morris, *The Future of Labour Law* (Oxford, Hart Publishing, 2004).

——, *The Right to Strike* (Oxford, Oxford University Press, 1991).

B Gernigon, A Odero, and H Guido, 'ILO Principles Concerning the Right to Strike' (1998) 137 *International Labour Review* 441.

J Hendy, 'Article 11 and the Right to Strike' in K D Ewing (ed), *Human Rights at Work* (London, Institute of Employment Rights, 2000).

—— 'Industrial Action and International Standards' in K D Ewing (ed), *Employment Rights at Work: Reviewing the Employment Relations Act 1999* (London, Institute of Employment Rights, 2001).

O Kahn Freund, *Labour and the Law*, 3rd edn by P Davies and M Freedland, (London, Stevens, 1983).

S Mills, 'The International Labour Organisation, the United Kingdom and Freedom of Association: An Annual Cycle of Condemnation' [1997] *European Human Rights Law Review* 35.

T Novitz, *International and European Protection of the Right to Strike* (Oxford, Oxford University Press, 2003).

Wikeley, Ogus, and Barendt's *The Law of Social Security* 5th edn by N J Wikeley (London, Butterworths, 2004).

Lord Wedderburn of Charlton, *Employment Rights in Britain and Europe* (London, Lawrence and Wishart, 1991), chapter 4.

10

Restructuring the Business

This chapter examines the legal protection afforded to workers in the event of managerial decisions that require major changes in the business. The employer may become insolvent, or the business may be sold to a new owner. Changing market conditions may force the employer to seek to reduce the number of employees or to alter their contractual terms. Most restructuring of business aims to improve the profits and the value of shares, at least in the short term, in solvent and successful companies. Whatever the cause of the restructuring, it is likely to have a significant adverse impact on jobs or terms and conditions of employment. What legal rights do employees have in respect of these decisions, and are these rights adequate to protect their interests?

Legal regulation in this sphere has been shaped by three dominant policy considerations. For the general purpose of wealth maximisation, the first policy respects the importance of permitting the managers of businesses to make decisions to improve the profitability of the business or to minimise costs and losses. The law recognises this policy by its general endorsement of freedom of contract. More specifically the law imposes a duty upon directors of companies to act in the best interests of the company, which is understood to mean usually the best interests of the shareholders or capital investors. Unless those interests are respected, investors will take their capital elsewhere. In this way the capital market disciplines the management of a company to maximise the profits of the company, and the law is reluctant to impede this process of wealth generation. This policy points the law against any restriction on management decisions about changes in the business, because legal rights that protect workers' interests, including the opportunity to have a say in such decisions, might prevent or obstruct such wealth-maximising decisions. The second policy recognises, however, that employees have certain interests deserving protection. This protection is afforded, of course, to the workers' contractual entitlements, but a broader range of interests may be recognised. These interests may include advance notification to employees about changes in the business, the opportunity to be consulted, protection of contractual rights when the business is sold to a new owner, and protection of an employee's interest in employment and economic security. The third policy concerns primarily the interests of the taxpayer, thus being of critical concern to governments. There is a public interest in reducing the social costs of changes in the business. These social costs include the costs to the government of providing economic support to the unemployed, the expense of retraining workers so that they can gain alternative employment, and all kinds of hidden costs such as health care and criminal justice that typically rise in areas of high unemployment. A government will also be concerned about the effects of social exclusion on displaced workers and their potential costs to remedy.

It should be apparent that these policy considerations may conflict sharply in particular instances. If the shareholders of a company agree with a management proposal that their best interests lie in closing a plant (with a view perhaps to relocating the production abroad), the first policy supports this decision and rejects the need for any legal intervention. But the second policy expresses the concern that the interests of the workforce in stable jobs and in participating in the running of the enterprise are being completely overridden. The social costs of the shareholders' decision are almost certainly treated as externalities by the company, that is costs that can be ignored when making the decision to relocate the plant because they will not fall on the company. The resulting costs to the community of unemployment, social alienation and social exclusion may, however, be far higher than the marginal benefits to the wealth of the shareholders. If this calculation applies, the case for regulatory intervention to compel businesses to take into account externalities becomes powerful, and points to the need for regulatory intervention that will restrain managerial decisions. In short, though this topic of changes in the business appears at the tail end of discussions of labour law, it exemplifies one of the core themes of the subject: an intrinsic conflict of interest between capital and labour, surrounded by a strong independent agenda for government that urges substantial market regulation.

Is it surprising that this field of labour law has been the one that has been intensively regulated by the European Union? The reason for this special interest at community level in an aspect of labour law lies in its possible impact upon competition between national economies. If regulation restricts the freedom of management to make decisions in the best interests of shareholders, it may discourage investment and impose additional costs on business. The Member States of the European Union have pursued a policy of avoiding the potential competitive disadvantages of any regulation that might lead to capital flight around the Community by establishing harmonisation in regulation. Harmonisation should establish a level playing field, so that investors will not base their decisions to invest on differences in regulation within the European market. Harmonisation should also prevent a 'race to the bottom' in the sense of deregulatory initiatives in order to attract inward capital investment. But this policy of harmonisation does not determine the precise level of protection for the interests of employees or how to manage the problem of social costs. The policy of harmonisation is compatible with high levels of intervention or very basic standards such as those set by judges under the common law. On the whole, however, European regulation has favoured high levels of intervention, that is a levelling up of standards. This policy may be based on the view that intervention serves the purpose of the reduction of social costs, though whether regulation achieves this ambition remains controversial.

Indeed, it is dubious whether regulation designed to protect the interests of employees in the event of changes in the business has a significant impact on the conduct of employers, the position of employees, and the competitive advantage of nations. Many attempts have been made by economists to determine whether legal regulation has an impact on labour markets. A straightforward hypothesis is that the higher the levels of severance pay that employers have to pay for dismissals, the lower the levels of employment in the economy, for these severance payments represent an additional labour cost that should depress demand. Although there is some statistical support for this hypothesis (EP Lazear, 'Job Security Provisions and Employment' (1990) 105 *Quarterly Journal of Economics* 699), the same statistics reveal that lengthy notice requirements, which are surely an equivalent cost, probably have the opposite effect (JT Addison and J-L Grosso, 'Job Security Provisions and Employment: Revised Estimates' (1996) 35 *Industrial Relations* 585). In comparative studies between countries in order to test the effect of differences in legal regulation, another puzzling result emerges. Even though Germany has a much more elaborate system of employment protection than the United States, the two countries appear to adjust in similar ways and at similar speeds to business cycles. The United Kingdom, with legal protections somewhere in the middle between Germany and the United States, exhibits stronger elasticities in levels of employment and hours (i.e. numbers employed and hours worked vary more significantly during business cycles), but these changes occur relatively slowly (CF Buechtemann, 'Introduction' in Cristoph F Buechtemann (ed), *Employment Security and Labour Market Behaviour* (Ithaca, NY, ILR Press, 1993)).

These economic studies, though fascinating, share two weaknesses. First, it is difficult to generalise about legal systems in a comparative way, in order to determine whether or not they afford the workers high levels of protection. A simple comparison of statutory rules does not reveal how they may be interpreted in practice or the extent to which they are enforced. In addition, many aspects of labour law may impinge on managerial decisions respecting changes in the business, and so without considering the totality of regulation one cannot grasp its possible impact. For example, in the USA, the social security system penalises employers who make economic dismissals by raising their contribution requirements, whereas this device is not used in the UK. Although the USA may figure in these comparative assessments as a jurisdiction that lacks regulation of economic dismissals, this additional tax burden may be far more influential than any regulation directed towards requiring severance payments. A second general weakness of these econometric studies is that, although they demonstrate that regulation may not be as important as might be commonly supposed, they do not reveal what factors are significant. We may surmise that complex institutional factors relating to managerial techniques play an important role, but the studies do not help to establish the validity of this idea. For example, in some countries such as Japan, it may be a central aspect of managerial technique to create a co-operative workforce by engaging in extensive consultation and by making a commitment to protect employment security. Variations in labour costs may be achieved, as in Japan, by making a large part of the salary bill dependent upon profit sharing, so that in the event of a downturn in business, there is a reduction in wages, but no dismissals or reductions in hours. The decision by management to approach changes in the business in such a way may reflect some aspect of the regulatory environment such as taxation. It may, alternatively, embody a conventional wisdom about successful techniques of management. In any case, even if legal regulation of economic dismissals does have adverse employment effects, there may be off-setting benefits in other respects such as more rapid earnings growth, greater equality of earnings, and the reduction of other social costs such as health care and crime (see R Buchele and J Christiansen, 'Do Employment and Income Security Cause Unemployment? A Comparative Study of the US and the E-4' (1998) 22 *Cambridge Journal of Economics* 117).

With that important caveat about the impact of regulation, we now examine the principal types of legal regulation of managerial decisions involving changes in the business that adversely affect the interests of employees. The discussion focuses on six aspects of this topic:

(1) variations of the terms of employment in order to create flexibility and efficiency gains;
(2) reduction of the workforce by dismissals for economic reasons in order to reduce costs;
(3) redeployment of workers to different jobs;
(4) the protection of rights of workers on the insolvency of the business;
(5) the protection of rights of workers on sales of the business to new owners;
(6) the participation of workers in decisions about all the above types of changes in the business.

It should be appreciated, however, that in many instances of restructuring, several or all of these topics may arise simultaneously or sequentially.

10.1 Variation of jobs

The principal response of most employers to changes in market conditions is likely to involve the desire to alter either working practices or the terms and conditions of employment. An employer may seek to reduce wages, to vary hours of work, or to require employees to be flexible in the tasks that they perform, which often means in practice to work harder. These measures may be responses to changed market conditions such as a decline in the market for a product or the need to introduce new products, or they may be simply a response to shareholder pressure to make the business more profitable. The introduction of functional flexibility into the workplace was perceived as a key management strategy for the improvement of productivity in manufacturing in the 1980s. It led to attacks on traditional craft demarcations between jobs and an insistence upon workers agreeing to be flexible in the work that they performed. This trend towards task enlargement and intensification of work achieves significant productivity gains for employers (for a survey see T Elger, 'Task Flexibility and the Intensification of Labour in UK Manufacturing in the 1980s' in A Pollert (ed), *Farewell to Flexibility?* (Oxford, Blackwell, 1991).

The central legal question is whether an employer can insist upon such changes, or whether the employees have rights to prevent such variations unless they agree to them. In addition, we shall consider whether the government should seek to assist employers to introduce such variations in terms and working conditions. These issues are largely governed by the common law of the contract of employment, but at the margins some regulation has an impact.

10.1.1 Flexibility under the contract of employment

We have already observed that contracts of employment are incomplete by design. Employers cannot be certain in advance about the precise tasks that will be required, their ordering of priorities, and how the work can be completed most efficiently. The contract of employment usually leaves gaps about these details to be filled by instructions by management. Often these gaps are filled in part by the works rules and staff handbooks, which, as we have seen, will be subject to revision. Without this flexibility in the use of labour power, the employer will be impeded in the pursuit of efficient production.

Added to this flexibility required by the employer, the employee also often expects the employment to be varied over time. If the employee enters a large firm with an internal labour market, the employee hopes to improve wages and skills by promotion and training. The employee may also expect to work at different locations. Such changes are part of the expectations of the parties when a person is recruited to a position at the bottom of the hierarchy or a management trainee in the internal labour market. Where the employee is a member of a recognised union, there will also be the expectation that the union will negotiate improvements to terms and conditions of employment. These expectations of variation present several legal difficulties in ascertaining the rights and obligations of the parties.

10.1.1.1 Unilateral variation of terms

The general contractual principle is that the parties are entitled to insist upon their original agreement made at the formation of a contract of employment until such time as, by agreement, the parties substitute a new contract or vary the terms of the contract for consideration. An employer cannot simply announce that it proposes to vary unilaterally the terms of employment, no matter how much notice is given. Faced with such an announcement, an employee is entitled either to treat it as a repudiatory breach of contract, that is a constructive dismissal, or to disregard the proposed variation and to affirm the existing contract. If the employee continues to work normally, however, this conduct may be regarded as acceptance by conduct of the new terms offered by the employer. To avoid that consequence, the employee needs to make it clear that he or she continues to work normally only under protest, and expects the employer to honour the original agreement. The employee may seek a declaration that the original agreement is still binding (e.g. *Burdett Coutts v Hertfordshire County Council* [1984] IRLR 92 (HC)), and also claim any shortfall in wages or other benefits resulting from the unilateral variation by the employer.

[10.1] *Rigby v Ferodo Ltd* **[1988] ICR 29 (HL)**

> The plaintiff was a lathe operator who had worked for the employer for 20 years, giving him an entitlement to 12 weeks' notice of termination. Owing to severe financial pressures on the business, management decided that it had no option but to reduce wages by 5 per cent in order to remain in business. Management sought to reach agreement with the unions for this reduction, but the plaintiff's union made no agreement other than to refrain from strike action. The employer then imposed the wage reduction on the workforce. The plaintiff continued to work, but by his conduct indicated that he did not accept the reduction in wages. After more than a year, the plaintiff commenced proceedings to claim the difference in wages on the basis of breach of contract at common law. The claim was successful before the House of Lords. The employer's reduction of wages was a fundamental breach of contract, but this action did not bring the contract to an end unless the employee had accepted the repudiation of the contract. Nor had the employer terminated the contract by notice. Neither had the employee accepted any variation of the contract by his conduct, because he had clearly objected to the variation. Thus the contract had persisted on its original terms, but the employer had withheld part of the wages. That shortfall of wages could be claimed.

In response to unilateral wage cuts, a worker can also use the statutory protection against deductions from wages (see above 2.2.1.2.). Unless the employer negotiates a new written contract of employment containing the wage reduction, the payment of a lesser sum will be regarded as a 'deduction' from wages that the employee can recover under ERA 1996, section 13 **[2.8]** in an employment tribunal. For example, in *Bruce v Wiggins Teape (Stationery) Ltd* [1994] IRLR 536 (EAT) employees successfully challenged the employer's unilateral withdrawal of a shift bonus as a deduction from wages.

These common law principles drawn from the ordinary law of contract, buttressed by the statutory protection against deductions, afford protection to employees against opportunist unilateral revisions of the terms of the contract by the employer. Yet these rules impose a static model on what is expected to be in many instances a flexible and evolving relationship. An employer may try avoid the static model of the common law by two mechanisms: reliance upon the discretion of management to direct production conferred by implication under the contract of employment; or the use of an express flexibility clause.

10.1.1.2 Scope of the employer's discretion

The first technique is to avoid much detail in the description of the work to be performed, leaving the matter to be determined by managerial discretion or the promulgation of works rules to which the employee must conform under the general implied obligation of obedience. The exercise of this discretion, provided that it falls within the powers of the employer conferred by contract, cannot easily be challenged as a breach of contract. Similarly, the fact that the variation has adverse consequences for the employee in terms of pay or hours will not provide the basis for a claim, provided the variation falls within the powers of the employer.

[10.2] *Hussman Manufacturing Ltd v Weir* **[1998] IRLR 288 (EAT)**

The employer exercised a power under the contract of employment to change the shift system, with the consequence that the claimant was transferred to a shift that attracted a lower rate of pay. The EAT rejected the argument that the reduction in pay amounted to a deduction contrary to section 13 of the Employment Rights Act 1996, because the wages, though lower, were those properly payable for the shift to which the employee had been transferred. There was therefore no unauthorised deduction from wages in this case of unilateral wage reduction because the contract conferred this power on the employer.

The extent to which employers may require workers to adapt to new working practices or tasks as part of the authority of management to issue instructions is examined in the following case.

[10.3] *Cresswell v Board of Inland Revenue* **[1984] ICR 508 (HC)**

The employer proposed to introduce a computerised system for records, the calculation of taxes owed, and sending out letters, in place of the traditional methods of paper files and writing on documents used by tax officers. The employees refused to co-operate with the introduction of the new technology in the absence of a guarantee that its introduction would not result in redundancies. The employers declined to give such a guarantee or to pay the employees unless they used the new technology. The plaintiff tax officers brought a test case seeking a declaration that the Revenue was in breach of contract. The terms of the contracts of employment did not specify the work to be performed except in the general terms of an obligations to perform the general duties appropriate to the particular grade of tax officer. The employees argued that the changes in working methods amounted to a change in the nature of the job, which necessarily involved a wholly new contract. The declaration was refused on the ground that the direction to adopt the new technology, known as COP 1, was not a breach of contract.

Walton J:
But there can really be no doubt as to the fact that an employee is expected to adapt himself to new methods and techniques introduced in the course of his employment: cf. *North Riding Garages Ltd. v Butterwick* [1967] 2 Q.B. 56 [below **[10.17]**]. Of course, in a proper case the employer must provide any necessary training or re-training . . . [It] will, in all cases, be a question of pure fact as to whether the re-training involves the acquisition of such esoteric skills that it would not be reasonable to expect the employee to acquire them. In an age when the computer has forced its way into the schoolroom and where electronic games are played by schoolchildren in their own homes as a matter of everyday occurrence, it can hardly be considered that to ask an employee to acquire basic skills as to retrieving information from a computer or feeding such information into a computer is something in the slightest esoteric or even, nowadays, unusual. In any event in the present case one remarkable feature, comparable to that of the dog which did not bark in the night, is that from first to last in all the voluminous evidence put in by the plaintiffs, there is no suggestion whatsoever that the plaintiffs themselves, or anybody else in any similar category in all the 14 districts covered by the present scheme, found any real difficulty in accepting the necessary instruction in the use of COP 1 and putting it into practice as they had been doing for some little time at the end of last year. Whatever the change in working methods may be it is one which, of course with proper instruction (which I think

the employer must be under a duty to provide and which has, of course, been provided in the present case), the three grades concerned have, one and all, taken in their stride. . . .

It appears to me that each of the three jobs, post-COP (and here I mean both COP 1 and COP 2) will be the same jobs as they were pre-COP, though in part done in a different way; that is to say, the clerical assistants will still be clerical assistants. They will, of course, now have to enter certain information into the computer, but it must be remembered that a clerk is defined in the *Shorter Oxford Dictionary* as: 'An officer who has charge of the records, correspondence, etc., and conducts the business, of any department . . .' A clerical assistant is one who assists, therefore, among other matters, in keeping the records and, depending upon precisely how these records are kept, so will his duties vary. One of the main functions of a computer is to store records and so it is well within the scope of the clerical assistant's job to help in keeping the necessary records by entering the information upon a computer. This does not, pace some of the wilder suggestions that have been made in this case, make him a computer operator any more than a customer who draws cash from a service till facility afforded by his bank is a computer operator because he is required to feed certain information into the service till as a pre-requisite to drawing the cash he requires. Of course, the transaction here is one way, but it is no more outside the scope of the duties of a clerical assistant than filing the details desired to be recorded upon a card; the essential step is the same in both cases. And when one comes to consider the tax officer and tax officer higher grade, the matter is, if anything, even clearer. Here, although I think also the words 'computer operator,' or, more picturesquely, 'slave to the machine' were bandied about during the course of the trial, it is extremely difficult to think that, if an entirely unprejudiced observer were to sit in the offices of any of the 14 districts for any length of time, observing intelligently all that went on, and was then asked, what job have these people got, he could not in all conscience be able to say that they were anything other than tax officer; that is to say, officers working the P.A.Y.E. tax system in all its manifold aspects.

Of course the changes in working methods and practices which COP brings in its train are great—although I think that the evidence has tended to exaggerate them. But that, as it seems to me, is not the point. COP merely introduces up to date modern methods for dealing with bulk problems: it leaves the jobs done by those who operate the new methodology precisely the same as before, although the content of some of the jobs, most notably that of the grade of clerical assistant, will have been considerably altered, but in no case altered anything like sufficiently to fall outside the original description of the proper functions of the grade concerned. Moreover, the contrary conclusion would fly in the face of common sense. Although doubtless, all of us, being conservative (with a small 'c') by nature desire nothing better than to be left to deepen our accustomed ruts, and hate change, a tax officer has no right to remain in perpetuity doing one defined type of tax work in one particular way. At any moment he may be required to switch, for example, to schedule D work; or, I assume, to some type of taxation work entirely outside the Income and Corporation Taxes Act 1970. It seems to me that if it is perfectly legitimate for the revenue to effect such changes, which would affect every single aspect of the working life of a tax officer, and not merely the way he is required to carry out one set of functions, it would be surprising in the extreme if it could not say that he was to carry out what he was doing—precisely and exactly what he was doing—but to come out of the horse and buggy age and use the computer to assist him to do it.

This decision, like many others, confirms that courts view the contract of employment as containing a broad residual discretion for management to direct the workforce to undertake new working methods. The express terms of the contract place the principal constraint upon this discretionary power. But it is also possible for a court to discover further constraints upon managerial discretion derived from implied terms of the contract of employment. These are terms to be implied in fact, that is on the basis of the presumed agreement between the parties based upon their joint intentions. In *Cresswell v Board of Inland Revenue* the court found such an implied term: the duty of the employer to provide instruction in how to use the new computers. In the next case, the general discretionary power to direct work is limited by an implied term to prevent the employer from directing the employer to work at any place beyond reasonable daily reach of the employee's home. The case is also important because it shows that an employer cannot vary the terms of the contract of employment by merely issuing a new set of written particulars under ERA 1996, section 1.

[10.4] *Jones v Associated Tunnelling Co Ltd* [1981] IRLR 477 (EAT)

The respondent company was a specialist tunnelling and bunkering contractor at collieries operated by the National Coal Board. Mr. Jones had worked as a tunneller for the company for about 15 years. He did not have a written contract of employment, but had been issued from time to time with statements of written particulars of employment. These statutory statements had varied from one to another, but they included a requirement to transfer from one site to another. On the completion of work at Hem Heath Colliery after about 10 years, Mr Jones was directed to work at another, about an equal distance from his home. He refused to do so and claimed a redundancy payment. In order to establish that he had been dismissed, the claimant had to demonstrate a constructive dismissal, that is a fundamental breach of contract by the employer. The claimant argued that the employer was in breach of a term that specified his place of work to be the Hem Heath Colliery and in breach of a term that limited his duties to tunnelling work. The industrial tribunal held that there had been no breach of contract, and the EAT rejected the employee's appeal.

Browne-Wilkinson J:
The starting point must be that a contract of employment cannot simply be silent on the place of work: if there is no express term, there must be either some rule of law that in *all* contracts of employment the employer is (or alternatively is not) entitled to transfer the employee from his original place of work or some term regulating the matter must be implied into each contract. We know of no rule of law laying down the position in relation to all contracts of employment, nor do we think it either desirable 'or possible' to lay down a single rule. It is impossible to conceive of any fixed rule which will be equally appropriate to the case of, say, an employee of a touring repertory theatre and the librarian of the British Museum. Therefore, the position must be regulated by the express or implied agreement of the parties in each case. In order to give the contract business efficacy, it is necessary to imply *some* term into each contract of employment.

The term to be implied must depend on the circumstances of each case. The authorities show that it may be relevant to consider the nature of the employer's business, whether or not the employee has in fact been moved during the employment, what the employee was told when he was employed, and whether there is any provision made to cover the employee's expenses when working away from daily reach of his home. These are only examples; all the circumstances of each case have to be considered: see *O'Brien v Associated Fire Alarms* (1969) 1 AER 93; *Stevenson v Teesside Bridge and Engineering Ltd* (1971) 1 AER 296; *Times Newspapers v Bartlett* (1976) 11 ITR 106.

Looking at the circumstances of this case, what would the parties have said had an officious bystander asked them 'At what sites can Mr Jones be asked to work?'. The employers might have replied 'Anywhere in the United Kingdom'. But the Industrial Tribunal's findings indicate that Mr Jones, as one would expect, would have objected to being transferred anywhere outside daily reach of his home. The employers were in business as contractors working at different sites; so the parties must have envisaged a degree of mobility. In 1969, Mr Jones himself was moved from his original place of work to Hem Heath Colliery without objection. All the statements of terms and conditions subsequently issued contain mobility clauses, albeit in varying terms. From these factors we think that the plain inference is that the employers were to have *some* power to move Mr Jones's place of work and that the reasonable term to imply (as the lowest common denominator of what the parties would have agreed if asked) is a power to direct Mr Jones to work at any place within reasonable daily reach of Mr Jones's home. Such a term would permit Mr Jones to be required to work at Florence Colliery. . . .

It is therefore not necessary for us to reach any concluded view as to whether the Industrial Tribunal was right in holding that, even if under the original contract Mr Jones's place of work could not be changed, by continuing to work without objection Mr Jones must be taken to have assented to a variation in his terms of employment including the introduction of the mobility clause. However, since the case may go further and the Court of Appeal may take a different view on the implied term, we must state our reservations about the Industrial Tribunal's view on such variations. The statutory 'statement of terms and conditions of employment' is not itself a contract but merely contains the employer's statement of what has previously been agreed. As such, the first of such statements to be issued is often compelling evidence of what terms have in fact been agreed. But where there are two or more statements which are not in identical terms, the later statement can only be evidence of an agreed variation of the original terms. Such variation may be either express or implied. If, as in the present case, there is no evidence of any oral discussion varying the original terms, the fact that a statement of terms and conditions containing different terms has been issued cannot be compelling evidence of an express oral variation. The most that can be said is that by continuing to work without objection after receiving such further statement, the employee may have impliedly agreed to the variation recorded in the second statement or is estopped from denying it.

In our view, to imply an agreement to vary or to raise an estoppel against the employee on the grounds that he has not objected to a false record by the employers of the terms actually agreed is a course which should be adopted with great caution. If the variation relates to a matter which has immediate practical application (eg, the rate of pay) and the employee continues to work without objection after effect has been given to the variation (eg, his pay packet has been reduced) then obviously he may well be taken to have impliedly agreed. But where, as in the present case, the variation has no immediate practical effect the position is not the same. It is the view of both members of this Tribunal with experience in industrial relations (with which the Chairman, without such experience, agrees) that it is asking too much of the ordinary employee to require him either to object to an erroneous statement of his terms of employment having no immediate practical impact on him or be taken to have assented to the variation. So to hold would involve an unrealistic view of the inclination and ability of the ordinary employee to read and fully understand such statements.

Even if he does read the statement and can understand it, it would be unrealistic of the law to require him to risk a confrontation with his employer on a matter which has no immediate practical impact on the employee. For those reasons, as at present advised, we would not be inclined to imply any assent to a variation from mere failure by the employee to object to the unilateral alteration by the employer of the terms of employment contained in a statutory statement.

We turn then to the work issue. This is really a question of fact. Mr Jones is a tunneller.

A bunker is a large underground storage chamber. A full description of the work involved in making a bunker is set out in the reasons of the Industrial Tribunal. The Industrial Tribunal, having heard the evidence, held that the work involved in making a bunker was not essentially different from ordinary tunnelling work and that therefore it was work of a kind which Mr Jones was contractually bound to do.

On the appeal, Mr Hughes has sought to persuade us that tunnelling and bunkering are two different trades. There was no evidence before the Industrial Tribunal to that effect: the only evidence was directed to showing that they were treated as separate trades. There was ample evidence to justify the Industrial Tribunal's conclusion that the work involved in bunkering was not so different from tunnelling as to render it outside Mr Jones's contractual obligation. The Industrial Tribunal is the body to decide questions of fact: it is not for us to interfere in such findings.

10.1.1.3 Flexibility clauses

Instead of relying upon the general residual discretionary power to direct labour contained in the contract of employment, the employer may alternatively bargain more explicitly for a duty to be flexible. The contract of employment can contain a 'flexibility clause', that is a term which gives the employer the express contractual right to vary the content of the job unilaterally. Such terms became increasingly common in contracts of employment during the 1980s and 1990s.

[10.5] W Brown, S Deakin, M Hudson, C Pratten and P Ryan, *The Individualisation of Employment Contracts in Britain* (London, Department of Trade and Industry, Employment Research Series No. 4, 1998) 45–46

[This study of 32 firms was designed to discover whether the derecognition of trade unions in some of the firms had led to significant differences in the contractual terms offered to individual employees. The study as a whole demonstrated that there was little difference in the types of contracts offered by firms with and without recognised unions except with respect to the extent to which management exercised a discretion of over individual rates of pay in non-union establishments. Flexibility clauses regarding the performance of work were common in all firms.]

Clauses were expressed in such a way as to reserve to the employer a unilateral right to vary the required contractual performance. This was regularly done for such matters as job duties and location, the employer reserving the right to change the employee's duties or place of work. Broad flexibility clauses of the following kind were common:

During your employment with the Company, you will be required to co-operate in the development of new working arrangements as necessary, including participating in training in order to improve both individual skills and the profitability of the Company. This will include being flexible in regard to the duties undertaken and mobile within the Company's establishment in which you are employed.

More bluntly, one agreement stated:

The Company may make reasonable changes to the terms and conditions of your employment. Such changes will be confirmed in writing.

Terms and conditions governing hours of work were also subject to flexibility. In one case a 'normal' working week of 37.5 hours was qualified by the statement, 'In addition, you will be required to undertake shift work as and when required'. In another, management reserved the right to insist on overtime work 'in order to meet prevailing needs such as deadlines, delivery dates, etc'.. In a further case, basic hours only were set by the contract itself, leaving starting and finishing times to the discretion of line managers . . . There were numerous other examples of contracts stipulating that employees were expected to work additional hours according to the company's needs, without entitlement to overtime pay.

The construction of a contract that contains a flexibility clause presents a court with a difficult problem of interpretation. On its face the flexibility clause may negate almost every other term of employment by granting the employer the right to change it. A court is unlikely to construe a flexibility clause so widely, unless the employer states extremely clearly that such basic items as hours of work and pay can be varied at its discretion.

[10.6] *Wandsworth London Borough Council v D'Silva* [1998] IRLR 193 (CA)

The employer notified employees of the adoption of a new procedure for handling long-term absence from work due to sickness. The principal change was the shortening of the period of absence before managers were required to initiate the procedure that might lead to termination of employment. Some staff brought a claim to test the legality of the change without their agreement. The Court of Appeal held that this aspect of sickness procedure was not a term of the contract, but stated the employer's policy or practice, which could be varied unilaterally. Other aspects of the procedure, such as the right to an appeal, did probably confer contractual rights. The test was whether the code of procedure was what was required to happen and was intended to confer rights upon employees. Lord Woolf MR made some further observations on the possibility of unilateral variation of contractual rights.

Lord Woolf:
The general position is that contracts of employment can only be varied by agreement. However, in the employment field an employer or for that matter an employee can reserve an ability to change a particular aspect of the contract unilaterally by notifying the other party as part of the contract that this is the situation. However, clear language is required to reserve to one party an unusual power of this sort. In addition, the court is unlikely to favour an interpretation which does more than enable a party to vary contractual provisions with which that party is required to comply. If, therefore, the provisions of the code which the council were seeking to amend in this case were of a contractual nature, then they could well be capable of unilateral variation as the counsel contends. In relation to the provisions as to appeals the position would be likely to be different. To apply a power of unilateral variation to the rights which an employee is given under this part of the code could produce an unreasonable result and the courts in construing a contract of employment will seek to avoid such a result.

Where the contract of employment contains a broad-ranging flexibility clause, in effect it confers a discretion upon the employer to vary the job unilaterally. It is possible that the courts will imply a limitation on how this discretion should be exercised, so that the power must be exercised reasonably or perhaps in good faith. The legal mechanism for constraining the use of flexibility clauses must again be discovered in implied terms.

[10.7] *United Bank Ltd v Akhtar* **[1989] IRLR 507 (EAT)**

A junior employee working in a branch was subject to an express mobility clause that enabled the bank to transfer employees to other branches. The bank purported to transfer the employee from Leeds to Birmingham on a few days' notice, and failed to respond to his requests for the transfer to be postponed so that he could move house or for information about any assistance that the bank might be able to give him in moving. The employee succeeded in a claim for unfair dismissal by establishing that the bank had committed a repudiatory breach of contract. The employers had broken an implied term that they would give reasonable notice of transfers, and an implied term that the discretion would not be exercised in such a way as to render it impossible for the employee to comply with the contractual obligation to move. These implied obligations were founded ultimately on the employer's duty not to destroy the trust and confidence on which the employment relation is based.

The conceptual problem with seeking to constrain the employer's exercise of power conferred by express flexibility clauses in contracts of employment through implied terms is that implied terms cannot be used to contradict express terms of the contract. In the following case, a majority of the Court of Appeal finds techniques for inserting an implied limitation on a discretionary power expressly conferred by the contract. The case also considers the possibility that some clauses in contracts of employment might be invalid under the Unfair Contract Terms Act 1977.

[10.8] *Johnstone v Bloomsbury Health Authority* **[1992] QB 333 (CA)**

A hospital doctor was employed under a contract which provided for a standard 40-hour week, but also required in paragraph 4(b) the doctor to be available, on call, for overtime of 48 hours on average. The employee claimed that the employer's requirement for long hours was damaging his health, and he sought a declaration that the employer could not lawfully require such long hours as would foreseeably damage his health, and damages for breach of contract. The employing hospital moved to strike out the action, so for the purpose of the hearing the court assumed that the plaintiff had established that his long hours of work were causing damage to his health. The Court of Appeal, Leggat LJ dissenting, awarded the declaration in the terms sought. The Court also agreed unanimously that paragraph 4(b) might be invalid under the Unfair Contract Terms Act, but that the clause could not be void as contrary to public policy.

Stuart Smith LJ:
It is not a question in this case of importing from the law of tort some hitherto unrecognised duty not provided for in the express contract terms or inconsistent with them. In this case it is common ground that the two duties or obligations run side by side. There was a duty on the part of the plaintiff to be available for duty for an average of 48 hours each week beyond the basic 40 hours (Duty A). There was a duty on the Authority to take reasonable care not to injure is health (Duty B). It is the interaction or reconciliation of these two duties which is in question here. Mr Beloff submits that Duty A must prevail over Duty B because the former is an express term of the contract and the latter is implied. But this is not an implication that arises because it is necessary to give business efficacy to the contract as in *The Moorcock* (1889) 14 PD 64; it arises by implication of law. While therefore Mr Beloff asks the question, how does Duty B cut down or override Duty A? One can equally ask how does Duty A cut down or override

Duty B? I can quite see that an express clause in a contract of employment could be so framed as to limit or exclude Duty B. If for example the employee agreed to take the risk that his employer would be negligent towards him in requiring him to work so many hours within the contract entitlement although it would foreseeably injure his health, and he waived any right to claim compensation for such negligence. This would be tantamount to an express term of volenti non fit injuria. I am quite unable to construe paragraph 4(b) of the contract as amounting to this; and Mr Beloff did not contend that it should be so construed. Moreover if it can be so construed, it falls to be considered in the light of the Unfair Contract Terms Act 1977 s.2(1), of which more hereafter. Mr Beloff submits that paragraph 4(b) of the contract in some way limits the ambit or scope of Duty B. I know of no authority that supports this contention and it seems to me to be contrary to principle. A workman whose contract requires him to work in a particular factory is not precluded from claiming damages for breach of duty to take care of him if he is exposed to noxious fumes in the factory and suffers injury as a result. A man who is engaged expressly to work on a particular machine or range of machinery is not thereby precluded from suing his employer if he sustains injury because the machine is dangerous. Take the case of a man whose contract requires him to work such long hours that he is exhausted and his attention or concentration fail so that he suffers an accident, it is no defence to the employer to say that the workman expressly agreed to work such hours. So much is trite law and finds succinct expression in the speech of Lord Thankerton in *Wilsons & Clyde Coal Co Ltd v English* [1938] AC 57 (HL). At p.67 he said:

'It appears clear, then, that, when the workman contracts to do the work, he is not to be held as having agreed to hold the master immune from the latter's liability for want of due care in the provision of a reasonably safe system of working'.

There is no difference between the duty to provide a safe system of working and the duty to take reasonable care for the safety of the employee. The former is merely an ingredient in the latter duty.

Moreover I cannot see, in the example I have just given, that it makes any difference that instead of the overtime being 'as required' the workman is contracted to work up to 88 hours a week. If these were the hours of a contract of a heavy goods driver, and he fell asleep at the wheel through exhaustion and suffered injury I entertain no doubt that, subject to any defence of contributory negligence, the employee would have a good claim against his employer for operating an unsafe system of work. There is no obligation on the employer to require the men to drive for 88 hours in the week, and if by so doing he exposes him to foreseeable risk of injury he will be liable.

It must be remembered that the duty of care is owed to the individual employee and different employees may have different stamina. If the Authority in this case knew or ought to have known that by requiring him to work the hours they did, they exposed him to risk of injury to his health, then they should not have required him to work in excess of those hours that he safely could have done.

In my opinion paragraph 4(b) gave the Authority the power to require the plaintiff to work up to 88 hours per week on average. But that power had to be exercised in the light of the other contractual terms and in particular their duty to take care for his safety. . . .

The Unfair Contract Terms Act 1977 s.2(1) provides:

'A person cannot by reference to any contract term or to a notice given to persons generally or to particular persons exclude or restrict his liability for death or personal injury resulting from negligence'.

There is no dispute that the Authority's liability, if any, is for personal injury resulting from negligence. See s.1(1) and (3). And the section operates in favour of the plaintiff, if it is applicable. By Schedule 1, para. 4 it is provided that s.2(1) and 2(2) do not extend to a contract of employment except in favour of the employee. I take this to mean that if there is in a contract of employment a term excluding or restricting the liability of the employer to the employee, the latter can rely on the provisions of s.2(1) and (2). . . .

If contrary to my opinion, the defendants are entitled to succeed on the submissions they advanced in support of the appeal in relation to the statement of claim, it is arguable that they can only do so because the effect of paragraph 4(b) of the contract must be construed as an express assumption of risk by the plaintiff (a plea of volenti non fit injuria) or because it operates to restrict or limit the ambit and scope of the duty of care owed by the Authority. If that is the correct analysis, then the substance and effect, though not the form, of the term is such that it can properly be argued to fall within section 1(1) of the Act. . . .

I have no doubt that it is a matter of grave public concern that junior doctors should be required to work such long hours without proper rest that not only their own health may be put at risk but that of their patients as well. That is the allegation in this case and it seems to me that for the purpose of a striking out application it must be assumed to be true. But it does not follow from that fact alone that clause 4(b) of this contract is contrary to public policy. The courts should be wary of extending the scope of the doctrine beyond the well-recognised categories: see *Fender v Mildmay* [1938] AC 1(HL) per Lord Atkin at p. 12. It should be even more reluctant to embark upon a wide-ranging inquiry into matters of public debate where it is plain that there are two views bona fide and firmly held, and where complex considerations of capacity of the NHS and public funding are involved. This is a matter which, in my view, is more appropriate for negotiation between the professional bodies representing the doctors and the managers of the NHS, or for Parliament, than for resolution by the courts.

Leggatt LJ:

It seems to me that the operation of the régime contemplated by the declaration sought would be fraught with difficulty. The number of hours that a person can work in a week without injuring his health will vary infinitely according to the health and constitution of that individual, the total number of hours worked, the length of continuous periods worked without rest, the nature of the work and many other matters. To this would then have to be added the difficulties of objective perception that the doctor concerned would be unable in any particular week to work for any longer than he already had. Taken to its logical conclusion, this approach might prevent the defendants from calling on a weakly doctor to work more than (say) 30 hours in a week lest his health be injured. Yet it is for 88 hours in total that the plaintiff contracted to make himself available. Before he accepted that obligation he knew what it would entail. It may indeed be scandalous that junior doctors should not now be offered more civilised terms of service in our hospitals; and the fact that past generations of doctors have accepted such onerous terms without demur is no reason why the terms now offered should not be more enlightened. But these are matters for negotiation by their association, or in default for amelioration by the legislature. They do not constitute means by which those bound by current contracts can be enabled by the ingenuity of their lawyers to derogate from obligations freely assumed. Those who cannot stand the heat should stay out of the kitchen.

The result is, in my judgement, that because the plaintiff undertook to make himself available for 48 hours on average a week in addition to his standard working week of 40 hours, the defendants were entitled to call on him for any number of hours in any week up to the amount of that extra period. . . .

In my judgement as a matter of law reliance on an express term cannot involve breach of an implied term. The defendants cannot be said by the mere fact of requiring the plaintiff to work no more hours than he had contracted to work, to be in breach of any contractual duty owed to him; and since the scope of the relevant duties owed was delimited by contract he can be in no better position by couching his claim in tort, or, as Mr Beloff puts it, 'Tort cannot trump contract.' In the result, if the plaintiff fell sick during the performance of his employment by the defendants because it was too arduous for him, he did not do so by reason of any relevant breach of duty on the defendants' part. I would therefore allow the appeal.

Browne-Wilkinson VC:
[I]f there is a term of contract which is in general terms (eg a duty to take reasonable care not to injure the employee's health) and another term which is precise and detailed (eg an obligation to work on particular tasks notwithstanding that they involve an obvious health risk expressly referred to in the contract) the ambit of the employer's duty of care for the employee's health will be narrower than it would be were there no such express terms. In the absence of such express term, an employer would be in breach of the normal obligation not knowingly to put the employee's health at risk. But the express term postulated would demonstrate that, in that particular contract, the duty was restricted to taking such care of the employee's health as was consistent with the employee working on the specified high risk tasks. The express and the implied terms of the contract have to be capable of coexistence without conflict. (I am of course ignoring the effect of the Unfair Contract Terms Act or any statutory duties overriding the contract.)

Therefore I agree with Leggatt LJ and disagree with Stuart-Smith LJ that in the present case the scope of the duty of care for the plaintiff's health owed by the Authority falls to be determined taking into account the express terms of clause 4(b) of the contract. If the contract, on its true construction, were to impose an absolute obligation to work 48 hours' overtime per week on average, it would, in my judgement, preclude an argument by the employee that the employer, in requiring 48 hours per week overtime, was in breach of his implied duty of care for the employee's health.

But this case is not the same as the example I have used above. Although clause 4(b) imposes an absolute duty on the plaintiff to work for 40 hours and in addition an obligation 'to be available' for a further 48 hours per week on average, the Authority has a discretion as to the number of hours it calls on the plaintiff to work 'overtime'. There is no incompatibility between the plaintiff being under a duty to be available for 48 hours' overtime and the Authority having the right, *subject to its ordinary duty not to injure the plaintiff*, to call on him to work up to 48 hours' overtime on average. There is, in the present contract, no incompatibility between the plaintiff's duty on the one hand and the Authority's right, subject to the implied duty as to health, on the other. The implied term does not contradict the express term of the contract.

The differences between these judgments may be crucial in determining the extent to which an employer's power to govern the workplace can be achieved through flexibility clauses. On the view of Stuart Smith LJ, no matter how specific the power to direct labour conferred by a flexibility clause, the exercise of the power is always subject to implied limitations based upon the implied terms inserted into contracts of employment by the common law. On the view of Browne-Wilkinson V-C, the discretionary power conferred expressly by the contract can be limited only by conflicting implied legal duties placed upon the employer when the terms confer a discretion or option upon the employer, not when the terms give the employer a right and the employee a correlative obligation. The difference between these approaches may be less significant in the context of most flexibility clauses, however, for the terms usually describe the power to redirect labour as conferring a discretion upon the employer.

Apart from these mechanisms of reliance on implied or express discretionary power to direct labour, through which the employer achieves flexibility in the use of labour, the employer must secure agreement to changes in the terms of employment. The agreement must be given by the other party to the contract, that is the employee. It follows, as we will see next, that it is not necessarily sufficient for the employer to secure the consent to change by a representative trade union through a collective agreement.

10.1.2 Variation by collective agreement

The effect of variations in collective agreements that have been expressly incorporated into contracts of employment depends upon the precise terms of the incorporation. The underlying principle of the law in the United Kingdom is that the employee must always consent to a variation of the terms of the contract of employment. It follows that variations in relevant collective agreements do not automatically cause variations in the terms of the individual contracts of employment.

If the contract of employment incorporates the relevant collective agreement in terms which expressly envisage that any alterations in the collective agreement will automatically vary the terms of the contract of employment, the variation of the collective agreement should be effective to vary the terms of the contract of employment. Here is an example of an effective clause, which creates an agency relation between the union and individual employees.

[10.9] W Brown, S Deakin, M Hudson, C Pratten and P Ryan, *The Individualisation of Employment Contracts in Britain* (London, Department of Trade and Industry, Employment Research Series No. 4, 1998) 47

> The Company recognises the [Union] as having sole Bargaining rights for you under this Contract of Employment. [The Union] is your agent and is empowered to negotiate variations to your terms and conditions of employment (including diminution of terms and conditions) on your behalf . . . The instrument through which the Company and [Union] establish all your terms and conditions of employment is the Collective Agreement . . . This Collective Agreement is hereby expressly and specifically incorporated into your Contract of Employment . . . If the Collective Agreement . . . is at any time replaced by a subsequent Collective Agreement between the Company and the [Union] your terms and conditions of employment shall be determined under that subsequent Agreement.

Unfortunately, the incorporation provisions in many contracts of employment do not expressly devise such an automatic variation mechanism. In the absence of an express automatic variation clause in the contract, a revised collective agreement may affect the terms of the contract of employment, either if the individual employee consents to it or if it can be held that the collective agreement became incorporated by means of a customary implied term.

Consent by employees to variations created by collective agreements is usually inferred from the conduct of an employee in continuing to work normally after a pay increase or variation of hours or duties. If the employee protests against the change, however, his refusal to accept the variation negotiated by the union prevents the employer from implementing it unilaterally. This legal position protects the employee against his union representatives negotiating unwelcome variations in his terms of employment, but it also undermines attempts by unions and management to engage in 'concession bargaining' or productivity agreements, because, in the absence of automatic incorporation of variations, individual employees are entitled to reject the outcome, or part of the outcome, of such collective agreements.

[10.10] *Lee v GEC Plessey Telecommunications Ltd* [1993] IRLR 383 (HC)

The collective agreement awarded a pay increase but also withdrew a generous severance or redundancy scheme, leaving any new scheme to be devised by further collective agreement. The employee obtained a declaration that the terms of the earlier agreement regarding severance pay remained in force in the contract of employment. The result might have been different if the employer had bargained in the collective agreement for a provision that withdrawal of the severance scheme was a condition of the pay increase, so that the employee could not have accepted the pay increase without by implication accepting also the abolition of the redundancy scheme.

The alternative argument for holding an employee to a revised collective agreement (in the absence of express incorporation of the variation in the contract of employment) is to insist that collective agreements have become a customary implied term of contracts of employment in that workplace. Under this approach, the general contract law test of implied terms has been applied: the custom must be reasonable, certain, and notorious. If this custom is established and has the effect that the terms of the individual contract of employment change in line with new collective agreements, the employee is bound by the revised terms.

[10.11] *Henry v London General Transport Services Ltd* [2002] EWCA Civ 488, [2002] ICR 910 (CA)

A trade union had negotiated with prospective owners of the business (a management buy-out by share transfer) a collective agreement that would impose reduced pay and less favourable conditions on its members. The union informed the employer that the new terms were acceptable to the workforce, and the vast majority of employees signed statements of changed terms and conditions. A minority of the workforce, including the 61 applicants in this case, wrote to the employer that they would continue to work only under protest about the new terms. Their legal claims were for unlawful deductions from wages contrary to ERA 1996, section 13 ([2.8] above). The principal question was whether the individual contracts of employment had been varied by the collective agreement, even though there was no express incorporation clause in the contracts of employment. The applicants argued that the union had failed to hold a ballot of the workforce prior to acceptance of the new terms of employment, which was contrary to custom in the workplace, so that the collective agreement had not been incorporated into their contracts of employment. The Employment Tribunal upheld the claim on the grounds that the collective agreement had not been incorporated and that by continuing to work for two years under protest the employes had not consented to the new terms. The EAT allowed the employer's appeal and remitted the case for a rehearing on the question of whether the custom in the workplace requiring a ballot prior to the incorporation of a new collective agreement into individual contracts of employment was reasonable, certain, and notorious. The Court of Appeal rejected the appeal by the applicants and remitted the case for a rehearing by the tribunal on two issues. First, the tribunal had not justified its conclusion that the employees had not consented to the new terms of employment even though they had worked normally in accordance with the new terms for two years before commencing legal proceedings. Second, the Court of Appeal required the tribunal to direct itself to the question of whether it was a custom of the workplace that the collective agreement would be incorporated even though no ballot had been held.

This case demonstrates that concession bargaining can be effective to change the terms of employment provided that there is a well-established practice of the collective agreement determining terms and conditions of employment at a particular workplace.

One last question with respect to variations in collective agreements concerns the effect of the employer's withdrawal from a collective agreement. If an employer derecognises a union, or simply declares that it will no longer be bound by a collective agreement, how does that affect the terms of individual contracts of employment? The answer seems to be that the terms of the collective agreement continue to bind the employer and employee until such time as the employer and employee agree new terms.

[10.12] *Robertson v British Gas Corp* [1983] ICR 351 (CA)

An important element of the employee's remuneration was comprised of bonus payments, the level of which was fixed by collective agreement. The employer notified the union that it was terminating the bonus scheme, that is withdrawing from the collective agreement, and the employer ceased to pay bonuses. The employees claimed arrears of pay based upon the abrogated bonus scheme. This claim was successful, because the court determined that the bonus scheme was part of the contracts of employment, and the employer's withdrawal of the scheme without the consent of the employees constituted a breach of contract.

Kerr LJ:
It is true that collective agreements such as those in the present case create no legally enforceable obligation between the trade union and the employers. Either side can withdraw. But their terms are in this case incorporated into the individual contracts of employment, and it is only if and when those terms are varied collectively by agreement that the individual contracts of employment will also be varied. If the collective scheme is not varied by agreement, but by some unilateral abrogation or withdrawal or variation to which the other side does not agree, then it seems to me that the individual contracts of employment remain unaffected. This is another way of saying that the terms of the individual contracts are in part to be found in the agreed collective agreements as they exist from time to time, and, if these cease to exist as collective agreements, then the terms, unless expressly varied between the individual and the employer, will remain as they were by reference to the last agreed collective agreement incorporated into the individual contracts.

Assuming that a new collective agreement does not succeed in altering the terms and conditions of employment of an individual employee in a particular case, what are the practical implications? In principle, the employee may insist upon his or her current terms and claim any shortfall in wages. If the employer fails to comply with the original terms, this breach of contract may amount to repudiation. Nevertheless, if the employer dismisses the employee or the employee claims constructive dismissal, the employee's prospects for success in a claim for unfair dismissal appear fairly bleak. The employer can present the employee's refusal to accept the collectively agreed terms as a substantial reason for dismissal. Following *Hollister v National Farmers' Union* [1979] ICR 542 CA (below **[10.21]**), a tribunal may decide that it was reasonable for an employer to dismiss for this reason.

10.1.3 Short-time working and employment subsidies

One response to adverse trading conditions is for employers to reduce the hours of work or to provide less piecework to be performed. Such a change may amount to a breach of contract if the employer fails to pay the contractual entitlement to wages. The employer can, however, insert an express term giving a right to make temporary lay-offs or to impose short-time working. It may be possible in some cases to justify an implied term in fact on the basis of the presumed intentions of the parties or customs of the particular trade. If a reduction of hours or temporary lay-off is a breach of contract, an employee may choose to resign, to claim constructive dismissal, and to seek compensation for breach of contract, unfair dismissal or redundancy. But the contract of employment may be drafted so as to place the risk of absence of work upon the employees: the agreement may be to pay for hours of work as required, or to pay for pieces produced as required. If the employer chooses to reduce hours of work or piecework in such cases, there would be no breach of contract. In an attempt to share the risk of the absence of work to be performed in such cases, a collective agreement may fix a minimum weekly rate of pay that is incorporated into relevant contracts of employment. For the majority of employment relations, however, the employer assumes the risk of absence of work through the contractual commitment to pay wages on a weekly or periodic basis, in which case the employer cannot reduce hours and wages without risking claims for constructive dismissal or for arrears of salary.

From the perspective of the reduction of social cost and the avoidance of social exclusion, governments may be tempted to introduce regulation for the purpose of encouraging employers and employees to agree to variations of the terms of employment as opposed to dismissals. It may be cheaper for the government to subsidise employment for a period of time than to pay social security benefits for the duration of a period of unemployment. In addition, the employer can be encouraged to retain the skilled and trained workforce, so that when demand for the product returns, the employer can resume efficient production. In response to cyclical patterns of economic growth and levels employment, it appears to be attractive for governments to even out the booms and busts of businesses by subsidies to employers to retain the workforce. In the United Kingdom, two such interventions have been attempted: guarantee payment schemes and short-time working schemes.

10.1.3.1 Guarantee pay

Under this legislation, there is no subsidy for employers, but if the employer reduces the number of working days for an employee, the employee is entitled to a minimum remuneration for the days of lay-off. This guarantee payment does not apply when the employer reduces the hours worked by other methods such as the elimination of overtime or a reduction of the hours worked each day.

[10.13] Employment Rights Act 1996, section 28

> **(1)** Where throughout a day during any part of which an employee would normally be required to work in accordance with his contract of employment the employee is not provided with work by his employer by reason of—
> (a) a diminution in the requirements of the employer's business for work of the kind which the employee is employed to do, or
> (b) any other occurrence affecting the normal working of the employer's business in relation to work of the kind which the employee is employed to do,
> the employee is entitled to be paid by his employer an amount in respect of that day.

Since many, perhaps most, contracts of employment oblige an employer to pay wages even if there is no work to be done, or to pay a minimum wage, this system of guarantee payments applies only to contracts where the risk of absence of work is placed squarely on the employee. This statutory entitlement forces the employer to provide some pay for the day in much the same way as some collective agreements require. The entitlement is, however, extremely meagre, for it applies only to a maximum of five workless days in a period of three months (ERA 1996, section 31(2)(3)), and the maximum payment in respect of any one day is £17.80, a figure which is well below the minimum wage.

What are the effects of this regulation? Some employees might otherwise be able to claim some income support from the social security system for periods of unemployment, so one purpose and a possible effect of the guarantee pay entitlement can be to reduce the cost to the taxpayer by transferring it onto the employer. The low amount of guarantee pay probably leaves the worker no better off than if the entitlement to social security benefits had remained. The liability to pay guarantee pay may also discourage employers from using the strategy of closing the business for odd days or a week in order to reduce labour costs, and instead steer them towards the negotiation for reduced hours of work every day and job sharing. The employer may be able to avoid the regulation entirely by negotiating a contract that has no fixed hours, such as a zero hours contract or casual work, so that the employee cannot claim under ERA 1996, section 28(1) that he would 'normally be required to work in accordance his contract of employment' (e.g. *Mailway (Southern) Ltd v Willsher* [1978] ICR 511 (EAT)). Another way to avoid the legislation is for the employer to require employees to agree to new terms of employment with reduced hours, so that if a four day week is negotiated, the fifth day is no longer within the definition of a workless day (*Clemens v Peter Richards Ltd* [1977] IRLR 332(EAT)). The guarantee payment system provides a small amount of protection of income for employees in respect of occasional reductions in work, but in so doing it imposes a slight disincentive for employers to adopt this approach to the reduction of working time as opposed to other techniques involving variation of the hours of work .

10.1.3.2 Short-time working subsidies

In contrast to this technique of requiring employers to provide income support on workless days, government policy at times of recession has sometimes been the opposite: to subsidise employers who keep employees at work instead of dismissing them. The high point of this intervention was established by the Employment Subsidies Act 1978, which enabled the government to create schemes to enable employers to keep persons in employment. Under this Act, the government introduced as an administrative measure the Temporary Short-time Working Compensation Scheme (88 *Employment Gazette* 478 (May 1980)). Employers were compensated for additional labour costs if, instead of dismissing part of the workforce for economic reasons, they introduced job sharing and short-time working. Employers were encouraged to introduce workless days as a way of handling reductions in output, in order to reduce the social costs of unemployment.

A problem with employment subsidies is that they detract from the level playing field sought by the EU, because employers may gain some competitive advantage in having part of the wage bill being paid. For this reason, these schemes eventually had to be withdrawn after pressure from the European Commission. Before that happened, the UK government had spent more than a billion pounds, and as many as three million employees had their dismissals for economic reasons at least temporarily averted. Employers were able to keep a skilled and trained workforce, which perhaps enabled a speedier recovery once the recession was over. From the perspective of social cost, the vital question is whether this expenditure was less than the alternative of support for the unemployed through the social security system. It was never clearly established that savings had been made, but such a calculation is extremely difficult when all the social costs of unemployment such as increased health care and a rise in certain types of criminal activity are included.

10.2 Workforce reductions

Government policy with respect to workforce reductions is torn in two directions. On the one hand, economic dismissals are to be encouraged in so far as they represent necessary adjustments to changing technologies, product markets, and competitive conditions, which will enable firms to survive and to increase their competitiveness and profits. Although economic dismissals may be popularly regarded as a sign of economic decline and recession, they occur in large numbers even in periods of economic growth as part of competitive pressures and displacement of workers from one industrial sector to another. For example, in 1998, a period of stability or modest growth in the UK economy, according to official statistics about 860,000 employees (or nine per thousand workers) were dismissed for redundancy, though about two-fifths found another job within three months (*Labour Market Trends* (May 1999), S63, table C.41). On the other hand, the State is concerned about the costs to society of widespread unemployment, the damage to local economies caused by plant closures, and the harm to individual workers caused by unemployment. Employees seldom welcome economic dismissals, of course, because any expectations of job security are dashed, and they are threatened with financial hardship and social exclusion. These fears no doubt lead to the pervasive use of euphemisms for dismissal in the management literature: downsizing, de-recruiting, de-layering, re-sizing, and right-sizing. Employers may not welcome economic dismissals either, not least because they damage the employer's credibility in offering good jobs, and will provoke among the retained workforce damaging reactions such as less commitment and heightened resistance to change. Nevertheless managers and shareholders usually regard economic dismissals in the face of technological change and competitive pressures as inevitable and desirable in terms of efficiency and productivity in the long run.

Legal regulation of economic dismissals reveals the ambiguous attitude of governments. The legislation, introduced originally as the Redundancy Payments Act 1965, provides employees with the right to claim compensation for economic dismissals. The redundancy payment, which is the same as the basic award for unfair dismissal, is calculated under a formula by reference to the weekly wage, years of service and the age of the worker. This right to a severance payment was presented by some proponents as a protection of the employee's expectation of job security by deterring employers from making workforce reductions and compensating employees for the loss of their jobs. Yet, at the same time, the government provided employers with a subsidy when making redundancy payments. The subsidy reduced the deterrent effect of the legislation against workforce reductions, because the government did not wish to discourage employers from making efficient adjustments to the workforce. The government believed that by compelling employers to adopt the practice of making severance payments, the practice of making redundancies would become more acceptable to both sides of industry, thus enabling businesses to become more competitive by the reduction of over-manning and the introduction of new technology. An early survey of employers and trade unions confirmed that three-quarters of employers believed that the legislation had made it easier to dismiss employees for redundancy (SR Parker, CG Thomas, ND Ellis and WEJ McCarthy, *Effects of the Redundancy Payments Act* (London, HMSO, 1971)). The subsidy to employers was gradually withdrawn in the 1980s, however, as the policy objective became increasingly one of discouraging economic dismissals, owing to the social costs of high levels of unemployment.

The right to claim a redundancy payment for an economic dismissal is excluded by various statutory provisions. Like other statutory claims for dismissal, the right is confined to employees (though there is power to make exceptions by regulation: ERA 1996, section 171). The qualifying period for the right is two years: ERA 1996, section 155. Employees over the 'normal retiring age' are excluded: ERA 1996, section 156. The right to a redundancy payment is, of course, excluded when the principal reason for dismissal concerned factors personal to the employee, such as misconduct. Where this misconduct is strike action in response to a notice of dismissal for

---

Redundancy Payment and Basic Award

The amount of a redundancy payment or a basic award in a claim for unfair dismissal is calculated by a formula that relates to age, wages, and years of service. Under ERA 1996 s. 162, employees over 40 receive one and a half week's pay for each year of employment, and one week's pay for each year between ages twenty-two and forty, and a half a week's pay for age below 21, up to a maximum of twenty years of employment. There is an upper limit on the amount of a week's pay, currently set at £240. What is the objective behind this calculation? The compensation looks backwards to determine the quantification, so that it cannot de designed precisely to compensate employees for future losses arising from dismissal, that is the hardship resulting from unemployment. The increased level of compensation for older employees recognises, however, that they find it more difficult to obtain another job. The length of service criterion perhaps recognises that dismissal after many years of service is a greater shock to employees, and may even symbolise some abstract idea that long-service employees have acquired some right analogous to a proprietary interest in their jobs. But this calculus can be criticised on the ground that by looking exclusively backwards rather than forwards to the likely effects of economic dismissal, it cannot provide an exact match between the economic and social losses and the level of compensation. In addition, by stressing length of service as the basis of compensation, it puts at a relative disadvantage those members of the labour force, especially women, who experience difficulty in accumulating length of service with a particular employer. For claims of unfair dismissal, the compensatory award provides forward-looking compensation, but this element is missing in economic dismissals, so that redundancy payments do not reflect the actual size of the economic and social costs experienced by the dismissed workforce. A rather different explanation of redundancy payments is that severance benefits represent a hypothetical insurance contract between the employees, under which they all agree to a reduction of wages, with a view to giving the savings to those workers who lose their jobs for economic reasons: O Fabel, S Welzmiller, and P Chribasik, 'Severance pay in Germany: a contract perspective', in G De Geest, J Siegers, and R Van den Bergh, *Law and Economics and the Labour Market* (Cheltenham, Elgar, 1999) 185.

---

redundancy, however, the claim for a redundancy payment is usually preserved: ERA 1996, section 140(2). In the face of a notice of dismissal for redundancy, an employee may decide to leave early in order to take up another job. The legislation tries to balance the interests of the employee in looking for a new job and the interests of the employer in carrying out the planned reduction of the workforce: if the employee leaves early, the employer can withdraw the redundancy payment, but the employee has a right to claim all or part of the redundancy payment on the ground that in the circumstances it would be 'just and equitable': ERA 1996, section 142.

As a necessary condition for making a claim for a redundancy payment, the employee normally has to demonstrate that employment has been terminated by a dismissal. For this purpose, the statutory concept of dismissal discussed in chapter 5.2 in connection with the law of unfair dismissal applies. In particular, it should be noted that calls for volunteers for redundancy or 'early retirement' amount to a request for an agreed termination of the contract, which falls outside the statutory concept of dismissal, so that the employees relinquishes any claim to a statutory redundancy payment: *Birch v Liverpool University* [1985] ICR 470 (CA), above **[5.32]**). As an exception to the statutory concept of dismissal, however, an employee may bring a claim for a redundancy payment under detailed statutory rules if he or she terminates the contract of employment, after having given notice, in response to prolonged lay-offs or periods of short-time working during which the employee is not paid or receives less than half pay: ERA 1996, sections 147–54.

The tensions in the policy behind the regulation of economic dismissals run through judicial interpretations of the legislation. A court that is sympathetic to the managerial objective of saving the business or improving efficiency might wish to minimise the employer's liability to make severance payments by a restrictive interpretation of the concept of redundancy. Yet a court with the same motivation might equally take the opposite stance, that is to award redundancy payments wherever possible, in order to encourage workers to accept the need for a workforce reduction, and, in the past, to enable the employer to obtain a subsidy. After 1971 (and especially after the introduction of the basic award in 1975), with the advent of the greater potential liability for unfair dismissal, a court with the same motivation would be even keener to make the employer liable to pay a redundancy payment, in order to help the employer to avoid the greater liability for compensation for unfair dismissal. In the cases that we shall consider below, it is often the employee who contests that he or she is redundant in the hope of obtaining the superior level of compensation for unfair dismissal.

Many of the cases that we shall consider, though in form a claim for unfair dismissal against an employer, involve a conflict of interest within the workforce about which workers should be selected for redundancy. Those who are selected for dismissal may express this claim in two ways. One is to admit that the dismissal was for redundancy, but to argue that the dismissal was nevertheless unfair owing to the employer's use of unfair procedures or selection criteria. The other route is to contest that the employee was redundant at all, and to argue instead that the employee was still required by the employer though other workers, who have not been dismissed, may have been redundant. If successful, this second argument may lead to the conclusion that the employer has not established a substantial reason for dismissal, so the dismissal was unfair. This second way of challenging selection for redundancy poses difficult questions for the courts on the meaning of the statutory concept of redundancy.

10.2.1 The concept of redundancy

An employee can claim a severance payment on dismissal, if the reason for dismissal was 'redundancy'.

[10.14] Employment Rights Act 1996, section 139

(1) For the purposes of this Act an employee who is dismissed will be taken to be dismissed by reason of redundancy if the dismissal is wholly or mainly attributable to—

(a) the fact that his employer has ceased or intends to cease—

(i) to carry on the business for the purposes of which the employee was employed by him, or

> (ii) to carry on that business in the place where the employee was so employed, or
> (b) the fact that the requirements of that business—
>   (i) for employees to carry out work of a particular kind, or
>   (ii) for employees to carry out work of a particular kind in the place where the employee was employed by the employer
>
> have ceased or diminished or are expected to cease or diminish.

This definition of the concept of redundancy is surprisingly complicated. It does not apply generally to dismissals for business or economic reasons, that is reasons unconnected with the personal conduct or circumstances of the dismissed employee. Such a broad definition of redundancy or economic dismissals is used, however, in the context of the duty to consult workforce representatives about economic dismissals (10.6 below).

[10.15] Trade Union and Labour Relations (Consolidation) Act 1992, section 195

> **(1)** In this chapter references to dismissal as redundant are references to dismissal for a reason not related to the individual concerned or for a number of reasons all of which are not so related.

Instead of this broad test, the statutory definition of redundancy for the purpose of claiming individual compensation introduces some further conditions: either a diminution in requirements 'for employees to carry out work of a particular kind' or a similar diminution in the 'place where the employee was so employed'. The latter condition provokes questions about where the employee worked. The former condition provokes questions about what kind of work the employee was required to perform, and whether the employer has a reduced demand for that kind of work. These questions are avoided by the broader definition of redundancy used for the purpose of triggering the employer's obligation to consult. In particular, it is clear that an employer's decision to alter the terms of employment of a group of workers unilaterally (a constructive dismissal) will fall within the broad concept of redundancy for the purpose of consultation, even though the employer has no intention to reduce the number of workers and therefore will probably not be liable to pay redundancy payments: *GMB v Man Truck & Bus UK Ltd* [2000] IRLR 636 (EAT).

In both definitions, however, it is clear that the tribunal is not required to decide whether the managerial decision was sensible, necessary, or justifiable. A tribunal is not permitted to assess whether in the circumstances the management strategy of making employees redundant furthered the business goals of the employers. The law requires courts and tribunals to respect the managerial decision to engage in restructuring; the only question is whether and how much compensation should be payable to individual workers who lose their jobs.

Although we shall focus on some of the complexities surrounding the statutory definition of redundancy in ERA 1996, section 139, we should recognise that most economic dismissals will be covered, and so the employer will be required to pay compensation. Typical instances of redundancy include plant closures, the reduction of the workforce in order to reduce labour costs, the reduction of the workforce as a result of the introduction of new technology or capital equipment, and the insolvency of the business. Here we examine three particularly contested topics related to the boundaries of the statutory concept of redundancy.

Perhaps the underlying source of this complexity in the application of the statutory concept of redundancy can best be understood by the contrast between 'employment security' and 'job security'. Protection for employment security suggests that compensation should be awarded only if the employee has been dismissed, not when the particular job performed or the terms and conditions have been varied though there is still work for the employee, perhaps involving different skills. Protection for job security would in contrast provide compensation whenever the employee's particular job was not longer required, even though the employee might have been offered alternative employment by the same employer. The phrase in the statute 'work of a particular kind' is susceptible to the interpretation that it requires compensation for job security, not just employment security. It therefore implies that a redundancy payment should be awarded where a particular job disappears, even though the employer immediately offers another job. This aim of protecting job security could be attributed plausibly to the legislation as a device to encourage employees to be flexible in the sense of giving up rigid job demarcations in return for compensation. But the courts have been reluctant to accept this interpretation and have instead preferred the view that redundancy payments should only be made when the employer is actually reducing the number of employees as opposed to reorganising the workforce. Furthermore, the view that the concept of redundancy protects job security is hard to square with the provisions considered below in 10.3, under which the employer can avoid paying compensation by making an offer of suitable alternative employment.

10.2.1.1 Reorganisation involving new job specification

We have noted already that the principal response of employers to changing business conditions is to seek to vary the terms of employment. These variations may involve minor reductions of hours or the elimination of overtime, or they may encompass a more fundamental restructuring of the business. In the 1990s, a common managerial response to competitive pressures involved 'de-layering', that is the elimination of many middle management positions, and the redesignation of some existing jobs at lower positions of responsibility in the hierarchy of the organisation. These business reorganisations often involve dismissals, either because the employer dismisses employees and invites them to apply for the new jobs, or because the employees refuse to agree to the variations in the terms of the contract of employment. It was established in early cases that variations in the terms of employment for reasons of efficiency did not necessarily amount to cases of redundancy.

[10.16] *Lesney Products & Co v Nolan* **[1977] ICR 235 (CA)**

> As sales of the factory's product fell, the employers introduced a new shift system. The night shift was eliminated, and day work was divided into two shifts. The amount of production and the number of workers required during the day remained the same, but the employers reduced costs by eliminating overtime payments through the new shift

system. Several employees refused to work the new day shift system, no doubt because it reduced their wages by about one third, owing to the loss of overtime payments, and were dismissed. Their claims for redundancy payments were upheld by an industrial tribunal, but the Court of Appeal allowed the employer's appeal. The dismissals were not for redundancy, because there was no drop in the amount of work required during the day.

Lord Denning MR:
[I]t is important that nothing should be done to impair the ability of employers to reorganise their work force and their times and conditions of work so as to improve efficiency. They may reorganise it so as to reduce overtime and thus to save themselves money, but that does not give the man a right to redundancy payment. Overtime might be reduced, for instance, by taking on more men: but that would not give the existing staff a right to redundancy payments. Also when overtime is reduced by a reorganisation or working hours, that does not give rise to a right to a redundancy payment, so long as the work to be done is the same.

This decision left open the possibility that major changes in the terms of employment, such as the creation of a completely new job specification, might amount to a redundancy. The old job would be eliminated and replaced by the new one, with a different title and varied duties and remuneration. The legal question was whether the elimination of the old job meant that the employer's requirements for employees to perform work of a particular kind had diminished. One answer, sometimes described as the job function approach, examines the work actually done by different employees, and concludes that the redundant employees are those whose 'jobs have gone'. A different answer is to look at the terms of the contracts of employment in order to decide which employees are no longer required. The 'job titles' indicate which employees are no longer required. The Court of Appeal in *Lesney Products v Nolan* appeared to suggest that the effect of contractual variation should be determined by reference to the work performed, that is a job function approach: if the employees were performing much the same work, albeit under different terms of employment, their dismissal for rejecting the new terms would not be a redundancy dismissal. In other decisions, however, courts appeared to place greater weight on the terms of the contract: if the terms remained the same, though the duties varied as a result of the reorganisation, the employee would not be redundant.

[10.17] *North Riding Garages v Butterwick* [1967] 2 QB 56 (QBD Div. Ct.)

The workshop manager of car repairs for a garage was dismissed after 30 years of service because he could not cope with new working methods required by the new owners of the business, which included increased paperwork and the provision of estimates in advance to customers. The Divisional Court (which at that time heard appeals from industrial tribunals) reversed the finding of redundancy on the ground that the garage continued to require a workshop manager, albeit one with different skills.

In recent cases, however, with the approval of the House of Lords in *Murray v Foyle Meats Ltd* (**[10.19]** below), the approach to business reorganisations involving variations in the work performed has rejected both the job function and the contract test. The issue is said simply to be whether there has been a reduction of the workforce as a result of a business reorganisation, and whether the dismissal under consideration was connected to that reduction. The terms of the contract or the actual job performed by an employee may be relevant to the question of causation, in the sense that the employee will not be redundant if the need for a workforce reduction occurs in another part of the business in which the employee has not worked and could not be required to work under the terms of the contract.

[10.18] *Safeway Stores Plc v Burrell* [1997] ICR 523 (EAT)

The employers engaged in a major restructuring of their supermarket business involving 'de-layering' of middle management and the reorganisation of departments. The applicant was employed as petrol station manager at the filling station located at the site of one of the supermarkets. The reorganisation plan involved the disappearance of the post of petrol station manager and its replacement by the grade of petrol station controller at a lower rate of pay. Much of the work required under the new job description remained the same as under the former position. Furthermore, although the former job description carried additional managerial responsibilities, in practice the employee had not performed them. The employee decided not to apply for the new post on the ground that his pay would be reduced, and he was given a redundancy payment. Subsequently he claimed unfair dismissal. By a majority, the employment tribunal decided that the employers had not demonstrated that the employee was redundant, because the new job involved much the same work as the employee had performed formerly in practice. On appeal against the finding of unfair dismissal, the EAT held that the tribunal had adopted the wrong test of redundancy and remitted the case for a rehearing. The correct test was to ask, first, whether there was diminution of the employer's requirement for employees, and second, was the dismissal caused by that diminution. The terms of the contract of employment were not relevant to those questions.

Peter Clark J:
Free of authority, we understand the statutory framework of [ERA 1996 s 139(1)(b)] to involve a three-stage process:
(1) was the employee dismissed? If so,
(2) had the requirements of the employer's business for employees to carry out work of a particular kind ceased or diminished, or were they expected to cease or diminish? If so,
(3) was the dismissal of the employee (the applicant before the industrial tribunal) caused wholly or mainly by the state of affairs identified at stage 2 above? . . .

From time to time the mistake is made of focusing on a diminution in the work to be done, not the employees who do it. One example will suffice. In *Carry All Motors Ltd v Pennington* [1980] IRLR 455 the applicant before the industrial tribunal, employed as a transport clerk, was dismissed by his employers following their decision that his depot was overstaffed; they concluded that the work of the transport manager and transport clerk could be carried out by one employee only. The transport manager was retained and the applicant dismissed.

On his complaint of unfair dismissal the employer relied on redundancy as the reason for dismissal. An industrial tribunal held that the requirement of the business for employees to carry out particular work had not ceased or diminished. The same work remained. Accordingly, there was no redundancy but simply a reorganisation. The dismissal was unfair.

On appeal the Employment Appeal Tribunal reversed the industrial tribunal's findings. It held that the question was not whether the requirement for particular work had diminished, but whether the requirement for employees to do that work had diminished. Since one employee was now doing the work formerly done by two, the statutory test of redundancy had been satisfied. In reaching that conclusion, the Employment Appeal Tribunal followed and applied the approach of the National Industrial Relations Court in the case of *Sutton v Revlon Overseas Corporation* [1973] IRLR 173.

In our view *Pennington* and *Sutton* correctly applied the law to the facts in those cases. It is necessary to look at the overall requirement for employees to do work of a particular kind; not at the amount of work to be done.

Business reorganisation

A complication has arisen where there is a business reorganisation followed by dismissals. The fact that there has been a reorganisation does not of itself answer the stage 2 question one way or the other. It is simply part of the factual background. It may be relevant to an alternative ground of some other substantial reason if that is advanced by the employers.

In *Robinson v British Island Airways Ltd* [1977] IRLR 477 the applicant employee worked as flight operations manager, reporting to the general manager operations and traffic. A reorganisation took place in the interests of efficiency and economy. The two former posts mentioned above were abolished and replaced by a single post of operations manager. That was a more important post than the two previous posts combined; both original postholders were dismissed and a new employee appointed operations manager. Before the industrial tribunal the applicant complained that he was not redundant and had been unfairly dismissed. The tribunal dismissed his complaint, holding that he had been dismissed fairly by reason of redundancy. The applicant's appeal to the Employment Appeal Tribunal was dismissed. In giving the judgment of this tribunal, Phillips J said this at 478,7:

> 'Cases concerning redundancy arising out of a reorganisation always cause difficulties. Certain passages in some of the judgments in *Johnson v Nottinghamshire Combined Police Authority* [1974] ICR 170 and *Lesney Products & Co. Ltd v Nolan* [1977] ICR 235 have been taken as suggesting that if a dismissal has been caused by a reorganisation the reason for dismissal cannot be redundancy. We do not think that this is the meaning of the passages, or what was intended. In truth a reorganisation may or may not end in redundancy; it all depends upon the nature and effect of the reorganisation. In *Johnson v Nottinghamshire Combined Police Authority* there was no redundancy because in the opinion of the Court of Appeal the change in the hours of work involved in that case did not change the particular kind of work being carried on. In *Lesney Products & Co Ltd. v Nolan* there was no redundancy because on the correct analysis of the facts (it was in the analysis of the facts that the appeal tribunal and the industrial tribunal were in error) there was no cessation or diminution of the requirement for employees to carry out work of a particular kind. The number of employees, and the nature of the work, remained the same, and all that changed was the ability to earn overtime. What has to be done in every case is to analyse the facts and to match the analysis against the words of ERA 1996, section 139. In doing this it is of no assistance to consider whether as a matter of impression there was or was not a 'redundancy situation.' The question is whether the definition is satisfied.'

Again, we adopt that analysis as a correct statement of the law, dealing, as it does, with the effect of the earlier Court of Appeal decisions in *Johnson* [1974] ICR 70 and *Lesney* [1977] ICR 235, themselves consistent with the previous decision of the Court of Appeal in *Chapman v Goonvean and Rostowrack China Clay Co. Ltd.* [1973] ICR 310, where withdrawal of a free bus service for seven employees, who were constructively dismissed and claimed redundancy payments, was held not to give rise to dismissals by reason of redundancy, since the work continued to be performed by an identical number of new employees, recruited to replace the seven who had left. . . .

[*The judge reviewed many authorities on the concept of redundancy.*]

The correct approach

Like the appeal tribunal in *Cowen v Haden Ltd.* [1983] ICR 1, we started by looking at the statute and construing the words free of authority. Similarly, we have looked at the authorities. Unlike that tribunal, we return to our original approach and conclude, first, that it was correct, and, secondly, that no binding authority causes us to abandon that position. We would summarise it as follows.

(1) There may be a number of underlying causes leading to a true redundancy situation; our stage 2. There may be a need for economies; a reorganisation in the interests of efficiency; a reduction in production requirements; unilateral changes in the employees' terms and conditions of employment. None of these factors are themselves determinative of the stage 2 question. The only question to be asked is: was there a diminution/cessation in the employer's requirement for *employees* to carry out work of a particular kind, or an expectation of such cessation/diminution in the future? At this stage it is irrelevant to consider the terms of the applicant employee's contract of employment. That will only be relevant, if at all, at stage 3 (assuming that there is a dismissal).

(2) At stage 3 the tribunal is concerned with causation. Was the dismissal attributable wholly or mainly to the redundancy? Thus—

(a) Even if a redundancy situation arises, as in *Nelson*, [*Nelson v British Broadcasting Corporation (No 2)* [1980] ICR 110, CA] if that does not cause the dismissal, the employee has not been dismissed by reason of redundancy. In *Nelson* the employee was directed to transfer to another job as provided for in his contract. He refused to do so. That was why he was dismissed.

(b) If the requirement for employees to perform the work of a transport clerk and transport manager diminishes, so that one employee can do both jobs, the dismissed employee is dismissed by reason of redundancy. See *Pennington*. The same explanation applies, on the facts, to the eventual decision in *Robinson*. In *Cowen v Haden Ltd* the requirement for employees to do the work of a divisional contracts surveyor ceased. The postholder was dismissed. That was a dismissal by reason of redundancy.

(c) Conversely, if the requirement for employees to do work of a particular kind remains the same, there can be no dismissal by reason of redundancy, notwithstanding any unilateral variation to their contracts of employment. See *Chapman*, *Lesney* and *Johnson*.

(d) The contract versus function test debate is predicated on a misreading of both the statute and the cases of *Nelson* and *Cowen v Haden Ltd*. Save for the limited circumstances arising from *Nelson* where an employee is redeployed under the terms of his contract of employment and refuses to move, and this causes his dismissal, the applicant/employee's terms and conditions of employment are irrelevant to the questions raised by the statute.

(e) This explains the concept of 'bumped redundancies'. Take this example: an employee is employed to work as a fork-lift truck driver, delivering materials to six production machines on the shop floor. Each machine has its own operator. The employer decides that it needs to run only five machines and that one machine operator must go. That is a stage 2 redundancy situation. Selection for dismissal is done on the LIFO principle within the department. The fork-lift truck driver is dismissed. Is he dismissed by reason of redundancy? The answer is yes. Although under both the contract and function tests he is employed as a fork-lift driver, and there is no diminution in the requirement for fork-lift drivers, nevertheless there is a diminution in the requirement for employees to carry out the operators' work and that has caused the employee's dismissal. See, for example, *W Gimbert & Sons Ltd v Spurett* [1967] 2 ITR 308; *Elliott Turbomachinery v Bates* [1981]

ICR 218. In our judgment, the principle of 'bumped' redundancies is statutorily correct, and further demonstrates the flaw in the 'contract test' adumbrated in *Pink [Pink v White and White & Co. (Earls Barton) Ltd [1985] IRLR 489 (EAT)]*.

(f) Our approach is also consistent with the decision of the Court of Appeal in *Murphy v Epsom College* [1984] IRLR 271. There, the applicant was one of two plumbers employed by a school. His work consisted mainly of general plumbing work. The employers decided to employ a heating technician to maintain their improved heating system. They then decided to dismiss one of the two plumbers and selected the employee for dismissal. The Court of Appeal upheld the majority view of the industrial tribunal that the reason for dismissal was redundancy. The employer originally had two plumbers; now it only required one. The employee was dismissed by reason of redundancy.

What does this decision imply about the application of the statutory concept of redundancy to business reorganisations? If the employer reduces the number of employees overall, provided that the dismissal of any individual is attributable to this workforce reduction rather than some other reason or motive, the dismissal should be regarded as a case of redundancy. In the case of *Safeway Stores Plc v Burrell*, therefore, the issue was whether the supermarket had reduced its number of employees or merely reorganised the same number of employees. As the de-layering did involve the reduction of managerial employees across the organisation, on this reasoning the applicant was dismissed for redundancy if the dismissal was part of that reorganisation. The terms of the contract of employment are relevant only to this question of causation: the employers were dismissing only middle managers, and the terms of Mr Burrell's employment placed him in that category. If the employer continues to require the same number of employees, albeit on different terms and conditions or performing different tasks, in general the conclusion should be that any dismissal is not on the ground of redundancy. This approach approves the result, though perhaps not the reasoning, in *Lesney Products v Nolan* and *North Riding Garages v Butterwick*. The unilateral variation of terms of employment, including new designations of jobs, new job descriptions, and alterations in hours and wages, does not in itself create a redundancy situation. Yet there does come a point when the variation of the job description becomes so great that a court will conclude that, even though the number of employees remains constant, the new job description is so different that in effect the old job has disappeared and a new one has been created. This is the explanation of *Murphy v Epson College* [1985] ICR 80 (CA), discussed at the end of the extract from *Safeway Stores Plc v Burrell*. In order to reach the determination that one job has disappeared altogether, it seems to be necessary to examine and compare the terms of employment of the two jobs. The effort in *Safeway Stores Plc v Burrell* to exclude consideration of the terms of the contract cannot therefore be followed entirely. The terms can be relevant both to the question of causation and also to the prior question whether the workforce has been reduced.

If this continuing relevance of the terms of employment is correct, however, it throws in doubt the straightforward disposal of the claim in *Safeway Stores Plc v Burrell*. Although the store reduced its number of managers in general, with respect to the petrol station operation, it still required someone to perform much the same job as that performed by Mr Burrell, albeit with a different job title and lower wages. To say that there is a redundancy in such a case requires the tribunal both to ignore the terms of employment and to rely on them. The terms must be ignored for the purpose of lumping together all the middle managers in order to demonstrate a workforce reduction. But then, paradoxically, the tribunal must rely upon the terms of the contract to demonstrate that despite the fact that Mr Burrell's job still needed to be done by someone, it no longer existed because the precise job title, though not the job function, had disappeared in the reorganisation. The reluctance of the EAT to examine either the job function or the terms of employment seems to mark a strong rejection of the idea that redundancy payments should protect job security. Instead, the emphasis on the issue of whether there was a dismissal, that is a reduction in the workforce, suggests that the court regards the protection of employment security as the principal objective of the redundancy payments scheme.

10.2.1.2 Flexibility clauses

Many employers insert into contracts of employment a flexibility clause. This term permits the employer to direct the employee to a wide range of tasks, even though in practice the employee is primarily employed to work on a particular job. If the employer decides to reduce the workforce, perhaps in response to a drop in product demand or to improve efficiency, the question arises which employees are redundant? Since in theory under the flexibility clause all employees are interchangeable, there is no apparent ground for determining which employees are redundant. Under the 'contractual approach', it is arguable that the insertion of a flexibility clause into the contracts of employment of the workforce means that no particular employee can be singled out as no longer required; all employees are equally vulnerable to job loss. Those employees who are actually selected for dismissal can use the flexibility clause to assert that they were not redundant, because there was still work to be done, which they could have been required to perform under their contracts of employment. If the dismissed employees were not redundant, or at least no more redundant than any other workers in the plant, they have a chance of obtaining the higher level of compensation for unfair dismissal. The courts have rejected this possibility.

[10.19] *Murray v Foyle Meats Ltd* **[1999] ICR 827 (HL)**

> The employers ran a meat slaughter business. In response to a decline in the market, the employers decided to eliminate one production line in the slaughter hall. After consultation with the union on the criteria of selection, the employers dismissed 35 'meat plant operatives' who worked in the slaughter hall as redundant. The employees of the company were all employed on similar contractual terms and were subject to flexibility clauses, so that they could (and sometimes did) work in other departments such as the boning hall or the loading bay. The dismissed employees argued that they were not redundant, because the employer still required workers under the same terms and conditions of employment, albeit working in different departments.

> *Lord Irvine LC:*
> The appellants say the company chose to engage all its employees on similar terms. 'Requirements for employees to carry out work of a particular kind' meant 'requirements for employees contractually engaged to carry out work of a particular kind'. In this respect, no distinction could be made between those who worked in the slaughter hall and those who worked elsewhere. It is therefore wrong of the company to select for

redundancy solely from those who normally worked in the slaughter hall. It should have selected from everyone working under the same contract of employment.

My Lords, the language of [Employment Rights Act 1996, section 139(1)(*b*)] is in my view simplicity itself. It asks two questions of fact. The first is whether one or other of various states of economic affairs exists. In this case, the relevant one is whether the requirements of the business for employees to carry out work of a particular kind have diminished. The second question is whether the dismissal is attributable, wholly or mainly, to that state of affairs. This is a question of causation. In the present case, the Tribunal found as a fact that the requirements of the business for employees to work in the slaughter hall had diminished. Secondly, they found that that state of affairs had led to the appellants being dismissed. That, in my opinion, is the end of the matter.

This conclusion is in accordance with the analysis of the statutory provisions by Judge Peter Clark in *Safeway Stores Plc. v Burrell* ([1997] ICR 523 (EAT), (above **[10.18]**) and I need to say no more than that I entirely agree with his admirably clear reasoning and conclusions. But I should, out of respect for the submissions of Mr Declan Morgan QC for the appellants, say something about the earlier cases which may have encouraged a belief that the statute had a different meaning.

In *Nelson v British Broadcasting Corporation* [1977] ICR 649 (CA), Mr Nelson was employed by the BBC under a contract which required him to perform any duties to which he might be assigned. In fact he worked for the General Overseas Service broadcasting to the Caribbean. In 1974 the BBC reduced its services to the Caribbean, as a result of which Mr Nelson's services in that capacity were no longer required. When he refused alternative employment, he was dismissed on grounds of redundancy. The Industrial Tribunal concluded that he had been dismissed for redundancy, apparently on the grounds that a term could be implied into Mr Nelson's contract of employment that he should carry out work on Caribbean programmes. The Court of Appeal rightly rejected the implication of such a term. But they went on to hold that Mr Nelson was therefore not redundant. This was wrong. Whatever the terms of Mr Nelson's contract, it was open to the Tribunal to find that he had been dismissed because the BBC's requirements for work on Caribbean programmes had diminished. This was a question of fact.

The basis for the fallacy is to be found in the judgment of Brandon LJ in *Nelson v British Broadcasting Corporation (No. 2)* [1980] ICR 110, when Mr Nelson's case came again before the Court of Appeal. He said (at p. 126) that Mr Nelson had been right in law in maintaining that 'because the work which he was employed to do continued to exist, he was not redundant.' In saying this Brandon LJ appears to have meant that because Mr Nelson was employed to do any work to which he might be assigned with the BBC and because the BBC was still carrying on business, he could not be redundant. In my opinion this cannot be right. The fact was that the BBC's requirements for employees in the General Overseas Service in general and for Caribbean broadcasts in particular had diminished. It must therefore have been open to the Tribunal to decide that Mr Nelson's dismissal was attributable to that state of affairs. Of course, the BBC did not necessarily have to respond in that way. They could, for example, have transferred Mr Nelson to broadcasts which were still being maintained at full strength (say, to West Africa) in the place of a less experienced employee and made the latter redundant instead. In that case, it would have been open to the Tribunal to find that the other employee had been dismissed on account of redundancy. . . . In each case, the factual question of whether the dismissal was 'attributable' to the statutory state of affairs is one for the Tribunal.

The judgments in the two *Nelson* cases have caused understandable difficulty for Industrial Tribunals. They have been treated as authority for what has been called the 'contract test', which requires consideration of whether there was a diminution in the kind of work for which, according to the terms of his contract, the employee had been engaged. I give one example. In *Pink v White and White & Co. (Earls Barton) Ltd* [1985] IRLR 489 (EAT), Mr Pink was engaged to work in a shoe factory as a 'making and finishing room operative.' In practice, he did more specialised work as sole layer/pre-sole fitter. Because of a reduction in demand, the employer's requirements for making and finishing room operatives in general diminished, but their need for sole layers and pre-sole fitters remained the same. Nevertheless, they selected Mr Pink for redundancy, apparently because he had been absent for lengthy periods and the employer had had to train someone else to do his work while he was away. The argument before the Employment Appeal Tribunal turned on whether the 'contract test' ought to be applied (i.e. did the company need less employees of the kind specified in Mr Pink's contract), in which case he was redundant, or the 'function test' (did it need less employees to do the kind of work he was actually doing), in which case he was not. It held that it was bound by *Nelson v British Broadcasting Corporation* [1977] ICR 649 to apply the contract test and held that Mr Pink was redundant. I have no doubt that on its facts the case was rightly decided, but both the contract test and the function test miss the point. The key word in the statute is 'attributable' and there is no reason in law why the dismissal of an employee should not be attributable to a diminution in the employer's need for employees irrespective of the terms of his contract or the function which he performed. Of course the dismissal of an employee who could perfectly well have been redeployed or who was doing work unaffected by the fall in demand may require some explanation to establish the necessary causal connection. But this is a question of fact, not law.

For these reasons, I would dismiss the appeal.

The effect of the decision in *Murray v Foyle Meats Ltd* is to obstruct employees from challenging their selection for economic dismissal on the ground that they were not redundant, or no more redundant than other workers, owing to the presence of a flexibility clause in their contracts of employment. In this context, the court attributes little or no meaning at all to the phrase 'work of a particular kind'. The question is simply whether the employer has a reduced demand for workers. If such a workforce reduction is required, then the second question is simply whether or not that business requirement caused the dismissal. If that causation test is satisfied, the employee has been dismissed for redundancy. In *Murray v Foyle Meats Ltd*, for example, once the employer had decided to discontinue one production line, whichever employees lost their jobs as a consequence, they would have been redundant. The question whether an employee was fairly selected for redundancy is kept separate. We shall examine below the potential for employees to challenge the fairness of selection for dismissal.

10.2.1.3 Place of work

The application of the concept of redundancy to plant closures is usually straightforward. But where an employer carries on business at several sites, and the reduction in the workforce applies at only one site, the issue can arise whether the dismissed employees are redundant. If the employer is transferring business from one site to another, with no reduction of the workforce overall, the issue of redundancy turns on whether or not the place of work of the dismissed employees was at only one site. The presence of a mobility clause in the contract that permits the employer to direct an employee to work at any site might suggest that the place of work extends to all the sites of the business. But the courts have disapproved such reliance on mobility clauses and have looked primarily at the performance of the contract in order to determine the place of work.

[10.20] *High Table Ltd v Horst* [1998] ICR 409 (CA)

The employer provided catering services to firms in the City of London and elsewhere. The applicant worked for four years from 10.a.m. to 4 p.m. on weekdays as a waitress under one catering service contract with Hill Samuel in the City. Her terms of employment included a mobility clause that stated that her normal place of work was at Hill Samuel, but that she could be transferred on a temporary or permanent basis to another location within reasonable daily travelling distance. Hill Samuel negotiated with the employer a new contract for catering services that reduced the number of waitresses required, though extended the hours of work of the remainder till 6pm. The employer wrote to the applicant stating that she would be dismissed for redundancy and given a redundancy payment, though expressing the hope that some suitable alternative employment might be found under another catering service contract. The applicant did not apply for a post at Hill Samuel with the additional hours, and was unsuccessful in her applications for posts under other catering service contracts. The applicant claimed unfair dismissal, but the employment tribunal held that she had been dismissed for redundancy and that the employers had not acted unfairly. On appeal to the Court of Appeal, the principal question was whether the employees were redundant. The applicant argued that there had not been a diminution of requirements for employees at her place of work, because the mobility clause entailed that her place of work might be anywhere in the City. Since the employer had jobs available in the City (which she had applied for unsuccessfully), her dismissal was not attributable to redundancy. The Court of Appeal rejected this argument, holding that for the purposes of the issue of redundancy her place of work had been Hill Samuel. The court confirmed the decision of the employment tribunal.

Peter Gibson LJ quoted with approval the test adopted by the EAT in *Bass Leisure Ltd v Thomas* [1994] IRLR 104, that the place where the employee was employed for the purpose of ERA 1996 s 139:

> 'is to be established by a factual inquiry, taking into account the employee's fixed or changing place or places of work and any contractual terms which go to evidence or define the place of employment and its extent, but not those (if any) which make provision for the employee to be transferred to another'.

Peter Gibson LJ continued:
I am in broad agreement with this interpretation of the statutory language. The question it poses—where was the employee employed by the employer for the purposes of the business?—is one to be answered primarily by a consideration of the factual circumstances which obtained until the dismissal. If an employee has worked in only one location under his contract of employment for the purposes of the employer's business, it defies common sense to widen the extent of the place where he was so employed merely because of the existence of a mobility clause. . . . If the work of the employee for his employer has involved a change of location, as would be the case where the nature of the work required the employee to go from place to place, then the contract of employment may be helpful to determine the extent of the 'place where the employee was employed. But it cannot be right to let the contract be the sole determinant, regardless of where the employee actually worked for the employer. The question what was the place of employment is one that can safely be left to the good sense of the industrial tribunal.

There appears to be a common theme in the cases selected above that the tribunals should avoid technicalities and detailed reference to the terms of employment in order to decide whether the statutory concept of redundancy has been satisfied. These technical points are often raised by employees who feel aggrieved at their treatment and selection for redundancy. They seek to persuade the tribunal that they were not dismissed for redundancy, in order to claim the superior measure of compensation for unfair dismissal. By insisting that a reduction in the number of employees suffices to support a finding of redundancy, and by asserting that flexibility and mobility clauses in the contract of employment are irrelevant to the statutory concept, the courts have in recent years placed considerable obstacles in the way of such technical arguments. Whether or not these interpretations ultimately disadvantage employees in their quest for higher levels of compensation is doubtful, as the next section reveals.

10.2.2 Some other substantial reason

If a dismissal for business reasons such as a reorganisation does not fall within the statutory concept of redundancy, the employer needs to defend the fairness of the dismissal on some other ground. Under the structure of the fairness enquiry, the employer has to put forward a 'substantial reason of a kind such as to justify the dismissal of an employee holding the position which the employee held': ERA 1996, section 98(1). Since the employer cannot rely upon the normal reasons that relate to the personal conduct of the employee such as lack of capability or misconduct, the employer must assert that the business reasons for the reorganisation and dismissals were themselves 'some other substantial reason' for dismissal. The courts have accepted that such business reasons can amount to some other substantial reason. The question then becomes whether it was reasonable to dismiss the employee for that reason under the general test of fairness contained in ERA 1996, section 98(4). If a tribunal concludes that it was reasonable to dismiss for that business reason, the employee will fail to obtain any compensation for loss of a job. The strategy adopted by employees of denying that they are redundant in the hope of obtaining higher compensation for unfair dismissal is therefore a risky one, because the employees may end up with no compensation at all, as illustrated in the next case.

[10.21] *Hollister v National Farmers' Union* **[1979] ICR 542 (CA)**

As a result of representations by other employees of the union in Cornwall, the union decided to reorganise its operations in that county to bring them into line with the arrangements for the rest of the country. These arrangements required employees to accept new contracts of employment, which offered improved remuneration in some respects, but less advantageous pension arrangements. The applicant refused to accept the new contract, and was dismissed. His claim for unfair dismissal was rejected by the industrial tribunal, a decision upheld by the Court of Appeal. The Court accepted that a business reorganisation could amount to 'some other substantial reason'.

Lord Denning MR:

The question which is being discussed in this case is whether the reorganisation of the business which the National Farmers' Union felt they had to undertake in 1976, coupled with Mr Hollister's refusal to accept the new agreement, was a substantial reason of such a kind as to justify the dismissal of the employee. Upon that there have only been one or two cases. One we were particularly referred to was *Ellis v Brighton Co-operative Society Ltd* [1976] IRLR 419 EAT, where it was recognised by the court that reorganisation of business may on occasion be a sufficient reason justifying the dismissal of an employee. They went on to say, at p. 420:

> 'Where there has been a properly consulted-upon reorganisation which, if it is not done, is going to bring the whole business to a standstill, a failure to go along with the new arrangements may well—it is not bound to, but it may well—constitute "some other substantial reason"'.

Certainly, I think, everyone would agree with that. But in the present case Arnold J expanded it a little so as not to limit it to where it came absolutely to a standstill but to where there was some sound, good business reason for the reorganisation. I must say I see no reason to differ from Arnold J's view on that. It must depend on all the circumstances whether the reorganisation was such that the only sensible thing to do was to terminate the employee's contract unless he would agree to a new arrangement.

What this decision makes clear is that dismissals in the context of business reorganisation can amount to 'some other substantial reason'. Notice in particular that an employee's refusal to accept a variation in the terms and conditions of his employment can provide the employer with a substantial reason for dismissal. This approach turns the employer's repudiatory breach of contract into a substantial reason for dismissal. The important question becomes whether there are limits on the inclusion of business reasons within the concept of 'some other substantial reason'. If the employee rejects the proposed variation because it increases hours or duties without additional remuneration, or perhaps simply involves a pay cut, must the employer demonstrate a compelling reason for insisting upon the change in terms, or is it sufficient for 'some other substantial reason' that the variation is more convenient or efficient? Given that employers will normally have some reason for seeking a change in terms of employment, unless some limits are placed on the concept of 'some other substantial reason', an employer could use the refusal to accept any variation as a ground for justifying a dismissal. Nevertheless, the courts have accepted that 'a sound good business reason' for insisting upon a variation in terms of employment may constitute 'some other substantial reason'.

It is important to recall, however, that the employee's claim of unfairness might still succeed on the ground that it was not reasonable to dismiss the employee for that reason. Can employees succeed after all in their claims for unfair dismissal on the ground that it was unreasonable to dismiss them for refusing to accept a disadvantageous variation in the terms of employment unless the very existence of the business depends upon their acceptance? The chances of success on the basis of the argument about reasonableness appear slim on the evidence of several cases.

[10.22] *Richmond Precision Engineering Ltd v Pearce* **[1985] IRLR 179 (EAT)**

Following the sale of the business and its relocation to the purchaser's premises, the employee was offered a new contract of employment that corresponded to the terms of employment offered to other employees of the purchasing company. The employee rejected the offer on the ground that it involved a slight reduction in his rate of pay, an increase in hours, a reduction in annual holiday entitlement, and loss of an occupational pension scheme and other fringe benefits. The employee succeeded in a claim for unfair dismissal before an industrial tribunal, but the EAT held that the complaint had not been established and reversed the industrial tribunal. The EAT held that the test was whether the terms of employment were ones which a reasonable employer could offer in all the circumstances, including consideration of the advantages and disadvantages to both parties. The mere fact that the employee would be worse off was not a sufficient reason for a finding of unfairness.

Beldam J:
The task of weighing the advantages to the employer against the disadvantages to the employee is merely one factor which the tribunal have to take into when determining the question in accordance with the equity and substantial merits of the case. Merely because there are disadvantages to the employee, it does not, by any means, follow that the employer has acted unreasonably in treating his failure to accept the terms which they have offered as a reason for dismissal.

[10.23] *Catamaran Cruisers Ltd v Williams* **[1994] IRLR 384 (EAT)**

The employers operated ferries and pleasure cruises on the River Thames in London. After new French owners had acquired the company, and in the face of a threat of insolvency, the representative trade union, the Transport and General Workers Union, agreed new terms for contracts of employment, and these were offered to employees. Some employees, including the seven applicants in this case, refused the new terms and were dismissed. The industrial tribunal found that the reason for the offer of new terms was a combination of financial exigency and the desire to improve the efficiency and profitability of the business. The tribunal held that the dismissals were unfair. On appeal, it was argued that the industrial tribunal had applied the wrong test to determine whether or not the dismissals for refusal to accept new terms and conditions were unfair. The EAT agreed that the tribunal had applied too strict a test, and remitted the case to the same tribunal for further investigation of the reasons for the employer's insistence upon new terms and conditions, and for the tribunals to apply a broader 'balancing test' under the general test of fairness in [ERA 1996, section 98 (4)]. (For the other ground of appeal see **[2.62]** above).

Tudor Evans J:
Turning to the second ground of appeal, in our opinion, neither *Richmond Precision Engineering Ltd v Pearce* [above] nor *St John of God (Care Services) Ltd v Brooks* [1992] ICR 715 (EAT) supports the proposition stated in paragraph 8 of the decision, that if the new terms of a contract of employment are much less favourable to the employee than the terms of the old contract, then the employee is not unreasonable in refusing to accept them and his dismissal will be unfair unless the business reasons are so pressing that it is vital for the survival of the employer's business that the new terms be accepted . . . [The EAT approved rather the balancing test of *Richmond Precision Engineering Ltd v Pearce*, quoted above].

Nor does it follow, as was said in *Evans v Elementa Holdings Ltd* [1982] IRLR 43 (EAT), that if it was reasonable for the employee to refuse the new terms then it was unreasonable for the employers to dismiss him for such refusal. Balcombe J (as he then was) in *Chubb Fire Security Ltd v Harper* [1983] IRLR 311 (EAT) at p. 313 declined, rightly in our view, to follow *Evans v Elementa Holdings Ltd,* holding:

> 'We must respectfully disagree with that conclusion. It may be perfectly reasonable for an employee to decline to work extra overtime, having regard to his family commitments. Yet, from the employment point of view, having regard to his business commitments, it may be perfectly reasonable to require an employee to work overtime'.

What has to be carried out in deciding the maters for decision under [ERA 1996 s. 98(4)] is a balancing process.

The prospects of success for employees in bringing claims for unfair dismissal in these circumstances of business reorganisation therefore appear slim indeed. Provided the employer can point to a 'sound business reason' for the need for the reorganisation, the employer will have established 'some other substantial reason' for the dismissal. On the question of the reasonableness of the dismissal for this reason, the tribunal must balance the strength and urgency of the business reasons for the proposed variations in terms of employment against the reasons that the employee has for rejecting them. It seems likely in the normal run of cases that the employer's business reasons will outweigh the employee's objections to disadvantageous alterations in the terms of employment. The employee may be acting reasonably in objecting to these changes, but the relevant issue is rather whether the employer is acting reasonably in insisting upon them despite the employee's objections. In effect, the courts insert a flexibility clause into every contract of employment by characterising employee's refusals to agree to changes as grounds for fair dismissal. Notice also how in the reference to overtime, the courts place little weight on the employee's interest in preserving an acceptable work/life balance.

These decisions provide strong support for the employer's power to reorganise the business through variation of job specifications and terms of employment. If the employer does not reduce the size of the workforce, there is little chance that the reorganisation will be classified as a redundancy. If the employees reject the new job specifications and terms because they are disadvantageous, the employer is likely to be able to persuade a tribunal that the dismissal was for a substantial reason and was fair. An employee would therefore obtain no compensation for losing his job when resisting organisational change. Thus, in the case of *Safeway Stores Plc* v. *Burrell*, discussed above, if the tribunal eventually found that Mr Burrell was not redundant, his chances of success in a claim for unfair dismissal would be small. The employer could rely on the delayering and Mr Burrell's refusal to accept the new contract as a substantial reason for dismissal, and insist that it was reasonable, following the balancing test in *Richmond Precision Engineering Ltd v Pearce*, to dismiss Mr Burrell for that reason.

10.2.3 Fairness of selection for redundancy

In practice, it seems that the only way in which an employee who loses his job for economic reasons can obtain the higher level of compensation provided by a claim for
unfair dismissal is to allege either unfair selection for redundancy or the failure to
follow a fair procedure. Procedural issues are considered separately below. Here the
question is whether the employee can obtain compensation for having been unfairly
chosen from among the workforce for dismissal.

In principle, a claim for unfair dismissal based upon unfair criteria for selection
among the pool of employees is possible. In effect, employers are required to be able
to justify their selection of some workers as opposed to others to be dismissed. The
first application of the principle in a higher court was in *Bessenden Properties Ltd v
Corness* Note (1974) [1977] ICR 821 (CA). The Court of Appeal found the
employer's selection for redundancy of a married women with longer service over two
junior single women to be unfair. (The dismissal would now also be a contravention
of the Sex Discrimination Act 1975, section 3). The legal principles applicable to
selection for redundancy are articulated most fully in the following case.
Browne-Wilkinson J based the principles upon the argument that the fairness of a
dismissal depends upon whether or not it conforms to 'good industrial practice', and
that good practice was well established in this field. The decision describes both procedural and substantive principles.

[10.24] *Williams v Compair Maxam Ltd* [1982] ICR 156 (EAT)

Following a dramatic fall in orders, the employer decided to reorganise the business and
reduce labour costs. The works manager asked departmental managers to 'pick a team' for
the department, so that the business could remain viable if those staff members were
retained. The departmental mangers chose employees to retain on the basis of personal
preference and what was in the best interests of the company. The union was not
consulted on the principles of selection. Other employees were dismissed for redundancy,
and they were given notice payments and further payments considerably in excess of their
statutory entitlements. Five dismissed workers claimed unfair dismissal, but the industrial
tribunal, by a majority, dismissed their claims, holding that it was reasonable for the
employer to decide to retain those employees whom the managers regarded as being those
who would keep the company viable in the long run. The successful ground of appeal,
discussed below, was that the tribunal had committed an error of law by reaching a
decision that was perverse; no tribunal properly directing itself could have reached such a
decision. The dismissals were unfair because they had been carried out in blatant
contravention of the standards of fair treatment generally accepted by fair employers.

Browne-Wilkinson J:
In considering whether the decision of an industrial tribunal is perverse in a legal sense,
there is one feature which does not occur in other jurisdictions where there is a right of
appeal only on a point of law. The industrial tribunal is an industrial jury which brings to
its task a knowledge of industrial relations both from the view point of the employer and
the employee. Matters of good industrial relations practice are not proved before an
industrial tribunal as they would be proved before an ordinary court: the lay members are
taken to know them. The lay members of the industrial tribunal bring to their task their

expertise in a field where conventions and practices are of the greatest importance. Therefore in considering whether the decision of an industrial tribunal is perverse, it is not safe to rely solely on the common sense and knowledge of those who have no experience in the field of industrial relations. A course of conduct which to those who have no practical experience with industrial relations might appear unfair or unreasonable, to those with specialist knowledge and experience might appear both fair and reasonable: and vice versa.

For this reason, it seems to us that the correct approach is to consider whether an industrial tribunal, properly directed in law and properly appreciating what is currently regarded as fair industrial practice, could have reached the decision reached by the majority of this tribunal. We have reached the conclusion that it could not.

For the purposes of the present case there are only two relevant principles of law arising from [ERA 1996 s 98(4)]. First, that it is not the function of the industrial tribunal to decide whether they would have thought it fairer to act in some other way: the question is whether the dismissal lay within the range of conduct which a reasonable employer could have adopted. The second point of law, particularly relevant in the field of dismissal for redundancy, is that the tribunal must be satisfied that it was reasonable to dismiss *an* employee; it must be shown that the employer acted reasonably in treating redundancy 'as a sufficient reason for dismissing *the* employee,' i.e. the employee complaining of dismissal. Therefore, if the circumstances of the employer make it inevitable that some employee must be dismissed, it is still necessary to consider the means whereby the applicant was selected to be the employee to be dismissed and the reasonableness of the steps taken by the employer to choose the applicant, rather than some other employee, for dismissal.

In law, therefore, the question we have to decide is whether a reasonable tribunal could have reached the conclusion that the dismissal of the applicants in this case law within the range of conduct which a reasonable employer could have adopted. It is accordingly necessary to try to set down in very general terms what a properly instructed industrial tribunal would know to be the principles which, in current industrial practice, a reasonable employer would be expected to adopt. This is not a matter on which the chairman of this appeal tribunal feels that he can contribute much, since it depends on what industrial practices are currently accepted as being normal and proper. The two lay members of this appeal tribunal hold the view that it would be impossible to lay down detailed procedures which *all* reasonable employers would follow in *all* circumstances: the fair conduct of dismissals for redundancy must depend on the circumstances of each case. But in their experience, there is a generally accepted view in industrial relations that, in cases where the employees are represented by an independent union recognised by the employer, reasonable employers will seek to act in accordance with the following principles:

1. The employer will seek to give as much warning as possible of impending redundancies so as to enable the union and employees who may be affected to take early steps to inform themselves of the relevant facts, consider possible alternative solutions and, if necessary, find alternative employment in the undertaking or elsewhere.

2. The employer will consult the union as to the best means by which the desired management result can be achieved fairly and with as little hardship to the employees as possible. In particular, the employer will seek to agree with the union the criteria to be applied in selecting the employees to be made redundant. When a selection has been made, the employer will consider with the union whether the selection has been made in accordance with those criteria.

3. Whether or not an agreement as to the criteria to be adopted has been agreed with the union, the employer will seek to establish criteria for selection which so far as possible

do not depend solely upon the opinion of the person making the selection but can be objectively checked against such things as attendance record, efficiency at the job, experience, or length of service.

4. The employer will seek to ensure that the selection is made fairly in accordance with these criteria and will consider any representations the union may make as to such selection.

5. The employer will seek to see whether instead of dismissing an employee he could offer him alternative employment.

The lay members stress that not all these factors are present in every case since circumstances may prevent one or more of them being given effect to. But the lay members would expect these principles to be departed from only where some good reason is shown to justify such departure. The basic approach is that, in the unfortunate circumstances that necessarily attend redundancies, as much as is reasonably possible should be done to mitigate the impact on the work force and to satisfy them that the selection has been made fairly and not on the basis of personal whim.

The crucial phrases in this judgement are that the criteria for selection should be 'objective' and that the criteria should be followed. The fairness standard does not endorse any particular criteria for selection, such as seniority (last in, first out). The employer can chose the relevant criteria, preferably following consultation with a recognised union, provided those criteria are transparent and verifiable.

These standards certainly establish a measure of judicial scrutiny of fairness in the context of selection for redundancy. Provided the employer declares what standards it is using, however, it is hard to challenge the content of those standards unless they really represent a concealed tests based upon personal preferences of managers or amount to indirect discrimination against a protected group. Furthermore, it is difficult to question the application of those standards to particular cases, because the employer is not usually required to justify the detailed application of the selection criteria.

[10.25] *British Aerospace Plc v Green & Others* [1995] ICR 1006 (CA)

The employers needed to reduce the workforce of 7,000 at one plant by 530 employees. The employers divided the workforce into 21 categories, determined how many workers in each category needed to be dismissed, and then carried out an individual assessment of the capabilities and experience of each of the 7,000 employees. Those employees who were awarded the lowest number of points under this system of assessment were chosen for dismissal. About 235 of the employees contested the fairness of the dismissals. The employers disclosed the points assessment forms of each employee who claimed unfair dismissal, but refused to disclose the forms of all employees or all employees in the relevant one of the 21 categories of workers. A number of sample or test cases were brought before the tribunal for rulings on procedural issues. The industrial tribunal ordered the employer to disclose the forms of retained employees, but the Court of Appeal allowed the employer's appeal against that procedural ruling. Disclosure of the assessments of retained employees would be ordered only where they became necessary in order to deal with a specific issue that had been raised, such as the allegation that the employer had unfairly applied the criteria of assessment to a particular employee.

Waite LJ:

It has been accepted from the outset of the unfair dismissal jurisdiction that the concept of fairness, when applied to the selection process for redundancy, is incapable of being expressed in absolute terms. There are no cut and dried formulae and no short cuts. The recognised objectives include the retention within the reduced workforce, once the redundancies have taken effect, of employees with the best potential to keep the business going and avoid the need for further redundancies in future; as well as the need to ensure that qualities of loyalty and long service are recognised and rewarded. These are objectives which are liable to conflict with each other. When they do, it becomes the task of the industrial tribunal to determine whether, in all the circumstances of each particular case, the employers have succeeded in providing a response to the tension between them which comes within the range of reasonableness. . . .

The industrial tribunal must, in short, be satisfied that redundancy selection has been achieved by adopting a fair and reasonable system and applying it fairly and reasonably as between one employee and another; and must judge that question objectively by asking whether the system and its application fall within the range of fairness and reasonableness (regardless of whether they would have chosen to adopt such a system or apply it in that way themselves).

Employment law recognises, pragmatically, that an over-minute investigation of the selection process by the tribunal members may run the risk of defeating the purpose which the tribunals were called into being to discharge—namely a swift, informal disposal of disputes arising from redundancy in the workplace. So in general the employer who sets up a system of selection which can reasonably be described as fair and applies it without any overt sign of conduct which mars its fairness will have done all that the law requires of him.

The issues of principle to which this case gives rise have been ably argued in this Court by leading counsel eminent in the employment law field. It is right to stress, in fairness to the chairman though without implying any criticism of those who appeared before her, that at the brief informal hearing at which her directions were given the chairman did not have the same opportunity of considering the matter in depth. Specifically, she did not have the benefit of the thorough review of the case law that was provided for us—a review which included, moreover, authorities which had not been decided or reported by the date of her hearing. That being acknowledged, however, the majority of the Employment Appeal Tribunal was nevertheless entirely right, in my judgment, to overrule the chairman's order for discovery of the retained assessment forms. I say that for the following reasons:

(1) The use of a marking system of the kind that was adopted in this case has become a well-recognised aid to any fair process of redundancy selection. By itself, of course, it does not render any selection automatically fair; every system has to be examined for its own inherent fairness, judging the criteria employed and the methods of marking in conjunction with any factors relevant to its fair application, including the degree of consultation which accompanied it. One thing, however, is clear: if such a system is to function effectively, its workings are not to be scrutinised officiously. The whole tenor of the authorities to which I have already referred is to show, in both England and Scotland, the courts and tribunals (with substantial contribution from the lay membership of the latter) moving towards a clear recognition that if a graded assessment system is to achieve its purpose it must not be subjected to an over-minute analysis. That applies both at the stage when the system is being actually applied, and also at any later stage when its operation is being called into question before an industrial tribunal. To allow otherwise would involve a serious risk that the system itself would lose the respect with which it is at present regarded on both sides of industry, and that tribunal hearings would become

hopelessly protracted. There were therefore strong reasons of policy against allowing disclosure of the retained assessments at this stage, and no special circumstances justifying a departure from that policy.

(2) The latitude which the tribunal procedure allows to an applicant in regard to the informal expression (and the progressive raising) of issues requires that discovery against the employer should be directed sparingly; and if necessary on a graduated basis—tranche by tranche as particular documents become relevant to any issue as and when it is specifically raised. That gradualist approach is clearly contemplated, and may even have been intended to be encouraged, by the use in county court rules O 14 R 8(1) of the phrase 'necessary at that stage of the action.' The chairman was therefore required to direct her mind to the question 'what discovery is necessary for disposing fairly of the application at the stage which it has reached at present, namely the selection of sample cases?' In answering it she was required to take account of the fact that the application of the system was not attacked in any specific respect, and that there was therefore at that stage no issue to which the retained assessments could be claimed to be relevant. To have forced their disclosure for the purposes of an exercise in comparison designed to provide individual applicants with grounds for specific allegations of anomaly or mistake in particular instances would have done nothing to ease the task in hand—which was limited to the selection of sample cases—and would have run a serious risk of subjecting these multiple applications to procedural chaos.

Early Retirement

A common practice for employers seeking to achieve workforce reductions is to offer older workers the possibility of 'early retirement'. If this offer is accepted, the employee is probably not 'dismissed' within the statutory concept (see: *Birch v University of Liverpool* above [5.32]). Even if the employee has been dismissed and can claim a redundancy payment, if the employee is entitled to occupational pension rights, the right to a redundancy payment in addition may be forfeited (ERA 1996, s.158; Redundancy Payments (Pensions) Regulations 1965 SI 1965/1932). One potential attraction to the employer is that the costs of compensation will be met from an occupational pension scheme rather than the employer's own resources. If the pension fund is in surplus (that is it can easily meet its existing commitments), the employer incurs no additional cost. The employee may receive a lump sum together with regular income perhaps amounting to a half of final salary. The employee can also seek other employment without forfeiting this income, though both sources of income will be taxed. Another advantage to employers is that they usually retain complete control over selection for redundancy by only permitting those employees whom they wish to dismiss to take early retirement. The UK government has encouraged this practice in the 1980s by subsidising 'job release' schemes under which employers replaced older workers with young (and cheap) unemployed workers. But this attitude towards older workers may appear increasingly unacceptable as a form of age discrimination. Considerable pressure may be brought to bear on older workers to accept these early retirement packages even though they would prefer to continue working. The disadvantages of these packages may not always be explained fully. For example, the pension may be fixed by reference to the final salary, which might have increased if the employee had continued to work. The question of whether the employer should be able to pay for the costs of redundancies out of the fund that was supposed to devoted to pensions rather than workforce reductions has also not been investigated adequately.

The precise implications of this decision have yet to be explored. The particular question is what sort of evidence does the claimant for unfair dismissal have to produce in order to obtain disclosure of assessments of retained employees. Does the claimant have to be able to point to some apparent bias in the application of the assessment criteria, or is sufficient merely to argue that such a possibility exists (which presumably, it always does)? In *John Brown Engineering Ltd v Brown* [1997] IRLR 90 (EAT), the employer was found to have acted unfairly by refusing to disclose to individual employees their personal assessments, because this refusal prevented employees from using the appeal procedure against dismissal that had been agreed with the union. However, the whole tenor of the decision of the Court of Appeal in the *British Aerospace* case is a warning to tribunals not to investigate the fairness of dismissals in connection with selection for redundancy, if the employer has apparently adopted a satisfactory objective system of selection. The legal justification for this abstention is placed upon the 'range of reasonable responses' test of fairness, a test, which we have seen, has been criticised in recent years for its tendency to tolerate all but the most extreme instances of unfairness in dismissals. The expressed policy justification for abstention from judicial review is to prevent the redundancy process from dragging out over a long time, and also to prevent the tribunals from undermining the perceived legitimacy of assessment systems by both sides of industry. It seems, therefore, that provided employers apparently conform to the normal standards of 'good industrial practice', the tribunals will resist attempts to scrutinise these standards in their details and their application to individuals. In short, employers can probably avoid the risk of challenges to the fairness of selection for redundancy by the precaution of incurring the expense of conducting an elaborate procedure of assessment.

10.3 Redeployment

Within larger businesses, the need to make redundancies may be limited to one aspect of the business, or one organisational division, or one company in a group of companies. In such cases, the employer may be able to offer alternative employment to a dismissed worker. It appears to be in the interests of both employer and employee to consider redeployment in every case, and the chance of avoiding the social cost of an economic dismissal must also render redeployment an attractive possibility for governments. The law provides some incentives for employers to redeploy workers, but does not clearly impose a legal duty to do so. We need to consider separately the legal position both where the employer does offer another job, that is redeployment, and where the employer fails to consider this possibility.

10.3.1 Offer of alternative employment

An employer can avoid liability to make a redundancy payment if the employer offers the dismissed worker another job, either on the same terms or suitable terms, and the employee unreasonably refuses the offer.

[10.26] Employment Rights Act 1996, section 141

(1) This section applies where an offer (whether in writing or not) is made to an employee before the end of his employment—
(a)   to renew his contract of employment, or
(b)   to re-engage him under a new contract of employment,
with renewal or re-engagement to take effect either immediately on, or after an interval of not more than four weeks after, the end of his employment.

(2) Where subsection (3) is satisfied, the employee is not entitled to a redundancy payment if he unreasonably refuses the offer.

(3) This subsection is satisfied where—
(a)   the provisions of the contract as renewed, or of the new contract, as to—
(i)   the capacity and place in which the employee would be employed, and
(ii)   the other terms and conditions of his employment,
would not differ from the corresponding provisions of the previous contract, or
(b)   those provisions of the contract as renewed, or of the new contract, would differ from the corresponding provisions of the previous contract but the offer constitutes an offer of suitable employment in relation to the employee.

(4) The employee is not entitled to a redundancy payment if—
(a)   his contract of employment is renewed, or he is re-engaged under a new contract of employment, in pursuance of the offer,
(b)   the provisions of the contract as renewed or new contract as to the capacity or place in which he is employed or the other terms and conditions of his employment differ (wholly or in part) from the corresponding provisions of the previous contract,
(c)   the employment is suitable in relation to him, and
(d)   during the trial period he unreasonably terminates the contract, or unreasonably gives notice to terminate it and it is in consequence terminated.

This offer can be made by the employer or an 'associated employer' (ERA 1996, section 146, above p 142). The requirement that a different job must be a suitable job has been interpreted to mean that the job should be substantially equivalent in terms of status, wages and types of duties: *Taylor v Kent County Council* [1969] 2 QB 560 (QBD Div. Ct.). The question when it is reasonable for an employee to refuse the offer of alternative employment (and thus preserve the claim for a redundancy payment) is explored in the following case.

[10.27] *Thomas Wragg & Sons Ltd v Wood* [1976] ICR 313 (EAT)

The employee was given six weeks' notice of dismissal for redundancy, but the day before the termination of his employment he received a written offer of another job, which he refused. It was not disputed that the alternative employment was suitable and that the offer was made within the statutory time limit. The industrial tribunal held that the employee had acted reasonably in refusing the offer of alternative employment and was entitled to a redundancy payment. The EAT dismissed the employer's appeal.

Lord McDonald:

The short point for decision, therefore, is whether or not the employee acted unreasonably in refusing the employers' offer of alternative employment, which indeed was the course which he adopted.

The tribunal have taken the view that the employee did not act unreasonably in refusing that offer. Their reasons for so concluding are summarised in their decision, in the following terms:

> 'The tribunal feels that [the employee] having committed himself to the new job, and having all the fears of a man of 56 who faces unemployment, and having received the offer not too late but . . . as late in the day as within 24 hours of the expiration of his notice, was not unreasonable in refusing the offer and, consequently, he succeeds in his claim'.

Counsel for the employers argued before us that this reason involved three factors and that two of those factors, as matter of law, should not be considered. The three factors were: first, that the employee had committed himself to accept a new job; secondly, that one of his reasons for refusing the employer's offer was fear of unemployment in the future in a contracting industry; and thirdly, the lateness of the offer of alternative employment.

So far as the second and third of those factors are concerned, counsel for the employers argued that those fell to be discounted completely as they were not factors which, in law, should be considered . . .

So far as the lateness of the offer is concerned, it was argued that if the statute had intended that this should be a factor falling to be taken into account in assessing reasonableness, it would have said so. On the contrary, the statute lays down a time limit and the offer was made within that time limit, albeit very late in the day. We would accept that if this was the only single factor which an employee relied upon to justify his refusal to accept an offer, and if no other factor existed, that would not be sufficient; but we do not consider that it is a matter which automatically falls to be ignored, if other considerations exist and, in particular, if the employee, as here, has sought and gained alternative employment and has accepted an offer such alternative employment from another employer.

Accordingly the two factors which have been criticised by counsel for the employers as being wholly irrelevant as matters of law are not, in our view, irrelevant to that extent. They are factors which we consider can be taken into account, provided other factors also exist.

It is clear in the present case that a third factor does exist and it is one which counsel for the employers accepted may competently be taken into account, although he argued that standing by itself it would not suffice. That factor, of course, is the acceptance by the employee of different employment before the expiry of his notice of dismissal . . .

In the case with which we are concerned today, this third factor is in our opinion one of great importance. The employee obviously acted with some diligence and was successful in obtaining other employment which was due to commence at the termination of his employment with the employer. In our opinion, in doing so he acted very sensibly and very reasonably. Faced at the end of his period of notice with the sudden offer of re-engagement by his employers, we consider that he did not act unreasonably in refusing that offer, having regard to the fact that he had already engaged himself in this other job.

If the employee takes up an offer of re-engagement, the employee enjoys a statutory four week 'trial period' in the new job. During the trial period the employee can opt to terminate the contract and still claim that a dismissal for redundancy has occurred:

ERA 1996, section 138. The right to a redundancy payment is lost, however, if a tribunal decides that the employee acted unreasonably in terminating the new contract: ERA 1996, section 141(4). It has also been held in *Turvey v C W Cheney & Son Ltd* [1979] ICR 341 (EAT) that, under the common law of contract, an employee can decide to give the alternative job a try for a reasonable period without committing himself to agreeing to the new contract of employment. Under this doctrine, the trial period can be lengthened, for first of all the employee may not agree to the new contract but simply give the work a try for a period of time at common law, and then agree to the new contract and enjoy the statutory four week 'trial period'. It is difficult to understand the basis of this common law trial period, when the employee is in a curious limbo of working at a new job but not under a contract. Perhaps the best explanation of the legal position is that the old contract has not yet been terminated, and during the notice period the employee consents to work at other duties temporarily.

10.3.2 Failure to consider redeployment

There is no express statutory duty placed upon employers to search for alternative employment for a redundant employee within the organisation or to offer dismissed workers any alternative employment that might be available. But failure to do so might provide an employee with grounds to challenge the fairness of selection for redundancy. This is the fifth principle stated by Browne-Wilkinson J in *Williams v Compare Maxam* (above). It was also endorsed by Lord Bridge in *Polkey v A E Dayton Services Ltd* [1988] ICR 142 (HL), who indicated that one aspect of fairness in making dismissals for redundancy was that the employer should take 'such steps as may be reasonable to avoid or minimise redundancy by redeployment within his own organisation'.

[10.28] *Thomas & Betts Manufacturing Ltd v Harding* **[1980] IRLR 255 (CA)**

> The applicant was employed initially as a packer, but later also worked on one of the production lines. When that production line was closed down, she was dismissed for redundancy. The applicant claimed unfair dismissal on the ground that there was still work for packers, and that, if necessary, a packer who had been employed for a shorter period of time should have been dismissed instead. The Industrial Tribunal upheld the claim for unfair dismissal on that ground, and the Court of Appeal found no error of law.

It has become a standard interpretation of the requirement of fairness in relation to redundancy dismissals that, as well as consideration of the issues of consultation and unfair selection, a tribunal should also consider whether the dismissal was unfair due to a failure by the employer to seek alternative employment for the employee: e.g. *Langston v Cranfield University* [1998] IRLR 172 (EAT).

A complementary legal duty that would assist redeployment in large organisations might be a requirement placed upon employers to notify the workforce of vacancies and opportunities for retraining. This duty is already envisaged for employees under fixed-term contracts. Under the Fixed-Term Employees (Prevention of Less Favourable Treatment) Regulations 2002, Regulation 3(2) requires the employer not to treat a fixed-term employee less favourably than the employer treats a comparable permanent employee with respect to the opportunity to receive training and to secure a permanent position. Furthermore Regulation 3(6) provides that the fixed-term employee has the right to be informed by his employer of available vacancies in the establishment. Although no such general legal duty to notify the workforce of vacancies applies to all employees, in practice larger employers do circulate such notices in order to assist compliance with the principle of equality of opportunity.

10.3.3 A positive duty?

The provisions described above create through exemptions and interpretations of individual rights relating to dismissal some financial incentives for employers to consider redeployment as an alternative to workforce reductions. What the law does not impose is a duty upon employers to go through such a process, supported by an automatic sanction for failure to do so. It might be hard to define the content of such a duty, because it might involve a careful consideration by the employer of business plans in many plants and across several countries, as well as an estimation of whether the employee might adapt to new kinds of work with the assistance of adequate training. Yet the absence of such a positive duty to consider redeployment does miss an opportunity both to reinforce some of the expectations that employers typically seek to generate in employees about the prospects for employment security and to help to minimise the social costs arising from workforce reductions. Perhaps a better way forward in view of the difficulty of defining the content of any positive duty is to require a mandatory procedure of consultation with representatives of the workforce with a view to establishing possibilities for redeployment. We have seen that EC law now promotes such a procedure in the revised Directive 98/59 on collective redundancies (above [8.59]). Article 2 requires consultation with workers' representatives about the possibilities for redeploying or retraining workers. The corresponding national legislation, however, in TULRCA 1992, section 188(2) (above [8.60]), merely refers to the need to consult about the possibility of avoiding the dismissals, and does not explicitly suggest discussions about redeployment and retraining. This difference of emphasis, as we shall see, reflects a broader divergence between UK law and that of many European countries, for in the latter legislation requires employers proposing to make redundancies to enter a 'social plan' with the workforce and the government with a view to resolving or reducing all aspects of the social costs involved.

10.4 Insolvency

When a business can no longer pay its debts, the investors and lenders to a company can initiate proceedings leading to the liquidation of the company and a distribution of its assets among creditors. A similar procedure of distribution of assets applies to an individual's bankruptcy. Because not all creditors can be paid out of the limited funds available, a crucial issue is which creditors can obtain priority over the others in the division of the assets, that is which creditors should be paid first. Employees occupy a special ranking order among creditors during insolvency proceedings in respect of the protection of the payment of their outstanding wages. Employees also benefit uniquely from guarantees of wage payments that are provided by the social security system. These principles conform to the ILO Convention 173, Protection of Workers' Claims (Employer's Insolvency) 1992. A central issue in this area of the law is whether employees are awarded too little or too much priority as between different groups of creditors.

As well as simply liquidating the assets of an insolvent company into cash in order to pay creditors, in recent years legal structures for insolvency proceedings have emphasised the possibility of keeping the business going, in order to reduce losses and perhaps even to avoid losses to creditors altogether. If such a 'corporate rescue' can be mounted, employees may both keep their jobs and receive any outstanding pay. The Enterprise Act 2002 introduced substantial reforms to the law of corporate insolvency with a view to increasing the opportunities for corporate rescue (V Finch, 'Re-Invigorating Corporate Rescue' [2003] *Journal of Business Law* 527). To some extent the interests of creditors in maximising the value of the pool of assets to be divided, the interests of workers in retaining their jobs, and the interests of government in minimising the social costs of changes in business coincide in the promotion of corporate rescues. But some conflicts of interest persist, and the issue becomes how should the decision to mount a rescue be reached?

Although this topic lies on the fringes of the interests of labour lawyers, in periods of recession it can have great practical importance. The topic also poses some profound theoretical questions central to the concerns of labour law. In order to justify a strengthening of employees' rights on insolvency, proponents often switch their terminology from that of the employee as 'unsecured creditor' who, owing to lack of bargaining power, needs assistance in achieving a fair distributive outcome, to that of employee as 'stakeholder'. The implicit suggestion of the 'stakeholder' rhetoric is that employees should be entitled by virtue of their contribution to the assets of the company to a share in those assets. Their position is implicitly contrasted with that of other unsecured creditors, such as contractors with the company, who have a claim for compensation, but not a type of proprietary claim, which is normally accorded priority. The rhetoric of stakeholding has many other applications in issues of corporate governance, but in the area of insolvency it enjoys a particular cutting edge, because it may influence the division of the company's assets.

10.4.1 Protection of wages

The protection of employees with respect to unpaid wages is achieved by two mechanisms. Employees are treated under general insolvency law as 'preferential creditors', so that some claims for wages have to be met before other creditors are paid. In addition, the State provides a limited guarantee of wages, so that if the employer's assets cannot meet the wage bill, the social security system will pay workers some compensation.

10.4.1.1 Preferential creditors

As a claim for 'preferential debt', an employee's claim for outstanding wages obtains a particular position in the priorities between creditors, as revised by the Enterprise Act 2002.

[10.29] Ranking Order of Creditors of Company in Insolvency

1. Secured creditors in the form of fixed charges over assets e.g. banks.
2. Preferential debts.
3. A proportion of the debts owed to floating charge holders e.g. banks.
4. Unsecured creditors e.g. other contractors; tort claimants, tax liabilities, and the remaining claims of floating charge holders.
5. Shareholders.

This priority for wages over some types of creditors may turn out not to be valuable. Ahead of the employees in the distribution of the company's assets are secured creditors with fixed charges, usually banks with equitable proprietary rights over most of the assets of the company, and also the expenses of the liquidator of the company. The list of preferential claims has been extended in the Insolvency Act 1986, Schedule 6 to include, as well as wages, many other items such as unpaid contributions to occupational pension schemes, accrued holiday pay, guarantee pay, payments for time off for trade union duties, and protective award payments. The claim for wages as a preferential debt is limited to a period of four months with an upper limit of the total that can be claimed of £800 (SI 1986/1996). One explanation of this upper limit is that it prevents highly paid managers, who may have been responsible for the collapse of the business, from obtaining priority over other creditors for their inflated wages.

10.4.1.2 Social security guarantee

Unlike other creditors, an employee also has recourse to the social security system to claim certain payments that have not been met by an insolvent employer. One set of regulations permits employees to recover any redundancy payments owed by the insolvent company: ERA 1996, sections 166–170. A slightly different set of rules permits employees to recover a wide range of payments due to them from their insolvent employer: ERA 1996, sections 182–190. These payments include up to eight weeks of wages, holiday pay, statutory guarantee pay, but not occupational pension contributions. A special regime applies to occupational pensions, which are protected against insolvency by a different guarantee mechanimsm enacted by the Pensions Act 2004. It is also possible for employees to recover some payments due on dismissal including compensation for lost wages during the notice period, the basic award for unfair dismissal, and the protective award for failure to consult with representatives of the workforce. An important exclusion from this list is the compensatory award for unfair dismissal, which usually represents the largest component of awards of compensation for dismissal. Employees may bring a claim for these guarantee payments against the Secretary of State before an employment tribunal. For such a claim to arise, the employer must either have been adjudged bankrupt, or, if the employer is a company, there must have been a winding up order, the appointment of a receiver, an administration order, or a voluntary arrangement under Part 1 of the Insolvency Act 1986 (ERA 1996, sections166, 183). There is an upper limit placed on recovery of payments referable to a period of a week of £270 . We saw an example of such a claim being contested in *McMeechan v Secretary of State for Employment* [1997] ICR 549 (CA), above **[2.64]**, where the Secretary of State unsuccessfully denied that a temporary agency worker was an employee (another condition for payments from the social security fund).

If the Secretary of State makes any payments to employees, the right to claim compensation against the insolvent employer is subrogated to the Secretary of State. On this ground, the Secretary of State may effectively pursue the employee's claims for a redundancy payment and other preferential debts in the insolvency proceedings against the assets of the employer.

This legislation mostly preceded, but is required in part by, European law.

[10.30] EC Directive 80/987 on the the protection of employees in the event of the insolvency of their employer (as amended by Directive 2002/74)

Article 3

1. Member States shall take the measures necessary to ensure that guarantee institutions guarantee, subject to Article 4, payment of employees' outstanding claims resulting from contracts of employment or employment relationships, including, where provided for by national law, severance pay on termination of employment relationships.
2. The claims taken over by the guarantee institution shall be the outstanding pay claims relating to a period prior to and/or, as applicable, after a given date determined by the Member States.

Although the Directive is narrower in scope than the UK legislation in some respects, employees can rely on the Directive as a guide to the legal interpretation of national legislation. The European Court of Justice has stressed the importance of the general principle of guaranteeing wages, and that derogations permitted by the Directive must be construed narrowly.

[10.31] Case C–125/97 *Regeling v Bestur van de Bedrijfsvereniging voor de Metaalnijverheid* [1999] IRLR 379 (ECJ)

A welder employed in the Netherlands received his pay only sporadically from January 1991 onwards until August when the contract was terminated after notice. The employer subsequently became bankrupt. The employee claimed his missing wages from the relevant guarantee institution in the Netherlands. The claim was rejected on the ground that the period in which pay was guaranteed, as permitted by the Directive, was 13 weeks preceding termination of employment, and during that period the employer had in fact paid sums in excess of wages (thereby trying to make up for earlier shortfalls). The ECJ upheld the employee's claim, stating that the employer's payments should be set off first against the outstanding wage debt, and only then be used to reduce the payments from the guarantee institution. To permit the employer's payments to reduce the obligation of the guarantee institution would be to undermine the minimum protection guaranteed by the Directive.

Judgment (extract):
The guarantee institutions are required, in principle, in accordance with Article 3(1) of the Directive, to guarantee payment of employees' outstanding claims relating to pay for the period prior to a given date. It is purely by way of derogation that Member States have the option, under Article 4(1), to limit that liability to pay to a given period fixed in accordance with the detailed rules laid down in Article 4(2). As the Advocate-General observes . . . that provision must be construed narrowly and in conformity with the social purpose of the Directive, which is to ensure a minimum level of protection for all workers.

This principle of giving the principle of guarantee great weight and interpreting exceptions narrowly was accepted, for instance, in *Mann v Secretary of State for Employment* [1999] IRLR 566 (HL). In that case it was observed that employees should be able to choose the particular eight weeks in respect of which they were claiming arrears of pay against the guarantee institution, thus choosing eight weeks in which they had not been paid at all instead of the last eight weeks when they might have received some payments.

The original justification for European regulation in this field of insolvency was the weak one of harmonisation of rules in order to create a competitive single market. It is conceivable that businesses might be tempted to invest in jurisdictions where their legal obligations towards employees in the event of insolvency are minimal, though why the additional liability of the State for such debts should alter the incentives is not explained. There is, however, a better reason for European regulation, which is to protect employees against disparate treatment by multinational enterprises. A company that has branches (but not subsidiary companies) in several Member States may register the corporation in the jurisdiction that places the least obligations upon it, and, in the event of insolvency, employees may have to launch claims for wages in that inhospitable territory. This rationale for the Directive was written into it subsequently by the ECJ in *Everson and Barrass v Secretary of State for Trade and Industry and Bell Lines Ltd (in liquidation)* [2000] IRLR 202 (ECJ), and Articles 8a and 8b of the amended Directive confirm the general proposition that employees can claim against the guarantee institution of the Member State in whose territory they work or habitually work

This measure forces the Secretary of State to pursue the government's subrogated remedies against the insolvent company in the foreign jurisdiction. Although there is a duty to share relevant information between the guarantee institutions in different countries, there is no system for set-offs or reimbursement between them. The amendments to the Directive, which must be implemented in national law by 2005, include some new restrictions on the extent to which national laws may restrict the obligations of the guarantee institution (M Sargeant, 'Protecting Employees with Insolvent Employers' (2003) 32 *Industrial Law Journal* 53). Potentially the most troublesome of these is Article 4 (3), which, though permitting national government to set ceilings on the payments made by the guarantee institutions, states that 'These ceilings must not fall below a level which is socially compatible with the social objective of this Directive.' That phrase reveals that the amended Directive is not merely about setting a level playing field in the common market, but has the ambition of securing to employees a satisfactory level of protection from guarantee institutions. The question posed for UK law is whether the ceiling of £270 per week for claims for outstanding wages satisfies the test of being 'socially compatible with the social objective' of the Directive.

The above patchwork of provisions represents an uneasy and perhaps not entirely coherent compromise of principles about the claims of employees in the event of insolvency. One principle suggests that employees, as both the group most likely to be seriously harmed by the employer's liquidation (because the risk of insolvency cannot be diversified) and the group least able to protect itself through contractual security rights, should be awarded the highest priority (or 'super-priority') in the distribution of assets. A competing principle suggests that employees should be treated in the same way as other unsecured creditors on the ground that the only fair way to spread the loss between employees and small business creditors is absolutely equally (*pari passu*, as insolvency lawyers say). A third principle holds that the State should provide a guarantee of wages and other sums due to employees out of general taxation as a type of social insurance, thereby removing employees from the contest in insolvency. The current insolvency rules satisfy none of those principles in their entirety. Employees are given a degree of priority, but not absolute priority, and at the same time the State guarantees some, but not all, money and benefits owed to the workforce by the insolvent employer.

10.4.2 Corporate rescue

The possibility of a corporate rescue is generally regarded favourably by the workforce. Employees have a chance of keeping their jobs, at least for the time being. But a successful rescue may require some adverse consequences such as wage cuts and a reduction of the workforce. It is usually hard, however, for the workforce to calculate where its best interests lie, because it is rarely given access to the relevant information about the company's prospects. For similar reasons, the policy of reducing social costs usually points towards the exploration of the possibility of corporate rescue. But other creditors, especially secured creditors, may share little sympathy with these objectives. They may want to retrieve their money as soon as possible, rather than wait for what might prove a better dividend at some uncertain future date. To promote corporate rescues, therefore, requires subtle regulation that produces the intended advantage to the workforce and society as a whole without harming the interests of creditors so much that they might become reluctant to assume that risk.

The Enterprise Act 2002 tries to promote corporate rescues by preventing banks in most cases from simply appointing a receiver to seize assets to the value of the floating charge it holds, and instead to require all creditors (other than holders of fixed charges) to follow an administration procedure under the supervision of a court. By an appointment by the floating charge holder or a court on the request of creditors of a company, an administrator takes over the management of the business of an insolvent company. The administrator is instructed to perform his functions with the following objectives in order of priority of (a) rescuing the company or as much of its business as possible as a going concern, if reasonably practicable, or (b) achieving a better result for the company's creditors as a whole than would be likely if the the company were wound up, or (c) realising property to make a distribution to secured or preferential creditors (Enterprise Act 2002 Schedule 16, para. 3, replacing Insolvency Act 1986 s.8(3)). While the insolvent company is in administration, which can last for a year, there is a moratorium so that none of the creditors can pursue their claims in the courts, though the administrator has the power to make interim payments to secured and preferred creditor. During this period of a year, the administrator may discover ways in which to keep all or part of the company in business as a going concern. These routes to corporate rescue may, however, affect adversely a large part of the workforce by including detrimental variations of terms of employment, plant closures, workforce reductions, and sales of parts of the business.

The first step to assist a corporate rescue is to induce the retained workforce to continue to work. Employees will be reluctant to help, however, unless they receive a better assurance that they will receive their wages than a promise from an insolvent company. The crucial question becomes therefore who is their employer or, more crudely, who will pay the wages and any compensation for subsequent dismissal? Under an administration order, section 19 Insolvency Act 1986 ranks any claims against the assets of the company by giving first priority to any claims based upon contracts entered into by the administrator and claims under contracts of employment adopted by the administrator to the extent of 'qualifying liabilities'. The administrator is given a period of 14 days during which to decide whether to 'adopt' contracts of employment with the existing workforce. Having reviewed the prospects for the company for two weeks, an administrator who decides to mount a rescue or at least keep part of the business going with a view to a sale, will rehire the relevant employees, acting as agent for the company. Employees have the assurance that their claims for payment once they have been adopted will have priority over all other creditors, including the administrator himself, except others with whom the administrator contracts for the purpose of the rescue. The 'qualifying liability', that is the extent to which employees enjoy this 'super-priority' over other creditors including the administrator, applies to wages, contributions to occupational pension schemes, holiday pay and sick pay. Employees are therefore given a strong inducement to carry on working for the insolvent company in administration, for their wages are fairly assured by their super-priority. But this super-priority does not apply to claims for compensation for dismissal, for which retained employees are in no better and no worse position than they were before the administrator took control; that is, they are ranked as unsecured creditors of the company, but have the entitlement to the social security guarantee for wages during the notice period and a redundancy payment (or basic award for unfair dismissal).

The reforms in insolvency law introduced by the Enterprise Act 2002 may help to encourage corporate rescues, but, apart from the abolition of the Crown as a preferential creditor, they do not significantly improve the position of employees compared to the former rules governing receiverships. The government has not taken powers to force a corporate rescue to be attempted, and nor has it extended the social security guarantee to cover all wages, even those above the ceiling, falling due during the rescue attempt. But the assurance of first priority of wages once the administrator has adopted the contracts of employment should generally suffice to induce the workforce to assist with the corporate rescue. At the second stage of the rescue, however, it is likely that the administrator will try to sell all or part of the business as a going concern in order to realise its assets for creditors. At this point, the employees may face a fresh round of dismissals and variations in their terms of employment in connection with the transfer of the undertaking.

10.5 Sales of the business

A change in ownership of a business often creates a period of uncertainty for employees. The new owners may wish to reorganise the business, vary terms of employment, close down some parts, and make economic dismissals. We have already noted that the sale may take place in the context of insolvency, forming part of a corporate rescue or the realisation of assets by a liquidator, administrator or a receiver. This section is concerned with special protections provided for employees on sales of the business in addition to the other rules concerning workforce reductions and variations of contract.

The position of employees depends on the method by which the sale of the business is achieved. If the sale of the business is effected by the sale of shares in a company, the employer in the form of a company retains the same identity, so all the contracts and other legal obligations of the parties remain the same. If the sale of the business is achieved by any other transaction, however, the ownership of the business is transferred to a new legal entity. The content of the transaction may include the sale of physical assets such as premises and machinery and the assignment of a lease and other rights. Often the most valuable element is the 'goodwill', that is, the business reputation and the existing customer base. On general legal principles, the new owner or employer is not bound by the legal obligations and contracts of the previous owner of the business except in so far as it expressly agrees to assume those obligations. The new owner of the business may decide to employ all or part of the existing workforce, being attracted towards their skill, training and experience, but under the common law these contracts would be new contracts of employment.

The European Acquired Rights Directive 77/187, now re-enacted by Directive 2001/23, which consolidates amendments, applies two principles to a sale of a business that should render it in effect the same in its implications for employees as a sale by share transfer. The objective of the Directive is to ensure that employees are not adversely effected in any way by the fact that the sale involves a change in the identity of the employer. The first principle is that on the sale of a business the workforce is automatically transferred to the new owner on their existing terms of employment. The second principle is that, if either the seller or the purchaser of the business dismisses any of the workforce in order to avoid the application of the first principle, those dismissals should be ineffective to achieve that result.

[10.32] Acquired Rights Directive 2001/23 Articles 3 and 4

Article 3

The transferor's rights and obligations arising from a contract of employment or from an employment relationship existing on the date of a transfer shall, by reason of such transfer, be transferred to the transferee . . .

Article 4

1. The transfer of the undertaking, business or part of the undertaking or business shall not in itself constitute grounds for dismissal by the transferor or the transferee. This provision shall not stand in the way of dismissals that may take place for economic, technical or organisational reasons entailing changes in the workforce. . . .
2. If the contract of employment or the employment relationship is terminated because the transfer involves a substantial change in working conditions to the detriment of the employee, the employer shall be regarded as having been responsible for termination of the contract of employment or the employment relationship.

The Directive was implemented by the Transfer of Undertakings (Protection of Employment) Regulations 1981 SI No 1794 (known as TUPE). An amended version of the Regulations in Draft form is due to be approved in 2005: DTI, *TUPE: Draft Revised Regulations: Public Consultation Document*, URN 05/926, March 2005. The questions of the precise meaning and application of these principles in the Directive, and whether TUPE 1981 implements them properly, have been the subject of considerable controversy and litigation.

The source of this controversy is not hard to find. The value of a business must depend on its debts and potential future revenues. To maximise the value of the business, the seller should protect the purchaser against outstanding claims for pay and compensation for dismissal, and should hand over to the purchaser the business as a going concern with only those employees that the transferee needs. The Directive and TUPE 1981 place considerable obstacles in the way of this business approach to sales. Many employers have sought loopholes in the regulations, usually without ultimate success. Our examination of this complex topic focuses on some of the standard problems that arise in connection with the regulation.

10.5.1 Dismissals before the sale

In order to improve the value of the business to be sold, a transferor may decide to reduce the size of the workforce or even to make the whole workforce redundant. Prior to the Regulations such dismissals would leave the purchaser free to decide which employees to rehire, leaving the cost of the dismissals to be met by the transferor. If the transferor was insolvent, those costs might well be met by the State. The

Regulations change the legal position, so that it is doubtful whether there is any advantage to the transferor to dismiss employees before a sale.

[10.33] Transfer of Undertakings (Protection of Employment) Regulations 1981, Regulation 8

8. (1) Where either before or after a relevant transfer, any employee of the transferor or transferee is dismissed, that employee shall be treated for the purposes of . . . [ERA 1996 Part X] as unfairly dismissed if the transfer or a reason connected with it is the reason or principal reason for his dismissal.

(2) Where an economic, technical or organisational reason entailing changes in the workforce of either the transferor or the transferee before or after a relevant transfer is the reason or principal reason for dismissing an employee—

(a) paragraph (1) shall not apply to his dismissal; but

(b) without prejudice to the application of . . . [ERA s. 98(4)] (test of fair dismissal), the dismissal shall for the purposes of . . . [ERA s. 98(1)] (substantial reason for dismissal) be regarded as having been for a substantial reason of a kind such as to justify the dismissal of an employee holding the position which that employee held.

This regulation has several effects. First, a dismissal connected with the sale might formerly have been regarded merely as a dismissal for redundancy, whereas Regulation 8 creates the possibility that an employee may obtain the higher level of compensation for unfair dismissal. It remains possible, of course, that dismissals prior to a sale of the business were not in fact connected to the transfer but were the result of some independent process of making redundancies or disciplinary dismissals, in which case TUPE has no application to the facts.

Secondly, the regulation declares that if the reason for the dismissal is connected to the transfer, the dismissal is automatically unfair, unless the employer can establish the defence in Regulation 8(2) that there was an 'economic, technical or organisational reason' for the dismissal. Dismissals that occur shortly before a sale will almost certainly fall within the category of dismissals for a reason connected to a transfer. The phrase 'economic, technical or organisational reason' (or 'eto') has not been interpreted to include the economic reason of improving the price of the sale, but has been applied more narrowly to a reason that is connected with the future conduct of the business as a going concern, which is likely to apply only to dismissals by the transferee (*Whitehouse v Charles A Blatchford & Sons Ltd* [2000] ICR 542 (CA)). Thus dismissals prior to and in connection with the transfer will most likely be regarded as automatically unfair. If the 'eto' defence applies, however, the dismissal is regarded as for a substantial reason, and the tribunal will only award compensation for unfair dismissal if it concludes that the dismissals were outside the range of reasonable responses of the transferor under section 98(4) ERA 1996. The proposed amended Regulations, whilst reorganising these provisions, leave the substance of the original regulations in place except for making it clear that, when the dismissal is for an 'eto' reason, the dismissal should be regarded as having been for redundancy when the statutory definition of redundancy is satisfied.

[10.34] Draft Transfer of Undertakings (Protection of Employment) Regulations 2005 Regulation 7

7. (1) Where either before or after a relevant transfer, any employee of the transferor or transferee is dismissed, that employee shall be treated for the purposes of Part X of the 1996 Act (unfair dismissal) as unfairly dismissed if the sole or principal reason for his dismissal is—

(a)   the transfer itself, or

(b)   a reason connected with the transfer that is not an economic, technical or organisational reason entailing changes in the workforce.

(2) The paragraph applies where the sole or principal reason for the dismissal is a reason connected with the transfer that is an economic, technical or organisational reason entialing changes in the workforce of either the transferor or the transferee before or after a relevant transfer.

(3) Where paragraph (2) applies

(a)   paragraph (1) shall not apply; but

(b)   without prejudice to the application of section 98(4) of the 1996 Act (test of fair dismissal), the dismissal shall for the purposes of section 98(1) of that Act (substnatial reason for dismissal) be regarded as having been for redundancy where section 98(2)(c) of that Act applies, or otherwise for a substantial reason of a kind such as to justify the dismissal of an employee holding the position what that employee held.

Thirdly, and this point is perhaps the most important, any dismissal by the seller of the business in connection with the transfer is deemed also to have been a dismissal by the purchaser. Thus employees can claim their unfair dismissal compensation against the purchaser, even though they were dismissed prior to the sale.

[10.35] Transfer of Undertakings (Protection of Employment) Regulations 1981, Regulation 5

5(1) Except where objection is made under paragraph (4A) below, a relevant transfer shall not operate so as to terminate the contract of employment of any person employed by the transferor in the undertaking or part transferred but any such contract which would otherwise have been terminated by the transfer shall have effect after the transfer as if originally made between the person so employed and the transferee.

(2) Without prejudice to paragraph (1) above, but subject to paragraph (4A) below, on the completion of a relevant transfer—

(a)   all the transferor's rights, powers, duties and liabilities under or in connection with any such contract shall be transferred by virtue of this Regulation to the transferee; and

(b)   anything done before the transfer is completed by or in relation to the transferor in respect of that contract or person employed in that undertaking or part shall be deemed to have been done by or in relation to the transferee.

(3) Any reference in paragraph (1) or (2) above to a person employed in an undertaking or part of one transferred by a relevant transfer is a reference to a person so employed immediately before the transfer.

The effect of Regulation 5 is that the transferee acquires all the outstanding obligations of the transferor with respect to the employees of the transferor, including
contractual obligations (except occupational pensions under Regulation 7), liabilities
to preferential creditors, compensation due for dismissal, and any other form of liability (except criminal liability) such as tort claims for personal injuries arising in
connection with the contract of employment. Thus there is no obvious finanacial
advantage to the transferee in acquiring the business after dismissals have reduced the
size of the workforce, because the transferee will probably be liable to pay compensation for unfair dismissal. As a consequence, the worth of the business is not increased
by dismissals. On the contrary, the purchaser of the business may best be advised to
retain the workforce, and, at later date, effect a reorganisation involving a workforce
reduction. Such economic dismissals may not be perceived to be made in connection
with the transfer, which would limit the dismissed employees to a claim for the
reduced compensatory measure of redundancy payments.

Because compliance with these rules required a fundamental change in business
culture and in the handling of what lawyers call 'acquisitions', the Regulations have
been ignored frequently and their application hotly contested. The next two cases
illustrate the application of the Regulations and establish important issues of interpretation of their effects.

[10.36] *Litster v Forth Dry Dock & Engineering Co Ltd* [1989] ICR 341 (HL)

A company went into a receivership but carried on trading for a few months when the
tangible assets were sold. About an hour before the sale, at the request of the purchasers,
the receivers summarily dismissed the workforce. 12 dismissed employees, who were not
subsequently re-engaged by the transferee, claimed unfair dismissal against both the
transferor and the transferee. The transferees argued that the regulations did not apply to
the dismissals at all, because (amongst many reasons put forward) the employees were not
employed 'immediately before' the transfer, as required by Regulation 5(3). The House of
Lords held that the Regulations did apply to dismissals connected to the transfer and that
the phrase 'immediately before' the transfer must be interpreted purposively in order to
achieve its objective of giving effect to the Acquired Rights Directive.

Lord Templeman:

The result of Article 4(1) is that the new owner intending to dismiss the workers cannot
achieve his purpose by asking the old owner to dismiss the workers immediately prior to
the transfer taking place. The new owner cannot dismiss the workers himself after the
transfer has taken place. Any such dismissal, whether by the old owner or the new owner,
would be inconsistent with the object of protecting the rights of the workers and is
prohibited by Article 4(1) . . .

The result of regulation 8(1) is the same as Article 4(1), namely, that if the new owner
wishes to dismiss the workers he cannot achieve his purpose either by procuring the old
owner to dismsis the workers, prior to the transfer taking place, or by himself dismsising
the workers after the date of the transfer. . . .

The appellants were dismissed at 3.30 p.m. on 6 February by Forth Dry Dock and the
business was transferred to Forth Estuary at 4.30 p.m. on the same day . . . Thus, it is said,
since the workforce of Forth Dry Dock were dismissed at 3.30 p.m., they were not
employed "immediately before the transfer" at 4.30 p.m. and therefore Regulation 5(1) did
not transfer any liability for the workforce from Forth Dry Dock to Forth Estuary. The

argument is inconsistent with the Directive. In *P Bork International A/S v Foreningen af Arbejdsledere I Danmark* (Case 101/87) [1989] IRLR 41, 44, the European Court of Justice ruled:

> 'the only workers who may invoke Directive [77/187] are those who have current employment relations or a contract of employment at the date of the transfer. The question whether or not a contract of employment or employment relationship exists at that date must be assessed under national law, subject, however, to the observance of the mandatory rules of the Directive concerning the protection of workers against dismissal by reason of the transfer. It follows that the workers employed by the undertaking whose contract of employment or employment relationship has been terminated with effect on a date before that transfer, in breach of Article 4(1) of the Directive, must be considered as still employed by the undertaking on the date of the transfer with the consequence, in particular, that the obligations of an employer towards them are fully transferred from the transferor to the transferee in accordance with Article 3(1) of the Directive.' . . .

[T]he courts of the United Kingdom are under a duty to follow the practice of the European Court of Justice by giving a purposive construction to Directives and to Regulations issued for the purpose of complying with Directives . . .

In the present case, . . . it seems to me . . . that paragraph 5(3) of the Regulation of 1981 was not intended and ought not to be construed so as to limit the operation of Regulation 5 to persons employed immediately before the transfer in point of time. Regulation 5(3) must be construed on the footing that it applies to a person employed immediately before the transfer or who would have been so employed if he had not been unfairly dismissed before the transfer for a reason connected with the transfer. It would, of course, still be open for a new owner to show that the employee had been dismissed for 'an economic, technical or organisational reason entailing changes in the workforce' [Regulation 8(2)], but no such reason could be advance in the present case where there was no complaint against the workers, they were not redundant and there were no relevant reasons entailing changes in the workforce.

If the transferor does dismiss all or part of the workforce in connection with the transfer of undertaking, what is the effect of the dismissals? In the light of the remarks of the ECJ in Case 101/87 *P Bork International A/S v Foreningen af Arbejdsledere I Danmark* [1989] IRLR 41 (ECJ), quoted by Lord Templeman above, it was suggested that the dismissals should have no legal effect at all: the dismissals should be void, or voidable, as in other European legal systems such as Germany, with the result that employees automatically would keep their jobs and become employees of the transferee. This view of the effect of the directive was rejected in the next case.

[10.37] *Wilson v St. Helens Borough Council; British Fuels Ltd v Baxendale* [1999] 2 AC 52 (HL)

Two cases were joined for appeal. In the *Wilson* case, in pursuance of a plan to reorganise the school system, teachers at a school were dismissed for redundancy by their old employer, the county council, but immediately afterwards accepted employment on different terms by the new school authority, the borough council. The main point of the appeal was whether the dismissals for redundancy before the transfer had been effective to terminate the contracts of employment of the teachers. If so, the teachers would have claims for dismissal against transferor and transferee, but could not claim that they were still employed under their former conditions of employment. The House of Lords held that the dismissals were effective to terminate the contracts of employment under national law, and that the Directive did not require the contrary result that the dismissals were void.

Lord Slynn:

In my opinion, the overriding emphasis in the European Court's judgments is that the existing rights of employees are to be safeguarded if there is a transfer. That means no more and no less than that the employee can look to the transferee to perform those obligations which the employee could have enforced against the transferor. The employer, be he transferor or transferee, cannot use the transfer as a justification for dismissal, but if he does dismiss it is a question for national law as to what those rights are. As I have already said, in English law there would as a general rule be no order for specific performance. The claim would be for damages for wrongful dismissal or for statutory rights including, it is true, reinstatement or re-engagement where applicable. It may be in other countries that an order for specific performance could be obtained under the appropriate domestic law and that on this approach different results would be achieved in different Member States. That I do not find surprising or shocking. The Directive is to 'approximate' the laws of the Member States. Its purpose is to 'safeguard' rights on a transfer. The 'rights' of an employee must depend on national rules of the law of contract or of legislation. There is no Community law of contract common to Member States, nor is there a common system or remedies. The object and purpose of the Directive is to ensure in all Member States that on a transfer an employee has against the transferee the rights and remedies which he would have had against the original employer. To that extent it reduces the differences which may exist in the event of a change of employers as to the enforcement by employees of existing rights. They must all provide for enforcement against the transferee of rights existing against the transferor at the time of transfer. It seems to me that the Court has clearly recognised that the precise rights to be transferred depend on national law. But neither the Regulations nor the Directive nor the jurisprudence of the Court create a community law right to continue in employment which does not exist under national law.

It is said that this is not an adequate remedy because some employees do not have statutory rights—e.g. those in the United Kingdom who have not been employed for a qualifying period—but that is inherent in the differences which exist in the laws of the Member States and seems to me to derive from the wording and limited purpose of the Directive.

Thus, where there is a transfer of an undertaking and the transferee actually takes on the employee the contract of employment is automatically transferred so that, in the absence of a permissible variation, the terms of the initial contract go with the employee, who though he may refuse to go, cannot as a matter of public policy waive the rights which the Directive and the Regulations confer on him. Where the transferee does not take on the employees who are dismissed on transfer the dismissal is not a nullity though the contractual rights formerly available against the transferor remain intact against the transferee. For the latter purpose, an employee dismissed prior to the transfer contrary to Article 4(1), i.e. on the basis of the transfer, is to be treated as still in the employment of the transferor at the date of transfer so as to satisfy the rule in [Case 19/83 *Wendelboe v L.J. Music ApS* [1985] ECR 457 (ECJ)] as consistently followed, *e.g.* in [Case 287/86 *Landsorganisationen I Danmark v Ny Molle Kro* [1989] IRLR 37 (ECJ)].

The Court has said that the employees' rights are safeguarded by 'enabling them to remain in employment with the new employer on the terms and conditions agreed with the transferor' (*Bork*) or by 'making it possible for them to continue to work for the new employer on the same conditions as those agreed with the transferor' [Cases 132, 138, 139/91 *Katsikas v Konstantinidis* [1993] ECR I–6577 (ECJ)], or, so far as possible, safeguarding employees' rights by "allowing them to remain in employment with the new employer on the terms and conditions agreed with the transferor" [Case 324/86 *Foreningen af Arbejdsledere I Danmark v Daddy's Dance Hall A/S* [1988] ECR 739 (ECJ) paragraph 9]. The emphasis is on the same terms and conditions applying if the employment is continued. I do not read, however, any of these expressions as meaning that the transferee is bound actually to take on an employee who has been dismissed, whether because of the transfer or for independent reasons, and to give him the same work as he had before. They mean that if he does take the employee he takes him on the terms of the employment with the transferor, i.e. there is a deemed novation by the two willing parties. If the transferee does not take the employee because the latter has already been dismissed by the transferor, or because he himself dismisses the employee on the transfer, then he must meet all of the transferor's contractual and statutory obligations unless (a) the employee objects to being employed by the transferee or (b) the or the principal reason for dismissal is an economic, technical or organisational reason entailing changes in the workforce when the employee is not to be treated as unfairly dismissed and when for the purposes of the 1978 Act and the 1976 Order the employee is to be regarded as having been dismissed for a substantial reason justifying the dismissal as fair.

This decision upholds the view that national law determines the detailed implementation of directives, and that, in particular, questions of termination of contracts of employment must be decided by reference to the law of the Member State. Under UK law, termination of the contract by dismissal is normally effective to bring the contract to an end. Thus dismissals prior to the sale will terminate contracts of employment, though leaving both transferor and transferee liable to pay compensation for unfair dismissal. It is also possible that a dismissed employee may seek an order for reinstatement as the remedy for unfair dismissal. The question then becomes whether it is practicable for the transferee to reinstate the worker (ERA 1996, section 114, section 5.5.2 above). The proposed draft TUPE regulations 2005 confirm these results, though a new Regulation 4 replaces the existing Regulation 5.

Dismissals before the sale of a business will often be carried out by an administrator or administrative receiver in control over a company that has become insolvent. The 1981 Regulations apply in general to corporate rescues, so that the transferee cannot avoid the potential cost of having to meet the expense of claims for dismissal. Either the employees can claim the compensation directly against the transferee, or the Secretary of State can recoup the cost of paying compensation from the transferee. This cost will affect the price of the sale of the business and perhaps make a sale as part of a rescue attempt less attractive to creditors. The employees are in effect gaining super-priority over other creditors of the insolvent company by having their dismissal claims met in full by the solvent purchaser, the cost presumably being deducted from the purchase price. A case can be made on grounds of minimising the social costs of economic dismissals for encouraging corporate rescues by insulating the transferee from these costs. The directive was revised to enable Member States to derogate from employees' acquired rights for the purpose of supporting corporate rescues.

[10.38] Acquired Rights Directive 2001/23 Article 5

5. 2. Where Articles 3 and 4 apply to a transfer during insolvency proceedings which have been opened in relation to a transferor . . . and provided that such proceedings are under the supervision of a competent public authority (which may be an insolvency practitioner determined by national law) a Member State may provide that—

(a)   notwithstanding Article 3(1), the transferor's debts arising from any contracts of employment . . . and payable before the transfer or before the opening of insolvency proceedings shall not be transferred to the transferee, provided that such proceedings give rise, under the law of that Member State, to protection at least equivalent to that provided for in . . . Directive 80/987 [the state guarantee] . . .; and, or alternatively, that

(b)   the transferee, transferor, or person or persons exercising the transferor's functions, on the one hand, and the representatives of the employees on the other hand may agree alterations, insofar as current law or practice permits, to the employee's terms and conditions of employment designed to safeguard employment opportunities by ensuring the survival of the undertaking, business or part of the undertaking or business.

In its draft Regulations intended to reform TUPE, the government has decided to take up these options. It proposes to permit recognised trade unions or workforce representatives to negotiate new terms and conditions provided that the variation promotes the survival of the undertaking (Draft Regulation 9, **[10.45]** below]. A new Draft Regulation 8 is designed to prevent transfers of some liabilities for dismissal and other outstanding debts from the insolvent transferor to the transferee.

[10.39] Draft Transfer of Undertakings (Protection of Employment) Regulations 2005 Regulation 8

8. (1) If at the time of a relevant transfer the transferor is subject to relevant insolvency proceedings paragraphs (2) to (6) apply.

(2) In this regulation "relevant employee" means an employee of the transferor—

(a)   whose contract of employment transfers to the transferee by virtue of the operation of these Regulations in relation to the relevant transfer, or

(b)   whose employment with the transferor is terminated before the time of the relevant transfer in the circumstances described in regulation 7(1).

(3) The relevant statutory schemes specified in paragraph (4)(b) and (d) shall apply irrespective of the fact that the qualifying requirement that the employment of an employee hwo is a relevant employee by virtue of paragraph (2)(a) has been terminated is not met and for those purposes the date of the transfer shall be treated as thed ate of the termination and the transferor shall be treated as the employer.

(4) In this regulation the "relevant statutory schemes" are:

(a)   Chapter VI of Part XI of the 1996 Act; [recovery of redundancy payments from the social security funds ERA 1996 ss. 166-170]

(b)   Part XII of the 1996 Act; [recovery of wages and other sums from the social security funds ERA 1996 ss. 182-190] . . .

(5) Regulation 4 [automatic transfer of contracts of employment] shall not operate to transfer liability for the sums payable to the relevant employee under the relevant statutory schemes.

(6) In this regulation "relevant insolvency proceedings" means insolvency proceeduings which have been opened in relation to the transferor not with a view to the liquidation of the assets of the transferor and which are under the supervision of an insolvency practitioner.

The effect of these rules is that employees of an insolvent company must claim their compensation for dismissal and wages from the Secretary of State or the assets of the insolvent company to the extent that those items of compensation are guaranteed by the social security system. For payments and compensation owed by the insolvent transferor that do not fall within the guarantee provisions, however, employees will be permitted claim their compensation from the transferee. For example, an employee who is dismissed by the insolvent company may claim a basic award or redundancy payment from the transferor or the Secretary of State, but if the dismissal is an unfair dismissal, as will be the case if it is connected to the transfer or their has been an unfair selection for redundancy, the compensatory award for unfair dismissal must be claimed against the solvent transferee. Similarly, outstanding wages of employees who are transferred as part of the corporate rescue can be claimed against the transferor and the social security system, but only up to the limits fixed by legislation. For sums owing above those limits, the employees can claim the excess from the transferee.

The likely effects of this Regulation on corporate rescues are uncertain, because it is unclear whether the automatic transfer of the costs of dismissal has impeded corporate rescues. The transfer of such costs may not discourage rescues, but merely reduce the sum available to the secured creditor on insolvency by reducing the price of the sale. The reduced price for the sale of a going concern may still have been superior to the alternative sum realised by a simple asset sale. Yet where the potential costs are indeterminate, as will be the case with respect to compensatory awards for unfair dismissal, the possibility of greater than expected liabilities may have a chilling effect on rescues. The effect of the proposed Regulation 8 is to permit the transferee to avoid many of the debts owed to employees, leaving the social security system to pick up a part of debts owed by the insolvent transferor to the workforce, thereby increasing the value of the business on sale to potential advantage of secured creditors. Since that option is only available in the case of corporate rescues, or more precisely is unavailable under Regulation 8(6) when there is a mere liquidation of the assets of the transferor, it may encourage creditors and administrators to view corporate rescues comparatively favourably. But the transferee still may encounter substantial costs in the form of wages owed and compensatory awards for unfair dismissal, which may discourage corporate rescues. In an attempt to counter that problem, the proposed draft TUPE regulations 2005 include new provisions in Regulations 11 and 12, which require the transferor to notify the transferee of outstanding liabilities towards employees. Failure to provide this information may result in the imposition of a penalty by the High Court of up to a mamimum of £75,000.

10.5.2 Dismissals after the sale

If the purchaser of the business takes on employees, but then decides to reduce the workforce, the Regulations will apply, provided that the dismissals are connected to the transfer. It is possible, of course, that if the dismissals occur after a period of time, a tribunal will decide that the dismissals were unconnected to the transfer, in which case they are likely to fall within the category of dismissals for redundancy. But if the workforce reduction is connected to the transfer, Regulation 8 applies to bring the dismissals within the law of unfair dismissal. The Regulations also apply to existing employees of the transferee who may be selected for dismissal (Regulation 8(3)).

Any dismissals in connection with the transfer will be automatically unfair unless the employer can demonstrate in accordance with Regulation 8(2) an economic, technical or organisational reason for the dismissals (the 'eto' defence). This broad exception seems likely to apply to most dismissals in such circumstances. Having acquired the business, the purchaser will look for savings in labour costs or efficient reorganisations. If those measures require dismissals, they will count as economic, technical or organisational reasons for dismissal. This broad scope of Regulation 8(2) can be justified because it places dismissed employees in the same position as if there had been no transfer at all.

If Regulation 8(2) applies, the 'eto' reason for dismissal is regarded as forming a substantial reason for the dismissal. The current Regulations do not specify what kind of substantial reason this is among those listed in ERA 1996, section 98(1)(b). The reason for dismissal is likely in fact to fall into the category of a dismissal for redundancy. The proposed Regulation 7(3) ([10.34] above) makes clear that an 'eto' reason may be regarded as a dismissal for redundancy (as an alternative to 'some other substantial reason') if the statutory definition of redundancy applies to case. In such cases, the dismissal will only be regarded as an unfair dismissal if the test of reasonableness in relation to procedure or selection applies (10.2.3, above). In such cases the employer must pay the redundancy payment, but will avoid additional compensation for unfair dismissal unless the tribunal finds that there was unfair selection for redundancy or an unfair procedure. In the unlikely event that the dismissal is held not to be for reason of redundancy, it must be classified as 'some other substantial reason', and the employer may be able to avoid the payment of any compensation if the tribunal decides that it was reasonable for the employer to dismiss the employee for that reason under ERA 1996, section 98(4).

10.5.3 Variation of terms by transferee

A frequent problem concerns the case where the new owner of the business proposes to vary the terms of the contracts of employment of the employees formerly employed by the transferor. Such variations may be unwelcome to employees, who may seek either to insist upon their previous terms or to resign and claim compensation for dismissal. In principle, such variations should be ineffective due to the automatic novation of contracts of employment established by Regulation 5 (above [10.35]). If an employee is transferred to the new owner, Regulation 5 deems the employment relation to be the same as if the new owner had been the original employer. If the employer attempts to alter the contract of employment in any respect, therefore, this must be regarded as an attempt to vary the contract unilaterally, which should have no legal effect without the consent of the employee. But if the employee consents to a new contract: is the variation effective? Regulation 12 declares that any provision of any agreement that purports to exclude or limit the effect of the Regulations should be void.

[10.40] *Crédit Suisse Ltd v Lister* [1999] ICR 794 (CA)

The employer sought to enforce by way of an injunction a covenant in the contract of employment that prevented the employee from working for a competing business for three months following termination of his employment. The employment relation had commenced when the employer purchased the business from a previous owner and had taken on 209 employees to whom the purchaser had offered incentives to stay. The new contracts of employment contained the restrictive covenant, which had not been present in the contracts with the transferor. The Court of Appeal held that the restrictive covenant was unenforceable. An employee's rights under his employment relation with the transferee could not be waived as a matter of public policy under TUPE and the Directive. It was irrelevant that the employee was receiving new rights that compensated him for the loss of the old. The employee could, however, enforce new rights that were advantageous.

This decision places a considerable obstacle in the way of purchasers of businesses who want to vary the terms of the retained employees. The transferee can offer 'sweeteners' in order to persuade employees to stay on, but cannot adversely affect the employee's legal rights in any way except for a limitation in relation to occupational pensions (see box p 1052). The new employer may argue, however, that the variations of the contract were not connected to the transfer, but were made for some other business reason. Under this argument, if it can be maintained that the transferor would have made these (or similar) variations to the contracts even if there had been no sale of the business, the variations are not prohibited. This reasoning was approved in the next case.

[10.41] *Wilson v St. Helens Borough Council; British Fuels Ltd v Baxendale* [1998] ICR 1141 (HL)

These cases were considered on another issue (above [10.37]). In the *Wilson* case, in pursuance of a plan to reorganise the school system, teachers at a school were dismissed for redundancy by their old employer, the county council, but immediately afterwards accepted employment on different terms by the new school authority, the borough council. The teachers worked under the new contracts for several months before complaining to a tribunal that in paying reduced wages the employers were in breach of Regulation 5, and that they should be able to recover the difference in wages as unauthorised deductions. On the question whether the variations were effective, the House of Lords expressed the view that the industrial tribunal had not committed an error of law in finding that the transfer had not been the reason for the variations.

Lord Slynn:
Accordingly it is not strictly necessary to deal with the second issue which has been raised as to whether variation of the terms of employment could lawfully be agreed between the parties. Since the matter has been fully argued, particularly in the case of *Wilson*, I express my opinion on the point. . . .

The employers contend that there can be an alteration of the terms and conditions of employment on or after a relevant transfer so that if the reasons are connected with the transfer the employee will be able to claim for unfair dismissal if he treats the imposition of the terms as a constructive dismissal. If he accepts the terms then that is the end of the matter. Here the employees had an option to stay with LCC or to go to St. Helens on new terms. They chose the latter alternative and only a year or so later sought to insist on the old terms. If the transferee cannot safely agree terms to bring his new employees into line with existing employees' standard terms and conditions, that will discourage employers from taking over new businesses or lead to the transferee dismissing transferred employees.

It seems to me clear, as Miss Booth QC contended, that the Industrial Tribunal in Wilson's case found on the evidence before it, and the Court of Appeal accepted, that the Home could not continue unless there were radical organisational changes which would reduce the cost of running the school. LCC could not or would not continue to carry the existing costs. St. Helens could not take over the running of the school with those costs and without organisational changes and reduced costs. Those changes were for an economic or organisational reason and entailed a change in the workforce since the number of employees at the school was considerably reduced, whether or not the "eto" defence can strictly be relied on in the present circumstances. The staff had the option of staying with LCC or going to St. Helens on the new terms to give effect to these economic and organisational reasons. In the circumstances the Industrial Tribunal and the Court of Appeal were entitled to find that the transfer of the undertaking did not constitute the reason for the variation. It was a variation of the terms of employment "to the same extent as it could have been with regard to the transferor" [Case 324/86 *Foreningen af Arbejdsledere I Danmark v Daddy's Dance Hall A/S* [1988] ECR 739 (ECJ) paragraph 17]. That seems to me to be sufficient on the facts to determine the appeal in Wilson's case. But I add that, although on a transfer, the employees' rights previously existing against the transferor are enforceable against the transferee and cannot be amended by the transfer itself, it does not follow there cannot be a variation of the terms of the contract for reasons which are not due to the transfer either on or after the transfer of the undertaking. It may be difficult to decide whether the variation is due to the transfer or attributable to some separate cause. If, however, the variation is not due to the transfer it can, in my opinion, on the basis of the authorities to which I have referred, validly be made . . .

There is no fixed time within which the terms of employment are protected from change by the Regulations, so the issue appears to turn on the question of causation. The Directive does specify in Article 3(3), however, that following a transfer, the transferee should continue to observe the terms and conditions agreed in any collective agreement until the termination or expiration of the collective agreement. As interpreted by Regulation 6 of TUPE, this protection means that the transferee is bound by the collective agreement to the same extent as the transferor, so that if the collective agreement determines the terms of employment by incorporation, the agreement still applies to those terms. But this Regulation does not place any restriction on the transferee trying to renegotiate the collective agreement immediately, even though that possibility seems contrary to the spirit of the Directive. The Directive now includes a permitted exception in cases of insolvency in Article 5.2(b) (above [10.35]), under which collective agreements may modify terms of employment for the purpose of corporate rescues that safeguard jobs, and we have noted that the government proposes to introduce that exception to the UK. The alternative route for introducing variations in terms of employment is the more drastic method used in *Wilson v St. Helens Borough Council*, that is to require the transferor to dismiss all the workforce and the transferee to offer jobs on new terms and conditions. Although this route is likely to incur the costs of paying compensation for unfair dismissal, it may be assessed as less expensive than an acquisition of the business and its workforce on the previous terms and conditions of employment.

When confronted with a variation in terms proposed by the transferee, the employee may chose to treat the unilateral variation as a constructive dismissal. The employee can then claim unfair dismissal against the transferee. Under the normal rules of constructive unfair dismissal (above 5.2.2), the transferee employer would claim that the dismissal was for a substantial reason, and the employment tribunal would have to assess whether it was reasonable for the employer to dismiss the employee for refusing to accept the variation in terms. The only difference here when TUPE 1981 applies is that a variation of terms of employment by the transferee 'in connection with the transfer' will render the constructive dismissal automatically unfair under Regulation 8(1). Under the original Regulations the defence to automatic unfairness provided by Regulation 8(2) when the dismissal is for economic, technical or organisational reasons does not apparently apply to mere variations of terms of employment: *Berriman v Delabole Slate Ltd* [1985] ICR 546 (CA). That interpretation creates a potential obstacle to corporate rescues, because employees could object to variations by the transferee by claiming constructive dismissal, and those dismissals would be automatically unfair no matter how advantageous and reasonable the variations might appear to the tribunal.

In the Draft Regulations of 2005, however, a new legislative scheme for handling variations of contracts by the transferee is proposed.

[10.42] Draft Transfer of Undertakings (Protection of Employment) Regulations 2005 Regulation 4

4 (4) In respect of a contract of employment that is, or will be, transferred by paragraph (1), and purported variation of the contract shall be void if the sole or principal reason for the variation is
(a)   the transfer itself, or
(b)   a reason connected with the transfer that is not an economic, technical or organisation reason entailing changes in the workforce.

(5) Paragraph (4) shall not prevent the employer and his employee, whose contract of employment is, or will be, transferred by paragraph (1), from agreeing a variation of that contract if the sole or principal reason for the variation is—
(a)   a reason connected with the transfer that is an economic, technical or organisational reason entailing changes in the workforce, or
(b)   a reason unconnected with the transfer.

If these Draft Regulations become law, the effect will be that a transferee may seek a binding agreement with its new employees to implement changes in terms that are motivated by an economic, technical or organisation reason. There is no requirement that all these changes should be beneficial to the individual employee. Thus an employee may agree with the transferee a new package of terms, some beneficial, others worse than before, and this agreement will be binding. This proposed regulation would therefore reverse the decision in *Crédit Suisse Ltd v Lister* in so far as that case only permitted beneficial variations to be binding. The proposed regulation also reverses the position established in *Wilson* v. *St. Helens Borough Council* that transferred staff could agree new terms and subsequently turn around and claim constructive dismissal that was automatically unfair. Under the new regulation, the agreement to be bound by new terms of employment would be binding, even if the changes are connected to the transfer of the undertaking. This acceptance of the possibility of variations in contracts does not prevent an employee from simply rejecting the proposed terms on the ground that they represent a substantial detrimental change, thereby entitling the employee to claim constructive unfair dismissal.

A final possibility is that the employee, on hearing about proposed changes by the transferee, or for some other reason disliking the prospect of being transferred, decides to resign or indicates an unwillingness to be transferred prior to the sale or transfer of undertaking. The legal effect of such a choice by an employee was unclear under the original Directive, but the ECJ held in Case C–132/91 *Katsikas v Konstantinidis* [1993] IRLR 179, that the Directive did not destroy the employee's right to refuse to transfer. The ECJ subsequently held in Case C–171/94 *Merckx v Ford Motors Co (Belgium)* [1996] IRLR 467 that national law should determine the legal consequences of an employee's objection to a transfer, except that where the objection is based upon a change in the level of remuneration or some other substantial detriment, following Article 4(2) of the Directive (above) the employer must be held responsible for the termination of employment. These decisions provoked amendments to TUPE, but left unclear the precise position of employees who objected to a transfer. Should the employee be regarded as having resigned, thereby losing any right to claim compensation for dismissal, or should the resignation be regarded as provoked by the transfer, and thus at least entitling the employee to a redundancy payment?

[10.43] Transfer of Undertakings (Protection of Employment) Regulations 1981 Regulation 5

5 (4A) Paragraphs (1) and (2) shall not operate to transfer his contract of employment and the rights, powers, duties and liabilities under or in connection with it if the employee informs the transferor or the transferee that he objects to becoming employed by the transferee.

(4B) Where an employee so objects the transfer of the undertaking or part in which he is employed shall operate so as to terminate his contract of employment with the transferor but he shall not be treated, for any purpose, as having been dismissed by the transferor.

(5) Paragraphs (1) and (4A) above are without prejudice to any right of an employee arising apart from these regulations to terminate his contract of employment without notice if a substantial change is made in his working conditions to his detriment; but no such right shall arise by reason only that, under that paragraph, the identity of his employer changes unless the employee shows that, in all the circumstances, the change is a significant change and is to his detriment.

At first sight, these provisions leave the employee who chooses to resign rather than move to the transferee in a poor position. Regulation 5(4A) permits the employee's resignation or rejection of the transfer to be effective, but Regulation 5(4B) appears to prevent any claim for dismissal either under statute or the common law. The next case prevented the Regulations from having the effect of worsening the employee's position compared to the common law.

[10.44] *University of Oxford v (1) Humphreys and (2) Associated Examining Board* **[2000] IRLR 183 (CA)**

> The university planned to transfer an examination business (the Oxford Delegacy) to the Associated Examining Board (AEB). An employee of the Delegacy, Mr Humphreys, notified the university that he objected to being employed by AEB because the transfer would involve a significant change in his working conditions to his detriment. Following the transfer, the employee claimed wrongful dismissal at common law. The potential measure of damages was substantial, because the employee had a contractual right not to be dismissed before retiring age except on grounds of misconduct or wilful disobedience to university statutes. The university argued that Mr Humphreys had no claim by virtue of Regulation 5(4B), or that any claim must be against the AEB. Mr Humphreys argued that his claim fell within Regulation 5(5). The Court of Appeal held that Regulation 5(4B) applied where the employee merely objected to a change in the identity of the employer, but when the reason for the objection was that the transfer would involve a substantial and detrimental change in an employee's terms and conditions of employment, Regulation 5(5) applied, rendering the case one of constructive dismissal. In effect, the Court of Appeal, following the ECJ in *Merckx v Ford Motors Co* (above), permits Regulation 5(5) to override Regulation 5(4B), even though Regulation 5(5) only refers to Regulation 5(4A), when the employee would have been able to claim constructive dismissal against the transferee, if the transfer had taken place. The court also held, however, that the claim must be against the transferor, since no transfer of employment had ever occurred by virtue of Regulation 5(4A).

An employee who refuses to transfer on the ground that the transferee offers disadvantageous terms can thus claim to have been dismissed by the transferor. The preceding case permitted a common law claim for wrongful dismissal, but the reasoning should also apply to statutory claims for unfair dismissal and redundancy payments. If that view is correct, the dismissal is likely to be automatically unfair under Regulation 8(1), since the dismissal counts as a dismissal before the sale in connection with a transfer.

The proposed Draft regulations introduce an exception to that conclusion when the disadvantageous new contract offered by the transferee has been negotiated with a recognised trade union or workforce representatives as part of a corporate rescue of an insolvent company.

[10.45] Draft Transfer of Undertakings (Protection of Employment) Regulations 2005 Regulation 9.

> 9. (1) If at the time of a relevant transfer the transferor is subject to relevant insolvency

proceedings these Regulations shall not prevent the transferor or transferee (or an insolvency practitioner) and appropriate representatives of assigned employees agreeing to permitted variations.

(2) For the purposes of this regulation "appropriate representatives" are—
(a)   if the employees are of a description in respect of which an indpendent trade union is recognised by their employer, representatives of the trade union, or
(b)   in any other case, whichever of the following employee representatives the employer chooses—
   (i)   employee representatives appointed or elected by the affected employees otherwise than for the purposes of this regulation, who (having regard to the purposes for and the method by which they were appointed or elected) have authority from those employees to agree permitted variations to contracts of employment on their behalf;
   (ii)   employee representatives elected by affected employees of the description in question for these particular purposes, in an election satisfying requirements identical to those contained in regulation 14 except those in regulation 14(1)(d) . . .

(6) Where assigned employees are represented by non-union representatives—
(a)   the agreement recording a permitted variation must be in writing and signed by each of the representatives who have made it or, where that is not reasonably practicable, by a duly authorised agent of that representative; and
(a)   the employer must, before the agreement is made available for signature, provide all employees to whom it is intended to apply on the date on which it is to come into effect with copies of the text of the agreement and such guidance as those employees might reasonably require in order to understand it fully.

(7) A permitted variation shall take effect as a term or condition of the assigned employee's contract of employment in place, wherever relevant, of any term or condition which it varies.

(8) In this regulation. . . "permitted variation" is a variation to the contract of employment of an assigned employee where—
(a)   the sole or principal reason for it is the transfer itself or a reason connected with the transfer that is not an economic, technical or organisational reason entailing chanes in the workforce, and
(b)   that is designed to safeguard employment opportunities by ensuring the survival of the undertaking, business or part of the undertaking or business the subject of the relevant transfer . . .

10.5.4 Outsourcing

One of the most contested questions has been whether or not any 'transfer of an undertaking' has taken place at all. It is sometimes thought that the Directive and Regulations apply only where the purchaser takes over the business in every aspect, including its plant, machinery, goodwill, and at least part of its workforce. But this view is misconceived. The Directive applies broadly to most sales. For instance, in *Kerry Foods Ltd v Creber* [2000] IRLR 10 (EAT), the TUPE 1981 Regulations applied to a sale merely of goodwill, stock and existing contracts, without any

---

Occupational Pension Rights

One of the potential great disappointments for employees on transfer to a new employer is a diminution or abolition of benefits under an occupational pension scheme. Rights under such a scheme are not automatically transferred as terms of the new job: TUPE Regulation 7; Directive 2001/23, Article 3(4). This exception to automatic transfer of contractual rights for 'old-age, invalidity or survivors' benefits under supplementary company pension schemes has been construed narrowly by the ECJ, so that it excludes only benefits paid from the time when an employee reaches the end of his normal working life as laid down by the general structure of the pension scheme, and not benefits paid in other circumstances, even if they are calculated under the same rules as the occupational pension scheme. Thus early retirement benefits paid in the event of dismissal of employees over a certain age but prior to the normal pensionable age will be automatically transferred with the contract of employment: Case C–4/01, *Martin v South Bank University* [2004] IRLR 74 (ECJ). The origin of the exclusion for occupational pension schemes lies in the difficulty of creating a Directive that might sensibly apply to all the variety of schemes throughout Europe. But the exclusion arguably makes sense within the British scheme that vests the funds of the pension in an entity that is separate from the transferor employer, so that the pension entitlements cannot be legally transferred without the consent of the trustees. What English law does achieve is to require that the employee's pension rights under the transferor's occupational scheme become vested or protected, so that they can eventually be claimed when the employee satisfies the normal conditions (Pension Schemes Act 1993). But the transferee employer is not under any obligation to offer the same or a similar occupational scheme. In some cases, the transferee employer may be willing to accept the new employees into its existing scheme and in effect arrange with the trustees of the transferor's scheme to take over the accrued benefits and liabilities, and there is a legal requirement in such cases that the benefits of the receiving scheme are at least equal in value (Occupational Pension Schemes (Preservation of Benefits) Regulations SI 167 1991). These rules do not apply to other forms of contractual promises by employers to contribute to personal pension schemes, which should be covered by TUPE Reg. 5. See the valuable analysis of these problems: B Hepple and K Mumgaard, 'Pension Rights in Business Transfers' (1998) 27 *Industrial Law Journal* 309. Where a transfer of an undertaking takes place in the context of an insolvent transferor, the new regulatory scheme under the Pensions Act 2004 provides a guarantee fund to protect the pension rights against the employer's insolvency.

---

transfer of premises, plant, machinery or the continuation of the workforce. The breadth of the factors to be considered has been stressed by the ECJ.

[10.46] Case 24/85 *Spijkers v Gebroeders Benedik Abattoir CV* [1986] ECR 1119 (ECJ)

The question whether or not there has been a transfer turns mainly on 'whether, having regard to all the facts characterising the transaction, the business was disposed of as a going concern, as would be indicated *inter alia* by the fact that its operation was actually continuing or resumed by the new employer, with the same or similar activities. In order to determine whether these conditions are met, it is necessary to consider all the facts characterising the transaction in question, including the type of undertaking or business, whether or not the business's tangible assets, such as buildings and moveable property, are transferred, the value of its intangible assets at the time of the transfer, whether or not the majority of its employees are taken over by the new employer, whether or not its customers are transferred and the degree of similarity between the activities carried on before and after the transfer and the period, if any, for which those activities were suspended.'

The most contentious applications of the concept of 'transfer of undertaking' have involved outsourcing. An employer may decide to contract out the work of part of its business to another employer. Cleaning and catering services are often provided by external contractors, but the technique of outsourcing can be applied to any type of work. The use of external contractors may reduce costs for a number of reasons including the better management skills of the contractor, economies of scale for the contractor, and the lower wage costs of the contractor. These savings in wages occur typically because the contractor is not governed by the rules of the core employer's internal labour market or relevant collective agreements. Outsourcing is one of the techniques that comprise the flexible firm (above 2.7.2). During the 1980s, the UK government promoted the use of outsourcing in the public sector, especially in the services provided by local authorities and the health service. Most of the savings from outsourcing can be achieved only if the employees accept new terms and conditions of employment. In many instances of outsourcing, the same workers continue at their jobs, though on adverse terms of employment such as longer hours and lower rates of pay. A crucial question for the strategy of the flexible firm and the government policy of contracting out public services was whether the Acquired Rights Directive applied to outsourcing. If the Directive applied, the new employer would have to pay the same rates of pay and continue any collective bargaining arrangements (see below 10.6.3), or face claims for unfair dismissal. During the 1980s the UK government denied that the Directive had any application to contracting out public services, but eventually as a result of a series of decisions of the ECJ, it had to be conceded that outsourcing might be covered in some instances by the Directive.

The central legal question in outsourcing is whether there has been a transfer of an undertaking or part of one. The ECJ declared that the answer to this question depended upon whether the 'entity' retained its 'identity' after the transfer. The task for a tribunal is first to identify an 'entity', that is an organised grouping of persons and of tangible and intangible assets that facilitates the performance of an economic activity or particular business purpose. Having found such an entity, the question is whether the entity has survived the transfer, that is retained its identity, excepting of course the fact that ownership and the identity of the employer has changed. The meaning of these phrases has been explained in numerous decisions of the ECJ, including the following, which involved the slightly more complex case when one con-tractor loses the work to another external contractor.

[10.47] Case 13/95 *Süzen v Zehnacker Gebäudereinigung GmbH Krankenhausservice* [1997] ICR 662 (ECJ)

The defendant employer had a contract to clean a private school. When the school terminated that contract and gave the work to another contractor, the defendant dismissed the cleaners including the claimant. The German labour court referred the question whether there could be a transfer of an undertaking to the ECJ, even though there had been no sale of tangible or intangible assets. The ECJ held that the question was whether the entity, that is an organised grouping of persons and assets pursuing an economic objective, had retained its identity. The mere fact that the new contractor provided the same service was insufficient. On the other hand, in labour intensive industries such as cleaning, it is not necessary for a transfer to involve the sale of tangible or intangible assets such as 'goodwill'; it is sufficient if the new employer carries out the same activity by taking over a major part, in terms of their numbers and skills, of the employees that formerly worked on that activity.

Judgment:

The aim of the Directive is to ensure continuity of employment relationships within a busienss, irrespective of any change of ownership. The decisive criterion for establishing the existence of a transfer within the meaning of the Directive is whether the entity in question retains its identity, as indicated inter alia by the fact that its operation is actually continued or resumed . . .

Whilst the lack of any contractual link between the transferor and the transferee, or, as in this case, between the two undertakings successively entrusted with the cleaning of a school, may point to the absence of a transfer within the meaning of the Directive, it is certainly not conclusive. . . .

[T]he Directive is applicable wherever, in the context of contractual relations, there is a change in the natural or legal person who is responsible for carrying on the business and who incurs the obligations of an employer towards employees of the undertaking. Thus, there is no need, in order for the Directive to be applicable, for there to be any direct contractual relationship between the transferor and the transferee: the transfer may also take place in two stages, through the intermediary of a third party such as the owner or the person putting up the capital.

For the Directive to be applicable, however, the transfer must relate to a stable economic entity whose activity is not limited to performing one specific works contract . . . The term entity thus refers to an organised grouping of persons and assets facilitating the exercise of an economic activity which pursues a specific objective.

In order to determine whether the conditions for the transfer of an entity are met, it is necessary to consider all the facts characterising the transaction in question, including in particular the type of undertaking or business, whether or not its tangible assets, such as buildings and moveable property, are transferred, the value of its intangible assets at the time of the transfer, whether or not the majority of its employees are taken over by the new employer, whether or not its customers are transferred, the degree of similarity between the activities carried on before and after the transfer, and the period, if any, for which those activities were suspended. However, all those circumstances are merely single factors in the overall assessment which must be made and cannot therefore be considered in isolation . . .

As observed by most of the parties who commented on this point, the mere fact that the service provided by the old and the new awardees of a contract is similar does not therefore support the conclusion that an economic entity has been transferred. An entity cannot be reduced to the activity entrusted to it. Its identity also emerges from other factors, such as its workforce, its management staff, the way in which its work is organised, its operating methods or indeed, where appropriate, the operational resources available to it.

The mere loss of a service contract to a competitor cannot therefore by itself indicate the existence of a transfer within the meaning of the Directive. In those circumstances, the service undertaking previously entrusted with the contract does not, on losing a customer, thereby cease fully to exist, and a business or part of a business belonging to it cannot be considered to have been transferred to the new awardee of the contract.

It must also be noted that, although the transfer of assets is one of the criteria to be taken into account by the national court in deciding whether an undertaking has in fact been transferred, the absence of such assets does not necessarily preclude the existence of such a transfer . . . Where in particular an economic entity is able, in certain sectors, to function without any significant tangible or intangible assets, the maintenance of its identity following the transaction affecting it cannot, logically, depend on the transfer of such assets . . .

Since in certain labour-intensive sectors a group of workers engaged in a joint activity on a permanent basis may constitute an economic entity, it must be recognised that such an entity is capable of maintaining its identity after it has been transferred where the new employer does not merely pursue the activity in question but also takes over a major part, in terms of their numbers and skills, of the employees specially assigned by his predecessor to that task. In those circumstances . . . the new employer takes over a body of assets enabling him to carry on the activities or certain activities of the transferor undertaking on a regular basis.

It is for the national court to establish, in the light of the foregoing interpretative guidance, whether a transfer has occurred in this case.

The answer to the questions from the national court must therefore be that Article 1(1) of the Directive is to be interpreted as meaning that the Directive does not apply to a situation in which a person who had entrusted the cleaning of his premises to a first undertaking terminates his contract with the latter and, for the performance of similar work, enters into a new contract with a second undertaking, if there is no concomitant transfer from one undertaking to the other of significant tangible or intangible assets or taking over by the new employer of a major part of the workforce, in terms of their numbers and skills, assigned by his predecessor to the performance of the contract.

This approach to the interpretation of the notion of an undertaking in the context of outsourcing was endorsed in amendments to the Directive made in 1998 that confirmed its possible application to outsourcing in both private and public sectors.

[10.48] Acquired Rights Directive 2001/23, Article 1

1.(a) This Directive shall apply to any transfer of an undertaking, business, or part of an undertaking or business to another employer as a result of a legal transfer or merger.

(b) Subject to subparagraph (a) and the following provisions of this Article, there is a transfer within the meaning of this Directive where there is a transfer of an economic entity which retains its identity, meaning an organised grouping of resources which has the objective of pursuing an economic activity, whether or not that activity is central or ancillary.

(c) This Directive shall apply to public and private undertakings engaged in economic activities whether or not they are operating for gain. An administrative reorganisation of public administrative authorities, or the transfer of administrative functions between public administrative authorities, is not a transfer within the meaning of this Directive.

Although it is now clear that outsourcing including a change of contractor through competitive tendering may be covered by the Directive, it is important to remember that the question whether the entity has retained its identity depends upon the consideration of numerous factors as set out in *Spijkers* **[10.46]** above. To reduce the uncertainty created by the difficulty of knowing what weight should be attached to all these relevant factors, the ECJ in the next case created a strong presumption that businesses which required physical plant or machinery as part of their 'entity' could not retain their identity if those tangible assets were not transferred.

[10.49] Case C–172/99 *Oy Liikenne AB v Liskojarvie and Juntunen* [2001] IRLR 171 (ECJ)

> A public authority in Helsinki awarded the franchise of running seven bus routes to a new contractor. The new contractor hired 33 out of the 45 drivers who had been dismissed by the previous contractor, and hired 18 new drivers. The new contractor used its own buses except for two buses that were temporarily hired from the former contractor. The new contractor bought some uniforms for drivers from the former contractor. The ECJ held that there had not been a transfer of an undertaking under the Directive. The degree of importance to be attached to the various factors described in *Spijkers* (above) and *Süzen* (above) varies according to the activity carried on, including its production or operating methods. In labour intensive businesses without any significant tangible or intangible assets, the fact that the new contractor took on a substantial proportion of the workforce of the transferee may be decisive in bringing the transaction within the Directive. In business entities that necessarily depend upon significant tangible assets such as buses for production, however, the absence of any sale of those tangible assets to the transferee must lead to the conclusion that the entity does not retain its identity even if some employees are hired by the transferee.

Relying on the apparent further guidance in *Süzen* ([10.47] above) that in labour intensive industries the absence of transfer of the workforce almost certainly negatived a finding of a transfer of an undertaking, even if the contract for services won by the employer was exactly the same, employers sometimes tried to avoid taking on any of the existing workforce at all in order to avoid the Regulations. After all, if the employees are not retained, what is left in a labour-intensive business service to give the entity its continuing identity? Of course, such an interpretation creates an opportunity for employers to avoid the Regulation and thereby to increase social costs by causing economic dismissals. This reading of the cases in the ECJ has been rejected by English courts. The Court of Appeal has insisted that *Süzen* does not mean that the absence of the transfer of any of the workforce necessarily excludes the possibility of a transfer of an undertaking, because under *Spijkers* it remains important to consider all the circumstances of the case. In a series of decisions concerning putative transfers from one contractor to another, the Court of Appeal has found that the tribunal did not err in concluding that there was a transfer of an undertaking even though the new contractor did not take on any of the existing workforce at all (*ECM (Vehicle Delivery Service) Ltd v Cox* [1999] ICR 1162 (CA); *ADI (UK) Ltd v Willer* [2001] IRLR 542 (CA). These results, as in the next case, are striking, for in effect the court discovers a transfer of an undertaking, even though no equipment and no staff were taken over by the transferee.

[10.50] *RCO Support Services Ltd v UNISON* **[2002] EWCA Civ 464, [2002] ICR 751 (CA)**

A hospital trust, which operated two hospitals, proceeded by stages to close down the 'in-patient' service at one (Walton) and replace it by new wards at the other (Fazakerley). After the in-patient service at Walton had been closed, the hardest legal issue in the case was whether there had been a transfer of an undertaking with respect to the ancillary cleaning staff formerly employed at Walton. The cleaners had been employed by a contractor Initial Hospital Services at Walton, but none of them accepted an offer from RCO, the cleaning contractors at Fazakerley, that if they would resign from their jobs with Initial they would be offered similar jobs on different terms of employment at Fazakerley. Upholding the decision of the employment tribunal and EAT, the Court of Appeal unanimously held that there had been a transfer of an undertaking even though no tangible assets or staff had in fact transferred to RCO.

Mummery LJ (giving the judgment of the court):

24 I agree that it has become clear from *Süzen* (**[10.47]** above) and later judgments that the Court of Justice now interprets Directive 77/187 as setting limits to its application in contracting out cases, which were not expressly identified in *Spikers* (**[10.46]** above) . . . and other earlier judgments of the Court of Justice. In particular, the mere fact that the putative transferee carries on the same activities or supplies the same services as the putative transferor had done does not by itself support the conclusion that an entity retains its identity . . .

25 I am, however, unable to accept RCO's submissions that the limits on the application of the Directive set in *Süzen* . . . mean that, as a matter of Community law, there can never be a transfer of an undertaking in a contracting out case if neither the assets nor workforce are transferred . . .

26 I do not read *Süzen* as singling out, to the exclusion of all other circumstances, the particular circumstances of none of the workforce being taken on and treating that as determinative of the transfer issue in every case. That interpretation of Directive 77/187 would run counter to what is described in RCO's submissions as the "multifactorial approach" to the retention of identity test in Spijkers . . . Whether or not the majority of employees are taken on by the new employer is only one of all the facts which must be considered by the national court in making an overall assessment of the facts characterising the transaction. Single factors must not be considered in isolation . . .

32. The fact that none of the workforce is taken on is relevant to, but not necessarily conclusive of, the issue of retention of identity. As it is a relevant factor, it is necessary for the employment tribunal to assess its significance by considering the context in which the decision was made. In the present case RCO positively said, in the context of a disagreement [with the union] as to whether the 1981 Regulations applied, that it would take on the cleaners employed by Initial at Walton, if they resigned from Initial . . . RCO's admitted willingness to take on the workfroce by way of re-employment on its terms and conditions, in preference to automatic employment on the terms and conditions applicable as a result of a transfer under the 1981 Regulations, was relevant to the crucial issue of retention of identity. The fact that RCO needed a workforce to operate the contract at Fazakerley; the fact that RCO was willing to re-employ at Fazakerley the workforce employed at Walton; and the fact that the workforce would have been taken on by RCO, if they had accepted RCO's offer to re-employ them on its terms and conditions;all this is relevant evidence pointing to, rather than away from, RCO's own recognition of the reality of the continuity of the entities and the retention of identity . . .

36. . . . I am inclined to accept the submissions of RCO that a subjective motive of the putative transferee to avoid the application of the Directive and the 1981 Regulations is

not the real point. The relevant exercise is that in Spijkers.., ie objective consideration and assessment of all the facts, including the circumstances of the decision not to take on the workforce.

It is not at all clear that this decision is consistent with the principles stated by the ECJ. If this transfer comprised an entity that consisted entirely of an organised group of workers without any tangible or intangible assets, the absence of a transfer of any of the workers seems to preclude the retention of the same identity following *Süzen*.The additional factor that RCO clearly intended to avoid the Directive by insisting that the cleaners should resign their jobs prior to the transfer is said not to be relevant, except in so far as it indicates that effectively the entity was likely to retain its identity after the transfer in the sense that the same work would be performed. Earlier decisions had indicated that such a motive of avoidance of the TUPE 1981 would tip the case in favour of a finding of a transfer of an undertaking: '[i]f the evidence discloses that a transaction has been deliberately structured with a view to avoiding the regulation applying, a tribunal is entitled to scrutinise with particular care whether that attempt has or has not been successful' (Lord Hamilton, *Lightways (Contractors) Ltd v Associated Holdings Ltd* [2000] IRLR 247 (Ct. Sess)). But if this factor is irrelevant, the decision in *RCO* does produce the result that an entity comprising a labour intensive activity without tangible or intangible assets can retain its identity even though no employees are transferred to the putative transferee in the sense that none ever work for the transferee. This ruling seems to expand the scope of the Directive into uncharted territory.

Nevertheless, this expansion seems to be endorsed by the proposed Draft Regulations. The aim of the new Regulation 3 is to make clearer when out-sourcing amounts to a transfer of an undertaking, and, by defining a broad scope for the application of the Regulations, which perhaps extends beyond the scope of the Directive, to avoid the need for UK courts and tribunals to match exactly the determinations of the ECJ with respect to the scope of the Directive.

[10.51] Draft Transfer of Undertakings (Protection of Employment) Regulations 2005 Regulation 3

3. (1) These Regulations apply to—
(a)   a transfer of an undertaking, business or part of an undertaking or business situated immediately before the transfer in the United Kingdom to another employer where there is a transfer of an economic entity which retains its identity;
(b)   a service provision change, that is a situation in which—
   (i)   activities cease to be carried out by a person ("a client") on his own behalf and are carried out instead by another person on the client's behalf ("a contractor"),
   (ii)   activities cease to be carried out by a contractor on a client's behalf (whether or not those activities had previously been carried out by the client on his own behalf) and are carried out instead by another person ("a subsequent contractor") on the client's behalf, or
   (iii)   activities cease to be carried out by a contractor or a subsequent contractor on a client's behalf (whether or not those activities had previously been carried out by the client on his own behalf) and are carried out instead by the client on his own behalf

and in which the conditions set out in paragraph (3) are satisfied.

(2) In this regulation "economic entity" means an organised grouping of resources which has the objective of pursuing an economic activity, whether or not that activity is central or ancillary.

(3) The conditions referred to in paragraph (1)(b) are that:
(a) before the service provision change—
  (i)   there is an organised grouping of employees situated immediately before the change in the United Kingdom which has as its principal purpose the carrying out of the activities concerned on behalf of the client.
  (ii) the client intends that the activities will, following the service provision change, be carried out by the transferee other than in connection with a single specific event or task; and
(b) the activities concerned—
  (i)   do not consist wholly or mainly of the procu rement or supply of goods for the client's use . . .

Standing back from these recent decisions and the proposed amendments to the TUPE Regulations, we can see that from the starting point where employers and the government did not think that the Acquired Rights Directive applied to outsourcing, we have now reached the point where it is regularly applied not only to outsourcing but also to the loss of the contract and its award to a new contractor. The Regulations may therefore prevent the use of outsourcing combined with frequent competitive tendering as a technique for cutting costs by driving down wages and other benefits. In the public sector, this result of cutting labour costs in local authority services was perhaps largely achieved during the 1980s, but the process of competitive tendering should no longer promise significant savings unless the new supplier can achieve superior management or capital intensive labour-saving production methods. In effect, the English courts have used the Acquired Rights Directive to place a brake on the aggressive use of outsourcing in the public and private sectors to cut costs by lowering pay and other benefits of some of the most poorly paid workers in the service sector.

10.6 Worker participation

Three key considerations point to the importance of promoting worker participation in decisions regarding changes in the business. First, any changes are likely to be implemented more effectively and efficiently if the workforce has consented to them and participated in the planning process. If the workforce understands the reasons for change and the objectives of the employer's proposals, it may support the changes, or at least not obstruct them. In particular, consultation may avoid the losses caused by industrial action directed against changes in the business by reducing the anger and fear provoked by sudden announcements of major upheavals. A second potential advantage of consultation with the workforce is that the discussions

Transfers in the Public Sector

The outsourcing and transfer of public sector jobs to the private sector has provoked considerable political controversy and fierce opposition from public sector unions. Not only are the transferred workers concerned about losing the protection of a strong recognised union and receiving worse terms and conditions of employment in the private sector, but also public sector workers express the worry that the ethos of service in the public sector will be undermined by the demands for profit in the private sector. As a result of the complex case law considered above, TUPE 1981 probably applies in general to transfers of undertakings from the public sector to the private sector (and back again). The ECJ has decided that the Acquired Rights Directive should not apply to internal reorganisations within the public sector (*Henke v Gemeinde Schierke* [1996] IRLR 701), and the new draft regulations in Regulation 3(5) confirm that exclusion. In order to avoid the uncertainty that has plagued the application of TUPE 1981 to all the variety of privatisation initiatives, the UK government has now adopted a Code of Practice governing staff transfers in the public sector (Cabinet Office, January 2000). Under this Code, notwithstanding the fact that TUPE may not apply to a particular contracting out of service activities, the principles of TUPE 1981 will be applied to nearly all transfers of activities including privatisation and other outsourcing and contracting-out exercises, reorganisations and transfers from one part of the public sector to another, and reorganisations and transfers within the civil service. The Code only permits avoidance of the application of automatic transfer of employees with their existing terms and conditions for 'genuinely exceptional reasons', such as where the features of the service subject to the contracting exercise are significantly different from the features previously performed within the public sector or by an existing contractor, as where a new technology is introduced. In such exceptional cases, the government undertakes where possible to redeploy retained staff within the public sector. An additional valuable protection provided by this Code is that public sector workers should also be offered by the transferee broadly comparable occupational pension arrangements. Similar rules have been applied to local government under powers conferred by the Local Government Act 2003, sections 101, 102. A further Code of Practice on Workforce Matters in Local Authority Service Contracts requires private sector transferees to offer new recruits (not formerly employed by either the transferor or the transferee) terms of employment that overall are no less favourable than those applied to transferred employees. This obligation is enforceable by the contract for the provision of the service with the local authority. Its objective is to avoid the development of a 'two-tier' workforce, that is, different terms of employment for transferred employee to those who are newly recruited by the transferee. See: G S Morris, 'The Future of the Public/Private Labour Law Divide', in C Barnard, S Deakin and G S Morris (eds), *The Future of Labour Law* (Oxford, Hart, 2004) 159, 170.

and negotiations may reveal better options for change. Representatives of the workforce may suggest ways in which efficiency could be improved without workforce reductions, or at least with fewer economic dismissals. Another possibility is 'concession bargaining', that is a temporary reduction in wage costs in return for the avoidance of redundancies or as part of a corporate rescue package. The reduction of economic dismissals fits with government objectives for the reduction of social costs associated with business reorganisations and plant closures. The third consideration that points to the importance of worker participation is that advance notice of impending changes permits individual employees to plan for a major change in their lives. The longer the warning that individuals receive of economic dismissals, the better their chances of finding a new job, of being able to move to where work may be available, of seeking retraining and learning new skills, of finding the capital to start up a business, or of planning to take early retirement. Not only will individuals bene-fit from advance warning, but also the employer and the government may be able to help them to make the adjustment. Again this advance planning will serve to reduce the social cost associated with economic dismissals. These compelling economic and practical considerations make a powerful case for worker participation, and they can be further supported by arguments of principle in favour of worker participation more generally that employers should treat their workforce with consideration and respect.

Some competing considerations may qualify these powerful arguments in favour of worker participation in restructuring. In some instances an employer may be reluc-tant to disclose business information that is regarded as commercially sensitive, that is of potential advantage to competitors. When contemplating a sale of the business, the employer may sometimes fear that disclosure of information will reduce its value. The employer may also calculate that surreptitious, incremental change will provoke less adverse reaction on the part of the workforce, though this view may of course be misconceived. Employers often invoke arguments of principle against any consulta-tion with the workforce at any time: ownership, it is said, entitles a person to do what he wants with his property without consulting anyone. Unless this last argument of principle is accepted, the other considerations merely point to some possible limita-tions on the timing and extent of consultation with the workforce. Most employers probably accept that on balance consultation with the workforce is to their advan-tage, and this disposition has perhaps permitted extensive and detailed legal regulation of this issue at European and national level. The question that needs to be asked about this regulation is whether it strikes the right balance between the compet-ing considerations. In particular, the history of regulation in the UK reveals a marked reluctance to delimit managerial discretion by imposing substantial obligations to consult the workforce. The question remains whether the current law meets European standards and pays sufficient attention to the consideration of the reduction of social costs that points strongly towards workforce participation.

The main elements of the current legal regulation comprise:

(a) a duty to consult individual employees about economic dismissals, backed by the potential sanction of compensation for unfair dismissal for failure to do so;

(b) a duty to consult representatives of the workforce prior to workforce reductions (collective redundancies or mass dismissals), backed by the sanction of addi-tional compensation to dismissed workers for failure to do so;

(c) a duty to consult representatives of the workforce prior to sales of the business (transfers of undertakings), backed by the sanction of additional compensation to dismissed workers for failure to do so;

(d) a duty to conform to collective agreements about procedures for handling and compensating redundancies, backed by various sanctions.

(e) a duty to provide information and consult workplace representatives about deci-sions likely to lead to substantial changes in work organisation or in contractual relations.

10.6.1 Individual consultation

No express statutory obligation requires employers to consult individual employees about impending economic dismissals. The legal duty has been created by the courts and tribunals through the law of unfair dismissal. The test of reasonableness has been used to require employers normally to engage in individual consultation prior to making a redundancy. If the employer fails to do so, the employee may succeed in obtaining a compensatory award for unfair dismissal in addition to a redundancy payment. The source of this legal obligation in the test of reasonableness is unsatisfactory, however, because it fails to lay down a clear requirement that is always applicable, and the sanction for breach of the standard varies with the measure of the compensatory award, so that it can become minimal if the employee is fortunate enough to obtain a new job quickly.

The leading decisions that explain the requirement of consultation with employees prior to redundancies have already been considered (above 5.4.3). It is worth repeating the statement of principles in this context in order to appreciate how consultation with an individual worker is linked to broader schemes of worker participation.

[10.52] *Williams v Compare Maxam* **[1982] ICR 156 (EAT)**

> *Browne-Wilkinson J:*
> [I]n cases where the employees are represented by an independent union recognised by the employer, reasonable employers will seek to act in accordance with the following principles:
>   1. The employer will seek to give as much warning as possible of impending redundancies so as to enable the union and employees who may be affected to take early steps to inform themselves of the relevant facts, consider possible alternative solutions and, if necessary, find alternative employment in the undertaking or elsewhere.
>   2. The employer will consult the union as to the best means by which the desired management result can be achieved fairly and with as little hardship to the employees as possible . . .

What is striking about these principles is how the requirement of procedural fairness in the law of unfair dismissal becomes a collective issue in the context of mass economic dismissals. Where there is a recognised trade union, the employer must inform and consult the union representatives as well as the individual employee. The law of unfair dismissal thus provides indirect support for collective worker participation in decisions about economic dismissals.

But this support for worker participation is qualified, because the potential to obtain a substantial compensatory award in addition to a redundancy payment has been blocked in many instances.

[10.53] *Polkey v A.E. Dayton Services Ltd* **[1988] ICR 142 (HL)**

> *Lord Bridge:*
> [I]n the case of redundancy, the employer will normally not act reasonably unless he

warns and consults any employees affected or their representative, adopts a fair basis on which to select for redundancy and takes such steps as may be reasonable to avoid or minimise redundancy by redeployment within his own organisation . . .

If it is held that taking the appropriate steps which the employer failed to take before dismissing the employee would not have affected the outcome, this will often lead to the result that the employee, though unfairly dismissed, will recover no compensation or, in the case of redundancy, no compensation in excess of his redundancy payment.

Thus even if a tribunal concludes that an employer should have consulted the individual employee or a representative trade union prior to a dismissal for redundancy, the tribunal still has the discretion not to award compensation if it believes that the consultation would not have affected the outcome. This limitation on the compensatory award subverts the procedural protection dramatically, because the employer can usually argue extremely plausibly that workforce reductions were inevitable, so that consultation would have made no difference to the outcome. The reduction perhaps to nil compensation on this ground is popularly (or perhaps notoriously) known as the '*Polkey* deduction'. This development in the case law of unfair dismissal is extremely unfortunate, for it subverts the procedural protection in almost every case of redundancy. It results from a false generalisation across all types of dismissal. In disciplinary dismissals, the employer may sometimes be able to convince a tribunal that the evidence of misconduct was so plain and so serious that no procedural steps could alter the outcome of dismissal. Nevertheless, with their experience of the need for procedural fairness or natural justice in the context of criminal and administrative law, the courts always view such claims sceptically. They know that without a proper investigation and hearing, there is a real danger of unfair decisions. In cases of redundancy dismissals, however, the employer has all or nearly all of the relevant information already, so that the employer can plausibly claim that dismissal was inevitable whatever consultation might have taken place. The employee has the difficult burden of trying to demonstrate that consultation might have revealed some other option such as redeployment. The *Polkey* deduction thus routinely destroys the sanction behind the support through the law of unfair dismissal for the principle of worker participation.

10.6.2 Mass dismissals

We have already considered the legal duty on employers to consult the workforce when proposing to make economic dismissals (above 8.5.4). It should be recalled that the core obligation contained in the Trade Union and Labour Relations (Consolidation) Act 1992, sections 188–198, which implements Directive 98/59 on the approximation of the laws relating to collective redundancies, has the following elements:

(a)   if the employer is proposing to dismiss 20 or more workers at one establishment for economic reasons,

(b)   the employer must consult in good time,

(c)   with representatives of the workforce, who may be the recognised trade union or (in the absence of a recognised union) elected representatives of the workforce,

(d) with a view to reaching agreement about ways in which dismissals may be avoided, reduced, or the consequences of dismissal may be mitigated.

If the employer fails to comply with the consultation requirement, an employment tribunal may award the dismissed employees (in addition to other compensation) a protective award, which consists of wages during the period in which proper consultation should have taken place. The employer is also under a separate duty to notify the government of collective dismissals, with a sanction of a fine: TULRCA 1992, sections 193–194.

Many of the controversies surrounding the interpretation of this legislation stem from its adaptation of European standards and practices in relation to workforce reductions. In other Member States, the first aim of legislation has been to obtain advance notification of mass economic dismissals to the local administrative bodies of the State, so that they may take measures designed to reduce social costs. Thus the emphasis upon the number of dismissals at an 'establishment' reflects the concern about economic dislocation in a locality, and is not directed towards the problem of promoting consultation at the right level of the organisation. The extent to which other European governments intervene varies, but in several instances the employer is required to co-operate with government authorities to carry out a 'social plan' aimed at reducing the adverse effects of mass redundancies. Hence Article 4.1 of Directive 98/59, which has no counterpart in the UK legislation, provides that projected economic dismissals should not take place for 30 days after the public authority has been notified, so that the authority can seek solutions to the problem. Similarly, the principle of consultation with representatives of the workforce reflects the legal arrangements in Germany and other States, where works councils have the power to block, at least temporarily, economic dismissals made without their consent. Without this institutional arrangement being available, the UK has tried to achieve an equivalent provision through *ad hoc* election of workers' representatives and financial compensation. But a small amount of extra severance pay to individuals cannot really be equivalent to the idea of a works council having the legal right to block the economic dismissals until every other avenue has been explored. These national measures will always appear inadequate from a European perspective, for in truth the Directive presupposes a degree of routine worker participation in the management of the enterprise that is unusual in the UK. That divergence between continental European and UK patterns of collective consultation will be narrowed by the implementation of the Information and Consultation Directive 2002/14 (below, 10.6.5). In sum, the Directive on collective redundancies contemplates a degree of governmental supervision of business decisions that seems alien to the sharp divisions customarily drawn in the UK between public and private spheres of responsibility.

Ultimately the crucial question about workplace participation in relation to collective redundancies is whether it changes any managerial decisions, and in particular whether it can reduce social costs. The advance notice of workforce reduction probably in itself reduces social costs, because employees can begin to look for another job or arrange for retraining. But does the requirement of consultation lead in some instances to the avoidance or reduction of economic dismissals? The evidence suggests that this is unlikely, or at best some jobs may be saved in a few instances. By the time that management announces its proposals, the issue of the need to make redundancies has usually been under consideration for some time and the decision in principle has been made. But there is evidence from one study that consultation with recognised trade unions may lead to deferrals of dismissals, alterations in the criteria of selection for dismissal, improved compensation packages, and more careful exploration of the possibility of redeployment elsewhere in the organisation (M Hall and P Edwards, 'Reforming the Statutory Consultation Procedure' (1999) 28 *Industrial Law Journal* 299).

10.6.3 Sales of the business

A similar legal duty to consult representatives of the workforce derived from the Acquired Rights Directive 2001/23 applies to sales of a business. The TUPE Regulations 1981, as amended, contain a duty upon the transferor and the transferee to consult a recognised trade union or, in the absence of a recognised trade union, other workforce representatives. This duty of consultation is described in slightly different terms as consultation with a view to seeking the agreement of the representatives of the workforce, and expressly includes a duty to consider representations. The sanction for the employer in failing to comply with this duty is the payment of compensation to 'affected employees' to the amount which a tribunal considers 'just and equitable having regard to the seriousness of the failure of the employer to comply with his duty', but not exceeding thirteen weeks' pay: TUPE 1981 Regulation 11(11).

[10.54] Transfer of Undertakings (Protection of Employment) Regulations 1981, Regulation 10

(1) In this Regulation . . . references to affected employees, in relation to a relevant transfer, are to any employees of the transferor or transferee (whether or not employed in the undertaking or the part of the undertaking to be transferred) who may be affected by the transfer or may be affected by measures taken in accordance with it; and references to the employer shall be construed accordingly.

(2) Long enough before a relevant transfer to enable the employer of any affected employees to consult all the persons who are appropriate representatives of any of those affected employees, the employer shall inform those representatives of—

(a) the fact that the relevant transfer is to take place, when, approximately, it is to take place and the reasons for it; and

(b) the legal, economic and social implications of the transfer for the affected employees; and

(c) the measures which he envisages he will, in connection with the transfer, take in relation to those employees or, if he envisages that no measures will be so taken, that fact; and

(d) if the employer is the transferor, the measures which the transferee envisages he will, in connection with the transfer, take in relation to such of those employees as, by virtue of Regulation 5 above, become employees of the transferee after the transfer or, if he envisages that no measures will be so taken, that fact.

(2A) For the purposes of this Regulation the appropriate representatives of any employees are—

(a)   if the employees are of a description in respect of which an independent trade union is recognised by their employer, representatives of the trade union, or

(b)   in any other case, which ever of the following employee representatives the employer chooses:—

    (i)   employee representatives appointed or elected by the affected employees otherwise than for the purposes of this Regulation, who (having regard to the purposes for and the method by which they were appointed or elected) have authority from those employees to receive information and to be consulted about the proposed dismissals on their behalf;

    (ii)   employee representatives elected by them, for the purposes of this Regulation, in an election satisfying the requirements of Regulation 10A(1).

(3) The transferee shall give the transferor such information at such a time as will enable the transferor to perform the duty imposed on him by virtue of paragraph (2)(d) above . . .

(5) Where an employer of any affected employees envisages that he will, in connection with the transfer, be taking measures in relation to any such employees he shall consult all the persons who are appropriate representatives of any of the affected employees in relation to whom he envisages taking measures with a view to seeking their agreement to measures to be taken.

(6) In the course of those consultations the employer shall—

(a)   consider any representations made by the appropriate representatives; and

(b)   reply to those representations and, if he rejects any of those representations, state his reasons.

(8A) If, after the employer has invited affected employees to elect representatives, they fail to do so within a reasonable time, he shall give to each affected employee the information set out in paragraph (2).

The main gap in coverage of this Regulation concerns sales of the business that take the legal form of a sale of shares or a take-over. These sales are excluded, because the legal and contractual rights of employees are unaffected by the change in ownership of shares. Yet a change in ownership in shares and control over a company will obviously raise important questions in the minds of the workforce about possible workforce reductions and restructuring, just as much as if there had been a sale of the assets of the business.

The principal importance of these consultation provisions concerns situations where the transferee employer is likely to introduce variations in terms and other changes in the organisation. Where the sale involves economic dismissals, either by the transferor or the transferee, the Regulations mostly duplicate the requirements of consultation for collective redundancies. The exception is where fewer than 20 employees will be dismissed, in which case the TUPE 1981 Regulations can be used to support a consultation requirement instead. The application of the consultation requirement to cases where the transferee proposes to introduce changes in the terms of employees and the organisation of the business presents the difficulty that the transferor may not know of these plans and the transferee will be unwilling to disclose them for reasons of commercial confidentiality. The transferor, whilst employer, has to give information about those plans, and the transferee is under a legal duty to disclose that information, but the transferor does not have to consult the workforce representatives about any such plans, because they are not the plans of the transferor. Nor can the transferor compel disclosure of such information. At best, the workforce may complain that the duty to supply information was breached by the transferor. The transferor may join the transferee to the proceedings for the purpose of paying compensation for that breach of duty on the ground that it was not reasonably practicable for the transferor to supply that information because the transferee did not disclose it to the transferor. Thus the transferee has a good chance of keeping its plans quiet and does not have to consult about these plans until immediately after the sale, at which time, of course, they will be implemented without delay. It must be doubted, therefore, whether these information and consultation requirements can have much effect in the case where they matter the most. It should be noted, however, that if the transferor is held liable to pay compensation for failure to inform and consult prior to the transfer, that liability to pay a compensatory award to employees will transfer as a liability connected to their contracts of employment under Regulation 5, so that the transferee may eventually find itself liable to pay compensation for the defaults of the transferor (whether or not it caused them): *Alamo Group (Europe) Ltd v Tucker* [2003] IRLR 266 (EAT). Under Article 3.1 of the Directive, national governments have the option to make both transferor and transferee jointly and severally liable for obligations arising prior to the transfer, a provision which, if implemented as expected in the proposed Draft TUPE regulations 2005, would enable tribunals to have a general power to link liability to responsibility for defaults in providing information and consultation.

10.6.4 Conformity to collective agreements

For employees who work under strong and effective collective bargaining relations, much of the above legal regulation may be rather beside the point. One topic on which unions usually press strongly for agreement is economic dismissals. The union will seek agreement on the procedures and selection methods to be followed by the employer in the event of redundancies. The union will also seek to augment levels of compensation payable to dismissed employees. The pattern of collective agreements in the UK, however, does not usually envisage that the union will have any power to block economic dismissals or even to be consulted with a view to reaching an agreement on the need to make economic dismissals.

Collective agreements about the procedures and selection criteria for redundancies are not legally enforceable for the same reason as any collective agreement is unlikely to be legally enforceable (TULCRA 1992, section 179, above **[2.14]**). The terms of the collective agreement may, however, confer legally enforceable rights upon individuals by being incorporated into their contracts of employment. We observed in *Alexander v Standard Telephones & Cables Ltd (No 2)*; *Wall v Standard Telephones & Cables Ltd (No 2)* [1991] IRLR 287 (HC) (above **[2.16]**) that the courts often view collective procedures designed to govern redundancy situations as not 'apt' for incorporation into the individual contract of employment. But in some cases, where a redundancy arrangement is expressly incorporated into contracts of employment and is sufficiently explicit in the rights that it confers upon employees, it should be possible to obtain a declaration or a remedy for breach of contract, including an interim injunction (e.g. *Anderson v Pringle of Scotland Ltd* [1998] IRLR 64 (Ct Sess, Outer House), if the employer ignores the procedure and selection criteria.

An employer's agreement as a result of collective negotiations to provide severance pay in excess of the statutory redundancy pay is a particularly valuable right that unions frequently negotiate. Assuming that the collective agreement fixes an amount or scale for compensation, a claim should become enforceable against the employer as a debt, provided that either the collective agreement on this issue becomes incorporated into contracts of employment or the employer makes separate severance agreements with each employee that incorporate the settlement achieved through collective bargaining.

From a comparative perspective, what is most striking about collective bargaining in the UK about restructuring of businesses is its typically narrow focus compared to some of the 'social plans' negotiated between businesses and unions in continental Europe. As well as severance or redundancy payments, such social plans attempt to reduce social costs by providing incentives for workers to seek alternative employment and to undertake training. A dismissed worker may receive an additional payment if another job is accepted within a short period of time; this measure encourages workers to accept lower paying jobs. Another common measure is for the employer to pay for approved training courses. Employers can also provide starting capital, technical and administrative advice, and training to workers who wish to start their own small businesses. Social plans also seek to redistribute work through reduced hours, job-sharing and part-time work. An example might be older workers sharing a job, whilst having their pension entitlement protected. (Examples of such

---

General Duty to Inform and Consult

Under the Information and Consultation of Employees Regulations 2004, based on the Information and Consultation Directive 2002/14 (8.6.3 above), a new layer of consultation requirements will shortly be introduced for larger businesses in 2005. These requirements differ from all the legal regulations reviewed above because they persist at all times, and are not merely triggered when the employer is contemplating mass dismissals or sales of the business. The typical pattern, as approved by the courts in the UK (above, 8.5.4.2), that consultation with representatives of the workers about mass dismissals does not have to commence until management has actually reached a decision to restructure and probably make redundancies, usually prevents meaningful discussions about possible ways in which to avoid economic dismissals. Under the new measures for information and consultation, however, employees or their representatives should be apprised at a much earlier stage that management may be contemplating restructuring and workforce adjustments.

These information and consultation arrangements, once they are in place and begin to operate as intended as part of the normal process of workplace governance in a 'spirit of co-operation', should provide workers for the first time with early warning signals of impending restructuring of the business. But whatever arrangements the employer chooses to adopt under these Regulations, there will still be no legal requirement for the employer to reach agreement with representatives of the workforce on the package of measures associated with the restructuring plans.

social plans are frequently reported in *European Industrial Relations Review*: e.g. 'Made to Measure: Restructuring at Levi Strauss' (1999) 305 *EIRR* 13–16.)

10.6.5 Conclusion

As a result of European Community Law, the notion that the workforce should routinely participate in managerial decisions that might affect their livelihoods seems less like a distant peak on the horizon of British industrial relations than hitherto. Gradually, the declaration of the Charter of Fundamental Rights of the European Union 2000, which in Article 27 (above **[1.2]**) asserts the workers' right to information and consultation in good time, is beginning to permeate the legal framework. The traditional culture of British management seems to be one of preferring to keep strategic decisions confidential and to regard business reorganisations as part of the managerial prerogative. We have observed many instances when the employer informs the workforce of economic dismissals, sales of the business, and insolvency only after it is too late for constructive consultation and negotiations. Although legal regulation has sought to change this attitude of management towards worker participation, one must doubt whether the law has yet had a significant impact. The courts have not always pressed home the legal regulation to its fullest potential. For example, the courts have interpreted the time at which consultation should take place for collective redundancies in cases such as *Griffin v South West Water Services Ltd* [1995] IRLR 15 (HC) as only after management has made the crucial decision rather than when it is being considered as a possibility. Similarly, the courts have often permitted employers to ignore collective agreements about procedures and criteria for selection for redundancy. Perhaps most striking of all is the '*Polkey* deduction', that is the rule that although it is unfair for an employer not to consult an individual employee and a recognised trade union before a dismissal for redundancy, the tribunals should award no compensation if consultation would not have prevented the dismissal. In the context of British industrial relations, that rule will nearly always be satisfied, because usually management will already have made an irreversible decision to dismiss for redundancy. Nevertheless, with the raft of measures on information and consultation agreed at EC level, it now seems possible that a culture of partnership may develop in Britain, so that business restructuring will no longer be so sudden, unexpected, and unplanned for by the workforce and public agencies.

10.7 Controlling capital

The fundamental problem addressed by the legal regulation considered in this chapter has been the extent to which changes in business should be controlled. In the past, the common law recognised the right of management to direct the workforce, to determine the size of the workforce, and to act in any way which management believed would best serve the interests of shareholders. The sole constraint on this power lay in the contracts of workers, which placed few limits on managerial discretion, and could in any case usually be terminated on short notice. The common law thus accorded priority to the policy of letting management alone in the hope and belief that in the long run market incentives would maximise the aggregate wealth of society. Modern regulation qualifies to some extent that traditional policy. But how far does the law control management's decisions with respect to restructuring and for what purposes?

With respect to constraints on how management might direct the workforce to perform new jobs and adapt to new technologies and working methods, any control exercised by legal regulation has surely proved slight. The advent of protection against dismissal, especially the possibility of claiming constructive dismissal for the employer's unilateral variation of terms of the contract of employment, suggested a measure of control over how far employers might impose new working conditions. But in the end these restrictions appear largely illusory. The employer can remove the legal controls by insisting upon flexibility clauses in contracts of employment and by reserving a broad managerial discretion. If the employer is entitled under the contract to direct the workforce to perform different jobs, there is no breach of contract or constructive dismissal. To put the seal on the preservation of the employer's power to vary jobs, the courts have concluded that an employee's refusal to accept new terms and conditions of employment could amount to justification for a fair dismissal for 'some other substantial reason'. In effect, any control over managerial discretion to vary working methods depends more or less, as it always did, on the bargaining power of the employee, not on any legal protection.

Nor was the redundancy payments legislation any more forceful in restricting the power of employers to carry out economic dismissals. Indeed, it must be doubted whether control fell within the original purpose of the legislation, which was surely intended to legitimate and subsidise workforce reductions for reasons of efficiency rather than to question the employer's decision. At no time was the employer required to justify the need to make redundancies or to demonstrate that economic dismissals were a proportionate response to the need for the business to reduce labour costs. Such a demand might have been warranted by the legitimate concern of governments to minimise the social costs associated with plant closures and mass unemployment. But in the United Kingdom legislation never attempted to provide a legal mechanism for that purpose.

In contrast, European law has compelled some hesitant regulation that places some controls over managerial decisions. The requirement for consultation with the workforce before mass economic dismissals and sales of the business entwines two justifications for regulation. It part, consultation is designed to minimise social costs by encouraging the parties to find ways to avoid economic dismissals. At the same time, this regulation also signals acceptance of a requirement for worker participation in major decisions that affect employment security. These foreign ideas about procedures for reaching such decisions with the workforce as 'stakeholders' fit uneasily with the traditional autonomy granted to employers in making business decisions. Yet these ideas have surely influenced the judicial development of principles governing the fairness of selection for redundancy, which received their most complete and persuasive statement from Browne-Wilkinson J in *Williams v Compare Maxam*. The misleading analogy drawn with the requirement of fair procedures prior to individual disciplinary dismissals permitted the EAT to assert a jurisdiction to set procedures prior to economic dismissals, which were then developed beyond individual consultation to include collective consultation and examination of the substantive grounds for selection for dismissal. The distinct unease that the courts feel with this judicial regulation of economic dismissals is revealed by the way in which compensation for unfair dismissal is minimised by the ready acceptance of a claim that a fair procedure would have been pointless, the so-called *Polkey* deduction. The fair procedure is, of course, pointless, because the legal regulation will never question whether the economic dismissal was required or justifiable by business considerations, so there is no pressure upon the employer to change its mind.

The deepest shock to the traditional respect paid to employers' decisions was to arrive, however, with the Acquired Rights Directive and its progeny TUPE. Governments, employers and insolvency practitioners simply could not believe that legislation could attempt both to prevent employers from carrying out dismissals in order to effect a sale and to prevent the purchaser from reorganising the business. They were astounded that, for the sake of protecting the contractual expectations of the workforce, legal controls might prevent employers from achieving the maximum value from the sales of businesses, prevent acquirers from introducing efficient reorganisations involving alterations in the terms of employment, and might block the use of outsourcing of parts of the business in order to take advantage of lower labour costs in the secondary labour market. Initially the courts shared this disbelief, but before long they accorded respect to the decisions of the ECJ which laid bare the purposes of the Directive. The strange result of the regulation is that, having been designed to equalise the position of workers whose business was sold compared to those whose companies were taken over by a share acquisition, the TUPE rules now protect the former group with the most intense regulation over employers' decisions with respect to changes in the business, and leave the latter group at the mercy of the new owners.

Perhaps underneath these tensions between European and national law lies a profound difference in attitude towards the circulation of capital. In order to protect employment and the economy, one approach is to help businesses to survive the vicissitudes of the business cycle through state subsidies at the price of locking them into doing business in the locality. An opposite approach is to encourage capital to seek its most profitable use in the belief that in the long run this policy will maximise wealth and provide the best growth and employment (but not job) security. Under the second approach, it is undesirable to interfere with the movement of capital by legal measures such as restrictions on sales of businesses, workforce reductions and the use of insolvency to permit capital to be recycled. Although governments tried in desperation to halt the collapse of industry in the UK in the 1980s through the use of employment subsidies, the dominant policy has always been the opposite, that is support for capital mobility. It may eventually prove to be the case that the pressures arising from globalisation of the economic system, especially financial investment, will prove irresistible and spell the demise of any legal attempts to prevent capital flight.

We can observe these pressures intensifying in the context of insolvency law. The mobility of capital requires inexpensive and expeditious insolvency procedures and the protection of corporate rescues from the pressing demands of creditors. But these requirements run up against many interest groups, such as banks, unsecured trade creditors, the government and workers. The employees' interests are ambiguous. Whilst employees want reassurance about the payment of their wages as creditors of the insolvent company, they may also wish to support the possibility of corporate rescue, which may require either concessions by workers participating in a rescue or a weakening of their protection as creditors. The insolvency regime may resolve this tension with the interests of employees by using the State as a guarantor of the interests of the workforce as creditor in order to disencumber corporate rescues and to support employment prospects in the long run.

Although the pressures from global capital movement may discourage legal interventions to control employers' decisions with respect to changes in the business, it is surely possible to justify some regulation even on narrow grounds of promoting allocative efficiency or the reduction of social cost. Severance payments, if modest, can legitimise workforce reductions, encourage employers to check that reductions will improve the efficient use of capital, and help to reduce social cost by compelling the employer to internalise some of the social costs of economic support for the workforce. The requirement to consult with the workforce may produce better proposals for the efficient use of capital that also serve to enhance employment security. These justifications fit into the policy of promoting the efficient use of capital. In addition, it is important to remember that economic analysis of the effects of regulation indicates that predictions about the inefficient use of capital caused by restrictions have been exaggerated.

One can also argue, however, that some controls over employers' decisions ought to be imposed for the sake of broader notions of social justice, not just allocative efficiency. The participation of the workforce in such decisions can embody respect for the principle that the ideal of democracy should not be confined to the public sphere, but should also apply to other powerful private institutions in society. The cushioning of dismissed workers against the vicissitudes of the circulation of capital can be justified as part of a strategy to establish economic security, as opposed to job security, for all citizens. Active manpower policies that assist displaced workers to find jobs can also form part of a strategy to tackle social exclusion. One of the fundamental purposes of labour law has always been to help to establish social cohesion in face of the disintegrative tendencies of market economies. Business restructuring presents labour law with a fundamental challenge to social cohesion or social solidarity, because as well as the loss of jobs it can involve the destruction of local communities and ways of life. The law in the United Kingdom has so far been relatively timid in tackling this form of challenge to social cohesion in comparison to our European neighbours. The result of this abstention may have been a competitive advantage in attracting inward capital investment, but the price may have been a subtle process of disintegration of social solidarity or civility.

FURTHER READING

J Armour and S Deakin, 'Insolvency and Employment Protection: The Mixed Effects of the Acquired Rights Directive' (2002) 22 *International Review of Law and Economics* 443.
H Collins, *Justice in Dismissal* (Oxford, Oxford University Press, 1992) chapter 6.

P L Davies, 'Acquired Rights, Creditors' Rights, Freedom of Contract, and Industrial Democracy' (1989) 9 *Yearbook of European Law* 21.

——, 'Employee Claims in Insolvency: Corporate Rescues and Preferential Claims' (1994) 23 *Industrial Law Journal* 141.

——, 'Preliminary Remarks', in S Sciarra (ed), *Labour Law in the Courts* (Oxford, Hart, 2001) 131-44.

V Finch, *Corporate Insolvency Law: Perspectives and Principles* (Cambridge, CUP, 2002) Chapter 16.

M R Freedland, 'Leaflet Law: The Temporary Short-time Working Compensation Scheme' (1980) 9 *Industrial Law Journal* 254.

R H Fryer, 'The Myths of the Redundancy Payments Act' (1973) 2 *Industrial Law Journal* 1.

B Hepple, M Partington and B Simpson, 'The Employment Protection Act and Unemployment Benefit: Protection for Whom?' (1977) 6 *Industrial Law Journal* 54.

A Kerr and M Radford, 'Acquiring Rights—Losing Power: A Case Study in Ministerial Resistance to the Impact of European Community Law' (1997) 60 *Modern Law Review* 23.

S Leader, 'Three Faces of Justice and the Management of Change' (2000) 63 *Modern Law Review* 55.

D Pollard, 'Adopted Employees in Insolvency—Orphans No More' (1995) 24 *Industrial Law Journal* 141.

—— 'Insolvent Companies and TUPE' (1996) 25 *Industrial Law Journal* 191.

E M Szyszczak, *Partial Unemployment: The Regulation of Short-Time Working in Britain* (London, Mansell, 1990).

C Villiers, 'Employees as Creditors: a Challenge for Justice in Insolvency Law' (1999) 20 *The Company Lawyer* 222.

Index

abroad, working, 47
ACAS:
    arbitration scheme, 508–9
    codes of practice
        disciplinary and grievance procedures,
            527, 753, 755, 756
        information rights, 814–15, 818, 821
        time off, 797, 801–10, 858
    conciliation, 25–6, 555–7, 960
    duties, 26
    and industrial disputes, 960–3
    and union recognition, 725, 771
access to justice, 29
Adam-Smith, D, 416
Addison, J T, 981
adoptive leave, 366–7, 375
advice:
    ACAS, 26
    citizens advice bureaux, 380–2
    compromise agreements, 495–6, 498
advocates, discrimination, 292
Age Concern, 348
age discrimination, 65, 275–7, 279–80, 507–8
agency workers:
    discrimination, 194
    employment status, 187–94, 754
    minimum wage, 194, 392
    regulation, 193–4
    taxation, 193–4
    working time, 403
Agricultural Wages Boards, 388
Akdenitz, Yuman, 611
Allen & Overy, 606
alternative dispute resolution:
    ACAS, 508–9
    forms, 23–30
Anderson, Lucy, 611
appeals:
    from Certification Officer, 659
    grievance procedures, 24
    Pension Ombudsman's decisions, 29
    to and from EAT, 31–2
apprentices, minimum wage, 392
arbitration:
    alternative to employment tribunals, 508–9
    industrial action, 962–3
    legal pluralism, 4
    procedures, 26–7
    public sector workers, 198

armed forces:
    employment status, 204
    industrial action, 200
    and minimum wage, 392
    prohibition to strike, 960
    sex discrimination, 299
Arrowsmith, J, 417, 418, 424, 427–8
Arthurs, H, 3–4
assault, context, 4
associated employers, 142
Atkinson, J, 167–8
atypical workers, 166–71, 215, 381–2
au pairs, and minimum wage, 392
Australia, 868, 971
Austria, collective bargaining, 727
authority of employers, 111–28
aviation, working time, 404

Banerji, N, 556
bank holidays, 426
Barclay's, 605
Barmes, Lizzie, 459
Barnard Report, 410, 417, 424
barristers, discrimination, 292
bastard defence, 333
Beckett, F, 847
Beckett, Margaret, 392
Beevor, Justin, 953
Belgium, 727
Benedictus, R, 937
Beveridge Report, 75
bias:
    disciplinary procedures, 698–700
    redundancy selection, 1024
blacklisting, 596–8, 600, 734
Blair, Tony, 898
BMW Rover, 832
Bolton, A, 40
Bonner, MIke, 604
bonuses, 455
Bowden, Caspar, 611
Bowers, J, 598, 644, 645
boycotts, 926–8, 973–4
Bradlaugh, Charles, 866
Bridlington principles, 687, 689, 694
Briscoe, I, 370–2
British Gas, 632
Brodie, Douglas, 119, 122
Brown, C, 337

Brown, Gordon, 596
Brown, W, 138, 989–90, 995
Bryson, A, 727–8, 844
Buchele, R, 982
Buechtermann, Cristoph, 981
bullying, 74
Burchell, B, 171
Burdon, Kit, 611
business plans, disclosure, 150
business restructuring:
    circumstances, 979
    and collective agreements, 1067–9
    control of capital, 1069–72
    EU law, 980, 1069, 1070
    individual consultation, 1062–3
    insolvency *see* insolvency
    policy considerations, 979–80
    redundancy *see* redundancy
    regulation, 982–3
    transfers *see* transfer of undertaking
    variation of work *see* variation of jobs
    worker participation, 1059–69
Byers, Stephen, 355

Cabinet Office Briefings, 342
Cable & Wireless, 608
call centres, 605
Campaign for Nuclear Disarmament, 596
Canada, 748, 749, 787, 812
capitalism, 1, 20–2, 1069–72
Caprim, 597
Caruso, D, 309
casual workers:
    disclosure of contract terms to, 140–1
    employment status, 162–6
    law reform, 195–6
    rights on dismissal, 503–5
CBI, 419, 424, 611, 848
CCTV, 602, 603, 606, 616, 623, 624, 631, 634
Central Arbitration Committee (CAC):
    approach, 27, 725
    decisions, 793–4, 837–8
    jurisdiction, 27, 960
        consultation procedures, 852, 855, 856
        derecognition of unions, 836
        European works councils, 859
        information rights, 813, 819–21
        union recognition, 769–79, 784–9
Chamberlain, A, 951–3
child labour:
    British labour market, 39–40
    EU Charter of Fundamental Rights, 8
    EU directive, 38
    ILO convention, 37–8
    legal history, 39
Child Poverty Action Group, 596

childcare, 368–72
children, working time, 407
China, 37
Choudhury, T, 227
Chribasik, P, 1002
Christian Aid, 596
Christiansen, J, 982
Churchill, Winston, 388, 554
citizens advice bureaux:
    and employment rights, 380–2
    and minimum wage, 398–400
    working time, 428–31
citizenship:
    and labour rights, 63–5
    and trade unions, 647–9
civil liability:
    labour regulation, 12–13
    use of courts, 30–2
Civil Service *see* public sector workers
class conflicts, 22
Clayton, P, 590–1
Cloke, K, 749
closed shop:
    abolition, 683
    agency shop agreements, 749
    agreements, 34
    Donovan Commission, 747
    and employers, 748
    free rider argument, 748, 749
    generally, 746–50
    and ILO, 746
    international comparisons, 749–50
    public policy, 748
    strikes in support of, 902
co-operation:
    employees' obligations, 111–28
    and hierarchy, 111–13
codes of conduct, 4, 41
collective agreements:
    and business restructuring, 1067–9
    contents, 102
    contracting out of unfair dismissal legisla-
        tion, 509–11
    definition, 102, 798
    enforceability, 15, 102–3
        by employees, 104–09
        by employers, 109–11
    and equal pay, 326–7
    generally, 102–11
    incorporation into contracts, 3, 103–11,
        163–4
    legal pluralism, 4
    legal status, 762–3
    no-strike agreements, 110, 960
    parental leave, 373
    peace obligations, 109–10

practice, 13
transfer of undertakings, 1047
variation of jobs, 995–8
working time, 840
collective bargaining:
changing patterns, 726–9
changing public policy, 723–6, 795–7
and closed shops, 747, 749
collective *laissez-faire,* 23
and common law, 30–1
dispute resolution, 20
effectiveness, 15
EU Charter of Fundamental Rights, 9
future, 61–2
Germany, 833–4
ILO Convention, 727, 729–30
inducements against, 751
and information rights, 812, 814
international instruments, 738–9
legal history, 14
and minority rights, 23
models, 794–5
negotiating procedures, 760–1
promotion, 14, 15, 18, 724, 725
regulation, 13–15, 18
and right to strike, 864
and trade unions, 723–9, 757–95
voluntary bargaining, 758
and women, 23
Collins, H, 122, 213
commercial agents, EU law, 187
Commission for Racial Equality:
function, 218
and occupational exceptions, 299–300,
302–3
and remedies, 336
Commissioner for Protection against Unlawful
Industrial Action, 966
common law, role, 4, 30–1
competition, EU law, 51
competitiveness, 56–8
compromise agreements, 495–8, 511
Conaghan, J, 23
conciliation, ACAS, 25–6, 555–7, 960
Confederation of British Industry, 419, 424,
611, 848
confidential information:
confidentiality clauses, 151
customer lists, 151
employees' obligations, 150–4
employers' obligations, 154–5
generally, 150–4
information in public domain, 153
legal professional privilege, 637, 815
personal data, 154
remedies, 153

and union rights' to information, 815–18
and whistleblowing, 636
workplace surveillance, 608
conflict of laws, 47
conflicts of interest, disclosure, 128
Connolly, M, 282–4
conspiracy, and industrial action, 870–1, 872
constructive dismissal:
breach of trust and confidence, 113–17,
485–7
fundamental breach, 484–8
generally, 482–8
and grievance procedures, 143–4
lock-outs, 959
variation of terms, 1048, 1049, 1050
consultation rights:
appropriate representatives, 823
business plans, 150
business restructuring, 1061
individual consultation, 1062–3
collective redundancies, 821–31, 1063–5
employee representatives, 844
employment status, 825
meaning of redundancy, 1004
numbers, 825–6
operation of legislation, 831–2
special circumstances, 824, 830–1
consultative committees, 62
and damages, 1062–3
disability adjustments, 291
employee representatives, 839–60
enforcement of Regulations, 854–7
failure to consult, 843
negotiated agreements, 850–2
procedures, 844–60
EU Charter of Fundamental Rights, 7, 9, 63
EU law, 46, 48, 62–3, 729, 822–3, 826, 839,
1069, 1070
form, 827, 829
health and safety, 16, 822, 840, 847–8
Information and Consultation Directive,
845–7
Information and Consultation of Employees
Regulations, 847–58, 1068
meaning of consultation, 826–9
remedies, 829–31
timing, 826–9
trade unions
generally, 821–32
priority of recognised unions, 840–2,
847–8
transfer of undertakings, 822, 843, 844,
1065–9
consumer picketing, 926–8
contempt of court, and industrial action, 914,
935–8

continuous employment:
  effective date of termination, 506–7
  qualifying periods, 501–7
    exceptions, 501, 515
    redundancy payments, 1001
    trade union victimisation, 734
  temporary cessation of work, 503–5
contract law:
  contract compliance, and trade union recognition, 796–7, 902
  and employment law, 4
  freedom to contract, 69–70
  illegality, 76
  information requirements, 129
  termination, 479
contracting out *see* outsourcing
contractors *see* self-employed
contracts of employment:
  balance of power, 3, 71, 112, 211–12, 445, 1070
  breach, strikes, 869, 944
  business efficacy, 88, 95
  centrality, 69, 195
  classification *see* employment status
  collective agreements *see* collective agreements
  contracts of services v contracts for services, 73, 157–66, 189, 499
  custom and practice, 3
  definition, 172–3
  disclosure requirements, 135–48
    EU law, 137–42
  express terms, 70
    false statements, 130
  freedom to contract, 69–70, 75, 171, 195–6, 211, 214
  frustration, 488–92
  gaps, 19–20
  generally, 69–75
  illegal contracts, 75, 76, 430
  implied contracts, 192–3
  implied terms, 70, 71–3
    breach by employees, 79–80
    co-operation, 111–28
    development, 128
    employees, 72, 111–28
    employers, 72
    fairness, 213–14
    flexibility, 1018
    good faith, 83, 113–26
    and job variation, 987
    loyalty, 72, 126–8, 151
    obedience to instructions, 72, 97, 112
    overarching principle, 72
    and smoking policies, 99–100

    trust and confidence, 72, 113–26, 134–5, 212, 756
  incorporation of documents
    collective agreements, 3, 103–4, 163–4
    disclosure, 138
    works rules, 3, 71, 95–102
  inducing breach, 869, 870, 871
  information *see* information rights
  legal institution, 73–5
  mutuality principle, 95
  nature, 2–3, 890–1
  and organisation of work, 95–102, 213
  public sector workers, 201, 203–4
  remuneration *see* remuneration
  specific performance, 468, 471–2
  standard model, 70–3
  statutory terms, 73
  termination *see* termination of employment

  umbrella contracts, 162–6
  unfair terms, 98, 991, 992
  variation *see* variation of jobs
  wage-work bargain, 71, 75–95
  weakness of legal framework, 211–15
  written statements, 135–48
    accuracy, 155
    changes, 145–8
  and wrongful dismissal, 436–7
control, self-employed status, 159–60
corporate veil, 186–7
corrective justice, 537–8
corruption, 118–22
Corus Steel, 832, 900
Council of Europe, Social Charter:
  fair remuneration, 387–8
  right to industrial action, 864
  social and economic rights, 35–6
  and trade union membership, 738, 739, 964
  and UK trade union legislation, 945, 947
criminal investigations, and data protection, 619
criminal liability:
  19th century workers, 14
  health and safety at work, 10–12
  industrial action in public sector, 200
  picketing, 921–6
  regulation method, 10–12
Crouch, C, 22, 33
Crown employment *see* public sector workers
Cully, M, 62
culture, and discrimination, 300
custom and practice:
  breach by employees, 79–80
  collective agreements, 103
  and contracts of employment, 3
  legal pluralism, 4
Cyprus, 412

damages:
    aggravated and exemplary damages, 338,
        515, 549, 942–3
    data protection regulation, 621
    disciplinary procedures, non-compliance,
        533, 555
    discrimination
        backdating, 338
        equal pay, 338
        exemplary damages, 338
        injury to feelings, 337–8
        levels, 337
        statutory provision, 336
    inadequacy, injunctions, 463–4, 469–75
    inducements against trade union member-
        ship, 751
    mental distress, 447–8
    stigma damages, 118–22
    unfair dismissal *see* unfair dismissal
    unlawful industrial action, 938–43
        exemplary damages, 942–3
        interest, 943
        vicarious liability of unions, 930
    victimisation, 460–1
    wrongful dismissal *see* wrongful dismissal
data protection:
    accuracy of data, 619
    and blacklisting, 596, 597, 600, 734
    compensation, 621
    consent, 635
    Directive, 611
    employment data, 154, 613–16
    enforcement, 619–21
    exemptions, 619
    fair processing code, 617–18
    generally, 611–28
    Information Commissioner
        duties, 619–20
        guidance, 615–16, 621–8
    national security, 618
    personal data, 154, 612
    principles, 616–19, 625–6
    rectification of data, 621
    rights of data subjects, 620–1
    sensitive personal data, 612, 617, 622, 623
        trade union membership, 734
    specified purposes, 618–19
    temp test, 616
    terminology, 612
    and workplace surveillance, 621–8
Davies, A C L, 5
Davies, H, 342
Davies, J, 288
Davies, Paul, 31, 47, 101, 112, 187–8, 212,
    790–1, 847–8
Davies, Simon, 602–6, 607

Daycare Trust, 368, 369
Deakin, S, 49–51, 56–7, 75, 138, 171, 389–91,
    410, 989–90, 995
declarations:
    discrimination, 337
    wrongful dismissal, 463–75
defamation, 130, 132
democracy, industrial democracy, 20, 81–3
Denmark, 376, 727
Department of Trade and Industry *see* DTI
diabetes, 285–8
Dickens, L, 539, 556–7
dignity, 6, 74, 607
disability discrimination
    see also discrimination
    burden of proof, 331–2, 334
    claims, time limits, 335
    comparators, 245–6
    direct discrimination, 236
    disability, meaning, 229–34
    EU Charter of Fundamental Rights, 9
    EU law, 291–2, 303
    harassment, 252
    indirect discrimination, 289
    justification, 285–9, 290
    meaning of discrimination, 245
    perceived disability, 231
    reasonable adjustments, 289–92
        consultation, 291
        examples, 290–1
        knowledge, 290, 291
    risk assessments, 285–6, 288
    scope of prohibition, 310
    victimisation, 257
Disability Rights Commission, 218
disabled:
    discrimination *see* disability discrimination
    meaning, 229–34
    welfare to work, 60
disciplinary procedures:
    bias, 698–700
    collective disputes, 532
    contractual status, 96, 98, 144–5
    definition, 755
    exceptional circumstances, 532–3
    fairness, 527–34
    implied fairness, 213–14
    implied terms, 445–9
    injunctions, 472–5
    policies, 519–20
    proportionality, 434
    right to be accompanied, 752–7
    statutory obligations, 530–2, 755
        damages for non-compliance, 533, 555
    suspension, remuneration, 90
    trade unions, 684–5, 693–705

UNISON, 695–7
wrongful dismissal, 445–52
discrimination:
  age *see* age discrimination
  agency workers, 194
  bastard defence, 333
  burden of proof, 331–5
  Burden of Proof Directive, 333
  claims
    funding by equality commissions, 332
    time limits, 335–6
  comparators, 240–6
  defences, 314
  detriment, meaning, 311–17
  direct discrimination, 235–56
    statutory provisions, 235–6
  disability *see* disability discrimination
  domestic employment, 306
  dress codes, 252–6
  ECHR, 220, 564, 584–6
  employee representatives, 844
  employer liability, 314–17
  employment status, 311
  equality of opportunity, 58–9
  EU Charter of Fundamental Rights, 9
  EU Treaty obligations, 49
  evidence, inferences, 332–3
  exceptions to prohibition, 292–306
  gender *see* sex discrimination
  and genetic testing, 607
  harassment, 246–56, 312, 314
  ILO conventions, 38
  incoherent legislation, 339
  indirect *see* indirect discrimination
  intentions and motivation, 236–40, 325
  law reform, 339
  legislation, 217
  minority rights, and collective bargaining, 23
  nationality discrimination, 46–9, 219–20, 224, 225
  occupational requirement exceptions, 293–306
  and parental leave, 374–5
  part-time workers *see* part-time workers
  pay *see* equal pay
  positive discrimination, 59, 306–9
  race *see* race discrimination
  religion and belief *see* religious discrimination
  remedies, 336–8
    compensation levels, 337
    heads of damages, 337
    injury to feelings, 337–8
  remuneration *see* equal pay
  scope of prohibition, 218, 310–17
  sex *see* equal pay; sex discrimination

  sexual orientation, 218, 222–4
  sources of law, 217. 219, 220
  trade union membership, 693–4, 730–4, 730–52
  trust and confidence, 117
  vicarious liability, 314–15
  victimisation, 256–62
  and workplace surveillance, 603
diseases, occupational diseases, 74
dismissal:
  constructive *see* constructive dismissal
  contracting out of statutory rights
    agreed termination, 494–8
    arbitration alternative, 508–9
    collective agreements, 509–11
    compromise agreements, 495–8, 511
    discharge by performance, 495
    employment status, 498–500
    generally, 492–511
    prohibition, 493
    retirement age, 507–8
    sham agreements, 499–500
    temporary work, 500–7
  date, meaning, 506–7, 955
  and emergency leave, 379–80
  employee representatives, 844, 857
  fairness *see* fairness of dismissal
  ILO Convention, 435
  and industrial action, 908, 944–58
    incidence, 977
    pre-1999 position, 945–7
    protected actions, 947–53
    protected periods, 948–9, 951–3
    replacement workers, 954
    unprotected actions, 953–8
  issues, 435
  maternity reasons, 356–7
  and minimum wage, 398, 399
  notice
    implied reasonable notice, 437–8
    statutory notice, 438–9
    summary dismissals, 439–45
  power, 433–4
  reasons
    principal reasons, 512–13
    substantial reasons, 513–14
    written statements, 135
  redundancy *see* redundancy
  statistics, 434
  statutory concept, 477–92
    definition, 478
    dismissal or resignation, 479–82
    frustration of contract, 488–92
    introduction, 477
    standards, 477

termination of fixed-term contracts, 478,
495, 513–14
statutory rights
contracting out, 492–511
and reasonableness, 557–9
v common law, 435, 448–9, 458, 475–7
transfer of undertakings *see* transfer of
undertakings
unfair dismissal *see* unfair dismissal
wrongful *see* wrongful dismissal
display screen equipment, 607–8
dispute settlement:
alternative dispute resolution, 23–30
arbitration, 26–7
Certification Officer, 29–30
civil courts, 30–2
class conflicts, 22
collective bargaining, 20
conciliation, 25–6
employment tribunals *see* employment
tribunals
grievance procedures *see* grievance
procedures
internal trade union disputes, 706–17
ombudsmen, 29
ownership and control, 20–2
public sector workers, 198
sources of conflict, 19–23
system, 19–32
TUC Disputes Committee, 30
workforce conflicts, 22–3
divorce, and women's income, 342, 348
doctors, working time, 403, 404, 411–12
Doeringer, P B, 101
domestic workers, working time, 404, 418
domicile, 47
Donovan Commission, 15, 656, 674, 707, 724,
747, 812, 867, 868
Doyle, Brian, 331–2
dress codes:
and human rights, 579, 582–3
sex discrimination, 252–6
Dromey, Jack, 600
drug testing, 606–7, 623, 628, 634, 635–6
DTI:
dismissal statistics, 434
Fairness at Work, 725–6, 766–7, 835, 947
flexible working, 382, 383–6, 726
maternity rights, 358, 360, 361
picketing code of practice, 917–19
religious discrimination, 228–9
retirement age, 508
sexual orientation guidelines, 305
trade union immunities, 897
unfair dismissal, 502
union recognition, 766–7

Code of Practice, 779–80, 781, 785
working time guidance, 410, 418–19, 421–2
Dumville, S L, 138
duty of care:
employees, 72, 80
employers
competent staff, 72
discrimination, 314–17
health and safety at work, 74, 991–4
implied term, 72
references, 134
systems of work, 148
workplace monitoring, 632–3

Economic League, 596
economic rights *see* social and economic rights

economy:
competitiveness, 56–8
labour market failures, 55
and labour regulation, 54–8
productivity, 56–7
social costs, 55–6
social exclusion, 58–61
Edwards, P, 831–2, 1065
Elger, T, 982
Elias, P, 944
Ellis, N D, 1001
email monitoring, 605, 608
emanation of states, 43, 45
emergency leave:
dismissals, 379–80
employee status, 378
EU Framework Agreement, 377–8
generally, 377–82
statutory entitlement, 378
emergency powers, 200, 965
employee representatives *see* worker
participation
employees *see* employment status
employers' liability, 72, 74
employment:
agencies *see* agency workers
contracts *see* contracts of employment
duration *see* continuous employment
law *see* labour law
meaning, 176–9
terms and conditions, meaning, 890–1
Employment Appeal Tribunal, 31–2
employment status:
and adoptive leave, 375
agency workers, 187–94, 754
armed forces, 204
atypical workers, 166–71, 215, 381–2
casual workers, 162–6
classification, 157–66

and contracts of employment, 73–4
contracts of services v contracts for services,
        73, 157–66, 189, 499
control, 159–60
Crown officers, 204
dependent entrepreneurs, 179–94
and disclosure of employment terms, 140–1
and discrimination prohibition, 311
and emergency leave, 378
employees, meaning, 157–66, 172–3
employment relationship, 173–4
flexibility, 166–71, 429–31
franchises, 180–6
generally, 155–96
issues, 155–7
law reform, 195–6
and minimum wage, 392
and parental leave, 375
Parliamentary staff, 204, 754
part-time workers, 351
professionals, 176–9, 767
public sector workers, 197, 199, 200–7
and redundancy rights, 825, 1001
Regulation powers, 194, 196
risk allocation, 159–62, 499
self-employed *see* self-employed
sham agreements, 499–500
and statutory rights on dismissal, 499–500,
        736
trainees, 177
and transfer of undertakings, 173–4
volunteers, 174
workers, meaning, 174–6, 392, 403–5, 754–5
working time, 403–5
employment tribunals:
    ACAS conciliation, 26
    arbitration alternative, 508–9
    chairmen sitting alone, 28
    composition, 27
    excluded claims, 27
    exhaustion of grievance procedures, 24–5
    hybrid nature, 28
    jurisdiction, 477
        deduction of wages, 86
        employment status, 498–500
        failure to consult on redundancy, 829
        flexible working, 382
        limitations, 476
        minimum wage, 13, 398
        qualifying periods *see* continuous
                employment
        retirement age, 507–8
        status *see* employment status
        trade union conflicts, 685
        worker representation issues, 755
        working time, 424

wrongful dismissal, 86
    legal representation, 29
    legalism, 28–9
    procedures, 28
    public authority status, 572–3
    and public sector workers, 202
    strategy, 24
    system, 27–9
Epstein, R, 510
Equal Opportunities Commission, 218, 336,
        343–5, 347–8, 359
equal pay:
    burden of proof, 317
    claims, time limits, 336
    and collective bargaining, 326–7
    comparators, 48, 317–23, 352
        equal value, 322–3
        EU law, 319–21
        hypotheticals, 317
        same employment, 317–19
    damages, 338
    EU obligations, 45–6, 48
    generally, 317–31
    indirect discrimination, 280
    intentions and motivation, 325
    material difference defence, 323–31
        burden of proof, 326–7, 330–1
        extrinsic forces, 323–4
        judicial credulity, 330
        market forces, 324–5, 327–9
    meaning of pay, 48
equality
    see also discrimination
    commissions, 218–19, 332
    Equal Treatment Directive, 219
    equality of opportunity, 58–9
    EU Charter of Human Rights, 7–8
    pay *see* equal pay
estoppel, 988
Ethical Investment Research Service, 597
EU Charter of Fundamental Rights:
    consultation rights, 7, 9, 63
    holistic approach, 64
    impact, 536
    social and economic rights, 48
    text, 6–9
    transnational standards, 34
    unfair dismissal, 7, 434–5, 515
    workers' rights, 7, 63, 1069
European Convention on Human Rights
    see also specific rights
    jurisprudence, 564, 575–86
    and labour law, 32, 562–4
    political discrimination, 598–601
    role, 34–5
    and whistleblowing, 644–5

and workplace surveillance, 628–33
European Court of Justice, appeals to, 31
European Industrial Relations Observatory, 727
European Social Charter *see* Council of
    Europe
European Union:
    Burden of Proof Directive, 333
    business restructuring, 980
    Charter of Rights *see* EU Charter of Fun-
        damental Rights
    collective redundancies, 822, 1028
    competition rules, 51
    Constitution, human rights, 6, 9
    consultation rights, 46, 48, 62–3, 727, 822–3,
        826, 839, 1069, 1070
    contracts of employment, disclosure require-
        ments, 137–42
    data protection, 611
    directives, direct and indirect effect, 43–5, 48
    disability discrimination, 291–2
        occupational exception, 303
    emanation of states, 43, 45
    employer insolvency, 1031–3
    employment agencies, 194
    employment relationship, 173–4
    and employment subsidies, 1000
    equal pay, 45–6, 319–21
    equal treatment
        burden of proof, 271–2
        Directive, 219
        non-discrimination principle, 49
        occupational exception, 293, 297–9
        positive discrimination, 59
        race equality, 225
    free movement of workers, 46–9
    gender reassignment, 220–1
    growing influence, 46–9
    health and safety, 16, 149
    indirect discrimination, 263, 277–80
    Information and Consultation Directive,
        845–7
    labour law competence, 34, 42–6
    maternity rights, 358, 361–4
    parental leave, 343, 372–3, 377–8
    part-time workers, 343, 348–50
    positive discrimination, 306, 307–9
    posted workers, 47
    pregnancy discrimination, 241–2
    purpose of regulation, 49–51
    Racial Equality Directive, 302, 303
    Regulations, 45
    self-employed commercial agents, 187
    Social Chapter, 348, 350
    Social Dialogue, 48, 63
    transfer of undertakings, 1035–6, 1043
        outsourcing, 1052–8

Treaty obligations, 45, 48
undertakings, meaning, 142
workers, meaning, 175–6, 193
working time, 401–2, 404–7, 411–16
Evans, S, 500, 502, 557–8
Ewing, K D, 34, 388, 453, 562–4, 588–9, 594,
    740, 787, 791, 792–3, 795, 836–9, 847,
    856–7, 938, 971–2

Fabel, O, 1002
Factory Acts, 12
factory inspectors, 10
Fagan, Colette, 346
fair hearings:
    ECHR, 563
    independent and impartial tribunals, 574
    procedural fairness, 573–5
    trade union disciplinary proceedings,
        698–700
Fair Wages policies, 796
Fair Wages Resolution, 796
Fairhurst, J, 404
fairness of dismissal:
    adequacy of tribunal jurisprudence, 534–6
        transfer of undertakings, 1045
    automatically unfair dismissals
        application, 514–15, 516, 536
        closed shops, 748
        maternity rights, 356–7
        part-time workers, 516
        participation in strikes, 908
        qualifying periods, 501
        strike dismissals, 947–53
        transfer of undertakings, 1037–44, 1048
    collective disputes, 532
    consistency, 519–20
    and disciplinary policies, 519–20
    equity, 520
    evidence of misconduct, 529
    exceptional circumstances, 532–3
    fairness test, 514
    and freedom of expression, 535
    generally, 511–36
    good faith, 123
    good industrial practice, 518–19, 521, 526
    human rights grounds, 570–3
        freedom of expression, 576–82
        jurisprudence, 575–86
    industrial action, 944–58
    maternity reasons, 356–7
    modified dismissal procedures, 531–2
    perversity, 522–6
    principal reasons, 512–13
    procedural fairness, 526–34
        Human Rights Act, 573–5
        judicial attitudes, 1070–1

lack of consultation on redundancy, 1062–4
mass dismissals, 1062
proportionality, 521–6
reasonable response test, 515–26
reasonableness, 557–9
redundancy reasons, 513–14, 1016–18
and alternative employment, 1027–8
selection for redundancy, 781–2, 1019–24
sexual orientation, 534–5
standards, 207, 214, 509, 511–12, 515
statutory minimum disciplinary procedures, 530–2
structure of fairness enquiries, 512–15
substantial reasons, 513–14
trade union related activities, 781–2
family-friendly policies, 61, 387, 401
family life *see* privacy rights
Fawcett Society, 348
fidelity *see* loyalty
Finch, V, 1029
Finland, 376, 387
firefighters, 960
fishermen, 392, 404
fixed-term contracts *see* temporary workers
flags of convenience, 901, 931
flexibility:
catchphrase, 402
contracting out of statutory rights, 492–3, 509–11
contracts of employment, 983–95
distancing strategies, 167
and DTI, 382, 383–6, 726
flexibility clauses, 989–95, 1011–13
flexible firm model, 166–9, 1052
functional flexibility, 167
homeworkers, 170
implied flexibility clauses, 1018
and labour law, 52–4
labour market, 166–71, 427–31
limits, 194–6
numerical flexibility, 167, 170
outsourcing, 167, 169, 1052
right to request flexible working, 382–7
sub-contracting, 167
variation of jobs, 983–95, 1011–13
Working Time Regulations, 402
forced labour, 6, 37
Ford, M, 631–2
Forde, M, 34
Forth, J, 844
Fosh, P, 647, 914
Fox, A, 21
France, 412, 727
franchises, 180–6
Fredman, Sandra, 197–8, 589

free movement of workers, 7, 9, 46–9
Freedland, Mark, 31, 72, 95, 101, 112, 169, 187–8, 207, 208–10, 212, 214–15, 790–1
freedom of assembly, picketing, 916, 923, 927
freedom of association:
and closed shops, 746, 747
ECHR, 564, 730
limits, 882
mutuality, 689
right of non-association, 749
right to strike, 888, 903, 976
and trade union membership, 563, 692, 718–19, 720, 738, 752
UK practice, 588–9
freedom of expression:
ECHR, 564, 576
and fairness of dismissal, 535, 576–82
picketing, 916, 927
references, 133
and whistleblowing, 644–5
freedom of thought, conscience and religion:
blacklisting, 596–8, 600
ECHR jurisprudence, 563–4, 582–3
and political activities, 587–601
restrictions on public sector workers, 591–5
freelance workers, 140–1, 170, 175
Friction Dynamics, 951–3, 970
fringe benefits, 454–6, 550
frustration of contract, 488–92

garden leave, 90–4
Gardner, J, 235
GCHQ, 740, 960
gender discrimination *see* sex discrimination
gender reassignment, 218, 220–1, 295–6
genetic testing, 607, 628
Genn, H & Y, 29
Germany:
business restructuring, 981
collective bargaining, 833–4
consultation rights, 1064
email monitoring, 608
forced labour, 37
Kapp Putsch, 866
parental Leave, 376
part-time work, 350
redundancy payments, 1002
working time, 412
works councils, 729, 833
globalisation, 32–3, 38
GM Luton, 900
GM Vauxhall, 832
golden parachutes, 441
good faith:
and confidential information, 152
employment relationship, 83, 113–26, 180

exercise of discretion, 122–3
and unfair dismissal, 123
whistleblowing, 639, 641–3
and wrongful dismissal, 476
Goodman, J, 500, 502, 557–8
Goriely, T, 84
Gospel, H, 819–21
Goss, D, 416
Gould, W B, 787
government ministers, 197
Greece, 376
grievance procedures:
appeals, 24
definition, 755, 756
disclosure requirements, 143
obligation to use, 24–4
right to be accompanied, 752–7
statutory obligations, 24–5, 755
Grosso, J-L, 981
group companies, 142
guarantee pay, 999–1000
Gunningham, N, 17

Hall, M, 831–2, 1065
Hanson, C G, 747
harassment, 246–56, 312, 314, 603
Hardy, Stan, 596–7
Hargreave, L, 500, 502, 557–8
Harris, J E, 101
Harrison, J L, 510
Hawthorne Experiment, 123, 124
Hayward, B, 501, 537, 556
health and safety at work:
1974 Act, 11–12
automatically unfair dismissal, 516
civil liability, 12
collective mechanism, 16
consultation rights, 16, 822
priority of recognised unions, 840, 847–8
costs, 12
criminal liability, 11–12
display screens, 149
duty of care, 74
effectiveness of regulation, 16–17
Factory Acts, 12
homeworkers, 170
improvement notices, 11
industrial injuries, 74
inspectors, 10, 11
manual handling operations, 149–50
and minimum wage, 400
overtime work, 991–4
prohibition notices, 11
regulation methods, 16
regulation powers, 11
risk assessments, 148–50

safety committees, 840
safety representatives, 16, 840
election, 843
time off, 843
training, 843
safety standards, 11
self-employed, 179–80
strengths and weaknesses, 12
systems of work, 148
Hencke, D, 847
Hendy, J, 791–2
Hepple, Bob, 41, 118, 227, 533, 569, 1052
Hewitt, Patricia, 610–11, 953
hierarchy, 111–13, 123
Hill, S, 124–6
Hilowitz, J, 41
Hobbs, S, 39–40, 410
holidays, 405–8, 426
Hollingworth, M, 600
homeworkers, 170, 754
homosexuality see sexual orientation
Honey, S, 171
Hudson, M, 989–90, 995
human rights
see also specific rights
1998 Act
approach, 64, 562, 565–8
declarations of incompatibility, 566–7
impact, 646
interpretation of legislation, 565–7
political discrimination, 598–601
procedural fairness, 573–5
public/private divide, 568–73
remedies, 568
and workplace surveillance, 633–6
EU Charter see EU Charter of Fundamental Rights
European Convention see European Convention on Human Rights
international law, 32, 34–5
and labour law, 5–9, 561, 562–4
ECHR jurisprudence, 575–86
and picketing, 927
and political activities, 587–601
blacklisting, 596–8
restrictions on public sector workers,
591–5
security vetting, 587–91
public sector workers, 211
and right to strike, 976
and trade unions, 720
unfair dismissal and, 570–3
and workplace surveillance, 601–36
Hunt, J, 536
Hunter, L, 168
Huysmans, Camille, 866

Hyman, R, 729

IBM, 608
immigration, discrimination, 239–40, 585–6, 587
imprisonment, frustration of contract, 488, 491
improvement notices, health and safety at work, 11
incentives:
    regulatory tool, 17
    welfare benefits at work, 59–61
income support, 969–70, 999
indirect discrimination:
    age limits, 275–7, 279–80
    burden of proof, 271–3
    collective disadvantage, 266–71
    disability discrimination, 289
    disparate impact, 265
    equal pay, 321
    gender reassignment, 221
    generally, 263–84
    individual disadvantage, 269–71
    justification, 273–84
    necessity defence, 282–4
    part-time workers, 277–79, 280–2
    pool selection, 267–71
    'provision, criterion or practice,' 266
    race discrimination, 263–5
    religion and belief, 263
    sex discrimination, 263
    sexual orientation, 263
    statistical evidence, 267–8
industrial action:
    arbitration, 962–3
    ballots see strike ballots
    call-out bans, 908
    Commissioner for Protection against Unlawful Industrial Action, 966
    conciliation, 961–2
    criminal liability, 200
    decline, 868
    deduction of wages, 78–9, 80–3, 86–7
    dismissal, 908, 944–58
        1980s cases, 946
        incidence, 977
        international law, 945–7
        protected actions, 947–53
        protected periods, 948–9, 951–3
        unprotected actions, 953–8
    dispute resolution, 960–3
    emergency powers, 200, 965
    forms, 863
    functions, 863–6
    immunities
        1906 Act, 870, 938, 971
        1974 Act, 875, 879, 939, 971

    ballot requirement, 897
    and liability, 893–6, 945
    meaning of trade disputes, 880–902
    present statutory immunity, 879–80
    secondary actions, 892–902
    UK approach, 971–2
    law reform, 971–2
    legal liability, 867
        breach of contract, 869, 944
        conspiracy to injure, 870–1, 872
        damages, 938–43
        generally, 869–80
        and immunity, 893–6
        inducing breach of contract, 869, 870, 871
        inducing breach of statutory duty, 877–9
        interference with business, 871
        interference with performance of commercial contracts, 874
        locus standi, 878, 966
        procuring breach of commercial contracts, 873
        tort boundaries, 869–79
        UK approach, 971–2
        unlawful means, 877–9
    meaning, 686–7
    notice, 904–5, 910–14
    overtime bans, 908
    peace obligations, 109–10
    picketing see picketing
    political ends, 865–6, 881–4, 974
    public sector workers, 200, 210, 884–8
    and redundancy, 959
    replacement workers, 954
    sanctions against strikers, 944–58
    sanctions against unions, 928–43
        authorisation by unions, 941
        contempt of court, 935–8
        damages, 938–43
        injunctions, 928–35
    secondary actions
        damages, 942–3
        generally, 875–6, 892–902
        Green Paper, 898
        ILO report, 973–4
        international solidarity actions, 899–902
        meaning, 863
        pre-1980, 893–6
        statutory withdrawal of immunity, 896–9
    state strategies, 958–70
        coercion, 963–70
        dispute resolution, 960–3
        encouraging strike breaking, 964–5
        social security penalties, 966–70
    strikes see strikes
    third party remedies, 878, 966

trade disputes
   House of Lords jurisprudence, 888–92
   international disputes, 899–902, 974
   meaning, 880–902, 962, 967, 972, 974
   privatised public sector, 884–8
   social and political ends, 865–6, 881–4,
      974
   unofficial actions, 902
   work to rule, 80–3, 97
   workers as citizens, 864–5, 882–3
industrial democracy, 20, 61–3
industrial injuries, 74
industrial pluralism, 20
Information Commissioner:
   duties, 619–20
   guidance, 615–16, 621–8
information rights:
   associated employers, 142
   business plans, 150
   confidentiality *see* confidential information

   deductions from wages, 135
   dismissal reasons, 135
   employee representatives
      business restructuring, 1061
      enforcement of Regulations, 854–7
      negotiated agreements, 850–2
      procedures, 844–60
   employment contract terms, 135–48
      accuracy, 155
      changes, 145–8
      effectiveness, 141
      EU law, 137–42
   EU Charter of Fundamental Rights, 9
   EU law, 48, 137–42, 845–7
   false and misleading information, 130–5
   generally, 129–55
   grievance procedures, 143
   group companies, 142
   Information and Consultation Directive,
      845–7
   Information and Consultation Regulations,
      847–58, 1068
   and informed choice, 136
   itemised pay statements, 135, 141
   legislative patchwork, 155
   references, 130–5
   risk assessments, 148–50
   trade unions, 681–2, 812–21
      ACAS code of practice, 814–15, 818, 821
      confidential information, 815–18
      critique, 819–21
      restrictions, 814–18
      statutory rights, 812–15
injunctions:
   Civil Procedure Rules, 929

   civil remedy, 30
   contempt of court, 935
   garden leave, 90
   industrial action, 928–35
   interim injunctions, 929–35
   springboard injunctions, 151
   wrongful dismissal, 463–75
injuries, industrial injuries, 74
injury to feelings, damages, 547–50
insolvency:
   administration, 1033–4
   corporate rescue, 1029, 1033–5
   employees as preferential creditors, 1029–30
   EU law, 1031–3
   ILO Convention, 1029
   protection of wages, 1029–33
   social security guarantees, 1030–3, 1072
      ceilings, 1033
      subrogation, 1031
   stakeholding rhetoric, 1029
   worker protection, 1028–35
Institute for Policy Studies, 342
Institute of Employment Rights, 692
insurance, employers' liability, 74
International Labour Organisation:
   child labour, 37
   and closed shops, 746
   collective bargaining, 727, 729–30
   conventions, 36
   Declaration of Fundamental Rights, 36–7
   dismissal, 435
   employer insolvency, 1029
   forced labour, 37
   freedom of association and trade disputes,
      945–7, 958, 964, 973–5
   and GCHQ, 740
   minimum wage, 388
   non-discrimination, 38
   part-time work, 350
   reports, 36
   trade unions, 648, 649, 719, 738, 835
   universal standards, 5, 33
   workers' representatives, 795
international law:
   child labour, 38–41
   European Union *see* European Union
   globalisation, 33
   governing law, 47
   human rights *see* human rights
   and labour law, 32–51
   right to strike, 975–7
   social and economic rights, 35–41
   transnational labour market, 42–51
International Transport Workers' Federation,
      900, 901, 931
Internet monitoring, 605, 608

intimidation, 942
investigatory powers, 609–11
Ireland, 376

Japan, 981
Jeffrey, M, 349–50
Jews, 218, 228
jobseeker's allowance:
    lower earnings limit, 348
    strikers, 966–7
    and unfair dismissal awards, 554
Johnstone, R, 17
joint industrial councils, 14, 723–4
Jones, Jack, 600
Joshi, H, 342
judicial review:
    court discretion, 204–7
    public sector employment, 200–3, 204–7
judiciary, 197

Kahn, P, 919
Kahn-Freund, Otto, 23, 103, 113, 725
Kaur, K, 62
Kelly, J, 729
Kendall, Liz, 386–7
Kilpatrick, C, 847–8

labour law:
    citizenship rights, 63–5
    civil law, 12–13
    common law, 4, 30
    costs of regulation, 10
    criminal law, 10–12
    disputes see dispute settlement
    effectiveness, 10, 12, 13, 15–17
    and flexibility, 52–4
    and human rights, 5–9
    incentives to comply, 17
    international aspects see international law
    and labour market failures, 55
    methods of regulation, 10–18
    nature, 1–6, 9
    objectives, 54–8, 1072
    pluralism, 3–4
    politics, 1
    prospects, 52–65
    public and private spheres, 63–5, 568–73
    scope see employment status
    and social costs, 55–6
    State role, 17–18, 958–70
    transnational law see international law
labour markets:
    British child labour, 39–40
    deregulation, 390
    external markets, 101
    failures, 55

flexibility, 166–71, 427–31
    internal labour markets, 101, 168, 983
    international market, 42–51
Labour Party, 656, 658, 659, 867, 870
Laski, Harold, 865–6, 970
Lazear, EP, 981
Leader, S, 23
legal professional privilege, 637, 815
Leighton, P E, 138
Lewis, J, 598, 644, 645
Lewis, P, 539, 556
Liberty, 600, 611
local government see public sector workers
lock-outs, 955, 957, 959
Lockwood, G, 819–21
Low Pay Commission, 391, 392
Low Pay Unit, 376, 596
loyalty, 72, 126–8, 151
Luxembourg, 412

MacInnes, J, 168
Mair, J, 359
Major, John, 589–90
Malta, working time, 412
management:
    authority, 111–28
    bargaining power, 3, 71, 112, 211–13, 445,
        1070
    hierarchy, 111–13, 123
    human resources management, 123
    and productivity, 123
    retail trade, 124–6
    Taylorism, 113
    working time, 418, 421
    works rules, 96–102
Manning, A, 345–6
manual handling operations, 149–50
Martin, R, 666, 914
Maternity Alliance, 386–7
Maternity Allowance, 348, 365
maternity leave:
    employment status, 375
    notice procedure, 359
    return from, 365–6
    rights during, 359–65
    statutory leave, 358–9
maternity rights:
    automatically unfair dismissal, 356–7, 516
        qualifying period, 501
    discrimination, 356–7, 361, 363–4
        comparators, 240–2, 244
        indirect discrimination, 274
    DTI guidance, 358, 360, 361
    during maternity leave, 359–65
    generally, 356–66
    maternity pay, 362–3, 364–5

redundancy, 357
sickness during pregnancy, 242
McCarthy, W E J, 1001
McColgan, Aileen, 293, 306, 376–7
McCrudden, C, 337
McEvoy, K, 590
McGregor, A, 168
McIntosh of Haringey, Lord, 904
McKechnie, J, 39–40
medical testing, 607, 627–8, 634
Mental Health Foundation, 342
Merkur Island, 901
MI5, 600
Miller, K, 749–50, 946
Millward, N, 727–8, 844
miners' strike 1984, 922, 925–6, 935, 936–7, 964
minimum wage:
    agency workers, 194
    application, 392
    catering sector, 399–400
    compensation rights, 12–13
    compliance officers, 398
    and contracts of employment, 73
    criminal liability, 12
    dismissals, 398, 399
    effect, 13, 398–401
    enforcement, 397–8
    excluded categories, 392
    generally, 387–401
    homeworkers, 170
    hours of work, 395–7
    inspections, 397, 398
    introduction, 389–91
    meaning of pay, 392, 393
    output work, 394
    pay reference periods, 393
    rates, 391
    records, 397
    time work, 394
    unmeasured work, 394, 396
    Wages Councils, 388–9
    welfare to work philosophy, 60
ministers, 197
misrepresentation, 130–5
Mizen, P, 40
mobile workers, working time, 404
Monks, John, 419, 847
Moore, S, 791, 792
MORI, 383, 606–7
Morris, A, 235
Morris, Bill, 951–3
Morris, D, 174
Morris, Gillian, 197–8, 210, 533, 569–70, 589,
    740, 957, 1060
Morris, H, 647, 914
Moss, Peter, 376

Mumgaard, K, 1052
Munday, R, 28–9
Mundlak, G, 510
Muslims, discrimination, 218, 227–8, 272
mutuality principle, 95, 113–26

NACAB, 380–2, 398–400, 428–31
Napier, B W, 938
Nash, D, 138
National Industrial Relations Court, 31
National Insurance, lower earnings limit, 347–8
national security:
    data protection, 618
    exemptions from discrimination prohibition,
        292
    political vetting, 587–91
    and trade union membership, 740
nationality discrimination, 46–9, 219–20, 224,
    225
Neathy, F, 417, 418, 424, 427–8
negligence, references, 131–2
neo-liberalism, 209
Netherlands, 341–2, 344, 376, 727, 900–1
New Public Management, 198
News International, 838–9, 868, 935, 938, 946
Northern Ireland:
    discrimination, 334, 336–7
    Equality Commission, 218
    political discrimination, 597–8
    security vetting, 590–1
Norton-Taylor, R, 600
Norway, parental Leave, 376
Norwich Union, 632
notice of dismissal:
    payments in lieu, 86, 441–2
    presumption of reasonable notice, 437–8
    statutory notice, 438–9
    summary dismissals, 439–45
Novitz, T, 951
NSPCC, 376

obedience:
    dismissal for disobedience, 442–3
    employees' implied contractual term, 72, 97,
        112
    employment relationship, 180
    hierarchy, 111–13
obscenity, dismissal, 443–5
occupational diseases, compensation, 74
O'Connell, Davidson, Julia, 180–6
Official Secrets Act, 636
Ogus, A, 17
O'Higgins, P, 5, 118
ombudsmen, 29
Omni Trak, 604
Orwell, George, 601

outsourcing:
    flexible firms, 167, 169, 1052
    internal contracting, 169
    public sector, 101, 198, 200, 210, 569, 884–8,
        1060
    transfer of undertakings, 1051–9, 1060
overtime work, enforceability, 109–10, 956,
        991–4
Oxenbridge, S, 138
Oxfam, 596

Palmer, T, 384–6
Pannick, David, 222–3, 296–7
parental leave:
    1999 Regulations, 372–5
    childcare issues, 368–72
    discrimination, prohibition, 374–5
    employment status, 375
    entitlement, 373
    EU law, 343, 372–3, 377–8
    evaluation, 375–7
    generally, 368–77
Parker, S R, 1001
parliamentary staff, employment status, 204,
        754
part-time workers:
    automatically unfair dismissal, 516
    contracts of employment, 73
    definition, 351
    Directive, 343, 348–50
    discrimination
        comparators, 351–2, 354
        justification, 353–4
        prohibition, 349, 350–1
    employment status, 351
    generally, 343–56
    growth, 166, 343
    guidance, 351, 353
    indirect discrimination, 277–79, 280–2
    low paid work, 342, 344–6, 390
    redundancy selection, 22
    Regulations 2000, 350–6
        effectiveness, 354–6
        scope, 351
    and social security system, 346–8
    transfers to part-time work, 249
    women, 343–4, 345–6
paternity leave, 367, 375
peace obligations, 109–10
Peccei, R, 124–6
pensions:
    occupational pensions
        and insolvency, 1030
        transfer of undertakings, 1052
    Ombudsman, 29
    part-time workers, 345

stakeholder pensions, 348
    trustees, time off, 356
    women, 342, 348
performance-related pay, 77, 101
Peters, M, 501, 537, 556
Petrongolo, B, 345–6
picketing:
    civil liability, 919–21
    Code of Practice, 917–19
    conflict of freedoms, 915–16
    consumer picketing, 926–8
    criminal offences, 921–6
        obstructing highway, 922–3
        obstructing police, 923–5
        public order, 921–2
        watching and besetting, 925–6
    generally, 915–28
    and human rights, 927
    lawful picketing, 899
    limits, 919–21
    location, 919–20
    miners' strike, 922, 925–6, 964–5
    numbers, 919, 924
    peaceful picketing, 916–17
    police powers, 918, 919
    purpose, 915, 920–1
    secondary picketing, 921
    statutory protection, 916–17
    unlawful picketing, 917
piece work, 77, 88–9
Pillinger, Jane, 387, 401
Piore, M J, 101
Pitt, G, 404
Pole, C, 40
police:
    impartiality, 594–5
    industrial action, 200
    political activities, 594–5, 600
    sex discrimination, exemptions, 292, 297–9
    strike prohibition, 960
politics:
    blacklisting, 596–8, 600
    and human rights, 587–601
    and industrial action
        international solidarity, 899–902
        political ends, 865–6, 881–4, 974
        privatised sector, 884–8
    restrictions on public sector workers
        Civil Service, 591–3, 600
        generally, 591–5
        local government, 593–4, 599–600
        police, 594–5, 600
    security vetting, 587–91
poor law, 969
pornography, 608, 632
Portugal, 376

positive discrimination, 59, 306–9
postal services, 960
posted workers, directive, 47
poverty trap, 391
Pratten, C, 989–90, 995
pregnancy *see* maternity rights
prison officers:
    employment status, 201–4
    industrial action, 200
    sex discrimination, exemptions, 292
    staff association, 836
privacy rights:
    domestic law, 568
    ECHR, 224, 563
    and employers' use of personal data, 154
    and employment tribunals, 534–5
    international law, 224, 563, 607
    and investigatory powers, 609–11
    meaning of private life, 630
    proportionality, 633
    scope, 535–6
    workers, 65
    and workplace surveillance, 602–36
private law, and public law:
    divide, 197–8, 569–70
    Human Rights Act, 568–73
    private bodies for public functions, 569–70
probationary workers, dismissal, 501–3
productivity, 56–7, 123, 124
professionals:
    meaning, 175, 176–9, 767
    and part-time work, 345
    working time, 422
prohibition notices, health and safety, 11
psychiatric harm:
    damages, 74
        and employment tribunals, 549
        principles, 461–2
        wrongful dismissal, 447–8, 457–62, 549
    stress, 74, 342
psychometric testing, 607
public authorities:
    data protection, 616
    employment tribunals, 572–3
    meaning, 568
    private bodies for public functions, 569–70
    reasons for actions, 674
    standards of behaviour, 673
public interest disclosures *see* whistleblowing
public law:
    implied terms, 445
    legitimate expectations, 829
    and private law, 197–8
        Human Rights Act, 568–73
        private bodies for public functions,
            569–70

and public sector workers, 197–211
    standards, 206, 207
public private partnerships, 796
public sector workers:
    contract compliance, 796–7
    contractual rights, 201, 203–4, 208–11
    Crown officers, 204
    employment status, 197, 199, 200–7, 754
    human rights, 211
    judicial review, 200–3, 204–7
    New Public Management, 198
    office holders, 173, 199, 200, 292
    outsourcing, 101, 198, 1060
        right to strike, 200, 210, 884–8
        and transfer of undertakings, 1051–9
    politics
        Civil Service Code, 591–3, 600
        local government employees, 593–4,
            599–600
        police, 594–5, 600
        purge and vetting, 587–91
        statutory restrictions, 591–5
    and public law, 197–211
        public/private sector approximation, 197,
            199–200
        retreat from, 200–7
    special status workers, 204
    special treatment, 210–11
publishing industry, 170

qualifying bodies, discrimination, 292

race discrimination
    see also discrimination
    burden of proof, 334
    claims, time limits, 335–6
    detriment, meaning, 312, 313–14
    direct discrimination, 235
    dress codes, 256
    ethnicity, 224, 225–6
    EU law, 225
    exceptions to prohibition, 292
    harassment, 251–2, 314
    indirect discrimination, 263–5
    injury to feelings, 337–8
    intentions and motivation, 239–40
    nationality, 224, 225
    occupational exceptions, 296–7, 299–303
    positive discrimination, 307
    racial grounds, 224–5
    racial groups, 224, 225–6
    remedies, 336–8
    scope of prohibition, 310
    trade union members, 680
    victimisation, 256–60
race to the bottom, 33–4, 980

Rastafarians, 218, 227, 228, 256
re-engagement:
    redundancy, 1024–7
    unfair dismissal, 538–43
reciprocity, employment relationship, 112
recognition of trade unions:
    changing public policy, 724–5
    and contract compliance, 796–7, 902
    derecognition, 789–90, 836, 838–9
        variation of jobs, 989–90
    employer counter-strategies, 792–3, 836–9
    generally, 725, 757–95
    independent trade unions, 767, 768, 834–6,
        839
    meaning of recognition, 797–800
    rights of recognised unions *see* trade union
        rights
    statutory procedure, 27
        access to workers, 775–80
        admissibility of applications, 769
        applications, 767–9
        automatic recognition, 773
        ballots, 773–80
        bargaining units, 771–3
        changes in bargaining units, 789–90
        Code of Practice, 779–80
        collective bargaining method, 785–7
        complexity, 765–6
        delay, 787–9
        derecognition, 789–90, 836
        employer campaigning, 783–5
        employer resistance, 780–5
        generally, 765–95
        intra-union competition, 769–71
        operation, 790–4
        scope, 766, 767, 768
        timetables, 787–9
        worker protection, 780–2
    trends, 728
    voluntary agreements, 757–65
        and employment contracts, 763–4
        legal status, 761–3
        model agreement, 758–61
        and transfer of undertakings, 764–5
recommendations, discrimination, 337
Reder, M W, 211–12
redundancy:
    alternative employment, 1021, 1024–7
        failure to consider, 1027–8
        trial periods, 1026–7
    business reorganisation, 1008–9
    and collective agreements, 105–09, 1067–9
    collective redundancies
        consultation rights, 821–31, 844, 1004,
            1063–5
        EU law, 46, 822, 1028
        meaning, 825–6
        special circumstances, 824, 830–1
    contracting out of statutory rights
        agreed termination, 494–8
        employment status, 498–500
        generally, 492–511
        retirement age, 507–8
        temporary work, 500–7
    definitions, 824
    early retirement, 1023
    fairness of dismissal, 513–14, 1016–18
        and alternative employment, 1027–8
    generally, 1000–28
    individual consultation, 1062–3
    and industrial action, 959
    justification, 1070
    loss of statutory right to, compensation, 546
    maternity reasons, 357
    meaning, 1003–18
        changed places of work, 1013–15
        other substantial reasons, 1015–18
        statutory definition, 1003–4
        variation of jobs, 1004–15
    payments
        basic awards, 1002
        conditions, 1001–3
        early leavers, 1002
        employment status, 1001
        lay-offs and short-time, 1003
        non-statutory payments, 1068
        qualifying period, 1001
        subsidies, 1001
    public policy, 1000–1
    qualifying period for statutory rights, 501–3
    selection criteria
        collective agreements, 1067–8
        consultation, 1020
        fairness, 1019
        LIFO, 105
        objectivity, 1021
        part-time workers, 22
        principles, 1019–21
    unfair selection, 1019–24
        damages, 1044
        trade union activities, 781–2
    victimisation, 424
references:
    breach of contract, 133–4
    confidentiality, 154
    defamation, 130, 132
    false information, 130–5
    freedom of speech, 133
    negligence, 131–2
regulation of investigatory powers, 609–11
reinstatement, unfair dismissal remedy, 537,
    538–43

religion *see* freedom of thought, conscience and religion
religious communities, 392, 418
religious discrimination:
    burden of proof, 334
    claims, time limits, 335
    dress codes, 256
    ECHR jurisprudence, 576–7, 587–8
    harassment, 314
    indirect discrimination, 263
    meaning of belief, 598
    occupational exception, 304
    positive discrimination, 307
    prohibition, 227–9
    refusal to employ, 601
    scope of prohibition, 310
remedies:
    consultation rights, 829–31
    discrimination, 336–8
        compensation, 336, 337
        declarations, 337
        individual remedies, 336
        injury to feelings, 337–8
        recommendations, 337
    Human Rights Act, 568
    inducements against trade union membership, 751
    industrial action
        against strikers, 944–58
        against unions, 928–43
        contempt of court, 914, 935–8
        damages, 938–43
        generally, 928–58
        interim injunctions, 928–35
        sequestration of assets, 938
        third parties, 966
    unfair dismissal, 537–57
    whistleblowing, 643–4
remuneration:
    contracts of employment, 71, 75–95
    deductions
        common law, 77–83
        enforced idleness, 90–4
        industrial action, 78–9, 80–3, 86–7, 944, 959
        and internal contracting, 169
        meaning, 86
        and notice requirements, 85
        remedies, 85–7
        retail stock shortages, 84
        statutory protections, 83–7
        trade union subscriptions, 811
        transparency, 83–5, 86
        unavailable work, 87–9
        unsatisfactory work, 77–87
        variation of wages, 984, 985

    written notifications, 135
discrimination *see* equal pay
employers' good faith, 117
Fair Wages policies, 796
Fair Wages Resolution, 796
garden leave, 90–1
guarantee pay, 999–1000
insolvency, protection on, 1029–33
internal labour markets, 101
itemised pay statements, 135, 141
low pay, 381, 389–90
meaning of pay, 392, 393
meaning of wages, 85–6
minimum wage *see* minimum wage
part-time workers, 342, 344–6
performance-related pay, 77, 101
suspension of workers, 90
time-served contracts, 77
variation, 983–4
representation, employment tribunals, 29
representatives *see* trade unions; worker participation
restraint of trade, garden leave, 90–4
restrictive covenants, 94
restructuring *see* business restructuring
retail trade, 84, 124–6, 180–6
retirement age:
    default age, 508
    and redundancy, 1001
    statutory rights on dismissal, 507–8
Rideout, R, 820
right to work, 8–9, 90, 92–3
risk assessments:
    disability, 285–6, 288
    health and safety, 148–50
Robson, William, 938
Romas, 239–40
Rosenthal, P, 124–6
Ross, N S, 21
Rousseau, N, 501, 537, 556
Rubenstein, Michael, 229
rule books *see* works rules
Ryan, P, 989–90, 995

safe systems of work, 73
Sainsbury, Lord, 378–9
salaries *see* remuneration
Sargeant, M, 1032
Scandinanvian countries, 341–2
Scanlon, Hugh, 600
Scottish Executive, 796
seafarers:
    1988 strike, 946, 957–8
    working time, 404
seasonal workers, 503–5
Seeds, K, 501, 537, 556

self-employed:
    as limited companies, 186–7
    control, 159–60
    dependent entrepreneurs, 179–94
    or employees, 157–66
    health and safety, 179–80
    professionals, 175, 176–9
    sham agreements, 499
    worker status, 176
separation of powers, 707
sequestration of assets, 938
sex discrimination
    see also discrimination
    burden of proof, 334–5
    claims, time limits, 335
    comparators, 242–3
    detriment, meaning, 311–13
    direct discrimination, 235–6
    dress codes, 252–6
    ECHR, 224
    ECHR jurisprudence, 585–6, 587
    exemptions, 292
    gender reassignment, 218, 220–2
        exemptions, 295–6
    harassment, 246–51
    indirect discrimination, 263, 282–4
    intentions and motivation, 236–9
    occupational requirement exceptions, 293–9
    positive discrimination, 307–9
    pregnancy, 240–2
    prohibition, 220
    remedies, 336–8
    remuneration *see* equal pay
    scope, 176
    scope of prohibition, 310
    trade union members, 680
    victimisation, 257, 261–2
sexual orientation:
    discrimination, 218, 222–4
        burden of proof, 334
        comparators, 244
        occupational exception, 304
        religious conviction exception, 304–6
    and fairness of dismissal, 534–5
    harassment, 248–50, 314
    indirect discrimination, 263
    positive discrimination, 307
    scope of prohibition, 310
    victimisation, 257
share fishermen, 392
shares, workers' remuneration, 17
short-time working, 998–1000, 1003
sickness:
    and continuous employment, 503
    dismissals, 488–92
Sikhs, 218, 225–6, 272

Simpson, B, 393, 396–7, 786
Skidmore, P, 254–5
slavery, 6
Smith, D, 337
Smith, P, 914
smoking policies, 99–100
social and economic rights:
    EU Charter of Fundamental Rights, 48
    European Social Charter, 35, 36
    and Human Rights Act, 68
    International Covenant, 975
    international law, 35–41
    and labour law, 1072
Social Charter *see* Council of Europe
Social Dialogue, 48, 63
social exclusion, 1, 58–61
social security:
    benefits, 380–2
    and contracts of employment, 74–5, 215
    and dismissal damages, 440
    and employment status, 157
    guarantees on insolvency, 1030–3
    incentives to employment, 59–61
    lower earnings limit, 347–8
    and minimum wage, 391
    and part-time work, 346–8
    strikers' benefits, 966–70
    and unfair dismissal awards, 554
    welfare to work, 59–61
software, copying, 633
solidarity, 892–3, 899–902
South Africa, 865, 883, 900, 901–2
Soviet Union, 37
Spain, 376, 412, 727
specific performance, 468, 471–2
Sproul, A, 168
staff associations, 834–9
staff handbooks *see* works rules
stakeholders, 1029, 1070
Stanworth, Celia and John, 170
statutory interpretation, and Human Rights
    Act, 565–7, 572–3
stigma damages, 118–22
strike ballots:
    costs, 909
    duration of mandates, 909–10
    enforcement of legislation, 903
    generally, 902–10
    Green Paper, 902–3
    law reform, 914–15
    post-ballot notice, 910–14
    pre-ballot notice, 904–5
    procedures, 907–8
    scrutineers, 909
    separate workplace ballots, 905–7
    statutory duty, 683, 904

strikes
see also industrial action
1926 General Strike, 894
ballots see strike ballots
decline, 868
dismissals, 908, 944–58
emergency powers, 200, 965
functions, 863–6, 867
general strikes, 866, 881–3, 894
and liberty, 865–6
meaning, 863
nature, 914
no-strike agreements, 110, 960
notice, 904–5, 910–14, 933–5
picketing see picketing
political aims, 865–6, 881–4
prohibition, categories of workers, 960
remedies see remedies
right not to strike, 682–7, 719, 903
right to strike, 14, 867
ballot requirement, 897
changing public sector, 884–8
and collective bargaining, 864
and corporate structures, 884, 974
freedom of association, 888, 903, 976
House of Lords jurisprudence, 888–92
and Human Rights Act, 976
international law, 975–7
meaning of trade disputes, 880–902
UK approach, 971–2
secondary actions, 892–902
state incitement to break, 964–5
summary dismissals:
compensation, 439–45
disciplinary procedures, 532–3
effective date of termination, 506–7
justifications, 440–5
surveillance:
regulation of investigatory powers, 609–11
telephone surveillance, 579, 609
workplace see workplace surveillance
Sweden, 309, 371, 376, 387

taxation:
agency workers, 193–4
employment status, 73–4, 157, 499–500
evasion, 76
performance-related pay, 101
and strikers' benefits, 970
tax credits, 60, 369
and tribunal awards, 537
Taylorism, 113
Tebbit, Norman, 939
telephone interceptions, 579, 609, 629–30
telephone monitoring, 604–5
teleworkers, 170

temporary workers:
agencies see agency workers
automatically unfair dismissal, 516
disclosure of nature of contracts, 140–1
employment status, 162–6
notice, 439
redundancy, alternative employment, 1028
statutory rights on dismissal, 500–7
non-renewal as dismissal, 478, 495,
513–14
qualifying period, 501–5
trend, 215
termination of employment:
dismissal see dismissal
effective date of termination, 506–7
frustration of contract, 488–92
notice
deductions of wages, 85
implied term, 72
payment in lieu, 86, 441–2
repudiation of contract, 463–9
Thomas, C G, 1001
time off:
adoptive leave, 366–7
emergency leave, 377–82
employee representatives, 843, 857, 858
generally, 356–87
maternity see maternity rights
miscellaneous duties, 356
parental leave see parental leave
paternity leave, 367
safety representatives, 843
trade union officials, 356
ACAS guide, 797, 801–10, 858
generally, 795–7, 800–12
reasonableness, 809–10
requests, 810
trade union duties, 800–4
training, 803–4
union activities, 806–9
union learning representatives, 804–6,
807
Timex Corporation, 946
torts:
and employment contracts, 70
Factory Acts, 12
industrial action, 869–79, 940–3, 950
industrial injuries, 74
intimidation, 942
negligence, 131–2
trade disputes see industrial action
trade secrets, 151
trade union rights, 62
accompanying workers, 752–7
consultation see consultation rights
facilities agreements, 811–12

information rights, 812–21
  ACAS code of practice, 814–15, 818, 821
  confidential information, 815–18
  critique, 819–21
  requests, 813
  restrictions, 814–18
  statutory rights, 812–15
priority of recognised unions, 840–2, 847–8
representation, 35–6
time off *see* time off
trade unions:
  abuse of power, 700–3
  accounts, 681–2
  activities
    appropriate time, 743–6
    consent of employers, 744–5
    meaning, 739–43
  authorisation of industrial action, 941
  blacklisting, 596, 597
  Bridlington principles, 687, 689, 694
  Certification Officer, 29–30
    accounting records, 682
    annual report, 708–10
    appeals from, 659
    decisions, 709–10
    and election of officers, 668
    jurisdiction, 658–9, 707–10
  changing nature of trade unionism, 719–21,
    727–8, 833
  changing public policy, 718–19
  and citizenship, 647–9
  closed shop *see* closed shop
  collective bargaining *see* collective
    bargaining
  competition between unions, 769–71
  constitutions, 659–65
    conflicts, 663–5
    restraints, 660–3
  contempt of court, 914, 935–8
  damages, vicarious liability, 930
  definition, 651
  disciplinary proceedings
    decisions, 700–5
    generally, 693–705
    and human rights, 720
    judicial guidelines, 698
    powers, 684–5, 693–4
    procedures, 694–700
    UNISON procedures, 695–7
  discrimination against members
    access to employment, 730–4
    automatically unfair dismissal, 516
    GCHQ, 740
    generally, 730–52
    meaning of union membership, 736–9
    qualifying period, 501, 734

  union activities, 739–46
  victimisation, 734–52
effectiveness, 15
election of officers
  candidates, 667–72
  common law, 672–89
  generally, 666–80
  statutory procedures, 666–72
functions, 723, 795
governance, 659–65
ILO conventions, 37, 648, 649, 719, 738
independent trade unions, 767, 768, 834–6,
  839
internal union disputes
  adjudication, 706–17
  CO decisions, 709–10
  CO jurisdiction, 707–10
  court jurisdiction, 710–17
  external review, 706–7
international dimension, 41
judicial restraint, 651–5
and Labour Party, 656, 658, 659
legal status, 651
membership
  blacklisting, 734
  contractual duties, 757
  disciplinary procedures, 684–5
  discrimination, 730–52
  exclusions, 687–93
  freedom of association, 563, 718–19, 720,
    738
  generally, 729–52
  inducements to give up, 739, 750–2
  information, 648, 681–2
  meaning, 736–9
  poaching, 687
  remedies, 685
  right not to strike, 682–7, 719
  right to non-membership, 746–50
  rights, 14, 680–93, 729–30
  sovereignty, 680
  subscriptions, check off, 811
nature, 649–59
objects, 650–5
political funds, 658–9
political objects, 656–8
positive discrimination, 307
recognition *see* recognition of trade unions
rights *see* trade union rights
rule books, 649, 650, 652
safety representatives, 16
sequestration of assets, 938
solidarity, 892–3, 899–902
state regulation, 648–9, 717–18
statutory restraints, 655–9
structures, 659–60

support for individual claims, 13
TUC Disputes Committee, 30
union learning representatives, 804–6, 807
and women, 23
and Working Time Regulations, 408–10
Trades Union Congress (TUC):
  Disputes Principles and Procedure, 770–1
  flexible working, 387
  intra-union competition, 770–1
  and minimum wage, 400–1
  and parental leave, 375, 377
  Social Partnership with CBI, 848
  working time, 416–18, 419–21, 425–6
  workplace surveillance, 611
trainees:
  employment status, 177
  and minimum wage, 392
training:
  consultation of trade unions on, 822
  employee representatives, 843
  positive discrimination, 307, 308
  safety representatives, 843
  trade union officials, 757, 803–6
transfer of undertakings:
  acquired rights, 1038–9, 1040–2
  Acquired Rights Directive, 1035–6, 1043,
    1055, 1071
  collective agreements, 1047
  consultation rights, 822, 843, 1065–9
    employee representatives, 844
  corporate rescue, 1042–4
  and employment status, 173–4
  ETO grounds for dismissal, 1037, 1045
  generally, 1035–59
  meaning of undertaking, 142
  methods, 1035
  occupational pension rights, 1052
  outsourcing, 1051–9, 1060
  post-transfer dismissals, 1044–5
  practice, 430–1
  pre-transfer dismissals, 1036–44
    deemed purchaser dismissals, 1038
    grounds, 1037–8
    timing, 1039–40
  public sector outsourcing, 1060
  and union recognition agreements, 764–5
  variation of terms, 1045–51
    constructive dismissal, 1048, 1049, 1050
    consultation, 1066–7
    trade union agreements, 1050–1
  waiver of rights, 1046
transnational corporations:
  codes of conduct, 41
  consultation obligations, 62–3
  European works councils, 845, 858–9
  globalisation, 33

human rights, 38, 41
transport, working time, 404
Tremlett, N, 556
trust and confidence:
  and constructive dismissal, 113–17, 485–7
  and corruption, 118–22
  discrimination, 117
  exercise of discretion, 122–3
  implied contractual term, 72, 113–26, 212,
    756
  mutuality, 113–26
  references, 134–5
  stigma damages, 118–22
  and wrongful dismissal, 447, 457–9, 469–75,
    476
Truter, G M, 833–4, 846, 847, 856–7
Turner, Adair, 419

umbrella contracts, 162–6
unavailability of work, 87–9, 959
undertakings, meaning, 142
Undy, R, 666, 914
unfair contracts terms:
  flexibility clauses, 991, 992
  works rules, 98
unfair dismissal:
  automatically unfair dismissal
    application, 514–15, 516, 536
    closed shops, 748
    compensation, 515
    and EU law, 536
    maternity rights, 356–7
    part-time workers, 516
    qualifying periods, 501
    strike dismissals, 947–53
    transfer of undertakings, 1037–44, 1045,
      1048
  conciliation, 555–7
  contracting out of statutory rights
    agreed termination, 494–8
    arbitration alternative, 508–9
    collective agreements, 509–11
    compromise agreements, 494–8, 511
    employment status, 498–500
    generally, 492–511
    prohibition, 493
    retirement age, 507–8
    temporary work, 501–7
  contributory fault, 551–2
  damages
    aggravated damages, 515, 549
    automatically unfair dismissal, 515
    basic awards, 543, 553
    conciliation, 555–7
    contributory fault, 551–2
    fringe benefits, 550

future loss of wages, 545–6, 550
generally, 543–55
injury to feelings, 547–50
and insolvency, 1031
just and equitable awards, 544–50
lack of consultation, 1062–3, 1064
levels, 537
loss of dismissal protection, 546
loss of wages, 545
non-compliance with statutory disciplin-
    ary procedure, 555
non-economic loss, 547–50
psychiatric illness, 549
and social security benefits, 554
unfair selection for redundancy, 1044
upper limits, 543, 552–3
economic analysis of law, 54, 510
EU Charter of Fundamental Rights, 7,
    434–5
fairness see fairness of dismissal
ILO Connvention, 435
and industrial action
    pre-1999 position, 945–7
    protected actions, 947–53
    replacement workers, 954
and parental leave, 375
practice, 557–8
purpose of legislation, 493
qualifying period, 139–41, 172, 501–3
remedies
    compensation, 543–55
    corrective justice, 537–8
    damages, 543–55
    generally, 537–57
    individual v collective, 515, 559
    re-engagement, 538–43
    reinstatement, 537, 538–43
scope see employment status
statutory rights, 493
structure of fairness enquiries, 512–15
victimisation, 424
UNISON, 695–7, 706, 797, 900
United Nations, 35
United States:
    business restructuring, 981
    closed shop, 748, 749
    collective bargaining, 727
    drug testing, 606
    information rights, 812
    recognition of trade unions, 765, 787
    Sacco & Vanzetti, 866
    strike dismissals, 954
    workplace surveillance, 603–5

variation of jobs:
    bargaining power, 212, 1070

collective agreements, 995–8
constructive dismissal, 1048, 1049, 1050
contracts of employment, 19–20, 212, 453
    disclosure requirements, 139–40, 983
    unilateral variation, 983–4
    written statements, 145–8
employer discretion, 984–9, 1070
flexibility, 983–95
flexibility clauses, 989–95, 1011–13
forms, 982
generally, 982–1000
place of work, 987–8
    mobility clauses, 991
    and redundancy, 1013–15
reasonableness, 1070
redundancy situation, 1004–15
short-time working, 998–1000
    guarantee pay, 999–1000
    subsidies, 998, 1000
transfer of undertakings, 1045–51, 1066–7
works rules, 99–101
vicarious liability:
    discrimination, 314–15
    employers, 72
    trade unions, 930
Vickers, Lucy, 644
victimisation, 256–62
    automatically unfair dismissal, 516
    damages, 460–1
    trade union members, 734–52
    weakness of legislation, 515
    whistleblowing, 643–4
    and working time, 424
volenti on fit injuria, 992, 993
voluntary associations, 673–4
volunteers, 174, 311, 392

Wachter, M L, 101
Wadham, John, 611
wage-work bargain, 71, 75–95
wages see remuneration
Wages Councils, 14–15, 388–9, 724–5
Wallington, P, 922, 925–6, 964, 965
Wardhaway solicitors, 608
Webb, Sidney and Beatrice, 112
Welzmiller, S, 1002
Western Electric Company, 123, 124
whistleblowing:
    and freedom of expression, 644
    generally, 636–45
    good faith, 639, 641–3
    medical scandals, 636
    and Official Secrets Act, 636
    pre-1998 Act, 636
    Public Interest Disclosure Act, 637–44
    qualifying disclosures, 637–43

remedies, 643–4
victimisation, 643–4
White, C, 590
Whitley, J H, 14
Whitley Council agreements, 204, 206, 325
Whitley Report, 723
Wikely, N, 65
Wilkinson, F, 49–51, 56–7, 389–91
Wilkinson, H, 370–2
Williamson, O E, 101
women:
    childcare, 368–72
    and collective bargaining, 23
    and divorce, 342
    family-friendly policies, 387, 401
    lifetime income, 342
    part-time workers, 343–4, 345–6
    pensions, 348
    work-life balance, 341, 342
Wood, S, 791, 792
Woolfson, C, 946
work-life balance, 61
    debate, 341–3
    gendered division, 341, 342
    issues, 380–2
    long hours, 341, 342, 377, 425
    maternity see maternity rights
    parents see parental leave
    working time see working time
work to rule, 80–3, 97
worker participation, 61–3
    business restructuring, 1059–69
    changing patterns, 726–9
    changing public policy, 860
    consultation see consultation rights
    debate, 1059–61
    decline, 844
    employee representatives
        election, 842–3
        facilities, 843, 858
        generally, 839–60
        negotiated agreements, 850–2
        procedures, 845–60
        protection, 843–4, 857–8
        support, 844
        time off, 843, 857, 858
    employer anti-union strategies, 792–3, 836–9
    EU law, 1069, 1070
    Germany, 833–4
    ILO convention, 795
    incoherence, 844–5
    information see information rights
    Information and Consultation Directive,
        845–7
    Information and Consultation of Employee
        Regulations

enforcement, 854–7
generally, 847–58
scope, 848–9
non-union representation, 833–60
principles, 1061
redundancy see redundancy
right to be accompanied, 752–7
staff associations, 834–9
trade unions see trade unions
transfer of undertakings, 1065–9
works councils see works councils
workers
    see also employment status
    dependent entrepreneurs, 179–94
    EU meaning, 175–6, 193
    meaning, 174–6, 392
        trade disputes, 887–8, 899
        trade union legislation, 736
        worker representation, 754–5
    part-time workers see part-time workers
    professionals, 176–9
    Regulation powers, 194, 196
working tax credits, 60, 369
working time:
    1998 Regulations, 402–8
        application, 403–5
        employment status, 403
        enforcement, 422–4
        operation, 408–10
    and contracts of employment, 73
    criminal liability, 12
    Directive, 43, 401–2
    DTI guidance, 410, 418–19, 421–2
    EU case law, 404–5
    excluded workers, 418–22
    flexibility, 427–8
    generally, 401–27
    holidays, 405–8, 426
    impact, 424–7
    long hours, 341, 342, 377, 425
    meaning, 410–12
    night work, 404
    on call workers, 410–12
    opting out, 377, 412, 413–18, 420
        UK abuse, 416–18, 425–6
    records, 422
    rest periods, 404
    victimisation, 424
    workforce agreements, 408–10, 840–2
    young workers, 407
workplace surveillance:
    confidential information, 608
    data protection see data protection
    drug testing, 606–7, 623, 628, 634, 635–6
    email and Internet, 605, 608
    genetic testing, 607, 628

and human rights, 601–36
   1998 Act, 633–6
   ECHR, 628–33
  medical testing, 607, 627–8, 634
  performance monitoring, 603, 604
  psychometric testing, 607
  techniques, 602–6
  telephone monitoring, 604–5
workplaces, meaning, 906
works councils:
  benefits, 834
  and business restructuring, 1064
  European Works Councils, 62, 516, 845,
    858–9
  financing, 834
  issues, 834
  mandatory councils, 833
works rules:
  legal status, 3, 96–102, 213
  meaning, 95–6
  practice, 71
  variation, 99–101
wrongful dismissal:
  breach of contract
    disciplinary procedures, 445–52
    express procedural terms, 449–52
    express substantuve conditions, 452–4
    implied procedural terms, 437–49
    implied reasonableness, 445
    implied substantive terms, 456–62

    notice entitlement, 437–9
    payments in lieu of notice, 441–2
  claims, jurisdiction, 86
  common law, 436–7
    approach, 558
    revival, 475–7
  damages, 437–62
    dating, 453–4
    economic loss, 459–60, 462
    fringe benefits, 454–6
    psychiatric harm, 447–8, 457–62
  declarations and injunctions, 463–75
    balance of convenience, 464
    breach of express terms, 463
    inadequacy of damages, 463–4, 469–75
    termination of employment relationship,
      463–9
  generally, 436–77
  summary dismissals, 439–40
    justifications, 440–5
Wynn, M, 363–4

young persons:
  British labour market, 39–40
  EU directive, 38
  legal history, 39
  working time, 407

Zappala, L, 194